2014 Wiley CPAexcel® EXAM REVIEW STUDY GUIDE

2014

Wiley

CPAexcel®
EXAM REVIEW
STUDY GUIDE

AUDITING AND ATTESTATION

O. Ray Whittington, CPA, PhD

WILEY

Cover Design by David Riedy
Cover image: © turtleteeth/iStockphoto

The following items, copyright © by the American Institute of Certified Public Accountants, Inc., are reprinted with permission:

1. Material from *Uniform CPA Examination Questions and Answers*, 1978 through 2000.

2. *Information for Uniform CPA Examination Candidates*, Board of Examiners, 2013.

Material from the Certified Internal Auditor Examination, Copyright © 1994 through 1997 by the Institute of Internal Auditors, Inc., are reprinted and/or adapted with permission.

Material from the Certified Management Accountant Examinations, Copyright © 1993 through 1997 by the Institute of Certified Management Accountants, are reprinted and/or adapted with permission.

Material adapted, with permission, from *Writing for Accountants*, Aletha Hendrickson, South-Western Publishing Co., 1993.

Published by John Wiley & Sons, Inc., Hoboken, New Jersey.
Published simultaneously in Canada.

For general information on our other products and services or for technical support, please contact our Customer Care Department within the US at 800-762-2974, outside the US at 317-572-3993 or fax 317-572-4002.

Wiley also publishes its books in a variety of electronic formats. Some content that appears in print may not be available in electronic books. For more information about Wiley products, visit our website at www.wiley.com

ISBN 978-1-118-73421-6 (paperback); 978-1-118-86351-0 (ebk); 978-1-118-86366-4 (ebk)

Printed in the United States of America

10 9 8 7 6 5 4 3 2 1

CONTENTS

INTRODUCTION

AUDITING AND ATTESTATION

APPENDICES

INDEX   737

PREFACE

Passing the CPA exam upon your first attempt is possible! The *Wiley CPAexcel Exam Review 2014 Study Guide: Auditing and Attestation* preparation materials provide you with the necessary materials (visit our website at www.wiley.com/cpa for more information). It's up to you to add the hard work and commitment. Together we can beat the pass rate on each section of about 50%. All Wiley CPAexcel products are continuously updated to provide you with the most comprehensive and complete knowledge base. Choose your products from the Wiley preparation materials and you can proceed confidently. You can select support materials that are exam-based and user-friendly. You can select products that will help you pass!

Remaining current is one of the keys to examination success. Here is a list of what's new in this edition of the *Wiley CPAexcel Exam Review 2014 Study Guide: Auditing and Attestation* **text.**

- The AICPA Content Specification Outlines on Auditing and Attestation for the Computerized CPA Examination beginning in 2014
- AICPA questions released in 2013
- The new task-based simulations
- Coverage of new audit and attestation standards, especially
  - Latest AICPA auditing, ethics, and quality control standards, including the new clarity standards
  - Latest Public Company Accounting Oversight Board auditing standards
  - International auditing standards

The objective of this work is to provide you with the knowledge to pass the Auditing and Attestation portion of the Uniform Certified Public Accounting (CPA) Exam. The text is divided up into eight areas of study called modules. Each module contains written text with discussion, examples, and demonstrations of the key exam concepts. Following each text area, actual American Institute of Certified Public Accountants (AICPA) unofficial questions and answers are presented to test your knowledge. We are indebted to the AICPA for permission to reproduce and adapt examination materials from past examinations. Author-constructed questions and simulations are provided for new areas or areas that require updating. All author-constructed questions and simulations are modeled after AICPA question formats. The multiple-choice questions are grouped into topical areas, giving candidates a chance to assess their areas of strength and weakness. Selection and inclusion of topical content is based upon current AICPA Content Specification Outlines. Only testable topics are presented. If the CPA exam does not test it, this text does not present it.

The CPA exam is one of the toughest exams you will ever take. It will not be easy. But if you follow our guidelines and focus on your goal, you will be thrilled with what you can accomplish.

Ray Whittington
November 2013

DON'T FORGET TO VISIT OUR WEBSITE AT WWW.WILEY.COM/CPA FOR SUPPLEMENTS AND UPDATES.

ABOUT THE AUTHOR

Ray Whittington, PhD, CPA, CMA, CIA, is the dean of the Driehaus College of Business at DePaul University. Prior to joining the faculty at DePaul, Professor Whittington was the Director of Accountancy at San Diego State University. From 1989 through 1991, he was the Director of Auditing Research for the American Institute of Certified Public Accountants (AICPA), and he previously was on the audit staff of KPMG. He previously served as a member of the Auditing Standards Board of the AICPA and as a member of the Accounting and Review Services Committee and the Board of Regents of the Institute of Internal Auditors. Professor Whittington has published numerous textbooks, articles, monographs, and continuing education courses.

ABOUT THE CONTRIBUTOR

Kurt Pany, PhD, CPA, is a Professor of Accounting at Arizona State University. His basic and advanced auditing courses provided the basis on which he received the Arizona Society of CPAs' Excellence in Teaching Award and an Arizona CPA Foundation Award for Innovation in the Classroom for the integration of computer and professional ethics applications. His professional experience includes serving for four years on the AICPA's Auditing Standards Board, serving as an academic fellow in the Auditing Division of the AICPA, and, prior to entering academe, working as a staff auditor for Deloitte and Touche.

INTRODUCTION

To maximize the efficiency of your review program, begin by studying (not merely reading) this chapter and the next three chapters of this volume. They have been carefully organized and written to provide you with important information to assist you in successfully completing the Auditing and Attestation section of the CPA exam. Beyond providing a comprehensive outline to help you organize the material tested on the Auditing and Attestation exam, Chapter 1 will assist you in organizing a study program to prepare for the exam. Self-discipline is essential.

Chapter 1: Beginning Your CPA Review Program

GENERAL COMMENTS ON THE EXAMINATION

The Uniform CPA Examination is delivered using computer-based testing (CBT). Computer-based testing has several advantages. You may take the exam one section at a time. As a result, your studies can be focused on that one section, improving your chances for success. In addition, the exam is no longer offered twice a year. In addition, you may take the exam on your schedule, eight months of the year, six days a week and in the morning or in the afternoon.
Successful completion of the Auditing and Attestation section is an attainable goal. Keep this point foremost in your mind as you study the first four chapters in this volume and develop your study plan.

Purpose of the Examination[1]

The Uniform CPA Examination is designed to test the entry-level knowledge and skills necessary to protect the public interest. An entry-level CPA is defined as one who has fulfilled the applicable jurisdiction's educational requirements and has the knowledge and skills typically possessed by a person with up to two years of experience. These knowledge and skills were identified through a Practice Analysis performed in 2008, which served as a basis for the development of the content specifications for the exam beginning in 2014.

The CPA examination is one of many screening devices to assure the competence of those licensed to perform the attest function and to render professional accounting services. Other screening devices include educational requirements, ethics examinations, and work experience.

The CPA examination appears to test the material covered in accounting programs of the better business schools. It also appears to be based upon the body of knowledge essential for the practice of public accounting and the audit of a medium-sized client. Since the examination is primarily a textbook or academic examination, you should plan on taking it as soon as possible after completing your required education.

Examination Content

Guidance concerning topical content of the computer-based exam in Auditing and Attestation can be found in a document prepared by the Board of Examiners of the AICPA entitled *Content and Skill Specifications for the Uniform CPA Exam.* We have included the content outline for Auditing and Attestation at the beginning of Chapter 5. The outline should be used as an indication of the topics' relative emphasis on the exam.

The Board's objective in preparing this detailed listing of topics tested on the exam is to help "in assuring the continuing validity and reliability of the Uniform CPA Examination." These outlines are an excellent source of guidance concerning the areas and emphasis to be given each area on future exams.

The new Content and Skill Specification Outlines for the CPA examination, including the testing of International Auditing Standards, went into effect January 1, 2011. In addition, the AICPA adopted CBT-e, which is a new computer platform. The major change from your standpoint is that simulations are smaller in size and a larger number of these "task-based simulations" are included on the Auditing and Attestation, Financial Accounting and Reporting, and Regulation exams. In addition, all simulations that test writing skills have been moved to the Business Environment and Concepts exam.

New accounting and auditing pronouncements, including those in the governmental and not-for-profit areas, are tested in the testing window starting six months after the pronouncement's *effective* date. If early application is permitted, a pronouncement is tested six months after the *issuance* date; candidates are responsible for the old pronouncement also until it is superseded. Federal laws are tested six months following their *effective date.* The AICPA posts content changes regularly on its Internet site at www.cpa-exam.org.

---

[1]More information may be obtained from the AICPA's *Uniform CPA Examination Candidate Bulletin,* which you can find on the AICPA's website at www.cpa-exam.org.

Nondisclosure and Computerization of Examination

Beginning May 1996, the Uniform CPA Examination became nondisclosed. For each exam section, candidates are required to agree to a *Statement of Confidentiality,* which states that they will not divulge the nature and content of any exam question. The exam is computer-based, and candidates take the exam at Prometric sites in the 55 jurisdictions in which the exam is offered. The CPA exam is offered continually during the testing windows shown below.

Testing Window (Exam Available)	January through February	April through May	July through August	October through November
AICPA Review and Update (Exam Unavailable)	March	June	September	December

One or more exam sections may be taken during any exam window, and the sections may be taken in any desired order. **However, no candidate will be allowed to sit for the same section more than once during any given testing window.** In addition, a candidate must pass all four sections of the CPA exam within a "rolling" eighteen-month period, which begins on the date he or she passes a section. In other words, you must pass the other three sections of the exam within eighteen months of when you pass the first section. If you do not pass all sections within the eighteen-month period, credit for any section(s) passed outside the eighteen-month period will expire and the section(s) must be retaken.

Types of Questions

The computer-based Uniform CPA Examination consists of two basic question formats.

1. Multiple-Choice—questions requiring the selection of one of four responses to a short scenario.
2. Task-Based Simulations—short case studies that are used to assess knowledge and skills in a context approximating that found on the job through the use of realistic scenarios and tasks, and access to normally available and familiar resources.

The multiple-choice questions are much like the ones that have constituted a majority of the CPA examination for years. **And the good news is that these types of questions constitute about 60% of the Auditing and Attestation section.**

Process for Sitting for the Examination

While there are some variations in the process from state to state, the basic process for sitting for the CPA examination may be described as follows:

1. Apply to take the examination (request, complete, and submit an application)
2. Pay the examination fees
3. Review the tutorial and sample tests
4. Receive your Notice to Schedule (NTS)
5. Schedule your examination(s)
6. Take your examination(s)
7. Receive your Score Report(s)

Applying to Take the Examination

The right to practice public accounting as a CPA is governed by individual state statutes. While some rules regarding the practice of public accounting vary from jurisdiction to jurisdiction, all State Boards of Accountancy use the Uniform CPA Examination and AICPA advisory grading service as one of the requirements to practice public accounting. The State Boards of Accountancy determine the requirements to sit for the exam (e.g., education requirements). For comparisons of requirements for various state boards and those policies that are uniform across jurisdictions you should refer to the website of the National Association of State Boards of Accountancy (NASBA) at www.nasba.org.

A frequent problem candidates encounter is failure to apply by the deadline. **Apply to sit for the examination early. Also, you should use extreme care in filling out the application and mailing required materials to your State Board of Accountancy.** If possible, have a friend review your completed application before mailing with check and other documentation. The name on your application must appear exactly the same as it appears on the identification you plan to use at the testing center. Candidates may miss a particular CPA examination window simply because of minor technical details that were overlooked (check not signed, items not enclosed, question not answered on application, etc.). **Because of the very high volume of applications received in the more populous states, the administrative staff does not have time to call or write to correct minor details and will simply reject your application.**

The NASBA website has links to the registration information for all 55 jurisdictions. It is possible for candidates to sit for the examination at a Prometric site in any state or territory. Candidates desiring to do so should refer to the registration information for the applicable State Board of Accountancy.

International Applicants

International administration of the CPA Exam is currently offered in Brazil, Japan, Bahrain, Kuwait, Lebanon, and the United Arab Emirates. If you live in one of these testing locations, or other select countries, you may be able to take the Exam without traveling to the U.S. The Exam is only offered in English, and is the same computerized test as the one administered in the U.S. You are required to meet the same eligibility requirements and complete the same licensure requirements as your U.S. counterparts.

Applicants from countries other than the U.S. must follow the same basic steps as U.S. applicants. This means they must select the jurisdiction in which they wish to qualify and file an application with the board of accountancy (or its designated agent) in that jurisdiction. Any special instructions for candidates who have completed their education outside the U.S. are included in the board of accountancy requirements. For more information on the international administration of the CPA Examination, visit the International section of the NASBA website.

Obtaining the Notice to Schedule

Once your application has been processed and you have paid all fees, you will receive a Notice to Schedule (NTS) from NASBA. The NTS will list the section(s) of the examination that you are approved to take. When you receive the NTS, verify that all information is correct. **Be certain that the name appearing on the NTS matches EXACTLY the name on the identification documents that you will use during check-in at the testing center. If the information is incorrect or the name does not match, immediately contact your board of accountancy or its designated agent to request a correction. You must bring your NTS with you to the examination.**

Exam Scheduling

Once you have been cleared to take the exam by the applicable state board, you will receive by mail a Notice to Schedule (NTS) and may then schedule to sit for one or more sections of the exam.

You have the following two options for scheduling your examination:

1. **Visit www.prometric.com/cpa on the Internet**

   This is the easiest and quickest way to schedule an examination appointment (or cancel and reschedule an appointment, if necessary). Simply go to the website, select "Schedule your test," and follow the directions. It is advised that you print and keep for your records the confirmation number for your appointment.

2. **Call 800-580-9648 (Candidate Services Call Center)**

   Before you call, you must have your NTS in front of you, and have in mind several times, dates, and locations that would work for you. You will not receive written confirmation of your appointment. Be sure to write down the date, time, location, and confirmation number for each of your appointments.

You should also be aware that if you have to cancel or reschedule your appointment, you may be subject to a cancellation/rescheduling fee. The AICPA's *Uniform CPA Examination Candidate Bulletin* lists the rescheduling and cancellation fees.

To assure that you get your desired location and time period, it is imperative that you schedule early. To get your first choice of dates, you are advised to schedule at least 45 days in advance. You will not be scheduled for an exam fewer than 5 days before testing.

ATTRIBUTES OF EXAMINATION SUCCESS

Your primary objective in preparing for the Auditing and Attestation section is to pass. Other objectives such as learning new and reviewing old material should be considered secondary. The six attributes of examination success discussed below are **essential**. You should study the attributes and work toward achieving/developing each of them **before** taking the examination.

1. **Knowledge of Material**

    Two points are relevant to "knowledge of material" as an attribute of examination success. **First,** there is a distinct difference between being familiar with material and knowing the material. Frequently candidates confuse familiarity with knowledge. Can you remember when you just could not answer an examination question or did poorly on an examination, but maintained to yourself or your instructor that you knew the material? You probably were only familiar with the material. On the CPA examination, familiarity is insufficient; you must know the material. Remember, the exam will test your ability to analyze data, make judgments, communicate, perform research, and demonstrate understanding of the material. Knowledgeable discussion of the material is required on the CPA examination. This text contains outlines of the topical areas in auditing including outlines of professional pronouncements, etc. Return to the original material (e.g., SAS, your auditing textbook, etc.) only if the outlines do not reinforce material you already know. **Second,** the Auditing and Attestation exam tests a literally overwhelming amount of material at a rigorous level. **Furthermore,** as noted earlier, the CPA exam will test new material, sometimes as early as six months after issuance. In other words, you are not only responsible for material you learned in your auditing and attestation course(s), but also for all new developments in auditing and attestation.

2. **Commitment to Exam Preparation**

    Your preparation for the CPA exam should begin at least two months prior to the date you plan to schedule your seating for an exam part. If you plan to take more than one part, you should start earlier. Over the course of your preparation, you will experience many peaks and valleys. There will be days when you feel completely prepared and there will also be days when you feel totally overwhelmed. This is not unusual and, in fact, should be expected.

    The CPA exam is a very difficult and challenging exam. How many times in your college career did you study months for an exam? Probably not too many. Therefore, candidates need to remain focused on the objective—succeeding on the CPA exam.

    Develop a personal study plan so that you are reviewing material daily. Of course, you should schedule an occasional study break to help you relax, but don't schedule too many breaks. Candidates who dedicate themselves to studying have a much greater chance of going through this process only one time. On the other hand, a lack of focus and piecemeal preparation will only extend the process over a number of exam sittings.

3. **Solutions Approach**

    The solutions approach is a systematic approach to solving the questions and task-based simulations found on the CPA examination. Many candidates know the material fairly well when they sit for the CPA exam, but they do not know how to take the examination. Candidates generally neither work nor answer questions efficiently in terms of time or grades. The solutions approach permits you to avoid drawing "blanks" on CPA exam questions; using the solutions approach coupled with grading insights (see below) allows you to pick up a sizable number of points on test material with which you are not familiar. Chapter 3 outlines the solutions approach for multiple-choice questions and task-based simulations.

4. **Grading Insights**

    Your score on each section of the exam is determined by the sum of points assigned to individual questions and simulations. Thus, you must attempt to maximize your points on each individual item.

    The multiple-choice questions within each section are organized into three groups which are referred to as testlets. Each multiple-choice testlet is comprised of approximately 30 multiple-choice questions. The multiple-choice testlets vary in overall difficulty. A testlet is labeled either "medium difficult" or "difficult" based on its makeup. A "difficult" testlet has a higher percentage of hard questions than a "medium difficult" testlets. Every candidate's first multiple-choice testlet in each section will be a "medium difficult" testlet. If a candidate scores well on the first testlet, he or she will receive a "difficult" second testlet. Candidates that do not perform well on the first testlet receive a second "medium difficult" testlet. Because the scoring procedure takes the difficulty of the testlet into account, candidates are scored fairly regardless of the type of testlets they receive.

    Each multiple-choice testlet contains "operational" and "pretest" questions. The operational questions are the only ones that are used to determine your score. Pretest questions are not scored; they are being tested for future use as operational questions. However, you have no way of knowing which questions are operational and which questions are pretest questions. Therefore, you must approach each question as if it will be used to determine your grade.

    Task-based simulations include more extensive scenarios and requirements. For example, the requirements may involve calculations, form completion, or research. The points assigned to the requirements will vary according to their difficulty. The task-based simulations make use of a number of commonly used tools such as spreadsheets and electronic research databases. Therefore, you need to become proficient in the use of these tools to maximize your score on the simulations.

CPA Exam scores are reported on a scale from 0 to 99. The total score is not a percent correct score. It is a combination of scores from the multiple-choice and simulation portions of the exam considering the relative difficulty of the items. A total score of 75 is required to pass each section.

The AICPA includes a tutorial and sample examinations on its website that allow you to get experience with the use of the actual computer tools used on the CPA exam. Also, more experience with computer testing can be obtained by using *Wiley CPAexcel Exam Review Test Bank*.

5. **Examination Strategy**

Prior to sitting for the examination, it is important to develop an examination strategy (i.e., an approach to working efficiently throughout the exam). Your ability to cope successfully with 4 hours of examination can be improved by

a. Recognizing the importance and usefulness of an examination strategy
b. Using Chapter 4, Taking the Examination, and previous examination experience to develop a "personal strategy" for the exam
c. Testing your "personal strategy" on example examinations under conditions similar to those at the testing centers (using similar tools and databases and with a time limit)

6. **Examination Confidence**

You need confidence to endure the physical and mental demands of 4 hours of test-taking under tremendous pressure. Examination confidence results from proper preparation for the exam which includes mastering the first five attributes of examination success. Examination confidence is necessary to enable you to overcome the initial frustration with questions for which you may not be specifically prepared.

This study manual, when properly used, contributes to your examination confidence. Build confidence by completing the questions contained herein.

Common Candidate Mistakes

The CPA Exam is a formidable hurdle in your accounting career. With a pass rate of about 45% on each section, the level of difficulty is obvious. The good news, though, is that about 75% of all candidates (first-time and re-exam) sitting for each examination eventually pass. The authors believe that the first-time pass rate could be higher if candidates would be more careful. Seven common mistakes that many candidates make are

1. Failure to understand the exam question requirements
2. Misunderstanding the supporting text of the problem
3. Lack of knowledge of material tested, especially recently issued pronouncements
4. Failure to develop proficiency with computer-based testing and practice tools such as electronic research databases and spreadsheets
5. Inability to apply the solutions approach
6. Lack of an exam strategy (e.g., allocation of time)
7. Sloppiness and logical errors

These mistakes are not mutually exclusive. Candidates may commit one or more of the above items. Remind yourself that when you decrease the number of common mistakes, you increase your chances of successfully becoming a CPA. Take the time to read carefully the exam question requirements. Do not jump into a quick start, only to later find out that you didn't understand what information the examiners were asking for. Read slowly and carefully. Take time to recall your knowledge. Respond to the question asked. Apply an exam strategy such as allocating your time among all question formats. Do not spend too much time on the multiple-choice testlets, leaving no time to spend on preparing your simulation responses. Write neatly and label all answer sections. Answer questions quickly but precisely, avoid common mistakes, and increase your score.

PURPOSE AND ORGANIZATION OF THIS REVIEW TEXTBOOK

This book is designed to help you prepare adequately for the Auditing and Attestation examination. There is no easy way to prepare for the successful completion of the CPA Examination; however, through the use of this manual, your approach will be systematic and logical.

The objective of this book is to provide study materials supportive to CPA candidates. While no guarantees are made concerning the success of those using this text, this book promotes efficient preparation by

1. Explaining how to **maximize your score** through analysis of examination grading and illustration of the solutions approach.
2. **Defining areas tested** through the use of the content specification outlines. Note that predictions of future exams are not made. You should prepare yourself for all possible topics rather than gambling on the appearance of certain questions.
3. **Organizing your study program** by comprehensively outlining all of the subject matter tested on the examination in eight easy-to-use study modules. Each study module is a manageable task which facilitates your exam preparation. Turn to Chapter 5 and peruse the contents to get a feel for the organization of this book.
4. **Providing CPA candidates with examination questions** organized by topic (e.g., internal control, audit reports, etc.). Questions have also been developed for new areas and in simulation format.
5. **Explaining the AICPA unofficial answers** to the examination questions included in this text. The AICPA publishes unofficial answers for all questions from exams administered prior to 1996 and for any released questions from exams administered on or after May 1996. However, no explanation is made of the approach that should have been applied to the examination questions to obtain these unofficial answers.

As you read the next few paragraphs which describe the contents of this book, flip through the chapters to gain a general familiarity with the book's organization and contents. Chapters 2, 3, and 4 are to help you maximize your score.

Chapter 2   Examination Grading
Chapter 3   The Solutions Approach
Chapter 4   Taking the Examination

Chapters 2, 3, and 4 contain material that should be kept in mind throughout your study program. Refer back to them frequently. Reread them for a final time just before you sit for the exam.

The Auditing and Attestation Modules contain

1. AICPA Content Specification Outlines of material tested on the Auditing and Attestation Examination
2. Multiple-choice questions
3. Task-based simulations
4. AICPA unofficial answers with the author's explanations for the multiple-choice questions
5. Author answers to task-based simulations

Also included in Appendix A of this text is a complete Sample Auditing and Attestation CPA Examination. The sample exam is included to help candidates gain experience in taking a "realistic" exam. While studying the modules, the candidates can become accustomed to concentrating on fairly narrow topics. By working through the sample examination near the end of their study programs, candidates will be better prepared for taking the actual examination. Because some task-based simulations require the use of research materials, it is useful to have the appropriate electronic research database (e.g., AICPA Resource: Accounting and Auditing) or printed versions of professional standards to complete the sample examination. AICPA Resource: Accounting and Auditing is available at discounted prices to student and faculty members of the AICPA. **Remember that this research material will not be available to answer the multiple-choice questions.**

Other Textbooks

This text is a comprehensive compilation of study guides and outlines; it should not be necessary to supplement them with textbooks and other materials for most topics. You probably already have an auditing textbook. In such a case, you must make the decision whether to replace it and trade familiarity (including notes therein, etc.), with the cost and inconvenience of obtaining the newer text containing a more updated presentation.

Before spending time and money acquiring a new book, begin your study program with the *Wiley CPAexcel Exam Review: Auditing and Attestation* to determine your need for a supplemental text.

Ordering Other Textual Materials

If you want to order AICPA materials, locate an AICPA educator member to order your materials, since educator members are entitled to a discount and may place website or telephone orders.

AICPA (CPA2Biz)

Telephone: 888-777-7077

website: www.CPA2Biz.com

A variety of supplemental CPA products is available from John Wiley & Sons, Inc. By using a variety of learning techniques, such as software, computer-based learning, and audio CDs, the candidate is more likely to remain focused during the study process and to retain information for a longer period of time. Visit our website at **www.wiley.com/cpa** for other products, supplements, and updates.

Working CPA Questions

The AICPA content outlines, study outlines, etc., will be used to acquire and assimilate the knowledge tested on the examination. This, however, should be only **one-half** of your preparation program. The other half should be spent practicing how to work questions. Some candidates probably spend over 90% of their time reviewing material tested on the CPA exam. Much more time should be allocated to working previous examination questions. Working examination questions serves two functions. First, it helps you develop a solutions approach as well as solutions that will maximize your score. Second, it provides the best test of your knowledge of the material.

The multiple-choice questions and answer explanations can be used in many ways. First, they may be used as a diagnostic evaluation of your knowledge. For example, before beginning to review audit sampling you may wish to answer 10 to 15 multiple-choice questions to determine your ability to answer CPA examination questions on audit sampling. The apparent difficulty of the questions and the correctness of your answers will allow you to determine the necessary breadth and depth of your review. Additionally, exposure to examination questions prior to review and study of the material should provide motivation. You will develop a feel for your level of proficiency and an understanding of the scope and difficulty of past examination diagnostic multiple-choice questions. Moreover, your review materials will explain concepts encountered in the diagnostic multiple-choice questions.

Second, the multiple-choice questions can be used as a poststudy or postreview evaluation. You should attempt to understand all concepts mentioned (even in incorrect answers) as you answer the questions. Refer to the explanation of the answer for discussion of the alternatives even though you selected the correct response. Thus, you should read the explanation of the unofficial answer unless you completely understand the question and all of the alternative answers.

Third, you may wish to use the multiple-choice questions as a primary study vehicle. This is probably the quickest but least thorough approach in preparing for the exam. Make a sincere effort to understand the question and to select the correct response before referring to the unofficial answer and explanation. In many cases, the explanations will appear inadequate because of your lack of familiarity with the topic. Always refer back to an appropriate study source, such as the outlines and text in this volume, your auditing textbook, AICPA pronouncements, etc.

The multiple-choice questions outnumber the task-based simulations by greater than 10 to 1 in this book. This is similar to the content of the new computer-based examination. One problem with so many multiple-choice questions is that you may overemphasize them. Candidates generally prefer to work multiple-choice questions because they are

1. Shorter and less time-consuming
2. Solvable with less effort
3. Less frustrating than task-based simulations

Another problem with the large number of multiple-choice questions is that you may tend to become overly familiar with the questions. The result may be that you begin reading the facts and assumptions of previously studied questions into the questions on your examination. Guard against this potential problem by reading each multiple-choice question with **extra** care.

Beginning with the introduction of the computer-based examination, the AICPA began testing with simulations. Simulations released by the AICPA, prepared by the author, and revised from prior CPA exam problems are incorporated in the modules to which they pertain.

The questions and solutions in this volume provide you with an opportunity to diagnose and correct any exam-taking weaknesses prior to sitting for the examination. Continually analyze your incorrect solutions to determine the cause of the error(s) during your preparation for the exam. Treat each incorrect solution as a mistake that will not be repeated (especially on the examination). Also attempt to generalize your weaknesses so that you may change, reinforce, or develop new approaches to exam preparation and exam taking.

After you have reviewed for the Auditing and Attestation section of the exam, work the complete Auditing and Attestation Sample Examination provided in Appendix A.

SELF-STUDY PROGRAM

CPA candidates generally find it difficult to organize and to complete their own self-study programs. A major problem is determining **what** and **how** to study. Another major problem is developing the self-discipline to stick to a study program. Relatedly, it is often difficult for CPA candidates to determine how much to study (i.e., determining when they are sufficiently prepared).

The following suggestions will assist you in developing a **systematic, comprehensive,** and **successful** self-study program to help you complete the Auditing and Attestation exam. Remember that these are only suggestions. You should modify them to suit your personality, available study time, and other constraints. Some of the suggestions may appear trivial, but CPA candidates generally need all the assistance they can get to systemize their study programs.

Study Facilities and Available Time

Locate study facilities that will be conducive to concentrated study. Factors which you should consider include

1. Noise distraction
2. Interruptions
3. Lighting
4. Availability (e.g., a local library is not available at 5:00 a.m.)
5. Accessibility (e.g., your kitchen table vs. your local library)
6. Desk or table space

You will probably find different study facilities optimal for different times (e.g., your kitchen table during early morning hours and local libraries during early evening hours).

Next review your personal and professional commitments from now until the exam to determine regularly available study time. Formalize a schedule to which you can reasonably commit yourself. At the end of this chapter you will find a detailed approach to managing your time available for the exam preparation program.

Self-Evaluation

The *Wiley CPAexcel Exam Review: Auditing and Attestation* self-study program is partitioned into eight topics or modules. Since each module is clearly defined and should be studied separately, you have the task of preparing for the Auditing and Attestation exam by tackling eight manageable tasks. Partitioning the overall project into eight modules makes preparation psychologically easier, since you sense yourself completing one small step at a time rather than seemingly never completing one or a few large steps.

By completing the following "Preliminary Estimate of Your Present Knowledge of Subject" inventory, organized by the eight modules in this program, you will tabulate your strong and weak areas at the beginning of your study program. This will help you budget your limited study time. Note that you should begin studying the material in each module by answering up to 1/4 of the total multiple-choice questions covering that module's topics. See instruction 4.A. in the next section. This "mini-exam" should constitute a diagnostic evaluation as to the amount of review and study you need.

No.	PRELIMINARY ESTIMATE OF YOUR PRESENT KNOWLEDGE OF SUBJECT				
	Module	Proficient	Fairly Proficient	Generally Familiar	Not Familiar
1	Professional Responsibilities				
2	Engagement Planning and Assessing Risk				
3	Understanding Internal Control and Assessing Control Risk				
4	Responding to Risk Assessment				
5	Reporting				
6	Accounting and Review Services				
7	Audit Sampling				
8	Auditing with Technology				

Time Allocation

The study program below entails an average of 75 hours (Step 5. below) of study time. The breakdown of total hours is indicated in the left margin.

[2 1/2 hrs.]	1.	Study Chapters 2–4 in this volume. These chapters are essential to your efficient preparation program. (Time estimate includes candidate's review of the examples of the solutions approach in Chapters 2 and 3.)
[1/2 hr.]	2.	Begin by studying the introductory material at the beginning of Chapter 5.
	3.	Study one module at a time. The modules are listed above in the self-evaluation section.
	4.	For each module:
[8 hrs.]	A.	First, review the listing of key terms at the end of the module. Then work 1/4 of the multiple-choice questions (e.g., if there are 40 multiple-choice questions in a module, you should work every 4th question). Score yourself. This diagnostic routine will provide you with an index of your proficiency and familiarity with the type and difficulty of questions. Time estimate: 3 minutes each, not to exceed 1 hour total.
[33 hrs.]	B.	Study the outlines and illustrations. Where necessary, refer to your auditing textbook and original authoritative pronouncements (this will occur more frequently for topics in which you have a weak background). The outlines for each module are broken into smaller sections that refer you to multiple choice questions to test your comprehension of the material. You may find this organization useful in breaking your study into smaller bites. Time estimate: 3 hours minimum per module with more time devoted to topics less familiar to you.
[16 hrs.]	C.	Work the remaining multiple-choice questions. Study the explanations of the multiple-choice questions you missed or had trouble answering. Time estimate: 3 minutes to answer each question and 2 minutes to study the answer explanation of each question missed.
[8 hrs.]	D.	Work at least 12 task-based simulations. Work additional problems as time permits. Time estimate: 10–15 minutes for each simulation and 10 minutes to review the answer for each problem worked.

[7 hrs.]	E. Work through the sample CPA examination presented at the end of this text. The exam should be taken in one sitting.
	
	     Take the examination under simulated exam conditions (i.e., in a strange place with other people present [your local municipal library or a computer lab]). Apply your solutions approach to each question and your exam strategy to the overall exam.
	
	     You should limit yourself to the time that you will have when taking the actual CPA exam section (4 hours for the Auditing and Attestation section). Spend time afterwards grading your work and reviewing your effort.
	
	Time estimate: To take the exam and review it later, approximately 7 hours.

	5. The total suggested time of 75 hours is only an average. Allocation of time will vary candidate by candidate. Time requirements vary due to the diverse backgrounds and abilities of CPA candidates. Allocate your time so you gain the most proficiency in the least time. Remember that while 75 hours will be required, you should break the overall project down into 6 or more manageable tasks. Do not study more than one module during each study session.

Using Notecards

Below are one candidate's notecards on Auditing and Attestation topics which illustrate how key definitions, formulas, lists, etc. can be summarized on index cards for quick review. Since candidates can take these anywhere they go, they are a very efficient review tool.

Auditability *Refers to auditor's ability to audit.* *Requires:* 1. *Adequate accounting records* 2. *Permission from client to understand internal control process* 3. *Management Integrity*	*Variable Sampling* | *Increases in*	*Effect on sample size*
Risk—incorrect acceptance	*D*
Risk—incorrect rejection	*D*
Tolerable misstatement	*D*
Expected population misstatement	*I*
Population size and variability	*I*	

Level of Proficiency Required

What level of proficiency must you develop with respect to each of the topics to pass the exam? You should work toward a minimum correct rate on the multiple-choice questions of 80%. Working toward a correct rate of 80% or higher will give you a margin.

    Warning: Disproportional study time devoted to multiple-choice questions (relative to simulations) can be disastrous on the exam. You should work a substantial number of task-based simulations under simulated exam conditions, even though multiple-choice questions are easier to work and are used to gauge your proficiency. The authors believe that practicing simulations will also improve your proficiency on the multiple-choice questions.

Multiple-Choice Feedback

One of the benefits of working through previous exam questions is that it helps you to identify your weak areas. Once you have graded your answers, your strong areas and weak areas should be clearly evident. Yet, the important point here is that you should not stop at a simple percentage evaluation. The percentage only provides general feedback about your knowledge of the material contained within that particular module. The percentage **does not** give you any specific feedback regarding the concepts which were tested. In order to get this feedback, you should look at the questions missed on an individual basis because this will help you gain a better understanding of **why** you missed the question.

    This feedback process has been facilitated by the fact that within each module where the multiple-choice answer key appears, two blank lines have been inserted next to the multiple-choice answers. As you grade the multiple-choice questions, mark those questions which you have missed. However, instead of just marking the questions right and wrong, you should now focus on marking the questions in a manner which identifies **why** you missed the question. As an example, a candidate could mark the questions in the following manner: ✓ for math mistakes, x for conceptual mistakes, and ? for areas which the candidate was unfamiliar with. The candidate should then correct these mistakes by reworking through the marked questions.

The objective of this marking technique is to help you identify your weak areas and thus, the concepts which you should be focusing on. While it is still important for you to get 80% correct when working multiple-choice questions, it is more important for you to understand the concepts. This understanding applies to both the questions answered correctly and those answered incorrectly. Remember, questions on the CPA exam will be different from the questions in the book; however, the concepts will be the same. Therefore, your preparation should focus on understanding concepts, not just getting the correct answer.

Conditional Candidates

If you have received conditional status on the examination, you must concentrate on the remaining section(s). Unfortunately, many candidates do not study after conditioning the exam, relying on luck to get them through the remaining section(s). Conditional candidates will find that material contained in Chapters 1–4 and the information contained in the appropriate modules will benefit them in preparing for the remaining section(s) of the examination.

PLANNING FOR THE EXAMINATION

Overall Strategy

An overriding concern should be an orderly, systematic approach toward both your preparation program and your examination strategy. A major objective should be to avoid any surprises or anything else that would rattle you during the examination. In other words, you want to be in complete control as much as possible. Control is of paramount importance from both positive and negative viewpoints. The presence of control on your part will add to your confidence and your ability to prepare for and take the exam. Moreover, the presence of control will make your preparation program more enjoyable (or at least less distasteful). On the other hand, a lack of organization will result in inefficiency in preparing and taking the examination, with a highly predictable outcome. Likewise, distractions during the examination (e.g., inadequate lodging, long drive) are generally disastrous.

In summary, establishing a systematic, orderly approach to taking the examination is of paramount importance. Follow these six steps:

1. Develop an overall strategy at the beginning of your preparation program (see below).
2. Supplement your overall strategy with outlines of material tested on the Auditing and Attestation section.
3. Supplement your overall strategy with an explicitly stated set of question and problem-solving procedures—the solutions approach.
4. Supplement your overall strategy with an explicitly stated approach to each examination session (see Chapter 4).
5. Evaluate your preparation progress on a regular basis and prepare lists of things "to do" (see Weekly Review of Preparation Program Progress below).
6. RELAX: You can pass the exam. About 40–45% of the candidates taking a section of the CPA examination pass. But if you take out the individuals that did not adequately prepare, these percentages increase substantially. You will be one of those who pass if you complete an efficient preparation program and execute well (i.e., solutions approach and exam strategy) while taking the exam.

The following outline is designed to provide you with a general framework of the tasks before you. You should tailor the outline to your needs by adding specific items and comments.

A. Preparation Program (refer to Self-Study Program discussed previously)

1. Obtain and organize study materials.
2. Locate facilities conducive for studying and block out study time.
3. Develop your solutions approach (including solving task-based simulations and multiple-choice questions).
4. Prepare an examination strategy.
5. Study the material tested recently and prepare answers to actual exam questions on these topics under examination conditions.
6. Periodically evaluate your progress.

B. Physical Arrangements

1. Apply to and obtain acceptance from your state board.
2. Schedule your testing location and time.

C. Taking the Examination (covered in detail in Chapter 4)

1. Become familiar with location of the testing center and procedures.
2. Implement examination strategies and the solutions approach.

Weekly Review of Preparation Program Progress

The following pages contain a hypothetical weekly review of program progress. You should prepare a similar progress chart. This procedure, taking only 5 minutes per week, will help you proceed through a more efficient, complete preparation program.

Make notes of materials and topics

1. That you have studied
2. That you have completed
3. That need additional study

Weeks to go	Comments on progress, "to do" items, etc.
10	1) Read chapters 1 - 4 2) Applied solutions approach to Multiple-Choice Questions and Task-Based Simulations on a sample basis 3) Read Professional Responsibility Mod
9	1) Read Engagement Planning and Assessing Risk Mod 2) Completed MC and Task-Based Simulations for Engagement Planning and Assessing Risk
8	1) Read Internal Control Mod 2) Completed MC and Task-Based Simulations for Internal Control
7	1) Refined solutions approach to Engagement Planning and Internal Control Task-Based Simulations 2) Read Responding to Risk Assessment Mod
6	1) Continued Responding to Risk Assessment Mod 2) Completed MC Questions and Task-Based Simulations in Responding to Risk Mod 3) Prepared Audit programs for receivables and payroll cycles 4) Contrasted Internal Control and Responding to Risk Assessment Mod
5	1) Read Reporting Mod 2) Prepared a standard unqualified report from memory 3) Completed MC questions, and Task-Based Simulations for Reporting Mod 4) Reviewed Engagement Planning, Internal Control, and Responding to Risk Assessment Mods
4	1) Finished Reporting Mod 2) Memorized outlines for report modifications and formats 3) Read Accounting and Review Services Mod 4) Completed MC and Task-Based Simulations in Accounting and Review Services
3	1) Read Audit Sampling Mod 2) Completed MC and Task-Based Simulations in Audit Sampling 3) Reviewed Professional Responsibilities Mod
2	1) Read Auditing with Technology Mod 2) Completed MC and Task-Based Simulations in Auditing with Technology 3) Reviewed SAS and SSARS 4) Reviewed all Mods
1	1) Reviewed all audit reports 2) Reviewed MC Questions for all Mods
0	1) Completed and graded sample exam 2) Reviewed all Mods, especially Reporting

Time Management of Your Preparation

As you begin your CPA exam preparation, you obviously realize that there is a large amount of material to cover over the course of the next two to three months. Therefore, it is very important for you to organize your calendar, and maybe even your daily routine, so that you can allocate sufficient time to studying. An organized approach to your preparation is much more effective than a last week cram session. An organized approach also builds up the confidence necessary to succeed on the CPA exam.

An approach which we have already suggested, is to develop weekly "to do" lists. This technique helps you to establish intermediate objectives and goals as you progress through your study plan. You can then focus your efforts on small tasks and not feel overwhelmed by the entire process. And as you accomplish these tasks you will see yourself moving one step closer to realizing the overall goal, succeeding on the CPA exam.

Note, however, that the underlying assumption of this approach is that you have found the time during the week to study and thus accomplish the different tasks. Although this is an obvious step, it is still a very important step. Your exam preparation should be of a continuous nature and not one that jumps around the calendar. Therefore, you should strive to find available study time within your daily schedule, which can be utilized on a consistent basis. For example, everyone has certain hours of the day which are already committed for activities such as jobs, classes, and, of course, sleep. There is also going to be the time you spend relaxing because CPA candidates should try to maintain some balance in their lives. Sometimes too much studying can be counterproductive. But there will be some time available to you for studying and working through the questions. Block off this available time and use it only for exam prep. Use the time to accomplish your weekly tasks and to keep yourself committed to the process. After a while your preparation will develop into a habit and the preparation will not seem as overwhelming as it once did.

NOW IS THE TIME TO MAKE YOUR COMMITMENT

Chapter 2: Examination Grading

All State Boards of Accountancy use the AICPA advisory grading service. As your grade is to be determined by this process, it is very important that you understand the AICPA grading process and its *implications for your preparation program and for the solution techniques you will use during the examination.*

The AICPA has a full-time staff of CPA examination personnel under the supervision of the AICPA Board of Examiners, which has responsibility for the CPA examination.

This chapter contains a description of the AICPA grading process including a determination of the passing standard.

Setting the Passing Standard of the Uniform CPA Examination

As a part of the development of any licensing process, the passing score on the licensing examination must be established. This passing score must be set to distinguish candidates who are qualified to practice from those who are not. After conducting a number of studies of methods to determine passing scores, the Board of Examiners decided to use candidate-centered methods to set passing scores for the computer-based Uniform CPA Examination. In candidate-centered methods, the focus is on looking at actual candidate answers and making judgments about which sets of answers represent the answers of qualified entry-level CPAs. To make these determinations, the AICPA convened panels of CPAs to examine candidate responses and set the passing scores for multiple-choice questions and simulations. The data from these panels provide the basis for the development of question and problem points (relative weightings). *A passing score on the computer-based examination is 75%.*

Grading the Examination

All of the responses on the Auditing and Attestation section of the computer-based CPA examination are objective in nature. Obviously, this includes the responses to the multiple-choice questions. However, it also includes the responses to the requirements of simulations. Requirements of simulations include responses involving check boxes, entries into spreadsheets, form completion, graphical responses, and drag and drop. All of these responses are computer graded. Therefore, no consideration is given to any comments or explanations outside of the structured responses.

Multiple-Choice Grading

Auditing and Attestation exams contain three multiple-choice testlets of 30 questions each. **A few of these questions will be pretest questions that will not be considered in the candidate's score, but there is no way of identifying those questions that are being pretested.** Also, the possible score on a question and on a testlet will vary based on the difficulty of the questions. The makeup of the second testlet provided to a candidate will be determined based upon the candidate's performance on the first testlet, and the makeup of the third testlet will be determined by the candidate's peformance on the first two testlets. Therefore, you should not be discouraged if you a get a difficult set of questions; it may merely mean that you performed very well on the previous testlet(s). Also, you will receive more raw points for hard and medium questions than for easy questions.

Your answers to the multiple-choice questions are graded by the computer. Your grade is based on the total number of correct answers weighted by their difficulty, and with no penalty for incorrect answers. As mentioned earlier, 5 of the multiple-choice questions are pretest items that are not included in the candidate's grade.

Tasked-Based Simulation Grading

As indicated previously, all of the responses to the simulations will be computer graded. They will typically involve checking a box, selecting a response from a list, or dragging and dropping an answer.

Requesting a Score Review

For an additional fee, you may request a score review. A score review is a verification of your score making certain that the approved answer key was used. Because the AICPA grades your exam at least twice as a part of its normal process, it is unlikely that you will get an adjustment to your score. You should contact the applicable board of accoutancy to request a score review.

NOW IS THE TIME TO MAKE YOUR COMMITMENT

Chapter 3: Solutions Approach

The solutions approach is a systematic problem-solving methodology. The purpose is to assure efficient, complete solutions to CPA exam questions, some of which are complex and confusing relative to most undergraduate accounting questions. This is especially true with regard to the new simulation type problems. Unfortunately, there appears to be a widespread lack of emphasis on problem-solving techniques in accounting courses. Most accounting books and courses merely provide solutions to specific types of problems. Memorization of these solutions for examinations and preparation of homework problems from examples is "cookbooking." "Cookbooking" is perhaps a necessary step in the learning process, but it is certainly not sufficient training for the complexities of the business world. Professional accountants need to be adaptive to a rapidly changing complex environment. For example, CPAs have been called on to interpret and issue reports on new concepts such as price controls, energy allocations, and new taxes. These CPAs rely on their problem-solving expertise to understand these problems and to formulate solutions to them.

The steps outlined below are only one of many possible series of solution steps. Admittedly, the procedures suggested are *very* structured; thus, you should adapt the suggestions to your needs. You may find that some steps are occasionally unnecessary, or that certain additional procedures increase your own problem-solving efficiency. Whatever the case, sustantial time should be allocated to developing an efficient solutions approach before taking the examination. You should develop your solutions approach by working questions and problems.

Note that the steps below relate to any specific question or simulation; overall examination or section strategies are discussed in Chapter 4. Remember, the Auditing and Attestation exam will consist of 3 multiple-choice testlets containing 30 questions each, and 1 simulation testlet consisting of 7 task-based simulations.

Multiple-Choice Screen Layout

The following is a computer screenshot that illustrates the manner in which multiple-choice questions will be presented:

As indicated previously, multiple-choice questions will be presented in three individual testlets of 30 questions each. Characteristics of the computerized testlets of multiple-choice questions include the following:

1. You may move freely within a particular testlet from one question to the next or back to previous questions until you click the "Exit" button. Once you have indicated that you have finished the testlet by clicking on the "Exit" button and reconfirmed, you can never return to that set of questions.
2. A button on the screen will allow you to "flag" a question for review if you wish to come back to it later.
3. A four-function computer calculator with an electronic tape is available as a tool.
4. The time remaining for the entire exam section is shown on the screen.
5. The questions will be shown at the bottom of the screen. You may navigate between questions by simply clicking on the question number.
6. The "Help" button will provide you with help in navigating and completing the testlet.

The screenshot above was obtained from the AICPA's sample exam at www.cpa-exam.org. Candidates are urged to complete the tutorial and other example questions on the AICPA's website to obtain additional experience with the computer-based testing.

Multiple-Choice Question Solutions Approach

1. **Work individual questions in order.**

   a. If a question appears lengthy or difficult, skip it until you can determine that extra time is available. Mark it for review to remind you to return to a question that you have skipped or need to review.

2. **Read the stem of the question without looking at the answers.**

   a. The answers are sometimes misleading and may cause you to misread or misinterpret the question.

3. **Read each question *carefully* to determine the topical area.**

   a. Study the requirements *first* so you know which data are important.
   b. Note keywords and important data.
   c. Identify pertinent information.
   d. Be especially careful to note when the requirement is an **exception** (e.g., "Which of the following is not a characteristic of variables sampling?").
   e. If a set of data is the basis for two or more questions, read the requirements of each of the questions first before beginning to work the first question (sometimes it is more efficient to work the questions out of order).
   f. Be alert to read questions as they are, not as you would like them to be. You may encounter a familiar looking item; do not jump to the conclusion that you know what the answer is without reading the question completely.

4. **Anticipate the answer before looking at the alternative answers.**

   a. Recall the applicable principle (e.g., circumstances requiring a consistency exception in the audit report).

5. **Read the answers and select the *best* alternative.**
6. **Click on the correct answer (or your educated guess).**
7. **After completing all of the questions including the ones flagged for review, click on the "Exit" button to close out the testlet. Remember once you have closed out the testlet you can never return to it.**

Multiple-Choice Question Solutions Approach Example

A good example of the multiple-choice question solutions approach follows.

Step 3:

Topical area? Auditor's assessment of control risk

Step 4:

Principle? Assessing control risk at below the maximum means that the auditor believes the particular controls are effective

Step 5:

    a. Incorrect—Would do if control risk at high level
    b. **Correct**—Which controls are relevant to FS
    c. Incorrect—Would do if control risk at high level
    d. Incorrect—Auditor does not control inherent risk

13. <u>Assessing control risk at a low level most likely would involve</u>

    a. Changing the timing of substantive tests by omitting the interim-date testing and performing the tests at year-end.
    b. Identifying specific internal control policies and procedures *relevant to* specific assertions.
    c. Performing more extensive substantive tests with larger sample sizes than originally planned.
    d. Reducing inherent risk for most of the assertions relevant to significant account balances.

Currently, all multiple-choice questions are scored based on the number correct, weighted by a difficulty rating (i.e., there is no penalty for guessing). The rationale is that a "good guess" indicates knowledge. Thus, you should answer all multiple-choice questions.

Task-Based Simulations

Simulations are case-based problems designed to

- Test integrated knowledge
- More closely replicate real-world problems
- Assess research and other skills

Any of the following types of responses might be required on task-based simulations:

- Drop-down selection
- Numeric and monetary inputs
- Formula answers
- Check box response
- Enter spreadsheet formulas
- Research results

The screenshot below illustrates a simulation that requires the candidate to select an answer from a drop-down list.

To complete the simulations, candidates are provided with a number of tools, including

- A four-function computer calculator with an electronic tape
- Scratch spreadsheet
- The ability to split windows horizontally or vertically to show two tabs on the screen (e.g., you can examine the situation tab in one window and a particular requirement in a second window)
- Access to professional literature databases to answer research requirements
- Copy and paste functions

In addition, the resource tab provides other resources that may be needed to complete the problem. For example, a resource tab might contain formulas for common ratios for answering an analytical procedures problem.

A window on the screen shows the time remaining for the entire exam and the "Help" button provides instructions for navigating the simulation and completing the requirements.

The AICPA has introduced a new simulation interface which is illustrated in this book. You are urged to complete the tutorial and other sample tests that are on the AICPA's website (www.cpa-exam.org) to obtain additional experience with the interface and computer-based testing.

Task-Based Simulations Solutions Approach

The following solutions approach is suggested for answering simulations:

1. **Review the entire background and problem.** Get a feel for the topical area and related concepts that are being tested. Even though the format of the question may vary, the exam continues to test your understanding of applicable principles or concepts. Relax, take a deep breath, and determine your strategy for conquering the simulation.
2. **Identify the requirements of the simulation.** This step will help you focus in more quickly on the solution(s) without wasting time reading irrelevant material.
3. **Study the items to be answered.** As you do this and become familiar with the topical area being tested, you should review the concepts of that area. This will help you organize your thoughts so that you can relate logically the requirements of the simulation with the applicable concepts.
4. **Use the scratch paper (which will be provided) and the spreadsheet and calculator tools to assist you in answering the simulation.**

The screenshots below explain how the spreadsheet operates.

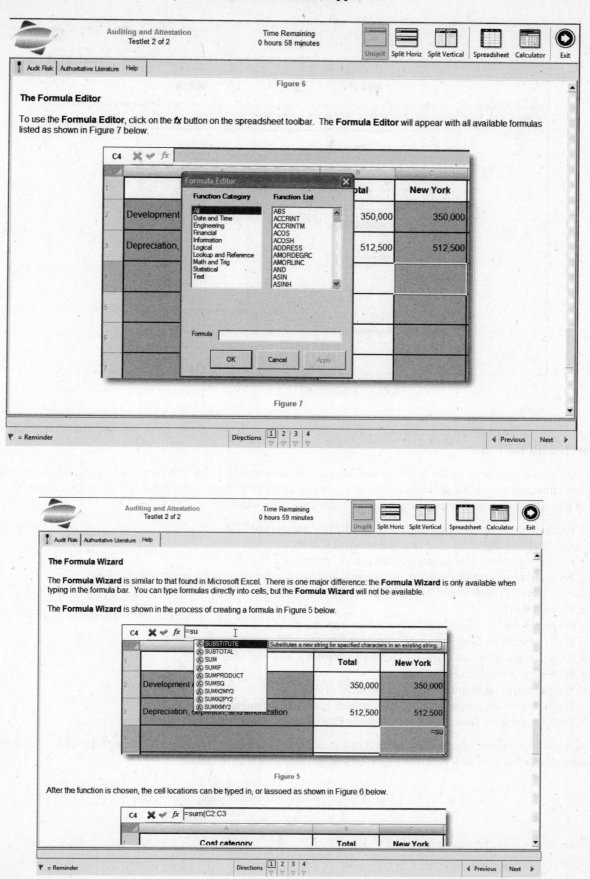

Figure 6

The Formula Editor

To use the **Formula Editor**, click on the *fx* button on the spreadsheet toolbar. The **Formula Editor** will appear with all available formulas listed as shown in Figure 7 below.

Figure 7

The Formula Wizard

The **Formula Wizard** is similar to that found in Microsoft Excel. There is one major difference: the **Formula Wizard** is only available when typing in the formula bar. You can type formulas directly into cells, but the **Formula Wizard** will not be available.

The **Formula Wizard** is shown in the process of creating a formula in Figure 5 below.

Figure 5

After the function is chosen, the cell locations can be typed in, or lassoed as shown in Figure 6 below.

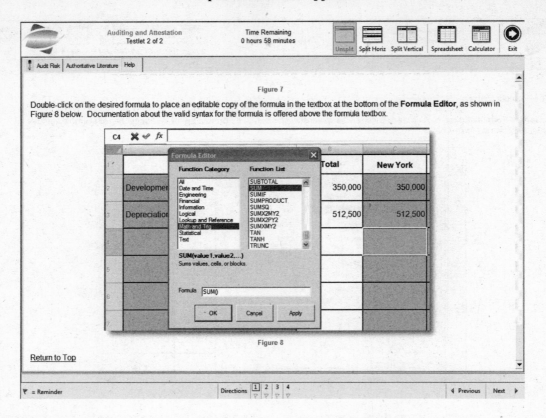

Research Simulations

One of the seven simulations on the Auditing and Attestation exam will be a research simulation. Research simulations require candidates to search the professional literature in electronic format and input the reference to the results. For the Auditing and Attestation exam the professional literature database includes

- AICPA Statements on Auditing Standards and Interpretations (AU-C)
- PCAOB Auditing Standards and Interpretations (PCAOB)
- AICPA Statements on Attestation Standards and Interpretations (AT)
- AICPA Statements on Standards for Accounting and Review Services and Interpretations (AR)
- AICPA Code of Professional Conduct (ET)
- AICPA Bylaws (BL)
- AICPA Statements on Standards for Valuation Services (VS)
- AICPA Statement on Standards for Consulting Services (CS)
- AICPA Statements on Standards for Quality Control (QC)
- AICPA Peer Review Standards (PR)
- AICPA Statement on Standards for Tax Services (TS)
- AICPA Statement on Responsibilities in Personal Financial Planning Practice (PFP)
- AICPA Statement on Standards for Continuing Professional Education Programs (CPE)

Shown below is a screenshot of a task-based research simulation for the Regulation section of the CPA examination. This screenshot is from the new research interface that was implemented in 2011.

The professional literature may be searched using the table of contents, a keyword search, or an advanced search. *If you use the search function, you must spell the term or terms correctly.* In using the table of contents, you simply click on the applicable standards and it expands to the next level of detail. By continuing to drill down you will get the topic or professional standard that provides the solution to the requirement.

The screenshot below illustrates the advanced search function.

Once you have found the correct passage in the literature, you must input the citation in the answer box. To facilitate this process you should use the split screen function to view the literature in one screen and the answer box in the other as shown below.

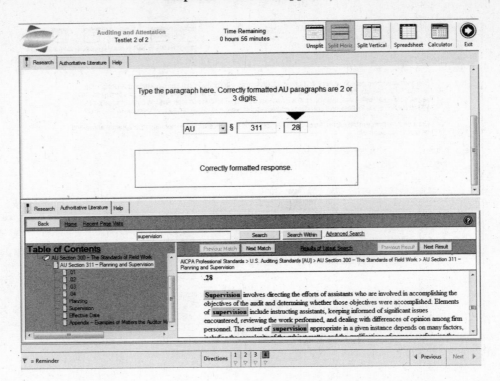

If possible, it is important to get experience using the AICPA Resource: Accounting and Auditing to sharpen your skills. In addition, CPA candidates can get a free six-month subscription to the online package of professional literature used in the computerized CPA examination. Other students and recent graduates may subscribe at a special price. Subscriptions are available at www.cpa-exam.org. If that is not available, you should use the printed copy of the professional standards to answer the simulation problems in the book.

Chapter 5 of this book contains guidance on how to perform research on the AICPA Professional Standards database.

Time Requirements for the Solutions Approach

Many candidates bypass the solutions approach, because they feel it is too time-consuming. Actually, the solutions approach is a time-saver and, more importantly, it helps you prepare better solutions to all questions and simulations.

Without committing yourself to using the solutions approach, try it step-by-step on several questions and simulations. After you conscientiously go through the step-by-step routine a few times, you will begin to adopt and modify aspects of the technique which will benefit you. Subsequent usage will become subconscious and painless. The important point is that you must try the solutions approach several times to accrue any benefits.

In summary, the solutions approach may appear foreign and somewhat cumbersome. At the same time, if you have worked through the material in this chapter, you should have some appreciation for it. Develop the solutions approach by writing down the steps in the solutions approach at the beginning of this chapter, and keep them before you as you work CPA exam questions and problems. Remember that even though the suggested procedures appear *very structured* and *time-consuming*, integration of these procedures into your own style of problem solving will help improve *your* solutions approach. The next chapter discusses strategies for the overall examination.

NOW IS THE TIME TO MAKE YOUR COMMITMENT

Chapter 4: Taking the Examination

This chapter is concerned with developing an examination strategy (e.g., how to cope with the environment at the test center, time management, etc.).

EXAMINATION STRATEGIES

Your performance during the examination is final and not subject to revision. While you may sit for the examination again if you are unsuccessful, the majority of your preparation will have to be repeated, requiring substantial, additional amounts of time. Thus, examination strategies (discussed in this chapter) that maximize your exam-taking efficiency are very important.

Getting "Psyched Up"

The CPA exam is quite challenging and worthy of your best effort. Explicitly develop your own psychological strategy to get yourself "up" for the exam. Pace your study program such that you will be able to operate at peak performance when you are actually taking the exam. A significant advantage of the computerized exam is that if you have scheduled early in a testing window and do not feel well, you can reschedule your sitting. However, once you start the exam, you cannot retake it in the same testing window, so do not leave the exam early. Do the best you can.

Lodging, Meals, Exercise

If you must travel to the test center, make advance reservations for comfortable lodging convenient to the test center. Do not stay with friends, relatives, etc. Both uninterrupted sleep and total concentration on the exam are a must. Consider the following in making your lodging plans:

1. Proximity to the test center
2. Availability of meals and snacks
3. Recreational facilities

Plan your meal schedule to provide maximum energy and alertness during the day and maximum rest at night. Do not experiment with new foods, drinks, etc., around your scheduled date. Within reasonable limits, observe your normal eating and drinking habits. Recognize that overconsumption of coffee during the exam could lead to a hyperactive state and disaster. Likewise, overindulgence in alcohol to overcome nervousness and to induce sleep the night before might contribute to other difficulties the following morning.

Tenseness should be expected before and during the examination. Rely on a regular exercise program to unwind at the end of the day. As you select your lodging for the examination, try to accommodate your exercise pleasure (e.g., running, swimming etc.).

To relieve tension or stress while studying, try breathing or stretching exercises. Use these exercises before and during the examination to start and to keep your adrenaline flowing. Remain determined not to have to sit for the section another time.

In summary, the examination is likely to be both rigorous and fatiguing. Expect it and prepare for it by getting in shape, planning methods of relaxation during the exam and in the evening before, and finally, building the confidence and competence to complete the exam (successfully).

Test Center and Procedures

If possible, visit the test center before the examination to assure knowledge of the location. Remember: no surprises. Having a general familiarity with the facilities will lessen anxiety prior to the examination. Talking to a recent veteran of the examination will give you background for the general examination procedures. **You must arrive at the testing center 30 minutes before your scheduled time.**

Upon completion of check-in at the test location, the candidate

- Is seated at a designated workstation
- Begins the exam after proctor launches the session
- Is monitored by a Test Center Administrator
- Is videotaped

If you have any remaining questions regarding examination procedure, call or write your state board or go to Prometric's website at www.prometric.com.

Allocation of Time

Budget your time. Time should be carefully allocated in an attempt to maximize points per minute. While you must develop your own strategy with respect to time allocation, some suggestions may be useful. Allocate 5 minutes to reading the instructions. When you begin the exam you will be given an inventory of the total number of testlets and simulations, including the suggested times. Budget your time based on this inventory.

Plan on spending 1½ minutes working each of the individual multiple-choice questions. The time allocated to the simulations will vary. Plan on spending 1½ to 1¾ hours on the simulations testlet of the exam.

Techniques for Time Management

The Auditing and Attestation section contains three testlets of multiple-choice questions with 30 questions each. As you complete each testlet keep track of how you performed in relation to the AICPA suggested time. The Auditing and Attestation section will also have one testlet of 7 task-based simulations. After you finish the multiple-choice testlets, budget your time for the simulations based on your remaining time and the AICPA suggested times. Remember that you alone control your progress towards successfully completing this exam.

Examination Rules

1. Prior to the start of the examination, you will be required to accept a *Confidentiality and Break Policy Statement.*
2. You must not bring any personal/unauthorized items into the testing room. Such items include but are not limited to outerwear, hats, food, drinks, purses, briefcases, notebooks, pagers, watches, cellular telephones, recording devices, and photographic equipment. You will be asked to empty and turn your pockets inside out prior to every entry into the test room to confirm that you have no prohibited items. Lockers are provided for storage of personal items.
3. Breaks may be taken at any time between testlets. **However, your exam time continues to run while you take the break.**
4. If you need access to an item stored in the test center during a break such as food or medicine, you must inform the Test Center Administrator before you retrieve the item. You are not allowed to access a prohibited item.
5. Any reference during the examination to books or other materials or the exchange of information with other persons shall be considered misconduct sufficient to bar you from further participation in the examination.
6. Penalties will be imposed on any candidate who is caught cheating before, during, or after the examination. These penalties may include expulsion from the examination, denial of applications for future examinations, and civil or criminal penalties.
7. You may not leave the examination room with any notes about the examination.

Refer to the brochure *Information for Uniform CPA Examination Candidates* for other rules.

CPA EXAM CHECKLIST

One week before you are scheduled to sit

___ 1. Reread outlines (your own or those in this volume) of most important SAS, underlining buzzwords.
___ 2. If time permits, work through a few questions in your weakest areas so that techniques/concepts are fresh in your mind.
___ 3. Assemble notecards and key outlines of major topical areas into a manageable "last review" notebook to be taken with you to the exam.

What to bring

___ 1. **Notice to Schedule (NTS)**—You must bring the proper NTS with you.

___ 2. **Identification**—Bring two valid forms of ID. One must be government issued. The name on the ID must match exactly the name on the NTS. The CPA Candidate bulletin lists valid primary and secondary IDs.

___ 3. **Hotel confirmation**—(if you must travel).

___ 4. **Cash**—Payment for anything by personal check is rarely accepted.

___ 5. **Major credit card**—American Express, Master Card, Visa, etc.

___ 6. **Alarm clock**—This is too important an event to trust to a hotel wake-up call that might be overlooked.

___ 7. **Clothing**—Should be comfortable and layered to suit the possible temperature range in the testing room.

___ 8. **Earplugs**—Even though examinations are being given, there may be constant activity in the testing room (e.g., people walking around, rustling of paper, clicking of keyboards, people coughing, etc.). The use of earplugs may block out some of this distraction and help you concentrate better.

___ 9. **Other**—Any "last review" materials.

Evenings before exams

1. Reviewing the evening before the exam could earn you the extra points needed to pass a section. Just keep this last-minute effort in perspective and do **not** panic yourself into staying up all night trying to cover every possible point. This could lead to disaster by sapping your body of the endurance needed to attack questions creatively during the next day.

2. Reread key outlines or notecards, reviewing important topics in which you feel deficient.

3. Go over mnemonics and acronyms you have developed as study aids. Test yourself by writing out the letters on paper while verbally giving a brief explanation of what the letters stand for.

4. Reread key outlines of important SAS.

5. **Set your alarm and get a good night's rest!** Being well rested will permit you to meet each day's challenge with a fresh burst of creative energy. You must arrive 30 minutes before your scheduled time.

Exam-taking strategy

1. Review the AICPA suggested times for the testlets to plan your time allocation during the exam.

2. Do not spend an excess amount of time on the introductory screens. If you take longer than 10 minutes on these screens, the test session will automatically terminate. If the exam session terminates, it will not be possible to restart the examination and you will have to reapply to take the section.

3. Report equipment/software issues to the test center staff immediately. Do not attempt to correct the problem yourself and do not use examination time thinking about it before reporting it. Remind the test center staff to file a report describing the problem. The test center staff should be able to handle any equipment or software problems. However, if you believe the problem was not handled appropriately, contact NASBA at candidatecare@nasba.org.

4. Report any concerns about test questions to test center staff after you have completed the session. The members of the test center staff know nothing about the CPA Examination content. The test center staff can report the issues to the AICPA. You should also report concerns about the questions in writing to the AICPA (fax to [609] 671-2922). If possible, the question and testlet numbers should be included in the fax.

5. In the event of a power outage or incident requiring a restart, the computer clock will stop and you will not lose examination time. Your responses up to the time of the restart will not be lost as responses are saved at frequent intervals throughout the examination.

6. If you have questions about the examination software functions (e.g., the transfer function), you should read the instructions and "help" tab information. The test center staff is not familiar with the functioning of the examination software and, therefore, will not be able to help you.

7. The crucial technique to use for multiple-choice questions is to read through each question stem **carefully,** noting keywords such as "audit risk," "management representation," "evidence," etc. Then **read each choice** carefully before you start eliminating inappropriate answers. Often the first or second answer may **sound** correct, but a later answer may be **more correct**! Be discriminating! Reread the question and choose the **best** answer.

8. If you are struggling with questions beyond a minute or two, use the strategy of dividing multiple-choice questions into two categories.

   a. Questions for which you **know** you lack knowledge to answer: Drawing from any responses you have, narrow answers down to as few as possible; then make an **educated guess**.

b. Questions for which you feel you should be getting the correct answer: Mark the question for review. Your mental block may clear, or you may spot a simple error in logic that will be corrected when you rereview the question.

9. Remember: **never** change a first impulse answer later unless you are absolutely certain you are right. It is a proven fact that your subconscious often guides you to the correct answer.

10. Begin the task-based simulations, carefully monitoring your time. Read the information and requirement tabs and organize your thoughts around the concepts, mnemonics, acronyms, and buzzwords that are responsive to the requirements. Constantly compare your progress with the time remaining. Fight the urge to **complete** one simulation at the expense of others.

11. Each test may include a simulation requirement or question for which you may feel unprepared. Accept the challenge and go after the points! Draw from all your resources. Ask yourself how professional standards would be applied to similar situations, scan the simulation questions for clues, look for relationships in **all** the available resources given in the problem, try "backing into" the questions from another angle, etc. Every simulation (no matter how impossible it may look at first glance) contains some points that are yours for the taking. Make your best effort. You may be on the right track and not even know it!

12. Constantly compare your progress with the time remaining. **Never** spend excessive amounts of time on one testlet or simulation.

13. The cardinal rule is **never,** but **never,** leave an answer blank.

After taking the examination

1. Retain the Confirmation of Attendance form issued after the examination because it provides valuable contact information.

2. Report any examination incident/concerns in writing, even if the issues were already reported to test center staff.

3. If you feel that the circumstances surrounding your test administration prevented you from performing at a level consistent with your knowledge and skills, immediately contact NASBA at candidatecare@nasba.org.

HAVE YOU MADE YOUR COMMITMENT?

Chapter 5: Exam Content Overview

The Auditing and Attestation section of the CPA exam tests the candidate's knowledge primarily of AICPA auditing standards and procedures as they relate to the CPA's functions in the examination of financial statements. However, the section also covers international auditing standards, accounting and review services, other attestation services, ethical standards issued by the AICPA, SEC, PCAOB, Department of Labor, and the GAO, and quality control standards. It also covers auditing standards for issuer (public) companies issued by the PCAOB and the Sarbanes-Oxley Act of 2002. You will increase your chances for success if you have a recent copy of the codification of the Statements on Auditing Standards, Statements on Standards for Accounting and Review Services, Statements on Standards for Attestation Engagements, Statements on Quality Control Standards, and the AICPA Code of Professional Conduct. The codified version, as opposed to the original pronouncements as issued, eliminates all superseded portions. The AICPA publishes the codification as the *AICPA Professional Standards*. Many university bookstores carry this source, as it is often required in undergraduate auditing courses. PCAOB standards are available on its website at www.pcaobus.org. An auditing textbook is also helpful.

This chapter reviews topics tested on the Auditing and Attestation section of the exam. Begin by performing a self-evaluation as suggested in the self-study program which appears in Chapter 1 of this volume. After studying each module in this volume, work all of the multiple-choice questions and task-based simulations.

Recognize that most candidates have difficulty with audit sampling and auditing with technology due to limited exposure in their undergraduate programs and in practice. Thus, you should work through the outlines presented in each study module and work the related questions.

The AICPA clarity standards recodify all of the existing auditing standards for nonpublic companies. These statements reorganized the auditing standards codification and accordingly affect research simulations that require identification of a particular requirement in the auditing standards.

AICPA CONTENT AND SKILLS SPECIFICATIONS

The AICPA Content and Skills Specifications for the Uniform CPA Exam set forth the coverage of topics on the Auditing and attestation exam. This outline was issued by the AICPA and is effective for exams beginning in 2014. The first part of the outline describes the topical coverage of the section, and the second part provides some insights into the skills tested on all sections of the Uniform CPA exam.

Content Specification Outlines (CSOs)

The Auditing and Attestation section tests knowledge and understanding of the following professional standards: Auditing standards promulgated in the United States of America (related to audits of an "Issuer" (a public company), a "Nonissuer" (an entity that is not a public company), governmental entities, not-for-profit entities, and employee benefit plans, standards related to attestation and assurance engagements, and standards for performing accounting and review services.

Candidates are expected to demonstrate an awareness of (1) the International Auditing and Assurance Standards Board (IAASB) and its role in establishing International Standards on Auditing (ISAs), (2) the differences between ISAs and US auditing standards, and (3) the audit requirements under US auditing standards that apply when they perform audit procedures on a US company that supports an audit report based upon the auditing standards of another country, or the ISAs.

This section also tests knowledge of professional responsibilities of certified public accountants, including ethics and independence.

Candidates are also expected to demonstrate an awareness of (1) the International Ethics Standards Board for Accountants (IESBA) and its role in establishing requirements of the International Federation of Accountants (IFAC) Code of Ethics for Professional Accountants, and (2) the independence requirements that apply when they perform audit procedures on a US company that supports an audit report based upon the auditing standards of another country, or the ISAs.

In addition to demonstrating knowledge and understanding of the professional standards, candidates are required to demonstrate the skills required to apply that knowledge in performing auditing and attestation tasks as certified public accountants. The outline below specifies the tasks and related knowledge in which candidates are required to demonstrate proficiency. Candidates are also expected to perform the following tasks:

- Demonstrate an awareness and understanding of the process by which standards and professional requirements are established for audit, attestation, and other services performed by CPAs, including the role of standard-setting bodies within the US and those bodies with the authority to promulgate international standards.

- Differentiate between audits, attestation and assurance services, compilations, and reviews.
- Differentiate between the professional standards for issuers and nonissuers.
- Identify situations that might be unethical or a violation of professional standards, perform research and consultations as appropriate, and determine the appropriate action.
- Recognize potentially unethical behavior of clients and determine the impact on the services being performed.
- Demonstrate the importance of identifying and adhering to requirements, rules, and standards that are established by licensing boards within their states, and which may place additional professional requirements specific to their state of practice.
- Appropriately apply professional requirements in practice, and differentiate between unconditional requirements and presumptively mandatory requirements.
- Exercise due care in the performance of work.
- Demonstrate an appropriate level of professional skepticism in the performance of work.
- Maintain independence in mental attitude in all matters relating to the audit.
- Research relevant professional literature.

The outline below specifies the knowledge in which candidates are required to demonstrate proficiency.

I. Auditing and Attestation: Engagement Acceptance and Understanding the Assignment (12%–16%)

A. Determine Nature and Scope of Engagement
B. Consider the Firm's Policies and Procedures Pertaining to Client Acceptance and Continuance
C. Communicate with the Predecessor Auditor
D. Establish an Understanding with the Client and Document the Understanding through an Engagement Letter or Other Written Communication with the Client
E. Consider Other Planning Matters

 1. Consider using the work of other independent auditors
 2. Determine the extent of the involvement of professionals possessing specialized skills
 3. Consider the independence, objectivity, and competency of the internal audit function

F. Identify Matters Related to Planning and Prepare Documentation for Communications with Those Charged with Governance

II. Auditing and Attestation: Understanding the Entity and Its Environment (Including Internal Control) (16%–20%)

A. Determine and Document Materiality
B. Conduct and Document Risk Assessment Discussions among Audit Team, Concurrently with Discussion on Susceptibility of the Entity's Financial Statement to Material Misstatement Due to Fraud
C. Consideration of Fraud

 1. Identify characteristics of fraud
 2. Document required discussions regarding risk of fraud
 3. Document inquiries of management about fraud
 4. Identify and assess risks that may result in material misstatements due to fraud

D. Perform and Document Risk Assessment Procedures

 1. Identify, conduct, and document appropriate inquiries of management and others within the entity
 2. Perform appropriate analytical procedures to understand the entity and identify areas of risk
 3. Obtain information to support inquiries through observation and inspection (including reading corporate minutes, etc.)

E. Consider Additional Aspects of the Entity and Its Environment, Including Industry, Regulatory, and Other External Factors; Strategies and Business Risks; Financial Performance
F. Consider Internal Control

 1. Perform procedures to assess the control environment, including consideration of the COSO framework and identifying entity-level controls
 2. Obtain and document an understanding of business processes and information flows
 3. Determine the effect of information technology on the effectiveness of an entity's internal control
 4. Perform risk assessment procedures to evaluate the design and implementation of internal controls relevant to an audit of financial statements
 5. Identify key risks associated with general controls in a financial IT environment, including change management, backup/recovery, and network access (e.g., administrative rights)
 6. Identify key risks associated with application functionality that supports financial transaction cycles, including application access control (e.g., administrative access rights); controls over interfaces, integrations, and e-commerce; significant algorithms, reports, validation, edit checks, error handling, etc.

7. Assess whether the entity has designed controls to mitigate key risks associated with general controls or application functionality
8. Identify controls relevant to reliable financial reporting and the period-end financial reporting process
9. Consider limitations of internal control
10. Consider the effects of service organizations on internal control
11. Consider the risk of management override of internal controls

G. Document an Understanding of the Entity and Its Environment, Including Each Component of the Entity's Internal Control, in Order to Assess Risks

H. Assess and Document the Risk of Material Misstatements

1. Identify and document financial statement assertions and formulate audit objectives including significant financial statement balances, classes of transactions, disclosures, and accounting estimates
2. Relate the identified risks to relevant assertions and consider whether the risks could result in a material misstatement to the financial statements
3. Assess and document the risk of material misstatement that relates to both financial statement level and specific assertions
4. Identify and document conditions and events that may indicate risks of material misstatement

I. Identify and Document Significant Risks That Require Special Audit Consideration

1. Significant recent economic, accounting, or other developments
2. Related parties and related party transactions
3. Improper revenue recognition
4. Nonroutine or complex transactions
5. Significant management estimates
6. Illegal acts

III. **Auditing and Attestation: Performing Audit Procedures and Evaluating Evidence (16%–20%)**

A. Develop Overall Responses to Risks

1. Develop overall responses to risks identified and use the risks of material misstatement to drive the nature, timing, and extent of further audit procedures
2. Document significant risks identified, related controls evaluated, and overall responses to address assessed risks
3. Determine and document performance materiality/level(s) of tolerable misstatement

B. Perform Audit Procedures Responsive to Risks of Material Misstatement; Obtain and Document Evidence to Form a Basis for Conclusions

1. Design and perform audit procedures whose nature, timing, and extent are responsive to the assessed risk of material misstatement
2. Integrating audits: in an integrated audit of internal control over financial reporting and the financial statements, design and perform testing of controls to accomplish the objectives of both audits simultaneously
3. Design, perform, and document tests of controls to evaluate design effectiveness
4. Design, perform, and document tests of controls to evaluate operating effectiveness
5. Perform substantive procedures
6. Perform audit sampling
7. Perform analytical procedures
8. Confirm balances and/or transactions with third parties
9. Examine inventories and other assets
10. Perform other tests of details, balances, and journal entries
11. Perform computer-assisted audit techniques (CAATs), including data query, extraction, and analysis
12. Perform audit procedures on significant accounting estimates
13. Auditing fair value measurements and disclosures, including the use of specialists in evaluating estimates
14. Perform tests on unusual year-end transactions
15. Audits performed in accordance with International Standards on Auditing (ISAs) or auditing standards of another country: determine if differences exist and whether additional audit procedures are required
16. Evaluate contingencies
17. Obtain and evaluate lawyers' letters
18. Review subsequent events
19. Obtaining and placing reliance on representations from management
20. Identify material weaknesses, significant deficiencies, and other control deficiencies

IV. **Auditing and Attestation: Evaluating Audit Findings, Communications, and Reporting (16%–20%)**

A. Perform Overall Analytical Procedures
B. Evaluate the Sufficiency and Appropriateness of Audit Evidence and Document Engagement Conclusions
C. Evaluate Whether Audit Documentation is in Accordance with Professional Standards
D. Review the Work Performed by Others, including Specialists and Other Auditors, to Provide Reasonable Assurance that Objectives are Achieved
E. Document the Summary of Uncorrected Misstatements and Related Conclusions

F. Evaluate Whether Financial Statements are Free of Material Misstatements

G. Consider the Entity's Ability to Continue as a Going Concern

H. Consider Other Information in Documents Containing Audited Financial Statements (e.g., Supplemental Information and Management's Discussion and Analysis)

I. Retain Audit Documentation as Required by Standards and Regulations

J. Prepare Communications

1. Reports on audited financial statements
2. Reports required by government auditing standards
3. Reports on compliance with laws and regulations
4. Reports on internal control
5. Reports on the processing of transactions by service organizations
6. Reports on agreed-upon procedures
7. Reports on financial forecasts and projections
8. Reports on pro forma financial information
9. Special reports
10. Reissue reports
11. Communicate internal control related matters identified in the audit
12. Communications with those charged with governance
13. Subsequent discovery of facts existing at the date of the auditor's report
14. Consideration after the report date of omitted procedures

V. Accounting and Review Services Engagements (12%–16%)

A. Plan the Engagement

1. Determine nature and scope of engagement
2. Decide whether to accept or continue the client and engagement including determining the appropriateness of the engagement to meet the client's needs and consideration of independence standards
3. Establish an understanding with the client and document the understanding through an engagement letter or other written communication with the client
4. Consider change in engagement
5. Determine if reports are to be used by third parties

B. Obtain and Document Evidence to Form a Basis for Conclusions

1. Obtain an understanding of the client's operations, business, and industry
2. Obtain knowledge of accounting principles and practices in the industry and the client
3. Perform analytical procedures for review services
4. Obtain representations from management for review services
5. Perform other engagement procedures
6. Consider departures from generally accepted accounting principles (GAAP) or other comprehensive basis of accounting (OCBOA)
7. Prepare documentation from evidence gathered
8. Retain documentation as required by standards
9. Review the work performed to provide reasonable assurance that objectives are achieved

C. Prepare Communications

1. Reports on compilations
2. Reports on reviews
3. Restricted use of reports
4. Communicating to management and others
5. Subsequent discovery of facts existing at the date of the report
6. Consider degree of responsibility for supplementary information

VI. Professional Responsibilities (16%–20%)

A. Ethics and Independence

1. Code of Professional Conduct (AICPA)
2. Requirements related to issuers, including the PCAOB, the SEC and the Sarbanes-Oxley Act of 2002, Titles II and III, Section 303
3. Government Accountability Office (GAO)
4. Department of Labor (DOL)
5. Code of Ethics for Professional Accountants (IFAC)

B. Other Professional Responsibilities

1. A firm's system of quality control
2. General role, structure, and requirements of the PCAOB Title I and Title IV of the Sarbanes-Oxley Act of 2002)

References—Auditing and Attestation

- AICPA Statements on Auditing Standards and Interpretations
- Public Company Accounting Oversight Board (PCAOB) Standards (SEC-Approved) and Related Rules, PCAOB Staff Questions and Answers, and PCAOB Staff Audit Practice Alerts
- US Government Accountability Office Government Auditing Standards
- Single Audit Act, as amended

- Office of Management and Budget (OMB) Circular A-133
- AICPA Statements on Quality Control Standards
- AICPA Statements on Standards for Accounting and Review Services and Interpretations
- AICPA Statements on Standards for Attestation Engagements and Interpretations
- AICPA Audit and Accounting Guides
- AICPA Code of Professional Conduct
- IFAC Code of Ethics for Professional Accountants
- Sarbanes-Oxley Act of 2002
- Department of Labor Guidelines and Interpretive Bulletins re: Auditor Independence
- SEC Independence Rules
- Employee Retirement Income Security Act of 1974
- The Committee of Sponsoring Organizations of the Treadway Commission (COSO): Internal Control—Integrated Framework
- Current textbooks on auditing, attestation services, ethics, and independence
- International Standards on Auditing (ISAs)

Skill Specification Outlines (SSOs)

The Skill Specification Outlines (SSOs) identify the skills to be tested on the Uniform CPA Examination. There are three categories of skills, and the weightings will be implemented through the use of different question formats in the exam. For each of the question formats, a different set of tools will be available as resources to the candidates, who will need to use those tools to demonstrate proficiency in the applicable skills categories.

Weights

The percentage range assigned to each skill category will be used to determine the quantity of each type of question, as described below. The percentage range assigned to each skill category represents the approximate percentage to which that category of skills will be used in the different sections of the CPA Examination to assess proficiency. The ranges are designed to provide flexibility in building the examination, and the midpoints of the ranges for each section total 100%. No percentages are given for the bulleted descriptions included in these definitions. The presence of several groups within an area or several topics within a group does not imply equal importance or weight will be given to these bullets on an examination.

Skills Category	Weights (FAR, REG, AUD)	Weights (BEC)
Knowledge and Understanding	50%–60%	80%–90%
Application of the Body of Knowledge	40%–50%	–
Written Communication	–	10%–20%

Knowledge and Understanding. Multiple-choice questions will be used as the proxy for assessing knowledge and understanding, and will be based upon the content topics as outlined in the CSOs. Candidates will not have access to the authoritative literature, spreadsheets, or database tools while answering these questions. A calculator will be accessible for the candidates to use in performing calculations to demonstrate their understanding of the principles or subject matter.

Application of the Body of Knowledge. Task-based simulations will be used as the proxy for assessing application of the body of knowledge and will be based upon the content topics as outlined in the CSOs. Candidates will have access to the authoritative literature, a calculator, spreadsheets, and other resources and tools which they will use to demonstrate proficiency in applying the body of knowledge.

Written Communication will be assessed through the use of responses to essay questions, which will be based upon the content topics as outlined in the CSOs. Candidates will have access to a word processor, which includes a spell-check feature.

Outlines

The outlines below provide additional descriptions of the skills that are represented in each category.

Knowledge and Understanding. Expertise and skills developed through learning processes, recall, and reading comprehension. Knowledge is acquired through experience or education and is the theoretical or practical understanding of a subject; knowledge is also represented through awareness or familiarity with information gained by experience of a fact or situation. Understanding represents a higher level than simple knowledge and is the process of using concepts to deal adequately with given situations, facts, or circumstances. Understanding is the ability to recognize and comprehend the meaning of a particular concept.

Application of the Body of Knowledge, Including Analysis, Judgment, Synthesis, Evaluation, and Research. Higher-level cognitive skills that require individuals to act or transform knowledge in some fashion. These skills are inextricably intertwined and thus are grouped into this single skill area.

- Assess the Business Environment

  - Business Process Evaluation: Assessing and integrating information regarding a business's operational structure, functions, processes, and procedures to develop a broad operational perspective; identify the need for new systems or changes to existing systems and/or processes.
  - Contextual Evaluation: Assessing and integrating information regarding client's type of business or industry.
  - Strategic Analysis—Understanding the Business: Obtaining, assessing, and integrating information on the entity's strategic objectives, strategic management process, business environment, the nature of and value to customers, its products and services, extent of competition within its market space, etc.
  - Business Risk Assessment: Obtaining, assessing, and integrating information on conditions and events that could impede the entity's ability to achieve strategic objectives.
  - Visualize Abstract Descriptions: Organize and process symbols, pictures, graphs, objects, and other information.

- Research

  - Identify the appropriate research question.
  - Identify key search terms for use in performing electronic searches through large volumes of data.
  - Search through large volumes of electronic data to find required information.
  - Organize information or data from multiple sources.
  - Integrate diverse sources of information to reach conclusions or make decisions.
  - Identify the appropriate authoritative guidance in applicable financial reporting frameworks and auditing standards for the accounting issue being evaluated.

- Application of Technology

  - Using electronic spreadsheets to perform calculations, financial analysis, or other functions to analyze data.
  - Integration of technological applications and resources into work processes.
  - Using a variety of computer software and hardware systems to structure, utilize, and manage data.

- Analysis

  - Review information to determine compliance with specified standards or criteria.
  - Use expectations, empirical data, and analytical methods to determine trends and variances.
  - Perform appropriate calculations on financial and nonfinancial data.
  - Recognize patterns of activity when reviewing large amounts of data or recognize breaks in patterns.
  - Interpretation of financial statement data for a given evaluation purpose.
  - Forecasting future financial statement data from historical financial statement data and other information.
  - Integrating primary financial statements: using data from all primary financial statements to uncover financial transactions, inconsistencies, or other information.

- Complex Problem Solving and Judgment

  - Develop and understand goals, objectives, and strategies for dealing with potential issues, obstacles, or opportunities.
  - Analyze patterns of information and contextual factors to identify potential problems and their implications.
  - Devise and implement a plan of action appropriate for a given problem.
  - Apply professional skepticism, which is an attitude that includes a questioning mind and a critical assessment of information or evidence obtained.
  - Adapt strategies or planned actions in response to changing circumstances.
  - Identify and solve unstructured problems.
  - Develop reasonable hypotheses to answer a question or resolve a problem.
  - Formulate and examine alternative solutions in terms of their relative strengths and weaknesses, level of risk, and appropriateness for a given situation.
  - Develop creative ways of thinking about situations, problems, and opportunities to create insightful and sound solutions.
  - Develop logical conclusions through the use of inductive and deductive reasoning.

- Apply knowledge of professional standards and laws, as well as legal, ethical, and regulatory issues.
- Assess the need for consultations with other professionals when gray areas, or areas requiring specialized knowledge, are encountered.

- Decision Making

  - Specify goals and constraints.
  - Generate alternatives.
  - Consider risks.
  - Evaluate and select the best alternative.

- Organization, Efficiency, and Effectiveness

  - Use time effectively and efficiently.
  - Develop detailed work plans, schedule tasks and meetings, and delegate assignments and tasks.
  - Set priorities by determining the relevant urgency or importance of tasks and deciding the order in which they should be performed.
  - File and store information so that it can be found easily and used effectively.

RESEARCHING AICPA PROFESSIONAL STANDARDS

Research components of simulations in the Auditing and Attestation section will involve a research database that includes

- AICPA Statements on Auditing Standards and Interpretations (AU-C)
- PCAOB Auditing Standards and Interpretations (PCAOB)
- Statements on Attestation Standards and Interpretations (AT)
- Statements on Standards for Accounting and Review Services and Interpretations (AR)
- AICPA Code of Professional Conduct (ET)
- AICPA Bylaws (BL)
- Statements on Standards for Valuation Services (VS)
- Statement on Standards for Consulting Services (CS)
- Statements on Standards for Quality Control (QC)
- Peer Review Standards (PR)
- Statement on Standards for Tax Services (TS)
- Statement on Responsibilities in Personal Financial Planning Practice (PFP)
- Statement on Standards for Continuing Professional Education Programs (CPE)

Database Searching

Searching a database consists of the following five steps:

1. Define the issue. What is the research question to be answered?
2. Select the database to search [e.g., (AU-C) the Statement on Auditing Standards and Interpretations].
3. Choose a keyword or table of contents search.
4. Execute the search. Enter the keyword(s) or click on the appropriate table of contents item and complete the search.
5. Evaluate the results. Evaluate the research to see if an answer has been found. If not, try a new search.

Advanced Searches

The advanced search screen allows you to use Boolean concepts to perform more precise searches. Examples of searches that can be performed in the advanced search mode include

1. Containing all these words—Allows you to retrieve sections that contain two or more specified words.
2. Not containing any of these words—Allows you to retrieve sections that do not contain specific words.
3. Containing one or more of these words—Allows you to retrieve sections that contain any one or more of the specified words.
4. Containing these words near each other—Allows you to retrieve sections that contain words near to each other.

The advanced search also allows you to select options for the search. One alternative allows you to retrieve alternative word terms. For example, using this approach with a search on the word "cost" would also retrieve sections containing the word "costing." A synonyms option allows you to retrieve sections that contain words that mean the same as the specified word. You also have the option to only search on the selected sections of the literature.

OVERVIEW OF THE ATTEST FUNCTION

In this overview section the general nature of the attest function is first discussed. Second, the general nature of the attest function as it relates to financial statement information is discussed. Third, a diagram is provided for understanding the nature of audits of financial statements. A section on generally accepted auditing standards (GAAS) and Statements on Auditing Standards (SASs) follows.

Attest Function—General Nature

In an attest engagement a CPA is engaged to issue or does issue an examination, a review, or an agreed-upon procedures report on *subject matter*, or an *assertion* about subject matter, that is the responsibility of another party.[1] The attest function adds value to information by having a third party (the CPA) provide assurance over subject matter prepared by a party responsible for that information. For example, in the United States, an attest engagement may be performed under generally accepted auditing standards or PCAOB standards (for historical financial statements and related information) or the attestation standards (for other information). An attestation engagement may be performed under either generally accepted accounting principles (for historical financial statements and related information) **or** the attestation standards (for other information).

As a starting point to thinking about the attest function, consider both the preparation of financial statements and the performance of an audit of those financial statements. The preparation of financial statements may be viewed as consisting of inputs (source documents) being processed (through use of journals, ledgers, etc.) to arrive at an output (the financial information itself). Or shown diagrammatically

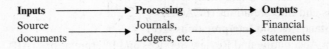

While CPAs often assist in the preparation of the financial statements, the attestation function conceptually begins with financial statements having been prepared by management. The purpose of a CPA financial statement audit is to provide assurance that financial statements which have been prepared by management follow a financial reporting framework—usually generally accepted accounting principles, but sometimes a special-purpose framework such as the cash or tax bases of accounting.

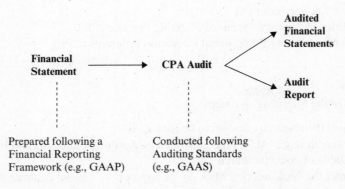

In performing an audit engagement, a CPA gathers various types of evidence relating to the propriety of the recording of economic events and transactions. For financial statements, this evidence will address the assertions that the assets listed in the balance sheet actually exist, that the company has title to these assets, and that the valuations assigned to these assets have been established in conformity with generally accepted accounting principles. The evidence gathered will also address whether the balance sheet contains all the liabilities of the company and that the notes to the financial statements include the needed disclosures. Similarly, a CPA will gather evidence about the income statement and the statement of cash flows. In short, the attest function provides assurance for the overall assertion that the financial statements follow generally accepted accounting principles.

---

[1]This "definition" is from the *Statements on Standards for Attestation Engagements*. Alternatively, the AICPA *Code of Professional Conduct* defines an attest engagement as an engagement that requires independence, as defined in AICPA *Professional Standards*.

It is helpful to generalize the discussion to information other than financial statements covered by the attestation standards as follows:

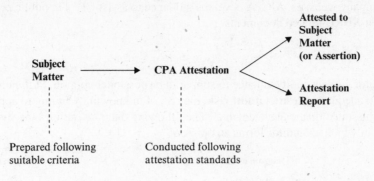

The attestation standards establish three forms of CPA attestation engagements—examinations, reviews, and the performance of agreed-upon procedures. An **examination,** referred to as an **audit** when it involves historical financial statements, normally results in a positive opinion that provides reasonable assurances, the highest form of assurance provided. When performing an examination, the CPAs select from all available evidence a combination that limits to a low level of risk the chance of material misstatement. A **review** is substantially less in scope than an audit and consists primarily of (1) application of analytical procedures, (2) making inquires of management, and (3) obtaining representations from management relating to the financial statements. It results in a report with limited assurance (also referred to as negative assurance since the CPA ordinarily concludes that he or she is not aware of any needed material modifications to the financial statements). For the third form of attestation engagement, a CPA and a specified party that wishes to use the information may mutually decide on specific **agreed-upon procedures** that the CPA will perform. Agreed-upon procedures engagements result in a report that describes the procedures performed and related findings.

CPAs may also provide services to clients in the form of **compilation**. The objective of a compilation of financial statements, as established in the accounting and review services standards, is to present information that is the representation of management without expressing any assurance on the statements; those standards categorize compilations as attest but not assurance engagements.

The Responding to Risk Assessment and Reporting Modules discuss these forms of association in further detail. For compilations note that the CPA's primary role is to prepare the financial statements. Accordingly, the CPA's report disclaims any opinion and gives no assurances with respect to whether the statements comply with the appropriate criteria. (The Responding to Risk Assessment and Reporting Modules discuss these forms of association in further detail.)

Expansions of the Attest Function

The overall need of individuals and organizations for credible information, combined with changes currently taking place in information technology, is leading to rapid changes in the role of the public accounting profession. CPA firms are already embracing a broader concept of the attest function that is being referred to as the **assurance function,** which includes providing assurance on a broad variety of types of financial or nonfinancial information.

Assurance services may be structured using the attest standards framework (i.e., examinations, reviews, or agreed-upon procedures engagements), or outside of that framework as the situation merits.

The AICPA Assurance Services Executive Committee has a mission of (1) identifying and prioritizing emerging trends and market needs for assurance, and (2) developing related assurance methodology guidance and tools as needed. Current services developed under this committee's oversight include

- **Trust Services (SysTrust and WebTrust).** These are a set of professional attestation and advisory services based on a core set of principles and criteria that address the risks and opportunities of IT-enabled systems and privacy programs. *SysTrust* is a service designed primarily to build trust and confidence among business depending on IT systems by addressing areas such as security, availability, confidentiality and processing integrity. WebTrust is a service designed to build trust and confidence among customers and businesses doing business on the Internet—it addresses area such as website security, privacy, availability, confidentiality and processing integrity.
- **PrimePlus/Elder Care Services.** These services focus on the specific needs and goals of older adults. In providing these services CPAs address a variety of areas, including accounting, cash flow planning and budgeting, pre- and post-retirement planning, insurance reviews, estate planning, and tax planning.

- **XBRL Services.** **EX**tensible **B**usiness **R**eporting **L**anguage is an international information format designed for business information. The SEC requires companies to provide financial statements in XBRL format, as well as posting such documents to company websites. AICPA develops guidance to assist CPAs in public practice who are requested to provide assurance on XBRL-related documents.

Diagram of an Audit

In the audit process an auditor gathers audit evidence to support a professional opinion. Sufficient appropriate audit evidence should be gathered to adequately restrict **audit risk,** the risk of unknowingly failing to appropriately modify the audit report on materially misstated financial statements.[2] The following diagram outlines the steps in the evidence gathering and evaluation process in which an auditor forms an opinion:

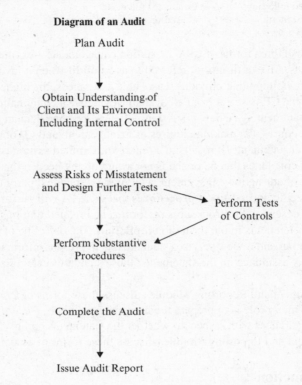

Diagram of an Audit

Plan Audit

↓

Obtain Understanding of
Client and Its Environment
Including Internal Control

↓

Assess Risks of Misstatement
and Design Further Tests → Perform Tests
of Controls

↓

Perform Substantive
Procedures ←

↓

Complete the Audit

↓

Issue Audit Report

Plan Audit. Audit planning involves developing an overall strategy for performing the audit. During planning auditors establish an understanding with their client as to the nature of services to be provided and the responsibilities of each party—this is ordinarily accomplished through use of an engagement letter. In addition, they develop an overall audit strategy, an audit plan, and an audit program.

Although the diagram suggests planning as an initial step, which indeed it is, planning continues throughout the entire audit as the auditor accumulates sufficient appropriate audit evidence to support the audit opinion. This is even more the case in a first year audit of a client in which an understanding of the client should be obtained to even be able to complete initial planning of the audit (e.g., to prepare the audit plan and audit program).

Obtain an Understanding of the Client and Its Environment, Including Internal Control. Auditors should attain a sufficient background to assess the risk of material misstatement of the financial statements and to design the nature, timing, and extent of further audit procedures. **Risk assessment procedures** are used here and include inquiries of management and others within the entity, analytical procedures, observation and inspection, and other procedures. At this stage it is an overall understanding of the client and its environment that is obtained, including its objectives and strategies and related business risks, the manner in which it measures and reviews its financial performance, and its internal control. This understanding helps the auditors to identify relevant assertions related to transaction classes, account balances, and disclosures with a high risk of material misstatement.

---

[2]The concept of audit risk is presented briefly in this section and is discussed in detail in Section A.2. of Module 2.

Obtaining an understanding of the nature of internal control is an essential part of this understanding as it allows the auditor to identify areas that may be misstated and to design other procedures based on characteristics of the existing system. Information on internal control comes from interviews with client personnel, observing the application of specific control, inspecting documents and reports, and tracing transactions through the information system, as well as reviewing audit working papers.

Assess Risks of Misstatement and Design Further Audit Procedures. Auditors use the information collected while obtaining their understanding of the client and its environment to identify classes of transactions (transaction classes), account balances, and disclosures that might be materially misstated. Assessing the risks of misstatement (the risk assessment) is performed both at the overall financial statement level and at the relevant assertion level and includes considering

- What could go wrong?
- How likely it is that it will go wrong?
- What are the likely amounts involved?

Risk assessment procedures provide the auditors with evidence on potential risks of material misstatement. The risks of material misstatement are composed of inherent and control risks for relevant assertions. Inherent risk is the susceptibility of a relevant assertion to material misstatement, assuming that there are no related controls. Inherent risk arises for a variety of reasons including the business risk faced by management, the possibility of material misstatement due to fraud, and significant measurement uncertainty in accounting estimates and in nonroutine transactions.

Control risk is the risk that a material misstatement could occur in a relevant assertion and not be prevented or detected on a timely basis by the entity's internal control. After analyzing the design and implementation of internal control, the auditors should decide whether the system appears adequate to prevent or detect and correct material misstatements. For example, if the auditors believe that internal control is weak for an important area (that is, control risk is high), they will assess the risk of material misstatement as high. On the other hand, if the system seems capable of preventing or detecting and correcting misstatements, the auditors may conclude that internal control *may* be strong. But in this case they should determine that it is strong by performing tests of controls.

Based on the assessed risks of misstatement for various transactions, account balances, and disclosures, and on various requirements to perform certain audit procedures regardless of the individual company risk assessment, the auditors will design and perform **further audit procedures**—tests of controls and substantive procedures.

Perform Tests of Controls. Tests of controls are performed to determine whether key controls are properly designed and *operating effectively.* To illustrate a test of a control, consider the control activity in which the accounting department accounts for the serial sequence of all shipping documents before preparing the related journal entries. The purpose of this control is to ensure that each shipment of merchandise is recorded in the accounting records (i.e., to ensure the completeness of recorded sales and accounts receivable).

Perform Substantive Procedures—General. Substantive procedures (also referred to as substantive tests) are used to "substantiate" account balances. Substantive procedures restrict detection risk, the risk that audit procedures will incorrectly lead to a conclusion that a material misstatement does not exist in an account balance when in fact such a misstatement does exist. While tests of controls, as noted above, provide evidence as to whether controls are operating effectively, substantive procedures provide evidence as to whether actual account balances and disclosures are proper. The auditor's reliance on substantive procedures to achieve an audit objective may be derived from (1) substantive analytical procedures, and (2) tests of details of account balances, transactions, and disclosures.

Substantive procedures—Analytical Procedures. Analytical procedures used as substantive procedures are used to obtain audit evidence about particular assertions related to account balances or classes of transactions. In these tests auditors gather evidence about relationships among various accounting and nonaccounting data such as industry and economic information. When unexpected changes occur (or expected changes do **not** occur) in these relationships, an auditor obtains an explanation and investigates. Ratio analysis is a frequently used analytical procedure. The auditor would, for example, calculate a ratio and compare it to expectations such as budgets, prior year data, and industry data.

Substantive procedures—Tests of Details of account balances, transactions and disclosures. The objective of these tests is to detect misstatements in the financial statements—more specifically, misstatements of relevant assertions relating to transactions, account balances, and disclosures. The details supporting financial statement accounts are tested to obtain assurance that material misstatements do not exist. Sending confirmations for year-end receivable accounts is an example of a substantive test of details.

Complete the Audit. Auditors perform a number of procedures near the end of the audit. For example, evidence is aggregated and evaluated for sufficiency. Analytical procedures are performed (again) to assist the auditor in assessing conclusions reached and for evaluating overall financial statement presentation. Final decisions are made as to required financial statement disclosures and as to the appropriate audit report.

Audit Report. A standard unqualified audit report is issued by CPAs when their examination and the results thereof are satisfactory. This report has an opinion referred to as "unmodified" in the AICPA and international standards, while referred to in the PCAOB standards as "unqualified." For simplicity sake we will use the term "unmodified," but you should realize that the opinion is referred to as "unqualified" when a public company audit is involved. Standard reports are presented in the Reporting Module.

The wording of audit reports is modified when the professional standards require or suggest that a matter be emphasized and when an unmodified opinion is not appropriate. Variations in the audit report include both those with unmodified opinions and those with modified opinions:

Audit reports with unmodified opinions:

- Standard report
- Emphasis of matter paragraph added to report
- Other matter paragraph added to report
- Report modified to refer to a component auditor

Audit reports with modified opinions:

- Qualified opinion
- Adverse opinion
- Disclaimer of opinion

These reports are presented in detail in the Reporting Module.

Generally Accepted Auditing Standards

The AICPA recently completed its clarity project, which resulted in a complete rewrite of its auditing standards. It is those standards that follow Module 8. The standards begin with the following principles underlying an audit of financial statements conducted in accordance with generally accepted auditing standards.

Principles Underlying an Audit Conducted in Accordance with Generally Accepted Auditing Standards	
Purpose of an audit	The purpose of an audit is to provide financial statement users with an opinion by the auditor on whether the financial statements are presented fairly, in all material respects, in accordance with the applicable financial reporting framework. An auditor's opinion enhances the degree of confidence that intended users can place in the financial statements.
Premise of an audit	An audit in accordance with generally accepted auditing standards is conducted on the premise that management and, where appropriate, those charged with governance, have responsibility a. For the preparation and fair presentation of the financial statements in accordance with the applicable financial reporting framework; this includes the design, implementation, and maintenance of internal control relevant to the preparation and fair presentation of financial statements that are free from material misstatement, whether due to fraud or error; and b. To provide the auditor with • All information, such as records, documentation, and other matters that are relevant to the preparation and fair presentation of the financial statements; • Any additional information that the auditor may request from management and, where appropriate, those charged with governance; and • Unrestricted access to those within the entity from whom the auditor determines it necessary to obtain audit evidence.
Personal responsibilities of the auditor	Auditors are responsible for having *appropriate competence and capabilities* to perform the audit; complying with relevant ethical requirements; and maintaining professional skepticism and exercising professional judgment, throughout the planning and performance of the audit.

Auditor actions in performing the audit	To *express an opinion,* the auditor obtains reasonable assurance about whether the financial statements as a whole are free from material misstatement, whether due to fraud or error.
	To *obtain reasonable assurance*, which is a high, but not absolute, level of assurance, the auditor
	• Plans the work and properly supervises any assistants.
	• Determines and applies appropriate materiality level or levels throughout the audit.
	• Identifies and assesses risks of material misstatement, whether due to fraud or error, based on an understanding of the entity and its environment, including the entity's internal control.
	• Obtains sufficient appropriate audit evidence about whether material misstatements exist, through designing and implementing appropriate responses to the assessed risks.
	The auditor is *unable to obtain absolute assurance* that the financial statements are free from material misstatement because of inherent limitations, which arise from
	• The nature of financial reporting;
	• The nature of audit procedures; and
	• The need for the audit to be conducted within a reasonable period of time and so as to achieve a balance between benefit and cost.
Reporting results of an audit	Based on an evaluation of the audit evidence obtained, the auditor expresses, in the form of a written report, *an opinion in accordance with the auditor's findings, or states that an opinion cannot be expressed.* The opinion states whether the financial statements are presented fairly, in all material respects, in accordance with the applicable financial reporting framework.

Traditionally, rather than the preceding principles, generally accepted auditing standards were established about the ten generally accepted auditing standards presented in the left column of the following figure.

The auditing standards of the PCAOB are structured about the ten standards.

The right side of the following figure provides the eleven attestation standards. The attestation standards relate to all attestation services performed by CPAs. The generally accepted auditing standards may be considered to be the appropriate interpretations as they relate to audits of financial statements. After you have memorized the generally accepted auditing standards, you will find that studying the attestation standards is easy since most are similar. Be familiar with the attestations standards since a question on them is likely.

GENERALLY ACCEPTED AUDITING STANDARDS AND ATTESTATION STANDARDS	
Generally Accepted Auditing Standards	**Attestation Standards**
General Standards	
1. The audit is to be performed by a person or persons having adequate technical **training** and proficiency as an auditor. 2. In all matters relating to the assignment, an **independence** in mental attitude is to be maintained by the auditor or auditors. 3. Due **professional care** is to be exercised in the performance of the audit and the preparation of the report.	1. The engagement shall be performed by a practitioner or practitioners having adequate technical **training** and proficiency in the attest function. 2. The engagement shall be performed by a practitioner or practitioners having adequate **knowledge** in the subject matter of the assertion. 3. The practitioner shall perform an engagement only if he or she has reason to believe that the subject matter is capable of reasonably consistent evaluation against criteria that are suitable and available to users. 4. In all matters relating to the engagement, an **independence** in mental attitude shall be maintained by the practitioner or practitioners. 5. Due **professional care** shall be exercised in the performance of the engagement.

Standards of Fieldwork	
1. The work is to be adequately **planned** and assistants, if any, are to be properly **supervised.** 2. A sufficient **understanding of internal control** is to be obtained to plan the audit and to determine the nature, timing and extent of tests to be performed. 3. Sufficient appropriate **evidential matter** is to be obtained through inspection, observation, inquiries and confirmations to afford a reasonable basis for an opinion regarding the financial statements under audit.	1. The work shall be adequately **planned** and assistants, if any, shall be properly supervised. 2. Sufficient **evidence** shall be obtained to provide a reasonable basis for the conclusion that is expressed in the report.

Standards of Reporting	
1. The report shall state whether the financial statements are presented in accordance with **generally accepted accounting principles** (GAAP). 2. The report shall identify those circumstances in which such principles have not been **consistently observed** in the current period in relation to the preceding period. 3. Informative **disclosures** in the financial statements are to be regarded as reasonably adequate unless otherwise stated in the report. 4. The report shall contain either an expression of **opinion** regarding the financial statements, taken as a whole, or an assertion to the effect that an opinion cannot be expressed. When an overall opinion cannot be expressed, the reasons therefor should be stated. In all cases where an auditor's name is associated with financial statements, the report should contain a clear-cut indication of the character of the auditor's work, if any, and the degree of responsibility the auditor is taking.	1. The report shall identify the subject matter or the assertion being reported on and state the character of the engagement. 2. The report shall state the practitioner's conclusion about the subject matter or the assertion in relation to the criteria against which the subject matter was evaluated. 3. The report shall state all of the practitioner's significant reservations about the engagement, the subject matter, and if applicable, the assertion related thereto. 4. The report shall state that the use of the report is restricted to specified parties under the following circumstances: • When the criteria used to evaluate the subject matter are determined by the practitioner to be suitable only for a limited number or parties who either participated in their establishment or can be presumed to have an adequate understanding of the criteria. • When the criteria used to evaluate the subject matter are available only to specified parties. • When reporting on subject matter and a written assertion has not been provided by the responsible party. • When the report is on an attest engagement to apply agreed-upon procedures to the subject matter.

PROFESSIONAL STANDARDS

The Professional Standards most directly related to the Auditing and Attestation section of the CPA exam (hereafter AUDIT) are

- Statements on Auditing Standards
- Public Company Accounting Oversight Board Pronouncements
- International Standards on Auditing
- Statements on Standards for Attestation Engagements
- Statements on Standards for Accounting and Review Services
- Statements on Quality Control Standards
- AICPA Code of Professional Conduct
- International Code of Ethics for Professional Accountants

A more complete list of references is presented following the Content Specification Outlines earlier in this module.

Statements on Auditing Standards

The Auditing Standards Board issues Statements on Auditing Standards that are considered GAAS. Unsuperseded sections of each SAS are included in the codification of auditing standards. Outlines of the entire codification are presented after Module 8 with an AU-C prefix. The manner in which you use these outlines depends upon your educational and practical auditing background. If you have previously read the SAS, you may be able to use the outlines directly without rereading the material. If you are unfamiliar with a section, to be safest you should read it and either simultaneously study the outline, or use the outline to review the major points. In some circumstances you may find that although you haven't read the detailed AU-C section, your educational and/or practical experience makes studying the outline adequate. At the beginning of each module in this chapter, a study program will refer you to the appropriate AU-C section. At that point you may read the AU-C either before beginning the module or when finished. Many Audit and Attestation exam questions can be directly answered by the AU-C outlines. One week before, you can use the outlines as a good review for the Audit and Attestation section. The module presentation provides a summary of the most important information, generally that which has received extremely heavy coverage on past exams.

The SAS (and attestation standards) use two categories of requirements to describe auditor responsibility for following a particular requirement.

- **Unconditional requirement**—The auditor must comply with the requirement in all cases in which the circumstances exist. SAS use the words *must* or *is required* to indicate an unconditional requirement.
- **Presumptively mandatory requirement**—Similarly, the auditor must comply with the requirement, but, in rare circumstances, the auditor may depart from such a requirement. In such circumstances, the auditor documents the departure, the justification for the departure, and how the alternative procedures performed in the circumstances were sufficient. SAS use the word *should* to indicate a presumptively mandatory requirement.[3]

As discussed in Chapter 3, the CPA exam requires the candidates to be able to conduct electronic research of the professional standards. While in most circumstances candidates should expect to use the index or a keyword search to find the relevant topic, knowledge of the overall codified layout of the standards may be helpful. The following table presents the AU-C sections in their codified order (in general the numbers correspond closely to the international standards):

STRUCTURE OF PROFESSIONAL STANDARDS—AUDITING STANDARDS BOARD

AU-C 200   **General Principles and Responsibilities**

200 Overall Objectives of the Independent Auditor and the Conduct of an Audit in Accordance with Generally Accepted Auditing Standards (110)	240 Consideration of Fraud in a Financial Statement Audit (316)
210 Terms of Engagement (120)	250 Consideration of Laws and Regulations in an Audit of Financial Statements (317)

AU-C 200   **General Principles and Responsibilities**

220 Quality Control for an Engagement Conducted in Accordance with Generally Accepted Auditing Standards (161)	260 The Auditor's Communication with Those Charged with Governance (380)
230 Audit Documentation (339)	265 Communicating Internal Control–Related Matters Identified in an Audit (325)

AU-C 300–499   **Risk Assessment and Response to Assessed Risks**

300 Planning an Audit (311)	330 Performing Audit Procedures in Response to Assessed Risks and Evaluating the Audit Evidence Obtained (318)
315 Understanding the Entity and Its Environment and Assessing the Risks of Material Misstatement (314)	402 Audit Considerations Relating to an Entity Using a Service Organization (324)
320 Materiality in Planning and Performing an Audit (312)	450 Evaluation of Misstatements Identified During the Audit (312)

---

[3]PCAOB standards supplement these two categories with a third category: **Responsibility to Consider**. For these responsibilities, whether the auditor implements these matters will depend on the exercise of professional judgment in the circumstances. PCAOB standards use words such as may, might or could to indicate a responsibility to consider.

AU-C 500   **Audit Evidence**

500   Audit Evidence (326)

501   Audit Evidence—Specific Considerations for Selected Items (337)

505   External Confirmations (330)

510   Opening Balances—Initial Audit Engagements, Including Reaudit Engagements (315)

520   Analytical Procedures (329)

530   Audit Sampling (350)

540   Auditing Accounting Estimates, Including Fair Value Accounting Estimates and Related Disclosures (342)

550   Related Parties (334)

560   Subsequent Events and Subsequently Discovered Facts (561)

570   Going Concern (341)

580   Written Representations (333)

585   Consideration of Omitted Procedures After the Report Release Date (AICPA only [390])

AU-C 600   **Using the Work of Others**

600   Special Considerations—Audits of Group Financial Statements (Including the Work of Component Auditors) (543)

610   Using the Work of Internal Auditors (322)

620   Using the Work of an Auditor's Specialist (336)

AU-C 700   **Audit Conclusions and Reporting**

700   Forming an Opinion and Reporting on Financial Statements (508)

705   Modifications to the Opinion in the Independent Auditor's Report (508)

706   Emphasis-of-Matter Paragraphs and Other-Matter Paragraphs in the Independent Auditor's Report (508)

708   Consistency of Financial Statements (AICPA only [420])

720   Other Information in Documents Containing Audited Financial Statements (550)

725   Supplementary Information in Relation to the Financial Statements as a Whole (AICPA only [551])

730   Required Supplementary Information (AICPA only [558])

AU-C 800   **Special Considerations**

800   Special Considerations—Audits of Financial Statements Prepared in Accordance with Special Purpose Frameworks (623)

805   Special Considerations—Audits of Single Financial Statements and Specific Elements, Accounts, or Items of a Financial Statement (623)

806   Reporting on Compliance with Aspects of Contractual Agreements or Regulatory Requirements in Connection with Audited Financial Statements (AICPA only [623])

810   Engagements to Report on Summary Financial Statements (552)

AU-C 900   **Special Considerations in the United States (AICPA only)**

905   Alert as to the Intended Use of the Auditor's Written Communication (532)

910   Financial Statements Prepared in Accordance with a Financial Reporting Framework Generally Accepted in Another Country (534)

925   Filings with the U.S. Securities and Exchange Commission Under the Securities Act of 1933 (711)

930   Interim Financial Information (722)

AU-C 900   **Special Considerations in the United States (AICPA only)**

915   Reports on Application of Requirements of an Applicable Financial Reporting Framework (625)

920   Letters for Underwriters and Certain Other Requesting Parties (634)

935   Compliance Audits (801)

The following sections (with abbreviated titles in some cases) may be particularly important for typical exams:

- AU-C 240   Consideration of Fraud in a Financial Statement Audit
- AU-C 260   The Auditor's Communication with Those Charged with Governance
- AU-C 265   Communicating Internal Control–Related Matters
- AU-C 315   Understanding the Entity and Its Environment
- AU-C 320   Materiality in Planning an Audit
- AU-C 330   Performing Audit Procedures in Response to Assessed Risks
- AU-C 450   Evaluation of Misstatements Identified during the Audit
- AU-C 570   Going Concern
- AU-C 700   Forming an Opinion and Reporting on Financial Statements
- AU-C 705   Modifications of the Opinion in the Independent Auditor's Report
- AU-C 706   Emphasis-of-Matter and Other-Matter Paragraphs in the Auditor's Report
- AU-C 708   Consistency of Financial Statements

Public Company Accounting Oversight Board Pronouncements

In 2002, in reaction to a number of corporate frauds, Congress passed the Sarbanes-Oxley Act authorizing the creation of the Public Company Accounting Oversight Board (PCAOB) to oversee the accounting profession. Establishment of the PCAOB eliminated a significant portion of the accounting profession's system of self-regulation. The Public Company Accounting Oversight Board was established in 2002. The five-member Board's duties include

- Registration of public accounting firms that prepare audit reports for financial statement issuers
- Establishment or adoption of auditing, quality control, ethics, independence and other standards relating to audit reports for issuers
- Conducting inspections of registered public accounting firms
- Performing other duties or functions to promote high professional standards for audits, enforcing compliance with the Sarbanes-Oxley Act, setting the budget, and managing operations

All accounting firms that audit SEC registrants must register with the Board. As part of that registration process, each firm pledges to cooperate with any inquiry made by the Board. The Board may impose monetary damages and may suspend firms and accountants from working on engagements for publicly traded companies. It may also make referrals to the Justice Department to consider criminal cases.

The Board creates auditing standards for the above areas of its listed duties, including audits and reviews of public company financial statements. Information relating to the PCAOB is presented in Modules 1 through 5. Public companies are also referred to as **issuers** indicating that they issue securities under the Securities Acts. The PCAOB adopted the AICPA auditing standards in existence on April 16, 2003 as the beginning of its own *Auditing Standards*. Most of those standards are still in effect for audits performed in accordance with PCAOB standards, as supplemented by subsequent PCAOB *Accounting Standards*. In this text we do not provide the interim standards as in substance they are very similar to those of the AICPA's Auditing Standards Board; rather, we highlight a number of significant differences between the sets of standards. We do provide brief summaries of the standards issued by the PCAOB following the outlines of the Auditing Standards Board.

Statements on Standards for Attestation Engagements (SSAE)

The Statements on Standards for Attestation Engagements relate to attestation engagements on subject matter other than financial statements. Outlines of the SSAE, which have an AT prefix, are presented following Module 8 and are discussed in the various modules, particularly Module 5. Their codified form may be summarized as

AT 20   Defining Professional Requirements in Statements on Standards for Attestation Engagements (SSAE)
AT 50   SSAE Hierarchy
AT 101   Attest Engagements
AT 201   Agreed-Upon Procedures Engagements
AT 301   Financial Forecasts and Projections
AT 401   Reporting on Pro Forma Financial Information
AT 501   An Examination of an Entity's Internal Control over Financial Reporting that is Integrated with an Audit of its Financial Statements

AT 601   Compliance Attestation
AT 701   Management's Discussion and Analysis
AT 801   Reporting on Controls at a Service Organization

Statements on Standards for Accounting and Review Services (SSARS)

The Statements on Standards for Accounting and Review Services provide the authoritative guidance on procedures and reporting of compilation and review engagements of nonissuer (nonpublic) entity financial statements. The outlines of the Codification of the SSARS is presented in Module 6.

Statements on Quality Control Standards (SQCS)

The Statements on Quality Control Standards apply to the accounting and auditing practices (including all attest services) of all firms. They serve as the standards a firm should be measured against when being evaluated through a peer review—an engagement in which other CPAs evaluate the quality of the firm's auditing and attestation work. In addition to peer reviews conducted under the SCQSs, quality reviews are performed under the Public Company Accounting Oversight Board.

AUDITING AND ATTESTATION

As indicated previously, this section consists of eight modules and two supplemental sections designed to facilitate your study for the Auditing and Attestation section of the Uniform CPA examination. The table of contents at the right describes the content of each module.

Module 1: Professional Responsibilities

Overview

This module presents requirements relating to a CPA's professional responsibilities related to ethics, including independence, as well as certain other responsibilities. The module begins with the AICPA *Code of Professional Conduct,* which consists of two sections: (1) Principles (the framework) and (2) Rules (govern performance of professional services). Integrated with these two sections are many related interpretations and rules that are also examined. The remainder of the module includes coverage of a number of other areas related to a CPA's professional responsibilities with which you should be familiar.

You should expect a significant number of questions from the AICPA *Code of Professional Conduct,* and somewhat fewer from each of the other areas. Also expect a simulation question in which you must show your research skills relating to finding particular information in the AICPA *Code of Professional Conduct* (codified using ET prefixes).

The primary reference here is the AICPA *Code of Professional Conduct.* This module incorporates an outline of its key provisions. Yet, access it electronically to gain a familiarity to allow you to efficiently respond to a simulation research question.

A. AICPA Requirements

1. Code of Professional Conduct—General

   a. The Code is applicable to all AICPA members, not merely those in public practice
   b. Compliance with the Code depends primarily on members' understanding and voluntary actions, and only secondarily on

   (1) Reinforcement by peers,
   (2) Public opinion, and
   (3) Disciplinary proceedings.

       (a) Possible disciplinary proceedings include from joint trial board panel **admonishment, suspension** (for up to two years), or **expulsion** from AICPA, or acquittal

   c. The Code provides **minimum** levels of acceptable conduct relating to all services performed by CPAs, unless wording of a standard specifically excludes some members

   (1) For example, some standards do not apply to CPAs not in public practice

   d. Overall structure of the Code goes from very generally worded standards to more specific and operational rules

   (1) Interpretations and rulings remaining from the prior Code are even more specific

   e. The Principles section consists of six Articles

      I. Responsibilities
     II. The Public Interest
    III. Integrity

      IV. Objectivity and Independence
      V. Due Care
      VI. Scope and Nature of Services

2. Code of Professional Conduct—Principles

   a. Outline of six Articles in Section 1 of the Code

Article I—Responsibilities. In carrying out their responsibilities as professionals, members should exercise sensitive professional and moral judgments in all their activities.

Article II—The Public Interest. Members should accept the obligation to act in a way that will serve the public interest, honor the public trust, and demonstrate commitment to professionalism.

    (1) A distinguishing mark of a professional is acceptance of responsibility to public.

       (a) The accounting profession's public consists of clients, credit grantors, governments, employers, investors, business and financial community, and others.

       (b) In resolving conflicting pressures among groups an accountant should consider the public interest (the collective well-being of the community).

Article III—Integrity. To maintain and broaden public confidence, members should perform all professional responsibilities with the highest sense of integrity.

    (1) Integrity can accommodate the inadvertent error and honest difference of opinion, but it cannot accommodate deceit or subordination of principle.

    (2) Integrity

       (a) Is measured in terms of what is right and just

       (b) Requires a member to observe **principles of objectivity, independence, and due care**

Article IV—Objectivity and Independence. A member should maintain objectivity and be free of conflicts of interest in discharging professional responsibilities. A member in public practice should be independent in fact and appearance when providing auditing and other attestation services.

    (1) Overall

       (a) Objectivity a state of mind

         [1] Objectivity imposes obligation to be impartial, intellectually honest, and free of conflicts of interest.

         [2] Independence precludes relationships that may appear to impair objectivity in rendering attestation services.

       (b) Regardless of the service performed, members should protect integrity of their work, maintain objectivity, and avoid any subordination of their judgment.

    (2) Members in public practice require maintenance of objectivity and independence (includes avoiding conflict of interest).

       (a) Attest services—require independence in fact and in appearance

    (3) Members not in public practice

       (a) Are unable to maintain appearance of independence, but should maintain objectivity

       (b) When employed by others to prepare financial statements, or to perform auditing, tax, or consulting services, should remain objective and candid in dealings with members in public practice

Article V—Due Care. A member should observe the profession's technical and ethical standards, strive continually to improve competence and the quality of services, and discharge professional responsibility to the best of the member's ability.

    (1) Competence is derived from both education and experience.

    (2) Each member is responsible for assessing his or her own competence and for evaluating whether education, experience, and judgment are adequate for the responsibility taken.

Article VI—Scope and Nature of Services. A member in public practice should observe the Principles of the Code of Professional Conduct in determining the scope and nature of services to be provided.

   (1) Members should

      (a) Have in place appropriate internal quality control procedures for services rendered
      (b) Determine whether scope and nature of other services provided to an audit client would create a conflict of interest in performance of audit
      (c) Assess whether activities are consistent with role as professionals

3. Code of Professional Conduct—Rules, Interpretations, and Rulings

   a. Combined outline of Section 2 of the code (rules) integrated with interpretation and rulings
     ET Section 100.01—Conceptual Framework for AICPA Independence Standards. The conceptual framework describes the risk-based approach to analyzing independence that is used by the AICPA Professional Ethics Executive Committee (PEEC). A member is not independent if there is an unacceptable risk to the member's independence. Risk is unacceptable if the relationship would compromise (or would be perceived as compromising by an informed third party) the member's professional judgment.

     (1) In using this framework, the member should identify and evaluate threats (both individually and in the aggregate) to independence. Types of threats include

        (a) *Self-review threat*—Reviewing evidence that results from the member's own work (e.g., preparing source documents for an audit client).
        (b) *Advocacy threat*—Actions promoting the client's interests or position (e.g., promoting a client's securities).
        (c) *Adverse interest threat*—Actions or interests between the member and the client that are in opposition (e.g., litigation between the client and the member).
        (d) *Familiarity threat*—Members having a close or longstanding relationship with client or knowing individuals or entities who performed nonattest services for the client, (e.g., a member of the attest engagement team whose spouse is in a key position at the client).
        (e) *Undue influence threat*—Attempts by a client's management (or others) to coerce the member or exercise excessive influence over the member (e.g., threat to replace the member over a disagreement regarding an accounting principle).
        (f) *Financial self-interest threat*—Potential benefit to a member from a financial interest in, or some financial relationship with, an attest client (e.g., having a direct financial interest in the client).
        (g) *Management participation threat*—Assuming the role of management or performing management functions for the attest client (e.g., serving as an officer of the client).

     (2) After considering the threats to independence, the member should consider the safeguards that mitigate or eliminate threats to independence. The three types of safeguards include

        (a) Safeguards created by the profession, legislation, or regulation (e.g., required continuing education on independence and ethics).
        (b) Safeguards implemented by the client (e.g., an effective governance structure, including an active audit committee).
        (c) Safeguards implemented by the firm (e.g., quality controls for attest engagements).

     Rule 101 Independence. A member in public practice shall be independent in the performance of professional services as required by standards promulgated by designated bodies.
     Interpretation 101-1. Independence is impaired if

     (1) During the period of the professional engagement a covered member

        (a) Had or was committed to acquire any direct or material indirect financial interest in the client.
        (b) Was a trustee of any trust or executor or administrator of any estate if such trust or estate had or was committed to acquire any direct or material indirect financial interest in the client.
        (c) Had a joint closely held investment that was material to the covered member.
        (d) Except as specifically permitted in interpretation 101-5, had any loan to or from the client, any officer or director of the client, or any individual owning 10% or more of the client's outstanding equity securities or other ownership interests.

(2) During the period of the professional engagement, a partner or professional employee of the firm, his or her immediate family, or any group of such persons acting together owned more than 5% of a client's outstanding equity securities or other ownership interests.

(3) During the period covered by the financial statements or during the period of the professional engagement, a partner or professional employee of the firm was simultaneously associated with the client as a

    (a) Director, officer, or employee, or in any capacity equivalent to that of a member of management;

    (b) Promoter, underwriter, or voting trustee; or

    (c) Trustee for any pension or profit-sharing trust of the client.

Application of the Independence Rules to a Covered Member's Immediate Family

(1) Except as stated in the following paragraph, a covered member's immediate family is subject to Rule 101 [ET Section 101.01], and its interpretations and rulings.

(2) The exceptions are that independence would not be considered to be impaired solely as a result of the following:

    (a) An individual in a covered member's immediate family was employed by the client in a position other than a key position.

    (b) In connection with his or her employment, an individual in the immediate family of one of the following covered members participated in a retirement, savings, compensation, or similar plan that is sponsored by a client or that invests in a client (provided such plan is normally offered to all employees in similar positions):

        [1] A partner or manager who provides ten or more hours of nonattest services to the client; or

        [2] Any partner in the office in which the lead attest engagement partner primarily practices in connection with the attest engagement.

(3) For purposes of determining materiality under Rule 101 [ET Section 101.01], the financial interests of the covered member and his or her immediate family should be aggregated.

Application of the Independence Rules to Close Relatives

(1) Independence would be considered to be impaired if

    (a) An individual participating on the attest engagement team has a close relative who had

        [1] A key position with the client; or

        [2] A financial interest in the client that

            [a] The individual or partner knows or has reason to believe was material to the close relative; or

            [b] Enabled the close relative to exercise significant influence over the client.

    (b) An individual in a position to influence the attest engagement or any partner in the office in which the lead attest engagement partner primarily practices in connection with the attest engagement has a close relative who had

        [1] A key position with the client; or

        [2] A financial interest in the client that

            [a] The individual or partner knows or has reason to believe was material to the close relative; and

            [b] Enabled the close relative to exercise significant influence over the client.

Application of the Independence Rules to Other Relatives and Friends

(1) Independence is only impaired when a reasonable person aware of all relevant facts relating to a situation would conclude that there is an unacceptable threat to independence (based on the AICPA Conceptual Framework for Independence Standards discussed earlier in this section).

Important Definitions

(1) **Covered member.** A covered member is

   (a) An individual on the attest engagement team;
   (b) An individual in a position to influence the attest engagement;
   (c) A partner or manager who provides nonattest services to the attest client beginning once he or she provides ten hours of nonattest services to the client within any fiscal year and ending on the later of the date:

   [1] The firm signs the report on the financial statements for the fiscal year during which those services were provided; or
   [2] He or she no longer expects to provide ten or more hours of nonattest services to the attest client on a recurring basis;

   (d) A partner in the office in which the lead attest engagement partner primarily practices in connection with the attest engagement;
   (e) The firm, including the firm's employee benefit plans; or
   (f) An entity whose operating, financial, or accounting policies can be controlled (as defined by generally accepted accounting principles [GAAP] for consolidation purposes) by any of the individuals or entities described in (a) through (e) or by two or more such individuals or entities if they act together.

(2) **Individual in a position to influence the attest engagement.** An individual in a position to influence the attest engagement is one who

   (a) Evaluates the performance or recommends the compensation of the attest engagement partner;
   (b) Directly supervises or manages the attest engagement partner, including all successively senior levels above that individual through the firm's chief executive;
   (c) Consults with the attest engagement team regarding technical or industry-related issues specific to the attest engagement; or
   (d) Participates in or oversees, at all successively senior levels, quality control activities, including internal monitoring, with respect to the specific attest engagement.

(3) **Period of the professional engagement.** The period of the professional engagement begins when a member either signs an initial engagement letter or other agreement to perform attest services or begins to perform an attest engagement for a client, whichever is earlier. The period lasts for the entire duration of the professional relationship (which could cover many periods) and ends with the formal or informal notification, either by the member or the client, of the termination of the professional relationship or by the issuance of a report, whichever is later. Accordingly, the period does not end with the issuance of a report and recommence with the beginning of the following year's attest engagement.

(4) **Key position.** A key position is a position in which an individual

   (a) Has primary responsibility for significant accounting functions that support material components of the financial statements;
   (b) Has primary responsibility for the preparation of the financial statements; or
   (c) Has the ability to exercise influence over the contents of the financial statements, including when the individual is a member of the board of directors or similar governing body, chief executive officer, president, chief financial officer, chief operating officer, general counsel, chief accounting officer, controller, director of internal audit, director of financial reporting, treasurer, or any equivalent position.

(5) **Close relative.** A close relative is a parent, sibling, or nondependent child.
(6) **Immediate family.** Immediate family is a spouse, spousal equivalent, or dependent (whether or not related).

Interpretation 101-2. A firm's independence is considered to be impaired if a partner or professional employee leaves the firm and is subsequently employed by or associated with a client in a key position, unless all of the following conditions are met:

(1) Amounts due to the former partner or professional employee for his or her previous interest in the firm and unfunded benefits are not material to the firm, and the amounts of payments are fixed,
(2) The former partner or professional employee is not in a position to influence the accounting firm's operations or financial policies,

(3) The former partner or professional employee is not associated with the firm (e.g., provides consulting services to the firm, the individual's name is included in the firm directory, etc.),

(4) The ongoing attest engagement team considers the risk of reduced audit effectiveness resulting from the fact that the partner or professional employee has prior knowledge of the audit plan,

(5) The firm assesses whether the existing attest engagement team members have appropriate experience and stature to effectively deal with the former partner or employee if significant interaction will occur, and

(6) The subsequent attest engagement is reviewed to determine whether the team members maintained the appropriate level of skepticism when evaluating the representations of the former partner or employee.

Interpretation 101-3. When a CPA performs nonattest services for an attest client it **may or may not** impair independence.

(1) This interpretation requires compliance with regulatory independence rules by regulators such as the SEC, the General Accounting Office (GAO), and the Department of Labor (DOL).

(2) Should not assume management responsibilities for attest clients.

    (a) Independence is not impaired if nonattest services are performed prior to the period of the professional audit engagement and relate to period before current audit.

    (b) Independence ordinarily is not impaired by attest related communications between the CPA and management regarding:

- Client's selection and application of accounting policies and discloses.
- Appropriateness of client's accounting methods.
- Adjusting journal entries member prepares or proposes.
- Form or content of the financial statements.

(3) When nonattest service are provided, the client must

    (a) Assume all management responsibilities

    (b) Oversee the service by designating an individual, preferably in senior management, who possesses suitable skill, knowledge and/or experience. The member should assess and be satisfied that such individual can perform the role.

    (c) Evaluate adequacy and results

    (d) Accept responsibility for results

    (e) Establish and maintain internal controls

(4) Must establish in writing understanding with client (board of directors, audit committee, or management) regarding

    (a) Engagement objectives

    (b) Services to be performed

    (c) Client's acceptance of its responsibilities

    (d) CPA's responsibilities

    (e) Any limitation of the engagement

(5) General activities that impair independence

    (a) Setting policies or strategic direction for the client.

    (b) Directing or accepting responsibility for actions of client employees (except as allowed for using the work of internal auditors)

    (c) Authorizing, executing, or consummating transactions

    (d) Preparing source documents

    (e) Having custody of assets

    (f) Deciding which recommendations are to be implemented or given priority

    (g) Reporting to those charged with governance on behalf of management

    (h) Accepting responsibility for managing a client's project

    (i) Accepting responsibility for preparing client financial statements

    (j) Serving as stock transfer agent, registrar, or general counsel

    (k) Accepting responsibility for designing, implementing or maintaining internal control

    (l) Performing evaluations of internal control as part of the company's monitoring activities.

(6) Independence is impaired by the performance of appraisal, valuation, and actuarial services if the results are material to the financial statements and the service involves a significant degree of subjectivity.

(7) Performing internal audit services for a client impairs independence unless the client accepts its responsibility for designing, implementing, and maintaining internal control and designates an officer to manage the internal audit function.

(8) The Sarbanes-Oxley Act of 2002 places additional restrictions on nonattest services for public company audit clients (see Section F).

Interpretation 101-4. CPA who is a director of a nonprofit organization where board is large and representative of community leadership is **not** lacking independence if

(1) Position purely honorary
(2) Position identified as honorary on external materials
(3) CPA participation restricted to use of name
(4) CPA does not vote or participate in management affairs

Interpretation 101-5. Loans from financial institution clients and related terminology

(1) Independence is not impaired by certain "grandfathered" and other loans from financial institution clients

   (a) Grandfathered loans that are permitted (home mortgages, other secured loans, loans immaterial to CPA) that were obtained

   [1] Prior to January 1, 1992, under standards then in effect
   [2] From a financial institution for which independence was not required, and the financial institution subsequently became an attest client
   [3] Obtained from a financial institution for which independence was not required, and the loan was sold to an attest client **or**
   [4] Obtained by a CPA prior to becoming a member of CPA firm of which the financial institution is an attest client

   (b) Other permitted loans from a financial institution attest client

   [1] Automobile loans and leases collateralized by automobile
   [2] Loans of surrender value under an insurance policy
   [3] Borrowings fully collateralized by cash deposits at same financial institution (e.g., "passbook loans")
   [4] Aggregate outstanding balances from credit card and overdraft accounts that are reduced to $10,000 on a current basis.

> **NOTE:** All of the above must be kept current and not renegotiated after the above dates. Also, the collateral on other secured loans must equal or exceed the remaining loan balance.

(2) Terminology

   (a) Loan—Financial transactions that generally provide for repayment terms and a rate of interest
   (b) Financial institution—An entity that makes loans to the general public as part of its normal business operations
   (c) Normal lending procedures, terms, and requirements—Comparable to those received by other borrowers during period, when considering

   [1] Amount of loan and collateral
   [2] Repayment terms
   [3] Interest rate, including "points"
   [4] Closing costs
   [5] General availability of such loans to public

Interpretation 101-6. Effect of threatened litigation

(1) Client-CPA actual or threatened litigation

    (a) Commenced by present management alleging audit deficiencies, impairs

    (b) Commenced by auditor against present management for fraud, deceit impairs

    (c) Expressed intention by present management alleging deficiencies in audit work impairs if auditor believes **strong possibility** of claim

    (d) Immaterial not related to audit **usually** does **not** impair (i.e., billing disputes)

(2) Litigation by client security holders or other third parties generally does not impair unless material client-CPA cross-claims develop.

(3) If independence is impaired, CPA should disassociate and/or disclaim an opinion for lack of independence.

Interpretation 101-7. (Deleted)

Interpretation 101-8. A CPA's financial interests in a nonclient may impair independence in a client of that CPA when that nonclient has financial interests in that client.

Interpretation 101-9. (Deleted)

Interpretation 101-10. Describes members' duties for independence when auditing entities included in governmental financial statements

(1) Generally, auditor of a material fund type, fund account group, or component unit of entity that should be disclosed in notes of general-purpose financial statements, but is not auditing primary government, should be independent with respect to those financial statements and primary government

(2) Also should be independent if, although funds and accounts are separately immaterial, they are material in the aggregate

Interpretation 101-11. Modified application of Rule 101 for engagements under the Statements on Standards for Attestation Engagements (SSAE)

The Rule 101 independence requirements apply to all attest engagements; exceptions in how they are applied for SSAE engagements:

(1) Those requiring independence other than agreed-upon procedures engagements:

    (a) Covered members must be independent of responsible party

    (b) When someone other than a responsible party engages the CPA, covered members need not be independent of that individual or entity

    (c) Nonattest services otherwise prohibited may be provided when such services do not relate to the specific subject matter of the SSAE engagement.

(2) Agreed-upon procedures (AUP) engagements. Only the following covered members and their immediate families are required to be independent with respect to the responsible party:

    (a) Individuals on AUP Team

    (b) Individuals who directly supervise or manage AUP engagement partner.

    (c) Individuals who consult with attest team on matters specific to AUP engagement.

Also, independence is impaired if firm had financial relationship covered by outline item (1) of Interpretation 101-1 that was material to the firm (i.e., the section on direct or material indirect financial interests, etc.)

Interpretation 101-12. Independence is impaired if during professional engagement or while expressing an opinion, member's firm had any material cooperative arrangement with client.

(1) Cooperative arrangement exists when member's firm and client participate jointly in business activity such as

    (a) Joint ventures to develop or market a product or service

    (b) Arrangements to provide services or products to a third party

    (c) Arrangements to combine services or products of the member's firm with those of client to market them with references to both parties

    (d) Arrangements under which member firm or client act as distributor of other's products or services

(2) Joint participation with client is not a cooperative arrangement and is thus allowed if all of the following three conditions are present.

  (a) Participation of the firm and client are governed by separate agreements
  (b) Neither firm nor client assumes any responsibility for the other
  (c) Neither party is an agent of the other

Interpretation 101-13. (Deleted)

Interpretation 101-14. If a firm is organized in an alternative practice structure, in which the attest function is part of a larger organization that leases the staff to the attest function, the independence provisions of the AICPA Code of Professional Conduct must be adhered to by all staff and management on attest engagement and every individual that is a direct superior of attest partners or managers. Indirect superiors of attest partners and managers cannot have any relationships prohibited by Interpretation 101-1A.

Interpretation 101-15. This interpretation provides definitions of direct and indirect financial interests that may impair independence.

(1) A **financial interest** is an ownership interest in an equity or a debt security issued by an entity, including derivatives directly related to the interest.

(2) A **direct financial interest** is

  (a) One owned directly by an individual or entity, under control of the individual or entity, or beneficially owned through an investment vehicle,
  (b) Under the control of an individual or entity, or
  (c) Beneficially owned through an investment vehicle, estate, trust or other intermediary when the beneficiary

    [1] Controls the intermediary, or
    [2] Has the authority to supervise or participate in the intermediary's investment decisions.

Interpretation 101-16 (Reserved)

Interpretation 101-17. A firm member of a network of firms is required to be independent of financial statement audit and review clients of the other members of the network for such clients for which the use of an audit report is not restricted; characteristics of a network include having a brand name, common control, profits/costs, common business strategy, significant professional resources, common quality controls.

Interpretation 101-18. Financial interests in, or other relationships with, affiliates of a financial statement attest client may impair independence with respect to that client. Examples of affiliates include entities (subsidiaries, partnerships, etc.) the attest client can control, material sister entities of the attest client, entities with a material direct financial interest in the attest client, an entity that controls the attest client, and the sponsor of the attest client's single-employer employee benefit plan. With respect to these entities, the CPA should apply the independence provisions of Rule 101 except in the following situations:

(1) A loan of a covered member from an officer, director, or 10-percent-or-more owner of an affiliate does not automatically impair independence. The member should evaluate the relationship by applying the Conceptual Framework for AICPA Independence Standards.

(2) A member or his or her firm may provide prohibited nonattest services to an affiliate providing it does not present a self-review threat to independence with respect to the attest client.

(3) Former employees of the affiliate may not affect independence if the position did not put them in a key position with respect to the attest client.

(4) Immediate family members and close relatives of a covered member may be employed at an affiliate in a key position provided that position does not put them in a key position with respect to the attest client.

Interpretation 101-19. Employment of a partner or professional staff member of a CPA firm with an educational institution does not impair the firm's independence with respect to the institution, providing that the partner or professional staff member:

(1) Does not hold a key position at the educational institution.
(2) Does not participate on the attest engagement team.
(3) Is not an individual in a position to influence the attest engagement.
(4) Is employed on a part-time and nontenure basis.
(5) Does not participate in the employee benefit plans sponsored by the educational institution.
(6) Does not assume any management responsibilities or set policies for the educational institution.

Rule 102 Integrity and Objectivity. In performance of **any** professional service, a member shall (a) maintain objectivity and integrity, (b) avoid conflicts of interest, and (c) not knowingly misrepresent facts or subordinate judgment.

(1) In tax matters, resolving doubt in favor of client does not, by itself, impair integrity or objectivity.

Interpretation 102-1. Knowingly making or permitting false and misleading entries in an entity's financial statements or records is a violation.

Interpretation 102-2. A conflict of interest may occur if a member performing a professional service has a **significant relationship** with another person, entity, product, or service that **could be viewed** as impairing the member's objectivity.

(1) If the member believes that the professional service can be performed with objectivity, and if the relationship is disclosed to and consent is obtained from the client, employer, or other appropriate parties, the rule does not prohibit performance of the professional service.
(2) Nothing in this interpretation overrides Rule 101 (on independence), its interpretations, and rulings.

Interpretation 102-3. When a member deals with his/her employer's external accountant, the member must be candid and not knowingly misrepresent facts or knowingly fail to disclose material facts.

Interpretation 102-4. If a member and his/her supervisor or any other person in the member's organization (hereafter, supervisor) have a difference of opinion relating to application of accounting principles, auditing standards or other relevant professional standards, the member should apply appropriate safeguards so as not to subordinate his/her judgment *when the member concludes the difference of opinion with the supervisor creates a threat to his/her integrity and objectivity*. In evaluating the significance of threats, the member should consider whether the result of the position taken by supervisor or other person (a) fails to comply with professional standards, (b) creates a material misrepresentation of fact, or (c) may violate applicable laws or regulations.

(1) If supervisor's position is not in compliance with professional standards but does not result in a material misrepresentation of fact or a violation of laws/regulations, the threats would not be considered significant (although member should discuss conclusions with person taking the position).
(2) If supervisor's position results in a material misrepresentation of fact or a violation of laws/regulations, threats would be considered significant and the member should discuss the matter with the supervisor. If the matter is still not resolved, the member should discuss concerns with higher levels of management in the member's organization. If the matter is still not resolved, the member should consider

   • Determining whether additional requirements exist under employer's internal policies and procedures.
   • Determining any other responsibilities to communicate to third parties.
   • Consulting with legal counsel.
   • Documenting his/her understanding of the facts, accounting principles, auditing standards and other relevant standards.

   The member may also conclude that a continuing relationship with the organization is inappropriate. Resignation, however, may not relieve member of responsibilities such as the above in the situation.

Interpretation 102-5. Those involved in educational services such as teaching full- or part-time at a university, teaching professional education courses, or engaged in research and scholarship are subject to Rule 102.

Interpretation 102-6. Sometimes members are asked by clients to act as advocates in support of clients' position on tax services, consulting services, accounting issues, or financial reporting issues. Member is still subject to Rule 102. Member is also still subject to Rules 201, 202, and 203. Member is also subject to Rule 101 for professional services requiring independence.

NOTE: While CPA candidates should read the rulings to better understand the ethics rules and interpretations, it is **not** necessary to memorize them; consider them to be illustrations. Gaps in sequence are due to deleted sections.

Rule 101, 102 Ethics Rulings

Independence and Integrity Ethics Rulings

2. A member may join a trade association that is a client, without impairing independence, but may not serve in a capacity of management.

8. Extensive accounting and consulting services, including interpretation of statements, forecasts, etc., do not impair independence.

11. Mere designation as executor or trustee, without actual services in either capacity, does not impair independence, but actual service does.

14. Independence of a member serving as director or officer of a local United Way or similar organization is not impaired with respect to a charity receiving funds from that organization unless the organization exercises managerial control over that charity.

17. The acquisition of equity or debt securities as a condition for membership in a country club does not normally impair independence; serving on the club's governing board or taking part in its management does impair independence.

20. Membership on governmental advisory committees does not impair independence with respect to that governmental unit.

21. Serving as a director of an entity impairs independence and therefore that member is not able to independently audit that entity's profit sharing and retirement trust.

31. A member's ownership of an apartment in a co-op apartment building would impair the member's and the firm's independence.

38. A member serves with a client bank in a co-fiduciary capacity with respect to an estate or trust. Independence with respect to the bank or the bank's trust department is not impaired, provided the assets in the estate or trust are not material to the total assets of the bank or the bank's trust department.

41. Independence is not impaired when a member's retirement plan is invested and managed by an insurance company in a separate account, not a part of the general assets of the insurance company.

52. Independence is impaired when prior year fees for professional services, whether billed or unbilled, remain unpaid for more than one year prior to the date of the report.

60. A member has been asked to audit the financial statements of an employee benefit plan that has one or more participating employers. Member independence with respect to the plan is impaired if a partner or professional employee of the CPA firm had significant influence over such employer, was in a key position with the employer, or was associated with the employer as a promoter, underwriter, or a voting trustee.

64. Independence with respect to a fund-raising foundation is impaired if a member serves on the board of directors of the entity for whose benefit the foundation exists (unless position is purely honorary).

67. If a client financial institution merely services a member's loan, independence is not impaired.

69. A member with a material limited partnership interest is not independent of other limited partnerships that have the same general partner. (The member is considered to have a joint closely held investment with the general partner.)

70. Maintaining state or federally insured deposits (e.g., checking accounts, savings accounts, certificates of deposit) in a financial institution does not impair independence; uninsured deposits do not impair independence if the uninsured amounts are immaterial.

71. CPA Firm A is not independent of an entity audited by Firm B. CPA Firm B may only use Firm A personnel in a manner similar to internal auditors without impairing Firm B's independence.

72. A member (and the member's firm) are not independent if the member serves on the advisory board of a client unless the advisory board (1) is truly advisory, (2) has no authority to make or appear to make management decisions, and (3) membership is distinct with minimal, if any, common membership with management and the board of directors.

74. A member must be independent to issue an audit opinion or a review report, but need not be independent to issue a compilation report (such lack of independence is disclosed).

75. Membership in a credit union does not impair audit independence if (1) the member qualifies as a credit union member on grounds other than by providing professional services, (2) the member does not exert significant influence over the credit union, (3) the member's loans (if any) from credit union are normal (see Interpretation 101-1), and (4) the conditions of Ruling 70 have been met.

81. A member's investment in a limited partnership impairs independence with respect to the limited partnership; when the investment is material, independence is impaired with respect to both the general partner of the limited partnership and any subsidiaries of the limited partnership.

82. When a member is the campaign treasurer for a mayoral candidate, independence is impaired with respect to the candidate's campaign organization, but independence is not impaired with respect to the candidate's political party or the municipality.

85. A member may serve as a bank director, but this is generally not desirable when s/he has clients that are bank customers; performing both services is allowed, however, if the relationship is disclosed and acceptable to all appropriate parties. Revealing confidential client information without client permission is a violation of the Code, even when the failure to disclose such information may breach the member's fiduciary responsibility as a director.

91. Independence is not impaired when a member has an "operating lease" from a client made under normal terms; independence is impaired by a "capital lease" from a client unless the "loan" related to the lease qualifies as "grandfathered."

92. A material joint investment in a vacation home with an officer, director, or principal stockholder of an attest client will impair independence.

93. When a member serves as a director or officer for the United Way or a similar organization and that organization provides funds to local charities that are the member's clients, a conflict of interest will not be considered to exist if the relationship is disclosed and consent is obtained from the appropriate parties.

94. Independence is not impaired if client in the engagement letter agrees to release, indemnify, defend, and hold harmless the member from any liability and costs from misrepresentations of management.

95. An agreement by the member and a client to use alternative dispute resolution techniques in lieu of litigation before a dispute arises does not impair independence.

96. A commencement of an alternative dispute resolution does not impair independence unless the member's and client's positions are materially adverse so that the proceedings are similar to litigation, such as binding arbitration.

98. A covered member's loan from a nonclient subsidiary impairs independence with respect to the client parent. However, a loan from a nonclient parent would not impair independence with respect to the client subsidiary, as long as the subsidiary is not material to its parent.

99. If a member is asked by a company to provide personal financial planning or tax services for its executives and the member may give the executives recommendations adverse to the company, before accepting and while doing this work, the member should consider Rule 102 on Integrity and Objectivity and Rule 301 on Confidential Client Information. The member can perform the work if s/he believes it can be done with objectivity.

100. A member who was independent when his/her report was issued, may resign the report or consent to its use at a later date when his/her independence is impaired, if no postaudit work is performed while impaired.

102. If a member indemnifies client for damages, losses or costs arising from lawsuits, claims, or settlements relating directly or indirectly to clients acts, this impairs independence.

106. Independence would be impaired if a member or the member's firm had significant influence over an entity that has significant influence over a client.

107. A covered member's participation in a health and welfare plan sponsored by a client would impair independence with respect to the client sponsor and the plan. However, if the covered member's participation results from permitted employment of the covered member's immediate family independence would not be considered impaired.

110. A covered member is associated with an entity in a position that allows him/her to exercise significant influence over the entity. The entity has a loan to or from a client. Independence would be impaired unless the loan is specifically permitted under Interpretation 101-5.

111. The performance of investment management or custodial services for an employee benefit plan would impair independence with respect to the plan. Independence would also be impaired with respect to the client sponsor of a defined benefit plan if the assets under management or in the custody of the member are material.

112. Rule 102, *Integrity and Objectivity,* requires the member to disclose to the client that the member uses a third-party service provider to perform certain of the services for the client.

113. Objectivity is impaired if a member receives a gift or entertainment from a client, unless the gift or entertainment is reasonable in the circumstances.

114. Objectivity is impaired if a covered member offers gifts or entertainment to an attest client, unless the gift or entertainment is clearly insignificant to the recipient.

Public Company Accounting Oversight Board (PCAOB) Independence Standards. The PCAOB adopted the AICPA rules, interpretations, and rulings relating to independence, integrity and objectivity as interim standards on April 16, 2003. Since then the PCAOB has adopted several additional independence standards. These standards apply to public accounting firms registered with the PCAOB when they are auditing an issuer (a public company).

(1) A registered public accounting firm must comply with all rules and standards of the PCAOB and also those set forth in the rules and regulations of the SEC under the federal securities laws.

(2) A registered public accounting firm is not independent of its audit client if the firm provides any service or product to the client for a contingent fee or a commission, or receives from the audit client a contingent fee or commission.

(3) A registered public accounting firm is not independent of its audit client if the firm provides any nonaudit service to the audit client related to marketing, planning, or opining in favor of

    (a) A ***confidential transaction*** (a tax transaction that is offered to a client under conditions of confidentiality and for which the client pays the public accounting firm a fee), or

    (b) ***Aggressive tax position transaction*** initially recommended by the public accounting firm.

(4) A registered public accounting firm is not independent of its audit client if the firm provides any tax service to a person in a financial reporting oversight role at the audit client, or an immediate family member of such person, unless

    (a) The person is in a financial reporting oversight role only because he or she serves as a member of the board of directors or similar body;

    (b) The person is in a financial reporting oversight role at the audit client only because of the person's relationship to an affiliate of the entity being audited, and

        [1] The affiliate's financial statements are not material to the consolidated financial statements, or
        [2] The affiliate is audited by another public accounting firm; or

    (c) The person was not in a financial reporting oversight role at the audit client before a hiring or some other change in employment and the tax services were

        [1] Provided pursuant to an engagement in process prior to the change in employment, and
        [2] Completed on or before 180 days after the change in employment.

(5) A registered public accounting firm must get preapproval from the audit committee to perform for an audit client any permissible tax service.

(6) A registered public accounting firm must communicate with the audit committee all relationships between the firm and the audit client that may reasonably be thought to bear on independence.

Rule 201 General Standards. Member shall comply with the following standards for all professional engagements:

(1) Only undertake professional services that one can reasonably expect to complete with professional competence

(2) Exercise due professional care

    (a) Member may need to consult with experts to exercise due care

(3) Adequately plan and supervise engagements

(4) Obtain sufficient relevant data to afford a reasonable basis for conclusions and recommendations

Interpretation 20161. Competence to complete an engagement includes

(1) Technical qualifications of CPA and staff

(2) Financial Accounting Standards Advisory Board for accounting principles for federal governmental entities

(3) Ability to supervise and evaluate work

(4) Knowledge of technical subject matter

(5) Capability to exercise judgment in its application

(6) Ability to research subject matter and consult with others

Interpretations 201-2, 3, 4. (Deleted)

Rule 202 Compliance with Standards. A member who performs auditing, review, compilation, consulting services, tax or other services shall comply with standards promulgated by bodies designated by Council.

NOTE: The designated bodies are

(1) Financial Accounting Standards Board for accounting principles for businesses
(2) Financial Accounting Standards Advisory Board for accounting principles for federal governmental entities
(3) Governmental Accounting Standards Board for accounting principles for state and local governmental entities
(4) Public Company Accounting Oversight Board for auditing, attestation, quality control, ethics and independence standards for companies covered by the Sarbanes-Oxley Act
(5) International Accounting Standards Board for international accounting standards
(6) AICPA designated bodies

    (a) Accounting and Review Services Committee
    (b) Auditing Standards Board
    (c) Management Consulting Services Executive Committee
    (d) Tax Executive Committee
    (e) Forensic and Valuation Executive Committee

Rule 203 Accounting Principles. Member cannot provide positive or negative assurance that financial statements are in conformity with GAAP if statements contain departures from GAAP having a material effect on statements taken as a whole except when unusual circumstances would make financial statements following GAAP misleading.

(1) Sources of GAAP: Financial Accounting Standards Board, financial Accounting Standards Advisory Board, Governmental Accounting Standards Board, International Accounting Standards Board.
(2) When unusual circumstances require a departure from GAAP, CPA must disclose in report the departure, its effects (if practicable), and reasons why compliance would result in a misleading statement.

Interpretation 203-1. CPAs are to allow departure from GAAP (without giving qualified or adverse opinion) only when results of applying will be misleading.
Examples of possible circumstances justifying departure are

(1) New legislation
(2) New form of business transaction

Interpretation 203-2. FASB, GASB and FASAB Interpretations are covered by Rule 203
Interpretation 203-3. (Deleted)
Interpretation 203-4. Rule 203 also applies to communications by employees such as reports to regulatory authorities, creditors, and auditors.
Interpretation 203-5. CPA may report on financial statements prepared using financial frameworks other than GAAP (e.g., principles of a particular country, principles used in a contract, statutory reporting provisions required by law). The financial statements or reports should not purport that GAAP were followed and should make clear the financial reporting framework used.

Rule 201, 202, 203 Ethics Rulings

8. A member selecting subcontractors for consulting services engagements is obligated to select subcontractors on the basis of professional qualifications, technical skills, etc.
9. A member should be in a position to supervise and evaluate work of a specialist in his employ.
10. If a member prepares financial statements as a stockholder, partner, director, or employee of an entity, any transmittal should indicate the member's relationship and should not imply independence.

If transmittal indicates financial statements are in accordance with GAAP, Rule 203 must be met. If financial statements are on member's letterhead, member should disclose lack of independence.

12. The CPA firm is responsible for providing adequate oversight of all services performed by a third-party provider for the firm's clients to ensure that the provider complies with professional standards.

Rule 301 Confidential Client Information. Member in public practice shall not disclose confidential client information without client consent except for

(1) Compliance with Rule 202 and 203 obligations
(2) Compliance with enforceable subpoena or summons
(3) AICPA review of professional practice
(4) Initiating complaint or responding to inquiry made by a recognized investigative or disciplinary body

Interpretation 301-1. (Deleted)
Interpretation 301-2. (Deleted)
Interpretation 301-3. A member who is considering selling his/her practice, or merging with another CPA, may allow that CPA to review confidential client information without the specific consent of the client.

(1) The member should take appropriate precautions (e.g., obtain a written confidentiality agreement) so that the prospective purchaser does not disclose such information.

> **NOTE:** This exception only relates to a review in conjunction with a purchase or merger. It **does not** apply to the review of working papers **after** a CPA has purchased another's practice. AU-C 510, discussed in detail later in this module, requires that the successor who wishes to review predecessor auditor working papers should request the client to authorize the predecessor to make such working papers available.

Rule 302 Contingent Fees.

(1) A member in public practice shall not

(a) Perform for a contingent fee any professional services when the member or member's firm also performs any of the following services for that client:

[1] Audits or reviews of financial statements
[2] Compilations when the member is independent and expects that a third party may use the financial statements
[3] Examinations of prospective financial information

(b) Prepare an original or amended tax return or claims for a tax refund for a contingent fee for any client

(2) Solely for purposes of this rule, (a) fees fixed by courts or other public authorities, or (b) in tax matters, fees determined based on the results of a judicial proceeding or findings of governmental agency, are not regarded as contingent and are therefore permitted.

Interpretation 302-1. Contingent fees in tax matters

(1) A contingent fee **would be permitted** in various circumstances in which the amounts due are not clear; examples are

(a) Representing a client in an examination by a revenue agent
(b) Filing amended tax returns based on a tax issue that is the subject of a test case **involving a different taxpayer** or where the tax authority is developing a position.
(c) Representing a taxpayer in getting a private ruling

(2) A contingent fee **would not be permitted** for preparing an amended tax return for a client claiming a refund that is clearly due to the client because of an inadvertent omission.

Rule 301, 302 Ethics Rulings

1. A member may utilize outside computer services to process tax returns as long as there is no release of confidential information.
2. With client permission, a member may provide P&L percentages to a trade association.
3. A CPA withdrawing from a tax engagement due to irregularities on the client's return should urge suc-cessor CPA to have client grant permission to reveal reasons for withdrawal.
6. A member may be engaged by a municipality to ver-ify taxpayer's books and records for the purpose of assessing property tax. The member must maintain confidentiality.
7. Members may reveal the names of clients without

client consent unless such disclosure releases confidential information.

14. A member has a responsibility to honor confidential relationships with nonclients. Accordingly, members may have to withdraw from consulting services engagements where the client will not permit the member to make recommendations without disclosing confidential information about other clients or nonclients.

15. If the member has conducted a similar consulting services study with a negative outcome, the member should advise potential clients of the previous problems providing that earlier confidential relationships are not disclosed. If the earlier confidential relationship may be disclosed (through client knowledge of other clients), the member should seek approval from the first client.

16. In divorce proceedings a member who has prepared joint tax returns for the couple should consider both individuals to be clients for purposes of requests for confidential information relating to prior tax returns. Under such circumstances the CPA should consider reviewing the legal implications of disclosure with an attorney.

17. A contingent fee or a commission is considered to be "received" when the performance of the related services is complete and the fee or commission is determined.

18. Identical to Ruling 85 under Rule 101.

19. A member's spouse may provide services to a member's attest client for a contingent fee and may refer products or services for a commission.

20. When a member learns of a potential claim against him/her, the member may release confidential client information to member's liability carrier used solely to defend against claim.

21. Identical to Ruling 99 under Rule 102.

23. A member may disclose confidential client information to the member's attorney or a court in connection with actual or threatened litigation.

24. A member's fee for investment advisory services for an attest client that is based on a percentage of the portfolio would be considered contingent and a violation of Rule 302, unless

    a. The fee is determined as a specified percentage of the portfolio,
    b. The dollar amount of the portfolio is determined at the beginning of each quarterly period (or longer) and is adjusted only for additions or withdrawals by the client, and
    c. The fee arrangement is not renewed with the client more frequently than on a quarterly basis.

25. A member who provides for a contingent fee investment advisory service, or refers for a commission products or services to the owners, officers, or employees of an attest client would not violate Rule 302 with respect to the client.

ET 400: Responsibilities to colleagues. No current rules or interpretations (section reserved).

Rule 501 Acts Discreditable. A member shall not commit an act discreditable to the profession.

Interpretation 501-1. A CPA's response to a client's request for records depends upon the nature of the records and certain circumstances:

(1) *Records provided by the client*—should be returned to client at the client's request.

(2) *CPA-prepared records that the CPA was not specifically engaged to prepare and are not in the client's books and records, with the result that the client's financial information is incomplete* (e.g., adjusting entries, closing entries and supporting schedules prepared as part of an engagement)—should be provided except that they may be withheld if there are fees due the CPA for the specific work product.

(3) *CPA work products (e.g., "deliverables" such as audit report, tax returns)*—should be provided to the client except that they may be withheld if

    (a) There are fees due on that work product
    (b) Work product is incomplete
    (c) Needed to comply with a professional standard (e.g., withholding an audit report due to outstanding audit issues)
    (d) There is threatened or outstanding litigation concerning the engagement or CPA's work.

(4) *CPA working papers*—prepared solely for the engagement either by the auditor (e.g., audit programs, analytical review procedures schedules) or by the client (at the request of CPA) are CPA's property and need not be provided.

NOTE: In all cases (1 through 4 above), if an authoritative regulatory body such as the CPA's state board of accountancy has a stricter rule, the CPA must follow it.

Interpretation 501-2. Discrimination on basis of race, color, religion, sex, age, or national origin is discreditable.

Interpretation 501-3. In audits of governmental grants, units, or other recipients of governmental monies, failure to follow appropriate governmental standards, procedures, etc. is discreditable.

Interpretation 501-4. Negligently making (or permitting or directing another to make) false or misleading journal entries is discreditable.

Interpretation 501-5. When a governmental body, commission, or other regulatory agency has requirements beyond those required by GAAS, members are required to follow them.

(1) Failure to follow these requirements is considered an act discreditable to the profession, unless the member discloses in the report that such requirements were not followed and the reasons therefor.

Interpretation 501-6. Member who solicits or discloses May 1996 or later Uniform CPA Examination question(s) and/or answer(s) without AICPA written authorization has committed an act discreditable to profession in violation of Rule 501.

Interpretation 501-7. A member who fails to comply with applicable federal, state, or local laws and regulations regarding the timely filing of his or her personal tax returns, or the timely remittance of all payroll and other taxes collected on behalf of others has committed an act discreditable to the profession.

Interpretation 501-8. In some engagements, government regulators prohibit indemnification or limitation of liability agreements. If the CPA engages in such agreements when they are prohibited, he or she has committed an act discreditable to the profession.

Interpretation 501-9. A CPA should maintain confidentiality of his or her employer's confidential information and any information obtained about an organization for which the CPA provides services on a voluntary basis. Disclosure of such information would be considered an act discreditable to the profession. Examples of situations in which the CPA may disclose confidential information include

(1) Disclosure is permitted by law and authorized by the employer.
(2) Disclosure is required by law.
(3) There is a professional responsibility to disclose the information.
(4) Disclosure is permitted on behalf of the employer.

Interpretation 501-10. A CPA is prohibited from promoting or marketing his or her abilities to provide professional services, or making claims about his or her experience or qualifications in a manner that is false, misleading, or deceptive.

Interpretation 501-11. A member who fails to follow state accountancy laws, rules and regulations regarding the use of the CPA credential in all jurisdictions in which the CPA practices is considered to have used the CPA credential in a manner that is false, misleading or deceptive and in violation of Rule 501.

Rule 502 Advertising and Other Forms of Solicitation. In public practice, shall not seek to obtain clients by false, misleading, deceptive advertising or other forms of solicitation.

Interpretation 502-1. (Deleted)

Interpretation 502-2. Advertising that is false, misleading or deceptive is prohibited, including advertising that

(1) Creates false or unjustified expectations
(2) Implies ability to influence a court, tribunal, regulatory agency or similar body or official
(3) Contains unrealistic estimates of future fees
(4) Would lead a reasonable person to misunderstand or be deceived

Interpretations 502-3, 4. (Deleted)

Interpretation 502-5. CPA may render services to clients of third parties as long as all promotion efforts are within Code.

Interpretation 502-6. A member who fails to follow state accountancy laws, rules and regulations regarding the use of the CPA credential in all jurisdictions in which the CPA practices is considered to have used the CPA credential in a manner that is false, misleading or deceptive and in violation of Rule 502.

Rule 503 Commissions and Referral Fees.

(1) A member in public practice may not accept a commission for recommending a product or service to a client when the member or member's firm also performs any of the following services for that client:

        (a) Audits or reviews of financial statements

        (b) Compilations when the member is independent and expects that a third party may use the financial statements

        (c) Examinations of prospective financial information

   (2) A member who receives a commission [not prohibited in (1) above] shall disclose that fact to the client.

   (3) A member who accepts a referral fee for recommending or referring any service of a CPA to any person or entity, or who pays a referral fee to obtain a client, shall disclose such acceptance or payment to the client.

Rule 504. (Deleted)

Rule 505 Form of Practice and Name. Member may practice public accounting in form of proprietorship, partnership, professional corporation, etc. and may not practice under a misleading name.

Interpretation 505-1. (Deleted)

Interpretation 505-2. Applicability of rules to members who operate a separate business that provides accounting services.

   (1) A member in public practice who participates in the operation of a separate business that performs accounting, tax, etc. services must observe all of the Rules of Conduct.

   (2) A member not otherwise in public practice must observe the Rules of Conduct if the member holds out as a CPA and performs for a client any professional services included in public accounting.

Interpretation 505-3. CPAs with attest practices that are organized as alternative practice structures must remain financially and otherwise responsible for the attest work.

Interpretation 505-4. A firm name would be considered misleading if it contains a representation that would be likely to cause a reasonable person to misunderstand, or be confused about, the legal form of the firm or who the owners or members of the firm are, such as a reference to a type of organization or abbreviation thereof that does not accurately reflect the form.

Interpretation 505-5. The sharing of a common brand name or common initials of a group of CPA firms within a network would not be considered misleading, provided the firm is a network firm.

Rule 591 Ethics Rulings and Other Responsibilities
Ethics Rulings

Due to rescinding the advertising and solicitation prohibition, the majority of the ethics rulings have been suspended.

3. A CPA employed by a firm with non-CPA practitioners must comply with the rules of conduct. If a partner of such a firm is a CPA, the CPA is responsible for all persons associated with the firm to comply with the rules of conduct.

134. Members who share offices, employees, etc., may not indicate a partnership exists unless a partnership agreement is in effect.

135. CPA firms that are members of an association cannot use letterhead that indicates a partnership rather than an association.

136. Where a firm consisting of a CPA and a non-CPA is dissolved, and an audit is continued to be serviced by both, the audit opinion should be signed by both individuals, such that a partnership is not indicated.

137. The designation "nonproprietary partner" should not be used to describe personnel as it may be misleading.

138. A member may be a partner of a firm of public accountants when all other personnel are not certified, and at the same time practice separately as a CPA.

141. A CPA in partnership with a non-CPA is ethically responsible for all acts of the partnership and those of the non-CPA partner.

145. Newly merged CPA firms may practice under a title that includes the name of a previously retired partner from one of the firms.

183. A CPA firm may designate itself "Accredited Personal Financial Specialists" on its letterhead and in marketing materials if all partners or shareholders of the firm currently have the AICPA-awarded designation.

184. Identical to Ruling 18 under Rule 302.

185. A member may purchase a product from a supplier and resell it to a client at a profit without disclosing the profit to the client.

186. A member may contract for support services from a computer-hardware maintenance servicer and bill them to a client at a profit without disclosing the profit to the client.

187. Identical to Ruling 19 under Rule 302.

188. When a member refers products to clients through distributors and agents, the member may not perform for those clients the services described in

Rule 503 [part (1) of the outline of Rule 503].

189. When individuals associated with a client entity have an internal dispute, and have separately asked a member for client records, the member need only supply them once, and to the individual who previously has been designated or held out as the client's representative.

190. A member who is in a partnership with non-CPAs may sign reports with the firm name and below it affix his own signature with the designation "Certified Public Accountant" providing it is clear that the partnership is not being held out as composed entirely of CPAs.

191. If a member (not an owner) of a firm is terminated, he/she may not take copies of the firm's client files without the firm's permission.

192. A member who provides for a contingent fee investment advisory services, or refers for a commission products or services to the owners, officers, or employees of an attest client would not violate Rule 302 or Rule 503 with respect to the client.

4. Responsibilities in Consulting Services

    a. In January of 1991 a new series of pronouncements on consulting services, *Statements on Standards for Consulting Services* (SSCS), became effective. This series of pronouncements replaces the three *Statements on Standards for Management Advisory Services*. These standards apply to CPAs in public practice who provide consulting services.

    b. Outline of SSCS 1 Definitions and Standards

        (1) Comparison of consulting and attest services

            (a) **Attest services**—Practitioner expresses a conclusion about the reliability of a written assertion that is the responsibility of another party (the asserter)

            (b) **Consulting services**—Practitioner develops the findings, conclusions and recommendations presented, generally only for the use and benefit of the client; the nature of the work is determined solely by agreement between the practitioner and the client

            (c) Performance of consulting services **for an attest client** requires that the practitioner maintain independence and does not in and of itself impair independence

> **NOTE:** While one must remain objective in performing consulting services, independence is not required unless the practitioner also performs attest (e.g., audit) services for that client.

        (2) Definitions

            (a) **Consulting services practitioner**—A CPA in public practice while engaged in the performance of a consulting service for a client

            (b) **Consulting process**—Analytical approach and process applied in a consulting service

                [1] This definition **excludes** services subject to other AICPA technical standards on auditing (SAS), other attest services (SSAE), compilations and reviews (SSARS), most tax engagements, and recommendations made during one of these engagements as a direct result of having performed these excluded services

            (c) **Consulting services**—Professional services that employ the practitioner's technical skills, education, observations, experiences, and knowledge of the consulting process

        (3) Types of consulting services

            (a) **Consultations**—Provide counsel in a short time frame, based mostly, if not entirely, on existing personal knowledge about the client

                [1] Examples: reviewing and commenting on a client business plan, suggesting software for further client investigation

            (b) **Advisory services**—Develop findings, conclusions and recommendations for client consideration and decision making

[1] Examples: Operational review and improvement study, analysis of accounting system, strategic planning assistance, information system advice

(c) **Implementation services**—Place an action plan into effect

[1] Examples: Installing and supporting computer system, executing steps to improve productivity, assisting with mergers

(d) **Transaction services**—Provide services related to a specific client transaction, generally with a third party

[1] Examples: Insolvency services, valuation services, information related to financing, analysis of a possible merger or acquisition, litigation services

(e) **Staff and other support services**—Provide appropriate staff and possibly other support to perform tasks specified by client

[1] Examples: Data processing facilities management, computer programming, bankruptcy trusteeship, controllership activities

(f) **Product services**—Provide client with a product and associated support services

[1] Examples: Sale, delivery, installation, and implementation of training programs, computer software, and systems development

(4) Standards for Consulting Services

(a) General Standards of Rule 201 of Code of Professional Conduct

[1] Professional competence
[2] Due professional care
[3] Planning and supervision
[4] Sufficient relevant data

(b) Additional standards established for this area (under Rule 202 of Code of Professional Conduct)

[1] Client interest—Must serve client interest while maintaining integrity and objectivity
[2] Understanding with client—Establish either in writing or orally
[3] Communication with client—Inform client of any conflicts of interest, significant reservations about engagement, significant engagement findings

(c) Professional judgment must be used in applying SSCS

[1] Example: Practitioner not required to decline or withdraw from a consulting engagement when there are mutually agreed upon limitations with respect to gathering relevant data

5. Responsibilities in Personal Financial Planning

a. Definition, scope and standards of personal financial planning

(1) Personal financial planning engagements are only those that involve developing strategies and making recommendations to assist a client in defining and achieving personal financial goals

(2) Personal financial planning engagements involve all of following

(a) Defining engagement objectives
(b) Planning specific procedures appropriate to engagement
(c) Developing basis for recommendations
(d) Communicating recommendations to client
(e) Identifying tasks for taking action on planning decisions

(3) Other engagements may also include

(a) Assisting client to take action on planning decisions
(b) Monitoring client's progress in achieving goals
(c) Updating recommendations and helping client revise planning decisions

(4) Personal financial planning does not include services that are limited to, for example

    (a) Compiling personal financial statements
    (b) Projecting future taxes
    (c) Tax compliance, including, but not limited to, preparation of tax returns
    (d) Tax advice or consultations

(5) CPA should act in conformity with AICPA Code of Professional Conduct

    (a) Rule 102, Integrity and Objectivity

        [1] A member shall maintain objectivity and integrity, be free of conflicts of interest, and not knowingly misrepresent facts or subordinate his/her judgment to others

    (b) Rule 201

        [1] A member shall undertake only those professional services that member can reasonably expect to be completed with professional competence, shall exercise due professional care in the performance of professional services, shall adequately plan and supervise performance of professional services, and shall obtain sufficient relevant data to afford a reasonable basis for conclusions or recommendations

    (c) Rule 301, Confidential Client Information

        [1] Member in public practice shall not disclose any confidential client information without specific consent of client

    (d) Rule 302, Contingent Fees

        [1] Rules must be followed

(6) When a personal financial planning engagement includes providing assistance in preparation of personal financial statements or financial projections, the CPA should consider applicable provisions of AICPA pronouncements, including

    (a) Statements on Standards for Accounting and Review Services
    (b) Statement on Standards for Attestation Engagements Financial Forecasts and Projections
    (c) Audit and Accounting Guide for Prospective Financial Information
    (d) Personal Financial Statements Guide

(7) The CPA should document his/her understanding of scope and nature of services to be provided

    (a) Consider engagement letter

(8) Personal financial planning engagement should be adequately planned

(9) Engagement's objectives form basis for planning engagement

    (a) Procedures should reflect materiality and cost-benefit considerations

(10) Relevant information includes understanding of client's goals, financial position, and available resources for achieving goals

    (a) External factors (such as inflation, taxes, and investment markets) and nonfinancial factors (such as client attitudes, risk tolerance, spending habits, and investment preferences) are also relevant information
    (b) Relevant information also includes reasonable estimates furnished by client's advisors, or developed by CPA

(11) Recommendations should ordinarily be in writing and include summary of client's goals and significant assumptions and description of any limitations on work performed

(12) Unless otherwise agreed, CPA is not responsible for additional services, for example,

    (a) Assisting client to take action on planning decisions
    (b) Monitoring progress in achieving goals
    (c) Updating recommendations and revising planning decisions

    b. Working with other advisers

       (1) If CPA does not provide a service needed to complete an engagement, s/he should restrict scope of engagement and recommend that client engage another adviser

       (2) If client declines to engage another adviser, CPA and client may still agree to proceed with engagement

    c. Implementation engagement functions and responsibilities

       (1) Implementation engagements involve assisting client to take action on planning decisions developed during personal financial planning engagement

       (2) Implementation includes activities such as selecting investment advisers, restructuring debt, creating estate documents, establishing cash reserves, preparing budgets, and selecting and acquiring specific investments and insurance products

       (3) When undertaking implementation engagement, CPA should apply existing professional standards and published guidance

---

NOW REVIEW MULTIPLE-CHOICE QUESTIONS 1 THROUGH 26

B. The Sarbanes-Oxley Act of 2002

  1. Title 1—Authorizes establishment of Public Company Accounting Oversight Board

    a. Consists of five members

       (1) Two members must be or have been CPAs

       (2) Three members cannot be or cannot have been CPAs

       (3) None of Board members may receive pay or profits from CPA firms

    b. Board regulates CPA firms ("registrants") that audit SEC registrants ("issuers")

       (1) Main functions are to

         (a) Register and conduct inspections of public accounting firms (this replaces peer reviews)

         (b) Set or adopt standards on auditing, quality control, independence, or preparation of audit reports (as per below, PCAOB adopted AICPA standards on an interim basis as of April 16, 2003)

       (2) Details—PCAOB

         (a) Enforces compliance with professional standards, securities laws relating to accountants and audits.

         (b) May regulate nonaudit services CPA firms perform for clients.

         (c) Performs investigations and disciplinary proceedings on registered public accounting firms.

         (d) May perform any other duties needed to promote high professional standards and to improve auditing quality.

    c. Accounting firms must have second partner review and approve each audit report.

    d. Accounting firms must report on an audit of internal control in addition to the audit of the financial statements for issuers.

    e. Most CPA working papers must be saved for seven years.

    f. Material additional services of auditors must receive preapproval by audit committee, and fees for those services must be disclosed to investors.

  2. Title II—Auditor Independence

    a. The act lists several specific service categories that the issuer's public accounting firm cannot legally perform

       (1) Bookkeeping or other services relating to financial statements or accounting records

       (2) Financial information systems design and/or implementation

       (3) Appraisal services

      (4) Internal audit outsourcing services

      (5) Management functions

      (6) Actuarial services

      (7) Investment or broker-dealer services

      (8) Certain tax services, such as tax planning for potentially abusive tax shelters

          Note that the Act does not restrict auditors from performing these services to nonaudit clients or to private companies. Also, the Act permits the auditor to perform nonaudit services not specifically prohibited (e.g., tax services) when approved by issuer's audit committee.

   b. The audit partner for the job and the audit partner who reviews the audit can do the audit services for only five consecutive years.

      (1) If public company has hired employee of an audit firm to be its CEO, CFO, or CAO within previous year, that audit firm cannot audit the company.

   c. The audit firm should report critical accounting policies, alternative treatments of transactions, etc. and other material written communications between the accounting firm and management to the audit committee.

3. Title III—Section 303

   a. It is unlawful for any officer or director to take any action to fraudulently influence, coerce, manipulate, or mislead any public accountant engaged in the performance of the audit.

4. Title IV

   a. Section 404 is particularly important to the overall process of CPA reporting on internal control.

      (1) It in essence led to CPA reporting on client internal control by establishing the following:

         (a) It is management's responsibility to establish adequate internal control

         (b) Management must assess its IC

         (c) The CPA firm attests to management's assessment of IC

   b. Section 406 requires every issuer shall report whether it has adopted a code of ethics for senior financial officers.

   c. CEOs and CFOs of most large companies are now required to certify financial statements filed with SEC

      (1) They certify that the information "fairly presents in all material respects the financial statements and result of operations" of the company.

C. Public Company Accounting Oversight Board

1. On April 16, 2003, the PCAOB adopted the following AICPA standards as its interim standards to be used on an initial transitional basis:

   a. Auditing Standards Board Standards (through SAS 95).

   b. Attestation Standards

   c. Quality Control Standards

   d. Ethics Standards 101 (Independence) and 102 (Integrity and objectivity) and several standards issued by the Independence Standards Board

2. The PCAOB has broad authority to oversee the public accounting profession by establishing rules in the above areas; in addition it

   a. Registers public accounting firms that audit issuers companies

   b. Performs inspections of the practices of registered firms

   c. Conducts investigations and disciplinary proceedings of registered firms

   d. Sanctions registered firms.

3. Inspections performed by the PCAOB

   a. The Sarbanes-Oxley Act requires that the PCAOB perform inspections of CPA firms that include at least the following three general components:

    (1) An inspection and review of selected audit and review engagements

    (2) An evaluation of the sufficiency of the quality control system of the CPA firm and the manner of documentation and communication of the system

    (3) Performance of such other testing of the audit, supervisory, and quality control procedures as are considered necessary

  b. Although inspections performed by the PCAOB staff meet the AICPA's practice review requirement for the public auditing practices of CPA firms, they differ from peer reviews conducted by CPA firms. Inspections generally focus on selected quality control issues and may also consider other aspects of practice management, such as how partner compensation is determined. Most of the inspection process is focused on evaluating a CPA firm's performance on a sample of individual audit and review engagements. In selecting the engagements for inspection, the PCAOB staff uses a risk assessment process to identify those engagements that have a higher risk of lack of compliance with professional standards. When an audit is selected, the inspection focuses on the high-risk aspects of that engagement, such as revenue recognition and accounting estimates. When a lack of compliance with professional standards is identified, the PCAOB staff attempts to determine the cause, which may lead to identification of a defect in the firm's quality control system.

  c. Each inspection results in a written report that is transmitted to the SEC and appropriate regulatory authorities. Also included is a letter of comments by the PCAOB inspectors, and any responses by the CPA firm. While the content of most of the reports are made available to the public, discussion of criticisms of a firm's quality control system are not made public unless the firm does not address the criticism within twelve months.

4. Several issues relating to PCAOB implementation of Sarbanes-Oxley independence requirements through rules passed include

- Prior to accepting an initial engagement (e.g., audit), the CPA firm must

  - Describe in writing to the audit committee all relationships between the CPA firm and the potential audit client (or persons in financial reporting oversight roles with the potential audit client) that may reasonably be thought to bear on independence.
  - Discuss any possible effects on independence of above relationships.
  - Document the substance of the discussion.

At least annually the above is updated.

- Recall that the Sarbanes-Oxley Act requires audit committee preapproval of permissible nonaudit services. The PCAOB has issued rules that require that when obtaining preapproval of *permissible tax services* or *permissible nonaudit services related to internal control over financial reporting,* the CPA firm must

  - Describe those services in writing to the audit committee.
  - Discuss any possible effects on independence with the audit committee.
  - Document the substance of the discussion.

- A CPA firm is not independent if it provides a client nonaudit services related to marketing, planning, or opinion in favor of the tax treatment of confidential transactions or aggressive tax position transactions (unless the proposed tax treatment is at least more likely than not to be allowable).

- A CPA firm is not independent if it provides any tax services to a person or a financial reporting oversight role to the audit client, or an immediate family member of such person. There are several exceptions if the person the services are provided for only serves as a member of the board of directors.

5. PCAOB Auditing Standards are discussed in subsequent modules; outlines and summary information follow the AU-C outlines.

D. International Standards—Ethical

The International Ethics Standards Board for Accountants (IESBA) is a standard-setting body within the International Federation of Accountants (IFAC) that issues ethical standards for accountants throughout the world. This group has issued the *Code of Ethics for Professional Accountants,* which is similar to the *Code of Professional Conduct* issued by the AICPA for accountants in the US. The IESBA code has three parts:

- Part A—Framework applies to all professional accountants
- Part B—Applies to professional accountants in public practice
- Part C—Applies to professional accountants in business

Part A—Framework

Section 110—Integrity. Professional accountants should be straightforward and honest in all professional and business relationships. Integrity implies fair dealing and truthfulness. The accountant should not be associated with reports or other communications where the accountant believes the information contains a materially false or misleading statement, contains statements or information furnished recklessly, or omits or obscures information required to be included where such omission or obscurity would be misleading.

Section 120—Objectivity. Professional accountants should not compromise their professional or business judgment.

Section 130—Professional Competence and Due Care. Professional accountants should maintain professional knowledge and skill at the level required to ensure that clients or employers receive competent professional service, and to act diligently in accordance with applicable technical and professional standards.

Section 140—Confidentiality. Professional accountants should refrain from disclosing confidential information unless there is a legal or professional obligation to do so, and using confidential information for personal advantage.

Section 150—Professional Behavior. Professional accountants should comply with laws and regulations and avoid actions that would discredit the profession. In marketing services the professional accountant shall be honest and truthful.

Part B—Accountants in Public Practice

Section 200—Professional Accountants in Public Practice. This section of the code begins with a framework that presents threats to ethical behavior and safeguards to help mitigate these threats.

Section 210—Professional Appointment. Before accepting a new client, a professional accountant should determine whether acceptance would create any threats to compliance with fundamental principles.

Section 220—Conflicts of Interest. A professional accountant should take reasonable steps to identify circumstances that could pose a conflict of interest.

Section 230—Second Opinions. When asked to provide a second opinion on applicable accounting, auditing, reporting or other standards to specific circumstances or transactions, a professional accountant should evaluate the significance of threats and apply necessary safeguards.

Section 240—Fees and Other Types of Remuneration. Commissions, referral fees, fees that are not adequate, and contingent fees may create threats to compliance with professional standards. Therefore, the professional accountant should make sure that necessary safeguards are in effect around fee determination.

Section 250—Marketing Professional Services. Solicitation of new work through advertising or other forms of marketing may create a threat to compliance with fundamental principles. The accountant in public practice should not bring the profession in disrepute when marketing professional services. Assertions in marketing should be honest and truthful.

Section 260—Gifts and Hospitality. Gifts and hospitality from a client may create a threat to independence. The accountant must evaluate the significance of the threat and apply necessary safeguards.

Section 270—Custody of Client Assets. A professional accountant in public practice shall not assume custody of client monies or other assets unless permitted by law.

Section 280—Objectivity—All Services. A professional accountant shall determine when providing professional services whether there are threats to objectivity. If so, the accountant should apply necessary safeguards.

Section 290—Independence—Audit and Review Engagements. The international ethics rules regarding independence in audit and review engagements are similar to the AICPA rules. Both require the concepts of independence in mind and in appearance. However, the international ethics rules have fewer definitive prohibitions. Like the AICPA Code, when there is no definitive prohibition, the following approach is used:

1. Identify threats to independence;
2. Evaluate the significance of the threats identified; and
3. Apply safeguards, when necessary, to eliminate the threats or reduce them to an acceptable level. If safeguards do not reduce the risk to an acceptable level, the firm should not accept or continue the engagement, or assign the particular individual to the engagement team. The firm should document these considerations and the conclusion. Threats to independence arise from self interest, self review, advocacy, familiarity, or intimidation.

    a. Like the AICPA *Code of Professional Conduct,* the international ethics rules indicate these types of threats can arise from

- Financial interests in the client;
- Having certain business relationships with the client;
- Serving as a director, officer, or employee of the client; and
- Performing certain non-assurance services to the client.

    b. Safeguards are of two categories: (1) those created by the profession, legislation, regulation, and (2) those implemented by the firm in the work environment. For example, legislation may prohibit the performance of certain nonassurance services for audit clients. The audit firm may decide not to assign a particular individual to an audit engagement to mitigate a threat to independence.

Section 291—Independence for Other Assurance Services. These requirements are similar to those established by the AICPA in the US. They relate to maintaining independence from the parties making the assertion on which the accountant is providing assurance.

Part C—Professional Accountants in Business

The rules that apply to professional accountants in business related to the following areas;

- Potential conflicts
- Preparation and reporting on information
- Acting with sufficient expertise
- Financial interests
- Inducements

E. International Standards—Auditing/Assurance

International auditing standards are developed by the **International Auditing and Assurance Standards Board (IAASB)** of the **International Federation of Accountants (IFAC),** a worldwide organization of approximately 160 national accounting bodies (e.g., the AICPA). IFAC was established to help foster a coordinated worldwide accounting profession with harmonized standards. Its boards also establish ethical and quality control standards for accounting professionals and accounting firms. International auditing standards are issued as a series of statements referred to as *International Standards on Auditing.*

    The pronouncements of the IAASB do not override the auditing standards of its members. Rather they are meant to help develop consistent worldwide professional standards. Members from countries that do not have their own standards may adopt IAASB standards as their own; members from countries that already have standards are encouraged to compare them to IAASB standards and to seek to eliminate any material inconsistencies. A report commissioned by the European Commission (the executive organization of the European Union) outlines a number of areas in which it suggests there are substantive differences between international and US PCAOB auditing standards. Remaining substantive differences from its list of areas at this point are

1. International standards do not require an audit of internal control, while PCAOB standards do so require.

2. International standards do not allow reference to another audit firm involved in a portion of the audit while PCAOB standards allow the principal auditor to so report (i.e., percentages or dollars audited by the other auditor are reported and the opinion is based in part upon the report of the other auditor).

3. International standards for documentation are less detailed than PCAOB standards, leaving more to professional judgment.

4. International standards in the area of going concern include time horizon of at least, but not limited to, twelve months, while PCAOB standards limit the foreseeable future for a going concern consideration of up to twelve months.

Additional differences not included in the above report as substantive differences include

Topic	International	US Standards (both AIPCA and PCAOB)
Compliance with GAAS	Auditors comply with requirements except in "exceptional circumstances" in which case alternate procedures are performed.	PCAOB standards establish three responsibility levels for compliance: (1) unconditional, (2) presumptively mandatory, and (3) responsibility to consider. Auditing Standards Board standards only include the first two categories (see Chapter 5 under **Statements on Auditing Standards**)
Confirmation of accounts receivable	Not required. In making a determination on whether to confirm, the auditor should consider the assessed risk of material misstatement at the assertion level and how the audit evidence from other planned audit procedures will reduce the risk of material misstatement at the assertion level to an acceptably low level.	Confirmation is presumptively required unless accounts receivable are immaterial, the use of confirmations would be ineffective or the combined assessed level of inherent and control risk is low.
Fraud definition	An intentional act by one or more individuals among management, those charged with governance, employees, or third parties, involving the use of deception to obtain an unjust or illegal advantage.	An intentional act that results in a material misstatement in financial statements that are the subject of an audit. **NOTE:** While the international definition is broader, it may have limited significance in that both an audit following International Standards and one following US Standards aim at obtaining reasonable assurance that the financial statements are free from material misstatement, whether due to fraud or error.
Fraud	Auditors should obtain a written representation from management that it has disclosed to the auditor the results of its assessment of the risk of fraud.	Not required. However, various representations on fraud are obtained (management's knowledge of its responsibility, management's knowledge of fraud, allegations of fraud).
Illegal acts	The auditor's concern is with whether laws and regulations may materially affect the financial statements. No explicit distinction is made between direct and indirect effect illegal acts.	The audit obtains reasonable assurance of detection of illegal acts that have a direct and material effect on financial statement amounts; if evidence about possible illegal acts with an indirect effect comes to the auditor's attention it is considered.
Use of the work of internal auditors	Auditors evaluate internal auditor objectivity, competence, and work performance before using their work.	In addition to the AICPA SAS requirement, auditors must determine that the internal audit function applies a systematic and disciplined approach, including quality control.
Sending letter of audit inquiry to lawyers	Only required when an auditor "assesses a risk of material misstatement."	Presumptively required.
Reviewing predecessor auditor's working papers for evidence on beginning balances	The standard states that this may provide sufficient appropriate audit evidence on opening balances.	This statement is not included in standards.
Terms of audit engagement change, and auditor is unable to agree on new terms	The auditor should withdraw and consider whether there is an obligation to contact other parties.	There is no explicit obligation to consider contacting other parties.
Opinion on financial statements.	Audit opinion may be on either (1) the fair presentation of the financial statements or (2) that the financial statements "give a true and fair view."	Audit opinion may only be on fair presentation of financial statements

Topic	International	US Standards (both AIPCA and PCAOB)
Audit report modification for consistency related to changes in accounting principles	Not required.	Audit reports are modified for changes in accounting principles with a material effect on the financial statements.
Inclusion of an emphasis of a matter paragraph in an audit report	Preferably after the opinion paragraph.	No such statement (may be before or after opinion paragraph).
Providing location the auditor practices in an audit report	Required.	Not required.
Dating the audit report for a subsequent event	When management amends financial statements for a subsequent event the auditor should perform necessary procedures and change the date of the audit report to no earlier than the date the financial statements were accepted as amended.	Auditors may "dual date" report (see Section A.2. of Reporting Module).
Communications to those charged with governance (internal control deficiencies and other matters related to the audit)	While report explicitly addressed to those charged with governance and/or management, the report does not include a restriction on use to these parties (nor does it prohibit such a limitation). Significant deficiencies identified, no category used to identify material weaknesses.	Report explicitly indicates that it is not intended to be, and should not be, used by anyone other than the specified parties (those charged with governance and/or management). Internal control deficiencies divided into two categories: (1) significant deficiencies and (2) material weaknesses.

Switching from auditing standards to accounting standards, you should know that the International Financial Reporting Standards (IFRS) are developed by the International Accounting Standards Board (IASB). These standards represent an alternative financial reporting framework to United States GAAP. When a client follows IFRS it has an effect on the audit process because of the differences between IFRS and US GAAP. Apart from some specific differences in rules, IFRS are considered to be more principle based than US GAAP. Therefore, IFRS generally require the application of more judgment.

F. Other

1. Securities and Exchange Commission (SEC)

   a. The mission of the SEC is to protect investors, maintain fair, orderly, and efficient markets, and facilitate capital formation.
   b. The SEC has the authority to establish standards relating to financial accounting, auditing and CPA professional conduct when involved with public-company financial statements

      (1) Some of those standards differ from AICPA requirements.
      (2) Currently, the SEC works with the PCAOB in this area.

   c. PCAOB pronouncements require SEC approval.
   d. Historically, SEC independence rules have been more restrictive than those than the AICPA in areas such as

      (1) The SEC requirements make clear that performing bookkeeping services impair audit independence; this is allowed under AICPA rules (thereby, only for nonpublic clients).
      (2) The SEC (and PCAOB) have required companies to disclose audit and nonaudit fees earned by CPA firms.

   e. Financial Reporting Releases (FRRs) are designed to communicate the SEC's positions on accounting principles and auditing practices.

2. Government Accountability Office (GAO)

   a. The GAO's mission is to support Congress in meeting its constitutional responsibilities and to help improvement the performance and ensure the accountability of the federal government.
   b. Work includes

    (1) Auditing agency operations to determine whether federal funds are being spent efficiently and effectively
    (2) Investigating allegations of illegal and improper activities
    (3) Reporting on how well government programs meet their objectives
    (4) Performing policy analyses and outlining various options for Congress
    (5) Issuing legal decision and opinions

  c. The GAO develops additional requirements for audits of organizations that receive federal financial assistance.

    (1) These are included in *Government Auditing Standards,* referred to as the "Yellow Book." (The *Government Auditing Standards* outline follow the PCAOB outlines)

  d. GAO independence requirements

    (1) In all matters relating to audit work, the audit organization and the individual auditor must be free of personal, external, and organizational impairments to independence, and must avoid the appearance of such impairments of independence. Many are similar to AICPA restrictions.
    (2) Some are more restrictive in some areas than those of the AICPA; examples are

      (a) CPA firm cannot allow personnel working on nonattest engagements to also work on the audit.
      (b) *Government Auditing Standards* places restrictions on the nature of nonattest services to be performed for an audit client

        [1] Nonattest services must be deemed not significant or material to the subject matter of the audit.

3. Department of Labor (DOL)

  a. The DOL's mission involves fostering and promoting the welfare of job seekers, wage earners, and retirees of the United States.
  b. The DOL conducts financial and performance audits following *Government Auditing Standards* relating to its mission, including audits of

    (1) Compliance with applicable laws and regulations
    (2) Evaluation of economy and efficiency of operations
    (3) Evaluation of effectiveness in achieving program results

  c. Employee benefit plans must be audited in accordance with the Employee Retirement Security Act of 1974 (ERISA), as enforced by DOL. Independence requirements are in general similar to those of the AICPA, except that

    (1) Accountant or firm may be engaged on a professional basis by the plan sponsor and the accountant may serve as an actuary.

  d. In some circumstances (e.g., definition of "member" for purposes of those who must maintain independence within a CPA firm) DOL requirements differ from AICPA requirements—in such cases they are generally more restrictive.

NOW REVIEW MULTIPLE-CHOICE QUESTIONS 27 THROUGH 47

KEY TERMS

Close relative. A parent, sibling, or nondependent child.
Covered member. A covered member is

  (a) An individual on the attest engagement team;
  (b) An individual in a position to influence the attest engagement;
  (c) A partner or manager who provides nonattest services to the attest client, beginning once he or she provides ten hours of nonattest services to the client within any fiscal year and ending on the later of the date.

[1] The firm signs the report on the financial statements for the fiscal year during which those services were provided; or

[2] He or she no longer expects to provide ten or more hours of nonattest services to the attest client on a recurring basis;

(d) partner in the office in which the lead attest engagement partner primarily practices in connection with the attest engagement;

(e) The firm, including the firm's employee benefit plans; or

(f) An entity whose operating, financial, or accounting policies can be controlled (as defined by generally accepted accounting principles [GAAP] for consolidation purposes) by any of the individuals or entities described in (a) through (e) or by two or more such individuals or entities if they act together.

Direct financial interest. A personal investment under the direct control of the investor. For example, an investment in the stock of a company.

Fraud. An intentional act by one or more individuals among management, those charged with governance, employees, or third parties, involving the use of deception that results in a misstatement in financial statements that are subject of an audit. For financial statement audits, fraud includes two types of intentional misstatements—misstatements arising from fraudulent financial reporting and misstatements arising from misappropriation of assets.

Independence. Defined in the Code of Professional Conduct as

1. *Independence of mind*—The state of mind that permits the performance of an attest service without being affected by influences that compromise professional judgment, thereby allowing an individual to act with integrity and exercise objectivity and professional skepticism.

2. *Independence in appearance*—The avoidance of circumstances that would cause a reasonable and informed third party, having knowledge of all relevant information, including safeguards applied, to reasonably conclude that the integrity, objectivity, or professional skepticism of a firm or a member of the attest engagement team had been compromised.

Immediate family. A spouse, spousal equivalent, or dependent (whether or not related).

Indirect financial interest. An investment in which the specific investment decisions are not under the control of the investor. For example, an investment in a professionally managed mutual fund.

Individual in a position to influence the attest engagement. An individual in a position to influence the attest engagement is one who

1. Evaluates the performance or recommends the compensation of the attest engagement partner;

2. Directly supervises or manages the attest engagement partner, including all successively senior levels above that individual through the firm's chief executive;

3. Consults with the attest engagement team regarding technical or industry-related issues specific to the attest engagement; or

4. Participates in or oversees, at all successively senior levels, quality control activities, including internal monitoring, with respect to the specific attest engagement.

Inspection (conducted by the PCAOB). A process that leads to an assessment of the degree of compliance of each registered public accounting firm and associated persons of that firm with the Sarbanes-Oxley Act of 2002, and the board's requirements in connection with its performance of audits, issuance of audit reports, and related matters.

International Accounting Standards Board. An independent, privately funded accounting standard-setter that is committed to developing a single set of high-quality, understandable, and enforceable global accounting standards.

International Auditing and Assurance Standards Board. A committee of the International Federation of Accountants, established to issue standards on auditing and reporting practices to improve the degree of uniformity of auditing practices and related services throughout the world.

International Federation of Accountants. A worldwide organization of national accounting bodies established to help foster a coordinated worldwide accounting profession with harmonized standards.

Interpretive publications. Auditing interpretations of GAAS, exhibits to GAAS, auditing guidance included in AICPA Audit and Accounting Guides, and AICPA Auditing Statements of Position.

Key position. A key position is a position in which an individual

1. Has primary responsibility for significant accounting functions that support material components of the financial statements;

2. Has primary responsibility for the preparation of the financial statements; or
3. Has the ability to exercise influence over the contents of the financial statements, including when the individual is a member of the board of directors or similar governing body, chief executive officer, president, chief financial officer, chief operating officer, general counsel, chief accounting officer, controller, director of internal audit, director of financial reporting, treasurer, or any equivalent position.

Peer review. A study and appraisal by an independent evaluator of a CPA firm's work.

Period of the professional engagement. The period of the professional engagement begins when a member either signs an initial engagement letter or other agreement to perform attest services or begins to perform an attest engagement for a client, whichever is earlier. The period lasts for the entire duration of the professional relationship (which could cover many periods) and ends with the formal or informal notification, either by the member or the client, of the termination of the professional relationship or by the issuance of a report, whichever is later. Accordingly, the period does not end with the issuance of a report and recommence with the beginning of the following year's attest engagement.

Professional judgment. The application of relevant training, knowledge, and experience, within the context provided by auditing, accounting, and ethical standards, in making informed decisions about the courses of action that are appropriate in the circumstances of the audit engagement.

Professional skepticism. An attitude that includes a questioning mind, being alert to conditions that may indicate possible misstatement due to fraud or error, and a critical assessment of audit evidence.

Professional services. All services performed by a member for a client, an employer, or on a volunteer basis, requiring accountancy or related skills.

Public Company Accounting Oversight Board (PCAOB). The five-member board established in 2002 to oversee the audit of public (issuer) companies that are subject to the securities laws. The board has authority to establish or adopt, or both, rules for auditing, quality control, ethics, independence, and other standards relating to the preparation of an audit report.

Public practice. Performance of professional services for a client by a member or a member's firm.

Quality control standards. AICPA standards designed to provide reasonable assurance that all of a CPA firm's engagements are conducted in accordance with applicable professional responsibilities.

Reporting accountant. An accountant, other than a continuing accountant, in public practice, as described in ET section 92.25 of the AICPA Code of Professional Conduct, who prepares a written report or provides oral advice on the application of the requirements of an applicable financial reporting framework to a specific transaction, or on the type of report that may be issued on a specific entity's financial statements. (A reporting accountant who is also engaged to provide accounting and reporting advice to a specific entity on a recurring basis is commonly referred to as an advisory accountant.)

Risk of material misstatement. The risk that the financial statements are materially misstated prior to the audit. This consists of two components, inherent risk and control risk.

Sarbanes-Oxley Act of 2002 (SOX). A set of reforms that strengthened penalties for corporate fraud, restricted the types of consulting CPAs can perform for audit clients, and created the Public Company Accounting Oversight Board to oversee CPAs and public accounting firms.

Multiple-Choice Questions (1–47)

A.1.–3. Code of Professional Conduct

1. Which of the following best describes what is meant by the term generally accepted auditing standards?

    a. Rules acknowledged by the accounting profession because of their universal application.

    b. Pronouncements issued by the Auditing Standards Board.

    c. Measures of the quality of the auditor's performance.

    d. Procedures to be used to gather evidence to support financial statements.

2. For which of the following can a member of the AICPA receive an automatic expulsion from the AICPA?

  I. Member is convicted of a felony.

  II. Member files his own fraudulent tax return.

  III. Member files fraudulent tax return for a client knowing that it is fraudulent.

    a. I only.

    b. I and II only.

    c. I and III only.

    d. I, II, and III.

3. Which of the following is an example of a safeguard implemented by the client that might mitigate a threat to independence?

    a. Required continuing education for all attest engagement team members.

    b. An effective corporate governance structure.

    c. Required second partner review of an attest engagement.

    d. Management selection of the CPA firm.

4. Which of the following is a "self review" threat to member independence?

    a. An engagement team member has a spouse that serves as CFO of the attest client.

    b. A second partner review is required on all attest engagements.

    c. An engagement team member prepares invoices for the attest client.

    d. An engagement team member has a direct financial interest in the attest client.

5. According to the standards of the profession, which of the following circumstances will prevent a CPA performing audit engagements from being independent?

    a. Obtaining a collateralized automobile loan from a financial institution client.

    b. Litigation with a client relating to billing for consulting services for which the amount is immaterial.

    c. Employment of the CPA's spouse as a client's director of internal audit.

    d. Acting as an honorary trustee for a not-for-profit organization client.

6. The profession's ethical standards most likely would be considered to have been violated when a CPA represents that specific consulting services will be performed for a stated fee and it is apparent at the time of the representation that the

    a. Actual fee would be substantially higher.

    b. Actual fee would be substantially lower than the fees charged by other CPAs for comparable services.

    c. CPA would **not** be independent.

    d. Fee was a competitive bid.

7. According to the ethical standards of the profession, which of the following acts is generally prohibited?

    a. Issuing a modified report explaining a failure to follow a governmental regulatory agency's standards when conducting an attest service for a client.

    b. Revealing confidential client information during a quality review of a professional practice by a team from the state CPA society.

    c. Accepting a contingent fee for representing a client in an examination of the client's federal tax return by an IRS agent.

    d. Retaining client records after an engagement is terminated prior to completion and the client has demanded their return.

8. According to the profession's ethical standards, which of the following events may justify a departure from a Statement of the Governmental Accounting Standards Board?

	New legislation	Evolution of a new form of business transaction
a.	No	Yes
b.	Yes	No
c.	Yes	Yes
d.	No	No

9. May a CPA hire for the CPA's public accounting firm a non-CPA systems analyst who specializes in developing computer systems?

    a. Yes, provided the CPA is qualified to perform each of the specialist's tasks.

    b. Yes, provided the CPA is able to supervise the specialist and evaluate the specialist's end product.

    c. No, because non-CPA professionals are **not** permitted to be associated with CPA firms in public practice.

    d. No, because developing computer systems is **not** recognized as a service performed by public accountants.

10. During an audit Bill Adams believes that his supervisor's position on an accounting matter, although consistent with the client's desires, materially departs from GAAP—the basis followed for the client's financial statements. Bill discussed his concerns with his supervisor and the matter is still not resolved. Following the AICPA Code of Professional Conduct, which of the following is **least** likely to be appropriate?

    a. Bill should consider consulting with legal counsel.
    b. Bill should determine whether there are responsibilities to communicate the matter to third parties.
    c. Bill should document his understanding of the situation in the working papers.
    d. Bill should use the discreditable acts framework to determine whether his supervisor is involved in an act discreditable to the profession.

11. According to the standards of the profession, which of the following activities would most likely **not** impair a CPA's independence?

    a. Providing advisory services for a client.
    b. Contracting with a client to supervise the client's office personnel.
    c. Signing a client's checks in emergency situations.
    d. Accepting a luxurious gift from a client.

12. Which of the following reports may be issued only by an accountant who is independent of a client?

    a. Standard report on an examination of a financial forecast.
    b. Report on consulting services.
    c. Compilation report on historical financial statements.
    d. Compilation report on a financial projection.

13. According to the standards of the profession, which of the following activities may be required in exercising due care?

	Consulting with experts	Obtaining specialty accreditation
a.	Yes	Yes
b.	Yes	No
c.	No	Yes
d.	No	No

14. Larry Sampson is a CPA and is serving as an expert witness in a trial concerning a corporation's financial statements. Which of the following is(are) true?

  I. Sampson's status as an expert witness is based upon his specialized knowledge, experience, and training.
  II. Sampson is required by AICPA ruling to present his position objectively.
  III. Sampson may regard himself as acting as an advocate.

    a. I only.
    b. I and II only.
    c. I and III only.
    d. III only.

15. According to the ethical standards of the profession, which of the following acts is generally prohibited?

    a. Purchasing a product from a third party and reselling it to a client.
    b. Writing a financial management newsletter promoted and sold by a publishing company.
    c. Accepting a commission for recommending a product to an audit client.
    d. Accepting engagements obtained through the efforts of third parties.

16. To exercise due professional care an auditor should

    a. Critically review the judgment exercised by those assisting in the audit.
    b. Examine all available corroborating evidence supporting managements assertions.
    c. Design the audit to detect all instances of illegal acts.
    d. Attain the proper balance of professional experience and formal education.

17. Kar, CPA, is a staff auditor participating in the audit engagement of Fort, Inc. Which of the following circumstances impairs Kar's independence?

    a. During the period of the professional engagement, Fort gives Kar tickets to a football game worth $75.
    b. Kar owns stock in a corporation that Fort's 401(k) plan also invests in.
    c. Kar's friend, an employee of another local accounting firm, prepares Fort's tax returns.
    d. Kar's sibling is director of internal audit at Fort.

18. On June 1, 20X8, a CPA obtained a $100,000 personal loan from a financial institution client for whom the CPA provided compilation services. The loan was fully secured and considered material to the CPA's net worth. The CPA paid the loan in full on December 31, 20X9. On April 3, 20X9, the client asked the CPA to audit the client's financial statements for the year ended December 31, 20X9. Is the CPA considered independent with respect to the audit of the client's December 31, 20X9 financial statements?

    a. Yes, because the loan was fully secured.
    b. Yes, because the CPA was not required to be independent at the time the loan was granted.
    c. No, because the CPA had a loan with the client during the period of a professional engagement.
    d. No, because the CPA had a loan with the client during the period covered by the financial statements.

19. Which of the following statements is(are) correct regarding a CPA employee of a CPA firm taking copies of information contained in client files when the CPA leaves the firm?

  I. A CPA leaving a firm may take copies of information contained in client files to assist another firm in serving that client.
  II. A CPA leaving a firm may take copies of information contained in client files as a method of gaining technical expertise.

a. I only.
b. II only.
c. Both I and II.
d. Neither I nor II.

20. Which of the following statements is correct regarding an accountant's working papers?

    a. The accountant owns the working papers and generally may disclose them as the accountant sees fit.
    b. The client owns the working papers but the accountant has custody of them until the accountant's bill is paid in full.
    c. The accountant owns the working papers but generally may not disclose them without the client's consent or a court order.
    d. The client owns the working papers but, in the absence of the accountant's consent, may not disclose them without a court order.

21. Which of the following is an authoritative body designated to promulgate attestation standards?

    a. Auditing Standards Board.
    b. Governmental Accounting Standards Board.
    c. Financial Accounting Standards Board.
    d. General Accounting Office.

A.4. Responsibilities in Consulting Services

22. According to the profession's standards, which of the following would be considered consulting services?

	Advisory services	Implementation services	Product services
a.	Yes	Yes	Yes
b.	Yes	Yes	No
c.	Yes	No	Yes
d.	No	Yes	Yes

23. According to the standards of the profession, which of the following events would require a CPA performing a consulting services engagement for a nonaudit client to withdraw from the engagement?

I. The CPA has a conflict of interest that is disclosed to the client and the client consents to the CPA continuing the engagement.
II. The CPA fails to obtain a written understanding from the client concerning the scope of the engagement.

    a. I only.
    b. II only.
    c. Both I and II.
    d. Neither I nor II.

24. Which of the following services may a CPA perform in carrying out a consulting service for a client?

I. Analysis of the client's accounting system.
II. Review of the client's prepared business plan.
III. Preparation of information for obtaining financing.

a. I and II only.
b. I and III only.
c. II and III only.
d. I, II, and III.

25. Under the Statements on Standards for Consulting Services, which of the following statements best reflects a CPA's responsibility when undertaking a consulting services engagement? The CPA must

    a. Not seek to modify any agreement made with the client.
    b. Not perform any attest services for the client.
    c. Inform the client of significant reservations concerning the benefits of the engagement.
    d. Obtain a written understanding with the client concerning the time for completion of the engagement.

A.5. Responsibilities in Personal Financial Planning

26. Which of the following services is a CPA generally required to perform when conducting a personal financial planning engagement?

    a. Assisting the client to identify tasks that are essential in order to act on planning decisions.
    b. Assisting the client to take action on planning decisions.
    c. Monitoring progress in achieving goals.
    d. Updating recommendations and revising planning decisions.

B. The Sarbanes-Oxley Act of 2002

27. Under the Sarbanes-Oxley Act, most audit working papers must be saved

    a. 5 years.
    b. 7 years.
    c. 10 years.
    d. Indefinitely as there is no time limitation provided.

28. Passage of the Sarbanes-Oxley Act led to the establishment of the

    a. Auditing Standards Board.
    b. Accounting Enforcement Releases Board.
    c. Public Company Accounting Oversight Board.
    d. Securities and Exchange Commission.

29. Under Title II of the Sarbanes-Oxley Act, the auditor of an issuer cannot legally perform which type of service for that issuer?

    a. Tax services.
    b. Review of interim information.
    c. Internal audit outsourcing services.
    d. Audit of internal control over financial reporting.

30. The audit partner in charge of an audit of a public company may only

a. Be in charge of the audit of that one company.
b. Perform the role as long as he or she also performs the "second partner review" for that audit.
c. Perform that role for five consecutive years.
d. Perform the role if he or she has proper AICPA issuer accreditation.

C. Public Company Accounting Oversight Board

31. Which of the following is correct concerning membership on the Public Company Accounting Oversight Board?

a. Only two of its members may be CPAs.
b. It is composed of 9 members.
c. All members must also currently be active in public accounting.
d. A majority of members must be or have been accounting educators.

32. The Public Company Accounting Oversight Board (PCAOB) is **not** responsible for standards related to

a. Accounting.
b. Attestation.
c. Auditing.
d. Quality control.

33. A PCAOB engagement that focuses on a selected quality control issue is most likely to be referred to as a(n)

a. Financial statement audit.
b. Inspection.
c. Peer review.
d. Quality control

34. Which statement below is correct concerning communicating the results of a PCAOB inspection?

a. The entire report issued by the PCAOB is publicly available.
b. The portion of the report issued on a CPA firm's quality control is not ordinarily publicly available.
c. The report issued is only available to Congress.
d. The report is available only to PCAOB members.

D. International Standards—Ethical

35. In relation to the AICPA Code of Professional Conduct, the IFAC *Code of Ethics for Professional Accountants*

a. Has more outright prohibitions.
b. Has fewer outright prohibitions.
c. Has no outright prohibitions.
d. Applies only to professional accountants in business.

36. Based on the IFAC *Code of Ethics for Professional Accountants,* threats to independence arise from all of the following except:

a. Self interest.
b. Advocacy.
c. The audit relationship.
d. Intimidation.

37. If an audit firm discovers threats to independence with respect to an audit engagement, the IFAC *Code of Ethics for Professional Accountants* indicates that the firm should

a. Immediately resign from the engagement.
b. Notify the appropriate regulatory body.
c. Document the issue.
d. Evaluate the significance of the threats and apply appropriate safeguards to reduce them to an acceptable level.

38. With respect to the acceptance of contingent fees for professional services, the IFAC *Code of Ethics for Professional Accountants* indicates that the accounting firm

a. Should not accept contingent fees.
b. Should establish appropriate safeguards around acceptance of a contingent fee.
c. Should accept contingent fees only for assurance services other than audits of financial statements.
d. Should accept contingent fees if it is customary in the country.

39. With regard to marketing professional services, the IFAC *Code of Ethics for Professional Accountants* indicates that

a. Direct marketing is prohibited.
b. Marketing is allowed if lawful.
c. Marketing should be honest and truthful.
d. Marketing of audit services is prohibited.

E. International Standards—Auditing/ Assurance

40. What body establishes international auditing standards?

a. The Public Company Accounting Oversight Board.
b. The International Federation of Accountants.
c. The World Bank.
d. The International Assurance Body.

41. Which of the following is not true about international auditing standards?

a. International auditing standards do not require an audit of internal control.
b. International auditing standards do not allow reference to division of responsibilities in the audit report.
c. International auditing standards require obtaining an attorney's letter.
d. International auditing standards are based on a risk assessment approach.

42. Which of the following is most likely to be required in an audit performed in conformity with international auditing standards?

a. Confirmation of accounts receivable.
b. Audit report modification for a change in accounting principles.
c. An opinion on internal control.
d. Audit report inclusion of the location in which the auditor practices.

F.2.   *Government Accountability Office (GAO)*

43. Independence standards of the GAO for audits in accordance with generally accepted government auditing standards describe three types of impairments of independence. Which of the following is not one of these types of impairments?

    a. Personal.
    b. Organizational.
    c. External.
    d. Unusual.

44. In accordance with the independence standards of the GAO for performing audits in accordance with generally accepted government auditing standards, which of the following is not an example of an external impairment of independence?

    a. Reducing the extent of audit work due to pressure from management to reduce audit fees.
    b. Selecting audit items based on the wishes of an employee of the organization being audited.
    c. Bias in the items the auditors decide to select for testing.
    d. Influence by management on the personnel assigned to the audit.

45. Under the independence standards of the GAO for performing audits in accordance with generally accepted government auditing standards, which of the following are overreaching principles for determining whether a nonaudit service impairs independence?

  I. Auditors must not perform nonaudit services that involve performing management functions or making management decisions.

II. Auditors must not audit their own work or provide nonaudit services in situations in which the nonaudit services are significant or material to the subject matter of the audit.
III. Auditors must not perform nonaudit services which require independence.

    a. I only.
    b. I and II only.
    c. I, II and III.
    d. II and III only.

F.3.   *Department of Labor (DOL)*

46. Which of the following bodies enforce the audit requirements of the Employee Retirement Security Act of 1974 (ERISA) with respect to employee benefit plans?

    a. The Department of Labor.
    b. The Department of Pension Management.
    c. The Securities and Exchange Commission.
    d. The Public Company Accounting Oversight Board.

47. The requirement for independence by the auditor regarding audits of employee benefit plans apply to the plan as well as

    a. Investment companies doing business with the plan.
    b. Members of the plan.
    c. The plan sponsor.
    d. The actuary firm doing services for the plan.

Multiple-Choice Answers and Explanations

Answers

1.	c	__ __	12.	a	__ __	23.	d	__ __	34.	b	__ __	45.	b	__ __
2.	d	__ __	13.	b	__ __	24.	d	__ __	35.	b	__ __	46.	a	__ __
3.	b	__ __	14.	b	__ __	25.	c	__ __	36.	c	__ __	47.	c	__ __
4.	c	__ __	15.	c	__ __	26.	a	__ __	37.	d	__ __			
5.	c	__ __	16.	a	__ __	27.	b	__ __	38.	b	__ __			
6.	a	__ __	17.	d	__ __	28.	c	__ __	39.	c	__ __			
7.	d	__ __	18.	b	__ __	29.	c	__ __	40.	b	__ __			
8.	c	__ __	19.	d	__ __	30.	c	__ __	41.	c	__ __			
9.	b	__ __	20.	c	__ __	31.	a	__ __	42.	d	__ __			
10.	d	__ __	21.	a	__ __	32.	a	__ __	43.	d	__ __	1st:	__/47 = __%
11.	a	__ __	22.	a	__ __	33.	b	__ __	44.	c	__ __	2nd:	__/47 = __%

Explanations

1. (c) The requirement is to identify the statement that best describes the meaning of generally accepted auditing standards. Answer (c) is correct because generally accepted auditing standards deal with measures of the quality of the performance of audit procedures (AU-C 200). Answer (d) is incorrect because procedures relate to acts to be performed, not directly to the standards. Answer (b) is incorrect because generally accepted auditing standards have been issued by predecessor groups, as well as by the Auditing Standards Board. Answer (a) is incorrect because there may or may not be **universal** compliance with the standards.

2. (d) All of these can result in the automatic expulsion of the member from the AICPA. Answer (a) is incorrect because although the conviction of a felony can result in automatic expulsion, likewise can the other two. Answers (b) and (c) are incorrect because all three can result in automatic expulsion from the AICPA.

3. (b) Answer (b) is correct because an effective corporate governance structure is a control that can be implemented by a client that increases independence of member shall maintain objectivity and integrity, avoid conflicts the attest team. Answer (a) is incorrect because it is a safeguard that is implemented by regulation or the CPA firm. Answer (c) is incorrect because it is a safeguard that is required by regulation or the CPA firm. Answer (d) is incorrect because it represents a threat rather than a safeguard.

4. (c) Answer (c) is correct because the team member would be reviewing his or her own work. Answer (a) is incorrect because this is an example of a familiarity threat. Answer (b) is incorrect because this is an example of a safeguard to threats to independence. Answer (d) is incorrect because this represents a financial self-interest threat to independence.

5. (c) According to the Code of Professional Conduct, Rule 101 regarding independence, a spouse may be employed by a client if s/he does not exert significant influence over the contents of the client's financial statements. This is a key position as defined by the Interpretation of Rule 101.

6. (a) According to Rule 102 of the Code of Professional Conduct, in performing any professional service, a member shall maintain objectivity and integrity, avoid conflicts of interest, and not knowingly misrepresent facts. Answer (a) is correct as this would be knowingly misrepresenting the facts. Answers (b) and (d) are incorrect as these are not intentional misstatements. Answer (c) is incorrect because while one must remain objective while performing consulting services, independence is not required unless the CPA also performs attest services for that client.

7. (d) The requirement is to determine which act is generally prohibited. Answer (d) is correct because "If an engagement is terminated prior to completion, the member is required to return only client records" (ET 501). Answer (a) is incorrect because issuing a modified report explaining a failure to follow a governmental regulatory agency's standards when conducting an attest service is not prohibited. Answer (c) is incorrect because accepting a contingent fee is allowable when representing a client in an examination by a revenue agent of the client's federal or state income tax return (ET 302). Answer (b) is incorrect because revealing confidential client information during a quality review of a professional practice by a team from the state CPA society is not prohibited (ET 301).

8. (c) According to Rule 203 of the Code of Professional Conduct, CPAs are allowed to depart from a GASB Statement only when results of the Standard would be misleading. Examples of possible circumstances justifying departure are new legislation and a new form of business transaction.

9. (b) The requirement is to determine whether a CPA may hire a non-CPA systems analyst and, if so, under what conditions. Answer (b) is correct because ET 291 allows such a situation when the CPA is qualified to supervise and evaluate the work of the specialist. Answer (a) is incorrect because the CPA need not be qualified to perform the specialist's tasks. Answer (c) is incorrect because non-CPA professionals are permitted to be associated with CPA firms in public practice. Answer (d) is incorrect because nonprofessionals may be hired, and because developing computer systems is recognized as a service performed by public accountants.

10. (d) The requirement is to determine which reply is not a responsibility when an accountant concludes that a difference of opinion with a supervisor exists relating to a significant accounting matter. Answer (d) is correct because the profession does not have a "discreditable acts framework" to be used in such a manner. Answers (a), (b) and (c) are incorrect because the Code of Professional Conduct requires that accountants consider consulting legal counsel (answer (b)), determining other communication responsibilities (answer (b)), and documenting his understanding (answer (c)). Bill should also consider whether additional requirements exist under his firm's internal policies.

11. (a) The requirement is to determine the activity that would most likely **not** impair a CPA's independence. Accounting and consulting services do not normally impair independence because the member's role is advisory in nature (ET 191). Answers (b) and (c) are incorrect because management functions are being performed (ET 191). Answer (d) is incorrect because accepting a luxurious gift impairs a CPA's independence (ET 191).

12. (a) The requirement is to identify the type of report that may be issued only by an independent accountant. Answer (a) is correct because AT 101 requires an accountant be independent for all attestation engagements. An attestation engagement is one in which the accountant expresses a conclusion about the reliability of assertions which are the responsibility of another party. A standard report on an examination of a financial forecast requires the auditor to express an opinion, which requires an accountant to be independent. Answer (b) is incorrect because CS 100 indicates that consulting services are fundamentally different from the attestation function, and therefore do not require independence of the accountant. Answers (c) and (d) are incorrect because AR 100 indicates that an accountant who is not independent is not precluded from issuing a report on a compilation of financial statements.

13. (b) Per ET 56, due care requires a member to discharge professional responsibilities with competence and diligence. Competence represents the attainment and maintenance of a level of understanding and knowledge that enables a member to render services with facility and acumen. It also establishes the limitations of a member's capabilities by dictating that consultation or referral may be required when a professional engagement exceeds the personal competence of a member or a member's firm. Accordingly, answer (b) is correct as it may be required to consult with experts in exercising due care. Due care does not require obtaining specialty accreditation.

14. (b) Under ruling 101 under Rule of Conduct 102, when a CPA is acting as an expert witness, s/he should **not** act as an advocate but should give his/her position based on objectivity. The expert witness does this based on specialized knowledge, training, and experience.

15. (c) The requirement is to determine which act is generally prohibited. Answer (c) is correct because "a member in public practice shall not for a commission recommend or refer to a client any product or service, or for a commission recommend

or refer any product or service to be supplied by a client, or receive a commission when the member or the member's firm perform for that client: (1) an audit of a financial statement; or (2) a compilation of a financial statement when the member expects that a third party will use the financial statement and the member's compilation report does not disclose a lack of independence; or (3) an examination of prospective financial information." Answer (a) is incorrect because a member may purchase a product and resell it to a client. Any profit on sale would not constitute a commission (ET 591).

16. (a) The principle of due care requires the member to observe the profession's technical and ethical standards, strive continually to improve competence and the quality of services, and discharge responsibility to the best of the member's ability. Answer (b) is incorrect as the auditor is not required to examine **all** corroborating evidence supporting management's assertions, but rather to examine evidence on a scope basis based on his/ her consideration of materiality and level of risk assessed. Answer (c) is incorrect as the auditor should be aware of the possibility of illegal acts, but an audit provides no assurance that all or any illegal acts will be detected. Answer (d) is not the best answer because competence is derived from both education and experience. The principle of due care requires the member to strive to improve competence, however, attaining the proper balance of professional experience and formal education is not a criterion for exercising due care.

17. (d) The fact that a close relative of Kar works for Fort impairs Kar's independence. Answer (a) is incorrect because the gift is of a token amount which does not impair Kar's independence. Answer (b) is incorrect because a joint financial investment must be material to impair independence, and this would generally not occur with respect to a retirement plan. Answer (c) is incorrect because preparation of the client's tax return is not a service that impairs independence.

18. (b) Independence was not required at the time the loan was obtained, and because it is fully secured it is grandfathered by 101-5. Answer (a) is incorrect because if the CPA is required to be independent, a mortgage loan would not be permitted even if it was fully secured. Answer (c) is incorrect because the CPA was not required to be independent of the client. Answer (d) is incorrect because the CPA was not required to be independent of the client.

19. (d) Both of the statements are incorrect; either would violate Rule 301 on confidential client information. Answer (a) is incorrect because statement I also is incorrect. Answer (b) is incorrect because statement II also is incorrect. Answer (c) is incorrect because statements I and II are both incorrect.

20. (c) Information in the CPA's working papers is confidential and may not be disclosed except with the client's consent or by court order. Answer (a) is incorrect because disclosure of the information would generally violate Rule 301 on confidential client information. Answers (b) and (d) are incorrect because the CPA owns the working papers.

21. (a) The requirement is to identify the listed authoritative body designated to promulgate attestation standards. Answer (a) is correct because only the Auditing Standards Board, the Accounting and Review Services Committee, and the Management Advisory Services Executive Committee have been authorized to promulgate attestation standards.

22. (a) Types of consulting services include consultations, advisory services, implementation services, transaction services, staff and other support services, and product services.

23. (d) According to the Statements on Standards for Consulting Services, independence is not required for performance of consulting services unless the CPA also performs attest services for that client. However, the CPA must remain objective in performing the consulting services. Furthermore, the understanding with the client for performing the services can be established either in writing or orally.

24. (d) CS 100 indicates that the nature and scope of consulting services is determined solely by the practitioner and the client, typically in which the practitioner develops findings, conclusions, and recommendations for the client. All three services listed would fall under the definition of consulting services.

25. (c) The AICPA Statement on Standards for Consulting Services, Section 100, describes general standards for all consulting services, in addition to those established under the AICPA Code of Professional Conduct. Section 100 addresses the areas of client interest, understanding with the client, and communication with the client. Specifically, this section states that the accountant should inform the client of significant reservations concerning the scope or benefits of the engagement.

26. (a) Personal financial planning engagements are only those that involve developing strategies and making recommendations to assist a client in defining and achieving personal financial goals. Personal financial engagements involve all of the following:

1. Defining engagement objectives
2. Planning specific procedures appropriate to engagement
3. Developing basis for recommendations
4. Communicating recommendations to client
5. Identifying tasks for taking action on planning decisions.

Other engagements may also include, but generally are not **required** to perform, the following:

1. Assisting client to take action on planning decisions
2. Monitoring client's progress in achieving goals
3. Updating recommendations and helping client revise planning decisions.

27. (b) The requirement is to determine how long audit working papers must be saved under the requirements of the Sarbanes-Oxley Act. Answer (b) is correct, 7 years. Answers (a), (c), and (d) are incorrect because a 7-year limit exists for most working papers.

28. (c) The requirement is to identify the organization established by the Sarbanes-Oxley Act. Answer (c) is correct because SOX did establish the Public Company Accounting Oversight Board. Answer (a) is incorrect because the Auditing Standards Board is the AICPA's auditing standards setting organization. Answer (b) is incorrect because

there is no organization titled the Accounting Enforcement Releases Board. Answer (d) is incorrect because the Securities and Exchange Commission was established in 1934 by the Securities Exchange Act.

29. (c) The requirement is to identify the type of service an auditor of an issuer cannot legally perform under Title II of the Sarbanes-Oxley Act. Answer (c) is correct because the auditor may not provide internal audit outsourcing services to the issuer. Answer (a) is incorrect because tax services may be performed. Answer (b) is incorrect because a review of interim information is required to be performed. Answer (d) is incorrect because, for large companies, the audit of internal control over financial reporting is required as a part of the integrated audit.

30. (c) The requirement is to identify a limitation for the audit partner in charge of an audit of a public company. Answer (c) is correct as the partner may only be in charge for five consecutive years. Answer (a) is incorrect since there is no such restriction. Answer (b) is incorrect because another partner must perform the second partner review function. Answer (d) is incorrect because the AICPA has no such accreditation.

31. (a) The requirement is to identify the correct statement concerning membership on the Public Company Accounting Oversight Board. Answer (a) is correct because the five-member board may have no more than two CPA members. Answer (b) is incorrect because the PCAOB is composed of 5 members. Answer (c) is incorrect because no members may be currently active in public accounting. Answer (d) is incorrect because there is no rule that a majority of members must be or must have been accounting educators.

32. (a) The requirement is to identify the type of standards for which the PCAOB is **not** responsible for. Answer (a) is correct because the PCAOB has no responsibility for promulgating or adopting accounting standards. Answer (b) is incorrect because the PCAOB does have responsibility for attestation standards relating to public companies. Answer (c) is incorrect because the PCAOB does have responsibility for auditing standards relating to public companies. Answer (d) is incorrect because the PCAOB does have responsibility for quality control standards relating to public companies.

33. (b) The requirement is to identify a PCOAB engagement that focuses on a selected quality control issue. Answer (b) is correct because this is ordinarily the focus of the PCAOB inspection. Answer (a) is incorrect because a financial statement audit focuses on the fairness of presentation of financial statements. Answer (c) is incorrect because peer reviews ordinarily focus upon an accounting firm's overall accounting and audit practice. Answer (d) is incorrect because there is no engagement referred to as quality control.

34. (b) The requirement is to identify the correct statement concerning communication of the results of a PCAOB inspection. Answer (b) is correct since the portion of the report issued on a CPA firm's quality control is not ordinarily publicly available. Answer (a) is incorrect because the portion of the report on a CPA firm's quality control is not ordinarily made available. Answer (c) is incorrect because most of the report (other than the portion on the CPA firm's quality control) is publicly available. Answer (d) is incorrect because most of the report (other than the portion on the CPA firm's quality control) is publicly available.

35. (b) The requirement is to identify the characteristic that differs between the two sets of ethical standards. Answer (b) is correct because the IFAC Code has fewer outright prohibitions than the AICPA Code. Answers (a) and (c) are incorrect because the IFAC Code has fewer outright prohibitions. Answer (d) is incorrect because the IFAC Code applies to all professional accountants.

36. (c) The requirement is to identify the item that is not a threat to independence. Answer (c) is correct because the audit relationship, in itself, is not a threat to independence. Answers (a), (b), and (d) are incorrect because they all represent types of threats to independence.

37. (d) The requirement is to identify the appropriate course of action when threats to independence are discovered. Answer (d) is correct because the firm should evaluate the significance of the threats and apply safeguards, if necessary, to reduce them to an acceptable level. Answer (a) is incorrect because the firm would only resign if appropriate safeguards could not reduce the threats to an acceptable level, or it is required based on a prohibition. Answer (b) is incorrect because the firm would not notify a regulatory body at this point. Answer (c) is incorrect because the firm would document the issue, but only after it is resolved.

38. (b) The requirement is to identify what the IFAC *Code of Ethics for Professional Accountants* provides with respect to contingent fees. Answer (b) is correct because the IFAC Code indicates that if the contingent fee presents a threat to apply fundamental principles, the firm should establish appropriate safeguards. Answer (a) is incorrect because a contingent fee may be accepted if threats can be reduced to an acceptable level. Answers (c) and (d) are incorrect because the IFAC Code does not contain these provisions.

39. (c) The requirement is to identify the IFAC Code provision regarding marketing. Answer (c) is correct because the IFAC Code indicates the marketing must be honest and truthful. Answers (a) and (d) are incorrect because no particular form of marketing is prohibited. Answer (b) is incorrect because marketing must be honest and truthful as well as legal.

40. (b) The requirement is to identify the body that establishes international auditing standards. Answer (b) is correct because the International Auditing and Assurance Standards Board of the International Federation of Accountants establishes international auditing standards. Answer (a) is incorrect because the Public Company Accounting Oversight Board establishes standards for the audit of public companies in the US. Answers (c) and (d) are incorrect because these bodies do not establish auditing standards.

41. (c) The requirement is to identify the item that is not true about international auditing standards. Answer (c) is correct

because international auditing standards require obtaining an attorney's letter only if the auditors assess a risk of material misstatement. Answers (a), (b) and (d) are incorrect because they are all true about international auditing standards.

42. (d) The requirement is to identify the most likely requirement in an audit performed in conformity with international auditing standards. Answer (d) is correct because audit reports based on international auditing standards must include the location in which the auditor practices (i.e., the city and country). Answer (a) is incorrect because whether accounts receivable are confirmed is based on the auditor's consideration of the assessed risk of material misstatement and how the audit evidence will, from other planned audit procedures, reduce that risk. Answer (b) is incorrect because audit report modification for a change in accounting principles is not required under international auditing standards. Answer (c) is incorrect because an opinion on internal control is not required under international auditing standards.

43. (d) The requirement is to identify the impairment that is not one of the three types of impairments described in the GAO standards. Answer (d) is correct because an unusual impairment is not one of the types of impairments described in the GAO standards. Answers (a), (b), and (c) are incorrect because they are the three types of impairments described in the GAO standards.

44. (c) The requirement is to identify the example that does not represent an external impairment of independence. Answer (c) is correct because this item is an example of a personal impairment of independence. Answers (a), (b) and (d) are incorrect because they are all examples of external impairments of independence.

45. (b) The requirement is to identify the overreaching principles for identifying whether nonaudit services impair independence. Answer (b) is correct because I and II are the two principles. Answer (a) is incorrect because II is also an overreaching principle. Answer (c) is incorrect because III is not an overreaching principle. Answer (d) is incorrect because I is an overreaching principle and III is not.

46. (a) The requirement is to identify the body that enforces the audit requirements of ERISA. Answer (a) is correct because the Department of Labor is responsible for enforcing the audit requirements. Answer (b) is incorrect because the Department of Pension Management does not exist. Answers (c) and (d) are incorrect because the SEC and the PCAOB deal with auditing requirements for entities with publicly traded securities (issuers).

47. (c) The requirement is to identify the party that independence standards also apply to when performing an audit of an employee benefit plan. Answer (c) is correct because the Department of Labor rules also apply to independence from the plan and the plan sponsor. Answers (a), (b) and (d) are incorrect because the independence standards do not apply to these parties.

Simulations

Task-Based Simulation 1

Assume that you are analyzing relationships for your firm to identify situations in which an auditor's independence may be impaired. For each of the following numbered situations, determine whether the auditor (a covered member in the situation) is considered to be independent. If the auditor's independence would **not** be impaired select No. If the auditor's independence would be impaired select Yes.

		Yes	No
1.	The auditor is a cosigner of a client's checks.	○	○
2.	The auditor is a member of a country club which is a client.	○	○
3.	The auditor owns a large block of stock in a client but has placed it in a blind trust.	○	○
4.	The auditor placed her checking account in a bank which is her client. The account is fully insured by a federal agency.	○	○
5.	The client has not paid the auditor for services for the past two years.	○	○
6.	The auditor is leasing part of his building to a client.	○	○
7.	The auditor joins, as an ordinary member, a trade association which is also a client.	○	○
8.	The auditor has an immaterial, indirect financial interest in the client.	○	○

Task-Based Simulation 2

The director of the audit committee of Hanmei Corp., a nonissuer (nonpublic) company, has indicated that the company may be interested in engaging your firm to perform various professional services. Consider each of the following potential services **by itself**, and determine whether a CPA firm may provide such a service. If a CPA firm may provide the service, fill in the circle under the first or second column of replies based upon whether independence is required. If the service may not be provided, fill in the circle under "May Not Provide." For each service you should have only one reply.

Service	May provide, independence is required	May provide, independence is not required	May not provide
1. Provide an opinion on whether financial statements are prepared following the cash basis of accounting.	○	○	○
2. Compile a forecast for the coming year.	○	○	○
3. Compile the financial statements for the past year and issue a publicly available report.	○	○	○

Service	May provide, independence is required	May provide, independence is not required	May not provide
4. Apply certain agreed-upon procedures to accounts receivable for purposes of obtaining a loan, and express a summary of findings relating to those procedures.	○	○	○
5. Review quarterly information and issue a report that includes limited assurance.	○	○	○
6. Perform an audit of the financial statements on whether they are prepared following generally accepted accounting principles.	○	○	○
7. Perform a review of a forecast the company has prepared for the coming year.	○	○	○
8. Compile the financial statements for the past year, but not issue a report since the financial statements are only for the company's use.	○	○	○
9. Calculate the client's taxes and fill out the appropriate tax forms.	○	○	○
10. Design a new payroll system for Hanmei and base billings on Hanmei's actual savings for the next three years.	○	○	○

Task-Based Simulation 3

Covered Member

You work with a CPA firm as an assistant. The senior on the XYZ audit has asked you to determine whether you are eligible to work on the XYZ audit since he knows that you own 100 shares of XYZ worth $700 in total. He has asked you to research the following:

Title choices

A.	AU-C
B.	PCAOB
C.	AT
D.	AR
E.	ET
F.	BL
G.	CS
H.	QC

	(A)	(B)	(C)	(D)	(E)	(F)	(G)	(H)
1. He thinks that he recalls the issue relates to whether you are or are not a "covered member." He would like you to find the definition of a covered member in the professional standards. Which title of the Professional Standards addresses this issue and will be helpful in responding to the senior?	○	○	○	○	○	○	○	○

2. Enter the exact section and paragraphs with helpful information.

3. Regardless of what you find, he would like you to determine whether a covered member may have such an immaterial financial investment in an audit client. What title, section, and paragraph addresses this issue?

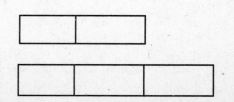

Task-Based Simulation 4

The firm of Willingham and Whiting, CPAs, has had requests from a number of clients and prospective clients as to providing various types of services. Please reply as to whether the appropriate independence rules (AICPA and/or PCAOB) allow the following engagements with
A—Allowable, given these facts.
N—Not allowable, given these facts.
(If both AICPA and PCAOB rules apply and one of them does not allow the services, answer N.)

Case	Request	Public or nonpublic client	Allowable (A) or not allowable (NA)?
1.	Provide internal audit outsourcing as well as perform the audit.	Public	
2.	Prepare the corporate tax return as well as perform the audit.	Public	
3.	Prepare the corporate tax return as well as perform the audit.	Nonpublic	
4.	Provide bookkeeping services as well as perform the audit; WW will not determine journal entries, authorize transactions, prepare or modify source documents.	Nonpublic	
5.	Provide financial information systems design and implementation assistance; WW provides no attest services for that company.	Public	
6.	Serve on the board of directors of the company; WW provides no attest services for that company.	Public	
7.	Implement an off-the-shelf accounting package as well as perform the audit.	Nonpublic	
8.	Provide actuarial services related to certain liabilities as well as perform the audit; the subjectively determined liabilities relate to a material portion of the financial statements.	Nonpublic	
9.	Provide actuarial services related to certain liabilities as well as perform the audit; the subjectively determined liabilities relate to material portion of the financial statements.	Public	
10.	Corporate executives of an audit client want to have WW provide tax planning for themselves (not the company).	Public	

Task-Based Simulation 5

Payroll System Engagement

Michael Edlinger is president of Edlinger Corporation, a nonpublic manufacturer of kitchen cabinets. He has been approached by Marla Wong, a partner with Wong and Co., CPAs, who suggests that her firm can design a payroll system for Edlinger that will either save his corporation money or be free. More specifically, Ms. Wong proposes to design a payroll system for Edlinger on a contingent fee basis. She suggests that her firm's fee will be 25 % of the savings in payroll for each of the next four years. After four years Edlinger will be able to keep all future savings. Edlinger Corporation's payroll system costs currently are approximately $200,000 annually, and the corporation has not previously been a client of Wong. Edlinger Corporation is audited by another CPA firm and Wong & Co. provides no other services to Edlinger Corporation. Select one of the following topics to answer question 1.

Selections

A. AU-C
B. PCAOB
C. AT
D. AR
E. ET
F. BL
G. CS
H. QC

	(A)	**(B)**	**(C)**	**(D)**	**(E)**	**(F)**	**(G)**	**(H)**
1. Which topic of the Professional Standards addresses this issue and will be helpful in determining whether Wong & Co. may perform this engagement under these terms without violating professional requirements?	○	○	○	○	○	○	○	○

2. Provide the appropriate paragraph citation that addresses this issue.

3. Interpret your findings in parts **1.** and **2.** and conclude on whether Wong & Co. may perform this service without violating professional standards.

___ Yes, this service may be performed without violating professional standards.
___ No, this service may not be performed without violating professional standards.

Task-Based Simulation 6

Professional Standards

You have worked with James & Co. CPAs for approximately 4 months. Jen Jefferson, who has just started with James & Co., has asked you to explain the nature of various professional standards to her. More specifically, she would like to have a better understanding of which standards to address, in which circumstances.

Select the appropriate title of standards for **1.** through **10.** below. Standards may be selected once, more than once, or not at all.

Title of Standards

A. AICPA Bylaws (BL)
B. Code of Professional Conduct (ET)
C. PCAOB Auditing Standards
D. Standards for Performing and Reporting on Peer Reviews (PR)
E. Statements on Auditing Standards (AU-C)
F. Statements on Quality Control Standards (SQCS)
G. Statements on Standards for Accounting and Review Services (SSARS)
H. Statements on Standards for Attestation Engagements (SSAE)
I. Statements on Standards for Consulting Services (CS)
J. Statements on Standards for Tax Services (TS)

Standards that provide guidance	(A)	(B)	(C)	(D)	(E)	(F)	(G)	(H)	(I)	(J)
1. For performance of a review of a nonpublic company's annual financial statements.	O	O	O	O	O	O	O	O	O	O
2. On whether a contingent fee may be billed to a client.	O	O	O	O	O	O	O	O	O	O
3. Related to firm requirements of CPA firms that are enrolled in an AICPA-approved practice-monitoring system.	O	O	O	O	O	O	O	O	O	O
4. For an examination of a client's financial forecast.	O	O	O	O	O	O	O	O	O	O
5. Relating to overall requirements when providing services for an advisory services engagement.	O	O	O	O	O	O	O	O	O	O
6. For the audit of a public company.	O	O	O	O	O	O	O	O	O	O
7. For the performance of an interim review of the quarterly financial statements of a nonpublic audit client.	O	O	O	O	O	O	O	O	O	O
8. For reporting on client pro forma financial information.	O	O	O	O	O	O	O	O	O	O
9. On whether an investment of a CPA impairs her independence with respect to a client.	O	O	O	O	O	O	O	O	O	O
10. On performing a compilation of a nonpublic company's quarterly statements.	O	O	O	O	O	O	O	O	O	O

Task-Based Simulation 7

Code of Professional Conduct

Assume that you are employed by DFW, CPAs. One of the partners has asked you to research the professional standards for the section that identifies the requirements regarding the acceptance of contingent fees for engagements.

Title choices

A. AU-C
B. PCAOB
C. AT
D. AR
E. ET
F. BL
G. CS
H. QC

	(A)	(B)	(C)	(D)	(E)	(F)	(G)	(H)
1. Which title of the Professional Standards addresses this issue and will be helpful in responding to the partner?	O	O	O	O	O	O	O	O

2. Enter the exact section and paragraphs with helpful information.

Simulation Solutions

Task-Based Simulation 1

		Yes	No
1.	The auditor is a cosigner of a client's checks.	●	○
2.	The auditor is a member of a country club which is a client.	○	●
3.	The auditor owns a large block of stock in a client but has placed it in a blind trust.	●	○
4.	The auditor placed her checking account in a bank which is her client. The account is fully insured by a federal agency.	○	●
5.	The client has not paid the auditor for services for the past two years.	●	○
6.	The auditor is leasing part of his building to a client.	●	○
7.	The auditor joins, as an ordinary member, a trade association which is also a client.	○	●
8.	The auditor has an immaterial, indirect financial interest in the client.	○	●

Explanations

1. (Y) Since the auditor is a cosigner on a client's check, the auditor could become liable if the client defaults. This relationship impairs the auditor's independence.

2. (N) Independence is not impaired because membership in the country club is essentially a social matter.

3. (Y) An auditor may not hold a direct financial interest in a client. Putting it in a blind trust does not solve the impairment of independence.

4. (N) If the auditor places his/her account in a client bank, this does not impair independence if the accounts are state or federally insured. If the accounts are not insured, independence is not impaired if the amounts are immaterial.

5. (Y) The auditor's independence is impaired when prior years' fees for professional services remain unpaid for more than one year.

6. (Y) The auditor's independence is impaired when s/he leases space out of a building s/he owns to a client.

7. (N) When the auditor does not serve in management, s/he may join a trade association who is a client.

8. (N) Independence is impaired for direct financial interests and material, indirect financial interests but not for immaterial, indirect financial interests.

Task-Based Simulation 2

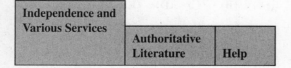

Service	May provide, independence is required	May provide, independence is not required	May not provide
1. Provide an opinion on whether financial statements are prepared following the cash basis of accounting	●	○	○
2. Compile a forecast for the coming year.	○	●	○
3. Compile the financial statements for the past year and issue a publicly available report.	○	●	○
4. Apply certain agreed-upon procedures to accounts receivable for purposes of obtaining a loan, and express a summary of findings relating to those procedures.	●	○	○
5. Review quarterly information and issue a report that includes limited assurance.	●	○	○
6. Perform an audit of the financial statements on whether they are prepared following generally accepted accounting principles.	●	○	○
7. Perform a review of a forecast the company has prepared for the coming year.	○	○	●
8. Compile the financial statements for the past year, but not issue a report since the financial statements are only for the company's use.	○	●	○
9. Calculate the client's taxes and fill out the appropriate tax forms.	○	●	○
10. Design a new payroll system for Hanmei and base billings on Hanmei's actual savings for the next three years.	○	●	○

Task-Based Simulation 3

(A) (B) (C) (D) (E) (F) (G) (H)

1. He thinks that he recalls the issue relates to whether you are or are not a "covered member." He would like you to find the definition of a covered member in the professional standards. Which title of the Professional Standards addresses this issue and will be helpful in responding to the senior?

○ ○ ○ ○ ○ ○ ○ ○

93	06

2. Enter the exact section and paragraphs with helpful information.

3. Regardless of what you find, he would like you to determine whether a covered member may have such an immaterial financial investment in an audit client. What title, section, and paragraph addresses this issue?

ET	101	02

Task-Based Simulation 4

Providing Various Services | **Authoritative Literature** | **Help**

1. Not allowable (PCAOB requirements prohibit)

2. Allowable

3. Allowable

4. Allowable

5. Allowable (Because no attest services are provided, the PCAOP allows this)

6. Not allowable

7. Allowable

8. Not allowable (AICPA rules prohibit this when amounts are subjectively determined and material)

9. Not allowable (Both AICPA nor PCAOB rules prohibit this when amounts are subjectively determined and material)

10. Not allowable

Task-Based Simulation 5

Research		
	Authoritative Literature	**Help**

	(A)	(B)	(C)	(D)	(E)	(F)	(G)	(H)
1. Which topic of the Professional Standards addresses this issue and will be helpful in determining whether Wong & Co. may perform this engagement under these terms without violating professional requirements?	○	○	○	○	○	○	○	○

2. Provide the appropriate paragraph citation that addresses this issue.

302	01

3. Interpret your findings in parts 1 and 2 and conclude on whether Wong & Co. may perform this service without violating professional standards.

   X   Yes, this service may be performed without violating professional standards.

           No, this service may not be performed without violating professional standards.

Task-Based Simulation 6

Research		
	Authoritative Literature	**Help**

Standards that provide guidance	(A)	(B)	(C)	(D)	(E)	(F)	(G)	(H)	(I)	(J)
1. For performance of a review of a nonpublic company's annual financial statements.	○	○	○	○	○	○	●	○	○	○
2. On whether a contingent fee may be billed to a client.	○	●	○	○	○	○	○	○	○	○

3. Related to firm requirements of CPA firms that are enrolled in an AICPA-approved practice-monitoring system.

4. For an examination of a client's financial forecast.

5. Relating to overall requirements when providing services for an advisory services engagement.

6. For the audit of a public company.

7. For the performance of an interim review of the quarterly financial statements of a nonpublic audit client.

8. For reporting on client pro forma financial information.

9. On whether an investment of a CPA impairs her independence with respect to a client.

10. On performing a compilation of a nonpublic company's quarterly statements.

Task-Based Simulation 7

Research		
	Authoritative Literature	Help

	(A)	(B)	(C)	(D)	(E)	(F)	(G)	(H)
1. Which title of the Professional Standards addresses this issue and will be helpful in responding to the partner?	○	○	○	○	●	○	○	○

2. Enter the exact section and paragraphs with helpful information.

302	1

Module 2: Engagement Planning, Obtaining an Understanding of the Client and Assessing Risks

Overview

This module presents requirements relating to planning, obtaining an understanding of the client, and assessing risks. Generally, multiple-choice questions are used to test the candidate's knowledge of areas such as

- Audit planning
- Obtaining an understanding of the client
- Auditor responsibility for the detection of misstatements (errors, fraud, and illegal acts)
- Assessing risks, including the components of audit risk

A simulation may require you to examine a situation, evaluate areas of risk related to a company, and to design appropriate audit procedures in response to that situation. The following sections of Statements on Auditing Standards pertain to this module:

AU-C 200	Responsibilities and Functions of the Independent Auditor
210	Relationship between the Auditor's Appointment and Planning
220	Quality Control for an Engagement Conducted in Accordance with GAAS
240	Consideration of Fraud in a Financial Statement Audit
250	Illegal Acts by Clients
300	Planning and Supervision
314	Substantive Tests prior to the Balance Sheet Date
315	Understanding the Entity and Its Environment and Assessing the Risks of Material Misstatement
510	Communications between Predecessor and Successor Auditors
520	Analytical Procedures
AT 101	Attestation Standards

A. Basic Concepts

1. **Financial statement assertions.** Management is responsible for the fair presentation of financial statements. In representing that the financial statements are fairly presented in conformity with generally accepted accounting principles, management implicitly or explicitly makes assertions relating to account balances at year-end (account balances), classes of transactions and events (transactions classes), and presentations and disclosures (disclosures). Those assertions, included in AU-C 500, are here presented at the transaction class, account balance, and disclosure levels.

Transactions Classes	Account Balances	Disclosures
Occurrence—Transactions and events that have been recorded have occurred and pertain to the entity.	*Existence*—Assets, liabilities, and equity interests exist.	*Occurrence*—Disclosed events and transactions have occurred.
	Rights and obligations—The entity holds or controls the rights to assets, and liabilities are the obligations of the entity.	*Rights and obligations*—Disclosed events pertain to the entity.
Completeness—All transactions and events have been recorded.	*Completeness*—All assets, liabilities, and equity interests have been recorded.	*Completeness*—All disclosures that should have been included have been included.

101

Accuracy—Amounts and other data relating to recorded transactions have been recorded appropriately.	*Valuation and allocation*—Assets, liabilities, and equity interests are included at appropriate amounts.	*Accuracy and valuation*—Information is disclosed fairly and at appropriate amounts.
Cutoff—Transactions and events have been recorded in the correct accounting period.		
Classification—Transactions and events have been recorded in the proper accounts.		*Classification and understandability*—Information is presented and described clearly.

Not all of these assertions are relevant in all circumstances. **Relevant assertions** are those that have a meaningful bearing on whether an account balance, transaction, or disclosure is fairly stated. For example, valuation may not be relevant to the cash account unless currency translation is involved; however, existence and completeness are always relevant.

In planning and performing an audit, the auditor considers these assertions for the various transaction classes, financial statement accounts, and disclosures. When, for example, all of these assertions have been met for an account, the account is in conformity with generally accepted accounting principles. Thus, errors and fraud may be viewed as having the effect of misstating one or more of the assertions. The Responding to Risk Assessment Module presents further illustration of these assertions.

NOW REVIEW MULTIPLE-CHOICE QUESTIONS 1 THROUGH 7

---

2. **Audit risk (AU-C 200).** An audit should be designed to limit audit risk to an appropriately low level. Audit risk, which may be assessed in quantitative or nonquantitative terms, consists of (1) the risk that an account and its related assertions contains material misstatements (composed of two components, referred to as inherent risk and control risk) and (2) the risk that the auditor will not detect such misstatements (referred to as detection risk). Mathematically, we may view this as follows:

$$\text{Audit Risk} = \text{Risk of material misstatement} \quad * \quad \text{Risk Auditor Fails to Detect Misstatements}$$

$$\text{Audit Risk} = \text{Inherent Risk} * \text{Control Risk} \quad * \quad \text{Detection Risk}$$

Inherent risk refers to the likelihood of material misstatement of an assertion, assuming no related internal control. This risk is assessed using various analytical techniques, available information on the company and its industry, as well as by using overall auditing knowledge. The risk differs by account and assertion. For example, cash is more susceptible to theft than an inventory of coal.

Control risk is the likelihood that a material misstatement will not be prevented or detected on a timely basis by internal control. This risk is assessed using the results of tests of controls. Tests of controls that provide audit evidence that controls operate effectively will ordinarily allow the auditor to assess control risk at a level below the maximum.

Detection risk is the likelihood that an auditor's procedures lead to an improper conclusion that no material misstatement exists in an assertion when in fact such a misstatement does exist. Substantive procedures are primarily relied upon to restrict detection risk. Auditors increase the nature, timing or extent of substantive procedures to decrease the assessed level of detection risk.

Relationship among inherent risk, control risk, and detection risk. Inherent risk and control risk differ from detection risk in that they exist independently of the audit, whereas detection risk relates to the effectiveness of the auditor's procedures. A number of questions are asked concerning the relationship among the three risks. Although the auditor may make either separate or combined assessments of inherent risk and control risk, you may find the audit risk formula that separates the risks helpful for such questions. First, assume that a given audit risk is to be accepted, say .05. Then, the product of inherent risk, control risk and detection risk is .05 as follows:

Audit Risk	=	Inherent Risk	*	Control Risk	*	Detection Risk
.05	=	Inherent Risk	*	Control Risk	*	Detection Risk

Accordingly, if any risk increases another must decrease to hold audit risk at .05. Therefore, when a question asks for the relationship between control risk and detection risk, for example, you would reply that it is inverse. Stated otherwise, if control risk (or inherent risk) increases, detection risk must decrease.

3. **Materiality (AU-C 320, 450).** Generally accepted accounting principles consider materiality to be "the magnitude of an omission or misstatement of accounting information that, in the light of surrounding circumstances, makes it probable that the judgment of a *reasonable person* relying on the information would have been changed or influenced by the omission or misstatement." AU-C 320 and 450 operationalize the concept of a *reasonable person* relying on the financial statements as **users.** Thus the evaluation of whether a misstatement could influence the economic decision of users involves consideration of the characteristics of those users. Users are assumed to have appropriate knowledge of business and accounting, be willing to study the information, understand that materiality judgments and uncertainty are involved. An auditor's consideration of user needs is as a group, not on specific individual users, whose needs may vary widely. Determining a materiality level helps auditors to (1) assess risks of material misstatements and plan the nature, timing, and extent of further audit procedures and (2) evaluate audit results.

The auditor plans the audit to obtain reasonable assurance of detecting misstatements that could be large enough, individually or when combined, to be quantitatively material to the financial statements. The process ordinarily begins with establishing a materiality for the financial statements as a whole. If specific account balances, classes of transactions or disclosures exist for which misstatements of lower amounts than the materiality for the financial statements as a whole are expected, the auditor should determine materiality level(s) to be applied to those accounts, classes of transactions and disclosures. Also, the auditor should revise materiality in the event of becoming aware of information during the audit that initially would have resulted in a different amount (or amounts) had that information been known. For example, if it appears that operating results are likely to be substantially different from anticipated results, the auditor may be required to revise materiality.

The many accounts and disclosures in the financial statements make simply using the amount(s) determined to be material over and over to determine the scope of audit procedures of individual procedures inappropriate since it overlooks the possibility that several individually immaterial misstatements may cause the financial statements to be materially misstated. For example, if $100,000 is considered material, individually immaterial understatements of two asset accounts by $60,000 and $80,000 respectively is, in total, a material misstatement. The professional standards establish the concept of **performance materiality** set by the auditors to reduce to an appropriately low level the possibility that the aggregate of uncorrected and undetected misstatements exceeds materiality for the financial statements—that is, performance materiality will ordinarily be set at an amount below the materiality level for the financial statements as a whole. Finally, **tolerable misstatement**, as discussed in Module 7, is a function of performance measure as related to the auditor's assessment of performance materiality and is normally set at, or less than performance materiality.[1] Audit documentation relating to materiality should include

- Materiality for the financial statements as a whole.
- If applicable, materiality level(s) for particular accounts, classes of transactions, or disclosures.
- Performance materiality.
- Any revisions of the above as the audit progressed.

The measures of materiality used for evaluation purposes will ordinarily differ from measures of materiality used for planning. This is the result of information encountered during the audit. For evaluation purposes, the auditor is aware of qualitative aspects of actual misstatements that s/he is not aware of during the planning stage. For example, an auditor will consider any fraud in which management is involved to be material, regardless of the amount involved.

---

[1] Performance materiality is a new concept in the ASB and international standards that is positioned between materiality at the engagement level and tolerable misstatement at the sample level. Differing approaches, ordinarily beyond the scope of CPA exam coverage, exist to setting performance materiality.

NOW REVIEW MULTIPLE-CHOICE QUESTIONS 8 THROUGH 21

4. **Errors and fraud (AU-C 240).** An audit should be planned and performed to obtain reasonable assurance about whether the financial statements are free of material misstatements, whether caused by error or fraud. While both errors and fraud may result in misstatements or omissions in the financial statements, they differ in that fraud is intentional. The two types of fraud considered in an audit are (1) **fraudulent financial reporting** that makes the financial statements misleading and (2) **misappropriation of assets** (i.e., theft, defalcation). The Summary of Auditor Responsibility for Errors, Fraud, and Illegal Acts table presents overall auditor responsibilities.

SUMMARY OF AUDITOR RESPONSIBILITY FOR ERRORS, FRAUD, AND ILLEGAL ACTS

	Errors	Fraud	Illegal acts	
			Direct effect	**Other laws**
Definition	Unintentional misstatements or omissions	Intentional misstatements or omissions	Violations of laws or governmental regulations having a material and direct effect on financial statement **amounts and disclosures**	Violations of laws or governmental regulations **not** having a material and direct effect on financial statement **amounts and disclosures**
Examples	Mistakes in processing accounting data, incorrect accounting estimates due to oversight, mistakes in application of accounting principles	Two types—**fraudulent financial reporting** (falsification of accounting records) and **misappropriation of assets** (embezzlement)	Tax laws, accrued revenue based on government contracts	Securities trading, occupational safety and health, food and drug administration, environmental protection, equal employment, price fixing
Detection responsibility	1. Assess risk of misstatement. 2. Based on assessment, design audit to provide reasonable assurance of detection of material misstatements. 3. Exercise due care in planning, performing, and evaluating results of audit procedures, and proper degree of professional skepticism to achieve reasonable assurance of detection.	(Same as for errors)	(Same as for errors)	1. Be aware of possibility that they may have occurred. 2. Inquire of management and those charged with governance re: compliance. 3. Inspect correspondence with licensing or regulatory authorities 4. If specific information comes to attention on an illegal act with a possible material indirect financial statement effect, apply audit procedures necessary to determine whether illegal act has occurred.
Reporting responsibility	1. Modify audit report for remaining departures from GAAP or scope limitations. 2. Report to audit committee (unless clearly inconsequential).	(Same as for errors)	(Same as for errors)	(Similar to errors)

	3. In audits in accordance with government auditing standards, consider notification of other parties (e.g., regulatory agencies). 4. Report in various other circumstances (e.g., Form 8-K, successor auditor, subpoena response).			
Primary standards	**AU-C 240**	**AU-C 240**	**AU-C 240, 250**	**AU-C 250**

You should be very familiar with the information presented in the rather lengthy outline of AU-C 240, as well as the outline of AU-C 250 on illegal acts (discussed in detail in the following section). While we summarize some of the most important concepts from them, reading this section of the module alone is insufficient. Although AU-C 240 does not refer to "steps" involved related to fraud, and indeed in practice the "steps" don't follow one another nicely, we summarize the layout of its guidance in the following table.

Consideration of Fraud

Step	Approach
Step 1. Staff discussion of the risk of material misstatement	• Brainstorm • Consider incentives/pressures, opportunities • Exercise professional skepticism
Step 2. Obtain information needed to identify risks of material misstatement due to fraud	• Make inquiries of management and others • Consider results of analytical procedures • Consider fraud risk factors • Consider other information
Step 3. Identify risks that may result in a material misstatement due to fraud	For risks identified, consider • Type of risk that may exist • Significance of risk (magnitude) • Likelihood of risk • Pervasiveness of risk
Step 4. Assess the identified risks after considering programs and controls	• Consider understanding of internal control • Evaluate whether programs and controls address the identified risks • Assess risks taking into account this evaluation
Step 5. Respond to the results of the assessment	As risk increases • Overall response: More experienced staff, more attention to accounting policies, less predictable procedures • For specifically identified risks: Consider need to increase nature, timing, and extent of audit procedures On all audits consider the possibility of management override of controls (adjusting journal entries, accounting estimates, unusual transactions)
Step 6. Evaluate audit evidence	• Assess risk of fraud throughout the audit • Evaluate analytical procedures performed as substantive procedures and at overall review stage • Evaluate risk of fraud near completion of fieldwork • Respond to misstatements that may be due to fraud
Step 7. Communicate about fraud	• Communicate all fraud to an appropriate level of management • Communicate all management fraud to audit committee • Communicate all material fraud to management and audit committee • Determine if significant deficiencies have been identified
Step 8. Document consideration of fraud	• Document steps 1–7 • If improper revenue recognition not considered a risk, describe why

AU-C 240 is the source of many questions. Here are some particularly important points included in the outline.

1. Because an audit is planned and performed to obtain reasonable, not absolute, assurance, even a properly performed audit may miss material misstatements.
2. The auditor should exercise professional skepticism—an attitude that includes (a) a questioning mind, being alert to conditions that may indicate possible misstatement due to fraud or error, and (b) a critical assessment of audit evidence. It requires that throughout the audit the auditor be alert for:

   - Audit evidence that contradicts other audit evidence.
   - Information that raises a question abut he reliability of documents and responses to inquiries.
   - Conditions indicating possible fraud.
   - Circumstances suggesting the need for additional audit procedures beyond those ordinarily required.

   Also, know that the PCAOB has raised concerns about whether auditors consistently and diligently apply professional skepticism, suggesting that inherent conditions in the audit engagement may create incentives and pressures that impede application of professional skepticism (e.g., long-term relationships, completing the audit too quickly to meet client demands, keeping audit costs low).
3. Make certain you can distinguish between **fraudulent financial reporting** in which the financial statements are intentionally misstated (cooked books) and **misappropriation of assets** when its assets are stolen.
4. Three conditions that are generally present when individuals commit fraud are incentive/pressure, opportunity, and attitude/rationalization.
5. The engagement partner and other key engagement team members are required to discuss the susceptibility of the company's financial statements to material misstatement—whether due to errors or fraud. The discussion should include an exchange of ideas or brainstorming about how and where the financial statements might be susceptible to material misstatement due to fraud, how management could perpetrate and conceal fraudulent financial reporting, and how assets of the company could be misappropriated.
6. Audits include a presumption that risks of fraud exist in revenue recognition (ordinarily overstatement) and that a risk of management override of internal control is present.
7. The responses to the results of the assessment as risk are an overall response, a response that specifically addresses identified risks, and a response for the possibility of management override. The response for management override (performed on all audits to some extent) includes

   - Testing the appropriateness of journal entries and adjustments
   - Reviewing accounting estimates for biases
   - Evaluating the rationale for significant unusual transactions

8. While fraud risk factors have been present in the past when fraud has occurred, they may or may not indicate fraud in any particular situation.
9. The existence of a fraud risk factor may or may not require modification of the audit program. For example, if a risk factor is identified and the current audit program already includes procedures to address the risk involved, modification of the program may not be necessary.
10. Fraud communication responsibility

    - All fraud involving management should be communicated to the audit committee
    - All material fraud should be communicated to the audit committee
    - The auditor should reach an understanding with the audit committee regarding other communications

At this point study the outline of AU-C 240 in detail.

5. **Laws and regulations** (AU-C 250). Auditor responsibility with respect to identifying client noncompliance with laws and regulations (hereafter, laws) depends upon the nature of the laws. The *Professional Standards* identify two types of laws—(1) those with a direct effect on the financial statement amounts and disclosures and (2) others.

   Certain laws have a **direct effect** on the financial statement amounts and disclosures. Examples are accounting for transactions under government contracts and the accrual of income tax and pension costs. Auditors should obtain an understanding of the legal and regulatory framework applicable to the entity and how the organization complies with that framework. Concerning illegal acts with a direct effect on financial statement amounts and disclosures, the auditors should obtain sufficient appropriate audit evidence to obtain **reasonable assurance** regarding those amounts and disclosures—the same responsibility the auditors have for material errors and fraud. Examples of audit procedures that may detect such illegal acts include inquiries of management and legal counsel, substantive procedures, and reading board of director meeting minutes and correspondence with licensing or regulatory authorities.

Other laws do not have a direct effect in the determination of amounts and disclosures, but compliance with them is required to stay in business, or to avoid material penalties. Examples of other laws include those relating to securities trading, occupational safety and health, food and drug administration, environmental protection, equal employment and price fixing or other anti-trust violations. For audit purposes, the difference between laws with a direct effect and other laws is that auditors have a higher level of responsibility relating to laws with a direct effect.

Other laws often deal with operating aspects of the business and do not have a direct effect on the determination of amounts in the financial statements. Auditors are required to perform specified audit procedures that may identify instances of noncompliance with other laws that may have a material effect on the financial statements, including:

- Inquiring of management and those charged with governance as to whether the entity is in compliance with such laws and
- Inspecting correspondence, if any, with relevant licensing or regulatory authorities.

Also, throughout the audit the auditors should remain alert for the possibility that other audit procedures bring forth instances of noncompliance or suspected noncompliance with any laws.

Additional audit procedures are required for all illegal acts (direct effect and other) when noncompliance is identified or suspected. In such a situation, the auditors should (1) obtain an understanding of the act and the circumstances in which it has occurred and (2) obtain further information to evaluate the possible effect on the financial statements. Unless all those charged with governance are involved in management and are aware of the matters identified, the auditor should communicate to them any identified or suspected noncompliance with laws identified, other than matters that are clearly inconsequential. When the violations are considered intentional and material, the auditors should communicate the matter to those charged with governance as soon as practicable.

If the auditors suspect that management or those charged with governance are involved in noncompliance, they should communicate the matter to the next higher level of authority in the organization, if it exists, such as the audit committee. Where no higher authority exists, or if the auditors believe that the communication may not be acted upon or who to report to, they should consider the need to obtain legal advice.

Violations of laws may affect the audit report as follows:

NOW REVIEW MULTIPLE-CHOICE QUESTIONS 22 THROUGH 65

B. Audit Planning

Situation	Audit Report Effect
1. Noncompliance with a material effect on financial statements not properly disclosed.	Departure from GAAP—qualified or adverse opinion.
2. Auditor is precluded by management or those charged with governance from obtaining sufficient appropriate audit evidence on whether noncompliance may have a material effect on the financial statements. Auditor unable to determine whether noncompliance has occurred due to limitations imposed by the circumstances.	Scope limitation—qualified opinion or disclaimer of opinion

CPAs should establish policies for deciding whether to accept (or continue serving) a client in order to minimize the likelihood of being associated with an organization whose management lacks integrity. The auditor should also adequately plan the audit. Much of the information on audit planning is included in AU-C 300.

Prior to acquiring a client, an auditor should attempt communication with the predecessor auditor and obtain a general understanding of the nature of the organization and its industry. The overall goal is to determine whether to attempt to acquire the client, and to gather adequate information so as to allow the auditor to develop a proposal to be presented to the prospective client.

1. **Communicate with predecessor auditors (AU-C 510).** Make certain that you are very familiar with the information presented in the outline. That standard requires a communication with the predecessor prior to acceptance of the engagement, and strongly recommends one after acceptance of the engagement (see Section C.1 of this module). Particularly heavily examined concepts relating to the communication prior to client acceptance are

   a. Initiating the communication is the responsibility of the successor.
   b. If the prospective client refuses to permit the predecessor to respond, or limits the predecessor's response, the successor should inquire as to the reasons and consider the implications in deciding whether to accept the engagement.
   c. The successor's inquiries of the predecessor should include

      (1) Information bearing on **integrity** of management
      (2) **Disagreements** with management as to accounting principles, auditing procedures or other similarly significant matters
      (3) **Communications** to audit committee regarding fraud, illegal acts, and internal control related matters
      (4) Predecessor's understanding of the **reasons for the change** in auditors

2. **Establishing an understanding with the client (engagement letters).** Auditors should establish an understanding with the client regarding the services to be performed—see AU-C 210. The auditor should document this understanding through a written communication with the client, ordinarily an engagement letter. The engagement letter is sent to the client, who normally indicates approval through returning a signed copy to the CPA.

   The understanding should include four general topics: (1) objectives of the engagement, (2) management's responsibilities, (3) auditor's responsibilities, and (4) limitations of the audit. If an auditor believes that an understanding has not been established, he or she should decline to accept or perform the audit.

   The following summary presents details of the required understanding with the client.

SUMMARY OF DETAILS OF AN UNDERSTANDING WITH THE CLIENT

General	Details
1. Objectives of the engagement	Expression of an opinion on the financial statements
2. Management's responsibilities	• Establishing and maintaining effective internal control over financial reporting • Identifying and ensuring that the entity complies with laws and regulations • Making financial records and related information available to the auditor • Providing a representation letter (see Responding to Risk Assessment Module) • Adjusting financial statements to correct material misstatements • Affirming in representation letter that effect of uncorrected misstatements aggregated by auditor is immaterial
3. Auditor's responsibilities	• Conducting audit in accordance with US GAAS • Ensuring that audit committee is aware of any significant deficiencies which come to auditor's attention
4. Limitations of the audit	• Obtains reasonable, rather than absolute, assurance • Material misstatement may remain undetected • If auditor is unable to form or has not formed an opinion, auditor may decline to express an opinion or decline to issue a report

Other (not required)	• Arrangements regarding:
	  – Conduct of engagement (timing, client assistance, etc.)
	  – Involvement of specialists or internal auditors
	  – Predecessor auditor
	  – Fees and billing
	  – Additional services to be provided relating to regulatory requirements
	  – Other additional services
	• Any limitation or other arrangement regarding the liability of the auditor or the client
	• Conditions under which access to the auditor's working papers may be granted to others

For recurring audits, the auditor should assess whether the terms of the audit need to be revised and a new engagement letter be utilized. If no modification is necessary, at a minimum, under AICPA requirements for nonpublic company audits, the auditor should remind management of the terms of the audit and document the reminder in the working papers. The PCAOB requires that an understanding be obtained for each engagement; this understanding should be documented in the working papers, preferably through a written communication (e.g., engagement letter) with the client.

3. **Preliminary engagement activities.** The auditor performs procedures to determine whether continuance of the client relationship is appropriate and to evaluate the auditor's compliance with ethical considerations (e.g., independence).

4. **Developing an overall strategy.** The nature, timing, and extent of planning will vary with the size and complexity of the audit client, experience with the client, and knowledge of the client's business. The overall audit strategy involves

   - Determining the characteristics of the engagement that define its scope (e.g., basis of reporting, industry-specific reporting requirements)
   - Determining reporting objectives of the engagement (e.g., deadlines for reporting, key dates)
   - Considering important factors that will determine the focus of the audit team's efforts (e.g., materiality levels, high-risk areas)

   The above items help the auditor to determine the appropriate resources necessary for the engagement. Once the audit strategy has been established, the auditor is able to start the development of a more detailed audit plan to address the various matters identified in the audit strategy.

5. **The audit plan.** The auditor should develop and document an audit plan in which the auditor determines the audit procedures to be used that, when performed, are expected to reduce audit risk to an acceptably low level. The audit plan should include a description of the nature, timing and extent of planned

   - Risk assessment procedures
   - Further audit procedures (tests of controls and substantive tests) at the relevant assertion level for account balances, transactions classes, and disclosures
   - Other audit procedures (e.g., seeking direct communication with the entity's lawyer)

6. **Audit program.** A written audit program should be developed and used to implement the audit plan. Audit programs are discussed in the Responding to Risk Assessment Module.

7. **Timing of audit procedures** Tests of controls and substantive tests can be conducted at various times. The timing of tests of controls is very flexible; they are often performed at an interim period, and subsequently updated through year-end.

   Auditors also have a certain amount of flexibility in planning the timing of substantive tests. These aspects should be considered.

   a. Factors to be considered before applying tests at an **interim date** before year-end
   b. Auditing procedures to be followed for the **remaining period** (the period after the interim date through year-end)
   c. **Coordination of the timing** of audit procedures

   Before applying procedures at an **interim date,** an auditor should consider the incremental audit risk involved as well as whether performance of such interim procedures is likely to be cost-effective. As an illustration of a substantive test applied at an interim date, consider the confirmation of receivables as of November 30, one month prior to the client's year-end.

   Appropriate auditing procedures should be applied to provide a reasonable basis for extending November 30 interim date results to the **remaining period** (December 1–31). When control risk is assessed at a level below the maximum, the auditor might be able to perform only limited substantive tests during the remaining period to obtain the assurance needed as of the balance sheet date.

   The auditor who intends to apply audit tests at an interim date should consider whether the accounting system will provide information on remaining period transactions that is sufficient to investigate (1) significant unusual transactions, (2) other causes of significant fluctuation (or expected fluctuations that did not occur), and (3) changes in the composition of the account balances.

   A properly performed audit involves **coordination of the timing** of procedures. This especially applies to (1) related-party transactions, (2) interrelated accounts and cutoffs, and (3) negotiable assets. For interrelated accounts and negotiable assets, the auditor is concerned that one might be substituted for another to allow the double counting of a given resource (e.g., sale of securities after they have been counted at year-end and inclusion of proceeds in year-end cash).

NOW REVIEW MULTIPLE CHOICE QUESTIONS 66 THROUGH 87

C. Obtain an Understanding of the Entity and Its Environment (AU-C 315).
The procedures followed to obtain an understanding of the entity are referred to as risk assessment procedures. Risk assessment procedures include

- Inquiries of management and others within the entity
- Observation and inspection
- Analytical procedures
- Other procedures, such as inquiries of others outside the entity (e.g., legal counsel, valuation experts) and reviewing information from external sources such as analysts, banks, etc.

The following is information on certain specific risk assessment procedures ordinarily performed.

1. **Communicate with predecessor auditors.** Earlier, we discussed the AU-C 510 requirement that potential successor auditors attempt communication with the predecessor **before** accepting a new client. We also emphasized that you should be very familiar with the outline of AU-C 510.

   Although strongly recommended, no second communication with the predecessor auditor is required **after** accepting a new client. This second communication would normally involve review of working papers related to opening balances and the consistency of application of accounting principles. With regard to working papers

   a. Documentation examined generally includes

      (1) Planning
      (2) Internal control
      (3) Audit results
      (4) Other matters of continuing accounting **and** auditing significance such as analyses of balance sheet accounts

   b. If in reviewing the working papers the successor identifies financial statement misstatements, the successor should request that the client inform the predecessor and arrange a meeting of the three parties.

   In addition, AU-C 510 includes a section on "reaudits" of previously audited financial statements. Reaudits may be necessary, for example, when a change in auditors has occurred and the predecessor refuses to reissue his or her audit report on previous year financial statements that are to be reissued (e.g., prior year statements in an SEC filing). In such cases the successor should request the working papers for the period of the reaudit; the extent to which the predecessor permits such access is considered a matter of judgment. Additional procedures beyond those performed by the predecessor are always necessary in such circumstances.

2. **Consideration of internal control.** In all audits, the CPA should obtain an understanding of internal control sufficient to assess the risk of material misstatement of the financial statements, and to design the nature, timing, and extent of further audit procedures. Internal control is discussed further in the Internal Control Module.

3. **Supervision requirements.** Supervision includes instructing assistants, being informed on significant problems, reviewing audit work, and dealing with differences of opinion among audit personnel. The complexity of the audit and qualifications of audit assistants affect the degree of supervision needed. The work of each assistant should be reviewed (1) to determine whether it was adequately performed and (2) to evaluate whether the results are consistent with the conclusions to be presented in the audit report. Procedures should be established for documenting any disagreements of opinions among staff personnel; the basis for resolution of such disagreements should also be documented.

4. **Analytical procedures.** AU-C 315 requires that analytical procedures be performed as a risk assessment procedure. Analytical procedures used during risk assessment may (1) enhance the auditor's understanding of the client's business and significant transactions and events that have occurred since the prior audit and (2) help the auditor to identify the existence of unusual transactions or events and amounts, ratios, and trends that might indicate matters that have audit implications. Such identified unusual or unexpected relationships may assist the auditor in identifying risks of material misstatement (including those due to fraud). However, often analytical procedures used during risk assessment use data aggregated at a high level and they may provide only a broad initial indication about possible existence of material misstatements. The following section provides an example of an approach used for testing analytical procedures on the CPA exam. Also, analytical procedures are discussed in further detail in the Responding to Risk Assessment Module.

4a. **Analytical procedures simulation illustration.** A number of simulation questions present two years of ratio information and require identification of a possible explanation for a change that occurred. For example:

Ratio	Year 1	Year 2
Accounts receivable turnover	7.00	5.00

Client Explanations (select 1)
• "Although sales remained the same, we were more profitable this year because we produced our product more efficiently." • "Our sales and accounts receivable increased at the same percentage as due to an effective advertising campaign." • "Although our sales remained at the same total for years 1 and 2, November and December of Year 2 were slow as our competition released a new version of its product. • "We made a large credit sale on December 31 of Year 2."

A complete simulation might include five or more ratios and a total of twelve or more possible explanations. Also, for some simulations the components of the ratio is provided (here, credit sales / accounts receivable), while for others candidates are expected to know the components of the ratio.

A key to these questions is considering underlying journal entries affecting the numerator and denominator of the ratio. Even with this knowledge, the nature of the double entry bookkeeping system sometimes results in changes in ratios that are less than intuitively obvious. For example, consider that a change in the accounts receivable turnover (credit sales / accounts receivable) may be due to a change in sales, accounts receivable or both. Thus, a credit sale is recorded with a debit to accounts receivable and a credit to sales. Accordingly, a credit sale that is not collected at year-end will affect both the numerator and the denominator, while a sale in which the receivable is collected prior to year-end will only affect sales, the numerator.

When addressing questions such as the above, rule out explanations have no effect on the ratio being considered—here explanations that do not affect sales or accounts receivable. For those that affect either or both of accounts receivable and sales, it becomes an issue of considering whether they have the net effect suggested (here, a decrease).

Client Explanation (re-presented)	Analysis
• "Although sales remained the same, we were more profitable this year because we produced our product more efficiently."	This doesn't have an obvious effect on either sales or accounts receivable as one would expect a decrease in the cost of goods sold and an increase in income (and retained earnings).
• "Our sales and accounts receivable increased at the same percentage due to an effective advertising campaign."	This explanation affects both sales and accounts receivable. But because they both increased at the same percentage rate one would not expect either a decrease or an increase in the accounts receivable turnover.
• "Although our sales remained at the same total for years 1 and 2, November and December of Year 2 were slow as our competition released a new version of its product."	This explanation possibly affects year-end accounts receivable; but total sales for the year remained at the same level for both years. If November and December sales were "slow," one would expect a decreased level of accounts receivable at year-end. This will increase in the accounts receivable turnover (not a decrease) because the denominator of the fraction decreases while the numerator (sales) remains at last year's level.
• "We made a large credit sales at the very end of Year 2 that led to an increase in sales as compared to Year 1."	This explanation affects both Year 2 year-end accounts receivable and total sales by the same amount—this will decrease the ratio(and could here explain the change from 7 to 5). For example, assume that the Year 1 accounts receivable turnover of 7 was achieved through sales of $700,000 and accounts receivable of $100,000. Now assume the same results in Year 2, supplemented by a last sale in Year 2 of $50,000. This would increase total sales to $750,000 and ending accounts receivable to $150,000—a turnover of 5. This explanation is correct as it will decrease the ratio. Note that the information provided does not indicate that the sale is uncollected as of year-end. It is implied by the "very end" of Year 2.

Questions of this sort require careful consideration of the various replies. The following generalizations are helpful in understanding the direction of changes in positive ratios (i.e., ratios greater than zero):

- Increasing the numerator of a ratio always increases the ratio.
- Increasing the denominator of a ratio always decreases the ratio.
- Increasing the numerator and denominator of a ratio by the same amount:

  → Decreases the ratio if the ratio is greater than 1—think of changing 4/3 (=1.33) to 5/4 (= 1.25).
  → Increases the ratio if the ratio is less than 1—think of changing 2/3(=.67) to 3/4 (= .75).

D. Assess the Risks of Material Misstatement and Design Further Audit Procedures

The auditor should perform the risk assessment to identify and assess the risks of material misstatement at the financial statement level and at the relevant assertion level for classes of transactions, account balances, and disclosures; the approach is one of

- Identifying risks
- Relating the risks to what can go wrong at the relevant assertion level
- Considering whether the risks are of a magnitude that could result in a material misstatement
- Considering the likelihood that risks could result in material misstatements

As a part of the risk assessment the auditor is required to identify significant risks that require special audit attention. Although determining the significant risks is a matter of professional judgment, the standards provide some guidance. Routine, noncomplex transactions that are subject to systematic processing are less likely to give rise to significant risks because they have lower inherent risks. Alternatively, significant risks are often derived from business risks that may result in a material misstatement. When evaluating risks, the auditor should consider

- Whether the risk is a risk of fraud
- Whether the risk is related to recent significant economic, accounting or other developments
- The complexity of transactions
- Whether the risk involves significant transactions with related parties
- The degree of subjectivity in the measurement of financial information
- Whether the risk involves significant nonroutine transactions and judgmental matters, or otherwise appear to be unusual

The "further audit procedures" that are designed are of two types—substantive procedures and tests of controls. When the risk assessment is based on an expectation that controls are operating effectively, the auditor should perform tests of controls to provide evidence on whether those controls are operating effectively—this is discussed further in the Internal Control Module.

Details on types of substantive tests are presented in the Responding to Risk Assessment Module.

E. Quality Control

1. The Statements on Quality Control Standards (SQCS) apply to the auditing and accounting (compilation and review) practice of CPA firms. While the generally accepted auditing standards and the *Code of Professional Conduct* are primarily directed at the **individual practitioner** level, the quality control standards apply to the CPA **firm** itself.

   Members of the AICPA who are in public practice and have financial reporting responsibilities should have a sample of their accounting (compilations and reviews) and auditing work reviewed by an independent party. To meet this requirement CPA firms undergo a **peer review** performed directly by a CPA, a CPA firm, or a team of CPAs. There are two types of peer reviews: *system review* and *engagement review*. A *system review* involves peer reviewers' study and appraisal of a CPA firm's system of quality control to perform accounting and auditing work; in essence, the quality control standards serve as the criteria for a system review. The approach of the peer reviewers in a system review is to obtain an understanding of the CPA firm through inquiry of CPA firm personnel, review of documentation about the quality control system (e.g., firm manuals), and selection of a sample of the CPA firm's engagements for review. Subsequently a report is issued by the peer reviewers. A pass rating provides reasonable assurance in that it includes the peer reviewers' opinion that the system is appropriately designed and is being complied with by the CPA firm in all material respects. A pass with deficiencies rating differs in that it indicates that in certain situations (outlined in the report) the system is not appropriately designed or complied with. A fail rating indicates that the peer reviewer has determined that the CPA firm's system is not suitably designed or being complied with.

   An *engagement review* is the second type of peer review. The peer reviewers select a sample of a CPA firm's actual accounting work, including accounting reports issued and CPA firm documentation to evaluate whether the reports and procedures are appropriate. This form of peer review is only available for CPA firms that do not perform audits, but do perform accounting work, including reviews and/or compilations. While, as is the case with a systems review, the report issued may be pass, pass with deficiencies, or fail as is the case with a systems review, the restricted nature of an engagement review results in a report in which the pass and pass with deficiencies reports include only limited (negative) assurance.

2. **Overall on a System of Quality Control**

   a. A system of quality control consists of policies designed to achieve the objective of the firm to establish and maintain a system of quality control (QC) to provide reasonable assurance that

      (1) The firm and its personnel comply with professional standards and applicable legal and regulatory requirements and
      (2) Reports issued by the firm or engagement partners are appropriate in the circumstances

   b. This standard is applicable to a CPA firm's accounting and auditing practice. Other professional pronouncement set out additional requirements and guidance for specific types of engagements.

3. Following are the elements of a firm's system of quality control:

   a. Leadership responsibilities for quality with the firm ("tone at the top")
   b. Relevant ethical requirements
   c. Acceptance and continuance of client relationships and specific engagements
   d. Human resources
   e. Engagement performance
   f. Monitoring

   > **NOTE:** The following sections (4 through 8) describe each of the above elements.

4. **Quality Control Element 1: Leadership responsibilities for quality within the firm ("Tone at the top").**

   a. Policies and procedures should be established to promote an internal culture based on the recognition that quality is essential in performing engagements.
   b. Any person with operational responsibility for quality control should have sufficient and appropriate experience and ability.

5. **Quality Control Element 2: Relevant ethical requirements.** The firm should establish policies and procedures to provide reasonable assurance that the firm and its personnel comply with relevant ethical requirements.

   a. The SQCS pay particular attention to the importance of providing reasonable assurance of maintaining independence.
   b. At least annually, the firm should obtain written confirmation of compliance with independence policies and procedures from firm personnel.

6. **Quality Control Element 3: Acceptance and continuance of client relationships and specific engagements.** Policies and procedures should provide reasonable assurance of accepting and continuing client relationships where the firm

   a. Is competent to perform the engagement
   b. Can comply with legal and ethical requirements
   c. Has considered client integrity

7. **Quality Control Element 4: Human resources.** The firm should establish policies and procedures to provide reasonable assurance that it has sufficient personnel with necessary capabilities, competence and commitment to ethical principles to (a) perform its engagements in accordance with appropriate standards and (b) enable it to issue appropriate reports. Such policies should address

   a. Recruiting
   b. Performance evaluation, compensation, and advancement
   c. Determining competencies and capabilities.

8. **Quality Control Element 5: Engagement performance.** The firm should establish policies and procedures to provide reasonable assurance that engagements are performed in accordance with appropriate standards and that appropriate reports are issued.

   a. Policies and procedures should address

      (1) Matters relevant to promoting consistency of engagement performance.
      (2) Supervision responsibilities
      (3) Review responsibilities

   b. The firm's review responsibility policies and procedures should be determined on the basis that suitably experienced team members review work performed by other engagement team members.

    c. The firm should establish policies and procedure for addressing and resolving differences of opinion within the audit team, with those consulted and, where applicable, between the engagement partner and the engagement quality control reviewer; such policies and procedures should:

        (1) Enable members of the engagement team to document disagreements and conclusions reached.

        (2) Require that conclusions reached be documented and implemented and the report not be released until the matter is resolved.

9. **Quality Control Element 6: Monitoring.** A firm should establish policies and procedures designed to provide it with reasonable assurance that the policies and procedures relating to the system of quality control are relevant, adequate, operating effectively, and complied with in practice.

    a. Deficiencies identified during monitoring do not necessarily indicate that the system of quality control is insufficient to provide it with reasonable assurance that it complies with appropriate standards and are not necessarily systemic, requiring prompt corrective action.

        (1) Firm should consider the seriousness of such deficiencies.

    b. At least annually, the firm should communicate monitoring results to relevant engagement partners and other appropriate individuals within the firm. This should allow those individuals to take prompt and appropriate corrective action.

    c. A peer review conducted under AICPA standards may substitute for the inspection of engagement working papers, reports and clients' financial statements for some or all engagements for the period covered by the peer review.

10. **Documentation**. The firm should establish policies and procedures requiring appropriate documentation to provide evidence of the operation of each elements of its system of quality control.

> **NOW REVIEW MULTIPLE-CHOICE QUESTIONS 88 THROUGH 116**

KEY TERMS

Accounting estimate. An approximation of a monetary amount in the absence of a precise means of measurement. This term is used for an amount measured at fair value where there is estimation uncertainty, as well as for other amounts that require estimation.

Analytical procedures. Evaluations of financial information through analysis of plausible relationships among both financial and nonfinancial data. Analytical procedures also encompass such investigation, as is necessary, of identified fluctuations or relationships that are inconsistent with other relevant information or that differ from expected values by a significant amount.

Assertions. Representations by management, explicit or otherwise, that are embodied in the financial statements, as used by the auditor to consider the different types of potential misstatements that may occur.

Audit evidence. Information used by the auditor in arriving at the conclusions on which the auditor's opinion is based. Audit evidence includes both information contained in the accounting records underlying the financial statements and other information:

    a. Sufficiency of audit evidence is the measure of the quantity of audit evidence. The quantity of the audit evidence needed is affected by the auditor's assessment of the risks of material misstatement and also by the quality of such audit evidence.

    b. Appropriateness of audit evidence is the measure of the quality of audit evidence; that is, its relevance and its reliability in providing support for the conclusions on which the auditor's opinion is based.

Audit plan. A description of the nature, timing, and extent of the audit procedures to be performed. It is often documented with an audit program.

Audit program. A detailed listing of the specific audit procedures to be performed in the course of an audit engagement. Audit programs are tailored to the risks and internal control of each engagement.

Audit risk. The risk that the auditor expresses an inappropriate audit opinion when the financial statements are materially misstated. Audit risk is a function of the risks of material misstatement and detection risk.

Audit strategy. The approach which involves determining overall characteristics of an audit that define its scope, its reporting objectives, timing of procedures and various important factors relating to the audit. When the overall audit strategy has been established, the auditors start the development of a more detailed audit plan to address the various matters identified in the audit strategy.

Control risk. The risk that a misstatement that could occur in an assertion about a class of transaction, account balance, or disclosure and that could be material, either individually or when aggregated with other misstatements, will not be prevented, or detected and corrected, on a timely basis by the entity's internal control.

Detection risk. The risk that the procedures performed by the auditor to reduce audit risk to an acceptably low level will not detect a misstatement that exists and that could be material, either individually or when aggregated with other misstatements.

Engagement letter. A formal letter sent by the auditors to the client at the beginning of an engagement summarizing such matters as the nature of the engagement, any limitations on the scope of the audit work, work to be performed by the client's staff, and the basis for the audit fee. The purpose of engagement letters is to avoid misunderstandings.

Fraud. An intentional act by one or more individuals among management, those charged with governance, employees, or third parties, involving the use of deception that results in a misstatement in financial statements that are subject of an audit. For financial statement audits, fraud includes two types of intentional misstatements—misstatements arising from fraudulent financial reporting and misstatements arising from misappropriation of assets.

Fraud risk factors. Events or conditions that indicate an incentive or pressure to perpetrate fraud, provide an opportunity to commit fraud, or indicate attitudes or rationalizations to justify a fraudulent action.

Fraudulent financial reporting (management fraud, cooking the books). Material misstatement of financial statements by management with the intent to mislead financial statement users.

Further audit procedures. The additional procedures that are performed based on the results of the auditors' risk assessment procedures. Such procedures include (1) tests of controls (if needed), (2) Detailed tests of transactions, balances, and disclosures and (3) substantive analytical procedures.

Historical financial information. Information expressed in financial terms in relation to a particular entity, derived primarily from that entity's accounting system, about economic events occurring in past time periods or about economic conditions or circumstances at points in time in the past.

Inherent risk. The susceptibility of an assertion about a class of transaction, account balance, or disclosure to a misstatement that could be material, either individually or when aggregated with other misstatements, before consideration of any related controls.

Materiality. The magnitude of an omission or misstatement of accounting information that, in the light of surrounding circumstances, makes it probable that the judgment of a reasonable person relying on the information would have been changed or influenced by the omission or misstatements.

Misappropriation of assets (defalcations). Theft of client assets by an employee or officer of the organization.

Misstatement. A difference between the amount, classification, presentation, or disclosure of a reported financial statement item and the amount, classification, presentation, or disclosure that is required for the item to be in accordance with the applicable financial reporting framework. Misstatements can arise from error or fraud. Misstatements also include those adjustments of amounts, classifications, presentations, or disclosures that, in the auditor's judgment, are necessary for the financial statements to be presented fairly, in all material respects.

a. **Factual misstatements.** Misstatements about which there is no doubt.

b. **Judgmental misstatements.** Differences arising from the judgments of management concerning accounting estimates that the auditor considers unreasonable or the selection or application of accounting policies that the auditor considers inappropriate.

c. **Projected misstatements.** The auditor's best estimate of misstatements in populations, involving the projection of misstatements identified in audit samples to the entire population from which the samples were drawn. For example, if statistical sampling was used with receivables, the difference between auditor estimated total audited value and the book value of receivables is the projected misstatement.

Noncompliance. Acts of omission or commission by the entity, either intentional or unintentional, which are contrary to the prevailing laws or regulations. Such acts involve transactions entered into by, or in the name of the entity, or on its behalf, by those charged with governance, management, or employees. Noncompliance does not include personal misconduct (unrelated to the business activities of the entity) by those charged with governance, management, or employees of the entity.

Performance materiality. The amount (or amounts) set by the auditor at less than materiality for the financial statements as a whole to reduce to an appropriately low level the probability that the aggregate of uncorrected and undetected misstatements exceeds materiality for the financial statements as a whole. It may also refer to the amount or amounts set by the auditor at less than the materiality level or levels for particular classes of transactions, account balances, or disclosures. See also **tolerable misstatement**.

Predecessor auditor. A CPA firm that formerly served as auditor but has resigned from the engagement or has been notified that its services have been terminated.

Professional judgment. The application of relevant training, knowledge, and experience, within the context provided by auditing, accounting, and ethical standards, in making informed decisions about the courses of action that are appropriate in the circumstances of the audit engagement.

Professional skepticism. An attitude that includes a questioning mind, being alert to conditions that may indicate possible misstatement due to fraud or error, and a critical assessment of audit evidence.

Quality control standards. AICPA standards designed to provide reasonable assurance that all of a CPA firm's engagements are conducted in accordance with applicable professional responsibilities.

Reasonable assurance. In the context of an audit of financial statements, a high, but not absolute, level of assurance.

Relevant assertion. A financial statement assertion that has a reasonable possibility of containing a misstatement or misstatements that would cause the financial statements to be materially misstated. The determination of whether an assertion is a relevant assertion is made without regard to the effect of controls.

Risk assessment procedures. The audit procedures performed to obtain an understanding of the entity and its environment, including the entity's internal control, to identify and assess the risks of material misstatement, whether due to fraud or error, at the financial statement and assertion levels.

Risk of material misstatement. The risk that the financial statements are materially misstated prior to the audit. This consists of two components, inherent risk and control risk.

Significant risk. An identified and assessed risk of material misstatement that, in the auditor's judgment, requires special audit consideration.

Substantive procedure. An audit procedure designed to detect material misstatements at the assertion level. Substantive procedures comprise tests of details (classes of transactions, account balances, and disclosures) and substantive analytical procedures.

Successor auditor. The auditors who have accepted an engagement to replace the CPA firm that formally served as auditor (the predecessor auditor).

Tests of controls. An audit procedure designed to evaluate the operating effectiveness of controls in preventing, or detecting/correcting material misstatements at the assertion level.

Tolerable misstatement. The application of **performance materiality** to a particular sampling procedure. Tolerable misstatement may be the same amount or an amount lower than performance materiality (for example, when the population from the sample selected is smaller than the account balance).

Multiple-Choice Questions (1–116)

A. Overview

1. Which of the following is a conceptual difference between the attestation standards and generally accepted auditing standards?

  a. The attestation standards do not apply to audits of historical financial statements, while the generally accepted auditing standards do.
  b. The requirement that the practitioner be independent in mental attitude is omitted from the attestation standards.
  c. The attestation standards do not permit an attest engagement to be part of a business acquisition study or a feasibility study.
  d. None of the standards of fieldwork in generally accepted auditing standards are included in the attestation standards.

2. Which of the following is not an attestation standard?

  a. Sufficient evidence shall be obtained to provide a reasonable basis for the conclusion that is expressed in the report.
  b. The report shall identify the subject matter on the assertion being reported on and state the character of the engagement.
  c. The work shall be adequately planned and assistants, if any, shall be properly supervised.
  d. A sufficient understanding of internal control shall be obtained to plan the engagement.

3. Which of the following is most likely to be unique to the audit work of CPAs as compared to work performed by practitioners of other professions?

  a. Due professional care.
  b. Competence.
  c. Independence.
  d. Complex body of knowledge.

4. The Public Company Accounting Oversight Board's third general standard states that due care is to be exercised in the performance of an audit. This standard is ordinarily interpreted to require

  a. Thorough review of the existing safeguards over access to assets and records.
  b. Limited review of the indications of employee fraud and illegal acts.
  c. Objective review of the adequacy of the technical training and proficiency of firm personnel.
  d. Critical review of the judgment exercised at every level of supervision.

5. After fieldwork audit procedures are completed, a partner of the CPA firm who has not been involved in the audit performs a second or wrap-up working paper review. This second review usually focuses on

  a. The fair presentation of the financial statements in conformity with GAAP.
  b. Fraud involving the client's management and its employees.
  c. The materiality of the adjusting entries proposed by the audit staff.
  d. The communication of internal control weaknesses to the client's audit committee.

A.1. Financial Statement Assertions

6. Financial statement assertions are established for account balances,

	Classes of transactions	Disclosures
a.	Yes	Yes
b.	Yes	No
c.	No	Yes
d.	No	No

7. Which of the following is not a financial statement assertion relating to account balances?

  a. Completeness.
  b. Existence.
  c. Rights and obligations.
  d. Valuation and competence.

A.2. Audit Risk

8. As the acceptable level of detection risk decreases, an auditor may

  a. Reduce substantive testing by relying on the assessments of inherent risk and control risk.
  b. Postpone the planned timing of substantive tests from interim dates to the year-end.
  c. Eliminate the assessed level of inherent risk from consideration as a planning factor.
  d. Lower the assessed level of control risk from the maximum level to below the maximum.

9. The risk that an auditor will conclude, based on substantive tests, that a material misstatement does not **exist in an**

account balance when, in fact, such misstatement does exist is referred to as

    a. Sampling risk.
    b. Detection risk.
    c. Nonsampling risk.
    d. Inherent risk.

10. As the acceptable level of detection risk decreases, the assurance directly provided from

    a. Substantive tests should increase.
    b. Substantive tests should decrease.
    c. Tests of controls should increase.
    d. Tests of controls should decrease.

11. Which of the following audit risk components may be assessed in nonquantitative terms?

	Control risk	Detection risk	Inherent risk
a.	Yes	Yes	No
b.	Yes	No	Yes
c.	Yes	Yes	Yes
d.	No	Yes	Yes

12. Inherent risk and control risk differ from detection risk in that they

    a. Arise from the misapplication of auditing procedures.
    b. May be assessed in either quantitative or nonquantitative terms.
    c. Exist independently of the financial statement audit.
    d. Can be changed at the auditor's discretion.

13. On the basis of the audit evidence gathered and evaluated, an auditor decides to increase the assessed level of control risk from that originally planned. To achieve an overall audit risk level that is substantially the same as the planned audit risk level, the auditor would

    a. Decrease substantive testing.
    b. Decrease detection risk.
    c. Increase inherent risk.
    d. Increase materiality levels.

14. Relationship between control risk and detection risk is ordinarily

    a. Parallel.
    b. Inverse.
    c. Direct.
    d. Equal.

A.3. Materiality

15. Which of the following would an auditor most likely use in determining the auditor's preliminary judgment about materiality?

    a. The anticipated sample size of the planned substantive tests.
    b. The entity's annualized interim financial statements.
    c. The results of the internal control questionnaire.
    d. The contents of the management representation letter.

16. Which of the following statements is not correct about materiality?

    a. The concept of materiality recognizes that some matters are important for fair presentation of financial statements in conformity with GAAP, while other matters are not important.
    b. An auditor considers materiality for planning purposes in terms of the largest aggregate level of misstatements that could be material to any one of the financial statements.
    c. Materiality judgments are made in light of surrounding circumstances and necessarily involve both quantitative and qualitative judgments.
    d. An auditor's consideration of materiality is influenced by the auditor's perception of the needs of a reasonable person who will rely on the financial statements.

17. Which of the following is a function of the risks of material misstatement and detection risk?

    a. Internal control.
    b. Corroborating evidence.
    c. Quality control.
    d. Audit risk.

18. Which of the following is correct concerning performance materiality on an audit?

    a. It will ordinarily be less than financial statement materiality.
    b. It should be established at beginning of an audit and not be revised thereafter.
    c. It should be established at separate amounts for the various financial statements.
    d. It need not be documented in the working papers.

19. Which of the following would an auditor most likely use in determining the auditor's preliminary judgment about materiality?

    a. The results of the initial assessment of control risk.
    b. The anticipated sample size for planned substantive tests.
    c. The entity's financial statements of the prior year.
    d. The assertions that are embodied in the financial statements.

20. Holding other planning considerations equal, a decrease in the amount of misstatement in a class of transactions that an auditor could tolerate most likely would cause the auditor to

    a. Apply the planned substantive tests prior to the balance sheet date.
    b. Perform the planned auditing procedures closer to the balance sheet date.
    c. Increase the assessed level of control risk for relevant financial statement assertions.
    d. Decrease the extent of auditing procedures to be applied to the class of transactions.

21. When issuing an unmodified opinion, the auditor who evaluates the audit findings should be satisfied that the

    a. Amount of known misstatement is documented in the management representation letter.
    b. Estimate of the total likely misstatement is less than a material amount.

c. Amount of known misstatement is acknowledged and recorded by the client.

d. Estimate of the total likely misstatement includes the adjusting entries already recorded by the client.

A.4. Errors and Fraud

22. Which of the following is an example of fraudulent financial reporting?

a. Company management changes inventory count tags and overstates ending inventory, while understating cost of goods sold.

b. The treasurer diverts customer payments to his personal due, concealing his actions by debiting an expense account, thus overstating expenses.

c. An employee steals inventory and the "shrinkage" is recorded in cost of goods sold.

d. An employee steals small tools from the company and neglects to return them; the cost is reported as a miscellaneous operating expense.

23. Which of the following best describes what is meant by the term "fraud risk factor?"

a. Factors whose presence indicates that the risk of fraud is high.

b. Factors whose presence often have been observed in circumstances where frauds have occurred.

c. Factors whose presence requires modification of planned audit procedures.

d. Material weaknesses identified during an audit.

24. Which of the following is correct concerning requirements about auditor communications about fraud?

a. Fraud that involves senior management should be reported directly to the audit committee regardless of the amount involved.

b. Fraud with a material effect on the financial statements should be reported directly by the auditor to the Securities and Exchange Commission.

c. Fraud with a material effect on the financial statements should ordinarily be disclosed by the auditor through use of an "emphasis of a matter" paragraph added to the audit report.

d. The auditor has no responsibility to disclose fraud outside the entity under any circumstances.

25. When performing a financial statement audit, auditors are required to explicitly assess the risk of material misstatement due to

a. Errors.

b. Fraud.

c. Illegal acts.

d. Business risk.

26. Audits of financial statements are designed to obtain assurance of detecting misstatement due to

	Errors	Fraudulent financial reporting	Misappropriation of assets
a.	Yes	Yes	Yes
b.	Yes	Yes	No
c.	Yes	No	Yes
d.	No	Yes	No

27. An auditor is unable to obtain absolute assurance that misstatements due to fraud will be detected for all of the following **except**

a. Employee collusion.

b. Falsified documentation.

c. Need to apply professional judgment in evaluating fraud risk factors.

d. Professional skepticism.

28. An attitude that includes a questioning mind and a critical assessment of audit evidence is referred to as

a. Due professional care.

b. Professional skepticism.

c. Reasonable assurance.

d. Supervision.

29. Professional skepticism requires that an auditor assume that management is

a. Honest, in the absence of fraud risk factors.

b. Dishonest until completion of audit tests.

c. Neither honest nor dishonest.

d. Offering reasonable assurance of honesty.

30. The most difficult type of misstatement to detect is fraud based on

a. The overrecording of transactions.

b. The nonrecording of transactions.

c. Recorded transactions in subsidiaries.

d. Related-party receivables.

31. When considering fraud risk factors relating to management's characteristics, which of the following is least likely to indicate a risk of possible misstatement due to fraud?

a. Failure to correct known significant deficiency on a timely basis.

b. Nonfinancial management's preoccupation with the selection of accounting principles.

c. Significant portion of management's compensation represented by bonuses based upon achieving unduly aggressive operating results.

d. Use of unusually conservative accounting practices.

32. Which of the following conditions identified during fieldwork of an audit is most likely to affect the auditor's assessment of the risk of misstatement due to fraud?

a. Checks for significant amounts outstanding at year-end.

b. Computer generated documents.

c. Missing documents.

d. Year-end adjusting journal entries.

33. Which of the following is most likely to be a response to the auditor's assessment that the risk of material misstatement due to fraud for the existence of inventory is high?

a. Observe test counts of inventory at certain locations on an unannounced basis.

b. Perform analytical procedures rather than taking test counts.

c. Request that inventories be counted prior to year-end.

d. Request that inventory counts at the various locations be counted on different dates so as to allow the same auditor to be present at every count.

34. Which of the following is most likely to be an example of fraud?

    a. Defalcations occurring due to invalid electronic approvals.

    b. Mistakes in the application of accounting principles.

    c. Mistakes in processing data.

    d. Unreasonable accounting estimates arising from oversight.

35. Which of the following characteristics most likely would heighten an auditor's concern about the risk of intentional manipulation of financial statements?

    a. Turnover of senior accounting personnel is low.

    b. Insiders recently purchased additional shares of the entity's stock.

    c. Management places substantial emphasis on meeting earnings projections.

    d. The rate of change in the entity's industry is slow.

36. Which of the following statements reflects an auditor's responsibility for detecting misstatements due to errors and fraud?

    a. An auditor is responsible for detecting employee errors and simple fraud, but not for discovering fraud involving employee collusion or management override.

    b. An auditor should plan the audit to detect misstatements due to errors and fraud that are caused by departures from GAAP.

    c. An auditor is not responsible for detecting misstatements due to errors and fraud unless the application of GAAS would result in such detection.

    d. An auditor should design the audit to provide reasonable assurance of detecting misstatements due to errors and fraud that are material to the financial statements.

37. Disclosure of fraud to parties other than a client's senior management and its audit committee or board of directors ordinarily is not part of an auditor's responsibility. However, to which of the following outside parties may a duty to disclose fraud exist?

	To the SEC when the client reports an auditor change	To a successor auditor when the successor makes appropriate inquiries	To a government funding agency from which the client receives financial assistance
a.	Yes	Yes	No
b.	Yes	No	Yes
c.	No	Yes	Yes
d.	Yes	Yes	Yes

38. Under Statements on Auditing Standards, which of the following would be classified as an error?

    a. Misappropriation of assets for the benefit of management.

    b. Misinterpretation by management of facts that existed when the financial statements were prepared.

    c. Preparation of records by employees to cover a fraudulent scheme.

    d. Intentional omission of the recording of a transaction to benefit a third party.

39. What assurance does the auditor provide that misstatements due to errors, fraud, and direct effect illegal acts that are material to the financial statements will be detected?

	Errors	Fraud	Direct effect of illegal acts
a.	Limited	Negative	Limited
b.	Limited	Limited	Reasonable
c.	Reasonable	Limited	Limited
d.	Reasonable	Reasonable	Reasonable

40. Because of the risk of material misstatement, an audit of financial statements in accordance with generally accepted auditing standards should be planned and performed with an attitude of

    a. Objective judgment.

    b. Independent integrity.

    c. Professional skepticism.

    d. Impartial conservatism.

41. Which of the following most accurately summarizes what is meant by the term "material misstatement?"

    a. Fraud and direct-effect illegal acts.

    b. Fraud involving senior management and material fraud.

    c. Material error, material fraud, and certain illegal acts.

    d. Material error and material illegal acts.

42. Which of the following statements best describes the auditor's responsibility to detect conditions relating to financial stress of employees or adverse relationships between a company and its employees?

    a. The auditor is required to plan the audit to detect these conditions on all audits.

    b. These conditions relate to fraudulent financial reporting, and an auditor is required to plan the audit to detect these conditions when the client is exposed to a risk of misappropriation of assets.

    c. The auditor is required to plan the audit to detect these conditions whenever they may result in misstatements.

    d. The auditor is not required to plan the audit to discover these conditions, but should consider them if he or she becomes aware of them during the audit.

43. When the auditor believes a misstatement is or may be the result of fraud but that the effect of the misstatement is not material to the financial statements, which of the following steps is required?

    a. Consider the implications for other aspects of the audit.

    b. Resign from the audit.

    c. Commence a fraud examination.

    d. Contact regulatory authorities.

44. Which of the following statements is correct relating to the auditor's consideration of fraud?

    a. The auditor's interest in fraud consideration relates to fraudulent acts that cause a material misstatement of financial statements.

    b. A primary factor that distinguishes fraud from error is that fraud is always intentional, while errors are generally, but not always, intentional.

    c. Fraud always involves a pressure or incentive to commit fraud, and a misappropriation of assets.

    d. While an auditor should be aware of the possibility of fraud, management, and not the auditor, is responsible for detecting fraud.

45. Which of the following factors or conditions is an auditor least likely to plan an audit to discover?

    a. Financial pressures affecting employees.

    b. High turnover of senior management.

    c. Inadequate monitoring of significant controls.

    d. Inability to generate positive cash flows from operations.

46. At which stage(s) of the audit may fraud risk factors be identified?

	Planning	Obtaining understanding	Conducting fieldwork
a.	Yes	Yes	Yes
b.	Yes	Yes	No
c.	Yes	No	No
d.	No	Yes	Yes

47. Management's attitude toward aggressive financial reporting and its emphasis on meeting projected profit goals most likely would significantly influence an entity's control environment when

    a. External policies established by parties outside the entity affect its accounting practices.

    b. Management is dominated by one individual who is also a shareholder.

    c. Internal auditors have direct access to the board of directors and the entity's management.

    d. The audit committee is active in overseeing the entity's financial reporting policies.

48. Which of the following is least likely to be required on an audit?

    a. Test appropriateness of journal entries and adjustment.

    b. Review accounting estimates for biases.

    c. Evaluate the business rationale for significant unusual transactions.

    d. Make a legal determination of whether fraud has occurred.

49. Which of the following is most likely to be an overall response to fraud risks identified in an audit?

    a. Supervise members of the audit team less closely and rely more upon judgment.

    b. Use less predictable audit procedures.

    c. Only use certified public accountants on the engagement.

    d. Place increased emphasis on the audit of objective transactions rather than subjective transactions.

50. Which of the following is least likely to be included in an auditor's inquiry of management while obtaining information to identify the risks of material misstatement due to fraud?

    a. Are financial reporting operations controlled by and limited to one location?

    b. Does it have knowledge of fraud or suspect fraud?

    c. Does it have programs to mitigate fraud risks?

    d. Has it reported to the audit committee the nature of the company's internal control?

51. Individuals who commit fraud are ordinarily able to rationalize the act and also have an

	Incentive	Opportunity
a.	Yes	Yes
b.	Yes	No
c.	No	Yes
d.	No	No

52. What is an auditor's responsibility who discovers management involved in what is financially immaterial fraud?

    a. Report the fraud to the audit committee.

    b. Report the fraud to the Public Company Oversight Board.

    c. Report the fraud to a level of management at least one below those involved in the fraud.

    d. Determine that the amounts involved are immaterial, and if so, there is no reporting responsibility.

53. Which of the following is most likely to be considered a risk factor relating to fraudulent financial reporting?

    a. Domination of management by top executives.

    b. Large amounts of cash processed.

    c. Negative cash flows from operations.

    d. Small high-dollar inventory items.

54. Which of the following is most likely to be presumed to represent fraud risk on an audit?

    a. Capitalization of repairs and maintenance into the property, plant, and equipment asset account.

    b. Improper revenue recognition.

    c. Improper interest expense accrual.

    d. Introduction of significant new products.

55. An auditor who discovers that a client's employees paid small bribes to municipal officials most likely would withdraw from the engagement if

- a. The payments violated the client's policies regarding the prevention of illegal acts.
- b. The client receives financial assistance from a federal government agency.
- c. Documentation that is necessary to prove that the bribes were paid does not exist.
- d. Management fails to take the appropriate remedial action.

56. Which of the following factors most likely would cause a CPA to not accept a new audit engagement?

- a. The prospective client has already completed its physical inventory count.
- b. The CPA lacks an understanding of the prospective client's operation and industry.
- c. The CPA is unable to review the predecessor auditor's working papers.
- d. The prospective client is unwilling to make all financial records available to the CPA.

57. Which of the following factors would most likely heighten an auditor's concern about the risk of fraudulent financial reporting?

- a. Large amounts of liquid assets that are easily convertible into cash.
- b. Low growth and profitability as compared to other entities in the same industry.
- c. Financial management's participation in the initial selection of accounting principles.
- d. An overly complex organizational structure involving unusual lines of authority.

A.5.   *Laws and Regulations*

58. An auditor who discovers that a client's employees have paid small bribes to public officials most likely would withdraw from the engagement if the

- a. Client receives financial assistance from a federal government agency.
- b. Evidence that is necessary to prove that the illegal acts were committed does not exist.
- c. Employees' actions affect the auditor's ability to rely on management's representations.
- d. Notes to the financial statements fail to disclose the employees' actions.

59. Which of the following illegal acts should an audit be designed to obtain reasonable assurance of detecting?

- a. Securities purchased by relatives of management based on knowledge of inside information.
- b. Accrual and billing of an improper amount of revenue under government contracts.
- c. Violations of antitrust laws.
- d. Price fixing.

60. Which of the following relatively small misstatements most likely could have a material effect on an entity's financial statements?

- a. An illegal payment to a foreign official that was not recorded.
- b. A piece of obsolete office equipment that was not retired.
- c. A petty cash fund disbursement that was not properly authorized.
- d. An uncollectible account receivable that was not written off.

61. During the annual audit of Ajax Corp., a publicly held company, Jones, CPA, a continuing auditor, determined that illegal political contributions had been made during each of the past seven years, including the year under audit. Jones notified the board of directors about the illegal contributions, but they refused to take any action because the amounts involved were immaterial to the financial statements. Jones should reconsider the intended degree of reliance to be placed on the

- a. Letter of audit inquiry to the client's attorney.
- b. Prior years' audit programs.
- c. Management representation letter.
- d. Preliminary judgment about materiality levels.

62. The most likely explanation why the auditor's examination cannot reasonably be expected to bring noncompliance with all laws by the client to the auditor's attention is that

- a. Illegal acts are perpetrated by management override of internal control.
- b. Illegal acts by clients often relate to operating aspects rather than accounting aspects.
- c. The client's internal control may be so strong that the auditor performs only minimal substantive testing.
- d. Illegal acts may be perpetrated by the only person in the client's organization with access to both assets and the accounting records.

63. If specific information comes to an auditor's attention that implies noncompliance with laws that could result in a material, but indirect effect on the financial statements, the auditor should next

- a. Apply audit procedures specifically directed to ascertaining whether noncompliance has occurred.
- b. Seek the advice of an informed expert qualified to practice law as to possible contingent liabilities.
- c. Report the matter to an appropriate level of management at least one level above those involved.
- d. Discuss the evidence with the client's audit committee, or others with equivalent authority and responsibility.

64. An auditor who discovers that client employees have committed an illegal act that has a material effect on the client's financial statements most likely would withdraw from the engagement if

- a. The illegal act is a violation of generally accepted accounting principles.

b. The client does not take the remedial action that the auditor considers necessary.

c. The illegal act was committed during a prior year that was not audited.

d. The auditor has already assessed control risk at the maximum level.

65. Under the Private Securities Litigation Reform Act of 1995, Baker, CPA, reported certain uncorrected illegal acts to Supermart's board of directors. Baker believed that failure to take remedial action would warrant a qualified audit opinion because the illegal acts had a material effect on Supermart's financial statements. Supermart failed to take appropriate remedial action and the board of directors refused to inform the SEC that it had received such notification from Baker. Under these circumstances, Baker is required to

a. Resign from the audit engagement within ten business days.

b. Deliver a report concerning the illegal acts to the SEC within one business day.

c. Notify the stockholders that the financial statements are materially misstated.

d. Withhold an audit opinion until Supermart takes appropriate remedial action.

B. Audit Planning

66. Which of the following would be least likely to be considered an audit planning procedure?

a. Use an engagement letter.

b. Develop the overall audit strategy.

c. Perform risk assessment.

d. Develop the audit plan.

67. Which of the following factors would most likely cause a CPA to decide not to accept a new audit engagement?

a. The CPA's lack of understanding of the prospective client's internal auditor's computer-assisted audit techniques.

b. Management's disregard of its responsibility to maintain an adequate internal control environment.

c. The CPA's inability to determine whether related-party transactions were consummated on terms equivalent to arm's-length transactions.

d. Management's refusal to permit the CPA to perform substantive tests before the year-end.

B.1 Communicate with Predecessor Auditors (Prior to Engagement Acceptance)

68. Before accepting an engagement to audit a new client, a CPA is required to obtain

a. An understanding of the prospective client's industry and business.

b. The prospective client's signature to the engagement letter.

c. A preliminary understanding of the prospective client's control environment.

d. The prospective client's consent to make inquiries of the predecessor auditor, if any.

69. Before accepting an audit engagement, a successor auditor should make specific inquiries of the predecessor auditor regarding

a. Disagreements the predecessor had with the client concerning auditing procedures and accounting principles.

b. The predecessor's evaluation of matters of continuing accounting significance.

c. The degree of cooperation the predecessor received concerning the inquiry of the client's lawyer.

d. The predecessor's assessments of inherent risk and judgments about materiality.

70. Before accepting an audit engagement, a successor auditor should make specific inquiries of the predecessor auditor regarding the predecessor's

a. Opinion of any subsequent events occurring since the predecessor's audit report was issued.

b. Understanding as to the reasons for the change of auditors.

c. Awareness of the consistency in the application of GAAP between periods.

d. Evaluation of all matters of continuing accounting significance.

B.2. Establishing an Understanding with the Client (Engagement Letters)

71. An auditor is required to establish an understanding with a client regarding the services to be performed for each engagement. This understanding generally includes

a. Management's responsibility for errors and the illegal activities of employees that may cause material misstatement.

b. The auditor's responsibility for ensuring that the audit committee is aware of any significant deficiencies in internal control that come to the auditor's attention.

c. Management's responsibility for providing the auditor with an assessment of the risk of material misstatement due to fraud.

d. The auditor's responsibility for determining preliminary judgments about materiality and audit risk factors.

72. Which of the following matters is generally included in an auditor's engagement letter?

a. Management's responsibility for the entity's compliance with laws and regulations.

b. The factors to be considered in setting preliminary judgments about materiality.

c. Management's vicarious liability for illegal acts committed by its employees.

d. The auditor's responsibility to search for significant internal control deficiencies.

73. During the initial planning phase of an audit, a CPA most likely would

    a. Identify specific internal control activities that are likely to prevent fraud.

    b. Evaluate the reasonableness of the client's accounting estimates.

    c. Discuss the timing of the audit procedures with the client's management.

    d. Inquire of the client's attorney as to whether any unrecorded claims are probable of assertion.

74. Which of the following statements would least likely appear in an auditor's engagement letter?

    a. Fees for our services are based on our regular per diem rates, plus travel and other out-of-pocket expenses.

    b. During the course of our audit we may observe opportunities for economy in, or improved controls over, your operations.

    c. Our engagement is subject to the risk that material misstatements or fraud, if they exist, will not be detected.

    d. After performing our preliminary analytical procedures we will discuss with you the other procedures we consider necessary to complete the engagement.

75. Which of the following documentation is not required for an audit in accordance with generally accepted auditing standards?

    a. A written audit plan setting forth the procedures necessary to accomplish the audit's objectives.

    b. An indication that the accounting records agree or reconcile with the financial statements.

    c. A client engagement letter that summarizes the timing and details of the auditor's planned fieldwork.

    d. The assessment of the risks of material misstatement.

76. An engagement letter should ordinarily include information on the objectives of the engagement and

	CPA responsibilities	Client responsibilities	Limitation of engagement
a.	Yes	Yes	Yes
b.	Yes	No	Yes
c.	Yes	No	No
d.	No	No	No

77. Arrangements concerning which of the following are **least** likely to be included in engagement letter?

    a. A predecessor auditor.

    b. Fees and billing.

    c. CPA investment in client securities.

    d. Other services to be provided in addition to the audit.

B.3.   Preliminary Engagement Activities

78. The auditor should document the understanding established with a client through a(n)

    a. Oral communication with the client.

    b. Written communication with the client.

    c. Written or oral communication with the client.

    d. Completely detailed audit plan.

79. Which of the following factors most likely would influence an auditor's determination of the auditability of an entity's financial statements?

    a. The complexity of the accounting system.

    b. The existence of related-party transactions.

    c. The adequacy of the accounting records.

    d. The operating effectiveness of control procedures.

B.4.   Developing an Overall Strategy

80. Which of the following is most likely to require special planning considerations related to asset valuation?

    a. Inventory is comprised of diamond rings.

    b. The client has recently purchased an expensive copy machine.

    c. Assets costing less than $250 are expensed even when the expected life exceeds one year.

    d. Accelerated depreciation methods are used for amortizing the costs of factory equipment.

81. A CPA wishes to determine how various publicly held companies have complied with the disclosure requirements of a new financial accounting standard. Which of the following information sources would the CPA most likely consult for information?

    a. AICPA *Codification of Statements on Auditing Standards*.

    b. AICPA *Accounting Trends and Techniques*.

    c. SEC Quality Control Review.

    d. SEC Statement 10-K Guide.

B.5.   The Audit Plan

82. An auditor should design the written audit program so that

    a. All material transactions will be selected for substantive testing.

    b. Substantive tests prior to the balance sheet date will be minimized.

    c. The audit procedures selected will achieve specific audit objectives.

    d. Each account balance will be tested under either tests of controls or tests of transactions.

83. The audit program usually cannot be finalized until the

    a. Consideration of the entity's internal control has been completed.

    b. Engagement letter has been signed by the auditor and the client.

    c. Significant deficiency has been communicated to the audit committee of the board of directors.

    d. Search for unrecorded liabilities has been performed and documented.

84. Audit programs should be designed so that

a. Most of the required procedures can be performed as interim work.
b. Inherent risk is assessed at a sufficiently low level.
c. The auditor can make constructive suggestions to management.
d. The audit evidence gathered supports the auditor's conclusions.

85. In designing written audit programs, an auditor should establish specific audit objectives that relate primarily to the

a. Timing of audit procedures.
b. Cost-benefit of gathering evidence.
c. Selected audit techniques.
d. Financial statement assertions.

B.7. Timing of Audit Procedures

86. With respect to planning an audit, which of the following statements is always true?

a. It is acceptable to perform a portion of the audit of a continuing audit client at interim dates.
b. An engagement should not be accepted after the client's year-end.
c. An inventory count must be observed at year-end.
d. Final staffing decisions must be made prior to completion of the planning stage.

87. The element of the audit planning process most likely to be agreed upon with the client before implementation of the audit strategy is the determination of the

a. Evidence to be gathered to provide a sufficient basis for the auditor's opinion.
b. Procedures to be undertaken to discover litigation, claims, and assessments.
c. Pending legal matters to be included in the inquiry of the client's attorney.
d. Timing of inventory observation procedures to be performed.

C. Obtain an Understanding of the Entity and Its Environment

88. To obtain an understanding of a continuing client's business, an auditor most likely would

a. Perform tests of details of transactions and balances.
b. Review prior year working papers and the permanent file for the client.
c. Read current issues of specialized industry journals.
d. Reevaluate the client's internal control environment.

89. On an audit engagement performed by a CPA firm with one office, at the minimum, knowledge of the relevant professional accounting and auditing standards should be held by

a. The auditor with final responsibility for the audit.
b. All professionals working upon the audit.

c. All professionals working upon the audit and the partner in charge of the CPA firm.
d. All professionals working in the office.

90. An auditor obtains knowledge about a new client's business and its industry to

a. Make constructive suggestions concerning improvements to the client's internal control.
b. Develop an attitude of professional skepticism concerning management's financial statement assertions.
c. Evaluate whether the aggregation of known misstatements causes the financial statements taken as a whole to be materially misstated.
d. Understand the events and transactions that may have an effect on the client's financial statements.

91. Which of the following procedures would an auditor least likely perform while obtaining an understanding of a client in a financial statement audit?

a. Coordinating the assistance of entity personnel in data preparation.
b. Discussing matters that may affect the audit with firm personnel responsible for nonaudit services to the entity.
c. Selecting a sample of vendors' invoices for comparison to receiving reports.
d. Reading the current year's interim financial statements.

C.1. Communicate with Predecessor Auditors (Subsequent to Engagement Acceptance)

92. Ordinarily, the predecessor auditor permits the successor auditor to review the predecessor's working paper analyses relating to

	Contingencies	Balance sheet accounts
a.	Yes	Yes
b.	Yes	No
c.	No	Yes
d.	No	No

93. In auditing the financial statements of Star Corp., Land discovered information leading Land to believe that Star's prior year's financial statements, which were audited by Tell, require substantial revisions. Under these circumstances, Land should

a. Notify Star's audit committee and stockholders that the prior year's financial statements cannot be relied on.
b. Request Star to reissue the prior year's financial statements with the appropriate revisions.
c. Notify Tell about the information and make inquiries about the integrity of Star's management.
d. Request Star to arrange a meeting among the three parties to resolve the matter.

94. A successor auditor should request the new client to authorize the predecessor auditor to allow a review of the predecessor's

	Engagement letter	Working papers
a.	Yes	Yes
b.	Yes	No
c.	No	Yes
d.	No	No

C.2.   Consideration of Internal Control

95. Which of the following procedures would an auditor most likely perform in planning a financial statement audit?

a. Inquiring of the client's legal counsel concerning pending litigation.
b. Comparing the financial statements to anticipated results.
c. Examining computer generated exception reports to verify the effectiveness of internal control.
d. Searching for unauthorized transactions that may aid in detecting unrecorded liabilities.

C.4.   Supervision Requirements

96. The in-charge auditor most likely would have a supervisory responsibility to explain to the staff assistants

a. That immaterial fraud is not to be reported to the client's audit committee.
b. How the results of various auditing procedures performed by the assistants should be evaluated.
c. What benefits may be attained by the assistants' adherence to established time budgets.
d. Why certain documents are being transferred from the current file to the permanent file.

97. The audit work performed by each assistant should be reviewed to determine whether it was adequately performed and to evaluate whether the

a. Auditor's system of quality control has been maintained at a high level.
b. Results are consistent with the conclusions to be presented in the auditor's report.
c. Audit procedures performed are approved in the professional standards.
d. Audit has been performed by persons having adequate technical training and proficiency as auditors.

C.4.   Perform Analytical Procedures

98. Analytical procedures used during risk assessment in an audit should focus on

a. Reducing the scope of tests of controls and substantive tests.
b. Providing assurance that potential material misstatements will be identified.

c. Enhancing the auditor's understanding of the client's business.
d. Assessing the adequacy of the available evidence.

99. A primary purpose of performing analytical procedures as risk assessment procedures is to identify the existence of

a. Unusual transactions and events.
b. Illegal acts that went undetected because of internal control weaknesses.
c. Related-party transactions.
d. Recorded transactions that were not properly authorized.

100. Which of the following nonfinancial information would an auditor most likely consider in performing analytical procedures during risk assessment?

a. Turnover of personnel in the accounting department.
b. Objectivity of audit committee members.
c. Square footage of selling space.
d. Management's plans to repurchase stock.

101. The accounts receivable turnover ratio increased during 20X2. This is consistent with:

a. Items shipped on consignment during December were recorded as credit sales; no cash receipts have yet been received on these consignments.
b. The company increased credit sales by 10% by allowing more lenient credit terms—30 days are now allowed whereas previously only 20 days were allowed.
c. A major credit sale on which title passed as of December 31, 20X2 was recorded in January of 20X3.
d. Sales for each month are approximately 25% higher than those of the preceding year.

102. A company's gross margin percentage increased in 20X2. This is consistent with which of the following occurring in 20X2?

a. An increase in the tax rate on income.
b. An increase in units sold.
c. A decrease in the rate of sales commissions paid to sales personnel.
d. Outsourcing of a part of the manufacturing process which resulted in no additional costs.

103. The following summarizes your client's inventory turnover for Years 1 and 2.

	Year 1	Year 2
Inventory turnover	7.00	6.00

This change is most consistent with

a. A number of expense items were erroneously included in cost of goods sold (but not in ending inventory).
b. While inventory levels remained the same in Year 2, total sales increased and a higher percentage of customers are paying their accounts.

c. Although sales for Year 2 were the same as for Year 1, inventory is a bit higher than normal because the last month of year 2's sales were lower than anticipated.

d. The year-end physical inventory count omitted a number of significant items. A periodic accounting inventory system is in use.

D. Assess the Risks of Material Misstatement and Design Further Audit Procedures

101. While assessing the risks of material misstatement auditors identify risks, relate risk to what could go wrong, consider the magnitude of risks and

a. Assess the risk of misstatements due to illegal acts.
b. Consider the complexity of the transactions involved.
c. Consider the likelihood that the risks could result in material misstatements.
d. Determine materiality levels.

102. Which of the following are considered further audit procedures that may be designed after assessing the risks of material misstatement?

	Substantive tests of details	Risk assessment procedures
a.	Yes	Yes
b.	Yes	No
c.	No	Yes
d.	No	No

103. Which of the following is **least** likely to be considered a risk assessment procedure?

a. Analytical procedures.
b. Confirmation of ending accounts receivable.
c. Inspection of documents.
d. Observation of the performance of certain accounting procedures.

104. In an audit of a nonissuer (nonpublic) company, the auditors identify significant risks. These risks often

a. Involve routine, high-volume transactions.
b. Do not require special audit attention.
c. Involve items with lower levels of inherent risk.
d. Involve judgmental matters.

E. Quality Control

105. The auditor with final responsibility for an engagement and one of the assistants have a difference of opinion about the results of an auditing procedure. If the assistant believes it is necessary to be disassociated from the matter's resolution, the CPA firm's procedures should enable the assistant to

a. Refer the disagreement to the AICPA's Quality Review Committee.
b. Document the details of the disagreement with the conclusion reached.
c. Discuss the disagreement with the entity's management or its audit committee.
d. Report the disagreement to an impartial peer review monitoring team.

E.4. Prospective Financial Statements

109. An examination of a financial forecast is a professional service that involves

a. Compiling or assembling a financial forecast that is based on management's assumptions.
b. Limiting the distribution of the accountant's report to management and the board of directors.
c. Assuming responsibility to update management on key events for one year after the report's date.
d. Evaluating the preparation of a financial forecast and the support underlying management's assumptions.

E.5. Quality Control

110. The nature and extent of a CPA firm's quality control policies and procedures depend on

	The CPA firm's size	The nature of the CPA firm's practice	Cost-benefit considerations
a.	Yes	Yes	Yes
b.	Yes	Yes	No
c.	Yes	No	Yes
d.	No	Yes	Yes

111. A CPA firm may communicate its quality control policies and procedures to its personnel in which manner(s):

	Orally	Written
a.	No	No
b.	No	Yes
c.	Yes	No
d.	Yes	Yes

112. Which of the following is **not** an element of quality control?

a. Acceptance and continuance of client relationships and specific engagements.
b. Human resources.
c. Internal control.
d. Monitoring.

113. Quality control for a CPA firm, as referred to in Statements on Quality Control Standards, applies to

a. Auditing services only.
b. Auditing and management advisory services.
c. Auditing and tax services.
d. Auditing and accounting and review services.

114. One of a CPA firm's basic objectives is to provide professional services that conform with professional standards. Reasonable assurance of achieving this basic objective is provided through

a. A system of quality control.
b. A system of peer review.
c. Continuing professional education.
d. Compliance with generally accepted accounting principles.

E.6.   *Public Company Accounting Oversight Board Requirements*

115. Which of the following is correct concerning PCAOB guidance that uses the term "should"?

    a.   The auditor must fulfill the responsibilities.

    b.   The auditor must comply with requirements unless s/he demonstrates that alternative actions were sufficient to achieve the objectives of the standard.

    c.   The auditor should consider performing the procedure; whether the auditor performs depends on the exercise of professional judgment in the circumstances.

    d.   The auditor has complete discretion as to whether to perform the procedure.

116. Which of the following sets of standards does the Public Company Accounting Oversight Board not have the authority to establish for audits of public companies?

    a.   Auditing standards.

    b.   Quality control standards.

    c.   Accounting standards.

    d.   Independence standards.

Multiple-Choice Answers and Explanations

Answers

1. a __ __	21. b __ __	41. c __ __	61. c __ __	81. b __ __	101. c
2. d __ __	22. a __ __	42. d __ __	62. b __ __	82. c __ __	102. b
3. c __ __	23. b __ __	43. a __ __	63. a __ __	83. a __ __	103. c
4. d __ __	24. a __ __	44. a __ __	64. b __ __	84. d __ __	104. c __ __
5. a __ __	25. b __ __	45. a __ __	65. b __ __	85. d __ __	105. b __ __
6. a __ __	26. a __ __	46. a __ __	66. c __ __	86. a __ __	106. b __ __
7. d __ __	27. d __ __	47. b __ __	67. b __ __	87. d __ __	107. d __ __
8. b __ __	28. b __ __	48. d __ __	68. d __ __	88. b __ __	108. b __ __
9. b __ __	29. c __ __	49. b __ __	69. a __ __	89. a __ __	109. d __ __
10. a __ __	30. b __ __	50. a __ __	70. b __ __	90. d __ __	110. a __ __
11. c __ __	31. d __ __	51. a __ __	71. b __ __	91. c __ __	111. d __ __
12. c __ __	32. c __ __	52. a __ __	72. a __ __	92. a __ __	112. c __ __
13. b __ __	33. a __ __	53. c __ __	73. c __ __	93. d __ __	113. d __ __
14. b __ __	34. a __ __	54. b __ __	74. d __ __	94. c __ __	114. a __ __
15. b __ __	35. c __ __	55. b __ __	75. c __ __	95. b __ __	115. b __ __
16. b __ __	36. d __ __	56. d __ __	76. a __ __	96. b __ __	116. c __ __
17. d __ __	37. d __ __	57. d __ __	77. c __ __	97. b __ __	
18. a __ __	38. b __ __	58. c __ __	78. b __ __	98. c __ __	
19. c __ __	39. d __ __	59. b __ __	79. c __ __	99. a __ __	1st: __/113 = __%
20. b __ __	40. c __ __	60. a __ __	80. a __ __	100. c __ __	2nd: __/113 = __%

Explanations

1. (a) The requirement is to identify a conceptual difference between the attestation standards and generally accepted auditing standards. Answer (a) is correct because AT 101 states that the attestation standards do not apply to audits of historical financial statements. Answer (b) is incorrect because an independent mental attitude is required for attestation engagements. Answer (c) is incorrect because an attest engagement may be related to a business acquisition study or a feasibility study. Answer (d) is incorrect because while there is no internal control fieldwork standard under the attestation standards, both a planning and an evidence standard of fieldwork are included.

2. (d) The requirement is to identify the reply which is not an attestation standard. Answer (d) is correct because the attestation standards do not include a requirement that a sufficient understanding of internal control be obtained to plan the engagement. There is no internal control standard because

the concept of internal control may not be relevant to certain assertions on which a CPA may be engaged to report (e.g., aspects of information about computer software). Answers (a), (b), and (c) are all incorrect because standards exist for evidence, reporting on the assertion or subject matter, and proper planning.

3. (c) The requirement is to identify the characteristic that is most likely to be unique to the audit work of CPAs as compared to work performed by practitioners of other professions. Answer (c) is correct because independence is absolutely required for the performance of audits; other professions do not in general require such independence. Answers (a), (b), and (d) are incorrect because the various professions require due professional care and competence and have a complex body of knowledge.

4. (d) The requirement is to determine what is meant by the third general standard's requirement of due care in the performance of an audit. Answer (d) is correct because due care requires critical review at every level of supervision of the work done and the judgment exercised by those assisting in the audit. Answer (a) is incorrect because the due care standard does not directly address safeguards over access to assets and records. Answer (b) is incorrect because due care does not relate to a limited review of employee fraud and illegal acts. Answer (c) is incorrect because the first general standard addresses technical training and proficiency as an auditor.

5. (a) The requirement is to identify the focus of a final wrap-up review performed by a second partner who has not been involved in the audit. Answer (a) is correct because this second or "cold" review aims at determining whether the financial statements result in fair presentation in conformity with GAAP and with whether sufficient appropriate evidence has been obtained. Answer (b) is incorrect because most frequently fraud involving the client's management and its employees have not been discovered and, even if they have been, the focus of the review is still on the fairness of presentation of the financial statements. Answers (c) and (d) are incorrect because decisions on materiality and communications with the audit committee are only two of the many matters the review may address in an effort to address fairness of presentation of the financial statements.

6. (a) The requirement is to identify the categories of financial statement assertions. Answer (a) is correct because the professional standards establish financial statement assertions for account balances, classes of transactions and disclosures. Answer (b) is incorrect because financial statement assertions are established for disclosures. Answer (c) is incorrect because financial statement assertions are established for classes of transactions. Answer (d) is incorrect because financial statement assertions are established for both classes of transactions and disclosures.

7. (d) The requirement is to identify the item that is not a financial statement assertion relating to account balances. Answer (d) is correct because valuation and allocation is an account balance assertion, not valuation and *competence*. Answer (a) is incorrect because completeness is an assertion relating to account balances. Answer (b) is incorrect because existence is an assertion relating to account balances. Answer (c) is incorrect because rights and obligations is an assertion relating to account balances.

8. (b) The requirement is to determine a likely auditor reaction to a decreased acceptable level of detection risk. Answer (b) is correct because postponement of interim substantive tests to year-end decreases detection risk by reducing the risk for the period subsequent to the performance of those tests; other approaches to decreasing detection risk include changing to more effective substantive tests and increasing their extent. Answer (a) is incorrect because increased, not reduced, substantive testing is required. Answer (c) is incorrect because inherent risk must be consid-ered in planning, either by itself or in combination with control risk. Answer (d) is incorrect because tests of con-trols must be performed to reduce the assessed level of control risk.

9. (b) The requirement is to identify the risk that an auditor will conclude, based on substantive tests, that a material error does not exist in an account balance when, in fact, such error does exist. Answer (b) is correct because detection risk is the risk that the auditor will not detect a material misstatement that exists in an assertion. Detection risk may be viewed in terms of two components (1) the risk that analytical procedures and other relevant substantive tests would fail to detect misstatements equal to tolerable misstatement, and (2) the allowable risk of incorrect acceptance for the substantive tests of details. Answer (a) is incorrect because sampling risk arises from the possibility that, when a test of controls or a substantive test is restricted to a sample, the auditor's conclusions may be different from the conclusions he or she would reach if the tests were applied in the same way to all items in the account balance or class of transactions. When related to substantive tests sampling risk is only a part of the risk that the auditor's substantive tests will not detect a material misstatement. Answer (c) is incorrect because nonsampling risk includes only those aspects of audit risk that are not due to sampling. Answer (d) is incorrect because inherent risk is the susceptibility of an assertion to a material misstatement, assuming that there are no related controls.

10. (a) The requirement is to identify an effect of a decrease in the acceptable level of detection risk. Answer (a) is correct because as the acceptable level of detection risk decreases, the assurance provided from substantive tests should increase. To gain this increased assurance the auditors may (1) change the nature of substantive tests to more effective procedures (e.g., use independent parties outside the entity rather than those within the entity), (2) change the timing of substantive tests (e.g., perform them at year-end rather than at an interim date), and (3) change the extent of substantive tests (e.g., take a larger sample). Answer (b) is incorrect because the assurance provided from substantive tests increases, it does not decrease. Answers (c) and (d) are incorrect because the acceptable level of detection risk is based largely on the assessed levels of control risk and in-herent risk. Accordingly, any tests of controls will already have been performed.

11. (c) The requirement is to determine whether inherent risk, control risk, and detection risk may be assessed in nonquantitative terms. Answer (c) is correct because all of these risks may be assessed in either quantitative terms such as percentages, or nonquantitative terms such as a range from a minimum to a maximum.

12. (c) The requirement is to determine a manner in which inherent risk and control risk differ from detection risk. Answer (c) is correct because inherent risk and control risk exist independently of the audit of the financial statements as functions of the client and its environment, whereas detection risk relates to the auditor's procedures and can be changed at his or her discretion. Answer (a) is incorrect because inherent risk and control risk are functions of the client and its environment and do not arise from misapplication of auditing procedures. Answer (b) is incorrect because inherent risk, control risk and detection risk may each be assessed in either quantitative or nonquantitative terms. Answer (d) is incorrect because inherent risk and control risk are functions of the client and its environment, they cannot be changed at the auditor's discretion. However, the assessed levels of inherent and control risk (not addressed in this question) may be affected by auditor decisions relating to the cost of gathering evidence to substantiate assessed levels below the maximum.

13. (b) The requirement is to determine the best way for an auditor to achieve an overall audit risk level when the audit evidence relating to control risk indicates the need to increase its assessed level. Answer (b) is correct because a decrease in detection risk will allow the auditor achieve an overall audit risk level substantially the same as planned. Answer (a) is incorrect because a decrease in substantive testing will increase, not decrease, detection risk and thereby increase audit risk. Answer (c) is incorrect because an increase in inherent risk will also increase audit risk. Answer (d) is incorrect because there appears to be no justification for increasing materiality levels beyond those used in planning the audit.

14. (b) The requirement is to determine the relationship between control risk and detection risk. Inverse is correct because as control risk increases (decreases) detection risk must decrease (increase).

15. (b) The requirement is to identify the information that an auditor would most likely use in determining a preliminary judgment about materiality. Answer (b) is correct because many materiality measures relate to an annual figure (e.g., net income, sales). Answer (a) is incorrect because the preliminary judgment about materiality is a factor used in determining the anticipated sample size, not the reverse as suggested by the reply. Answers (c) and (d) are incorrect because materiality will not normally be affected by the results of the internal control questionnaire or the contents of the management representation letters.

16. (b) The requirement is to identify the statement that is not correct concerning materiality. Answer (b) is the proper reply because the auditor considers materiality for planning purposes in terms of the smallest, not the largest, aggregate amount of misstatement that could be material to any one of the financial statements. Answers (a), (c), and (d) all represent correct statements about materiality.

17. (d) The requirement is to identify which reply is a function of the risks of material misstatement and detection risk. Answer (d) is correct because audit risk is the risk that auditor expresses an inappropriate audit opinion when the financial statements are misstated, and it is a function of the risks of material misstatement and detection risk. Answer (a) is incorrect because while a consideration of internal control is required during an audit, internal control is not a function of these risks. Answer (b) is incorrect because while corroborating evidence is obtained to measure these risks, it is not a function of them. Answer (c) is incorrect because quality control relates to requirements placed upon the CPAs while conducting an audit.

18. (a) The requirement is to determine the correct statement with respect to performance materiality on an audit. Answer (a) is correct because performance materiality is largely established to help provide assurance that several immaterial misstatements do not combine to a material undetected amount of misstatement; accordingly, it ordinarily is established at a level lower than that of materiality for the financial statements. Answer (b) is incorrect because performance materiality may be revised throughout the audit, particularly when circumstances depart from those which had been expected while planning the audit. Answer (c) is incorrect because performance materiality is ordinarily established for the financial statements as a whole, and if applicable, materiality levels for particular classes of transactions, account balances, or disclosures. Answer (d) is incorrect because performance materiality must be documented in the working papers.

19. (c) The requirement is to identify the information that an auditor would be most likely to use in making a preliminary judgment about materiality. Answer (c) is correct because auditors often choose to use a measure relating to the prior year's financial statements (e.g., a percentage of total assets, net income, or revenue) to arrive at a preliminary judgment about materiality. Answer (a) is incorrect because materiality is based on the magnitude of an omission or misstatement and not on the initial assessment of control risk. Answer (b) is incorrect because while an auditor's materiality judgment will affect the anticipated sample size for planned substantive tests, sample size does not affect the materiality judgment. Answer (d) is incorrect because the assertions embodied in the financial statements remain the same from one audit to another.

20. (b) The requirement is to identify the most likely effect of a decrease in the tolerable amount of misstatement (tolerable misstatement) in a class of transactions. Answer (b) is correct because auditing standards state that decreasing the tolerable amount of misstatement will require the auditor to do one or more of the following: (1) perform auditing procedures closer to the balance sheet date (answer [b]); (2) select a more effective auditing procedure; or (3) increase the extent of a particular auditing procedure. Answer (a) is incorrect because in such a circumstance substantive tests are more likely to be performed at or after the balance sheet date than prior to the balance sheet date. Answer (c) is incorrect because decreasing the tolerable amount of misstatement will not necessarily lead to an increase in the assessed level of control risk. Answer (d) is incorrect because the extent of auditing procedures will be increased, not decreased.

21. (b) The requirement is to identify the necessary condition for an auditor to be able to issue an unmodified opinion. Answer (b) is correct because if the estimate of likely misstatement is equal to or greater than a material amount a material departure from generally accepted accounting principles exists and thus AU-C 705 requires either a qualified or adverse opinion in such circumstances. Answer (a) is incorrect because the amount of known misstatement (if any) need not be documented in the management representation letter. Answer (c) is incorrect because it ordinarily is not necessary for the client to acknowledge and record immaterial known misstatements. Answer (d) is incorrect because the total likely misstatement need not include the adjusting entries already recorded by the client.

22. (a) The requirement is to identify the example of fraudulent financial reporting. Answer (a) is correct because fraudulent financial reporting involves intentional misstatements or omissions of amounts or disclosures in financial statements to deceive financial statement users and changing the inventory count tags results in such a misstatement. Answers (b), (c), and (d) are all incorrect because they represent the misappropriation of assets. See AU-C 240, which divides fraudulent activities into misstatement arising from fraudulent financial reporting and misstatements arising from misappropriation of assets (sometimes referred to as defalcation).

23. (b) The requirement is to identify the best description of what is meant by a "fraud risk factor." Answer (b) is correct because AU-C 240 suggests that while fraud risk factors do not necessarily indicate the existence of fraud, they often have been observed in circumstances where frauds have occurred. Answer (a) is incorrect because the risk of fraud may or may not be high when a risk factor is present. Answer (c) is incorrect because the current audit program may in many circumstances appropriately address a fraud risk factor. Answer (d) is incorrect because a fraud risk factor may or may not represent a material weakness.

24. (a) The requirement is to identify the reply which represents an auditor communication responsibility relating to fraud. Answer (a) is correct because all fraud involving senior management should be reported directly to the audit committee. Answer (b) is incorrect because auditors are only required to report fraud to the Securities and Exchange Commission under particular circumstances. Answer (c) is incorrect because auditors do not ordinarily disclose fraud through use of an "emphasis of a matter" paragraph added to their report. Answer (d) is incorrect because under certain circumstances auditors must disclose fraud outside the entity.

25. (b) The requirement is to identify the risk relating to material misstatement that auditors are required to assess. Answer (b) is correct because auditors must specifically assess the risk of material misstatements due to fraud and consider that assessment in designing the audit procedures to be performed. Answer (a) is incorrect because while AU-C 315 also requires an assessment of the overall risk of material misstatement (whether caused by error or fraud) there is no requirement to explicitly assess the risk of material misstatement due to errors. Answer (c) is incorrect because the auditor need not explicitly assess the risk of misstatement due to illegal acts. Answer (d) is incorrect because no assessment of business risk is required.

26. (a) The requirement is to determine whether audits are designed to provide reasonable assurance of detecting misstatements due to errors, fraudulent financial reporting, and/or misappropriation of assets. Answer (a) is correct because AU-C 240 requires that an audit obtain reasonable assurance that material misstatements, whether caused by error or fraud, be detected. Fraudulent financial reporting and the misappropriation of assets are the two major types of fraud with which an audit is relevant.

27. (d) The requirement is to identify the reply which is not a reason why auditors are unable to obtain absolute assurance that misstatements due to fraud will be detected. Answer (d) is correct because while an auditor must exercise professional

skepticism when performing an audit it does not represent a limitation that makes is impossible to obtain absolute assurance. Answers (a), (b), and (c) are all incorrect because they represent factors considered in the professional literature for providing reasonable, and not absolute assurance.

28. (b) The requirement is to determine which concept requires an attitude that includes a questioning mind and a critical assessment of audit evidence. Answer (b) is correct because AU-C 200 states that professional skepticism includes these qualities. Answer (a) is incorrect because due professional care is a broader concept that concerns what the independent auditor does and how well he or she does it. Answer (c) is incorrect because reasonable assurance is based on the concept that an auditor is not an insurer and his or her report does not provide absolute assurance. Answer (d) is incorrect because supervision involves the directing of the efforts of assistants who are involved in accomplishing the objectives of the audit and determining whether those objectives were accomplished.

29. (c) The requirement is to determine what presumption concerning management's honesty that professional skepticism requires. Answer (c) is correct because professional skepticism requires that an auditor neither assume dishonesty nor unquestioned honesty. Answers (a) and (b) are incorrect because neither honesty in the absence of fraud risk factor nor dishonesty are assumed. Answer (d) is incorrect because the concept of reasonable assurance is not directed towards management's honesty.

30. (b) The requirement is to identify the type of fraudulent misstatement that is most difficult to detect. Answer (b) is correct because transactions that have not been recorded are generally considered most difficult because there is no general starting point for the auditor in the consideration of the transaction. Answers (a), (c), and (d) all represent recorded transactions which, when audited, are in general easier to detect.

31. (d) The requirement is to identify the least likely indicator of a risk of possible misstatement due to fraud. Answer (d) is correct because one would expect unusually aggressive, rather than unusually conservative accounting practices to indicate a risk of misstatement due to fraud. Answers (a), (b), and (c) are all incorrect because they represent risk factors explicitly included in AU-C 240, which provides guidance on fraud.

32. (c) The requirement is to determine the reply which represents information most likely to affect the auditor's assessment of the risk of misstatement due to fraud. Answer (c) is correct because AU-C 240 states that missing documents may be indicative of fraud. Answer (a) is incorrect because checks for significant amounts are normally expected to be outstanding at year-end. Answer (b) is incorrect because almost all audits involve computer generated documents and their existence is not considered a condition indicating possible fraud. Answer (d) is incorrect because while last-minute adjustments that significantly affect financial results may be considered indicative of possible fraud, year-end adjusting journal entries alone are to be expected.

33. **(a)** The requirement is to identify the most likely response to the auditor's assessment that the risk of material misstatement due to fraud for the existence of inventory is high. Answer (a) is correct because observing test counts of inventory on an unannounced basis will provide evidence as to whether record inventory exists. Answer (b) is incorrect because replacing test counts with analytical procedures is not likely to be particularly effective. Answers (c) and (d) are incorrect because the inventories might well be counted at year-end, all on the same date, rather than prior to year-end and at differing dates.

34. **(a)** The requirement is to identify the reply that is most likely to be an example of fraud. Answer (a) is most likely, since "defalcation" is another term for misstatements arising from misappropriation of assets, a major type of fraud. Answers (b), (c), and (d) are all incorrect because mistakes in the application of accounting principles or in processing data, and unreasonable accounting estimates arising from oversight are examples of misstatements rather than fraud.

35. **(c)** The requirement is to identify the characteristic most likely to heighten an auditor's concern about the risk of intentional manipulation of financial statements. Answer (c) is correct because the placement of substantial emphasis on meeting earnings projections is considered a risk factor. Answer (a) is incorrect because high turnover, not low turnover, is considered a risk factor. Answer (b) is incorrect because insider purchases of additional shares of stock are less likely to be indicative of intentional manipulation of the financial statements than is undue emphasis on meeting earnings projections. Answer (d) is incorrect because a rapid rate of change in an industry, not a slow rate, is considered a risk factor.

36. **(d)** The requirement is to identify an auditor's responsibility for detecting errors and fraud. Answer (d) is correct because AU-C 200 requires that an auditor design the audit to provide reasonable assurance of detecting misstatements due to errors and fraud that are material to the financial statements. Answer (a) is incorrect because audits provide reasonable assurance of detecting material errors and fraud. Answer (b) is incorrect because it doesn't restrict the responsibility to material errors and fraud. Answer (c) is incorrect because it is less precise than answer (d), which includes the AU-C 200 responsibility on errors and fraud.

37. **(d)** The requirement is to identify the circumstances in which an auditor may have a responsibility to disclose fraud to parties other than a client's senior management and its audit committee or board of directors. Answer (d) is correct because AU-C 240 states that such a responsibility may exist to the SEC when there has been an auditor change to a successor auditor or to comply with SEC 1995 Private Securities Reform Act communication requirement, when the successor auditor makes inquiries, and to a government agency from which the client receives financial assistance. In addition, that section states that an auditor may have such a disclosure responsibility in response to a subpoena, a circumstance not considered in this question.

38. **(b)** Errors refer to unintentional mistakes in financial statements such as misinterpretation of facts. Answers (a), (c),

and (d) all represent fraud which are defined as intentional distortions of financial statements.

39. **(d)** The requirement is to identify the level of assurance an auditor provides with respect to detection of material errors, fraud, and direct effect illegal acts. Answer (d) is correct because AU-C 200 requires the auditor to design the audit to provide reasonable assurance of detecting material errors, fraud and direct effect illegal acts. (A "direct effect" illegal act is one that would have an effect on the determination of financial statement amounts.)

40. **(c)** The requirement is to identify the proper attitude of an auditor who is performing an audit in accordance with generally accepted auditing standards. Answer (c) is correct because the auditor should plan and perform the audit with an attitude of professional skepticism, recognizing that the application of the auditing procedures may produce evidence indicating the possibility of misstatements due to errors or fraud. Answer (a) is incorrect because while the CPA must exhibit objective judgment, "professional skepticism" more accurately summarizes the proper attitude during an audit. Answer (b) is incorrect because while a CPA must be independent and have integrity, this is not the "attitude" used to plan and perform the audit. Answer (d) is incorrect because the audit is not planned and performed with impartial conservatism.

41. **(c)** The requirement is to identify the meaning of the term "material misstatement" when used in the professional standards. Answer (c) is correct because AU-C 240 states that a material misstatement may occur due to errors, fraud, and illegal acts with a direct effect on financial statement amounts.

42. **(d)** The requirement is to identify an auditor's responsibility for detecting financial stress of employees or adverse relationships between a company and its employees. Answer (d) is correct because AU-C 240 states that, while the auditor is not required to plan the audit to discover information that is indicative of financial stress of employees or adverse relationships between the company and its employees, such conditions must be considered when an auditor becomes aware of them. Answers (a), (b), and (c) are all incorrect because the auditor does not plan the audit to detect these conditions.

43. **(a)** The requirement is to identify an auditor's responsibility when he or she believes that a misstatement is or may be the result of fraud, but that the effect of the misstatements is immaterial to the financial statements. Answer (a) is correct because AU-C 240 states that in such circumstances the auditor should evaluate the implications of the fraud, especially those dealing with the organizational position of the person(s) involved.

44. **(a)** The requirement is to identify the correct statements relating to the auditor's consideration of fraud. Answer (a) is correct because AU-C 240 states that the auditor's interest relates to fraudulent acts that cause a material misstatement of financial statements. Answer (b) is incorrect because errors are unintentional. Answer (c) is incorrect because fraud does not necessarily involve the misappropriation of assets (it may involve fraudulent financial reporting). Answer (d) is incorrect because an auditor must design an audit to obtain reasonable assurance of detecting misstatements, regardless of whether they are caused by errors or fraud.

45. (a) The requirement is to identify the factor or condition that an audit is least likely to be planned to discover. Answer (a) is correct because it represents a financial stress, and auditors are not required to plan audits to discover information that is indicative of financial stress of employees or adverse relationships between the entity and its employees. Answers (b), (c), and (d) are all incorrect because they represent examples of risk factors that should be considered in an audit and are included in AU-C 240.

46. (a) The requirement is to determine when audit risk factors may be identified. Answer (a) is correct because AU-C 240 states that fraud risk factors may be identified during planning, obtaining an understanding, or while conducting fieldwork; in addition, they may be identified while considering acceptance or continuance of clients and engagements.

47. (b) The requirement is to identify the circumstance in which it is most likely that management's attitude toward aggressive financial reporting and toward meeting projected profit goals would most likely significantly influence an entity's control environment. Answer (b) is correct because when management is dominated by one individual, that individual may be able to follow overly aggressive accounting principles.

48. (d) The requirement is to identify the procedure least likely to be required on an audit. Answer (d) is correct because fraud is a broad legal concept and auditors do not make legal determinations of whether fraud has occurred. Answers (a), (b), and (c) are incorrect because considering journal entries, estimates, and unusual transactions are ordinarily required audit procedures to address the risk of management override of controls. See AU-C 240 for information on the auditor's responsibility for the consideration of fraud in a financial statement audit.

49. (b) The requirement is to identify the most likely response when a risk of fraud has been identified on an audit. Answer (b) is correct because AU-C 240 indicates that overall responses to the risk of material misstatements due to fraud include (1) assigning personnel with particular skills relating to the area and considering the necessary extent of supervision to the audit, (2) increasing the consideration of management's selection and application of accounting principles, and (3) making audit procedures less predictable. Answer (a) is incorrect because closer supervision, not less close supervision, is more likely to be appropriate. Answer (c) is incorrect because individuals with specialized skills may be needed who are not CPAs. Answer (d) is incorrect because subjective transactions (e.g., accounting estimates) often provide more risk than objective transactions.

50. (a) The requirement is to identify the least likely inquiry of management relating to identifying the risk of material misstatement due to fraud. Answer (a) is correct because financial operations of many companies are not ordinarily controlled by and limited to one location. Answers (b), (c), and

(d) are all incorrect because they are included in AU-C 240 as inquiries that should be made of management.

51. (a) The requirement is to identify the attributes ordinarily present when individuals commit fraud. Answer (a) is correct because AU-C 240 suggests that the three conditions generally present when fraud occurs are that individuals have an (1) incentive or pressure, (2) opportunity, and (3) ability to rationalize. Answers (b), (c), and (d) are all incorrect because they suggest that one of the three elements is not ordinarily present.

52. (a) The requirement is to determine an auditor's reporting responsibility when he or she has discovered that management is involved in a financially immaterial fraud. Answer (a) is correct because AU-C 240 requires that all management fraud, regardless of materiality, be reported to the audit committee. Answer (b) is incorrect because fraud is not directly reported to the Public Company Accounting Oversight Board. Answer (c) is incorrect because if anything, in addition to the audit committee, the fraud is reported to a level of management at least one level above those involved in a fraud. Answer (d) is incorrect because there is a reporting responsibility for financially immaterial management fraud.

53. (c) The requirement is to identify the most likely risk factor relating to fraudulent financial reporting. Answer (c) is correct because negative cash flows from operations may result in pressure upon management to overstate the results of operations. Answer (a) is incorrect because one would expect a company's top executives to dominate management— domination by one or a few might be considered a risk factor. Answers (b) and (d) are incorrect because large amounts of cash being processed and small high-dollar inventory items are more directly related to the misappropriation of assets than they are to fraudulent financial reporting.

54. (b) The requirement is to identify the most likely fraud risk factor on an audit. Answer (b) is correct because the possibility of improper revenue recognition is ordinarily presumed on audits. Answers (a), (c), and (d) all represent potential risks, but risks that are not ordinarily presumed on an audit. See AU-C 240 for information on the auditor's responsibility for the consideration of fraud in a financial statement audit.

55. (d) The requirement is to identify the circumstances relating to the discovery of the payment of small bribes to municipal officials that is most likely to cause an auditor to withdraw from an engagement. Answer (d) is correct because AU-C 250 states that management failure to take the appropriate remedial action is particularly problematical since it may affect the auditor's ability to rely on management representation and may therefore lead to withdrawal. Answers (a), (b), and (c) all represent circumstances which the auditor will consider, but are not ordinarily considered as serious as failure to take the appropriate remedial action.

56. (d) The requirement is to identify the factor most likely to cause a CPA not to accept a new audit engagement. Answer (d) is correct because a part of the understanding an auditor must obtain with a client is that management is responsible for making all financial records and related information available.

Accordingly, if the client refuses to make such information available the auditor is unlikely to accept the audit client. Answer (a) is incorrect because a circumstance-imposed scope limitations such as completion of the physical inventory count results in a situation in which the auditor may consider using alternative procedures (including making some test counts) to determine whether inventory counts are proper. Answer (b) is incorrect because an auditor may obtain an understanding of the client's operations and industry while performing the audit. Answer (c) is incorrect because while a review of the predecessor auditor's working papers is ordinarily desirable, it is not required.

57. (d) The requirement is to identify the factor most likely to heighten an auditor's concern about the risk of fraudulent financial reporting. Answer (d) is correct because AU-C 240, which presents a variety of risk factors, suggests that an overly complex organizational structure is such a risk factor. Answer (a) is incorrect because large amounts of liquid assets that are easily convertible into cash represent more of a risk relating to misappropriation of assets rather than to fraudulent financial reporting. Answer (b) is incorrect because high growth, rather than low growth, is considered a risk factor. Answer (c) is incorrect because one would expect financial management's participation in the initial selection of accounting principles.

58. (c) The requirement is to identify the situation in which an auditor would be most likely to withdraw from an engagement when he or she has discovered that a client's employees have paid small bribes to public officials. Answer (c) is correct because AU-C 250 states that resignation should be considered when an illegal act does not receive proper remedial action, because such inaction may affect the auditor's ability to rely on management representations and the effects of continued association with the client. Answer (a) is incorrect because the receipt of federal funds in such a situation is not as likely to result in auditor withdrawal as is answer (c). Answer (b) is incorrect because it seems inconsistent with the premise of the question in that, if no evidence exists, the auditor is unlikely to know that bribes have been paid. Answer (d) is incorrect because such small bribes will not ordinarily need to be disclosed. Alternatively, if the auditor believes that there is such a need, the lack of such disclosure represents a departure from generally accepted accounting principles and either a qualified or adverse opinion is appropriate.

59. (b) The requirement is to identify the illegal act that an audit should be designed to obtain reasonable assurance of detecting. Answer (b) is correct because the accrual and billing of an improper amount of revenue under government contracts is an illegal act with a direct effect on the determination of financial statement amounts, and audits are designed to detect such illegal acts. Answers (a), (c), and (d) are all incorrect because they represent illegal acts with an indirect financial statement effect and an audit provides no assurance that such acts will be detected or that any contingent liabilities that may result will be disclosed. See AU-C 250 for detailed guidance on auditor responsibility with respect to direct and indirect illegal acts.

60. (a) The requirement is to identify the small misstatement that is most likely to have a material effect on an entity's financial statements. Answer (a) is correct because an illegal payment of an otherwise immaterial amount may be material if there is a reasonable possibility that it may lead to a material contingent liability or a material loss of revenue.

61. (c) The requirement is to determine what an auditor might reconsider when a client's board of directors has refused to take any action relating to an auditor's disclosure that the company has made immaterial illegal contributions. Answer (c) is correct because in such a circumstance the failure to take remedial action may cause an auditor to decrease reliance on management representations. Answer (a) is incorrect because the reply by the attorney is likely to disclose any claims, litigation or assessments that the client has improperly omitted from the letter of audit inquiry. Answer (b) is incorrect because the prior years' audit programs are not being relied upon for this year's audit. Answer (d) is incorrect because the preliminary judgment about materiality levels would not be expected to change.

62. (b) The requirement is to identify a reason why audits cannot reasonably be expected to bring all illegal acts to the auditor's attention. Answer (b) is correct because illegal acts relating to the operating aspects of an entity are often highly specialized and complex and often are far removed from the events and transactions reflected in financial statements. Answer (a) is partially correct since management override represents a limitation of the effectiveness of internal control. Yet, auditors are more likely to identify such transactions because they relate to events and transactions reflected in the financial statements. Answer (c) is incorrect because many illegal acts are not subject to the client's internal control. Answer (d) is incorrect because illegal acts may be perpetrated without access to both assets and accounting records.

63. (a) The requirement is to determine an auditor's responsibility when information comes to his/her attention that implies the existence of possible illegal acts with a material, but indirect effect on the financial statements. Answer (a) is correct because AU-C 250 requires the auditor to apply audit procedures specifically designed to determine whether an illegal act has occurred when such information comes to his/her attention. Answers (b), (c), and (d) are all incorrect because they represent procedures the auditor would perform after initial procedures had confirmed the existence of the possible illegal act(s).

64. (b) The requirement is to determine the circumstance in which it is most likely that a CPA would withdraw from an audit engagement after having discovered that client employees have committed an illegal act. Answer (b) is correct because the auditor may conclude that withdrawal is necessary when the client does not take the remedial action, even when the illegal act is not material to the financial statements. Answers (a) and (c) are incorrect because whether generally accepted accounting principles have been violated and whether the illegal act occurred during a prior year that was not audited may or may not have an effect on the decision to withdraw from the engagement. Answer (d) is incorrect because the assessed level of control risk will not have a direct relationship on the decision to withdraw from the engagement.

65. (b) The requirement is to identify a CPA's responsibility under the Securities Litigation Reform Act of 1995 for uncorrected illegal acts which have been communicated to the board of directors which refuses to inform the SEC of their existence. Answer (b) is correct because CPAs are required under the law to deliver a report on those illegal acts to the SEC within one business day in such circumstances. Answer (a) in incorrect because there is no requirement to resign, although the auditor may decide to do so. Answer (c) is incorrect because the Act sets up reporting to the SEC, not to the stockholders. Answer (d) is incorrect because withholding of the audit opinion is not suggested in the Act.

66. (c) The requirement is to identify the procedure least likely to be considered an audit planning procedure. Answer (c) is correct because performing the risk assessment occurs subsequent to audit planning. Answer (a) is incorrect because an engagement letter is used to establish an understanding with the client, and this is a planning procedure. Answer (b) is incorrect because auditors develop the overall audit strategy during audit planning. Answer (d) is incorrect because the audit plan is developed during planning.

67. (b) The requirement is to identify the factor most likely to cause a CPA to decide not to accept a new audit engagement. Answer (b) is correct because a certain level of internal control is essential for financial statement reporting, and management's disregard in this area may lead the CPA to reject the engagement. Answer (a) is incorrect both because a CPA may not need an understanding of the prospective client's internal auditor's computer-assisted audit technique to form an opinion on the financial statements, and because if such understanding is necessary, it can be obtained subsequent to engagement acceptance. Answer (c) is incorrect because AU-C 550 indicates that a CPA often will be unable to determine whether related-party transactions were consummated on terms equivalent to arm's-length transactions. Answer (d) is incorrect because while management's refusal to permit the performance of substantive tests before the year-end may present a problem, the auditor may be able to effectively perform such tests after year-end.

68. (d) The requirement is to identify a requirement prior to accepting an engagement to audit a new client. Answer (d) is correct because AU-C 210 requires that an auditor attempt to obtain client permission to contact the predecessor prior to accepting a new engagement. Answers (a), (b), and (c) are incorrect because they may all be obtained subsequent to accepting an engagement.

69. (a) The requirement is to determine the nature of the inquiries that a successor auditor should make of the predecessor auditor prior to accepting an audit engagement. Answer (a) is correct because the inquiries should include specific questions to management on (1) disagreements with management as to auditing procedures and accounting principles (reply [a]), (2) facts that might bear on the integrity of management and (3) the predecessor's understanding as to the reasons for the change of auditors. Answers (b), (c), and (d) are incorrect because, if made at all, they will be after the engagement has been accepted.

70. (b) The requirement is to identify the correct statement regarding a successor auditor's inquiries of the predecessor auditor. Answer (b) is correct because the successor should request information such as (1) facts that might bear on the integrity of management, (2) disagreements with management as to accounting principles, auditing procedures, or other significant matters, and (3) the predecessor's understanding of the reasons for the change of auditors. Answers (a), (c), and (d) all relate to matters not required to be discussed prior to accepting an audit engagement.

71. (b) The requirement is to identify the item ordinarily included when an auditor establishes an understanding with a client regarding the services to be performed. Answer (b) is correct because auditing standards require that an auditor ensure that the audit committee is aware of any significant deficiencies which come to the CPA's attention. Answer (a) is incorrect because while an understanding will include a statement that management is responsible for the entity's financial statements, an explicit statement about errors and illegal activities of employees is not ordinarily included. Answer (c) in incorrect because management does not provide the auditor with an assessment of the risk of material misstatement due to fraud. Answer (d) is incorrect because no such statement about an auditor's responsibility for determining preliminary judgments about materiality and audit risk factors is ordinarily included in establishing an understanding. See AU-C 210 for information on establishing an understanding with a client.

72. (a) The requirement is to identify the matter generally included in an auditor's engagement letter. Answer (a) is correct because AU-C 210, which outlines requirements for engagement letters, indicates that an engagement letter should include an indication that management is responsible for identifying and ensuring that the company complies with the laws and regulations applicable to its activities. Answer (b) is incorrect because such detailed information on materiality is not generally included in an engagement letter. Answer (c) is incorrect because management liability (if any) for illegal acts committed by employees is not generally included in an engagement letter. Answer (d) is incorrect because while an auditor is required to obtain an understanding of internal control, he or she is not required to search for significant internal control deficiencies.

73. (c) The requirement is to identify the most likely procedure during the initial planning phase of an audit. Answer (c) is correct because during initial planning the timing of procedures will be discussed due to the need for client assistance with many of these procedures. Answer (a) is incorrect because the timing of audit procedures will occur subsequent to the initial planning stage of an audit. Answer (b) is incorrect because the evaluation of reasonableness of the client's accounting estimates will occur after planning—see AU-C 540. Answer (d) is incorrect because the inquiry of a client's attorney will occur subsequently to initial planning—see AU-C 501.

74. (d) The requirement is to identify the statement that is least likely to appear in an auditor's engagement letter. Answer (d) is correct because auditors ordinarily will not discuss with management the details of procedures that are necessary to perform the audit. Answers (a), (b), and (c) are incorrect because engagement letters will include a statement on the risk of not detecting material errors and fraud, and may include information on fees and observed opportunities for economy.

75. (c) The requirement is to identify the item for which the generally accepted auditing standards do not require documentation. Answer (c) is correct because while a CPA firm will include an engagement letter in the working papers, it will not detail the auditor's planned fieldwork. Answer (a) is incorrect because SAS 300 requires a written audit plan. Answer (b) is incorrect because AU-C 230 requires that the working papers document the agreement or reconciliation of the accounting records with the financial statements. Answer (d) is incorrect because AU-C 315 requires the auditor to document the assessment of the risks of material misstatement.

76. (a) The requirement is to determine what types of items are ordinarily included in an engagement letter in addition to the objectives of the engagement. Answer (a) is correct because AU-C 210 also requires inclusion of information on CPA responsibilities, client responsibilities, and limitations of the engagement.

77. (c) The requirement is to determine the reply which is least likely to be included in an engagement letter. Answer (c) is correct because AU-C 210, which provides information on obtaining an understanding with the client, does not suggest any arrangement concerning CPA investment in client securities; indeed such investments are prohibited by the Code of Professional Conduct. Answers (a), (b), and (d) all represent arrangements which AU-C 210 suggests may be included in an engagement letter (or other form of understanding with a client).

78. (b) The requirement is to identify form(s) of documentation of the understanding obtained with a client. Answer (b) is correct because the professional standards require that an auditor document the understanding through a written communication with the client. Answer (a) is incorrect because an oral communication is not sufficient. Answer (c) is incorrect because the communication should be in writing. Answer (d) is incorrect because the understanding is not documented in a *completely detailed audit plan*—a term of questionable meaning.

79. (c) The requirement is to identify the factor that most likely would influence an auditor's determination of the auditability of an entity's financial statements. Answer (c) is correct because inadequate accounting records may cause an auditor to conclude that it is unlikely that sufficient appropriate evidence will be available to support an opinion on the financial statements; accordingly, an auditor may determine that the financial statements are not auditable. Answer (a) is incorrect because an auditor should be able to obtain the knowledge necessary to audit a complex accounting system. Answer (b) is incorrect because while related-party transactions may raise transaction valuation issues due to the lack of an "arm's-length transaction," the problem is normally not so severe as to make the entity not auditable. Answer (d) is incorrect because a lack of operating effectiveness of controls

may often be overcome through an increase in the scope of substantive tests.

80. (a) The requirement is to identify the area that is most likely to require special audit planning considerations. Answer (a) is correct because an inventory comprised of diamond rings is likely to require that the auditor plan ahead to involve a specialist to assist in valuation issues. Answer (b) is incorrect because valuation of an asset such as a new copy machine is not ordinarily expected to provide valuation difficulties. Answer (c) is incorrect because the expensing purchases of such small assets is ordinarily acceptable due to the immateriality of the transactions. Answer (d) is incorrect because accelerated depreciation methods are ordinarily acceptable.

81. (b) The requirement is to identify the information source that a CPA would most likely consult for information on how various publicly held companies have complied with the disclosure requirements of a new financial accounting standard. Answer (b) is correct because AICPA *Accounting Trends and Techniques*, which is issued annually, summarizes such disclosures of 600 industrial and merchandising corporations. Answer (a) is incorrect because the AICPA *Codification of Statements on Auditing Standards* codifies the various Statements on Auditing Standards and does not include information on individual company compliance with disclosure requirements. Answer (c) is incorrect because Quality Control Review standards are established by the AICPA and because they do not include information on individual company compliance with disclosure requirements. Answer (d) is incorrect because Form 10-K itself provides information on preparing Form 10-K and this form does not include information on individual company compliance with disclosure requirements.

82. (c) The requirement is to determine why an auditor should design a written audit program. Answer (c) is correct because an audit program sets forth in detail the audit procedures that are necessary to accomplish the objectives of the audit. Answer (a) is incorrect because audit programs address topics beyond selecting material transactions and this is not their primary focus. Answer (b) is incorrect because a program may include numerous substantive tests to be performed prior to the balance sheet date. Answer (d) is incorrect because immaterial accounts often are not tested and because tests of transactions, tests of balances, and analytical procedures are used to test account balances; account balances are not directly tested through tests of controls.

83. (a) The requirement is to determine a point at which an audit program may be finalized. Answer (a) is correct because the consideration of internal control helps the auditor to assess control risk and to plan the audit; accordingly, the audit program is not generally finalized prior to the consideration of internal control. Answer (b) is incorrect because, while generally desirable, engagement letters are not required on audits. Answer (c) is incorrect because significant deficiency may be communicated at various times subsequent to finalization of the audit program. Answer (d) is incorrect because audit programs are often finalized prior to the performance of the search for unrecorded liabilities.

84. (d) The requirement is to determine the manner in which audit programs should be designed. Answer (d) is correct because an audit program should be designed so that the audit evidence gathered is sufficient to support the auditor's conclusions. Answer (a) is incorrect because, often, most audit procedures will not be performed as interim work. Answer (b) is incorrect because inherent risk need not be assessed at a low level. Answer (c) is incorrect because while providing constructive suggestions to management is desirable, the audit program is not based on developing constructive suggestions.

85. (d) The requirement is to determine what specific audit objectives are addressed when designing an audit program. Answer (d) is correct because in obtaining evidence in support of financial statement assertions, the auditor develops specific audit objectives in the light of those assertions. Answers (a), (b), and (c) are all incorrect because these replies do not relate specifically to the audit objectives as do the financial statement assertions.

86. (a) The requirement is to identify the statement that is always true with respect to planning an audit. Answer (a) is correct because it is acceptable for an auditor to perform a certain portion of the audit at an interim date; for example, performing a portion of planning prior to year-end is always acceptable for a continuing client. Also, when a new client has engaged an auditor prior to year-end, a portion of the audit may be conducted prior to year-end. Answer (b) is incorrect because an engagement may be accepted after the client's year-end. Answer (c) is incorrect because alternative procedures may be possible when an inventory count was not observed at year-end. Answer (d) is incorrect because final staffing decisions need not be made prior to completion of the planning stage of an audit.

87. (d) The requirement is to identify the element of the audit planning process most likely to be agreed upon with the client before implementation of the audit strategy. Answer (d) is correct because the auditor will ordinarily observe the counting of inventory and this will require a degree of coordination between the performance of audit procedures and client count procedures. Answer (a) is incorrect because the client will not determine the evidence to be gathered to provide a sufficient basis for the auditor's opinion. Answers (b) and (c) are incorrect because these procedures will be determined subsequent to implementation of the audit strategy.

88. (b) The requirement is to determine the manner in which an auditor plans an audit of a continuing client. Answer (b) is correct because a review of prior year working papers and the permanent file may provide useful information about the nature of the business, organizational structure, operating characteristics, and transactions that may require special attention. Answer (a) is incorrect because tests of details of transactions and balances occur subsequent to planning. Answer (c) is incorrect because while reading specialized industry journals will help the auditor to obtain a better understanding of the client's industry, it is likely to be less helpful than reviewing the working papers. Answer (d) is incorrect because a reevaluation of the client's internal control environment occurs subsequent to the ordinal planning of the audit.

89. (a) The requirement is to determine who, at a minimum, must have knowledge of the relevant professional accounting and auditing standards when an audit is being performed. Answer (a) is correct because AU-C 200 requires that, at a minimum, the auditor with final responsibility have such knowledge. Answers (b), (c), and (d) are all incorrect because they suggest a higher minimum requirement.

90. (d) The requirement is to determine why an auditor obtains knowledge about a new client's business and its industry. Answer (d) is correct because obtaining a level of knowledge of the client's business and industry enables the CPA to obtain an understanding of the events, transactions, and practices that, in the CPA's judgment, may have a significant effect on the financial statements. Answer (a) is incorrect because providing constructive suggestions is a secondary, and not the primary, reason for obtaining knowledge about a client's business and industry. Answer (b) is incorrect because while a CPA must develop an attitude of professional skepticism concerning a client, this attitude is not obtained by obtaining knowledge about the client's business and industry. Answer (c) is incorrect because in-formation on the business and industry of a client will provide only limited information in determining whether financial statements are materially misstated, and numerous other factors are considered in evaluating audit findings.

91. (c) The requirement is to identify the least likely procedure to be performed in planning a financial statement audit. Answer (c) is correct because selecting a sample of vendors' invoices for comparison to receiving reports will occur normally as a part of the evidence accumulation process, not as a part of the planning of an audit. Answer (a) is incorrect because coordination of the assistance of entity personnel in data preparation occurs during planning. Answer (b) is incorrect because while planning the audit, CPAs may discuss matters that affect the audit with firm personnel responsible for providing nonaudit services to the entity. Answer (d) is incorrect because any available current year interim financial statements will be read during the planning stage.

92. (a) The requirement is to identify whether a predecessor auditor should permit a successor auditor to review working paper analyses relating to contingencies, balance sheet accounts, or both. Answer (a) is correct because AU-C 210 states that a predecessor auditor should ordinarily permit the successor to review working papers, including documentation of planning, internal control, audit results, and other matters of continuing accounting and auditing significance, such as the working paper analysis of balance sheet accounts and those relating to contingencies.

93. (d) The requirement is to determine a successor auditor's responsibility when financial statements audited by a predecessor auditor are found to require substantial revisions. Answer (d) is correct because when a successor auditor becomes aware of information that indicates that financial statements reported on by the predecessor may require revision, the successor should request that the client arrange a meeting among the three parties to discuss and attempt to resolve the matter. Answer (a) is incorrect because the successor is not required to notify the audit committee and stockholders. Answer (b) is incorrect because the client should first communicate with the predecessor before revising the financial statements. Answer (c) is incorrect because a meeting of the three parties is arranged by the client and because the situation may or may not have anything to do with the integrity of management.

94. (c) The requirement is to determine whether a successor auditor should request a new client to authorize the predecessor auditor to allow a review of the predecessor's engagement letter, working papers, or both. Answer (c) is correct because AU-C 510 states that it is advisable that a successor auditor request to be allowed to review the predecessor's working papers.

95. (b) The requirement is to identify the audit procedure that an auditor will most likely perform during risk assessment for a financial statement audit. Answer (b) is correct because AU-C 315 requires that an auditor perform analytical procedures such as comparing the financial statements to anticipated results during the planning stage of an audit. Answers (a), (c), and (d) are all incorrect because these procedures will all occur subsequent to planning.

96. (b) The requirement is to identify the information that is most likely to be communicated by a supervisor to staff assistants. Answer (b) is correct because staff assistants must be aware of how their procedures should be evaluated in order to perform these procedures effectively. Answer (a) is incorrect because some immaterial fraud may be reported to the client's audit committee. Answer (c) is incorrect because the emphasis in an audit must be on performing the audit effectively and not merely on adhering to time budgets. Answer (d) is incorrect because decisions regarding transferring documents from the current file to the permanent file are generally of less importance than the procedure suggested by answer (b).

97. (b) The requirement is to determine why the work of each assistant should be reviewed. Answer (b) is correct because AU-C 300 suggests that the work performed by each assistant should be reviewed to determine whether it was adequately performed and to evaluate whether the results are consistent with the conclusions to be presented in the auditor's report. Answer (a) is incorrect because CPA firms, not individual auditors within the firms, have systems of quality control. Answer (c) is incorrect because the professional standards do not in general approve specific audit procedures. Answer (d) is incorrect because while determining that the audit has been performed by persons having adequate technical training and proficiency as auditors is important, it should be addressed prior to the commencement of fieldwork.

98. (c) The requirement is to determine the proper focus of analytical procedures used during risk assessment of an audit. Answer (c) is correct because analytical procedures used during risk assessment may enhance the auditor's understanding of the client's business and significant transactions and events that have occurred since the prior audit and also may help to identify the existence of unusual transactions or events and amounts, ratios, and trends that might indicate matters that have audit implications.

99. (a) The requirement is to identify a primary purpose of performing analytical procedures during an audit's risk assessment. Answer (a) is correct because analytical procedures used during risk assessment may enhance the auditor's understanding of the client's business and significant transactions and events that have occurred since the prior audit and also may help to identify the existence of unusual transactions or events and amounts, ratios, and trends that might indicate matters that have audit implications. Answers (b), (c), and (d) are all incorrect because while analytical procedures may lead to the discovery of illegal acts, related-party transactions, and unauthorized transactions, this is not the primary objective.

100. (c) The requirement is to identify the type of nonfinancial information an auditor would most likely consider in performing analytical procedures during the risk assessment phase of an audit. Answer (c) is correct because the square footage of selling space may be used in considering the overall reasonableness of sales. Answer (a) is incorrect because while the turnover of personnel in the accounting department may provide a measure of risk relating to the accounting function, it is not ordinarily used in performing analytical procedures. Similarly, answer (b) is incorrect because while the objectivity of audit committee members is an important consideration, it is not ordinarily used in performing analytical procedures. Answer (d) is also incorrect because management's plans to repurchase stock is not directly related to analytical procedures. See AU-C 315 and AU-C 520 for information on analytical procedures.

101. (c) The requirement is to identify the reply which is consistent with an increase in the accounts receivable turnover ratio (credit sales / accounts receivable). Answer (c) is correct because not including the sale in either the 20X2 sales or year-end accounts receivable increases the ratio. For example, assume that the actual total year sales are $100,000 and year-end receivables are $20,000—a turnover of 5—when the sale, assume for $5,000, is included in 20X2. Subtracting the $5,000 from 20X2 sales and receivables results in a turnover ratio of 6.33 ($95,000 / $15,000)—an increase. Answer (a) is incorrect because the consignment increases the numerator and denominator by an equal amount—this decreases the ratio. Answer (b) is incorrect because the denominator of the ratio is likely to increase disproportionately when 30 days rather than 20 days are allowed—this results in a decrease in the ratio. Answer (d) is incorrect because one would expect a pro-rata increase in accounts receivable, thus resulting in no change to the ratio.

102. (b) The requirement is to identify which reply is consistent with an increase in a company's gross margin percentage ([sales − cost of goods sold] / sales). Answer (b) is correct because fixed overhead costs will not increase with the increase in units—thus allowing costs of goods sold to increase less proportionately to the increase in units sold. Answers (a) and (c) are incorrect because income taxes and sales commissions are not included in the gross margin calculation. Answer (d) is incorrect because cost of goods sold should remain the same due to the outsourcing.

103. (c)   The requirement is to identify the reply that is most consistent with a decrease in the inventory turnover (cost of goods sold / inventory). Answer (c) is correct because an increase in inventory with no change in cost of goods sold will decrease the ratio. Answer (a) is incorrect because an increase in cost of goods sold will increase the ratio. Answer (b) is incorrect because the increased sales would be expected to increase the turnover ratio in year 2 since the increased sales, with no increase in inventory levels, results in an increase in the inventory turnover (through an increase in cost of goods sold), not a decrease—more clients paying their accounts does not directly affect the ratio. Answer (d) is incorrect because this will increase the turnover ratio since cost of goods sold will be overstated and inventory will be understated.

104. (c)   The requirement is to identify the next step in assessing the risks of material misstatement after auditors identify risks, relate risks to what could go wrong, and consider the magnitude of risks. Answer (c) is correct because the professional standards suggest that auditors should then consider the likelihood that risks involved could result in material misstatements. Answer (a) is incorrect because the assessment is not limited to illegal acts. Answer (b) is incorrect because the complexity of transactions is not next to be considered. Answer (d) is incorrect because determining materiality levels occurs prior to this stage of the audit.

105. (b)   The requirement is to identify whether substantive tests of details and/or risk assessment procedures are considered further audit procedures that may be designed after assessing the risks of material misstatement. Further audit procedures are composed of substantive procedures (tests of details and analytical procedures) and tests of controls. Answer (b) is correct because while substantive tests of details are further audit procedures, risk assessment procedures are not. Answer (a) is incorrect because risk assessment procedures are not further audit procedures. Answer (c) is incorrect because substantive tests of details are further audit procedures and because risk assessment procedures are not. Answer (d) is incorrect because substantive tests of details are further audit procedures.

106. (b)   The requirement is to identify the procedure that is least likely to be considered a risk assessment procedure. Answer (b) is correct because confirmation is a substantive test, rather than a risk assessment procedure. Answers (a), (b), and (c) are all risk assessment procedures, as are certain inquiries of others outside the entity.

107. (d)   Answer (d) is correct because significant risks often involve accounting estimates or complex accounting that involves significant judgments. Answer (a) is incorrect because routine, high-volume transactions typically have lower risk. Answer (b) is incorrect because significant risks do require special audit attention. Answer (c) is incorrect because significant risks involve items with high levels of inherent risk.

108. (b)   The requirement is to determine the proper method for handling a difference of opinion between auditors concerning interpretation of the results of an auditing procedure. Answer (b) is correct because the quality control standards require documentation of the considerations

involved in the resolution of differences of opinion. Answer (a) is incorrect because the AICPA does not, in general, rule on disagreements of this nature. Answer (c) is incorrect because the disagreement relates to an auditing procedure and therefore in most such circumstances the entity's management or its audit committee will have no particular expertise. Answer (d) is incorrect because the disagreement need not necessarily be reported to a peer review "monitoring" team.

109. (d)   The requirement is to identify what is included in the examination of a financial forecast. Answer (d) is correct because an examination of a forecast includes an evaluation of its preparation and the support underlying management's assumptions. As discussed in AT 301, an examination also includes evaluating the representation of the prospective financial statements for conformity with AICPA presentation guidelines and the issuance of an examination report. Answer (a) is incorrect because the service need not include the compiling or assembling of the financial forecast. Answer (b) is incorrect because distribution of financial forecasts need not be limited. Answer (c) is incorrect because the CPA assumes no responsibility to update management on key events. See AT 301 for information on prospective financial information.

110. (a)   The requirement is to determine the factors that affect the nature and extent of a CPA firm's quality control policies and procedures. Answer (a) is correct because the nature and extent of a firm's quality control policies and procedures depend on a number of factors, including its size, the degree of operating autonomy allowed to its personnel and practice offices, the nature of its practice, its organization, and appropriate cost-benefit considerations.

111. (d)   The requirement is to identify the manners in which a CPA firm may communicate its quality control policies and procedures to its personnel. Answer (d) is correct because the requirements relating to quality control standard documentation state that either orally or written are acceptable. Answers (a), (b) and (c) all include one or more inappropriate "no" replies.

112. (c)   The requirement is to identify the reply that is not one of the elements of quality control. Answer (c) is correct because there is no quality control element on internal control. Acceptance of client relationships and specific engagements (a), human resources (b), and monitoring (d) are all elements of quality control. In addition, the following also are elements of quality control: leadership responsibilities for engagement performance, quality within the firm, and relevant ethical requirements.

113. (d)   The requirement is to determine the types of services to which Statements on Quality Control Standards apply. Answer (d) is correct because the standards explicitly limit application to auditing and accounting and review services. Although the quality control standards may be applied to other segments of a firm's practice (e.g., management advisory services and tax), the standards do not require it.

114. (a)   The requirement is to determine how a CPA firm obtains reasonable assurance of providing professional services that conform with professional standards. Answer (a) is correct because a system of quality control is designed to provide a CPA firm with reasonable assurance of meeting its responsibility to provide professional services that conform with professional standards. Answer (b) is incorrect because a peer review provides information on whether a CPA firm is following an appropriate system of quality control. Answer (c) is incorrect because it is less complete than answer (a) since continuing professional education helps achieve the specific quality control element of professional development. Answer (d) is incorrect because the financial statements comply with generally accepted accounting principles, not the professional services provided by the CPA firm.

115. (b) The requirement is to identify the correct statement concerning PCAOB guidance that uses the term "should." Answer (a) is correct because the term "should" means that the auditor must comply with the requirements unless he or she can demonstrate that alternative actions were sufficient to achieve the objectives of the standards. Answer (a) is incorrect because terms such as "must," "shall," and "is required to" are

used to indicate that the auditor must fulfill the responsibilities. Answer (c) is incorrect because terms such as "may," "might," and "could" are used when the auditor should consider performing the audit procedure. Answer (d) is incorrect because no particular terms are used for the situation in which the auditor has complete discretion whether to perform the procedure.

116. (c) The requirement is to determine the set of standards that the PCAOB does not have authority to establish. Answer (c) is correct because the FASB establishes accounting standards for both public and nonpublic companies. Answer (a) is incorrect because the PCAOB has authority to issue auditing standards. Answer (b) is incorrect because the PCAOB has the authority to issue quality control standards. Answer (d) is incorrect because the PCAOB has the authority to issue independence standards.

Task-Based Simulation 1

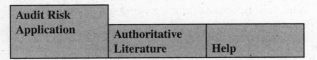

Green, CPA, is considering audit risk, including fraud risk, at the financial statement level in planning the audit of National Federal Bank (NFB) Company's financial statements for the year ended December 31, 2005. Audit risk at the financial statement level is influenced by the risk of material misstatements, which may be indicated by a combination of factors related to management, the industry, and the entity. In assessing such factors Green has gathered the following information concerning NFB's environment.

Company profile

NFB is a federally insured bank that has been consistently more profitable than the industry average by marketing mortgages on properties in a prosperous rural area, which has experienced considerable growth in recent years. NFB packages its mortgages and sells them to large mortgage investment trusts. Despite recent volatility of interest rates, NFB has been able to continue selling its mortgages as a source of new lendable funds.

NFB's board of directors is controlled by Smith, the majority stockholder, who also acts as the chief executive officer. Management at the bank's branch offices has authority for directing and controlling NFB's operations and is compensated based on branch profitability. The internal auditor reports directly to Harris, a minority shareholder, who also acts as chairman of the board's audit committee.

The accounting department has experienced little turnover in personnel during the five years Green has audited NFB. NFB's formula consistently underestimates the allowance for loan losses, but its controller has always been receptive to Green's suggestions to increase the allowance during each engagement.

Recent developments

During 20X5, NFB opened a branch office in a suburban town thirty miles from its principal place of business. Although this branch is not yet profitable due to competition from several well-established regional banks, management believes that the branch will be profitable by 20X7. Also, during 20X5, NFB increased the efficiency of its accounting operations by installing a new, sophisticated computer system.

Based only on the information above, indicate by marking the appropriate button whether the following factors indicate an increased or decreased audit risk. Also, indicate whether the factor is a fraud risk factor.

Factor	Increased audit risk	Decreased audit risk	Fraud risk factor
1. Branch management authority	O	O	O
2. Government regulation	O	O	O
3. Company profitability	O	O	O
4. Demand for product	O	O	O
5. Interest rates	O	O	O
6. Availability of mortgage funds	O	O	O
7. Involvement of principal shareholder in management	O	O	O
8. Branch manager compensation	O	O	O
9. Internal audit reporting relationship	O	O	O
10. Accounting department turnover	O	O	O
11. Continuing audit relationship	O	O	O
12. Internal controls over accounting estimates	O	O	O
13. Response to proposed accounting adjustments	O	O	O
14. New unprofitable branch	O	O	O
15. New computer system	O	O	O

Task-Based Simulation 2

Green, CPA, is considering audit risk, including fraud risk, at the financial statement level in planning the audit of National Federal Bank (NFB) Company's financial statements for the year ended December 31, 20X5. Audit risk at the financial statement level is influenced by the risk of material misstatements, which may be indicated by a combination of factors related to management, the industry, and the entity. In assessing such factors Green has gathered the following information concerning NFB's environment.

Company profile

NFB is a federally insured bank that has been consistently more profitable than the industry average by marketing mortgages on properties in a prosperous rural area, which has experienced considerable growth in recent years. NFB packages its mortgages and sells them to large mortgage investment trusts. Despite recent volatility of interest rates, NFB has been able to continue selling its mortgages as a source of new lendable funds.

NFB's board of directors is controlled by Smith, the majority stockholder, who also acts as the chief executive officer. Management at the bank's branch offices has authority for directing and controlling NFB's operations and is compensated based on branch profitability. The internal auditor reports directly to Harris, a minority shareholder, who also acts as chairman of the board's audit committee.

The accounting department has experienced little turnover in personnel during the five years Green has audited NFB. NFB's formula consistently underestimates the allowance for loan losses, but its controller has always been receptive to Green's suggestions to increase the allowance during each engagement.

Recent developments

During 20X5, NFB opened a branch office in a suburban town thirty miles from its principal place of business. Although this branch is not yet profitable due to competition from several well-established regional banks, management believes that the branch will be profitable by 20X7. Also, during 20X5, NFB increased the efficiency of its accounting operations by installing a new, sophisticated computer system.

Assume you are preparing for the audit personnel discussion of potential risks of material misstatement due to fraud for the NFB audit. While any matters below might be discussed, indicate by marking the appropriate four highest risks based on the information contained in the simulation description and requirements of professional standards.

Risk	High-risk item
1. Computer fraud risk	○
2. Risk related to management override of internal control	○
3. Fraud by branch management	○
4. Fraud by accounting personnel	○
5. Misstatement of accounting estimates	○
6. Fraud by loan processing clerks	○
7. Fraud by internal auditors	○
8. The risk of fraudulent misstatement of revenues	○

Task-Based Simulation 3

Assume that you have been hired to perform the audit of Hanmei's financial statements. When planning such an audit, you often may need to refer to various of the profession's auditing standards. For each of the following circumstances in Column A, select the topic from the Professional Standards that is likely to provide the most guidance in the planning of the audit. A topic may be selected once, more than once, or not at all.

Topic

A. Analytical Procedures
B. Materiality
C. Communications between Predecessor and Successor Auditors
D. Consideration of Fraud in a Financial Statement Audit
E. Understanding the Entity and Its Environment and Assessing the Risks of Material Misstatement

F. Consideration of Laws and Regulations
G. Management Representations
H. Part of the Audit Performed by Other Independent Auditors
I. Related Parties

Transactions	(A)	(B)	(C)	(D)	(E)	(F)	(G)	(H)	(I)
1. Possible risk factors related to misappropriation of assets.	O	O	O	O	O	O	O	O	O
2. The relationship between materiality used for planning versus evaluation purposes.	O	O	O	O	O	O	O	O	O
3. Hanmei Corp. has transactions with the corporation president's brother.	O	O	O	O	O	O	O	O	O
4. Comparing a client's unaudited results for the year with last year's audited results.	O	O	O	O	O	O	O	O	O
5. Auditing and reporting guidance on the possible need to reaudit previous year results due to the disbanding of the firm that performed last year's audit.	O	O	O	O	O	O	O	O	O
6. Requirements relating to identifying violations of occupational safety and health regulations.	O	O	O	O	O	O	O	O	O
7. Audit report considerations when audit of a subsidiary of the client will be performed by Williams & Co., CPAs.	O	O	O	O	O	O	O	O	O
8. The need to "brainstorm" among audit team members about how accounts could be intentionally misstated.	O	O	O	O	O	O	O	O	O
9. Details on considering design effectiveness of controls.	O	O	O	O	O	O	O	O	O
10. The importance of considering the possibility of overstated revenues (for example, through premature revenue recognition).	O	O	O	O	O	O	O	O	O

Task-Based Simulation 4

Risk Analysis		
	Authoritative Literature	
		Help

DietWeb Inc. (hereafter DietWeb) was incorporated and began business in March of 20X1, seven years ago. You are working on the 20X8 audit—your CPA firm's fifth audit of DietWeb.

The company's mission is to provide solutions that help individuals to realize their full potential through better eating habits and lifestyles. Much of 20X1 and 20X2 was spent in developing a unique software platform that facilitates the production of individualized meal plans and shopping lists using a specific mathematical algorithm, which considers the user's physical condition, proclivity to exercise, food preferences, cooking preferences, desire to use prepackaged meals or dine out, among others. DietWeb sold its first online diet program in 20X2 and has continued to market memberships through increasing online advertising arrangements through the years. The company has continued to develop this program throughout the years and finally became profitable in 20X6.

DietWeb is executing a strategy to be a leading online provider of services, information and products related to nutrition, fitness and motivation. In 20X8, the company derived approximately 86% of its total revenues from the sale of approximately 203,000 personalized subscription-based online nutrition plans related to weight management, to dietary regimens such as vegetarianism and to specific medical conditions such as Type 2 diabetes. Given the personal nature of dieting, DietWeb assures customers of complete privacy of the information they provide. To this point DietWeb's management is proud of its success in assuring the privacy of information supplied by its customers—this is a constant battle given the variety of intrusion attempts by various Internet hackers.

DietWeb nutrition plans are paid in advance by customers and offered in increments of thirteen weeks with the customers having the ability to cancel and receive a refund of the unused portion of the subscription—this results in a significant level of "deferred revenue" each period. Although some DietWeb members are billed through use of the postal system, most DietWeb members currently purchase programs and products using credit cards, with renewals billed automatically, until cancellation. One week of a basic DietWeb membership costs less than one-half the cost of a weekly visit to the leading classroom-based diet program. The president, Mr. William Readings, suggests that in addition to its superior cost-effectiveness, the DietWeb online diet program is successful relative to classroom-based programs due to its customization, ease of use, expert support, privacy, constant availability, and breadth of choice. The basic DietWeb membership includes

- Customized meal plans and workout schedules and related tools such as shopping lists, journals, and weight and exercise tracking.
- Interactive online support and education including approximately 100 message boards on various topics of interest to members and a library of dozens of multimedia educational segments presented by experts including psychologists, mental health counselors, dietitians, fitness trainers, a spiritual advisor and a physician.
- 24/7/365 telephone support from a staff of approximately 30 customer service representatives, nutritionists and fitness personnel.

Throughout its nine-year history, Mr. William Readings has served as chief executive officer. The other three founders of the company are also officers. A fifth individual, Willingsley Williamson, also a founder, served as Chief Financial Officer until mid-20X8 when he left the company due to a difference of opinion with Mr. Readings. The four founders purchased Mr. Williamson's stock and invested an additional approximately $1.2 million in common stock during 20X8 so as to limit the use of long-term debt.

The company's board of directors is currently composed of the four individuals who remain active in the company; these four individuals also serve as the company's audit committee; Mr. Readings chairs both the board and the audit committee. Previously, Mr. Readings had also served on the board and the audit committee. With Mr. Williamson's departure, Ms. Jane Jennings, another of the founders, became the company's CFO.

The nutrition and diet industry in many ways thrives because individuals are becoming more aware of the negative health and financial consequences of being overweight, and consider important both weight loss and healthy weight maintenance. A study by two respected researchers concluded that obesity was linked to higher rates of chronic illness than living in poverty, than smoking, or than drinking. In addition, the American Cancer Society reported that as many as 14% of cancer deaths in men and 20% of cancer deaths in women could be related to being overweight.

The financial costs of excess weight are also high. A 20X8 study based on data from a major automobile manufacturer's health-care plan showed that an overweight adult has annual health-care costs that are 7.3% higher than a person in a healthy weight range, while obese individuals have annual health-care costs that are 69% higher than a person of a healthy weight. With health-care cost inflation running in the double digits in the United States since 20X4, supporters of the industry believe that the implementation of effective weight management tools will attract more attention from insurers, employers, consumers, and the government. As of January 20X9 five nutrition- or fitness-related bills were being considered in Congress, and several states had enacted or were considering enacting legislation relating to the sale of "junk" food in public schools. In addition, the US Food and Drug Administration, Department of Health and Human Services, and Federal Trade Commission are contemplating new labeling requirements for packaged food and restaurant food, new educational and motivational programs related to healthy eating and exercise, and increased regulation of advertising claims for food.

In response to consumers' growing demand for more healthful eating options, quick-service and full-service restaurants have introduced new offerings including salads, sandwiches, burgers, and other food items designed for the weight-conscious person. At the retail level, sales of natural and organic foods have been growing more rapidly than the overall food and over-the-counter drug market for the last several years. Nutritional supplement sales in the US, for instance, are estimated to have grown 34% between 20X4 and 20X8, while natural and organic foods are estimated to be growing at a rate of approximately 15% annually. Also, the industry has a tendency to change quickly as "dieting fads" regularly are introduced; some remain popular for years, some for only months.

Approximately 60% of the US adult population, or 120 million adults, are overweight and, of those, the Calorie Control Council estimates only about 50 million are dieting in a given year. About 15% of these dieters are using a commercial weight loss center, generating revenues of approximately $1.5 billion annually. DietWeb targets dieters who are online, which represents about two-thirds of the total universe at current Internet penetration rates, or 34 million adults, about 5 million of whom are spending approximately $1 billion at weight loss centers.

At the same time, the online dieting segment of the market is growing rapidly. The online diet industry in the US generated in excess of $100 million in 20X8, compared to revenues of approximately $75 million in 20X2. The industry includes other online nutrition and diet-oriented websites.

Another group of competitors to DietWeb are commercial weight loss centers, an industry that has shown marked decline in the last decade. According to Market Analysis Enterprises, the number of commercial weight loss centers in the US declined approximately 50% between 20X2 and 20X8, from over 8,600 to approximately 4,400. DietWeb competes against this segment on the basis of lower price, superior value, convenience, availability, the ability to personalize a meal plan on an ongoing basis, its extensive support capabilities, and the breadth of its meal plan options.

(A) (B) (C) (D)

1. Of the following, which is likely to be one of DietWeb's major risks of doing business on the Internet in the future?   ○ ○ ○ ○

    A. Maintaining privacy of customer information.
    B. Maintaining the ability to pay Federal Communication Commission Internet use fees.
    C. Inability to provide 24/7/365 support.
    D. Inability to reach customers beyond the United States.

(A) (B) (C) (D)

2. Which of the following is likely to be the most significant business risk for DietWeb?   ○ ○ ○ ○

    A. Internal control limitations due to the small size of the company.
    B. Inability of the Internet to provide adequate support for such a business due to its instability.
    C. Entrance of new competitors onto the Internet.
    D. Misstatements of revenues due to difficulties in determining appropriate year-end cutoffs.

(A) (B) (C) (D)

3. Which of the following is most accurate concerning DietWeb's audit committee?   ○ ○ ○ ○

    A. It should be considered very independent in that the company's founders serve on it.
    B. Mr. Readings' chairmanship of the audit committee creates a situation in which the audit committee serves a strong independent role due to his closeness to company operations.
    C. Because all committee members are members of management, the audit committee lacks independence.
    D. The audit committee does not have enough members in that the size of the board of directors should be less than that of the audit committee.

(A) (B) (C) (D)

4. Which of the following indicates an increased risk of misstatement due to fraud?   ○ ○ ○ ○

    A. Resignation of Mr. Williamson.
    B. Domination of management by company founders.
    C. Issuance of debt during 20X8.
    D. Competition with non-Internet weight loss organizations.

(A) (B) (C) (D)

5. Which of the following is the most significant risk facing DietWeb that might cause it to not be able to continue increasing sales?   ○ ○ ○ ○

    A. A decreasing market in the United States for dietary products.
    B. DietWeb must respond to "dieting fads" on a timely basis.
    C. The constantly decreasing number of individuals in the United States.
    D. Obsolescence of the Internet.

Task-Based Simulation 5

Financial Statement Analysis		
	Authoritative Literature	**Help**

    DietWeb Inc. (hereafter DietWeb) was incorporated and began business in March of 20X1, seven years ago. You are working on the 20X8 audit—your CPA firm's fifth audit of DietWeb. Analyze the following financial statements and reply to each of the questions that follow.

DietWeb, Inc.
BALANCE SHEET
December 31, 20X8 and 20X7
(in thousands)

	20X8	20X7
Assets		
Current assets		
Cash and cash equivalents	$3,032	$1,072
Trade receivables	485	450
Prepaid advertising expenses	59	609
Prepaid expenses and other current assets	175	230
Total current assets	3,751	2,361
Fixed assets, net	3,321	3,926
Total assets	$7,072	$6,287
Liabilities and shareholders' equity		
Current liabilities		
Accounts payable	$1,070	$ 909
Current maturities of notes payable	42	316
Deferred revenue	1,973	1,396
Other current liabilities	171	12
Total current liabilities	3,256	2,633
Long-term debt, less current maturity	34	176
Accrued liabilities	792	690
Deferred tax liability	15	145
Total liabilities	4,097	3,644
Shareholders' equity		
Common stock	6,040	4,854
Retained earnings	(3,065)	(2,211)
Total shareholders' equity	2,975	2,643
Total liabilities plus shareholders' equity	$7,072	$6,287

DietWeb, Inc.
INCOME STATEMENT
Two Years Ended December 31, 20X8 and 20X7
(in thousands)

	20X8	20X7
Revenue	$19,166	$14,814
Costs and expenses		
Cost of revenue	2,326	1,528
Product development	725	653
Sales and marketing	13,903	8,710
General and administrative	2,531	2,575
Depreciation and amortization	629	661
Impairment of intangible assets	35	–
Total costs and expenses	20,149	14,127
Net income before taxes	(983)	687
Income tax benefit	129	125
Net income (loss)	$(854)	$ 812

DietWeb, Inc.
STATEMENT OF CASH FLOWS
Year Ended December 31, 20X8

	20X8	20X7
Cash flows from operations		
Net income (loss)	$(854)	812
Adjustments to net income		
Depreciation	629	660
Increase in receivables	(35)	(47)
Decrease (Increase) in prepaid advertising	550	(650)
Decrease in other current assets	55	74
Increase (Decrease) in accounts payable	161	(540)
Increase in accrued liabilities	102	43
Increase (Decrease) in deferred revenue	432	(665)
Increase in common stock issued	1,186	-
Increase in other current liabilities	159	43
Net cash provided (used) by operations	2,385	(270)
Cash flows from investing activities		
Purchase of property and equipment	(320)	2,016
Cash flows from financing activities		
New debt	613	40
Debt payments	(718)	(918)
Net cash provided (used) by financing activities	(105)	(878)
Net increase in cash and cash equivalents	$1,960	868
Cash and equivalents at beginning of year	$1,072	204
Cash and equivalents at end of year	$3,032	1,072

(A) (B) (C) (D)
○ ○ ○ ○

1. The most likely misstatement in the financial statements is

   A. The increase in cash in 20X8.
   B. Treatment of impaired intangible assets as an expense in 20X8.
   C. Treatment of common stock issued as an adjustment to net income (loss) under cash flow from operations.
   D. An income tax benefit on the income statement as contrasted to income tax expense.

(A) (B) (C) (D)
○ ○ ○ ○

2. Which of the following is the most unexpected change on the balance sheet, if one assumes the revenue increase in 20X8 is correct?

   A. Decrease in prepaid advertising expenses.
   B. Increase in accounts payable.
   C. Decrease in deferred revenues.
   D. Increase in common stock.

(A) (B) (C) (D)
○ ○ ○ ○

3. Which of the following is most likely to lead the auditors to question whether DietWeb has the ability to continue as a going concern?

   A. The net loss incurred in 20X8.
   B. The decrease in cash that occurred in 20X8.
   C. Increases in fixed assets during 20X8.
   D. Mr. Readings serving as both CEO and chairman of the board of directors.

(A) (B) (C) (D)
○ ○ ○ ○

4. Which of the following classifications is likely to be incorrect?

   A. Classification of prepaid expenses as assets.
   B. Classification of accrued liabilities as a noncurrent liability.
   C. A deferred tax liability with a positive balance.
   D. Retained earnings including a negative balance.

(A) (B) (C) (D)

5. Which of the following changes that have been recorded seems most unexpected?   ○ ○ ○ ○

   A. The decrease in fixed assets.
   B. The decrease in prepaid expenses and other current assets.
   C. An increase in cash during a year in which there is a net loss.
   D. An increase in accrued liabilities, given the large increase in sales.

Task-Based Simulation 6

You are working with William Bond, CPA, and you are considering the risk of material misstatement in planning the audit of Toxic Waste Disposal (TWD) Company's financial statements for the year ended December 31, 20X1. TWD is a privately owned entity that contracts with municipal governments to remove environmental waste. Based only on the information below, indicate whether each of the following factors would most likely increase (I), decrease (D), or have no effect on the risk of material misstatement (N).

		(I)	(D)	(N)
1.	Because municipalities have received increased federal and state funding for environmental purposes, TWD returned to profitability for the first year following three years with losses.	○	○	○
2.	TWD's Board of Directors is controlled by Mead, the majority stockholder, who also acts as the chief executive officer.	○	○	○
3.	The internal auditor reports to the controller and the controller reports to Mead.	○	○	○
4.	The accounting department has experienced a high rate of turnover of key personnel.	○	○	○
5.	TWD's bank has a loan officer who meets regularly with TWD's CEO and controller to monitor TWD's financial performance.	○	○	○
6.	TWD's employees are paid biweekly.	○	○	○
7.	TWD has such a strong financial presence in its history so as to allow it often to dictate the terms or conditions of transactions with its suppliers.	○	○	○
8.	During 20X1, TWD changed its method of preparing its financial statements from the cash basis to generally accepted accounting principles.	○	○	○
9.	During 20X1, TWD sold one-half of its controlling interest in United Equipment Leasing (UEL) Co. TWD retained significant influence over UEL.	○	○	○
10.	During 20X1, litigation filed against TWD from an action ten years ago that alleged that TWD discharged pollutants into state waterways was dropped by the state. Loss contingency disclosures that TWD included in prior years' financial statements are being removed from the 20X1 financial statements.	○	○	○
11.	During December 20X1, TWD signed a contract to lease disposal equipment from an entity owned by Mead's parents. This related-party transaction is not disclosed in TWD's notes to the 20X1 financial statements.	○	○	○
12.	During December 20X1, TWD completed a barter transaction with a municipality. TWD removed waste from the municipally owned site and acquired title to another contaminated site at below market price. TWD intends to service this new site in 20X2.	○	○	○
13.	During December 20X1, TWD increased its casualty insurance coverage on several pieces of sophisticated machinery from historical cost to replacement cost.	○	○	○
14.	Inquiries about the substantial increase in revenue TWD recorded in the fourth quarter of 20X1 disclosed a new policy. TWD guaranteed to several municipalities that it would refund the federal and state funding paid to TWD if any municipality fails a federal or state site clean-up inspection in 20X2.	○	○	○
15.	An initial public offering of TWD's stock is planned for late 20X2.	○	○	○

Task-Based Simulation 7

Identifying Risks		
	Authoritative Literature	Help

Planning

You are beginning the 20X8 audit of Toastco, a nonpublic company that manufactures various kitchen products. This is your firm's sixth annual audit of Toastco.

Toastco's most profitable product is a deluxe toaster that is designed for those who want "a truly outstanding toaster." The toaster was first marketed through *Sky Mall Magazine,* which offers specialty-type products to airplane passengers. Demand has grown so that at this point the company advertises the product much more broadly through a variety of media. Sales have been outstanding from the start and continue to increase. The recorded level of sales for 20X8 indicates that the company now controls approximately 5% of the toaster market, which represents 55% of company sales. In addition to the toaster, the company manufactures other products, including toaster ovens, coffee makers, food blenders, and electric can openers. Most of the manufacturing process is performed in several plants in Asia.

The highly successful toaster is the product of Bill Williams, who became Toastco's chief executive officer in 20X3. Bill and several other officers invested heavily in the company at that time with the intent of ultimately selling common stock to the public. His and those individuals' lives are centered about the firm and making it a success. Consistently, Toastco is of critical importance to each of these individuals financially.

Recently you discussed the coming audit with Bill. You quickly found that he was elated that the company had earned $1.21 per share, one cent more than he had assured the bank that had provided Toastco with extensive financing during 20X8. He suggested that some had feared that Toastco wouldn't make it after somewhat weak second and third quarters, but that he knew all along that a strong fourth quarter was ahead and that it would "bring us through." He also pointed out that sales are up about 38% compared to the previous year and income by 54%. Furthermore, he indicated that an initial public offering of securities was planned for approximately eighteen months from now.

Toastco's outstanding performance for the past several years is in large part due to the highly profitable toaster, with other products gaining sales at approximately the industry's growth rate. In fact, Bill indicated that the toaster has become even more profitable this year due to reengineering of its production process and components, which brought costs of production down and decreased sales returns and allowances.

Bill also suggested to you that the $42,216,000 bank loan received during the year has been primarily used to increase inventories and fixed assets to support the rapidly rising demand for the toaster, as well as Toastco's other products. He pointed out that the company could never have achieved its projected earnings per share goal without the bank's support. This bank support has also allowed Toastco to work on developing what Bill refers to as "our next super product … an improved can opener that works well with all sizes of cans and doesn't leave a mess."

Finally, Bill said that there was some sad news. The Chairman of the Board of Directors, John Whing, an independent director, had been forced to step down for health reasons. Bill had replaced Mr. Whing as Chairman of the Board, and Toastco Vice President Sam Adamson filled the empty seat on the board of directors. The seven-member board is now composed of Bill (who will begin serving as Chairman), Sam Adamson, two others from management, and the three independent directors. The audit committee has not been affected by the change, as the three independent directors continue to serve in that role.

Industry Information

In the portions of the kitchen product industry in which Toastco operates, demand is influenced by economic trends such as increases or decreases in consumer disposable income, availability of credit, and housing construction. Competition is very active in all products and comes from a number of principal manufacturers and suppliers. An important factor is the degree of product differentiation achieved through innovation and new product features. Other significant factors include product quality and cost, brand recognition, customer responsiveness, and appliance service capability.

Overall, for the industry, sales have been and are expected to remain relatively stable with a slight increase—increases have approximated 3% industry-wide per year during the past five years, and are expected to continue at that rate of increase for the next five years. Much of the manufacturing of these products takes place in Asia, and to a lesser extent in South America. Increasingly, Asian companies are becoming directly involved in marketing their own household products.

(A) (B) (C) (D)

1. Which of the following identifies an aspect of the company's business model, strategies, and/or business environment that is most likely to increase Toastco's inherent risk?   ○ ○ ○ ○

    A. Manufacturing in Asia.
    B. An expected industry growth rate in sales of approximately 3%.
    C. Product obsolescence or loss of product differentiation advantages.
    D. Overstated accounts receivable due to internal control deficiencies.

(A) (B) (C) (D)

2. Which of the following identifies a situation most likely to increase the risk of misstatement arising from fraudulent financial reporting?   ○ ○ ○ ○

    A. The household products industry seems stable, and is not rapidly growing.
    B. Toastco reported a strong fourth quarter that brought it up to expectations for earnings per share.
    C. Toastco controls approximately 5% of the market for toasters.
    D. Toastco has one relatively profitable product, and a number of products that are not as profitable.

(A) (B) (C) (D)

3. Which of the following identifies an aspect of the company's business model, strategies, and/or business environment that is most likely to increase the risk of misstatement arising from fraudulent financial reporting?   ○ ○ ○ ○

    A. Toastco sells more than one type of product.
    B. The president's wealth is based on the success of Toastco.
    C. The audit committee is composed entirely of independent directors.
    D. Toastco continues to hire your firm for its fifth year.

Ratio Analysis

Below are two sets of ratios that were identified as significant in the current and prior years' audits of Toastco. For each pair, compare the values of each ratio. Then select an audit finding that is consistent with these metrics. Each of the audit findings may be used once, more than once, or not at all. Ratios using balance sheet numbers are based on end of year balances.

Ratio	20X8	20X7
Gross margin percentage	0.154	0.166
Current ratio	2.619	3.688

Substantive procedure

    A. Increases in costs of purchases were not completely passed on to customers through higher selling prices.
    B. Increases in trade receivables.
    C. Owners' equity increased due to retention of profits.
    D. A larger percentage of sales occurred during the last month of 20X8, as compared to 20X7.
    E. Interest expense decreased during 20X8.
    F. The percentage tax included in the provision for income taxes for 20X8 was less than the percentage in 20X7.
    G. A significant amount of long-term debt became current.

(A) (B) (C) (D) (E) (F) (G)

1. An audit finding most consistent with the change in the gross margin percentage   ○ ○ ○ ○ ○ ○ ○

2. An audit finding most consistent with the change in the current ratio   ○ ○ ○ ○ ○ ○ ○

Ratio	20X8	20X7
Inventory turnover	10.52	7.95
Return on equity	0.40	0.67

Audit findings

H. Increases in costs of purchases were not completely passed on to customers through higher selling prices.
I.   Increases in trade receivables.
J.   Owners' equity increased due to retention of profits.
K. A larger percentage of sales occurred during the last month of 20X8, as compared to 20X7.
L.   Interest expense decreased during 20X8.
M. The percentage tax included in the provision for income taxes for 20X8 was less than the percentage in 20X7.

	(H)	(I)	(J)	(K)	(L)	(M)
3. An audit finding consistent with the change in inventory turnover for Toastco	O	O	O	O	O	O
4. An audit finding consistent with the change in the return on equity	O	O	O	O	O	O

Task-Based Simulation 8

Observed Ratio Changes		
	Authoritative Literature	Help

Items 1 through 6 represent an auditor's observed changes in certain financial statement ratios or amounts from the prior year's ratios or amounts. For each observed change, select the most likely explanation or explanations from List B. Select only the number of explanations as indicated. Answers on the list may be selected once, more than once, or not at all.

List B

A. Items shipped on consignment during the last month of the year were recorded as sales.
B. A significant number of credit memos for returned merchandise that were issued during the last month of the year were not recorded.
C. Year-end purchases of inventory were overstated by incorrectly including items received in the first month of the subsequent year.
D. Year-end purchases of inventory were understated by incorrectly excluding items received before the year-end.
E. A larger percentage of sales occurred during the last month of the year, as compared to the prior year.
F. A smaller percentage of sales occurred during the last month of the year, as compared to the prior year.
G. The same percentage of sales occurred during the last month of the year, as compared to the prior year.
H. Sales increased at the same percentage as cost of goods sold, as compared to the prior year.
I.   Sales increased at a greater percentage than cost of goods sold increased, as compared to the prior year.
J.   Sales increased at a lower percentage than cost of goods sold increased, as compared to the prior year.
K. Interest expense decreased, as compared to the prior year.
L.   The effective income tax rate increased, as compared to the prior year.
M. The effective income tax rate decreased, as compared to the prior year.
N. Short-term borrowing was refinanced on a long-term basis at the same interest rate.
O. Short-term borrowing was refinanced on a long-term basis at lower interest rates.
P. Short-term borrowing was refinanced on a long-term basis at higher interest rates.

Auditor's observed changes	(A)	(B)	(C)	(D)	(E)	(F)	(G)	(H)	(I)	(J)	(K)	(L)	(M)	(N)	(O)	(P)
1. Inventory turnover increased substantially from the prior year. (Select 4 explanations)	O	O	O	O	O	O	O	O	O	O	O	O	O	O	O	O
2. Accounts receivable turnover decreased substantially from the prior year. (Select 3 explanations)	O	O	O	O	O	O	O	O	O	O	O	O	O	O	O	O

3. Allowance for doubtful accounts increased from the prior year, but allowance for doubtful accounts as a percentage of accounts receivable decreased from the prior year. (Select 3 explanations)

    O O O O O O O O O O O O O O O O

4. Long-term debt increased from the prior year, but interest expense increased a larger-than-proportionate amount than long-term debt. (Select 1 explanation)

    O O O O O O O O O O O O O O O O

5. Operating income increased from the prior year although the entity was less profitable than in the prior year. (Select 2 explanations)

    O O O O O O O O O O O O O O O O

6. Gross margin percentage was unchanged from the prior year although gross margin increased from the prior year. (Select 1 explanation)

    O O O O O O O O O O O O O O O O

Task-Based Simulation 9

Assertions and Audit Procedures		
	Authoritative Literature	**Help**

You are a staff auditor with Williams and Co. CPAs. Bill Jones, a new hire, has come to you with questions concerning "assertions" and "audit procedures." For **1.** through **6.** match each assertion with the statement that most closely approximates its meaning. Each statement may be used only once.

Statement

A. There is such an asset

B. The company legally owns the assets

C. All assets have been recorded

D. Transactions are recorded in the correct accounting period

E. Assets are recorded at proper amounts

F. Assets are properly classified

Assertion	(A)	(B)	(C)	(D)	(E)	(F)
1. Completeness	O	O	O	O	O	O
2. Cutoff	O	O	O	O	O	O
3. Existence and occurrence	O	O	O	O	O	O
4. Presentation and disclosure	O	O	O	O	O	O
5. Rights and obligations	O	O	O	O	O	O
6. Valuation	O	O	O	O	O	O

Auditors perform audit procedures to obtain audit evidence that will allow them to draw reasonable conclusions as to whether the client's financial statements follow generally accepted accounting principles. Match each audit procedure with its type. Each type of audit procedure is used, one of them twice.

Type of audit procedure

A. Analytical procedures

B. Tests of controls

C. Risk assessment procedures (other than analytical procedures)

D. Test of details of account balances, transactions, or disclosures

Audit procedures	(A)	(B)	(C)	(D)
1. Prepare a flowchart of internal control over sales.	O	O	O	O
2. Calculate the ratio of bad debt expense to credit sales.	O	O	O	O
3. Determine whether disbursements are properly approved.	O	O	O	O
4. Confirm accounts receivable.	O	O	O	O
5. Compare current financial information with comparable prior periods.	O	O	O	O

Task-Based Simulation 10

Audit Risk and Its Components		
	Authoritative Literature	Help

You recently graduated from college and joined a CPA firm as a junior assistant. You have been assigned to audit Wiglo, Inc. At lunch one of Wiglo's accountants said to you that he is having some trouble with basic audit concepts, and this bothers him since he thinks he may want to take the CPA exam at some point in the future. He has the following questions for you to which you should reply with a "yes" if it is correct, and a "no" if it is incorrect.

	Yes	No
1. Am I right that the risk of material misstatement is composed of the three components of audit risk?	O	O
2. Is inherent risk the possibility of material misstatement before considering the client's internal control?	O	O
3. In our company I think our control risk is lower this year than it was last year; does that mean that there is an increase in the risk of material misstatement?	O	O
4. Is it right to say that there would be no detection risk if we didn't have an audit?	O	O
5. Auditors simply assess detection risk rather than restrict it, right?	O	O
6. Am I right that absent any other changes, an increase in the risk of material misstatement results in an increase in audit risk?	O	O
7. Does the term "audit risk" refer to the possibility that the auditors may unknowingly fail to appropriately modify their opinion on financial statements that are materially or immaterially misstated?	O	O
8. Do both inherent risk and control risk exist independently of the audit of financial statements?	O	O

Task-Based Simulation 11

Research: Supervision		
	Authoritative Literature	Help

You graduated from college recently and joined a CPA firm as an assistant. You have been assigned to the audit of PJ Wholesale, Inc. The CEO of the nonpublic company cannot understand why a supervisor from your firm needs to review your audit work, given that you have a formal accounting education and took auditing courses in college.

Title choices
A. AU-C
B. PCAOB
C. AT
D. AR
E. ET
F. BL
G. CS
H. QC

(A) (B) (C) (D) (E) (F) (G) (H)

1. ·Which title of the Professional Standards addresses this issue and will be helpful in responding to the CEO?   ○ ○ ○ ○ ○ ○ ○ ○

2. Enter the exact section and paragraph(s) with helpful information.

Task-Based Simulation 12

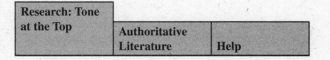

Research: Tone at the Top | Authoritative Literature | Help

Bill Jensen, CPA, has just become partner of Wigg & Co. CPAs. He is concerned that the "tone at the top" of the firm could use some improvement in the messages it sends to employees concerning the firm's culture. He has asked you to find any professional standards that address the need for *a CPA firm* to have a proper tone at the top.

Title choices

A.   AU-C
B.   PCAOB
C.   AT
D.   AR
E.   ET
F.   BL
G.   CS
H.   QC

(A) (B) (C) (D) (E) (F) (G) (H)

1. Which title of the Professional Standards addresses this issue and will be helpful in responding to the partner?   ○ ○ ○ ○ ○ ○ ○ ○

2. Enter the exact section and paragraphs with helpful information.

Task-Based Simulation 13

Effects on Audit Risk Components | Authoritative Literature | Help

Bestwood Furniture, Inc., a private company that produces wood furniture, is undergoing a year 2 audit. The situations in the table below describe changes Bestwood made during year 2 that may or may not contribute to audit risk. For each situation, select from the list provided the impact, if any, that the situation has on a specific component of audit risk for the year 2 audit. A selection may be used once, more than once, or not at all.

Impact on component of audit risk

A.   Decreases control risk
B.   Decreases detection risk
C.   Decreases inherent risk
D.   Increases control risk
E.   Increases detection risk
F.   Increases inherent risk
G.   No impact on audit risk

Situation	(A)	(B)	(C)	(D)	(E)	(F)	(G)
1. During year 2, the company instituted a new procedure whereby the internal audit department distributes payroll checks to employees for selected payroll cycles.	O	O	O	O	O	O	O
2. During year 2, the company centralized authority for changes in accounting software programs by placing sole responsibility for such changes with the programmer who makes the changes, replacing a system in which an individual other than the programmer reviews such changes.	O	O	O	O	O	O	O
3. Early in year 2, the company extended its existing warranty program on certain of its major products in an effort to increase revenue.	O	O	O	O	O	O	O

Task-Based Simulation 14

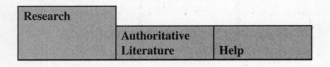

Quality Control Standards

Assume that you are employed by Wilson & Wilson CPAs. One of the partners has asked you to research the professional standards for the reference that identifies the requirements for documentation of a firm's quality control policies and procedures.

Title choices

A. AU-C
B. PCAOB
C. AT
D. AR
E. ET
F. BL
G. CS
H. QC

	(A)	(B)	(C)	(D)	(E)	(F)	(G)	(H)
1. Which title of the Professional Standards addresses this issue and will be helpful in responding to the partner?	O	O	O	O	O	O	O	O

2. Enter the exact section and paragraphs with helpful information.

Simulation Solutions

Task-Based Simulation 1

Audit Risk Application		
	Authoritative Literature	Help

Factor	Increased audit risk	Decreased audit risk	Fraud risk factor
1. Branch management authority	●	○	●
2. Government regulation	○	●	○
3. Company profitability	○	●	○
4. Demand for product	○	●	○
5. Interest rates	●	○	○
6. Availability of mortgage funds	○	●	○
7. Involvement of principal shareholder in management	○	●	○
8. Branch manager compensation	●	○	●
9. Internal audit reporting relationship	○	●	○
10. Accounting department turnover	○	●	○
11. Continuing audit relationship	○	●	○
12. Internal controls over accounting estimates	●	○	●
13. Response to proposed accounting adjustments	○	●	○
14. New unprofitable branch	●	○	●
15. New computer system	●	○	○

Task-Based Simulation 2

Risk of Material Misstatement		
	Authoritative Literature	Help

Risk	High risk item
1. Computer fraud risk	○
2. Risk related to management override of internal control	●
3. Fraud by branch management	●
4. Fraud by accounting personnel	○
5. Misstatement of accounting estimates	●
6. Fraud by loan processing clerks	○
7. Fraud by internal auditors	○
8. The risk of fraudulent misstatement of revenues	●

Task-Based Simulation 3

Research Topics
| Authoritative Literature | Help |

	(A)	(B)	(C)	(D)	(E)	(F)	(G)	(H)	(I)
Transactions									
1. Possible risk factors related to misappropriation of assets.	○	○	○	●	○	○	○	○	○
2. The relationship between materiality used for planning versus evaluation purposes.	○	●	○	○	○	○	○	○	○
3. Hanmei Corp. has transactions with the corporation president's brother.	○	○	○	○	○	○	○	○	●
4. Comparing a client's unaudited results for the year with last year's audited results.	●	○	○	○	○	○	○	○	○
5. Auditing and reporting guidance on the possible need to reaudit previous year results due to the disbanding of the firm that performed last year's audit.	○	○	●	○	○	○	○	○	○
6. Requirements relating to identifying violations of occupational safety and health regulations.	○	○	○	○	○	●	○	○	○
7. Audit report considerations when audit of a subsidiary of the client will be performed by Williams & Co., CPAs.	○	○	○	○	○	○	○	●	○
8. The need to "brainstorm" among audit team members about how accounts could be intentionally misstated.	○	○	○	●	○	○	○	○	○
9. Details on considering design effectiveness of controls.	○	○	○	○	●	○	○	○	○
10. The importance of considering the possibility of overstated revenues (for example, through premature revenue recognition).	○	○	○	●	○	○	○	○	○

Task-Based Simulation 4

Risk Analysis
| Authoritative Literature | Help |

	(A)	(B)	(C)	(D)
1. Of the following, which is likely to be one of DietWeb's major risks of doing business on the Internet in the future?	●	○	○	○
2. Which of the following is likely to be the most significant business risk for DietWeb?	○	○	●	○
3. Which of the following is most accurate concerning DietWeb's audit committee?	○	○	●	○
4. Which of the following indicates an increased risk of misstatement due to fraud?	●	○	○	○
5. Which of the following is the most significant risk facing DietWeb that might cause it to not be able to continue increasing sales?	○	●	○	○

Explanations

1. (A) The requirement is to identify DietWeb's major listed risk of doing business on the Internet. Answer (A) is correct because DietWeb must carefully maintain the privacy of their customers' information—both due to law and due to DietWeb's assurance provided to its customers. Answer (B) is incorrect because there are no major Federal Communications Commission Internet use fees. Answer (C) is incorrect because the case indicates no particular problem in providing 24/7/365 support. Answer (D) is incorrect because the Internet is able to reach customers beyond the United States.

2. (C) The requirement is to identify the most significant business risk listed for DietWeb. Answer (C) is correct because barriers to entrance on the Internet are ordinarily not high. Another organization might develop similar (or more accepted) software, and/or charge lower prices than those charged by DietWeb. Answer (A) is incorrect because internal control limitations need not necessarily be a major problem, and because internal control relates to control risk more directly than to the company's business risk. Answer (B) is incorrect because while Internet instability may cause difficulties, few would consider it as significant a problem as new competitors. Answer (D) is incorrect because determining appropriate year-end cutoffs is not likely to create major difficulties.

3. (C) The requirement is to identify the most accurate statement concerning DietWeb's audit committee. Answer (C) is correct because the audit committee has no members who are independent of management. Answer (A) is incorrect because the audit committee has no members who are independent of management. Answer (A) is incorrect because the company founders are not independent. Answer (B) is incorrect because Mr. Readings' chairmanship of the audit committee is likely to result in a weak, not a strong audit committee. Answer (D) is incorrect because the size of the board of directors virtually always exceeds that of the audit committee—is not equal to or less than in size.

4. (A) The requirement is to identify a factor that indicates an increased risk of misstatement due to fraud. Answer (A) is correct because the simulation provides no explanation of the nature of the disagreement that led to Mr. Williamson's resignation from an apparently very desirable job. Answer (B) is incorrect because many small companies are dominated by company founders and those companies do not generally misstate earnings due to fraud. Answer (C) is incorrect because the issuance of debt need not indicate fraud. Answer (D) is incorrect because competition itself need not lead to an increased risk of misstatement due to fraud.

5. (B) The requirement is to identify the most significant risk facing DietWeb that might cause it not to be able to continue increasing sales. Answer (B) is correct because the industry information makes clear that the market changes rapidly—only companies that can respond in a timely basis are likely to be able to maintain and improve sales. Answers (A) and (C) are incorrect because there is no indication that the United States will face a decreasing market for dietary products or that the population is decreasing. Answer (D) is incorrect because at this point there is no indication of obsolescence of the Internet.

Task-Based Simulation 5

Financial Statement Analysis		
	Authoritative Literature	Help

	(A)	(B)	(C)	(D)
1. The most likely misstatement in the financial statements is	○	○	●	○
2. Which of the following is the most unexpected change on the balance sheet, if one assumes the revenue increase in 20X8 is correct?	●	○	○	○
3. Which of the following is most likely to lead the auditors to question whether DietWeb has the ability to continue as a going concern?	●	○	○	○
4. Which of the following classifications is likely to be incorrect?	○	●	○	○
5. Which of the following changes that have been recorded seems most unexpected?	●	○	○	○

Explanations

1. (C) The requirement is to identify a likely misstatement in the financial statements. Answer (C) is correct because common stock issued should be treated under financing rather than operations. Answer (A) is incorrect because an increase in cash may well occur—even during a year in which the company encounters a loss. Answer (B) is incorrect because there is no indication that the impairment expense is inappropriate. Answer (D) is incorrect because previous years' pattern of income and losses may create a situation in which a net income tax benefit occurs.

2. (A) The requirement is to identify, of the balance sheet changes listed, the most unexpected one. Answer (A) is unexpected in that prepaid advertising expenses decreased by more than ninety percent—at a time when the company increased its sales and marketing expenses so significantly. Answer (B) is incorrect because the relatively small increase in accounts payable may be expected given the increase in revenues. Answer (C) is incorrect because one would expect such an increase in deferred revenues as revenues increase. Answer (D) is incorrect since the company simply issued more stock—as indicated in the company profile.

3. (A) The requirement is to identify the factor that might lead the auditors to question whether DietWeb has the ability to continue as a going concern. Answer (A) is correct because the current net loss may raise a question as to future profitability. Answer (B) is incorrect because there was an increase in cash, not a decrease. Answer (C) is incorrect because fixed assets decreased rather than increased during 20X8. Answer (D) is incorrect because Mr. Reading's serving as CEO indicates no particular problem.

4. (B) The requirement is to identify an incorrect classification in the financial statements. Answer (B) is correct because accrued liabilities are in general current, not noncurrent, liabilities. Answer (A) is incorrect because prepaid expenses are ordinarily assets. Answer (C) is incorrect because one would expect the deferred tax liability to have a positive balance. Answer D is incorrect because the retained earnings negative balance may be explained by early year losses.

5. (A) The requirement is to identify the most unexpected change. Answer (A) is most unexpected because the expanded scale of operations would lead one to expect an increase in fixed assets, not a decrease. Answer (B) is incorrect because small changes in prepaid expense and other current assets are expected. Answer (C) is incorrect because it is not surprising that cash may increase when there is a net loss—particularly in a year when common stock has been issued. Answer (C) is incorrect because an increase in accrued liabilities is consistent with an increase in the scale of operations as indicated by a large increase in sales.

Task-Based Simulation 6

Risk of Material Misstatement Analysis		
	Authoritative Literature	Help

AU-C 200, 240, and 320 all require that auditors consider factors influencing the risk of material misstatement and that the risk of material misstatement be considered during the planning phase of an audit engagement.

1. (D) Since TWD returned to profitable operation, its healthier financial condition leads to a decrease in the risk of material misstatement.

2. (I) The risk of material misstatement increases when management is dominated by a single person. Since Mead controls the Board of Directors, is a majority stockholder, and is the CEO, it would appear that Mead dominates management.

3. (I) The risk of material misstatement increases when the internal auditor reports to top management rather than to the audit committee because it is less likely that the internal auditor will be able to objectively perform the function.

4. (I) The risk of material misstatement increases when the key management positions (particularly senior accounting personnel) encounter turnover.

5. (D) The loan officer's continual monitoring of TWD decreases the risk of material misstatement.

6. (N) Timing of payroll cycles would normally have no impact on the risk of material misstatement.

7. (I) A strong financial presence or ability to dominate a certain industry sector that allows a company to dictate terms or conditions to suppliers or customers may result in inappropriate or non-arm's-length transactions.

8. (I) A change to generally accepted accounting principles will increase the risk of material misstatement because the change in basis requires management to prepare a number of entries that have not been made in the past; these entries may be made improperly. Also, difficulties in determining beginning accrual basis balances increases the risk of misstatement.

9. (I) The sale of one-half of the company's controlling interest in United Equipment Leasing is an entry that is out of the ordinary course of business, and accordingly, increases the risk of material misstatement.

10. (D) Litigation results in contentious and difficult accounting valuation issues because an accountant must attempt to determine the likelihood of loss and the amount.

11. (I) The risk of material misstatement increases when significant related-party transactions occur and management has an aggressive attitude towards reporting of the transactions.

12. (I) The risk of material misstatement increases in situations where there are unusual and difficult accounting issues present. It would appear that the barter transaction with a below-market purchase would be considered an unusual transaction.

13. (N) The amount of insurance coverage would have little impact on the risk of material misstatement.

14. (I) The risk of material misstatement increases as it appears that management has taken an aggressive attitude toward reporting this transaction. In addition, this appears to be an unusual and difficult accounting issue involving revenue recognition.

15. (I) Experience has shown that a number of entities have intentionally misstated reported financial condition and operating results in situations in which a public (or private) placement of securities is planned. Accordingly, an initial public offering of stock increases the risk of material misstatement.

Task-Based Simulation 7

Identifying Risks		
	Authoritative Literature	Help

(A) (B) (C) (D)

1. Which of the following identifies an aspect of the company's business model, strategies, and/or business environment that is most likely to increase Toastco's inherent risk? ○ ○ ● ○

2. Which of the following identifies a situation most likely to increase the risk of misstatement arising from fraudulent financial reporting? ○ ● ○ ○

3. Which of the following identifies an aspect of the company's business model, strategies, and/or business environment that is most likely to increase the risk of misstatement arising from fraudulent financial reporting? ○ ● ○ ○

Explanations

1. **(C)** The requirement is to identify the factor that is most likely to increase Toastco's inherent risk. Answer (C) is correct because Toastco relies significantly upon the toaster, and since obsolescence of that product could cause very major difficulties for the company. Answer (A) is incorrect because the manufacturing continues to be in Asia and there is no indication of a related problem. Answer (B) is incorrect because the growth of 3%, while high, does not increase inherent risk. Answer (D) is incorrect because overstated accounts receivable due to internal control deficiencies relates to control risk, not inherent risk.

2. **(B)** The requirement is to determine the aspect of Toastco that is most likely to increase the risk of misstatement arising from fraudulent financial reporting. Answer (B) is correct because the president, Bill Williams, felt pressure to meet the earnings per share number he had promised the bank due to weak second and third quarters. Therefore the high earnings in the fourth quarter represent a risk. Answer (A) is incorrect because the stability of the industry presents no particular risk. Answer (C) is incorrect because Toastco's market share by itself does not seem to pose a risk of misstatement. Answer (D) is incorrect because while Toastco would certainly be in a safer position with more profitable products, this is not as significant a fraud risk as is the pressure to achieve the earnings per share target.

3. **(B)** The requirement is to determine an aspect of a company that is most likely to increase the risk of misstatement arising from fraudulent financial reporting. Answer (B) is correct because the president's investment in Toastco creates a situation in which losses in value of the company will profoundly affect him—particularly given his desire to take the company public. Answer (A) is incorrect because selling more than one type of product may or may not affect the risk of misstatement. Answer (C) is incorrect because it is desirable to have the audit committee composed entirely of independent directors. Answer (D) is incorrect because the fact that this is a continuing engagement has no direct tie to the risk of misstatement.

Ratio Analysis

(A) (B) (C) (D) (E) (F) (G)

1. An audit finding most consistent with the change in the gross margin percentage ● ○ ○ ○ ○ ○ ○

2. An audit finding most consistent with the change in the current ratio ○ ○ ○ ○ ○ ○ ●

Explanations

1. **(A)** The requirement is to identify an audit finding most consistent with a decrease in the gross margin percentage—gross margin/sales. Answer (A) is correct because the inability to pass on increases in costs will decrease the gross margin because cost of goods sold as a percentage of sales will increase.

2. **(G)** The requirement is to identify an audit finding that is consistent with a decrease in the current ratio—current assets/current liabilities. Answer (G) is correct because the long-term debt becoming current increases the denominator of the current ratio, which decreases the ratio.

	(H)	(I)	(J)	(K)	(L)	(M)
3. An audit finding consistent with the change in inventory turnover for Toastco	○	○	○	●	○	○
4. An audit finding consistent with the change in the return on equity	○	○	●	○	○	○

Explanations

3. (K) The requirement is to identify the finding that is consistent with an increase in the inventory turnover ratio— cost of goods sold/inventory. Answer (D) is correct because a larger percentage of sales in the last month is likely to result in a lower ending inventory, thus increasing the inventory turnover ratio since the denominator of the fraction becomes smaller.

4. (J) The requirement is to identify the reply that is consistent with a decrease in the return on equity ratio—net income/shareholders' equity. Answer (C) is correct because retention of profits increases the shareholders' equity, thereby decreasing the ratio.

Task-Based Simulation 8

Observed Ratio Changes		
	Authoritative Literature	Help

Auditor's observed changes	(A)	(B)	(C)	(D)	(E)	(F)	(G)	(H)	(I)	(J)	(K)	(L)	(M)	(N)	(O)	(P)
1. Inventory turnover increased substantially from the prior year. (Select 4 explanations)	●	●	○	●	●	○	○	○	○	○	○	○	○	○	○	○
2. Accounts receivable turnover decreased substantially from the prior year. (Select 3 explanations)	●	●	○	○	○	●	○	○	○	○	○	○	○	○	○	○
3. Allowance for doubtful accounts increased from the prior year, but allowance for doubtful accounts as a percentage of accounts receivable decreased from the prior year. (Select 3 explanations)	●	●	○	○	●	○	○	○	○	○	○	○	○	○	○	○
4. Long-term debt increased from the prior year, but interest expense increased a larger-than-proportionate amount than long-term debt. (Select 1 explanation)	○	○	○	○	○	○	○	○	○	○	○	○	○	○	○	●
5. Operating income increased from the prior year although the entity was less profitable than in the prior year. (Select 2 explanations)	○	○	○	○	○	○	○	○	○	○	○	●	○	○	○	●
6. Gross margin percentage was unchanged from the prior year although gross margin increased from the prior year. (Select 1 explanation)	○	○	○	○	○	○	○	●	○	○	○	○	○	○	○	○

Explanations

1. (A, B, D, E,) The requirement is to identify three explanations for an increase in the inventory turnover when compared to the prior year. The inventory turnover is calculated by dividing the cost of goods sold by the inventory. An increase may occur either through (1) an overstatement of the cost of goods sold (the numerator), (2) an understatement of inventory (the denominator), or (3) a combination of changes. Answer (A) is correct because the recording of the consignment shipment as a sale will overstate cost of goods sold and understate the ending inventory. Answer (B) is correct because not recording the credit memos will result in understatement of inventory. Answer (D) is correct because the understatement of purchases of inventory will understate the ending inventory. Answer (E) is correct because a larger percentage of sales in the last month of the year is likely to result in a lower ending inventory.

Answer (C) is incorrect because overstating the year-end purchases will result in overstatement of inventory, and thereby decrease the inventory turnover. Answers (F) through (J) are all incorrect because such changes in sales will not affect the inventory turnover ratio. Answers (K) through (P) are all incorrect because the interest expense, income tax rate, and the short-term borrowing do not affect the inventory turnover. Note that this question relies upon an unstated assumption that the year-end inventory is not adjusted to a year-end physical count.

2.   **(A, B, E)**   The requirement is to identify three explanations for a decrease in the accounts receivable turnover when compared to the prior year. The accounts receivable turnover is calculated by dividing sales by accounts receivable. A decrease may occur through (1) an understatement of sales (the numerator), (2) an overstatement of accounts receivable (the denominator), or (3) a combination of misstatements of sales and accounts receivable that decrease the ratio. Answer (A) is correct because recording the consignment as sales overstates both sales and accounts receivable by an identical amount, thus decreasing the ratio; the decrease is due to the entry debiting accounts receivable and crediting sales for the same amount. Answer (B) is correct because not recording the credit memo overstates both sales and accounts receivable by an identical amount, thus decreasing the ratio; this identical amount of decrease is due to the lack of a debit to sales returns and allowances and a credit to accounts receivable. Note that answers (A) and (B) are correct in any situation in which the ratio is greater than 1.0; when the ratio is less than 1.0 they result in an increase in the ratio. Answer (E) is correct because while the sales for the year remain at the expected level, accounts receivable at year-end will be at a higher than average level due to the year-end sales.

Answers (C) and (D) are incorrect because the level of inventory does not affect the ratio. Answers (F) and (G) are incorrect because a larger, not a smaller or the same, percentage of sales near year-end decreases the ratio. Answers (H), (I) and (J) are incorrect because one would expect accounts receivable to increase at the same rate as the increase in sales. Answers (K) through (P) are all incorrect because interest expense, income tax rate, and the short-term borrowing do not affect the accounts receivable turnover.

3.   **(A, B, E)**   The requirement is to identify three explanations for an increase in the allowance for doubtful accounts, but a decrease in the allowance for doubtful accounts as a percentage of accounts receivable. The allowance for doubtful accounts as a percentage of accounts receivable is calculated by dividing the allowance for doubtful accounts by accounts receivable. The percentage may decrease due to (1) a decrease in the allowance for doubtful accounts, (2) an increase in the accounts receivable, or (3) a combination of misstatements that decrease the ratio; here, however, we are told that reason (1), a decrease in the allowance, has not occurred. Answer (A) is correct because recording the consignment as a sale results in an increase in accounts receivable which decreases the ratio. Answer (B) is correct because not recording the credit memos overstates accounts receivable, thereby decreasing the ratio. Answer (E) is correct because the larger percentage of sales occurring during the last month of the year results in accounts receivable at year-end that will be at a higher than average level due to the year-end sales.

Answers (C) and (D) are incorrect because the level of inventory does not affect the ratio. Answers (F) and (G) are incorrect because a larger, not a smaller or the same, percentage of sales near year-end decreases the ratio. Answers (H), (I), and (J) are incorrect because one would expect accounts receivable and the allowance for doubtful accounts to increase at approximately the same rate as the increase in sales. Answers (K) through (P) are all incorrect because interest expense, income tax rate, and the short-term borrowing do not affect the accounts receivable turnover.

4.   **(P)**   The requirement is to identify a reason why long-term debt increased, but interest expense increased a larger-than-proportionate amount than long-term debt. Answer (P) is correct because the higher interest rates on long-term debt will result in higher interest expense. Answers (A) through (M) are all incorrect because they relate neither to long-term debt nor interest expense. Answers (N) and (O) are incorrect because refinancing at the same or a lower interest rate will result in smaller-than-proportionate amounts of interest expense.

5.   **(L, P)**   The requirement is to identify two reasons why operating income might increase, yet the company would be less profitable. Since operating income increased and net income decreased, the explanation must be items that are listed on the income statement between operating income and net income—interest expense and federal income taxes. The net of these two expenses must have increased to result in a situation in which the entity was less profitable. Answer (L) is correct because an increase in the effective income tax rate could decrease the profit when compared to the prior year. Answer (P) is correct because higher interest rates decrease profits. Answers (A) through (J) are all incorrect because they pertain to details of operating income. Answers (K) and (M) are incorrect because a decrease in interest expense or the income tax rate would increase net income. Answer (N) is incorrect because refinancing at the same rate will not affect net income. Answer (O) is incorrect because refinancing at a lower interest rate will increase profits.

6.   **(H)**   The requirement is to identify one reason why the gross margin percentage may remain unchanged, despite an increase in gross margin from the prior year. Answer (H) is correct because when sales increase at the same percentage as cost of goods sold, the gross margin percentage remains unchanged, and yet the increased sales will result in an increase in the gross margin. Answers (A) through (D) are all incorrect because they will result in a change in the gross margin percentage. Answers (E), (F), and (G) are all incorrect because no increase in sales is indicated and no information on the gross margin is provided. Answers (I) and (J) are incorrect because they suggest a decrease and an increase in the gross margin, respectively. Answers (K) through (P) are all incorrect because interest expense, income tax rate, and debt do not affect gross margin.

Task-Based Simulation 9

Assertions and Audit Procedures	Authoritative Literature	Help

Assertion	(A)	(B)	(C)	(D)	(E)	(F)
1. Completeness	○	○	○	○	○	○
2. Cutoff	○	○	○	●	○	○
3. Existence and occurrence	●	○	○	○	○	○
4. Presentation and disclosure	○	○	○	○	○	●
5. Rights and obligations	○	●	○	○	○	○
6. Valuation	○	○	○	○	●	○

Audit procedures	(A)	(B)	(C)	(D)
1. Prepare a flowchart of internal control over sales.	○	○	●	○
2. Calculate the ratio of bad debt expense to credit sales.	●	○	○	○
3. Determine whether disbursements are properly approved.	○	●	○	○
4. Confirm accounts receivable.	○	○	○	●
5. Compare current financial information with comparable prior periods.	●	○	○	○

Task-Based Simulation 10

Audit Risk and Its Components	Authoritative Literature	Help

1. **(No)** The risk of material misstatement is composed of inherent risk and detection risk.

2. **(Yes)**

3. **(No)** A decrease in control risk, absent other changes, results in a decrease in the risk of material misstatement.

4. **(Yes)** Detection risk is a function of the audit and its procedures. If there is no audit there is no measure of detection risk.

5. **(No)** This is backwards. Auditors restrict detection risk through the performance of more substantive procedures. Auditors assess inherent risk and control risk.

6. **(Yes)**

7. **(No)** The error is the "or immaterially." Audit risk deals with material misstatements.

8. **(Yes)**

Task-Based Simulation 11

Research: Supervision	Authoritative Literature	Help

	(A)	(B)	(C)	(D)	(E)	(F)	(G)	(H)
1. Which title of the Professional Standards addresses this issue and will be helpful in responding to the CEO?	●	○	○	○	○	○	○	○

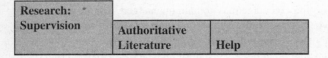

2. Enter the exact section and paragraph with helpful information

210	03

Task-Based Simulation 12

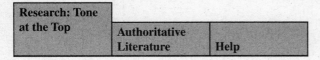

1. Which title of the Professional Standards addresses this issue and will be helpful in responding to the partner?

2. Enter the exact section and paragraphs with helpful information.

(A) (B) (C) (D) (E) (F) (G) (H)
○ ○ ○ ○ ○ ○ ○ ●

10	15–18

Task-Based Simulation 13

Effects on Audit Risk Components		
	Authoritative Literature	Help

Situation

(A) (B) (C) (D) (E) (F) (G)

1. During year 2, the company instituted a new procedure whereby the internal audit department distributes payroll checks to employees for selected payroll cycles.

● ○ ○ ○ ○ ○ ○

2. In year 2, the auditor noted that the company's newly hired purchasing agent was not obtaining competitive bids for all major purchase requisitions.

○ ○ ○ ● ○ ○ ○

3. Early in year 2, the company extended its existing warranty program on certain of its major products in an effort to increase revenue.

○ ○ ○ ○ ○ ● ○

Task-Based Simulation 14

Research		
	Authoritative Literature	Help

(A) (B) (C) (D) (E) (F) (G) (H)

1. Which title of the Professional Standards addresses this issue and will be helpful in responding to the partner?

2. Enter the exact section and paragraph(s) with helpful information.

○ ○ ○ ○ ○ ○ ○ ●

220	17, A12–A18

Module 3: Understanding Internal Control and Assessing Control Risk

Overview

AU-C 315 and AU-C 330 provide auditors with information in which a client's internal control affects financial statement audits. The guidance first is about obtaining an understanding of the entity including its internal control to help auditors to assess the risk of material misstatement and to design the nature, timing and extent of further audit procedures—this material is in Sections C through E of the outline of AU-C 315.

Next, AU-C 330 provides auditors with guidance on the nature of further audit procedures as they relate to internal control (i.e., tests of controls).

The following "Diagram of an Audit," originally presented in the auditing overview section, shows the relationship of internal control to an audit:

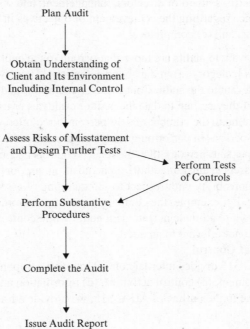

Diagram of an Audit

Plan Audit

↓

Obtain Understanding of Client and Its Environment Including Internal Control

↓

Assess Risks of Misstatement and Design Further Tests → Perform Tests of Controls

↓

Perform Substantive Procedures

↓

Complete the Audit

↓

Issue Audit Report

This module covers obtaining an understanding of internal control and tests of controls. It also develops the relationships among internal control and further audit tests—tests of controls, and substantive tests. Every CPA examination includes numerous questions on internal control and its relationship to various portions of the audit. Multiple-choice questions frequently require specification of a control that would, if present and operating properly, detect a stated weakness or error. Objective questions also have appeared regarding organization responsibility (e.g., who should distribute payroll checks?). A simulation may include a requirement to complete a flowchart of a transaction cycle, evaluate strengths and weaknesses of a system, and/or determine appropriate tests of controls and substantive tests.

In Section A of this module we begin with the key concepts related to an entity's internal control. In Section B we review the approach suggested by the professional standards for considering internal control in a financial statement audit.

Information on audits of internal control is presented in Section C. The Section D discussion is meant to provide you with information that will help you to respond to "applied type" questions that involve actual accounting cycles. Section E involves communications with audit committees, the effects of an internal audit function on an audit, and reports on the processing of transactions by service organizations.

The following sections of Statements of Auditing Standards pertain to internal control and are discussed in this module.

AU-C 260	The Auditor's Communication with Those Charged with Governance
265	Communication of Internal Control Related Matters Noted in an Audit
315	Understanding the Entity and Its Environment and Assessing the Risks of Material Misstatement
330	Performing Audit Procedures in Response to Assessed Risks and Evaluating the Audit Evidence Obtained
402	Reports on the Processing of Transactions by Service Organizations
610	The Auditor's Consideration of the Internal Audit Function in an Audit of Financial Statements
AT 501	An Examination of an Entity's Internal Control over Financial Reporting That Is Integrated with an Audit of Its Financial Statements

A. The Nature of Internal Control

AU-C 315 and AU-C 330 present information on (1) the nature of internal control and (2) the auditor's consideration of internal control. In this section we begin by discussing material related to the first area—the nature of internal control. Finally, we present several important, related topics.

1. Definition of Internal Control

AU-C 315 uses the concepts included in the 1992 *Internal Control—Integrated Framework*, published by the Committee of Sponsoring Organizations of the Treadway Commission (the COSO Commission). Although the framework was updated in 2013, the revisions have at this point not resulted in changes to either AICPA or PCAOB standards. In the following sections we include the COSO concepts currently included in the auditing standards. Internal control is defined by COSO as

> a process. effected by an entity's board of directors, management, and other personnel, designed to provide reasonable assurance regarding the achievement of objectives in the following categories: (a) reporting, (b) operations, and (c) compliance.

The controls generally most relevant to audits are those that pertain to the entity's objective of preparing financial statements for external purposes [category (a) in the above definition]. Thus, typically, controls over **financial reporting** are relevant to the audit. Controls over operations and compliance objectives [categories (b) and (c) above] may be relevant if they pertain to data the auditor evaluates or uses in applying auditing procedures. For example, while controls relating to the number of salespersons hired often would not be relevant to the audit, if the auditor uses the number of salespersons in performing analytical procedures to help determine the reasonableness of sales (e.g., by calculating sales per salesperson), then the related controls become relevant.

While the safeguarding of assets against unauthorized acquisition, use, or disposition is an essential part of internal control, the auditor's responsibility with respect to safeguarding of assets is limited to those relevant to the reliability of financial reporting. For example, the company's use of passwords for limiting access to accounts receivable data files may be relevant to a financial statement audit, while controls to prevent the excess use of materials in production generally are not relevant to an audit.

2. Major Components of Internal Control

You need to know that AU-C 315 divides internal control into five components, and the nature of each—(a) control environment, (b) risk assessment, (c) control activities, (d) information and communication, and (e) monitoring. Although you should study these in the outline of AU-C 315, we provide a brief summary of each of them at this point.

a. **Control environment.** The control environment factors set the tone of an organization, influencing the control consciousness of its people. The seven control environment factors, which you may remember using the mnemonic IC HAMBO, are

I—Integrity and ethical values
C—Commitment to competence
H—Human resource policies and practices
A—Assignment of authority and responsibility
M—Management's philosophy and operating style
B—Board of directors or audit committee participation
O—Organizational structure

b. **Risk assessment.** For financial reporting purposes an entity's risk assessment is its identification, analysis, and management of risks relevant to the preparation of financial statements following GAAP (or some other comprehensive basis). The following are considered risks that may affect an entity's ability to properly record, process, summarize, and report financial data:

(1) Changes in the operating environment (e.g., increased competition)
(2) New personnel
(3) New information systems
(4) Rapid growth
(5) New technology
(6) New lines, products, or activities
(7) Corporate restructuring
(8) Foreign operations
(9) Accounting pronouncements

c. **Control activities.** The third component of internal control is composed of the various policies and procedures that help ensure that necessary actions are taken to address risks to achieving the entity's objectives. Those policies and procedures include

P—Performance reviews (reviews of actual performance against budgets, forecasts, one another, etc.)
I—Information processing (controls that check accuracy, completeness, and authorization of transactions)
P—Physical controls (activities that assure the physical security of assets and records)
S—Segregation of duties (separate authorization, recordkeeping, and custody)

d. **Information and communication.** The fourth component includes the accounting system, consisting of the methods and records established to **record, process, summarize, and report** entity transactions and to maintain accountability of the related assets and liabilities. To be effective, the information and communication system should accomplish the following goals for transactions:

(1) Identify and record all valid transactions
(2) Describe on a timely basis
(3) Measure the value properly
(4) Record in the proper time period
(5) Properly present and disclose
(6) Communicate responsibilities to employees

e. **Monitoring.** Monitoring assesses the quality of internal control performance over time. Monitoring activities may be **ongoing, separate evaluations**, or a **combination** thereof. Ongoing monitoring activities are often designed into recurring activities such as sales and purchases. **Separate evaluations** are often performed by internal auditors or other personnel and often include communication of information about strengths and weaknesses and recommendations for improving internal control. Monitoring activities may also be performed by external parties (e.g., customers implicitly corroborate billing data by paying invoices).

The 2013 COSO *Internal Control—Integrated Framework* revision provides 17 internal control principles (summarized):

Control Environment

- Demonstrates a commitment to integrity and ethical values.
- Exercises oversight responsibility (by a board of directors that demonstrates independence from management).
- Establishes proper structures, reporting lines, authorities and responsibilities.
- Demonstrates a commitment to competence.
- Enforces accountability of individuals.

Risk Assessment

- Specifies clear objectives.
- Identifies and analyzes risks to achievement of its objectives.
- Considers the potential for fraud in assessing risks.
- Identifies and assesses changes that could affect internal control.

Control Activities

- Selects and develops appropriate control activities to mitigate risks to achievement of objectives.
- Selects and develops general control activities over technology.
- Deploys control activities that establish what is expected and place policies into action.

Information and Communication

- Obtains or generates and uses relevant information to support internal control.
- Communicates information internally to support internal control.
- Communicates information externally to support internal control.

Monitoring

- Conducts evaluations of whether components of internal control are present and functioning.
- Evaluates and communicates internal control deficiencies in a timely manner to appropriate parties.

Notice that the above principles are consistent with the nature of internal control as presented in Section A.2 above from AU-C 315.

3. **Related Topics**

   a. **Financial statement assertions.** As presented in the Engagement Planning Module, and discussed in further detail in the Responding to Risk Assessment Module, assertions are management representations that are embodied in the transaction class, account balance, and disclosure components of financial statements. For example, for account balances, the assertions include existence, rights/obligations, completeness, and valuation/allocation. The approach embodied in the auditing standards is one of suggesting that for each transaction class, account, or disclosure the auditor determines relevant assertions and then considers the related controls. A control seldom relates to all important assertions. A control over processing sales orders might, for example, be effective at determining the **existence of receivables** (e.g., there was a sale), but would not directly address receivables **valuation** (because collection may be questionable), or **completeness** (whether all receivables have been recorded).

   b. **Limitations of internal control.** As we have suggested earlier, internal control provides reasonable, but not absolute, assurance that specific entity objectives will be achieved. Even the best internal control may break down due to

   (1) Human judgment in decision making can be faulty
   (2) Breakdowns can occur because of human failures such as simple errors or mistakes
   (3) Controls, whether manual or automated, can be circumvented by collusion
   (4) Management has the ability to override internal control
   (5) Cost constraints (the cost of internal control should not exceed the expected benefits expected to be derived)
   (6) Custom, culture, and the corporate governance system may inhibit fraud, but they are not absolute deterrents

   > **NOTE:** Be familiar with these limitations.

   c. **Accounting vs. administrative control.** Previously, the AICPA Professional Standards distinguished between administrative and accounting controls, stating that auditors generally emphasize the latter. While the distinction no longer remains for purposes of the professional standards, it does remain in certain laws, such as the Foreign Corrupt Practices Act.

   d. **Foreign Corrupt Practices Act.** A law passed by Congress in 1977 with provisions

   (1) Requiring every corporation registered under the Securities Exchange Act of 1934 to maintain a system of strong internal accounting control (as defined above),
   (2) Requiring corporations [defined in (1)] to maintain accurate books and records, and

(3) Making it illegal for individuals or business entities to make payments to foreign officials to secure business.

Violations of the Act can result in fines (up to $1 million for SEC registrants and $10,000 for individuals) and imprisonment (up to five years) of the responsible individuals. Thus, strong internal accounting control is required under federal law.

e. **Committee of Sponsoring Organizations (COSO).** This committee is composed of representatives from various professional organizations, including the AICPA, the Institute of Management Accountants, the Financial Executives Institute, the Institute of Internal Auditors, and the American Accounting Association. Its mission is to provide thought leadership through the development of comprehensive frameworks and guidance on enterprise risk management, internal control and fraud deterrence designed to improve organizational performance and governance and to reduce the extent of fraud in organizations.

COSO's internal control framework is examined on both the Auditing and Business Environment and Concepts (BEC) sections of the CPA exam. Its enterprise risk management framework is included in the BEC section. Discussion of both frameworks beyond that in this module is included in BEC Module 40.

f. **Sarbanes-Oxley Act of 2002 (SOX).** As indicated in Chapter 5, the SOX created a variety of new regulations and eliminated a significant portion of the accounting profession's system of self-regulation. Three particularly relevant sections are

(1) **Section 302:** Makes officers responsible for maintaining effective internal control and requires the principal executive and financial officers to disclose all significant internal control deficiencies to the company's auditors and audit committee.

(2) **Section 404:** Requires that management acknowledge its responsibility for establishing adequate internal control over financial reporting and provide an assessment in the annual report of the effectiveness of internal control. Also requires that CPAs attest to management's report on internal control as part of the audit of the financial statements—discussed further in Section D.2 of this module.

(3) **Section 906:** Requires that management certify reports filed with the SEC (primarily annual 10-K and quarterly 10-Qs) that the reports comply with relevant securities laws and also fairly present, in all material respects, the financial condition and results of operations of the company.

NOW REVIEW MULTIPLE-CHOICE QUESTIONS 1 THROUGH 9

B. The Auditor's Consideration of Internal Control

AU-C 315 presents the auditor's consideration of internal control (this begins at Section B in the AU-C 315 outline). Recall that after planning the audit, auditors

- Obtain an understanding of the entity and its environment, including its internal control
- Assess the risks of material misstatement and design further audit procedures
- Perform further audit procedures, including tests of controls and substantive tests

Internal control is a part of each of these stages. Auditors obtain an understanding of internal control to aid them in their assessment of the risks of material misstatement and to design further audit procedures. Tests of controls, performed to determine whether controls operate effectively, are further audit procedures. While the auditor's consideration of internal control may become quite involved, we will summarize the auditor's approach using the above steps.

If the auditor is performing an audit of a public company, the approach to internal control will be somewhat different. Section C covers the auditor's approach to the audit of a public company.

The relationships among these steps are presented in the flowchart below. We now discuss them in detail.

**SUMMARY FLOWCHART OF INTERNAL CONTROL CONSIDERATION
DURING A FINANCIAL STATEMENT AUDIT**

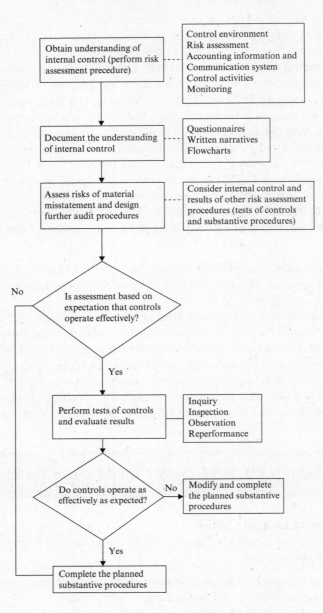

1. **Obtain an understanding of internal control.** As discussed in Module 2, this understanding is obtained as a part of the overall understanding of the entity and its environment. Here we emphasize the internal control portion and its interaction with other audit procedures.

    The auditor performs risk assessment procedures to obtain an understanding of the five components of internal control sufficient to assess the risk of material misstatement of the financial statements, and to design the nature, timing and extent of further audit procedures. Risk assessment procedures for internal control include

    • Inquiries of management and others within the entity
    • Observing the application of specific controls
    • Inspecting documents and records
    • Tracing transactions through the information system

    The knowledge obtained through risk assessment procedures is used to

    • Identify types of potential misstatements
    • Consider factors that affect the risk of material misstatement
    • Design tests of controls and substantive procedures

Auditor experience in previous years with the entity may also help auditors to assess the risk of material misstatement.

At this point in the audit, the above procedures are performed primarily to help the auditor to understand the design and whether the controls have been *implemented* (previously referred to as placed in operation). AU-C 315 distinguishes between determining that controls have been implemented vs. evaluating their operating effectiveness. In determining whether controls have been implemented, the auditor determines that the entity is using them. This is all that is necessary for obtaining an understanding of internal control.

In evaluating operating effectiveness, the auditor goes further and considers (1) how the control was applied; (2) the consistency with which it was applied; and (3) by whom (or what means) it is applied. Tests of controls (described in detail in Section B.3 below) address the effectiveness of the design and operation of a control. Tests of controls are necessary when the auditor's risk assessment relies upon an assumption that controls operate effectively.

AU-C 315 provides information on the level of understanding necessary for the (a) control environment, (b) risk assessment, (c) control activities, (d) information and communication, and (e) monitoring.

a. **Control environment.** The auditor should obtain sufficient knowledge to understand management's and the board of directors' **attitude, awareness,** and **actions** concerning the control environment. The substance of the policies, procedures, and actions is more important than the form. Thus, for example, a budget reporting system that provides adequate reports that are not used is of little value.

b. **Risk assessment.** The auditor should obtain sufficient knowledge to understand how management considers risks relevant to financial reporting objectives and decides about actions to address those risks. This knowledge generally includes obtaining an understanding of how management identifies risks, estimates the significance of risks, assesses the likelihood of their occurrence, and relates them to financial reporting.

c. **Control activities.** The auditor should obtain an understanding of those control activities relevant to planning the audit. While obtaining an understanding of the other components of internal control, the auditor obtains knowledge about some control activities. For example, while obtaining an understanding of accounting for cash disbursements, an auditor is likely to become aware of whether bank accounts are reconciled (a control activity). An auditor should use professional judgment to determine the extent of additional knowledge needed to plan the audit. Ordinarily, audit planning does not require an understanding of control activities related to each account or to every assertion.

d. **Information and communication.** The auditor needs to obtain a level of knowledge of the information system and communication to understand (1) the major transaction classes, (2) how those transactions are initiated, (3) the available accounting records and support, (4) the manner of processing of transactions, (5) the financial reporting process used to prepare financial statements, and (6) the means the entity uses to communicate financial reporting roles and responsibilities.

e. **Monitoring.** The auditor should obtain sufficient knowledge of the major types of monitoring activities the entity uses to monitor internal control over financial reporting, including how those activities are used to initiate corrective action.

The following illustration summarizes the nature of the internal control components and the auditor's planning responsibility.

**SUMMARY OF INTERNAL CONTROL COMPONENTS AND
THE AUDITOR'S REQUIRED UNDERSTANDING TO PLAN THE AUDIT**

	Summary of Components	Auditor's Required Understanding to Plan Audit
Overall Internal Control for Financial Reporting	Objective is to prepare financial statements for external purposes that are fairly presented in conformity with GAAP (or another comprehensive basis)	Obtain knowledge about design and whether controls have been implemented; the understanding should be adequate to allow the auditor to (1) Identify types of potential misstatements (2) Consider factors affecting risk of material misstatements (3) Design effective substantive tests

Control Environment	Factors • Integrity and ethical values • Commitment to competence • Human resource policies and practices • Assignment of authority and responsibility • Management's philosophy and operating style • Board of directors or audit committee participation • Organizational structure	Obtain sufficient knowledge to understand management and board of directors (1) Attitudes (2) Awareness (3) Actions
Risk Assessment	The identification, analysis, and management of risks relevant to the preparation of financial statements following GAAP	Obtain understanding of how management (1) Identifies risks (2) Estimates the significance of the risks (3) Assesses the likelihood of occurrence
Control Activities	Policies and procedures that pertain to • Performance reviews • Information processing • Physical controls • Segregation of duties	Obtain additional understanding as necessary to plan the audit. Ordinarily, an understanding of control activities related to each account or to every assertion is not necessary.
Information and Communication	Methods to record, process, summarize, and report transactions, which include • Identify and record all valid transactions • Describe on a timely basis • Measure the value properly • Record in the proper time period • Properly present and disclose • Communicate responsibilities to employees	Obtain understanding of (1) Major transaction classes (2) How transactions are initiated (3) Available accounting records and support (4) Manner of processing of transactions (5) Financial reporting process used to prepare financial statements (6) Means the entity uses to communicate financial reporting roles and responsibilities
Monitoring	Methods to consider whether controls are operating as intended	Obtain sufficient understanding of major types of monitoring activities

Procedures for obtaining an understanding. The auditor relies primarily upon a combination of (1) previous experience with the entity, (2) inquiries, (3) inspection of documents and records, and (4) observation of entity activities to obtain the needed understanding of the internal control. At this point in the audit, these procedures are performed primarily to help the auditor to understand the design and whether the controls have been **implemented**.

AU-C 315 points out that while obtaining an understanding of the design of a control, including whether it has been implemented, an auditor may either by plan or by chance obtain some information on operating effectiveness. For example, while making inquiries about the design of the client's budgeting system and whether it has been implemented, an auditor may have obtained evidence on the effectiveness of the control in preventing or detecting expense misclassifications. Thus, its operating effectiveness has been tested. In this manner, in essence, some **tests of controls** may have been concurrently performed with obtaining an understanding of internal control.

Documentation of understanding of internal control. The auditor's documentation of his/her understanding of internal control for purposes of planning the audit is influenced by the size and complexity of the entity, as well as the nature of the entity's internal control. For a small client a memorandum may be sufficient. For a larger client, flowcharts, questionnaires, and decision tables may be needed. The more complex the internal control and the more extensive the procedures performed by the auditor, the more extensive should be the documentation. The advantages and disadvantages of using questionnaires, memoranda, and/or flowchart methods are as follows:

Method	Advantages	Disadvantages
Questionnaire	1. Easy to complete 2. Comprehensive list of questions make it unlikely that important portions of internal control will be overlooked 3. Weaknesses become obvious (generally those questions answered with a "no")	1. May be answered without adequate thought being given to questions 2. Questions may not "fit" client adequately
Memoranda	1. Tailor-made for engagement 2. Requires a detailed analysis and thus forces auditor to understand functioning of structure	1. May become very long and time-consuming 2. Weaknesses in structure not always obvious 3. Auditor may overlook important portions of internal control
Flowchart	1. Graphic representation of structure 2. Usually makes it unlikely that important portions of internal control will be overlooked 3. Good for electronic systems 4. No long wording (as in case of memoranda)	1. Preparation is time-consuming 2. Weaknesses in structure not always obvious (especially to inexperienced auditor)

NOTE: Flowcharts, including symbols, are discussed in the Auditing with Technology Module.

In addition to questionnaires, memoranda, and flowcharts, auditors may prepare "decision tables" to document their understanding of internal control. Decision tables are graphic methods of describing the logic of decisions. Various combinations of **conditions** are matched to one of several **actions**. In an internal control setting, the various important controls are reviewed and, based on the combination of answers received, an action is taken, perhaps a decision on whether to perform tests of controls. The following extremely simplified table will provide you with the information you need for the CPA exam (note, for example, in the case of segregation of functions, a series of detailed segregation conditions—not one summary—would be used).

	Rules						
Conditions	1	2	3	4	5	6	7
(1) Segregation of function adequate	y	y	y	y	n	n	n
(2) Adequate documents	y	y	n	n	y	y	n
(3) Independent checks on performance	y	n	y	n	y	n	-
Actions	1	2	3	4	5	6	7
(1) Perform all relevant tests of controls	x						
(2) Perform limited tests of controls		x	x		x		
(3) Perform no tests of controls				x		x	x

Note that for decision rule 7, after the first two conditions have each received a reply of "no" it doesn't matter what the third condition is—tests of controls will not be used. Also, while a decision table is an efficient means of describing the logic of an internal control process, it does not provide an analysis of document flow as does a flowchart.

2. **Assess risks of material misstatement and design further audit procedures.** In Section D of Module 2 we discussed in general terms the process of assessing the risks of material misstatement and designing further audit procedures (tests of controls and substantive procedures). On an overall basis the auditors should perform the

risk assessment to identify and assess the risks of material misstatement at the financial statement level and at the relevant assertion level for classes of transactions, account balances, and disclosures; the approach is one of

- Identifying risks
- Relating the risks to what can go wrong at the relevant assertion level
- Considering whether the risks are of a magnitude that could result in a material misstatement
- Considering the likelihood that risks could result in material misstatements

The effectiveness of internal control is important in many situations since particular controls may lessen the likelihood that risks could result in material misstatements (the final bullet). As an example, consider an auditor who identifies a risk of overstated sales. Further, assume that the client has implemented a control with the objective of only allowing proper sales to be recorded. Here the likelihood of material misstatements is affected by the operating effectiveness of the control. In this type of situation the auditors will consider the appropriate combination of tests of controls and substantive procedures to perform.

The decision sequence for considering internal control for the assertions related to classes of transactions, account balances and disclosures depends upon whether controls such as that described in the preceding paragraph appear effective. If the control appears effective, tests of controls will be performed

- When the auditor's risk assessment *includes an expectation of operating effectiveness* of controls because the likelihood of material misstatement is lower if the control operates effectively, *or*
- When substantive procedures alone do not provide sufficient audit evidence.

In the first situation, an auditor's risk assessment will include an expectation of operating effectiveness when the auditor believes that such operating effectiveness decreases the likelihood of material misstatement and that testing such controls is likely to be cost effective. But, since tests of controls alone are not normally sufficient, the further audit procedures will be composed of a combination of tests of controls and substantive procedures. Thus, the decision to perform tests of controls will be made when the auditor believes that a combination of tests of controls and a decreased scope of substantive procedures is likely to be more cost effective than performing more extensive substantive procedures or when this is the only viable approach. The overall approach here, as it relates to controls is to (1) identify controls that are relevant to specific assertions that are likely to prevent or detect material misstatements, and (2) perform tests of controls to evaluate the effectiveness of those controls.

Alternatively, the risk assessment may **not** include an expectation that controls operate effectively. This will be the case when (1) controls appear weak, or (2) the auditor believes that performing extensive substantive procedures is likely to be more cost effective than performing a combination of tests of controls and a decreased scope of substantive procedures. When the risk assessment does not include an expectation that controls operate effectively, further audit procedures will consist entirely of substantive procedures. No evidence on the operating effectiveness of the controls need then be gathered; that is, no tests of controls will be performed. If a separate assessment of control risk is made, control risk is at the maximum level and the auditor will design substantive tests placing no reliance upon the controls operating effectively.

When designing further audit procedures the auditor may design a test of controls to be performed concurrently with a substantive procedure test of details on the same transaction. The objective of tests of controls is to evaluate whether a control operated effectively. The objective of tests of details is to support relevant assertions or detect material misstatements at the assertion level. Although these objectives differ, both may be accomplished concurrently through performance of a test of controls and a test of details on the same transaction; this is known as a **dual-purpose test.** For example, an auditor may examine an invoice to determine whether it has been properly approved (a test of a control) and to provide substantive evidence of a transaction (a test of details).

At this point in the audit, the auditor has obtained the needed understanding of internal control. During this process the effectiveness of some controls may have been tested (i.e., some tests of controls may have been performed). If this is the case, the auditors in essence are already using a combination approach involving both tests of controls and substantive tests.

3. **Perform tests of controls.** Tests of controls are used to test either the effectiveness of the design or operation of a control. Approaches include
   a. **Inquiries** of appropriate personnel
   b. **Inspection** of documents and reports
   c. **Observation** of the application of controls
   d. **Reperformance** of the control by the auditor (when evaluating operation)

To illustrate the nature of tests of controls, assume that the client has implemented the control of requiring a second person to review the quantities, prices, extensions, and footing of each sales invoice. The purpose of this control is to prevent material misstatements in the billing of customers and the recording of sales transactions. By using the first approach, inquiry, the auditor would discuss with appropriate client personnel the manner in which the control functions. Generally, because of the indirect nature of the information obtained, inquiry alone is not considered to provide credible enough evidence to conclude on operating effectiveness of controls.

The remaining approaches, inspection, observation, and reperformance, may be illustrated by assuming that a sample of sixty sales invoices has been selected from throughout the year. The auditor might inspect the invoices and determine whether evidence exists that the procedures have been performed (e.g., invoices bearing initials of the individual who reviewed them). Another option is to observe applications of the procedures being applied to the invoices. Note that for controls that leave no documentary trail (e.g., segregation of functions in certain circumstances) inquiry and observation may become the only feasible approaches. Finally, the auditors may reperform the procedure by comparing quantities shown on each invoice to the quantities listed on the related shipping documents, by comparing unit prices to the client's price lists, and by verifying the extensions and footings.

Timeliness of evidence. For reasons of efficiency and practicality, auditors often perform tests of controls at an interim date prior to year-end and then update them to the extent considered necessary at year-end. Also, pertaining to observation approach, note that for many situations only a limited number of observations of individuals performing controls are practical. The auditor should realize that generalizing tests of controls results beyond the periods sampled is risky. It is for this reason that auditors should consider whether additional tests should be performed over untested periods to provide assurance that controls functioned over the entire period.

Audit evidence on operating effectiveness from a prior period. Is an auditor allowed to use the results of prior years' tests of controls in the current audit? PCAOB auditing standards do not allow this. Auditing Standards Board standards allow this in limited circumstances. If the auditor of a nonpublic company plans to use audit evidence about the operating effectiveness of controls obtained in prior audits, the auditor should obtain audit evidence about whether changes in those specific controls have occurred subsequent to the prior audit. When controls have changed since they were last tested, the auditor should test the operating effectiveness of such controls in the current audit. In circumstances in which controls have not changed since they were last tested, the auditor should test the operating effectiveness of such controls at least once in every three years. That is, the auditor should test a control at least once in every third year in an annual audit.

IT controls. Ordinarily an auditor tests a control multiple times to arrive at a conclusion concerning operating effectiveness (e.g., 60 sales invoices). When a control is performed by the computer, must an auditor test the automated control numerous times to conclude on operating effectiveness? No. Generally IT processing is inherently consistent; therefore, the auditor may be able to limit the testing to one or a few instances of the control operation. Note here, however, that an auditor should have confidence that the control operated in the same manner throughout the period (e.g., a computer program didn't inappropriately disable it during part of the period). Also, the timing of tests of controls (and substantive procedures) may be affected by irretrievability of certain client data after a certain period of time.

Evaluating the results of tests of controls. Based on the results of the tests of controls the auditor will determine whether it is necessary to modify substantive procedures. If tests of control reveal that the system operates as expected, there will generally be no need to change the scope of planned substantive procedures. Conversely, if the system does not operate as effectively as expected (control risk is higher than expected), the scope of substantive procedures for the relevant assertion(s) involved will increase (thereby decreasing detection risk).

The entire approach for the consideration of internal control (understand, assess the risks and design further audit procedures, perform tests of controls) may be illustrated through use of an example. Assume that you have been told by the controller that two secretaries are present and open all mail together each morning. These secretaries are supposed to prepare a list of all cash receipts, which is then to be forwarded to the accounts receivable clerk. The cash, according to the controller, is then given to the cashier who deposits it each day. Because you work in the area where the secretaries work, you have observed them following these procedures and conclude that the process seems to have been implemented. To keep the example simple, assume that base on this and other audit evidence you gathered while obtaining an understanding of internal control over receivables, controls seem strong. Assume that to this point you have performed no tests of controls. Thus, you should document your understanding of the structure and make a decision as to whether controls should be tested. Because no tests of controls have been performed, you initial assessment is that you have no evidence on operating effectiveness (control risk is at the maximum level).

Subsequently, you decide to perform tests of controls with the objective of determining whether the structure is actually in operation and may be relied upon. Also, assume you have decided that, if the results of your tests of controls indicate that the controls are operating as described, one substantive procedure will be performed. You intend to confirm 30 of the firm's 250 accounts receivable to verify their existence. That is, despite strong internal control, substantive procedures should generally still be performed.

However, now assume that when you performed your tests of controls by observing the opening of the mail, you discovered that the secretaries, in circumstances in which one is "busy," had decided to minimize their work by having the other individually perform the task periodically. Also, you discovered that the secretaries, when only a "limited" amount of cash is received, decided to omit the step of preparing a list of cash receipts and simply forwarded the receipts to the accounts receivable clerk who then forwarded them to the cashier who deposited them periodically.

You have discovered that the controls over cash receipts are **not** as strong as was indicated when you were gaining an understanding of internal control. In this situation, you might decide that a higher than acceptable likelihood exists that an embezzlement of cash receipts could occur; that is, control risk is high. You might then decide to increase the scope of your substantive procedures; you could, for example, confirm more accounts than originally had been planned. You might also decide to expand your investigation of bad debt write-offs to determine that accounts have not been collected and subsequently have been fraudulently written off. Note that if you had originally obtained a more accurate description of the actual functioning of the internal control over cash receipts, you might have decided to omit the tests of controls and have relied entirely upon substantive procedures, thus resulting in complete reliance upon substantive procedures.

4. **Summary.** The approach presented above may be summarized as follows:

Step 1. Obtain and document understanding of internal control

(1) Study the control environment, risk assessment, control activities, information and communication, and monitoring

(2) Document understanding of system—use flowcharts, memoranda, questionnaires, decision tables, etc.

Step 2. Assess risk of material misstatement and design further audit procedures

(1) Risk assessment procedures are performed to assess the risk of material misstatement

(2) Risk assessment procedures include inquiries of management and others within the entity, analytical procedures, observation and inspection, and other inquiries

(3) Appropriate further procedures are designed—tests of controls and substantive procedures

Step 3. Perform tests of controls and evaluate results

(1) Tests whether controls are operating effectively (through inquiry, inspection, observation, and reperformance)

(2) Test of control results
As expected—the planned substantive procedures will be performed
Not as expected—the scope of planned substantive procedures will be modified and those procedures will be performed

---

NOW REVIEW MULTIPLE-CHOICE QUESTIONS 10 THROUGH 42

C. Audits (Examinations) of Internal Control

The Sarbanes-Oxley Act of 2002 created a requirement for an integrated audit of SEC registrants that provides assurance about the fairness of financial statements *and* about the effectiveness of internal control over financial reporting. The financial statement audit portion of the integrated audit is similar to any other financial statement audit, but its integrated nature means that auditors rely much more on internal control and less on substantive procedures.

Section 404 of the Sarbanes-Oxley act of 2002 requires internal control reporting by management and the auditor.

* Section 404a: Requires management to include its assessment of internal control in the annual report filed with the SEC.
* Section 404b: Requires the CPA firm to audit internal control and express an opinion on the effectiveness of internal control. As implemented, the Act applies to companies with a market capitalization of $75,000,000 or more.

Guidance to meet the auditor's responsibilities for reporting upon internal control of a public audit client ("an issuer") as a part of an integrated audit is provided by PCAOB Standard 5; guidance for a nonpublic company ("a nonissuer") is provided by Statements on Attestation Standards and Interpretations (AT) 501. While integrated audits are required for public companies with a market capitalization of $75,000,000 or more, they are not required for nonpublic companies unless required by some other regulatory body. Both PCAOB Standard 5 and AT 501 require when performing an audit of internal control that the auditor examine the design and operating effectiveness of internal control over financial reporting (hereafter IC or internal control) to provide a sufficient basis to issue an opinion on the effectiveness of IC in preventing or detecting material misstatements of the financial statements. Also, the report issued may be either a separate report on IC or combined with the audit report on the financial statements.

PCAOB Standard 5 and AT 501 are very similar to one another. Our approach here is to first present an outline of PCAOB Standard 5 (which essentially includes a summary of most of the key information in AT 501), and then provide a brief section presenting some of the differences between the two standards. The following serves as an overall outline of Standard 5 and a summary of the most important points of that standard and of AT 501.

1. General

   a. Objective of audit of IC—express an opinion on the effectiveness of the company's IC

      (1) To form a basis for such an opinion, the auditor should plan and perform the audit to obtain reasonable assurance about whether material weaknesses exist as of the date of management's assessment.

      (2) The existence of one or more material weaknesses leads to a conclusion that IC is not effective.

   b. The general group of the 10 GAAS that remain in the PCAOB standards are applicable (adequate training, independence, due professional care); the fieldwork and reporting standards for an audit of IC are established in Standard 5.

   c. Important terms

      (1) Deficiencies in IC

         (a) Deficiency—The design or operation of a control does not allow management or employees, in the normal course of performing their assigned functions, to prevent or detect misstatements on a timely basis. A deficiency is also referred to as a control deficiency in Standard 5.

         (b) Significant deficiency—A deficiency, or combination of deficiencies, in IC that is less severe than a material weakness, yet important enough to merit attention by those responsible for oversight of the company's financial reporting.

         (c) Material weakness—A deficiency, or combination of deficiencies, in IC such that there is *a reasonable possibility* that a material misstatement of the company's annual or interim financial statements will not be prevented or detected on a timely basis.

           [1] A reasonable possibility is either "reasonably possible" or "probable" as those terms are used in SFAS 5, *Accounting for Contingencies*.

           [2] Note that this definition of material weakness is slightly different from the AICPA definition.

      (2) **Control objective**—A specific target against which to evaluate the effectiveness of controls. A control objective for IC generally relates to a relevant assertion and states a criterion for evaluating whether the company's control procedures in a specific area provide reasonable assurance that a misstatement in that relevant assertion is prevented or detected on a timely basis.

      (3) **Management's assessment**—The assessment required under provisions of the Sarbanes-Oxley Act (Item 308(a)3 of Regulations S-B and S-K) that is included in management's annual report on internal control over financial reporting.

      (4) **Relevant assertion**—A financial statement assertion that has a reasonable possibility of containing misstatements that could cause the financial statements to be materially misstated (determination made without regard to the effect of controls).

      (5) **Significant accounts and disclosures**—An account or disclosure for which there is a reasonable possibility of material misstatement. The determination is based on inherent risk, without regard to the effect of controls.

d. In summary, the standard may be viewed as having the following structure:

- Plan the audit
- Use a top-down approach to identify controls to test
- Test design and operating effectiveness of controls
- Evaluate identified deficiencies
- Wrap-up
- Report on internal control

> **NOTE:** Sections 2. through 7. of this outline describe the above bulleted points.

2. Plan the audit

a. The opinion on internal control is as to whether internal control is effective at a point in time—the "as of date"—as contrasted to a period of time (e.g., the entire year). The as of date is the last day of the company's fiscal period.

b. Similar to a typical audit of financial statements, the auditor should obtain an understanding of the company's industry, regulations affecting the company, the company's business, and recent changes in operations and internal control.

c. Risk assessment underlies the entire audit process

   (1) As risk of material misstatement increases, so should the auditor's attention to that area.
   (2) The risk that a company's IC will fail to prevent or detect misstatement caused by *fraud* usually is higher than the risk of failure to prevent or detect *errors*.

d. Scaling the audit (for smaller and/or less complex companies)—size and complexity affect how companies achieve control objectives. Scaling is a natural extension of the risk-based approach to audits.

e. Addressing the risk of fraud

   (1) The auditor should take into account the AU-C 240 fraud risk assessment results.
   (2) Controls that might address risk of fraud and management override include controls over

      (a) Significant, unusual transactions
      (b) Journal entries and adjustments made in the period-end financial reporting process
      (c) Related-party transactions
      (d) Significant management estimates
      (e) Incentives or pressures of management to falsify or inappropriately manage financial results

> **NOTE:** Be familiar with the above, as a lack of controls in these areas may result in fraud and/or management override.

f. In an IC audit, to use the work of others (e.g., internal auditors and other client personnel), the auditor should

   (1) Assess their competence and objectivity; do not use the work of those with low competence and/or low objectivity
   (2) In general, use the work in lower risk areas

g. Entity-level controls vary in nature and precision.

   (1) Some entity-level controls have an important but indirect effect on the likelihood of misstatement (e.g., certain control environment controls such as tone at the top). These controls might affect the other controls the auditor decides to test, and the nature, timing and extent of procedures performed on other controls.
   (2) Some entity-level controls monitor the effectiveness of other controls, but not at a level of precision that would address the assessed risk that misstatements will be prevented or detected (e.g., controls that monitor the operation of other controls). These entity-level controls, when operating effectively, might allow the auditor to reduce testing of the other controls.

(3) Some entity-level controls by themselves adequately prevent or detect misstatements. If an entity-level control sufficiently addresses the risk of misstatement, the auditor need not test additional controls related to that risk.

h. The auditor should use the same materiality considerations as s/he would use in planning the annual financial statement audit.

3. Use a top-down approach to identify controls to test.

a. A top-down approach, beginning at the financial statement level, should be used to select controls to test.

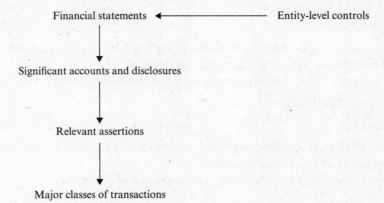

Financial statements ◄──────────── Entity-level controls

Significant accounts and disclosures

Relevant assertions

Major classes of transactions

b. Entity-level controls

(1) Controls related to the control environment; particularly whether

(a) Management's philosophy and operating style promotes effective IC
(b) Sound integrity and ethical values are developed and understood
(c) The board of directors or audit committee understands and exercises oversight responsibility over financial reporting and IC

(2) Controls over management override
(3) The company's risk assessment process
(4) Centralized processing and controls
(5) Controls to monitor results of operations
(6) Controls to monitor other controls (e.g., internal auditing, the audit committee, self-assessment programs)
(7) Controls over the period-end financial reporting process
(8) Policies that address significant business control and risk management practices

c. The auditor should evaluate the period-end financial reporting process (e.g., entering transaction totals to the general ledger, selection of accounting policies, adjustments, preparing financial statements).

d. Identifying significant accounts and disclosures

(1) Consider

(a) Size and composition of account
(b) Susceptibility to misstatement
(c) Volume of activity, complexity, homogeneity of transactions
(d) Nature of account
(e) Accounting and reporting complexities
(f) Exposure to losses in account
(g) Possibility of significant contingent liabilities
(h) Related-party transactions
(i) Changes from the prior period in accounts or disclosures

(2) The auditor should identify significant accounts and disclosures and their relevant assertions; relevant assertions include

(a) Existence or occurrence
(b) Completeness
(c) Valuation or allocation

       (d) Rights and obligations
       (e) Presentation and disclosure

  e. To obtain a further understanding of the likely sources of misstatement, and as a part of selecting the controls to test, the auditor should achieve the following objectives:

    (1) Understand the flow of transactions
    (2) Verify that he or she has identified points at which a material misstatement could arise
    (3) Identify controls implemented by management to address potential misstatements
    (4) Identify controls to prevent or detect unauthorized acquisition, use or disposition of assets that could result in a material misstatement

  f. Selecting controls to test

    (1) Test those that are important to a conclusion about whether company's controls sufficiently address the assessed risk of misstatement for each relevant assertion.
    (2) It is not necessary to test redundant controls, unless redundancy is itself a control objective.

4. Test design and operating effectiveness of controls

  a. Design effectiveness

    (1) Determine whether, if operating properly, control(s) would satisfy company's control objectives and prevent or detect material misstatements
    (2) Procedures include inquiry, observation, and inspection of documents

  b. Operating effectiveness.

    (1) Determine whether control is operating as designed and whether person performing the control possesses the necessary authority and competence.
    (2) Procedures include inquiry, observation, inspection, and reperformance.
    (3) Walk-throughs may be used to test operating effectiveness; walk-throughs

      (a) Involve following a transaction from origination through the company processes until it is reflected in the financial statements
      (b) Usually consist of a combination of inquiry of appropriate personnel, observation of the company's operations, inspection of relevant documentation, and reperformance of the control

        [1] Included in inquires are questions of company personnel about their understanding of what is required by the company's procedures and controls

      (c) Might provide sufficient evidence on operating effectiveness, depending on the risk associated with the control being tested, the specific procedures performed as a part of the walk-through and the results of those procedures

  c. Auditors are not responsible for obtaining sufficient evidence to support an opinion about the effectiveness of each individual control; rather, their objective is to express an overall opinion on IC.
  d. When the auditor identifies deviations from established controls, s/he should determine the effect of the deviations on his/her assessment of the risk associated with the control and on operating effectiveness.

    (1) Any individual control does not necessarily have to operate without deviation to be considered effective.

  e. Timing of testing controls

    (1) Testing controls over a greater period of time provides more evidence of the effectiveness of control.
    (2) Testing performed closer to the date of management's assessment provides more evidence than testing performed earlier.

  f. The more extensively a control is tested, the greater the evidence obtained from that test.
  g. When the auditor obtains evidence about operating effectiveness at an interim date (e.g., October 31 for a December 31 year-end client), s/he should determine what additional evidence is needed for the remaining period (referred to as "roll-forward procedures"); the needed additional evidence depends upon

    (1) Details of the control itself and results of tests performed
    (2) Sufficiency of evidence of effectiveness obtained at interim date
    (3) Length of remaining period
    (4) Possibility of significant changes in IC since interim date

  h. In subsequent years' audits, the auditor should incorporate knowledge obtained during past audits of IC.

    (1) Risk associated with the control should be considered.
    (2) The amount of work performed in previous audits, results, and whether there have been changes should also considered.

5. Evaluate identified deficiencies.

  a. Although the audit is designed to identify material weaknesses, any deficiencies the auditor has identified should be considered; the severity of a deficiency depends on

    (1) Whether there is reasonable possibility that the control will fail to prevent or detect a misstatement
    (2) The magnitude of the potential misstatement

  b. Details on evaluating deficiencies

    (1) Factors affecting the magnitude include

      (a) Financial statement amounts or total transactions exposed to the deficiency
      (b) Volume of activity exposed to the deficiency in the current period

    (2) The maximum amount that an account balance can be overstated is generally the recorded amount, while understatements can be larger.
    (3) The auditor should consider the effect of compensating controls which might detect such a misstatement; if an adequate compensating control exists, the deficiency is not a material weakness.
    (4) The auditor need **not** identify a material, misstatement for a deficiency to be considered a material weakness—rather, there should be a reasonable possibility of a material misstatement.

  c. Indicators of material weaknesses

    (1) Identification of fraud, whether or not material, on the part of senior management
    (2) Restatement of previously issued financial statements to reflect a correction of a misstatement
    (3) Identification by the auditor of a material misstatement that would not have been detected by the company's IC
    (4) Ineffective oversight of external reporting and IC by the audit committee

> **NOTE:** Make certain that you know the above 4 indicators.

6. Wrap-up

  a. The auditor should form an opinion.
  b. Written representations from the client should be obtained.
  c. Communicating certain matters

    (1) Material weaknesses—Communicate, in writing, to management and the audit committee prior to issuing the auditor's report on IC.

      (a) If oversight by the audit committee of external financial reporting and IC is ineffective, the auditor should communicate in writing to the board of directors.

    (2) Significant deficiencies—Communicate in writing to management and the audit committee.
    (3) Significant deficiencies and deficiencies (those that are not material weaknesses)—Communicate in writing to management and inform the audit committee when such a communication has been made.

      (a) Significant deficiencies and deficiencies previously communicated to management in writing by the auditor, internal auditors, or others in the organization, need not be repeated to *management*.
      (b) Significant deficiencies that are not corrected and were previously communicated to the audit committee should be recommunicated. The auditor may recommunicate them by referring to the prior communication.

    (4) The auditor should not issue a report stating that no significant deficiencies or deficiencies were noted during the audit.

> **NOTE:** Make certain that you know all of the above communication requirements.

7. Report on internal control

   a. Report should include

     (1) Title with word *independent*
     (2) Statement that management is responsible for IC
     (3) Identification of management's report on IC
     (4) Statement that the auditor's responsibility is to express an opinion on IC
     (5) Definition of IC
     (6) Audit conducted in accordance with standards of PCAOB
     (7) Standards of PCAOB require auditor to plan and perform audit to obtain reasonable assurance
     (8) Audit includes obtaining an understanding of IC, assessing risk that a material weakness exists, testing and evaluating the design and operating effectiveness of IC, and performing other necessary procedures
     (9) The auditor believes the audit provides a reasonable basis for his/her opinion.
     (10) Paragraph on inherent limitation of IC
     (11) Auditor's opinion on whether company maintained effective IC
     (12) Manual or printed signature of firm
     (13) City and state of firm
     (14) Date of report

   b. Separate reports on the financial statements and IC or a combined report are acceptable.
   c. Report date—no earlier than date on which auditor has obtained sufficient competent evidence to support opinion.
   d. Material weaknesses result in an adverse opinion.
   e. The auditor should inquire of management as to any subsequent events affecting IC and should obtain written representation.
   f. Other reporting situations

     (1) Management's report on IC is incomplete or improperly represented—auditor should include an explanatory paragraph describing
     (2) Scope limitation—withdraw from engagement or disclaim an opinion

       (a) If the auditor concludes that a material weakness exists and a disclaimer is being issued, the report should include the definition of material weakness and a description of any material weakness identified.

     (3) Opinion based, in part, on report of another auditor—follow advice from AU-C 600
     (4) If management's report on IC includes information beyond that normally presented, the auditor ordinarily should disclaim an opinion on that information.

       (a) If that information includes a material misstatement of fact, the auditor should notify management and the audit committee.

8. The following is an example of a combined unqualified audit report on the financial statements and IC.

Report of Independent Registered Public Accounting Firm

To the Audit Committee and Stockholders of Carver Company

   [Introductory paragraph]

   We have audited the accompanying balance sheets of Carver Company as of December 31, 20X8 and 20X7, and the related statements of income, stockholders' equity and comprehensive income, and cash flows for each of the years in the three-year period ended December 31, 20X8. We also have audited Carver Company's internal control over financial reporting as of December 31, 20X8, based on [Identify control criteria, for example, "criteria established in Internal Control—Integrated Framework issued by the Committee of Sponsoring Organizations of the Treadway Commission (COSO)."]. Carver Company's management is responsible for these financial statements, for maintaining effective internal control over financial reporting, and for its assessment of the effectiveness of internal control over financial reporting, included in the accompanying [title of management's report]. Our responsibility is to express an opinion on these financial statements and an opinion on the company's internal control over financial reporting based on our audits.

[Scope paragraph]

We conducted our audits in accordance with the standards of the Public Company Accounting Oversight Board (United States). Those standards require that we plan and perform the audits to obtain reasonable assurance about whether the financial statements are free of material misstatement and whether effective internal control over financial reporting was maintained in all material respects. Our audits of the financial statements include examining, on a test basis, evidence supporting the amounts and disclosures in the financial statements, assessing the accounting principles used and significant estimates made by management, and evaluating the overall financial statement presentation. Our audit of internal control over financial reporting included obtaining an understanding of internal control over financial reporting, assessing the risk that a material weakness exists, and testing and evaluating the design and operating effectiveness of internal control based on the assessed risk. Our audits also included performing such other procedures as we considered necessary in the circumstances. We believe that our audits provide a reasonable basis for our opinions.

[Definition paragraph]

A company's internal control over financial reporting is a process designed to provide reasonable assurance regarding the reliability of financial reporting and the preparation of financial statements for external purposes in accordance with generally accepted accounting principles. A company's internal control over financial reporting includes those policies and procedures that (1) pertain to the maintenance of records that, in reasonable detail, accurately and fairly reflect the transactions and dispositions of the assets of the company; (2) provide reasonable assurance that transactions are recorded as necessary to permit preparation of financial statements in accordance with generally accepted accounting principles, and that receipts and expenditures of the company are being made only in accordance with authorizations of management and directors of the company; and (3) provide reasonable assurance regarding prevention or timely detection of unauthorized acquisition, use, or disposition of the company's assets that could have a material effect on the financial statements.

[Inherent limitations paragraph]

Because of its inherent limitations, internal control over financial reporting may not prevent or detect mis-statements. Also, projections of any evaluation of effectiveness to future periods are subject to the risk that controls may become inadequate because of changes in conditions, or that the degree of compliance with the policies or procedures may deteriorate.

[Opinion paragraph]

In our opinion, the financial statements referred to above present fairly, in all material respects, the financial position of Carver Company as of December 31, 20X8 and 20X7, and the results of its operations and its cash flows for each of the years in the three-year period ended December 31, 20X8, in conformity with accounting principles generally accepted in the United States of America. Also in our opinion, Carver Company maintained, in all material respects, effective in-ternal control over financial reporting as of December 31, 20X8, based on [Identify control criteria, for example, "criteria established in Internal Control—Integrated Framework issued by the Committee of Sponsoring Organizations of the Treadway Commission (COSO).]

Willington & Co., CPAs
Bisbee, Arizona, United States of America
February 20X9

9. **Differences between PCAOB Standard 5 and AT 501.** The following are differences between PCAOB 5 and AT 501 that you should be aware of:

- PCAOB 5 refers to this as an "audit," while AT 501 refers to it as an "examination."
- Both standards are structured about reporting on internal control at a point in time (the "as of " date), but AT 501 also allows an auditor to examine effectiveness of internal control for a period of time (e.g., for the year 20X7).
- Both standards provide for reporting on the subject matter (internal control), but AT 501 also allows for reporting on management's assertion. However, when a material weakness exists in an AT 501 engagement, the auditor should report on the subject matter.
- Both standards require that the auditor not issue a report stating that no significant deficiencies exist, but only AT 501 explicitly requires that no such report be issued stating that no material weaknesses were identified during the examination.

- The stage referred to as "wrapping-up" by PCAOB 5 (step 6 in the preceding outline) is referred to as "concluding procedures" by AT 501.
- The reports issued on IC are very similar, but differ in that PCAOB 5 states that the audit was conducted in accordance with standards of the PCAOB while AT 501 states that the examination was conducted in accordance with attestation standards established by the AICPA.

10. **Reporting on Whether a Previously Reported Material Weakness Continues to Exist (PCAOB Standard 4).** After the existence of a material weakness has lead to an adverse opinion in an internal control audit report, the company is ordinarily motivated to eliminate the weakness as quickly as is reasonably possible. When management believes that the material weakness continues to exist.

    The overall approach under PCAOB Standard 4 is one in which management gathers evidence, including documentation that the material weakness no longer exists, and then prepares a written report so indicating. The auditors then plan and perform an engagement emphasizing the controls over the material weakness. The report issued indicates the auditor's opinion that the material weakness "no longer exists" or "exists" as of the date of management's assertion. At this point you should study the outline of PCAOB Standard 4.

NOW REVIEW MULTIPLE-CHOICE QUESTIONS 43 THROUGH 77

D. Accounting Cycles

We now consider CPA exam questions that require an understanding of a transaction cycle.[1] These questions may, for example, require a candidate to perform one or more of the following:

- Identify an audit test that will meet some specified objective (or financial statement assertion).
- Identify internal control strengths/weaknesses.
- Complete a flowchart which includes a number of symbols without descriptors.
- Evaluate an internal control questionnaire.

These questions may be difficult because a candidate (1) may not have an understanding of the various source documents and accounting records and how they relate to one another in an accounting system, and (2) does not know what types of detailed controls should exist. To help you prepare for these questions we are presenting information on both directional testing (which is also helpful for evidence questions) and a summary of transaction cycles.

    Directional Testing. As a starting point, you should understand the notion of directional testing. Directional testing has a from and to. The basic idea is that testing from source documents forward to recorded entries accomplishes a different objective than testing from recorded entries back to source documents.

    Diagrammatically, directional testing suggests

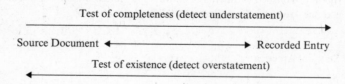

In sentence form, the rules are

1. Tracing forward (source document to recorded entry) primarily tests completeness of recording, and has a primary objective of detecting understatements.
2. Vouching (tracing backwards—recorded entry to source document) primarily tests existence and has a primary objective of detecting overstatements.

    To understand the basic concept here, think about sales invoices (a source document) and the sales journal (the recorded entry).

---

[1] What is the relationship between an accounting cycle and a class of transactions? This is a largely definitional issue with no firm agreement. Many consider an accounting cycle to be broad—for example, we discuss later in this module the "purchase, payables, and cash disbursements cycle." Within that cycle are both purchase and cash disbursement transactions. While some would consider this one transaction cycle, most would consider the purchases and the cash disbursement as classes of transactions.

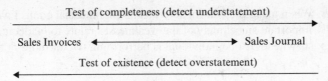

Test of completeness (detect understatement)

Sales Invoices ←——————————→ Sales Journal

Test of existence (detect overstatement)

An auditor may select a group of sales invoices and compare them to the sales journal. On the other hand, the auditor may also vouch sales journal entries back to the sales invoices (and other support such as shipping documents, customer purchase orders). If an auditor is testing for understated sales, it would be best to start with possible sales, not those that were already recorded in the sales journal. Thus, for finding understatements of sales, a CPA would sample from the sales invoices (which are prepared when a sale occurs) in an effort to determine whether individual sales are being recorded. On the other hand, when testing for overstated sales, the CPA would test from the sales recorded in the sales journal back to sales invoices (as well as other source documents such as shipping documents, customer purchase orders). This is because for each recorded sale there should be support. We will apply the concept of directional testing in our discussion of the detailed transaction cycles.

Financial Accounting Reporting Cycle. In the overview section we suggested that an accounting system may be viewed as follows:

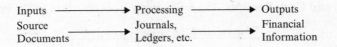

| Inputs | → | Processing | → | Outputs |
| Source Documents | | Journals, Ledgers, etc. | | Financial Information |

At this point review "The Financial Reporting Cycle" on the following page and simply look it over and note the various source documents (inputs), and accounting records such as journals and ledgers which are used to process the inputs (processing), and financial statements (outputs). Recall that our objectives are to (1) learn an approach for addressing questions pertaining to internal control weaknesses and for preparing internal control questionnaires, and (2) learn how to answer other questions pertaining to the effectiveness of audit tests.

When you consider a simulation question pertaining to internal control weaknesses an organized approach is to

1. Read the simulation to identify the type of transaction cycle
2. Obtain an understanding of how the accounting system works by carefully reading the simulation in detail (and possibly informally flowcharting it if the description is very detailed)
3. Consider the control activities (PIPS—**P**erformance reviews, **I**nformation processing, **P**hysical controls, and **S**egregation of duties), but particularly segregation of duties
4. Recall typical weaknesses (presented subsequently) for the transaction cycle involved to find additional internal control weaknesses

Steps 1 and 2 are clearly necessary since you need to understand the simulation and its requirements. When performing the second step, realize that on an overall basis, controls are aimed at safeguarding both assets and financial records. Also, be aware of each department's operational objective (e.g., the shipping department ships goods). Also, know that one way to consider controls is to classify them by function.

Functions of controls. Although the word "controls" has different meanings in different contexts, from an internal control perspective controls within a business organization serve to ensure that information is processed correctly. Controls can in general be viewed as having a function of either (1) preventing misstatements, (2) detecting and correcting misstatements that have occurred, although a particular control may have elements of each. Preventive controls are typically most effective since they are designed to prevent a misstatement from occurring (e.g., two persons opening the mail which includes cash receipts may prevent embezzlement). Detective and corrective controls most frequently occur together. They detect and correct a misstatement that has already occurred (e.g., bank account reconciliation by an individual not otherwise involved with cash receipts or cash disbursements). While these controls are typically less expensive to implement than preventive controls, they may detect misstatements too late. They may detect that an employee embezzled $1,000,000, but may only be corrective in the sense that an embezzlement loss journal entry is made in cases where the employee has disappeared. For purposes of the CPA exam, ask yourself how effective each of the detective and corrective controls is—their effectiveness depends on the details of the system being examined.

Segregation of duties. When using the control activities to find internal control weaknesses (step 3), segregation of duties is especially important since many of the weaknesses relate to inadequate segregation. Recall that inadequate segregation exists whenever one individual is performing two or more of the following:

- Authorization
- Recordkeeping
- Custodianship

For example, when a cashier (custodian) authorizes the write-off of bad debts (authorization), a weakness exists. Also, know that for good internal control reconciliation of an account with some other information should be performed by an individual otherwise independent of the function. To illustrate, the individual preparing checks should not perform the reconciliation of the bank account.

We now analyze in detail each of the following accounting cycles:

1. Sales, Receivables, and Cash Receipts
2. Purchases, Payables, and Cash Disbursements
3. Inventories and Production
4. Personnel and Payroll
5. Financing
6. Investing

1. **Sales, Receivables, and Cash Receipts.** The following is a possible flow of documents:

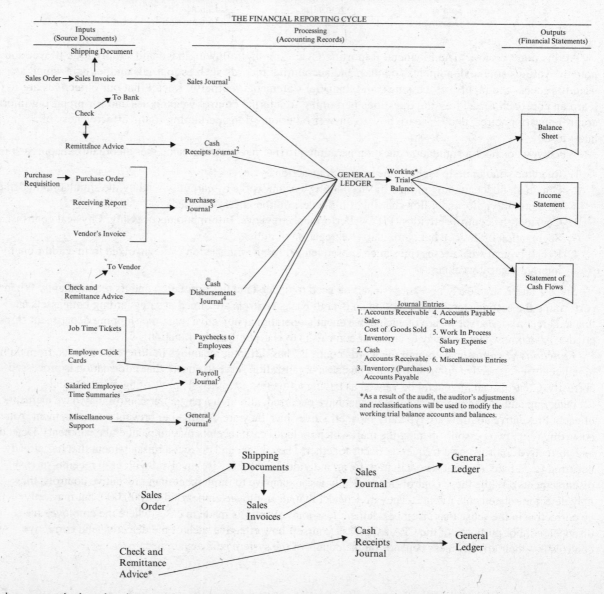

* Checks are sent to banks and remittance advices (or a list of remittance advices) are used to prepare journal entries.

Assume that the firm's sales personnel prepare sales orders for potential sales (many other possibilities, such as the customer filling out the sales order, are found in practice). The sale is approved by the credit department, the goods are shipped, and the billing department (a part of accounting) prepares a sales invoice (a copy of which becomes the customer's "bill"). After the sales invoice is prepared, the sales journal, the general ledger, and the accounts receivable subsidiary ledger are posted. The customer pays the account with a check, and a remittance advice is enclosed to describe which invoice the check is paying. As a preventive control, two individuals open the mail that includes these customer remittances. The checks are listed and sent to the cashier who daily deposits them in the bank (recall that the checks should not go to the accounting department, as that would give the accounting department custody of assets [checks in this case] as well as recordkeeping responsibility). Another copy of the list of checks and the remittance advices is sent to accounting to be used to post the cash receipts journal, which is subsequently posted to the general and accounts receivable subsidiary ledgers.

Major Controls
Sales

(1) Credit granted by a credit department
(2) Sales orders and invoices prenumbered and controlled
(3) Sales returns are presented to receiving clerk who prepares a receiving report which supports prenumbered sales return credit memoranda

Accounts Receivable

(1) Subsidiary ledger reconciled to control ledger regularly
(2) Individual independent of receivable posting reviews statements before sending to customers
(3) Monthly statements sent to all customers
(4) Write-offs approved by management official independent of recordkeeping responsibility (e.g., the treasurer is appropriate)

Cash Receipts

(1) Cash receipts received in mail listed by individuals with no recordkeeping responsibility

    (a) Cash goes to cashier
    (b) Remittance advices go to accounting

(2) Over-the-counter cash receipts controlled (cash register tapes)
(3) Cash deposited daily
(4) Employees handling cash are bonded
(5) **Lockbox,** a post office box controlled by the company's bank at which cash remittances from customers are received. The bank collects customer remittances, immediately credits the cash to the company's bank account, and forwards the remittance advices to the company. A lockbox system is considered an extremely effective control because company employees have no access to cash and bank employees have no access to the company's accounting records.
(6) Bank reconciliation prepared by individuals independent of cash receipts recordkeeping

Sales, Receivables, and Cash Receipts CPA Exam Questions

1. Which assertion is being most directly addressed when an auditor selects a sample of sales invoices and compares them to the subsequent journal entries recorded in the sales journal?

a. Occurrence.
b. Classification.
c. Accuracy.
d. Completeness.

(d) This question is about directional testing. The step will help the auditor to determine that **all** sales invoices have been properly recorded. Accordingly answer (d) is correct since completeness relates most directly to whether **all** items are recorded. Answer (a), occurrence, would be a good reply for the opposite direction of testing—from sales journal entries to sales invoices. Answer (b), classification, would be to a limited extent also tested by tracing from the sales journal to the sales invoices. But, one would also wish to examine other documents such as contracts relating to classification. Little evidence is obtained here on accuracy, answer (c), in that recorded transactions are not being selected for testing.

2. When a client's physical count of inventories is lower than the inventory quantities shown on its perpetual records, the situation would most likely be caused by unrecorded

a. Sales.
b. Sales returns.
c. Purchases.
d. Purchase discounts.

(a) The question is asking what situation could cause the actual inventory to be lower than the amount recorded in the perpetual records. If sales had not been recorded, the perpetual records would not reflect the shipment of inventory; this would result in an overstatement of inventory in the accounting records. Answers (b) and (c) would address cases for which the physical count is higher than the perpetual records since physical goods would be in inventory with no recordkeeping having been performed. Purchase discounts, answer (d), relates to the cost of items as contrasted to the quantity.

3. How would you test credit sales for understatement?

ANSWER: Compare a sample of approved sales orders to the subsequent posting in the sales journal (and through to the general ledger). You are interested in finding out whether the approved sales order made it all the way to the general ledger. Note that you may find overstatements by this audit procedure (e.g., a $10 sale recorded for a higher amount) but that the primary emphasis is in finding understatements.

4. How would you test credit sales for overstatements?

ANSWER: Opposite of 3. above.

5. Are you mainly testing for over or understatements of cash when you agree remittance advices to the cash receipts journal?

ANSWER: Understatements. That is, did the cash that the firm received get recorded?

6. What could cause a remittance advice with no subsequent cash receipt entry?

ANSWER: An embezzlement.

7. Should there be a sales invoice for each sales order?

ANSWER: No. Sales in process and sales not approved will not be invoiced.

Illustrative Task-Based Simulation

Illustrative Simulation A, which follows, involves internal control strengths and deficiencies over the revenue cycle. Consider the following:

Illustrative Simulation A

Items 1 through 11 present various internal control strengths or internal control deficiencies. For each item, select from the list below the appropriate response.

A. Internal control strength for the revenue cycle (including cash receipts).
B. Internal control deficiency for the revenue cycle (including cash receipts).
C. Internal control strength unrelated to the revenue cycle.

Items to be answered

1. Credit is granted by a credit department.
2. Sales returns are presented to a sales department clerk who prepares a written, prenumbered shipping report.
3. Statements sent monthly to customers.
4. Write-offs of accounts receivable are approved by the controller.
5. Cash disbursements over $10,000 require two signatures on the check.
6. Cash receipts received in the mail are received by a secretary with no recordkeeping responsibility.
7. Cash receipts received in the mail are forwarded unopened with remittance advices to accounting.
8. The cash receipts journal is prepared by the treasurer's department.
9. Cash is deposited weekly.
10. Support for disbursement checks is canceled after payment by the treasurer.
11. Bank reconciliation is prepared by individuals independent of cash receipts recordkeeping.

Solution to Illustrative Simulation A

1. (A) The function of a credit department is to follow the company's credit policies to make decisions on the granting of credit.

2. (B) Sales returns should be presented to the receiving clerk (not a sales department clerk) who should prepare a receiving report (not a shipping report).

3. (**A**) Sending monthly statements to customers represents a control strength as errors and fraud may be discovered.

4. (**B**) Write-offs of accounts receivable should be approved by a management official independent of recordkeeping responsibility, not by the controller who is responsible for recordkeeping. Frequently, the treasurer approves write-offs.

5. (**C**) While requiring two signatures on large checks is a good control over expenditures, it relates much more directly to the purchases/disbursements cycle than to the revenue cycle.

6. (**A**) Mailed cash receipts should be received by an individual with no recordkeeping responsibility—a secretary with no recordkeeping responsibility is appropriate. That individual should open the mail and prepare a list of the receipts. The cash should be forwarded with a copy of the listed receipts to a cashier (or the individual who makes deposits) and the remittance advices should be forwarded with another copy of the listed receipts to accounting.

7. (**B**) As indicated in the answer explanation to item 6, the cash receipts should be opened by an individual with no recordkeeping responsibility. The cash should be forwarded with a copy of the listed receipts to a cashier (or the individual who makes deposits) and the remittance advices should be forwarded with another copy of the listed receipts to accounting.

8. (**B**) The cash receipts journal should be prepared by the department responsible for recordkeeping—accounting—under the leadership of the controller.

9. (**B**) Cash should ordinarily be deposited **daily**.

10. (**C**) This control relates to the purchases/disbursements cycle.

11. (**A**) Bank reconciliations should be prepared by individuals independent of cash receipts (and cash disbursements) recordkeeping.

NOW REVIEW MULTIPLE-CHOICE QUESTIONS 78 THROUGH 93

---

2. **Purchases, Payables, and Cash Disbursements.** The following is a possible flow of documents:

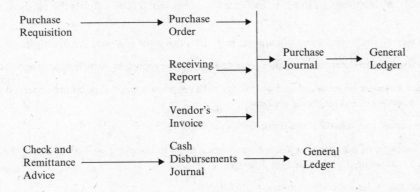

Assume that the purchase requisition is an internal document sent by the department in need of the supplies to the purchasing department. The purchasing department determines the proper quantity and vendor for the purchase and prepares a purchase order. One copy of the purchase order is sent to the vendor. Another copy is sent to the receiving department to allow receiving personnel to know that items received have been ordered; however, the copy of the purchase order sent to receiving will not have a quantity of items on it so as to encourage personnel to count the goods when they are received. When the goods are received, a receiving report is prepared by the receiving department and forwarded to the accounting department. A vendor's invoice or "bill" is received by the accounting department from the vendor. When the accounting department has the purchase order, receiving report, and vendor's invoice, the payment is approved and then recorded in the purchases journal since evidence exists that the item was ordered, received, and billed. A check and remittance advice is subsequently sent to the vendor in accordance with the terms of the sale. The purchase order, receiving report, and vendor's invoice are stamped paid to prevent duplicate payments.

Major Controls

Purchases

    (1) Prenumbered purchase orders used

    (2) Separate purchasing department makes purchases

    (3) Purchasing personnel independent of receiving and recordkeeping

    (4) Suppliers' monthly statements compared with recorded payables

Accounts Payable

    (1) Accounts payable personnel independent of purchasing, receiving, and disbursements

    (2) Clerical accuracy of vendors' invoices tested

    (3) Purchase order, receiving report, and vendor's invoice matched

Cash Disbursements

    (1) Prenumbered checks with a mechanical check protector used

    (2) Two signatures on large check amounts

    (3) Checks signed only with appropriate support (purchase order, receiving report, vendor's invoice). Treasurer signs checks and mails them

    (4) Support for checks canceled after payment

    (5) Voided checks mutilated, retained, and accounted for

    (6) Bank reconciliations prepared by individual independent of cash disbursements recordkeeping

    (7) Physical control of unused checks

Purchases, Payables, and Cash Disbursement Questions

1. Which documents need to be present before payment is approved?

    ANSWER: Purchase order, receiving report, vendor's invoice. (This shows that the firm ordered the goods, received the goods, and has been billed for the goods.)

2. How can a firm control disbursements so that if a duplicate invoice is sent by the supplier the payment will not be made a second time?

    ANSWER: Cancel the required supporting documents in 1. after the invoice is paid the first time.

3. What audit test could be used to determine whether recorded purchases represent valid business expenses?

    ANSWER: Compare a sample of recorded disbursements with properly approved purchase orders, purchase requisitions, vendor's invoices, and receiving reports.

4. What audit procedure would test whether actual purchases are recorded?

    ANSWER: Select a sample of purchase requisitions and agree them to the purchase orders and to the purchases journal (as well as to subsequent general ledger posting).

5. Should there be a purchase order for each purchase requisition?

    ANSWER: No. Several requisitions may be summarized on one purchase order and some requisitions may not be approved.

The above are meant to assist you in obtaining an overall understanding of auditing procedures and internal control. Note that entire courses (and majors) in systems analysis address these issues. The purpose of the above is to give the individual who has a very limited systems background a starting point for analysis.

Task-Based Simulation

Illustrative Simulation B, a purchase/disbursements simulation, is typical of a number of questions which have presented a flowchart with certain information on operations omitted—the candidate is to determine what description belongs in the blocks, circles, etc. which simply contain a number or letter. This type of question does **not** require a knowledge of internal control weaknesses. What is necessary is an understanding of how accounting systems generally work.

First, you should know the common flowchart symbols (presented in the Auditing with Technology Module under "Flowcharting"). This information will be helpful to you because when you see, for example, a trapezoid, you will know that a manual operation has been performed. Additionally, for such simulations, you should consider the department the missing information is in and that department's purpose (e.g., the purchasing department purchases appropriate goods from vendors at acceptable prices). Finally, consider both the step preceding and succeeding the missing information to provide you with a clue as to what is being represented.

Starting with A in the purchasing department, we note that an approved requisition has been received from stores. Step A represents some form of manual operation (due to the existence of a trapezoid) out of which a 5-copied purchase order as well as the requisition come. The only possible manual operation here is the preparation of a 5-part purchase order. At this point, the various copies are either filed or sent elsewhere (the circles represent connectors to other portions of the flowchart or possibly represent a document leaving the system). In this case, we see the various copies being filed and sent to receiving and vouchers payable. Step B represents a copy being sent elsewhere. When we consider the fact that the purpose of the purchasing department is to purchase the items, it becomes obvious that this copy should be sent to the vendor—otherwise no order would occur.

Because a receiving report appears for the first time under step C, it obviously represents the preparation of a receiving report. Next are connectors D and E. We know that the use of the circle indicates that something—probably a document or form of some sort—has been received. For D, a clue is given in that requisition 1 has also been received. We know that this is from purchasing by recalling that requisition 1 and purchase order 5 were sent to vouchers payable—this is shown on the flowchart under purchasing. Similarly, we know that receiving sent a copy of the receiving report to vouchers payable and that E and G relate to it. Thus, through understanding the nature of the various symbols and by considering preceding and succeeding information, we are able to determine the nature of the omitted information. The following is the complete solution to this simulation:

Purchases and Disbursements Flowchart

A. Prepare purchase order
B. To vendor
C. Prepare receiving report
D. From purchasing
E. From receiving
F. Purchase order No. 5
G. Receiving report No. 1

H. Prepare and approve voucher
I. Unpaid voucher file, filed by due date
J. Treasurer
K. Sign checks and cancel voucher package documents
L. Canceled voucher package

Illustrative Simulation B

The Following illustrates a manual system for executing purchases and cash disbursements transactions.

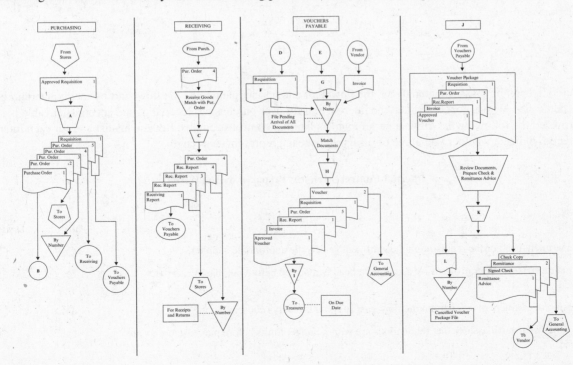

Required:

Indicate what each of the letters (A) through (L) represent. Do not discuss adequacies or inadequacies in the system of internal control.

Illustrative Simulation C asks candidates to identify internal control strengths. Work through it.

Illustrative Simulation C

The following flowchart depicts the activities relating to the purchasing, receiving, and accounts payable departments of Model Company, Inc. Assume that you are a supervising assistant assigned to the Model Company audit.

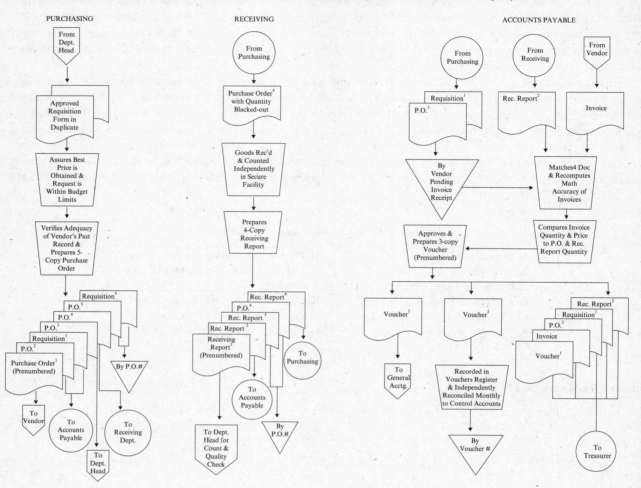

Joe Werell, a beginning assistant, analyzed the flowchart and has supplemented the flowchart by making certain inquiries of the controller. He has concluded that the internal control over purchasing, receiving, and accounts payable is strong and has provided the following list of what he refers to as internal control strengths. Review his list and for each internal control strength indicate whether you agree or disagree that each represents a strength.

Internal Control Strengths Prepared by Joe Werell

Purchasing	Agree	Disagree
1. The department head of the requisitioning department selects the appropriate supplier.	○	○
2. Proper authorization of requisitions by department head is required before purchase orders are prepared.	○	○
3. Purchasing department makes certain that low-cost supplier is always chosen.	○	○
4. Purchasing department assures that requisitions are within budget limits before purchase orders are prepared.	○	○
5. The adequacy of each vendor's past record as a supplier is verified.	○	○

Receiving   *Agree*   *Disagree*

6. Secure facilities limit access to the goods during the receiving activity.   ○   ○

7. Receiving department compares its count of the quantity of goods received with that listed on its   ○   ○
    copy of the purchase order.

8. A receiving report is required for all purchases, including purchases of services.   ○   ○

9. The requisitioning department head independently verifies the quantity and quality of the goods   ○   ○
    received.

10. Requisitions, purchase orders, and receiving reports are matched with vendor invoices as to quantity   ○   ○
    and price.

Accounts Payable   *Agree*   *Disagree*

11. Accounts payable department recomputes the mathematical accuracy of each invoice.   ○   ○

12. The voucher register is independently reconciled to the control accounts monthly by the originators   ○   ○
    of the related vouchers.

13. All supporting documentation is marked "paid" by accounts payable immediately prior to making it   ○   ○
    available to the treasurer.

14. All supporting documentation is required for payment and is made available to the treasurer.   ○   ○

15. The purchasing, receiving, and accounts payable functions are segregated.   ○   ○

Solution to Illustrative Simulation C

1. Disagree. Someone independent of requisitioning should
    select the supplier.

2. Agree.

3. Disagree. Often, factors in addition to cost are considered
    (e.g., quality, dependability).

4. Agree.

5. Agree.

6. Agree.

7. Disagree. A comparison of quantities is not possible
    because quantity is blacked out on the purchase order pro-
    vided to receiving.

8. No receiving report is ordinarily necessary for purchases of
    services.

9. Agree.

10. Agree.

11. Agree.

12. Disagree. The reconciliation should be performed by an
    independent party.

13. Disagree. Documentation should be marked "paid" by the
    individual making the payment.

14. Agree.

15. Agree.

3. **Inventories and Production.** Inventories and production fit under the first two cycles. However, due to the unique nature of inventories, separate coverage is warranted. Two cases will be considered here: a nonmanufacturing firm and a manufacturing firm.

   Assume you are auditing a retailer who purchases products from a wholesaler and then sells the goods to the public. As in the acquisitions and payments cycle, purchase requisitions and purchase orders are used and controlled to purchase the inventory items that are of a "finished goods" nature. Likewise, when ordered goods are received, a receiving report is filled out by personnel in the receiving department. Perpetual inventory records are maintained for large dollar items. The firm has calculated economic reorder points and quantities. When quantities on hand reach the reorder point, a purchase requisition is prepared and sent to the purchasing department that places the order.

   At the end of the year, a physical inventory is taken during which items on hand are counted. In the case of items for which perpetual records exist, the perpetuals are corrected for any errors—large errors should be explained. For items without perpetual records, the total on hand is used to adjust the cost of goods sold at year-end (Beginning inventory + Purchases – Ending inventory = Cost of goods sold).

   The case of the manufacturing firm is somewhat more involved. Recall that basically three types of inventory accounts are involved. First, supplies and raw materials are purchased from suppliers in much the same manner as described above for the nonmanufacturing firm. Second, work in process is the combination of raw materials, direct labor, and factory overhead. Third, when the items in process have been completed, they are inspected and transferred at their cost (typically standard cost) to finished goods. Finally, when the goods are sold, the entry is to credit finished goods and to debit cost of goods sold.

Work in process is controlled through use of a standard cost system as described in elementary cost accounting courses. Recall that raw materials are those that typically can be directly identified with the product (e.g., transistors in a radio). Direct labor is also identified with the product (e.g., assembly line labor). Overhead includes materials not specifically identified with the product (amount of glue used) and supervisory, nonadministrative labor. Variances may be calculated for all three components—raw materials, direct labor, and overhead. Variances will be allocated between cost of goods sold and ending inventory (finished goods and work in process) based on the proportion of items sold and those remaining in inventory, although any "abnormal" waste will be directly expensed. This allocation is necessary because generally accepted accounting principles require that the firm report inventory based on the lower of actual cost or market—not standard cost.

Major Inventory and Production Controls

(1) Perpetual inventory records for large dollar items
(2) Prenumbered receiving reports prepared when inventory received; receiving reports accounted for
(3) Adequate standard cost system to cost inventory items
(4) Physical controls against theft
(5) Written inventory requisitions used
(6) Proper authorization of purchases and use of prenumbered purchase orders

Inventories and Production CPA Exam Multiple-Choice Questions

1. To verify debits to the perpetual inventory records an auditor would sample from the recorded debits to a sample of

   a. Purchase approvals.
   b. Purchase requisitions.
   c. Purchase invoices.
   d. Purchase orders.

1. (c) The question is asking what an auditor would sample **to** when testing debits in the perpetual inventory records. The invoice from the vendor (purchase invoice) will include both the quantity and cost of items sent to the client company. Note that none of the other replies will include the quantities actually shipped. Answer (a) would address a question relating to internal control over purchases. Answer (b) would address: "When verifying that recorded purchases of inventory were requisitioned by stores, an auditor would be most interested in examining a sample of. . .?" Answer (d) would address: "When verifying that recorded purchases of inventory have been properly ordered, an auditor would be most interest in examining a sample of. . .?"

2. The best procedure to allow an auditor to determine that a client has completely included merchandise it owns in its ending inventory is to review and test the

   a. Terms of the open purchase orders.
   b. Purchase cutoff.
   c. Commitments.
   d. Purchase invoices received around year-end.

2. (b) The question is asking how best to address the completeness of inventory. Purchase cutoff procedures include the other choices and are thus more complete. Answers (a) and (c) would be good answers for a question such as "To determine the amount of future purchase commitments a client has, an auditor should test the. . .?" Answer (d) would address: "An effective procedure for determining that a proper year-end cutoff of purchases has occurred is to test the. . .?"

4. **Personnel and Payroll.** The following is a possible flow of documents:

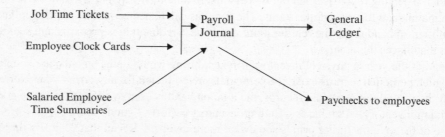

Assume that a separate personnel department maintains complete, up-to-date records for each employee. Included in such records is information on level of education, basic payroll information, experience, and authorization for any changes in pay rates. Assume that the firm's factory direct labor personnel use a time clock to punch in each morning and out each evening. Their employee clock card thus shows the total hours worked each day. These direct labor personnel also fill out job time tickets for each job they work on each day. At the end of each week their supervisor compares job time tickets with employee clock cards that have already been signed by the employees. Assume also that salaried and other employees fill out weekly time summaries indicating hours worked. All of the above information is sent to the payroll accounting department whose responsibility is to prepare the payroll journal and to prepare the unsigned payroll checks. The checks are then signed by the treasurer and distributed by an independent paymaster who has no other payroll functions. The summary payroll entry is then posted to the general ledger in the accounting department.

The internal auditing department periodically compares the payroll department's file on each employee with that in the personnel department's file to determine that no unauthorized changes in payroll records have been made. Employees with cash handling and recordkeeping responsibilities should be covered by fidelity bonds, a form of insurance which protects an employer against losses caused by dishonest employees (fidelity bonds also serve as a control when new employees are hired since the insurer will typically perform a background check on prospective employees).

Major Personnel and Payroll Controls

(1) Segregate: Timekeeping
                 Payroll Preparation
                 Personnel
                 Paycheck Distribution
(2) Time clocks used where possible
(3) Job time tickets reconciled to time clock cards
(4) Time clock cards approved by supervisors (overtime and regular hours)
(5) Treasurer signs paychecks
(6) Unclaimed paychecks controlled by someone otherwise independent of the payroll function (locked up and eventually destroyed if not claimed). In cases in which employees are paid cash (as opposed to checks) unclaimed pay should be deposited into a special bank account.
(7) Personnel department promptly sends termination notices to the payroll department.

Personnel and Payroll CPA Exam Multiple-Choice Questions

1. From the perspective of good internal control, which of the following is the most appropriate individual to distribute payroll checks?

    a. The payroll clerk.
    b. A personnel employee.
    c. Accounts receivable clerk.
    d. Employee supervisors.

1. **(c)** When considering internal control, a person not otherwise involved in personnel or payroll procedures, an "independent paymaster," should distribute paychecks. Of the choices provided, the accounts receivable clerk [answer (c)] is best. Answers (a) and (b) are improper because the payroll clerk prepares the payroll and the personnel department is involved in hiring and terminating employees. Employee supervisors are inappropriate due to the potential problem of employees who have quit, but for which paychecks are still, improperly, being prepared. Note that the key for this question is **not** that the accounts receivable clerk should distribute checks, but that an individual otherwise independent of the process should perform the function. Previous CPA questions, for example, have included the receptionist as an appropriate individual to distribute checks.

2. If an auditor is concerned about whether all individuals being paid are bona fide employees, would s/he sample from source documents to the payroll journal, or from the payroll journal to source documents?

2. The direction of testing will be **from** the payroll journal that represents the population of employees who are being paid **to** support. This support will include personnel records, employees' Form W-4, and clock cards or time tickets. In addition, the auditor might observe the distribution of the paychecks, or observe employees listed in the payroll journal at work. Note here that the auditor should sample from the population representing the firm's paid employees, here the payroll journal, to determine whether they are all bona fide.

Illustrative Simulation

Illustrative Simulation Problem D, which follows, provides an illustration of the relationship between controls and tests of controls in the payroll area.

Illustrative Simulation D

You are working in the payroll area of the Remlo Company Audit. For each of the listed controls, select the **best** test of a control to determine whether the control is operating effectively. Each test of a control may be used only once (or not at all).

Controls

1. The Human Resources Department authorizes all hires.

2. The Human Resources Department authorizes all pay rate changes.

3. Authorized **decreases** in pay rate have been reflected in subsequent remuneration.

4. Factory workers on the payroll exist as working employees of the company.

5. The individual signing the payroll checks (the maker) is properly authorized.

6. Individual payroll checks are signed by the authorized check maker.

7. The payroll bank account is reconciled by an individual who is not involved in preparation of payroll checks.

8. Employee overtime is approved by the employee's supervisor.

9. Sales commissions are properly calculated.

Tests of Controls

A. Agree pay rate change authorizations to subsequent pay rates in the payroll journal.

B. Compare current employee time cards to the subsequent payroll journal.

C. Compare payroll budgets to the preceding period budget.

D. Compare the total payroll costs per the payroll journal to the amounts as posted to ledger accounts.

E. Confirm the payroll account using the Standard Form to Confirm Account Balance Information with Financial Institutions.

F. Confirm with the bank that all checks have been issued bearing the signature of the proper check maker.

G. Confirm with the bank the individual responsible for account reconciliation.

H. Examine employee time cards for proper authorization.

I. Observe and make inquiries about the performance of the reconciliation and payroll check preparation function.

J. Obtain a list of authorized check signers (makers) from the bank.

K. Recalculate employee gross pay using supporting information.

L. Select a sample of cancelled payroll checks and determine that the maker's signature is proper.

M. Select a sample of employees on the payroll and determine that each has a properly approved hiring authorization form in his or her personnel file.

N. Select a sample of employee names from the payroll register and briefly interview each on a surprise basis.

O. Select a sample of hiring authorization forms and agree each to an employee in the payroll journal.

P. Vouch changes in pay rates as per two periods to pay rate change authorizations.

Solution to Illustrative Simulation Problem D

1. (M) To test whether all hires are authorized, selecting a sample of employees on the payroll to determine whether they have the proper documentation is the best approach. Notice that reply (O), selecting a sample of hiring authorization forms and agreeing each to employees in the payroll journal tests in the wrong direction. If one starts with a hiring authorization form one is not going to identify an employee without such a form. Reply (O) would more directly address whether those with hiring authorization forms are being paid—not typically a problem given individuals' tendency to complain if they are not paid.

2. (P) To test whether pay rate changes have been authorized, one should identify situations in which there is an actual change in pay and determine whether it was authorized. Reply (P) provides a good test since it identifies such a change and tests whether there is a pay rate change authorization.

3. (A) To determine whether authorized pay **decreases** have been properly processed, one should begin with the authorized decreases and test whether they have been recorded. In this case, the only documents likely to serve as the source documents are the pay rate change authorization forms.

4. (N) To determine whether factory workers being paid are actually at work, one would expect to test from source documents relating to paychecks (or the payroll journal) to some evidence that the person is on the job, whether it be evidence of work performed or the employee him or herself. Reply (N) is in the proper direction in that those on the payroll register are being paid, and should be on the job.

5. (J) The list of authorized check signers is maintained by the bank. Also, the board of directors may authorize signers. Since none of the replies deal with the Board of Directors the confirmation obtaining a list of authorized check signers from the bank is the best option.

6. (L) To determine whether the authorized check maker is signing the checks, one should examine individual checks. Notice that this control would ordinarily be tested following testing of the preceding control.

7. (I) Observation and inquiry about reconciliation and the payroll check preparation functions will serve to test this segregation.

8. (H) To determine whether overtime is approved by the employee's supervisor, one should understand the approval process. But in a question such as this, one should find a reply that implies authorization, as does reply (H).

9. (K) The proper calculation of sales commission requires a comparison of sales with pay. The general reply (K) on recalculating gross pay accomplishes this task.

5. **Financing.** This cycle includes issuance and repurchase of debt (bank loans, mortgages, bonds payable) and capital stock, and payment of interest and dividends. Debt and capital stock transactions should be authorized by the board of directors. Often an independent trustee issues bonds, monitors company compliance with the provisions of the debt agreement, and pays interest.

For capital stock transactions, corporations may either employ an independent stock registrar and a stock transfer agent, or handle their own transactions. Normally, internal control is stronger when a stock registrar and a stock transfer agent are utilized. A stock registrar's primary responsibility is to verify that stock is issued in accordance with the authorization of the board of directors and the articles of incorporation; the stock transfer agent's primary responsibility is maintaining detailed stockholder records and carrying out transfers of stock ownership.

Major Financing Controls Frequently Missing in CPA Exam Questions

(1) Debt and equity transactions are properly approved by the company's board of directors.
(2) An independent trustee handles bond transactions.
(3) A stock registrar and a stock transfer agent handle capital stock transactions.
(4) Canceled stock certificates are defaced to prevent their reissuance.

6. **Investing.** This cycle includes investments in the debt and equity of other organizations, and purchases of property, plant, and equipment. Investments may be categorized as marketable securities and long-term investments. Purchases are recorded at cost, and reported at the lower of cost or market, as guided by SFAS 12.

Major Investment Controls Frequently Missing in CPA Exam Questions

(1) Segregation of duties among the individuals authorizing purchases and sales of securities, maintaining custody of the securities, and maintaining the records of securities
(2) Use of an independent agent such as a stockbroker, bank or trust company to maintain custody of securities
(3) Securities not in the custody of an independent agent maintained in a bank safe-deposit box under the joint control of the treasurer and one other company official; both individuals should be present to gain access
(4) Registration of securities in the name of the company
(5) Detailed records of all securities and related revenue from interest and dividends
(6) Periodical physical inspection of securities by individuals with no responsibility for the authorization, custody, or recordkeeping for investments

Property, plant, and equipment acquisitions require board of directors' approval for purchases over a certain amount. Otherwise, the purchase is handled similarly to a merchandise purchase. As in the case of merchandise purchases, the item is recorded as an addition when some form of purchase authorization is present with a vendor's invoice and a receiving report. The company then selects an appropriate life and depreciation method (e.g., straight-line, sum-of-the-years' digits, double-declining balance). Depreciation entries are made in the general journal with a debit to depreciation expense (manufacturing overhead for manufacturing equipment) and a credit to accumulated depreciation. The company should also have controls to determine that repair and maintenance expenses have not been capitalized.

Asset retirements are recorded by removing the asset and accumulated depreciation from the general ledger—a gain (loss) may occur on the transaction. In the case of an exchange of assets, the firm has policies to determine that GAAP is properly followed in recording the transaction.

Major Property, Plant, and Equipment Controls Frequently Missing in CPA Exam Questions

(1) Major asset acquisitions are properly approved by the firm's board of directors and properly controlled through capital budgeting techniques.
(2) Detailed records are available for property assets and accumulated depreciation.
(3) Written policies exist for capitalization vs. expensing decisions.
(4) Depreciation properly calculated.
(5) Retirements approved by an appropriate level of management.
(6) Physical control over assets to prevent theft.
(7) Periodic physical inspection of plant and equipment by individuals who are otherwise independent of property, plant, and equipment (e.g., internal auditors).

7. **Overall Internal Control Questionnaires (checklists).** The following internal control questionnaires (in checklist form) outline the controls that are typically necessary in various transaction cycles and accounts. While the lists are clearly too lengthy to memorize, review them and obtain a general familiarity. **Candidates with little actual business experience will probably find them especially helpful for questions that require analysis of internal control deficiencies.** Study in detail the questionnaire checklists on cash receipts (#3), cash disbursements (#4), and on payroll (#14)—as indicated above, a large percentage of the internal control weakness type questions relate to these three areas.

The checklists are organized into subtopics—generally by category of balance sheet account (e.g., cash, receivables, fixed assets, liabilities, shareholders' equity, etc.). The related nominal accounts should be considered with the real accounts (e.g., depreciation and fixed assets, sales and accounts receivable).

1. General

   Chart of accounts
   Accounting procedures manual
   Organizational chart to define responsibilities
   Absence of entries direct to ledgers
   Posting references in ledgers
   Review of journal entries
   Use of standard journal entries
   Use of prenumbered forms
   Support for all journal entries
   Access to records limited to authorized
     persons
   Rotation of accounting personnel
   Required vacations
   Review of system at every level
   Appropriate revision of chart of accounts
   Appropriate revision of procedures

   Separation of recordkeeping from operations
   Separation of recordkeeping from
     custodianship
   Record retention policy
   Bonding of employees
   A conflict of interest policy

2. Cash funds

   Imprest system
   Reasonable amount
   Completeness of vouchers
   Custodian responsible for fund
   Reimbursement checks to order of custodian
   Surprise audits
   No employee check cashing
   Physically secure
   Custodian has no access to cash receipts
   Custodian has no access to accounting records

3. Cash receipts

    Detail listing of mail receipts
    Restrictive endorsement of checks
    Special handling of postdated checks
    Daily deposit
    Cash custodians bonded
    Cash custodians apart from negotiable
        instruments
    Bank accounts properly authorized
    Handling of returned NSF items
    Comparison of duplicate deposit slips with
        cash book
    Comparison of duplicate deposit slips with
        detail AR
    Banks instructed not to cash checks to company
    Control over cash from other sources
    Separation of cashier personnel from
        accounting duties
    Separation of cashier personnel from
        credit duties
    Use of cash registers
    Cash register tapes
    Numbered cash receipt tickets
    Outside salesmen cash control
    Daily reconciliation of cash collections

4. Cash disbursements

    Numbered checks
    Sufficient support for check
    Limited authorization to sign checks
    No signing of blank checks
    All checks accounted for
    Detail listing of checks
    Mutilation of voided checks
    Specific approval for unusually large checks
    Proper authorization of persons signing
        checks
    Control over signature machines
    Check listing compared with cash book
    Control over interbank transfers
    Prompt accounting for interbank transfers
    Checks not payable to cash
    Physical control of unused checks
    Cancellation of supporting documents
    Control over long outstanding checks
    Reconciliation of bank account
    Independence of person reconciling bank
        statement
    Bank statement direct to person reconciling
    No access to cash records or receipts by
        check signers

5. Investments

    Proper authorization of transactions
    Under control of a custodian
    Custodian bonded

Custodian separate from cash receipts
    Custodian separate from investment records
    Safety-deposit box
    Record of all safety-deposit visits
    Access limited
    Presence of two required for access
    Periodic reconciliation of detail with control
    Record of all aspects of all securities
    Availability of brokerage advices, etc.
    Periodic internal audit
    Securities in name of company
    Proper segregation of collateral
    Physical control of collateral
    Periodic appraisal of collateral
    Periodic appraisal of investments
    Adequate records of investments for
        application of equity method

6. Accounts receivable and sales

    Sales orders prenumbered
    Credit approval
    Credit and sales departments independent
    Control of back orders
    Sales order and sales invoice comparison
    Shipping invoices prenumbered
    Names and addresses on shipping invoice
    Review of sales invoices
    Control over returned merchandise
    Credit memoranda prenumbered
    Matching of credit memoranda and receiving
        reports
    Control over credit memoranda
    Control over scrap sales
    Control over sales to employees
    Control over COD sales
    Sales reconciled with cash receipts and AR
    Sales reconciled with inventory change
    AR statement to all customers
    Periodic preparation of aging schedule
    Control over collections of written-off
        receivables
    Control over AR write-offs (e.g., proper
        authorization)
    Control over AR written off (i.e., review for
        possible collection)
    Independence of sales, AR, receipts, billing,
        and shipping personnel

7. Notes receivable

    Proper authorization of notes
    Detailed records of notes
    Periodic detail to control comparison
    Periodic confirmation with makers
    Control over notes discounted
    Control over delinquent notes
    Physical safety of notes

Periodic count of notes
Control over collateral
Control over revenue from notes
Custodian of notes independent from cash
and recordkeeping

8. Inventory and cost of sales

Periodic inventory counts
Written inventory instructions
Counts by noncustodians
Control over count tags
Control over inventory adjustments
Use of perpetual records
Periodic comparison of G/L and perpetual
records
Investigation of discrepancies
Control over consignment inventory
Control over inventory stored at warehouses
Control over returnable containers left with
customers
Preparation of receiving reports
Prenumbered receiving reports
Receiving reports in numerical order
Independence of custodian from
recordkeeping
Adequacy of insurance
Physical safeguards against theft
Physical safeguards against fire
Adequacy of cost system
Cost system tied into general ledger
Periodic review of overhead rates
Use of standard costs
Use of inventory requisitions
Periodic summaries of inventory usage
Control over intra-company inventory
transfers
Purchase orders prenumbered
Proper authorization for purchases
Review of open purchase orders

9. Prepaid expenses and deferred charges

Proper authorization to incur
Authorization and support of amortization
Detailed records
Periodic review of amortization policies
Control over insurance policies
Periodic review of insurance needs
Control over premium refunds
Beneficiaries of company policies
Physical control of policies

10. Intangibles

Authorization to incur
Detailed records
Authorization to amortize
Periodic review of amortization

11. Fixed assets

Detailed property records
Periodic comparison with control accounts
Proper authorization for acquisition
Written policies for acquisition
Control over expenditures for self-
construction
Use of work orders
Individual asset identification plates
Written authorization for sale
Written authorization for retirement
Physical safeguard from theft
Control over fully depreciated assets
Written capitalization—expense policies
Responsibilities charged for asset and
depreciation records
Written, detailed depreciation records
Depreciation adjustments for sales and
retirements
Control over intra-company transfers
Adequacy of insurance
Control over returnable containers

12. Accounts payable

Designation of responsibility
Independence of AP personnel from
purchasing, cashier, receiving functions
Periodic comparison of detail and control
Control over purchase returns
Clerical accuracy of vendors' invoices
Matching of purchase order, receiving report,
and vendor invoice
Reconciliation of vendor statements with
AP detail
Control over debit memos
Control over advance payments
Review of unmatched receiving reports
Mutilation of supporting documents at
payment
Review of debit balances
Investigation of discounts not taken

13. Accrued liabilities and other expenses

Proper authorization for expenditure and
incurrence
Control over partial deliveries
Postage meter
Purchasing department
Bids from vendors
Verification of invoices
Imprest cash account
Detailed records
Responsibility charged
Independence from G/L and cashier functions
Periodic comparison with budget

14. Payroll

   Authorization to employ
   Personnel data records
   Tax records
   Time clock
   Supervisor review of time cards
   Review of payroll calculations
   Comparison of time cards to job sheets
   Imprest payroll account
   Responsibility for payroll records
   Compliance with labor statutes
   Distribution of payroll checks
   Control over unclaimed wages
   Profit-sharing authorization
   Responsibility for profit-sharing computations

15. Long-term liabilities

   Authorization to incur
   Executed in company name
   Detailed records of long-term debt
   Reports of independent transfer agent
   Reports of independent registrar
   Otherwise adequate records of creditors
   Control over unissued instruments

   Signers independent of each other
   Adequacy of records of collateral
   Periodic review of debt agreement
      compliance
   Recordkeeping of detachable warrants
   Recordkeeping of conversion features

16. Shareholders' equity

   Use of registrar
   Use of transfer agent
   Adequacy of detailed records
   Comparison of transfer agent's report with
      records
   Physical control over blank certificates
   Physical control over treasury certificates
   Authorization for transactions
   Tax stamp compliance for canceled certificates
   Independent dividend agent
   Imprest dividend account
   Periodic reconciliation of dividend account
   Adequacy of stockholders' ledger
   Review of stock restrictions and provisions
   Valuation procedures for stock issuances
   Other paid-in capital entries
   Other retained earnings entries

NOW REVIEW MULTIPLE-CHOICE QUESTIONS 94 THROUGH 136

E Other Considerations

1. **Additional Financial Statement Audit Communications**

   a. **Communication of internal control related matters.** AU-C 265 requires auditors to communicate significant deficiencies and material weaknesses to management and to those charged with governance.[2] At this point study the outline of AU-C 265. This and the communication in the following section are referred to as "by-product" reports since they result from an audit, but are not the primary report of an audit (i.e., they are not the audit report). Make certain that you know the following points related to the AU-C 265 communication:

   • Summary of likelihood and potential amount involved

Deficiency	Severity	Required Communication to Management and Those Charged with Governance?
Control Deficiency	Design or operation of control does not allow management or employees, in the normal course of performing their assigned functions, to prevent or detect and correct misstatements on a timely basis.	No
Significant Deficiency	Less severe than a material weakness, yet important enough to merit attention by those charged with governance.	Yes
Material Weakness	A reasonable possibility that a material misstatement will not be prevented, or detected and corrected on a timely basis.	Yes

---

[2]Those charged with governance are the person(s) with responsibility for overseeing the strategic direction of the entity and obligations related to the accountability of the entity. This often is the audit committee.

- The report issued should be **written** and include

  - Purpose of consideration of IC was to express an opinion on the financial statements, **not** to express an opinion on IC.
  - Auditor is not expressing an opinion on IC effectiveness.
  - Consideration of IC not designed to identify all significant deficiencies or material weaknesses.
  - Definition of material weakness and significant deficiency.
  - Separately describe significant deficiencies and material weaknesses identified.
  - Indication that the communication is for management, those charged with governance and others within the organization; it **should not be used by others**.

- While a written report indicating that no significant deficiencies were identified should **not** be issued, a report indicating that no material weaknesses were identified **may** be issued. Notice that this differs from an AT 501 internal control engagement (discussed in Section C of this module) in which a report directly stating that no material weaknesses were identified **cannot** be issued.
- Communications are best if issued by the audit report release date (the date the auditor grants client permission to use report), but should be issued not later than 60 days following the audit report release date.
- A previously communicated significant deficiency or material weakness that has not been corrected should be recommunicated; it may be communicated by simply referring to the prior communication and its date.

b. **The auditor's communication with those charged with governance.** AU-C 260 requires that a communication (orally or in writing) of certain information occur between the auditor and those charged with governance of the company being audited (e.g., the board of directors, audit committee). Recall that the audit committee is a group of outside (non management) directors whose functions typically include

- Nominating, terminating, and negotiating CPA firm audit fees
- Discussing broad, general matters concerning the type, scope, and timing of the audit with the public accounting firm
- Discussing internal control weaknesses with the public accounting firm
- Reviewing the financial statements and the public accounting firm's audit report
- Working with the company's internal auditors

The following summarizes the required matters communicated:

Audit responsibilities under GAAS

1. Responsibility to form and express an opinion
2. An audit does not relieve management for those charged with governance of their responsibilities.

Planned scope and timing of the audit—An overview of the planned scope and timing of the audit; this may assist those charged with governance in understanding the consequences of the auditor's work for their oversight activities and the auditor to understand better the entity and its environment.

Significant findings from the audit

1. Qualitative aspects of the entity's significant accounting practices
2. Significant difficulties encountered during the audit
3. Uncorrected misstatements
4. Disagreements with management
5. Management's consultations with other accountants
6. Significant issues discussed, or subject to correspondence with management
7. Auditor independence issues
8. If those charged with governance are not involved in managing the entity, the following should also be communicated

   - Material corrected misstatements resulting from audit
   - Representations requested from management
   - Other significant issues

The PCAOB requires communications similar to those of AU-C 260. In addition, the following may go beyond those of AU-C 260 in that the PCAOB requires:

- Communication of difficult or contentious matters about which the auditor consulted when the auditor considers it relevant to the audit committee.
- Communication of two categories of accounting policies and practices:

  - Significant—important on an overall basis.
  - Critical—tailored to specific events of the current year (a subset of significant).

  AU-C only speaks of significant accounting policies and practices.

- That when departure from standard audit report expected, the auditor communicate the matter.
- Specific going concern communications as per the above bullet, but also situations in which the auditor concludes that there is no need for a going concern modification due to management's plans.
- That the communication occur prior to the issuance of the auditor's report while AU-C 260 requires only timely disclosure.

A simulation question might make the Professional Standards available and ask the candidate to prepare a report on internal control deficiencies or on matters to be communicated to those charged with governance. While you might use either the index or keyword approach to identify the appropriate standards, bear in mind that the two primary sections here are AU-C 260 and AU-C 265. At this point you should study the outline of AU-C 260.

NOW REVIEW MULTIPLE-CHOICE QUESTIONS 137 THROUGH 151

---

2. **Effects of an Internal Audit Function.** AU-C 610 discusses the effect of an internal audit function on the CPA's audit.

   Internal auditors have two primary effects on the audit: (1) their existence and work may **affect the nature, timing, and extent of audit procedures**, and (2) CPAs may use internal auditors to **provide direct assistance** in performing procedures. The CPA should assess both the **competence** and **objectivity** of internal auditors. Competence is evaluated by considering education, experience, professional certification, audit policies, and various work policies. Objectivity is assessed by considering organizational status within the company, and policies for assuring that internal auditors are objective with respect to the areas being audited. Section B of the outline of Section AU-C 610 presents more detailed information on the heavily tested area of internal auditor competence and objectivity.

   Internal auditors may affect the CPA's understanding of internal control, control risk assessment, and substantive procedures. You should know that for assertions with high audit risk, the internal auditor's work alone cannot eliminate the need for CPA's tests. A number of questions may be expected on this topic. At this point, you should study the section outline.

3. **Reports on Processing of Transactions by Service Organizations (AT 801 and AU-C 402)**

   A service organization provides services to user entities. Those services are likely to be relevant to the user entities' internal control over financial reporting. For example, a payroll processing service organization's controls related to the timely remittance of payroll deductions to government authorities may be relevant to a user entity because late remittances could incur interest and penalties. Auditors of user entities are concerned with service organization controls. Accordingly, service organizations often obtain from their CPAs a report on those elements of internal control that are relevant to the users and their auditors—related guidance is in AT 801. Guidance on how the users' auditor should consider those reports is presented in AU-C 402.

To the XYZ Loan Servicer:

We have examined the accompanying description of the loan servicing application of XYZ Loan Servicer. Our examination included procedures to obtain reasonable assurance about whether (1) the accompanying description presents fairly, in all material respects, the aspects of XYZ Loan Servicer's policies and procedures that may be relevant to a user organization's internal control, (2) the control structure policies and procedures included in the description were suitably designed to achieve the control objectives specified in the description, if those policies and procedures were complied with satisfactorily, and (3) such policies and procedures had been implemented as of December 31, 20X2. The control objectives were specified by the State of Arizona Loan Servicing Authority. Our examination was performed in accordance with standards established by the American Institute of Certified Public Accountants and included those procedures we considered necessary in the circumstances to obtain a reasonable basis for rendering an opinion.

We did not perform procedures to determine the operating effectiveness of policies and procedures for any period. Accordingly, we express no opinion on the operating effectiveness of any aspects of XYZ Loan Servicer's policies and procedures, individually or in the aggregate.

In our opinion, the accompanying description of the aforementioned application presents fairly, in all material respects, the relevant aspects of XYZ Loan Servicer's policies and procedures that had been implemented as of December 31, 20X2. Also, in our opinion, the policies and procedures, as described, are suitably designed to provide reasonable assurance that the specified control objectives would be achieved if the described policies and procedures were complied with satisfactorily.

The description of policies and procedures at XYZ Loan Servicer is as of December 31, 20X2, and any projection of such information to the future is subject to the risk that, because of change, the description may no longer portray the system in existence. The potential effectiveness of specific policies and procedures at the service organization is subject to inherent limitations and, accordingly, misstatements or fraud may occur and not be detected. Furthermore, the projection of any conclusions, based on our findings, to future periods is subject to the risk that changes may alter the validity of such conclusions.

This report is intended solely for use by the management of XYZ Loan Servicer, its customers, and the independent auditors of its customers.

Two types of service auditor reports are described in detail in this section. The first addresses whether service organization controls have been implemented. The following is an example of such a report.

The second, issued when the effectiveness of controls has been tested, includes the information presented in the first type of report plus an opinion on the operating effectiveness of those controls. Of the two reports, only the second type provides the user auditor a basis for reducing the assessment of control risk. At this point, you may wish to study the outlines of AT 801 and AU-C 402.

Section G.3.g of the Reporting Module discusses the reports discussed in this section and two other types of service organization control (SOC) reports. Those discussed here are referred to as SOC 1 reports in that section.

> **NOW REVIEW MULTIPLE-CHOICE QUESTIONS 152 THROUGH 165**

KEY TERMS

Assertions. Representations by management, explicit or otherwise, that are embodied in the financial statements, as used by the auditor to consider the different types of potential misstatements that may occur.

Control risk. The risk that a misstatement that could occur in an assertion about a class of transaction, account balance, or disclosure and that could be material, either individually or when aggregated with other misstatements, will not be prevented, or detected and corrected, on a timely basis by the entity's internal control.

Deficiency in internal control. A deficiency in internal control exists when the design or operation of a control does not allow management or employees, in the normal course of performing their assigned functions, to prevent, or detect and correct, misstatements on a timely basis. A *deficiency in design* exists when (a) a control necessary to meet the control objective is missing or (b) an existing control is not properly designed so that, even if the control operates as designed, the control objective would not be met. A *deficiency in operation* exists when a properly designed control does not operate as designed, or when the person performing the control does not possess the necessary authority or competence to perform the control effectively.

Foreign Corrupt Practices Act of 1977. Federal legislation prohibiting payments to foreign officials for the purpose of securing business. The act also requires all companies under SEC jurisdiction to maintain a system of internal control to provide reasonable assurance that transactions are executed only with the knowledge and authorization of management.

Internal control. A process—effected by those charged with governance, management, and other personnel—designed to provide reasonable assurance about the achievement of the entity's objectives with regard to the reliability of financial reporting, effectiveness and efficiency of operations, and compliance with applicable laws and regulations. Internal control over safeguarding of assets against unauthorized acquisition, use, or disposition may include controls relating to financial reporting and operations objectives.

Internal control checklist. One of several methods of describing internal control in audit working papers. Checklists are usually designed so that "no" answers prominently identify weaknesses in internal control.

Internal control flowchart. One of several methods of describing internal control in audit working papers. A symbolic representation of a system or series of procedures with each procedure shown in sequence.

Internal control questionnaire. One of several methods of describing internal control in audit working papers. Questionnaires may either ask (1) open-ended questions or (2) "yes/no questions (in which case it in essence becomes the same as an internal control checklist).

Internal control written narrative. One of several methods of describing internal control in audit working papers. A written summary of internal control for inclusion in audit working paper—generally a memo.

Material weakness. A deficiency, or a combination of deficiencies, in internal control, such that there is a reasonable possibility that a material misstatement of the entity's financial statements will not be prevented, or detected and corrected, on a timely basis.

Report on management's description of a service organization's system and the suitability of the design of controls. A report that comprises

1. Management's description of the service organization's system.
2. A written assertion by management of the service organization about whether, in all material respects, and based on suitable criteria

   a. Management's description of the service organization's system fairly presents the service organization's system that was designed and implemented as of a specified date.
   b. The controls related to the control objectives stated in management's description of the service organization's system were suitably designed to achieve those control objectives as of the specified date.

3. A service auditor's report that expresses an opinion on the matters in 2.a.–2.b.

Report on management's description of a service organization's system and the suitability of the design and operating effectiveness of controls (referred to in this section as a *type 2 report*). A report that comprises

1. Management's description of the service organization's system.
2. A written assertion by management of the service organization, about whether in all material respects, and based on suitable criteria,

   a. The description of the service organization's system fairly presents the service organization's system that was designed and implemented throughout the specified period.
   b. The controls related to the control objectives stated in the description of the service organization's system were suitably designed throughout the specified period to achieve those control objectives.
   c. The controls related to the control objectives stated in the description of the service organization's system operated effectively throughout the specified period to achieve those control objectives.

3. A service auditor's report that

   a. Expresses an opinion about the matters in 2.a.–2.c.
   b. Includes a description of the service auditor's tests of controls and the results thereof.

> **NOTE:** The two primary differences between a type 1 and type 2 report are that (1) a type 2 report deals with controls over a time period (often a year) while a type 1 deals with controls at a point in time and (2) only a type 2 report addresses operating effectiveness.

Sarbanes-Oxley Act of 2002 (SOX). A set of reforms that strengthened penalties for corporate fraud, restricted the types of consulting CPAs can perform for audit clients, and created the Public Company Accounting Oversight Board to oversee CPAs and public accounting firms.

Service auditor. A practitioner who reports on controls at a service organization.

Service organization. An organization or segment of an organization that provides services to user entities that are likely to be relevant to user entities' internal control as it relates to financial reporting.

Service organization's system. The policies and procedures designed, implemented and documented by management of the service organization to provide user entities with the services covered by the service auditor's report. Management's description of the service organization's system identifies the services covered, the period to which the description relates (or in the case of a type 1 report, the date to which the description relates), the control objectives specified by management or an outside party, the party specifying the control objectives (if not specified by management), and the related controls.

Significant deficiency. A deficiency, or a combination of deficiencies, in internal control that is less severe than a material weakness, yet important enough to merit attention by those charged with governance.

Substantive procedure. An audit procedure designed to detect material misstatements at the assertion level. Substantive procedures comprise tests of details (classes of transactions, account balances, and disclosures) and substantive analytical procedures.

Those charged with governance. The person(s) or organization(s) (for example, a corporate trustee) with responsibility for overseeing the strategic direction of the entity and the obligations related to the accountability of the entity. This includes overseeing the financial reporting process. Those charged with governance may include management personnel; for example, executive members of a governance board or an owner-manager.

Tests of controls. An audit procedure designed to evaluate the operating effectiveness of controls in preventing, or detecting/correcting material misstatements at the assertion level.

User auditor. An auditor who audits and reports on the financial statements of a user entity.

User entity. An entity that uses a service organization and whose financial statements are being audited.

Walk-through. A procedure in which an auditor follows a transaction from origination through the company's processes, including information systems, until it is reflected in the company's financial records, using the same documents and information technology that company personnel use. Walkthrough procedures usually include a combination of inquiry, observation, inspection of relevant documentation, and reperformance of controls.

Multiple-Choice Questions (1–165)

A.1. Definition of Internal Control

1. Which of the following most likely would **not** be considered an inherent limitation of the potential effectiveness of an entity's internal control?

   a. Incompatible duties.
   b. Management override.
   c. Mistakes in judgment.
   d. Collusion among employees.

2. When considering internal control, an auditor should be aware of the concept of reasonable assurance, which recognizes that

   a. Internal control may be ineffective due to mistakes in judgment and personal carelessness.
   b. Adequate safeguards over access to assets and records should permit an entity to maintain proper accountability.
   c. Establishing and maintaining internal control is an important responsibility of management.
   d. The cost of an entity's internal control should not exceed the benefits expected to be derived.

3. Proper segregation of functional responsibilities calls for separation of the functions of

   a. Authorization, execution, and payment.
   b. Authorization, recording, and custody.
   c. Custody, execution, and reporting.
   d. Authorization, payment, and recording.

A.2. Major Components of Internal Control

4. An entity's ongoing monitoring activities often include

   a. Periodic audits by the audit committee.
   b. Reviewing the purchasing function.
   c. The audit of the annual financial statements.
   d. Control risk assessment in conjunction with quarterly reviews.

5. The overall attitude and awareness of an entity's board of directors concerning the importance of internal control usually is reflected in its

   a. Computer-based controls.
   b. System of segregation of duties.
   c. Control environment.
   d. Safeguards over access to assets.

6. Management philosophy and operating style most likely would have a significant influence on an entity's control environment when

   a. The internal auditor reports directly to management.
   b. Management is dominated by one individual.
   c. Accurate management job descriptions delineate specific duties.

   d. The audit committee actively oversees the financial reporting process.

7. Which of the following factors are included in an entity's control environment?

	Audit committee	Integrity and ethical values	Organizational
a.	Yes	Yes	No
b.	Yes	No	Yes
c.	No	Yes	Yes
d.	Yes	Yes	Yes

8. Which of the following is **not** a component of an entity's internal control?

   a. Control risk.
   b. Control activities.
   c. Monitoring.
   d. Control environment.

A.3. Related Topics

9. Which of the following is a provision of the Foreign Corrupt Practices Act?

   a. It is a criminal offense for an auditor to fail to detect and report a bribe paid by an American business entity to a foreign official for the purpose of obtaining business.
   b. The auditor's detection of illegal acts committed by officials of the auditor's publicly held client in conjunction with foreign officials should be reported to the Enforcement Division of the Securities and Exchange Commission.
   c. If the auditor of a publicly held company concludes that the effects on the financial statements of a bribe given to a foreign official are not susceptible to reasonable estimation, the auditor's report should be modified.
   d. Every publicly held company must devise, document, and maintain internal control sufficient to provide reasonable assurances that internal control objectives are met.

B.1. Obtain Understanding of the Client and Its Internal Control

10. An auditor suspects that certain client employees are ordering merchandise for themselves over the Internet without recording the purchase or receipt of the merchandise. When vendors' invoices arrive, one of the employees approves the invoices for payment. After the invoices are paid, the employee destroys the invoices and the related vouchers. In gathering evidence regarding the fraud, the auditor most likely would select items for testing from the file of all

   a. Cash disbursements.
   b. Approved vouchers.
   c. Receiving reports.
   d. Vendors' invoices.

11. Which of the following procedures most likely would provide an auditor with evidence about whether an entity's internal control activities are suitably designed to prevent or detect material misstatements?

    a. Reperforming the activities for a sample of transactions.
    b. Performing analytical procedures using data aggregated at a high level.
    c. Vouching a sample of transactions directly related to the activities.
    d. Observing the entity's personnel applying the activities.

12. Which statement is correct concerning the relevance of various types of controls to a financial audit?

    a. An auditor may ordinarily ignore a consideration of controls when a substantive audit approach is taken.
    b. Controls over the reliability of financial reporting are ordinarily most directly relevant to an audit, but other controls may also be relevant.
    c. Controls over safeguarding of assets and liabilities are of primary importance, while controls over the reliability of financial reporting may also be relevant.
    d. All controls are ordinarily relevant to an audit.

13. In an audit of financial statements in accordance with generally accepted auditing standards, an auditor is required to

    a. Document the auditor's understanding of the entity's internal control.
    b. Search for significant deficiencies in the operation of internal control.
    c. Perform tests of controls to evaluate the effectiveness of the entity's internal control.
    d. Determine whether controls are suitably designed to prevent or detect material misstatements.

14. In obtaining an understanding of an entity's internal control relevant to audit planning, an auditor is required to obtain knowledge about the

    a. Design of the controls pertaining to internal control components.
    b. Effectiveness of controls that have been implemented.
    c. Consistency with which controls are currently being applied.
    d. Controls related to each principal transaction class and account balance.

15. An auditor should obtain sufficient knowledge of an entity's information system to understand the

    a. Safeguards used to limit access to computer facilities.
    b. Process used to prepare significant accounting estimates.
    c. Controls used to assure proper authorization of transactions.
    d. Controls used to detect the concealment of fraud.

16. When obtaining an understanding of an entity's internal control, an auditor should concentrate on the substance of controls rather than their form because

    a. The controls may be operating effectively but may **not** be documented.
    b. Management may establish appropriate controls but **not** enforce compliance with them.
    c. The controls may be so inappropriate that **no** reliance is contemplated by the auditor.
    d. Management may implement controls whose costs exceed their benefits.

17. Decision tables differ from program flowcharts in that decision tables emphasize

    a. Ease of manageability for complex programs.
    b. Logical relationships among conditions and actions.
    c. Cost benefit factors justifying the program.
    d. The sequence in which operations are performed.

18. During the consideration of internal control in a financial statement audit, an auditor is **not** obligated to

    a. Search for significant deficiencies in the operation of the internal control.
    b. Understand the internal control and the information system.
    c. Determine whether the control activities relevant to audit planning have been implemented.
    d. Perform procedures to understand the design of internal control.

19. A primary objective of procedures performed to obtain an understanding of internal control is to provide an auditor with

    a. Knowledge necessary to assess the risks of material misstatements.
    b. Evidence to use in assessing inherent risk.
    c. A basis for modifying tests of controls.
    d. An evaluation of the consistency of application of management's policies.

20. Which of the following statements regarding auditor documentation of the client's internal control is correct?

    a. Documentation must include flowcharts.
    b. Documentation must include procedural write-ups.
    c. No documentation is necessary although it is desirable.
    d. No one particular form of documentation is necessary, and the extent of documentation may vary.

21. In obtaining an understanding of an entity's internal control, an auditor is required to obtain knowledge about the

	Operating effectiveness of controls	Design of controls
a.	Yes	Yes
b.	No	Yes
c.	Yes	No
d.	No	No

B.2. Assess the Risk of Material Misstatement and Design Further Audit Procedures

22. Which of the following may not be required on a particular audit of a nonissuer (nonpublic) company?

   a. Risk assessment procedures.
   b. Tests of controls.
   c. Substantive procedures.
   d. Analytical procedures.

23. Control risk should be assessed in terms of

   a. Specific controls.
   b. Types of potential fraud.
   c. Financial statement assertions.
   d. Control environment factors.

24. After assessing control risk, an auditor desires to seek a further reduction in the assessed level of control risk. At this time, the auditor would consider whether

   a. It would be efficient to obtain an understanding of the entity's information system.
   b. The entity's controls have been implemented.
   c. The entity's controls pertain to any financial statement assertions.
   d. Additional audit evidence sufficient to support a further reduction is likely to be available.

25. Assessing control risk at a low level most likely would involve

   a. Performing more extensive substantive tests with larger sample sizes than originally planned.
   b. Reducing inherent risk for most of the assertions relevant to significant account balances.
   c. Changing the timing of substantive tests by omitting interim-date testing and performing the tests at year-end.
   d. Identifying specific controls relevant to specific assertions.

26. An auditor assesses control risk because it

   a. Is relevant to the auditor's understanding of the control environment.
   b. Provides assurance that the auditor's materiality levels are appropriate.
   c. Indicates to the auditor where inherent risk may be the greatest.
   d. Affects the level of detection risk that the auditor may accept.

27. When an auditor increases the assessed level of control risk because certain control activities were determined to be ineffective, the auditor would most likely increase the

   a. Extent of tests of controls.
   b. Level of detection risk.
   c. Extent of tests of details.
   d. Level of inherent risk.

28. An auditor uses the knowledge provided by the understanding of internal control and the assessed level of the risk of material misstatement primarily to

   a. Determine whether procedures and records concerning the safeguarding of assets are reliable.
   b. Ascertain whether the opportunities to allow any person to both perpetrate and conceal fraud are minimized.
   c. Modify the initial assessments of inherent risk and preliminary judgments about materiality levels.
   d. Determine the nature, timing, and extent of substantive tests for financial statement assertions.

29. An auditor may compensate for a weakness in internal control by increasing the

   a. Level of detection risk.
   b. Extent of tests of controls.
   c. Preliminary judgment about audit risk.
   d. Extent of analytical procedures.

30. Which of the following statements is correct concerning an auditor's assessment of control risk?

   a. Assessing control risk may be performed concurrently during an audit with obtaining an understanding of the entity's internal control.
   b. Evidence about the operation of internal control in prior audits may not be considered during the current year's assessment of control risk.
   c. The basis for an auditor's conclusions about the assessed level of control risk need not be documented unless control risk is assessed at the maximum level.
   d. The lower the assessed level of control risk, the less assurance the evidence must provide that the control procedures are operating effectively.

31. Regardless of the assessed level of control risk, an auditor would perform some

   a. Tests of controls to determine the effectiveness of internal control policies.
   b. Analytical procedures to verify the design of internal control.
   c. Substantive tests to restrict detection risk for significant transaction classes.
   d. Dual-purpose tests to evaluate both the risk of monetary misstatement and preliminary control risk.

B.3. Perform Further Audit Procedures—Tests of Controls

32. How frequently must an auditor test operating effectiveness of controls that appear to function as they have in past years and on which the auditor wishes to rely in the current year?

   a. Monthly.
   b. Each audit.
   c. At least every second audit.
   d. At least every third audit.

33. Before assessing control risk at a level lower than the maximum, the auditor obtains reasonable assurance that controls are in use and operating effectively. This assurance is most likely obtained in part by

a. Preparing flowcharts.
b. Performing substantive tests.
c. Analyzing tests of trends and ratios.
d. Inspection of documents.

34. An auditor generally tests the segregation of duties related to inventory by

a. Personal inquiry and observation.
b. Test counts and cutoff procedures.
c. Analytical procedures and invoice recomputation.
d. Document inspection and reconciliation.

35. The objective of tests of details of transactions performed as tests of controls is to

a. Monitor the design and use of entity documents such as prenumbered shipping forms.
b. Determine whether controls have been implemented.
c. Detect material misstatements in the account balances of the financial statements.
d. Evaluate whether controls operated effectively.

36. After obtaining an understanding of internal control and assessing the risk of material misstatement, an auditor decided to perform tests of controls. The auditor most likely decided that

a. It would be efficient to perform tests of controls that would result in a reduction in planned substantive tests.
b. Additional evidence to support a further reduction in the risk of material misstatement is **not** available.
c. An increase in the assessed level of the risk of material misstatement is justified for certain financial statement assertions.
d. There were many internal control weaknesses that could allow misstatements to enter the accounting system.

37. In assessing control risk, an auditor ordinarily selects from a variety of techniques, including

a. Inquiry and analytical procedures.
b. Reperformance and observation.
c. Comparison and confirmation.
d. Inspection and verification.

38. Which of the following types of evidence would an auditor most likely examine to determine whether controls are operating as designed?

a. Confirmations of receivables verifying account balances.
b. Letters of representations corroborating inventory pricing.
c. Attorneys' responses to the auditor's inquiries.
d. Client records documenting the use of computer programs.

39. Which of the following is **not** a step in an auditor's assessment of control risk?

a. Evaluate the effectiveness of internal control with tests of controls.

b. Obtain an understanding of the entity's information system and control environment.
c. Perform tests of details of transactions to detect material misstatements in the financial statements.
d. Consider whether controls can have a pervasive effect on financial statement assertions.

40. To obtain audit evidence about control risk, an auditor selects tests from a variety of techniques including

a. Inquiry.
b. Analytical procedures.
c. Calculation.
d. Confirmation.

41. Which of the following is **least** likely to be evidence the auditor examines to determine whether controls are operating effectively?

a. Records documenting usage of computer programs.
b. Canceled supporting documents.
c. Confirmations of accounts receivable.
d. Signatures on authorization forms.

42. Which of the following procedures concerning accounts receivable would an auditor most likely perform to obtain evidence in support of an assessed level of control risk below the maximum?

a. Observing an entity's employee prepare the schedule of past due accounts receivable.
b. Sending confirmation requests to an entity's principal customers to verify the existence of accounts receivable.
c. Inspecting an entity's analysis of accounts receivable for unusual balances.
d. Comparing an entity's uncollectible accounts expense to actual uncollectible accounts receivable.

C.1. *Management's Responsibility*

43. The internal control provisions of the Sarbanes-Oxley Act of 2002 apply to which companies in the United States?

a. All companies.
b. SEC registrants.
c. All issuer (public) companies and nonissuer (nonpublic) companies with more than $100,000,000 of net worth.
d. All nonissuer companies.

44. The framework most likely to be used by management in its internal control assessment under requirements of the Sarbanes-Oxley Act of 2002 is the

a. COSO internal framework.
b. COSO enterprise risk management framework.
c. FASB 37 internal control definitional framework.
d. AICPA internal control analysis manager.

45. Which of the following best describes a CPA's engagement to report on an entity's internal control over financial reporting?

a. An attestation engagement to form an opinion on the effectiveness of its internal control.
b. An audit engagement to provide negative assurance on the entity's internal control.
c. A prospective engagement to project, for a period of time **not** to exceed one year, and report on the expected benefits of the entity's internal control.
d. A consulting engagement to provide constructive advice to the entity on its internal control.

46. An engagement to examine internal control will generally

a. Require procedures that duplicate those already applied in assessing control risk during a financial statement audit.
b. Increase the reliability of the financial statements that have already been audited.
c. Be more extensive in scope than the assessment of control risk made during a financial statement audit.
d. Be more limited in scope than the assessment of control risk made during a financial statement audit.

C.2. *Management's Assessment*

47. Which of the following is correct concerning the level of assistance auditors may provide in assisting management with its assessment of internal control?

a. No assistance of any type may be provided.
b. No limitations on assistance exist.
c. Only very limited assistance may be provided.
d. As less risk is assumed by the auditors, a higher level of assistance is appropriate.

48. Which of the following need **not** be included in management's report on internal control under Section 404a of the Sarbanes-Oxley Act of 2002?

a. A statement that the company's auditor has issued an attestation report on management's assertion.
b. Identification of the framework for evaluating internal control.
c. Management's assessment of the effectiveness of internal control.
d. Management's statement of responsibility to establish and maintain internal control that has no significant deficiencies.

C.3. *Control Definitions*

49. Which of the following is an accurate statement about internal control weaknesses?

a. Material weaknesses are also control deficiencies.
b. Significant deficiencies are also material weaknesses.
c. Control deficiencies are also material weaknesses.
d. All control deficiencies must be communicated to the audit committee.

50. In an integrated audit, which of the following is defined as a weakness in internal control that is less severe than a material weakness but important enough to warrant attention by those responsible for oversight of the financial reporting function?

a. Control deficiency.
b. Unusual weakness.
c. Unusual deficiency.
d. Significant deficiency.

51. A material weakness is a significant deficiency (or combination of significant deficiencies) that results in a reasonable possibility that a misstatement of at least what amount will not be prevented or detected?

a. An amount greater than zero.
b. An amount greater than zero, but at least inconsequential.
c. An amount greater than inconsequential.
d. A material amount.

52. The minimum likelihood of loss involved in the consideration of a control deficiency is

a. Remote.
b. More than remote.
c. Probable.
d. Not explicitly considered.

C.4. *Evaluating Internal Control*

53. Assume that a company has a control deficiency regarding the processing of cash receipts. Reconciliation of cash accounts by a competent individual otherwise independent of the cash function might make the likelihood of a significant misstatement due to the control deficiency remote. In this situation, reconciliation may be referred to as what type of control?

a. Compensating.
b. Preventive.
c. Adjustive.
d. Nonroutine.

54. According to Public Company Accounting Oversight Board Standard 5, what type of transaction involves establishing a loan loss reserve?

a. Substantive transaction.
b. Routine transaction.
c. Nonroutine transaction.
d. Estimation transaction.

55. How do the scope, procedures, and purpose of an examination of internal control compare to those for obtaining an understanding of internal control and assessing control risk as part of an audit?

	Scope	Procedures	Purpose
a.	Similar	Different	Similar
b.	Different	Similar	Similar
c.	Different	Different	Different
d.	Different	Similar	Different

C.5. *The Audit of Internal Control*

56. A procedure that involves tracing a transaction from its origination through the company's information systems until it is reflected in the company's financial report is referred to as a(n)

a. Analytical analysis.
b. Substantive procedure.
c. Test of a control.
d. Walk-through.

57. For purposes of an audit of internal control performed under Public Company Accounting Oversight Board standards, the "as of date" is ordinarily

a. The first day of the year.
b. The last day of the fiscal period.
c. The last day of the auditor's fieldwork.
d. The average date for the entire fiscal period.

58. Consider an issuer (public) company whose purchases are made through the Internet and by telephone. Which of the following is correct?

a. These types of purchases represent control objectives for the audit of internal control.
b. These purchases are the assertions related to the purchase class of transactions.
c. These types of purchases represent two major classes of transactions within the purchases process.
d. These two types of transactions represent routine transactions that must always be investigated in extreme detail.

59. For an issuer (public) company audit of internal control, walkthroughs provide the auditor with *primary evidence* to

	Evaluate the effectiveness of the design of controls	Confirm whether controls have been implemented
a.	Yes	Yes
b.	Yes	No
c.	No	Yes
d.	No	No

60. Which is **most** likely to be a question asked of employee personnel during a walk-through in an audit of the internal control of an issuer (public) company?

a. Have you ever been asked to override the process?
b. Do you believe that you are underpaid?
c. What do you do when you find a fraudulent transaction?
d. Who trained you for this job?

61. How large must the *actual loss identified by the auditor* be for a control deficiency to possibly be considered a material weakness?

	Immaterial	Material
a.	Yes	Yes
b.	Yes	No
c.	No	Yes
d.	No	No

62. For purposes of an audit of internal control performed under Public Company Accounting Oversight Board requirements, an account is significant if there is more than a

a. Reasonably possible likelihood that it could contain immaterial or material misstatements.

b. Reasonably possible likelihood that it could contain material misstatements.
c. Remote likelihood that it could contain material misstatements.
d. Remote likelihood that it could contain more than inconsequential misstatements.

63. A control deficiency that is more than a significant deficiency is most likely to result in what form of audit opinion relating to internal control?

a. Adverse.
b. Qualified.
c. Unqualified.
d. Unqualified with explanatory language.

64. Which of the following is most likely to be considered a material weakness in internal control for purposes of an internal control audit of an issuer (public) company?

a. An ineffective oversight of financial reporting by the audit committee.
b. Restatement of previously issued financial statements due to a change in accounting principles.
c. Inadequate segregation of recordkeeping from accounting.
d. Weaknesses in control activities.

65. Inability to evaluate internal control due to a circumstance-caused scope limitation relating to a significant account in a Sarbanes-Oxley 404 internal control audit is most likely to result in a(n)

a. Adverse opinion.
b. Qualified opinion.
c. Unqualified opinion with explanatory language.
d. All of the above are equally likely.

66. Which of the following is most likely to indicate a significant deficiency relating to a client's antifraud programs?

a. A broad scope of internal audit activities.
b. A "whistle-blower" program that encourages anonymous submissions.
c. Audit committee passivity when conducting oversight functions.
d. Lack of performance of criminal background investigations for likely customers.

67. An auditor identified a material weakness in December. The client was informed and corrected it shortly after the "as of date" (December 31); the auditor agrees that the correction eliminates the material weakness as of January 31. The appropriate report under a PCAOB Standard 5 audit of internal control is

a. Adverse.
b. Unqualified.
c. Unqualified with explanatory language relating to the material weakness.
d. Qualified.

68. In an integrated audit, which of the following lead(s) to an adverse opinion on internal control?

	Material weaknesses	Significant deficiencies
a.	Yes	Yes
b.	Yes	No
c.	No	Yes
d.	No	No

69. In an integrated audit, what must the auditor communicate to the audit committee?

	Known material weaknesses	All control deficiencies
a.	Yes	Yes
b.	Yes	No
c.	No	Yes
d.	No	No

70. In which manner are significant deficiencies communicated by the auditors to the audit committee under Public Company Accounting Oversight Board Standard 5?

    a. The communication may either be orally or in written form.
    b. The communication must be oral, and not in written form.
    c. The communication must be in written form.
    d. No such communication is required as only material weaknesses must be communicated.

71. Which is correct concerning the external auditors' use of the work of others in an audit of internal control performed for a public company?

    a. It is not allowed.
    b. The work of internal auditors may be used, but only when those internal auditors report directly to the audit committee.
    c. Ordinarily the work of internal auditors and others is used primarily in low-risk areas.
    d. There is no limitation and is likely to reduce auditor liability since the auditors will then share legal responsibility with those who have performed the service.

72. In an integrated audit, which must the auditor communicate in writing to management?

    a. Only material weaknesses.
    b. Material weaknesses and significant deficiencies.
    c. Material weaknesses, significant deficiencies and other control deficiencies.
    d. Material weaknesses, significant deficiencies, other control deficiencies, and all suspected and possible employee law violations.

73. Which of the following is correct when applying a top-down approach to identify controls to test in an integrated audit?

    a. For certain assertions, strong entity-level controls may allow the auditor to omit additional testing beyond those controls.
    b. Starting at the top—controls over specific assertions—the auditor should link to major accounts and reporting items.

    c. The goal is to focus on details of accounting controls, while avoiding consideration of overall entity-level controls.
    d. The goal is to focus on all controls related to assertions, omitting consideration of controls related to the financial statements.

74. Which of the following is not included in a standard unqualified opinion on internal control over financial reporting performed under PCAOB requirements?

    a. Because of inherent limitations, internal control over financial reporting may not prevent or detect misstatements.
    b. In our opinion, [company name] maintained, in all material respects, effective internal control over financial reporting.
    c. Our audit included obtaining an understanding of internal control over financial reporting.
    d. The [company name] management and audit committee is responsible for maintaining effective internal control over financial reporting.

C.7. Report on Internal Control

75. In reporting on an entity's internal control over financial reporting, a practitioner should include a paragraph that describes the

    a. Documentary evidence regarding the control environment factors.
    b. Changes in internal control since the prior report.
    c. Potential benefits from the practitioner's suggested improvements.
    d. Inherent limitations of any internal control.

76. When an independent auditor reports on internal control based on criteria established by governmental agencies, the report should

    a. Not include the agency's name in the report.
    b. Indicate matters covered by the study and whether the auditor's study included tests of controls with the procedures covered by the study.
    c. Not express a conclusion based on the agency's criteria.
    d. Assume responsibility for the comprehensiveness of the criteria established by the agency and include recommendations for corrective action.

77. When an examination has been performed on the effectiveness of entity's internal control over financial reporting and a material weakness has been noted, the practitioner's report should express an opinion on

    a. The assertion.
    b. The subject matter to which the assertion relates.
    c. Neither of the above.
    d. Both of the above.

D.1. Sales, Receivables, and Cash Receipts

78. Which of the following procedures would an auditor most likely perform to test controls relating to management's assertion about the completeness of cash receipts for cash sales at a retail outlet?

    a. Observe the consistency of the employees' use of cash registers and tapes.
    b. Inquire about employees' access to recorded but undeposited cash.
    c. Trace deposits in the cash receipts journal to the cash balance in the general ledger.
    d. Compare the cash balance in the general ledger with the bank confirmation request.

79. Sound internal control dictates that immediately upon receiving checks from customers by mail, a responsible employee should

    a. Add the checks to the daily cash summary.
    b. Verify that each check is supported by a prenumbered sales invoice.
    c. Prepare a duplicate listing of checks received.
    d. Record the checks in the cash receipts journal.

80. Tracing shipping documents to prenumbered sales invoices provides evidence that

    a. No duplicate shipments or billings occurred.
    b. Shipments to customers were properly invoiced.
    c. All goods ordered by customers were shipped.
    d. All prenumbered sales invoices were accounted for.

81. Which of the following controls most likely would reduce the risk of diversion of customer receipts by an entity's employees?

    a. A bank lockbox system.
    b. Prenumbered remittance advices.
    c. Monthly bank reconciliations.
    d. Daily deposit of cash receipts.

82. An auditor suspects that a client's cashier is misappropriating cash receipts for personal use by lapping customer checks received in the mail. In attempting to uncover this embezzlement scheme, the auditor most likely would compare the

    a. Dates checks are deposited per bank statements with the dates remittance credits are recorded.
    b. Daily cash summaries with the sums of the cash receipts journal entries.
    c. Individual bank deposit slips with the details of the monthly bank statements.
    d. Dates uncollectible accounts are authorized to be written off with the dates the write-offs are actually recorded.

83. Upon receipt of customers' checks in the mailroom, a responsible employee should prepare a remittance listing that is forwarded to the cashier. A copy of the listing should be sent to the

    a. Internal auditor to investigate the listing for unusual transactions.
    b. Treasurer to compare the listing with the monthly bank statement.

    c. Accounts receivable bookkeeper to update the subsidiary accounts receivable records.
    d. Entity's bank to compare the listing with the cashier's deposit slip.

84. Which of the following procedures most likely would not be a control designed to reduce the risk of misstatements in the billing process?

    a. Comparing control totals for shipping documents with corresponding totals for sales invoices.
    b. Using computer programmed controls on the pricing and mathematical accuracy of sales invoices.
    c. Matching shipping documents with approved sales orders before invoice preparation.
    d. Reconciling the control totals for sales invoices with the accounts receivable subsidiary ledger.

85. Which of the following audit procedures would an auditor most likely perform to test controls relating to management's assertion concerning the completeness of sales transactions?

    a. Verify that extensions and footings on the entity's sales invoices and monthly customer statements have been recomputed.
    b. Inspect the entity's reports of prenumbered shipping documents that have **not** been recorded in the sales journal.
    c. Compare the invoiced prices on prenumbered sales invoices to the entity's authorized price list.
    d. Inquire about the entity's credit granting policies and the consistent application of credit checks.

86. Which of the following controls most likely would assure that all billed sales are correctly posted to the accounts receivable ledger?

    a. Daily sales summaries are compared to daily postings to the accounts receivable ledger.
    b. Each sales invoice is supported by a prenumbered shipping document.
    c. The accounts receivable ledger is reconciled daily to the control account in the general ledger.
    d. Each shipment on credit is supported by a prenumbered sales invoice.

87. An auditor tests an entity's policy of obtaining credit approval before shipping goods to customers in support of management's financial statement assertion of

    a. Valuation or allocation.
    b. Completeness.
    c. Existence or occurrence.
    d. Rights and obligations.

88. Which of the following controls most likely would help ensure that all credit sales transactions of an entity are recorded?

    a. The billing department supervisor sends copies of approved sales orders to the credit department for comparison to authorized credit limits and current customer account balances.
    b. The accounting department supervisor independently reconciles the accounts receivable subsidiary ledger to the accounts receivable control account monthly.

c. The accounting department supervisor controls the mailing of monthly statements to customers and investigates any differences reported by customers.

d. The billing department supervisor matches prenumbered shipping documents with entries in the sales journal.

89. Which of the following controls most likely would be effective in offsetting the tendency of sales personnel to maximize sales volume at the expense of high bad debt write-offs?

a. Employees responsible for authorizing sales and bad debt write-offs are denied access to cash.

b. Shipping documents and sales invoices are matched by an employee who does not have authority to write off bad debts.

c. Employees involved in the credit-granting function are separated from the sales function.

d. Subsidiary accounts receivable records are reconciled to the control account by an employee independent of the authorization of credit.

90. Proper authorization of write-offs of uncollectible accounts should be approved in which of the following departments?

a. Accounts receivable.

b. Credit.

c. Accounts payable.

d. Treasurer.

91. Employers bond employees who handle cash receipts because fidelity bonds reduce the possibility of employing dishonest individuals and

a. Protect employees who make unintentional misstatements from possible monetary damages resulting from their misstatements.

b. Deter dishonesty by making employees aware that insurance companies may investigate and prosecute dishonest acts.

c. Facilitate an independent monitoring of the receiving and depositing of cash receipts.

d. Force employees in positions of trust to take periodic vacations and rotate their assigned duties.

92. During the consideration of a small business client's internal control, the auditor discovered that the accounts receivable clerk approves credit memos and has access to cash. Which of the following controls would be most effective in offsetting this weakness?

a. The owner reviews errors in billings to customers and postings to the subsidiary ledger.

b. The controller receives the monthly bank statement directly and reconciles the checking accounts.

c. The owner reviews credit memos after they are recorded.

d. The controller reconciles the total of the detail accounts receivable accounts to the amount shown in the ledger.

93. When a customer fails to include a remittance advice with a payment, it is common practice for the person opening the mail to prepare one. Consequently, mail should be opened by which of the following four company employees?

a. Credit manager.

b. Receptionist.

c. Sales manager.

d. Accounts receivable clerk.

D.2. Purchases, Payables, and Cash Disbursements

94. To provide assurance that each voucher is submitted and paid only once, an auditor most likely would examine a sample of paid vouchers and determine whether each voucher is

a. Supported by a vendor's invoice.

b. Stamped "paid" by the check signer.

c. Prenumbered and accounted for.

d. Approved for authorized purchases.

95. In testing controls over cash disbursements, an auditor most likely would determine that the person who signs checks also

a. Reviews the monthly bank reconciliation.

b. Returns the checks to accounts payable.

c. Is denied access to the supporting documents.

d. Is responsible for mailing the checks.

96. In assessing control risk for purchases, an auditor vouches a sample of entries in the voucher register to the supporting documents. Which assertion would this test of controls most likely support?

a. Completeness.

b. Existence or occurrence.

c. Valuation or allocation.

d. Rights and obligations.

97. Which of the following controls is **not** usually performed in the vouchers payable department?

a. Matching the vendor's invoice with the related receiving report.

b. Approving vouchers for payment by having an authorized employee sign the vouchers.

c. Indicating the asset and expense accounts to be debited.

d. Accounting for unused prenumbered purchase orders and receiving reports.

98. With properly designed internal control, the same employee most likely would match vendors' invoices with receiving reports and also

a. Post the detailed accounts payable records.

b. Recompute the calculations on vendors' invoices.

c. Reconcile the accounts payable ledger.

d. Cancel vendors' invoices after payment.

99. An entity's internal control requires for every check request that there be an approved voucher, supported by a prenumbered purchase order and a prenumbered receiving report. To determine whether checks are being issued for unauthorized expenditures, an auditor most likely would select items for testing from the population of all

a. Purchase orders.
b. Canceled checks.
c. Receiving reports.
d. Approved vouchers.

100. Which of the following questions would most likely be included in an internal control questionnaire concerning the completeness assertion for purchases?

a. Is an authorized purchase order required before the receiving department can accept a shipment or the vouchers payable department can record a voucher?
b. Are purchase requisitions prenumbered and independently matched with vendor invoices?
c. Is the unpaid voucher file periodically reconciled with inventory records by an employee who does not have access to purchase requisitions?
d. Are purchase orders, receiving reports, and vouchers prenumbered and periodically accounted for?

101. For effective internal control, the accounts payable department generally should

a. Stamp, perforate, or otherwise cancel supporting documentation after payment is mailed.
b. Ascertain that each requisition is approved as to price, quantity, and quality by an authorized employee.
c. Obliterate the quantity ordered on the receiving department copy of the purchase order.
d. Establish the agreement of the vendor's invoice with the receiving report and purchase order.

102. Internal control is strengthened when the quantity of merchandise ordered is omitted from the copy of the purchase order sent to the

a. Department that initiated the requisition.
b. Receiving department.
c. Purchasing agent.
d. Accounts payable department.

103. A client erroneously recorded a large purchase twice. Which of the following internal control measures would be most likely to detect this error in a timely and efficient manner?

a. Footing the purchases journal.
b. Reconciling vendors' monthly statements with subsidiary payable ledger accounts.
c. Tracing totals from the purchases journal to the ledger accounts.
d. Sending written quarterly confirmations to all vendors.

104. With well-designed internal control, employees in the same department most likely would approve purchase orders, and also

a. Reconcile the open invoice file.
b. Inspect goods upon receipt.
c. Authorize requisitions of goods.
d. Negotiate terms with vendors.

D.3.   *Inventories and Production*

105. In obtaining an understanding of a manufacturing entity's internal control over inventory balances, an auditor most likely would

a. Analyze the liquidity and turnover ratios of the inventory.
b. Perform analytical procedures designed to identify cost variances.
c. Review the entity's descriptions of inventory policies and procedures.
d. Perform test counts of inventory during the entity's physical count.

106. Which of the following controls most likely would be used to maintain accurate inventory records?

a. Perpetual inventory records are periodically compared with the current cost of individual inventory items.
b. A just-in-time inventory ordering system keeps inventory levels to a desired minimum.
c. Requisitions, receiving reports, and purchase orders are independently matched before payment is approved.
d. Periodic inventory counts are used to adjust the perpetual inventory records.

107. A client maintains perpetual inventory records in both quantities and dollars. If the assessed level of control risk is high, an auditor would probably

a. Insist that the client perform physical counts of inventory items several times during the year.
b. Apply gross profit tests to ascertain the reasonableness of the physical counts.
c. Increase the extent of tests of controls of the inventory cycle.
d. Request the client to schedule the physical inventory count at the end of the year.

108. Which of the following controls most likely addresses the completeness assertion for inventory?

a. Work in process account is periodically reconciled with subsidiary records.
b. Employees responsible for custody of finished goods do **not** perform the receiving function.
c. Receiving reports are prenumbered and periodically reconciled.
d. There is a separation of duties between payroll department and inventory accounting personnel.

109. Sound internal control dictates that defective merchandise returned by customers should be presented initially to the

a. Salesclerk.
b. Purchasing clerk.
c. Receiving clerk.
d. Inventory control clerk.

110. Alpha Company uses its sales invoices for posting perpetual inventory records. Inadequate controls over the invoicing function allow goods to be shipped that are not invoiced. The inadequate controls could cause an

a. Understatement of revenues, receivables, and inventory.
b. Overstatement of revenues and receivables, and an understatement of inventory.

c. Understatement of revenues and receivables, and an overstatement of inventory.

d. Overstatement of revenues, receivables, and inventory.

111. Which of the following is a question that the auditor would expect to find on the production cycle section of an internal control questionnaire?

a. Are vendors' invoices for raw materials approved for payment by an employee who is independent of the cash disbursements function?

b. Are signed checks for the purchase of raw materials mailed directly after signing without being returned to the person who authorized the invoice processing?

c. Are all releases by storekeepers of raw materials from storage based on approved requisition documents?

d. Are details of individual disbursements for raw materials balanced with the total to be posted to the appropriate general ledger account?

112. The objectives of internal control for a production cycle are to provide assurance that transactions are properly executed and recorded, and that

a. Production orders are prenumbered and signed by a supervisor.

b. Custody of work in process and of finished goods is properly maintained.

c. Independent internal verification of activity reports is established.

d. Transfers to finished goods are documented by a completed production report and a quality control report.

D.4. Personnel and Payroll

113. An auditor vouched data for a sample of employees in a payroll register to approved clock card data to provide assurance that

a. Payments to employees are computed at authorized rates.

b. Employees work the number of hours for which they are paid.

c. Segregation of duties exist between the preparation and distribution of the payroll.

d. Controls relating to unclaimed payroll checks are operating effectively.

114. Which of the following is a control that most likely could help prevent employee payroll fraud?

a. The personnel department promptly sends employee termination notices to the payroll supervisor.

b. Employees who distribute payroll checks forward unclaimed payroll checks to the absent employees' supervisors.

c. Salary rates resulting from new hires are approved by the payroll supervisor.

d. Total hours used for determination of gross pay are calculated by the payroll supervisor.

115. In determining the effectiveness of an entity's controls relating to the existence or occurrence assertion for payroll transactions, an auditor most likely would inquire about and

a. Observe the segregation of duties concerning personnel responsibilities and payroll disbursement.

b. Inspect evidence of accounting for prenumbered payroll checks.

c. Recompute the payroll deductions for employee fringe benefits.

d. Verify the preparation of the monthly payroll account bank reconciliation.

116. An auditor most likely would assess control risk at a high level if the payroll department supervisor is responsible for

a. Examining authorization forms for new employees.

b. Comparing payroll registers with original batch transmittal data.

c. Authorizing payroll rate changes for all employees.

d. Hiring all subordinate payroll department employees.

117. Which of the following controls most likely would prevent direct labor hours from being charged to manufacturing overhead?

a. Periodic independent counts of work in process for comparison to recorded amounts.

b. Comparison of daily journal entries with approved production orders.

c. Use of time tickets to record actual labor worked on production orders.

d. Reconciliation of work-in-process inventory with periodic cost budgets.

118. In meeting the control objective of safeguarding of assets, which department should be responsible for

	Distribution of paychecks	Custody of unclaimed paychecks
a.	Treasurer	Treasurer
b.	Payroll	Treasurer
c.	Treasurer	Payroll
d.	Payroll	Payroll

119. Proper internal control over the cash payroll function would mandate which of the following?

a. The payroll clerk should fill the envelopes with cash and a computation of the net wages.

b. Unclaimed pay envelopes should be retained by the paymaster.

c. Each employee should be asked to sign a receipt.

d. A separate checking account for payroll be maintained.

120. The purpose of segregating the duties of hiring personnel and distributing payroll checks is to separate the

a. Authorization of transactions from the custody of related assets.

b. Operational responsibility from the recordkeeping responsibility.

c. Human resources function from the controllership function.

d. Administrative controls from the internal accounting controls.

121. To minimize the opportunities for fraud, unclaimed cash payroll should be

    a. Deposited in a safe-deposit box.
    b. Held by the payroll custodian.
    c. Deposited in a special bank account.
    d. Held by the controller.

122. The auditor may observe the distribution of paychecks to ascertain whether

    a. Pay rate authorization is properly separated from the operating function.
    b. Deductions from gross pay are calculated correctly and are properly authorized.
    c. Employees of record actually exist and are employed by the client.
    d. Paychecks agree with the payroll register and the time cards.

123. Which of the following departments most likely would approve changes in pay rates and deductions from employee salaries?

    a. Personnel.
    b. Treasurer.
    c. Controller.
    d. Payroll.

D.5. Financing

124. Which of the following questions would an auditor most likely include on an internal control questionnaire for notes payable?

    a. Are assets that collateralize notes payable critically needed for the entity's continued existence?
    b. Are two or more authorized signatures required on checks that repay notes payable?
    c. Are the proceeds from notes payable used for the purchase of noncurrent assets?
    d. Are direct borrowings on notes payable authorized by the board of directors?

125. The primary responsibility of a bank acting as registrar of capital stock is to

    a. Ascertain that dividends declared do **not** exceed the statutory amount allowable in the state of incorporation.
    b. Account for stock certificates by comparing the total shares outstanding to the total in the shareholders subsidiary ledger.
    c. Act as an independent third party between the board of directors and outside investors concerning mergers, acquisitions, and the sale of treasury stock.
    d. Verify that stock is issued in accordance with the authorization of the board of directors and the articles of incorporation.

126. Where no independent stock transfer agents are employed and the corporation issues its own stocks and maintains stock records, canceled stock certificates should

    a. Be defaced to prevent reissuance and attached to their corresponding stubs.
    b. Not be defaced but segregated from other stock certificates and retained in a canceled certificates file.
    c. Be destroyed to prevent fraudulent reissuance.
    d. Be defaced and sent to the secretary of state.

D.6. Investing

127. Which of the following is **not** a control that is designed to protect investment securities?

    a. Custody over securities should be limited to individuals who have recordkeeping responsibility over the securities.
    b. Securities should be properly controlled physically in order to prevent unauthorized usage.
    c. Access to securities should be vested in more than one individual.
    d. Securities should be registered in the name of the owner.

128. Which of the following controls would a company most likely use to safeguard marketable securities when an independent trust agent is **not** employed?

    a. The investment committee of the board of directors periodically reviews the investment decisions delegated to the treasurer.
    b. Two company officials have joint control of marketable securities, which are kept in a bank safe-deposit box.
    c. The internal auditor and the controller independently trace all purchases and sales of marketable securities from the subsidiary ledgers to the general ledger.
    d. The chairman of the board verifies the marketable securities, which are kept in a bank safe-deposit box, each year on the balance sheet date.

129. A weakness in internal control over recording retirements of equipment may cause an auditor to

    a. Inspect certain items of equipment in the plant and trace those items to the accounting records.
    b. Review the subsidiary ledger to ascertain whether depreciation was taken on each item of equipment during the year.
    c. Trace additions to the "other assets" account to search for equipment that is still on hand but **no** longer being used.
    d. Select certain items of equipment from the accounting records and locate them in the plant.

130. Which of the following questions would an auditor **least** likely include on an internal control questionnaire concerning the initiation and execution of equipment transactions?

    a. Are requests for major repairs approved at a higher level than the department initiating the request?
    b. Are prenumbered purchase orders used for equipment and periodically accounted for?
    c. Are requests for purchases of equipment reviewed for consideration of soliciting competitive bids?
    d. Are procedures in place to monitor and properly restrict access to equipment?

131. Which of the following controls would be most effective in assuring that the proper custody of assets in the investing cycle is maintained?

    a. Direct access to securities in the safe-deposit box is limited to only one corporate officer.
    b. Personnel who post investment transactions to the general ledger are **not** permitted to update the investment subsidiary ledger.
    c. The purchase and sale of investments are executed on the specific authorization of the board of directors.
    d. The recorded balances in the investment subsidiary ledger are periodically compared with the contents of the safe-deposit box by independent personnel.

132. A company holds bearer bonds as a short-term investment. Responsibility for custody of these bonds and submission of coupons for periodic interest collections probably should be delegated to the

    a. Chief Accountant.
    b. Internal Auditor.
    c. Cashier.
    d. Treasurer.

133. Which of the following controls would an entity most likely use to assist in satisfying the completeness assertion related to long-term investments?

    a. Senior management verifies that securities in the bank safe-deposit box are registered in the entity's name.
    b. The internal auditor compares the securities in the bank safe-deposit box with recorded investments.
    c. The treasurer vouches the acquisition of securities by comparing brokers' advices with canceled checks.
    d. The controller compares the current market prices of recorded investments with the brokers' advices on file.

134. Which of the following controls would an entity most likely use in safeguarding against the loss of marketable securities?

    a. An independent trust company that has no direct contact with the employees who have recordkeeping responsibilities has possession of the securities.
    b. The internal auditor verifies the marketable securities in the entity's safe each year on the balance sheet date.
    c. The independent auditor traces all purchases and sales of marketable securities through the subsidiary ledgers to the general ledger.
    d. A designated member of the board of directors controls the securities in a bank safe-deposit box.

135. When there are numerous property and equipment transactions during the year, an auditor who plans to assess control risk at a low level usually performs

    a. Tests of controls and extensive tests of property and equipment balances at the end of the year.
    b. Analytical procedures for current year property and equipment transactions.
    c. Tests of controls and limited tests of current year property and equipment transactions.
    d. Analytical procedures for property and equipment balances at the end of the year.

D.7. *Overall Internal Control Questionnaires (Checklists)*

136. In general, material fraud perpetrated by which of the following are most difficult to detect?

    a. Cashier.
    b. Keypunch operator.
    c. Internal auditor.
    d. Controller.

E.1.a. *Communication of Internal Control Related Matters*

137. Which of the following is **not** an accurate statement about communication of internal control related matters to management on a nonissuer (nonpublic) company?

    a. The auditor must communicate both material weaknesses and significant deficiencies.
    b. The auditor must communicate in writing.
    c. Previously communicated weaknesses that have not been corrected need not be recommunicated.
    d. A communication indicating that no significant deficiencies were identified should not be issued.

138. Which of the following matters would an auditor most likely consider to be a material weakness to be communicated to those charged with governance of an audit client?

    a. Management's failure to renegotiate unfavorable long-term purchase commitments.
    b. Recurring operating losses that may indicate going concern problems.
    c. Ineffective oversight of financial reporting by those charged with governance.
    d. Management's current plans to reduce its ownership equity in the entity.

139. Which of the following statements is correct concerning significant deficiencies in an audit?

    a. An auditor is required to search for significant deficiencies during an audit.
    b. All significant deficiencies are also considered to be material weaknesses.
    c. An auditor may communicate significant deficiencies during an audit or after the audit's completion.
    d. An auditor may report that **no** significant deficiencies were noted during an audit.

140. An auditor's letter issued on significant deficiencies relating to an entity's internal control observed during a financial statement audit should

    a. Include a brief description of the tests of controls performed in searching for significant deficiencies and material weaknesses.
    b. Indicate that the significant deficiencies should be disclosed in the annual report to the entity's shareholders.
    c. Include a paragraph describing management's assertion concerning the effectiveness of internal control.
    d. Indicate that the audit's purpose was to report on the financial statements and **not** to express an opinion on internal control.

141. Which of the following statements is correct concerning an auditor's required communication of significant deficiencies?

    a. A significant deficiency previously communicated during the prior year's audit that remains uncorrected causes a scope limitation.

    b. An auditor should perform tests of controls on significant deficiencies before communicating them to the client.

    c. An auditor's report on significant deficiencies should include a restriction on the distribution of the report.

    d. An auditor should communicate significant deficiencies after tests of controls, but before commencing substantive tests.

142. Which of the following statements is correct concerning significant deficiencies noted in an audit?

    a. Significant deficiencies are material weaknesses in the design or operation of specific internal control components.

    b. The auditor is obligated to search for significant deficiencies that could adversely affect the entity's ability to record and report financial data.

    c. Significant deficiencies need not be recommunicated each year if management has acknowledged its understanding of such deficiencies.

    d. The auditor should separately communicate those significant deficiencies considered to be material weaknesses.

143. Which of the following representations should **not** be included in a report on internal control related matters noted in an audit?

    a. Significant deficiencies related to internal control exist.

    b. There are no significant deficiencies in the design or operation of internal control.

    c. Corrective follow-up action is recommended due to the relative significance of material weaknesses discovered during the audit.

    d. The auditor's consideration of internal control would not necessarily disclose all significant deficiencies that exist.

144. Which of the following statements concerning material weaknesses and significant deficiencies is correct?

    a. An auditor should not identify and communicate material weaknesses separately from significant deficiencies.

    b. Compensating controls may limit the severity of a material weakness or significant deficiency.

    c. Upon discovery an auditor should immediately report all material weaknesses and significant deficiencies identified during an audit.

    d. All significant deficiencies are material weaknesses.

145. During the audit the independent auditor identified the existence of a weakness in the client's internal control and communicated this finding in writing to the client's senior management and those charged with governance. The auditor should

    a. Consider the weakness a scope limitation and therefore disclaim an opinion.

    b. Consider the effects of the condition on the audit.

    c. Suspend all audit activities pending directions from the client's audit committee.

    d. Withdraw from the engagement.

E.1.b. *The Auditor's Communication with Those Charged with Governance*

146. In identifying matters for communication with those charged with governance of an audit client, an auditor most likely would ask management whether

    a. The turnover in the accounting department was unusually high.

    b. It consulted with another CPA firm about accounting matters.

    c. There were any subsequent events of which the auditor was unaware.

    d. It agreed with the auditor's assessed level of control risk.

147. Which of the following statements is correct concerning an auditor's required communication with those charged with governance of an audit client?

    a. This communication is required to occur before the auditor's report on the financial statements is issued.

    b. This communication should include discussion of any significant disagreements with management concerning the financial statements.

    c. Any significant matter communicated to the audit committee also should be communicated to management.

    d. Significant audit adjustments proposed by the auditor and recorded by management need **not** be communicated to those charged with governance.

148. An auditor would **least** likely initiate a discussion with those charged with governance of an audit client concerning

    a. The methods used to account for significant unusual transactions.

    b. The maximum dollar amount of misstatements that could exist without causing the financial statements to be materially misstated.

    c. Indications of fraud and illegal acts committed by a corporate officer that were discovered by the auditor.

    d. Disagreements with management as to accounting principles that were resolved during the current year's audit.

149. Which of the following statements is correct about an auditor's required communication with those charged with governance of an audit client?

    a. Any matters communicated to the entity's audit committee also are required to be communicated to the entity's management.

    b. The auditor is required to inform those charged with governance about significant misstatements discovered by the auditor and subsequently corrected by management.

c. Disagreements with management about the application of accounting principles are required to be communicated in writing to those charged with governance.
d. Weaknesses in internal control previously reported to those charged with governance need not be recommunicated.

150. Which of the following matters is an auditor required to communicate to an entity's audit committee?
I. Disagreements with management about matters significant to the entity's financial statements that have been satisfactorily resolved.
II. Initial selection of significant accounting policies in emerging areas that lack authoritative guidance.

a. I only.
b. II only.
c. Both I and II.
d. Neither I nor II.

151. Should an auditor communicate the following matters to those charged with governance of an audit client?

	Significant audit adjustments recorded by the entity	Management's consultation with other accountants about significant accounting matters
a.	Yes	Yes
b.	Yes	No
c.	No	Yes
d.	No	No

E.2. Effects of an Internal Audit Function

152. In assessing the competence of an internal auditor, an independent CPA most likely would obtain information about the

a. Quality of the internal auditor's working paper documentation.
b. Organization's commitment to integrity and ethical values.
c. Influence of management on the scope of the internal auditor's duties.
d. Organizational level to which the internal auditor reports.

153. For which of the following judgments may an independent auditor share responsibility with an entity's internal auditor who is assessed to be both competent and objective?

	Assessment of inherent risk	Assessment of control risk
a.	Yes	Yes
b.	Yes	No
c.	No	Yes
d.	No	No

154. The work of internal auditors may affect the independent auditor's
I. Procedures performed in obtaining an understanding of internal control.
II. Procedures performed in assessing the risk of material misstatement.

III. Substantive procedures performed in gathering direct evidence.

a. I and II only.
b. I and III only.
c. II and III only.
d. I, II, and III.

155. An internal auditor's work would most likely affect the nature, timing, and extent of an independent CPA's auditing procedures when the internal auditor's work relates to assertions about the

a. Existence of contingencies.
b. Valuation of intangible assets.
c. Existence of fixed asset additions.
d. Valuation of related-party transactions.

156. During an audit an internal auditor may provide direct assistance to an independent CPA in

	Obtaining an understanding of internal control	Performing tests of controls	Performing substantive tests
a.	No	No	No
b.	Yes	No	No
c.	Yes	Yes	No
d.	Yes	Yes	Yes

157. When assessing the internal auditor's competence, the independent CPA should obtain information about the

a. Organizational level to which the internal auditors report.
b. Educational background and professional certification of the internal auditors.
c. Policies prohibiting the internal auditors from auditing areas where relatives are employed.
d. Internal auditors' access to records and information that is considered sensitive.

158. In assessing the competence and objectivity of an entity's internal auditor, an independent auditor would **least** likely consider information obtained from

a. Discussions with management personnel.
b. External quality reviews of the internal auditor's activities.
c. Previous experience with the internal auditor.
d. The results of analytical procedures.

159. If the independent auditors decide that the work performed by the internal auditor may have a bearing on their own procedures, they should consider the internal auditor's

a. Competence and objectivity.
b. Efficiency and experience.
c. Independence and review skills.
d. Training and supervisory skills.

160. In assessing the objectivity of internal auditors, an independent auditor should

a. Evaluate the quality control program in effect for the internal auditors.

b. Examine documentary evidence of the work performed by the internal auditors.

c. Test a sample of the transactions and balances that the internal auditors examined.

d. Determine the organizational level to which the internal auditors report.

E.3.   Reports on the Processing of Transactions by Service Organizations

161. Dunn, CPA, is auditing the financial statements of Taft Co. Taft uses Quick Service Center (QSC) to process its payroll. Price, CPA, is expressing an opinion on a description of the controls implemented at QSC regarding the processing of its customers' payroll transactions. Dunn expects to consider the effects of Price's report on the Taft engagement. Price's report should contain a(n)

a. Description of the scope and nature of Price's procedures.

b. Statement that Dunn may assess control risk based on Price's report.

c. Assertion that Price assumes no responsibility to determine whether QSC's controls are suitably designed.

d. Opinion on the operating effectiveness of QSC's internal controls.

162. Payroll Data Co. (PDC) processes payroll transactions for a retailer. Cook, CPA, is engaged to express an opinion on a description of PDC's internal controls implemented as of a specific date. These controls are relevant to the retailer's internal control, so Cook's report may be useful in providing the retailer's independent auditor with information necessary to plan a financial statement audit. Cook's report should

a. Contain a disclaimer of opinion on the operating effectiveness of PDC's controls.

b. State whether PDC's controls were suitably designed to achieve the retailer's objectives.

c. Identify PDC's controls relevant to specific financial statement assertions.

d. Disclose Cook's assessed level of control risk for PDC.

163. The auditor who audits the processing of transactions by a service organization may issue a report on controls

	Implemented	Operating effectiveness
a.	Yes	Yes
b.	Yes	No
c.	No	Yes
d.	No	No

164. Computer Services Company (CSC) processes payroll transactions for schools. Drake, CPA, is engaged to report on CSC's policies and procedures implemented as of a specific date. These policies and procedures are relevant to the schools' internal control, so Drake's report will be useful in providing the schools' independent auditors with information necessary to plan their audits. Drake's report expressing an opinion on CSC's policies and procedures implemented as of a specific date should contain a(n)

a. Description of the scope and nature of Drake's procedures.

b. Statement that CSC's management has disclosed to Drake all design deficiencies of which it is aware.

c. Opinion on the operating effectiveness of CSC's policies and procedures.

d. Paragraph indicating the basis for Drake's assessment of control risk.

165. Lake, CPA, is auditing the financial statements of Gill Co. Gill uses the EDP Service Center, Inc. to process its payroll transactions. EDP's financial statements are audited by Cope, CPA, who recently issued a report on EDP's internal control. Lake is considering Cope's report on EDP's internal control in assessing control risk on the Gill engagement. What is Lake's responsibility concerning making reference to Cope as a basis, in part, for Lake's own opinion?

a. Lake may refer to Cope only if Lake is satisfied as to Cope's professional reputation and independence.

b. Lake may refer to Cope only if Lake relies on Cope's report in restricting the extent of substantive tests.

c. Lake may refer to Cope only if Lake's report indicates the division of responsibility.

d. Lake may **not** refer to Cope under the circumstances above.

Multiple-Choice Answers and Explanations

Answers

1.	a	35.	d	69.	b	103.	b	137.	c
2.	d	36.	a	70.	c	104.	d	138.	c
3.	b	37.	b	71.	c	105.	c	139.	c
4.	b	38.	d	72.	c	106.	d	140.	d
5.	c	39.	c	73.	a	107.	d	141.	c
6.	b	40.	a	74.	d	108.	c	142.	d
7.	d	41.	c	75.	d	109.	c	143.	b
8.	a	42.	a	76.	b	110.	c	144.	b
9.	d	43.	b	77.	b	111.	c	145.	b
10.	a	44.	a	78.	a	112.	b	146.	b
11.	d	45.	a	79.	c	113.	b	147.	b
12.	b	46.	c	80.	b	114.	a	148.	b
13.	a	47.	c	81.	a	115.	a	149.	b
14.	a	48.	d	82.	a	116.	c	150.	a
15.	b	49.	a	83.	c	117.	c	151.	a
16.	b	50.	d	84.	d	118.	a	152.	a
17.	b	51.	d	85.	b	119.	c	153.	d
18.	a	52.	d	86.	a	120.	a	154.	d
19.	a	53.	a	87.	a	121.	c	155.	c
20.	d	54.	d	88.	d	122.	c	156.	d
21.	b	55.	d	89.	c	123.	a	157.	b
22.	b	56.	d	90.	d	124.	d	158.	d
23.	c	57.	b	91.	b	125.	d	159.	a
24.	d	58.	c	92.	c	126.	a	160.	d
25.	d	59.	a	93.	b	127.	a	161.	a
26.	d	60.	a	94.	b	128.	b	162.	a
27.	c	61.	a	95.	d	129.	d	163.	a
28.	d	62.	c	96.	b	130.	d	164.	a
29.	d	63.	a	97.	d	131.	d	165.	d
30.	a	64.	a	98.	b	132.	d		
31.	c	65.	b	99.	b	133.	b		
32.	d	66.	c	100.	d	134.	a		
33.	d	67.	a	101.	d	135.	c	1st: __/165= __%
34.	a	68.	b	102.	b	136.	d	2nd: __/165= __%

Explanations

1. (a) The requirement is to identify the reply that most likely would not be considered an inherent limitation of the potential effectiveness of an entity's internal control. Answer (a) is correct because incompatible duties may generally be divided among individuals in such a manner as to control the problem. Answers (b), (c), and (d) are all incorrect because management override, mistakes of judgment, and collusion among employees are all inherent limitations of internal control.

2. (d) The requirement is to identify the meaning of the concept of reasonable assurance. Answer (d) is correct because reasonable assurance recognizes that the cost of internal control should not exceed the benefits expected to be derived.

3. (b) The requirement is to identify the functions that should be segregated for effective internal control. Answer (b) is correct because authorizing transactions, recording transactions, and maintaining custody of assets should be segregated.

4. (b) The requirement is to identify the most likely type of ongoing monitoring activity. Answer (b) is correct because ongoing monitoring involves assessing the design and operation of controls on a timely basis and taking necessary corrective actions and such an approach may be followed in reviewing the purchasing function. Answer (a) is incorrect because periodic audits are not ordinarily performed by the audit committee, a subcommittee of the Board of Directors. Answer (c) is incorrect because the audit of the annual financial statements is not ordinarily considered monitoring as presented in the professional standards. Answer (d) is incorrect because the meaning of the reply, control risk assessment in conjunction with quarterly reviews, is uncertain.

5. (c) The requirement is to identify where the overall attitude and awareness of an entity's board of directors concerning the importance of internal control is normally reflected. Answer (c) is correct because the control environment reflects the overall attitude, awareness, and actions of the board of directors, management, owners, and others concerning the importance of control and its emphasis in the entity.

6. (b) The requirement is to identify the circumstance in which management philosophy and operating style would have a significant influence on an entity's control environment. Answer (b) is correct because management philosophy and operating style, while always important, is particularly so when management is dominated by one or a few individuals because it may impact numerous other factors. Answer (a) is incorrect because the impact of the internal auditor reporting directly to management is likely to be less than that of answer (a). Answer (c) is incorrect because while accurate management job descriptions are desirable, they do not have as significant of an effect on management philosophy and operating style as does domination by an individual. Answer (d) is incorrect because an active audit committee might temper rather than lead to a more significant influence of management philosophy and operating style.

7. (d) The requirement is to determine which of the factors listed are included in an entity's control environment. Answer (d) is correct because the audit committee, integrity and ethical values, and organization structure are all included.

8. (a) The requirement is to identify the reply that is not a component of an entity's internal control. Answer (a) is correct because while auditors assess control risk as a part of their consideration of internal control, it is not a component of an entity's internal control. Answers (b), (c), and (d) are incorrect because the control environment, risk assessment, control activities, information and communication, and monitoring are the five components of an entity's internal control (AU-C 315).

9. (d) The Foreign Corrupt Practices Act makes payment of bribes to foreign officials illegal and requires publicly held companies to maintain systems of internal control sufficient to provide reasonable assurances that internal control objectives are met.

10. (a) The requirement is to determine the most likely population from which an auditor would sample when vendors' invoices and related vouchers relating to purchases made by employees have been destroyed. Answer (a) is correct because the disbursement will be recorded and the auditor may thus sample from that population. Answers (b) and (d) are incorrect because the related vouchers and vendors' invoices are destroyed. Answer (c) is incorrect because there is no recording of the receipt of the merchandise.

11. (d) The requirement is to identify the procedure an auditor would perform to provide evidence about whether an entity's internal control activities are suitably designed to prevent or detect material misstatements. Answer (d) is correct because AU-C 315 indicates an auditor will observe the entity's personnel applying the procedures to determine whether controls have been implemented. Answer (a) is incorrect because reperforming the activities is a test of control to help assess the operating effectiveness of a control. Answer (b) is incorrect because analytical procedures are not performed to determine whether controls are suitably designed. Answer (c) is incorrect because vouching a sample of transactions is a substantive test not directly aimed at determining whether controls are suitably designed. See AU-C 315 for a discussion of an auditor's responsibility for determining whether controls have been implemented vs. their operating effectiveness.

12. (b) The requirement is to identify the correct statement relating to the relevance of various types of controls to a financial statement audit. Answer (b) is correct because, generally, controls that are relevant to an audit pertain to the entity's objective of preparing financial statements for external purposes. Answer (a) is incorrect because AU-C 315 makes clear that an auditor may not ignore consideration of controls under any audit approach. Answer (c) is incorrect because control over financial reporting are of primary importance. Answer (d) is incorrect because many operational and compliance related controls are not ordinarily relevant to an audit.

13. (a) The requirement is to identify the statement that represents a requirement when an audit of financial statements in accordance with generally accepted accounting principles is performed. Answer (a) is correct because AU-C 315 requires that the auditor document the understanding of the entity's internal control. Answer (b) is incorrect because while an auditor might find significant deficiencies in the operation of internal control, no such search is required. Answer (c) is incorrect because an auditor might use a substantive approach in performing an audit and thereby perform few (if any) tests of controls. Answer (d) is incorrect because while auditors must obtain knowledge of internal control sufficiently to identify types of potential misstatements, they are not required to obtain the detailed knowledge of internal control suggested by this reply.

14. (a) The requirement is to identify the knowledge that an auditor must obtain when obtaining an understanding of an entity's internal control sufficient for audit planning. Answer (a) is correct because an auditor must obtain an understanding that includes knowledge about the design of relevant controls and records and whether the client has placed those controls in operation. Answers (b) and (c) are incorrect because auditors may choose not to obtain information on operating effectiveness of controls and their consistency of application. Answer (d) is incorrect because there is no such explicit requirement relating to controls; see AU-C 315 for the necessary understanding of internal control.

15. (b) AU-C 315 states that the auditor should obtain sufficient knowledge of the information (including accounting) system to understand the financial reporting process used to prepare the entity's financial statements, including significant accounting estimates and disclosures. It also states that this knowledge is obtained to help the auditor to understand (1) the entity's classes of transactions, (2) how transactions are initiated, (3) the accounting records and support, and (4) the accounting processing involved from initiation of a transaction to its inclusion in the financial statements.

16. (b) The requirement is to determine why an auditor should concentrate on the substance of procedures rather than their form when obtaining an understanding of an entity's controls. Answer (b) is correct because management may establish appropriate controls but not act on them, thus creating a situation in which the form differs from the substance. Answer (a) is incorrect because documentation is not directly related to the issue of substance over form. Answer (c) is incorrect because inappropriate controls is only a part of an auditor concern; for example, a control may be appropriate, but it may not be operating effectively. Answer (d) is incorrect because while an auditor might suggest to management that the cost of certain controls seems to exceed their likely benefit, this is not the primary reason auditors are concerned with the substance of controls.

17. (b) Decision tables include various combinations of conditions that are matched to one of several actions. In an internal control setting, the various important controls are reviewed and, based on the combination of answers received, an action such as a decision on whether to perform tests of controls is determined. Program flowcharts simply summarize the steps involved in a program. Answer (a) is incorrect because decision tables do not emphasize the ease of manageability for complex programs. Answer (c) is incorrect because while decision tables may be designed using various cost benefit factors relating to the various conditions and actions, they do not justify the program. Answer (d) is incorrect because program flowcharts, not decision tables, emphasize the sequence in which operations are performed.

18. (a) The requirement is to identify the procedure that is not required to be included in an auditor's consideration of internal control. Answer (a) is correct because the auditor need not obtain evidence relating to operating effectiveness when control risk is to be assessed at the maximum level. Answer (b) is incorrect because an auditor must obtain an understanding of the internal control environment and the information system. Answers (c) and (d) are incorrect because an auditor is obligated to obtain information on the design of internal control and on whether control activities have been implemented.

19. (a) The requirement is to identify the primary objective of procedures performed to obtain an understanding of internal control. Answer (a) is correct because the auditor obtains a sufficient understanding of internal control to assess the risks of material misstatement and to design the nature, timing, and extent of further audit procedures. Answer (b) addresses inherent risk, the susceptibility of an assertion to material misstatement, assuming that there are no related controls. Answer (b) is incorrect since the concept of inherent risk assumes no internal control and is therefore not the primary objective. Answer (c) is incorrect because answer (a) is more complete and because decisions on modifying tests of controls are often made at a later point in the audit. Answer (d) is incorrect because the consistency of application of management's policies relates more directly to tests of controls than to obtaining an understanding of internal control.

20. (d) The requirement is to determine the correct statement with respect to the auditor's required documentation of the client's internal control. An auditor may document his/her understanding of the structure and his/her conclusions about the design of that structure in the form of answers to a questionnaire, narrative memorandums, flowcharts, decision tables, or any other form that the auditor considers appropriate

in the circumstances. Answers (a) and (b) are, thus, incorrect because they suggest restrictions which do not exist in practice. Answer (c) is incorrect since at a minimum a list of reasons for nonreliance must be provided.

21. (b) In obtaining an understanding of internal control, the auditor should perform procedures to provide sufficient knowledge of the design of the relevant controls and whether they have been implemented. Information on operating effectiveness need not be obtained unless control risk is to be assessed at a level below the maximum.

22. (b) Answer (b) is correct because tests of controls are only required when the auditor relies on the controls or substantive tests alone are not sufficient to audit particular assertions. Answers (a), (c), and (d) are incorrect because these procedures are required on every audit.

23. (c) The requirement is to identify the terms in which control risk should be assessed. Answer (c) is correct because AU-C 315 requires that control risk be assessed in terms of financial statement assertions.

24. (d) The requirement is to identify a situation in which an auditor may desire to seek a further reduction in the assessed level of control risk. Answer (d) is correct because such a reduction is only possible when additional evidence, evaluated by performing additional tests of controls, is available. Answer (a) is incorrect because auditors at this point will ordinarily already have obtained the understanding of the information system to plan the audit. Furthermore, an understanding of internal control is needed on all audits. Answer (b) is incorrect because auditors must determine that controls have been implemented in all audits. Answer (c) is incorrect because a significant number of controls always pertain to financial statement assertions.

25. (d) Assessing control risk at a low level involves (1) identifying specific controls relevant to specific assertions that are likely to prevent or detect material misstatements in those assertions, and (2) performing tests of controls to evaluate the effectiveness of such controls. Answer (a) is incorrect because assessing control risk at a low level may lead to less extensive, not more extensive substantive tests. Answer (b) is incorrect because the actual level of inherent risk is not affected by the level of control risk. Also, one would not expect a change in the assessed level of control risk to result in a change in the assessed level of inherent risk. Answer (c) is incorrect because assessing control risk at a low level may lead to interim-date substantive testing rather than year-end testing.

26. (d) The requirement is to determine why an auditor assesses control risk. Answer (d) is correct because the assessed levels of control risk and inherent risk are used to determine the acceptable level of detection risk for financial statement assertions.

27. (c) Increases in the assessed level of the risk of material misstatement lead to decreases in the acceptable level of detection risk. Accordingly, the auditor will need to increase the extent of substantive tests such as tests of details. Answer (a) is incorrect because tests of controls are performed to reduce the assessed level of control risk only when controls are believed to be effective. Answer (b) is incorrect because the level of detection risk must be decreased, not increased. Answer (d) is incorrect because the level of inherent risk pertains to the susceptibility of an account to material misstatement independent of related controls.

28. (d) The requirement is to determine the primary purpose for which an auditor uses the knowledge provided by the understanding of internal control and the assessed level of the risk of material misstatement. Answer (d) is correct because the auditor uses such knowledge in determining the nature, timing, and extent of substantive tests for financial statement assertions. Answer (a) is incorrect because it is incomplete. For example, while auditors are concerned with the safeguarding of assets, they also need to determine whether the financial statement information is accurate. Answer (b) is incorrect for reasons similar to (a) in that determining whether opportunities are available for committing and concealing fraud is incomplete since this knowledge is also used to ascertain whether the chance of errors is minimized. Answer (c) is incorrect because knowledge provided by the understanding of internal control and the assessed level of control risk is not used to modify initial assessments of inherent risk and preliminary judgments about materiality levels. This knowledge is unrelated to those processes.

29. (d) The requirement is to identify a way that an auditor may compensate for a weakness in internal control. Answer (d) is correct because increasing analytical procedures decreases detection risk in a manner which may counterbalance the condition in internal control. In effect, the weakness in internal control is compensated for by increased substantive testing. See the outline of AU-C 200 for the relationships among audit risk and its component risks—inherent risk, control risk, and detection risk. Answer (a) is incorrect because increasing both control risk (through a weakness in internal control) and detection risk increases audit risks. In addition, control risk and detection risk do not compensate for one another. Answer (b) is incorrect because increasing the extent of tests of controls is unlikely to be effective since the condition is known to exist. Answer (c) is incorrect because it is not generally appropriate to increase the judgment as to audit risk based on the results obtained.

30. (a) The requirement is to identify the correct statement concerning an auditor's assessment of control risk. Answer (a) is correct because AU-C 315 indicates that assessing control risk may be performed concurrently during an audit with obtaining an understanding of internal control. Answer (b) is incorrect because evidence about the operation of internal control obtained in prior audits may be considered during the current year's assessment of control risk. Answer (c) is incorrect because the basis for an auditor's conclusions about the assessed level of control risk needs to be documented when control risk is assessed at levels other than the maximum level. Answer (d) is incorrect because a lower level of control risk requires more assurance that the control procedures are operating effectively.

31. (c) The requirement is to determine the correct statement concerning the assessed level of control risk. Answer (c) is correct because ordinarily the assessed level of control risk

cannot be sufficiently low to eliminate the need to perform any substantive tests to restrict detection risk for significant transaction classes. Answer (a) is incorrect because tests of controls are unnecessary when control risk is assessed at the maximum level. Answer (b) is incorrect because analytical procedures are not designed to verify the design of internal control. Answer (d) is incorrect because dual-purpose tests (i.e., those that serve as both substantive tests and tests of controls) are not required to be performed, and because the term "preliminary control risk" is unclear.

32. (d) The requirement is to identify how frequently controls that the auditor wishes to rely upon must be tested. Answer (d) is correct because the professional standards require auditors to test controls at least every third year. Answer (a) is incorrect because controls need not be tested monthly. Answer (b) is incorrect because ordinarily controls need not be tested with each audit. Answer (c) is incorrect because auditors may test such controls every third year, not every second year.

33. (d) The requirement is to identify the type of audit test most likely to provide assurance that controls are in use and operating effectively. Answer (d) is correct because inspection of documents is a form of a test of controls, and such tests are used to obtain reasonable assurance that controls are in use and operating effectively. Answer (a) is incorrect because auditors prepare flowcharts to document a company's internal control, not to obtain assurance that controls are in use and operating effectively. Answer (b) is incorrect because substantive tests relate to the accuracy of accounts and assertions rather than testing controls directly. Answer (c) is incorrect because analyzing tests of trends and ratios is an analytical procedure that does not directly test controls.

34. (a) The requirement is to identify the appropriate procedures for testing the segregation of duties related to inventory. Answer (a) is correct because AU-C 315 suggests that when no audit trail exists (as is often the case for the segregation of duties) an auditor should use the observation and inquiry techniques.

35. (d) The requirement is to identify the objective of tests of details of transactions performed as tests of controls. Answer (d) is correct because the purpose of tests of controls is to evaluate whether internal control operates effectively. Answer (a) is incorrect because while monitoring the design and use of entity documents may be viewed as a test of controls, it is not the objective. Answer (b) is incorrect because determining whether internal control is implemented is not directly related to tests of controls; see AU-C 315 for the distinction between "implemented" and "operating effectiveness." Answer (c) is incorrect because substantive tests, not tests of controls, are focused on detection of material misstatements in the account balances of the financial statements.

36. (a) The requirement is to identify a circumstance in which an auditor may decide to perform tests of controls. Answer (a) is correct because tests of controls will be performed when they are expected to result in a cost effective reduction in planned substantive tests. Answer (b) is incorrect because tests of controls are only performed when they are likely to support a further reduction in the assessed level of the risk of material misstatement. Answer (c) is incorrect because tests of controls are designed to decrease the assessed level of the risk of material misstatement, not increase it. Answer (d) is incorrect because internal control weaknesses normally result in more substantive testing and less tests of controls.

37. (b) The requirement is to identify the most appropriate procedures for assessing control risk. Auditors perform tests of controls to obtain evidence on the operating effectiveness of controls to assess control risk. Answer (b) is correct because tests of controls include inquiries of appropriate entity personnel, inspection of documents and reports, observation of the application of the policy or procedure, and reperformance of the application of the policy or procedure.

38. (d) The requirement is to identify the type of evidence an auditor most likely would examine to determine whether controls are operating as designed. Answer (d) is correct because inspection of client records documenting the use of computer programs will provide evidence to help the auditor evaluate the effectiveness of the design and operation of internal control; the client's control over use of its computer programs in this case is documentation of the use of the programs. In order to test this control, the auditor will inspect the documentation records. See AU-C 330 for information on the nature of tests of controls. Answer (a) is incorrect because the confirmation process is most frequently considered a substantive test, not a test of a control. Answer (b) is incorrect because letters of representations provide corroborating information on various management representations obtained throughout the audit and therefore only provides limited evidence on internal control. Answer (c) is incorrect because attorneys' responses to auditor inquiries most frequently pertain to litigation, claims, and assessments.

39. (c) The requirement is to identify the procedure that is **not** a step in an auditor's assessment of control risk. Answer (c) is correct because performing tests of details of transactions to detect material misstatements pertains more directly to detection risk rather than inherent or control risk. Answer (a) is incorrect because auditors evaluate the effectiveness of internal control with tests of controls. Answer (b) is incorrect because obtaining an understanding of the entity's information system and control environment is a preliminary step for considering control risk. Answer (d) is incorrect because auditors will consider the effect of internal control on the various financial statement assertions.

40. (a) The requirement is to identify an approach that auditors use to obtain audit evidence about control risk. Answer (a) is correct because auditors test controls to provide evidence for their assessment of control risk through inquiries of appropriate personnel, inspection of documents and records, observation of the application of controls, and reperformance of the application of the policy or procedure. Answers (b), (c), and (d) are incorrect because analytical procedures, calculation, and confirmation relate more directly to substantive testing and are not primary methods to test controls for purposes of assessing control risk.

41. (c) The requirement is to identify the **least** likely type of evidence the auditor will examine to determine whether

controls are operating effectively. Answer (c) is correct because confirmation of accounts receivable is a substantive test, not a test of a control. Answer (a) is incorrect because records documenting the usage of computer programs may be tested to determine whether access is appropriately controlled. Answer (b) is incorrect because examining canceled supporting documents may help the auditor to determine that the structure will not allow duplicate billing to result in multiple payments. Answer (d) is incorrect because proper signatures will help the auditor to determine whether the authorization controls are functioning adequately.

42. (a) The requirement is to identify the accounts receivable auditing procedure that an auditor would most likely perform to obtain support for an assessed level of control risk below the maximum. Since an auditor uses the results of tests of controls to support an assessed level of control risk below the maximum, we are attempting to identify a test of a control. Answer (a) is correct because observing an entity's employee prepare the schedule of past due accounts receivable is a test of a control to evaluate the effectiveness the process of preparing an accurate schedule of past due accounts; if the process is found to be effective it may lead to a reduction in the assessed level of control risk. Answer (b) is incorrect because the confirmation of accounts receivable is a substantive test, not a test of a control. Answer (c) is incorrect because the inspection of accounts receivable for unusual balances and comparing uncollectible accounts expense to actual accounts expense is ordinarily an analytical procedure performed as a substantive test. Answer (d) is incorrect because comparing uncollectible accounts expense to actual uncollectible accounts is ordinarily a substantive test.

43. (b) The requirement is to identify the type of companies to which the internal control provisions of the Sarbanes-Oxley Act of 2002 apply. Answer (b) is correct because the provisions apply to public companies that are registered with the Securities and Exchange Commission. Answer (a) is incorrect because nonissuer companies are not directly affected by the control provisions. Answer (c) is incorrect; there is no $100,000,000 requirement. Answer (d) is incorrect because nonissuer companies are not directly affected by the internal control provisions of the Act.

44. (a) The requirement is to identify the most likely framework to be used by management in its internal control assessment. Answer (a) is correct as the COSO internal control framework is by far the most frequently used one. Answer (b) is incorrect because while a COSO enterprise risk management framework does exist, it is not ordinarily used by management in its internal control assessment. Answers (c) and (d) are incorrect because there is no such thing as a "FASB 37 internal control definitional framework" or an "AICPA internal control analysis manager."

45. (a) The requirement is to identify the statement that best describes a CPA's engagement to report on an entity's internal control over financial reporting. Answer (a) is correct because the objective of an attestation engagement is to form an opinion on the effectiveness of internal control. Answer (b) is incorrect because no such negative assurance is provided based on an "audit" of the entity's internal control. Answer (c) is incorrect because such engagements do not project expected benefits of the entity's internal control. Answer (d) is incorrect because such engagements are attestation engagements, not consulting engagements.

46. (c) The requirement is to determine the correct statement regarding an engagement to examine internal control. Answer (c) is correct because the procedures relating to internal control will be more extensive when reporting on internal control as compared to procedures performed for a financial statement audit. This difference occurs because during financial statement audits the auditor may decide not to perform tests of controls and may simply assess control risk at the maximum level. Conversely, in an engagement to report on internal control an auditor must perform additional tests of controls. Answer (a) is incorrect because such duplication of procedures may not be necessary. Answer (b) is incorrect because a report on internal control will not in general increase the reliability of the financial statements. Answer (d) is incorrect because, as indicated, the scope of procedures relating to internal control is more extensive, not more limited, than the assessment of control risk made during a financial statement audit.

47. (c) The requirement is to identify the correct statement concerning the level of assistance that auditors may provide in assisting management with its assessment of internal control. Answer (c) is correct since only limited assistance may be provided so as not to create a situation in which the auditors are auditing their own work. Answer (a) is incorrect since some assistance may be provided. Answer (b) is incorrect because there are limitations on the level of assistance. Answer (d) is incorrect because the tie between risk and assistance seems inappropriate and in the wrong direction; also, this type of tradeoff between risk and assistance is not included in PCAOB Standard 5.

48. (d) The requirement is to identify which of the following need **not** be included in management's report on internal control under Section 404a of the Sarbanes-Oxley Act of 2002. Answer (d) is correct because, while the report must indicate that it is management's responsibility to establish and maintain adequate internal control, it need not also indicate that such control has no significant deficiencies. Answers (a), (b), and (c) are all incorrect because they include information that must be contained in management's report.

49. (a) Answer (a) is correct because all material weaknesses are control deficiencies. Answer (b) is incorrect because a significant deficiency may or may not be a material weakness. Answer (c) is incorrect because not all control deficiencies are material weaknesses. Answer (d) is incorrect because only significant deficiencies and material weaknesses must be communicated.

50. (d) The requirement is to identify the term that is defined as a weakness in internal control that is less severe than a material weakness but important enough to warrant attention by those responsible for oversight of the financial reporting function. Answer (d) is correct because this is the definition of a significant deficiency. Answer (a) is incorrect because a *control deficiency* exists when the design or operation of a control does not allow management, or employees, in the normal course of performing their functions to prevent or detect misstatements on a timely basis. Answer (b) is incorrect because an *unusual weakness* is not used in the standards for integrated audits. Answer (c) is incorrect because the term unusual deficiency is not used in the standards for integrated audits.

51. (d) The requirement is to identify the amount involved with a material weakness. Answer (d) is correct because a material amount is involved. Answers (a), (b), and (c) are all incorrect because they suggest smaller amounts.

52. (d) The requirement is to identify the minimum likelihood of loss involved in the consideration of a control deficiency. Answer (d) is correct because a control deficiency is a condition in which the operation of a control does not allow management, or employees, in the normal course of performing their functions to prevent or detect misstatements on a timely basis—it does not explicitly consider likelihood of loss. Answer (a) is incorrect because the minimum likelihood of loss is not considered. Answer (b) is incorrect because the control deficiency occurrence of loss need not be more than remote. Answer (c) is incorrect because whether the minimum likelihood of loss is probable is not considered.

53. (a) The requirement is to identify the type of control that reconciliation of cash accounts represents. Answer (a) is correct in that it is a compensating control which supplements a basic underlying control, in this case basic information processing controls related to cash. Answer (b) is incorrect because a preventive control prevents errors or fraud from occurring. Answer (c) is incorrect because the term "adjustive" control is not ordinarily used. Answer (d) is incorrect because "nonroutine" is ordinarily considered a type of transaction (e.g., the year-end close process), not a type of control.

54. (d) The requirement is to identify the type of transaction that establishing loan loss reserves is. Answer (d) is correct because *estimation transactions* are activities involving management's judgments or assumptions, such as determining the allowance for doubtful accounts, establishing warranty reserves, and assessing assets for impairment. Answer (a) is incorrect because the term substantive transaction is not used in PCAOB standards. Answer (b) is incorrect because routine transactions are those for recurring activities, such as sales, purchases, cash receipts and disbursements, and payroll. Answer (c) is incorrect because nonroutine transactions occur only periodically, such as the taking of physical inventory, calculating depreciation expense, or adjusting for foreign currencies; nonroutine transactions generally are not a part of the routine flow of transactions.

55. (d) The requirement is to identify the relationship between an examination of internal control and obtaining an understanding of internal control and assessing control risk as part of an audit. Answer (d) is correct because, while the scope and purpose differ between the two types of engagements, the procedures followed are similar. See AT 501 (or PCAOB Standard 5) for information on reporting on an audit of internal control.

56. (d) The requirement is to identify the procedure that involves tracing a transaction from origination through the company's information systems until it is reflected in the company's financial report. Answer (d) is correct because this is the approach followed in a walk-through. Answer (a) is incorrect because analytical analysis is a general term that simply suggests a general analysis. Answer (b) is incorrect because a substantive procedure addresses the correctness of a particular financial statement amount or disclosure. Answer (c) is incorrect because a test of a control addresses the operating effectiveness of a control.

57. (b) The requirement is to identify the "as of date" for purposes of an audit of internal control performed under PCAOB standards. Answer (b) is correct because the "as of" date is the last day of the fiscal period; it is this date on which the auditor concludes as to the effectiveness of internal control. Answers (a) and (c) are incorrect because neither the first day of the year nor the last day of the auditor's fieldwork is the appropriate date on which to evaluate internal control. Answer (d) is incorrect because the "as of date" is a particular date, not an average.

58. (c) The requirement is to identify the correct statement concerning a company that makes purchases both through the Internet and by telephone. Answer (c) is correct because both types of purchases are a part of the purchases process and represent major classes of transactions, as per PCAOB Standard 5. Answer (a) is incorrect because the purchase types themselves are not control objectives for internal control (control objectives address issues such as the completeness of the recording of sales). Answer (b) is incorrect because purchases are not assertions. Answer (d) is incorrect because purchase transactions may or may not be investigated in extreme detail.

59. (a) The requirement is to identify the circumstance(s) in which walk-throughs provide the auditor with primary evidence. A walk-through involves literally tracing a transaction from its origination through the company's information systems until it is reflected in the financial reports. Answer (a) is correct because a walk-through provides evidence to (1) confirm the auditor's understanding of the flow of transactions and the design of controls, (2) evaluate the effectiveness of the design of controls, and (3) to confirm whether controls have been implemented. Answer (b) is incorrect because walk-throughs provide the auditors with primary evidence to confirm whether controls have been implemented. Answer (c) is incorrect because walk-throughs provide primary evidence to evaluate the effectiveness of design in internal control. Answer (d) is incorrect both because walk-throughs provide primary evidence to (1) evaluate the effectiveness of the design of controls and (2) confirm whether the controls have been implemented.

60. (a) The requirement is to identify the most likely question to be asked of employee personnel during a walk-through. Answer (a) is correct because a question on whether an employee has ever been asked to override the process is included in the example questions to be asked by the auditor. Answer (b) is incorrect because auditors do not in general ask whether the employee believes he or she is

underpaid. Answer (c) is incorrect because a direct question on fraudulent transactions like this, while possible, ordinarily is not suggested. Answer (d) is incorrect because the auditor will not usually ask who trained the person. Note that all four questions might be asked, but only one is among those recommended in Standard 5.

61. (a) The requirement is to identify how large the actual loss identified must be for a control deficiency to possibly be considered a material weakness. Answer (a) is correct because a material weakness is determined by whether there is more than a remote likelihood of a material loss occurring due to the control deficiency; the actual loss identified need not be material. Answer (b) is incorrect because it suggests that a material amount identified will not be considered a material weakness. Answer (c) is incorrect because it states that when the identified amount is immaterial it is never a material weakness. Answer (d) is incorrect because it suggests that when an immaterial or material actual loss is discovered, the situation would not be assessed as a possible material weakness.

62. (c) The requirement is to identify the circumstance that makes an account significant for purposes of a PCAOB audit of internal control. Answer (c) is correct because Standard 5 requires only more than a remote likelihood of material misstatement. Answer (a) is incorrect because the standard requires only a remote likelihood and because it is limited to material misstatements. Answer (b) is incorrect because the standard requires more than a remote likelihood, not more than a reasonably possible likelihood. Answer (d) is incorrect because material misstatements are involved, not misstatements that are more than inconsequential.

63. (a) The requirement is to identify the appropriate report when a control deficiency that is more than a significant deficiency is identified. Answer (a) is correct because a control deficiency that is more than a significant deficiency is a material weakness, and because a material weakness leads to an adverse opinion on internal control. Answer (b) is incorrect because qualified opinions are not issued when a material weakness exists. Answer (c) is incorrect because an unqualified opinion is not issued when a material weakness exists. Answer (d) is incorrect because explanatory language added to an unqualified report is not appropriate when a material weakness exists.

64. (a) The requirement is to identify the deficiency that is most likely to be considered a material weakness in internal control for purposes of an internal control audit of a public company. Answer (a) is correct because ineffective oversight of financial reporting by the audit committee is among the list of circumstances that PCAOB Standard 5 suggests are strong indicators of the existence of a material weakness. Restatement of previously issued financial statements as a result of a *change in accounting principles* is ordinarily not considered even a significant deficiency. Answer (c) is incorrect because the reply "inadequate segregation of recordkeeping from accounting" makes no real sense because accounting is involved with recordkeeping. Answer (d) is incorrect because control activity weaknesses often do not represent material weaknesses.

65. (b) The requirement is to identify the most appropriate report when a circumstance-caused scope limitation results in inability to evaluate internal control for a significant account involved in the audit. Answer (b) is correct because PCAOB Standard 5 indicates that either a qualified opinion or a disclaimer is appropriate, and because the disclaimer is not listed as an option. Answer (a) is incorrect because an adverse opinion is not appropriate. Answer (c) is incorrect because an unqualified opinion with explanatory language is not appropriate when the auditor is unable to evaluate internal control for a significant account. Answer (d) is incorrect because answers (a) and (c) are not appropriate.

66. (c) The requirement is to identify the most likely significant deficiency relating to a client's antifraud programs. Answer (c) is correct because an active audit committee, not a passive audit committee is needed. Answer (a) is incorrect because a broad scope of internal audit activities is ordinarily a strength, not a deficiency. Answer (b) is incorrect because a whistle-blower program that encourages anonymous submissions is required. Answer (d) is incorrect because it is not ordinarily necessary to perform criminal background investigations for likely customers.

67. (a) The requirement is to identify the appropriate audit report when a material weakness is corrected subsequent to year-end, but before the audit report is issued. Answer (a) is correct because PCAOB Standard 5 requires an adverse audit report when a material weakness exists at year-end, the "as of date." Answer (b) is incorrect because an unqualified opinion is not appropriate. Answer (c) is incorrect because an unqualified opinion with explanatory language is not adequate. Answer (d) is incorrect because a qualified opinion is not appropriate when a material weakness exists at year-end.

68. (b) The requirement is to specify whether material weaknesses and/or significant deficiencies lead to an adverse opinion on internal control in an integrated audit. Answer (b) is correct because only material weaknesses lead to an adverse opinion. Answer (a) is incorrect because significant deficiencies do not result in an adverse opinion. Answer (c) is incorrect because material weaknesses do result in adverse opinions but significant deficiencies do not. Answer (d) is incorrect because material weaknesses do result in adverse opinions.

69. (b) The requirement is to specify what types of deficiencies must be communicated by the auditor to the audit committee. Answer (b) is correct because the auditor must communicate material weaknesses and other significant deficiencies, but not all control deficiencies. Answer (a) is incorrect because control deficiencies that are not significant need not be communicated to the audit committee (unless the auditor has made an agreement to communicate them). Answers (c) and (d) are incorrect because known material weaknesses must be communicated to the audit committee and control deficiencies that are not significant deficiencies need not be communicated.

70. (c) The requirement is to determine the manner in which significant deficiencies are communicated by the auditor to the audit committee under PCAOB Standard 5.

Answer (c) is correct because the Standard requires a written communication. Answer (a) is incorrect because a written communication is required. Answer (b) is incorrect because the communication must be in a written form, not in an oral form. Answer (d) is incorrect because both material weaknesses and significant deficiencies must be communicated.

71. (c) The requirement is to identify the correct statement concerning the external auditors' use of the work of others when performing an audit of internal control of a public company. Answer (c) is correct because, after assuring themselves as to the competence and objectivity of the internal auditors and others, the external auditors may use their work—particularly in low-risk areas and when that work is supervised and/or reviewed. Answer (a) is incorrect because using the work of internal auditors and others is allowed. Answer (b) is incorrect because there is no such requirement of reporting to the audit committee, although this is one indication of internal auditor objective. Answer (d) is incorrect because there are limitations, and because it is uncertain whether liability will be shared.

72. (c) The requirement is to identify the information that must be communicated in writing to management. Answer (c) is correct because in an integrated audit all material weaknesses, significant deficiencies, and other control deficiencies must be reported to management. Answers (a) and (b) are incorrect because they are incomplete. Answer (d) is incorrect because "all suspected and possible employee law violations" need not be communicated.

73. (a) The requirement is to identify a correct statement about applying a top-down approach to identify controls to test in an integrated audit. Answer (a) is correct because certain effective entity-level controls may allow the auditor to omit additional testing beyond those controls. Answer (b) is incorrect because starting with assertions does not represent starting at the top (starting at the top includes consideration of the financial statements and entity-level controls first). Answer (c) is incorrect because consideration of entity-level controls cannot be avoided. Answer (d) is incorrect because not all controls related to assertions need to be focused upon, and because one may not omit controls related to the financial statements.

74. (d) The requirement is to identify the statement not included in a standard unqualified opinion on internal control performed under PCAOB requirements. Answer (d) is correct because the report indicates that management is responsible for maintaining effective internal control over financial reporting, not management and the audit committee. Answers (a), (b) and (c) are all incorrect because they represent statements included in the audit report.

75. (d) The requirement is to identify the statement that should be included in a CPA's report on a client's internal control over financial reporting. Answer (d) is correct because AT 501 requires that the report include a comment on the inherent limitations of any internal control.

76. (b) The requirement is to describe the contents of a report on the study of internal control that is based on criteria established by governmental agencies. Answer (b) is correct because the report should indicate matters covered by the consideration and whether the auditor's consideration included tests of controls with the procedures covered by his/her consideration. Additionally, the report should describe the objectives and limitations of internal control and the accountant's evaluation thereof; state the accountant's conclusion, based on the agency's criteria; and describe the purpose of the report and state that it should not be used for any other purpose. Answer (a) is incorrect because the agency's name should be included. Answer (c) is incorrect because a conclusion may be made relative to the agency's criteria. Answer (d) is incorrect because the accountant should not assume responsibility for the comprehensiveness of the criteria.

77. (b) AT 501 states that when a deviation from the control criteria being reported upon exists (here a material weakness in internal control) the CPA should report directly upon the subject matter and not upon the assertion.

78. (a) The requirement is to identify the procedure an auditor most likely would perform to test controls relating to management's assertion about the completeness of cash receipts for cash sales at a retail outlet. Answer (a) is correct because the use of cash registers and tapes helps assure that all such sales are recorded. Answer (b) is incorrect because the cash has already been recorded. Answer (c) is incorrect because the procedure only deals with recorded deposits, and therefore the completeness assertion is not addressed as directly as in answer (a). Answer (d) is incorrect because one would not expect the cash balance in the general ledger to agree with the bank confirmation request amount due to items in transit and outstanding at the point of reconciliation.

79. (c) The requirement is to identify the proper procedure to be performed immediately upon receipt of checks by mail. Sound internal control requires the use of adequate documentation to ensure that all transactions are properly recorded. This helps the company attain the financial statement assertion of completeness. Answer (c) is correct because the preparation of a duplicate listing of checks received provides the company with a source document of all the checks received that day. One list is then forwarded to the employee responsible for depositing the checks at the end of the day and the other list is sent to the accounting department so that they can post the amount to the cash receipts journal. Answer (a) is incorrect because the daily cash summary will ordinarily be prepared at the end of the day when all checks have been received. Answer (b) is incorrect because checks need not be compared to a sales invoice. Answer (d) is incorrect because the employee opening the mail should not also perform the recordkeeping function of recording the checks in the cash receipts journal.

80. (b) The requirement is to determine the type of evidence obtained when tracing shipping documents to prenumbered sales invoices. Answer (b) is correct because the shipping documents relate to shipments to customers, and tracing them to sales invoices will provide evidence on whether sales invoices were prepared. Answer (a) is incorrect because duplicate shipments or billings will not in general be detected by tracing individual shipping documents to prenumbered sales invoices. Answer (c) is incorrect because an auditor will trace from customer orders to shipping documents to determine whether all goods ordered were shipped. Answer (d) is incorrect because an auditor will account for the sequence of sales invoices to determine whether all sale invoices were accounted for.

81. (a) The requirement is to identify the control most likely to reduce the risk of diversion of customer receipts by an entity's employees. Answer (a) is correct because a bank lockbox system eliminates employee contact with cash receipts, and thereby greatly reduces the risk of diversion by employees. Answer (b) is incorrect because remittance advices are ordinarily prenumbered using the numbering schemes of the various customers and not of the client; also, even if a prenumbering system is instituted, difficulties remain in assuring that all receipts are recorded. Answer (c) is incorrect because a monthly bank reconciliation is only likely to be effective when receipts are deposited and then abstracted. Answer (d) is incorrect because while the daily deposit of cash receipts may reduce the risk of employee diversion of receipts, the procedure is not as effective as the bank lockbox system, which eliminates employee contact with the receipts.

82. (a) The requirement is to identify the best listed procedure for detecting the lapping of cash receipts by the client's cashier through use of customer checks received in the mail. Answer (a) is correct because lapping will result in a delay in the recording of specific remittance credits on the financial records, but the checks will be deposited in the bank as they are received. Answer (b) is incorrect because the daily cash summaries will include the same sums as the cash receipts journal entries. Answer (c) is incorrect because the bank deposit slips will be identical to any details included in the monthly bank statements. Answer (d) is incorrect because while the write-off of a receivable may help the individual involved in the lapping to avoid repayment, no lag is to be expected between authorization of the write-off and the date it is actually recorded.

83. (c) The requirement is to determine the individual or organization to which a list of remittances should be forwarded to in addition to the cashier. Answer (c) is correct because the accounts receivable bookkeeper will use the listing to update the subsidiary accounts receivable records. Answer (a) is incorrect because internal auditors will not normally investigate each day's listing of remittances for unusual transactions. Answer (b) is incorrect because the treasurer will not in general compare daily listings to the monthly bank statement. Answer (d) is incorrect because the list will not be sent to the bank.

84. (d) The requirement is to identify the procedure that most likely would **not** be a control designed to reduce the risk of errors in the billing process. Answer (d) is correct because the reconciliation of the control totals for sales invoices with the accounts receivable subsidiary ledger will follow billing; thus billing errors will have already occurred. Answer (a) is incorrect because identification of differences in shipping documents and sales invoices will allow for a correction of any errors and proper billing. Answer (b) is incorrect because computer programmed controls will assure the accuracy of the sales invoice. Answer (c) is incorrect because the matching of shipping documents with the approved sales orders will allow the preparation of a correct invoice.

85. (b) The requirement is to identify the audit procedure an auditor most likely would perform to test controls relating to management's assertion concerning the completeness of sales transactions. Answer (b) is correct because inspection of shipping documents that have **not** been recorded in the sales journal will possibly reveal items that have been sold (as evidenced by a shipping document) but for some reason have not been recorded as sales. Answers (a), (c), and (d) are all incorrect because verification of extension and footings, comparing invoiced prices, and inquiring about credit granting policies all relate more directly to the valuation assertion than to the completeness assertion.

86. (a) The requirement is to identify the control that most likely would assure that all billed sales are correctly posted to the accounts receivable ledger. Answer (a) is correct because the daily sales summary will include all "billed" sales for a particular day. Comparing this summary to the postings to the accounts receivable ledger will provide evidence on whether billed sales are correctly posted. Answer (b) is incorrect because comparing sales invoices to shipping documents provides evidence on whether invoiced sales have been shipped. Answer (c) is incorrect because reconciling the accounts receivable ledger to the control account will not provide assurance that all billed sales were posted in that both the receivable ledger and the control account may have omitted the sales. Answer (d) is incorrect because comparing shipments with sales invoices provides evidence on whether all shipments have been invoiced, not on whether all billed sales are correctly posted.

87. (a) The requirement is to determine the financial statement assertion being most directly tested when an auditor tests an entity's policy of obtaining credit approval before shipping goods to customers. Answer (a) is correct because testing credit approval helps assure that goods are shipped to customers who are likely to be able to pay; accordingly the valuation assertion for receivables is being directly tested. Answer (b) is incorrect because completeness deals with whether all transactions and accounts are recorded. Answer (c) is incorrect because existence deals with whether assets exist at a given date and whether recorded transactions have occurred during a given period. Answer (d) is incorrect because rights and obligations deal with whether assets are the rights of the entity and liabilities are the obligations of the entity at a given date.

88. (d) The requirement is to identify the control that most likely would help ensure that **all** credit sales transactions are recorded. Answer (d) is correct because the matching of shipping documents with entries in the sales journal will provide assurance that all shipped items (sales) have been completely recorded. Answer (a) is incorrect because comparison of approved sales orders to authorized credit limits and balances will help ensure that customer credit limits are not exceeded, rather than the complete recording of credit sales. Answer (b) is incorrect because reconciliation

of the accounts receivable subsidiary ledger to the accounts receivable control account will provide only a limited amount of control over the complete recording of sales. The control is incomplete since, for example, a sale that has not been recorded in either the subsidiary or control accounts will not be detected. Answer (c) is incorrect because monthly statements generally will not be sent to customers to whom no sales have been recorded.

89. (c) The requirement is to identify the control that will be most effective in offsetting the tendency of sales personnel to maximize sales volume at the expense of high bad debt write-offs. Answer (c) is correct because segregation of the authorization of credit from the sales function will allow an independent review of the creditworthiness of customers. Answer (a) is incorrect because while denying access to cash by employees responsible for sales and bad debt write-offs may deter embezzlements, the problem of high bad debt write-offs is likely to remain. Answer (b) is incorrect because while so segregating the matching of shipping documents and sales invoices may help assure that items are shipped properly and subsequently recorded, it will not significantly affect bad debts. Answer (d) is incorrect because while independent reconciliation of control and subsidiary accounts receivable records may defer embezzlements, bad debt write-offs will not be affected.

90. (d) The requirement is to determine the department that should approve bad debt write-offs. The department responsible for bad debt write-offs should be independent of the sales, credit, and the recordkeeping for that function, and should have knowledge relating to the accounts. Answer (d) is correct because, in addition to being independent of the various functions, the treasurer's department is likely to have knowledge to help make proper decisions of this nature. Answers (a) and (b), accounts receivable and the credit department, are incorrect because neither department is independent of this function. Answer (c) is incorrect because while accounts payable is independent of the function, its personnel are less likely than those of the treasurer's department to have the necessary information relating to the accounts that should be written off.

91. (b) The requirement is to identify a reason that employers bond employees who handle cash receipts. Answer (b) is correct because employee knowledge that bonding companies often prosecute those accused of dishonest acts may deter employees' dishonest acts. Answer (a) is incorrect because bonding protects the employer from dishonest acts, not the employee from unintentional errors. Answer (c) is incorrect because the bonding company does not serve the role of independent monitoring of cash. Answer (d) is incorrect because while rotation of positions and forcing employees to take periodic vacations are effective controls for preventing fraud, they are not accomplished through bonding.

92. (c) The requirement is to identify the control which would offset a weakness that allowed the accounts receivable clerk to approve credit memos and to have access to cash. Note that such a weakness may lead to a fraud in which the accounts receivable clerk receives and keeps cash payments while issuing a fraudulent credit memo as the basis for a credit to the customer's account. Answer (c) is correct because the owner's review of credit memos could help establish that fraudulent memos had not been issued for receivables which had in actuality been collected by the clerk; for example, when reviewing credit memos the owner would expect to see a receiving report for sales returns for which credit memos have been generated. Answer (a) is incorrect because the bookkeeper may be able to maintain the records in such a manner as to avoid billing errors related to the fraud, and therefore a review of billings and postings may not reveal such fraud. Answer (b) is incorrect because month-end reconciliation of checking accounts with the monthly bank statement will not reflect cash that has been improperly diverted by the accounts receivable clerk. Answer (d) is incorrect because the accounts receivable clerk should be able to maintain the detail and ledger amount in balance and thereby avoid detection.

93. (b) The requirement is to determine who should prepare a remittance advice when the customer fails to include one with a remittance. Remittances should be opened by an individual such as a receptionist who is independent of the sales function. That individual will prepare any needed remittance advices. The credit manager [answer (a)], and the sales manager [answer (c)], are incorrect because they perform an authorization function related to sales. Answer (d) is incorrect because the accounts receivable clerk performs a recordkeeping function for sales.

94. (b) The requirement is to identify the audit procedure relating to paid vouchers that will provide assurance that each voucher is submitted and paid only once. Answer (b) is correct because when the check signer stamps vouchers "paid" it is unlikely to be paid a second time since that individual will notice the stamp on the voucher the second time it is submitted for payment.

95. (d) The requirement is to determine the appropriate responsibility for the person who signs checks. Answer (d) is correct because the individual who signs checks should be responsible for mailing them so as to avoid a variety of fraud in which the checks are improperly converted into cash by company employees. Answer (a) is incorrect because the individual who reconciles the bank accounts should have no other responsibilities with respect to cash. Answer (b) is incorrect because accounts payable does not need the checks and, if they receive them, those checks may be converted into cash which is then stolen. Answer (c) is incorrect because the person who signs the checks should determine that proper supporting documents exist and should cancel that documentation after the payment is made.

96. (b) The requirement is to determine the financial statement assertion that a test of controls of vouching a sample of entries in the voucher register to the supporting documents most directly addresses. Answer (b) is correct because the existence or occurrence assertion addresses whether recorded entries are valid and the direction of this test is from the recorded entry in the voucher register to the supporting documents. Answer (a) is incorrect because completeness addresses whether all transactions and accounts are included and would involve tests tracing from support for purchases to

the recorded entry. Answers (c) and (d) are incorrect because vouching the entries provides only limited evidence on valuation and rights.

97. (d) The requirement is to determine the control that is **not** usually performed in the vouchers payable department. Answer (d) is correct because the vouchers payable department will not in general have access to unused prenumbered purchase orders and receiving reports. Answer (a) is incorrect because the vouchers payable department will match the vendor's invoice with the related receiving report to determine that the item for which the company has been billed has been received. Answer (b) is incorrect because the vouchers payable department will approve vouchers for payment when all documentation is proper and present. Answer (c) is incorrect because the vouchers payable department will code the voucher with accounts to be debited.

98. (b) The requirement is to identify the function that is consistent with matching vendors' invoices with receiving reports. Answer (b) is correct because while matching invoices and receiving reports, the employee might effectively recompute the calculations on the vendors' invoices to determine that the amounts are proper. Answers (a) and (c) are incorrect. The individual who matches the invoices and receiving reports will often also approve them for payment. Therefore, this individual should not also post accounts payable records or reconcile the accounts payable ledger. Answer (d) is incorrect because the individual who controls the signing of the checks should cancel the invoices after payment.

99. (b) The requirement is to identify the population from which items should be selected to determine whether checks are being issued for unauthorized expenditures. Answer (b) is correct because a sample of canceled checks should be selected and compared with the approved vouchers, a prenumbered purchase order and prenumbered receiving reports. A canceled check that does not have such support may have been unauthorized. Answers (a), (c), and (d) are all incorrect because selecting items from purchase orders, receiving reports, or approved vouchers will not reveal circumstances in which a check was issued without that supporting document. For example, when selecting a sample from purchase orders, one would not discover a situation in which a check had been issued without a purchase order.

100. (d) The requirement is to determine which question would most likely be included in an internal control questionnaire concerning the completeness assertion for purchases. Answer (d) is correct because prenumbering and accounting for purchase orders, receiving reports, and vouchers will allow a company to determine that purchases are completely recorded. For example, in examining a receiving report the client might discover that the purchase was not recorded. Answer (a) is incorrect because requiring a purchase order before a shipment is accepted will address whether or not the shipment has been ordered. Answer (b) is incorrect because matching purchase requisitions with vendor invoices does not directly address whether the purchase is recorded. Answer (c) is incorrect because the unpaid voucher file represents items that have already been recorded, and thus will not directly address the completeness of the recording of purchases.

101. (d) The requirement is to identify the proper control pertaining to the accounts payable department. Answer (d) is correct because the accounts payable department should establish the agreement of the vendor's invoice with the purchase order and receiving report to provide assurance that the item was both ordered and received. Answer (a) is incorrect because the individual signing the check (e.g., the treasurer), not the accounts payable department, should stamp, perforate, or otherwise cancel supporting documentation after a check is signed. Answer (b) is incorrect because purchase requisitions will not normally include detailed price information. Answer (c) is incorrect because the quantity ordered on the receiving department copy of the purchase order will already be obliterated when the purchase order is completed by the purchasing department.

102. (b) The requirement is to determine which copy of the purchase order should omit indication of the quantity of merchandise ordered. Answer (b) is correct because if the receiving department personnel are unaware of the quantities ordered, they will provide an independent count of quantities received. Answer (a) is incorrect because the department that initiated the requisition needs the merchandise, and therefore, should know what has been ordered. Answer (c) is incorrect because the purchasing agent is involved with purchasing the items and therefore must be aware of the quantity involved. Answer (d) is incorrect because the accounts payable department must reconcile the quantity received and the quantity billed to the quantity that was authorized to be purchased per the purchase order.

103. (b) The requirement is to identify the audit procedure which would most likely detect a client error in recording a large purchase. Answer (b) is correct because reconciling the vendors' monthly statements with the subsidiary ledger for payables should disclose a difference in the month following the error. Answer (a), footing the purchases journal, is unlikely to detect the error since the journal's totals will have been mathematically accumulated properly. Answer (c) is incorrect because the incorrect total will be reflected in both the purchases journal and in the ledger accounts. Answer (d) is incorrect because such confirmations will only detect the error quarterly which is neither timely nor efficient.

104. (d) The requirement is to identify a function that is compatible with the approval of purchase orders. Answer (d) is correct because the purchases department will normally approve purchase orders (generated from user departments or stores) and negotiate terms of purchase with vendors. Answer (a) is incorrect because while the purchases department may reconcile the open invoice file, this is primarily a recordkeeping function that will often be performed by the accounting department. Answer (b) is incorrect because most frequently the receiving department will inspect goods upon receipt. Answer (c) is incorrect because user groups or stores will authorize requisitions of goods. Keep in mind the principle of segregation of functions. Recordkeeping, authorization, and custodial functions should all be segregated.

105. (c) The requirement is to identify the most likely procedure an auditor would perform in obtaining an understanding of a manufacturing entity's internal control for inventory balances. Answer (c) is correct because a review of the entity's descriptions of inventory policies and procedures will help the auditor to obtain the necessary understanding about the design of relevant policies, procedures, and records, and whether they have been implemented by the entity. Answers (a) and (b) are incorrect because analyses of liquidity and turnover ratios are analytical procedures designed to identify cost variances that will help the auditor primarily to determine the nature, timing and extent of auditing procedures that will be used to obtain evidence for specific account balances or classes of transactions. Answer (d) is incorrect because test counts of inventory are generally obtained as a substantive procedure.

106. (d) The requirement is to identify the control that most likely would be used to maintain accurate inventory records. Answer (d) is correct because periodic inventory counts will assure that perpetual inventory records are accurate and, because employees will know that inventory differences are investigated, they will be less likely to steal any inventory. Answer (a) is incorrect because comparing the perpetual inventory records with current costs of items will reveal situations in which costs have changed, but is unlikely to help in the maintenance of accurate inventory records. Answer (b) is incorrect because while a just-in-time inventory ordering system may help assure that inventory records are accurate (as well as kept at low levels), such a system generally also requires periodic inventory counts to maintain accurate inventory records. Answer (c) is incorrect because matching requisitions, receiving reports, and purchase orders only helps assure that items received are paid for; the matching process does not assure accurate inventory records.

107. (d) The requirement is to determine a likely effect on the audit of inventory if the assessed level of control risk is high. Answer (d) is correct because a high assessed level of control risk may result in changing the timing of substantive tests to year-end rather than at an interim date. If the assessed level of control risk is low, the auditor could perform interim substantive tests and rely upon internal control to provide valid year-end records. However, because the assessed level of control risk is high, the controls cannot be relied upon. Also, the nature of substantive tests may change from less effective to more effective procedures (e.g., use of independent parties outside the entity rather than internal) and an increase in the extent of procedures (e.g., larger sample sizes). Answer (a) is incorrect because, as indicated, an auditor will generally seek a year-end count of inventory. Answer (b) is incorrect because gross profit tests will not in general have the required precision when control risk is high. Answer (c) is incorrect because tests of controls are likely to substantiate an auditor's view that control risk is high, and it is therefore unlikely that their performance will be cost-effective.

108. (c) The requirement is to identify the control which is most likely to address the completeness assertion for inventory. Answer (c) is correct because by prenumbering receiving reports and by reconciling them with inventory records, one is able to test completeness by determining whether all receipts have been recorded. Answer (a) is incorrect because reconciling the subsidiary records with the work in process will only identify discrepancies between the records, it will not identify whether all transactions that should be in the inventory records are represented in the records. Answer (b) is incorrect because while the segregation of receiving from custody of finished goods is important, it less directly addresses completeness than does answer (a). Answer (d) is incorrect because separating the duties between the payroll department and inventory accounting personnel does not directly address completeness of inventory.

109. (c) The requirement is to determine the proper internal control for handling customer returns of defective merchandise. Answer (c) is correct because the receiving department can count the goods, and list them on a sales return notice to determine that all such returns are properly recorded. This serves as a control because the normal procedures of the receiving function include establishing the original accountability and recordkeeping for items received. Answers (a), (b), and (d) all represent functions not typically involved in the receiving function and thus involve a higher risk relating to establishing accountability.

110. (c) The requirement is to identify the effect on revenues, receivables, and inventory of inadequate controls over the invoicing function that allows goods to be shipped without being invoiced. Items shipped without invoicing will result in a situation in which the accounting department is unaware of the sale. Therefore, debits to accounts receivable and credits to sales will not be recorded, resulting in an understatement of both revenues and receivables. Similarly, because accounting is unaware of the sale, no entry to reduce inventory will be made, resulting in an overstatement of inventory.

111. (c) The requirement is to identify the question that an auditor would expect to find on the **production** cycle section of an internal control questionnaire. Answer (c) is correct because approved requisitions will help maintain control over raw materials released to be used in the production cycle. Answers (a), (b), and (d) are all incorrect because approval of vendors' invoices for payment, mailing of checks after signing, and comparing individual disbursements to totals all pertain more directly to the disbursement cycle.

112. (b) The requirement is to determine an objective of internal control for a production cycle in addition to providing assurance that transactions are properly executed and recorded. Answer (b) is correct because, in addition to providing assurance as to proper execution and recording, an objective for the production cycle (as well as other cycles) is the safeguarding of assets, here work in process and finished goods. Answers (a), (c), and (d) are incorrect because they represent detailed controls established to help achieve the overall objectives. They are all much more specific than the overall objectives.

113. (b) The requirement is to identify a purpose of vouching data for a sample of employees in a payroll register to approved clock card data. Answer (b) is correct because the clock card data provides the auditor with evidence on whether

employees worked the number of hours for which the payroll register indicates they were paid. Answer (a) is incorrect because clock card data often does not include authorized pay rates. Answer (c) is incorrect because the procedure does not directly address the segregation of duties since no information is provided concerning the distribution of the payroll. Answer (d) is incorrect because unclaimed payroll checks are not being analyzed.

114. (a) The requirement is to identify the control that most likely could help prevent employee payroll fraud. Answer (a) is correct because prompt notification of the payroll supervisor concerning terminations will lead to timely removal of terminated employees from the payroll. Accordingly, no payroll checks will be prepared for such terminated employees. Answer (b) is incorrect because unclaimed payroll checks should not be returned to the supervisors who might inappropriately cash them. Answer (c) is incorrect because since the payroll department is involved in recordkeeping, it should not approve salary rates. Answer (d) is incorrect because calculation of total hours by the payroll supervisor is unlikely to prevent employee payroll fraud.

115. (a) The requirement is to determine the best procedure for determining the effectiveness of an entity's controls relating to the existence or occurrence assertion for payroll transactions. Answer (a) is correct because proper segregation of duties between personnel and payroll disbursement eliminates many frauds in which "phantom" employees are being paid. Answer (b) is incorrect because accounting for the prenumbered payroll checks addresses completeness more directly than it does existence or occurrence. Answer (c) is incorrect because recomputing payroll deductions for employee fringe benefits, without additional analysis, provides only a very limited test of existence or occurrence. Answer (d) is incorrect because verifying the preparation of the monthly payroll account bank reconciliation is unlikely to provide evidence on the existence or occurrence assertion, although some possibility does exist if signatures on checks are analyzed in detail.

116. (c) The requirement is to identify the situation in which it is most likely that an auditor would assess control risk for payroll at a high level. Answer (c) is correct because the payroll department, which is essentially a recordkeeping function, should not also authorize payroll rate changes. Under strong internal control recordkeeping, authorization, and custody over assets should be segregated. Answer (a) is incorrect because examining authorization forms for new employees is consistent with the payroll department's recordkeeping function. Answer (b) is incorrect because comparing payroll registers with original batch transmittal data is a control relating to recordkeeping. Answer (d) is incorrect because while the actual hiring of employees is normally done in the personnel department, allowing the payroll department supervisor to hire subordinates, with proper approval, is not as inconsistent with payroll's recordkeeping function as is authorizing rate changes for all employees.

117. (c) The requirement is to identify the control most likely to prevent direct labor hours from being charged to manufacturing overhead. Answer (c) is correct because time tickets may be coded as to whether direct labor on various projects was involved. Accordingly, using time tickets will help identify direct labor costs. Answer (a) is incorrect because while periodic counts of work in process may provide a control over physical units of production, the counts will not in general provide assurance that direct labor hours are properly charged to the product rather than to manufacturing overhead. Answer (b) is incorrect because comparing daily journal entries with production orders will not in general identify costs that have been omitted from direct labor due to the level of aggregation of the entries. Answer (d) is incorrect because the reconciliation of work in process inventory with budgets will provide only very limited detection ability relating to the charging of direct labor to manufacturing overhead.

118. (a) The requirement is to determine the individual(s) who should distribute paychecks and have custody of unclaimed paychecks. Answer (a) is correct because these custody functions should not be performed by the payroll department which is a recordkeeping function. Under proper internal control recordkeeping, custody, and authorization of transactions should be segregated.

119. (c) If payment of wages were to be in cash, each employee receiving payment should be required to sign a receipt for the amount of pay received. Thus, there would be control over the total amount disbursed as well as amounts disbursed to each individual employee. Answer (a) is incorrect because if a signed receipt is not received from each employee paid, there would be no proof of payment. Even though the pay envelopes include both cash and a computation of net wages, the employees should have the opportunity to count the cash received before signing a payroll receipt. Answer (b) is incorrect because unclaimed pay envelopes should not be retained by the paymaster, but rather deposited in a bank account by the cashier. Answer (d) is incorrect because the wage payment will be made in cash and not by check. Accordingly, a receipt must be obtained for each cash payment.

120. (a) The requirement is to identify the purpose of segregating the duties of hiring personnel and of distributing payroll checks. Answer (a) is correct because the hiring of personnel is an authorization function while the distribution of checks is a custody function. Thus, in order to properly segregate authorization from custody, these duties should not be performed by the same individual. The combination of these two functions in the same position would create the possibility of the addition of a fictitious employee to the payroll and subsequent misappropriation of paychecks. Answer (b) is incorrect because the functions involved are not primarily operational or recordkeeping. Answer (c) is incorrect because the treasury function, and not the controllership function, will normally be responsible for distributing payroll checks. Answer (d) is incorrect because segregation of duties does not directly address administrative controls vs. internal accounting controls.

121. (c) The requirement is to determine the best method to minimize the opportunities for fraud for unclaimed cash in a **cash** payroll system. For a **cash** payroll the best control is to get the unclaimed cash out of the firm's physical control and into the bank. Answer (a) is incorrect because maintaining the accountability for cash which is in a safe-deposit box is difficult. Answers (b) and (d) are incorrect because the cash need not be kept by the firm.

122. (c) The requirement is to identify a reason why an auditor may observe the distribution of paychecks. Answer (c) is correct because an employee's presence to collect the paycheck provides evidence that the employee actually exists and is currently employed by the client. Answer (a) is incorrect because the distributions of payroll checks would not reveal whether payrate authorization is properly separated from the operating function. Answer (b) is incorrect because the paycheck distribution does not provide information on whether deductions from gross pay have been calculated properly. Answer (d) is incorrect because observation of the paycheck distribution process does not of itself provide assurance that the paychecks agree with the related payroll register and time cards.

123. (a) The requirement is to determine the department most likely to approve change in pay rates and deductions from employee salaries. Answer (a) is correct because the personnel department, which has the primary objective of planning, controlling and coordinating employees, will determine that proposed salary increases (often recommended by supervisors of employees) are consistent with the company's salary guidelines and will approve changes in deductions. Answers (b) and (c) are incorrect because the treasurer and controller will in general initiate the pay rate change process for only those employees within their departments and will not generally approve changes for employees outside their departments. Answer (d) is incorrect because the payroll functions is a recordkeeping function which will modify employee pay rates based on approved changes from personnel. Payroll should not have authority regarding pay rates and deductions.

124. (d) The requirement is to determine the most likely question that would be included on an internal control questionnaire for notes payable. Answer (d) is correct because companies frequently require that direct borrowings on notes payable be authorized by the board of directors; accordingly, auditors will determine whether proper policy has been followed. Answer (a) is incorrect because internal control questionnaires do not in general include questions on whether assets that collateralize notes payable are critically needed. Answer (b) is incorrect because the internal control questionnaire for disbursements is more likely to address the required authorized signatures on checks than will the internal control questionnaire for notes payable. Answer (c) is incorrect because while it is often good business practice to use proceeds from long-term notes to purchase noncurrent assets, this is not required and is not included on an internal control questionnaire.

125. (d) The requirement is to identify the primary responsibility of a bank acting as registrar for capital stock. Answer (d) is correct because the primary responsibility of the stock registrar is to prevent any overissuance of stock, and thereby verify that the stock is issued properly.

Answer (a) is incorrect because registrar will not in general determine that the dividend amounts are proper. Answer (b) is incorrect because the transfer agent will maintain records of total shares outstanding as well as detailed stockholder records, and carry out transfers of stock ownership. Answer (c) is incorrect because registrars do not perform the role described relating to mergers, acquisitions, and the sale of treasury stock.

126. (a) Canceled stock certificates should be defaced and attached to corresponding stubs as is done with voided checks. The objective of the control is to prevent reissuance. Answer (b) is incorrect because failure to deface permits reissuance. Answer (c) is incorrect because destruction of the certificates would preclude their control (i.e., their existence after defacing provides assurance that they cannot be reissued). If the certificates were destroyed, one or more might be reissued without any proof that such occurred. Answer (d) is incorrect because the Secretary of State has no interest in receiving defaced and canceled stock certificates.

127. (a) The requirement is to identify the reply which is **not** a control that is designed to protect investment securities. Answer (a) is not a control since the custody of securities should be assigned to individuals who **do not** have accounting responsibility for securities; as with other assets, authorization, recordkeeping, and custody should be separated. Answer (b) is incorrect because securities should be properly controlled physically in order to prevent unauthorized usage. Answer (c) is incorrect because access to securities should ordinarily be vested in two individuals so as to assure their safekeeping. Answer (d) is incorrect because securities should be registered in the name of the owner.

128. (b) The requirement is to identify the best control for safeguarding marketable securities when an independent trust agent is not employed. Answer (b) is correct because requiring joint control over securities maintained in a safe-deposit box assures that, absent collusion, assets are safeguarded. Answer (a) is incorrect because a review of investment decisions by the investment committee will have a very limited effect on *safeguarding* marketable securities. Answer (c) is incorrect because the simple tracing of marketable securities from the subsidiary ledgers to the general ledger does not directly safeguard marketable securities since, for example, unrecorded transactions may occur. Answer (d) is incorrect because, even if the chairman of the board did verify marketable securities on the balance sheet date, the control will only be effective at that point in time.

129. (d) The requirement is to identify the best audit procedure when a weakness in internal control over reporting of retirements exists. Answer (d) is correct because selecting certain items of equipment from the accounting records and attempting to locate them will reveal situations in which the accounting records still have them recorded subsequent to their retirement. Answer (a) is incorrect because inspecting items that still exist is not likely to lead to discovery of unrecorded retirements. Answer (b) is incorrect because depreciation may continue to be taken on equipment that has been retired, but not recorded. Answer (c) is incorrect because it is doubtful that such retirements have been reclassified as "other assets."

130. (d) The requirement is to identify the question that is **least** likely to be included on an internal control questionnaire concerning the initiation and execution of equipment transactions. Answer (d) is correct because procedures to monitor and properly restrict access to equipment do not relate directly to the initiation and execution of equipment transactions. Answer (a) is incorrect because requests for major repairs relate to initiation of a transaction which should be controlled. Answer (b) is incorrect because prenumbered purchase orders may be used to control all purchases, including purchases of equipment. Answer (c) is incorrect because the significant amounts of money involved with purchases of equipment suggest the need for the solicitation of competitive bids.

131. (d) The requirement is to identify the control that would be most effective in assuring that the proper custody of assets in the investing cycle is maintained. Answer (d) is correct because comparing recorded balances in the investment subsidiary ledger with physical counts will help assure that recorded assets are those over which the company has custody. This is an example of the control activity of comparison of assets with recorded accountability. Answer (a) is incorrect because internal control is improved when two individuals, not one, must be present for entry to the safe-deposit box. Answer (b) is incorrect because while the segregation of duties within the recordkeeping may in certain circumstances be desirable, it does not directly address custody over assets. Answer (c) is incorrect because only extremely major investments generally need be authorized by the board of directors.

132. (d) The requirement is to determine who should have responsibility for custody of short-term bearer bond investments and the submission of coupons for periodic collections of interest. The treasurer authorizes such transactions. Answer (a) is incorrect because the chief accountant, who is in charge of the recordkeeping function, should not also maintain custody of the bonds. Answer (b) is incorrect because the internal auditor should not be directly involved as such involvement would make an independent review of the system impossible. Answer (c) is incorrect because the cashier function is more directly involved with details such as endorsing, depositing, and maintaining records of cash receipts.

133. (b) The requirement is to identify the control that would be most likely to assist an entity in satisfying the completeness assertion related to long-term investments. Answer (b) is correct because completeness deals with whether all transactions are recorded, and the comparison of securities in the bank safe-deposit box with recorded investments may reveal securities which are in the safe-deposit box but are not recorded. Answer (a) is incorrect because verification of security registration helps establish the rights assertion not the completeness assertion. Answer (c) is incorrect because vouching the acquisition of securities by comparing brokers' advices with canceled checks helps to establish the existence assertion not the completeness assertion. Answer (d) is incorrect because a comparison of the current market prices of recorded investments with brokers' advices addresses the valuation assertion not the completeness assertion.

134. (a) The requirement is to identify the best control for safeguarding marketable securities against loss. Answer (a) is correct because use of an independent trust company allows the effective separation of custody and recordkeeping for the securities. Answer (b) is incorrect because a verification of marketable securities at the balance sheet date may have only a limited effect on safeguarding the securities throughout the year. Answer (c) is incorrect because tracing all purchases and sales of marketable securities will not affect securities that have disappeared for which no entries have been made. Also, it is unlikely that an entity will rely upon the independent auditor in this manner. Answer (d) is incorrect because maintenance of control over custody by a member of the board of directors may provide less complete control than the use of an independent trust company.

135. (c) The requirement is to determine the appropriate combination of audit tests when there are numerous property and equipment transactions during the year and the auditor plans to assess control risk at a low level. Answer (c) is correct because, to justify an assessment of control risk at a low level, tests of controls will be required. This will allow auditors to perform only limited tests of current year property and equipment transactions. Answer (a) is incorrect because tests of controls will be performed to allow the auditor to perform limited, not extensive, tests of property and equipment balances at the end of the year. Answers (b) and (d) are incorrect because analytical procedures on either year-end balances or transactions will not justify a low assessed level of control risk.

136. (d) The requirement is to determine the type of fraud which is most difficult to detect. Answer (d), a fraud committed by the controller, is most difficult to detect because the controller is in control of the recordkeeping function and thus may be able to commit a fraud and then manipulate the accounting records so as to make its discovery unlikely. Answer (a) is incorrect because while a cashier may be able to embezzle funds, s/he will not have access to the accounting records and thus discovery of the embezzlement will be likely. Answer (b) is incorrect because a keypunch operator will not in general have access to assets. Answer (c) is incorrect because an internal auditor will not generally be able to manipulate the accounting records and generally has limited access to assets.

137. (c) Answer (c) is correct because weaknesses that were communicated in the past and not corrected must be recommunicated to management and those charged with governance. Answers (a), (b), and (d) are all accurate statements about audit requirements.

138. (c) The requirement is to identify the matter an auditor would most likely consider to be a material weakness to be communicated to those charged with governance. Answer (c) is correct because ineffective oversight of financial reporting by those charged with governance is an indicator of a material weakness—AU-C 265. Answers (a), (b), and (d) are all incorrect because a failure to renegotiate unfavorable long-term purchase commitments, recurring operating losses, and plans to reduce ownership equity do not fall within the definition of a material weakness.

139. (c) The requirement is to identify the correct statement concerning significant deficiencies identified in an audit. Answer (c) is correct because an auditor may communicate significant deficiencies either during an audit or after the audit's completion. Answer (a) is incorrect because an auditor need not search for significant deficiencies. Answer (b) is incorrect because all significant deficiencies are not also material weaknesses. Answer (d) is incorrect because an auditor may not issue a written report that **no** significant deficiencies were noted during an audit.

140. (d) The requirement is to identify the statement that should be included in an auditor's letter on significant deficiencies. Answer (d) is correct because AU-C 265 indicates that such a letter to the audit committee should (1) indicate that the audit's purpose was to report on the financial statements and **not** to express an opinion on internal control, (2) include the definition of a significant deficiency, and (3) restrict distribution of the report.

141. (c) The requirement is to identify the correct statement concerning an auditor's required communication of significant deficiencies. Answer (c) is correct because distribution of an auditor's report on significant deficiencies should be restricted to management and the audit committee. Answer (a) is incorrect because lack of correction of a significant deficiency does not necessarily result in a scope limitation. Answer (b) is incorrect because tests of controls need not be performed relating to significant deficiencies. Answer (d) is incorrect because although timely communication of significant deficiencies may be important, depending upon the nature of the significant deficiency identified, the auditor may choose to communicate it either after the audit is concluded or during the course of the audit.

142. (d) The requirement is to identify the correct statement about significant deficiencies noted in an audit. Answer (d) is correct because the auditor should separately identify and communicate material weaknesses and significant deficiencies (AU-C 265). Answer (a) is incorrect because significant deficiencies are less severe than material weaknesses. Answer (b) is incorrect because the auditor is not obligated to search for significant deficiencies. Answer (c) is incorrect because such deficiencies should be recommunicated.

143. (b) The requirement is to determine the representation that should **not** be included in a report on internal control related matters noted in an audit. Answer (b) is correct because the auditors should not issue a report on internal control stating that no significant deficiencies were identified during the audit. Answer (a) is incorrect because significant deficiencies should be disclosed. Answer (c) is incorrect because an auditor may recommend corrective follow-up action. Answer (d) is incorrect because an auditor may disclose the fact that the consideration of internal control would **not** necessarily disclose all significant deficiencies that exist.

144. (b) The requirement is to identify the correct statement regarding material weaknesses and significant deficiencies. Answer (b) is correct because a compensating control is a control that lessens the severity of a deficiency (AU-C 265). Answer (a) is incorrect because material weaknesses should be reported separately from significant deficiencies. Answer (c) is incorrect because while the auditor may choose to communicate material weakness and significant deficiencies immediately, the communication may occur at other times. Answer (d) is incorrect because significant deficiencies are less severe than material weaknesses.

145. (b) The requirement is to determine an auditor's responsibility after s/he has discovered and orally communicated information on a weakness in internal control to the client's senior management and those charged with corporate governance. Answer (b) is correct because the auditor, as outlined throughout AU-C 330, considers and documents his/her understanding of internal control to assist in planning and determining the proper nature, timing, and extent of substantive tests. Answer (a) is incorrect because no scope limitation is indicated although an internal control condition does exist. Similarly, answers (c) and (d) are incorrect because audit activities need not be suspended and the auditor need not withdraw from the engagement.

146. (b) The requirement is to determine the matter that an auditor would communicate to those charged with governance. Answer (b) is correct because AU-C 260 requires that when the auditor is aware of such consultation with another CPA, s/he should discuss with the audit committee his/her views about significant matters that were the subject of such consultation; accordingly, such a discussion with management is to be expected. While the information suggested in answers (a), (c), and (d) may all be communicated to the audit committee, they are not included as required disclosures under AU-C 260. See AU-C 260 for the various matters that must be communicated to those charged with governance.

147. (b) The requirement is to identify the correct statement concerning an auditor's required communication with those charged with governance. Answer (b) is correct because the communication should include such information on disagreements. See AU-C 260 for this and other required communications with those charged with governance. Answer (a) is incorrect because the communication may occur before or after issuance of the auditor's report. Answer (c) is incorrect because not all matters need be communicated to management. Answer (d) is incorrect because significant adjustments need to be communicated to those charged with governance.

148. (b) The requirement is to identify the discussion that it is least likely that an auditor will initiate with those charged with governance. Answer (b) is correct because auditors do not generally initiate a discussion on materiality, although they do occasionally respond to such questions. See AU-C 260 for auditor communications with those charged with governance.

149. (b) The requirement is to identify the correct statement about an auditor's required communication with those charged with governance. Answer (b) is correct because the communication must include significant misstatements discovered, even if corrected by management. Answer (a) is incorrect because while such communications may be communicated to management, there is no such requirement. Answer (c) is incorrect because disagreements with management, as well as the other required disclosures, may

be communicated either orally or in writing. Answer (d) is incorrect because an auditor must recommunicate such weaknesses in internal control. Also, see AU-C 260 for the matters communicated to those charged with governance.

150. (a) The requirement is to determine whether disagreements with management and initial selection of significant accounting policies need to be communicated to those charged with corporate governance. Answer (a) is correct because disagreements should be communicated directly to those charged with corporate governance. Answer (b) is incorrect because direct communication by the auditor is not required for selection of accounting principles. Management may engage in this communication with those charged with corporate governance. Answer (c) is incorrect because the auditor only needs to make sure that management has communicated with the committee concerning initial selection of significant accounting policies in emerging areas that lack authoritative guidance. Answer (d) is incorrect because disagreements should be communicated directly to those charged with corporate governance.

151. (a) The requirement is to determine the information that an auditor should communicate to those charged with corporate governance. Answer (a) is correct because both significant audit adjustments and management's consultation with other accountants about significant accounting matters should be communicated to an audit committee. See AU-C 260 for these and other matters that should be so communicated.

152. (a) The requirement is to identify the most likely information a CPA would obtain in assessing the competence of an internal auditor. Answer (a) is correct because in assessing competence, an internal auditor will consider the quality of working paper documentation as well as a variety of other factors outlined in AU-C 610. Answer (b) is incorrect because an organization's commitment to integrity and ethical values, while important, does not bear as directly upon internal auditor competence. Answers (c) and (d) are incorrect because the influence of management and the organizational level to which the internal auditor reports are factors used to assess internal auditor objectivity. AU-C 610 provides overall guidance on the use of internal auditors.

153. (d) The requirement is to determine whether the independent auditor may share responsibility with an entity's internal auditor for assessing inherent risk and control risk. AU-C 610 requires that judgments about inherent and control risk always be those of the independent auditor. It also requires that judgments about the materiality of misstatements, the sufficiency of tests performed, the valuation of significant accounting estimates, and other matters affecting the auditor's report should always be those of the independent auditor. See AU-C 610 for information on the external auditor's consideration of the internal audit function.

154. (d) The work of internal auditors may affect the nature, timing and extent of the audit, including (1) procedures the auditor performs when obtaining an understanding of the entity's internal control, (2) procedures the auditor performs when assessing risk, and (3) substantive procedures the auditor performs.

155. (c) The requirement is to identify the circumstance in which an internal auditor's work would most likely affect the nature, timing, and extent of a CPA's auditing procedures. When considering the effect of the internal auditors' work, the CPA considers (1) the materiality of financial statement amounts, (2) the risk of material misstatement of the assertions, and (3) the degree of subjectivity involved in the evaluation of the audit evidence. Answer (c) is correct because the existence of fixed asset additions involves little subjectivity. Answers (a) and (b) are incorrect because the existence of contingencies and the valuation of intangible assets are subjective and the risk of misstatement may be high. Answer (d) is incorrect because the valuation of related-party transactions may be very subjective due to the lack of an "arm's-length" transaction.

156. (d) AU-C 610 states that internal auditors may assist the CPA in obtaining an understanding of internal control, in performing tests of controls, and in performing substantive tests.

157. (b) The requirement is to identify the type of information used by a CPA to assess the competence of internal auditors. Answer (b) is correct because, along with various other factors, AU-C 610 indicates that the CPA should obtain evidence on the educational background and professional certification of the internal auditors when considering competence. Answers (a) and (c) are incorrect because analysis of organizational level to which the internal auditors report and policies on relatives are considered when assessing internal auditor objectivity. Answer (d) is incorrect because access to sensitive records will not provide a CPA with information on competence.

158. (d) The requirement is to identify the **least** likely source of information to the CPA on an entity's internal auditor's competence and objectivity. Answer (d) is correct because analytical procedures do not ordinarily provide information on the internal auditor. See AU-C 520 for information on analytical procedures.

159. (a) The requirement is to identify the characteristics of an internal auditor which must be considered by an independent auditor who decides that the internal auditor's work might have a bearing on his/her procedures. Answer (a) is correct because independent auditors must consider internal auditor competence, objectivity, and work performance. Answer (b) is incorrect because an independent auditor is less concerned about internal auditor efficiency, although internal auditor experience will be considered in the assessment of competence. Answers (c) and (d), while partially correct, are less complete than answer (a).

160. (d) The requirement is to determine how a CPA should assess the objectivity of an internal auditor. Answer (d) is correct because when assessing the objectivity of an internal auditor the CPA should consider organizational status and policies for maintaining objectivity. Answers (a), (b), and (c) are all incorrect because evaluating the quality control program, and examining and testing an internal auditor's work all relate more directly to assessing internal auditor competence rather than to objectivity. See AU-C 610 for these

and other factors considered when assessing internal auditor competence.

161. (a) The requirement is to identify the information provided in a service auditor's report which includes an opinion on a description of controls implemented. Answer (a) is correct since such a report includes a description of the scope and nature of the CPA's procedures. Answers (b), (c), and (d) are all incorrect because they suggest information not included in such a report. See AU-C 402 for information on the audit of service organizations.

162. (a) The requirement is to identify a CPA's reporting responsibility when reporting on internal control implemented for a service organization that processes payroll transactions. Answer (a) is correct because since the CPA is only expressing an opinion on whether controls have been implemented, a disclaimer should be provided on operating effectiveness. Answer (b) is incorrect because no specific statement is made with respect to earlier objectives. Answer (c) is incorrect because controls relevant to financial statement assertions are not so identified. Answer (d) is incorrect because the assessed level of control risk is not disclosed. See AU-C 402 for information on processing of transactions by service organizations.

163. (a) The requirement is to determine whether an auditor who audits the processing of transactions by a service organization may issue a report on either, or both, of whether controls have been implemented and control operating effectiveness. Answer (a) is correct because AU-C 402 indicates that such "service auditors" may issue either of the two types of reports.

164. (a) The requirement is to identify the proper information to be included in a service auditor's report on whether a client's controls have been implemented. Answer (a) is correct because such a report should include a description of the scope and nature of the client's procedures.

165. (d) The requirement is to determine the propriety of a computer "user" auditor (Lake) making reference to a service auditor's (Cope) report. Answer (d) is correct because the user auditor should not make reference to the report of the service auditor. See AU-C 402 for reports on the processing of transactions by service organizations.

Task-Based Simulation 1

Cash Receipts and Billing		
	Authoritative Literature	Help

An auditor's working papers include the narrative description of the cash receipts and billing portions of Southwest Medical Center's internal control. Evaluate the information in the situation as being either (1) a strength, (2) a weakness, (3) not a strength or a weakness.

Southwest is a health-care provider that is owned by a partnership of five physicians. It employs eleven physicians, including the five owners, twenty nurses, five laboratory and X-ray technicians, and four clerical workers. The clerical workers perform such tasks as reception, correspondence, cash receipts, billing, accounts receivable, bank deposits, and appointment scheduling. These clerical workers are referred to in the situation as office manager, clerk #1, clerk #2, and clerk #3. Assume that the narrative is a complete description of the system.

About two-thirds of Southwest's patients receive medical services only after insurance coverage is verified by the office manager and communicated to the clerks. Most of the other patients pay for services by cash or check when services are rendered, although the office manger extends credit on a case-by-case basis to about 5% of the patients.

When services are rendered, the attending physician prepares a prenumbered service slip for each patient and gives the slip to clerk #1 for pricing. Clerk #1 completes the slip and gives the completed slip to clerk #2 and a copy to the patient.

Using the information on the completed slip, clerk #2 performs one of the following three procedures for each patient:

- Clerk #2 files an insurance claim and records a receivable from the insurance company if the office manager has verified the patient's coverage, or
- Clerk #2 posts a receivable from the patient on clerk #2's PC if the office manager has approved the patient's credit, or
- Clerk #2 receives cash or a check from the patient as the patient leaves the medical center, and clerk #2 records the cash receipt.

At the end of each day, clerk #2 prepares a revenue summary.

Clerk #1 performs correspondence functions and opens the incoming mail. Clerk #1 gives checks from insurance companies and patients to clerk #2 for deposit. Clerk #2 posts the receipt of patients' checks on clerk #2's PC patient receivable records and insurance companies' checks to the receivables from the applicable insurance companies. Clerk #1 gives mail requiring correspondence to clerk #3.

Clerk #2 stamps all checks "for deposit only" and each day prepares a list of checks and cash to be deposited in the bank. (This list also includes the cash and checks personally given to clerk #2 by patients.) Clerk #2 keeps a copy of the deposit list and gives the original to clerk #3.

Clerk #3 personally makes the daily bank deposit and maintains a file of the daily bank deposits. Clerk #3 also performs appointment scheduling for all of the doctors and various correspondence functions. Clerk #3 also maintains a list of patients whose insurance coverage the office manager has verified.

When insurance claims or patient receivables are not settled within sixty days, clerk #2 notifies the office manager. The office manager personally inspects the details of each instance of nonpayment. The office manger converts insurance claims that have been rejected by insurance companies into patient receivables. Clerk #2 records these patient receivables on clerk #2's PC and deletes these receivables from the applicable insurance companies. Clerk #2 deletes the patient receivables that appear to be uncollectible from clerk #2's PC when authorized by the office manager. Clerk #2 prepares a list of patients with uncollectible balances and gives a copy of the list to clerk #3, who will not allow these patients to make appointments for future services.

Once a month an outside accountant posts clerk #2's daily revenue summaries to the general ledger, prepares a monthly trial balance and monthly financial statements, accounts for prenumbered service slips, files payroll forms and tax returns, and reconciles the monthly bank statements to the general ledger. This accountant reports directly to the physician who is the managing partner.

All four clerical employees perform their tasks on PCs that are connected through a local area network. Each PC is accessible with a password that is known only to the individual employee and the managing partner. Southwest uses a standard software package that was acquired from a software company and that cannot be modified by Southwest's employees. None of the clerical employees have access to Southwest's check-writing abilities.

For each of the following conditions indicate whether it is a strength, weakness, or neither.

Condition	Strength	Weakness	Neither
1. Southwest is involved only in medical services and has not diversified its operations.	○	○	○
2. Insurance coverage for patients is verified and communicated to the clerks by the office manager before medical services are rendered.	○	○	○
3. The physician who renders the medical services documents the services on a prenumbered slip that is used for recording revenue and as a receipt for the patient.	○	○	○
4. Cash collection is centralized in that Clerk #2 receives the cash (checks) from patients and records the cash receipt.	○	○	○
5. Southwest extends credit rather than requiring cash or insurance in all cases.	○	○	○
6. The office manager extends credit on a case-by-case basis rather than using a formal credit search and established credit limits.	○	○	○
7. The office manager approves the extension of credit to patients and also approves the write-offs of uncollectible patient receivables.	○	○	○
8. Clerk #2 receives cash and checks and prepares the daily bank deposit.	○	○	○
9. Clerk #2 maintains the accounts receivable records and can add or delete information on the PC.	○	○	○
10. Prenumbered service slips are accounted for on a monthly basis by the outside accountant who is independent of the revenue generating and revenue recording functions.	○	○	○
11. The bank reconciliation is prepared monthly by the outside accountant who is independent of the revenue generating and revenue recording functions.	○	○	○
12. Computer passwords are only known to the individual employees and the managing partner who has no duties in the revenue recording functions.	○	○	○
13. Computer software cannot be modified by Southwest's employees.	○	○	○
14. None of the employees who perform duties in the revenue generating and revenue recording are able to write checks.	○	○	○

Task-Based Simulation 2

The following flowchart depicts part of a client's purchases and cash disbursements cycle. Some of the flowchart symbols are labeled to indicate operations, controls, and records. For each symbol numbered 1 through 12, select one response from the answer lists below. Each response in the lists may be selected once or **not** at all.

Operations and controls

A. Approve receiving report
B. Prepare and approve voucher
C. Prepare purchase order
D. Prepare purchase requisition
E. Prepare purchases journal
F. Prepare receiving report
G. Prepare sales journal
H. Prepare voucher
I. Sign checks and cancel voucher package documents

Connectors, documents, departments, and files

J. Accounts payable
K. Canceled voucher package
L. From purchasing
M. From receiving
N. From vouchers payable

O. Purchase order No. 5
P. Receiving report No. 1
Q. Stores
R. To vendor
S. Treasurer
T. Unpaid voucher file, filed by due date

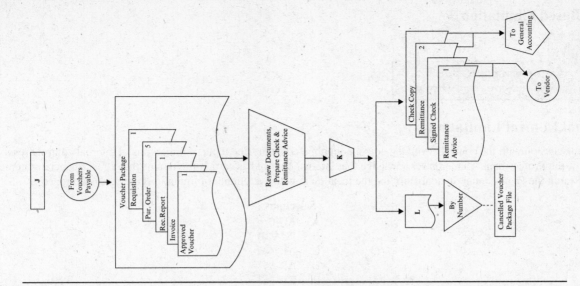

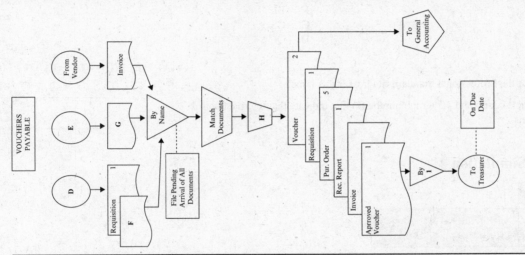

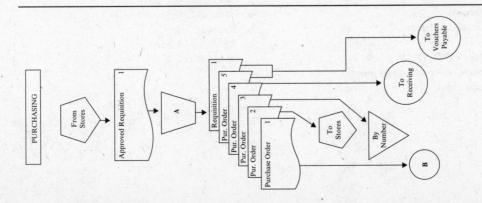

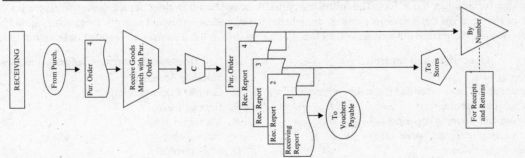

Task-Based Simulation 3

Internal Control Limitations

In a discussion with the controller of Gemcon, a nonpublic company, the topic of limitations of internal control arose. Relatedly, the Professional Standards acknowledge that internal control has certain limitations that affect financial statement audits. Search the Professional Standards to find the location at which a number of limitations are discussed together.

Selections

A. AU-C
B. PCAOB
C. AT
D. AR
E. ET
F. BL
G. CS
H. QC

	(A)	(B)	(C)	(D)	(E)	(F)	(G)	(H)
1. Which title of the Professional Standards addresses this issue?	○	○	○	○	○	○	○	○

2. Enter the exact section and paragraph number(s) that indicate that internal control has limitations.

Task-Based Simulation 4

You are working for Smith & Co. CPAs. The following partially completed flowchart depicts part of Welcore Inc., your client's revenue cycle. Some of the flowchart symbols are labeled to indicate controls and records. For each symbol numbered **1** though **13**, select one response from the answer lists below. Each response in the lists may be selected once or **not** at all.

Operations and controls

A. Enter shipping data
B. Verify agreement of sales order and shipping document
C. Write off accounts receivable
D. To warehouse and shipping department
E. Authorize account receivable write-off
F. Prepare aged trial balance
G. To sales department
H. Release goods for shipment
I. To accounts receivable department
J. Enter price data
K. Determine that customer exists
L. Match customer purchase order with sales order
M. Perform customer credit check
N. Prepare sales journal
O. Prepare sales invoice

Documents, journals, ledgers, and files

P. Shipping document
Q. General ledger master file
R. General journal
S. Master price file
T. Sales journal
U. Sales invoice
V. Cash receipts journal
W. Uncollectible accounts file
X. Shipping file
Y. Aged trial balance
Z. Open order file

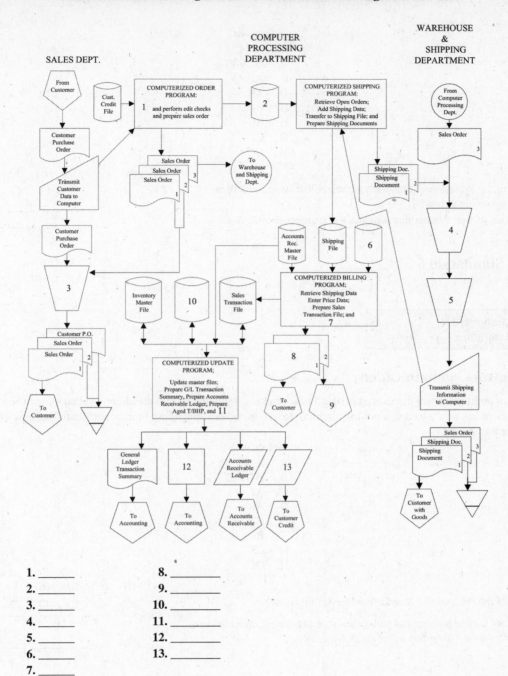

1. _____
2. _____
3. _____
4. _____
5. _____
6. _____
7. _____

8. _____
9. _____
10. _____
11. _____
12. _____
13. _____

Task-Based Simulation 5

Internal Control Reporting

The president of Welcore Inc., a nonpublic audit client of your firm, has indicated to you that he believes that he may "take the company public in a year or two." He asked you whether, in addition to your report on the financial statements, your firm can issue a report on internal control that he could make available to any individual or organization he so desired. He indicated that he would like to have two reports—as do public companies—one on the financial statements and one on the company's internal control.

Selections

A. AU-C
B. PCAOB
C. AT
D. AR
E. ET
F. BL
G. CS
H. QC

	(A)	(B)	(C)	(D)	(E)	(F)	(G)	(H)
	○	○	○	○	○	○	○	○

1. Which title of the Professional Standards addresses this issue and will be helpful in responding to him?

2. Enter the exact section number that provides the appropriate guidance.

Task-Based Simulation 6

Internal Control Communications

On the Adams audit your firm discovered certain immaterial audit judgments that the client's management chose not to record. Management has now asked you not to communicate anything regarding these omitted entries to the audit committee—after all, they are immaterial.

Selections

A. AU-C
B. PCAOB
C. AT
D. AR
E. ET
F. BL
G. CS
H. QC

	(A)	(B)	(C)	(D)	(E)	(F)	(G)	(H)
	○	○	○	○	○	○	○	○

1. Which title of the Professional Standards addresses this issue?

2. Enter the exact section number and paragraphs that address communication of these uncorrected misstatements to the audit committee.

Task-Based Simulation 7

Internal Control-Related Matters Communication | **Authoritative Literature** | **Help**

You have been asked by the audit partner to draft a letter to the client on internal control related matters. You were informed that the written communication regarding significant deficiencies and material weaknesses indentified during an audit of financial statements should include certain statements.

For each of the significant deficiencies and material weaknesses reflected in the table below, double-click on each of the associated shaded cells and select from the list provided the appropriate disposition of each statement in regard to the letter to the client on internal control related matters. Each selection may be used once, more than once, or not at all.

Selection List

Included

Excluded

Included, but only with client management's approval

Communicated orally with no need to document the communication

Internal controls	Related matters
State that the purpose of the audit was to express an opinion on the financial statements, and to express an opinion on the effectiveness of the entity's internal control over financial reporting.	
Identify, if applicable, items that are considered to be material weaknesses.	
State that the author is not expressing an opinion on the effectiveness of internal control.	
Include the definition of the term *significant deficiency*.	
Include the definition of the term *material weakness*, where relevant.	
State that the author is expressing an unqualified opinion on the effectiveness of internal control.	
State that the communication is intended solely for management and external parties.	
Identify the matters that are considered to be significant deficiencies.	

Task-Based Simulation 8

Integrated audits

Assume that you are assigned to the audit of Regis Corporation, an issuer company. Your firm is performing its first integrated audit for the company, and the partner on the engagement has asked you to research professional standards to identify the controls that address the risk of fraud.

Selections

A. AU-C

B. PCAOB

C. AT

D. AR

E. ET

F. BL

G. CS

H. QC

	(A)	(B)	(C)	(D)	(E)	(F)	(G)	(H)
1. Which title of the Professional Standards addresses this issue?	○	○	○	○	○	○	○	○

2. Enter the exact Auditing Standard Number or section and paragraph with helpful information.

Simulation Solutions

Task-Based Simulation 1

Condition	Strength	Weakness	Neither
1. Southwest is involved only in medical services and has not diversified its operations.	○	○	●
2. Insurance coverage for patients is verified and communicated to the clerks by the office manager before medical services are rendered.	●	○	○
3. The physician who renders the medical services documents the services on a prenumbered slip that is used for recording revenue and as a receipt for the patient.	●	○	○
4. Cash collection is centralized in that Clerk #2 receives the cash (checks) from patients and records the cash receipt.	○	●	○
5. Southwest extends credit rather than requiring cash or insurance in all cases.	○	○	●
6. The office manager extends credit on a case-by-case basis rather than using a formal credit search and established credit limits.	○	●	○
7. The office manager approves the extension of credit to patients and also approves the write-offs of uncollectible patient receivables.	○	●	○
8. Clerk #2 receives cash and checks and prepares the daily bank deposit.	○	●	○
9. Clerk #2 maintains the accounts receivable records and can add or delete information on the PC.	○	●	○
10. Prenumbered service slips are accounted for on a monthly basis by the outside accountant who is independent of the revenue generating and revenue recording functions.	●	○	○
11. The bank reconciliation is prepared monthly by the outside accountant who is independent of the revenue generating and revenue recording functions.	●	○	○
12. Computer passwords are only known to the individual employees and the managing partner who has no duties in the revenue recording functions.	●	○	○
13. Computer software cannot be modified by Southwest's employees.	●	○	○
14. None of the employees who perform duties in the revenue generating and revenue recording are able to write checks.	●	○	○

Task-Based Simulation 2

Purchases and Disbursements / Authoritative Literature / Help

1. **(C)** *Prepare purchase order*—A trapezoid represents a manual operation. Here, a purchase order enters the flowchart after this step; accordingly, a purchase order is being prepared.

2. **(R)** *To vendor*—A circle represents a connector, a symbol indicating that a document is entering or leaving that portion of the flowchart. Here a copy of the purchase order is sent to the vendor to order the goods. This must be the case, because otherwise the vendor would not be informed of the order.

3. **(F)** *Prepare receiving report*—A trapezoid represents a manual operation. Here, a receiving report enters the flowchart after this step; accordingly, a receiving report is being prepared. Also, note above this step that goods are received, the point at which one would expect preparation of a receiving report.

4. **(L)** *From purchasing*—A circle represents a connector, a symbol indicating that a document is entering or leaving that portion of the flowchart. The document here is from purchasing because below the connector is requisition No. 1, which purchasing has sent with the purchase order No. 5 to vouchers payable, as evidenced by the connector in the bottom far right under purchasing.

5. **(M)** *From receiving*—A circle represents a connector, a symbol indicating that a document is entering or leaving that portion of the flowchart. The document here is from receiving because under the receiving portion of the flowchart, approximately 3/4 of the way down, we see a connector indicating that receiving report No. 1 is being sent to vouchers payable. Also, toward the bottom under the vouchers payable portion of the flowchart, we see that receiving report No. 1 is indeed in the system.

6. **(O)** *Purchase order No. 5*—We know from item 4 that this document was sent from purchasing, and we know that purchasing has sent to vouchers payable requisition No. 1 and purchase order No. 5. Since requisition No. 1 is labeled on the flowchart, this must be purchase order No. 5.

7. **(P)** *Receiving report No. 1*—We know from item 5 that this document was sent from receiving, and since we know that receiving has sent receiving report No. 1 to vouchers payable this must be that document.

8. **(B)** *Prepare and approve voucher*—A trapezoid represents a manual operation. Here, an approved voucher enters the flowchart after this step; accordingly, a voucher is being prepared and approved in this step.

9. **(T)** *Unpaid voucher file, filed by due date*—The triangle symbol represents a file. Entering this file are the approved but unpaid vouchers with the support of their invoices, receiving reports, purchase orders and purchase requisitions. Because these vouchers are sent to the treasurer in order of due date (the bottom, right symbol under vouchers payable) this file is the unpaid voucher file, filed by due date.

10. **(S)** *Treasurer*—Because the unpaid vouchers (the "voucher package") was sent from vouchers payable to the treasurer, this is the treasurer.

11. **(I)** *Sign checks and cancel voucher package documents*—A trapezoid represents a manual operation. Here, the operation prior to 11 involves a review of documents and preparation of a check and a remittance advice. After this operation the documents changed are a "canceled voucher package file" and a "signed check;" accordingly, checks are being signed and the voucher package is being canceled.

12. **(K)** *Canceled voucher package*—After step 11, the check copy, remittance advice No. 1, the signed check, and remittance advice No. 2 exit on the far right. Accordingly, item 12 is the voucher package, now canceled as evidenced by the description below the triangular file symbol.

Task-Based Simulation 3

	(A)	(B)	(C)	(D)	(E)	(F)	(G)	(H)
1. Which title of the Professional Standards addresses this issue?	●	○	○	○	○	○	○	○

2. Enter the exact section and paragraph numbers that describe the limitations.	330	45

Task-Based Simulation 4

1. **(M)** *Perform customer credit check*—The customer credit file is being accessed, making it likely that a credit check is occurring.

2. **(Z)** *Open order file*—The processing to the right of #2 begins with "open orders," making this an open order file.

3. **(L)** *Match customer purchase order with sales order*—Two copies of the sales order are being combined with the customer purchase order through a manual operation (the trapezoid).

4. **(B)** *Verify agreement of sales order and shipping document*—This manual operation (trapezoid) includes two copies of the shipping document being combined with the sales order.

5. **(H)** *Release goods for shipment*—The department is the warehouse and shipping department, and out of this operation is "shipping information"; accordingly goods are being released for shipment.

6. **(S)** *Master price file*—The operation below #6 includes entering price data; since the first two files being accessed are the accounts receivable master file and the shipping file, this third file must include prices.

7. **(O)** *Prepare sales invoice*—Since a document is being prepared through this computerized billing program, it is the sales invoice.

8. **(U)** *Sales invoice*—A sales invoice is normally sent to the customer.

9. **(I)** *To accounts receivable department*—This copy of the sales invoice informs accounts receivable that the sale has been both processed and shipped.

10. **(Q)** *General ledger master file*—Because the processing step below includes updating of master files, this is the general ledger master file.

11. **(N)** *Prepare sales journal*—Sales transactions are being processed; accordingly a sales journal is prepared.

12. **(T)** *Sales journal*—From above, a sales journal was prepared; the accounting department will receive the sales journal.

13. **(Y)** *Aged trial balance*—In the processing step above, an aged trial balance of accounts receivable is prepared; the credit department will receive such a report.

Task-Based Simulation 5

(A) (B) (C) (D) (E) (F) (G) (H)

1. Which title of the Professional Standards addresses this issue and will be helpful in responding to him?   ○ ○ ● ○ ○ ○ ○ ○

2. Enter the exact section number that provides the appropriate guidance. | 501 |

Task-Based Simulation 6

(A) (B) (C) (D) (E) (F) (G) (H)

1. Which title of the Professional Standards addresses this issue?   ● ○ ○ ○ ○ ○ ○ ○

2. Enter the exact section number and paragraphs that address communication of these uncorrected misstatements to the audit committee. | 260 | 13, A29 |

Task-Based Simulation 7

AU-C 265 includes the matters required to be included in the written communication regarding significant deficiencies and material weaknesses indentified during an audit as

- State that the purpose of the audit was to express an opinion on the financial statements, but not to express an opinion on the effectiveness of the entity's internal control over financial reporting.
- State that the auditor is not expressing an opinion on the effectiveness of internal control.

- Include the definition of the terms *significant deficiency* and, where relevant, *material weakness*.
- Identify the matters that are considered to be significant deficiencies and, if applicable, those that are considered to be material weaknesses.
- State that the communication is intended solely for the information and use of management, those charged with governance, and others within the organization and is not intended to be and should not be used by anyone other than those specified parties. If an entity is required to furnish such auditor communications to a governmental authority, specific reference to such governmental authorities may be made.

Internal controls	Related matters	Comment
State that the purpose of the audit was to express an opinion on the financial statements, and to express an opinion on the effectiveness of the entity's internal control over financial reporting.	Excluded	The latter part of the sentence is incorrect since no opinion on internal control effectiveness is issued.
Identify, if applicable, items that are considered to be material weaknesses.	Included	Required
State that the author is not expressing an opinion on the effectiveness of internal control.	Included	Required
Include the definition of the term *significant deficiency*.	Included	Required
Include the definition of the term *material* weakness, where relevant.	Included	Required
State that the author is expressing an unqualified opinion on the effectiveness of internal control.	Excluded	The auditor expresses no opinion on internal control.
State that the communication is intended solely for management and external parties.	Excluded	The communication is not intended for external parties.
Identify the matters that are considered to be significant deficiencies.	Included	Required

Task-Based Simulation 8

1. Which title of the Professional Standards addresses this issue?

(A)	(B)	(C)	(D)	(E)	(F)	(G)	(H)
○	●	○	○	○	○	○	○

2. Enter the exact Auditing Standard Number or section and paragraph with helpful information.

5	14

Module 4: Responding to Risk Assessment: Evidence Accumulation and Evaluation

Overview

The entire financial statement audit may be described as a process of evidence accumulation and evaluation. This process enables the auditor to formulate an informed opinion as to whether the financial statements are presented fairly in accordance with US generally accepted accounting principles. The following "Diagram of an Audit" was first presented and explained in the auditing overview section.

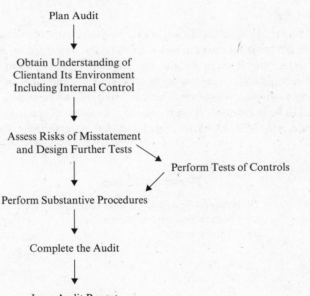

Diagram of an Audit

Plan Audit

↓

Obtain Understanding of Clientand Its Environment Including Internal Control

↓

Assess Risks of Misstatement and Design Further Tests

→ Perform Tests of Controls

↓

Perform Substantive Procedures

↓

Complete the Audit

↓

Issue Audit Report

After assessing the risks of material misstatement, the auditors design and perform further audit procedures—tests of controls and substantive procedures. The internal control module discussed tests of controls. This module emphasizes substantive procedures. It first covers audit evidence as a concept and discusses types of audit evidence generated through performance of substantive procedures, both (1) substantive analytical procedures and (2) tests of details of transactions, account balances, and disclosures. It concludes with audit procedures involved in completing the audit.

Numerous questions on audit evidence appear on each CPA exam. Multiple-choice questions frequently ask the candidate to select the audit procedure most likely to detect misstatements that have occurred in given situations, and to distinguish among various concepts such as

1. Appropriate vs. sufficient evidence
2. Analytical procedures vs. tests of details of transactions, account balances, and disclosures
3. Audit objectives vs. audit procedures

A simulation question may require the candidate to select appropriate audit procedures for a particular account and to research the professional standards on some aspect of that account (e.g., when are negative confirmation requests appropriate). Alternatively, the candidate may be required to calculate various ratios using a spreadsheet and to then interpret those ratios.

This module covers information included in the Evidence and Procedures Section of the AICPA Content Specification Outline with the following exceptions: (1) Use of the Computer in Performing the Audit is covered in the Auditing with Technology Module; and (2) Use of Statistical Sampling in Performing the Audit is covered in the Audit Sampling Module.

The following sections of Statements on Auditing Standards pertain to audit evidence:

AU-C 500	Audit Evidence
501	Audit Evidence—Specific Considerations for Selected Items
505	The Confirmation Process
520	Analytical Procedures
540	Auditing Accounting Estimates, Including Fair Value Accounting Estimates and Related Disclosures
550	Related-Party Transactions
560	Subsequent Events and Subsequently Discovered Facts
580	Written Representations
585	Consideration of Omitted Procedures after the Report Date
620	Using the Work of a Specialist
730	Supplementary Information
930	Interim Financial Information
935	Compliance Audits

Read the various sections and study the outlines for each of the above SAS separately. After studying each outline, attempt to summarize in your own words the "sum and substance" of the pronouncement. If you cannot explain the pronouncement in your own words, you do not understand it. Go back and study it again.

A. Evidence—General

When performing audits of financial statements or attest examinations, auditors should obtain sufficient appropriate evidence to provide a reasonable basis for the conclusion to be issued in the report. Audit evidence is all the information used by the auditor in arriving at the conclusions on which the audit opinion is based. It includes information contained in the accounting records underlying the financial statements and other information.

As background pertaining to financial statements, bear in mind that when management prepares financial statements that are supposed to be in conformity with generally accepted accounting principles, certain assertions (implicit or explicit) are made. AU-C 500 identifies and classifies these assertions which we originally presented in Module 2 as

Account Balances	Transaction Classes	Disclosures
Existence—Assets, liabilities, and equity interests exist.	*Occurrence*—Transactions and events that have been recorded have occurred and pertain to the entity.	*Occurrence*—Disclosed events and transactions have occurred.
Rights and obligations—The entity holds or controls the rights to assets, and liabilities are the obligations of the entity.		*Rights and obligations*—Disclosed events pertain to the entity.
Completeness—All assets, liabilities, and equity interests have been recorded.	*Completeness*—All transactions and events have been recorded.	*Completeness*—All disclosures that should have been included have been included.
Valuation and allocation—Assets, liabilities, and equity interests are included at appropriate amounts.	*Accuracy*—Amounts and other data relating to recorded transactions have been recorded appropriately.	*Accuracy and valuation*—Information is disclosed fairly and at appropriate amounts.
	Cutoff—Transactions and events have been recorded in the correct accounting period.	
	Classification—Transactions and events have been recorded in the proper accounts.	*Classification and understandability*—Information is presented and described clearly.

Later in this module we will discuss audit programs in detail. In those audit programs, which emphasize account balances, we will summarize the assertions into one list (based primarily upon account balances) as follows:

Presentation and disclosure—accounts are described and classified in accordance with generally accepted accounting principles, and financial statement disclosures are complete, appropriate, and clearly expressed.

Existence and occurrence—assets, liabilities, and equity interests exist, and recorded transactions and events have occurred.

Rights and obligations—the company holds rights to the assets, and liabilities are the obligations of the company.

Completeness and cutoff—all assets, liabilities, equity interests, and transactions that should have been recorded have been recorded, and all transactions and events are recorded in the appropriate accounting period.

Valuation, allocation, and accuracy—all transactions, assets, liabilities, and equity interests are included in the financial statements at proper amounts.

(PERCV—as in, "I perceive the need to pass the CPA exam.")

Note the relationship between existence and completeness. The existence assertion relates to whether the recorded amount is bona fide (e.g., recorded receivables are legitimate). Completeness, on the other hand, addresses the issue of whether all transactions have been recorded (e.g., are all receivables recorded?). An auditor should test for both existence and completeness. This concept of "directional testing" is discussed in Section D of the Internal Control Module.

The Statement on Attestation Standards suggests two basic types of evidence collection procedures: (1) search and verification, and (2) internal inquiries and comparisons. Search and verification procedures include procedures such as inspecting assets, confirming receivables, and observing the counting of inventory. Internal inquiry and comparison procedures include discussions with firm representatives and analytical procedures such as ratio analysis.

As described in greater detail in the Reporting Module, accountants perform (1) examinations, (2) reviews, (3) agreed-upon procedures, and (4) compilation accounting engagements. Of these forms of association, an examination offers the highest level of assurance. (An "audit" is considered to be an examination of financial statements.) In examinations, accountants select from among all available audit procedures to determine whether the appropriate assertions (generally PERCV in the case of financial statements) have been met.

A review offers limited assurance (also referred to as negative assurance) with respect to information. It is composed primarily of internal inquiries and comparisons. However, when evidence with respect to an assertion seems incomplete or inaccurate, search and verification procedures may be performed.

Agreed-upon procedures result in a report in which a summary of findings is provided. The extent of the procedures is specified by the user, but should exceed the attester's mere reading of the assertions.

Compilations, which are considered accounting and attest services, result in a report that provides no explicit assurance on the information. While the accountant who performs a compilation should understand the nature of the client's business and its accounting records, s/he is not required to make any inquiries or perform any other verification procedures beyond reading the information. As is the case with all other forms of association, material known misstatements or omissions should be disclosed in the accountant's report that is expanded to disclose the situation.

Three presumptions (asked directly and indirectly on several previous exams) relate to the validity of evidence: (1) evidence from independent sources provides more assurance than evidence secured solely from within the entity, (2) information from direct personal knowledge is more persuasive than information obtained indirectly, and (3) assertions developed under effective internal control are more reliable than those developed in the absence of internal control.

1. **Sufficient Appropriate Audit Evidence.** Auditors should obtain sufficient appropriate audit evidence to reduce audit risk to a low level. What do the terms sufficient and appropriate mean? Section AU-C 500 points out that *sufficiency* is the measure of the quantity of audit evidence that should be obtained. *Appropriateness* is the measure of the quality of that audit evidence—both its *relevance* and *reliability* in providing support for, or detecting misstatements. *Relevance* relates to the assertion being addressed. For example, analyzing the confirmation with a client's customers of accounts receivable may provide evidence on the existence of receivables at year-end, yet only limited information relating to whether the client has completely recorded all receivable accounts. The *reliability* of evidence is dependent on the circumstances in which it is obtained. While generalizations are difficult and subject to exceptions, audit evidence is *ordinarily* more reliable when it is

   • Obtained from knowledgeable independent sources *outside the client company* rather than nonindependent sources

- Generated internally through a system of *effective controls* rather than ineffective controls
- Obtained *directly* by the auditor rather than indirectly or by inference (e.g., observation of application of a control is more reliable than an inquiry to the client concerning the control)
- *Documentary* in form (paper, electronic, or other) rather than an oral representation
- Provided by *original documents* rather than copies or facsimiles

AU-C 500 suggests that in the great majority of cases the auditor finds it necessary to rely on evidence that is persuasive rather than conclusive. An acceptable level of audit risk does not indicate that **all** uncertainty be eliminated for sufficient evidence to have been gathered. The auditor should be able to form an opinion within a reasonable length of time, at a reasonable cost. However, the difficulty or expense involved in testing a particular item is not in itself a valid reason for omitting a test. Auditors use professional judgment to determine the extent of tests necessary to obtain sufficient evidence. In exercising this professional judgment, auditors consider both the materiality of the item in question (e.g., dollar size) as well as the inherent risk of the item (e.g., cash, due to its liquidity, may have a higher inherent risk than do certain property, plant, and equipment items).

The following example distinguishes between appropriate vs. sufficient evidence. Assume that an auditor has highly credible evidence on one account receivable for $400 out of a total receivable balance of $1,000,000. While this evidence is appropriate, most auditors would suggest that it is not sufficient evidence for the $1,000,000 balance; to be sufficient, more evidence verifying the account's **total** value should be collected.

Obtaining sufficient appropriate evidence is particularly difficult when auditing client accounting estimates (e.g., allowance for doubtful accounts, loss reserves, pension expenses). AU-C 540 suggests that the auditor's objectives relating to estimates are to determine that all estimates (1) have been developed, (2) are reasonable, and (3) follow GAAP. Typically these estimates are needed because the valuation of some accounts is based on future events or because certain evidence cannot be accumulated on a timely, cost-effective basis. Know that the three basic approaches for evaluating the reasonableness of these estimates are (1) to review and test management's process of deriving the estimate (consider the reasonableness and accuracy of management's approach), (2) develop one's own expectation of the accounting estimate and compare it to management's, and (3) review subsequent events or transactions occurring prior to the completion of fieldwork which bear on the estimate.

2. **Types of Audit Evidence.** Recall from Module 2 that at the account level audit risk is composed of the risk of material misstatement (inherent risk and control risk) and the risk that the auditor's procedures do not detect a material misstatement). The auditor should obtain audit evidence to draw reasonable conclusions on which to base the audit opinion by performing audit procedures. The following are the basic procedures used in an audit:

   - **Risk assessment procedures**—Used to obtain an understanding of the entity and its environment, including its internal control. Risk assessment procedures are discussed in detail in Module 2.
   - **Tests of controls**—When necessary, or when the auditor has decided to do so, used to test the operating effectiveness of controls at the relevant assertion level. Tests of controls are discussed in detail in Module 3.
   - **Substantive procedures**—Used to detect material misstatements in transactions, account balances, and disclosures. Substantive procedures include substantive analytical procedures and test of details of account balances, transactions, and disclosures.

Tests of controls and substantive procedures are referred to as "further procedures" in that they are designed based on the risk assessment and follow that stage. Substantive procedures are used to restrict detection risk. As the acceptable level of detection risk decreases, the assurance provided by substantive procedures should increase. This increased assurance may be obtained by modifying the nature, timing, and/or extent of substantive procedures as follows:

   - **Nature**—Use more effective procedures, such as tests directed toward independent parties rather than toward parties within the entity.
   - **Timing**—Perform tests at year-end rather than at an interim date.
   - **Extent**—Use a larger sample size.

Audit evidence includes the information contained in the *accounting records* underlying the financial statements and *other information*. *Accounting records,* which alone do not provide sufficient appropriate audit evidence on which to base an audit opinion, generally include the records of initial entries and supporting records, such as

   - Documents, including checks and records of electronic fund transfers, invoices, contracts
   - General and subsidiary ledgers, journal entries, and other adjustments to the financial statements that are not reflected in formal journal entries
   - Records such as worksheets and spreadsheets supporting cost allocations, computations, reconciliations, and disclosures

Other information that the auditor may use as audit evidence includes

- Minutes of meetings
- Confirmations from third parties
- Industry analysts' reports
- Comparable data about competitors (benchmarking)
- Controls manuals
- Information obtained by the auditor from such audit procedures as inquiry, observation, and inspection
- Other information developed by or available to the auditor that permits the auditor to reach conclusions through valid reasoning

Since the quality of audit evidence depends upon the financial statement assertion under consideration, the auditor should use professional judgment when deciding which type of evidence is most appropriate in a specific situation. Conceptually, the auditor should attempt to gather a sufficient quantity of appropriate evidence at a minimum cost.

Audit procedures (acts to be performed) are used as risk assessment procedures, tests of controls, and substantive procedures. The following is a list of types of procedures:

- *Inspection of records or documents* (e.g., invoice for an equipment purchase transaction)
- *Inspection of tangible assets* (e.g., inventory items)
- *Observation* (e.g. observation of inventory count, observation of control activities)
- *Inquiry* (e.g., written inquiries and oral inquiries)
- *Confirmation* (e.g., accounts receivable)
- *Recalculation* (e.g., checking the mathematical accuracy of documents or records.)
- *Reperformance* (e.g., reperforming the aging of accounts receivable)
- *Analytical procedures* (e.g., scanning numbers for reasonableness, calculating ratios)

Numerous other terms have been used in both the professional standards and in auditing texts. Some of the more frequent terms that you will find in written audit programs include the following:

Agree (schedule balances to general ledger)
Analyze (account transactions)
Compare (beginning balances with last year's audited figures)
Count (cash, inventory, etc.)
Examine (authoritative documents)
Foot (totals)
Prove (totals)
Read (minutes of directors' meetings)
Reconcile (cash balance)
Review (disclosure, legal documents)
Scan (for unusual items)
Trace (from support to recorded entry)
Vouch (from recorded entry to support)

The auditor may obtain the assistance of client personnel to perform certain tasks (e.g., prepare schedules) providing the auditor adequately tests the work performed by these individuals.

> **NOW REVIEW MULTIPLE-CHOICE QUESTIONS 1 THROUGH 14**

B. Evidence—Specific (Substantive Procedures)

As noted earlier, the objective of an audit is to express an opinion on whether the company's financial statements are fairly presented in conformity with generally accepted accounting principles. Substantive procedures are designed to assist the auditor in reaching this goal by determining whether the specific balances of financial statement accounts, transactions, and disclosures are in conformity with generally accepted accounting principles. While tests of controls are used to test the "means" of processing (internal control), substantive procedures are used to directly test the "ends" of processing—the financial statements.

When evaluating evidence, auditors estimate the amount of misstatements within the financial statements, and determine whether it exceeds a material amount. The auditor estimates the likely misstatement in the financial statements and attempts to determine whether an unacceptably high audit risk exists. Note that in the evaluation of audit evidence, because of the information obtained during the audit, the auditor may revise his/her preliminary estimate of materiality (see discussion in Module 2).

1. **Types of Substantive Procedures.** Substantive procedures are of two types: (1) Substantive analytical procedures, (2) Tests of details of transactions, account balances, and disclosures.

    a. **Analytical procedures.** Analytical procedures consist of evaluations of financial information made by a study of plausible relationships among financial and nonfinancial data. Analytical procedures are used as follows:

    Risk assessment (also referred to as analytical procedures used to plan the audit)—Identify aspects of the entity of which the auditor was unaware and assist in assessing the risks of material misstatement. As such these tests help the auditor to determine the nature, timing, and extent of tests.

    Substantive procedures—Obtain relevant and reliable audit evidence to substantiate accounts for which overall comparisons are helpful.

    Near the end of the audit—Assess conclusions reached and evaluate overall financial statement presentation.

> **NOTE:** GAAS requires the use of analytical procedures during risk assessment and near the end of the audit. Analytical procedures are **not** a required substantive procedure.

The following table summarizes some important characteristics of analytical procedures performed at the three stages of an audit. Make certain that you know all of the information presented on it.

Stage of audit	Required?	Purpose	Comment
Risk Assessment	Yes	To identify aspects of the entity of which the auditor was unaware and assist in assessing the risks of material misstatement in order to provide a basis for designing and implementing responses in the assessed risks.	Generally use data aggregated at a high level
Substantive Procedures	No	To obtain evidence about particular assertions related to account balances or classes of transactions	Effectiveness depends upon (a) Nature of assertion (b) Plausibility and predictability of relations (c) Reliability of data (d) Precision of expectation
Near end of audit	Yes	To corroborate audit evidence obtained during the audit and to assist the auditor in drawing reasonable conclusions on which to base the audit opinion.	Includes reading financial statements to consider (a) Adequacy of evidence gathered for unusual or unexpected balances identified during planning or during course of audit (b) Unusual or unexpected balances or relationships not previously identified

Perhaps the most familiar example of analytical procedures used in auditing is the calculation of ratios. However, analytical procedures range from simple comparisons of information through the use of complex models such as regression and time series analysis. The typical approach is

    (1) Develop an expectation for the account balance
    (2) Determine the amount of difference from the expectation that can be accepted without investigation
    (3) Compare the company's account balance (or ratio) with the expected account balance
    (4) Investigate significant differences from the expected account balance

When developing an expectation, the auditor should attempt to identify plausible relationships. These expectations may be derived from

(1) The information itself in prior periods
(2) Anticipated results such as budgets and forecasts
(3) Relationships among elements of financial information within the period
(4) Industry information
(5) Relevant **nonfinancial** information

Relationships differ in their predictability. Be familiar with the following principles:

(1) Relationships in a dynamic or unstable environment are less predictable than those in a stable environment.
(2) Relationships involving balance sheet accounts are less predictable than income statement accounts (because balance sheet accounts represent balances at one arbitrary point in time).
(3) Relationships involving management discretion are sometimes less predictable (e.g., decision to incur maintenance expense rather than replace plant).

Recall from earlier in this module (section A) that the reliability of evidence varies based on whether it is obtained from (1) independent sources, (2) personal knowledge, or (3) developed under strong internal control. In addition, in the case of analytical procedures be aware that use of data that has been subjected to audit testing and data available from a variety of sources increases the reliability of the data used in the analysis.

Principal limitations concerning analytical procedures include

(1) The guidelines for evaluation may be inadequate (e.g., Why is an industry average good? Why should the ratio be the same as last year?).
(2) It is difficult to determine whether a change is due to a misstatement or is the result of random change in the account.
(3) Cost-based accounting records hinder comparisons between firms of different ages and/or asset compositions.
(4) Accounting differences hinder comparisons between firms (e.g., if one firm uses LIFO and another uses FIFO the information is not comparable).
(5) Analytical procedures present only "circumstantial" evidence in that a "significant" difference will lead to additional audit procedures as opposed to direct detection of a misstatement.

b. **Tests of details of transactions, balances, and disclosures.** These tests are used to examine the actual details making up the various account balances and disclosures. For example, if receivables total $1,000,000 at year-end, tests of details may be made of the individual components of the total account. Assume the $1,000,000 is the accumulation of 250 individual accounts. As a test of details, an auditor might decide to confirm a sample of these 250 accounts. Based on the results of the auditor's consideration of internal control and tests of controls, the auditor might determine that 60 accounts should be confirmed. Thus, when responses are received and when the balances have been reconciled, the auditor has actually tested the detail supporting the account; the **existence** of the accounts has been confirmed. As an additional test (and also as an alternative procedure when confirmation replies have not been received from debtors), the auditor may examine cash receipts received subsequent to year-end on individual accounts. This substantive procedure provides evidence pertaining to both the **existence** and the **valuation** of the account.

> **NOTE:** In gathering sufficient appropriate audit evidence, auditors seek an efficient and effective combination of (1) tests of controls, (2) analytical procedures, and (3) tests of details to afford a reasonable basis for an opinion.

2. **Substantive Procedure Audit Programs.** An audit program is a detailed list of the audit procedures to be performed in the course of an audit. It is helpful to understand the nature of audit programs for various accounts to help reply to a variety of multiple choice questions and, possibly, to a simulation. The professional standards require a written audit program for each audit.

As noted earlier under "Evidence—Specific (Substantive Procedures)," financial statements that purport to be in conformity with generally accepted accounting principles contain certain assertions: presentation and disclosure, existence or occurrence, rights and obligations, completeness and cutoff, and valuation, allocation, or accuracy (PERCV). Auditors gather evidence to form an opinion with respect to assertions. But all assertions do not apply to all financial statement items. Relevant assertions are those that, without regard to the effect of controls, have a reasonable possibility of containing a misstatement that could cause the financial statements to be materially misstated. For example, existence and completeness assertions may always be relevant to the cash account; however, valuation often is not unless currency translation is involved.

The experienced auditor should be able to prepare an audit program for an audit area (e.g., inventory) to test whether these assertions are supportable. The process is one in which specific audit objectives are developed (also either explicitly or implicitly) based on the assertions being made in the financial statements. Finally, audit procedures to meet these audit objectives are formulated and listed in an audit program. These relationships may be illustrated as

Financial Statements

↓

Assertions

↓

Audit Objectives

↓

Audit Procedures

↓

Audit Program

For purposes of the CPA exam, consider two possible approaches for auditing an account

(1) Direct tests of ending balance ("tests of balances")
(2) Tests of inputs and outputs during the year ("tests of details of transactions")

An auditor may emphasize the first approach to directly test ending balances for high turnover accounts such as cash, accounts receivable, accounts payable, etc. (e.g., confirm year-end balances). The second approach, tests of transactions (inputs and outputs during the year), is used most extensively for lower turnover accounts (e.g., fixed assets, long-term debt, etc.). For example, for fixed assets, a low turnover account, the emphasis will be on vouching additions or retirements—not on auditing the entire account for a continuing audit engagement. Bear in mind, however, that during an audit it is **not** an either/or proposition—a **combination of approaches** with an emphasis of one approach over the other will generally be used.

The tables that appear at the end of this section present summarized substantive audit programs for the major balance sheet accounts. Although the programs are constructed to present the pertinent procedures under only one assertion, be aware that many audit procedures provide support for multiple assertions. The purpose is to use the PERCV assertions to organize your thoughts about audit programs.

Recall from Section A of this module and Section C of the Internal Control Module on directional testing, that some objective questions may ask which assertion a procedure applies most directly to (e.g., analysis of inventory turnover rates most directly applies to valuation). You must use your understanding of the assertions for the specific procedure presented in that type of question. Section C of this module should help you understand the nature of various audit procedures. Below, for each assertion, we present a brief "overall concept" discussion to help you with such objective questions, followed by one or more typical procedures.

Presentation and Disclosure:

Overall Concept: Think in terms of whether proper disclosures (particularly financial statement notes) are presented and that financial statement amounts are properly classified (e.g., debt between current and noncurrent portions).

Typical Procedure

- *Consider completeness of disclosures.* Consider specific disclosure requirements for the account, as well as for related accounts. Example: for receivables, you would recall from your accounting courses such possibilities as factoring, pledging, or discounting.

Existence or Occurrence:

Overall concept: Think in terms of whether *recorded* transactions and balances actually exist. This assertion is not directly related to the amount recorded (that's the valuation assertion), but with whether transactions that were recorded should have been recorded.

Typical Procedures:

- *Confirmation.* Often an account will lend itself to confirmation (e.g., bank for cash, debtor for receivables, stock registrar and transfer agent for stock authorized and outstanding). Because the confirmation process begins with recorded amounts it ordinarily addresses the existence assertion more than the completeness assertion.
- *Inspection.* Examples include cash on hand, inventory, loan agreements.
- *Vouch transactions.* A typical procedure is to start with a recorded transaction such as a recorded purchase in the purchases journal and to vouch it back to the receiving report to determine that the item does exist. Existence and completeness (below) relate directly to "directional testing" as presented in Section C of the Internal Control Module.

Rights and Obligations:

Overall Concept: Think in terms of whether the client owns the rights to the assets and liabilities are its obligations. Again, do not emphasize recorded amounts for this assertion.

Typical Procedures:

- *Vouch transactions.* The emphasis of vouching for this assertion is on whether the client owns (owes) the recorded item.
- *Authorization.* Consider whether there are transactions that require specific authorization. Authorization of transactions relates to whether proper rights and obligations have been established.

Completeness and Cutoff:

Overall Concept: Think in terms of whether *all* transactions and events have been recorded for completeness, not with whether recorded transactions are proper. Relating to assets, appropriate procedures are those which attempt to *determine whether certain transactions that should have been recorded were not recorded.*

Typical Procedures

- *Trace from source documents to recorded entries.* A typical procedure is to start with a source document such as a receiving report for a purchase and determine that the transaction is recorded in the purchases journal.
- *Analytical procedures.* Always include a step on analytical procedures. Also, mention specific procedures for the account being audited. Section C of this module provides examples for the various accounts.
- *Omissions.* Consider how transactions (adjustment) could improperly have been omitted from the account. Examples here include inventory count sheets not included, accruals not made, debt not recorded.
- *Cutoff.* Auditors should consider whether transactions have been reported in the proper period. Think about the transactions affecting the account to determine the proper cutoff. For example, cash cutoffs will relate to receipts and disbursements of cash, while receivables will relate to credit sales and cash receipts.

> **NOTE:** Be careful here. Cutoff applies to both the existence/occurrence and completeness assertions. If a multiple-choice question is asked, the specific details of the question determine the most directly related assertion.

Valuation, Allocation, and Accuracy:

Overall Concept: Think in terms of whether the proper amounts are recorded. Whereas *existence* addresses whether recorded transactions and events should be recoded and *completeness* addresses whether all transactions and events that should have been recorded have been recorded, *valuation* addresses the amounts involved with the related items.

Typical Procedures:

- *Foot schedules.* Consider the actual schedules involved with the account and include a step to foot and cross-foot them.
- *Agree schedules balances to general ledger balances.*

- *Agree financial statement balances to schedules.* Because financial statements are derived from accounting information, the general and subsidiary ledgers as well as other accounting records should be summarized. Examples: accounts receivable, inventory count sheets.
- *Consider valuation method of account.* Consider the accounting method used, and whether it has been properly applied. Most accounts have a number of steps here. Examples: Receivables should be valued net of an appropriate allowance, inventory costing methods (e.g., LIFO, FIFO), and application of the lower of cost or market rule. Always integrate your accounting knowledge with auditing procedures here.
- *Consider related accounts.* When you are considering an audit program for a balance sheet account, know that it ordinarily will include procedures used to audit the related income statement accounts. Examples: analytical procedures for bad debt expense may provide evidence as to the valuation of receivables; recalculating interest expense may provide evidence as to the existence of long-term debt; and recalculating depreciation and applying analytical procedures to repairs and maintenance expense may provide evidence as to the completeness and/or valuation of property, plant, and equipment.

Audit objectives. The CPA exam may ask for the auditor's "objectives" in the audit of an account. In general there will be one or more "objectives" relating to each of the financial statement assertions. For example, in the case of long-term debt, the following could serve as objectives:

1. Determine whether internal control over long-term debt is adequate
2. Determine whether long-term debt disclosures comply with GAAP (presentation and disclosure)
3. Determine whether recorded long-term debt exists at year-end (existence or occurrence)
4. Determine whether long-term debt represents an obligation to the firm at year-end (rights and obligations)
5. Determine whether all long-term debt has been completely recorded at year-end (completeness)
6. Determine whether all long-term debt has been properly valued at year-end (valuation)

Areas in which a SAS prescribes procedures. The Professional Standards include a number of areas in which specific procedures are either required or suggested. A simulation question may require you to find them. Although you need not memorize the AU-C section, know that such procedures have been presented in areas such as the following:

Specific types of transactions

Noncompliance with Laws and Regulations	AU-C 250
Related Parties	AU-C 550
Litigation (Loss Contingencies)	AU-C 501

Information with which "limited" procedures are required

Other Information in Documents Containing Audited Statements	AU-C 720
Interim Reviews	AU-C 930
Compilations	AR 80
Reviews	AR 90

Required supplemental information

General Procedures	AU-C 730

Areas in which "audit" procedures are required

Receivables	AU-C 505
Inventories	AU-C 501
Investment Securities	AU-C 501
Subsequent Events and Subsequently Discovered Facts	AU-C 560

Other

Group Audits	AU-C 600
Public Warehouses	AU-C 901 , AU-C 501

While we discuss these areas throughout the various modules, the Summary of Prescribed Audit Procedures: Other Areas (see the following pages) presents lists of the primary procedures for several of the areas for which you may expect an exam question. Do not try to memorize the procedures for each of the areas. Instead, review them well before the exam and then again shortly before the exam. A simulation question might ask you to find certain of these procedures and paste them to your answer.

NOW REVIEW MULTIPLE-CHOICE QUESTIONS 15 THROUGH 33

SUMMARY AUDIT PROCEDURES[1]: CASH, RECEIVABLES, INVENTORY

	Cash	**Receivables**	**Inventory**
Presentation and Disclosure	1. Review disclosures for compliance with GAAP 2. Inquire about compensating balance requirements and restrictions	1. Review disclosures for compliance with GAAP 2. Inquire about pledging, discounting 3. Review loan agreements for pledging, factoring	1. Review disclosures for compliance with GAAP 2. Inquire about pledging 3. Review purchase commitments
Existence or Occurrence	3. Confirmation 4. Count cash on hand 5. Prepare bank transfer schedule	4. Confirmation 5. Inspect notes 6. Vouch (examine shipping documents, invoices, credit memos)	4. Confirmation of consigned inventory and inventory in warehouses 5. Observe inventory count
Rights and Obligations	6. Review bank statements	7. Inquire about factoring of receivables	6. Inquire about inventory from vendors on consignment
Completeness and Cutoff	7. Review cutoffs (receipts and disbursements) 8. Perform analytical procedures 9. Review bank reconciliation 10. Obtain bank cutoff statement to verify reconciling items on bank reconciliation	8. Review cutoffs (sales, cash receipts, sales returns) 9. Perform analytical procedures	7. Review cutoffs (sales, sales returns, purchases, purchase returns) 8. Perform test counts and compare with client's counts/summary 9. Inquire about consigned inventory 10. Perform analytical procedures 11. Account for all inventory tags and count sheets
Valuation, Allocation and Accuracy	11. Foot summary schedules 12. Reconcile summary schedules to general ledger 13. Test translation of any foreign currencies	10. Foot subsidiary ledger 11. Reconcile subsidiary ledger to general ledger 12. Examine subsequent cash receipts 13. Age receivables to test adequacy of allowance for doubtful accounts 14. Discuss adequacy of allowance for doubtful accounts with management and compare to historical experience	12. Foot and extend summary schedules 13. Reconcile summary schedules to general ledger 14. Test inventory costing method 15. Determine that inventory is valued at lower of cost or market 16. Examine inventory quality (salable condition) 17. Test inventory obsolescence

SUMMARY AUDIT PROCEDURES:

MARKETABLE SECURITIES, PROPERTY, PLANT, AND EQUIPMENT, PREPAIDS

	Marketable securities	**Property, plant, equipment**	**Prepaids**
Presentation and Disclosure	1. Review disclosures for compliance with GAAP 2. Inquire about pledging 3. Review loan agreements for pledging 4. Review management's classification of securities	1. Review disclosures for compliance with GAAP 2. Inquire about liens and restrictions 3. Review loan agreements for liens and restrictions	1. Review disclosures for compliance with GAAP 2. Review adequacy of insurance coverage

---

[1]Audit procedures are described in detail in Section C.

	Marketable securities	Property, plant, equipment	Prepaids
Existence or Occurrence	5. Confirmation of securities held by third parties 6. Inspect and count 7. Vouch (to available documentation)	4. Inspect additions 5. Vouch additions 6. Review any leases for proper accounting 7. Perform search for unrecorded retirements	3. Confirmation of deposits and insurance 4. Vouch (examine) insurance policies (miscellaneous support for deposit)
Rights and Obligations	(See Existence or Occurrence)	8. Review minutes for approval of additions	(See Existence or Occurrence)
Completeness and Cutoff	8. Review cutoffs (examine transactions near year-end) 9. Perform analytical procedures 10. Reconcile dividends received to publish records	9. Perform analytical procedures 10. Vouch major entries to repairs and maintenance expense	5. Review cutoffs 6. Perform analytical procedures
Valuation, Allocation and Accuracy	11. Foot summary schedules 12. Reconcile summary schedules to general ledger 13. Test amortization of premiums and discounts 14. Determine the market value for trading and available-for-sale securities 15. Review audited financial statements of major investees	11. Foot summary schedules 12. Reconcile summary schedules to general ledger 13. Recalculate depreciation	7. Foot summary schedules 8. Reconcile summary schedules to general ledger 9. Recalculate prepaid portions

SUMMARY AUDIT PROCEDURES:

PAYABLES (CURRENT), LONG-TERM DEBT, OWNERS' EQUITY

	Payables (current)	Long-term debt	Owners' equity
Presentation and Disclosure	1. Review disclosures for compliance with GAAP 2. Review purchase commitments	1. Review disclosures for compliance with GAAP 2. Inquire about pledging of assets 3. Review debt agreements for pledging and events causing default	1. Review disclosures for compliance with GAAP 2. Review information on stock options, dividend restrictions
Existence or Occurrence	3 Confirmation 4. Inspect copies of notes and note agreements 5. Vouch payables (examine purchase order, receiving reports, invoices)	4. Confirmation 5. Inspect copies of notes and note agreements 6. Trace receipt of funds (and payment) to bank account and cash receipts journal	3. Confirmation with registrar and transfer agent (if applicable) 4. Inspect stock certificate book (when no registrar or transfer agent) 5. Vouch capital stock entries
Rights and Obligations	(See Existence or Occurrence)	7. Review minutes for proper authorization	6. Review minutes for proper authorization 7. Inquire of legal counsel on legal issues 8. Review Articles of Incorporation and bylaws for propriety of equity securities

Completeness and Cutoff	6. Review cutoffs (purchases, purchase returns, disbursements) 7. Perform analytical procedures 8. Perform search for unrecorded payables (examine unrecorded invoices, receiving reports, purchase orders) 9. Inquire of management as to completeness	8. Review cutoffs (examine transactions near year-end) 9. Perform analytical procedures 10. Inquire of management as to completeness 11. Review bank confirmations for unrecorded debt	9. Perform analytical procedures 10. Inspect treasury stock certificates
Valuation, Allocation and Accuracy	10. Foot subsidiary ledger 11. Reconcile subsidiary ledger to general ledger 12. Recalculate interest expense (if any) 13. For payroll, review year-end accrual 14. Recalculate other accrued liabilities	12. Foot summary schedules 13. Reconcile summary schedules to general ledger 14. Vouch entries to account 15. Recalculate interest expense and accrued interest payable	11. Agree amounts to general ledger 12. Vouch dividend payments 13. Vouch all entries to retained earnings 14. Recalculate treasury stock transactions

3. **Documentation (AU-C 230 and PCAOB 3).** Make certain that you are familiar with the information in the outline of AU-C 230. You should know that

   a. The overall objective of audit documentation is to provide (1) a sufficient and appropriate record of the basis for the auditor's report and (2) evidence that the audit was planned and performed in accordance with GAAS (and applicable legal and regulatory requirements).

   b. Audit documentation should be prepared so as to enable an experienced auditor, with no previous connection to the audit, to understand procedures performed, audit evidence obtained, and conclusions reached.

   c. While it is not necessary to document every matter considered during an audit, oral explanations alone (absent working paper documentation) are not sufficient to support the work of the auditor.

   d. Audit documentation should include a written audit program (or set of audit programs) for every audit.

   e. Documentation relating to documents inspected by the auditor should allow an experienced auditor to determine which ones were tested.

   f. The auditor should identify any information that contradicts or is inconsistent with auditor's final conclusion regarding significant matter and how the matter was addressed in forming a conclusion, but need not retain documentation that is incorrect or superseded. Documentation of the contradiction or inconsistency may include procedures performed, records documenting consultations, differences in professional judgment among team members or between team members and others consulted.

   g. If information is added to the working papers after the issuance of the audit report, documentation should include (1) when and by whom changes were made and reviewed, (2) specific reasons for changes, and (3) the effect, if any, of the changes on the auditor's conclusion.

   h. The documentation completion period is 60 days following the report release date. That means that changes resulting from the process of assembling and completing the audit file may be made within 60 days following the date the audit report was released to the client. The fact that these changes have been made need not be documented. Examples of such changes include routine file-assembling procedures, deleting discarded documentation, sorting, and signing off file completion checklists. However, the auditor may not add new information to the working papers unless it is documented per g. above.

   i. After the documentation completion date, the auditor should not delete or discard audit documentation. Additions are treated as per g. above.

   j. The retention period (how long audit documentation should be kept) should not be less than five years from the report release date (longer if legal and regulatory requirements so require).

   k. Audit documentation is the property of the auditor and is confidential.

SUMMARY OF PRESCRIBED AUDIT PROCEDURES: OTHER AREAS

Professional Standard Section	Illegal acts	Related parties—identifying transactions	Related parties—determining existence	Litigation, claims, and assessments	Required supplemental information	Subsequent events
	AU 317	AU 334	AU 334	AU 337	AU 558	AU 560
1. Discuss with Management	a. Policies for prevention b. Policies for identifying, evaluating, and accounting c. Inquire as to existence **NOTE:** Audits do not include procedures designed specifically to detect illegal acts. However, normal audit procedures may bring illegal acts to the auditor's attention.	a. Inquire as to existence	a. Policies for identifying and accounting b. Obtain list of related parties c. Inquire as to existence	a. Policies for identifying, evaluating, and accounting for b. Obtain description	a. Measurement methods, significant assumptions, consistency with prior periods	a. Contingent liabilities b. Significant changes in capital stock, debt, working capital c. Current status of estimated items d. Unusual items after balance sheet date
2. Examine	a. Consider laws and regulations b. Normal tests of controls (compliance tests) and substantive test examination procedures	a. SEC filings b. Minutes of Board of Directors and others c. Conflict of interest statements	a. SEC filings b. Pensions, other trusts, and identify officers thereof c. Stockholder listings (for closely held firms) d. Prior year audit workpapers	a. Correspondence and invoices from lawyers b. Minutes—stockholders, directors, others c. Read contracts, agreements, etc. d. Other documents.	a. Compare with financial statements and other information	a. Latest interim statements b. Minutes of stockholders, directors, etc.
3. Other Procedures	a. Coordinate with loss contingency procedures b. Consideration of internal control c. Read minutes d. Overall substantive tests e. Include in representation letter	a. Review business with major customers, suppliers, etc. b. Consider services being provided (received) at unreasonable prices c. Review accounting records for large, unusual transactions d. Review confirmations e. Review invoices from lawyers f. Consideration of internal control g. Provide audit personnel with names of known related parties		a. Contact predecessor and other auditors b. Review material investment transactions c. Know that such transactions are more likely for firms in financial difficulty	a. Letters of audit inquiry to clients's lawyers	a. Add to representation letter b. Perform further inquiries if information seems incorrect c. Apply any other required procedures for specific area being considered	a. Include in representation letter b. Coordinate with loss contingency procedures c. Cutoff procedures (sales, purchases)

PCAOB Standard 3 contains documentation requirements for audits and reviews of issuer (public) companies—you should review the outline of Standard 3, which follows the AU-C Outlines. The requirements differ from AICPA standards in these significant ways.

1. The documentation should demonstrate that the engagement complied with PCAOB standards.
2. The documentation completion period is 45 days (not 60 days) following the report release date.
3. The retention period is seven years (rather than five years).

Additionally, candidates should be aware of the following terms:

Working Trial Balance—A listing of ledger accounts with current year-end balances (as well as last year's ending balances), with columns for adjusting and reclassifying entries as well as for final balances for the current year. Typically both balance sheet and income statement accounts are included.

Lead Schedules—Schedules that summarize like accounts, the total of which is typically transferred to the working trial balance. For example, a client's various cash accounts may be summarized on a lead schedule with only the total cash being transferred to the working trial balance.

Index—The combination of numbers and/or letters given to a workpaper page for identification and organization purposes. For example, cash workpaper may be indexed A-1.

Cross-Reference—When the same information is included on two workpapers, auditors indicate on each workpaper the index of the other workpaper containing the identical information. For example, if Schedule A-1 includes a bank reconciliation with total outstanding checks listed, while Schedule A-2 has a detailed list of these outstanding checks plus the total figure, the totals on the two workpapers will be cross-referenced to one another.

Current Workpaper Files—Files that contain corroborating information pertaining to the current year's audit program (e.g., cash confirmation)

Permanent Workpaper Files—Files that contain information that is expected to be used by the auditor on many future audits of a client (e.g., copies of articles of incorporation and bylaws, schedules of ratios by year, analyses of capital stock accounts, debt agreements, and internal control)

NOW REVIEW MULTIPLE-CHOICE QUESTIONS 34 THROUGH 47

C. Other Specific Audit Evidence Topics

1. Cash

a. Special audit considerations for cash

(1) Kiting. Kiting is a form of fraud that overstates cash by causing it to be simultaneously included in two or more bank accounts. Kiting is possible because a check takes several days to clear the bank on which it is drawn (the "float period"). Following is an example of how kiting can be used to conceal a prior embezzlement in a company that has two bank accounts (one in Valley State Bank and one in First City Bank).

Date	Situation
12/15	Bookkeeper writes himself a $10,000 check on the Valley account, and cashes it—no journal entry is made
12/16	Bookkeeper loses the money gambling in Bullhead City
12/31	Bookkeeper, fearing the auditors will detect the fraud, conceals the shortage by

1. Writing a $10,000 unrecorded check on First City account and depositing it in the Valley account. This will cover up the shortage because Valley will credit the account for the $10,000, and the check will not clear the First City account until January—no journal entry is made until after year-end.
2. When the First City bank reconciliation is prepared at 12/31, the check is not listed as outstanding.

Kiting may be detected by preparing a bank transfer schedule, by preparing a four-column bank reconciliation for the Valley account, or by obtaining a cutoff statement for the First City account.

(2) **Bank transfer schedule.** A bank transfer schedule shows the dates of all transfers of cash among the client's various bank accounts. Know that its primary purpose is to help auditors to **detect kiting**. The

schedule is prepared by using bank statements for the periods before and after year-end **and** by using the firm's cash receipts and disbursements journals. The following is an example of a bank transfer schedule that will help an auditor to detect the kiting described in (1) above:

| | | Date | | | Date | |
Amount	Bank drawn on	Books	Bank	Bank deposited in	Books	Bank
$10,000	First City	1/2	1/2	Valley	1/2	12/31

Note that analysis of the schedule reveals that at December 31, the cash is double counted: it is included in both the Valley account (the bank gave credit for the deposit on 12/31) and in the First City account. Another misstatement that may arise is caused when the date per books for deposit and withdrawal are in different periods (e.g., 12/31 and 1/1).

(3) **Bank reconciliations.** Auditors generally prepare either a two- or a four-column bank reconciliation for the difference between the cash per bank and per books. The four-column approach (also called a proof of cash) **will** allow the auditor to reconcile

(a) All cash receipts and disbursements recorded on the books to those on the bank statement and
(b) All deposits and disbursements recorded on the bank statement to the books.

A four-column reconciliation **will not** allow the auditor to verify whether

(a) Checks written have been for the wrong amounts and so recorded on both the books and the bank statement and
(b) Unrecorded checks or deposits exist that have not cleared the bank.

In the earlier kiting example, note that the Valley four-column reconciliation will detect the kiting because the 12/15 credit for the check used in the embezzlement will have been included in the Valley bank statement disbursements, but not on the books as of 12/31. This is because the embezzlement will result in a $10,000 unreconciled difference between the book and bank totals in the disbursements column of the reconciliation. The First City reconciliation, by itself, will not assist in detection of the kiting because both book and bank entries occur after year-end.

(4) **Bank cutoff statements.** A cutoff statement is a bank statement for the first 8-10 business days after year-end. Know that its primary purpose is to help auditors to **verify reconciling items** on the year-end bank reconciliation. Tests performed using a cutoff statement include verifying that outstanding checks have been completely and accurately recorded as of year-end, and that deposits in transit have cleared within a reasonable period. The statement is sent directly by the bank to the auditor. In the above kiting example, the cutoff statement for the First City account will allow the auditor to detect the fraud since it will include the December 31 unrecorded check.

(5) **Standard confirmation form.** Auditors use a standard form to obtain information from financial institutions (Standard Form to Confirm Account Balance Information with Financial Institutions). The form requests information on two types of balances—**deposits** and **loans**. The form requests financial institutions to indicate any exceptions to the information noted, and to confirm any additional account or loan balance information that comes to their attention while completing the form. Know that the form is designed to substantiate evidence primarily on the **existence** assertion, and not to discover or provide assurance about accounts not listed on the form (evidence on the completeness assertion is not elicited).

b. **Typical substantive audit procedures for cash**

(1) Review disclosures for compliance with generally accepted accounting principles.
(2) Inquire of management concerning compensating balance requirements and restrictions on cash. A compensating balance is an account with a bank in which a company has agreed to maintain a specified minimum amount; compensating balances are typically required under the terms of bank loan agreements. Such restrictions on cash, when material, should be disclosed in the financial statements.
(3) Send confirmation letters to financial institutions to verify existence of the amounts on deposit. See Section a.(5) above.
(4) Count cash on hand at year-end to verify its existence.
(5) Prepare a bank transfer schedule for the last week of the audit year and the first week of the following year to disclose misstatements of cash balances resulting from kiting. See Section a. above.
(6) Review the cutoff of cash receipts and cash disbursements around year-end to verify that transactions affecting cash are recorded accurately and in the proper period.

(7) Review bank statements to verify that book balances represent amounts to which the client has rights.

(8) Perform analytical procedures to test the reasonableness of cash balances. Tests here may include comparisons to prior year cash balances. These procedures help verify the existence and completeness as well as the accuracy of cash transactions.

(9) Review year-end bank reconciliations to verify that cash has been properly stated as of year-end. See Section a. above.

(10) Obtain a bank cutoff statement to verify whether the reconciling items on the year-end bank reconciliation have been properly reflected. See Section a. above.

(11) Foot summary schedules of cash and agree their total to the amount which will appear on the financial statements.

(12) Reconcile summary schedules of cash to the general ledger.

(13) Test translation of any foreign currencies.

2. **Receivables (AU-C 505)**

a. **Special audit considerations for receivables**

(1) **Lapping.** Lapping is an embezzlement scheme in which cash collections from customers are stolen and the shortage is concealed by delaying the recording of subsequent cash receipts. A simplified lapping scheme is shown below.

Date	Situation	Bookkeeping entry		
1/7	Jones pays $500 on account	No entry, bookkeeper cashes check and keeps proceeds		
1/8	Smith pays $200 on account	Cash	500	
	Adam pays $300 on account	Accounts Receivable—Jones		500
1/9	Brock pays $500 on account	Cash	500	
		Accounts Receivable—Smith		200
		Accounts Receivable—Adam		300
1/10	Bookkeeper determines Brock is unlikely to purchase from company in the future	Allowance for Doubtful Accts.	500	
		Accounts Receivable—Brock		500

Lapping most frequently occurs when one individual has responsibility for both recordkeeping and custody of cash. Although the best way to control lapping is to segregate duties and thereby make its occurrence difficult, it may be detected by using the following procedures:

(a) Analytical procedures—calculate age of receivables and turnover of receivables (lapping increases the age and decreases turnover)

(b) Confirm receivables—investigate all exceptions noted, emphasize accounts that have been written off and old accounts. For all accounts watch for postings of cash receipts which have taken an unusually long time. For example, when a reply to a confirmation suggests that the account was paid on December 29, investigate when the posting occurred.

(c) Deposit slips

1] Obtain authenticated deposit slips from bank and compare names, dates, and amounts on remittance advices to information on deposit slips (where possible).

2] Perform surprise inspection of deposits, and compare deposit slip with remittances.

(d) Bookkeeping system

1] Compare remittance advices with information recorded.

2] Verify propriety of noncash credits to accounts receivable.

3] Foot cash receipts journal, customers' ledger accounts, and accounts receivable control account.

4] Reconcile individual customer accounts to accounts receivable control account.

5] Compare copies of monthly statements with customer accounts.

(2) **Confirmations.** Confirmation of accounts receivable is a generally accepted auditing procedure. Auditors are to confirm receivables unless (1) accounts receivable are immaterial, (2) confirmations would be ineffective as an audit procedure, or (3) the combined assessment of inherent and control risk is low, and that assessment, with other substantive evidence, is sufficient to reduce audit risk to an acceptably low level.

Receivable confirmations primarily test the **existence** assertion, and only to a limited extent the completeness and valuation assertions. Know the difference between the **positive** and **negative** forms of confirmation request.

The positive form requests a reply from debtors. Some positive forms request the recipient to indicate either agreement or disagreement with the information stated on the request. Other positive forms, "blank forms," do not state the amount (or other information), but request the respondent to fill in the balance or furnish other information, and when used, often result in lower response rates.

The negative form requests the recipient to respond only if he or she disagrees with the information stated on the request. Negative confirmation requests may be used when

(a) The combined assessed level of inherent risk and control risk is low,
(b) A large number of small balances is involved, and
(c) The auditor has no reason to believe that recipients are unlikely to give them adequate consideration.

Note that when no reply is received to the negative form, the assumption is made that the debtor agrees with the amount and that evidence as to the existence assertion has been collected. When no reply is received to a positive confirmation, a second request is normally mailed to the debtor; if no reply to the second request is received, the auditor normally performs **alternative procedures** (e.g., examination of shipping documents, subsequent cash receipts, sales agreements). However, the auditor may consider **not performing alternative procedures** when (1) no unusual qualitative factors or systematic characteristics related to responses have been identified, and (2) the nonresponses in total, when projected as 100% misstatements to the population, are immaterial.

b. **Typical substantive audit procedures for receivables**

(1) Review disclosures for compliance with generally accepted accounting principles.
(2) Inquire of management about pledging, or discounting of receivables to verify that appropriate disclosure is provided.
(3) Review loan agreements for pledging and factoring of receivables to verify that appropriate disclosure is provided.
(4) Confirm accounts and notes receivable by direct communication with debtors to verify the existence and gross valuation of the accounts. See Section C.2.a. above.
(5) Inspect notes on hand and confirm those not on hand by direct communication with holders. For notes receivable, the auditor will generally be able to inspect the actual note. This procedure is particularly important in situations in which the note is negotiable (i.e., salable) to third parties.
(6) Vouch receivables to supporting customer orders, sales orders, invoices, shipping documents, and credit memos to verify the existence of accounts, and occurrence and accuracy of sales transactions.
(7) Review the cutoff of sales and cash receipts around year-end to verify that transactions affecting accounts receivable are recorded in the proper period. A sale is properly recorded when title passes on the items being sold. Title passes for items sold FOB shipping point when the item is shipped from inventory; title passes for items sold FOB destination when the item is received by the purchaser. You should realize that a proper credit sales cutoff generally affects at least four components of the financial statements: accounts receivable, sales, cost of goods sold, and inventory. Cash receipts should be recorded when the check (or cash) is received from a customer.
(8) Inquire about factoring of receivables to verify that the client maintains rights to the accounts.
(9) Perform analytical procedures for accounts receivable, sales, notes receivable, and interest revenue. Typical ratios include: (a) the gross profit rate, (b) accounts receivable turnover, (c) the ratio of accounts receivable to credit sales, (d) the ratio of accounts written off to the ending accounts receivable, and (e) the ratio of interest revenue to notes receivable. These procedures typically provide evidence to support the existence, completeness, accuracy, and valuation assertions.
(10) Foot the accounts and notes receivable subsidiary ledgers to verify clerical accuracy.
(11) Reconcile subsidiary ledgers to the general ledger control accounts to verify clerical accuracy.
(12) Examine cash receipts subsequent to year-end to test the adequacy of the allowance for doubtful accounts to determine appropriate valuation.
(13) Age accounts receivable to test the adequacy of the allowance for doubtful accounts. An aging schedule is used to address the receivable valuation assertion. Such a schedule summarizes receivables by their age (e.g., 0-30 days since sale, 31-60 days since sale...). Estimates of the likely amount of bad debts in each age group are then made (typically based on historical experience) to estimate whether the amount in the allowance for doubtful accounts is adequate at year-end.

(14) Discuss the adequacy of the allowance for doubtful accounts with management and the credit department and compare it to historical experience to verify valuation.

(15) Consider changes in the economy or the company's customers that might affect the valuation of accounts receivable.

NOW REVIEW MULTIPLE-CHOICE QUESTIONS 48 THROUGH 74

---

3. **Inventory (AU-C 501)**

   a. **Special audit consideration for inventory**

      (1) **Observation.** Observation by the auditor of the client's counting of inventory is a generally accepted auditing procedure and departure from it should be justified. During the inventory observation the auditor seeks to determine that recorded inventory items do not exist (addressing the existence assertion), that all items are recorded (completeness), and that the client has properly considered the condition of the items (valuation). You should be familiar with various situations that may affect the auditor's observation.

         (a) When a client uses statistical methods in determining inventory quantities, the auditor should be satisfied that the sampling plan has statistical validity.

         (b) The existence of good internal control, including an accurate perpetual inventory system, may allow an effective count to be made prior to year-end. In such circumstances, the auditor will rely upon internal control and tests of updating of inventory through year-end to determine that year-end inventory exists and is properly valued. The auditor may verify the accuracy of the perpetual inventory records by examining receiving reports and vendor invoices.

         (c) For a first-year client the auditor will probably not have been present for the count of the beginning inventory, a necessary input to determining cost of goods sold. If adequate evidence is available (e.g., acceptable predecessor workpapers), no report modification may be necessary. When adequate evidence is not available, the auditor may be required to qualify his/her audit report due to the scope limitation. Any resulting misstatement affects both current and prior year income and is therefore likely to result in qualification of the opinion on the income statement. The balance sheet at year-end will be unaffected due to the self-correcting nature of such an error.

         (d) Related to (c), a first-year client may have engaged the auditor subsequent to year-end and the auditor may also have missed the year-end inventory count. In addition, other events may make it impossible for the auditor to be present for the client's count of inventory. In such circumstances, alternate procedures may sometimes be used to establish the accuracy of the count (e.g., good internal control); however, these alternate procedures **should include some physical counts of inventory items** and should include appropriate tests of intervening transactions.

   b. **Typical substantive audit procedures for inventory**

      (1) Review disclosures for compliance with generally accepted accounting principles.

      (2) Inquire of management about pledging of inventory and verify the adequacy of disclosure.

      (3) Review purchase and sales commitments to verify whether there may be a need to either accrue a loss and/or provide disclosure. Generally, commitments are not disclosed in the financial statements unless uneconomic commitments result in a need to accrue significant losses (due to current price changes).

      (4) Confirm consigned inventory and inventory in warehouses. Some companies store inventory items in public warehouses. In such a situation, the auditor should confirm in writing with the custodian that the goods are being held. Additionally, if such holdings are significant, the auditor should apply one or more of the following procedures:

         (a) Review the client's control procedures relating to the warehouseman.

         (b) Obtain a CPA's report on the warehouseman's internal control.

         (c) Observe physical counts of the goods.

         (d) If warehouse receipts have been pledged as collateral, confirm with lenders details of the pledged receipts.

      (5) Observe the taking of the physical inventory and make test counts to verify the existence (and to a limited extent the ownership and valuation) of inventory. See Section C.3.a. above.

(6) Review cutoffs of sales, sales returns, purchases, and purchase returns around year-end to verify that transactions affecting inventory are recorded in the proper period. Know here that the objective is to include in inventory those items for which the client has legal title.

(7) Perform test counts during the observation of the taking of the inventory and compare them to the client's counts and subsequently to the accumulated inventory to verify the accuracy of the count and its accumulation. See Section C.3.a. above.

(8) Inquire of management as to the existence of consigned inventory to verify the adequacy of its disclosure. Know that inventory consigned out remains the property of the client until it is sold. Inventory consigned to the client should not be included in the physical count since it belongs to the consignor.

(9) Perform analytical procedures to test the reasonableness of inventory. Analytical procedures include calculation of gross profit margins by product, and inventory turnover rates. Analytical procedures are particularly effective at identifying obsolete inventory and, therefore, are useful in determining its proper valuation.

(10) Account for all inventory tags and count sheets to verify that inventory has been completely recorded.

(11) Foot and extend summary inventory schedules to verify clerical accuracy.

(12) Reconcile inventory summary schedules to the general ledger to verify clerical accuracy.

(13) Test the inventory cost method to verify that it is in conformity with generally accepted accounting principles. Here the auditor will determine the method of pricing used and whether it is acceptable and consistent with the prior years (e.g., LIFO, FIFO).

(14) Test the pricing of inventory to verify that it is valued at the lower of cost or market and that inventory and cost of goods sold transactions are accurately recorded. As a general rule, inventories should not be carried in excess of their net realizable value. The accuracy of pricing is determined by reference to vendor invoices (for wholesalers and retailers) and to vendor invoices, requisitions, and labor reports (for manufacturers). In certain circumstances a specialist may be needed to assist in valuation of inventory (see Section 13, Using the Work of a Specialist, below).

(15) Examine inventory quality and condition to assess whether there may be evidence suggesting that it is in unsatisfactory condition.

(16) Perform any necessary additional tests of inventory obsolescence to verify the valuation of inventory.

4. **Investment Securities (AU-C 501)**
(Review outline of AU-C 501 at this point)

a. **Special audit considerations for investment securities**

(1) **GAAP requirements.** Recall the criteria for deciding whether the cost adjusted for fair value, equity, or consolidated basis should be used for the investments (see outlines of APB 18 and SFAS 94). Also recall the distinction in accounting treatment under SFAS 115 for debt securities and equity securities where significant influence does not exist. Accounting for derivative instruments is presented in SFAS 133.

(2) **Audit approach.** Evidence related to the **existence** assertion is obtained by inspecting any securities that are held by a client (often in a safe deposit box) and by confirming securities held by custodians (e.g., a bank or trust company). A client employee should be present during the inspection to avoid confusion over any missing securities. In examining the security certificates, the auditor determines whether securities held are identical to the recorded securities (certificate numbers, number of shares, face value, etc.).

Evidence pertaining to **valuation** (carrying amount) for long-term investments for an investee may be obtained by examining investee (a) audited financial statements, (b) unaudited financial statements (insufficient evidence in and of itself), (c) market quotations, and (d) other evidence.

(3) **Simultaneous verification.** Because of the liquid nature of securities, the auditor's inspection is generally performed at year-end simultaneously with the audit of cash, bank loans (e.g., a revolving credit agreement), and other related items.

(4) **Client controls.** The liquid nature of marketable securities makes certain controls, such as the following, desirable:

(a) The treasurer should authorize purchases and sales up to a certain value. After that value has been reached, transactions should be authorized by the board of directors.

(b) Two individuals should be present when access to the securities is necessary.

(c) Recorded balances for investments should periodically be compared with the actual securities held by individuals independent of the function.

b. **Typical substantive audit procedures for investment securities**

(1) Review disclosures for compliance with generally accepted accounting principles.

(2) Inquire of management about pledging of investment securities and verify that appropriate disclosure is provided.

(3) Review loan agreements for pledging of investment securities and verify that appropriate disclosure is provided.

(4) Review management's classification of securities held for investment.

(5) Obtain confirmation of securities in the custody of others to verify their existence.

(6) Inspect and count securities on hand and compare serial numbers with those shown on the records and, if appropriate, with prior year audit working papers. This procedure addresses the existence of the securities and provides evidence that no fraud involving "substitution" (e.g., unauthorized sale and subsequent repurchase) of securities has occurred during the year. When an auditor is unable to inspect and count securities held in a safe-deposit box at a bank until after the balance sheet date, a bank representative should be asked to confirm that there has been no access between the balance sheet date and the security count date.

(7) Vouch purchases and sales of securities during the year. This audit procedure will provide evidence relating to all financial statement assertions. Included here will be recomputation of gains and losses on security sales.

(8) Review the cutoff of cash receipts and disbursements around year-end to verify that transactions affecting investment securities transactions are recorded accurately and in the proper period.

(9) Perform analytical procedures to test the reasonableness of investment securities. A typical analytical procedure is to verify the relationship between interest and dividend income to the related securities. The auditor will also be able to recompute the interest and dividend income if so desired.

(10) Reconcile amounts of dividends received to published dividend records generally available from databases maintained on the Internet to verify the completeness and accuracy of dividend revenue.

(11) Foot and extend summary investment security schedules to verify clerical accuracy.

(12) Reconcile summary inventory schedules to the general ledger to verify clerical accuracy.

(13) Test amortization of premiums and discounts to verify that investments are properly valued.

(14) Determine the market value of securities classified as trading or available-for-sale at the date of the balance sheet.

(15) Review audited financial statements of major investments to test whether they are properly valued at year-end.

5. **Property, Plant, and Equipment (PP&E)**

a. **Special audit considerations for PP&E**

(1) **Accounting considerations.** Many PP&E acquisitions involve trades of used assets. Module 11, Section C, points out that under SFAS 153 most nonmonetary exchanges of these assets are recorded using the fair value of the asset exchanged.

Assets constructed by a company for its own use should be recorded at the cost of direct material, direct labor, and applicable overhead. Recall that interest may be capitalized.

PP&E should be tested for impairment when facts and circumstances indicate that the asset's value may be impaired.

(2) **Overall approach.** The reasonableness of the entire account balance should be audited in detail for a client that has not previously been audited. When a predecessor auditor exists, the successor will normally review that auditor's workpapers.

For a continuing audit client, the audit of PP&E consists largely of an analysis of the year's acquisitions and disposals (an input and output approach). Subsequent to the first year, the account's slow rate of turnover generally permits effective auditing of the account in less time than accounts of comparable size.

(3) **Relationship with repairs and maintenance.** A number of CPA questions address this area. A PP&E acquisition may improperly be recorded in the repair and maintenance expense account. Therefore, an analysis of repairs and maintenance may detect **understatements** of PP&E. Alternatively, an analysis of PP&E may disclose repairs and maintenance that have improperly been capitalized, thereby resulting in **overstatements** of PP&E. Expenditures that make the asset more productive or extend its useful life should be capitalized in the asset account (betterment) or as a debit to accumulated depreciation (life extension).

(4) **Unrecorded retirements.** Disposals may occur due to retirements or thefts of PP&E items. Simple retirements of equipment are often difficult to detect since no journal entry may have been recorded to reflect the event. Unrecorded or improperly recorded retirements (and thefts) may be discovered through examination of changes in insurance policies, consideration of the purpose of recorded acquisition, examination of property tax files, discussions, observation, or through an examination of debits to accumulated depreciation and of credits to miscellaneous revenue accounts. Inquiry of the plant manager may disclose unrecorded retirements and/or obsolete equipment.

b. **Typical substantive audit procedures for PP&E**

(1) Review disclosures for compliance with generally accepted accounting principles.

(2) Inquire of management concerning any liens and restrictions on PP&E. PP&E may be pledged as security on a loan agreement. Such restrictions are disclosed in the notes to the financial statements.

(3) Review loan agreements for liens and restrictions on PP&E and verify that appropriate disclosure is provided.

(4) Inspect major acquisitions of PP&E to verify their existence.

(5) Vouch additions and retirements to PP&E to verify their existence, accuracy, and the client's rights to them. Typically large PP&E transactions support will include original documents such as contracts, deeds, construction work orders, invoices, and authorization by the directors. This procedure will also help to identify transactions that should be expensed rather than capitalized.

(6) Review any leases for proper accounting to determine whether the related PP&E assets should be capitalized.

(7) Perform search for unrecorded retirements and for obsolete equipment. See Section C.5.a. above.

(8) Review minutes of the board of directors (and shareholders) to verify that additions have been properly approved.

(9) Perform analytical procedures to test the reasonableness (existence, completeness, and valuation) of PP&E. Typical analytical procedures involve a (a) comparison of total cost of PP&E divided by cost of goods sold, (b) comparison of repairs and maintenance on a monthly and annual basis, and (c) comparison of acquisitions and retirements for the current year with prior years.

(10) Obtain or prepare an analysis of repairs and maintenance expense and vouch transactions to discover items that should have been capitalized. See Section C.5.a. above.

(11) Foot PP&E summary schedules to verify clerical accuracy.

(12) Reconcile summary PP&E schedules to the general ledger to verify clerical accuracy.

(13) Recalculate depreciation to establish proper valuation of PP&E. In addition, the existence of recurring losses on retired assets may indicate that depreciation charges are generally insufficient.

(14) Consider any conditions that indicate that assets may be impaired to determine that the assets are properly valued. Indications of possible impairment include discontinuance of a business segment or type of product, excessive capacity, loss of major customers, etc.

c. **Intangible assets** are audited similar to PP&E. They are generally valued at cost and amortized over their useful lives. However, goodwill is not amortized; instead it is tested for impairment at least annually. Research and development expenditures are not capitalized. They are expensed as incurred.

6. **Prepaid Assets**

a. **Special audit considerations for prepaid assets**

(1) **Overall.** Prepaid assets typically consist of items such as insurance and deposits. Insurance policies may be examined and the prepaid portion of any expenditure may be recalculated. Additionally, policies may be confirmed with the company's insurance agent and/or payments may be vouched. Deposits and other prepaid amounts are typically immaterial. When they are considered material, an auditor may confirm their existence, recalculate prepaid portions, and examine any available support.

(2) **Self-insurance.** The lack of insurance on an asset (or inadequate insurance) will not typically result in report modification, although this may be disclosed in the notes to the financial statements. Also, an auditor may serve an advisory role by pointing out assets that, unknown to management, may have inadequate insurance.

b. **Typical substantive audit procedures for prepaid assets**

(1) Review disclosures for compliance with generally accepted accounting principles.

(2) Review the adequacy of insurance coverage.

(3) Confirm deposits and insurance with third party to verify their existence and valuation.

(4) Vouch additions to accounts (examine insurance policies and miscellaneous other support for deposit) to verify existence and accuracy.

(5) Perform analytical procedures to test the reasonableness of prepaid assets. A primary procedure here is comparison with prior year balances and obtaining explanations for any significant changes.

(6) Foot prepaid summary schedules to verify accuracy.

(7) Reconcile summary schedules to the general ledger to verify proper accuracy and valuation.

(8) Recalculate prepaid portions of prepaid assets to verify proper valuation.

NOW REVIEW MULTIPLE-CHOICE QUESTIONS 75 THROUGH 98

---

7. **Payables (Current)**

   a. **Special audit considerations for payables**

   (1) **Confirmation.** Confirmations may be sent to vendors. However, such confirmation procedures are sometimes omitted due to the availability of externally generated evidence (e.g., both purchase agreements and vendors' invoices) and due to the inability of confirmations to adequately address the completeness assertion. (Auditors are primarily concerned about the possibility of understated payables; a major payable will not in general be confirmed if the client completely omits it from the trial balance of payables.)

   Accounts payable confirmations are most frequently used in circumstances involving (1) bad internal control, (2) bad financial position, and (3) situations when vendors do not send month-end statements. However, when an auditor has chosen to confirm payables despite the existence of vendor statements, the confirmation will generally request the vendor to send the month-end statement to the auditor. For this reason, the balance per the client's books is not included on such a confirmation.

   Confirmations are sent to (1) major suppliers, (2) disputed accounts, and (3) a sample of other suppliers. Major suppliers are selected because they represent a possible source of large understatement: the client will normally have established large credit lines. The size of the recorded payable at year-end is of less importance than for receivables. While as a practical matter large year-end recorded balances will normally be confirmed, the emphasis on detecting understated payables may lead the auditor to also confirm accounts with relatively low recorded year-end balances. Also, if the payables to be confirmed are selected from a list of vendors instead of from the recorded year-end payables, the completeness assertion as well as the existence assertion may be addressed.

   (2) The **search for unrecorded liabilities.** The search for unrecorded liabilities is an effort to discover any liabilities that may have been omitted from recorded year-end payables (completeness). Typical procedures include the following:

   (a) Examination of vendors' invoices and statements both immediately prior to and following year-end

   (b) Examination, after year-end, of the following to test whether proper cutoffs have occurred:

     1] Cash disbursements
     2] Purchases
     3] Unrecorded vouchers (receiving reports, vendors' invoices, purchase orders)

   (c) Analytical procedures

   (d) Internal control is analyzed to evaluate its likely effectiveness in preventing and detecting the occurrence of such misstatements.

   b. **Typical substantive audit procedures for payables**

   (1) Review disclosures for compliance with generally accepted accounting principles.

   (2) Review purchase commitments to determine whether there may be a need to either accrue a loss and/or provide disclosure (see also step 3 of inventory program).

   (3) Confirm accounts payable by direct correspondence with vendors. Confirmation of payables provides evidence relating to the occurrence, obligation, completeness, accuracy, and valuation assertions. See Section C.7.a. above.

   (4) Inspect copies of notes and note agreements.

(5) Vouch balances payable to selected creditors by inspecting purchase orders, receiving reports, and invoices to verify existence, accuracy, valuation, and to a lesser extent, completeness.

(6) Review the cutoff of purchases, purchase returns, and disbursements around year-end to verify that transactions are recorded in the proper period.

(7) Perform analytical procedures to test the reasonableness of payables. Examples here are ratios such as accounts payable divided by purchases, and accounts payable divided by total current liabilities.

(8) Perform search for unrecorded payables to determine whether liabilities have been completely recorded. See Section C.7.a. above.

(9) Inquire of management as to the completeness of payables.

(10) Foot the subsidiary accounts payable ledger to test clerical accuracy.

(11) Reconcile the subsidiary ledger to the general ledger control account to verify clerical accuracy.

(12) Recalculate interest expense on interest-bearing debt.

(13) Recalculate year-end accrual for payroll. A typical procedure here is to allocate the total days in the payroll subsequent to year-end between the old and new years and to determine whether the accrual is reasonable.

(14) Recalculate other accrued liabilities. The approach for accruals is largely one of (1) testing computations made by the client in setting up the accrual, and (2) determining that the accruals have been treated consistently with the past. Note that the audit approach here is somewhat different than for accounts payable that, because one or more transactions usually directly indicate the year-end liability, do not require such a computation. Examples of accounts requiring accrual include property taxes, pension plans, vacation pay, service guarantees, commissions, and income taxes payable.

8. **Long-Term Debt**

   a. **Special audit considerations for long-term debt**

   (1) **Overall approach.** Despite the fact that this account's turnover rate is low, considerable analysis is performed on its ending balance. Confirmations are frequently used; recall that when the debt is owed to banks, confirmation is obtained with the standard bank confirmation. In addition, minutes of director and/or stockholder meetings will be reviewed to determine whether new borrowings have been properly authorized.

   The proceeds of any new borrowings are traced to the cash receipts journal, deposit slips, and bank statements. Repayments are traced to the cash disbursements journal, canceled checks, and canceled notes. If a debt trustee is used, it will be possible to obtain information through use of a confirmation whether the repayments have been made.

   b. **Typical substantive audit procedures for long-term debt**

   (1) Review disclosures for compliance with generally accepted accounting principles.

   (2) Inquire of management concerning pledging of assets related to debt.

   (3) Review debt agreements for details on pledged assets and for events that may result in default on the loan.

   (4) Confirm long-term debt with payees or appropriate third parties (including any applicable sinking fund transactions).

   (5) Obtain and inspect copies of debt agreements to verify whether provisions have been met and disclosed.

   (6) Trace receipt of funds (and payments) to the bank account and to the cash receipts journal to verify that the funds were properly received (or disbursed) by the company.

   (7) Review the cutoff of cash receipts and disbursements around year-end to verify that transactions affecting debt are recorded in the proper period.

   (8) Review minutes of board of directors' and/or shareholders' meetings to verify that transactions have been properly authorized and, if necessary, that an opinion of an attorney has been obtained regarding the legality of the debt.

   (9) Perform analytical procedures to verify the overall reasonableness of long-term debt and interest expense.

   (10) Inquire of management as to the completeness of debt.

   (11) Review bank confirmations for any indication of unrecorded debt.

   (12) Foot summary schedules of long-term debt to test clerical accuracy.

   (13) Reconcile summary schedules of long-term debt to the general ledger to verify clerical accuracy.

   (14) Vouch entries in long-term debt accounts to test existence, obligation, and accuracy of debt.

   (15) Recalculate interest expense and accrued interest payable to determine accuracy of the amounts.

9. **Owners' Equity**

   a. **Special audit considerations for owners' equity**

      (1) **Control of capital stock transactions.** Clients use one of two approaches for capital stock transactions. First, a stock certificate book may be used which summarizes shares issued through use of "stubs" which remain after a certificate has been removed. The certificates for outstanding shares are held by the stockholders; canceled certificates (for repurchased stock or received when a change in stock ownership occurs) are held by the client. When a stock certificate book is used auditors reconcile outstanding shares, par value, etc., with the "stubs" in the book. Confirmations are sometimes sent to stockholders. Since capital stock transactions are generally few in number, the audit of this area takes relatively less audit time.

      The second approach, typically used by large clients, is to engage a registrar and a stock transfer agent to manage the company's stock transactions. The primary responsibility of the registrar is to verify that stock which is issued is properly authorized. Stock transfer agents maintain detailed stockholder records and carry out transfers of stock ownership. The number of shares authorized, issued, and outstanding will usually be confirmed to the auditor directly by the registrar and stock transfer agent.

      (2) **Retained earnings.** Little effort will be exerted in auditing the retained earnings of a continued client. The audit procedures for dividends will allow the auditor to verify the propriety of that debit to retained earnings. The entry to record the year's net income (loss) is readily available. Finally, the nature of any prior period adjustments is examined to determine whether they meet the criteria for an adjustment to retained earnings. Recall that the type of adjustment typically encountered is a correction of prior years' income.

   b. **Typical substantive audit procedures for stockholders' equity**

      (1) Review disclosures for compliance with generally accepted accounting principles.
      (2) Review Articles of Incorporation, bylaws, and minutes for provisions relating to stock options, and dividends restriction.
      (3) Confirm stocks authorized, issued, and outstanding with the independent registrar and stock transfer agent (if applicable).
      (4) For a corporation that acts as its own stock registrar and transfer agent, reconcile the stock certificate book to transactions recorded in the general ledger.
      (5) Vouch transactions and trace receipt of funds (and payment) to the bank account and to the cash receipts journal to verify that the funds were properly received (or disbursed) by the company.
      (6) Review minutes of the board of directors' and/or shareholders' meetings to verify that stock transactions and dividends have been properly authorized.
      (7) Inquire of the client's legal counsel to obtain information concerning any unresolved legal issues.
      (8) Review the Articles of Incorporation and bylaws for the propriety of equity transactions.
      (9) Perform analytical procedures to test the reasonableness of dividends.
      (10) Inspect treasury stock certificates to verify that transactions have been completely recorded and that client has control of certificates.
      (11) Agree amounts that will appear on the financial statements to the general ledger.
      (12) Vouch dividend payments to verify that amounts have been paid.
      (13) Vouch all entries affecting retained earnings.
      (14) Recalculate treasury stock transactions.

10. **Revenue**

   a. **Special audit considerations for revenue**

      (1) **Overall approach.** Most revenue accounts are verified in conjunction with the audit of a related asset or liability account. For example

Balance Sheet Account	Revenue Account
Accounts receivable	Sales
Notes receivable	Interest
Investments	Interest, dividends, gains on sales
Property, plant, and equipment	Rent, gains on sales

      (2) Module 9 discusses revenue recognition. Most frequently sales are recorded during the period in which title has passed, or services have been rendered to customers who have made firm, enforceable commitments to purchase such goods or services. SEC Staff Accounting Bulletin 101 provides a more specific, helpful overall set of criteria for revenue recognition.

    (a) Persuasive evidence of an arrangement exists.

    (b) Delivery has occurred or services have been rendered.

    (c) The seller's price to the buyer is fixed or determinable.

    (d) Collectibility is reasonably assured.

(3) **Potential problem areas for revenues**

    (a) **Bill and hold transactions.** Transactions in which a customer agrees to purchase goods but the seller retains physical possession until the customer requests shipment to designated locations. Because delivery has not yet occurred, such transactions do not ordinarily qualify. The primary requirements to qualify for revenue recognition are that the buyer make an absolute commitment to purchase, has assumed the risks and rewards of the product, and is unable to accept delivery because of some compelling reason.

    (b) **Side agreements.** Agreements used to alter the terms and conditions of recorded sales transactions, often to convince customers to accept delivery of goods and services. Side agreements are frequently hidden from the board of directors and may create obligations that relieve the customer of the risks and rewards of ownership. Accordingly, side agreement terms *may* preclude revenue recognition.

    (c) **Channel stuffing (trade loading).** A marketing practice that suppliers sometimes use to boost sales by inducing distributors to buy substantially more inventory than they can promptly resell. Inducements may range from deep discounts on the inventory to threats of losing the distributorship if inventory is not purchased. Channel stuffing may result in the need to increase the level of anticipated sales returns.

    (d) **Related-party transactions.** A variety of potential misstatements may occur due to transactions with related parties. For example, sales of the same inventory back and forth among affiliated companies may "freshen" receivables.

  b. **Substantive procedure approach for revenues not verified in the audit of balance sheet accounts**

    (1) Perform analytical procedures related to revenue accounts.

    (2) Obtain or prepare analyses of selected revenue accounts.

    (3) Vouch selected transactions and determine that they represent proper revenue for the period.

11. **Expenses**

  a. **Special audit considerations for expenses**

    (1) **Overall approach.** Most expense accounts are verified in conjunction with the audit of a related asset or liability account. For example

Balance Sheet Account	Expense Account
Accounts receivable	Uncollectible accounts
Inventories	Purchases, cost of goods sold, payroll
Property, plant, and equipment	Depreciation, repairs, and maintenance
Accrued liabilities	Commissions, fees, product warranty expenses

  b. **Substantive procedure approach for expenses not verified in the audit of balance sheet accounts**

    (1) Perform analytical procedures related to the expense accounts.

    (2) Obtain or prepare analyses of selected expense accounts.

    (3) Vouch selected transactions.

NOW REVIEW MULTIPLE-CHOICE QUESTIONS 99 THROUGH 120

12. **Client Representation Letters (AU-C 580).** Review the outline and note that representation letters are required for audits. In reviewing the outline be generally familiar with the various representations obtained by auditors. Expect multiple-choice questions on matters such as the following:

  a. The representation letter should be addressed to the auditor, in a letter dated no earlier than the date of the auditor's report.

b. The representation letter should be signed by the chief executive officer and the chief financial officer.

c. Representations from management are not a substitute for the application of other necessary auditing procedures.

d. Representations should be obtained for all periods being reported upon, even if management was not present during all of those periods.

e. Management refusal to furnish written representations **precludes** an unqualified opinion, and ordinarily results in a disclaimer, although a qualified opinion may be appropriate in some circumstances.

13. **Using the Work of a Specialist (AU-C 620).** Read the outline of this standard. Auditors increasingly are finding it necessary to use the work of specialists in areas such as postemployment and postretirement benefits, environmental cleanup obligations, fair value disclosures and derivatives, as well as in more traditional areas such as the valuation of inventory (e.g., diamonds). A specialist is an individual or organization possessing expertise in a field other than accounting and auditing. A specialist may be hired by the client (the "client's specialist") or by the auditors (the "auditors' specialist). While it is desirable for the specialist to be unrelated to the client, it is not required. Bear in mind that a major difference between the client's and the auditors' specialist is the fact that the client's specialist may be less objective, given he or she is employed by the client.

Regardless of whether a client or auditor specialist is involved, the auditors should evaluate the specialist's professional qualifications, understand the objectives and scope of the specialist's work, the appropriateness of using the specialist's work, and the form and content of the specialist's findings. Several other key points from AU-C 620 include

a. For purposes of this standard, internal auditors are **not** considered specialists.

b. To assess the qualifications of the specialist, the CPA should consider specialist professional certification, reputation, and experience in the type of work under consideration.

c. Auditors should obtain an adequate understanding of the methods or assumptions used by the specialist to determine that they are not unreasonable in the circumstances in relation to the findings and conclusions of the specialist. Also, if the work of the specialist involves the use of source data that is significant to the work of the specialist, the auditor should evaluate its relevance, completeness, and accuracy.

d. While the work of a client's specialist may be used, the CPA should carefully evaluate the relationship and consider whether it might impair the specialist's objectivity. If objectivity may be impaired, additional procedures should be performed, possibly including using another specialist.

e. The specialist is not referred to in the auditor's report unless such a reference would help report users to understand the need for an explanatory paragraph or a departure from an unmodified opinion. (If the work of the specialist is consistent with the client's financial statements, no reference is permitted.)

NOW REVIEW MULTIPLE-CHOICE QUESTIONS 121 THROUGH 137

14. **Loss Contingencies and Inquiry of a Client's Lawyer (AU-C 501).** Accounting standards (e.g., FAS 5) require disclosures relating to loss contingencies, as well as adjusting journal entries for those which are probable and estimable. Loss contingencies arise due to occurrences such as

- Litigation
- Income tax disputes
- Various guarantees made by the client
- Accounts receivable sold or assigned with recourse
- Environmental issues

While auditors obtain information on many of these issues through inquiry of management, reading related correspondence, and various analyses of transactions, the client's lawyer is the primary source for corroboration of information obtained from the client concerning loss contingencies. If the auditor assesses a risk of material misstatement regarding litigation, claims, or assessments, the auditor should seek direct communication with the entity's external legal counsel who have devoted substantive attention to the matter. At this point, read the outline of AU-C 501.

The process relating to the attorney is one in which the client prepares a list and describes claims, litigation, assessments, and unasserted claims pending against the firm. This information is sent by the auditor to the attorney who is to review it and provide additional input, if possible.

Refusal of the lawyer to reply is a scope limitation that may affect the audit report. If the lawyer is unable to estimate the effect of litigation, claims, and assessments on the financial statements, it may result in an uncertainty that would also have an effect on the audit report. In the case of unasserted claims that the client has not disclosed, the lawyer is **not** required to note them in his/her reply to the auditor.

15. **Fair Values (AU-C 501).** Generally accepted accounting principles require companies to use "fair value" for measuring, presenting, and disclosing various accounts (e.g., investments, intangible assets, impaired assets, derivatives). Fair value is generally considered to be the amount at which an asset (or liability) could be bought or sold in a current transaction between willing parties.

The determination of fair value is easiest when there are published price quotations in an active market (e.g., a stock exchange). Determining fair value is more difficult when an active market does not exist for items such as various investment properties or complex derivative financial instruments. In such circumstances fair value may be calculated through the use of a valuation model (e.g., a model based on forecasts and discounting of future cash flows). Auditing fair values is similar to that of other estimates (see topic A.1 of this module) in that a combination of three approaches is often used—(1) review and test management's process, (2) independently develop as estimate, or (3) review subsequent events.

When reviewing management's process (approach 1), the auditors consider whether the assumptions used by management are reasonable, whether the valuation model seems appropriate, and whether management has used relevant information that is reasonably available. Developing one's own estimate (approach 2) offers the advantage of allowing the auditors to compare that estimate with that developed by management. Reviewing subsequent events (approach 3) allows the auditors to use information obtained subsequent to year-end to help evaluate the reasonableness of management's estimate. Often auditors will use a combination of the approaches. Regardless of the approach(es) followed, the auditors should evaluate whether the disclosures of fair values required by GAAP have been properly presented.

16. **Related-Party Transactions (AU-C 550; AU-C 334).** Review the outline of AU-C 550. The main issue with related-party transactions concerns the price at which a transaction occurs. This price may not be the one that would have resulted from an "arm's-length bargaining." Note the procedures suggested in Section 334 for discovering related-party transactions. Further note that it is generally not possible for the auditor to determine whether such a transaction would have occurred if no related party had existed, and, if so, the price thereof.

17. **Subsequent Events and Subsequent Discovery of Facts Existing at the Date of the Audit Report (AU-C 560).** This section deals with accounting issues (e.g., how to measure and disclose certain events) as well as audit responsibility with respect to subsequent events. Section 560 classifies subsequent events into two types.

a. Those events that provide additional evidence with respect to conditions that existed at the date of the balance sheet (for which the financial statements are to be adjusted for any changes in estimates)
b. Those events that provide evidence with respect to conditions that did **not** exist at the date of the balance sheet but arose subsequent to that date (for which there is to be footnote disclosure)
The following diagram depicts the two types of subsequent events.

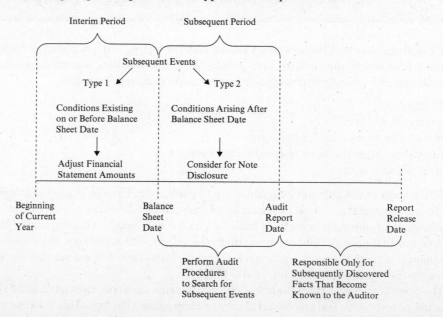

Subsequent Events. The auditor should perform audit procedures to obtain sufficient appropriate audit evidence that subsequent events that require adjustment or disclosure have been identified, including:

- Obtaining an understanding of management's procedures for identifying subsequent events.
- Inquiring of management about subsequent events.
- Reading minutes (e.g., stockholders and board of directors' meetings).
- Reading the latest subsequent interim financial statements, if available.

Subsequently Discovered Facts that Become Known to the Auditor *before* **the Report Release Date.** While the auditor is not required to perform audit procedures after the date of the auditor's report, if a subsequently discovered fact becomes known before the report release date, the auditor should discuss it with management (and those charged with governance) and determine whether the financial statements should be amended. If such amendment occurs, the auditor should either date the auditor's report as of the later date (and extend audit procedures for subsequent events) or dual date the auditor's report with the second date relating to the subsequently discovered facts. If management refuses to amend the financial statements, a departure from GAAP exists that may lead to a qualified or adverse opinion.

Subsequently Discovered Facts that Become Known to the Auditor *after* **the Report Release Date.** The auditor should discuss the matter with management and determine whether the financial statements need to be amended. If they are amended, the auditor should:

- Either extend the audit procedures or dual date the report as in the preceding section.
- Determine that proper steps are taken to inform anyone who might be using the misstated financial statements.
- If the auditor's opinion differs from that previously expressed, describe the situation in an emphasis of matter or other matter paragraph. That paragraph should include the date of the previous report, type of opinion, reasons for the different opinion and that the auditor's opinion differs from that in the previous opinion.

If management refuses to take the necessary steps to correct the situation, the auditor should take appropriate action to seek to prevent reliance on the auditor's report.

Predecessor Auditor's Reissuance of the Auditor's Report on Comparative Financial Statements. The predecessor should read the subsequent period financial statements, compare with prior year financial statements, and obtain a representation letter from management.

18. **Omitted Procedures Discovered after the Report Date (AU-C 585).** Subsequent to issuance of an audit report, an auditor may realize that one or more necessary procedures were omitted from the audit. When this occurs, the auditor should first assess its importance. If omission is considered important (i.e., it affects present ability to support the previously expressed opinion) and if the auditor believes individuals are relying or are likely to rely on the financial statements, the procedures or alternate procedures should be promptly applied. If the procedure is then applied and misstatements are detected, the auditor should review his/her responsibilities under AU-C 560 on subsequent discovery of facts existing at the date of the auditor's report. If the client does not allow the auditor to apply the necessary procedure(s), the auditor should consult his/her attorney as to appropriate action.

19. **Audit of the Statement of Cash Flows.** The statement of cash flows is prepared from the other financial statements and from analyses of increases and decreases in selected account balances. Since the amounts included in the statement of cash flows are audited in conjunction with the audit of balance sheet and income statement accounts, only limited substantive procedures are necessary.

   The statement of cash flows divides cash receipts and cash disbursements into three categories: operating, investing, and financing. In addition to comparing this information to the balance sheet and income statement, the auditors should determine whether it has been properly classified among the three categories. For example, cash flow from operations should not be overstated through inclusion of funds from either investing or financing. The auditors should also determine that the concept of cash or cash equivalents analyzed in the statement agrees with an amount shown on the balance sheet. Finally, the auditors should determine that a statement of cash flows is presented for each year for which an income statement is presented.

NOW REVIEW MULTIPLE-CHOICE QUESTIONS 138 THROUGH 163

D. Completing the Audit

1. **Procedures Completed near the End of the Audit.** A number of audit procedures (most discussed in sections B and C) are involved in completing the audit. These procedures, completed on or near the last day of fieldwork, include

   - Search for unrecorded liabilities.
   - Review minutes of meetings of shareholders, board of directors, and the audit committee.
   - Perform final review stage analytical procedures.
   - Perform procedures, including the inquiry of client's lawyers, to identify loss contingencies.
   - Perform review for subsequent events.
   - Obtain representation letter.
   - Evaluate audit findings (see 2. below).
   - Review adequacy of disclosures using a **disclosure checklist** that lists all specific disclosures required by GAAP and the SEC, if appropriate.
   - Review of working papers performed by manager, partner, and possibly a **second partner review** performed by a partner who is not otherwise involved in the engagement but to provide an independent review of the work performed. The review process helps provide assurance that audit risk is an appropriately low level, working paper documentation is adequate, and that the evidence supports the opinion being rendered.
   - Communicate with the audit committee.

2. **Evaluate Audit Findings.** Throughout the course of the audit, the auditors will propose adjusting entries for all **material misstatements** (whether caused by error or fraud) that are discovered in the client's financial records. Any material misstatement that the auditors find should be corrected; otherwise, they cannot issue an unqualified opinion on the financial statements. Unrecorded misstatements are combined as **total likely misstatement** in the financial statements and considered. At this point turn to Section D of the outline of AU-C 450 to review details on how these misstatements are considered.

3. **Engagement Quality Review.** PCAOB Auditing Standard No. 7 requires that an engagement quality reviewer perform a review of the audit and the related conclusions reached in forming the audit's overall conclusions and in preparing the audit report. In essence, this is a final review of the audit, performed by a competent reviewer who isn't a member of the audit team and who should maintain objectivity when performing the review. The audit report may only be issued after the engagement quality reviewer provides concurring approval of issuance.

   The quality review process is one in which the quality reviewer evaluates the significant judgments made by the engagement team throughout the audit. This includes considering significant ricks identified by the engagement team, reviewing the engagements team's evaluation of firm independence in relation to the engagement, reviewing the financial statements, and considering other areas of the audit. The engagement quality reviewer may provide concurring approval to issue the audit report only if he or she is not aware of a significant engagement deficiency. Documentation of an engagement quality review should contain sufficient information to enable an experienced auditor having no previous connection with the engagement to understand the procedures performed by the quality reviewer.

   The AICPA *Quality Control Standards* for nonpublic company engagements require that a CPA firm establish criteria to determine which of its engagements should undergo a quality control review. Thus, the audit of a nonpublic client that meets the firm's criteria will have a quality review prior to audit report issuance. In addition, and related, various laws require certain nonpublic companies to have quality control reviews. A result of this overall situation is that many, but not all, audits of nonpublic companies also undergo a quality control review.

E. Other Related Topics

Operational Auditing. Operational audits, generally performed by internal auditors, typically evaluate the effectiveness and efficiency of various operational processes. As such they are similar to "performance audits" as presented in the outline of *Government Auditing Standards*. In fact, the topic "operational auditing" was dropped from the AICPA Content Specification Outline when compliance auditing was added.

As an example of an operational audit, consider an auditor's examination of the sales, receivables, and cash receipts cycle to consider whether policies and procedures concerning the effectiveness and efficiency of related management decision-making processes. A financial statement audit, on the other hand, would deal more directly with controls relating to the entity's ability to record, process, summarize, and report financial data consistent with the assertions in the financial statements.

NOW REVIEW MULTIPLE-CHOICE QUESTIONS 164 THROUGH 169

KEY TERMS

Accounting estimate. An approximation of a monetary amount in the absence of a precise means of measurement. This term is used for an amount measured at fair value where there is estimation uncertainty, as well as for other amounts that require estimation. Where this section addresses only accounting estimates involving measurement at fair value, the term fair value accounting estimates is used.

Analytical procedures. Evaluations of financial information through analysis of plausible relationships among both financial and nonfinancial data. Analytical procedures also encompass such investigation, as is necessary, of identified fluctuations or relationships that are inconsistent with other relevant information or that differ from expected values by a significant amount.

Appropriateness (of audit evidence). The measure of the quality of audit evidence; that is, its relevance and its reliability in providing support for the conclusions on which the auditor's opinion is based.

Arm's length transaction. A transaction conducted on such terms and conditions between a willing buyer and a willing seller who are unrelated and are acting independently of each other and pursuing their own best interests.

Assertions. Representations by management, explicit or otherwise, that are embodied in the financial statements, as used by the auditor to consider the different types of potential misstatements that may occur.

Audit evidence. Information used by the auditor in arriving at the conclusions on which the auditor's opinion is based. Audit evidence includes both information contained in the accounting records underlying the financial statements and other information:

1. Sufficiency of audit evidence is the measure of the quantity of audit evidence. The quantity of the audit evidence needed is affected by the auditor's assessment of the risks of material misstatement and also by the quality of such audit evidence.
2. Appropriateness of audit evidence is the measure of the quality of audit evidence; that is, its relevance and its reliability in providing support for the conclusions on which the auditor's opinion is based.

Control risk. The risk that a misstatement that could occur in an assertion about a class of transaction, account balance, or disclosure and that could be material, either individually or when aggregated with other misstatements, will not be prevented, or detected and corrected, on a timely basis by the entity's internal control.

Detection risk. The risk that the procedures performed by the auditor to reduce audit risk to an acceptably low level will not detect a misstatement that exists and that could be material, either individually or when aggregated with other misstatements.

Exception (to external confirmation request). A response that indicates a difference between information requested to be confirmed, or contained in the entity's records, and information provided by the confirming party.

External confirmation. Audit evidence obtained as a direct written response to the auditor from a third party (the confirming party), either in paper form or by electronic or other medium (for example, through the auditor's direct access to information held by a third party).

1. The auditor's direct access to information held by the confirming party may meet the definition of an external confirmation when for example, the auditor is provided by the confirming party with the electronic access codes or information necessary to access a secure website where data that addresses the subject matter of the confirmation is held.
2. The auditor's access to information held by the confirming party may also be facilitated by a third party provider. Where access codes or information necessary to access data held by a third party is provided to the auditor by management (i.e., not by the confirming party), evidence obtained by the auditor from access to such information does not meet the definition of an external confirmation.

Fraud. An intentional act by one or more individuals among management, those charged with governance, employees, or third parties, involving the use of deception that results in a misstatement in financial statements that are the subject of an audit. For financial statement audits, fraud includes two types of intentional misstatements—misstatements arising from fraudulent financial reporting and misstatements arising from misappropriation of assets.

Fraud risk factors. Events or conditions that indicate an incentive or pressure to perpetrate fraud, provide an opportunity to commit fraud, or indicate attitudes or rationalizations to justify a fraudulent action.

Fraudulent financial reporting (management fraud, cooking the books). Material misstatement of financial statements by management with the intent to mislead financial statement users.

Further audit procedures. The additional procedures that are performed based on the results of the auditors' risk assessment procedures. Such procedures include (1) tests of controls (if needed), (2) Detailed tests of transactions, balances, and disclosures, and (3) substantive analytical procedures.

Internal auditing. An independent, objective assurance and consulting activity designed to add value and improve an organization's operations. It helps an organization accomplish its objective by bring a systematic, disciplined approach to evaluate and improve the effectiveness of risk management, control, and governance processes.

Negative confirmation request. A request that the confirming party respond directly to the auditor only if the confirming party disagrees with the information provided in the request.

Nonresponse. A failure of the confirming party to respond, or fully respond, to a positive confirmation request, or a confirmation request returned undelivered.

Omitted procedure. An auditing procedure that the auditor considered necessary in the circumstances existing at the date of the audit of financial statements, but which was not performed.

Positive confirmation request. A request that the confirming party respond directly to the auditor providing the requested information or indicating whether the confirming party agrees or disagrees with the information in the request.

Related-party transaction. A transaction in which one party has the ability to influence significantly the management or operating policies of the other party, to the extent that one of the transacting parties might be prevented from pursuing fully its own separate interests.

Risk assessment procedures. The audit procedures performed to obtain an understanding of the entity and its environment, including the entity's internal control, to identify and assess the risks of material misstatement, whether due to fraud or error, at the financial statement and assertion levels.

Relevant assertion. A financial statement assertion that has a reasonable possibility of containing a misstatement or misstatements that would cause the financial statements to be materially misstated. The determination of whether an assertion is a relevant assertion is made without regard to the effect of controls.

Risk of material misstatement. The risk that the financial statements are materially misstated prior to the audit. This consists of two components, inherent risk and control risk.

Scanning. A type of analytical procedure involving the auditor's use of professional judgment to review accounting data to identify significant or unusual items.

Specialist. An individual or organization possessing expertise in a field other than accounting or auditing, whose work in that field is used by the auditor to assist the auditor in obtaining sufficient appropriate audit evidence.

Subsequent events. Events occurring between the date of the financial statements and the date of the auditor's report that require adjustment of, or disclosure in, the financial statements.

Subsequently discovered facts. Facts that become known to the auditor after the date of the auditor's report that, had they been known to the auditor at that date, may have caused the auditor to amend the auditor's report.

Substantive procedure. An audit procedure designed to detect material misstatements at the assertion level. Substantive procedures comprise tests of details (classes of transactions, account balances, and disclosures) and substantive analytical procedures.

Sufficiency (of audit evidence). The measure of the quantity of audit evidence. The quantity of the audit evidence needed is affected by the auditor's assessment of the risks of material misstatement and also by the quality of such audit evidence.

Written representation. A written statement by management provided to the auditor to confirm certain matters or to support other audit evidence. Written reorientations, for purposes of his section, do not include financial statements, the assertions therein, or supporting books and records.

Multiple-Choice Questions (1–169)

A.1. Sufficient Appropriate Audit Evidence

1. Which of the following best describes what is meant by the term generally accepted auditing standards?

    a. Procedures to be used to gather evidence to support financial statements.
    b. Measures of the quality of the auditor's performance.
    c. Pronouncements issued by the Auditing Standards Board.
    d. Rules acknowledged by the accounting profession because of their universal application.

2. Which of the following is not an assertion relating to classes of transactions?

    a. Accuracy.
    b. Consistency.
    c. Cutoff.
    d. Occurrence.

3. Which of the following is a general principle relating to the reliability of audit evidence?

    a. Audit evidence obtained from indirect sources rather than directly is more reliable than evidence obtained directly by the auditor.
    b. Audit evidence provided by copies is more reliable than that provided by facsimiles.
    c. Audit evidence obtained from knowledgeable independent sources outside the client company is more reliable than audit evidence obtained from nonindependent sources.
    d. Audit evidence provided by original documents is more reliable than audit evidence generated through a system of effective controls.

4. Which of the following types of audit evidence is the most persuasive?

    a. Prenumbered client purchase order forms.
    b. Client work sheets supporting cost allocations.
    c. Bank statements obtained from the client.
    d. Client representation letter.

5. Which of the following presumptions is correct about the reliability of audit evidence?

    a. Information obtained indirectly from outside sources is the most reliable audit evidence.
    b. To be reliable, audit evidence should be convincing rather than persuasive.
    c. Reliability of audit evidence refers to the amount of corroborative evidence obtained.
    d. Effective internal control provides more assurance about the reliability of audit evidence.

6. Which of the following statements relating to the appropriateness of audit evidence is always true?

    a. Audit evidence gathered by an auditor from outside an enterprise is reliable.
    b. Accounting data developed under satisfactory conditions of internal control are more relevant than data developed under unsatisfactory internal control conditions.
    c. Oral representations made by management are **not** valid evidence.
    d. Evidence gathered by auditors must be both valid and relevant to be considered appropriate.

7. Which of the following types of audit evidence is the **least** persuasive?

    a. Prenumbered purchase order forms.
    b. Bank statements obtained from the client.
    c. Test counts of inventory performed by the auditor.
    d. Correspondence from the client's attorney about litigation.

8. In evaluating the reasonableness of an entity's accounting estimates, an auditor normally would be concerned about assumptions that are

    a. Susceptible to bias.
    b. Consistent with prior periods.
    c. Insensitive to variations.
    d. Similar to industry guidelines.

A.2. Types of Evidence

9. Which of the following is not a basic procedure used in an audit?

    a. Risk assessment procedures.
    b. Substantive procedures.
    c. Tests of controls.
    d. Tests of direct evidence.

10. Which of the following procedures would an auditor ordinarily perform first in evaluating management's accounting estimates for reasonableness?

    a. Develop independent expectations of management's estimates.
    b. Consider the appropriateness of the key factors or assumptions used in preparing the estimates.
    c. Test the calculations used by management in developing the estimates.
    d. Obtain an understanding of how management developed its estimates.

11. In evaluating the reasonableness of an accounting estimate, an auditor most likely would concentrate on key factors and assumptions that are

    a. Consistent with prior periods.
    b. Similar to industry guidelines.
    c. Objective and **not** susceptible to bias.
    d. Deviations from historical patterns.

12. In evaluating an entity's accounting estimates, one of an auditor's objectives is to determine whether the estimates are

    a. Not subject to bias.
    b. Consistent with industry guidelines.
    c. Based on objective assumptions.
    d. Reasonable in the circumstances.

13. In testing the existence assertion for an asset, an auditor ordinarily works from the

    a. Financial statements to the potentially unrecorded items.
    b. Potentially unrecorded items to the financial statements.
    c. Accounting records to the supporting evidence.
    d. Supporting evidence to the accounting records.

14. A client uses a suspense account for unresolved questions whose final accounting has not been determined. If a balance remains in the suspense account at year-end, the auditor would be most concerned about

    a. Suspense debits that management believes will benefit future operations.
    b. Suspense debits that the auditor verifies will have realizable value to the client.
    c. Suspense credits that management believes should be classified as "Current liability."
    d. Suspense credits that the auditor determines to be customer deposits.

B.1.a.   Analytical Procedures

15. Which of the following would **not** be considered an analytical procedure?

    a. Estimating payroll expense by multiplying the number of employees by the average hourly wage rate and the total hours worked.
    b. Projecting an error rate by comparing the results of a statistical sample with the actual population characteristics.
    c. Computing accounts receivable turnover by dividing credit sales by the average net receivables.
    d. Developing the expected current year sales based on the sales trend of the prior five years.

16. What type of analytical procedure would an auditor most likely use in developing relationships among balance sheet accounts when reviewing the financial statements of a nonpublic entity?

    a. Trend analysis.
    b. Regression analysis.
    c. Ratio analysis.
    d. Risk analysis.

17. An auditor may achieve audit objectives related to particular assertions by

    a. Performing analytical procedures.
    b. Adhering to a system of quality control.
    c. Preparing auditor working papers.
    d. Increasing the level of detection risk.

18. An entity's income statements were misstated due to the recording of journal entries that involved debits and credits to an unusual combination of expense and revenue accounts. The auditor most likely could have detected this fraudulent financial reporting by

    a. Tracing a sample of journal entries to the general ledger.
    b. Evaluating the effectiveness of internal control.
    c. Investigating the reconciliations between controlling accounts and subsidiary records.
    d. Performing analytical procedures designed to disclose differences from expectations.

19. Auditors try to identify predictable relationships when using analytical procedures. Relationships involving transactions from which of the following accounts most likely would yield the highest level of evidence?

    a. Accounts receivable.
    b. Interest expense.
    c. Accounts payable.
    d. Travel and entertainment expense.

20. Analytical procedures used in the overall review stage of an audit generally include

    a. Gathering evidence concerning account balances that have **not** changed from the prior year.
    b. Retesting control procedures that appeared to be ineffective during the assessment of control risk.
    c. Considering unusual or unexpected account balances that were **not** previously identified.
    d. Performing tests of transactions to corroborate management's financial statement assertions.

21. Which of the following tends to be most predictable for purposes of analytical procedures applied as substantive procedures?

    a. Relationships involving balance sheet accounts.
    b. Transactions subject to management discretion.
    c. Relationships involving income statement accounts.
    d. Data subject to audit testing in the prior year.

22. A basic premise underlying the application of analytical procedures is that

    a. The study of financial ratios is an acceptable alternative to the investigation of unusual fluctuations.
    b. Statistical tests of financial information may lead to the discovery of material misstatements in the financial statements.
    c. Plausible relationships among data may reasonably be expected to exist and continue in the absence of known conditions to the contrary.
    d. These procedures **cannot** replace tests of balances and transactions.

23. For all audits of financial statements made in accordance with generally accepted auditing standards, the use of analytical procedures is required to some extent

	In the risk assessment stage	As a substantive procedure	Near-audit completion
a.	Yes	No	Yes
b.	No	Yes	No
c.	No	Yes	Yes
d.	Yes	No	No

24. An auditor's analytical procedures most likely would be facilitated if the entity

    a. Segregates obsolete inventory before the physical inventory count.

    b. Uses a standard cost system that produces variance reports.

    c. Corrects material weaknesses in internal control before the beginning of the audit.

    d. Develops its data from sources solely within the entity.

25. Analytical procedures performed near the end of an audit suggest that several accounts have unexpected relationships. The results of these procedures most likely would indicate that

    a. Irregularities exist among the relevant account balances.

    b. Internal control activities are **not** operating effectively.

    c. Additional tests of details are required.

    d. The communication with the audit committee should be revised.

26. Which of the following comparisons would an auditor most likely make in evaluating an entity's costs and expenses?

    a. The current year's accounts receivable with the prior year's accounts receivable.

    b. The current year's payroll expense with the prior year's payroll expense.

    c. The budgeted current year's sales with the prior year's sales.

    d. The budgeted current year's warranty expense with the current year's contingent liabilities.

27. To be effective, analytical procedures performed near the end of an audit engagement should be performed by

    a. The staff accountant who performed the substantive auditing procedures.

    b. The managing partner who has responsibility for all audit engagements at that practice office.

    c. A manager or partner who has a comprehensive knowledge of the client's business and industry.

    d. The CPA firm's quality control manager or partner who has responsibility for the firm's peer review program.

B.1.b. Tests of Details of Transactions and Balances

28. Which of the following is the best example of a substantive procedure?

    a. Examining a sample of cash disbursements to test whether expenses have been properly approved.

    b. Confirmation of balances of accounts receivable.

    c. Comparison of signatures on checks to a list of authorized signers.

    d. Flowcharting of the client's cash receipts system.

29. The objective of tests of details of transactions performed as substantive procedures is to

    a. Comply with generally accepted auditing standards.

    b. Attain assurance about the reliability of the accounting system.

    c. Detect material misstatements in the financial statements.

    d. Evaluate whether management's policies and procedures operated effectively.

30. In the context of an audit of financial statements, substantive procedures are audit procedures that

    a. May be eliminated under certain conditions.

    b. Are designed to discover significant subsequent events.

    c. May be either tests of transactions, direct tests of financial balances, or analytical tests.

    d. Will increase proportionately with the auditor's reliance on internal control.

31. The auditor will most likely perform extensive tests for possible understatement of

    a. Revenues.

    b. Assets.

    c. Liabilities.

    d. Capital.

B.2. Preparing Substantive Procedure Audit Programs

32. Which of the following procedures would an auditor most likely perform in auditing the statement of cash flows?

    a. Compare the amounts included in the statement of cash flows to similar amounts in the prior year's statement of cash flows.

    b. Reconcile the cutoff bank statements to verify the accuracy of the year-end bank balances.

    c. Vouch all bank transfers for the last week of the year and first week of the subsequent year.

    d. Reconcile the amounts included in the statement of cash flows to the other financial statements' balances and amounts.

33. In determining whether transactions have been recorded, the direction of the audit testing should be from the

    a. General ledger balances.

    b. Adjusted trial balance.

    c. Original source documents.

    d. General journal entries.

B.3.   *Documentation*

34. Which statement is correct concerning the deletion of audit documentation?

   a. Superseded audit documentation should always be deleted from the audit file.

   b. After the audit file has been completed, the auditor should not delete or discard audit documentation.

   c. Auditors should use professional skepticism in determining which audit documentation should be deleted.

   d. Audit documentation should never be deleted from the audit file.

35. Ignoring any particular legal or regulatory requirement, audit documentation should be retained

   a. A minimum of five years.

   b. As long as lead schedules have relevance to forthcoming audits.

   c. Until 3 years after the client selects another auditor.

   d. Working papers must be maintained indefinitely.

36. Which of the following pairs of accounts would an auditor most likely analyze on the same working paper?

   a. Notes receivable and interest income.

   b. Accrued interest receivable and accrued interest payable.

   c. Notes payable and notes receivable.

   d. Interest income and interest expense.

37. An auditor's working papers serve mainly to

   a. Provide the principal support for the auditor's report.

   b. Satisfy the auditor's responsibilities concerning the Code of Professional Conduct.

   c. Monitor the effectiveness of the CPA firm's quality control procedures.

   d. Document the level of independence maintained by the auditor.

38. The permanent file of an auditor's working papers generally would **not** include

   a. Bond indenture agreements.

   b. Lease agreements.

   c. Working trial balance.

   d. Flowchart of internal control.

39. An auditor ordinarily uses a working trial balance resembling the financial statements without footnotes, but containing columns for

   a. Cash flow increases and decreases.

   b. Audit objectives and assertions.

   c. Reclassifications and adjustments.

   d. Reconciliations and tick marks.

40. Which of the following is least likely to be a factor in the auditor's decision about the extent of the documentation of a particular audit area?

   a. The risk of material misstatement.

   b. The extent of the judgment involved in performing the procedures.

   c. The nature and extent of exceptions identified.

   d. Whether or not the client has an internal audit function.

41. Which of the following is required documentation in an audit in accordance with generally accepted auditing standards?

   a. A flowchart or narrative of the accounting system describing the recording and classification of transactions for financial reporting.

   b. An audit program setting forth in detail the procedures necessary to accomplish the engagement's objectives.

   c. A planning memorandum establishing the timing of the audit procedures and coordinating the assistance of entity personnel.

   d. An internal control questionnaire identifying controls that assure specific objectives will be achieved.

42. Which of the following factors most likely would affect an auditor's judgment about the quantity, type, and content of the auditor's working papers?

   a. The assessed level of control risk.

   b. The likelihood of a review by a concurring (second) partner.

   c. The number of personnel assigned to the audit.

   d. The content of the management representation letter.

43. The audit working paper that reflects the major components of an amount reported in the financial statements is the

   a. Interbank transfer schedule.

   b. Carryforward schedule.

   c. Supporting schedule.

   d. Lead schedule.

44. Which of the following documentation is required for an audit in accordance with generally accepted auditing standards?

   a. A flowchart or an internal control questionnaire that evaluates the effectiveness of the entity's controls.

   b. A client engagement letter that summarizes the timing and details of the auditor's planned fieldwork.

   c. An indication in the working papers that the accounting records agree or reconcile with the financial statements.

   d. The basis for the auditor's conclusions when the assessed level of control risk is at the maximum level for all financial statement assertions.

45. No deletions of audit documentation are allowed after the

   a. Client's year-end.

   b. Documentation completion date.

   c. Last date of significant fieldwork.

   d. Report release date.

46. Under the requirements of the PCAOB, audit documentation must contain sufficient information to allow what type of auditor to understand the nature, timing, extent, and results of procedures performed?

   a. An experienced audit team member.

   b. An experienced auditor having no previous connection with the engagement.

   c. Any certified public accountant.

   d. An auditor qualified as a peer review specialist.

47. Audit documentation for audits performed under the requirements of the Public Company Accounting Oversight Board should be retained for

- a. The shorter of five years, or the period required by law.
- b. Seven years.
- c. The longer of seven years, or the period required by law.
- d. Indefinitely.

C.1. Evidence—Cash

48. Which of the following sets of information does an auditor usually confirm on one form?

- a. Accounts payable and purchase commitments.
- b. Cash in bank and collateral for loans.
- c. Inventory on consignment and contingent liabilities.
- d. Accounts receivable and accrued interest receivable.

49. The usefulness of the standard bank confirmation request may be limited because the bank employee who completes the form may

- a. Not believe that the bank is obligated to verify confidential information to a third party.
- b. Sign and return the form without inspecting the accuracy of the client's bank reconciliation.
- c. Not have access to the client's cutoff bank statement.
- d. Be unaware of all the financial relationships that the bank has with the client.

50. An auditor most likely would limit substantive audit tests of sales transactions when control risk is assessed as low for the occurrence assertion concerning sales transactions and the auditor has already gathered evidence supporting

- a. Opening and closing inventory balances.
- b. Cash receipts and accounts receivable.
- c. Shipping and receiving activities.
- d. Cutoffs of sales and purchases.

Items 51 and 52 are based on the following:

The information below was taken from the bank transfer schedule prepared during the audit of Fox Co.'s financial statements for the year ended December 31, 2005. Assume all checks are dated and issued on December 30, 20X5.

| | Bank accounts | | Disbursement date | | Receipt date | |
Check no.	From	To	Per books	Per bank	Per books	Per bank
101	National	Federal	Dec. 30	Jan. 4	Dec. 30	Jan. 3
202	County	State	Jan. 3	Jan. 2	Dec. 30	Dec. 31
303	Federal	American	Dec. 31	Jan. 3	Jan. 2	Jan. 2
404	State	Republic	Jan. 2	Jan. 2	Jan. 2	Dec. 31

51. Which of the following checks might indicate kiting?

- a. #101 and #303.
- b. #202 and #404.
- c. #101 and #404.
- d. #202 and #303.

52. Which of the following checks illustrate deposits/ transfers in transit at December 31, 20X5?

- a. #101 and #202.
- b. #101 and #303.
- c. #202 and #404.
- d. #303 and #404.

---

53. An auditor should trace bank transfers for the last part of the audit period and first part of the subsequent period to detect whether

- a. The cash receipts journal was held open for a few days after the year-end.
- b. The last checks recorded before the year-end were actually mailed by the year-end.
- c. Cash balances were overstated because of kiting.
- d. Any unusual payments to or receipts from related parties occurred.

54. To gather evidence regarding the balance per bank in a bank reconciliation, an auditor would examine all of the following **except**

- a. Cutoff bank statement.
- b. Year-end bank statement.
- c. Bank confirmation.
- d. General ledger.

55. Which of the following cash transfers results in a misstatement of cash at December 31, 2005?

| | Bank Transfer Schedule | | | |
| | Disbursement | | Receipt | |
Transfer	Recorded in books	Paid by bank	Recorded in books	Received by bank
a.	12/31/X5	1/4/X6	12/31/X5	12/31/X5
b.	1/4/X6	1/5/X6	12/31/X5	1/4/X6
c.	12/31/X5	1/5/X6	12/31/X5	1/4/X6
d.	1/4/X6	1/11/X6	1/4/X6	1/4/X6

56. A cash shortage may be concealed by transporting funds from one location to another or by converting negotiable assets to cash. Because of this, which of the following is vital?

- a. Simultaneous confirmations.
- b. Simultaneous bank reconciliations.
- c. Simultaneous verification.
- d. Simultaneous surprise cash count.

57. The primary purpose of sending a standard confirmation request to financial institutions with which the client has done business during the year is to

    a. Detect kiting activities that may otherwise **not** be discovered.
    b. Corroborate information regarding deposit and loan balances.
    c. Provide the data necessary to prepare a proof of cash.
    d. Request information about contingent liabilities and secured transactions.

58. An auditor observes the mailing of monthly statements to a client's customers and reviews evidence of follow-up on errors reported by the customers. This test of controls most likely is performed to support management's financial statement assertion(s) of

	Presentation and disclosure	Existence or occurrence
a.	Yes	Yes
b.	Yes	No
c.	No	Yes
d.	No	No

Items 59 and 60 are based on the following:

Miles Company
BANK TRANSFER SCHEDULE
December 31, 2005

Check no.	Bank accounts From	To	Amount	Date disbursed per Books	Bank	Date deposited per Books	Bank
2020	1st Natl.	Suburban	$32,000	12/31	1/5◆	12/31	1/3▲
2021	1st Natl.	Capital	21,000	12/31	1/4◆	12/31	1/3▲
3217	2nd State	Suburban	6,700	1/3	1/5	1/3	1/6
0659	Midtown	Suburban	5,500	12/30	1/5◆	12/30	1/3▲

59. The tick mark ◆ most likely indicates that the amount was traced to the

    a. December cash disbursements journal.
    b. Outstanding check list of the applicable bank reconciliation.
    c. January cash disbursements journal.
    d. Year-end bank confirmations.

60. The tick mark ▲ most likely indicates that the amount was traced to the

    a. Deposits in transit of the applicable bank reconciliation.
    b. December cash receipts journal.
    c. January cash receipts journal.
    d. Year-end bank confirmations.

C.2. Evidence—Receivables

61. Which of the following statements is correct concerning the use of negative confirmation requests?

    a. Unreturned negative confirmation requests rarely provide significant explicit evidence.
    b. Negative confirmation requests are effective when detection risk is low.
    c. Unreturned negative confirmation requests indicate that alternative procedures are necessary.
    d. Negative confirmation requests are effective when understatements of account balances are suspected.

62. When an auditor does **not** receive replies to positive requests for year-end accounts receivable confirmations, the auditor most likely would

    a. Inspect the allowance account to verify whether the accounts were subsequently written off.

    b. Increase the assessed level of detection risk for the valuation and completeness assertions.
    c. Ask the client to contact the customers to request that the confirmations be returned.
    d. Increase the assessed level of inherent risk for the revenue cycle.

63. In confirming a client's accounts receivable in prior years, an auditor found that there were many differences between the recorded account balances and the confirmation replies. These differences, which were not misstatements, required substantial time to resolve. In defining the sampling unit for the current year's audit, the auditor most likely would choose

    a. Individual overdue balances.
    b. Individual invoices.
    c. Small account balances.
    d. Large account balances.

64. Confirmation is most likely to be a relevant form of evidence with regard to assertions about accounts receivable when the auditor has concerns about the receivables'

    a. Valuation.
    b. Classification.
    c. Existence.
    d. Completeness.

65. An auditor should perform alternative procedures to substantiate the existence of accounts receivable when

    a. No reply to a positive confirmation request is received.
    b. No reply to a negative confirmation request is received.
    c. Collectibility of the receivables is in doubt.
    d. Pledging of the receivables is probable.

66. Which of the following procedures would an auditor most likely perform for year-end accounts receivable confirmations when the auditor did **not** receive replies to second requests?

    a. Review the cash receipts journal for the month prior to the year-end.
    b. Intensify the study of internal control concerning the revenue cycle.
    c. Increase the assessed level of detection risk for the existence assertion.
    d. Inspect the shipping records documenting the merchandise sold to the debtors.

67. In which of the following circumstances would the use of the negative form of accounts receivable confirmation most likely be justified?

    a. A substantial number of accounts may be in dispute and the accounts receivable balance arises from sales to a few major customers.
    b. A substantial number of accounts may be in dispute and the accounts receivable balance arises from sales to many customers with small balances.
    c. A small number of accounts may be in dispute and the accounts receivable balance arises from sales to a few major customers.
    d. A small number of accounts may be in dispute and the accounts receivable balance arises from sales to many customers with small balances.

68. To reduce the risks associated with accepting e-mail responses to requests for confirmation of accounts receivable, an auditor most likely would

    a. Request the senders to mail the original forms to the auditor.
    b. Examine subsequent cash receipts for the accounts in question.
    c. Consider the e-mail responses to the confirmations to be exceptions.
    d. Mail second requests to the e-mail respondents.

69. To reduce the risks associated with accepting fax responses to requests for confirmations of accounts receivable, an auditor most likely would

    a. Examine the shipping documents that provide evidence for the existence assertion.
    b. Verify the sources and contents of the faxes in telephone calls to the senders.
    c. Consider the faxes to be nonresponses and evaluate them as unadjusted differences.
    d. Inspect the faxes for forgeries or alterations and consider them to be acceptable if none are noted.

70. In auditing accounts receivable, the negative form of confirmation request most likely would be used when

    a. The total recorded amount of accounts receivable is immaterial to the financial statements taken as a whole.
    b. Response rates in prior years to properly designed positive confirmation requests were inadequate.
    c. Recipients are likely to return positive confirmation requests without verifying the accuracy of the information.
    d. The combined assessed level of inherent risk and control risk relative to accounts receivable is low.

71. Under which of the following circumstances would the use of the blank form of confirmations of accounts receivable most likely be preferable to positive confirmations?

    a. The recipients are likely to sign the confirmations without devoting proper attention to them.
    b. Subsequent cash receipts are unusually difficult to verify.
    c. Analytical procedures indicate that few exceptions are expected.
    d. The combined assessed level of inherent risk and control risk is low.

72. In confirming accounts receivable, an auditor decided to confirm customers' account balances rather than individual invoices. Which of the following most likely would be included with the client's confirmation letter?

    a. An auditor-prepared letter explaining that a nonresponse may cause an inference that the account balance is correct.
    b. A client-prepared letter reminding the customer that a nonresponse will cause a second request to be sent.
    c. An auditor-prepared letter requesting the customer to supply missing and incorrect information directly to the auditor.
    d. A client-prepared statement of account showing the details of the customer's account balance.

73. Which of the following statements would an auditor most likely add to the negative form of confirmations of accounts receivable to encourage timely consideration by the recipients?

    a. "This is **not** a request for payment; remittances should **not** be sent to our auditors in the enclosed envelope."
    b. "Report any differences on the enclosed statement directly to our auditors; **no** reply is necessary if this amount agrees with your records."
    c. "If you do **not** report any differences within fifteen days, it will be assumed that this statement is correct."
    d. "The following invoices have been selected for confirmation and represent amounts that are overdue."

74. Which of the following strategies most likely could improve the response rate of the confirmation of accounts receivable?

    a. Including a list of items or invoices that constitute the account balance.
    b. Restricting the selection of accounts to be confirmed to those customers with relatively large balances.
    c. Requesting customers to respond to the confirmation requests directly to the auditor by fax or e-mail.
    d. Notifying the recipients that second requests will be mailed if they fail to respond in a timely manner.

C.3. Evidence—Inventory

75. An auditor most likely would make inquiries of production and sales personnel concerning possible obsolete or slow-moving inventory to support management's financial statement assertion of

    a. Valuation.
    b. Rights.
    c. Existence.
    d. Presentation.

76. While observing a client's annual physical inventory, an auditor recorded test counts for several items and noticed that certain test counts were higher than the recorded quantities in the client's perpetual records. This situation could be the result of the client's failure to record

    a. Purchase discounts.
    b. Purchase returns.
    c. Sales.
    d. Sales returns.

77. To gain assurance that all inventory items in a client's inventory listing schedule are valid, an auditor most likely would trace

    a. Inventory tags noted during the auditor's observation to items listed in the inventory listing schedule.
    b. Inventory tags noted during the auditor's observation to items listed in receiving reports and vendors' invoices.
    c. Items listed in the inventory listing schedule to inventory tags and the auditor's recorded count sheets.
    d. Items listed in receiving reports and vendors' invoices to the inventory listing schedule.

78. To measure how effectively an entity employs its resources, an auditor calculates inventory turnover by dividing average inventory into

    a. Net sales.
    b. Cost of goods sold.
    c. Operating income.
    d. Gross sales.

79. Which of the following auditing procedures most likely would provide assurance about a manufacturing entity's inventory valuation?

    a. Testing the entity's computation of standard overhead rates.
    b. Obtaining confirmation of inventories pledged under loan agreements.
    c. Reviewing shipping and receiving cutoff procedures for inventories.
    d. Tracing test counts to the entity's inventory listing.

80. A client maintains perpetual inventory records in both quantities and dollars. If the assessed level of control risk is high, an auditor would probably

    a. Increase the extent of tests of controls of the inventory cycle.
    b. Request the client to schedule the physical inventory count at the end of the year.
    c. Insist that the client perform physical counts of inventory items several times during the year.
    d. Apply gross profit tests to ascertain the reasonableness of the physical counts.

81. An auditor concluded that no excessive costs for idle plant were charged to inventory. This conclusion most likely related to the auditor's objective to obtain evidence about the financial statement assertions regarding inventory, including presentation and disclosure and

    a. Valuation.
    b. Completeness.
    c. Existence.
    d. Rights.

82. An auditor selected items for test counts while observing a client's physical inventory. The auditor then traced the test counts to the client's inventory listing. This procedure most likely obtained evidence concerning management's assertion of

    a. Rights.
    b. Completeness.
    c. Existence.
    d. Valuation.

83. An auditor most likely would analyze inventory turnover rates to obtain evidence concerning management's assertions about

    a. Existence.
    b. Rights.
    c. Presentation.
    d. Valuation.

84. An auditor usually examines receiving reports to support entries in the

    a. Voucher register and sales returns journal.
    b. Sales journal and sales returns journal.
    c. Voucher register and sales journal.
    d. Check register and sales journal.

85. When auditing inventories, an auditor would **least** likely verify that

    a. The financial statement presentation of inventories is appropriate.
    b. Damaged goods and obsolete items have been properly accounted for.
    c. All inventory owned by the client is on hand at the time of the count.
    d. The client has used proper inventory pricing.

C.4. Evidence—Investment Securities

86. An auditor who physically examines securities should insist that a client representative be present in order to

    a. Detect fraudulent securities.
    b. Lend authority to the auditor's directives.
    c. Acknowledge the receipt of securities returned.
    d. Coordinate the return of securities to the proper locations.

87. In establishing the existence and ownership of a long-term investment in the form of publicly traded stock, an auditor should inspect the securities or

    a. Correspond with the investee company to verify the number of shares owned.
    b. Inspect the audited financial statements of the investee company.
    c. Confirm the number of shares owned that are held by an independent custodian.
    d. Determine that the investment is carried at the lower of cost or market.

88. When an auditor is unable to inspect and count a client's investment securities until after the balance sheet date, the bank where the securities are held in a safe-deposit box should be asked to

    a. Verify any differences between the contents of the box and the balances in the client's subsidiary ledger.
    b. Provide a list of securities added and removed from the box between the balance sheet date and the security-count date.
    c. Confirm that there has been **no** access to the box between the balance sheet date and the security-count date.
    d. Count the securities in the box so the auditor will have an independent direct verification.

89. In testing long-term investments, an auditor ordinarily would use analytical procedures to ascertain the reasonableness of the

    a. Completeness of recorded investment income.
    b. Classification between current and noncurrent portfolios.
    c. Valuation of marketable equity securities.
    d. Existence of unrealized gains or losses in the portfolio.

C.5. Evidence—Property, Plant, and Equipment

90. Analysis of which account is **least** likely to reveal evidence relating to recorded retirement of equipment?

    a. Accumulated depreciation.
    b. Insurance expense.
    c. Property, plant, and equipment.
    d. Purchase returns and allowances.

91. Which of the following explanations most likely would satisfy an auditor who questions management about significant debits to the accumulated depreciation accounts?

    a. The estimated remaining useful lives of plant assets were revised upward.

    b. Plant assets were retired during the year.
    c. The prior year's depreciation expense was erroneously understated.
    d. Overhead allocations were revised at year-end.

92. In testing for unrecorded retirements of equipment, an auditor most likely would

    a. Select items of equipment from the accounting records and then locate them during the plant tour.
    b. Compare depreciation journal entries with similar prior year entries in search of fully depreciated equipment.
    c. Inspect items of equipment observed during the plant tour and then trace them to the equipment subsidiary ledger.
    d. Scan the general journal for unusual equipment additions and excessive debits to repairs and maintenance expense.

93. An auditor analyzes repairs and maintenance accounts primarily to obtain evidence in support of the audit assertion that all

    a. Noncapitalizable expenditures for repairs and maintenance have been recorded in the proper period.
    b. Expenditures for property and equipment have been recorded in the proper period.
    c. Noncapitalizable expenditures for repairs and maintenance have been properly charged to expense.
    d. Expenditures for property and equipment have **not** been charged to expense.

94. The auditor is most likely to seek information from the plant manager with respect to the

    a. Adequacy of the provision for uncollectible accounts.
    b. Appropriateness of physical inventory observation procedures.
    c. Existence of obsolete machinery.
    d. Deferral of procurement of certain necessary insurance coverage.

95. Treetop Corporation acquired a building and arranged mortgage financing during the year. Verification of the related mortgage acquisition costs would be least likely to include an examination of the related

    a. Deed.
    b. Canceled checks.
    c. Closing statement.
    d. Interest expense.

96. In testing plant and equipment balances, an auditor may inspect new additions listed on the analysis of plant and equipment. This procedure is designed to obtain evidence concerning management's assertions of

	Existence or occurrence	Presentation and disclosure
a.	Yes	Yes
b.	Yes	No
c.	No	Yes
d.	No	No

C.6.   *Evidence—Prepaid Assets*

97. In auditing intangible assets, an auditor most likely would review or recompute amortization and determine whether the amortization period is reasonable in support of management's financial statement assertion of

    a. Valuation or allocation.
    b. Existence or occurrence.
    c. Completeness.
    d. Rights and obligations.

98. When auditing prepaid insurance, an auditor discovers that the original insurance policy on plant equipment is not available for inspection. The policy's absence most likely indicates the possibility of a(n)

    a. Insurance premium due but **not** recorded.
    b. Deficiency in the coinsurance provision.
    c. Lien on the plant equipment.
    d. Understatement of insurance expense.

C.7.   *Evidence—Payables (Current)*

99. Which of the following procedures would an auditor most likely perform in searching for unrecorded liabilities?

    a. Trace a sample of accounts payable entries recorded just before year-end to the unmatched receiving report file.
    b. Compare a sample of purchase orders issued just after year-end with the year-end accounts payable trial balance.
    c. Vouch a sample of cash disbursements recorded just after year-end to receiving reports and vendor invoices.
    d. Scan the cash disbursements entries recorded just before year-end for indications of unusual transactions.

100. When using confirmations to provide evidence about the completeness assertion for accounts payable, the appropriate population most likely would be

    a. Vendors with whom the entity has previously done business.
    b. Amounts recorded in the accounts payable subsidiary ledger.
    c. Payees of checks drawn in the month after the year-end.
    d. Invoices filed in the entity's open invoice file.

101. Auditor confirmation of accounts payable balances at the balance sheet date may be unnecessary because

    a. This is a duplication of cutoff tests.
    b. Accounts payable balances at the balance sheet date may not be paid before the audit is completed.
    c. Correspondence with the audit client's attorney will reveal all legal action by vendors for nonpayment.
    d. There is likely to be other reliable external evidence to support the balances.

102. Which of the following is a substantive procedure that an auditor most likely would perform to verify the existence and valuation of recorded accounts payable?

    a. Investigating the open purchase order file to ascertain that prenumbered purchase orders are used and accounted for.

    b. Receiving the client's mail, unopened, for a reasonable period of time after the year-end to search for unrecorded vendors' invoices.
    c. Vouching selected entries in the accounts payable subsidiary ledger to purchase orders and receiving reports.
    d. Confirming accounts payable balances with known suppliers who have zero balances.

103. In auditing accounts payable, an auditor's procedures most likely would focus primarily on management's assertion of

    a. Existence.
    b. Presentation and disclosure.
    c. Completeness.
    d. Valuation.

C.8.   *Evidence—Long-Term Debt*

104. When a CPA observes that the recorded interest expense seems to be excessive in relation to the balance in the bonds payable account, the CPA might suspect that

    a. Discount on bonds payable is understated.
    b. Bonds payable are understated.
    c. Bonds payable are overstated.
    d. Premium on bonds payable is overstated.

105. An auditor most likely would inspect loan agreements under which an entity's inventories are pledged to support management's financial statement assertion of

    a. Presentation and disclosure.
    b. Valuation or allocation.
    c. Existence or occurrence.
    d. Completeness.

106. In auditing long-term bonds payable, an auditor most likely would

    a. Perform analytical procedures on the bond premium and discount accounts.
    b. Examine documentation of assets purchased with bond proceeds for liens.
    c. Compare interest expense with the bond payable amount for reasonableness.
    d. Confirm the existence of individual bond holders at year-end.

107. The auditor can best verify a client's bond sinking fund transactions and year-end balance by

    a. Confirmation with individual holders of retired bonds.
    b. Confirmation with the bond trustee.
    c. Recomputation of interest expense, interest payable, and amortization of bond discount or premium.
    d. Examination and count of the bonds retired during the year.

C.9.   *Evidence—Owners' Equity*

108. An auditor usually obtains evidence of stockholders' equity transactions by reviewing the entity's

    a. Minutes of board of directors meetings.
    b. Transfer agent's records.

   c. Canceled stock certificates.
   d. Treasury stock certificate book.

109. When control risk is assessed as low for assertions related to payroll, substantive procedures of payroll balances most likely would be limited to applying analytical procedures and

   a. Observing the distribution of paychecks.
   b. Footing and crossfooting the payroll register.
   c. Inspecting payroll tax returns.
   d. Recalculating payroll accruals.

110. Which of the following circumstances most likely would cause an auditor to suspect an employee payroll fraud scheme?

   a. There are significant unexplained variances between standard and actual labor cost.
   b. Payroll checks are disbursed by the same employee each payday.
   c. Employee time cards are approved by individual departmental supervisors.
   d. A separate payroll bank account is maintained on an imprest basis.

111. In auditing payroll, an auditor most likely would

   a. Verify that checks representing unclaimed wages are mailed.
   b. Trace individual employee deductions to entity journal entries.
   c. Observe entity employees during a payroll distribution.
   d. Compare payroll costs with entity standards or budgets.

112. In performing tests concerning the granting of stock options, an auditor should

   a. Confirm the transaction with the Secretary of State in the state of incorporation.
   b. Verify the existence of option holders in the entity's payroll records or stock ledgers.
   c. Determine that sufficient treasury stock is available to cover any new stock issued.
   d. Trace the authorization for the transaction to a vote of the board of directors.

113. During an audit of an entity's stockholders' equity accounts, the auditor determines whether there are restrictions on retained earnings resulting from loans, agreements, or state law. This audit procedure most likely is intended to verify management's assertion of

   a. Existence or occurrence.
   b. Completeness.
   c. Valuation or allocation.
   d. Presentation and disclosure.

114. When a client company does **not** maintain its own stock records, the auditor should obtain written confirmation from the transfer agent and registrar concerning

   a. Restrictions on the payment of dividends.
   b. The number of shares issued and outstanding.
   c. Guarantees of preferred stock liquidation value.
   d. The number of shares subject to agreements to repurchase.

115. An audit program for the examination of the retained earnings account should include a step that requires verification of the

   a. Market value used to charge retained earnings to account for a two-for-one stock split.
   b. Approval of the adjustment to the beginning balance as a result of a write-down of an account receivable.
   c. Authorization for both cash and stock dividends.
   d. Gain or loss resulting from disposition of treasury shares.

116. An auditor most likely would perform substantive procedures of details on payroll transactions and balances when

   a. Cutoff tests indicate a substantial amount of accrued payroll expense.
   b. The assessed level of control risk relative to payroll transactions is low.
   c. Analytical procedures indicate unusual fluctuations in recurring payroll entries.
   d. Accrued payroll expense consists primarily of unpaid commissions.

117. An auditor usually tests the reasonableness of dividend income from investments in publicly held companies by computing the amounts that should have been received by referring to

   a. Dividend record books produced by investment advisory services.
   b. Stock indentures published by corporate transfer agents.
   c. Stock ledgers maintained by independent registrars.
   d. Annual audited financial statements issued by the investee companies.

C.10. Revenue

118. The most likely risk involved with a bill and hold transaction at year-end is a(n)

   a. Accrued liability may be overstated as of year-end.
   b. Buyer may have made an absolute purchase commitment.
   c. Sale may inappropriately have been recorded as of year-end.
   d. Buyer may have assumed the risk and reward of the purchased product.

119. Which of the following accounts is the practice of "channel stuffing" for sales most likely to most directly affect, and thereby result in additional audit procedures?

   a. Accrued liabilities.
   b. Allowance for sales returns.
   c. Cash.
   d. Marketable investments.

C.11. Expenses

120. Recorded entries in which of the following accounts are most likely to relate to the property, plant, and equipment completeness assertion?

   a. Allowance for doubtful accounts.
   b. Marketable securities.

c. Sales.

d. Repairs and maintenance expense.

C.12. Client Representation Letters

121. For which of the following matters should an auditor obtain written management representations?

a. Management's cost-benefit justifications for **not** correcting internal control weaknesses.

b. Management's knowledge of future plans that may affect the price of the entity's stock.

c. Management's compliance with contractual agreements that may affect the financial statements.

d. Management's acknowledgment of its responsibility for employees' violations of laws.

122. To which of the following matters would materiality limits **not** apply in obtaining written management representations?

a. The availability of minutes of stockholders' and directors' meetings.

b. Losses from purchase commitments at prices in excess of market value.

c. The disclosure of compensating balance arrangements involving related parties.

d. Reductions of obsolete inventory to net realizable value.

123. The date of the management representation letter should coincide with the date of the

a. Balance sheet.

b. Latest interim financial information.

c. Auditor's report.

d. Latest related-party transaction.

124. Which of the following matters would an auditor most likely include in a management representation letter?

a. Communications with the audit committee concerning weaknesses in internal control.

b. The completeness and availability of minutes of stockholders' and directors' meetings.

c. Plans to acquire or merge with other entities in the subsequent year.

d. Management's acknowledgment of its responsibility for the detection of employee fraud.

125. The current chief executive and financial officers have only been employed by ABC Company for the past five months of year 2. ABC Company is presenting comparative financial statements on Years 1 and 2, both of which were audited by William Jones, CPA. For which year(s) should Jones obtain written representations from these two individuals?

	Year 1	Year 2
a.	No	No
b.	No	Yes
c.	Yes	No
d.	Yes	Yes

126. Which of the following statements ordinarily is included among the written client representations obtained by the auditor?

a. Compensating balances and other arrangements involving restrictions on cash balances have been disclosed.

b. Management acknowledges responsibility for illegal actions committed by employees.

c. Sufficient audit evidence has been made available to permit the issuance of an unqualified opinion.

d. Management acknowledges that there are **no** material weaknesses in the internal control.

127. When considering the use of management's written representations as audit evidence about the completeness assertion, an auditor should understand that such representations

a. Complement, but do **not** replace, substantive procedures designed to support the assertion.

b. Constitute sufficient evidence to support the assertion when considered in combination with reliance on internal control.

c. Are **not** part of the audit evidence considered to support the assertion.

d. Replace reliance on internal control as evidence to support the assertion.

128. A written representation from a client's management which, among other matters, acknowledges responsibility for the fair presentation of financial statements, should normally be signed by the

a. Chief executive officer and the chief financial officer.

b. Chief financial officer and the chairman of the board of directors.

c. Chairman of the audit committee of the board of directors.

d. Chief executive officer, the chairman of the board of directors, and the client's lawyer.

129. A limitation on the scope of the auditor's examination sufficient to preclude an unqualified opinion will always result when management

a. Prevents the auditor from reviewing the working papers of the predecessor auditor.

b. Engages the auditor after the year-end physical inventory count is completed.

c. Fails to correct a significant deficiency of internal control that had been identified during the prior year's audit.

d. Refuses to furnish a management representation letter to the auditor.

130. A purpose of a management representation letter is to reduce

a. Audit risk to an aggregate level of misstatement that could be considered material.

b. An auditor's responsibility to detect material misstatements only to the extent that the letter is relied on.

c. The possibility of a misunderstanding concerning management's responsibility for the financial statements.

d. The scope of an auditor's procedures concerning related-party transactions and subsequent events.

131. "There have been no communications from regulatory agencies concerning noncompliance with, or deficiencies in, financial reporting practices that could have a material effect on the financial statements." The foregoing passage is most likely from a

- a. Report on internal control.
- b. Special report.
- c. Management representation letter.
- d. Letter for underwriters.

C.13. Using the Work of a Specialist

132. Which of the following statements is correct concerning an auditor's use of the work of a specialist?

- a. The work of a specialist who is related to the client may be acceptable under certain circumstances.
- b. If an auditor believes that the determinations made by a specialist are unreasonable, only a qualified opinion may be issued.
- c. If there is a material difference between a specialist's findings and the assertions in the financial statements, only an adverse opinion may be issued.
- d. An auditor may **not** use a specialist in the determination of physical characteristics relating to inventories.

133. In using the work of a specialist, an auditor may refer to the specialist in the auditor's report if, as a result of the specialist's findings, the auditor

- a. Becomes aware of conditions causing substantial doubt about the entity's ability to continue as a going concern.
- b. Desires to disclose the specialist's findings, which imply that a more thorough audit was performed.
- c. Is able to corroborate another specialist's earlier findings that were consistent with management's representations.
- d. Discovers significant deficiencies in the design of the entity's internal control that management does **not** correct.

134. Which of the following statements is correct about the auditor's use of the work of a specialist?

- a. The specialist should **not** have an understanding of the auditor's corroborative use of the specialist's findings.
- b. The auditor is required to perform substantive procedures to verify the specialist's assumptions and findings.
- c. The client should **not** have an understanding of the nature of the work to be performed by the specialist.
- d. The auditor should obtain an understanding of the methods and assumptions used by the specialist.

135. In using the work of a specialist, an auditor referred to the specialist's findings in the auditor's report. This would be an appropriate reporting practice if the

- a. Client is **not** familiar with the professional certification, personal reputation, or particular competence of the specialist.
- b. Auditor, as a result of the specialist's findings, adds an explanatory paragraph emphasizing a matter regarding the financial statements.

- c. Client understands the auditor's corroborative use of the specialist's findings in relation to the representations in the financial statements.
- d. Auditor, as a result of the specialist's findings, decides to indicate a division of responsibility with the specialist.

136. In using the work of a specialist, an understanding should exist among the auditor, the client, and the specialist as to the nature of the specialist's work. The documentation of this understanding should cover

- a. A statement that the specialist assumes **no** responsibility to update the specialist's report for future events or circumstances.
- b. The conditions under which a division of responsibility may be necessary.
- c. The specialist's understanding of the auditor's corroborative use of the specialist's findings.
- d. The auditor's disclaimer as to whether the specialist's findings corroborate the representations in the financial statements.

137. Which of the following is **not** a specialist upon whose work an auditor may rely?

- a. Actuary.
- b. Appraiser.
- c. Internal auditor.
- d. Engineer.

C.14. Inquiry of a Client's Lawyer

138. A lawyer's response to an auditor's inquiry concerning litigation, claims, and assessments may be limited to matters that are considered individually or collectively material to the client's financial statements. Which parties should reach an understanding on the limits of materiality for this purpose?

- a. The auditor and the client's management.
- b. The client's audit committee and the lawyer.
- c. The client's management and the lawyer.
- d. The lawyer and the auditor.

139. The refusal of a client's attorney to provide information requested in an inquiry letter generally is considered

- a. Grounds for an adverse opinion.
- b. A limitation on the scope of the audit.
- c. Reason to withdraw from the engagement.
- d. Equivalent to a significant deficiency.

140. Which of the following is an audit procedure that an auditor most likely would perform concerning litigation, claims, and assessments?

- a. Request the client's lawyer to evaluate whether the client's pending litigation, claims, and assessments indicate a going concern problem.
- b. Examine the legal documents in the client's lawyer's possession concerning litigation, claims, and assessments to which the lawyer has devoted substantive attention.

c. Discuss with management its policies and procedures adopted for evaluating and accounting for litigation, claims, and assessments.

d. Confirm directly with the client's lawyer that all litigation, claims, and assessments have been recorded or disclosed in the financial statements.

141. The primary reason an auditor requests letters of inquiry be sent to a client's attorneys is to provide the auditor with

a. The probable outcome of asserted claims and pending or threatened litigation.

b. Corroboration of the information furnished by management about litigation, claims, and assessments.

c. The attorneys' opinions of the client's historical experiences in recent similar litigation.

d. A description and evaluation of litigation, claims, and assessments that existed at the balance sheet date.

142. Which of the following is **not** an audit procedure that the independent auditor would perform concerning litigation, claims, and assessments?

a. Obtain assurance from management that it has disclosed all unasserted claims that the lawyer has advised are probable of assertion and must be disclosed.

b. Confirm directly with the client's lawyer that all claims have been recorded in the financial statements.

c. Inquire of and discuss with management the policies and procedures adopted for identifying, evaluating, and accounting for litigation, claims, and assessments.

d. Obtain from management a description and evaluation of litigation, claims, and assessments existing at the balance sheet date.

143. The scope of an audit is **not** restricted when an attorney's response to an auditor as a result of a client's letter of audit inquiry limits the response to

a. Matters to which the attorney has given substantive attention in the form of legal representation.

b. An evaluation of the likelihood of an unfavorable outcome of the matters disclosed by the entity.

c. The attorney's opinion of the entity's historical experience in recent similar litigation.

d. The probable outcome of asserted claims and pending or threatened litigation.

144. A CPA has received an attorney's letter in which no significant disagreements with the client's assessments of contingent liabilities were noted. The resignation of the client's lawyer shortly after receipt of the letter should alert the auditor that

a. Undisclosed unasserted claims may have arisen.

b. The attorney was unable to form a conclusion with respect to the significance of litigation, claims, and assessments.

c. The auditor must begin a completely new examination of contingent liabilities.

d. An adverse opinion will be necessary.

145. Which of the following statements extracted from a client's lawyer's letter concerning litigation, claims, and assessments most likely would cause the auditor to request clarification?

a. "I believe that the possible liability to the company is nominal in amount."

b. "I believe that the action can be settled for less than the damages claimed."

c. "I believe that the plaintiff's case against the company is without merit."

d. "I believe that the company will be able to defend this action successfully."

C.15.   *Fair Values*

146. When auditing the fair value of an asset or liability, valuation issues ordinarily arise at the point of

	Initial recording	Subsequent to initial recording
a.	Yes	Yes
b.	Yes	No
c.	No	Yes
d.	No	No

147. Which of the following is **least** likely to be an approach followed when auditing the fair values of assets and liabilities?

a. Review and test management's process of valuation.

b. Confirm valuations with audit committee members.

c. Independently develop an estimate of the value of the account.

d. Review subsequent events relating to the account.

C.16.   *Related-Party Transactions*

148. Which of the following auditing procedures most likely would assist an auditor in identifying related-party transactions?

a. Inspecting correspondence with lawyers for evidence of unreported contingent liabilities.

b. Vouching accounting records for recurring transactions recorded just after the balance sheet date.

c. Reviewing confirmations of loans receivable and payable for indications of guarantees.

d. Performing analytical procedures for indications of possible financial difficulties.

149. After determining that a related-party transaction has, in fact, occurred, an auditor should

a. Add a separate paragraph to the auditor's standard report to explain the transaction.

b. Perform analytical procedures to verify whether similar transactions occurred, but were **not** recorded.

c. Obtain an understanding of the business purpose of the transaction.

d. Substantiate that the transaction was consummated on terms equivalent to an arm's-length transaction.

150. When auditing related-party transactions, an auditor places primary emphasis on

    a. Ascertaining the rights and obligations of the related parties.

    b. Confirming the existence of the related parties.

    c. Verifying the valuation of the related-party transactions.

    d. Evaluating the disclosure of the related-party transactions.

151. Which of the following statements is correct concerning related-party transactions?

    a. In the absence of evidence to the contrary, related-party transactions should be assumed to be outside the ordinary course of business.

    b. An auditor should determine whether a particular transaction would have occurred if the parties had **not** been related.

    c. An auditor should substantiate that related-party transactions were consummated on terms equivalent to those that prevail in arm's-length transactions.

    d. The audit procedures directed toward identifying related-party transactions should include considering whether transactions are occurring, but are **not** being given proper accounting recognition.

152. An auditor most likely would modify an unqualified opinion if the entity's financial statements include a footnote on related-party transactions

    a. Disclosing loans to related parties at interest rates significantly below prevailing market rates.

    b. Describing an exchange of real estate for similar property in a nonmonetary related-party transaction.

    c. Stating that a particular related-party transaction occurred on terms equivalent to those that would have prevailed in an arm's-length transaction.

    d. Presenting the dollar volume of related-party transactions and the effects of any change in the method of establishing terms from prior periods.

C.17. Subsequent Events

153. Which of the following procedures would an auditor most likely perform in obtaining evidence about subsequent events?

    a. Determine that changes in employee pay rates after year-end were properly authorized.

    b. Recompute depreciation charges for plant assets sold after year-end.

    c. Inquire about payroll checks that were recorded before year-end but cashed after year-end.

    d. Investigate changes in long-term debt occurring after year-end.

154. Which of the following events occurring after the issuance of an auditor's report most likely would cause the auditor to make further inquiries about the previously issued financial statements?

    a. An uninsured natural disaster occurs that may affect the entity's ability to continue as a going concern.

    b. A contingency is resolved that had been disclosed in the audited financial statements.

    c. New information is discovered concerning undisclosed lease transactions of the audited period.

    d. A subsidiary is sold that accounts for 25% of the entity's consolidated net income.

155. Zero Corp. suffered a loss that would have a material effect on its financial statements on an uncollectible trade account receivable due to a customer's bankruptcy. This occurred suddenly due to a natural disaster ten days after Zero's balance sheet date, but one month before the issuance of the financial statements and the auditor's report. Under these circumstances,

	The financial statements should be adjusted	The event requires financial statement disclosure, but no adjustment	The auditor's report should be modified for a lack of consistency
a.	Yes	No	No
b.	Yes	No	Yes
c.	No	Yes	Yes
d.	No	Yes	No

156. After an audit report containing an unqualified opinion on a nonissuer (nonpublic) client's financial statements was issued, the client decided to sell the shares of a subsidiary that accounts for 30% of its revenue and 25% of its net income. The auditor should

    a. Determine whether the information is reliable and, if determined to be reliable, request that revised financial statements be issued.

    b. Notify the entity that the auditor's report may **no** longer be associated with the financial statements.

    c. Describe the effects of this subsequently discovered information in a communication with persons known to be relying on the financial statements.

    d. Take **no** action because the auditor has **no** obligation to make any further inquiries.

157. A client acquired 25% of its outstanding capital stock after year-end and prior to completion of the auditor's fieldwork. The auditor should

    a. Advise management to adjust the balance sheet to reflect the acquisition.

    b. Issue pro forma financial statements giving effect to the acquisition as if it had occurred at year-end.

    c. Advise management to disclose the acquisition in the notes to the financial statements.

    d. Disclose the acquisition in the opinion paragraph of the auditor's report.

158. Which of the following procedures would an auditor most likely perform to obtain evidence about the occurrence of subsequent events?

    a. Confirming a sample of material accounts receivable established after year-end.

    b. Comparing the financial statements being reported on with those of the prior period.

    c. Investigating personnel changes in the accounting department occurring after year-end.

    d. Inquiring as to whether any unusual adjustments were made after year-end.

159. Which of the following procedures should an auditor generally perform regarding subsequent events?

    a. Compare the latest available interim financial statements with the financial statements being audited.

    b. Send second requests to the client's customers who failed to respond to initial accounts receivable confirmation requests.

    c. Communicate material weaknesses in internal control to the client's audit committee.

    d. Review the cutoff bank statements for several months after the year-end.

C.18. Omitted Procedures Discovered after the Report Date

160. On February 25, a CPA issued an auditor's report expressing an unqualified opinion on financial statements for the year ended January 31. On March 2, the CPA learned that on February 11, the entity incurred a material loss on an uncollectible trade receivable as a result of the deteriorating financial condition of the entity's principal customer that led to the customer's bankruptcy. Management then refused to adjust the financial statements for this subsequent event. The CPA determined that the information is reliable and that there are creditors currently relying on the financial statements. The CPA's next course of action most likely would be to

    a. Notify the entity's creditors that the financial statements and the related auditor's report should **no** longer be relied on.

    b. Notify each member of the entity's board of directors about management's refusal to adjust the financial statements.

    c. Issue revised financial statements and distribute them to each creditor known to be relying on the financial statements.

    d. Issue a revised auditor's report and distribute it to each creditor known to be relying on the financial statements.

161. An auditor is considering whether the omission of a substantive procedure considered necessary at the time of an audit may impair the auditor's present ability to support the previously expressed opinion. The auditor need **not** apply the omitted procedure if the

    a. Financial statements and auditor's report were not distributed beyond management and the board of directors.

    b. Auditor's previously expressed opinion was qualified because of a departure from GAAP.

    c. Results of other procedures that were applied tend to compensate for the procedure omitted.

    d. Omission is due to unreasonable delays by client personnel in providing data on a timely basis.

162. On March 15, 20X2, Kent, CPA, issued an unqualified opinion on a client's audited financial statements for the year ended December 31, 20X1. On May 4, 20X2, Kent's internal inspection program disclosed that engagement personnel failed to observe the client's physical inventory. Omission of this procedure impairs Kent's present ability to support the unqualified opinion. If the stockholders are currently relying on the opinion, Kent should first

    a. Advise management to disclose to the stockholders that Kent's unqualified opinion should **not** be relied on.

    b. Undertake to apply alternative procedures that would provide a satisfactory basis for the unqualified opinion.

    c. Reissue the auditor's report and add an explanatory paragraph describing the departure from generally accepted auditing standards.

    d. Compensate for the omitted procedure by performing tests of controls to reduce audit risk to a sufficiently low level.

163. Six months after issuing an unqualified opinion on audited financial statements, an auditor discovered that the engagement personnel failed to confirm several of the client's material accounts receivable balances. The auditor should first

    a. Request the permission of the client to undertake the confirmation of accounts receivable.

    b. Perform alternative procedures to provide a satisfactory basis for the unqualified opinion.

    c. Assess the importance of the omitted procedures to the auditor's ability to support the previously expressed opinion.

    d. Inquire whether there are persons currently relying, or likely to rely, on the unqualified opinion.

D. Completing the Audit

164. Which of the following procedures is **least** likely to be performed before the balance sheet date?

    a. Testing of internal control over cash.

    b. Confirmation of receivables.

    c. Search for unrecorded liabilities.

    d. Observation of inventory.

165. Which of the following most likely would be detected by an auditor's review of a client's sales cutoff?

    a. Shipments lacking sales invoices and shipping documents.

    b. Excessive write-offs of accounts receivable.

    c. Unrecorded sales at year-end.

    d. Lapping of year-end accounts receivable.

166. Cutoff tests designed to detect credit sales made before the end of the year that have been recorded in the subsequent year provide assurance about management's assertion of

    a. Presentation.

    b. Completeness.

    c. Rights.

    d. Existence.

D.1. Procedures Completed near the End of the Audit

167. Which of the following procedures would an auditor most likely perform during an audit engagement's overall review stage in formulating an opinion on an entity's financial statements?

a. Obtain assurance from the entity's attorney that all material litigation has been disclosed in the financial statements.
b. Verify the clerical accuracy of the entity's proof of cash and its bank cutoff statement.
c. Determine whether inadequate provisions for the safeguarding of assets have been corrected.
d. Consider whether the results of audit procedures affect the assessment of the risk of material misstatement due to fraud.

E. Other Related Topics

168. Operational auditing is primarily oriented toward

a. Future improvements to accomplish the goals of management.
b. The accuracy of data reflected in management's financial records.
c. The verification that a company's financial statements are fairly presented.
d. Past protection provided by existing internal control.

169. A typical objective of an operational audit is to determine whether an entity's

a. Internal control is adequately operating as designed.
b. Operational information is in accordance with generally accepted governmental auditing standards.
c. Financial statements present fairly the results of operations.
d. Specific operating units are functioning efficiently and effectively.

Multiple-Choice Answers and Explanations

Answers

1. b	31. c	61. a	91. b	121. c	151. d
2. b	32. d	62. c	92. a	122. a	152. c
3. c	33. c	63. b	93. d	123. c	153. d
4. c	34. b	64. c	94. c	124. b	154. c
5. d	35. a	65. a	95. a	125. d	155. d
6. d	36. a	66. d	96. b	126. a	156. d
7. a	37. a	67. d	97. a	127. a	157. c
8. a	38. c	68. a	98. c	128. a	158. d
9. d	39. c	69. b	99. c	129. d	159. a
10. d	40. d	70. d	100. a	130. c	160. b
11. d	41. b	71. a	101. d	131. c	161. c
12. d	42. a	72. d	102. c	132. a	162. b
13. c	43. d	73. c	103. c	133. a	163. c
14. a	44. c	74. a	104. b	134. d	164. c
15. b	45. b	75. a	105. a	135. b	165. c
16. c	46. b	76. d	106. c	136. c	166. b
17. a	47. c	77. c	107. b	137. c	167. d
18. d	48. b	78. b	108. a	138. d	168. a
19. b	49. d	79. a	109. d	139. b	169. d
20. c	50. b	80. b	110. a	140. c	
21. c	51. b	81. a	111. d	141. b	
22. c	52. b	82. b	112. d	142. b	
23. a	53. c	83. d	113. d	143. a	
24. b	54. d	84. a	114. b	144. a	
25. c	55. b	85. c	115. c	145. b	
26. b	56. c	86. c	116. c	146. a	
27. c	57. b	87. c	117. a	147. b	
28. b	58. c	88. c	118. c	148. c	
29. c	59. b	89. a	119. b	149. c	1st: __/169 = __%
30. c	60. a	90. d	120. d	150. d	2nd: __/169 = __%

Explanations

1. (b) The requirement is to identify the statement that best describes the meaning of generally accepted auditing standards. Answer (b) is correct because generally accepted auditing standards deal with measures of the quality of the performance of audit procedures. Answer (a) is incorrect because procedures relate to acts to be performed, not directly to the standards. Answer (c) is incorrect because generally accepted auditing standards have been issued by predecessor groups, as well as by the Auditing Standards Board. Answer (d) is incorrect because there may or may not be **universal** compliance with the standards.

2. (b) The requirement is to identify the reply that is **not** an assertion for classes of transactions. The assertions for classes of transactions are occurrence, completeness, accuracy, cutoff and classification. Answer (b) is correct since consistency is not an assertion for classes of transactions. Answer (a), (c), and (d) are all incorrect because accuracy, cutoff and occurrence are class of transaction assertions.

3. (c) The requirement is to identify the type of evidence that is generally most reliable. Answer (c) is correct because audit evidence obtained from knowledgeable independent sources outside the client company is more reliable than audit evidence obtained from nonindependent sources (e.g., company sources who may be biased). Answer (a) is incorrect because audit evidence obtained from direct sources is more reliable. Answer (b) is incorrect because it is not clear as to whether copies or facsimile copies are more reliable. Answer (d) is incorrect because it is unclear whether audit evidence provided by original documents is more reliable than that provided through a system of effective controls—indeed, they may be one and the same.

4. (c) The requirement is to identify the most persuasive type of evidence. Answer (c) is correct because a bank statement represents evidence prepared outside of the entity and is considered an audit evidence source which provides the auditor with a high level of assurance. Answers (a), (b), and (d) are incorrect because prenumbered client purchase order forms, client work sheets and a representation letter all represent internally generated documents, generally considered less persuasive than externally generated documents.

5. (d) The requirement is to identify a correct presumption about the reliability of audit evidence. Answer (d) is correct because AU-C 500 indicates that effective internal control provides more assurance about the reliability of audit evidence than ineffective control. Answer (a) is incorrect because information obtained directly is considered more reliable than that obtained indirectly. Answer (b) is incorrect because audit evidence is normally persuasive rather than convincing. Answer (c) is incorrect because reliability of audit evidence relates to the appropriateness of audit evidence.

6. (d) The requirement is to determine the correct statement with respect to the appropriateness of audit evidence. To be appropriate, evidence must be both reliable and relevant. Answer (a) is incorrect because while externally generated evidence is generally considered to provide greater assurance of reliability, there are important exceptions, (e.g., the confirmation is erroneously returned with no exception when one actually exists). Answer (b) is incorrect because while evidence so gathered is typically considered to provide greater assurance concerning reliability, no similar generalization can be made about its relevance. Answer (c) is incorrect because oral representations from management, when corroborated by other forms of evidence, are considered valid evidence.

7. (a) The requirement is to identify the **least** persuasive type of evidence. Answer (a) is correct because evidence secured solely from within the entity, here prenumbered purchase order forms, is considered less persuasive than evidence obtained from independent sources. Answer (b) is incorrect because a bank statement (even though received from the client) is externally created and therefore more persuasive than audit evidence secured solely from within the entity. Answer (c) is incorrect because evidence obtained directly by the auditor through observation is considered relatively persuasive. Answer (d) is incorrect because correspondence from the client's attorney about litigation is obtained directly from independent sources and is therefore more persuasive than audit evidence secured from within the entity.

8. (a) The requirement is to identify an area of concern to auditors when evaluating the reasonableness of an entity's accounting estimates. Answer (a) is correct because AU-C 500 states that in evaluating the reasonableness of estimates auditors normally concentrate on assumptions that are subjective and susceptible to bias. Answer (b) is incorrect because all things being equal, an auditor would expect assumptions that are consistent with prior periods. Answer (c) is incorrect because assumptions that are insensitive to variations in underlying data have little predictive ability. Answer (d) is incorrect because, often, one would expect assumptions similar to industry guidelines.

9. (d) The requirement is to identify the reply that is not a basic procedure used in an audit. Answer (d) is correct because the term "test of direct evidence" is not used in the professional standards. Answer (a) is incorrect because risk assessment procedures are used while obtaining an understanding of the client. Answer (b) is incorrect because

substantive procedures test account balances. Answer (c) is incorrect because tests of controls test the operating effectiveness of controls.

10. (d) The requirement is to identify the procedure an auditor would perform first in evaluating management's accounting estimates for reasonableness. Answer (d) is correct because in evaluating reasonableness, the auditor should first obtain an understanding of how management developed the estimate. Answers (a), (b), and (c) are all incorrect because developing independent expectations, considering appropriateness of key factors or assumptions, and testing calculations occur after obtaining the understanding. See AU-C 500 for information on auditing accounting estimates.

11. (d) The requirement is to identify a factor that an auditor would concentrate upon when evaluating the reasonableness of an accounting estimate. Answer (d) is correct because AU-C 500 states that the auditor normally concentrates on key factors and assumptions that are deviations from historical patterns, as well as those that are significant to the accounting estimate, sensitive to variations, and subjective and susceptible to misstatement and bias. Answer (a) is incorrect because deviations from historical patterns, not consistent patterns, are concentrated upon. Answer (b) is incorrect because factors and assumptions that are similar to industry guidelines are often reasonable. Answer (c) is incorrect because subjective factors and assumptions that are susceptible to bias are concentrated upon, not objective ones that are **not** susceptible to bias. See AU-C 500 for information on the manner in which auditors consider accounting estimates.

12. (d) The requirement is to identify one of an auditor's objectives when evaluating an entity's accounting estimates. Answer (d) is correct because when evaluating accounting estimates an auditor's objectives are to obtain sufficient appropriate audit evidence that (1) all material accounting estimates have been developed, (2) those accounting estimates are reasonable, and (3) those accounting estimates are in conformity with GAAP.

13. (c) The requirement is to determine the proper test for the existence assertion of an asset. Answer (c) is correct because testing **from** accounting records **to** the supporting evidence discloses whether recorded transactions occurred and whether the asset exists. Answer (a) is incorrect because testing for the completeness assertion addresses whether there are unrecorded items. Also, the aggregated nature of the financial statements makes the use of potentially unrecorded items unlikely as a method of identifying unrecorded items. Answer (b) is incorrect because testing potentially unrecorded items to the financial statements addresses the completeness assertion. Answer (d) is incorrect because testing from the supporting evidence to the accounting records addresses the completeness assertion. See the outline of AU-C 500 for information on the financial statement assertions.

14. (a) The requirement is to determine which balance remaining in a "suspense" account would be of most concern to an auditor. Answer (a) is correct because suspense debits that management believes will benefit future operations must be audited carefully to determine whether they have value and should be classified as an asset. Answer (b) is incorrect because when an auditor has already determined that a suspense debit has value it becomes a relatively straightforward issue of the item's proper classification. Answer (c) is incorrect because the conservative approach taken in audits is likely to cause the auditor to have somewhat more concern about suspense purported to be assets [i.e., answer (a)], than for those classified as current liabilities. Answer (d) is incorrect because when the auditor determines that the suspense credits represent customer deposits, establishing a proper accounting will ordinarily be relatively simple.

15. (b) The requirement is to identify the procedure that would **not** be considered an analytical procedure. Analytical procedures consist of evaluations of financial information made by a study of plausible relationships among both financial and nonfinancial data. Answer (b) is correct because projecting an error rate from a statistical sample to an actual population is not a comparison of a plausible relationship. Answers (a), (c), and (d) are all incorrect because they all include a study of plausible relationships.

16. (c) The requirement is to identify the type of analytical procedure an auditor would most likely use in developing relationships among balance sheet accounts when reviewing the financial statements of a nonpublic entity. Answer (c) is correct because balance sheet accounts may be analyzed through a number of ratios (e.g., current ratio). Answer (a) is incorrect because trend analysis is often more appropriate for income statement analysis. Answer (b) is incorrect because regression analysis, while used in practice, is not used as frequently as is ratio analysis. Answer (d) is incorrect because risk analysis in and of itself is not a type of analytical procedure. See AR 100 for information on reviews of nonissuer (nonpublic) entities.

17. (a) The requirement is to identify how an auditor may achieve audit objectives related to particular assertions. Answer (a) is correct because an auditor may perform analytical procedures to achieve an audit objective related to a particular assertion. Answer (b) is incorrect because a system of quality control provides the CPA firm with reasonable assurance of conforming with professional standards. Answer (c) is incorrect because while working papers provide support for the audit report and aid in the conduct and supervision of the audit, they do not in and of themselves achieve audit objectives (see AU-C 230 for information on audit working papers). Answer (d) is incorrect because increasing the level of detection risk does not in and of itself achieve audit objectives.

18. (d) The requirement is to identify the procedure most likely to detect a fraud involving misstatement of income statements due to the recording of journal entries with unusual combinations of debits and credits to expense and revenue accounts. Answer (d) is correct because an objective of analytical procedures is identification of unusual transactions and events, and amounts, ratios and trends that might indicate misstatements. Answer (a) is incorrect because the limited number of journal entries traced to the general ledger in a sample is unlikely to include the erroneous journal entries. Answer (b) is incorrect because while an evaluation of the effectiveness of internal control might help detect such

misstatements, it is somewhat doubtful due to the fact that it is likely that few journal entries are involved. Answer (c) is incorrect because there is no indication that the fraud involves differences between controlling accounts and subsidiary records.

19. (b) The requirement is to identify the account that would yield the highest level of evidence through the performance of analytical procedures. As higher levels of assurance are desired from analytical procedures, more predictable relationships are required to develop the auditor's expectation. Relationships involving income statement accounts tend to be more predictable than relationships involving only balance sheet accounts, and relationships involving transactions not subject to management discretion are generally more predictable. Answer (b) is correct because interest expense relates to the income statement, and because interest expense is subject to only limited management discretion, given the existence of the related debt. Answers (a) and (c) are incorrect because accounts receivable and accounts payable are balance sheet accounts. Answer (d) is incorrect because travel and entertainment expense is normally subject to management discretion. See AU-C 520 for more information on the use of analytical procedures.

20. (c) The requirement is to determine what is included when analytical procedures are used in the overall review stage of an audit. Answer (c) is correct because the overall review stage includes reading the financial statements and notes and considering the adequacy of evidence gathered in response to unusual or unexpected balances. Answer (a) is incorrect because analytical procedures are not particularly aimed at gathering evidence on account balances that have not changed. Answer (b) is incorrect because analytical procedures do not directly test control procedures. Answer (d) is incorrect because tests of transactions to corroborate management's financial statement assertions are performed when considering internal control and for substantive procedures of transactions. See AU-C 520 for information on analytical procedures.

21. (c) The requirement is to determine the most predictable relationship for purposes of analytical procedures applied as substantive procedures. Answer (c) is correct because AU-C 520 indicates that relationships involving income statement accounts tend to be more predictable than relationships involving only balance sheet accounts. Answer (a) is incorrect because, as indicated, relationships involving income statements are considered more predictable. Answer (b) is incorrect because relationships involving transactions subject to management discretion are often less predictable. For example, management might incur maintenance expense rather than replace plant and equipment, or they may delay advertising expenditures. Answer (d) is incorrect because prior year data is sometimes not a reliable predictor of subsequent year's data.

22. (c) The requirement is to identify a basic premise underlying the application of analytical procedures. Answer (c) is correct because, as indicated in AU-C 520, a basic premise underlying the application of analytical procedures is that plausible relationships among data may reasonably be expected to exist and continue in the absence of known conditions to the contrary. Answer (a) is incorrect because the study of financial ratios is an approach to identifying unusual fluctuations, not an acceptable alternative to investigating them. Answer (b) is incorrect because analytical procedures may be either statistical or nonstatistical. Answer (d) is incorrect because analytical procedures may be used as substantive procedures, and may result in modification of the scope of tests of balances and transactions.

23. (a) The requirement is to identify the stages of an audit for which the use of analytical procedures is required. AU-C 315 and AU-C 520 require the use of analytical procedures at both the risk assessment and near completion of the audit, but not as a substantive procedure.

24. (b) The requirement is to determine the reply that would facilitate an auditor's analytical procedures. Answer (b) is correct because use of a standard cost system (a form of budgeting) produces variance reports that will allow the auditor to compare the financial information with the standard cost system data to identify unusual fluctuations. See AU-C 520 for the approach used. Answer (a) is incorrect because segregating obsolete inventory before the inventory count is related to the auditor's physical inventory observation and will not necessarily affect analytical procedures. Answer (c) is incorrect because correcting a material weakness in internal control before the beginning of the audit generally will have minimal, if any, effect on the historical information used for analytical procedures. Answer (d) is incorrect because data from independent sources outside the entity is more likely to be reliable than purely internal sources.

25. (c) The requirement is to identify the most likely effect on an audit of having performed analytical procedures near the end of an audit which suggest that several accounts have unexpected relationships. Answer (c) is correct because when unexpected relationships exist, additional tests of details are generally required to determine whether misstatements exist. Answer (a) is incorrect because irregularities (fraud) may or may not exist. Answer (b) is incorrect because internal control activities may or may not be operating effectively. Answer (d) is incorrect because ordinarily the situation need not be communicated to the audit committee.

26. (b) The requirement is to identify the comparison an auditor most likely would make in evaluating an entity's costs and expenses. Answer (b) is correct because payroll expense is an income statement expense and because it may be expected to have a relationship with that of the prior year. Answer (a) is incorrect because the accounts receivable account is not a cost or expense. Answer (c) is incorrect because comparing budgeted sales with actual sales of the current year is more likely to be performed than comparing budgeted sales with those of prior years. Answer (d) is incorrect because comparing the budgeted current year's warranty expense with the current year's contingent liabilities is less direct than that in answer (b), and because one would be more likely to compare current year budgeted warranty expense with actual warranty expense.

27. (c) The requirement is to identify the best individual to perform analytical procedures near the end of an audit. At this point the objective of analytical procedures is to assist the auditor in assessing the conclusions reached and in the evaluation of the overall financial statement presentation. Answer (c) is correct because an experienced individual with business and industry knowledge is likely to be able to fulfill this function. Answer (a) is incorrect because a staff accountant who has performed the substantive auditing procedures may not be able to objectively perform the analytical procedure and may not have the necessary experience to perform the function. Answer (b) is incorrect because the managing partner of the office may not be close enough to the audit to perform the function effectively. Answer (d) is incorrect because the individual in charge of quality control and the peer review program should be as independent as possible of the audits he or she is considering. See AU-C 520 for guidance on analytical procedures.

28. (b) The requirement is to identify the best example of a substantive procedure. Answer (b) is correct because confirmation of balances of accounts receivable will provide a test of the ending account balance and is therefore a detailed test of a balance, a type of substantive procedure. Answers (a) and (c) are incorrect because examining approval of cash disbursements and comparison of signatures on checks to a list of authorized check signers are tests of controls. Answer (d) is incorrect because flowcharting a client's cash receipts system is a method used to document the auditor's understanding of internal control.

29. (c) The requirement is to identify the objective of tests of details of transactions performed as substantive procedures. Answer (c) is correct because AU-C 330 states that the objective of tests of details of transactions performed as substantive procedures is to detect material misstatements in the financial statements. Answer (a) is incorrect because while performing tests of details of transactions as substantive procedures complies with generally accepted auditing standards, this is not their objective. Answers (b) and (d) are incorrect because neither attaining assurance about the reliability of the accounting system nor the evaluation of the operating effectiveness of management's policies and procedures are the objective of tests of details of transactions performed as substantive procedures.

30. (c) The requirement is to find the statement which describes substantive audit tests. Answer (c) is correct because substantive procedures are defined as tests of transactions, direct tests of financial balances, or analytical procedures. Answer (a) is incorrect because substantive procedures may not be eliminated due to the limitations of internal control. Answer (b) is incorrect since substantive procedures primarily directly test ending financial statement balances, not subsequent events. Answer (d) is incorrect because substantive procedures **decrease** with increased reliance on internal control.

31. (c) The requirement is to determine the account for which the auditor is most likely to perform extensive tests for possible understatement. An analysis of past audits, in which existing financial statement errors were not discovered prior to the issuance of the financial statements, reveals that the great majority of the errors resulted in overstated profits. Therefore, the risk to a CPA is that the client is overstating profits. Answer (c) is correct because it is the only item whose understatement results in overstated profits. Answers (a), (b), and (d) are incorrect because understatement of these items would result in understated profits.

32. (d) The requirement is to determine the most likely approach for auditing the statement of cash flows. Answer (d) is correct because the statement of cash flows includes accounts considered during the audit of the balance sheet and income statements and, accordingly, the most frequent approach is to reconcile amounts. Answers (a), (b), and (c) are all incorrect because they suggest approaches not typically followed when auditing the statement of cash flows.

33. (c) The requirement is to determine the direction of audit testing to determine whether transactions have been recorded. Answer (c) is correct because to determine whether transactions have been recorded the auditor will test **from** the original source documents **to** the recorded entries. Answers (a), (b), and (d) are incorrect because when testing from the general ledger, the adjusted trial balance, or from general journal entries the auditor is dealing with the entries that have been recorded, not whether all transactions have been recorded.

34. (b) The requirement is to identify the correct statement concerning the deletion of audit documentation. Answer (b) is correct because after the audit file has been completed (ordinarily 60 days or less after the issuance of the audit report), no portions of audit documentation should be deleted. Answer (a) is incorrect because after completion of the audit file no documentation should be deleted or discarded. Answer (c) is incorrect because professional skepticism is not the basis for determining deletions. Answer (d) is incorrect because prior to the file completion date most superseded documentation may be deleted (an exception is that information that reflects a disparate point of view should be retained).

35. (a) The requirement is to determine how long audit documentation must be retained. Answer (a) is correct because AU-C 230 requires that they be maintained a minimum of five years. Answers (b), (c), and (d) all present other, incorrect time periods.

36. (a) The requirement is to identify the most likely pair of accounts to be analyzed on the same working paper. Answer (a) is correct because an auditor will often consider interest income with notes receivable because the interest is earned on those notes and therefore closely related. Answer (b) is incorrect because interest receivable relates to an asset account (notes receivable) while accrued interest payable relates to a liability account (notes payable) and accordingly one would expect separate working papers. Answer (c) is incorrect because notes payable and receivable are entirely separate accounts. Answer (d) is incorrect because interest income relates to interest-bearing securities while interest expense relates to debt accounts.

37. (a) The requirement is to identify a primary purpose of an auditor's working papers. AU-C 230 states that working papers serve mainly to provide the principal support for the auditor's report and to aid the auditor in the conduct and supervision of the audit.

38. (c) The requirement is to identify the **least** likely item to be included in the permanent file of an auditor's working papers. Answer (c) is correct because permanent files include information affecting a number of years' audits, and the working trial balance relates most directly to the current and, to a limited extent, the subsequent year's audit. Answers (a), (b), and (d) are all incorrect because bond indenture agreements, lease agreements, and a flowchart of internal control affect more years' audits than does a specific year's working trial balance.

39. (c) The requirement is to determine a difference between an auditor's working trial balance and financial statements without footnotes. Answer (c) is correct because a working trial balance includes columns for reclassification and adjustments. Answers (a), (b), and (d) are all incorrect because while they suggest information that might be included on a working trial balance, they will not be included in the form of additional columns.

40. (d) AU-C 230 states that the degree of documentation for a particular audit area should be affected by (1) the risk of material misstatement, (2) extent of judgment, (3) nature of the auditing procedures, (4) significance of the evidence obtained, (5) nature and extent of the exceptions identified, and (6) the need to document a conclusion that is not obvious from the documentation of the work.

41. (b) The requirement is to identify the required documentation in an audit. Answer (b) is correct because AU-C 300 requires a written audit program setting forth in detail the procedure necessary to accomplish the engagement's objectives. Answer (a) is incorrect because while flowcharts and narratives are acceptable methods of documenting an auditor's understanding of internal control, they are not required. Answer (c) is incorrect because a planning memorandum is not required. Answer (d) is incorrect because completion of an internal control questionnaire is not required.

42. (a) The requirement is to identify a factor that would most likely affect the auditor's judgment about the quantity, type, and content of the working papers. Answer (a) is correct because the Professional Standards state that the assessed level of control risk will affect the quantity, type and content of working papers. AU-C 230 provides a listing of this and other factors. For example, the quantity, type and content of working papers will be affected by whether tests of controls have been performed.

43. (d) The requirement is to identify the type of audit working paper that reflects the major components of an amount reported in the financial statements. Answer (d) is correct because lead schedules aggregate the major components to be reported in the financial statements. Answer (a) is incorrect because an interbank transfer schedule summarizes transfers between banks among accounts. Answer (b) is incorrect because the term "carryforward schedule" is not frequently used. Answer (c) is incorrect because supporting schedules present the details supporting the information on a lead schedule. For example, a detailed bank reconciliation for a cash account might serve as a supporting schedule for an account on the cash lead schedule.

44. (c) The requirement is to identify the documentation that is required for an audit in accordance with generally accepted auditing standards. Answer (c) is correct because AU-C 230 requires that the working papers show that the accounting records agree or reconcile with the financial statements. Answer (a) is incorrect because neither a flowchart nor an internal control questionnaire is required. Answer (b) is incorrect because the *Professional Standards* do not require the use of an engagement letter. Answer (d) is incorrect because when control risk is assessed at the maximum level, the auditor's understanding of internal control needs to be documented, but the basis for the conclusion that it is at the maximum level need not be documented.

45. (b) The requirement is to identify the point at which no deletions of audit documentation are allowed. Answer (b) is correct because the professional standards indicate that audit documentation may not be deleted after the documentation completion date. Answer (a) is incorrect because documentation may be deleted between the client's year-end date and the documentation completion date. Answer (c) is incorrect because the last date of significant fieldwork is prior to the documentation completion date. Answer (d) is incorrect because the report release date is up to 60 days prior to the documentation completion date; 45 days for issuer (public) company audits.

46. (b) The requirement is to determine the type of auditor that should be able to understand audit documentation of the nature, timing, extent, and results of audit procedures performed. Answer (b) is correct because PCAOB Standard 3 requires that audit documentation be understandable to an experienced auditor having no prior connection with the engagement. Answer (a) is incorrect because the requirement is not limited to audit team members. Answer (c) is incorrect because the requirement is more limited than to any certified public accountant. Answer (d) is incorrect both because there is no certification of a peer review specialist and because this is not a requirement.

47. (c) The requirement is to identify the period for which audit documentation should be retained for issuer (public) company audits. Answer (c) is correct because PCAOB Standard 3 requires that audit documentation be retained for the longer of seven years or the period required by law. Answer (a) is incorrect both because of the seven-year requirement, and because it is the longer of seven years or the period required by law. Answer (b) is incorrect because while seven years is the general requirement, a longer period may be required by law. Answer (d) is incorrect because audit documentation need not be retained indefinitely.

48. (b) The requirement is to identify the information that an auditor usually confirms on one form. Answer (b) is correct because the standard form to confirm account balance information with financial institution requests information on both the cash in bank and collateral for loans. Answers (a), (c), and (d) are all incorrect because they suggest pairs of information that are not usually confirmed on one form.

49. (d) The requirement is to determine a reason that the usefulness of the standard bank confirmation request may be limited. Answer (d) is correct because the bank employee who completes the form often will not have access to all the financial relationships that the bank has with the client. Answer (a) is incorrect because bank employees who complete the form realize that they may verify confidential information with the auditor. Answer (b) is incorrect because while it is correct that the employee who completes the confirmation form will not generally inspect the accuracy of the bank reconciliation, this does not limit the confirmation's usefulness. Answer (c) is incorrect because the employee who completes the form does not need to have access to the client's cutoff bank statement to complete the confirmation.

50. (b) The requirement is to determine the type of evidence that is likely to result in an auditor limiting substantive audit tests of sales transactions when control risk is assessed as low for the occurrence assertion for sales. Answer (b) is correct because an auditor may analyze the completeness of sales using cash receipts and accounts receivable (for example, an auditor may add year-end receivables to cash receipts and subtract beginning receivables to obtain an estimate of sales). Answer (a) is incorrect because the opening and closing inventory balances will only provide indirect evidence on sales through calculation of the cost of goods sold. Answer (c) is incorrect because while shipping as of year-end will help assure an accurate cutoff of sales, the receiving activity has no necessary relationship to the sales figure. Answer (d) is incorrect because while the cutoff of sales will provide evidence on the completeness of sales, the purchases portion of the reply is not appropriate.

51. (b) The requirement is to determine the two checks that might indicate kiting, a form of fraud that overstates cash by simultaneously including it in two or more bank accounts. Answer (b) is correct because checks #202 and #404 include cash in two accounts at year-end. The cash represented by check #202 is included in both State Bank and County Bank cash as of December 31. This is because its receipt is recorded prior to year-end, but its disbursement is recorded after year-end. (For the cash receipts journal to remain in balance prior to year-end, some account must have been credited on December 30 to offset the debit to cash.) Check #404 also represents a situation in which the cash is included in two accounts as of year-end; the check may represent a situation in which a shortage in the account is concealed through deposit of the check that is not recorded on the books at year-end. Check #101 does not result in a misstatement of cash since the books recorded both the debit and credit portions of the entry before year-end, while both banks recorded them after year-end. Check #303 represents a situation in which funds are disbursed on the Federal account as of year-end, but not received into the American account (per bank or per books) until after year-end; check #303 accordingly understates cash and the nature of the debit for the entry on December 31 is unknown. Answer (a) is incorrect because neither check #101 nor #303 overstates cash. Answer (c) is incorrect because check #101 does not overstate cash. Answer (d) is incorrect because check #303 understates cash.

52. (b)   The requirement is to determine the checks which represent deposits in transit at December 31, 2001. Deposits in transit are those that have been sent to the bank prior to year-end, but have not been received by the bank as of year-end. Answer (b) is correct because both check #101 and check #303 have been disbursed per books as of year-end, but have not yet been received by the bank as of December 31. Checks #202 and #404 have been received by the bank as of year-end and accordingly are not in transit. Answer (a) is incorrect because check #202 has been received before year-end. Answer (c) is incorrect because both checks #202 and #404 have been received before year-end. Answer (d) is incorrect because check #404 has been received before year-end.

53. (c)   The requirement is to identify why auditors trace bank transfers for the last part of the audit period and the first part of the subsequent period. Answer (c) is correct because auditors use a bank transfer schedule to analyze transfers so as to detect kiting that overstates cash balances. Answers (a) and (b) are incorrect because the process of analyzing transfers is not an efficient way to determine whether the cash receipts journal was held open or when the year's final checks were mailed. Auditors use a bank cutoff statement rather than a bank transfer schedule to help detect these situations. Answer (d) is incorrect because the process of analyzing transfers is unlikely to identify any unusual payments or receipts from related parties.

54. (d)   The requirement is to determine the source of evidence which does **not** contain information on the balance per bank in a bank reconciliation. Answer (d) is correct because the general ledger contains only the client's cash balance, not the balance per bank. Answer (a) is incorrect because the beginning balance on a cutoff statement represents the year-end bank balance. Answer (b) is incorrect because the primary purpose of a year-end bank statement is to present information on the balance per bank. Answer (c) is incorrect because the first question on a standard bank confirmation form requests information on the year-end balance per bank.

55. (b)   The requirement is to identify the cash transfer which will result in a misstatement of year-end cash. Answer (b) is correct because the receipt is recorded on the books prior to year-end, while the disbursement is recorded subsequent to year-end. Therefore, the cash on the books is overstated. Answers (a), (c), and (d) are incorrect because they do not reveal a cutoff error. Answer (a) is incorrect because both the disbursement and receipt are recorded on the books prior to year-end; note that one would expect to see an outstanding check on the disbursing bank reconciliation as of year-end. Answer (c) is incorrect because both the disbursement and receipt are recorded on the books prior to year-end; one would expect the disbursing bank reconciliation to show an outstanding check and the receiving bank to show a deposit in transit as of year-end. Answer (d) is incorrect because the entire transaction is recorded after year-end.

56. (c)   The requirement is to determine an approach for detecting the concealing of a cash shortage by transporting funds from one location to another or by converting negotiable assets to cash. Answer (c) is correct because the timing of the performance of auditing procedures involves the proper synchronizing of their application and thus comprehends the possible need for simultaneous examination of, for example, cash on hand and in banks, securities owned, bank loans, and other related items.

57. (b)   The requirement is to identify the primary purpose of sending a standard confirmation request to financial institutions with which the client has done business during the year. Answer (b) is correct because CPAs generally provide the account information on the form and ask for balance corroboration. The form explicitly states that the CPAs do not request, nor expect, the financial institution to conduct a comprehensive, detailed, search of its records for other accounts. Answer (a) is incorrect because a standard confirmation request will not detect kiting, a manipulation causing an amount of cash to be included simultaneously in the balance of two or more bank accounts. Answer (c) is incorrect because bank statements available from the client allow the CPA to prepare a proof of cash. Answer (d) is incorrect because the standard form does not request information about contingent liabilities and secured transactions.

58. (c)   The requirement is to determine the assertion (or assertions) being tested by a test of a control in which an auditor observes the mailing of monthly statements to a client's customers and reviews evidence of follow-up on errors reported by the customers. Answer (c) is correct because observing the mailing of monthly statements and follow-up of errors will provide evidence to the auditor as to whether the receivables **exist** at a given date; the tests do not directly address the presentation and disclosure assertion since little evidence is obtained about whether financial statement components are properly classified, described, and disclosed. See AU-C 500 for a discussion of the various financial statement assertions. Answer (a) is incorrect because the presentation and disclosure assertion is not addressed. Answer (b) is incorrect because the presentation and disclosure assertion is not addressed and because the existence or occurrence assertion is addressed. Answer (d) is incorrect because the existence or occurrence assertion is addressed.

59. (b)   The requirement is to determine the most likely audit step summarized by the tick mark placed under "date disbursed per bank." Answer (b) is correct because the checks were written in December but cleared in January and should therefore be listed as outstanding on the year-end outstanding check list of the applicable bank reconciliation. Answer (a) is incorrect because the tick marks are beside the date per bank, and not per books. Answer (c) is incorrect because the December cash disbursements journal, and not the January cash disbursements journal, will include these disbursements. Answer (d) is incorrect because the year-end bank confirmations do not include information on outstanding checks.

60. (a)   The requirement is to determine the most likely audit step summarized by the tick mark placed under "date deposited per bank." Answer (a) is correct because deposits recorded on the books as of 12/31 should be included as deposits in transit on the applicable bank reconciliation. Answer (b) is incorrect because the tick mark is placed beside the "bank" column, and not the books column. Answer (c) is incorrect because the December cash receipts journal, and not the January cash receipts journal should include the deposit. Answer (d) is incorrect because the year-end bank confirmations will not include deposits in transit.

61. (a) The requirement is to identify the correct statement concerning the use of negative confirmation requests. Answer (a) is correct because AU-C 505 states that unreturned negative confirmation requests rarely provide significant evidence concerning financial statements assertions other than certain aspects of the existence assertion. Answer (b) is incorrect because positive, not negative, confirmation requests are normally used when a low level of detection risk is to be achieved. Answer (c) is incorrect because alternative procedures are not generally performed on unreturned negative confirmation requests since it is assumed that the respondent did not reply because of agreement with the balance on the confirmation request. Answer (d) is incorrect because respondents may not reply when misstatements are in their favor.

62. (c) The requirement is to identify the most likely action taken by an auditor when no reply is received to positive confirmation requests. Answer (c) is correct because asking the client to contact customers to ask that confirmation requests be returned may increase response rates. Answer (a) is incorrect because the lack of a reply to a confirmation request does not necessarily indicate that the account needs to be written off. Answer (b) is incorrect because accounts receivable confirmations deal more directly with existence than with valuation or completeness and because alternative procedures may provide the auditor with the desired assurance with respect to the nonrespondents. Answer (d) is incorrect because the assessed level of inherent risk will not normally be modified due to confirmation results.

63. (b) The requirement is to determine the best sampling unit for confirmation of accounts receivable when many differences between the recorded account balances and the confirmation replies have occurred in the past. Answer (b) is correct because the misstatements may have occurred because respondents are not readily able to confirm account balances. AU-C 505 suggests that in such circumstances certain respondents' accounting systems may facilitate the confirmation of single transactions (individual invoices) rather than of entire account balances.

64. (c) The requirement is to identify the assertion most directly addressed by accounts receivable confirmations. AU-C 500 presents information on financial statement assertions. Answer (c) is correct because a confirmation addresses whether the entity replying to the confirmation believes that a debt exists. Answer (a) is incorrect because while confirmations provide limited information on valuation, they do not directly address whether the entity replying will pay the debt (or whether the account has been factored). Answer (b) is incorrect because limited classification information is received via confirmations. Answer (d) is incorrect because confirmations are generally sent to recorded receivables, and are of limited assistance in the determination of whether all accounts are recorded (completeness).

65. (a) The requirement is to determine when alternative procedures should be performed in order to substantiate the existence of accounts receivable. Answer (a) is correct because the auditor should employ alternative procedures for nonresponses to positive confirmations to satisfy himself/herself as to the existence of accounts receivable. Those procedures may include examination of evidence of subsequent cash receipts, cash remittance advices, sales and shipping documents, and other records. Answer (b) is incorrect because with negative confirmations the debtor is asked to respond only if s/he disagrees with the information on the confirmation; thus, no reply is assumed to indicate agreement. Answers (c) and (d) are incorrect because while **additional** procedures may be required when collectibility is questionable, **alternative** procedures are those used in lieu of confirmation.

66. (d) The requirement is to identify the most likely alternate procedure when replies have not been received to either first or second accounts receivable confirmation requests. Answer (d) is correct because the inspection of shipping records will provide evidence that the merchandise was actually shipped to the debtor. Answer (a) is incorrect because, a review of the cash receipts journal **prior** to year-end is unlikely to provide evidence on account recorded as unpaid as of year-end. Also, the procedure would only detect one specific type of misstatement, that in which payments were recorded in the cash receipts journal, but not credited to the customers' accounts. Answer (b) is incorrect because the lack of a reply to the confirmation provides no particular evidence that the scope of procedures related to internal control should be modified. Answer (c) is incorrect because the lack of a reply need not necessarily lead to a presumption that the account is misstated. See AU-C 505 for procedures typically performed for year-end accounts receivable confirmation requests for which no reply is received.

67. (d) The requirement is to identify the circumstances in which use of the negative form of accounts receivable confirmation most likely would be justified. Negative confirmations are used when (1) the combined assessed level of inherent and control risk is low, (2) a large number of small balances is involved, and (3) the auditor has no reason to believe that the recipients of the requests are unlikely to give them consideration. Positive confirmations are used when those conditions are not met as well as in other circumstances in which it seems desirable to request a positive response, such as when accounts are in dispute. Answer (d) is best because small balances are involved and few accounts are in dispute. Answer (a) is incorrect because it refers to a substantial number of accounts in dispute and sales are to a few major customers. Answer (b) is incorrect because it refers to a substantial number of accounts in dispute. Answer (c) is incorrect because it refers to sales to a few major customers.

68. (a) The requirement is to identify a method to reduce the risk associated with accepting e-mail responses to accounts receivable confirmation requests. Answer (a) is correct because a response by mail will confirm the e-mail response. Answer (b) is incorrect because while such subsequent cash receipts will ordinarily be examined, this represents an alternative, complementary approach to confirmation. Answer (c) is incorrect because the auditor need not consider e-mail responses to be confirmations with exception. Answer (d) is incorrect because a second request is more likely to elicit either no response or another e-mail response.

69. (b) The requirement is to determine the most likely procedure to reduce the risks associated with accepting fax responses to requests for confirmations of accounts receivable. Answer (b) is correct because verification of the sources and contents through telephone calls will address whether the information on the fax (which may have been sent from almost anywhere) is correct. Answer (a) is incorrect because an examination of the shipping documents is less complete than is verification of the entire balance. Answer (c) is incorrect because such faxes need not be treated as nonresponses. Answer (d) is incorrect because inspection of the faxes is unlikely to reveal forgeries or alterations, even when such circumstances have occurred.

70. (d) The requirement is to identify the circumstance in which the negative form of confirmation request most likely would be used. Answer (d) is correct because AU-C 505 states that negative confirmations may be used when (1) the combined assessed level of inherent and control risk is low [answer (d)], (2) a large number of small balances is involved, and (3) the auditor has no reason to believe that the recipients of the requests are unlikely to give them consideration. Answer (a) is incorrect because when the accounts receivable are immaterial, a decision may be made to send no confirmations. Answer (b) is incorrect because an inadequate rate is not an acceptable reason to send negative confirmations. Answer (c) is incorrect because negative confirmations are only of value when the auditor has no reason to believe that the recipients of the requests are unlikely to give them consideration.

71. (a) The requirement is to identify the circumstance in which an auditor would use the blank form of confirmations (one which includes no amount and asks the respondent to supply the amount due) rather than positive confirmations. Answer (a) is correct because if a recipient simply signs a blank confirmation and returns it the confirmation will have no amount on it and the auditor will know that additional procedures are necessary. Answers (b) and (c) are incorrect because there is no necessary relationship between the use of blank confirmations and subsequent cash receipt verification difficulty and analytical procedures results. Answer (d) is incorrect because when the combined assessed level of inherent risk and control risk is low it is unlikely to lead to the blank form of confirmation. In fact, when that risk is low, and when adequate other substantive procedures of details, no confirmation may be necessary. See AU-C 505 for information on the confirmation process.

72. (d) The requirement is to identify the most likely information that would be included in a client's confirmation letter that is being used to confirm accounts receivable balances rather than individual invoices. Answer (d) is correct since including details of the account is likely to make it easier for the customer to respond in a meaningful manner. Answer (a) is incorrect because no such auditor-prepared letter will be

included and because only in the case of the negative form of confirmation does a nonresponse lead to an inference that the account balance is correct. Answer (b) is incorrect because confirmation requests do not ordinarily include a letter suggesting that a second request will be sent. Answer (c) is incorrect because the auditor does not enclose a letter requesting that the information be supplied. See AU-C 505 for information on the confirmation process.

73. (c) The requirement is to identify a statement that an auditor would be most likely to add to the negative form of confirmation of accounts receivable to encourage a timely consideration by the recipient. Answer (c) is correct because providing such information might increase timely consideration in that the recipient may realize the importance of a reply when the information is incorrect. Answers (a) and (b) are incorrect because while a confirmation request may include these statements, the statements are unlikely to encourage timely consideration of the request. Answer (d) is incorrect because many accounts that are not overdue are sampled, and because even for those overdue such a statement is not ordinarily included with the confirmation request.

74. (a) The requirement is to identify the strategy most likely to improve the response rate for confirmation of accounts receivable. Answer (a) is correct because including a list of items or invoices that constitute the account balance makes it easier for the potential respondent to reply. Answer (b) is incorrect because customers with relatively large balances may or may not be more likely to reply. Answers (c) and (d) are incorrect because there is no research available indicating that requesting a fax or e-mail reply, or threatening a second request is likely to improve response rate.

75. (a) The requirement is to determine the financial statement most directly related to the procedure of making inquiries concerning possible obsolete or slow-moving inventory. Answer (a) is correct because inquiries concerning possible obsolete or slow-moving inventory deal with whether the inventory is being carried at the proper value and this is most directly related to the valuation assertion. The other assertions are less directly related. Answer (b) is incorrect because the rights assertion deals with whether assets are the rights of the entity and liabilities are the obligations of the entity at a given date. Answer (c) is incorrect because the existence assertion deals with whether assets exist at a given date. Answer (d) is incorrect because the presentation assertion deals with whether particular components of the financial statements are properly classified. See AU-C 500 for information on the financial statement assertions.

76. (d) The requirement is to identify the type of omitted journal entry that would result in inventory test counts that are higher than the recorded quantities in the client's perpetual records. Answer (d) is correct because a failure to record sales returns results in a situation in which the item is returned by a customer and included in the inventory count, but not recorded in the perpetual records; accordingly the test counts are higher than the recorded quantities. Answer (a) is incorrect because purchase discounts do not affect quantities in inventory. Answers (b) and (c) are incorrect because a failure to record purchase returns or sales result in a situation in which less inventory will be counted (since the items are no longer physically in inventory) than is recorded on the perpetual records.

77. (c) The requirement is to identify a procedure that will provide assurance that all inventory items in a client's inventory listing schedule are valid. Answer (c) is correct because tracing **from** the inventory listing schedule **to** inventory tags and **to** the auditor's recorded count sheets will provide assurance that the listed items actually exist. Answer (a) is incorrect because tracing from inventory tags to items in the inventory listing schedule tests the completeness of the inventory listing sheet, not whether all of the items it lists are valid. Answer (b) is incorrect because it does not directly test the client's inventory listing schedule. Answer (d) is incorrect because tracing items listed in receiving reports and vendors' invoices to the inventory listing schedule will provide assurance on the completeness of the inventory listing sheet; it will also be a difficult procedure to accomplish due to the fact that a number of these items will not be in inventory due to sales. See AU-C 500 for information on the testing of the various financial statement assertions.

78. (b) The requirement is to identify the factor that average inventory is divided into to calculate inventory turnover. Answer (b) is correct because the average inventory is divided into the cost of goods sold to calculate the inventory turnover.

79. (a) The requirement is to identify the auditing procedure that most likely would provide assurance about a manufacturing entity's inventory valuation. Answer (a) is correct because testing the overhead computation will provide evidence on whether inventory has been included in the financial statements at the appropriate amount. Answer (b) is incorrect because obtaining confirmation of inventories pledged under loan agreements relates more directly to the presentation assertion. Answers (c) and (d) are incorrect because reviewing shipping and receiving cutoff procedures for inventories and tracing test counts to the inventory listing relate more directly to the existence and completeness assertions.

80. (b) The requirement is to identify an action that an auditor might take when the assessed level of control risk is high for inventory. Answer (b) is correct because a high level of control risk will generally result in a low acceptable level of detection risk, which may be achieved by changing the timing of substantive procedures to year-end, changing the nature of substantive procedures to more effective procedures, and/or by changing the extent of substantive procedures. Answer (a) is incorrect because control risk has been assessed and tests of controls, if any, will already have been completed. Answer (c) is incorrect because a year-end count of inventory is more appropriate when control risk is high. Answer (d) is incorrect because gross profit tests will generally provide less assurance than is required in circumstances such as this when control risk is assessed at a high level.

81. (a) The requirement is to identify the financial statement assertion (other than presentation and disclosure) most directly related to an auditor's conclusion that no excessive costs for idle plant were charged to inventory. Answer (a) is

correct because the assertion deals with whether the inventory has been included in the financial statements at the appropriate amount, and therefore that no excessive costs were charged to inventory. Answer (b) is incorrect because the completeness assertion deals with whether all inventory items that should be presented are so included. Answer (c) is incorrect because existence deals with whether the inventory actually exits at the given date. Answer (d) is incorrect because rights deal with whether the inventory is owned by the client. For more information on management's financial statement assertions, see AU-C 500.

82. (b) The requirement is to identify the financial statement assertion most directly related to an auditor's tracing of inventory test counts to the client's inventory listing. Answer (b) is correct because the completeness assertion deals with whether all transactions are included. Tracing from the inventory items observed to the inventory listing will help determine whether all the transactions are included and the inventory listing is complete. Answer (a) is incorrect because the rights assertion deals with whether assets are the rights of the entity and this is not being tested when an auditor traces test counts to an inventory listing. Answer (c) is incorrect because existence deals with whether the inventory existed at the date of the count. To test existence the auditor would sample from the inventory listing and compare quantities to the test counts. Answer (d) is incorrect because valuation deals with whether the inventory is properly included in the balance sheet at the appropriate dollar amount and this is not being tested here. See AU-C 500 for more information on management's financial statement assertions.

83. (d) The requirement is to determine the assertion most directly related to an auditor's analysis of inventory turnover rates. Answer (d) is correct because an analysis of inventory turnover rates will provide the auditor with evidence on slow-moving, excess, defective, and obsolete items included in inventories. These items may be improperly valued.

84. (a) The requirement is to determine which types of entries will be supported when the auditor examines receiving reports. Answer (a) is correct because receiving reports will be prepared when goods are received through purchase (as recorded in the voucher register) and when goods are received through sales returns (as recorded in the sales returns journal). Answers (b), (c), and (d) are incorrect because entries in sales journals result in items being shipped, not received. Note, however, that answers (b), (c), and (d) are partially correct because the sales returns journal, voucher register, and check register all result from transactions related to the receipt of goods.

85. (c) The requirement is to identify the response which does **not** represent one of the independent auditor's objectives regarding the examination of inventory. Answer (c) is correct because verifying that all inventory owned by the client is on hand at the time of the count is not an objective. For example, purchased items in transit at year-end, for which title has passed, should be included in inventory. Similarly, inventory out on consignment should also be included in inventory. Answer (a) is incorrect because proper presentation of inventory pertains to the presentation and disclosure assertion and therefore would be subject to auditor verification. Answers (b) and (d) are incorrect because proper accounting for damaged and obsolete items and proper inventory pricing pertain to the valuation assertion and therefore would be subject to auditor verification. See AU-C 500 for details on financial statement assertions.

86. (c) The requirement is to determine why an auditor should insist that a client representative be present when he or she physically examines securities. Answer (c) is correct because requiring that a client representative acknowledge the receipt of the securities will eliminate any question concerning the CPA's responsibility for any subsequent misplacement or misappropriation of the securities. Answer (a) is incorrect because the client's representative will not in general help the CPA to detect fraudulent securities. Answers (b) and (d) are incorrect because while the client's representative will help the CPA to gain access to the securities and may coordinate their return, these are not the auditor's primary purpose.

87. (c) The requirement is to identify the best procedure other than inspection to establish the existence and ownership of a long-term investment in a publicly traded stock. Answer (c) is correct because confirmation of the number of shares owned that are held by an independent custodian is effective at testing existence. Answer (a) is incorrect because auditors do not in general correspond with the investee company and because that company may or may not have detailed information on the identity of shareholders at any point in time. Answer (b) is incorrect because while inspection of the audited financial statements of the investee company may provide limited information on valuation of the investment, it does not directly address existence; note that this procedure is of limited use here since the stock is publicly traded and obtaining its value through stock price quotations should not be difficult. Answer (d) is incorrect because this procedure addresses the valuation of the securities. In addition, under SFAS 115, investments are no longer carried at the lower of cost or market. See AU-C 500 for more information on management's financial statement assertions.

88. (c) The requirement is to determine the best procedure when an auditor has been unable to inspect and count a client's investment securities (held in a safe-deposit box) until after the balance sheet date. Answer (c) is correct because banks maintain records on access to safe-deposit boxes. Thus, the confirmation of no access during the period will provide the auditor with evidence that the securities in the safe-deposit box at the time of the count were those available at year-end. Answers (a) and (b) are incorrect because the bank will not generally be able to provide a list of securities added and removed from the box (typically, only records on access are maintained by the bank). Therefore, the bank will have no information on reconciling items between the subsidiary ledger and the securities on hand. Answer (d) is incorrect because it is the responsibility of the auditor and the client, not the bank, to count the securities maintained in a safe-deposit box.

89. (a) The requirement is to determine the most likely use of analytical procedures when testing long-term investments. Answer (a) is correct because the predictable relationship between long-term investments and investment income creates a situation in which analytical procedures may provide substantial audit assurance. Answer (b) is incorrect because the classification between current and noncurrent portfolios may be expected to fluctuate in an unpredictable manner as investment goals and the environment change. Answers (c) and (d) are incorrect because the valuation of marketable equity securities at the lower of cost or market and unrealized gains or losses do not result in a predictable relationship on which analytical procedures may provide effective results.

90. (d) The requirement is to identify the account whose analysis is **least** likely to reveal evidence relating to **recorded** retirements of equipment. Answer (d) is correct because the purchase returns and allowances account deals with returns and allowances for purchases of merchandise, not equipment. Answer (a) is incorrect because analysis of accumulated depreciation will reveal the retirement through charges made to the accumulated depreciation account. Answer (b) is incorrect because companies will ordinarily modify insurance coverage when assets are retired. Answer (c) is incorrect because the property, plant, and equipment account will reflect the retirement.

91. (b) The requirement is to identify a likely explanation for a situation in which significant debits have been posted to the accumulated depreciation expense. Answer (b) is correct because debits to accumulated depreciation are properly recorded upon retirement of a plant asset. Answer (a) is incorrect because changing the useful lives of plant assets does not affect accumulated depreciation. Answer (c) is incorrect because understatement of the prior year's depreciation expense does not result in an adjustment to accumulated depreciation. Answer (d) is incorrect because overhead allocations do not ordinarily affect accumulated depreciation.

92. (a) The requirement is to identify the best procedure for testing unrecorded retirements of equipment. Answer (a) is correct because selecting items from the accounting records and attempting to locate them will reveal unrecorded retirements when the item cannot be located. Answer (b) is incorrect because depreciation entries will continue when retirements have not been recorded. Answer (c) is incorrect because the direction of the test is incorrect since beginning with the item is unlikely to reveal a situation in which an unrecorded retirement has occurred. Answer (d) is incorrect because scanning the general journal for **recorded** entries is unlikely to reveal **unrecorded** retirements of equipment.

93. (d) The requirement is to determine why an auditor analyzes repairs and maintenance accounts. Answer (d) is correct because clients often erroneously charge expenditures for property and equipment acquisitions as expenses rather than capitalize them as assets. An analysis of repairs and maintenance accounts will reveal such errors. Answer (a) is incorrect because while auditors will want to determine that noncapitalizable expenses for repairs and maintenance have been recorded in the proper period, analyzing only the recorded entries is an incomplete test since entries occurring after year-end will also need to be examined. Answer (b) is incorrect because procedures relating to the property and equipment account will be performed to determine whether such entries have been recorded in the proper period. Answer (c) is incorrect because analyzing the repairs and maintenance accounts only considers recorded entries and not whether all noncapitalizable expenditures for repairs and maintenance have been properly charged to expense.

94. (c) The requirement is to determine the information an auditor is most likely to seek from the plant manager. The plant manager comes into day-to-day contact with the machinery when producing a product; that contact is likely to provide information on its condition and usefulness. Answers (a) and (d) are incorrect because the plant manager will generally not have detailed knowledge as to the adequacy of the provision for uncollectible accounts or the amount of insurance which is desirable. Answer (b) is incorrect because the plant manager will have limited knowledge concerning physical inventory observation procedures and their appropriateness.

95. (a) The requirement is to identify the document least likely to provide evidence regarding mortgage acquisition costs. Deeds generally consist of a legal conveyance of rights to use real property. Frequently the sales price is not even specified and the related mortgage acquisition costs are much less likely to be stated in a deed. Answer (b) is incorrect because cancelled checks would provide verification of mortgage acquisition costs. Answer (c) is incorrect because the closing statement would provide a detailed listing of the costs of acquiring the real property, including possible mortgage acquisition costs. Answer (d) is incorrect because examination of interest expense would also relate to the mortgage acquisition costs.

96. (b) The requirement is to determine the assertion(s) involved when an auditor is inspecting new additions on a list of property, plant, and equipment. Answer (b) is correct because an auditor who inspects new additions relating to property and equipment balances addresses existence or occurrence, but not presentation and disclosure; presentation and disclosure relates more directly to proper classification and note disclosures rather than account balances.

97. (a) The requirement is to determine the financial statement assertion most directly related to the procedure of reviewing or recomputing amortization of intangible assets. Answer (a) is correct because the amortization of intangible assets deals with whether the accounts are properly valued, the valuation assertion. The other assertions are less directly related. Answer (b) is incorrect because the existence or occurrence assertion deals with whether assets or liabilities exist at a given date and whether recorded transactions have occurred during a given period. Answer (c) is incorrect because the completeness assertion deals with whether all transactions and accounts that should be presented in the financial statements are so included. Answer (d) is incorrect because the rights and obligations assertion deals with whether assets are the rights of the entity and liabilities are the obligations of the entity at a given date. See AU-C 500 for information on the financial statement assertions.

98. (c) The requirement is to determine the most likely reason for the absence of the original insurance policy on plant equipment. Answer (c) is correct because the holder of the lien may also in certain circumstances maintain the original insurance policy. Answer (a) is incorrect because an insurance premium which is due but not recorded is unlikely to account for the lack of the original insurance policy. Answer (b) is incorrect because while coinsurance provisions are outlined in the policy, they are unlikely to be a reason that the policy is not available for inspection. Answer (d) is incorrect because there is no obvious relationship between the understatement of insurance expense and the presence or absence of an insurance policy.

99. (c) The requirement is to identify the best audit procedures for identifying unrecorded liabilities. Answer (c) is correct because unrecorded liabilities eventually become due and must be paid. Accordingly, a review of cash disbursements after the balance sheet date is an effective procedure for detecting unrecorded payables. Answer (a) is incorrect because tracing a sample of accounts payable that have been recorded is not likely to result in identification of unrecorded liabilities. Answer (b) is incorrect because purchase orders issued after year-end will not result in liabilities as of year-end. Answer (d) is incorrect because disbursement entries recorded before year-end generally relate to accounts payable that have been paid before year-end.

100. (a) The requirement is to identify the appropriate population when using accounts payable confirmations directed towards obtaining evidence on the completeness assertion. Answer (a) is correct because to address completeness the auditor attempts to determine that all accounts payable are reflected, and a company potentially may be liable to any of its vendors. Answer (b) is incorrect because confirming based on recorded amounts addresses existence more directly than completeness. Answer (c) is incorrect because basing the sample on payees after year-end only deals with those payables that have been paid as of that point. Answer (d) is incorrect because open invoices are a less complete population than are vendors. See AU-C 505 for information on the confirmation process, and AU-C 500 for information on management's financial statement assertions.

101. (d) The requirement is to determine why confirmation of accounts payable is unnecessary. Accounts payable are usually not confirmed because there is better evidence available to the auditor, (i.e., examination of cash payments subsequent to the balance sheet date). If the auditor reviews all cash payments for a sufficient time after the balance sheet date for items pertaining to the period under audit and finds no such payments which were not recorded as liabilities at year-end, the auditor is reasonably assured that accounts payable were not understated. Answer (a) is a nonsense answer. Answer (b) is incorrect because AP balances could be paid during year-end audit work after the balance sheet date. Answer (c) is incorrect because whether or not legal action has been taken against the client is irrelevant to the confirmation procedure.

102. (c) The requirement is to identify the substantive procedure to be performed to verify the existence and valuation of recorded accounts payable. Answer (c) is correct because the vouching of various payable accounts to purchase orders and receiving reports will provide evidence that the debt was incurred and the related goods received, thereby providing evidence on the existence of the debt and its amount, or valuation. Answer (a) is incorrect because determining whether prenumbered purchase orders are used and accounted for relates more directly to the completeness with which purchases and accounts payable were recorded. Answers (b) and (d) are incorrect because the question addresses the existence and valuation of **recorded** accounts payable, not unrecorded payables or payables with a zero balance.

103. (c) The requirement is to determine management's accounts payable assertion that an auditor will primarily focus on. Experience has indicated that overstated income is more of a risk than is understated income. Answer (c) is correct because the completeness assertion focuses upon whether payables have been omitted, thereby overstating income. Answer (a) is incorrect because the existence assertion deals with whether recorded accounts payable are overstated, thereby understating income. Answer (b) is incorrect because payables often require no particularly troublesome presentations and disclosures. Answer (d) is incorrect because payables are most frequently simply valued at the cost of the related acquisition. See AU-C 500 for more information on management's financial statement assertions.

104. (b) The requirement is to identify a likely reason for a recorded interest expense that seems excessive in relation to the balance in the bonds payable account. Answer (b) is correct because understated bonds payable will result in a lower account balance than is proper and thereby create a situation in which the interest expense appears excessive. Answers (a) and (d) are incorrect because an understated discount or an overstated premium on bonds payable result in situations in which the recorded interest expense seems lower than expected since the net bonds payable are overstated. Answer (c) is incorrect because understatements, not overstatements, of bonds payable will result in what appears to be an excessive rate of interest expense.

105. (a) The requirement is to determine the financial statement assertion most directly related to an auditor's inspection of loan agreements under which an entity's inventories are pledged. Answer (a) is correct because the presentation and disclosure assertion deals with whether particular components of the financial statements—such as loan agreement covenants—are properly classified, described, and disclosed. The other assertions are less directly related. Answer (b) is incorrect because the valuation or allocation assertion deals with whether asset, liabilities, revenue, and expense components have been included in the financial statements at the appropriate amounts. Answer (c) is incorrect because the existence or occurrence assertion deals with whether assets or liabilities exist at a given date and whether recorded transactions have occurred during a given period. Answer (d) is incorrect because the completeness assertion deals with whether all transactions and accounts that should be presented in the financial statements are so included. See AU-C 500 for information on the financial statement assertions.

106. (c) The requirement is to identify a procedure an auditor would perform in auditing long-term bonds payable.

Answer (c) is correct because comparing interest expense with the bond payable amount will provide evidence as to reasonableness. Such a procedure may reveal either interest not expensed or debt not properly recorded. Answer (a) is incorrect because analytical procedures will not in general be performed on bond premiums and discounts since these accounts may easily be verified by examining details of the entry recording the debt issuance and any subsequent amortization. Answer (b) is incorrect because an examination of the documentation of assets purchased with bond proceeds is only necessary when such a use of the funds is a requirement of the debt issuance. Answer (d) is incorrect because confirmation of bonds outstanding will often be with the trustee rather than with individual bondholders.

107. (b) The requirement is to determine how an auditor can best verify a client's bond sinking fund transactions and year-end balance. Answer (b) is correct because confirmation with the bond trustee represents externally generated evidence received directly by the auditor. Such evidence is considered very reliable. Answer (a) is incorrect because individual holders of retired bonds will have no information on actual bond sinking fund transactions or year-end balances. Answer (c) is incorrect because, while recomputing interest expense, interest payable, and amortization of bond discount or premiums are desirable procedures, they do not directly address bond sinking fund transactions and year-end balances. Answer (d) is similar to answer (c) in that it is desirable but does not address the actual bond sinking fund transactions and year-end balance.

108. (a) The requirement is to determine how an auditor ordinarily obtains evidence of stockholders' equity transactions. Answer (a) is correct because the board of directors will, in general, authorize changes in stockholders' equity. Answer (b) is less complete in that for small clients there may be no transfer agent, and because the transfer agent deals most directly with transfers of outstanding stock. Answer (c) is incorrect because canceled stock certificates are ordinarily available only for small clients. Answer (d) is incorrect because companies do not ordinarily have a "treasury stock certificate book."

109. (d) The requirement is to identify the most likely audit procedure, in addition to analytical procedures, when control risk for payroll is assessed as low. Answer (d) is correct because accrual of payroll at year-end is not an entry made frequently throughout the year and accordingly recording of the entry is often not controlled by the payroll portion of the internal control structure. Answers (a), (b), and (c) are incorrect because observing the distribution of paychecks, the footing and crossfooting of the payroll register, and inspection of payroll tax returns are recurring operations that will have been considered when assessing control risk at a low level.

110. (a) The requirement is to identify the circumstance that most likely would cause an auditor to suspect an employee payroll fraud scheme. Answer (a) is correct because significant unexplained variances between standard and actual labor cost may lead an auditor to suspect fraud. Answer (b) is incorrect because one would expect payroll checks to be distributed by the same employees each payday. Answer (c) is incorrect because time cards are ordinarily approved by individual departmental supervisors. Answer (d) is incorrect because the maintenance of a separate payroll bank account is considered a control, not an indication of fraud.

111. (d) The requirement is to identify the procedure that an auditor most likely would perform when auditing payroll. Answer (d) is correct because a comparison of payroll costs with entity standards or budgets will generally be included in the audit program as a test of overall payroll reasonableness. Answer (a) is incorrect because unclaimed wages will not be mailed unless an employee so requests and this often will not be tested by an auditor. Answer (b) is incorrect because total employee deductions will be traced to journal entries. Answer (c) is incorrect because observing entity employees during a payroll distribution is generally only included in an audit program when internal control is weak; accordingly, it is more likely that a comparison of payroll costs with entity standards or budgets [answer (d)] will be included.

112. (d) The requirement is to identify the procedure that is most likely when an auditor is performing tests concerning the granting of stock options. Answer (d) is correct because authorizing the issuance of stock options is ordinarily a decision made by the board of directors. Answer (a) is incorrect because the Secretary of State of the state of incorporation will not have this information on stock options. Answer (b) is incorrect because the existence of the option holders is not ordinarily a significant question. Answer (c) is incorrect because stock to be issued relating to options may be either from treasury stock or new issuances; accordingly, sufficient treasury stock need not be available.

113. (d) The requirement is to identify the assertion to which determining whether there are restrictions on retained earnings relates most directly. Answer (d) is correct because such restrictions will result in disclosures and thus the presentation and disclosure assertion is most directly being verified. Answer (a) is incorrect because the existence or occurrence assertion addresses whether assets or liabilities of the entity exist at a given date and whether recorded transactions have occurred during a given period. Answer (b) is incorrect because the completeness assertion addresses whether all transactions and accounts that should be presented in the financial statements are so included. Answer (c) is incorrect because the valuation or allocation assertion addresses whether asset, liability, revenue, and expense components have been included in the financial statements at appropriate amounts. See AU-C 500 for a discussion of financial statement assertions.

114. (b) The requirement is to identify the information an auditor should confirm with a client's transfer agent and registrar. Answer (b) is correct because when a client employs a transfer agent and registrar, there will be no stock certificate book to examine, and accordingly, information on shares issued and outstanding should be confirmed. Answers (a), (c), and (d) are incorrect because the transfer agent and registrar often will not have information on dividend restrictions, guarantees of preferred stock liquidation values, and the number of shares subject to agreements to repurchase.

115. (c) The requirement is to determine a likely step in the audit program for retained earnings. The legality of a dividend depends in part on whether it has been properly authorized (state laws differ on specific requirements). Thus, the auditor must determine that proper authorization exists, as both cash and stock dividends affect retained earnings. Answer (a) is incorrect since only a memo entry is required for a stock split. Answer (b) is incorrect because the write-down of an account receivable will not, in general, be recorded in retained earnings. Answer (d) is incorrect because gains from the disposition of treasury shares are recorded in paid-in capital accounts.

116. (c) The requirement is to determine when an auditor would be most likely to perform substantive procedures of details on payroll transactions and balances. Answer (c) is correct because analytical procedures result in further investigation when unexpected differences occur. This investigation will generally involve substantive procedures of details of transactions and balances. AU-C 520 provides detailed information on analytical procedures. Answer (a) is incorrect because a substantial amount of accrued payroll expense as indicated by a cutoff test will not necessarily result in additional substantive procedures. Answer (b) is incorrect because a low assessed level of control risk is likely to result in less substantive procedures. Answer (d) is incorrect because the nature of accrued payroll expense being unpaid commissions need not necessarily result in more substantive procedures.

117. (a) The requirement is to determine a source an auditor uses to test the reasonableness of dividend income from investments in publicly held companies. Answer (a) is correct because dividend record books produced by investment advisory services provide summaries of dividends paid for various securities, and an auditor is able to compare the reasonableness of a client's recorded dividend income from investments with this information. Answers (b) and (c) are incorrect because auditors do not, in general, determine the reasonableness of dividend income by examining stock "indentures" or "stock ledgers." Answer (d) is incorrect because while annual financial statements of investee companies may include such information, examining such financial statements is not generally an efficient approach for testing the reasonableness of dividend income. Also, the current year financial statements of the investees often are not available when the auditor is performing the current audit.

118. (c) The requirement is to identify the most likely risk involved with a bill and hold transaction at year-end. Answer (c) is correct because a bill and hold transaction results in the recording of a sale prior to delivery of the goods—accordingly, sales may be inappropriately recorded. Answer (a) is incorrect because accrued liabilities are not ordinarily affected by bill and hold transactions. Answers (b) and (d) are incorrect because an absolute purchase commitment and the assuming of risk and reward relating to the product represent conditions which increase the likelihood that recording of a sale for such a transaction is appropriate.

119. (b) The requirement is to identify the most likely listed effect of "channel stuffing." Answer (b) is correct because channel stuffing is a marketing practice that suppliers sometimes use to boost sales by inducing distributors to buy substantially more inventory than they can promptly resell; accordingly, increased sales returns in the future are likely. Answers (a), (c) and (d) are incorrect because accrued liabilities, cash, and marketable investments are less likely to be affected by channel stuffing, which results in entries increasing accounts receivable, cost of goods sold, and sales, while decreasing inventory.

120. (d) The requirement is to identify the account in which a recorded entry is most likely to relate to the property, plant, and equipment completeness assertion. The completeness assertion addresses whether all transactions have been recorded in an account (here, property, plant, and equipment). Answer (d) is correct because the purchase of property, plant, and equipment may inappropriately have been recorded in the repairs and maintenance account rather than in property, plant, and equipment; this is a frequent bookkeeping error since the individual recording the entry may frequently see similar invoices which do represent repairs and maintenance expense. Answers (a), (b), and (c) are all incorrect because the allowance for doubtful accounts, marketable securities, and sales has no apparent relationship to the completeness of recording of property, plant, and equipment.

121. (c) The requirement is to identify the matter on which an auditor should obtain written management representations. Answer (c) is correct because written representations are ordinarily obtained on noncompliance with aspects of contractual agreements that may affect the financial statements. Answer (a) is incorrect because auditors do not ordinarily obtain a cost-benefit justification from management related to internal control weaknesses. Answer (b) is incorrect because written representations are not ordinarily obtained on such future plans. Answer (d) is incorrect because management may or may not be responsible for employee violations of laws, and because such a representation is not ordinarily obtained. See AU-C 580 for information on client representations.

122. (a) The requirement is to determine a matter to which materiality limits do **not** apply in obtaining written management representations. Answer (a) is correct because materiality considerations do not apply to management's acknowledgment of its responsibility for fair presentation of financial statements, the availability of all financial records, the completeness and availability of all minutes and meetings of stockholders, directors, and committees of directors, and communication from regulatory agencies. Answers (b), (c), and (d) are all incorrect because materiality considerations relate to losses from purchase commitments, compensating balances, and obsolete inventory. AU-C 580 discusses client representations.

123. (c) The requirement is to determine the proper date for a client's representation letter. AU-C 580 states that the representation letter should be dated as of the date of the auditor's report.

124. (b) The requirement is to identify the matter that an auditor most likely would include in a management representation letter. Auditors will generally request assurance as to the completeness and availability of minutes of stockholders' and directors' meetings. See AU-C 580 for written representations ordinarily obtained by the auditor.

125. (d) The requirement is to determine the year(s) on which a CPA must obtain written representations from management, when comparative financial statements are being issued, but current management has only been employed for a portion of one of those years. AU-C 580 states that if current management was not present during all periods reported upon, the auditor should nevertheless obtain written representations from current management on all such periods.

126. (a) The requirement is to identify the information ordinarily included among the written client representations obtained by the auditor. Answer (a) is correct because AU-C 580 includes information on compensating balances in the list of representations normally obtained. Answer (b) is incorrect because management need not acknowledge a responsibility for employee illegal actions. Answer (c) is incorrect because the auditor, not the client, determines whether sufficient audit evidence has been made available. Answer (d) is incorrect because, for purposes of a financial statement audit, management need not attempt to determine whether material weaknesses in internal control exist.

127. (a) The requirement is to determine the correct statement with respect to the use of a management representation letter as audit evidence about the completeness assertion. Answer (a) is correct because such written representations are meant to complement, but not replace, substantive procedures. Answer (b) is incorrect because the complementary nature of such representations is **not** considered sufficient, even when combined with reliance upon internal control. The inherent limitations of internal control do not permit the auditor to **replace** substantive procedures with complete reliance on internal control. Answer (c) is incorrect because the written representations are considered complementary evidence in support of various assertions. Answer (d) is incorrect because such written representations are not considered to be replacements for reliance upon internal control.

128. (a) The requirement is to determine who should sign a letter of representation. AU-C 580 states that, normally, the chief executive officer and the chief financial officers should sign the letter of representation.

129. (d) The requirement is to identify the scope limitation which **in all cases** is sufficient to preclude an unqualified opinion. Answer (d) is correct because the professional standards state that management refusal to furnish written representations constitutes a limitation on the scope of the auditor's examination sufficient to preclude an unqualified opinion. Answer (a) is incorrect because management's refusal to allow the auditor to review the predecessor's work may not necessarily result in report modification. Answer (b) is incorrect because alternate procedures may be available that will make report modification unnecessary when the auditor has been engaged after completion of the year-end physical count. Answer (c) is incorrect because management may choose not to correct a significant deficiencies in internal control without a resulting limitation on the scope of the audit.

130. (c) The requirement is to identify a purpose of a management representation letter. Answer (c) is correct because a management representation letter is meant to reduce the possibility of a misunderstanding concerning management's responsibility for the financial statements. Answer (a) is incorrect because reducing audit risk to an aggregate level of misstatement that could be considered material is not a logically sound statement. Answer (b) is incorrect because the management representation letter does not modify an auditor's responsibility to detect material misstatements. Answer (d) is incorrect because management representation letters are not a substitute for other procedures.

131. (c) The requirement is to identify the most likely source of a statement suggesting that there have been no communications from regulatory agencies. Answer (c) is correct because information such as this is ordinarily included in a management representation letter. Answers (a), (b), and (d) are incorrect because such a disclosure is not ordinarily included in a report on internal control, a special report, or a letter for an underwriter. See AU-C 580 for guidance on representation letters.

132. (a) The requirement is to identify the correct statement concerning an auditor's use of the work of a specialist. Answer (a) is correct because the work of a specialist who is related to the client may be acceptable under certain circumstances. Answer (b) is incorrect because if the auditor believes that the findings of the specialist are unreasonable, it is generally appropriate to obtain the findings of another specialist. Answer (c) is incorrect because a material difference between a specialist's findings and those included in the financial statements may result in the need for an explanatory paragraph, a qualified opinion, a disclaimer, or an adverse opinion. Answer (d) is incorrect because an auditor may use a specialist in the determination of various physical characteristics of assets.

133. (a) The requirement is to identify a circumstance in which an auditor may refer to the findings of a specialist in the auditor's report. Answer (a) is correct because the auditor may refer to the specialist when the specialist's findings result in inclusion of an explanatory paragraph to an audit report, in this case on going concern status. Answers (b), (c), and (d) are all incorrect because a specialist is only referred to in an audit report when that specialist's findings identify a circumstance requiring modification of the audit report. Auditors do not modify audit reports to simply inform the user that a specialist was involved.

134. (d) The requirement is to identify the statement that is correct about the auditor's use of the work of a specialist. Answer (d) is correct because the auditor should obtain an understanding of the nature of the work performed by the specialist. Answer (a) is incorrect because ordinarily a specialist will have a basic understanding of the auditor's corroborative use of the findings. Answer (b) is incorrect because the auditor need not perform substantive procedures to verify the specialist's assumptions and findings. Answer (c) is incorrect because the client may have an understanding of the nature of the work performed by the specialist. See AU-C 620 for information on the auditor's use of the work of a specialist.

135. (b) The requirement is to identify the circumstance in which an auditor may appropriately refer to the findings of a specialist. Answer (b) is correct because an auditor may refer to a specialist when the report is being modified due to the specialist's findings. Answers (a) and (c) are incorrect because a client's familiarity with a specialist or understanding of the auditor's use of the findings of a specialist does not result in modification of the audit report. Answer (d) is incorrect because an auditor does not divide responsibility with a specialist.

136. (c) The requirement is to identify the statement that an auditor must document when using the work of a specialist. Answer (c) is correct because the specialist's understanding of the auditor's corroborative use of his or her findings must be documented. See AU-C 620 for this and other documentation requirements. Answer (a) is incorrect because no statement concerning an update of the specialist's report is required to be documented. Answer (b) is incorrect because a division of responsibility relates to circumstances in which other auditors, not specialists, are involved. Answer (d) is incorrect because an auditor will not normally issue a disclaimer related to whether the specialist's findings corroborate the representations in the financial statements. The specialist's report is only referred to when there is a material difference between the specialist's findings and the representations in the financial statements. See AU-C 620 for information on the effect of a specialist's work on an auditor's report.

137. (c) The requirement is to determine which individual is **not** considered a **specialist** upon whose work an independent auditor may rely. The professional standards relating to using the work of a specialist do not apply to using the work of an internal auditor. Answers (a), (b), and (d), actuary, appraiser, and engineer, respectively, are all examples of specialists per the professional standards. Note here that the question and its reply do not imply that a CPA cannot use the work of an internal auditor. What is being suggested is that an internal auditor is not considered a specialist under the professional standards.

138. (d) The requirement is to identify which parties should reach an understanding on the limits of materiality for purposes of a lawyer's response to an auditor's inquiry concerning litigation, claims, and assessments. Answer (d) is correct because AU-C 501 states that a lawyer's response to an inquiry may be limited to material items, provided the lawyer and the auditor have reached an understanding on the limits of materiality for this purpose. Answer (a) is incorrect because it includes the client's management. Answer (b) is incorrect because it includes the client's audit committee and omits the auditor. Answer (c) is incorrect because it includes the client's management and omits the auditor.

139. (b) The requirement is to identify the correct statement concerning the refusal of a client's attorney to provide information requested in an inquiry letter. Answer (b) is correct because AU-C 501 indicates that this is a limitation on the scope of the audit. Answer (a) is incorrect because the lack of information is unlikely to lead to an adverse opinion since no information has been provided indicating that the financial statements are misstated. Answer (c) is incorrect because withdrawal is not generally necessary due to the client's attorney's failure to provide information. Answer (d) is incorrect because significant deficiencies pertain to weaknesses in internal control.

140. **(c)** The requirement is to identify the audit procedure that an auditor most likely would perform concerning litigation, claims, and assessments. Answer (c) is correct because auditors must discuss with management its policies and procedures for evaluating and accounting for litigation, claims and assessments. See AU-C 501 for this and other requirements. Answer (a) is incorrect because the client's lawyer is not ordinarily asked to make an assessment about whether the client has a going concern problem (see AU-C 570) for information on an auditor's consideration of a client's ability to continue as a going concern). Answer (b) is incorrect because an auditor will not ordinarily examine legal documents in the client's lawyer's possession. Answer (d) is incorrect because an auditor will not ordinarily confirm with the client's lawyer that all litigation, claims, and assessment have been recorded.

141. **(b)** The requirement is to identify the primary reason that an auditor should request a client to send a letter of inquiry to its attorneys. Answer (b) is correct because a letter of audit inquiry to the client's attorney is the auditor's primary means of obtaining corroboration of the information furnished by management concerning litigation, claims, and assessments. Answer (a) is incorrect because it will often be impossible to determine the probable outcome of asserted claims and pending or threatened litigation. Answer (c) is incorrect because no such opinions on historical experiences are generally available. Answer (d) is incorrect because the description of litigation, claims, and assessments is generally prepared by the client.

142. **(b)** The requirement is to identify the procedure that is **not** performed regarding litigation, claims, and assessments. Answer (b) is correct because the CPA does not confirm directly with the client's lawyer that all claims have been recorded in the financial statements. Answers (a), (c), and (d) are all incorrect because they represent information obtained from management regarding litigation, claims, and assessments as summarized in AU-C 501.

143. **(a)** The requirement is to identify the appropriate limitation for an attorney's response to a client's letter of audit inquiry. Answer (a) is correct because AU-C 501 states that an attorney may appropriately limit his response to matters to which s/he has given substantive attention in the form of legal consultation or representation. Answers (b), (c), and (d) are incorrect because AU-C 501 presents a variety of other requests in addition to information on the likelihood of an unfavorable outcome of the matters disclosed by the entity, similar litigation, and probable outcomes.

144. **(a)** If a client's lawyer resigned shortly after the receipt of an attorney's letter which indicated no significant disagreements with the client's assessment of contingent liabilities, the auditor should inquire why the attorney resigned. The auditor's concern is whether any undisclosed unasserted claims have arisen. Per AU-C 501, a lawyer may be required to resign if his

advice concerning reporting for litigation, claims, and assessments is disregarded by the client. Accordingly, the resignation shortly after issuance of an attorney's letter may indicate a problem. Answer (b) is incorrect because the attorney issued a letter indicating no significant disagreement with the client's assessment of contingent liabilities. Answers (c) and (d) are incorrect because AU-C 501 only suggests that the auditor should consider the need for inquiries (i.e., AU-C 501) does not require a complete new exam of contingent liabilities or an adverse opinion).

145. **(b)** The requirement is to identify the lawyer's letter comment that is most likely to cause the auditor to request clarification. Answer (b) is correct because a statement that the action can be settled for less than the damages claimed is unclear as to the details of the attorney's belief. Answers (a), (c), and (d) are all incorrect because they represent responses that may be clearly interpreted by the auditor. See AU-C 501 for information on assessing lawyer's evaluations of the likely outcome of litigation.

146. **(a)** The requirement is to determine whether valuation issues arise at initial recording, subsequent to initial recording, or at both times when considering fair value of an asset or liability. Answer (a) is correct because AU-C 500 makes clear that valuation issues arise at both times. Answers (b), (c), and (d) are all incorrect because they suggest that there are no valuation issues at one or both of these time periods.

147. **(b)** The requirement is to identify the **least** likely approach for auditing the fair values of assets and liabilities. Answer (b) is correct because it is doubtful that audit committee members will have information on the valuation. Answers (a), (c), and (d) are all incorrect because they represent the three approaches presented for auditing fair values (as well as other estimates).

148. **(c)** The requirement is to identify the auditing procedure that would most likely assist an auditor in identifying related-party transactions. Answer (c) is correct because reviewing confirmations of loans receivable and payable for indications of guarantees may reveal unusual transactions that involve related parties. See AU-C 550 for procedures related to identifying transactions with related parties. Answer (a) is incorrect because inspecting the correspondence with lawyers for evidence of unreported contingent liabilities does not generally relate directly to related-party transactions. Answer (b) is incorrect because nonrecurring transactions are more indicative of related-party transactions. Answer (d) is incorrect because analytical procedures performed to identify possible financial difficulties do not relate directly to related-party transactions.

149. **(c)** The requirement is to determine an auditor's responsibility after having determined that a related-party transaction has occurred. Answer (c) is correct because after identifying the existence of such an act, the auditor should obtain an understanding of the business purpose of the transaction. See AU-C 550 for this and other responsibilities. Answer (a) is incorrect because the mere existence of a related-party transaction may or may not lead to audit report modification. Answer (b) is incorrect because the performance of analytical procedures is not required. Answer (d) is incorrect because except for routine transactions, it will generally not be possible to determine whether the transaction would have taken place, or whether it was consummated on terms equivalent to an arm's-length transaction.

150. (d) The requirement is to identify the correct statement concerning related-party transactions. Answer (d) is correct because AU-C 550 requires that the auditor should place primary emphasis on the adequacy of disclosure. Answer (a) is incorrect because ascertaining rights and obligations is only part of the auditor's total responsibility and not the primary emphasis. Answer (b) is incorrect because while auditors attempt to determine the existence of related parties, this is not the primary emphasis. Answer (c) is incorrect because verifying the valuation of related-party transactions will often not be possible.

151. (d) The requirement is to identify the correct statement concerning related-party transactions. Answer (d) is correct because AU-C 550 requires that procedures directed toward identifying related-party transactions should be performed, even if the auditor has no reason to suspect their existence. Answer (a) is incorrect because, in the absence of evidence to the contrary, related-party transactions need not be assumed to be outside the ordinary course of business. Answer (b) is incorrect because the auditor will not in general be able to determine whether a particular transaction would have occurred if the parties had **not** been related. Answer (c) is incorrect because, if proper disclosures are made, the related-party transactions are not required to be recorded on terms equivalent to arm's-length transactions.

152. (c) The requirement is to identify the circumstance in which an auditor most likely would modify an unqualified opinion if the entity's financial statements include a footnote on related-party transactions. Answer (c) is correct because it generally will not be possible to determine whether a particular transaction was consummated on terms equivalent to those with unrelated parties. Therefore, the auditor may be required to express a qualified or an adverse opinion when such an unsubstantiated disclosure is included. Answers (a), (b), and (d) are all incorrect because they represent situations that may be disclosed in related-party transaction disclosures.

153. (d) The requirement is to identify the most likely procedure to be performed in obtaining evidence about subsequent events. Answer (d) is correct because changes in long-term debt occurring after year-end may require note disclosure. Answers (a) and (b) are incorrect because auditors will not generally test changes in employee pay rates after year-end or recompute depreciation expense for plant assets sold. Answer (c) is incorrect because payroll checks issued near year-end may frequently be cashed after year-end and their investigation will not in general be directly related to obtaining evidence about subsequent events. See AU-C 560 for the responsibilities of auditors with respect to subsequent events.

154. (c) The requirement is to identify the event occurring after the issuance of an auditor's report that would most likely cause the auditor to make further inquiries about the previously issued financial statements. Answer (c) is correct because when an auditor becomes aware of information which relates to the financial statements previously reported upon, but which was not known at the date of the report, he or she should undertake to determine whether the information is reliable and whether the facts existed at the date of the audit report; in this circumstance it seems that the lease transactions existed as of the date of the audit report. Answer (a) is incorrect because the natural disaster occurred subsequent to the issuance of the audit report. Answer (b) is incorrect because the contingency had been properly disclosed. Answer (d) is incorrect because the sale of the subsidiary occurred subsequent to the issuance of the audit report.

155. (d) The requirement is to determine proper accounting and auditing treatment of uncollectibility of an account receivable resulting from a customer's bankruptcy due to a natural disaster occurring after a client's balance sheet date. Answer (d) is correct because a customer's major casualty loss after year-end will result in a financial statement note disclosure with no adjustment and no audit report modification due to consistency.

156. (d) The requirement is to determine an auditor's responsibility when subsequent to issuance of an audit report a client sells the shares of a major subsidiary. Answer (d) is correct because no action need be taken since the event arose after the issuance of the auditor's report. Answers (a), (b), and (c) are all incorrect because they outline responsibilities which are not appropriate in this circumstance. See AU-C 560 for a discussion of auditor responsibility when subsequent to the issuance of the auditor's report the auditor becomes aware of a fact that **existed at the date of the auditor's report**.

157. (c) The requirement is to determine the auditor's responsibility with respect to a client acquisition of 25% of its outstanding capital stock after year-end and prior to the completion of the auditor's fieldwork. Answer (c) is correct because the transaction described is a type 2 subsequent event (since the acquisition provided evidence of a condition which came into existence after year-end) and therefore the proper accounting approach would be note disclosure rather than adjustment. Answer (a) is incorrect because adjustments are only appropriate for type 1 subsequent events (events which provide evidence that the condition was in existence at year-end). Answer (b) is incorrect because the auditor does not issue financial statements for the client. Answer (d) is incorrect because the opinion paragraph of the report need not be modified; if any report modification were considered necessary, it would be an explanatory paragraph emphasizing the matter.

158. (d) The requirement is to identify a procedure that an auditor would perform to obtain evidence about the occurrence of subsequent events. Answer (d) is correct because an auditor will inquire of officers and other executives having responsibility for financial and accounting matters whether any unusual adjustments have been made during the period from the balance sheet date to the date of inquiry. See AU-C 560 for auditing procedures performed to identify subsequent events.

159. (a) The requirement is to determine a procedure that an auditor should generally perform regarding subsequent events. Answer (a) is correct because the *Professional Standards* state that the auditor generally should compare the latest available interim financial statements with the financial statements being audited. See AU-C 560 (for this and other requirements. Answer (b) is incorrect because second accounts receivable confirmation requests will be sent well before the auditor's review of subsequent events. Answer (c) is incorrect because the communication of material weaknesses is not a subsequent event procedure. See AU-C 265 for the required communication of **significant deficiencies**. Answer (d) is incorrect because auditors generally only receive cutoff statements for the period immediately after year-end, not for multiple months.

160. (b) The requirement is to identify an auditor's responsibility when a client refuses to adjust recently issued financial statements for a subsequent event related to the bankruptcy of the entity's principal customer. Answer (b) is correct because if the client refuses to make disclosures, AU-C 560 requires the auditor to notify each member of the board of directors of such refusal and that he or she will take steps to prevent future reliance upon the audit report. Ordinarily the auditor will then notify the clients and regulatory agencies that the report should no longer be associated with the financial statements, and when possible, notify persons known to be relying upon the financial statements. Answer (a) is incorrect because it is less likely that all of the creditors will be informed. Answer (c) is incorrect because the financial statements are the responsibility of management, and the auditor will not revise or distribute them. Answer (d) is incorrect because no revised report will be issued.

161. (c) The requirement is to identify the circumstance in which an auditor who finds that he or she has omitted a substantive procedure at the time of an audit may decide not to apply that procedure. Answer (c) is correct because when results of other procedures tend to compensate for the procedure it may be omitted. Answer (a) is incorrect because, even when distribution of the financial statement has been limited to management and the board of directors, it may be necessary to perform the procedure. Answer (b) is incorrect because the type of report issued does not affect the need to perform the procedure. Answer (d) is incorrect because delays by the client in providing data are not an acceptable reason not to perform that procedure.

162. (b) The requirement is to determine professional responsibility when, subsequent to issuance of an audit report, an auditor has determined that a necessary audit procedure has been omitted. Answer (b) is correct because an auditor must apply procedures that would provide a satisfactory basis for the opinion issued. Answer (a) is incorrect because stockholders need not be informed at this point that the audit report should **not** be relied upon. Answer (c) is incorrect because the auditor's report will not be reissued unless the financial statements are restated. Answer (d) is incorrect because tests of controls will not compensate for the omitted procedure. See AU-C 585 (390) for overall procedures relating to considering omitted procedures after an audit report has been issued.

163. (c) The requirement is to identify an auditor's first responsibility upon discovering six months after completion of an audit that engagement personnel failed to confirm several of the client's material accounts receivable balances. Answer (c) is correct because the auditor must first assess the importance of the omitted procedures to the auditor's ability to support the previously expressed opinion. Answers (a) and (b) are incorrect because prior to attempting any such confirmation or performing alternative procedures, an assessment of whether the procedures are needed is to be performed. Answer (d) is incorrect because a consideration of whether anyone is relying on, or is likely to rely on, the unqualified opinion is made after assessing the importance of the omitted procedure.

164. (c) The requirement is to determine the procedure **least** likely to be performed before the balance sheet date. Answer (c) is correct because the search for unrecorded liabilities relies upon a review of documents unrecorded at year-end, as well as inspection of purchases and disbursements recorded after year-end, to determine whether a proper cutoff of transactions between periods has occurred. Answer (a) is incorrect because auditors are able to test internal control over cash prior to year-end. Answers (b) and (d) are incorrect because in cases of good internal control, receivables may be confirmed and inventory observed prior to year-end.

165. (c) The requirement is to determine the most likely type of transaction that would be detected by an auditor's review of a client's sales cutoff. Answer (c) is correct because the auditor's review will include a study of sales recorded late in December and early in January. This will be accomplished by reviewing the period when the revenue was earned by shipment of goods or performance of services, as compared to the period in which the revenue was recorded. Accordingly, the review of sales recorded in January may reveal unrecorded sales for the preceding year. Answer (a) is incorrect because shipments lacking sales invoices and shipping documents will be very difficult to identify; also, this reply is more limited than answer (c). Answer (b) is incorrect because excessive write-offs of accounts receivable will not usually be detected when testing the sales cutoff. Answer (d) is incorrect because it is unlikely that lapping in the application of cash receipts will be detected by sales cutoff testing. More frequently, procedures such as confirmations, analytical procedures, and an analysis of deposit tickets reveal lapping.

166. (b) The requirement is to identify the assertion being tested by cutoff tests designed to detect credit sales made before the end of the year that have improperly been recorded in the subsequent year. Answer (b) is correct because the completeness assertion deals with whether all transactions have been included in the proper period. Answer (a) is incorrect because the presentation or disclosure assertion deals with whether particular components of the financial statements are properly classified, described, and disclosed. Answer (c) is incorrect because the rights and obligations assertion deals with whether assets are the rights of the entity and liabilities are the obligations of the entity at a given date. Answer (d) is incorrect because the existence or occurrence assertion deals with whether assets or liabilities of the entity exist at a given date and whether recorded transactions have occurred during a given period. In this question, the existence assertion would be tested if the auditor sampled from sales recorded prior to year-end to determine whether the sale occurred before or after year-end.

167. (d) The requirement is to identify the procedure an auditor would most likely perform during the overall review stage of formulating an opinion on an entity's financial statements. Answer (d) is correct because a consideration of results relating to the assessment of the risk of material misstatement due to fraud may reveal that the audit has inadequately addressed that risk; in such a case additional procedures would be required. Answer (a) is incorrect because such assurance from the entity's attorney is ordinarily obtained prior to the overall review stage of an audit. Answer (b) is incorrect because the verification of the accuracy of the proof of cash is ordinarily performed prior to the overall review and because little verification of the bank cutoff statement is usually necessary since it is ordinarily received directly by the auditor from the bank. Answer (c) is incorrect because such provisions for the safeguarding of assets may be corrected well after the conclusion of the audit.

168. (a) The requirement is to identify the correct statement with respect to the primary orientation of operational auditing. Answer (a) is correct because operational audits deal primarily with evaluating the efficiency and effectiveness with which operations function, often with the intention of making improvements to accomplish the goals of management. Answers (b) and (c) are incorrect because financial statement audits are oriented toward such determinations, not operational audits. Answer (d) is incorrect because examinations of internal control are not performed on operational audits.

169. (d) The requirement is to identify a typical objective of an operational audit. Answer (d) is correct because operational audits typically address efficiency and effectiveness. Answer (a) is incorrect because while the adequacy of internal control design may be addressed during an operational audit, this is less complete than answer (d). Answer (b) is incorrect because operational audits may or may not be related to compliance with generally accepted governmental auditing standards. Answer (c) is incorrect because financial statement audits, not operational audits, address whether results of operations are fairly presented.

Simulations

Task-Based Simulation 1

Audit Investments and Accounts Receivable		
	Authoritative Literature	Help

Items 1 through 7 represent audit objectives for the investments and accounts receivable. To the right of each set of audit objectives is a listing of possible audit procedures for that account. For each audit objective, select the audit procedure that would primarily respond to the objective. Select only one procedure for each audit objective. A procedure may be selected only once, or not at all.

Audit procedures for investments

A. Trace opening balances in the subsidiary ledger to prior year's audit working papers.
B. Determine that employees who are authorized to sell investments do not have access to cash.
C. Examine supporting documents for a sample of investment transactions to verify that prenumbered documents are used.
D. Determine that any impairments in the price of investments have been properly recorded.
E. Verify that transfers from the current to the noncurrent investment portfolio have been properly recorded.
F. Obtain positive confirmations as of the balance sheet date of investments held by independent custodians.
G. Trace investment transactions to minutes of the Board of Directors meetings to determine that transactions were properly authorized.

Audit objectives for investments	(A)	(B)	(C)	(D)	(E)	(F)	(G)
1. Investments are properly described and classified in the financial statements.	O	O	O	O	O	O	O
2. Recorded investments represent investments actually owned at the balance sheet date.	O	O	O	O	O	O	O
3. Trading investments are properly valued at fair market value at the balance sheet date.	O	O	O	O	O	O	O

Audit procedures for accounts receivable

A. Analyze the relationship of accounts receivable and sales and compare it with relationships for preceding periods.
B. Perform sales cutoff tests to obtain assurance that sales transactions and corresponding entries for inventories and cost of goods sold are recorded in the same and proper period.
C. Review the aged trial balance for significant past due accounts.
D. Obtain an understanding of the business purpose of transactions that resulted in accounts receivable balances.
E. Review loan agreements for indications of whether accounts receivable have been factored or pledged.
F. Review the accounts receivable trial balance for amounts due from officers and employees.
G. Analyze unusual relationships between monthly accounts receivable balances and monthly accounts payable balances.

Audit objectives for accounts receivable	(A)	(B)	(C)	(D)	(E)	(F)	(G)
4. Accounts receivable represent all amounts owed to the entity at the balance sheet date.	O	O	O	O	O	O	O
5. The entity has legal right to all accounts receivable at the balance sheet date.	O	O	O	O	O	O	O
6. Accounts receivable are stated at net realizable value.	O	O	O	O	O	O	O
7. Accounts receivable are properly described and presented in the financial statements.	O	O	O	O	O	O	O

Task-Based Simulation 2

Confirmation of Accounts Receivable

Bill Smith, the president of Alex Inc., a nonpublic audit client, has suggested to you that his previous auditor did not confirm accounts receivable and he sees no reason why you should do so.

Selections

A. AU-C
B. PCAOB
C. AT
D. AR
E. ET
F. BL
G. CS
H. QC

	(A)	**(B)**	**(C)**	**(D)**	**(E)**	**(F)**	**(G)**	**(H)**
1. Which title of the Professional Standards addresses this issue and will be helpful in responding to him?	O	O	O	O	O	O	O	O

2. Enter the exact section and paragraph(s) with helpful information.

Task-Based Simulation 3

Illegal Acts and Related-Party Transactions — Authoritative Literature — Help

In applying audit procedures and evaluating the results of those procedures, auditors may encounter specific information that may raise a question concerning the existence of illegal acts and related-party transactions. Indicate whether each of the following is more likely related to an illegal act (IA) or a related-party transaction (RP).

Statement	**IA**	**RP**
1. A note payable has an interest rate well below the market rate at the time at which the loan was obtained.	O	O
2. The company has a properly documented loan but the loan has no scheduled repayment terms.	O	O
3. Unexplained payments have been made to government officials.	O	O
4. The company exchanged certain real estate property for similar real estate property.	O	O
5. Large cash receipts near year-end have been received based on cash sales for which there is no documentation.	O	O

Task-Based Simulation 4

An auditor may use confirmations of accounts receivable. Reply as to whether the following statements are correct or incorrect with respect to the confirmation process when applied to accounts receivable.

Statement	Correct	Incorrect
1. The confirmation requests should be mailed to respondents by the CPAs.	○	○
2. A combination of positive and negative request forms must be used if receivables are significant.	○	○
3. Second requests are ordinarily sent for positive form confirmations requests when the first request is not returned.	○	○
4. Confirmations address existence more than they address completeness.	○	○
5. Confirmation of accounts receivable is a generally accepted auditing standard.	○	○
6. Absent a few circumstances, there is a presumption that the auditor will confirm accounts receivable.	○	○
7. Auditors should always confirm the total balances of accounts rather than individual portions. (e.g., if the balance is made up of three sales, all three should be confirmed).	○	○
8. Auditors may ignore individually immaterial accounts when confirming accounts receivable.	○	○
9. The best way to evaluate the results of the confirmation process is to total the misstatements identified and to compare that total to the account's tolerable error amounts.	○	○
10. Accounts receivable are ordinarily confirmed on a standard form developed by the American Institute of Certified Public Accountants and the Financial Executives Institute.	○	○

Task-Based Simulation 5

Auditors often observe the counting of their clients' inventories. Reply as to whether the following statements are correct or incorrect with respect to the inventory observation.

Statement	Correct	Incorrect
1. With strong internal control, the inventory count may be at the end of the year or at other times.	○	○
2. When a client has many inventory locations, auditors ordinarily need not be present at each location.	○	○
3. All auditor test counts must be documented in the working papers.	○	○
4. Auditors' observation of the counting of their clients' inventories addresses the existence of inventory, and not the completeness of the count.	○	○
5. When the client manufactures a product, direct labor and overhead ordinarily become a part of inventory item costs.	○	○
6. Inventory is ordinarily valued at the lower of standard cost or market.	○	○
7. Inventory items present as "consigned in" should not be included in the clients' inventory value.	○	○
8. Auditor recording of test counts ordinarily replaces the need for client "tagging" of inventory.	○	○
9. Ordinarily, an auditor need not count all items in the inventory.	○	○
10. At the completion of the count, an auditor will ordinarily provide the client with copies of his or her inventory test counts to help assure inventory accuracy.	○	○

Task-Based Simulation 6

Auditing Derivatives

The partner in charge of the nonpublic company audit you are currently working on is concerned about overall audit requirements relating to derivatives that are measured based on fair value. More specifically, she has asked you to find the section and paragraph that addresses an auditor's overall responsibilities in that area.

Selections

A. AU-C
B. PCAOB
C. AT
D. AR
E. ET
F. BL
G. CS
H. QC

	(A)	(B)	(C)	(D)	(E)	(F)	(G)	(H)
1. Which title of the Professional Standards addresses this issue and will be helpful in responding to her?	O	O	O	O	O	O	O	O

2. Enter the exact section and paragraph(s) with helpful information.

Task-Based Simulation 7

Items 1 through 6 represent the items that an auditor ordinarily would find on a client-prepared bank reconciliation. The accompanying **List of Auditing Procedures** represents substantive auditing procedures. For each item, select one or more procedures, as indicated, that the auditor most likely would perform to gather evidence in support of that item. The procedures on the **List** may be selected once, more than once, or not at all.

Assume

- The client prepared the bank reconciliation on 10/2/X5.
- The bank reconciliation is mathematically accurate.
- The auditor received a cutoff bank statement dated 10/7/X5 directly from the bank on 10/11/X5.
- The 9/30/X5 deposit in transit, outstanding checks #1281, #1285, #1289, and #1292, and the correction of the error regarding check #1282 appeared on the cutoff bank statement.
- The auditor assessed control risk concerning the financial statement assertions related to cash at the maximum.

List of Auditing Procedures

A. Trace to cash receipts journal.

B. Trace to cash disbursements journal.

C. Compare to 9/30/01 general ledger.

D. Confirm directly with bank.

E. Inspect bank credit memo.

F. Inspect bank debit memo.

G. Ascertain reason for unusual delay.

H. Inspect supporting documents for reconciling item not appearing on cutoff statement.

I. Trace items on the bank reconciliation to cutoff statement.

J. Trace items on the cutoff statement to bank reconciliation.

General Company
BANK RECONCILIATION
1ST NATIONAL BANK OF US BANK ACCOUNT
September 30, 20X5

1. Select 2 Procedures	Balance per bank		$ 28,375
2. Select 5 Procedures	Deposits in transit		
	9/29/X5	$4,500	
	9/30/X5	1,525	6,025
			34,400
3. Select 5 Procedures	Outstanding checks		
	# 988 8/31/X5	2,200	
	#1281 9/26/X5	675	
	#1285 9/27/X5	850	
	#1289 9/29/X5	2,500	
	#1292 9/30/X5	7,225	(13,450)
			20,950
4. Select 1 Procedure	Customer note collected by bank		(3,000)
5. Select 2 Procedures	Error: Check #1282, written on 9/26/X5 for $270 was erroneously charged by bank as $720; bank was notified on 10/2/X5		450
6. Select 1 Procedure	Balance per books		$18,400

Task-Based Simulation 8

Audit Procedures		
	Authoritative Literature	Help

Items 1 through 12 represent possible errors and fraud that you suspect may be present at General Company. The accompanying List of Auditing Procedures represents procedures that the auditor would consider performing to gather evidence concerning possible errors and fraud. For each item, select one or two procedures, as indicated, that the auditor most likely would perform to gather evidence in support of that item. The procedures on the list may be selected once, more than once, or not at all.

List of Auditing Procedures

A. Compare the details of the cash receipts journal entries with the details of the corresponding daily deposit slips.

B. Scan the debits to the fixed asset accounts and vouch selected amounts to vendors' invoices and management's authorization.

C. Perform analytical procedures that compare documented authorized pay rates to the entity's budget and forecast.

D. Obtain the cutoff bank statement and compare the cleared checks to the year-end bank reconciliation.

E. Prepare a bank transfer schedule.

F. Inspect the entity's deeds to its real estate.

G. Make inquiries of the entity's attorney concerning the details of real estate transactions.

H. Confirm the terms of borrowing arrangements with the lender.

I. Examine selected equipment repair orders and supporting documentation to determine the propriety of the charges.

J. Send requests to confirm the entity's accounts receivable on a surprise basis at an interim date.

K. Send a second request for confirmation of the receivable to the customer and make inquiries of a reputable credit agency concerning the customer's creditworthiness.

L. Examine the entity's shipping documents to verify that the merchandise that produced the receivable was actually sent to the customer.

M. Inspect the entity's correspondence files for indications of customer disputes for evidence that certain shipments were on consignment.

N. Perform edit checks of data on the payroll transaction tapes.

O. Inspect payroll check endorsements for similar handwriting.

P. Observe payroll check distribution on a surprise basis.

Q. Vouch data in the payroll register to documented authorized pay rates in the human resources department's files.

R. Reconcile the payroll checking account and determine if there were unusual time lags between the issuance and payment of payroll checks.

S. Inspect the file of prenumbered vouchers for consecutive numbering and proper approval by an appropriate employee.

T. Determine that the details of selected prenumbered vouchers match the related vendors' invoices.

U. Examine the supporting purchase orders and receiving reports for selected paid vouchers.

Possible misstatements due to errors and fraud

1. The auditor suspects that a kiting scheme exists because an accounting department employee who can issue and record checks seems to be leading an unusually luxurious lifestyle. (**Select only 1 procedure**)

2. An auditor suspects that the controller wrote several checks and recorded the cash disbursements just before year-end but did not mail the checks until after the first week of the subsequent year. (**Select only 1 procedure**)

3. The entity borrowed funds from a financial institution. Although the transaction was properly recorded, the auditor suspects that the loan created a lien on the entity's real estate that is not disclosed in its financial statements. (**Select only 1 procedure**)

4. The auditor discovered an unusually large receivable from one of the entity's new customers. The auditor suspects that the receivable may be fictitious because the auditor has never heard of the customer and because the auditor's initial attempt to confirm the receivable has been ignored by the customer. (**Select only 2 procedures**)

5. The auditor suspects that fictitious employees have been placed on the payroll by the entity's payroll supervisor, who has access to payroll records and to the paychecks. (**Select only 1 procedure**)

6. The auditor suspects that selected employees of the entity received unauthorized raises from the entity's payroll supervisor, who has access to payroll records. (**Select only 1 procedure**)

7. The entity's cash receipts of the first few days of the subsequent year were properly deposited in its general operating account after the year-end. However, the auditor suspects that the entity recorded the cash receipts in its books during the last week of the year under audit. (**Select only 1 procedure**)

8. The auditor suspects that vouchers were prepared and processed by an accounting department employee for merchandise that was neither ordered nor received by the entity. (**Select only 1 procedure**)

9. The details of invoices for equipment repairs were not clearly identified or explained to the accounting department employees. The auditor suspects that the bookkeeper incorrectly recorded the repairs as fixed assets. (**Select only 1 procedure**)

10. The auditor suspects that a lapping scheme exists because an accounting department employee who has access to cash receipts also maintains the accounts receivable ledger and refuses to take any vacation or sick days. (**Select only 2 procedures**)

11. The auditor suspects that the entity is inappropriately increasing the cash reported on its balance sheet by drawing a check on one account and not recording it as an outstanding check on that account and simultaneously recording it as a deposit in a second account. (**Select only 1 procedure**)

12. The auditor suspects that the entity's controller has overstated sales and accounts receivable by recording fictitious sales to regular customers in the entity's books. (**Select only 2 procedures**)

Task-Based Simulation 9

Substantive Procedures for Property, Plant and Equipment	Authoritative Literature	Help

DietWeb Inc. (hereafter DietWeb) was incorporated and began business in March of 20X1, seven years ago. You are working on the 20X8 audit—your CPA firm's fifth audit of DietWeb. For each audit objective, select a substantive procedure that would help to achieve that objective. Each of the procedures may be used once, more than once, or not at all.

Substantive procedure

A. Trace opening balances in the summary schedules to the prior year's audit working papers.
B. Review the provision for depreciation expense and determine that depreciable lives and methods used in the current year are consistent with those used in the prior year.
C. Determine that responsibility for maintaining the property and equipment records is segregated from the responsibility for custody of property and equipment.
D. Examine deeds and title insurance certificates.
E. Perform cutoff test to verify that property and equipment additions are recorded in the proper period.
F. Determine that property and equipment is adequately insured.
G. Physically examine all recorded major property and equipment additions.
H. Analyze repairs and maintenance expense.

Audit objectives	(A)	(B)	(C)	(D)	(E)	(F)	(G)	(H)
1. DietWeb has legal rights to property and equipment acquired during the year.	O	O	O	O	O	O	O	O
2. DietWeb recorded property and equipment acquired during the year that did not actually exist at the balance sheet date.	O	O	O	O	O	O	O	O
3. DietWeb's property and equipment was properly valued at the balance sheet date.	O	O	O	O	O	O	O	O
4. DietWeb recorded all property and equipment assets that were purchased near year-end.	O	O	O	O	O	O	O	O
5. DietWeb recorded all property retirements that occurred during the year.	O	O	O	O	O	O	O	O
6. DietWeb capitalized all acquisitions that occurred during the period.	O	O	O	O	O	O	O	O

Task-Based Simulation 10

Risk Analysis	Authoritative Literature	Help

You are working with William Bond, CPA, and you are considering the risk of material misstatement in planning the audit of Toxic Waste Disposal (TWD) Company's financial statements for the year ended December 31, 20X0.

Assume that you have identified the following risks at the account level relating to TWD's property and equipment. Identify the most closely related financial statement assertion and the audit procedure that might be planned to most likely address the risk. Financial statement assertions and audit procedures may be used once, more than once, or not used at all.

Related financial statement assertion	**Audit procedures**
A. Existence or occurrence	**H.** Determine that the responsibility for maintaining the property and equipment records is segregated from the responsibility for custody of property and equipment.
B. Completeness	
C. Rights and obligations	
D. Valuation or allocation	**I.** Examine deeds and title insurance certificates.
E. Presentation and disclosure	**J.** Perform cutoffs tests to verify that property and equipment additions are recorded in the proper period.
F. Trace opening balances in the summary schedules to the prior year's audit working papers.	
	K. Determine that property and equipment are adequately insured.
G. Review the provision for depreciation expense and determine that depreciable lives and methods used in the current year are consistent with those used in the prior year.	**L.** Physically examine all major property and equipment additions.

Risk identified	Related financial statement assertion						Audit procedures					
	(A)	**(B)**	**(C)**	**(D)**	**(E)**	**(F)**	**(G)**	**(H)**	**(I)**	**(J)**	**(K)**	**(L)**
1. TWD may not have legal title to certain property and equipment recorded as acquired during the year.	O	O	O	O	O	O	O	O	O	O	O	O
2. Recorded property and equipment acquisitions may include nonexistent assets.	O	O	O	O	O	O	O	O	O	O	O	O
3. Recorded net property and equipment are for proper amounts.	O	O	O	O	O	O	O	O	O	O	O	O

Task-Based Simulation 11

Audit Objectives and Procedures		
	Authoritative Literature	Help

For each audit objective listed below select the most appropriate audit procedure for raw materials inventory (**Items 1–3**) and for Accounts Receivable (**Items 4–6**). Audit procedures may be used once, more than once, or not at all.

List of audit procedures for raw materials inventory

A. Compare standard costs of inventories with standardized market values.
B. Determine that all direct labor and overhead has been expensed and not included in inventory valuation.
C. Examine vendors' invoices.
D. Perform analytical procedures comparing inventory to various industry averages.
E. Review drafts of financial statement note disclosures.
F. Select a sample of items during the physical count and determine that the client has included items on inventory count sheets.
G. Select a sample of recorded items on count sheets and determine that the items are on hand.

	(A)	**(B)**	**(C)**	**(D)**	**(E)**	**(F)**	**(G)**
1. Determine that company legally owns inventories.	O	O	O	O	O	O	O
2. Establish the completeness of inventories.	O	O	O	O	O	O	O
3. Determine that the cost of inventories is proper.	O	O	O	O	O	O	O

List of audit procedures for accounts receivable

A. Analyze relationships between accounts receivable balances and changes in the current portion of long-term debt.
B. Compare accounts receivable on the accounts receivable lead schedule with those on supporting audit schedules.
C. Compare total 20X8 annual sales with those of 20X7.
D. Examine December 20X8 sales journal and determine that sales are properly recorded in December.
E. Examine January 20X9 sales journal and determine that sales are properly recorded in January.
F. Inquire of credit manager about the collectability of various receivables.
G. Review disclosure checklist for recommended and required accounts receivable disclosures.

	(A)	(B)	(C)	(D)	(E)	(F)	(G)
4. Determine that all accounts receivable are properly recorded as of year-end.	O	O	O	O	O	O	O
5. Determine that accounts receivable are properly valued at net realizable value.	O	O	O	O	O	O	O
6. Note disclosures related to accounts receivable are proper.	O	O	O	O	O	O	O

Task-Based Simulation 12

The auditor determines that each of the following objectives will be part of the audit of Enright Corporation. For each audit objective, select a substantive procedure that would help to achieve the audit objectives. Each of the procedures may be used once, more than once, or not at all.

Substantive procedure

A. Review minutes of board of directors meetings and contracts, and make inquiries of management.
B. Test inventory transactions between a preliminary physical inventory date and the balance sheet date.
C. Obtain confirmation of inventories pledged under loan agreement.
D. Review perpetual inventory records, production records, and purchasing records for indication of current activity.
E. Reconcile physical counts to perpetual records and general ledger balances and investigate significant fluctuation.
F. Examine sales after year-end and open purchase order commitments.
G. Examine paid vendors' invoices, consignment agreements, and contracts.
H. Analytically review and compare the relationship of inventory balance to recent purchasing, production, and sales activity.

	(A)	(B)	(C)	(D)	(E)	(F)	(G)	(H)
1. Identify inventory transactions involving related parties.	O	O	O	O	O	O	O	O
2. Determine that items counted are included in the inventory listing.	O	O	O	O	O	O	O	O
3. Determine that a proper cutoff of purchases has occurred at year-end.	O	O	O	O	O	O	O	O
4. Determine that financial statements include proper disclosures relating to inventory.	O	O	O	O	O	O	O	O
5. Determine that recorded inventory is owned.	O	O	O	O	O	O	O	O

Task-Based Simulation 13

Spreadsheet Completion
Authoritative Literature
Help

Analytical procedures are evaluations of financial information made by a study of plausible relationships among financial and nonfinancial data. Understanding and evaluating such relationships are essential to the audit process.

The following spreadsheet with the financial statements were prepared by Holiday Manufacturing Co. for the year ended December 31, 20X1. Also presented are various financial statement ratios for Holiday as calculated from the prior year's financial statements. Sales represent net credit sales. The total assets and the receivables and inventory balances at December 31, 20X1, were the same as at December 31, 20X0.

	A	B	C	D	E	F	G
1	**Holiday Manufacturing Co.**						
2	**Balance Sheet**						
3	**December 31, 20X1**						
4							
5	Cash		$ 240,000		Accounts Payable		$ 160,000
6	Receivables		400,000		Notes payable		100,000
7	Inventory		600,000		Other current liabilities		140,000
8	Total current assets		$1,240,000		Total current liabilities		400,000
9							
10	Plant and equipment—net		760,000		Long-term debt		350,000
11					Common stock		750,000
12					Retained earnings		500,000
13	Total assets		$2,000,000		Total liabilities and capital		$2,000,000
14							
15							
16	Income Statement						
17	Year ended December 31, 20X1						
18							
19	Sales				$3,000,000		
20	Cost of goods sold						
21	Materials		800,000				
22	Labor		700,000				
23	Overhead		300,000		1,800,000		
24	Gross margin				1,200,000		
25							
26	Selling expenses		240,000				
27	General and admin. exp.		300,000		540,000		
28	Operating income				660,000		
29	Less: interest expense				40,000		
30	Income before taxes				620,000		
31	Less: federal income taxes				220,000		
32	Net income				$ 400,000		
33							
34							
35							
36	Ratios		**12/31/X1**		**12/31/X0**		
37	Current ratio		**(1)**		2.5		
38	Quick ratio		**(2)**		1.3		
39	Accounts receivable turnover		**(3)**		5.5		
40	Inventory turnover		**(4)**		2.5		
41	Total asset turnover		**(5)**		1.2		
42	Gross margin %		**(6)**		35%		
43	Net operating margin %		**(7)**		25%		
44	Times interest earned		**(8)**		10.3		
45	Total debt to equity %		**(9)**		50%		

Insert spreadsheet formulas into the worksheet to allow the direction calculation of each ratio (**1 through 9**). Use cell location rather than amounts.

Simulation Solutions

Task-Based Simulation 1

Audit Investments and Accounts Receivable	Authoritative Literature	Help

Audit objectives for investments	(A)	(B)	(C)	(D)	(E)	(F)	(G)
1. Investments are properly described and classified in the financial statements.	○	○	○	○	●	○	○
2. Recorded investments represent investments actually owned at the balance sheet date.	○	○	○	○	○	●	○
3. Trading investments are properly valued at fair market value at the balance sheet date.	○	○	○	●	○	○	○

Explanations

1. (E) The verification of transfers from the current to the noncurrent investment portfolio will provide assurance that the investments are properly classified in the financial statements.

2. (F) Positive confirmation replies as of the balance sheet date for investments held by independent custodians will provide assurance that the recorded investments are in fact owned by the audit client.

3. (D) Because trading investments should be valued at fair market value, determining whether any impairments in the price of investments have been recorded will provide assurance that investments are properly valued.

Audit objectives for accounts receivable	(A)	(B)	(C)	(D)	(E)	(F)	(G)
4. Accounts receivable represent all amounts owed to the entity at the balance sheet date.	○	●	○	○	○	○	○
5. The entity has legal right to all accounts receivable at the balance sheet date.	○	○	○	○	●	○	○
6. Accounts receivable are stated at net realizable value.	○	○	●	○	○	○	○
7. Accounts receivable are properly described and presented in the financial statements.	○	○	○	○	○	●	○

Explanations

4. (B) Performance of sales cutoff tests will provide assurance that sales transactions and the related receivables are recorded in the proper period. Thus, sales cutoff tests will provide assurance that all amounts owed to the entity at the balance sheet date are recorded in that period.

5. (E) A review of loan agreements, paying special attention to accounts receivable that have been factored, will provide assurance as to whether the entity has a legal right to all accounts receivable at the balance sheet date.

6. (C) An analysis of the aged trial balance for significant past due accounts will provide evidence with respect to accounts that may be uncollectible. Accordingly, the procedure will address the net realizable value of accounts receivable.

7. (F) Because material amounts due from officers and employees should be segregated from other receivables, a review of the trial balance for amounts due from officers and employees will provide assurance that accounts receivable are properly described and presented in the financial statements.

Task-Based Simulation 2

Audit objectives for investments	(A)	(B)	(C)	(D)	(E)	(F)	(G)	(H)
1. Which title of the Professional Standards addresses this issue and will be helpful in responding to him?	●	○	○	○	○	○	○	○

2. Enter the exact section and paragraph(s) with helpful information.	330	20, A54–A56

Task-Based Simulation 3

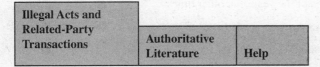

Statement	IA	RP
1. A note payable has an interest rate well below the market rate at the time at which the loan was obtained.	○	●
2. The company has a properly documented loan but the loan has no scheduled repayment terms.	○	●
3. Unexplained payments have been made to government officials.	●	○
4. The company exchanged certain real estate property for similar real estate property.	○	●
5. Large cash receipts near year-end have been received based on cash sales for which there is no documentation.	●	○

Task-Based Simulation 4

Accounts Receivable Confirmations
Authoritative Literature / Help

Statement	Correct	Correct
1. The confirmation requests should be mailed to respondents by the CPAs.	●	○
2. A combination of positive and negative request forms must be used if receivables are significant.	○	●
3. Second requests are ordinarily sent for positive form confirmations requests when the first request is not returned.	●	○
4. Confirmations address existence more than they address completeness.	●	○
5. Confirmation of accounts receivable is a generally accepted auditing standard.	○	●
6. Absent a few circumstances, there is a presumption that the auditor will confirm accounts receivable.	●	○
7. Auditors should always confirm the total balances of accounts rather than individual portions (e.g., if the balance is made up of three sales, all three should be confirmed).	○	●
8. Auditors may ignore individually immaterial accounts when confirming accounts receivable.	○	●

9. The best way to evaluate the results of the confirmation process is to total the misstatements identified and to compare that total to the account's tolerable error amounts.   ○   ●

10. Accounts receivable are ordinarily confirmed on a standard form developed by the American Institute of Certified Public Accountants and the Financial Executives Institute.   ○   ●

Task-Based Simulation 5

Statement	**Correct**	**Incorrect**
1. With strong internal control, the inventory count may be at the end of the year or at other times.	●	○
2. When a client has many inventory locations, auditors ordinarily need not be present at each location.	●	○
3. All auditor test counts must be documented in the working papers.	○	●
4. Auditors' observation of the counting of their clients' inventories addresses the existence of inventory, and not the completeness of the count.	○	●
5. When the client manufactures a product, direct labor and overhead ordinarily become a part of inventory item costs.	●	○
6. Inventory is ordinarily valued at the lower of standard cost or market.	○	●
7. Inventory items present as "consigned in" should not be included in the client's inventory value.	●	○
8. Auditor recording of test counts ordinarily replaces the need for client "tagging" of inventory.	○	●
9. Ordinarily, an auditor need not count all items in the inventory.	●	○
10. At the completion of the count, an auditor will ordinarily provide the client with copies of his or her inventory test counts to help assure inventory accuracy.	○	●

Task-Based Simulation 6

Research		
	Authoritative Literature	**Help**

	(A)	(B)	(C)	(D)	(E)	(F)	(G)	(H)
1. Which title of the Professional Standards addresses this issue and will be helpful in responding to her?	●	○	○	○	○	○	○	○

2. Enter the exact section and paragraph(s) with helpful information.

501	06, A11–A18*

*All of paragraphs above not required, simply the overall location.

Task-Based Simulation 7

1. **(D, I)** The balance per bank may be traced to a standard form used to confirm account balance information with financial institutions and to the cutoff statement (on which will appear the beginning balance).

2. **(A, G, H, I, J)** One of the deposits in transit does not appear on the cutoff bank statement (the 9/29/05 deposit for $4,500). Accordingly, that deposit should be traced to the cash receipts journal (procedure A), the reason for the delay should be investigated (procedure G), and supporting documents should be inspected (procedure H). Both deposits should be traced to and from the bank reconciliation and the cutoff statement (procedures I and J).

3. **(B, G, H, I, J)** One of the checks does not appear on the cutoff statement (check #988 dated 8/31/05 for $2,200). Accordingly, that check should be traced to the cash disbursements journal (procedure B), the reason for the delay should be investigated (procedure G), and supporting documents should be inspected (procedure H). All checks should be traced to and from the bank reconciliation and cutoff statement (procedures I and J).

4. **(E)** The credit memo from the bank for the note collected should be investigated.

5. **(E, I)** The credit for the check that was charged by the bank for an incorrect amount should be investigated on both the bank credit memo and on the cutoff statement.

6. **(C)** The only source of the balance per books is the cash general ledger account as of 9/30/05.

Task-Based Simulation 8

1. **(E)** Kiting involves manipulations causing an amount of cash to be included simultaneously in the balance of two or more bank accounts. Kiting schemes are based on the float period—the time necessary for a check deposited in one bank to clear the bank on which it was drawn. To detect kiting, a bank transfer schedule is prepared to determine whether cash is improperly included in two accounts.

2. **(D)** A comparison of the cleared checks to the year-end bank reconciliation will identify checks that were not mailed until after the first week of the subsequent year because most of those checks will not be returned with the cutoff statement and will appear to remain outstanding an abnormally long period of time.

3. **(H)** Among the terms confirmed for such a borrowing arrangement will be information on liens.

4. **(K, L)** A reply to the second request, or information from the credit agency, may confirm the existence of the new customer. Also, examination of shipping documents will reveal where the goods were shipped, and ordinarily to which party.

5. **(P)** Observing the payroll check distribution on a surprise basis will assist in detection since the auditor will examine details related to any paychecks not picked up by employees.

6. **(Q)** Vouching data in the payroll register to document authorized pay rates will reveal situations in which an employee is earning income at a rate that differs from the authorized rate.

7. **(A)** A comparison of the details of the cash receipts journal to the details on the daily deposit slips will reveal a circumstance since the details will have been posted to accounts during the last week of the year under audit.

8. **(U)** When vouchers are processed for merchandise not ordered or received, there will be no supporting purchase orders and receiving reports and this will alert the auditor to the problem.

9. **(B)** Scanning the debits to the fixed asset accounts and vouching selected amounts will reveal repairs that have improperly been capitalized.

10. **(A, J)** Lapping involves concealing a cash shortage by delaying the recording of journal entries for cash receipts. Since lapping includes differences between the details of postings to the cash receipts journal and corresponding deposit slips, com-

paring these records will reveal it. Also, confirmation requests may identify lapping when payments of receivables (as indicated by confirmation replies) appear to have taken too much time to be processed.

11. (E) C Increasing cash by drawing a check in this manner is a form of kiting (see answer 1). Preparation of a bank transfer schedule will assist the auditor in identifying such transactions.

12. (J, L) Confirmations will identify overstated accounts receivable when customers disagree with the recorded balance due. Also, the related overstated sales will not have shipping documents indicating that a shipment has occurred.

Task-Based Simulation 9

Substantive Procedures for Property, Plant and Equipment	Authoritative Literature	Help

	(A)	(B)	(C)	(D)	(E)	(F)	(G)	(H)
1. DietWeb has legal rights to property and equipment acquired during the year.	○	○	○	●	○	○	○	○
2. DietWeb recorded property and equipment acquired during the year that did not actually exist at the balance sheet date.	○	○	○	○	○	○	●	○
3. DietWeb's property and equipment was properly valued at the balance sheet date.	○	●	○	○	○	○	○	○
4. DietWeb recorded all property and equipment assets that were purchased near year-end.	○	○	○	○	●	○	○	○
5. DietWeb recorded all property retirements that occurred during the year.	○	○	○	○	○	○	●	○
6. DietWeb capitalized all acquisitions that occurred during the period.	○	○	○	○	○	○	○	●

Explanations

1. (D) The requirement is to identify the best substantive procedure to determine that DietWeb has legal rights to the property and equipment acquired during the year. Answer (D) is correct because the deeds and title insurance certificates will provide evidence that the company owns the property and equipment.

2. (G) The requirement is to identify the best substantive procedure to determine that DietWeb recorded property and equipment actually exists. Answer (G) is correct because physically examining the items will provide this evidence.

3. (B) The requirement is to identify a substantive procedure to test whether DietWeb's net property and equipment was properly valued at the balance sheet date. Answer (B) is correct because reviewing depreciation expense (and the related allowance for doubtful accounts) will indicate whether the net value is proper.

4. (E) The requirement is to identify how an auditor may test whether DietWeb recorded all property and equipment assets that were purchased during the year. Answer (E) is correct because performance of a cutoff test will indicate whether additions made during the year were properly recorded.

5. (G) The requirement is to identify a substantive procedure to test whether DietWeb recorded all property retirements that occurred during the year. Answer (G) is correct because examining the major recorded property and equipment items may identify situations in which an item has been retired (often due to its replacement) and is no longer available for physical examination.

6. (H) The requirement is to identify a substantive procedure to test whether DietWeb capitalized acquisitions. Answer (H) is correct because an analysis of repairs and maintenance accounts will reveal a situation in which such an acquisition has inappropriately been recorded as an expense and not capitalized.

Task-Based Simulation 10

Risk Analysis		
	Authoritative Literature	Help

Risk identified	Related financial statement assertion					Audit procedures						
	(A)	(B)	(C)	(D)	(E)	(F)	(G)	(H)	(I)	(J)	(K)	(L)
1. TWD may not have legal title to certain property and eqauipment recorded as acquired during the year.	○	○	●	○	○	○	○	○	●	○	○	○
2. Recorded property and equipment acquisitions may include nonexistent assets.	●	○	○	○	○	○	○	○	○	○	○	●
3. Recorded net property and equipment are for proper amounts.	○	○	○	●	○	○	●	○	○	○	○	○

Explanations

1. (C, I) Legal titles relates most directly to the client having rights over the assets; an examination of deeds and title insurance certificates will provide assurance that the client has a legal right to the property and equipment acquired during the year.

2. (A, L) The recording of nonexistent assets relates most directly to existence of assets; physical examination of the major additions will address whether they exist.

3. (D, G) The proper recording of the net of property and equipment relates most directly to the valuation or allocation of the accounts; reviewing the provision for depreciation expense will address whether accumulated depreciation has been properly updated.

Task-Based Simulation 11

Audit Objectives and Procedures		
	Authoritative Literature	Help

	(A)	(B)	(C)	(D)	(E)	(F)	(G)
1. Determine that company legally owns inventories.	○	○	●	○	○	○	○
2. Establish the completeness of inventories.	○	○	○	○	○	●	○
3. Determine that the cost of inventories is proper.	○	○	●	○	○	○	○

Explanations

1. (C) Because ownership information is included on invoices, examining vendors' invoices will provide evidence that the company legally owns inventory raw material items.

2. (F) Selecting a sample of items and agreeing to the physical count sheet will establish that those items have been included in the count, and this will address completeness of inventories.

3. (C) Examining vendors' invoices will provide evidence as to the cost of the inventory items.

	(A)	(B)	(C)	(D)	(E)	(F)	(G)
4. Determine that all accounts receivable are properly recorded as of year-end.	O	O	O	O	●	O	O
5. Determine that accounts receivable are properly valued at net realizable value.	O	O	O	O	O	●	O
6. Note disclosures related to accounts receivable are proper.	O	O	O	O	O	O	●

Explanations

4. (E) When examining the January 20X9 sales journal the auditor may identify sales that should have been recorded in December of 20X8.

5. (F) Auditors will generally inquire of the credit manager as to his or her beliefs concerning the collectability of various receivables, and thereby obtain evidence on the net realizable value of accounts receivable. Often one would expect an answer such as "analyze aging of receivables." Since that was not present here, (F) is the best reply.

6. (G) A disclosure checklist is used to determine that the disclosure requirements of generally accepted accounting principles have been met.

Task-Based Simulation 12

Inventory Audit Objectives and Procedures	Authoritative Literature	Help

	(A)	(B)	(C)	(D)	(E)	(F)	(G)	(H)
1. Identify inventory transactions involving related parties.	●	O	O	O	O	O	O	O
2. Determine that items counted are included in the inventory listing.	O	O	O	O	●	O	O	O
3. Determine that a proper cutoff of purchases has occurred at year-end.	O	O	O	O	O	●	O	O
4. Determine that financial statements include proper disclosures relating to inventory.	O	O	●	O	O	O	O	O
5. Determine that recorded inventory is owned.	O	O	O	O	O	O	●	O

Explanations

1. (A) The requirement is to identify a procedure for identifying inventory transactions involving related parties. The best procedure listed is review minutes of Board of Directors' meeting and contracts, and to make inquiries of management; these are all procedures used to identify related-party transactions.

2. (E) The requirements is to identify a procedure for determining that items counted are included in the count sheet. The best procedure is to reconcile physical counts to perpetual records and general ledger balances and investigate significant fluctuations. This will allow the auditor to identify items not included.

3. (F) The requirement is to determine that a proper cutoff of purchases has occurred at year end. The best procedure listed is to review sales after year-end and open purchase order commitments—this will help determine whether transactions recorded after year-end should have been recorded prior to year-end. Another procedure, not listed, is to perform the procedure on transactions recorded right before year-end.

4. (C) The requirement is to determine that the financial statements include proper disclosures relating to inventory. Answer C is correct because inventories pledged under loan agreement should be disclosed.

5. (G) The requirement is to determine that recorded inventory is owned. Examining invoices is best because invoice will present information on the purchase.

Task-Based Simulation 13

Spreadsheet Completion		
	Authoritative Literature	Help

	A	B	C	D	E	F	G
1	**Holiday Manufacturing Co.**						
2	**Balance Sheet**						
3	**December 31, 20X1**						
4							
5	Cash		$ 240,000		Accounts Payable		$ 160,000
6	Receivables		400,000		Notes payable		100,000
7	Inventory		600,000		Other current liabilities		140,000
8	Total current assets		$1,240,000		Total current liabilities		400,000
9							
10	Plant and equipment—net		760,000		Long-term debt		350,000
11					Common stock		750,000
12					Retained earnings		500,000
13	Total assets		$2,000,000		Total liabilities and capital		$2,000,000
14							
15							
16	Income Statement						
17	Year ended December 31, 20X1						
18							
19	Sales				$3,000,000		
20	Cost of goods sold						
21	Materials		800,000				
22	Labor		700,000				
23	Overhead		300,000		1,800,000		
24	Gross margin				1,200,000		
25							
26	Selling expenses		240,000				
27	General and admin. exp.		300,000		540,000		
28	Operating income				660,000		
29	Less: interest expense				40,000		
30	Income before taxes				620,000		
31	Less: federal income taxes				220,000		
32	Net income				$ 400,000		
33							
34							
35							
36	Ratios		**12/31/X1**		**12/31/X0**		
37	Current ratio		**(1)**		2.5		
38	Quick ratio		**(2)**		1.3		
39	Accounts receivable turnover		**(3)**		5.5		
40	Inventory turnover		**(4)**		2.5		
41	Total asset turnover		**(5)**		1.2		
42	Gross margin %		**(6)**		35%		
43	Net operating margin %		**(7)**		25%		
44	Times interest earned		**(8)**		10.3		
45	Total debt to equity %		**(9)**		50%		

	Ratio		Spreadsheet Formula	Calculation
1. (H)	Current ratio =	$\dfrac{\text{Current assets}}{\text{Current liabilities}}$	= C8/G8	$\dfrac{\$1,240,000}{\$400,000} = 3.1$
2. (E)	Quick ratio =	$\dfrac{\text{Quick assets*}}{\text{Current liabilities}}$ *Cash + Accounts receivable. Also marketable securities would be included if the company owned any.	= (C5+C6)/G8	$\dfrac{\$240,000 + \$400,000}{\$400,000} = \dfrac{\$640,000}{\$400,000} = 1.6$
3. (K)	Accounts receivable turnover =	$\dfrac{\text{Sales}}{\text{Accounts receivable}}$	= E19/C6	$\dfrac{\$3,000,000}{\$400,000} = 7.5$
4. (G)	Inventory turnover =	$\dfrac{\text{Cost of goods sold}}{\text{Inventory}}$	= E23/C7	$\dfrac{\$1,800,000}{\$600,000} = 3.0$
5. (D)	Total asset turnover =	$\dfrac{\text{Sales}}{\text{Total assets}}$	= E19/C13	$\dfrac{\$3,000,000}{\$2,000,000} = 1.5$
6. (T)	Gross margin percentage =	$\dfrac{\text{Gross margin}}{\text{Sales}}$	= E24/E19	$\dfrac{\$1,200,000}{\$3,000,000} = 40\%$
7. (P)	Net operating margin % =	$\dfrac{\text{Operating income}}{\text{Sales}}$	= E28/E19	$\dfrac{\$660,000}{\$3,000,000} = 22\%$
8. (N)	Times interest earned =	$\dfrac{\text{Operating income}}{\text{Interest expense}}$	= E28/E29	$\dfrac{\$660,000}{\$40,000} = 16.5$
9. (U)	Total debt to equity percentage =	$\dfrac{\text{Total debt*}}{\text{Owners' equity**}}$ *Total current liabilities + Long-term debt. **Common stock + Retained earnings	= (G8+G10)/ (G11+G12)	$\dfrac{\$400,000 + \$350,000}{\$750,000 + \$500,000} = \dfrac{\$750,000}{\$1,250,000} = 60\%$

Module 5: Reporting

Overview

The report represents the end product of the auditor's association with the client's financial statements. The following "Diagram of an Audit," originally presented in the auditing overview section, shows the relationship of the audit report to the entire financial statement audit.

This module covers auditor reporting responsibility relating to audits and other forms of association ("Issue Audit Report," the final step in the diagram). The emphasis is upon financial statement audit reports, but it also includes information on other attestation reports. Compilations and reviews are presented in Module 6.

Diagram of an Audit

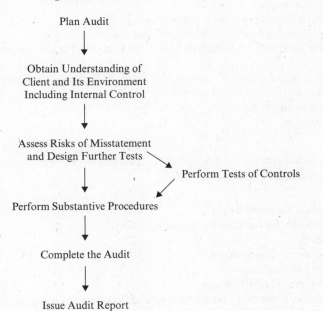

Plan Audit

↓

Obtain Understanding of
Client and Its Environment
Including Internal Control

↓

Assess Risks of Misstatement
and Design Further Tests

→ Perform Tests of Controls

↓

Perform Substantive Procedures

↓

Complete the Audit

↓

Issue Audit Report

When thinking about reporting, it is useful to consider four primary forms of accountant association with information:

- **Examinations** (referred to as audits in the case of financial statements) provide a report with a positive opinion with reasonable assurance on whether assertions follow the appropriate criteria.
- **Reviews** provide a report that includes limited assurance. Limited assurance is also referred to as "negative assurance" because a phrase such as "I am not aware of any material modifications that should be made" is included in the report. The procedures of a review are largely limited to internal inquiries and analytical procedures and are thus

343

significantly more limited than an examination. Reviews of interim information under the Statements on Auditing Standards are discussed in this module, while reviews of financial information under the Statements on Standards for Accounting and Review Services are presented in the following module.

- **Agreed-upon procedures** result in a report that provides a summary of findings. Because agreed-upon procedures are ordinarily less in scope than examination, the report disclaims a positive opinion on the financial statements—it provides a list of procedures performed and related findings. One ordinarily performs agreed-upon procedures upon specific accounts and not on an entire set of financial statements.
- **Compilations** provide a report with no assurance. The objective of performing a compilation is assisting management in presenting financial information in the form of financial statements, without undertaking to obtain any assurance that there are no material modifications that need to be made. Compilations are discussed in the following module.

Candidate knowledge of reports is heavily tested on every examination. While most of the report questions refer to financial statement audit reports, a significant number refer to the other types of reports that CPAs issue in other circumstances. Multiple-choice questions present a circumstance that calls for a departure from the standard unmodified report and ask specifically what type of report is to be issued. A simulation question may require preparation of a report using electronic access to the appropriate professional standards.

All of the following sections of the clarity Statements on Auditing Standards (codified as AU-C) apply to reports.

570	The Auditor's Consideration of an Entity's Ability to Continue as a Going Concern.
600	Special Considerations—Audits of Group Financial Statements
700	Forming an Opinion and Reporting on Financial Statements
705	Modifications to the Opinion in the Independent Auditor's Report
706	Emphasis-of-Matter Paragraphs and Other-Matter Paragraphs in the Independent Auditor's Report
708	Consistency of Financial Statements
720	Other Information in Documents Containing Audited Financial Statements
725	Supplementary Information in Relation to the Financial Statements as a Whole
730	Required Supplementary Information
800	Special Considerations—Audits of Financial Statements Prepared in Accordance with Special Purpose Frameworks
805	Special Considerations—Audits of Single Financial Statements and Specific Elements, Accounts, or Items of a Financial Statement
806	Reporting on Compliance with Aspects of Contractual Agreements or Regulatory Requirements in Connection with Audited Financial Statements
810	Engagements to Report on Summary Financial Statements
905	Alert as to the Intended Use of the Auditor's Written Communication
910	Financial Statements Prepared in Accordance with a Financial Reporting Framework Generally Accepted in Another Country
915	Reports on Application of Requirements of an Applicable Financial Reporting Framework
920	Letters for Underwriters and Certain Other Requesting Parties
925	Filings under Federal Securities Statutes
930	Interim Financial Information
935	Compliance Audits

The Statements on Standards for Attestation Engagements (codified as AT) apply to a variety of attest services and include guidance for reporting on those services.

20	Defining Professional Responsibilities
50	Statements on Standards for Attestation Engagements (SSAE) Hierarchy
101	Attestation Standards
201	Agreed-Upon Procedures Engagements
301	Financial Forecast and Projections
401	Reporting on Pro Forma Financial Statements
501	Reporting on an Entity's Internal Control over Financial Reporting
601	Compliance Attestation
701	Management's Discussion and Analysis
801	Reporting on Controls at a Service Organization

The AU-C and AT sections are very detailed. In this module, we present an overview of the information contained in those sections. In order to simplify the discussion, the topics are covered in a sequence that is different than that of the codified professional standards. The purpose of this module is to give you an overview of the information that will make it easier for you to understand the actual professional standards. You should also carefully study the various outlines.

A. Audit Reports: Standard Unmodified Reports

Overview. Auditors often issue a "standard" report with an unmodified (unqualified) opinion[1] on a complete set of general purpose financial statements (i.e., balance sheet, income statement, statement of cash flows). They may do this when they conclude that (a) the financial statements are prepared, in all material respects, in accordance with the applicable financial reporting framework (most frequently GAAP in this country) and (b) it is not necessary to include an emphasis-of-matter or other-matter paragraph in the audit report (see section B. below).

1. **Background.** The nature of the report issued depends upon whether the client is a nonpublic or a public company. In this section we divide our discussion in that manner.

2. **Nonpublic Companies (Nonissuers).** Most CPA exam questions pertain to audits of financial statements. The following standard short-form report for a nonpublic company was originally presented in the overview section:

Independent Auditor's Report

To the Board of Directors and Stockholders of ABC Company

We have audited the accompanying consolidated financial statements of ABC Company and its subsidiaries, which comprise the consolidated balance sheets as of December 31, 20X1 and 20X0, and the related consolidated statements of income, changes in stockholders' equity and cash flows for the years then ended, and the related notes to the financial statements.

Management's Responsibility for the Financial Statements

Management is responsible for the preparation and fair presentation of these consolidated financial statements in accordance with accounting principles generally accepted in the United States of America; this includes the design, implementation and maintenance of internal control relevant to the preparation and fair presentation of consolidated financial statements that are free from material misstatement, whether due to fraud or error.

Auditor's Responsibility

Our responsibility is to express an opinion on these consolidated financial statements based on our audits. We conducted our audits in accordance with auditing standards generally accepted in the United States of America. Those standards require that we plan and perform the audit to obtain reasonable assurance about whether the consolidated financial statements are free of material misstatement.

An audit involves performing procedures to obtain audit evidence about the amounts and disclosures in the consolidated financial statements. The procedures selected depend on the auditor's judgment, including the assessment of the risks of material misstatement of the consolidated financial statements, whether due to fraud or error. In making those risk assessments, the auditor considers internal control relevant to the entity's preparation and fair presentation of the consolidated financial statements in order to design audit procedures that are appropriate in the circumstances, but not for the purpose of expressing an opinion on the effectiveness of the entity's internal control. Accordingly, we express no such opinion. An audit also includes evaluating the appropriateness of accounting policies used and the reasonableness of significant accounting estimates made by management, as well as evaluating the overall presentation of the consolidated financial statements.

We believe that the audit evidence we have obtained is sufficient and appropriate to provide a basis for our audit opinion.

Opinion

In our opinion, the consolidated financial statements referred to above present fairly, in all material respects, the financial position of ABC Company and its subsidiaries as of December 31, 20X1 and 20X0, and the results of their operations and their cash flows for the years then ended in accordance with accounting principles generally accepted in the United States of America.

Smith & Co., LLP
Phoenix Arizona
February 5, 20X2

---

[1]Historically unmodified opinions have been referred to as unqualified opinions. Currently AICPA and international standards use the term unmodified, while the PCAOB standards continue to use the term unqualified. We will use the term unmodified, but recognize that this is equivalent to unqualified.

Some key details relating to the report include[2]

Required Title ("Independent" should be in title)

Addressee (company, board of directors and/or stockholders—**not** management)

Introductory paragraph

1. Identify the entity audited.
2. Financial statements have been audited.
3. Titles of financial statements.
4. Date or period covered by financial statements.

Management's responsibility for the financial statements (section with this heading)

1. Management's responsibility for preparation and fair presentation of the financial statements following applicable financial reporting framework.
2. Responsibility includes design, implementation and maintenance of IC to allow preparation and fair presentation of financial statements that are free of material misstatement from errors or fraud.

Auditor's responsibility (section with this heading)

1. Express an opinion based on audit
2. Audit conducted in accordance with GAAS of USA
3. Standards require auditor to plan and perform audit to obtain reasonable assurance financial statements free of material misstatement.
4. Discuss nature of audit procedures.
5. Audit evidence sufficient and appropriate for opinion.

Opinion (section with this heading)

1. Financial statements present fairly, in all material respects, financial position and results of operations and cash flows in accordance with applicable financial reporting framework.
2. Identify the financial reporting framework.

Manual or printed signature (firm name)

Auditor's address (city and state)

Date (no earlier than date auditor has obtained sufficient appropriate audit evidence).

3. **Public Companies (Issuers)**

a. The Sarbanes-Oxley Act of 2002 created a requirement for an integrated audit that provides assurance about the fairness of financial statements *and* about the effectiveness of internal control over financial reporting—the internal control module discusses audit reports on internal control. As implemented the audit of internal control requirement applies only to public companies with a market capitalization of $75,000,000 or more.

The audit report on financial statements is different from that of a nonpublic (nonissuer) company in that it includes:

- The title "Report of Independent Registered Public Accounting Firm."
- Referral to the standards of the PCAOB rather than generally accepted auditing standards.
- Less detailed discussions of management and auditor responsibilities.
- A paragraph referring to the auditor's report on internal control. (This reference is obviously only required when the reports on the financial statements and internal control are separate.)

b. The following is a sample audit report on the financial statements of a public company.

---

[2]Auditors sometimes have reporting responsibilities related to other legal and regulatory requirements. For example, for audits performed under Government Auditing Standards the auditor may be required to report on internal control over financial reporting and on compliance with laws, regulations, and other matters. It is when the relevant law or regulation requires or permits the auditor to report within the auditor's report on the financial statements that this becomes relevant. In such a situation the overall report is divided by two headings:

- **Report on Financial Statements.** This heading is added following the addressee, prior to the first paragraph of the report.
- **Report on Other Legal and Regulatory Requirements.** This heading and the related report follow the opinion paragraph on the financial statements.

The examples in the following portions of this module follow the format for U.S. nonpublic company audit reports. While in most areas U. S. nonpublic reporting requirements are similar to those under both international standards and U.S. public company standards, in several areas where they differ we so indicate.

Report of Independent Registered Public Accounting Firm

We have audited the accompanying balance sheets of X Company as of December 31, 20X3 and 20X2, and the related statements of operations, stockholders' equity, and cash flows for each of the three years in the period ended December 31, 20X3. These financial statements are the responsibility of the Company's management. Our responsibility is to express an opinion on these financial statements based on our audits.

We conducted our audits in accordance with the standards of the Public Company Accounting Oversight Board (United States). Those standards require that we plan and perform the audit to obtain reasonable assurance about whether the financial statements are free of material misstatement. An audit includes examining, on a test basis, evidence supporting the amounts and disclosures in the financial statements. An audit also includes assessing the accounting principles used and significant estimates made by management, as well as evaluating the overall financial statement presentation. We believe that our audits provide a reasonable basis for our opinion.

In our opinion, the financial statements referred to above present fairly, in all material respects, the financial position of the Company as of [at] December 31, 20X3 and 20X2, and the results of its operations and its cash flows for each of the three years in the period ended December 31, 20X3, in conformity with US generally accepted accounting principles.

We also have audited, in accordance with the standards of the Public Company Accounting Oversight Board (United States), the effectiveness of X Company's internal control over financial reporting as of December 1, 20X3, based on criteria established in Internal Control—Integrated Framework issued by the Committee of Sponsoring Organizations of the Treadway Commission and our report dated February 24, 20X4, expressed an unqualified opinion thereon.

[*Signature*]
[*City and State or Country*]
[*Date*]

We structure our discussion of circumstances resulting in modification of the standard report around: unmodified opinions with an emphasis-of-matter paragraph (Section B), modified opinions (Section C), opinions on group financial statements (Section D), and unmodified opinions with an other-matter paragraph (Section E). Since several circumstances may result in either an unmodified or a modified opinion (e.g., substantial doubt about going concern status and uncertainties) we emphasize that circumstance in the category in which the report is most frequently issued.

> **NOW REVIEW MULTIPLE-CHOICE QUESTIONS 1 THROUGH 16**

B. Audit Reports: Unmodified Opinion with Emphasis-of-Matter Paragraphs

Overview. Our discussion is divided into the circumstances that may result in inclusion of such paragraphs as follows:

1. Background
2. Substantial Doubt about Ability to Continue as a Going Concern
3. Inconsistency in Application of Accounting Principles
4. Uncertainties
5. Other Circumstances at the Discretion of the Auditor

1. **Background.** Emphasis-of-matter paragraphs[3] are added to audit reports in two situations: (1) when the professional standards require that, when material, the matter be brought to the attention of users in the auditor's report in all instances and (2) when the auditor on a discretionary basis includes the matter in the audit report. When an emphasis-of-matter paragraph is inserted the auditor should:

- Include it *after* the opinion paragraph.
- Use the heading "Emphasis-of-matter" or other appropriate heading.

---

[3]The terms "emphasis-of-matter paragraph" and "other-matter" paragraphs are used in AICPA and international auditing standards. The PCAOB uses the term "explanatory paragraph."

- Include in the paragraph a clear reference to the matter emphasized and where that matter is in the financial statements.
- Indicate that the auditor's opinion is not modified with respect to the matter emphasized.

In the following two circumstances (substantial doubt about ability to continue as a going concern and inconsistency in application of GAAP) GAAS require that the auditor include an emphasis-of-matter paragraph (or other report modification).

The following summarizes the issuance of the audit reports discussed in this section when the underlying accounting is proper (e.g., no departure from GAAP also exists):

Nature of Matter	Audit Report Modification
Substantial doubt about ability to continue as a going concern	Unmodified opinion with emphasis-of-matter paragraph or disclaimer (no criteria provided for deciding which is appropriate)
Inconsistency in application of accounting principles	Unmodified opinion with emphasis-of-matter paragraph.
Uncertainties	Unmodified opinion with emphasis-of-matter paragraph or disclaimer (multiple uncertainties may lead to a disclaimer)
Other circumstances at the discretion of the auditor	Unmodified opinion with emphasis-of-matter paragraph.

2. **Substantial Doubt about Ability to Continue as a Going Concern (AU-C 570).** The use of accruals by generally accepted accounting principles relies on an assumption that an entity will continue indefinitely as a going concern. For example, capitalizing assets and depreciating them over future periods is justified on the basis that the costs will be "matched" against future revenues.

Auditors are required to consider whether there is *substantial doubt as to whether an entity will continue as a going concern for a reasonable period of time not to exceed one year from the date of the financial statements* (hereafter, simply, substantial doubt). The approach is one of considering whether the results of procedures performed during the audit identify conditions or events that could indicate substantial doubt. The following are examples of such conditions and events:

- Negative trends (e.g., recurring losses, negative cash flows)
- Other indication of possible financial difficulties (e.g., default on loan, arrearages in dividends, denial of usual credit from suppliers)
- Internal matters (e.g., work stoppages, uneconomic long-term commitments).
- External matters (e.g., legal proceedings, legislation, loss of a principal customer or supplier, flood).

AU-C 570 suggests that procedures that may identify conditions or events such as the above include

(1) Analytical procedures.
(2) Review of subsequent events.
(3) Review of compliance with debt agreements.
(4) Reading of minutes of stockholders, board of directors and other important board committees.
(5) Inquiry of legal counsel.
(6) Confirmation with related and third parties of the details of arrangement to provide or maintain financial support.

When audit procedures indicate that substantial doubt could exist, the auditor should obtain management's plans (including significant prospective financial information) for dealing with the conditions and events and assess the likelihood that these plans can effectively be implemented. That consideration may include:

- Plans to dispose of assets.
- Plans to borrow money or restructure debt.
- Plans to reduce or delay expenditures.
- Plans to increase ownership equity.

NOTE: Make certain you have the above three concepts clear—(1) conditions or events indicating that there could be substantial doubt; (2) audit procedures that may identify those conditions and events, and (3) management's plans for dealing with the conditions and events.

If after evaluating management's plans substantial doubt exists, the auditor should either add an emphasis-of-matter paragraph to the report (following the opinion paragraph) or disclaim an opinion. In either case the report should explicitly include the phrases "substantial doubt" and "going concern." If analysis of management's plans convinces the auditor that substantial doubt does not exist, he or she still should consider the adequacy of financial statement note disclosures related to the matter. The following diagram summarizes the entire decision process.

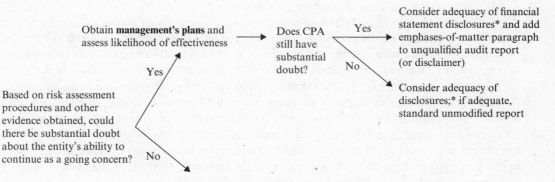

3 **Inconsistency in Application of GAAP (AU-C 708).** In the United States, inconsistency in application of GAAP (a change in accounting principles) that has a material effect on the comparability of a company's financial statements ordinarily results in a report with an unmodified opinion followed by an emphasis-of-matter paragraph. This holds for both public and nonpublic companies.[4]

The general rule under both GAAS and PCAOB Standards is that it is an inconsistency in application of accounting principles that results in the addition of an emphasis-of-matter paragraph, while changes in accounting estimates and minor reclassifications of accounts from one year to the next do not.

The periods considered for the auditor's consideration of consistency depend on the periods covered by the auditor's report on the financial statement:

- When the auditor's opinion covers only the current period, the auditor should evaluate whether the current-period financial statements are consistent with those of the preceding period, regardless of whether the financial statements of the preceding period are presented.
- When the auditor's opinion covers two or more periods, the auditor should evaluate consistency between such periods and the consistency of such periods with the period prior thereto if such prior period is presented with the financial statements being reported upon.

When a client company makes a **change in accounting principles** the nature of, justification for, and effect of the change are reported in a note to the financial statements for the period in which the change is made. Auditors evaluate such a change by applying "four tests" to determine that the:

(1) Newly adopted principle is generally accepted,
(2) Method of accounting for the effect of the change is in conformity with GAAP,
(3) Disclosures related to the change are adequate, and
(4) Management has justified that the new accounting principle is preferable.

When the auditors believe that the new principle meets the above four tests, an emphasis-of-matter paragraph is added to the audit report to highlight the lack of consistent application of acceptable accounting principles; but the opinion remains unmodified. Following is an example of an emphasis-of-matter paragraph which would follow the opinion paragraph:

---

[4]International auditing standards allow, but do not require, an emphasis-of-matter paragraph relating to a properly accounted for change in accounting principles.

Emphasis of matter

As discussed in Note 5 to the consolidated financial statements, the Company adopted Statement of Financial Accounting Standards Update No. XXX, *Provide Title,* as of December 31, 20X8. Our opinion is not modified with respect to this matter.

When the auditors believe that the new principle does not meet one or more of the earlier presented four tests, a departure from generally accepted accounting principles exists. In such a circumstance the auditors should issue either a qualified or an adverse opinion.

A client's correction of a material misstatement in previously issued financial statements also results in addition of an emphasis-of-matter paragraph to the audit report. The paragraph is only included in the year of correction and includes a statement that the previously issued financial statements have been restated for correction of a material misstatement and a reference to the entity's disclosure of the correction in the financial statements.

Changes in the accounting for the reporting entity that are *not the result of a transaction or event result* in the addition of an emphasis-of-matter paragraph to the audit report. Examples are presenting consolidated financial statements in place of individual entity financial statements, changing specific subsidiaries that make up a group and changing entities included in combined financial statements). Changes in the accounting for a reporting entity that *are the result of a transaction or event do not result* in the addition of an emphasis-of-matter paragraph to the audit report; examples are the creation, cessation, or complete or partial purchase or disposition of a subsidiary or other business unit.

Among other situations that ordinarily *do not* result in an emphasis-of-matter paragraph on consistency are changes in accounting estimates (e.g., changing the life of a fixed asset) and changes in principles with an immaterial effect (even if expected to be material in the future). Finally, because consistency is a between-periods concept, a consistency modification is not appropriate for a company in the first year of its existence. Two other important points relating to consistency.

- Differing accounting principles may be used for different portions of an account. For example, a client may choose to use FIFO for valuation of a portion of its inventory and LIFO for the remainder. Similarly, for fixed assets, differing depreciation methods may be used for differing classes (types) of assets. No emphasis-of-matter paragraph is necessary in this situation.

- The audit report includes no explicit mention of consistency when there has been no change in principle.

The most frequent changes in principle relating to consistency are summarized below.

Type of change	Emphasis of matter paragraph
I. Change in Accounting Principle	
1. GAAP to GAAP	Yes
2. Non-GAAP to GAAP	Yes
3. GAAP to non-GAAP	Yes*
I. Change in Accounting Principle	
4. For newly acquired assets in an existing class of assets (whether 1, 2, or 3 above)	Yes
5. For a new class of asset (whether 1, 2, or 3 above)	No
II. Change in Accounting Estimate	
1. Judgmental adjustments	No
2. Inseparable estimate and principle change	Yes
III. Change in Entity	
1. Changes not involving a transaction	Yes
2. Changes involving a transaction	No
IV. Correction of Error	
1. Error in principle	Yes
2. Error not involving application of a principle	Yes
V. Change in Statement Format	
1. Classifications and reclassifications	No

*Note that Section I.3. will also result in a departure from GAAP exception.

4. **Uncertainties (AU-C 706).** Uncertainties are situations in which conclusive audit evidence concerning the ultimate outcome cannot be expected to exist at the time of the audit since that outcome will occur in the future. Although not required, auditors may choose to modify their reports for uncertainties. As an example of an uncertainty consider a lawsuit against the client the ultimate results of which are uncertain. Realize that all financial statements are affected by some uncertainties. Uncertainty relating to a future outcome that is particularly significant is the situation that is expected to lead to an emphasis-of-matter paragraph (e.g., unusually important litigation or regulatory action in process against the client). The emphasis-of-matter paragraph added to the auditor's report will refer to the financial statement note describing the uncertainty, state that the outcome of the matter is uncertain, and indicate that the auditors' opinion is not qualified with respect to the matter.

While an unmodified opinion with an emphasis-of-matter paragraph is the most frequent resolution for a particularly important uncertainty, there is a situation in which a disclaimer may be issued. When multiple uncertainties cause the auditor may conclude that it is not possible to form an opinion on the financial statements as a whole due to the interaction and cumulative possible effects of the uncertainties a disclaimer may be appropriate.

5. **Other Circumstances at the Discretion of the Auditor (AU-C 706).** Examples of other discretionary circumstances (in addition to uncertainties) in which auditors may include an emphasis-of-matter paragraph are:

- A major catastrophe that affects the entity's financial position.
- Significant transactions with related parties.
- Unusually important subsequent events.

NOW REVIEW MULTIPLE-CHOICE QUESTIONS 17 THROUGH 39

C. **Circumstances Resulting in Audit Reports with Modified Opinions**
Overview. Our discussion is divided into the circumstances that result in issuance of modified opinions as follows:

1. Background
2. Materially Misstated Financial Statements (Departures from GAAP)
3. Inability to Obtain Sufficient Appropriate Audit Evidence (Scope Limitations)
4. Other Circumstances Resulting in Disclaimers Of Opinion

1. **Background.** Modified opinions are required in two circumstances (primarily AU-C 705):

- *Materially misstated financial statements (a "departure from GAAP")*—The auditor concludes that the financial statements as a whole are materially misstated.
- Inability to obtain sufficient appropriate audit evidence (a "scope limitation")—The auditor is unable to obtain sufficient appropriate audit evidence to conclude that the financial statements as a whole are free from material misstatements.

There are three types of modified opinions:

- *Qualified opinion.* A qualified opinion is issued in both of the circumstances: (1) materially misstated financial statements and (2) an inability to obtain sufficient appropriate audit evidence. The likely effects, while material, are not considered pervasive.
- Adverse opinion. An adverse opinion is issued in the first circumstance, when financial misstatements are materially misstated and the effects of the misstatements are both material and pervasive.
- Disclaimer of opinion. A disclaimer of opinion is issued in the second circumstance, when inability to obtain sufficient appropriate audit evidence has occurred and the possible effects are both material and pervasive.[5] A disclaimer states that the auditor does not express an opinion on the financial statements.

Audit reports with a modified opinion include a basis for modification paragraph that describes the matter giving rise to the modification. The paragraph is placed immediately before the opinion paragraph and has the heading "Basis for Qualified Opinion," "Basis for Adverse Opinion," or "Basis for Disclaimer of Opinion," as appropriate. Also, the title of the opinion paragraph becomes "Qualified Opinion," "Adverse Opinion," or "Disclaimer of Opinion," as appropriate.

---

[5]Also, recall from Section B that a disclaimer may be issued relating to multiple uncertainties and when substantial doubt about ability to remain a going concern.

The degree of pervasiveness of a misstatement (or possible misstatement) determines the type of audit report to be issued. Effects become more pervasive when, in the auditor's judgment, they meet one or more of the following three criteria:

- The misstatements or possible misstatements are not confined to specific elements, accounts, or items of the financial statements.
- If confined, they represent or could represent a substantial proportion of the financial statements.
- In relation to disclosures, are fundamental to users' understanding of the financial statements.

The following table summarizes the issuance of audit reports with modified opinions for departures from GAAP and scope limitations:

Nature of matter giving rise to the modification	Auditor's judgment about the pervasiveness of the effects or possible effects on the financial statements		
	Not material (accordingly, not pervasive)	Material but not pervasive	Material and pervasive
Misstated financial statements (Departure from GAAP)	Unmodified	Qualified	Adverse
Inability to obtain audit evidence (Scope limitation)	Unmodified	Qualified	Disclaimer

As indicated in the above table, materially misstated financial statements result in either a qualified opinion or adverse opinion, while the inability to obtain sufficient appropriate audit evidence results in either a qualified opinion or a disclaimer of opinion.

The following sections discuss modified opinions for misstated financial statements and the inability to obtain sufficient appropriate audit evidence.

2. **Materially Misstated Financial Statements (Departures from GAAP) (AU-C 705).** Materially misstated financial statements due to departures from GAAP result in either a qualified opinion or an adverse opinion; both types of reports include a basis for modification paragraph preceding the opinion paragraph. Examples of departures from GAAP include the use of an unacceptable inventory valuation method (e.g., current sales value) or incorrectly treating a capital lease as an operating lease.

As per our earlier comments, the type of report depends on the pervasiveness of the misstatements. When the effects of such departures become pervasive an adverse opinion is issued. The following are examples of opinion paragraphs for qualified and adverse opinions:

Qualified Opinion

In our opinion, except for the effects of the matter described in the Basis for Qualified Opinion paragraph, the financial statements the financial statements referred to above present fairly, in all material respects, the financial position of ABC Company as of December 31, 20X1, and the results of its operations and its cash flows for the year then ended in accordance with accounting principles generally accepted in the United States of America.

Adverse Opinion

In our opinion, because of the significance of the matter discussed in the Basis for Adverse Opinion paragraph, the consolidated financial statements referred to above do not present fairly the financial position of ABC Company and its subsidiaries as of December 31, 20X1, or the results of their operations or their cash flows for the year then ended.

If there is a material misstatement that relates to specific amounts in the financial statements, the auditor should include a basis for modification paragraph, which should precede the opinion paragraph. The basis for modification paragraph should include a description and, unless impracticable, quantification of the financial effects of the misstatement. If it is not practicable to quantify the financial effects the auditor should so state in the basis for modification paragraph. Similarly, if the departure from GAAP consists of inadequate disclosure of required information, the correct information, if practicable, should be included in a paragraph. When the information is not available, the basis for modification paragraph of the report should so state.

When an adverse opinion is being issued, an auditor may be asked to add a comment in the audit report indicating that certain identified accounts or disclosures in the financial statements are fairly presented. The auditor should not comply with this type of request since such "piecemeal opinions" are considered inappropriate because they might overshadow or contradict the overall adverse opinion.

Be familiar with a circumstance relating to departures from GAAP: omission of the statement of cash flows. When a company presents financial statements that purport to present financial position **and** results of operations (e.g., balance sheet **and** an income statement) GAAP requires that a statement of cash flows also be presented. The omission of a statement of cash flows in such a circumstance is a departure from GAAP. The auditor need not present the missing statement of cash flows in a basis for modification paragraph of the audit report.

3. **Inability to Obtain Sufficient Appropriate Audit Evidence (Scope Limitations) (AU-C 705).** The inability to obtain sufficient appropriate audit evidence due to scope limitations results in either a qualified opinion or a disclaimer depending upon whether the auditor concludes that the possible effects on the financial statements are pervasive. In both cases, the opinion paragraph indicates that the opinion modification is based on the possible effects of the matter on the financial statements, and not due to the scope limitation itself; for example, opinion paragraphs for the two possible types of modified opinions might be worded as:

Qualified Opinion

In our opinion, except for the possible effects of the matter described in the Basis for Qualified Opinion paragraph, the financial statements referred to above present fairly, in all material respects, the financial position of ABC Company as of December 31, 20X1, and the results of its operations and its cash flows for the year then ended in accordance with accounting principles generally accepted in the United States of America.

Disclaimer of Opinion

Because of the significance of the matter described in the Basis for Disclaimer of Opinion paragraph, we have not been able to obtain sufficient appropriate audit evidence to provide a basis for an audit opinion. Accordingly, we do not express an opinion on these financial statements.

Three types of scope limitations include:

- Circumstances beyond the control of the client (e.g., important accounting records were destroyed).
- Circumstances relating to the nature and timing of the auditor's work (e.g., the auditors were hired too late to observe the client's beginning inventory).
- The client (e.g., the client refused to allow the auditors to send confirmations to customers).

Client imposed limitations provide a particular problem since they may have other implications for the audit, such as for the auditor's assessment of fraud risks and consideration of whether to continue on the engagement or to withdraw. If a client imposed limitation occurs and management refuses to remove it, the auditor should communicate this to those charged with governance.

When a scope limitation occurs, the auditors attempt to obtain sufficient appropriate audit evidence by performing alternative procedures. If those procedures provide sufficient appropriate audit evidence no report modification is needed. If they do not, a decision needs to be made as to whether a qualified opinion is necessary or whether the possible effects on the financial statements are so pervasive as to require a disclaimer of opinion.

Know that scope limitations may result in different opinions on individual financial statements. For example, if the auditor of a first-year client has been unable to verify the accuracy of the beginning inventory, the scope limitation will affect the current year's income statement (through cost of goods sold) but not the year-end balance sheet. In such a situation, the auditor might issue an unmodified opinion on the balance sheet and a disclaimer on the income statement.

Also be aware of the distinction between scope limitations and limited reporting objectives. The auditor may, when requested, report on only one statement (e.g., the balance sheet); this is a limited reporting objective.

If access to information underlying the financial statements is not limited, such a situation does not involve a scope limitation. The auditor may report on the financial statement. Two other points:

- As is the case with issuance of an adverse opinion, when issuing a disclaimer the auditor may not include a "piecemeal opinion" that identifies certain accounts that are properly stated.
- Several multiple-choice questions have required knowledge of the "circumstance for which it is **not** appropriate to refer a reader of an auditor's report to a financial statement note for details." The proper answer is generally a scope limitation since details of audit scope are not presented in the financial statement notes.

4. **Other Circumstances Resulting in Disclaimers of Opinion** (as discussed earlier).

   a. Substantial doubt about ability to remain as a going concern. While this circumstance ordinarily results in a report with an emphasis-of-matter paragraph and an unmodified opinion, a disclaimer may be issued.

   b. Uncertainties. In circumstances involving multiple uncertainties, the auditor may issue a disclaimer of opinion. Ordinarily uncertainties result in a report with an emphasis-of-matter paragraph and an unmodified opinion.

D. Audit Reports: Group Financial Statements

Overview. AU-C 600 addresses the situation in which one or more components of a company are audited by different audit firms.

1. **Background.** The following is an example of a group audit in which a *component auditor* has audited one of a company's three subsidiaries while the *group engagement team*[6] audited the other two as well as the parent company of the organization's financial statements.

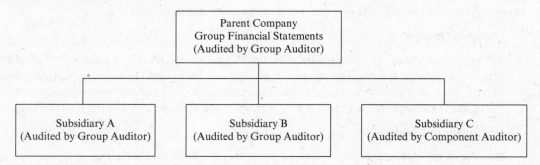

In the above illustration the group auditor ordinarily will issue an audit report on Parent Company. That report is based upon Parent Company's own financial information as well as that of Subsidiaries A, B and C. The primary issue here relates to how the group auditor should consider Subsidiary C in obtaining sufficient appropriate audit evidence to issue an audit report on Parent Company's group financial statements. Also realize that while an audit report on the overall group financial statements ordinarily is issued, audit reports on the individual subsidiaries may or may not be issued based upon the overall situation. The following serve as two examples of situations in which a separate audit report on a subsidiary may be required:

- A bank that has provided a loan to one of the subsidiaries may request audited financial statements of that subsidiary
- A portion of a subsidiary's stock may be publicly traded, thus requiring an audit report on the subsidiary alone.

2. **Group Audit Requirements.** The group engagement partner is responsible for (1) the direction, supervision and performance of the group audit and (2) determining whether the auditor's report on the group financial statements that is issued is appropriate. As a part of this responsibility the group audit partner should determine whether sufficient appropriate audit evidence on the component(s) and on the consolidation process can reasonably be expected to be obtained. Important here is that the necessary evidence should be obtained either by the group engagement team or the component auditor. The group engagement team should obtain an understanding of

- Whether the component auditor is competent and understands and will comply with all ethical requirements, particularly independence.
- The extent to which the group engagement team will be involved with the component auditor.
- Whether the group engagement team will be able to obtain necessary information on the consolidation process from the component auditor.
- Whether the component auditor operates in a regulatory environment that actively oversees auditors.

---

[6]The terminology used here relates to AICPA and international standards. The terms "principal auditor" and "other auditor" are still used in PCAOB auditing standards.

Additional audit procedures required of the group engagement team depend upon whether the work of the component auditor is to be referred to in the group audit report.[7] When the group engagement partner plans to make reference in the audit report to the component auditor, this is done through dividing responsibility between the group engagement team and the component auditor in the auditor's responsibility and opinion sections of the group audit report. Briefly, the choice in wording the audit report is:

a. *Make no reference to the component auditors.* If the group engagement partner makes no reference in the group audit report to the portions of the engagement performed by the component auditors, the group auditors assume full responsibility for the entire audit. Two examples of when this approach is usually followed include when the group auditors have difficulties relating to the earlier presented four bulleted items and when the group auditors are responsible for the hiring of the component auditors. If the group auditors elect to make no reference, they will issue the standard auditors' report with no additional wording.

b. *Make reference to the component auditors.* If the group engagement partner makes reference to the work done by component auditors, this *divides* the responsibility for the engagement *among the participating CPA firms.* This type of report is sometimes called a *shared responsibility opinion*, even though it is signed only by the group auditors. This type of report is usually issued when the other auditors were engaged by the client with no guidance from the group auditors.

In either alternative, the group audit report should be signed by the group engagement partner (in the firm's name).

REPORTING ON GROUP AUDITS

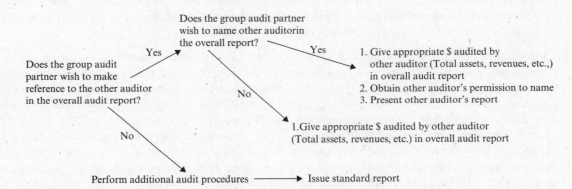

The "perform additional audit procedures" step above applies when the group engagement partner decides not to make reference to the component auditor (i.e., the group auditor assumes responsibility for the work of the component auditor). The amount and nature of work required of the group engagement team relating to that component depends upon whether that component is considered to be a *significant component*; a significant component is one identified by the group engagement team that is of financial significance to the group or that due to its nature, is likely to include significant risks of material misstatements of the group financial statements. The following summarizes the audit work ordinarily needed for components:

Component nature	Audit procedures
Not significant	The group engagement team should perform analytical procedures at the group level. Audit additional components *if* sufficient appropriate audit evidence has not been obtained.
Significant due to its individual financial significance to the group.	1. The group auditor or component auditor should perform audit of component, adapted as necessary to the needs of the group engagement team, using the materiality of the component. 2. The group engagement team should be involved in the risk assessment and should: • Discuss with the component auditor or the component management the component's business activities of significance to the group. • Discuss with the component auditor the susceptibility of the component to material misstatement. • Review the component auditor's documentation of identified significant risks of material misstatement of the group financial statements.

---

[7]International auditing standards do not allow referral to the component auditor as the group audit firm must assume full responsibility for the audit.

Component nature	Audit procedures
Significant because it is likely to include significant risks of material misstatement of the group financial statements.	1. The group auditor or the component auditor should perform one or more of: • Audit component, adapted as necessary to the needs of the group engagement team, using the materiality of the component. • Audit one or more component account balances, classes of transactions or disclosures that relate to the significant risks. • Perform specified audit procedures relating to the likely significant risks of material misstatement of the group financial statements. 2. Requirement 2 above.

When reference is made to the component auditor in the group audit report, two circumstances require special attention in the audit report:

1. When the component's financial statements are prepared using a different financial reporting framework from that used for the group financial statements, that different framework should be disclosed and the group auditor must take responsibility for evaluating the appropriateness of the adjustments to convert those financial statements to the financial reporting framework used by the group.
2. When the component auditor has performed the audit using other than GAAS (or PCAOB standards), the group audit report indicates that the component's financial statements were audited by other auditors in accordance with (describe standards) and that additional audit procedures were performed as necessary by the group auditor to conform with US GAAS (PCAOB standards).

Regardless of whether the component auditor is referred to in the audit report (i.e., the group auditor does or does not take responsibility), the group engagement team should obtain an understanding of group controls and the consolidation process. The group engagement team should design and perform further audit procedures on the consolidation process to respond to the assessed risks of material misstatement of the group financial statements. This should include evaluating whether all components have been properly included in the group financial statements.

Any significant unresolved difficulties relating to the component auditor create a situation in which the group engagement team should obtain sufficient appropriate audit evidence without using the work of the component auditor. Finally, note that in situations in which the component auditor's report is modified, the group audit report may or may not be modified. This is because the matter, while material to the component's financial statements, will not necessarily be material to the overall group financial statements.

> **NOW REVIEW MULTIPLE-CHOICE QUESTIONS 40 THROUGH 65**

E. Audit Reports: Unmodified Opinions with Other-Matter Paragraphs

Overview. Following background information, our discussion of audit reports with unmodified opinions and an other-matter paragraph is divided into the circumstances that may result in inclusion of such paragraphs:

1. Background
2. Comparative Financial Statements (certain circumstances)
3. Other Information in Documents Containing Audited Financial Statements
4. Required Supplementary Information
5. Supplementary Information in Relation to the Financial Statements as a Whole.
6. Alerts as to Report Intended Use (Restricting The Use of an Auditor's Report)
7. Additional Circumstances
8. Summary of Placement of Additional Paragraphs

1. **Background.** The following sections present guidance on a variety of situations that may result in other-matter paragraphs. As described below, other information in documents containing audited financial statements (e.g., an annual report) and required supplementary information (e.g., interim information included with annual financial information) require such paragraphs in certain circumstances. Other-matter paragraphs are similar

to emphasis-of-matter paragraphs in that they are included after the opinion paragraph of the report; they are given a heading such as "other-matter." They differ from emphasis-of-matter paragraphs in that they refer to a matter not in the audited financial statements.

2. **Comparative Financial Statements.** Many companies present comparative financial statements that include the current year and one or more prior periods; for example, public companies are required to provide such information in various forms they must file with the SEC. Ordinarily, this presents no particular problem—as illustrated in the earlier audit reports on comparative financial statements presented in Sections A.2 and A.3 of this module provide examples. Nonetheless, other-matter paragraphs are included in audit reports on comparative financial statements in a number of circumstances, including:

   a. **Prior period financial statements not audited (that is, they are reviewed, compiled, or there is no CPA association).** An other-matter paragraph is added indicating the nature of CPA association with the prior period financial statements (or indicating that there is no association).

   b. **Opinion on prior period statements different from opinion previously issued.** As an example assume that in year 1 a qualified opinion was issued due to a departure from GAAP. If in year 2 comparative financial statements on years 1 and 2 are being presented and both years follow GAAP (i.e., the year 1 departure is eliminated by the client) an other-matter paragraph would be added to the audit report. That paragraph would include the date of the previous report, the type of opinion previously issued, the reasons for the different opinion, and that the opinion is amended.

   c. **Prior period financial statements audited by a predecessor auditor.** The successor auditor has a choice here as to whether to ask the predecessor to reissue the audit report on the preceding period(s). Assume, two years of financial statements are being presented. If the predecessor's audit report is reissued, the financial statements will have two audit reports—one for year 1 (predecessor's report) and one for year 2 (successor's report). Before reissuing the prior year's audit report the predecessor auditor should perform limited procedures such as reading the current financial statements, comparing them to the prior period financial statements and obtaining representation letters from both the client's management and the successor auditor.

   If the predecessor auditor's report is **not** reissued, an other-matter paragraph is added to the successor auditor's report indicating

   • That the financial statements of the prior period were audited by a predecessor auditor.
   • The type of opinion expressed by the predecessor and, if the opinion was modified, the reasons therefor.
   • The nature of an emphasis-of-matter paragraph or other-matter paragraph included in the predecessor auditor's report, if any.
   • The date of that report.

   Finally, make certain that you distinguish between the two situations that we have presented involving multiple audit firms—predecessor auditor situations and group audit situations. A predecessor auditor situation involves, for example, *two years* of financial statements with *a different CPA firm each year*. A group audit situation (described earlier in Section D of this outline) involves, for example, *one year* of financial statements with *two CPA firms involved with that one audit*.

3. **Other Information in Documents Containing Audited Financial Statements (AU-C 720).** This is financial and nonfinancial information other than required supplementary information (see following section) that is included in a document that contains audited financial statements. The document containing audited financial statements is often an annual report, which includes information such as a report by management, financial summaries, employment data, planned capital expenditures, financial ratios, names officers and directors, and selected quarter information. Auditors are required to *read* this information for inconsistencies, if any, with the audited financial statements.

   If the auditor identifies no inconsistencies, *no additional paragraph is added to the audit report.* Thus, the report contains no indication that the auditors have read the other information when no inconsistencies are identified. If *inconsistencies* between the financial statements and the other information are identified, the auditor will first request the client to revise any incorrect information. If the client refuses to revise the incorrect information, one or both of the following must be true:

   • Financial statements are incorrect—This will lead to a qualified opinion or an adverse opinion since it is a departure from GAAP (see Section C.2).
   • Other information is incorrect—This will lead to a report with an unmodified opinion with an other-matter paragraph, withholding the auditor's report, or withdrawing from the engagement.

The auditor may note *no inconsistency*, but may believe that the other information *seems* incorrect. In such cases the auditor discusses the matter with the client, consults with other parties such as legal counsel, and uses judgment as to the resolution of the matter.

4. **Required Supplementary Information (AU-C 730).** This information is required by a designated accounting standards setter (e.g., FASB) to accompany a company's basic financial statements. As an example, large public companies are required to disclose selected interim financial information with their annual financial statements. Procedures that auditors should perform include

   a. *Inquire* of management about methods of preparing information--including whether it was prepared following prescribed guidelines, whether methods of measurement or presentation have changed from the prior period, and whether there were any significant assumptions or interpretations underlying the measurement or presentation of information

   b. *Compare information* for consistency with

      (1) Management's responses to the inquiries.
      (2) The basic financial statements
      (3) Other knowledge obtained during the audit.

   c. *Obtain written representations* from management acknowledging its responsibility for (1) the information being measured within guidelines, (2) consistency of methods followed, and (3) significant assumptions.

      If an auditor does not identify likely misstatements, proper reporting varies between public and nonpublic company audits. The PCAOB standards do not include any disclosure in this situation for public company audits. Alternatively, audits in conformity with the Auditing Standards Board requirements require an other-matter paragraph such as the following:

   Accounting principles generally accepted in the United States of America require that the [identify the supplementary information] on page xx be presented to supplement the basic financial statements. Such information, although not a part of the basic financial statements, is required by the FASB who considers it to be an essential part of the financial reporting and for placing the basic financial statements and related notes in an appropriate operational, economic, or historical context. We have applied limited procedures to the required supplementary information in accordance with auditing standards generally accepted in the USA, which consisted of inquiries of management about the methods of preparing the information and comparing the information for consistency with management's responses o our inquiries, the basic financial statements, and other knowledge we obtained during our audit of the basic financial statements. We do not express an opinion or provide any assurance on the information because the limited procedures do not provide us with sufficient evidence to express an opinion or provide any assurance.

      Note that for nonpublic companies this differs from the other information of point E3, for which there is no reporting responsibility when the other information seems consistent with the financial statements. Here, a paragraph is added to nonpublic company audit report regardless of results obtained.

      When the supplementary information is omitted or improperly stated, that information is added to the other-matter paragraph. The opinion paragraph of the report is not modified since the supplementary information is not considered a part of the audited information. Realize that the audit report refers to the information regardless of whether it is properly or improperly stated.

5. **Supplementary Information in Relation to the Financial Statements as a Whole (AU-C 725).** The subject matter addressed in this section is information that can be derived from and relate directly to the underlying accounting and other records used to prepare the financial statements (a portion of the subject matter of preceding sections E.3 and E.4). Examples of such information are consolidating information, historical summaries of accounts, and statistical data. With this service auditors are engaged to perform procedures to allow them to provide assurance on whether supplementary information is fairly stated, in all material respects, in relation to the financial statements as a whole. The information may be presented in a document containing audited financial statements or may be separate from the financial statements. As presented in the outline of AU-C 725, the auditor's procedures for this service go well beyond those of the preceding two sections, including:

   • Inquiring of management about the purpose of the information and criteria used to prepare it.
   • Determining the propriety of the form and content of the information.

- Obtaining an understanding of how he information was prepared.
- Comparing and reconciling information to underlying accounting and other records.
- Inquiring of management concerning significant assumptions.
- Evaluating the appropriateness and completeness of the information.
- Obtaining written representations.

When the information is found to be fairly stated in relation to the financial statements, an other-matter paragraph such as the following is added:

Our audit was conducted for the purpose of forming an opinion on the financial statements as a whole. The [identify the supplementary information] is presented for purposes of additional analysis and is not a required part of the financial statements. Such information was derived from and relates directly to the underlying accounting and other records used to prepare the financial statements. Such information is the responsibility of management and was derived from and relates directly to the underlying and other records used to prepare the financial statements. The information has been subjected to the auditing procedures applied in the audit of the financial statements and certain additional procedures, including comparing and reconciling such information directly to the underlying accounting and other records used to prepare the financial statements and other additional procedures prescribed by auditing standards generally accepted in the United States of America. In our opinion, the information is fairly stated in all material respects in relation to the financial statements as a whole.

If the auditors conclude that the information is not fairly stated in all material respects, the paragraph so states. The opinion paragraph of the audit report is not modified since the supplementary information is not considered a part of the audited information.

6. **Alerts as to Report Intended Use (Restricting the Use of an Auditor's Report) (AU-C 905).** An auditor may be required to or may choose to alert readers of financial statements that the report is intended for only certain users through the use of an audit report through inclusions of an other-matter paragraph. That paragraph should indicate that:

- The report is intended solely for the information and use of the specified parties.
- Identify the specified parties.
- Indicate that the report is not intended to be used by anyone other than the specified parties.

As indicated in the Internal Control Module, two byproduct reports, communicating internal control related matters and the auditor's communication with those charged with governance, are restricted reports. All agreed-upon procedures engagements result in restricted reports.

7. **Additional Circumstances Involving Other-Matter Paragraphs**

Circumstance	**Content of other-matter paragraph**
Special purpose financial statements prepared in accordance with a *contractual* or *regulatory* basis of accounting.	Restrict use of audit report to those within entity, parties to the contractor agreement, or the regulatory agencies to whose jurisdiction the entity is subject. (In the case of regulatory basis financial statement, issuance of a general use audit report is also possible.)
In rare circumstances an auditor may legally be unable to withdraw from an engagement even when a pervasive limitation of the scope of the audit has been imposed by management.	Explain why it is not possible for the auditor to withdraw (also disclaim an opinion).
An entity prepares sets of financial statements in accordance with more than one general-purpose framework (for example, one set of financial statements following GAAP and another following IFRS)	The auditor may issue reports on each and refer to the fact that another set of financial statements has been prepared using the other general-purpose framework and the auditor also has reported on those financial statements.

8. **Summary of Placement of Additional Paragraphs**

AICPA and International Standards

Type of paragraph	Placement
Basis for Modification (Basis for Qualified Opinion, Basis for Adverse Opinion and Basis for Disclaimer of Opinion)	Immediately preceding opinion section.
Emphasis-of-Matter	After opinion section.
Other-Matter	After opinion section and after emphasis-of-matter section if one is in report.

The PCAOB uses the term "explanatory paragraph" instead of the terms for the above three types of paragraphs. PCAOB explanatory paragraphs follow the following rules:

- For qualified, disclaimer or adverse opinions—paragraph precedes opinion paragraph
- Consistency and going concern—paragraph follows opinion paragraph.
- Others—either before or after opinion paragraph.

F. Audit Reports: Additional Situations

Overview. The two additional situations discussed in this section are (1) Audits of Financial Statements Prepared in Accordance with Special Purpose Financial Reporting Frameworks and (2) Audits of Single Financial Statements, and Specific Elements, Accounts, or Items of Financial Statements

1. **Audits of Financial Statements Prepared in Accordance with Special Purpose Financial Reporting Frameworks (AU-C 800).** The *Professional Standards* define the following special purpose financial reporting frameworks: (a) cash basis, (b) tax basis, (c) contractual basis, (d) regulatory basis (two forms–restricted use and general use), and (e) other basis.[8]

When considering accepting an engagement in which a special purpose financial reporting framework is used, the auditors should obtain an understanding of the purpose of the financial statements, the intended users, and steps taken by management to determine that the framework is acceptable in the circumstances. In addition, management should acknowledge in the representations letter that it understands its responsibilities with respect to the framework. When planning and performing the audit, the auditors adapt AU-C sections that are relevant as necessary in the circumstances.

An audit report on financial statements prepared using a special purpose financial reporting framework departs from the standard form in several ways. Most important, the report should include an emphasis-of-matter paragraph alerting users that the financial statements are prepared in accordance with the special purpose financial reporting framework and refer to the financial statement note that describes the framework. The paragraph should also state that the special purpose framework is a basis of accounting other than GAAP, and describe the basis of accounting being used or refer to a financial statement note that provides such a description. The essence of the report is the expression of an opinion as to whether the financial statements fairly present what they purport to present according to the special purpose framework being used.

The auditors should be cautious about the titles given to the financial statements. Titles such as "balance sheet," "income statement," and "statement of cash flows" are generally associated with financial statements presented in accordance with GAAP. Consequently, the professional standards require more descriptive titles for statements that are presented on some other basis. For example, a cash-basis "balance sheet" is more appropriately titled "statement of assets and liabilities arising from cash transactions." Perhaps the most common financial statements prepared on a basis other than GAAP are cash-basis statements. The body of an unmodified report on cash-basis statements is shown below with the distinctive wording emphasized.

---

[8]AICPA and international auditing standards use the term special purpose financial reporting frameworks (or special purpose frameworks); PCAOB materials refer to cash, tax and regulatory bases of accounting as *other comprehensive basis of accounting*.

We have audited the accompanying financial statements of ABC Partnership, which comprise the *statement of assets and liabilities arising from cash transactions* as of December 31, 20X1 and the *related statement of revenue collected and expenses paid* for the year then ended.

Management's Responsibility for the Financial Statements

Management is responsible for the preparation and fair presentation of these financial statements in *accordance with the cash receipts and disbursements basis of accounting described in Note X*; this includes determining that the cash receipts and disbursements basis of accounting is an acceptable basis for the preparation of the financial statements in the circumstances. Management is also responsible for the design, implementation, and maintenance of internal control relevant to the preparation and fair presentation of financial statements that are free from material misstatement, whether due to fraud or error.

Auditor's Responsibility

Our responsibility is to express an opinion on these financial statements based on our audit. We conducted our audit in accordance with auditing standards generally accepted in the United States of America. Those standards require that we plan and perform the audit to obtain reasonable assurance about whether the financial statements are free from material misstatement.

An audit involves performing procedures to obtain audit evidence about the amounts and disclosures in the financial statements. The procedures selected depend on the auditor's judgment, including the assessment of the risks of material misstatement of the financial statements, whether due to fraud or error. In making those risk assessments, the auditor considers internal control relevant to the partnership's preparation and fair presentation of the financial statements in order to design audit procedures that are appropriate in the circumstances, but not for the purpose of expressing an opinion on the effectiveness of the partnership's internal control. An audit also includes evaluating the appropriateness of accounting policies used and the reasonableness of significant accounting estimates made by management, as well as evaluating the overall presentation of the financial statements.

We believe that the audit evidence we have obtained is sufficient and appropriate to provide a basis for our audit opinion.

Opinion

In our opinion, the financial statements referred to above present fairly, in all material respects, the *assets and liabilities arising from cash transactions* of ABC Partnership as of December 31, 20X1, and its revenue collected and expenses paid during the year then ended in accordance with *the cash receipts and disbursements basis of accounting* described in Note X.

Basis of Accounting

Without modifying our opinion, we draw attention to Note X to the financial statements, which describes the basis of accounting. The financial statements are prepared on the cash receipts and disbursements basis of accounting, which is a basis of accounting other than generally accepted accounting principles.

If the special purpose financial statements are prepared in accordance with a contractual or regulatory basis of accounting, the auditors' report should also include an other-matter paragraph restricting the use of the auditor's report to those within the entity, the parties to the contract or agreement, or the regulatory agencies to whose jurisdiction the entity is subject. The following represents a paragraph:

Our report is intended solely for the information and use of ABC Company and Regulator DEF and is not intended to be and should not be used by parties other than ABC Company or Regulator DEF.

The following table provides overall reporting requirements relating to the various special purpose frameworks.

	Cash Basis or Tax Basis	Contractual Basis	Regulatory Basis	Regulatory Basis (General Use Statements)	Other Basis
Opinion(s)	Single opinion on special purpose framework	Single opinion on special purpose framework	Single opinion on special purpose framework	Dual opinion on special purpose framework and on GAAP	Single opinion on special purpose framework
Description of purpose for which special purpose financial statements are prepared	No	Yes	Yes	Yes	Yes
Emphasis-of-matter paragraph alerting readers re: special purpose framework.	Yes	Yes	Yes	No	Yes
Other-matter paragraph with alert restricting use	No	Yes	Yes	No	Yes If required by Section 905
Additional requirements unique to category.		The auditors should obtain an understanding of significant management interpretations of the contract.	If a specific layout, form or wording is required that the auditor has no basis to make, the auditor should reword the form or attach an appropriately worded separate report.		

2. **Audits of Single Financial Statements, and Specific Elements, Accounts, or Items of Financial Statements (AU-C 805).** Auditors may be engaged to audit a single financial statement or a specific element, account, or item (hereafter, element) of a financial statement. For example, a company may have entered into agreements such as:

   a. A loan agreement that includes a requirement that the balance sheet (but not other financial statements) be audited annually.

   b. A lease with a requirement that annual company revenues be audited as rent is based in part on the lessee's revenue.

      When auditing a single financial statement or a specific element of a financial statement, the auditors should adapt GAAS to the extent necessary in the circumstances. The auditors should perform procedures on interrelated items as necessary to meet the objectives of the audit For example, sales and receivables; inventory and payables; and building and equipment and depreciation each are interrelated. Thus, when auditing a single financial statement or a specific element of a financial statement, the auditor may not be able to consider the financial statement or the element in isolation. Accordingly, the auditor should perform procedures on interrelated items as necessary to meet the objective of the audit.

      When the CPAs are engaged to audit a particular account or element they modify the standard audit report to indicate the information audited, the basis of accounting used, and whether the information is presented fairly on that basis. For example, the following represents the opinion paragraph of an audit of accounts receivable.

      In our opinion, the schedule of accounts receivable referred to above presents fairly, in all material respects, the accounts receivable of ABC Company as of December 31, 20X1 in accordance with accounting principles generally accepted in the United States of America relevant to preparing such a statement.

      In some situations the auditors may be engaged to report on incomplete information that is otherwise in accordance with GAAP. For example:

   • A governmental agency may require a schedule of gross income and certain expenses of a company's real estate operation in which income and expenses are measured in accordance with GAAP, but expenses are defined to exclude certain items such as interest, depreciation and income taxes.

   • An acquisition agreement may specify a schedule of gross assets and liabilities of the company measured in accordance with GAAP, but limited to the assets to be sold and liabilities to be transferred according to the agreement.

      In such a situation the auditor's report should include an emphasis-of-matter paragraph stating the purpose of the presentation, referring to the note into information that describes the basis of presentation, and state that the presentation is not intended to be a complete presentation of the organization's assets, liabilities, revenues or expenses.

Auditors may be asked to audit a single financial statement or element in circumstances in which they have audited the complete set of financial statements. For example, perhaps an audit of the financial statements has been performed and the client also needs an audit of accounts receivable due to requirements included in a loan agreement it has entered with a bank. In such circumstances:

- A separate opinion should be issued on each engagement.
- Different materiality measures will ordinarily be used for the two engagements (e.g., materiality for a particular element may be lower than for the overall financial statements).
- When both the complete set of financial statements and the single financial statement (or element) are being published together, the auditor should be satisfied that there is a clear differentiation between them.
- When the auditors' report on the complete set of financial statements is modified in some manner, the auditor should consider its effect on the single financial statement (or element) report. When the matter relates to the specific element, that report is likely to also be modified. When it does not relate to the specific element, it may be possible to issue an unmodified report on the element if the two reports are not published together and the specific element does not constitute a major portion of the complete set of financial statements.

NOW REVIEW MULTIPLE-CHOICE QUESTIONS 66 THROUGH 92

G. Accountant Association Other Than Audits

Overview. The forms of accountant association other than audits discussed in this section include (1) other forms of association with historical financial statements (2) other reports based on GAAS and (3) other reports based on the attestation standards.

1. **Other Forms of Accountant Association with Historical Financial Statements.** Here we discuss four primary "other" forms of accountant association. The candidate should be very familiar with each of these forms of association.

    a. **Compiled or reviewed statements performed under Statements on Standards for Accounting and Review Services (AR 100-600).** Information on CPA involvement in this area is presented in Module 6.

    b. **Reviewed interim (quarterly) statements (AU-C 930).** The reviews referred to in a. above are most frequently for reviews of annual financial statements. Reviews are also performed on interim (ordinarily, quarterly) financial information. Public companies ("issuers") are required to have interim reviews, while nonpublic companies ("nonissuers") may choose to have reviews.

    AU-C 930 outlines a service very similar to reviews in *Statements on Standards for Accounting and Review Services* (SSARS, codified as AR sections—discussed in detail in the next module). Rather than provide a detailed outline of AU-C 930, we provide one that summarizes significant differences between SSARS reviews and interim reviews. At this point you should study that outline.

    The objective of a review of interim information is to provide the accountant with a basis for communicating whether he or she is aware of any material modifications that should be made to the interim financial information for it to conform with the applicable financial reporting framework (e.g., GAAP). Particularly important to this area are:

    - Overall, the procedures should be sufficient to provide a reasonable basis for obtaining limited (negative) assurance that there are no material modifications needed.
    - The accountant should obtain an understanding of the industry and knowledge of the client (the business itself and accounting principles followed).
    - While the Accounting and Review Services module includes much more information on the nature of reviews, know that interim reviews involve performing analytical procedures, making inquiries of management (and others within the organization), and the obtaining an understanding of internal control. The understanding of internal control should be sufficient to identify types of potential misstatements and to allow the auditor to select appropriate inquiries and analytical procedures. As discussed in the Accounting and Review Services module, this understanding of internal control is not required under reviews performed under SSARS.

The following is the standard review report for a public company:

Report of Independent Registered Public Accounting Firm

We have reviewed the accompanying [*describe the interim financial information*] of ABC Company and consolidated subsidiaries as of September 30, 20X1, and for the three-month and nine-month periods then ended. This interim financial information is the responsibility of the company's management.

We conducted our review in accordance with standards of the Public Company Accounting Oversight Board. A review of interim financial information consists principally of applying analytical procedures and making inquiries of persons responsible for financial and accounting matters. It is substantially less in scope than an audit conducted in accordance with generally accepted auditing standards, the objective of which is the expression of an opinion regarding the financial statements taken as a whole. Accordingly, we do not express such an opinion.

Based on our review, we are not aware of any material modifications that should be made to the accompanying interim financial information for it to be in conformity with US generally accepted accounting principles.

---

c. **Summary financial statements (AU-C 810).** Occasionally, a client prepared document will include **summary financial statements** (condensed financial statements) developed from audited financial statements. These statements typically include considerably less detail than the audited financial statements. The CPAs who issued the report on the audited financial statements may be asked to report on the summary statements. Unless they have issued an adverse opinion or a disclaimer of opinion on the audited financial statements, the CPAs may accept an engagement related to the summary financial statements. In these circumstances the CPAs determine whether the criteria applied by management in the preparation of the summary financial statements are acceptable and whether those criteria have been properly applied. While the audited financial statements need not accompany the summary financial statements, those statements should be readily available to any user who wishes to obtain them (e.g., available on the company's website). When the CPAs have concluded that the summary financial information is properly presented, they issue an opinion stating that the summary financial statements are consistent, in all material respects, with the financial statements from which they have been derived, in accordance with the applied criteria.

d. **Financial statements prepared using a financial reporting framework generally accepted in another country (AU-C 910).** A U.S.-based company may prepare financial statements for use in other countries. For example, a company may have a subsidiary in Germany and may prepare financial statements for that subsidiary as part of an effort to raise capital in Germany. AU-C 910 addresses the auditors' responsibility in this situation. When auditing the information, the auditors should comply with standards of the AICPA (or PCAOB for a public company) to the extent the standards are appropriate. In addition, the auditors should obtain an understanding of the other country's financial reporting framework. Also, if the terms of the engagement require the auditor to apply either the auditing standards of that country or the international standards, the auditor should obtain an understanding of and apply those standards.

The audit report issued depends upon whether the financial statements will be used in the United States. When the financial statements are intended for use only outside the United States, the auditors should issue one report, using either:

- A United States form of report that indicates that the financial statements have been prepared in accordance with a financial reporting framework generally accepted in another country, or
- The other country audit report.

A second report is issued when the financial statements are intended both for use outside and inside the United States. For nonpublic companies, this report includes an emphasis-of-matter paragraph stating the financial reporting framework used and that it differs from GAAP; an unmodified opinion may be issued relating to the financial reporting framework used. For public companies, the PCAOB requires that an opinion also be added on whether the financial statements follow GAAP.

2. **Other Reports—Auditing Standards Based**

a. **Letters for underwriters (AU-C 920).** When a company wishes to issue new securities to the public, the underwriters of the securities will generally ask the company's auditor to provide "comfort" on the financial and accounting data in the prospectus that is not covered by an accountant's report of some form (e.g., an audit report on the financial statements). In comfort letters, the CPAs will provide positive assurance that they are independent and that their audit followed SEC standards. They will provide negative assurance or a summary of findings on various types of accounting related matters such as the following: unaudited condensed and summarized interim information, pro forma financial information, change subsequent to the balance sheet date, and on various tables of data. Quickly review the outline of AU-C 920.

b. **Application of requirements of an applicable financial reporting framework (AU-C 915).** This section applies to situations in which an accountant (referred to as a "reporting accountant") other than the company's auditor is asked to issue a written report on

- whether a specific transaction meets the requirements of an applicable financial reporting framework, or
- the type of report that may be issued on an entity's financial statements.
- It also applies to oral advice when the reporting accountant concludes that the advice is considered important to the above.
- In determining whether to accept such an engagement, the reporting accountant should consider the circumstances under which the report (or oral advice) is requested, the purpose of the request, and the intended use of the report (or oral advice).
- Before providing a report on accounting principles, AU-C 915 requires the reporting accountant to take steps to assure a complete understanding of the form and substance of the transaction, ordinarily including consulting with the entity's auditor (referred to as the "continuing accountant"). An exception to the requirement to communicate with the auditor exists if the engagement relates to a specific transaction and the reporting accountant is engaged to provide recurring accounting and reporting advice and (1) does not believe a second opinion is being requested, (2) has full access to management, and (3) believes that the necessary relevant information has been obtained. The reporting accountant's report should describe the appropriate application of the matter and is restricted to the specified parties involved. Several additional points here are:

1. The reporting accountant is not required to be independent of the entity.
2. The reporting accountant should accept an engagement for a written report only when the transaction involves facts or circumstances of a specific entity—no written report should be issued on a hypothetical transaction.
3. Responsibility for proper accounting treatment rests with management.

3. **Other Reports—Attestation Standards Based.** CPAs[9] also become involved with a variety of other types of information which result in the following reports:

a. Attestation engagements—general (AT 101)
b. Agreed-upon procedures engagements (AT 201)
c. Financial forecasts and projections (AT 301)
d. Pro forma financial information (AT 401)
e. Management discussion and analysis (AT 701)
f. Trust Services
g. Service Organization Control (SOC) Reports (AT 801)

Points a. and b. provide overall general guidance for attestation engagements of all types. For example, the overall eleven attestation standards are presented in AT 101, and the overall standards for agreed-upon procedures engagements in AT 201.

The remaining points (c. through g.) relate to specific guidance for attestation engagements related to a particular topic (e.g., AT 301 [topic c. above] relates to providing assurance on forecasts). Thus, the individual performing an attestation engagement for a financial forecast has two sources of guidance—the general and the specific. In situations in which an attestation engagement is being performed on a type of information for which a detailed standard has not been provided, the CPA uses that information provided in AT 101 and AT 201. In addition to the above detailed types of engagements, recall that auditors may issue reports on internal control over financial reporting (AT 501); this topic is summarized in the Internal Control Module. Also, information on compliance attestation (AT 601) is presented later in this module.

a. **Attestation engagements—general (AT 101).** AT 101 provides the framework for all attest engagements. Attestation standards apply to engagements in which CPAs are engaged to issue or do issue an examination, a review, or an agreed-upon procedures report on subject matter, or an assertion about subject matter, that is the responsibility of another party. It is important to distinguish between the subject matter and the assertion about the subject matter.

---

[9]The attestation standards use the term "practitioner" throughout.

The **subject matter** of an attestation engagement may take many forms, including

- Historical or prospective performance or condition (e.g., historical prospective financial information, performance measurements, and backlog data),
- Physical characteristics (e.g., narrative descriptions, square footage of facilities),
- Historical events (e.g., price of a market basket of goods on a certain date),
- Analyses (e.g., breakeven analyses),
- Systems or processes (e.g., internal control), or
- Behavior (e.g., corporate governance, compliance with laws and regulations, and human resource practices).

An **assertion** is a declaration about whether the subject matter is presented in accordance with certain criteria. For example, management might assert that the price of a market basket of goods at its store was the lowest in the city as of a certain date. While such an assertion is generally obtained, in those circumstances in which it is not, the attest report should be restricted in those few circumstances in which a written assertion is not obtained.

CPAs may ordinarily report on either the assertion about the subject matter, **or** on the subject matter itself either as of a point in time or for a period of time. Continuing with our market basket engagement example, if reporting on the assertion, the CPAs' opinion would include assurance about management's assertion concerning the prices. Alternatively, when reporting on the subject matter, the CPAs' opinion would include assurance directly on the price of that market basket. An exception to allowing reporting on either the subject matter or on the assertion is when the examination reveals material departures from the suitable criteria. In such circumstance the CPA should report directly upon the subject matter, and not on the assertion.

If the CPAs are reporting on an assertion about the subject matter, the assertion is presented with the subject matter or in the CPAs' report. If the CPAs are reporting **directly** on the subject matter, the assertion normally is included only in a representation letter that the CPAs obtain from the responsible party.

Recall the eleven attestation standards presented in Chapter 5. Those standards provide a general framework for all such engagements. You should consider several important concepts related to those standards, including criteria and types of engagements.

Criteria. Criteria are standards or benchmarks that are used to evaluate the subject matter of the engagements. Criteria are important in reporting the CPAs' conclusion to the users because they convey the basis on which the conclusion was formed. For example, generally accepted accounting principles are ordinarily used as the frame of reference—criteria—to evaluate the financial statements.

A CPA should evaluate the criteria being followed. As indicated in the third general standard, the criteria used in an attestation engagement should be **suitable** and **available** to the users. **Suitable criteria** should have an appropriate combination of the following characteristics: objective, measurable, complete, and relevant. The following are general rules relating to criteria suitability:

- Criteria are ordinarily suitable if they are developed by regulatory agencies or other bodies composed of experts that use due process, including exposing the proposed criteria for public comment.
- Criteria developed by management or industry groups without due process may be suitable, but the CPA should carefully evaluate them in relation to the characteristics described in the previous paragraph.
- Criteria that are overly subjective should not be used in an attestation engagement. For example, an assertion that a particular software product is the *best on the market* is too subjective for an attestation engagement. There are no generally accepted criteria for what constitutes the *best* software product. Some criteria may be suitable in evaluating subject matter for only those specified parties who established them (e.g., management and the CPA) and are not suitable for general use.

In addition to meeting the requirement that they be *suitable*, the criteria should also be available to users. This requirement of availability actually has two parts in that not only should the criteria be available, they should be understandable to users. Criteria should be available in one or more of the following ways:

- Publicly
- Inclusions—with the subject matter or in the assertion
- Inclusion in CPA's report
- Well understood by most users (e.g., the distance between A and B is 20 feet)
- Available only to specified parties (in this case the CPA's report is restricted to those parties)

Forms of engagements. As indicated earlier in this module, the forms of attestation engagements are **examinations, reviews,** or the performance of **agreed-upon procedures**.

An examination is designed to provide the highest level of assurance that CPAs provide—the same level of assurance about other types of subject matter as an audit provides for financial statements. When performing an examination, CPAs select from all available procedures to gather sufficient evidence to allow the issuance of a report with a positive opinion about whether the subject matter being examined follows some established or stated criteria. Sufficient evidence exists when it is enough to drive attestation risk to an appropriate **low level**.

At the completion of the examination, the CPAs issue an appropriate report. The following is an example of a standard unqualified examination report **directly on the subject matter**:

Independent Accountant's Report

We have examined the accompanying schedule of investment performance statistics of Yorn Investment Fund for the year ended December 31, 20X2. This schedule is the responsibility of Yorn Investment Fund's management.

Our responsibility is to express an opinion on this schedule based on our examination.

Our examination was conducted in accordance with attestation standards established by the American Institute of Certified Public Accountants and, accordingly, included examining, on a test basis, evidence supporting the schedule and performing such other procedures as we considered necessary in the circumstances. We believe our examination provides a reasonable basis for our opinion.

In our opinion, the schedule of investment performance statistics referred to above presents, in all material respects, the performance of Yorn Investment Fund for the year ended December 31, 20X2, in conformity with the measurement and disclosure criteria set forth by the Association of Investment Management Research, Inc., as described in Note 1.

Jane Zhang, CPA, LLP
January 22, 20X3

This standard report, however, is not appropriate in all cases. The following illustrates circumstances that result in modification of the standard unqualified report.

Situation	Report modification
1. Criteria are agreed upon or only available to specified users	A statement of limitations on the use of the report
2. Departure of subject matter from criteria	Qualified or adverse opinion depending on materiality of the departure
3. Limitation on scope of engagement	Qualified opinion or disclaimer
4. When reporting on subject matter and a written assertion is not obtained from the responsible party	A statement of limitations on the use of the report

Reviews. A review engagement involves performing limited procedures, such as inquiries and analytical procedures. In performing a review, the CPAs endeavor to gather sufficient evidence to drive attestation risk to a **moderate level**. Accordingly, the resulting report provides only limited assurance that the information is fairly presented. **Limited assurance** is also referred to as **negative assurance** because the CPAs' report disclaims an opinion on the reviewed information, but includes a statement such as "We are not aware of any material modifications that should be made in order for the information to be in conformity with the criteria." Of course, when uncorrected material departures from the criteria are noted, the report should be modified to so indicate. The following is an example of an unmodified review report **directly on the subject matter**:

Independent Accountant's Report

We have examined the accompanying schedule of investment performance statistics of King Investment Fund for the year ended December 31, 20X2. This schedule is the responsibility of King Investment Fund's management.

Our examination was conducted in accordance with attestation standards established by the American Institute of Certified Public Accountants. A review is substantially less in scope than an examination, the objective of which is the expression of an opinion on the schedule. Accordingly, we do not express such an opinion.

Based on our review, nothing came to our attention that caused us to believe that the accompanying schedule of investment performance statistics of King Investment Fund for the year ended December 31, 20X2, is not presented, in all material respects, in accordance with the measurement and disclosure criteria set forth by the Association of Investment Management Research, Inc., as described in Note 1.

George Williams & Associates, LLP
January 15, 20X3

The following lists circumstances that result in modification of the CPAs' review report.

Situation	Report modification
1. Criteria are agreed upon or only available to specified users	A statement of limitations on the use of the report
2. Departure of subject matter from criteria	Modified report describing the departure
3. Limitation on scope of the engagement	Report cannot be issued
4. When reporting on subject matter and a written assertion is not obtained from the responsible party	A statement of limitations on the use of the report

At this point you should carefully study the outline of AT 101.

b. **Agreed-upon procedures engagements (AT 201).** AT 201 provides guidance for agreed-upon procedures engagements. The section applies to both engagements relating to historical financial information and engagements related to information other than historical financial statements. Agreed-upon procedures reports include a list of procedures performed (or reference thereto) and the related findings. Because specified parties have agreed upon the nature of the procedures, the reports for such engagements are intended only for those parties. Consequently, reports on agreed-upon procedures are referred to as **restricted use** reports, as contrasted to **general use** reports, such as those on examinations and reviews. As previously indicated, examination and review reports ordinarily may be used by all third parties. Only when the criteria have been agreed upon by the parties involved and such criteria are not generally understandable to those not involved with the information should an examination or review report be restricted. Examples of the later type of engagement include the application of agreed-upon procedures to an entity's internal control over financial reporting, compliance with various laws and regulations, or on a schedule of statistical production data. At this point you should carefully study the outline of AT 201.

c. **Financial forecasts and projections (AT 301).** AT 301 presents three forms of accountant association with forecasts or projections—compilation, examination, and application of agreed-upon procedures.

The following are the standard report forms suggested for compilation and examination of forecasts or projections:

Compilation Report

We have compiled the accompanying forecasted balance sheet, statements of income, retained earnings, and cash flows of XYZ Company as of December 31, 20XX, and for the year then ending, in accordance with standards established by the American Institute of Certified Public Accountants.

A compilation is limited to presenting in the form of a forecast information that is the representation of management and does not include evaluation of the support for the assumptions underlying the forecast. We have not examined the forecast and, accordingly, do not express an opinion or any other form of assurance on the accompanying statements or assumptions. Furthermore, there will usually be differences between the forecasted and actual results, because events and circumstances frequently do not occur as expected, and those differences may be material. We have no responsibility to update this report for events and circumstances occurring after the date of this report.

Examination Report

We have examined the accompanying forecasted balance sheet, statements of income, retained earnings, and cash flows for XYZ Company as of December 31, 20XX, and for the year then ended. XYZ Company's management is responsible for the forecast. Our responsibility is to express an opinion on the forecast based on our examination.

Our examination was conducted in accordance with attestation standards established by the American Institute of Certified Public Accountants and, accordingly, included such procedures as we considered necessary to evaluate both the assumptions used by management and the preparation and presentation of the forecast. We believe that our examination provides a reasonable basis for our opinion.

In our opinion, the accompanying forecast is presented in conformity with guidelines for presentation of a forecast established by the American Institute of Certified Public Accountants, and the underlying assumptions provide a reasonable basis for management's forecast. However, there will usually be differences between the forecasted and actual results, because events and circumstances frequently do not occur as expected, and those differences may be material. We have no responsibility to update this report for events and circumstances occurring after the date of this report.

Departures from the standard report for forecasts/projections are very similar to those for historical financial statement audit reports. While it is not necessary that you read the entire Statement (on forecasts/projections), you should at this point turn to the outline of AT 301. Several **extremely** important points relative to that outline are

(1) An accountant should not be associated with forecasts/projections that do not disclose assumptions.
(2) Forecasts may be for general or limited use, while projections are for limited use only (see Section A.1. of outline for AT 301 for discussion).
(3) Independence is **not** required for compilations (recall this is also the case for financial statement compilations).
(4) Concerning assurance provided: Know that a compilation report provides no assurance (again, this is also the case with financial statement compilations); an examination report provides positive assurance with respect to the reasonableness of assumptions; and an agreed-upon procedures report provides a summary of findings.

d. **Reporting on pro forma financial information (AT 401).** High levels of business combinations and various types of changes in capitalization created a significant demand for auditor association with "pro forma financial information" which adjusts earlier historical financial information prospectively for the effects of an actual or proposed transaction (or event). Accountants may either review or examine the information. The following is an example of an examination report:

Pro Forma Financial Information

Independent Auditor's Report

We have examined the pro forma adjustments reflecting the transaction described in Note 1 and the application of those adjustments to the historical amounts in the accompanying pro forma condensed balance sheet of X Company as of December 31, 20X0, and the pro forma condensed statement of income for the year then ended. The historical condensed financial statements are derived from the historical financial statements of X Company, which were audited by us, and of Y Company, which were audited by other accountants, appearing elsewhere herein. Such pro forma adjustments are based upon management's assumptions described in Note 2. X Company's management is responsible for the pro forma financial information. Our responsibility is to express an opinion on the pro forma financial information based on our examination.

Our examination was conducted in accordance with attestation standards established by the American Institute of Certified Public Accountants and, accordingly, included such procedures as were considered necessary in the circumstances. We believe that our examination provides a reasonable basis for our opinion.

The objective of this pro forma financial information is to show what the significant effects on the historical financial information might have been had the transaction [or event] occurred at an earlier date. However, the pro forma condensed financial statements are not necessarily indicative of the results of operations or related effects on financial position that would have been attained had the above-mentioned transaction [or event] actually occurred earlier.

[Additional paragraph(s) may be added to emphasize certain matters relating to the attest engagement of the subject matter.]

In our opinion, management's assumptions provide a reasonable basis for presenting the significant effects directly attributable to the above-mentioned transaction described in Note 1, the related pro forma adjustments give appropriate effect to those assumptions, and the pro forma column reflects the proper application of those adjustments to the historical financial statement amounts in the pro forma condensed balance sheet as of December 31, 20X0, and the pro forma condensed statement of income for the year then ended.

Review reports, as is the case with reviews of historical financial information, indicate that they are less in scope than examinations, and provide negative assurance (e.g., "I am not aware of any material modifications that should be made. . .").

Scope restrictions, departures from AICPA standards, etc., are treated in a manner similar to that for reviews and audits of historical financial statements. At this point, review the outline of the section that precedes the SAS outline.

e. **Management discussion and analysis (AT 701).** AT 701 provides guidance for performing review and examination of management's discussion and analysis (MD&A). MD&A is included in reports filed with the SEC (e.g., Form 10K and 10Q) and in annual reports sent directly to shareholders. In addition, a number of companies that do not report to the SEC prepare such information. This service allows a CPA to provide assurance ("negative assurance" for a review, and "reasonable assurance" for an examination) on a client's MD&A. At this point you should review carefully the outline of AT 701, including the summary tables that follow that outline.

f. **Trust Services.** Trust Services—jointly developed with the Canadian Institute of Chartered Accountants (CICA)—are designed to provide information system business assurance and advisory services that instill confidence in an organization, system, or other entity by improving the quality or context of information for decision makers. They were developed by the AICPA's Assurance Services Executive Committee (discussed in Overview).

Trust Services view a system as consisting of five key components organized to achieve a specified objective—infrastructure, software, people, procedures, and data. It may be as simple as a personal-computer-based payroll application with only one user, or as complex as a multiapplication, multicomputer banking system accessed by many users both within and outside the banks involved.

In a Trust Services engagement, management prepares and communicates a system description that can be included on the company's website, attached to the practitioners' report, or communicated to users in some other manner. It should clearly articulate the boundaries of the system so as to allow individuals to understand both the scope of management's assertions related to it and the CPA's report.

In performing a Trust Services engagement the CPA (practitioner) performs procedures to determine that management's description of the system is fairly stated, and obtains evidence that the controls over the system are designed and operating effectively to meet the Trust Services **Principles** and **Criteria**—the suitable criteria required for an attest engagement. The CPA reports on whether the system meets one or more of the following **principles** over a particular reporting period:

1. **Security.** The system (infrastructure, software, people, procedures, and data) is protected against unauthorized access (both physical and logical).
2. **Availability.** The system is available for operation and use as committed or agreed.
3. **Processing Integrity.** System processing is complete, accurate, timely and authorized.
4. **Online Privacy.** Private information obtained as a result of electronic commerce is collected, used, disclosed, and retained as committed or agreed.
5. **Confidentiality.** Information designated as confidential is protected as committed or agreed.

For each principle reported upon by the auditor, the auditor considers each of the following four criteria:

1. **Policies.** The entity has defined and documented its policies relevant to the particular principle. These policies are written statements that communicate management's intent, objectives, requirements, responsibilities, and/ or standards for a particular subject.
2. **Communications.** The entity has communicated its defined policies to authorized users.
3. **Procedures.** The entity utilizes procedures to achieve the objectives in accordance with its defined policies.
4. **Monitoring.** The entity monitors the system and takes action to maintain compliance with its defined policies.

Key points related to a Trust Services engagement

1. Management ordinarily provides the CPA with a written assertion on the system and the CPA may report either on management's assertion or the subject matter of the engagement (one or more of the principles). When the CPA reports on the assertion, the assertion should accompany the CPA's report or the first paragraph of the report should contain a statement of the assertion. The CPA's report and management's assertion should specify the period covered—that may be for a period of time (ordinarily one year or less) or at a point in time.
2. If one or more criteria relating to a principle have not been achieved, the CPA issues a qualified or adverse report. If management refuses to provide a written assertion, a disclaimer of opinion is ordinarily appropriate.
3. When reporting on more than one principle, the CPA may issue either a combined report on all principles, or individual reports.
4. Either an examination or an agreed-upon procedures engagement may be performed for a Trust Services engagement.
5. At present CPAs offer two types of trust services—WebTrust and SysTrust.

   a. **WebTrust** provides assurance on electronic commerce (including websites). The CPA is engaged to examine *both* that a client *complied* with the Trust Services criteria (e.g., the company uses procedures in accordance with its defined policies) and that it *maintained effective controls* over the system based on Trust Services criteria (e.g., the company's procedures are effective).
   b. **SysTrust** provides assurance on any defined electronic system. In a SysTrust engagement the CPA is engaged to examine only that a client *maintained effective controls* over the system based on the Trust Services criteria.

6. Both WebTrust and SysTrust are designed to incorporate a seal management process by which a seal (logo) may be included on a client's website as an electronic representation of the practitioner's unqualified WebTrust report. If the client wishes to use the seal (logo), the engagement should be updated at least annually. Also, the initial reporting period should include at least two months. Following are sample reports for WebTrust and SysTrust.

Independent Practitioner's WebTrust Report on Consumer Protection

To the Management of ABC Company:

We have examined ABC Company's compliance with the AICPA/CICA Trust Services Criteria for consumer protection, and based on these criteria, the effectiveness of controls over the Online Privacy and Processing Integrity of the Customer Order Placement System during the period January 1, 20X2, through June

30, 20X2. The compliance with these criteria and maintaining the effectiveness of these controls is the responsibility of ABC Company's management. Our responsibility is to express an opinion based on our examination.

Within the context of AICPA/CICA Trust Services, consumer protection addresses the controls over personally identifiable information and the processing of electronic commerce transactions. The AICPA/CICA Trust Services On-line Privacy and Processing Integrity Criteria are used to evaluate whether ABC Company's controls over consumer protection of its Customer Order Placement System are effective. Consumer protection does not address the quality of ABC Company's goods, nor their suitability for any customer's intended purpose.

Our examination was conducted in accordance with attestation standards established by the American Institute of Certified Public Accountants and, accordingly, included (1) obtaining an understanding of ABC Company's relevant on-line privacy and processing integrity controls; (2) testing and evaluating the operating effectiveness of the controls; (3) testing compliance with the Online Privacy and Processing Integrity Criteria; and (4) performing such other procedures as we considered necessary in the circumstances. We believe that our examination provides a reasonable basis for our opinion.

In our opinion, ABC Company complied, in all material respects, with the criteria for consumer protection and maintained, in all material respects, effective controls over the Customer Order Placement System to provide reasonable assurance that

- Personal information obtained as a result of electronic commerce was collected, used, disclosed, and retained as committed or agreed, and
- System processing was complete, accurate, timely and authorized during the period of January 1, 20X2, through June 30, 20X2, based on the AICPA/CICA Trust Services Criteria for consumer protection.

Because of inherent limitations in controls, error or fraud may occur and not be detected. Furthermore, the projection of any conclusions, based on our findings, to future periods is subject to the risk that the validity of such conclusions may be altered because of changes made to the system or controls, the failure to make needed changes to the system or controls, or a deterioration in the degree of effectiveness of the controls.

The WebTrust Seal of Assurance on ABC Company's website constitutes a symbolic representation of the contents of this report and it is not intended, nor should it be construed, to update this report or provide any additional assurance.

This report does not include any representation as to the quality of ABC Company's goods nor their suitability for any customer's intended purpose.

[*Name of CPA Firm, City, State, Date*]

Independent Practitioner's SysTrust Report

To the Management of ABC Company:

We have examined the effectiveness of ABC Company's control described in Schedule X, over the security of its Cash Disbursements System during the period January 1, 20X2, to June 30, 20X2, based on the AICPA/CICA Trust Services Security Criteria. Maintaining the effectiveness of these controls is the responsibility of ABC Company's management. Our responsibility is to express an opinion based on our examination.

Our examination was conducted in accordance with attestation standards established by the American Institute of Certified Public Accountants and, accordingly, included (1) obtaining an understanding of ABC Company's relevant on-line privacy and processing integrity controls; (2) testing and evaluating the operating effectiveness of the controls; (3) testing compliance with the Online Privacy and Processing Integrity Criteria; and (4) performing such other procedures as we considered necessary in the circumstances. We believe that our examination provides a reasonable basis for our opinion.

In our opinion, ABC Company maintained, in all material respects, effective controls described in Schedule X, over the security of the Cash Disbursements System to provide reasonable assurance that the Cash Disbursements System was protected against unauthorized access (both physical and logical) during the period January 1, 20X2 to June 30, 20X2, based on the AICPA/CICA Trust Services Security Criteria.

Because of inherent limitations in controls, error or fraud may occur and not be detected. Furthermore, the projection of any conclusions, based on our findings, to future periods is subject to the risk that the validity of such conclusions may be altered because of changes made to the system or controls, the failure to make needed changes to the system or controls, or a deterioration in the degree of effectiveness of the controls.

The SysTrust Seal on ABC Company's website constitutes a symbolic representation of the contents of this report and it is not intended, nor should it be construed, to update this report or provide any additional assurance.

[*Name of CPA Firm, City, State, Date*]

organization control (SOC) reports. Service organizations provide processing services to custom- decide to outsource their processing of particular data. Examples of service organizations include data flexible spending account servicers, and medical claims processers. The AICPA has established three examination services that result in the following three types of CPA reports on service organization (SOC):

- SOC 1: Restricted use reports on controls at a service organization relevant to a user entity's internal control over financial reporting.
- SOC 2: Restricted use reports on controls at a service organization related to security, availability, processing integrity, confidentiality, and/or privacy.
- SOC 3: General use SysTrust reports related to security, availability, processing integrity, confidentiality, and/or privacy.

SOC 1 Reports. Section E3 of the Understanding Internal Control and Assessing Control Risk module discusses SOC 1 reports. These reports are intended primarily for the use of user auditors and the company that uses the services of the service organization. AT 801 provides guidance to CPAs providing SOC 1 reports and AU-C 402 addresses the use of such reports.

SOC 2 Reports. SOC 2 reports are performed under AT Section 101, Attest Engagements and address one or more of the Trust Services principles of security, availability, processing integrity, confidentiality, and/or privacy. SOC 2 reports are designed to provide

- Organizations that outsource tasks and functions a mechanism for improving governance and oversight of service providers.
- Service organizations the ability to communicate the suitability of the design and operating effectiveness of their controls.

In a SOC 2 engagement, management prepares a detailed description of the service organization's system, including controls designed to achieve the criteria for one or more of the Trust Services Principles. In essence, the CPA reports on the fairness of the description. Service organizations can distribute the report to their customers and other intended recipients, such as regulators and business partners.

SOC 3 Reports. SOC 3 reports are in essence Trust Services reports for service organizations. These reports provide users with an assertion by management that it maintained effective controls to meet the Trust Services criteria, a short description of its system, and a CPA's report on either management's assertion or on the effectiveness of controls that meet the Trust Services criteria as described earlier in this chapter. The following figure compares the various types of service organization reports.

	SOC 1	SOC 2	SOC 3
Professional Standards	• AT 801 (SSAE No. 16) • AICPA Guide *Applying SSAE No. 16 Reporting on Controls at a Service Organization* • AU-402	• AT 101 • AICPA Guide, *Reporting on Controls at a Service Organization Relevant to Security, Availability, Processing Integrity, Confidentiality, or Privacy*	• AT 101 • AICPA Technical Practice Aid, *Trust Services Principles, Criteria and Illustrations*
Primary Purpose	Report on service organization controls over financial reporting, particularly on those controls likely to be relevant to user entities' financial statements. These reports are primarily for auditors of companies that outsource processing to a service organization.	Report on service organization controls related to compliance with the Trust Services Principles and Criteria (controls over security, availability, processing integrity, confidentiality, and/or privacy).	
Assertion provided by service organization management	A specific, detailed assertion on the part of the system the CPA is reporting upon.		A more general assertion on the organization having met one or more of the AICPA Trust Services Criteria.

	SOC 1	SOC 2	SOC 3
Report	Detailed Type 1 or Type 2 report on controls tested.*	Detailed Type 1 or Type 2 report on service organization's compliance with one or more Trust Service Principles.*	A less detailed report on whether service organization maintained effective controls based on the Trust Services Criteria.
Use of Report	Restricted use report primarily for user auditors (auditors auditing the financial statements of companies that use the service auditor).	Restricted use report primarily for service organization and user stakeholders such as customers, regulators, business partners, suppliers, and directors.	General use report (for use by anyone).

Type 1 reports address whether the description of the controls is fairly presented and whether the controls described are suitably designed. A Type 2 report includes the information in a Type 1 report and an opinion on whether the controls were operating effectively.

NOW REVIEW MULTIPLE-CHOICE QUESTIONS 93 THROUGH 145

H. Reporting on Compliance

Overview. Compliance auditing involves testing and reporting on whether an organization has complied with the requirements of various laws, regulations, contracts, and grants. Congress and various regulatory agencies have adopted compliance auditing requirements for a variety of governmental and other organizations. While not a new type of auditing, it has become more significant in the last decade. A primary purpose of compliance auditing is to provide assurance that requirements of various federal programs have been met. Currently, the major engagements are (1) compliance with contractual agreements based on having performed a financial statement audit, (2) compliance attestation engagements, or (3) compliance auditing of federal financial assistance programs.

1. **Reporting on Compliance with Aspects of Contractual Agreements or Regulatory Requirements in Connection with Audited Financial Statements (AU-C 806).** After completing an audit of financial statements, auditors may be asked to test whether the audited entity is in compliance with some form of agreement. The auditor's objective in such an engagement is to provide *negative assurance* on the entity's compliance with aspects of agreements or regulatory requirement *in connection with the audit* of the financial statements. For example, an auditor may provide negative assurance to a bank on whether a client is in conformity with restrictions contained in a debt agreement (e.g., maintain a particular level of working capital). Auditors who have audited the financial statements may issue a report on compliance (1) when the covenants relate to the financial statements (2) those covenants have been subjected to audit procedures and (3) the auditor's audit report on the financial statement has other than an adverse opinion or a disclaimer of opinion. The auditor's report on compliance

   * States that the financial statements were audited.
   * Refers to the specific covenant or paragraphs of the agreement and provides negative assurance relative to compliance (i.e., "nothing came to our attention that caused us to believe that XYZ Company failed to comply with the terms of...").
   * Describes any significant interpretations made by management relating to the agreement.

   When the auditor has identified one or more items of noncompliance, those items are identified in the report.

2. **Compliance Attestation Engagements (AT 601).** AT 601 provides guidance to CPAs on providing assurance—either through agreed-upon procedures or through examination engagements—concerning an organization's compliance with requirements of certain laws, regulations, rules, contracts, or grants (referred to as compliance with **specified requirements**). This form of association goes beyond that described in 1 above. The following are examples of agreed-upon procedures engagements (which occur much more frequently than examinations):

EXAMPLE 1

The Federal Depository Insurance Corporation (FDIC) Improvement Act of 1991 requires that CPAs be engaged by certain financial institutions to perform agreed-upon procedures engagements to test financial institution compliance with certain "safety and soundness" laws designated by the FDIC.

EXAMPLE 2

The Environmental Protection Agency (EPA) requires that CPAs (or internal auditors) be engaged to perform agreed-upon procedures engagements to test certain entities' compliance with an EPA regulation that gasoline contains at least 2.0% oxygen.

As an alternative to performing agreed-upon procedures in engagements such as the above, a CPA may perform agreed-upon procedures on the portion of the internal control that is designed to provide reasonable assurance of compliance with such specified requirements. Using the second illustration, a control over compliance engagement would analyze controls related to providing management with reasonable assurance that gasoline contains at least 2.0% oxygen.

Basic to compliance attestation engagements **is a written management assertion** concerning compliance. In this assertion, management ordinarily states that it believes that the company is in compliance with the specified requirements or acknowledges certain instances of noncompliance. This written assertion is included in a representation letter addressed by management to the auditor, and may also be included in a separate management report. For example, in the second earlier example, the written management assertion relates to its compliance with the EPA regulation; alternatively, structured on internal control, the assertion relates to internal control over compliance with the EPA regulation. The CPA performs procedures to test whether the written assertion is correct. AT 601 establishes standards for agreed-upon procedures engagements on compliance and internal control, and for examination engagements on compliance. The statement does not permit review engagements.

a. **Agreed-upon procedures engagements (AT 201)**

  (1) **Applicability**—These engagements may be related either to management's assertion about compliance with specified requirements or to management's assertion about the effectiveness of its internal control over compliance.

  (2) **Engagement scope**—The scope of these engagements is often fixed by the regulatory agency involved (e.g., the EPA in the second example presented earlier). The CPA is required to obtain an understanding of the compliance requirements addressed in management's assertion and should obtain a representation letter from management.

  (3) **Reporting**—As with other agreed-upon procedures engagements, the report is a limited distribution report, in this case restricted to the audit committee, management, and the parties for whom the procedures were performed (e.g., the EPA). The accountant provides a summary of findings in the report. The report should include any material noncompliance noted, regardless of whether the CPA became aware of it as a direct result of the procedures performed or in some other manner (e.g., through a discussion with an internal auditor). The following is an example of an agreed-upon procedures report:

Independent Practitioner's Report

To XYZ Company:

    We have performed the procedures enumerated below, which were agreed to by the Minnesota Department of Education, solely to assist the specified parties in evaluating XYZ Company's compliance with Section F.2. of Minnesota Department of Education Regulation 76A of *Employment Health Requirements* during the period ended December 31, 20XX. Management is responsible for XYZ Company's compliance with those requirements. This agreed-upon procedures engagement was conducted in accordance with attestation standards established by the American Institute of Certified Public Accountants. The sufficiency of these procedures is solely the responsibility of those parties specified in this report. Consequently, we make no representation regarding the sufficiency of the procedures described below either for the purpose for which this report has been requested or for any other purpose.

[Include paragraphs to enumerate procedures and findings.]

We were not engaged to, and did not, perform an examination, the objective of which would be the expression of an opinion on compliance. Accordingly, we do not express such an opinion. Had we performed additional procedures, other matters might have come to our attention that would have been reported to you.

This report is intended solely for the information of the audit committee, management, and the parties listed in the first paragraph, and is not intended to be and should not be used by anyone other than those specified parties.

b. **Examination engagements**

(1) **Applicability**—These engagements relate to management's written assertion about the entity's compliance with specified requirements. (AT 601 does not provide guidance for examinations of the internal control over compliance. General guidance for such engagements is provided in AT 101.)

(2) **Engagement scope**—The procedures and scope of an examination of compliance are similar to those of an audit of financial statements. Following are the major stages:

  (a) Obtain an understanding of specified compliance requirements.
  (b) Plan the engagement.
  (c) Consider relevant portions of internal control over compliance (when control risk is to be assessed below maximum, tests of controls should be performed).
  (d) Obtain sufficient evidence through substantive tests of compliance with specified requirements.
  (e) Consider whether any subsequent events affect compliance.
  (f) Form an opinion about whether management's assertion about the entity's compliance with specified requirements is fairly stated in all material respects based on established or agreed-upon criteria.

(3) **Reporting**—The CPA's report may either be (1) directly upon compliance, or (2) on management's assertion. The following is an unqualified report directly upon compliance:

Independent Practitioner's Report

To XYZ Company:

We have examined XYZ Company's compliance with Section F.2. of Minnesota Department of Education Regulation 76A of *Employment Health Requirements* during the period ended December 31, 20XX. Management is responsible for XYZ Company's compliance with those requirements. Our responsibility is to express an opinion on XYZ Company's compliance based on our examination.

Our examination was conducted in accordance with attestation standards established by the American Institute of Certified Public Accountants, and, accordingly, included examining, on a test basis, evidence about XYZ Company's compliance with those requirements and performing such other procedures as we considered necessary in the circumstances. We believe that our examination provides a reasonable basis for our opinion. Our examination does not provide a legal determination on XYZ Company's compliance with specified requirements.

In our opinion, XYZ Company complied, in all material respects, with the aforementioned requirements for the year ended December 31, 20XX.

This report is intended solely for the information and use of XYZ Company and the State of Minnesota and is not intended to be and should not be used by anyone other than these specified parties.

As is the case with other attestation reports, if an opinion other than unqualified is being issued the CPA should follow the first reporting option, reporting directly upon compliance. The following table presents the primary circumstances:

Circumstance	Examination Report Effect
1. Entity did not comply	Qualified or adverse opinion with an explanatory paragraph added before the opinion paragraph
2. Material uncertainty relating to future events makes determination of compliance insusceptible to reasonable estimation	Qualified opinion or disclaimer of opinion with an explanatory paragraph added before the opinion paragraph
3. Scope restriction	When client-imposed, generally disclaim an opinion; when circumstance-imposed, consider qualified opinion or disclaimer of opinion
4. Involvement of another CPA firm	When the principal CPA does not wish to take responsibility for the other CPA's work, the other CPA's report is referred to.

3. **Compliance Auditing, Government Auditing Standards and the Single Audit Act.** Governments frequently establish requirements that entities undergo a "compliance audit" to address their compliance with applicable requirements relating to various laws, regulations, contracts, and grants. The scope of compliance audits differs from one another, ordinarily due to differing requirements of the particular situation involved. Yet, the overall goal is for the auditor to provide assurance about whether the law, regulation, contract or grant has been administered in accordance with applicable laws and regulations. Further guidance for compliance auditing is provided by AU-C 935 and *Government Auditing Standards (GAS),* also referred to as the "Yellow Book," published by the Comptroller General of the United States (the top executive within the General Accountability Office).

AU-C 935 applies when an auditor is engaged, or required by law or regulation, to perform a compliance audit in accordance with any of the following:

- GAAS
- Standards for financial statements under Government Auditing Standards
- A governmental audit requirement that requires an auditor to express an opinion on compliance (e.g., a requirement of organizations governed by the US Department of Housing and Urban Development)

Read the outline of AU-C 935.

Government Auditing Standards provides what it refers to a as "generally accepted government auditing standards (GAGAS)—read the summary information relating to Government Auditing Standards presented following the outline of AU-C 935.

To provide a perspective on this area, we discuss compliance auditing in three contexts—GAAS audits, Government Auditing Standard audits, and audits performed under the Single Audit Act.

a. **Audits conducted in accordance with GAAS**

(1) **Applicability**—This form of audit is generally performed for governmental entities for which no law requires either a *GAS* or Single Audit. It is also performed for certain nongovernmental entities that have received federal financial assistance.

(2) **Audit scope**—Recall from Section A of the Engagement Planning Module that auditors have a responsibility to design all audits to provide reasonable assurance of detecting misstatements resulting from violations of laws and regulations that have a direct and material effect on line item amounts (hereafter "direct effect") in the financial statements; this responsibility remains the same for these audits. Because entities that receive financial aid should comply with a number of laws that, if violated, result in illegal acts with a direct effect on the financial statements, an audit should provide reasonable assurance of their detection.

To identify laws having a direct effect on an organization's financial statements, auditors (1) discuss laws with management, other administrators, and government auditors, (2) review relevant grant and loan agreements, (3) review minutes of the legislative body of the governmental organization, and (4) obtain written representations from management about the completeness of laws identified. They then assess the risk that financial statement amounts might be materially misstated by violations of laws and design and perform appropriate substantive tests of compliance with the laws.

The objectives, scope, methodology, and results of the audit should be summarized in audit working papers in a legible manner and should contain evidence of supervisory reviews of the work conducted. These working papers should "stand alone" without the need for any supplementary explanations to describe the nature of the audit and should include a written audit program, with proper cross-referencing to the working papers.

(3) **Reporting**—The standard audit report is normally issued. If material noncompliance is detected, it should be disclosed in the financial statements or treated as a departure from GAAP in the audit report, thus requiring a qualified or an adverse opinion. **No** compliance report (see next section) is issued, and a report on internal control is only issued when significant deficiencies have been identified.

b. **Audits conducted in accordance with generally accepted government auditing standards (GAGAS)**

   (1) **Applicability**—These audits are required for certain organizations that receive federal financial assistance. Whether a governmental organization is so required depends upon requirements of the federal financial assistance programs in which it participates and whether it is required to have a Single Audit (see c. below).

   (2) **Audit scope**—In addition to GAAS requirements, depending upon the nature of the entity being audited, additional auditor responsibilities may exist. (See outline of *Government Auditing Standards* following AU-C 935 outline.)

   (3) **Reporting**—While GAGAS require reporting on the **financial statements** (i.e., the "audit report"), **internal control,** and on **compliance with laws and regulations,** other government audits may not require a report on internal control. The AU-C 935 reporting requirements outline reports for reporting on compliance alone, combining a report on compliance and internal control, and reporting on internal control over compliance.

c. **Audits conducted in accordance with the Single Audit Act.** Audits in accordance with the Single Audit Act of 1984 (as amended in 1996) are more extensive than GAAS or GAS audits. This act, passed by Congress, is implemented by the Office of Management and Budget (OMB) through its Circular A-133 and its related Compliance Supplement. Circular A-133 is the OMB's key policy document that implements the Single Audit Act. The Compliance Supplement is the document that provides guidance to auditors who are engaged to test for compliance with program requirements.

   Audits in accordance with the Single Audit Act include requirements that supplement the GAS audit procedures. The auditors' report(s) may be presented in the form of either combined or separate reports, but should include the following:

   (1) Opinion (or disclaimer) on whether financial statements conform to GAAP.
   (2) Opinion on schedule of expenditures of federal awards. The schedule summarized program expenditures for all programs. The auditors' report includes an opinion as to whether the information is presented fairly, in all material respects, in relation to the financial statements taken as a whole.
   (3) Report on internal control related to the financial statements and major programs. Under the single audit requirements, auditors are responsible for understanding internal control over major programs and reporting the results of their tests; significant deficiencies and material weaknesses should be disclosed. Auditors are required to obtain an understanding of the recipient's internal control over financial reporting and over federal programs sufficient to plan the audit to support a low assessed level of control risk for major programs. While this provision does not require that auditors achieve a low assessed level of risk, it does require auditors to test the controls over federal programs to determine whether they are effective.

   The internal control report (or internal control portion of a combined report) includes the following:

First paragraph

- Management is responsible for establishing and maintaining effective internal control over compliance with requirements of laws.
- We considered internal control over compliance that could have a direct and material effect on a major federal program.

Second paragraph

- Our consideration would not necessarily disclose all material weaknesses.

- Definition of material weakness
- Material weaknesses noted (or statement that none were noted)

Third paragraph

- Other matters (less than material weaknesses) noted

Fourth paragraph

- Report is for information of audit committee, management, and federal awarding agencies.
- Report is a matter of public record and its distribution is not limited.

Opinion paragraph

- Entity complied, in all material respects, with types of requirements described above for each of its major programs.
- Auditing procedures disclosed immaterial instances of noncompliance described in the accompanying Schedule of Findings and Questioned Costs.

(4) **Report on major financial assistance program compliance.** A major program is one that is determined by using a risk-based approach that considers both the amount of the program's expenditures and the risk of material noncompliance. In general, the major programs should constitute at least 50% of the total federal expenditures by the organization.

Under the Single Audit Act, compliance procedures are performed for the specific requirements of all major programs. The specific requirements that should be audited are those that, if not complied with, could have a material effect on a major program. These requirements relate to such matters as activities allowed, allowable costs, cash management, and eligibility. In testing compliance under the Single Audit Act, a lower level of planning materiality is used because auditors should consider compliance from the perspective of a material effect on each major federal assistance program. When evaluating whether an instance of noncompliance with law is material, auditors should consider the frequency of noncompliance and whether it results in a material amount of questioned costs. Questioned costs are those costs not allowed by the program, not adequately supported with documentation, unnecessary, or unreasonable.

The compliance report (or compliance portion of a combined report) in general follows the format of the standard unqualified report, with modifications including the following:

Introductory paragraph

- We have audited in compliance with requirements of Circular A-133.
- Compliance is the responsibility of management.
- Our responsibility is to express an opinion on compliance.

Scope paragraph

- Conducted audit in compliance with US GAAS, *Government Auditing Standards*, and OMB Circular A-133

Opinion paragraph

- Entity complied, in all material respects, with types of requirements described above for each of its major programs.
- Auditing procedures disclosed immaterial instances of noncompliance described in the accompanying Schedule of Findings and Questioned Costs.

(5) **A summary report on audit results relating to financial statements, internal control, and compliance.** This report includes a summary of the auditors' findings relating to the financial statements, internal control, compliance matters, questioned costs, or suspected fraud.

NOW REVIEW MULTIPLE-CHOICE QUESTIONS 146 THROUGH 167

KEY TERMS

Adverse opinion. The opinion expressed when the auditor concludes that the financial statements are materially and pervasively misstated and accordingly are **not** prepared in accordance with the applicable financial reporting framework (ordinarily GAAP).

Agreed-upon procedures. An attest engagement in which the CPAs agree to perform procedures for a specified party and to issue a report that is restricted to use by that party (and management).

Audit report on financial statements. A document designed to communicate the nature of the audit, including responsibilities taken, limitations, and a conclusion as to the fairness of presentation of the financial statements.

Comparative financial statements. A complete set of financial statements for one or more prior periods included with current year financial statements of the current period.

Compliance audit. An audit that emphasizes performing audit procedures to test an organization's compliance with laws and regulations.

Condensed (summary) financial statements. Historical financial information that is derived from the financial statements but contains less detail, while still providing a structured representation consistent with the financial statements.

Consistency. The concept of using the same accounting principles from year to year so that the successive financial statements issued by a business entity will be comparable.

Continuing accountant. An accountant who has been engaged to report on the financial statements of a specific entity.

Date of the auditor's report. A date no earlier than the date on which the auditor has obtained sufficient appropriate audit evidence, including evidence that the audit documentation has been reviewed.

Date of the financial statements. The date of the end of the latest period covered by the financial statements.

Disclaimer of opinion. An auditor's conclusion in an audit report that he or she is unable to form an opinion on whether the financial statements are prepared in accordance with the applicable financial reporting framework (ordinarily GAAP). This conclusion most frequently occurs due to a lack of sufficient appropriate audit evidence. It may also occur due to uncertainties, including going concern uncertainties.

Emphasis-of-matter paragraph. A paragraph included in the auditor's report that is required by GAAS, or is included at the auditor's discretion, and that refers to a matter appropriately presented or disclosed in the financial statement that, in the auditor's professional judgment, is of such importance that it is fundamental to users' understanding of the financial statements.

Examination. An attest engagement designed to provide the highest level of assurance that CPAs provide on an assertion. An examination of financial statements is referred to as an audit.

Explanatory paragraph. For a public company, a paragraph inserted in an audit report in which the auditors describe the reasons for giving a report other than a standard report.

Fraud. An intentional act by one or more individuals among management, those charged with governance, employees, or third parties, involving the use of deception that results in a misstatement in financial statements that are subject of an audit. For financial statement audits, fraud includes two types of intentional misstatements—misstatements arising from fraudulent financial reporting and misstatements arising from misappropriation of assets.

General-purpose financial statements. Financial statements prepared in accordance with a general-purpose framework.

General-purpose framework. A financial reporting framework designed to meet the common financial information needs of a wide range of users.

Hypothetical transaction. A transaction or financial reporting issue that does not involve facts or circumstances of a specific entity.

Integrated audit. As required by the Sarbanes-Oxley Act and the Public Company Accounting Oversight Board, an audit that includes providing assurance on both the financial statements and internal control over financial reporting. Integrated audits are required of large publicly traded companies in the United States.

Issuer. A company whose stock is traded on a public market or a company in the process of registering its stock for public sale.

Letter for underwriter. A letter issued by the independent auditors to the underwriters of securities registered with the SEC under the Securities Act of 1933. Letters for underwriters deal with matters such as the auditor's independence and the compliance of unaudited data with requirements of the SEC. These letters are also referred to as "comfort letters."

Modified opinion. A qualified opinion, an adverse opinion, or a disclaimer of opinion.

Negative assurance. A conclusion by CPAs that, after applying limited investigative techniques to certain information, they are not aware of the need to modify the presentation of the information. Negative assurance is equivalent to limited assurance.

Nonissuer. A company whose securities are *not* registered under requirements of the Securities and Exchange Commission; ordinarily, a "nonissuer" is a nonpublic company. This is in contrast to an issuer, a company whose securities are registered under the requirements of the Securities and Exchange Commission.

Nonpublic company. A company other than one whose securities are traded on a public market or one that makes a filing with a regulatory agency in preparation for the sale of securities on a public market.

Other auditor. Within the context of a situation in which more than one auditing firm is involved with an audit, the auditor that has performed some of the audit work, but is not the principal auditor.

Other comprehensive basis of accounting. A basis for financial reporting other than GAAP, including (1) any basis required by a governmental regulatory agency, (2) income tax basis, (3) cash basis, and (4) a definite set of criteria having substantial support.

Other-matter paragraph. A paragraph included in the auditor's report that is required by GAAS, or is included at the auditor's discretion, and that refers to a matter other than those presented or disclosed in the financial statements that, in the auditor's professional judgment is relevant to users' understanding of the audit, the auditor responsibilities or the auditor's opinion.

Pervasive. The effects on financial statements of misstatements or possible effects of misstatements that are undetected due to an inability to obtain sufficient appropriate audit evidence. Pervasive effects on the financial statements are those that, in the auditor's judgment are not confined to specific elements, accounts or items of the financial statements or if so confined, represent or could represent a substantial proportion of the financial statements or in relation to disclosures, are fundamental to users' understanding of the financial statements.

Predecessor auditor. A CPA firm that formerly served as auditor but has resigned from the engagement or has been notified that its services have been terminated.

Principal auditor. Auditors who use the work and reports of other auditors who have audited the financial statements of one or more subsidiaries, branches, or other segments of the principal auditor's client.

Qualified opinion. The opinion expressed when the auditor concludes that the financial statements are prepared in all material respects, in accordance with the applicable financial reporting framework (ordinarily GAAP) except for the effects of some limitation in the scope of the audit or some departure from GAAP.

Reasonable assurance. In the context of an audit of financial statements, a high, but not absolute, level of assurance.

Shared responsibility opinion. An audit report in which the principal auditors decide to refer to an other auditor involved with the audit of some component of the company.

Single Audit Act. Legislation passed by the US Congress that establishes uniform requirements for audits of federal financial assistance provided to state and local government.

Special report. An auditors' report issued on any of the following: (1) financial statements prepared on a comprehensive basis of accounting other than GAAP, (2) elements of financial statements, (3) compliance with regulatory or contractual requirements, (4) financial presentations to comply with contractual agreements or regulatory provisions, or (5) audited information presented in prescribed forms.

Standard audit report. The wording of an unqualified audit report that includes no modifications for matters such as substantial doubt about going concern status, a change in accounting principle, emphasis of a matter described in the financial statements, or a shared responsibility opinion.

Successor auditor. The auditors who have accepted an engagement to replace the CPA firm that formerly served as auditor (the predecessor auditor).

Unmodified opinion. The opinion expressed when the auditor concludes that the financial statements are prepared in all material respects, in accordance with the applicable financial reporting framework.

Multiple-Choice Questions (1–167)

A.1.   Audit Reports: Standard Unmodified Reports—Background

1. The existence of audit risk is recognized by the statement in the auditor's standard report that the auditor

- a. Obtains reasonable assurance about whether the financial statements are free of material misstatement.
- b. Assesses the accounting principles used and also evaluates the overall financial statement presentation.
- c. Realizes some matters, either individually or in the aggregate, are important while other-matters are not important.
- d. Is responsible for expressing an opinion on the financial statements, which are the responsibility of management.

2. When an accountant performs more than one level of service (for example, a compilation and a review, or a compilation and an audit) concerning the financial statements of a nonissuer (nonpublic) entity, the accountant generally should issue the report that is appropriate for

- a. The lowest level of service rendered.
- b. The highest level of service rendered.
- c. A compilation engagement.
- d. A review engagement.

3. Which of the following statements is correct concerning an auditor's responsibility for controlling the **distribution by the client** of a restricted-use report?

- a. An auditor must make clear to the client that it is illegal to distribute such a report beyond to specified parties.
- b. When an auditor is aware that a client has distributed a restricted-use report to inappropriate third parties, the auditor should immediately inform the client to cease and desist.
- c. An auditor controls distribution through insisting that the client not duplicate the restricted-use report for any purposes.
- d. An auditor is not responsible for controlling the distribution of such reports.

4. March, CPA, is engaged by Monday Corp., a client, to audit the financial statements of Wall Corp., a company that is not March's client. Monday expects to present Wall's audited financial statements with March's auditor's report to 1st Federal Bank to obtain financing in Monday's attempt to purchase Wall. In these circumstances, March's auditor's report would usually be addressed to

- a. Monday Corp., the client that engaged March.
- b. Wall Corp., the entity audited by March.
- c. 1st Federal Bank.
- d. Both Monday Corp. and 1st Federal Bank.

A.2.   Nonpublic Companies (Nonissuers)

5. Which of the following statements is a basic element of the auditor's standard report?

- a. The disclosures provide reasonable assurance that the financial statements are free of material misstatement.
- b. The auditor evaluated the overall internal control.
- c. An audit includes assessing significant estimates made by management.
- d. The financial statements are consistent with those of the prior period.

6. In May 20X9, an auditor reissues the auditor's report on the 20X7 financial statements at a continuing client's request. The 20X7 financial statements are not restated and the auditor does not revise the wording of the report. The auditor should

- a. Dual date the reissued report.
- b. Use the release date of the reissued report.
- c. Use the original report date on the reissued report.
- d. Use the current period auditor's report date on the reissued report.

7. For a nonpublic company, which section (paragraph) of the audit report includes a statement that the auditor believes that the audit evidence obtained is sufficient?

- a. Introductory.
- b. Opinion.
- c. Auditor's responsibility.
- d. Management's responsibility.

8. For a nonpublic company audit report, a statement that the auditor has audited the financial statements followed by the titles of the financial statements is included in the

- a. Management's responsibility section of the audit report.
- b. The opening paragraph of the auditor's standard report.
- c. The auditor's responsibility section of the audit report.
- d. The opinion paragraph of the auditor's standard report.

9. Which of the following phrases should be included in the opinion paragraph when an auditor expresses a qualified opinion?

	When read in conjunction with Note X	With the foregoing explanation
a.	Yes	No
b.	No	Yes
c.	Yes	Yes
d.	No	No

10. How does an auditor make the following representations when issuing the standard public company auditor's report on comparative financial statements?

	Examination of evidence on a test basis	Consistent application of accounting principles
a.	Explicitly	Explicitly
b.	Implicitly	Implicitly
c.	Implicitly	Explicitly
d.	Explicitly	Implicitly

11. An auditor concludes that extreme doubt exists about the integrity of management and the representations obtained from management relating to the fairness of the financial statements and the completeness of the record of transactions. If the auditor retains the client, which audit report is most likely to be appropriate?

    a. Unmodified with emphasis-of-matter paragraph.
    b. Standard unmodified.
    c. Disclaimer.
    d. Adverse

12. Wilson, CPA, completed gathering sufficient appropriate audit evidence for the audit of Abco's December 31, 20X8 financial statements on March 6, 20X9. A subsequent event requiring adjustment to the 20X8 financial statements occurred on April 10, 20X9 and came to Wilson's attention on April 24, 20X9. If the adjustment is made without disclosure of the event, Wilson's report ordinarily should be dated

    a. March 6, 20X9.
    b. April 10, 20X9.
    c. April 24, 20X9.
    d. Using dual dating.

13. An auditor issued an audit report that was dual dated for a subsequent event occurring after the completion of field-work but before issuance of the auditor's report. The auditor's responsibility for events occurring subsequent to the completion of fieldwork was

    a. Extended to subsequent events occurring through the date of issuance of the report.
    b. Extended to include all events occurring since the completion of fieldwork.
    c. Limited to the specific event referenced.
    d. Limited to include only events occurring up to the date of the last subsequent event referenced.

A.3. Public Companies (Issuers)

14. Which of the following **best** describes the reference to the expression "taken as a whole" in the PCAOB's fourth generally accepted auditing standard of reporting?

    a. It applies equally to a complete set of financial statements and to each individual financial statement.
    b. It applies only to a complete set of financial statements.
    c. It applies equally to each item in each financial statement.

    d. It applies equally to each material item in each financial statement.

15. A financial statement audit report issued for the audit of an issuer (public) company concludes that the financial statements follow

    a. Generally accepted accounting principles.
    b. Public Company Accounting Oversight Board standards.
    c. Generally accepted auditing standards.
    d. International accounting standards.

16. Which of the following is not correct concerning information included in an audit report of financial statements issued under the requirements of the Public Company Accounting Oversight Board?

    a. The report should include the title "Report of Independent Registered Public Accounting Firm."
    b. The report should refer to the standards of the PCAOB.
    c. The report should include a paragraph referring to the auditor's report on compliance with laws and regulations.
    d. The report should contain the city and state or country of the office that issued the report.

B.2. Substantial Doubt about Ability to Continue as a Going Concern

17. An auditor concludes that there is substantial doubt about an entity's ability to continue as a going concern for a reasonable period of time. If the entity's financial statements adequately disclose its financial difficulties, the auditor's report is required to include an emphasis-of-matter paragraph that specifically uses the phrase(s)

	"Reasonable period of time, not to exceed 1 year"	"Going concern"
a.	Yes	Yes
b.	Yes	No
c.	No	Yes
d.	No	No

18. Mead, CPA, had substantial doubt about Tech Co.'s ability to continue as a going concern when reporting on Tech's audited financial statements for the year ended June 30, 20X1. That doubt has been removed in 20X1. What is Mead's reporting responsibility if Tech is presenting its financial statements for the year ended June 30, 20X2, on a comparative basis with those of 20X2?

    a. The emphasis-of-matter paragraph included in the 20X2 auditor's report should not be repeated.
    b. The emphasis-of-matter paragraph included in the 20X2 auditor's report should be repeated in its entirety.
    c. A different emphasis-of-matter paragraph describing Mead's reasons for the removal of doubt should be included.
    d. A different emphasis-of-matter paragraph describing Tech's plans for financial recovery should be included.

19. When an auditor concludes there is substantial doubt about a continuing audit client's ability to continue as a going concern for a reasonable period of time, the auditor's responsibility is to

 a. Issue a qualified or adverse opinion, depending upon materiality, due to the possible effects on the financial statements.
 b. Consider the adequacy of disclosure about the client's possible inability to continue as a going concern.
 c. Report to the client's audit committee that management's accounting estimates may need to be adjusted.
 d. Reissue the prior year's auditor's report and add an emphasis-of-matter paragraph that specifically refers to "substantial doubt" and "going concern."

20. Green, CPA, concludes that there is substantial doubt about JKL Co.'s ability to continue as a going concern. If JKL's financial statements adequately disclose its financial difficulties, Green's auditor's report should

	Include an emphasis-of-matter paragraph following the opinion paragraph	Specifically use the words "going concern"	Specifically use the words "substantial doubt"
a.	Yes	Yes	Yes
b.	Yes	Yes	No
c.	Yes	No	Yes
d.	No	Yes	Yes

21. In which of the following circumstances would an auditor most likely add an emphasis-of-matter paragraph to the audit report while **not** affecting the auditor's unmodified opinion?

 a. The auditor is asked to report on the balance sheet, but not on the other basic financial statements.
 b. There is substantial doubt about the entity's ability to continue as a going concern.
 c. Management's estimates of the effects of future events are unreasonable.
 d. Certain transactions cannot be tested because of management's records retention policy.

22. After considering an entity's negative trends and financial difficulties, an auditor has substantial doubt about the entity's ability to continue as a going concern. The auditor's considerations relating to management's plans for dealing with the adverse effects of these conditions most likely would include management's plans to

 a. Increase current dividend distributions.
 b. Reduce existing lines of credit.
 c. Increase ownership equity.
 d. Purchase assets formerly leased.

23. Which of the following conditions or events most likely would cause an auditor to have substantial doubt about an entity's ability to continue as a going concern?

 a. Significant related-party transactions are pervasive.
 b. Usual trade credit from suppliers is denied.

 c. Arrearages in preferred stock dividends are paid.
 d. Restrictions on the disposal of principal assets are present.

24. Cooper, CPA, believes there is substantial doubt about the ability of Zero Corp. to continue as a going concern for a reasonable period of time. In evaluating Zero's plans for dealing with the adverse effects of future conditions and events, Cooper most likely would consider, as a mitigating factor, Zero's plans to

 a. Discuss with lenders the terms of all debt and loan agreements.
 b. Strengthen controls over cash disbursements.
 c. Purchase production facilities currently being leased from a related party.
 d. Postpone expenditures for research and development projects.

25. Which of the following conditions or events most likely would cause an auditor to have substantial doubt about an entity's ability to continue as a going concern?

 a. Cash flows from operating activities are negative.
 b. Research and development projects are postponed.
 c. Significant related-party transactions are pervasive.
 d. Stock dividends replace annual cash dividends.

26. Which of the following auditing procedures most likely would assist an auditor in identifying conditions and events that may indicate substantial doubt about an entity's ability to continue as a going concern?

 a. Inspecting title documents to verify whether any assets are pledged as collateral.
 b. Confirming with third parties the details of arrangements to maintain financial support.
 c. Reconciling the cash balance per books with the cut-off bank statement and the bank confirmation.
 d. Comparing the entity's depreciation and asset capitalization policies to other entities in the industry.

27. Which of the following audit procedures would most likely assist an auditor in identifying conditions and events that may indicate there could be substantial doubt about an entity's ability to continue as a going concern?

 a. Review compliance with the terms of debt agreements.
 b. Confirmation of accounts receivable from principal customers.
 c. Reconciliation of interest expense with debt outstanding.
 d. Confirmation of bank balances.

28. Davis, CPA, believes there is substantial doubt about the ability of Hill Co. to continue as a going concern for a reasonable period of time. In evaluating Hill's plans for dealing with the adverse effects of future conditions and events, Davis most likely would consider, as a mitigating factor, Hill's plans to

 a. Accelerate research and development projects related to future products.
 b. Accumulate treasury stock at prices favorable to Hill's historic price range.

c. Purchase equipment and production facilities currently being leased.

d. Negotiate reductions in required dividends being paid on preferred stock.

29. The adverse effects of events causing an auditor to believe there is substantial doubt about an entity's ability to continue as a going concern would most likely be mitigated by evidence relating to the

a. Ability to expand operations into new product lines in the future.

b. Feasibility of plans to purchase leased equipment at less than market value.

c. Marketability of assets that management plans to sell.

d. Committed arrangements to convert preferred stock to long-term debt.

B.3. Inconsistency in Application of GAAP

30. For which of the following events would an auditor issue a report that omits any reference to consistency?

a. A change in the method of accounting for inventories.

b. A change from an accounting principle that is **not** generally accepted to one that is generally accepted.

c. A change in the useful life used to calculate the provision for depreciation expense.

d. Management's lack of reasonable justification for a change in accounting principle.

31. An auditor would express an unmodified opinion and add an emphasis-of-matter paragraph for

	An unjustified accounting change	A material weakness in the internal control
a.	Yes	Yes
b.	Yes	No
c.	No	Yes
d.	No	No

32. Under which of the following circumstances would a disclaimer of opinion **not** be appropriate?

a. The auditor is unable to determine the amounts associated with an employee fraud scheme.

b. Management does **not** provide reasonable justification for a change in accounting principles.

c. The client refuses to permit the auditor to confirm certain accounts receivable or apply alternative procedures to verify their balances.

d. The chief executive officer is unwilling to sign the management representation letter.

33. Digit Co. uses the FIFO method of costing for its international subsidiary's inventory and LIFO for its domestic inventory. Under these circumstances, the auditor's report on Digit's financial statements should express an

a. Unmodified opinion.

b. Opinion qualified because of a lack of consistency.

c. Opinion qualified because of a departure from GAAP.

d. Adverse opinion.

34. In the first audit of a new client, an auditor was able to extend auditing procedures to gather sufficient evidence about consistency. Under these circumstances, the auditor should

a. Not report on the client's income statement.

b. Not refer to consistency in the auditor's report.

c. State that the consistency standard does **not** apply.

d. State that the accounting principles have been applied consistently.

35. When management does **not** provide reasonable justification that a change in accounting principle is preferable and it presents comparative financial statements, the auditor should express a qualified opinion

a. Only in the year of the accounting principle change.

b. Each year that the financial statements initially reflecting the change are presented.

c. Each year until management changes back to the accounting principle formerly used.

d. Only if the change is to an accounting principle that is not generally accepted.

36. When an entity changes its method of accounting for income taxes, which has a material effect on comparability, the auditor should refer to the change in an emphasis-of-matter paragraph added to the auditor's report. This paragraph should identify the nature of the change and

a. Explain why the change is justified under generally accepted accounting principles.

b. Describe the cumulative effect of the change on the audited financial statements.

c. State the auditor's explicit concurrence with or opposition to the change.

d. Refer to the financial statement note that discusses the change in detail.

37. An entity changed from the straight-line method to the declining balance method of depreciation for all newly acquired assets. This change has no material effect on the current year's financial statements, but is reasonably certain to have a substantial effect in later years. If the change is disclosed in the notes to the financial statements, the auditor should issue a report with a(n)

a. "Except for" qualified opinion.

b. Emphasis-of-matter paragraph.

c. Unmodified opinion.

d. Consistency modification.

B.4. Uncertainties

38. An uncertainty facing the firm relating to the possible future results of litigation filed against client is most likely to result in which of the following types of audit report?

a. Adverse with a basis for adverse opinion paragraph.

b. Qualified due to a scope limitation.

c. Qualified with a basis for qualification paragraph.

d. Unqualified with emphasis-of-matter paragraph.

B.5. *Other Circumstances at the Discretion of the Auditor*

39. An auditor includes a separate paragraph in an otherwise unmodified report to emphasize that the entity being reported on had significant transactions with related parties. The inclusion of this separate paragraph

   a. Is considered an "except for" qualification of the opinion.
   b. Violates generally accepted auditing standards if this information is already disclosed in footnotes to the financial statements.
   c. Necessitates a revision of the opinion paragraph to include the phrase "with the foregoing explanation."
   d. Is appropriate and would not negate the unmodified opinion.

C.1. *Circumstances Resulting in Audit Reports with Modified Opinions—Background*

40. An auditor may **not** issue a qualified opinion when

   a. An accounting principle at variance with GAAP is used.
   b. The auditor lacks independence with respect to the audited entity.
   c. A scope limitation prevents the auditor from completing an important audit procedure.
   d. The auditor's report refers to the work of a specialist.

41. In an accountant's review of interim financial information, the accountant typically performs each of the following, **except**

   a. Reading the available minutes of the latest stockholders' meeting.
   b. Applying financial ratios to the interim financial information.
   c. Inquiring of the accounting department's management.
   d. Confirming major receivable accounts.

C.2. *Materially Misstated Financial Statements (Departures from GAAP)*

42. When an auditor expresses an adverse opinion, the opinion paragraph should include

   a. The principal effects of the departure from generally accepted accounting principles.
   b. A direct reference to a separate paragraph disclosing the basis for the opinion.
   c. The substantive reasons for the financial statements being misleading.
   d. A description of the uncertainty or scope limitation that prevents an unmodified opinion.

43. An auditor concludes that a client's illegal act, which has a material effect on the financial statements, has not been properly accounted for or disclosed. Depending on the materiality of the effect on the financial statements, the auditor should express either a(n)

   a. Adverse opinion or a disclaimer of opinion.
   b. Qualified opinion or an adverse opinion.
   c. Disclaimer of opinion or an unmodified opinion with a separate emphasis-of-matter paragraph.
   d. Unmodified opinion with a separate emphasis-of-matter paragraph or a qualified opinion.

44. Which of the following phrases would an auditor most likely include in the auditor's report when expressing a qualified opinion because of inadequate disclosure?

   a. Subject to the departure from US generally accepted accounting principles, as described above.
   b. With the foregoing explanation of these omitted disclosures.
   c. Except for the omission of the information discussed in the preceding paragraph.
   d. Does not present fairly in all material respects.

45. In which of the following circumstances would an auditor be most likely to express an adverse opinion?

   a. The chief executive officer refuses the auditor access to minutes of board of directors' meetings.
   b. Tests of controls show that the entity's internal control is so poor that it **cannot** be relied upon.
   c. The financial statements are **not** in conformity with a FASB requirement regarding the capitalization of leases.
   d. Information comes to the auditor's attention that raises substantial doubt about the entity's ability to continue as a going concern.

46. When an auditor qualifies an opinion because of inadequate disclosure, the auditor should describe the nature of the omission in a basis for qualification paragraph and modify the

	Introductory paragraph	Auditor responsibility paragraphs	Opinion paragraph
a.	Yes	No	No
b.	Yes	Yes	No
c.	No	Yes	Yes
d.	No	No	Yes

47. If a publicly held company issues financial statements that purport to present its financial position and results of operations but omits the statement of cash flows, which of the following types of opinion is most likely to be appropriate?

   a. Disclaimer of opinion.
   b. Qualified opinion.
   c. Review report with negative assurance.
   d. Unmodified opinion with a separate emphasis-of-matter paragraph.

48. In which of the following situations would an auditor ordinarily choose between expressing an "except for" qualified opinion or an adverse opinion?

   a. The auditor did not observe the entity's physical inventory and is unable to become satisfied as to its balance by other auditing procedures.

b. The financial statements fail to disclose information that is required by generally accepted accounting principles.

c. The auditor is asked to report only on the entity's balance sheet and not on the other basic financial statements.

d. Events disclosed in the financial statements cause the auditor to have substantial doubt about the entity's ability to continue as a going concern.

49. In which of the following situations would an auditor ordinarily choose between expressing a qualified opinion or an adverse opinion?

a. The auditor did not observe the entity's physical inventory and is unable to become satisfied about its balance by other auditing procedures.

b. Conditions that cause the auditor to have substantial doubt about the entity's ability to continue as a going concern are inadequately disclosed.

c. There has been a change in accounting principles that has a material effect on the comparability of the entity's financial statements.

d. The auditor is unable to apply necessary procedures concerning an investor's share of an investee's earnings recognized on the equity method.

C.3. Inability to Obtain Sufficient Appropriate Audit Evidence (Scope Limitations)

50. In the first audit of a client, an auditor was not able to gather sufficient evidence about the consistent application of accounting principles between the current and the prior year, as well as the amounts of assets or liabilities at the beginning of the current year. This was due to the client's record retention policies. If the amounts in question could materially affect current operating results, the auditor would

a. Be unable to express an opinion on the current year's results of operations and cash flows.

b. Express a qualified opinion on the financial statements because of a client-imposed scope limitation.

c. Withdraw from the engagement and refuse to be associated with the financial statements.

d. Specifically state that the financial statements are not comparable to the prior year due to an uncertainty.

51. In which of the following circumstances would an auditor **not** express an unmodified opinion?

a. There has been a material change between periods in accounting principles.

b. Quarterly financial data required by the SEC has been omitted.

c. The auditor wishes to emphasize an unusually important subsequent event.

d. The auditor is unable to obtain audited financial statements of a consolidated investee.

52. Due to a scope limitation, an auditor disclaimed an opinion on the financial statements taken as a whole, but the auditor's report included a statement that the current asset portion of the entity's balance sheet was fairly stated. The inclusion of this statement is

a. Not appropriate because it may tend to overshadow the auditor's disclaimer of opinion.

b. Not appropriate because the auditor is prohibited from reporting on only one basic financial statement.

c. Appropriate provided the auditor's scope paragraph adequately describes the scope limitation.

d. Appropriate provided the statement is in a separate paragraph preceding the disclaimer of opinion paragraph.

53. Park, CPA, was engaged to audit the financial statements of Tech Co., a new client, for the year ended December 31, 2009. Park obtained sufficient audit evidence for all of Tech's financial statement items except Tech's opening inventory. Due to inadequate financial records, Park could not verify Tech's January 1, 2009 inventory balances. Park's opinion on Tech's 2009 financial statements most likely will be

	Balance sheet	**Income statement**
a.	Disclaimer	Disclaimer
b.	Unmodified	Disclaimer
c.	Disclaimer	Adverse
d.	Unmodified	Adverse

54. An auditor who qualifies an opinion because of an insufficiency of audit evidence should describe the limitations in a basis for modification paragraph. The auditor should also refer to the limitation in the

	Auditor's responsibility section	**Opinion paragraph**	**Notes to the financial statements**
a.	Yes	No	Yes
b.	No	Yes	No
c.	Yes	Yes	No
d.	Yes	Yes	Yes

55. Harris, CPA, has been asked to audit and report on the balance sheet of Fox Co. but not on the statements of income, retained earnings, or cash flows. Harris will have access to all information underlying the basic financial statements. Under these circumstances, Harris may

a. Not accept the engagement because it would constitute a violation of the profession's ethical standards.

b. Not accept the engagement because it would be tantamount to rendering a piecemeal opinion.

c. Accept the engagement because such engagements merely involve limited reporting objectives.

d. Accept the engagement but should disclaim an opinion because of an inability to apply the procedures considered necessary.

56. When disclaiming an opinion due to a client-imposed scope limitation on a nonpublic company's financial statements, an auditor should indicate in a separate paragraph why the audit did not comply with generally accepted auditing standards. The auditor should also omit which of the two sections (paragraphs) below?

	Auditor responsibility	Opinion
a.	No	Yes
b.	Yes	Yes
c.	Yes	No
d.	No	No

57. An auditor decides to issue a qualified opinion on an entity's financial statements because a major inadequacy in its computerized accounting records prevents the auditor from applying necessary procedures. The opinion paragraph of the auditor's report should state that the qualification pertains to

a. A client-imposed scope limitation.
b. A departure from generally accepted auditing standards.
c. The possible effects on the financial statements.
d. Inadequate disclosure of necessary information.

58. A scope limitation sufficient to preclude an unmodified opinion always will result when management

a. Prevents the auditor from reviewing the working papers of the predecessor auditor.
b. Engages the auditor after the year-end physical inventory is completed.
c. Requests that certain material accounts receivable **not** be confirmed.
d. Refuses to acknowledge its responsibility for the fair presentation of the financial statements in conformity with GAAP.

D.1. The Group Audit Situation and Terminology

59. In which of the following situations would an auditor ordinarily issue an unmodified audit opinion without an emphasis-of-matter paragraph?

a. The auditor wishes to emphasize that the entity had significant related-party transactions.
b. The auditor decides to make reference to the report of an auditor who audited a component of group financial statements.
c. The entity issues financial statements that present financial position and results of operations, but omits the statement of cash flows.
d. The auditor has substantial doubt about the entity's ability to continue as a going concern, but the circumstances are fully disclosed in the financial statements.

D.2. Group Audit Requirements

60. A group engagement partner decides not to refer to the audit of another CPA who audited a component of the overall group financial statements. After making inquiries about the other CPA's professional reputation and independence, the principal auditor most likely would

a. Add an emphasis-of-matter paragraph to the auditor's report indicating that the subsidiary's financial statements are not material to the consolidated financial statements.
b. Document in the engagement letter that the principal auditor assumes no responsibility for the other CPA's work and opinion.
c. Obtain written permission from the other CPA to omit the reference in the principal auditor's report.
d. Perform additional audit procedures based on the significance of the subsidiary.

61. The auditor's responsibility section of a nonpublic company's auditor's report contains the following sentences:

We did not audit the financial statements of EZ Inc., a wholly owned subsidiary, which statements reflect total assets and revenues constituting 27% and 29%, respectively, of the related consolidated totals. Those statements were audited by other auditors whose report has been furnished to us, and our opinion, insofar as it relates to the amounts included for EZ Inc., is based solely on the report of the other auditors.

These sentences

a. Indicate a division of responsibility.
b. Assume responsibility for the other auditor.
c. Require a departure from an unmodified opinion.
d. Are an improper form of reporting.

62. An auditor may issue the standard audit report when the

a. Auditor refers to the findings of a specialist.
b. Financial statements are derived and summarized from complete audited financial statements that are filed with a regulatory agency.
c. Financial statements are prepared on the cash receipts and disbursements basis of accounting.
d. Group engagement partner assumes responsibility for the work of a component auditor.

63. In the auditor's report, the group engagement partner decides not to make reference to a component auditor who audited a client's subsidiary. The group engagement partner could justify this decision if, among other requirements, he or she

a. Issues an unmodified opinion on the consolidated financial statements.
b. Learns that the component auditor issued an unmodified opinion on the subsidiary's financial statements.
c. Is unable to review the audit programs and working papers of the component auditor.
d. Is satisfied as to the independence and professional reputation of the other CPA.

64. When financial statements of a company that follows GASB standards would be misleading due to unusual circumstances depart from those standards, the auditor should explain the unusual circumstances in a separate paragraph and express an opinion that is

    a. Unmodified.
    b. Qualified.
    c. Adverse.
    d. Qualified or adverse, depending on materiality.

65. A client follows US GAAP for its domestic operations and foreign GAAP for a foreign subsidiary. The foreign subsidiary is audited by a component auditor, while the group auditor audits the remainder of the corporation and issues an audit report on consolidated operations. Which auditor(s) is (are) responsible for evaluating the appropriateness of the adjustment of the foreign GAAP statements to US GAAP?

	Group auditor	Component auditor
a.	Yes	Yes
b.	Yes	No
c.	No	Yes
d.	No	No

E.2. Comparative Financial Statements

66. When reporting on comparative financial statements, an auditor ordinarily should change the previously issued opinion on the prior year's financial statements if the

    a. Prior year's financial statements are restated to conform with generally accepted accounting principles.
    b. Auditor is a predecessor auditor who has been requested by a former client to reissue the previously issued report.
    c. Prior year's opinion was unmodified and the opinion on the current year's financial statements is modified due to a lack of consistency.
    d. Prior year's financial statements are restated following a pooling of interests in the current year.

67. Jewel, CPA, audited Infinite Co.'s prior year financial statements. These statements are presented with those of the current year for comparative purposes without Jewel's auditor's report, which expressed a qualified opinion. In drafting the current year's auditor's report, Crain, CPA, the successor auditor, should

    I. Not name Jewel as the predecessor auditor.
    II. Indicate the type of report issued by Jewel.
    III. Indicate the substantive reasons for Jewel's qualification.

    a. I only.
    b. I and II only.
    c. II and III only.
    d. I, II, and III.

68. Before reissuing the prior year's auditor's report on the financial statements of a former client, the predecessor auditor should obtain a letter of representations from the

	Former client's management	Successor auditor
a.	Yes	Yes
b.	Yes	No
c.	No	Yes
d.	No	No

69. When single-year financial statements are presented, an auditor ordinarily would express a standard audit report if the

    a. Auditor is unable to obtain audited financial statements supporting the entity's investment in a foreign affiliate.
    b. Entity declines to present a statement of cash flows with its balance sheet and related statements of income and retained earnings.
    c. Auditor wishes to emphasize an accounting matter affecting the comparability of the financial statements with those of the prior year.
    d. Prior year's financial statements were audited by another CPA whose report, which expressed an unmodified opinion, is not presented.

70. A client is presenting comparative (two-year) financial statements. Which of the following is correct concerning reporting responsibilities of a continuing auditor?

    a. The auditor should issue one audit report that is on both presented years.
    b. The auditor should issue two audit reports, one on each year.
    c. The auditor should issue one audit report, but only on the most recent year.
    d. The auditor may issue either one audit report on both presented years, or two audit reports, one on each year.

71. The predecessor auditor, who is satisfied after properly communicating with the successor auditor, has reissued a report because the audit client desires comparative financial statements. The predecessor auditor's report should make

    a. Reference to the report of the successor auditor only in the scope paragraph.
    b. Reference to the work of the successor auditor in the scope and opinion paragraphs.
    c. Reference to both the work and the report of the successor auditor only in the opinion paragraph.
    d. No reference to the report or the work of the successor auditor.

72. Compiled financial statements for the prior year presented in comparative form with audited financial statements for the current year should be clearly marked to indicate their status and

    I. The report on the prior period should be reissued to accompany the current period report.
    II. The report on the current period should include as a separate paragraph a description of the responsibility assumed for the prior period's financial statements.

    a. I only.
    b. II only.

c. Both I and II.

d. Either I or II.

E.3. Other Information in Documents Containing Audited Financial Statements

73. An auditor concludes that there is a material inconsistency in the other information in an annual report to shareholders containing audited financial statements. If the auditor concludes that the financial statements do **not** require revision, but the client refuses to revise or eliminate the material inconsistency, the auditor may

     a. Revise the auditor's report to include a separate emphasis-of-matter paragraph describing the material inconsistency.

     b. Issue an "except for" qualified opinion after discussing the matter with the client's board of directors.

     c. Consider the matter closed since the other information is **not** in the audited financial statements.

     d. Disclaim an opinion on the financial statements after explaining the material inconsistency in a separate basis for disclaimer paragraph.

74. When audited financial statements are presented in a client's document containing other information, the auditor should

     a. Perform inquiry and analytical procedures to ascertain whether the other information is reasonable.

     b. Add an emphasis-of-matter paragraph to the auditor's report without changing the opinion on the financial statements.

     c. Perform the appropriate substantive auditing procedures to corroborate the other information.

     d. Read the other information to determine that it is consistent with the audited financial statements.

75. An auditor may express an opinion on an entity's accounts receivable balance even if the auditor has disclaimed an opinion on the financial statements taken as a whole provided the

     a. Report on the accounts receivable discloses the reason for the disclaimer of opinion on the financial statements.

     b. Distribution of the report on the accounts receivable is restricted to internal use only.

     c. Auditor also reports on the current asset portion of the entity's balance sheet.

     d. Report on the accounts receivable is presented separately from the disclaimer of opinion on the financial statements.

E.4. Required Supplementary Information

76. In an audit of a nonissuer company, which statement is correct concerning required supplementary information by a designated accounting standards setter?

     a. The auditor has no responsibility for required supplementary information as long as it is outside the basic financial statements.

     b. The auditor's only responsibility for required supplementary information is to determine that such information has **not** been omitted.

     c. The auditor should apply certain limited procedures to the required supplementary information, and report deficiencies in, or omissions of, such information.

     d. The auditor should apply tests of details of transactions and balances to the required supplementary information, and report any material misstatements in such information.

77. If management declines to present supplementary information required by the Governmental Accounting Standards Board (GASB), the auditor should issue a(n)

     a. Adverse opinion.

     b. Qualified opinion with an other-matter paragraph.

     c. Unmodified opinion.

     d. Unmodified opinion with an additional other-matter paragraph.

E.5. Supplementary Information in Relation to the Financial Statements as a Whole

78. If an auditor is asked to provide an opinion relating to information accompanying the financial statements in a document, the opinion will ordinarily be upon whether the information is fairly stated in

     a. Accordance with US generally accepted auditing standards.

     b. Conformity with US generally accepted accounting principles.

     c. All material respects in relation to the basic financial statements taken as a whole.

     d. Accordance with attestation standards expressing a conclusion about management's assertions.

E.6. Alerts as to Report Intended Use (Restricting the Use of an Auditor's Report)

79. Which of the following types of reports is most likely to include an alert as to its use being restricted to certain specified parties?

     a. Audit report.

     b. Review report.

     c. Compilation report.

     d. Agreed-upon procedures report.

80. Which of the following is **least** likely to be a restricted use report?

     a. A report on internal control significant deficiencies noted in an audit.

     b. A required communication with the audit committee.

     c. A report on financial statements prepared following a financial reporting framework other than generally accepted accounting principles.

     d. A report on compliance with aspects of contractual agreements.

E.7. Additional Circumstances Involving Other-Matter Paragraphs

81. An auditor expressed a qualified opinion on the prior year's financial statements because of a lack of adequate disclosure. These financial statements are properly restated in the current year and presented in comparative form with the current year's financial statements. The auditor's updated report on the prior year's financial statements should

    a. Be accompanied by the auditor's original report on the prior year's financial statements.
    b. Continue to express a qualified opinion on the prior year's financial statements.
    c. Make **no** reference to the type of opinion expressed on the prior year's financial statements.
    d. Express an unmodified opinion on the restated financial statements of the prior year.

82. Before reporting on the financial statements of a US entity that have been prepared in conformity with another country's accounting principles, an auditor practicing in the US should

    a. Understand the accounting principles generally accepted in the other country.
    b. Be certified by the appropriate auditing or accountancy board of the other country.
    c. Notify management that the auditor is required to disclaim an opinion on the financial statements.
    d. Receive a waiver from the auditor's state board of accountancy to perform the engagement.

83. The financial statements of KCP America, a US entity, are prepared for inclusion in the consolidated financial statements of its non-US parent. These financial statements are prepared in conformity with the accounting principles generally accepted in the parent's country and are for use only in that country. How may KCP America's auditor report on these financial statements?

    I.   A US-style report (unmodified).
    II. A US-style report modified to report on the accounting principles of the parent's country.
    III. The report form of the parent's country.

	I	II	III
a.	Yes	No	No
b.	No	Yes	No
c.	Yes	No	Yes
d.	No	Yes	Yes

E.8. Summary of Placement of Additional Paragraphs

84. An auditor should disclose the substantive reasons for expressing an adverse opinion in a basis for modification paragraph

    a. Preceding the scope paragraph.
    b. Preceding the opinion paragraph.
    c. Following the opinion paragraph.
    d. Within the notes to the financial statements.

F.1. Audits of Financial Statements Prepared in Accordance with Special-Purpose Financial Reporting Frameworks

85. When an auditor reports on financial statements prepared on an entity's income tax basis, the auditor's report should

    a. Disclaim an opinion on whether the statements were examined in accordance with generally accepted auditing standards.
    b. Not express an opinion on whether the statements are presented in conformity with the financial reporting framework used.
    c. Include an explanation of how the results of operations differ from the cash receipts and disbursements basis of accounting.
    d. State that the basis of presentation is a financial reporting framework other than GAAP.

86. Helpful Co., a nonprofit entity, prepared its financial statements on an accounting basis prescribed by a regulatory agency solely for filing with that agency. Green audited the financial statements in accordance with generally accepted auditing standards and concluded that the financial statements were fairly presented on the prescribed basis. Green should issue a report with a(n)

    a. Qualified opinion.
    b. Adverse opinion
    c. Disclaimer of opinion.
    d. Unmodified opinion.

87. An auditor's report on financial statements prepared in conformity with the cash basis of accounting should include a separate emphasis-of-matter paragraph that

    a. Justifies the reasons for departing from generally accepted accounting principles.
    b. States whether the financial statements are fairly presented in conformity with GAAP.
    c. Refers to the note to the financial statements that describes the basis of accounting.
    d. Explains how the results of operations differ from financial statements prepared in conformity with generally accepted accounting principles.

88. An auditor's report would refer to a basis of accounting other than GAAP in which of the following situations?

    a. Interim financial information of a publicly held company that is subject to a limited review.
    b. Compliance with aspects of regulatory requirements related to audited financial statements.
    c. Application of accounting principles to specified transactions.
    d. Limited use prospective financial statements such as a financial projection.

89. Delta Life Insurance Co. prepares its financial statements on an accounting basis insurance companies use pursuant to the rules of a state insurance commission. If Wall, CPA, Delta's auditor, discovers that the statements are **not** suitably titled, Wall should

a. Disclose any reservations in an emphasis-of-matter paragraph and qualify the opinion.
b. Apply to the state insurance commission for an advisory opinion.
c. Issue a special statutory basis report that clearly disclaims any opinion.
d. Explain in the notes to the financial statements the terminology used.

90. Financial information is presented in a printed form that prescribes the wording of the independent auditor's report. The form is not acceptable to the auditor because the form calls for statements that are inconsistent with the auditor's responsibility. Under these circumstances, the auditor most likely would

a. Withdraw from the engagement.
b. Reword the form or attach a separate report.
c. Express a qualified opinion with an explanation.
d. Limit distribution of the report to the party who designed the form.

F.2.   Audits of Single Financial Statements, and Specific Elements, Accounts, or Items of Financial Statements

91. Field is an employee of Gold Enterprises. Hardy, CPA, is asked to express an opinion on Field's profit participation in Gold's net income. Hardy may accept this engagement only if

a. Hardy also audits Gold's complete financial statements.
b. Gold's financial statements are prepared in conformity with GAAP.
c. Hardy's report is available for distribution to Gold's other employees.
d. Field owns controlling interest in Gold.

92. A CPA is permitted to accept a separate engagement (**not** in conjunction with an audit of financial statements) to audit an entity's

	Schedule of accounts receivable	Schedule of royalties
a.	Yes	Yes
b.	Yes	No
c.	No	Yes
d.	No	No

G.1.b. Reviewed Interim (Quarterly) Statements

93. When an independent CPA has reviewed the interim financial statements of a public client, which procedure is least likely to have been performed?

a. Obtaining written representations from management for all interim financial information presented.
b. Observing the interim count of inventory.

c. Reading the financial statements for obvious material misstatements.
d. Performing analytical procedures related to sales.

94. The objective of a review of interim financial information of a public entity (issuer) is to provide an accountant with a basis for reporting whether

a. Material modifications should be made to conform with generally accepted accounting principles.
b. A reasonable basis exists for expressing an updated opinion regarding the financial statements that were previously audited.
c. Summary financial statements or pro forma financial information should be included in a registration statement.
d. The financial statements are presented fairly in accordance with generally accepted accounting principles.

95. An independent accountant's report is based on a review of interim financial information. If this report is presented in a registration statement, a prospectus should include a statement clarifying that the

a. Accountant's review report is not a part of the registration statement within the meaning of the Securities Act of 1933.
b. Accountant assumes **no** responsibility to update the report for events and circumstances occurring after the date of the report.
c. Accountant's review was performed in accordance with standards established by the Securities and Exchange Commission.
d. Accountant obtained corroborating evidence to determine whether material modifications are needed for such information to conform with GAAP.

96. A modification of the CPA's report on a review of the interim financial statements of a publicly held company would be necessitated by which of the following?

a. An uncertainty.
b. Lack of consistency.
c. Reference to another accountant.
d. Inadequate disclosure.

97. Which of the following procedures ordinarily should be applied when an independent accountant conducts a review of interim financial information of a publicly held entity?

a. Verify changes in key account balances.
b. Read the minutes of the board of directors' meetings.
c. Inspect the open purchase order file.
d. Perform cut-off tests for cash receipts and disbursements.

98. Which of the following is **least** likely to be a procedure included in an accountant's review of interim financial information of a public entity?

a. Compare disaggregated revenue data by month to that of the previous interim period.
b. Read available minutes of meetings of stockholders.
c. Observe counting of physical inventory.

d. Inquire of management concerning significant journal entries and other adjustments.

99. An accountant's review report on interim financial information of a public entity is most likely to include a

    a. Statement that the interim financial information was examined in accordance with standards of the Public Company Accounting Oversight Board.

    b. Statement that the interim financial information is the responsibility of the entity's shareholders.

    c. Description of the procedures for a review.

    d. Statement that a review of interim financial information is less in scope than a compilation conducted in accordance with AICPA standards.

G.1.c. Summary Financial Statements

100. An auditor may report on summary financial statements that are derived from complete financial statements if the

    a. Summary financial statements are distributed to stockholders along with the complete financial statements.

    b. Auditor described the additional procedures performed on the summary financial statements.

    c. Auditor indicates whether the information in the summary financial statements is fairly stated in all material respects in relation to the complete financial statements from which it has been derived.

    d. Summary financial statements are presented in comparative form with the prior year's summary financial statements.

101. An auditor is engaged to report on selected financial data that are included in a document containing audited financial statements. Under these circumstances, the report on the selected data should

    a. Be limited to data derived from the audited financial statements.

    b. Be distributed only to senior management and the board of directors.

    c. State that the presentation is a financial reporting framework other than GAAP.

    d. Indicate that the data are not fairly stated in all material respects.

G.2.a. Letters for Underwriters

102. A registration statement filed with the SEC contains the reports of two independent auditors on their audits of financial statements for different periods. The predecessor auditor who audited the prior period financial statements generally should obtain a letter of representation from the

    a. Successor independent auditor.

    b. Client's audit committee.

    c. Principal underwriter.

    d. Securities and Exchange Commission.

103. Which of the following statements is correct concerning letters for underwriters, commonly referred to as comfort letters?

    a. Letters for underwriters are required by the Securities Act of 1933 for the initial public sale of registered securities.

    b. Letters for underwriters typically give negative assurance on unaudited interim financial information.

    c. Letters for underwriters usually are included in the registration statement accompanying a prospectus.

    d. Letters for underwriters ordinarily update auditors' opinions on the prior year's financial statements.

104. Comfort letters ordinarily are signed by the client's

    a. Independent auditor.

    b. Underwriter of securities.

    c. Audit committee.

    d. Senior management.

105. Comfort letters ordinarily are addressed to

    a. Creditor financial institutions.

    b. The client's audit committee.

    c. The Securities and Exchange Commission.

    d. Underwriters of securities.

106. When an accountant issues to an underwriter a comfort letter containing comments on data that have **not** been audited, the underwriter most likely will receive

    a. Negative assurance on capsule information.

    b. Positive assurance on supplementary disclosures.

    c. A limited opinion on pro forma financial statements.

    d. A disclaimer on prospective financial statements.

107. When an independent audit report is incorporated by reference in a SEC registration statement, a prospectus that includes a statement about the independent accountant's involvement should refer to the independent accountant as

    a. Auditor of the financial reports.

    b. Management's designate before the SEC.

    c. Certified preparer of the report.

    d. Expert in auditing and accounting.

108. Which of the following matters is covered in a typical comfort letter?

    a. Negative assurance concerning whether the entity's internal control procedures operated as designed during the period being audited.

    b. An opinion regarding whether the entity complied with laws and regulations under Government Auditing Standards and the Single Audit Act of 1984.

    c. Positive assurance concerning whether unaudited condensed financial information complied with generally accepted accounting principles.

    d. An opinion as to whether the audited financial statements comply in form with the accounting requirements of the SEC.

109. When unaudited financial statements are presented in comparative form with audited financial statements in a document filed with the Securities and Exchange Commission, such statements should be

	Marked as "unaudited"	Withheld until audited	Referred to in the auditor's report
a.	Yes	No	No
b.	Yes	No	Yes
c.	No	Yes	Yes
d.	No	Yes	No

110. In connection with a proposal to obtain a new audit client, a CPA in public practice is asked to prepare a report on the application of accounting principles to a specific transaction. The CPA's report should include a statement that

a. The engagement was performed in accordance with Statements on Standards for Accounting and Review Services.
b. Responsibility for the proper accounting treatment rests with the preparers of the financial statements.
c. The evaluation of the application of accounting principles is hypothetical and may **not** be used for opinion-shopping.
d. The guidance is provided for management's use only and may not be communicated to the prior or continuing auditor.

G.2.b. Application of Accounting Principles

111. In connection with a proposal to obtain a new client, an accountant in public practice is asked to prepare a written report on the application of accounting principles to a specific transaction. The accountant's report should include a statement that

a. Any difference in the facts, circumstances, or assumptions presented may change the report.
b. The engagement was performed in accordance with Statements on Standards for Consulting Services.
c. The guidance provided is for management use only and may **not** be communicated to the prior or continuing auditors.
d. Nothing came to the accountant's attention that caused the accountant to believe that the accounting principles violated GAAP.

112. Blue, CPA, has been asked to render an opinion on the application of accounting principles to a specific transaction by an entity that is audited by another CPA. Blue, who previously has provided no services to the entity, may accept this engagement, but should

a. Consult with the continuing CPA to obtain information relevant to the transaction.
b. Report the engagement's findings to the entity's audit committee, the continuing CPA, and management.
c. Disclaim any opinion that the hypothetical application of accounting principles conforms with generally accepted accounting principles.

d. Notify the entity that the report is for the restricted use of management and outside parties who are aware of all relevant facts.

113. Which of the following statements is **not** included in an accountant's report on the application of accounting principles?

a. The engagement was performed following standards established by the American Institute of Certified Public Accountants.
b. The report is based on a hypothetical transaction not involving facts or circumstances of this particular entity.
c. The report is intended solely for the information and use of specified parties.
d. Responsibility for the proper accounting treatment rests with the preparers of the financial statements.

G.3.a. Attestation Engagements—General

114. Which of the following services would be most likely to be structured as an attest engagement?

a. Advocating a client's position in tax matter.
b. A consulting engagement to develop a new database system for the revenue cycle.
c. An engagement to issue a report addressing an entity's compliance with requirements of specified laws.
d. The compilation of a client's forecast information.

115. An unmodified attestation report ordinarily may refer to

a. Only the assertion.
b. Only the subject matter to which the assertion relates.
c. Either the assertion or the subject matter to which the assertion relates.
d. Neither the assertion nor the subject matter to which the assertion relates.

116. A practitioner is issuing a standard unmodified examination report under the attestation standards. The CPA's conclusion may be on

	Subject matter	Management's written assertion
a.	Yes	Yes
b.	Yes	No
c.	No	Yes
d.	No	No

117. Conditions exist that result in a material deviation from the criteria against which the subject matter was evaluated during an examination. The CPA's conclusion may be on

	Subject matter	Written assertion
a.	Yes	Yes
b.	Yes	No
c.	No	Yes
d.	No	No

118. When performing an attestation engagement, which of the following is **least** likely to be present?

    a. Practitioner's written assertion.
    b. Responsible party.
    c. Subject matter.
    d. Suitable criteria.

119. Suitable criteria in an attestation engagement may be available

	Publicly	In CPA's report
a.	Yes	Yes
b.	Yes	No
c.	No	Yes
d.	No	No

120. Which of the following is **least** likely to result in a restricted use attest report?

    a. Criteria suitable only for a limited number of parties.
    b. Subject matter available only to specified parties.
    c. A written assertion has not been obtained.
    d. Criteria developed by an industry association.

121. Which of the following is **least** likely to be included in an agreed-upon procedures attestation engagement report?

    a. The specified party takes responsibility for the sufficiency of procedures.
    b. Use of the report is restricted.
    c. Limited assurance on the information presented.
    d. A summary of procedures performed.

122. A summary of findings rather than assurance is most likely to be included in

    a. Agreed-upon procedures report.
    b. Compilation report.
    c. Examination report.
    d. Review report.

G.3.b. Agreed-Upon Procedures Engagements

123. Which of the following is **not** correct concerning "specified parties" of an agreed-upon procedures report under either the auditing or attestation standards?

    a. They must agree on the procedures to be performed.
    b. They must take responsibility for the adequacy of the procedures performed.
    c. They must sign an engagement letter.
    d. After completion of the engagement, another party may be added as a specified user.

G.3.c. Financial Forecasts and Projections

124. When an accountant examines projected financial statements, the accountant's report should include a separate paragraph that

    a. Describes the limitations on the usefulness of the presentation.

    b. Provides an explanation of the differences between an examination and an audit.
    c. States that the accountant is responsible for events and circumstances up to one year after the report's date.
    d. Disclaims an opinion on whether the assumptions provide a reasonable basis for the projection.

125. An accountant may accept an engagement to apply agreed-upon procedures to prospective financial statements provided that

    a. Use of the report is restricted to the specified parties.
    b. The prospective financial statements are also examined.
    c. Responsibility for the adequacy of the procedures performed is taken by the accountant.
    d. Negative assurance is expressed on the prospective financial statements taken as a whole.

126. An accountant's compilation report on a financial forecast should include a statement that

    a. The forecast should be read only in conjunction with the audited historical financial statements.
    b. The accountant expresses only limited assurance on the forecasted statements and their assumptions.
    c. There will usually be differences between the forecasted and actual results.
    d. The hypothetical assumptions used in the forecast are reasonable in the circumstances.

127. Accepting an engagement to examine an entity's financial projection most likely would be appropriate if the projection were to be distributed to

    a. All employees who work for the entity.
    b. Potential stockholders who request a prospectus or a registration statement.
    c. A bank with which the entity is negotiating for a loan.
    d. All stockholders of record as of the report date.

128. A CPA in public practice is required to comply with the provisions of the Statements on Standards for Attestation Engagements (SSAE) when

	Testifying as an expert witness in accounting and auditing matters given stipulated facts	Compiling a client's financial projection that presents a hypothetical course of action
a.	Yes	Yes
b.	Yes	No
c.	No	Yes
d.	No	No

129. An accountant's compilation report on a financial forecast should include a statement that the

    a. Compilation does not include evaluation of the support of the assumptions underlying the forecast.
    b. Hypothetical assumptions used in the forecast are reasonable.

c. Range of assumptions selected is one in which one end of the range is less likely to occur than the other.

d. Prospective statements are limited to presenting, in the form of a forecast, information that is the accountant's representation.

130. Which of the following is a prospective financial statement for general use upon which an accountant may appropriately report?

a. Financial projection.
b. Partial presentation.
c. Pro forma financial statement.
d. Financial forecast.

131. Which of the following is **not** included in a compilation report on prospective financial statements?

a. A statement that the practitioner assumes no responsibility to update the report for events and circumstances occurring after the date of the report.

b. A caveat that the prospective results may not be achieved.

c. A statement that a compilation is limited in scope and does not enable the practitioner to express an opinion or any other form of assurance on the information.

d. Distribution of the report is restricted to specified parties.

132. When an accountant examines a financial forecast that fails to disclose several significant assumptions used to prepare the forecast, the accountant should describe the assumptions in the accountant's report and issue a(n)

a. "Except for" qualified opinion.
b. "Subject to" qualified opinion.
c. Unmodified opinion with a separate emphasis-of-matter paragraph.
d. Adverse opinion.

G.3.d. *Reporting on Pro Forma Financial Information*

133. Given one or more hypothetical assumptions, a responsible party may prepare, to the best of its knowledge and belief, an entity's expected financial position, results of operations, and changes in financial position. Such prospective financial statements are known as

a. Pro forma financial statements.
b. Financial projections.
c. Partial presentations.
d. Financial forecasts.

134. An accountant's report on a review of pro forma financial information should include a

a. Statement that the entity's internal control was not relied on in the review.

b. Disclaimer of opinion on the financial statements from which the pro forma financial information is derived.

c. Caveat that it is uncertain whether the transaction or event reflected in the pro forma financial information will ever occur.

d. Reference to the financial statements from which the historical financial information is derived.

G.3.e. *Management Discussion and Analysis*

135. Which of the following is **not** an objective of a CPA's examination of a client's management discussion and analysis (MD&A) prepared pursuant to Securities and Exchange Commission rules and regulations?

a. The historical amounts have been accurately derived, in all material respects, from the entity's financial statements.

b. The presentation is in conformity with rules and regulations adopted by the Securities and Exchange Commission.

c. The underlying information, determinations, estimates and assumptions of the entity provide a reasonable basis for the disclosures contained herein.

d. The presentation includes the required elements of MD&A.

136. Which of the following is an assertion embodied in management's discussion and analysis (MD&A)?

a. Valuation.
b. Reliability.
c. Consistency with the financial statements.
d. Rights and obligations.

137. Which of the following statements is correct relating to an auditor's review engagements on an entity's management discussion and analysis (MD&A)?

a. A review consists principally of applying analytical procedures and search and verification procedures.

b. The review report of a public entity should be restricted to the use of specified parties.

c. No consideration of internal control is necessary.

d. The report issued will ordinarily include a summary of findings, but no negative assurance.

G.3.f. *Trust Services*

138. Trust Service engagements are performed under the provisions of

a. Statements on Assurance Standards.
b. Statements on Standards for Attestation Engagements.
c. Statements on Standards for Trust Engagements
d. Statements on Auditing Standards.

139. The WebTrust seal of assurance relates most directly to

a. Financial statements maintained on the Internet.
b. Health care facilities.
c. Risk assurance procedures.
d. Websites.

140. A CPA's examination report relating to a WebTrust engagement is most likely to include

a. An opinion on whether the site is "hackproof."
b. An opinion on whether the site meets the WebTrust criteria.
c. Negative assurance on whether the site is electronically secure.
d. No opinion or other assurance, but a summary of findings relating to the website.

141. An engagement in which a CPA considers security, availability, processing integrity, online privacy, and/or confidentiality over any type of defined electronic system is most likely to considered which of the following types of engagements?

a. Internal control over financial reporting.
b. SysTrust.
c. Web siteAssociate.
d. WebTrust.

142. A client's refusal to provide a written assertion in a Trust Services engagement is most likely to result in which of the following types of opinions?

a. Adverse.
b. Disclaimer.
c. Qualified.
d. Unmodified with explanatory language.

G.3.g. Service Organization Control (SOC) Reports

143. Which of the following is correct relating to service organization control (SOC) reports referred to as "SOC 2" reports?

a. They are primarily to assist financial statement auditors when processing services have been outsourced to a service provider.
b. They are generally available to anyone.
c. They relate most directly to internal control over financial reporting.
d. They are meant for management of service organizations, user entities and certain other specified entities.

144. The type of service organization control (SOC) report that is for general use is

a. SOC 1.
b. SOC 2.
c. SOC 3.
d. SOC 4.

145. The AICPA has outlined auditor reports based on three services that may be provided on service organization controls (SOC). The type most likely to result in a restricted use report on controls at a service organization related to security, availability, processing integrity, confidentiality, and/or privacy is

a. SOC 2
b. SOC SYS
c. SOC 6
d. SOC OC

H.2.a. Agreed-Upon Procedures Engagements

146. Which of the following types of engagements is **not** permitted under the professional standards for reporting on an entity's compliance?

a. Agreed-upon procedures on compliance with the specified requirements of a law.
b. Agreed-upon procedures on the effectiveness of internal control over compliance with a law.
c. Review on compliance with specified requirements of a law.
d. Examination on compliance with specified requirements of a law.

147. Mill, CPA, was engaged by a group of royalty recipients to apply agreed-upon procedures to financial data supplied by Modern Co. regarding Modern's written assertion about its compliance with contractual requirements to pay royalties. Mill's report on these agreed-upon procedures should contain a(n)

a. Disclaimer of opinion about the fair presentation of Modern's financial statements.
b. List of the procedures performed (or reference thereto) and Mill's findings.
c. Opinion about the effectiveness of Modern's internal control activities concerning royalty payments.
d. Acknowledgment that the sufficiency of the procedures is solely Mill's responsibility.

148. A CPA's report on agreed-upon procedures related to an entity's compliance with specified requirements should contain

a. A statement of limitations on the use of the report.
b. An opinion about whether management's assertion is fairly stated.
c. Negative assurance that control risk has not been assessed.
d. An acknowledgment of responsibility for the sufficiency of the procedures.

H.2.b. Examination Engagements

149. When reporting on an examination of a company's compliance with requirements of specified laws, the practitioner has identified an instance of material noncompliance. Management has agreed to include this instance in its written assertion. The examination report should include

a. No modification from the standard form.
b. An opinion paragraph that is unmodified, and an emphasis-of-matter paragraph.
c. A qualified or adverse opinion.
d. A disclaimer of opinion.

H.3.a. Compliance Audits Conducted in Accordance with GAAS

150. In auditing a not-for-profit entity that receives governmental financial assistance, the auditor has a responsibility to

a. Issue a separate report that describes the expected benefits and related costs of the auditor's suggested changes to the entity's internal control.

b. Assess whether management has identified laws and regulations that have a direct and material effect on the entity's financial statements.

c. Notify the governmental agency providing the financial assistance that the audit is **not** designed to provide any assurance of detecting misstatements and fraud.

d. Render an opinion concerning the entity's continued eligibility for the governmental financial assistance.

151. Hill, CPA, is auditing the financial statements of Helping Hand, a not-for-profit organization that receives financial assistance from governmental agencies. To detect misstatements in Helping Hand's financial statements resulting from violations of laws and regulations, Hill should focus on violations that

a. Could result in criminal prosecution against the organization.

b. Involve significant deficiencies to be communicated to the organization's trustees and the funding agencies.

c. Have a direct and material effect on the amounts in the organization's financial statements.

d. Demonstrate the existence of material weaknesses.

152. A governmental audit may extend beyond an examination leading to the expression of an opinion on the fairness of financial presentation to include

	Program results	Compliance	Economy and efficiency
a.	Yes	Yes	No
b.	Yes	Yes	Yes
c.	No	Yes	Yes
d.	Yes	No	Yes

153. When auditing an entity's financial statements in accordance with Government Auditing Standards (the "*Yellow Book*"), an auditor is required to report on

I. Noteworthy accomplishments of the program.
II. The scope of the auditor's testing of internal controls.

a. I only.
b. II only.
c. Both I and II.
d. Neither I nor II.

154. When auditing an entity's financial statements in accordance with Government Auditing Standards (the "*Yellow Book*"), an auditor is required to report on

I. Recommendations for actions to improve operations.
II. The scope of the auditor's tests of compliance with laws and regulations.

a. I only.
b. II only.
c. Both I and II.
d. Neither I nor II.

H.3.b. Compliance Audits Conducted in Accordance with Generally Accepted Government Auditing Standards (GAGAS)

155. Which of the following statements is a standard applicable to financial statement audits in accordance with Government Auditing Standards (the "*Yellow Book*")?

a. An auditor should report on the scope of the auditor's testing of compliance with laws and regulations.

b. An auditor should assess whether the entity has reportable measures of economy and efficiency that are valid and reliable.

c. An auditor should report recommendations for actions to correct problems and improve operations.

d. An auditor should determine the extent to which the entity's programs achieve the desired results.

156. Which of the following statements is a standard applicable to financial statement audits in accordance with Government Auditing Standards (the "*Yellow Book*")?

a. An auditor should report on the scope of the auditor's testing of internal controls.

b. All instances of abuse, waste, and mismanagement should be reported to the audit committee.

c. An auditor should report the views of responsible officials concerning the auditor's findings.

d. Internal control activities designed to detect or prevent fraud should be reported to the inspector general.

157. In reporting under Government Auditing Standards, an auditor most likely would be required to report a falsification of accounting records directly to a federal inspector general when the falsification is

a. Discovered after the auditor's report has been made available to the federal inspector general and to the public.

b. Reported by the auditor to the audit committee as a significant deficiency in internal control.

c. Voluntarily disclosed to the auditor by low-level personnel as a result of the auditor's inquiries.

d. Communicated by the auditor to the auditee and the auditee fails to make a required report of the matter.

158. Although the scope of audits of recipients of federal financial assistance in accordance with federal audit regulations varies, these audits generally have which of the following elements in common?

a. The auditor is to determine whether the federal financial assistance has been administered in accordance with applicable laws and regulations.

b. The materiality levels are lower and are determined by the government entities that provided the federal financial assistance to the recipient.

c. The auditor should obtain written management representations that the recipient's internal auditors will report their findings objectively without fear of political repercussion.

d. The auditor is required to express both positive and negative assurance that illegal acts that could have a material effect on the recipient's financial statements are disclosed to the inspector general.

159. An auditor most likely would be responsible for communicating significant deficiencies in the design of internal control

    a. To the Securities and Exchange Commission when the client is a publicly held entity.
    b. To specific legislative and regulatory bodies when reporting under Government Auditing Standards.
    c. To a court-appointed creditors' committee when the client is operating under Chapter 11 of the Federal Bankruptcy Code.
    d. To shareholders with significant influence (more than 20% equity ownership) when significant deficiencies are deemed to be material weaknesses.

160. Wolf is auditing an entity's compliance with requirements governing a major federal financial assistance program in accordance with Government Auditing Standards. Wolf detected noncompliance with requirements that have a material effect on the program. Wolf's report on compliance should express

    a. No assurance on the compliance tests.
    b. Reasonable assurance on the compliance tests.
    c. A qualified or adverse opinion.
    d. An adverse or disclaimer of opinion.

161. Which of the following is a specific documentation requirement that an auditor should follow when auditing in accordance with Government Auditing Standards?

    a. The auditor should obtain written representations from management acknowledging responsibility for correcting instances of fraud, abuse, and waste.
    b. Before the report is issued, evidence of supervisory review of the audit.
    c. The auditor should document the procedures that assure discovery of all illegal acts and contingent liabilities resulting from noncompliance.
    d. The auditor's working papers should contain a caveat that all instances of material misstatements and fraud may not be identified.

162. In performing a financial statement audit in accordance with Government Auditing Standards, an auditor is required to report on the entity's compliance with laws and regulations. This report should

    a. State that compliance with laws and regulations is the responsibility of the entity's management.
    b. Describe the laws and regulations that the entity must comply with.
    c. Provide an opinion on overall compliance with laws and regulations.
    d. Indicate that the auditor does not possess legal skills and cannot make legal judgments.

163. In reporting under Government Auditing Standards, an auditor most likely would be required to communicate management's misappropriation of assets directly to a federal inspector general when the fraudulent activities are

    a. Concealed by management by circumventing specific internal controls designed to safeguard those assets.
    b. Reported to the entity's governing body and the governing body fails to make a required report to the federal inspector general.
    c. Accompanied by fraudulent financial reporting that results in material misstatements of asset balances.
    d. Perpetrated by several levels of management in a scheme that is likely to continue in future years.

H.3.c. Compliance Audits Conducted in Accordance with the Single Audit Act

164. In auditing compliance with requirements governing major federal financial assistance programs under the Single Audit Act, the auditor's consideration of materiality differs from materiality under generally accepted auditing standards. Under the Single Audit Act, materiality is

    a. Calculated in relation to the financial statements taken as a whole.
    b. Determined separately for each major federal financial assistance program.
    c. Decided in conjunction with the auditor's risk assessment.
    d. Ignored, because all account balances, regardless of size, are fully tested.

165. Kent is auditing an entity's compliance with requirements governing a major federal financial assistance program in accordance with the Single Audit Act. Kent detected noncompliance with requirements that have a material effect on that program. Kent's report on compliance should express a(n)

    a. Unmodified opinion with a separate emphasis-of-matter paragraph.
    b. Qualified opinion or an adverse opinion.
    c. Adverse opinion or a disclaimer of opinion.
    d. Limited assurance on the items tested.

166. When performing an audit of a city that is subject to the requirements of the Uniform Single Audit Act of 1984, an auditor should adhere to

    a. Governmental Accounting Standards Board General Standards.
    b. Governmental Finance Officers Association *Governmental Accounting, Auditing, and Financial Reporting Principles.*
    c. General Accounting Office Government Auditing Standards.
    d. Securities and Exchange Commission Regulation S-X.

167. A CPA has performed an examination of the general-purpose financial statements of Big City. The examination scope included the additional requirements of the Single Audit Act. When reporting on Big City's internal accounting and administrative controls used in administering a federal financial assistance program, the CPA should

a. Communicate those weaknesses that are material in relation to the general-purpose financial statements.

b. Express an opinion on the systems used to administer major federal financial assistance programs and express negative assurance on the systems used to administer nonmajor federal financial assistance programs.

c. Communicate those weaknesses that are material in relation to the federal financial assistance program.

d. Express negative assurance on the systems used to administer major federal financial assistance programs and express no opinion on the systems used to administer nonmajor federal financial assistance programs.

Multiple-Choice Answers and Explanations

Answers

1.	a	35.	b	69.	d	103.	b	137.	b
2.	b	36.	d	70.	a	104.	a	138.	b
3.	d	37.	c	71.	d	105.	d	139.	d
4.	a	38.	d	72.	d	106.	a	140.	b
5.	c	39.	d	73.	a	107.	d	141.	b
6.	c	40.	b	74.	d	108.	d	142.	b
7.	c	41.	d	75.	d	109.	a	143.	d
8.	b	42.	b	76.	c	110.	b	144.	c
9.	d	43.	b	77.	d	111.	a	145.	a
10.	d	44.	c	78.	c	112.	a	146.	c
11.	c	45.	c	79.	d	113.	b	147.	b
12.	a	46.	d	80.	c	114.	c	148.	a
13.	c	47.	b	81.	d	115.	c	149.	c
14.	a	48.	b	82.	a	116.	a	150.	b
15.	a	49.	b	83.	d	117.	b	151.	c
16.	c	50.	a	84.	b	118.	a	152.	b
17.	c	51.	d	85.	d	119.	a	153.	b
18.	a	52.	a	86.	d	120.	d	154.	b
19.	b	53.	b	87.	c	121.	c	155.	a
20.	a	54.	c	88.	b	122.	a	156.	a
21.	b	55.	c	89.	a	123.	c	157.	d
22.	c	56.	d	90.	b	124.	a	158.	a
23.	b	57.	c	91.	a	125.	a	159.	b
24.	d	58.	d	92.	a	126.	c	160.	c
25.	a	59.	b	93.	b	127.	c	161.	b
26.	b	60.	d	94.	a	128.	c	162.	a
27.	a	61.	a	95.	a	129.	a	163.	b
28.	d	62.	d	96.	d	130.	d	164.	b
29.	c	63.	d	97.	b	131.	d	165.	b
30.	c	64.	a	98.	c	132.	d	166.	c
31.	d	65.	b	99.	c	133.	b	167.	c
32.	b	66.	a	100.	c	134.	d		
33.	a	67.	d	101.	a	135.	b	1st:	__/167 = __%
34.	b	68.	a	102.	a	136.	c	2nd:	__/167 = __%

Explanations

1. (a) The requirement is to identify the statement in the standard audit report that indicates the existence of audit risk. Answer (a) is correct because the existence of audit risk is recognized by the statement in the auditor's standard report that the auditor obtained "reasonable assurance." Answer (b) is incorrect because while the standard report does indicate that the CPA assesses the accounting principles used and the overall financial statement presentation, this does not indicate the existence of audit risk. Answer (c) is incorrect because while the standard report does indicate that the audit relates to whether the financial statements are free of material misstatement, it does not discuss materiality and the audit risk associated with materiality. Answer (d) is incorrect because while the financial statements are the responsibility of management and the CPA's responsibility is to express an opinion, the indication that the CPA expresses an opinion does not address audit risk and is less precise than the statement that the auditor obtains reasonable assurance.

2. (b) The requirement is to determine an accountant's reporting responsibility when more than one level of service concerning the financial statements of a nonissuer (nonpublic) entity has been performed. Answer (b) is correct because the professional standards that the accountant report on the highest level of service rendered. Answer (a) is incorrect because the highest, and not the lowest, level is reported on. Answer (c) is incorrect because regardless of the other type of service performed, the compilation level is always the lowest level and therefore should not be the basis of the report. Answer (d) is incorrect because in circumstances in which an audit has been performed, an audit report, not a review report, is appropriate.

3. (d) The requirement is to determine an auditor's responsibility for controlling the distribution by the client of a restricted-use report. Answer (d) is correct because the professional standards state that an auditor is not responsible for controlling the distribution of such reports. Answer (a) is incorrect because while an auditor should consider informing a client that restricted-use reports are not intended for such distribution, there is no such requirement and such distribution may or may not be legal. Answer (b) is incorrect because the auditor need not inform the client to cease and desist. Answer (c) is incorrect because an auditor need not insist that the client not duplicate the restricted-use report.

4. (a) The requirement is to determine the proper addressee of a report in a circumstance in which one company has hired a CPA to audit another company's financial statements. Answer (a) is correct because while audit reports are ordinarily addressed to the company whose financial statements are being audited, when a CPA audits the financial statements of a company that is not his or her client (as is the case here) the report is addressed to the company that hired the CPA.

5. (c) The requirement is to identify the statement that is included in the auditor's standard report. Answer (c) is correct because the auditor's standard report states that an audit includes assessing significant estimates made by management; the other replies provide information not directly mentioned in a standard report.

6. (c) The requirement is to determine the proper date of a reissued audit report on financial statements that have **not** been restated. Answer (c) is correct because use of the original date on the reissued audit report removes any implication that records, transactions or events after the date of the audit report have been examined or reviewed.

7. (c) The requirements to identify which section of the audit report the auditor speaks of the adequacy of audit evidence. Answer (a) is correct because in the auditor's responsibility section the auditors states a belief that the audit evidence obtained is sufficient and appropriate to provide a basis for the audit opinion.

8. (b) The requirement is to identify the correct statement concerning where a statement that the auditor has audited the financial statements which are then listed is included in the audit report. Answer (b) is correct because the opening (introductory) paragraph of the auditor's standard report states that the auditor has audited the financial statements and then lists them. Answer (a) is incorrect because of the explicit statement in the introductory paragraph. Answers (c) and (d) are incorrect because the introductory paragraph, not

the auditor's responsibility section or the opinion paragraph, includes the statement and lists the financial statements.

9. (d) The requirement is to determine whether the terms "when read in conjunction with Note X," and "with the foregoing explanation" should be included in the opinion paragraph of a qualified opinion. The professional standards state that an audit report with a qualified opinion should **not** include either phrase in the opinion paragraph.

10. (d) The requirement is to determine the representations made explicitly and implicitly when issuing a public company standard auditor's report on comparative financial statements. Answer (d) is correct because that audit report explicitly states that the examination of evidence is made on a test basis and implicitly assumes consistent application of accounting principles. Answer (a) is incorrect because consistency of application of accounting principles is not indicated explicitly. Answer (b) is incorrect because examination of evidence on a test basis is referred to explicitly. Answer (c) is incorrect because examination of evidence on a test basis is explicitly referred to and because consistent application of accounting principles is not explicitly referred to.

11. (c) The requirement is to determine the proper audit report when an auditor has doubt as to the integrity of management and the representations obtained from management and has not decided to resign. Answer (c) is correct because the professional standards consider this as a scope limitation and accordingly its significant nature makes a disclaimer most likely. Answer (a) is incorrect because an unmodified opinion is not appropriate due to the lack of sufficient appropriate audit evidence due to the doubt concerning management's integrity. Answer (b) is incorrect because the lack of confidence in management's integrity makes an unmodified opinion inappropriate. Answer (d) is incorrect because the auditor is not aware of significant misstatements that would lead to an adverse opinion.

12. (a) The requirement is to determine the appropriate date for an audit report when a subsequent event requiring adjustment of financial statements, without disclosure of the event, comes to the auditor's attention. The professional standards state that the date sufficient appropriate audit evidence has been collected should be used in such circumstances.

13. (c) The requirement is to determine an auditor's responsibility for subsequent events when an audit report has been dual dated for a subsequent event. Answer (c) is correct because, when dual dating is used, auditor responsibility for events subsequent to the completion of fieldwork is limited to the specific event referred to in the notes to the financial statement. Answers (a), (b), and (d) are all incorrect because they establish more responsibility than required by the professional standards. Note, however, that if the auditor chooses to date the report as of the date of the subsequent event, his/her responsibility for other subsequent events extends to the date of the audit report.

14. (a) The requirement is to determine the meaning of the expression "taken as a whole" in the fourth generally accepted auditing standard of reporting. The professional standards state that "taken as a whole" applies equally to a complete set of financial statements and to an individual financial statement.

15. (a) The requirement is to determine the accounting principles that an issuer (public) company audit report refers to. Answer (a) is correct because the financial statements follow generally accepted accounting principles. Answer (b) is incorrect because, while the audit is performed in accordance with PCAOB standards, the financial statements do not follow those standards. Answer (c) is incorrect because the financial statements do not follow generally accepted auditing standards. Answer (d) is incorrect because the financial statements ordinarily follow generally accepted accounting principles, not International Accounting Standards.

16. (c) The requirement is to identify the incorrect statement concerning information included in an audit report of financial statements issued under the requirements of the PCAOB. Answer (c) is correct since the report should refer to the auditor's report on internal control, not on compliance with laws and regulations. Answer (a) is incorrect because the report should include the title "Report of Independent Registered Public Accounting Firm." Answer (b) is incorrect because the report should refer to the standards of the PCAOB. Answer (d) is incorrect because the report should contain the city and state or country of the office that issued the report.

17. (c) The requirement is to determine whether the term "reasonable period of time, not to exceed one year" and/or "going concern" is included in an emphasis-of-matter paragraph relating to going concern status. Answer (c) is correct because while the term "going concern" must be included, the first term is not included in such a report.

18. (a) The requirement is to determine an auditor's reporting responsibility when reporting on comparative financial statements in which the first year presented originally received a going concern modification on a matter that has now been resolved, thus removing the auditor's substantial doubt. Answer (a) is correct because if substantial doubt has been removed in the current period, the emphasis-of-matter paragraph included in the auditor's report on the financial statements of the prior period should not be repeated. Answers (b), (c), and (d) are all incorrect because they suggest the need for an emphasis-of-matter paragraph.

19. (b) The requirement is to determine the auditor's responsibility when s/he concludes that there is substantial doubt about an entity's ability to continue as a going concern for a reasonable period of time. Answer (b) is correct because when the auditor concludes there is substantial doubt, s/he should consider the possible effects on the financial statements, and the adequacy of the related disclosures. Answer (a) is incorrect because either an unmodified opinion with an emphasis-of-matter paragraph or a disclaimer is generally appropriate, not a qualified or adverse opinion. Answer (c) is incorrect because the substantial doubt of going concern status does not require adjusting accounting estimates. Answer (d) is incorrect because the prior year's audit report need not be reissued with an emphasis-of-matter paragraph.

20. (a) The requirement is to determine an auditor's reporting responsibility when there is substantial doubt about a client's ability to continue as a going concern. Answer (a) is correct because the audit report must include an emphasis-of-matter paragraph following the opinion paragraph, and must use the terms "going concern" and "substantial doubt."

21. (b) The requirement is to identify the situation in which an emphasis-of-matter paragraph may be added to an unmodified report. Answer (b) is correct because substantial doubt about the entity's ability to continue as a going concern leads to either an unmodified report with an emphasis-of-matter paragraph or a disclaimer of opinion. Answer (a) is incorrect because an auditor may issue an opinion on a balance sheet without reporting on the other basic financial statements. Answer (c) is incorrect because unreasonable estimates lead to either a qualified or an adverse opinion. Answer (d) is incorrect because inadequate management record retention policies are a scope limitation that may result in a qualified opinion or a disclaimer.

22. (c) The requirement is to identify the management plan an auditor would most likely positively consider when a question concerning an entity's ability to continue as a going concern exists. Answer (c) is correct because increasing the ownership equity will bring in funds to possibly overcome the negative trends and financial difficulties. Answers (a), (b), and (d) are all incorrect because increasing dividend distributions, reducing lines of credit, and purchasing assets will all use funds, they will not provide funds. See AU-C 570 for guidance on an auditor's consideration of an entity's ability to continue as a going concern.

23. (b) The requirement is to identify the condition or event most likely to cause an auditor to have substantial doubt about an entity's ability to continue as a going concern. Answer (b) is correct because denial of usual trade from suppliers is ordinarily an indicator that the company is in weak financial condition. Answer (a) is incorrect because while such related-party transactions may be considered risky, there is less likely to be a question concerning going concern status than suggested by answer (a). Answer (c) is incorrect because the payment of such stock dividends does not indicate financial weakness. Answer (d) is incorrect because restrictions on the disposal of principal assets is a condition often present in various loan agreements.

24. (d) The requirement is to identify the most likely mitigating factor a CPA would consider when a client's ability to continue as a going concern is in question. Answer (d) is correct because the ability to postpone expenditures for research and development projects may mitigate the circumstance. Answer (a) is incorrect because there is no guarantee that Zero's discussions with its lenders will lead to a restructuring of the debt and loan agreements. Only existing or committee agreements to restructure the debt would be considered a mitigating factor. Answer (b) is incorrect because weak internal control over cash disbursements may or may not have caused the going concern problem. Answer (c) is incorrect because an entity with a going concern problem is unlikely to be able to purchase such production facilities.

25. (a) The requirement is to identify the condition or event that is most likely to cause an auditor to have substantial doubt about an entity's ability to continue as a going concern. Answer (a) is correct because the professional standards (as well as logic) includes negative cash flows as one of its examples of such conditions and events. Answer (b) is incorrect because while the postponement of research and development projects may sometimes be due to extreme financial difficulties, often it is not. Answers (c) and (d) are incorrect because neither significant related-party transactions nor stock dividends need not indicate substantial doubt about an entity's ability to continue as a going concern. See AU-C 570 for information on an auditor's consideration of an entity's ability to continue as a going concern.

26. (b) The requirement is to identify the condition or event that might indicate to an auditor substantial doubt about an entity's ability to continue as a going concern. Answer (b) is correct because confirmation with related and third parties of the details of arrangements to provide or maintain financial support is a procedure that would assist an auditor in identifying a question concerning going concern status. See AU-C 570 for this and other such conditions and events indicating doubt about an entity's ability to continue as a going concern. Answer (a) is incorrect because the pledging of assets as collateral is a normal business transaction and it need not necessarily indicate a question of going concern status. Answer (c) is incorrect because reconciling the cash balances with the cutoff bank statement is an acceptable audit procedure, but will not normally identify a going concern question. Answer (d) is incorrect because comparing an entity's depreciation and asset capitalization policies will not normally indicate a question of going concern status.

27. (a) The requirement is to identify the audit procedure most likely to assist an auditor in identifying conditions and events that may indicate there could be substantial doubt about an entity's ability to continue as a going concern. Answer (a) is correct because a review of compliance with terms of debt and loan agreements may reveal conditions of noncompliance due to poor financial condition. See the outline of AU-C 570 for a list of procedures that may identify such conditions and events. Answers (b), (c), and (d) are all incorrect because, while they might in some circumstances reveal a question concerning the company's ability to continue as a going concern, they are not considered to be as effective as answer (a).

28. (d) The requirement is to identify the factor which a CPA would most likely consider as mitigating substantial doubt about the ability of an entity to continue as a going concern. Answer (d) is correct because management's ability to negotiate reductions of required dividends will decrease required cash outflows, and thereby increase the likelihood that the entity will be able to continue as a going concern. AU-C 570 provides examples of information that might mitigate such concern. Answers (a), (b), and (c) are all incorrect because they involve spending cash, rather than reducing outflows of cash.

29. (c) The requirement is to identify the circumstance most likely to mitigate an auditor's substantial doubt about an entity's ability to continue as a going concern. Answer (c) is correct because the marketable assets that management

intends to sell may potentially provide the necessary financial resources to mitigate the substantial doubt about the entity's ability to continue as a going concern. Answer (a) is incorrect because the ability to expand operations into new product lines is a suspect circumstance, given the substantial doubt about the entity's ability to continue as a going concern. Answer (b) is incorrect because it also requires cash resources which may not be available. Answer (d) is incorrect because converting preferred stock to long-term debt will not generally alleviate a question concerning an entity's ability to continue as a going concern.

30. (c) The requirement is to identify the circumstances in which an auditor would issue a report that omits any reference to consistency. Answer (c) is correct because a change in the useful life of assets is a change in estimate, and a change in estimate does not result in a consistency modification. Answers (a) and (b) are incorrect because they both represent a change in accounting principle, and a change in accounting principle requires a consistency modification. Answer (d) is incorrect because management's lack of reasonable justification for a change in accounting principle is a departure from generally accepted accounting principles, and the description of the departure will discuss the inconsistency.

31. (d) The requirement is to determine whether an unjustified accounting change, a material weakness in internal control, or both, would cause an auditor to express an unmodified opinion with an emphasis-of-matter paragraph. Answer (d) is correct because an unjustified accounting change will result in either a qualified or an adverse opinion and a material weakness will ordinarily result in no report modification (see AU-C 265 for information on the treatment of material weaknesses); accordingly, an unmodified opinion with an emphasis-of-matter paragraph added to the auditor's report is not appropriate in either case.

32. (b) The requirement is to identify the circumstance in which a disclaimer of opinion is **not** appropriate. Answer (b) is correct because when management does **not** provide reasonable justification of a change in accounting principles either a qualified or an adverse opinion is appropriate, not a disclaimer. Answers (a), (c), and (d) are all incorrect because they represent scope limitations that lead to either a qualified opinion or a disclaimer of opinion.

33. (a) The requirement is to determine the effect on an audit report of a client's decision to use differing inventory costing methods for various portions of its inventory. Answer (a) is correct because a standard unmodified opinion may ordinarily be issued (see AU-C 708 for a discussion of the consistency standard). Answer (b) is incorrect because there is no lack of consistency between accounting periods. Answer (c) is incorrect because there is no departure from GAAP. Answer (d) is incorrect because adverse opinions are only issued when a departure from GAAP exists that makes the financial statements misleading.

34. (b) The requirement is to identify an auditor's reporting responsibility when performing a first audit of a new client and when the auditor was able to extend auditing procedures to gather sufficient evidence about consistency. Answer (b) is correct because, when the auditor has obtained assurance as to the consistency of application of accounting principles between the current and preceding year, no mention of consistency is included in the audit report. Answer (a) is incorrect because the auditor may report on the client's income statement. Answer (c) is incorrect because the consistency standard does apply. Answer (d) is incorrect because the auditor does not refer to consistency when accounting principles have been applied consistently.

35. (b) The requirement is to determine auditor reporting responsibility when management does not provide reasonable justification for a change in accounting principle and presents comparative financial statements. Answer (b) is correct because the auditor should continue to express his/her exception with the financial statements for the year of change as long as they are presented and reported on. Answer (a) is incorrect because the auditor must express his/her exception for as long as the financial statements for the year of change are presented and reported on. Answer (c) is incorrect because the auditor need not qualify the report until management changes back to the accounting principle formerly used. Answer (d) is incorrect because the qualification is necessary despite the fact that the principle is generally accepted.

36. (d) The requirement is to determine the information that must be presented when a client has changed accounting principles. Answer (d) is correct because in addition to identifying the nature of the change, the auditor must refer to the financial statement note that discusses the change in detail. Answer (a) is incorrect because while the auditor must believe that the change is justified, it is not necessary to explain it in the report. Answer (b) is incorrect because the cumulative effect of the change need not be described in the audit report. Answer (c) is incorrect because the auditor need not make explicit concurrence with the change.

37. (c) The requirement is to determine the proper reporting option for a change in accounting principles with an immaterial current year effect, but which is expected to have a substantial effect in subsequent years. Answer (c) is correct because the auditor need not recognize the change in the audit report and may issue a standard unmodified opinion.

38. (d) The requirement is to identify the proper audit report relating to an uncertainty arising due to litigation. Answer (d) is correct because an uncertainty may result in either a an unqualified opinion with an emphasis-of-matter paragraph or a disclaimer. Answer (a) is incorrect because an adverse opinion is not appropriate. Answers (c) and (d) are incorrect because a qualified opinion is not appropriate.

39. (d) The requirement is to identify the proper statement about an audit report that includes a separate paragraph in an otherwise unmodified report that emphasizes that the entity being reported on had significant transactions with related parties. Answer (d) is correct because such emphasis of a matter does not negate the unmodified opinion. Answer (a) is incorrect because the report is considered unmodified. Answer (b) is incorrect because such emphasis of a matter does not violate generally accepted auditing standards if this information is disclosed in notes to the financial statements.

Answer (c) is incorrect because the report should **not** include the phrase "with the foregoing explanation."

40. (b) The requirement is to identify the situation in which an auditor may **not** issue a qualified opinion. Answer (b) is correct because the auditor who lacks independence must disclaim an opinion, not qualify an opinion. Answer (a) is incorrect because a departure from GAAP will result in either a qualified opinion or an adverse opinion. Answer (c) is incorrect because scope limitations result in either a qualified opinion or a disclaimer of opinion. Answer (d) is incorrect because a specialist may be referred to when an auditor is issuing a qualified opinion, an adverse opinion, or a disclaimer of opinion.

41. (d) The requirement is to identify the procedure **not** ordinarily included in an accountant's review of interim financial information. Answer (d) is correct because reviews consist largely of inquiries of management and analytical procedures and not corroborating external evidence such as confirmations. Answer (a) is incorrect because the reading of minutes is ordinarily a part of a review. Answer (b) is incorrect because "applying financial ratios" is a form of analytical procedures that may be included in a review. Answer (c) is incorrect because inquiries of accounting department management personnel are appropriate in a review.

42. (b) The requirement is to identify the information that should be included in the opinion paragraph of an audit report with an adverse opinion. Answer (b) is correct because the opinion paragraph should include a direct reference to a separate paragraph disclosing the basis for the opinion. Answer (a) is incorrect because the principal effects, if available, should be described in a separate emphasis-of-matter paragraph, and not in the opinion paragraph. Answer (c) is incorrect because while a separate paragraph provides a description of the substantive reasons for the adverse opinion, the opinion paragraph does not. Answer (d) is incorrect because neither an uncertainty nor a scope limitation leads to an adverse opinion.

43. (b) The requirement is to identify the appropriate types of audit reports when an illegal act with a material effect on the financial statements has not been properly accounted for or disclosed. Answer (b) is correct because omission of required disclosures, a departure from generally accepted accounting principles, leads to either a qualified or an adverse opinion. Answer (a) is incorrect because a disclaimer of opinion is not appropriate when the auditor knows of such misstatements. Answer (c) is incorrect because neither a disclaimer of opinion nor an unmodified opinion with a separate emphasis-of-matter paragraph is appropriate. Answer (d) is incorrect because an unmodified opinion with a separate emphasis-of-matter paragraph is not appropriate.

44. (c) The requirement is to identify the phrase that an auditor would include in an audit report with a qualified opinion because of inadequate disclosure. Answer (c) is correct because the phrase "except for the omission of the information discussed in the opinion paragraph" is the proper phrase. Answers (a), (b), and (d) are all incorrect because they are phrases not allowed in reports with qualified opinions.

45. (c) The requirement is to identify the circumstance that would most likely result in an auditor expressing an adverse opinion. Answer (c) is correct because departures from GAAP, such as inappropriately reporting leases, result in either a qualified or an adverse opinion. Answer (a) is incorrect because client refusal to provide access to minutes is a client imposed scope limitation that will normally result in a disclaimer of opinion. Answer (b) is incorrect because weak internal control will not in general result in an adverse opinion; if controls are so weak that an audit cannot effectively be completed, a disclaimer of opinion or withdrawal may be appropriate. Answer (d) is incorrect because substantial doubt about going concern status results in either an unmodified opinion with an emphasis-of-matter paragraph or a disclaimer of opinion.

46. (d) The requirement is to identify the paragraphs of an audit report that are modified when an auditor qualifies an opinion because of inadequate disclosure. In addition to requiring the inclusion of a separate basis for qualification matter paragraph, AU-C 705 indicates that only the opinion paragraph should be modified.

47. (b) The requirement is to determine the appropriate report modification that results when the management of a publicly held company issues financial statements that purport to present its financial position and results of operations but omits the statement of cash flows. Answer (b) is correct because failure to include a statement of cash flows in such a circumstance is considered a departure from GAAP and the appropriate choice here is a qualified opinion.

48. (b) The requirement is to identify the circumstance in which an auditor will choose between expressing an "except for" qualified opinion and an adverse opinion. Answer (b) is correct because omissions of required information, a departure from generally accepted accounting principles, leads to either a qualified or an adverse opinion. Answer (a) is incorrect because a scope limitation such as the failure to observe a client's physical inventory leads to either a qualified opinion or a disclaimer of opinion. Answer (c) is incorrect because an auditor may issue an unmodified opinion on one statement. Answer (d) is incorrect because substantial doubt about an entity's ability to continue as a going concern leads to either an unmodified report with explanatory language or a disclaimer of opinion.

49. (b) The requirement is to identify the situation in which an auditor will ordinarily choose between expressing a qualified opinion or an adverse opinion. Answer (b) is correct because departures from generally accepted accounting principles result in either a qualified opinion or an adverse opinion—such lack of disclosure is a departure from generally accepted accounting principles. Answer (a) is incorrect because the inability to observe the physical inventory and inability to become satisfied about its balance represents a scope limitation that will result in either a qualified opinion or a disclaimer of opinion. Answer (c) is incorrect because a change in accounting principles leads to an unmodified opinion with an emphasis-of-matter paragraph added to the report. Answer (d) is incorrect because inability to apply

necessary procedures represents a scope limitation that will result in either a qualified opinion or a disclaimer of opinion.

50. (a) The requirement is to identify the type of opinion that should be issued on the financial statements when an auditor has been unable to obtain sufficient evidence relating to the consistent application of accounting principles between the current and prior year. Answer (a) is correct because the scope limitation will affect the year's beginning balances and thereby affect the current year's results of operations and cash flows. Answer (b) is incorrect because the year-end balance sheet will be unaffected by the scope limitation (any retained earnings misstatement of the preceding year will be offset in the current year). Answer (c) is incorrect because the auditor need not withdraw in such circumstances. Answer (d) is incorrect because this situation represents a scope limitation, and not an uncertainty.

51. (d) The requirement is to identify the circumstance in which an auditor would **not** express an unmodified opinion. Answer (d) is correct because an inability to obtain the audited financial statements of a consolidated investee represents a scope limitation, and a significant scope limitation results in either a qualified opinion or a disclaimer of opinion. Answer (a) is incorrect because a material change between periods in accounting principles will result in an emphasis-of-matter paragraph being added to a report with an unmodified opinion. Answer (b) is incorrect because the omission of the SEC required quarterly financial data, which is considered "unaudited," results in a report with an unmodified opinion with an emphasis-of-matter paragraph. Answer (c) is incorrect because an auditor's emphasis of an unusually important subsequent event results in a report with an unmodified opinion with an emphasis-of-matter paragraph.

52. (a) The requirement is to determine the propriety of including a statement that the current asset portion of an entity's balance sheet was fairly stated in an audit report that disclaims an opinion on the overall financial statements. Answer (a) is correct because expressions of opinion as to certain identified items in financial statements (referred to as "piecemeal opinions") should not be expressed when the auditor has disclaimed an opinion or has expressed an adverse opinion. Such opinions tend to overshadow or contradict the disclaimer or adverse opinion. Answer (b) is incorrect because an auditor may report on one basic financial statement. Answers (c) and (d) are incorrect because providing such assurance is **not** appropriate.

53. (b) The requirement is to identify the type of opinion that should be issued on the balance sheet and the income statement when an auditor did not observe a client's taking of the beginning physical inventory and was unable to become satisfied about its accuracy by using other auditing procedures. Answer (b) is correct because the scope limitation will not affect the year-end balance sheet account balances. However, because evidence with respect to the beginning inventory is lacking, verification of cost of goods sold, an income statement element, is impossible. Although year-end retained earnings will not be affected, both the current and prior years' retained earnings statements will be affected (by an offsetting amount) by the cost of goods sold misstatement. If no other problems arise, the auditor will be able to issue an unmodified opinion on the balance sheet and a disclaimer on the income statement (and on the retained earnings statement). Answer (a) is incorrect because an unmodified opinion may be issued on the balance sheet. Answer (c) is incorrect because an unmodified opinion may be issued on the balance sheet with a disclaimer on the income statement. Answer (d) is incorrect because a disclaimer should be issued on the income statement.

54. (c) The requirement is to determine whether the auditor responsibility section, opinion paragraph, and/or notes to the financial statements should refer to an audit scope limitation. Answer (c) is correct because the suggested report presented for a scope limitation includes modification of both the scope and opinion paragraphs. In addition, it is not appropriate for the scope of the audit to be explained in a note to the financial statements.

55. (c) The requirement is to identify a CPA's responsibility when asked to report on only one financial statement. Answer (c) is correct because the auditor may accept the engagement because the situation involves limited reporting objectives, not a limitation on the scope of audit procedures. Answers (a), (b), and (d) are incorrect because the auditor is able to accept such an engagement and because the auditor is able to apply the procedures considered necessary.

56. (d) The requirement is to determine whether either the auditor's responsibility section, the opinion paragraph, or both should be deleted when an auditor is disclaiming an opinion due to a client-imposed scope limitation. Answer (d) is correct because neither the auditor responsibility section nor the opinion paragraph is deleted, although they are both modified Answer (a) is incorrect because it suggests that the opinion paragraph is omitted. Answer (b) is incorrect because it states that both the auditor responsibility paragraph and the opinion paragraph are omitted. Answer (c) is incorrect because it states that the opinion paragraph is omitted.

57. (c) The requirement is to identify the information included in the opinion paragraph of an auditor's report that is qualified due to a major inadequacy in the computerized accounting records. Answer (c) is correct because the opinion paragraph indicates that the exception is due to the possible effects on the financial statements. Answer (a) is incorrect because the opinion paragraph will not include a reference to client-imposed scope limitations. Answer (b) is incorrect because no indication of a departure from generally accepted auditing standards is provided in the opinion paragraph and this situation is not a departure from GAAS. Answer (d) is incorrect because there is no indication that there is inadequate disclosure of necessary information.

58. (d) The requirement is to identify the circumstance in which a scope limitation is sufficient to preclude an unmodified opinion. Answer (d) is correct because AU-C 580 states that management's refusal to furnish such a written representation constitutes a limitation on the scope of an audit sufficient to preclude an unmodified opinion. Answers (a), (b), and (c) are all incorrect because while they represent scope limitations, they may sometimes not result in a report that is other than unmodified.

59. (b) The requirement is to determine the situation in which an auditor would ordinarily issue an unmodified audit opinion without an emphasis-of-matter paragraph. Answer (b) is correct because when an auditor makes reference to the report of another auditor no additional paragraph is added to the report. Answer (a) is incorrect because emphasizing that the entity had significant related-party transactions is normally accomplished through the addition of an emphasis-of-matter paragraph. Answer (c) is incorrect because the omission of a statement of cash flows when an entity issues financial statements that present financial position and result of operations results in a qualified audit opinion with basis for qualified opinion paragraph. Answer (d) is incorrect because substantial doubt about the entity's ability to continue as a going concern normally results in either an unmodified opinion with an emphasis-of-matter paragraph or a disclaimer of opinion.

60. (d) The requirement is to determine a group engagement partner's responsibility, in addition to making inquiries of the other auditor's reputation and independence, after having decided **not** to refer to the audit of the component (other) auditor. Answer (d) is correct because when a decision is made **not** to make reference to the component auditor—that is, to take responsibility for that auditor's work—the group auditor should perform additional procedures dependent upon the significance of the component. Answer (a) is incorrect because no emphasis-of-matter paragraph is added to the audit report. Answer (b) is incorrect because the group engagement partner is assuming responsibility for the component auditor's work when a decision is made not to refer to the component auditor's report. Answer (c) is incorrect because written permission is not required when the group engagement partner is taking responsibility for the work of the other auditor.

61. (a) The requirement is to determine the meaning of sentences added to the auditor responsibility section of an auditor's report that states that another auditor audited a portion of the entity. Answer (a) is correct because the professional standards provide that such a statement indicates a division of responsibility. Answer (b) is incorrect because when the other auditor is referred to the CPA, the CPA is not assuming responsibility for the other auditor. Answer (c) is incorrect because an unmodified opinion may be issued. Answer (d) is incorrect because the sentences are proper.

62. (d) The requirement is to identify the situation in which an auditor may issue the standard audit report. Answer (d) is correct because a standard report may be issued in circumstances in which the principal auditor assumes responsibility for the work of another auditor. Answer (a) is incorrect because the standard report does not include reference to a specialist. Thus, reference to a specialist within a report by definition causes modification of the standard report. Answer (b) is incorrect because the auditor is required to issue a modified report on condensed financial statements. Answer (c) is incorrect because audit reports on financial statements prepared using a financial reporting framework other than GAAP require departures from the standard form.

63. (d) The requirement is to determine a group engagement partner's reporting responsibility when a decision has been made to not make reference to a component auditor who has audited a client's subsidiary. Answer (d) is correct because, regardless of whether the component auditor is referred to, the group engagement partner must be satisfied as to the independence and professional reputation of the other CPA. Answer (a) is incorrect because the group engagement partner need not issue an unmodified opinion on the consolidated financial statements. Answer (b) is incorrect because it is not necessary that the component auditor issue an unmodified opinion on the subsidiary's financial statements. Answer (c) is incorrect because the group engagement partner should consider a variety of procedures depending upon the significance of the subsidiary when a decision is made to not make reference to the component auditor.

64. (a) The requirement is to determine the type of opinion to be issued when financial statements of an entity that follows GASB standards include a justified departure from GAAP. Answer (a) is correct because the auditor should issue an unmodified opinion and should include a separate emphasis-of-matter paragraph explaining the departure from GAAP. Answers (b), (c), and (d) are incorrect because when the auditor believes that the departure is justified, neither a qualified nor adverse opinion is appropriate.

65. (b) The requirement is to determine which auditor(s) is (are) responsible for evaluating the appropriateness of the adjustment of foreign financial statements consolidated with US GAAP financial statements in a group audit situation. Answer (b) is correct because the group auditor is responsible. Answer (a) is incorrect because the component auditor is not responsible. Answer (c) is incorrect because the group auditor is responsible and the component auditor is not. Answer (d) is incorrect because the group auditor is responsible.

66. (a) The requirement is to identify the circumstance in which an auditor reporting on comparative financial statements would ordinarily change the previously issued opinion on the prior year's financial statements. Answer (a) is correct because when an auditor has previously expressed a qualified or an adverse opinion on financial statements of a prior period and those financial statements have been restated, the auditor's updated report is changed. Answer (b) is incorrect because, ordinarily, the reissued report by a predecessor auditor will be the same as that originally issued. Answer (c) is incorrect because the prior year's opinion will remain unmodified if the current year's audit report is modified due to a lack of consistency. Answer (d) is incorrect because restatement of prior year's financial statements following a pooling of interest will not lead to a change in the previously issued opinion.

67. (d) The requirement is to determine the information to be included in an audit report on comparative financial statements when a predecessor auditor's report is not being reissued. Answer (d) is correct because an other-matter paragraph should be added to the successor's report and it should indicate (1) that the financial statements of the prior period were audited by another auditor (whose name is not presented), (2) the date of the predecessor's report, (3) the type of report issued by the predecessor, and (4) if the report was other than a standard report, the substantive reasons therefor.

68. (a) The requirement is to determine whether the predecessor auditor should obtain a representation letter from management, the successor auditor, or both, before reissuing the prior year's audit record. Answer (a) is correct because the predecessor auditor should obtain a representation letter from both management and the successor auditor.

69. (d) The requirement is to identify the circumstance in which a standard unmodified report may be issued when single-year financial statements are presented. Answer (d) is correct because when the prior year's financial statements are not being presented, the CPA need not refer to them or include the predecessor auditor's report. Answer (a) is incorrect because inability to audit an investment in a foreign affiliate is a scope limitation that is likely to result in either a qualified opinion or a disclaimer. Answer (b) is incorrect because a qualified opinion is appropriate when an entity declines to present a statement of cash flows with its balance sheet and related statements of income and retained earnings. Answer (c) is incorrect because the emphasis of an accounting matter by an auditor results in inclusion of an emphasis-of-matter paragraph to the unmodified audit report.

70. (a) The requirement is to identify the correct form of an audit report on comparative financial statements when a continuing auditor has audited the two years of financial statements being presented. Answer (a) is correct because one audit report should be issued that includes the years involved. Answer (b) is incorrect because one report, not two reports, should be issued. Answer (c) is incorrect because both years should be reported upon. Answer (d) is incorrect because auditors do not have the option of issuing two audit reports in this circumstance.

71. (d) The requirement is to determine the manner in which a predecessor auditor who has reissued a report for comparative financial statements should refer to the successor auditor. The predecessor auditor should not refer in the reissued report to the report or work of the successor auditor.

72. (d) The requirement is to determine the proper reporting procedure for comparative financial statements for which the prior year is compiled, and the current year is audited. When compiled financial statements are presented in comparative form with audited financial statements, the report on the prior period may be reissued to accompany the current period report. In addition, the report on the current period may include a separate paragraph describing responsibility assumed for the prior period financial statements.

73. (a) The requirement is to identify the auditor's reporting responsibility for a material inconsistency between the audited financial statements and the other information in an annual report to shareholders containing audited financial statements. Answer (a) is correct because AU-C 720 states that if a material inconsistency exists and the client refuses to revise the other information, the auditor should include an emphasis-of-matter paragraph that explains the inconsistency. The auditor may also withhold the use of the audit report or the auditor may withdraw from the engagement. Answer (b) is incorrect because the financial statements are not misstated. Answer (c) is incorrect because the auditor must review the other information to ensure that it is consistent with the financial statements. Answer (d) is incorrect because the financial statements are not misstated and therefore a disclaimer of opinion is inappropriate.

74. (d) The requirement is to determine an auditor's responsibility when audited financial statements are presented in a document containing other information. Answer (d) is correct because the auditor is required to read the other information to determine that it is consistent with the audited financial statements. Answers (a) and (c) are incorrect because no such inquiry, analytical procedures, or other substantive auditing procedures are required. Answer (b) is incorrect because, unless the information seems incorrect or inconsistent with the audited financial statements, no emphasis-of-matter paragraph needs to be added to the auditor's report.

75. (d) The requirement is to identify the manner in which an auditor may express an opinion on an entity's accounts receivable when that auditor has disclaimed an opinion on the financial statements taken as a whole. Answer (d) is correct because such a report is considered a "specified elements, accounts, or items report," and should include the opinion on the accounts receivable separately from the disclaimer of opinion on the financial statement. Answer (a) is incorrect because reason for the disclaimer of opinion need not be provided. Answer (b) is incorrect because distribution of such a report is not restricted to internal use only. Answer (c) is incorrect because the auditor need not report on the current asset portion of the entity's balance sheet to issue such a report.

76. (c) The requirement is to identify an auditor's responsibility for required supplementary information that is placed outside the basic financial statements. Answer (c) is correct because AU-C 730 requires that the auditor apply limited procedures to the information and report deficiencies in, or the omission of, the information. Answer (a) is incorrect because the auditor does have some responsibility for the supplementary information. Answer (b) is incorrect because the auditor must apply limited procedures to information presented and report deficiencies in the information in addition to determining whether it has been omitted. Answer (d) is incorrect because tests of details of transactions and balances need not be performed.

77. (d) The requirement is to determine the proper audit report when management declines to present supplementary information required by the Governmental Accounting Standards Board. Answer (d) is correct because omission of required supplementary information, which when presented is not considered audited, leads to an unmodified opinion with an other-matter paragraph. Answers (a) and (b) are incorrect because neither an adverse opinion nor a qualified opinion is appropriate since the supplementary information is not audited. Answer (c) is incorrect because it is incomplete since an unmodified opinion with an additional other-matter paragraph is required.

78. (c) The requirement is to identify the correct statement that may be included in an auditor's report when an auditor provides an opinion on information accompanying the basic

financial statements. Answer (c) is correct because the report indicates whether the accompanying information is fairly stated in all material respects in relation to the basic financial statements taken as a whole. Answer (a) is incorrect because the information is not presented in accordance with generally accepted auditing standards. Answer (b) is incorrect because the information is in addition to that required by generally accepted accounting principles. Answer (d) is incorrect because it is not in accordance with attestation standards.

79. (d) The requirement is to identify the type of report that is most likely to include an alert to readers that its use is restricted to certain specified users. Answer (d) is correct because all agreed-upon procedures reports are so restricted. Although audit, review, or compilations reports may be so restricted, there is no requirement that they be.

80. (c) The requirement is to identify the report that is **least** likely to be a restricted-use report. Answer (c) is correct because reports on most financial reporting frameworks other than GAAP are not restricted. Answers (a) and (b) are incorrect because reports on significant deficiencies and reports to audit committees are restricted under the professional standards. Answer (d) is incorrect because a report on compliance is restricted.

81. (d) The requirement is to determine auditor reporting responsibility when prior period financial statements which received a qualified opinion due to a lack of adequate disclosure have been restated to eliminate the lack of disclosure. Answer (d) is correct because an auditor should express an unmodified opinion on the restated financial statements of the prior year (with an emphasis-of-matter paragraph describing the circumstance). Answer (a) is incorrect because the auditor's original report is not reissued. Answer (b) is incorrect because the qualified opinion is eliminated. Answer (c) is incorrect because reference to the type of opinion expressed is included in the reissued report's emphasis-of-matter paragraph.

82. (a) The requirement is to identify audit reporting requirements when reporting on financial statements of a US entity prepared in accordance with another country's accounting principles. Answer (a) is correct because AU-C 910 states that the auditor should understand the accounting principles generally accepted in the other country. Answer (b) is incorrect because the auditor does not have to obtain certification outside of the United States. Answer (c) is incorrect because the auditor does not have to disclaim an opinion. Answer (d) is incorrect because the auditor does not have to receive a waiver from the auditor's state board of accountancy.

83. (d) The requirement is to determine the appropriate types of reports that may be issued when the financial statements of a US subsidiary are prepared following the principles of a non-US parent company's country for inclusion in that parent company's non-US consolidated financial statements. AU-C 910 allows either a modified US style report or the report form of the parent's country. A US style unmodified report is not appropriate.

84. (b) The requirement is to determine the proper placement of a basis for modification paragraph disclosing the substantive reasons for expressing an adverse opinion. AU-C 705 requires that such paragraphs precede the opinion paragraph.

85. (d) The requirement is to determine the information that should be included in an audit report on financial statements prepared on the income tax basis of accounting. AU-C 800 presents the form of the report to be issued. Answer (d) is correct because AU-C 800 requires that the report indicate that the income tax basis of accounting is a financial reporting framework other than GAAP.

86. (d) The requirement is to identify the appropriate type of audit report to be issued for a nonprofit entity's financial statements prepared following an accounting basis prescribed by a regulatory agency solely for filing with that agency. Answer (d) is correct because an unmodified opinion is appropriate given that the financial statements are fairly presented; the report will include a paragraph indicating that a basis other than GAAP is being followed. Answer (a) is incorrect because an unmodified report may be issued if there are no departures from the prescribed basis. The report would not be qualified because the financial statements were prepared using an accounting basis prescribed by a regulatory agency. Answer (b) is incorrect because an adverse opinion is not appropriate when the information is properly presented. Answer (c) is incorrect because a disclaimer of opinion need not be issued.

87. (c) The requirement is to identify the disclosure included in a separate emphasis-of-matter paragraph of an auditor's report on financial statements prepared in conformity with the cash basis of accounting. Answer (c) is correct because the emphasis-of-matter paragraph refers to the note to the financial statements that describes the basis of accounting. AU-C 800 presents complete details on such reports. Answer (a) is incorrect because the report need not justify the reasons for following a basis other than generally accepted accounting principles. Answer (b) is incorrect because the emphasis-of-matter paragraph contains no statement on fair presentation, and because the opinion paragraph states whether the presentation is in conformity with the basis described in the appropriate financial statement note. Answer (d) is incorrect because no explanation of how the results of operations differ from financial statements prepared in conformity with generally accepted accounting principles is necessary.

88. (b) The requirement is to identify a situation in which an auditor's report would refer to a basis of accounting other than GAAP AU-C 800 defines reports on compliance with aspects of regulatory requirements related to audited financial statements as special-purpose financial reporting frameworks and requires such identification.

89. (a) The requirement is to determine the type of report to issue when a client who uses a special-purpose financial reporting framework has not appropriately titled its financial statements. Answer (a) is correct because any such exceptions or reservation should be described in an emphasis-of-matter paragraph and possibly a qualified (or adverse) opinion should

be issued. Answer (b) is incorrect because no such application to the state insurance commission is necessary. Answer (c) is incorrect because a disclaimer of opinion is not appropriate when known misstatements exist. Answer (d) is incorrect because, as indicated, more than describing the terminology is necessary.

90. (b) The requirement is to identify an auditor's reporting responsibility when a printed form prescribes the wording of the independent auditor's report that will accompany it, but that wording is not acceptable to the auditor. AU-C 800 suggests that the auditor reword the report (or attach a separate report) in this situation.

91. (a) The requirement is to identify a requirement for a CPA to express an opinion on a profit participation plan relating to an entity's net income. Answer (a) is correct because if a specified element is, or is based upon, an entity's net income or stockholders' equity, the CPA should have audited the complete financial statements in order to express an opinion on the element. Answer (b) is incorrect because the financial statements need not be prepared in conformity with GAAP, as other bases of accounting may be followed. Answer (c) is incorrect because the report need not be made available for distribution to other employees. Answer (d) is incorrect because the individual in the profit participation plan need not own a controlling interest in the company.

92. (a) The requirement is to determine whether a CPA is permitted to accept an engagement to audit either a schedule of accounts receivable, a schedule of royalties, or both. Answer (a) is correct because auditors may audit "specified elements, accounts or items of a financial statement," including either a schedule of accounts receivable or a schedule of royalties. Answer (b) is incorrect because an auditor may audit a schedule of royalties. Answer (c) is incorrect because an auditor may audit a schedule of accounts receivable. Answer (d) is incorrect because an auditor may audit both a schedule of accounts receivable and a schedule of royalties.

93. (b) The requirement is to identify the least likely procedure included in an interim review of the financial statements of a public client. Answer (b) is correct because an interim review ordinarily does not include such substantive tests of balances. Answer (a) is incorrect because a CPA should obtain such written representations. Answer (c) is incorrect because the CPA will read the financial statements for obvious material misstatements. Answer (d) is incorrect because the primary procedures included in such a review are analytical procedures and inquiries.

94. (a) The requirement is to identify the objective of a review of interim financial information. Answer (a) is correct because the objective of a review of interim financial information is to provide a basis for reporting on whether material modification should be made for such information to conform with generally accepted accounting principles. Answer (b) is incorrect because no updated opinion is being issued. Answer (c) is incorrect because summary financial statements or pro forma financial information are not being considered in this question. Answer (d) is incorrect because the statements may or may not be presented in conformity with generally accepted accounting principles.

95. (a) The requirement is to identify the correct statement with respect to an independent accountant's review report on interim financial information presented in a registration statement. Answer (a) is correct because an accountant's review report is **not** a part of the registration statement within the meaning of Section 11 of the Securities Act of 1933. Answer (b) is incorrect because under certain conditions an accountant is required to update the report. Answers (c) and (d) are incorrect because the prospectus includes neither a statement that the review was performed in accordance with SEC standards, nor a statement that the accountant obtained corroborating evidence.

96. (d) The requirement is to determine the circumstances which will lead to a modification of an interim report. Departures from generally accepted accounting principles, which include adequate disclosure, require modification of the accountant's report. Normally neither an uncertainty [answer (a)] nor a lack of consistency [answer (b)] would cause a report modification. Reference to another accountant [answer (c)] is not considered a modification.

97. (b) The requirement is to identify the procedure that would ordinarily be applied when an accountant conducts a review of the interim financial information of a publicly held entity. Answer (b) is correct because the accountant will ordinarily read the minutes of meetings of stockholders, the board of directors, and committees of the board of directors to identify actions that may affect the interim financial information. Answers (a), (c), and (d) are all incorrect because they represent verification procedures typically beyond the scope of a review of interim financial information.

98. (c) The requirement is to identify the least likely procedure to be included in an accountant's review of interim financial information of an issuer (public) entity. Answer (c) is correct because a review consists principally of performing analytical procedures and making inquiries, not procedures such as observation, inspection, and confirmation. Answers (a), (b), and (d) are all incorrect because they include review procedures included in the professional standards

99. (c) The requirement is to identify the most likely information included in a review report. Answer (c) is correct because the professional standards require that the report include a description of procedures performed. Answer (a) is incorrect because the information was reviewed, not examined, in accordance with standards of the PCAOB. Answer (b) is incorrect because the interim financial information is the responsibility of the entity's management, not the shareholders. Answer (d) is incorrect because a review is less in scope than an audit, not than a compilation.

100. (c) The requirement is to determine the circumstance under which an auditor may report on summary financial statements that are derived from complete audited financial statements. Answer (c) is correct because a report may be issued when the information in the summary financial statements is fairly stated in all material respects in relation to the financial statements. Answer (a) is incorrect because the

summary financial statements need not be distributed with the complete financial statements. Answer (b) is incorrect because the report need not indicate the nature of any additional procedures. Answer (d) is incorrect because prior year summary financial information is not necessary. See AU-C 810 for information on summary financial statements.

101. (a) The requirement is to determine the appropriate response relating to selected financial data that are included in a document containing audited financial statements. Answer (a) is correct because the selected data should be limited to data derived from the audited financial statements. Answer (b) is incorrect because distribution of the report need not be limited to senior management and the board of directors. Answer (c) is incorrect because the selected data need not follow a financial reporting framework other than GAAP. Answer (d) is incorrect because the report will ordinarily state that the selected data are fairly stated in all material respects in relation to the consolidated financial statements.

102. (a) The requirement is to determine a predecessor auditor's responsibility when the financial statements he or she audited are being included in an SEC registration statement filing. Answer (a) is correct because AU-C 920 requires that the predecessor (1) read pertinent portions of the document, and (2) obtain a letter of representation from the successor auditor.

103. (b) The requirement is to identify the statement that is correct concerning letters for underwriters. Answer (b) is correct because letters for underwriters typically provide negative assurance on unaudited interim financial information. Answer (a) is incorrect because letters for underwriters are not required by the Securities Act of 1933. Answer (c) is incorrect because letters for underwriters are not included in registrations statements. Answer (d) is incorrect because auditors' opinions on the prior year's financial statement are not updated.

104. (a) The requirement is to determine who ordinarily signs a comfort letter. Answer (a) is correct because a comfort letter (also known as letter to an underwriter) is sent by the independent auditor to the underwriter.

105. (d) The requirement is to identify to whom comfort letters are ordinarily addressed. Answer (d) is correct because comfort letters, also referred to as letters for underwriters, are ordinarily addressed to underwriters.

106. (a) The requirement is to determine the type of opinion or assurance provided by an accountant who issues a comfort letter containing comments on data that have **not** been audited. Answer (a) is correct because when procedures short of an audit are applied to information such as capsule information, a comfort letter will generally provide negative assurance. Answer (b) is incorrect because CPAs do not provide positive assurance on supplementary disclosures. Answer (c) is incorrect because no "limited opinion" is issued on pro forma or other information. Answer (d) is incorrect because no disclaimer will be included on the prospective financial statements.

107. (**d**)   The requirement is to determine the appropriate reference to an independent accountant in a prospectus (relating to an SEC registration statement) that includes a statement about his/her involvement with an independent audit report. AU-C 920 indicates that the independent accountant is an expert in auditing and accounting.

108. (**d**)   The requirement is to identify the information included in a typical comfort letter. Answer (d) is correct because in a comfort letter auditors provide an opinion as to whether the audited financial statements comply in form with the accounting requirements of the SEC. Answer (a) is incorrect because negative assurance concerning whether the entity's internal control procedures operated as designed during the period is not provided. Answer (b) is incorrect because a comfort letter does not include an opinion on whether the entity complied with Government Auditing Standards and the Single Audit Act. Answer (c) is incorrect because negative, not positive, assurance is provided on unaudited summary financial information.

109. (**a**)   The requirement is to determine the proper treatment of unaudited financial statements presented in comparative form with audited financial statements in a document filed with the Securities and Exchange Commission. Answer (a) is correct because those statements should be marked "unaudited," not withheld until they are audited, and not referred to in the auditor's report.

110. (**b**)   The requirement is to identify the requirement relating to a CPA's report when reporting on the application of accounting principles to a specific transaction. Answer (b) is correct because AU-C 915 requires that the report include a statement that responsibility for the proper accounting treatment rests with the preparers of the financial statements. Answer (a) is incorrect because the report states that the engagement was performed in accordance with applicable AICPA standards, not Statements on Standards for Accounting and Review Services. Answer (c) is incorrect as no such statement about opinion-shopping is included. Answer (d) is incorrect because the information may be communicated to a prior or continuing auditor.

111. (**a**)   The requirement is to determine an auditor's reporting responsibility when asked by a prospective client to render an opinion on the application of accounting principles to a specific transaction. Answer (a) is correct because AU-C 915 indicates that the report must include a statement that any difference in the facts, circumstances, or assumptions presented may change the report, as well as various other disclosures. Answer (b) is incorrect because the report indicates that the engagement was performed in accordance with AICPA standards, not Statements on Standards for Consulting Services. Answer (c) is incorrect because the report need **not** indicate that the guidance is for management use only and may not be communicated to the prior or continuing auditors. Answer (d) is incorrect because the report does not include negative assurance ("nothing came to our attention"). See AU-C 915 for performance and reporting requirements relating to reports on the application of accounting principles.

112. (**a**)   The requirement is to determine an auditor's responsibility when asked to render an opinion on the application of accounting principles to a specific transaction by an entity that is audited by another CPA. Answer (a) is correct because the accountant ordinarily must consult with the continuing CPA to attempt to obtain information relevant to the transaction; an exception to this rule exists under certain circumstances in which the accountant provides recurring services for the entity. Answer (b) is incorrect because the engagement's findings need not be reported to all of the groups listed—the entity's audit committee, the continuing CPA, and management. Answer (c) is incorrect because the accountant need not disclaim an opinion. Answer (d) is incorrect because the report's distribution need not be restricted to management and outside parties who are aware of all relevant facts.

113. (**b**)   Answer (b) is correct because AU-C 915 indicates that an accountant should not undertake such an engagement when the report would be based on such a hypothetical transaction. Answers (a), (c), and (d) are all incorrect because they include information included in an accountant's report on the application of accounting principles.

114. (**c**)   The requirement is to select the service that is most likely to be structured as an attest engagement. Answer (c) is correct because CPAs may provide assurance as to compliance with requirements of specified laws through a variety of services, including agreed-upon procedures engagements and various compliance audits. Answers (a) and (b) are incorrect because advocating a client's tax position and consulting on a new database system are examples of professional services **not** typically structured as attest services. Answer (d) is incorrect because compilations are not a form of attest engagement.

115. (**c**)   Answer (c) is correct because AT 101 indicates that an unmodified may ordinarily refer to that assertion or to the subject matter to which the assertion relates. Answer (a) is incorrect because it suggests reporting only on the assertion. Answer (b) is incorrect because it suggests reporting only on the subject matter. Answer (d) is incorrect because it suggests that reporting on neither the assertion nor the subject matter is appropriate. Note, however, that AT 101 also states that when a deviation from the criteria being reported upon exits (e.g., a material weakness in internal control" the CPA should report directly upon the subject matter and not upon the assertion.

116. (**a**)   The requirement is to identify the correct statement. When a standard unmodified examination report is being issued, that report may be upon the subject matter or the written assertion. Answers (b), (c), and (d) are all incorrect because they suggest that the report may not be upon either the subject matter, the written assertion, or both.

117. (**b**)   The requirement is to determine whether a CPA's conclusion may be upon the subject matter, the written assertion, or both when conditions exist that result in a material deviation from the criteria against which the subject matter was evaluated during an examination. Answer (b) is correct because in such circumstances the conclusion should be directly upon the subject matter. Answer (a) is incorrect because it suggests that the conclusion may be upon the written assertion. Answer (c) is incorrect because it states that the conclusion may not be upon the subject matter and may be upon the written assertion. Answer (d) is incorrect because it states that the conclusion may not be upon the subject matter.

118. (a) The requirement is to determine the element that is **least** likely to be present when a practitioner performs an attest engagement. Answer (a) is correct because while an assertion is generally present, it is from the responsible party, not from the practitioner. Answer (b) is incorrect because ordinarily there is a responsible party. Answers (c) and (d) are incorrect because both subject matter, and suitable criteria are required.

119. (a) The requirement is to determine whether suitable criteria in an attestation engagement may be available publicly, and/or in the CPA's report. Answer (a) is correct because suitable criteria may be available publicly in the CPA's report, included with the subject matter or in the assertion, well understood by users (e.g., the distance between A and B is twenty feet) or available only to specified parties. Answers (b), (c), and (d) are all incorrect because they suggest that suitable criteria may not be available publicly, in the CPA's report, or both.

120. (d) The requirement is to identify the situation that is **least** likely to result in a restricted use attest report. Answer (d) is correct because criteria developed by an industry association may or may not result in a restricted use attest report. Answers (a), (b), and (c) always result in a restricted use report.

121. (c) The requirement is to identify the information that is **least** likely to be included in an agreed-upon procedures attestation report. Answer (c) is correct because an agreed-upon procedures report provides a summary of procedures performed and findings, not limited assurance. Answer (a) is incorrect because the specified party does not take responsibility for the sufficiency of procedures. Answer (b) is incorrect because the report's use is restricted. Answer (d) is incorrect because a summary of procedures performed is included.

122. (a) The requirement is to identify the type of report that is most likely to include a summary of findings rather than assurance. Answer (a) is correct because agreed-upon procedures reports include a summary of findings. Answer (b) is incorrect because a compilation report does not provide a summary of findings. Answer (c) is incorrect because an examination report includes positive assurance and not a summary of findings. Answer (d) is incorrect because a review report includes limited (negative) assurance, not a summary of findings.

123. (c) The requirement is to identify the statement that is **not** correct concerning "specified parties" of an agreed-upon procedures report under either the auditing or attestation standards. Answer (c) is correct because while a practitioner should establish a clear understanding regarding the terms of the engagement, preferably in an engagement letter, no such engagement letter is required. Answers (a) and (b) are incorrect because the specified parties must agree on the procedures to be performed and take responsibility for their adequacy. Answer (d) is incorrect because an additional party may be added as a specified party after completion of the engagement.

124. (a) The requirement is to determine the information to be included in a separate paragraph included in an accountant's report on the examination of projected financial statements. Answer (a) is correct because AT 301 requires that such a report include a separate paragraph that describes the limitations on the usefulness of the presentation. See AT 301 for information that should be included in an examination report of prospective financial statements. Answer (b) is incorrect because the report includes no such statement attempting to distinguish between an examination and an audit. Answer (c) is incorrect because the report includes no such disclosure and because the accountant is **not** responsible for events and circumstances up to one year after the report's date. Answer (d) is incorrect because the report suggests that the assumptions do provide a reasonable basis.

125. (a) The requirement is to identify the circumstance in which an accountant may accept an engagement to apply agreed-upon procedures to prospective financial statements. Answer (a) is correct because AT 301 states that an accountant may accept an engagement to apply agreed-upon procedures to prospective financial statements provided that (1) the specified parties involved have participated in establishing the nature and scope of the engagement and take responsibility for the adequacy of the procedures to be performed, (2) use of the report is to be restricted to specified parties involved, and (3) the prospective financial statements include a summary of significant assumptions. Answer (b) is incorrect because the prospective financial statements need not be examined. Answer (c) is incorrect because responsibility for the adequacy of the procedures is taken by the specified parties. Answer (d) is incorrect because a summary of findings may be provided based on the agreed-upon procedures.

126. (c) The requirement is to identify the statement which should be included in an accountant's compilation report on financial forecasts. Answer (c) is correct because when the accountant is preparing a standard compilation report on prospective financial statements, AT 301 requires that the accountant include a statement indicating that the prospective results may not be achieved.

127. (c) The requirement is to identify the appropriate distribution of an entity's financial projection. A financial projection is sometimes prepared to present one or more hypothetical courses of action for evaluation in response to a question such as "What would happen if...?" It is based on a responsible party's assumptions reflecting conditions it expects would exist and the course of action it expects would be taken, given one or more hypothetical assumptions. Projections are "limited use" financial statements meant for the responsible party (generally management) and third parties with whom the responsible party is negotiating directly. Answer (c) is correct because a bank might be expected to receive such a projection. Answers (a), (b), and (d) are all incorrect because projections are meant for "limited use" and not to be broadly distributed to groups such as all employees or potential or current stockholders. AT 301 provides overall guidance on the area of financial forecasts and projections.

128. (c) The requirement is to determine whether either testifying as an expert witness, compiling a financial projection, or both are engagements governed by the provisions of the Statement on Standards for Attestation Statements. Answer (c) is correct because the attestation standards explicitly exclude expert witness work, but include the compilation of a financial projection; note that in most areas compilations are not included in attestation standard coverage, but in the area of prospective financial statement (forecasts as well as projections) coverage is included. Answer (a) is incorrect because it states that expert witness work is included. Answer (b) is incorrect both because it states that expert witness work is included and that compiling a projection is not included. Answer (d) is incorrect because it states that compilations of projections are not included.

129. (a) The requirement is to identify the statement that should be included in a compilation report on a financial forecast. Answer (a) is correct because the report should state that the compilation does **not** include evaluation of the support of the assumptions underlying the forecast. Answer (b) is incorrect because no such statement is included in a compilation report, and because hypothetical assumptions pertain to financial projections, not financial forecasts. Answer (c) is incorrect because the report makes no statement concerning the range of assumptions. Answer (d) is incorrect because the statement is not included in the report, and because the prospective statements are management's, not the accountant's, representation.

130. (d) The requirement is to identify the type of general use prospective financial statement on which the accountant may appropriately report. Answer (d) is correct because financial forecasts are considered prospective financial statements, and they are appropriate for general use. Answer (a) is incorrect because financial projections are only appropriate for the party responsible for preparing them or for third parties with whom the responsible party is negotiating directly. Answers (b) and (c) are incorrect because partial presentations and pro forma financial statements are not considered prospective financial statements.

131. (d) The requirement is to identify the statement that is not included in a compilation report on prospective financial statements. Answer (d) is correct because distribution of such a report is not necessarily restricted to specified parties. Answers (a), (b), and (c) are all incorrect because such statements are included in a compilation report.

132. (d) The requirement is to determine the appropriate type of audit report to be issued when an accountant examines a financial forecast that fails to disclose several significant assumptions used to prepare the forecast. AT 301 states that an adverse opinion is appropriate when significant assumptions are not disclosed.

133. (b) The requirement is to identify the type of prospective financial statement that includes one or more hypothetical ("what if?") assumptions. Answer (b) is correct because financial projections include one or more hypothetical assumptions. Answer (a) is incorrect because pro forma financial presentations are designed to demonstrate the effect of a future or hypothetical transaction by showing how it might have affected the historical financial statements if it

had been consummated during the period covered by those statements. Answer (c) is incorrect because partial presentations are presentations that do not meet the minimum presentation guidelines of AT 301. Answer (d) is incorrect because financial forecasts present, to the best of the responsible party's knowledge and belief, an entity's expected financial position, results of operations, and changes in financial information.

134. (d) The requirement is to determine the statement that should be included in an accountant's report on a review of pro forma financial information. Answer (d) is correct because the report must include a reference to the financial statements from which the historical financial information is derived and a statement as to whether such financial statements were audited or reviewed.

135. (b) The requirement is to determine the reply that is **not** an objective of a CPA's examination of a client's MD&A. Answer (b) is correct because an examination of a client's MD&A does not directly address overall conformity with such rules and regulations. Answers (a), (c), and (d) are the three objectives of an MD&A examination agreement.

136. (c) The requirement is to identify an assertion embodied in MD&A. Answer (c) is correct because the attestation standards on MD&A indicate that consistency with the financial statements is an assertion—in addition, occurrence, completeness, and presentation and disclosure are embodied assertions. Answers (a), (b), and (d) are all incorrect because valuation, reliability, and rights and obligations are not considered to be assertions embodied in the MD&A.

137. (b) Answer (b) is correct because the MD&A review of an issuer (public) entity should be restricted to the use of specified parties. Answer (a) is incorrect because a review consists principally of applying analytical procedures, rather than also including search and verification procedures. Answer (c) is incorrect because a consideration of relevant portion of internal control is necessary to identify types of potential misstatements and to select the inquiries and analytical procedures. Answer (d) is incorrect because a review report ordinarily provides negative assurance, not a summary of findings.

138. (b) The requirement is to identify the standards under which Trust Services engagements are performed. Answer (b) is correct because the Statements on Standards for Attestation engagements address such engagements. More information on Trust Services engagements (WebTrust and SysTrust) is available on the AICPA's website—www.aicpa.org. Answers (a) and (c) are incorrect because such standards do not exist. Answer (d) is incorrect because Statements on Auditing Standards do not address Trust Services engagements.

139. (d) The requirement is to identify what the Web-Trust seal of assurance relates most directly to. Answer (d) is correct because the WebTrust seal is designed to provide assurance on website security, availability, processing integrity, online privacy and confidentiality. Answers (a), (b), and (c) are all incorrect since WebTrust isn't specially aimed at financial statements, health care facilities, or risk assurance procedures.

140. (b) The requirement is to determine the type of opinion or assurance most likely to be included in a CPA's report relating to WebTrust engagements. Answer (b) is correct because the WebTrust examination report provides an opinion on whether the site meets the Trust Services criteria for one or more of the Trust Services Principles. Answer (a) is incorrect because no opinion on being "hackproof" is issued. Answer (c) is incorrect because negative assurance is not provided. Answer (d) is incorrect because an agreed-upon procedures engagement, not an examination engagement results in a summary of findings.

141. (b) The requirement is to identify the type of engagement that considers security, availability, processing integrity, online privacy and/or confidentiality over any type of defined electronic system. Answer (b) is correct because SysTrust engagements consider any type of defined electronic system. Answer (a) is incorrect because an engagement to consider internal control over financial reporting does not directly address these attributes. Answer (c) is incorrect because there is no such engagement as a website Associate. Answer (d) is incorrect because WebTrust deals more directly with company websites.

142. (b) The requirement is to identify the most likely report when a client refuses to provide a written assertion in a Trust Services engagement. Answer (b) is correct because this represents a scope limitation, and client imposed scope limitations are most likely to result in a disclaimer of opinion. Answer (a) is incorrect because an adverse opinion is appropriate when a CPA believes that the information is so misstated as to be misleading. Answer (c) is incorrect because client imposed scope limitations generally result in disclaimers, not qualified opinions. Answer (d) is incorrect because an unmodified opinion is most likely not appropriate in such a circumstance.

143. (d) The requirement is to identify the item that is true about SOC 2 reports. Answer (d) is correct as such reports are meant for management of service organizations, user entities and certain other specified entities. Answer (a) is incorrect because it is SOC 1 reports that are meant primarily to assist financial statement auditors. Answer (b) is incorrect because the reports are not meant to be generally available. Answer (c) is incorrect because they relate more directly to the SysTrust principles than they do to internal control over financial reporting.

144. (c) Answer (c) is correct because a SOC 3 report is a general-use report. Answers (a) and (b) are incorrect because SOC 1 and SOC 2 reports are restricted-use reports. Answer (d) is incorrect because no SOC 4 report exists.

145. (a) The requirement is to identify the type of service organization control report most likely to result in a restricted use report on security, availability, processing integrity, confidentiality, and/or privacy. Answer (a) is correct as a SOC 2 report is restricted and on such content. Answers (b), (c) and (d) are all incorrect because no such reports exist. The AICPA has issued three service organizations control reports:

- SOC 1: Restricted use reports on controls at a service organization relevant to a user entity's internal control over financial reporting.
- SOC 2: Restricted use reports on controls at a service organization related to security, availability, processing integrity, confidentiality, and/or privacy.
- SOC 3: General use SysTrust reports related to security, availability, processing integrity, confidentiality, and/or privacy.

146. (c) The requirement is to identify the type of association **not** permitted under the compliance attestation standards. AT 601 does not allow the CPA to perform a review over compliance.

147. (b) The requirement is to identify the information provided in an agreed-upon procedures report on compliance with contractual requirements to pay royalties. Answer (b) is correct because agreed-upon procedures reports include a list of the procedures performed (or reference thereto) and findings. Answer (a) is incorrect because no such disclaimer of opinion is provided in an agreed-upon procedures report. Answer (c) is incorrect because no opinion is included in an agreed-upon procedures report. Answer (d) is incorrect because an agreed-upon procedures report includes a statement disclaiming an opinion on the sufficiency of procedures, not an acknowledgement of the sufficiency of the procedures. See AT 201 for guidance on agreed-upon procedures engagements.

148. (a) The requirement is to identify the statement that is included in a CPA's report on agreed-upon procedures on management's assertion about an entity's compliance with specified requirements. Answer (a) is correct because such an agreed-upon procedures report includes a statement of limitations on the use of the report because it is intended solely for the use of specified parties. See AT 601 for information that should be included in such an agreed-upon procedures report. Answer (b) is incorrect because no "opinion" is included. Answer (c) is incorrect because a summary of findings, not negative assurance is provided. Answer (d) is incorrect because the CPA makes no representation regarding the sufficiency of procedures.

149. (c) The requirement is to identify the correct statement concerning an examination report when management has properly disclosed an instance of material noncompliance. AT 601 states that the opinion should be qualified or adverse. Note that AT 601 requires the CPA's report to relate directly to the subject matter when the opinion is modified.

150. (b) The requirement is to determine an auditor's responsibility when auditing a not-for-profit entity that receives governmental financial assistance. Answer (b) is correct because AU-C 806 requires that the auditor assess whether management has identified laws and regulations that have a direct and material effect on the entity's financial statements; AU-C 806 also presents procedures to be followed in assessing such laws and regulations. Answer (a) is incorrect because such a separate report describing expected benefits and costs does not need to be issued. Answer (c) is incorrect because the CPA will not notify the governmental agency that the audit is not designed to provide assurance. Answer (d) is incorrect because the CPA does not express an opinion on the entity's continued eligibility for governmental financial assistance. AU-C 806 presents requirements relating to compliance auditing for governmental entities and recipients of governmental financial assistance.

151. (c) The requirement is to determine the focus of an auditor's attention in detecting misstatements resulting from violations of laws and regulations when auditing a not-for-profit organization that receives financial assistance from governmental agencies. Answer (c) is correct because the focus of such procedures should be on violations that have a direct and material effect on the amounts in the organization's financial statements (AU-C 806). Answers (a), (b), and (d) all represent a focus that is not as accurate as that provided in answer (c).

152. (b) The requirement is to determine the proper scope of a governmental audit. The General Accounting Office's *"Yellow Book"* suggests that in addition to financial statements, such an audit may include consideration of (1) program results, (2) compliance with laws and regulations, and (3) economy and efficiency.

153. (b) The requirement is to identify whether an auditor performing an audit in accordance with Government Auditing Standards (the *"Yellow Book"*) is required to report on noteworthy accomplishments of the program, the scope of the auditor's testing of internal controls, or both. Answer (b) is correct because the *"Yellow Book"* requires reporting only upon the scope of the auditor's testing of internal controls. Answers (a), (c), and (d) all include an incorrect combination of reporting replies.

154. (b) The requirement is to identify whether an auditor performing an audit in accordance with Government Auditing Standards (the *"Yellow Book"*) is required to report on recommendations for actions to improve operations, the scope of tests of compliance with laws and regulations, or both. Answer (b) is correct because the *"Yellow Book"* requires reporting upon the scope of the auditor's tests of compliance with laws and regulations. Answers (a), (c), and (d) all include an incorrect combination of reporting replies.

155. (a) The requirement is to identify the correct statement with respect to a financial statement audit conducted in accordance with Government Auditing Standards (the *"Yellow Book"*). Answer (a) is correct because the auditor issues a report on compliance with laws and internal control, and a report on the financial information. Answer (b) is incorrect because a financial statement audit does not address economy and efficiency in the manner suggested. Answer (c) is incorrect because recommendations for actions to correct problems and improve operations are not ordinarily included. Answer (d) is incorrect because a financial statement audit does not address whether programs are achieving the desired results.

156. (a) The requirement is to identify the correct statement with respect to a financial statement audit conducted in accordance with Government Auditing Standards (the *"Yellow Book"*). Answer (a) is correct because the auditor issues a report on compliance with laws and internal control, and a

report on the financial information. Answer (b) is incorrect because not all instances of abuse, waste and mismanagement are so reported. Answer (c) is incorrect because the views of officials are not reported. Answer (d) is incorrect because internal control activities designed to detect or prevent fraud are not reported to the inspector general.

157. (d) The requirement is to identify the circumstance in which an auditor is required to report a falsification of accounting records directly to a federal inspector general. Answer (d) is correct because under Government Auditing Standards a falsification of accounting records must ordinarily be communicated by the auditor to the auditee and, if the auditee fails to make appropriate disclosure, by the auditor to a federal inspector general. Answers (a), (b), and (c) all provide inaccurate descriptions of auditor reporting responsibility. See Government Auditing Standards (the *"Yellow Book"*) for information on reporting under Government Auditing Standards.

158. (a) The requirement is to identify a common aspect of various types of audits of recipients of federal financial assistance in accordance with federal audit regulations. Answer (a) is correct because audits of recipients of federal financial assistance include reports on (1) the financial statements, and (2) a separate or combined report on internal control and on compliance with laws and regulations. Answer (b) is incorrect because materiality levels are not ordinarily lower or always determined by the governmental entity. Answer (c) is incorrect because the auditor need not obtain such written management representations. Answer (d) is incorrect because requirements for reporting illegal acts may vary depending upon the type of audit being performed. AU-C 806 provides requirements related to auditing entities that have received governmental financial assistance. In addition, guidance is provided by Government Auditing Standards (GAS), also referred to as the *"Yellow Book,"* published by the Comptroller General of the United States.

159. (b) The requirement is to identify to whom an auditor most likely would be responsible for communicating significant deficiencies in the design of internal control. Answer (b) is correct because in audits under Government Auditing Standards, significant deficiencies in the design of internal control are communicated to legislative and regulatory bodies (AU-C 806). Answer (a) is incorrect because the Securities and Exchange Commission does not ordinarily receive information on such deficiencies. Answer (c) is incorrect because while a court-appointed creditors' committee might in some circumstances receive information on such deficiencies, this practice is not as frequent as is done under Government Auditing Standards. Answer (d) is incorrect because shareholders do not normally receive reports on significant deficiencies or material weaknesses (see AU-C 265).

160. (c) The requirement is to determine the opinion which an auditor should express in a report on compliance when s/he has detected material instances of noncompliance within the program. AU-C 806 defines these instances of material noncompliance as failures to follow requirements, or violations of regulations or grants which cause the auditor to conclude that the total of the misstatements resulting from these failures or violations is material to the financial statements. Therefore, answer (c) is correct because the auditor should issue a qualified or an adverse opinion. Answer (a) is incorrect because the auditor is required under Governmental Auditing Standards to provide reasonable assurance on the entity's compliance with the applicable laws and regulations. Answer (b) is incorrect because the auditor must disclose the instances of noncompliance. Answer (d) is incorrect because the auditor should not disclaim an opinion as a result of noncompliance.

161. (b) The requirement is to determine a documentation requirement that an auditor should follow when auditing in accordance with (also referred to as the "*Yellow Book*"). Answer (b) is correct because Government Auditing Standards require documentation of supervisory review before the report is issued.

162. (a) The requirement is to identify the statement that should be included in an auditor's report on an entity's compliance with laws and regulations when performing an audit in accordance with Government Auditing Standards. Answer (a) is correct because such compliance reports require a statement that management is responsible for compliance with laws, regulations, contracts, and grants. See AU-C 806 for this requirement and others.

163. (b) The requirement is to determine when an auditor reporting under would most likely be required to communicate management's misappropriation of assets directly to a federal inspector general. Answer (b) is correct because Government Auditing Standards requires that when a governing body fails to make a required report on such acts the auditors should communicate the matter to the external body specified in the law or regulation. Answer (a) is incorrect because such concealment will not necessarily lead to

communication to a federal inspector general. Answer (c) is incorrect because material misstatement does not necessarily lead to such communication. Answer (d) is incorrect because the expected duration of the scheme is not what leads to reporting to a federal inspector general.

164. (b) The requirement is to identify the auditor's proper measure of materiality for major federal financial assistance programs under the Single Audit Act. AU-C 806 requires that it be determined separately for each major program.

165. (b) The requirement is to identify the appropriate compliance report under the Single Audit Act when a CPA has detected noncompliance with requirements that have a material effect on that program. AU-C 806 states that under such circumstances the auditor should express a qualified or adverse opinion.

166. (c) The requirement is to identify the source of authoritative guidance for performing audits of a city that is subject to the requirements of the Uniform Single Audit Act of 1984. Answer (c) is correct because while the AICPA's generally accepted auditing standards must be followed to the extent they are pertinent, the General Accounting Office Government Auditing Standards must also be adhered to. The other replies all relate to standards not directly related to the Uniform Single Audit Act.

167. (c) The requirement is to identify the correct statement which would communicate weaknesses in internal control used in administering a federal financial assistance program when a CPA has examined the general purpose financial statements of a municipality. The AICPA Accounting and Audit Guide, *Audits of State and Local Governmental Units*, requires the communication of weaknesses that are material in relation to the federal financial assistance program.

Simulations

Task-Based Simulation 1

The audit of a nonpublic client, Park Publishing Co. for the year ended September 30, 20X2, is near completion. Your senior, Dave Moore, at Tyler & Tyler CPAs, has asked you to draft the audit report, considering the following:

- During fiscal year 20X2, Park changed its depreciation method. The engagement partner concurred with this change in accounting principle and its justification, and Moore wants it properly reflected in the auditors' report; the change is discussed in Note 7 to the financial statements.
- The 20X2 financial statements are affected by an uncertainty concerning a lawsuit over patent infringement, the outcome of which cannot presently be estimated. Moore has suggested the need for an emphasis-of-matter paragraph in the auditors' report related to this matter which is discussed in Note 4 to the financial statements.
- The financial statements for the year ended September 30, 20X1, are to be presented for comparative purposes. Wilson & Wilson previously audited these statements and expressed a standard unmodified opinion.

1. Identify the paragraphs in the Professional Standards that provide guidance regarding the periods included in the auditor's evaluation of consistency. First present the paragraph(s) for the actual requirement and then the related application and other explanatory material guidance.
2. Identify the paragraph in Professional Standards that provides an example report of an auditor's report with an emphasis-of-matter paragraph because of pending litigation.
3. Wilson & Wilson's audit report will not be reissued. Identify the paragraphs in the Professional Standards that provide the requirements as to what the auditor should include in an other-matter paragraph concerning the 20X1 audit of Wilson & Wilson.

Task-Based Simulation 2

Assume that items 1 through 8 are situations that Jones, CPA, has encountered during his audit of Welles Incorporated, a nonpublic company. List A represents the types of opinions the auditor ordinarily would issue and List B represents a portion of the needed report modifications—whether an additional paragraph will be included. For each situation, select one response from List A and one from List B. Select as the best answers for each item the action the auditor would normally take. The types of opinions in List A and the report modifications in List B may be selected once, more than once, or not at all.

Assume

- The auditor is independent.
- The auditor previously expressed an unmodified opinion on the prior year's financial statements.
- Only single-year (not comparative) statements are presented for the current year.
- The conditions for an unmodified opinion exist unless contradicted by the facts.
- The conditions stated in the items to be answered are material, unless otherwise indicated.
- Each item to be answered is independent of the others.
- No report modifications are to be made except in response to the factual situation.
- The auditor will not treat a situation as an "emphasis of a matter" in what remains an unmodified audit report unless it is one of those circumstances specifically illustrated in the Professional Standards as an example of a matter an auditor may wish to emphasize.

List A	List B
Types of opinions	**Report modifications**

A. Either an "except for" qualified opinion or an adverse opinion

B. Either a disclaimer of opinion or an "except for" qualified opinion

C. Either an adverse opinion or a disclaimer of opinion

D. An "except for" qualified opinion

E. An unmodified opinion

F. An adverse opinion

G. A disclaimer of opinion

H. Basis for modification paragraph.

I. Emphasis-of-matter paragraph.

J. Other-matter paragraph

K. No additional paragraph.

L. Describe the circumstances within the **opinion** paragraph

	Types of opinions (A–G)	Additional Paragraph (H–L)

1. Jones hired an actuary to assist in corroborating Welles' complex pension calculations concerning accrued pension liabilities that account for 35% of the client's total liabilities. The actuary's findings are reasonably close to Welles' calculations and support the financial statements.

2. Welles holds a note receivable consisting of principal and accrued interest payable in 20X4. The note's maker recently filed a voluntary bankruptcy petition, but Welles failed to reduce the recorded value of the note to its net realizable value, which is approximately 20% of the recorded amount.

3. Jones was engaged to audit a client's financial statements after the annual physical inventory count. The accounting records were not sufficiently reliable to enable him to become satisfied as to the year-end inventory balances.

4. Jones found an immaterial adjustment relating to inventory. Welles has refused to adjust the financial statements to reflect this immaterial item.

5. Welles' financial statements do not disclose certain long-term lease obligations. Jones determined that the omitted disclosures are required by FASB.

6. Jones decided not to take responsibility for the work of another CPA who audited a wholly owned subsidiary of Welles. The total assets and revenues of the subsidiary represent 27% and 28%, respectively, of the related consolidated totals.

7. Welles changed its method of accounting for the cost of inventories from FIFO to LIFO. Jones concurs with the change although it has a material effect on the comparability of the financial statements.

8. Due to losses and adverse key financial ratios, Jones has substantial doubt about Welles' ability to continue as a going concern for a reasonable period of time. The client has adequately disclosed its financial difficulties in a note to its financial statements. Also, Jones has ruled out the use of a disclaimer of opinion.

Task-Based Simulation 3

Contacting a Predecessor Auditor

You recently graduated from college and have worked with Tice & Co. CPAs for several months. A partner in Tice has indicated that the firm has a potential nonpublic new audit client and that he would like to research the matters that subject to an auditor's inquiry of a predecessor auditor prior to accepting a new engagement.

Selections

A. AU-C
B. PCAOB
C. AT
D. AR
E. ET
F. BL
G. CS
H. QC

(A) (B) (C) (D) (E) (F) (G) (H)

1. Which title of the Professional Standards addresses this issue and will be helpful in responding to the partner?

    ○ ○ ○ ○ ○ ○ ○ ○

2. Enter the exact section and paragraph with the appropriate guidance.

Task-Based Simulation 4

Standard Report Elements

The senior on your job has pointed out to you that the CPA firm always signs the audit report both for nonpublic companies with its signature and its location (Yuma, Arizona) and that she suggests that she thinks it isn't necessary to provide the location.

1. Identify the title, section, and paragraph of the auditing standards that provide the basic elements that must be included in the auditor's standard report.

2. Is she correct or incorrect concerning inclusion of the location?

    Yes   No

    ○   ○

Task-Based Simulation 5

Audit Report Details		
	Authoritative Literature	Help

On September 30, 20X2, White & Co. CPAs was engaged to audit the consolidated financial statements of National Motors Inc. for the year ended December 31, 20X2. The consolidated financial statements of National had not been audited the prior year. National's inadequate inventory records precluded White from forming an opinion as to the proper application of generally accepted accounting principles to inventory balances on January 1, 20X2. Therefore, White decided not to express an opinion on the results of operations for the year ended December 31, 20X2. National decided not to present comparative financial statements.

Rapid Parts Company, a consolidated subsidiary of National, was audited for the year ended December 31, 20X2, by Green & Co. CPAs. Green completed its audit procedures on February 28, 20X3, and submitted an unmodified opinion on Rapid's financial statements on March 7, 20X3. Rapid's statements reflect total assets and revenues constituting $700,000 and $2,000,000, respectively, of the consolidated totals of National. White decided not to assume responsibility for the work of Green. Green's report on Rapid does not accompany National's consolidated statements.

The following lists potential effects on White's audit report.

Effect on the Audit Report

A. Disclaim on balance sheet, income statement and statement of cash flows.
B. Disclaim only on results of operations.
C. Qualified audit opinion on results of operations.
D. Modification of report to set forth a division of responsibility for the audit.
E. Issuance of two separate reports.
F. Date the report March 28, 20X3.
G. Date the report April 4, 20X3.
H. Management of National Motors.
I. National Motors' Board of Directors.
J. Managements of both National Motors and Rapid Parts.
K. White & Co. only.
L. White & Co. and Green & Co.

For each circumstance described below select the most appropriate statement that reflects the effect or details of the audit report.

	(A) (B) (C) (D) (E) (F) (G) (H) (I) (J) (K) (L)
1. National's inadequate inventory records precluded White from forming an opinion as to the proper application of generally accepted accounting principles to inventory balances on January 1, 20X2.	O O O O O O O O O O O O
2. Rapid Parts Company, a consolidated subsidiary of National, was audited for the year ended December 31, 20X2, by Green & Co. CPAs.	O O O O O O O O O O O O
3. White has completed its audit procedures on March 28, 20X3, and planned to submit its auditor's report to National on April 4, 20X3.	O O O O O O O O O O O O
4. The most appropriate addressee of the audit report.	O O O O O O O O O O O O
5. National's audit report should be signed by	O O O O O O O O O O O O

Simulation Solutions

Task-Based Simulation 1

1. The appropriate guidance regarding reporting on the periods covered is AU-C 708.06 with interpretative guidance at AU-C 708.A2–.A3.
2. The appropriate guidance regarding emphasis of a matter is found in AU-C 706.A13.
3. The appropriate guidance regarding reporting on comparative financial statements is found in AU-C 700.54.

Task-Based Simulation 2

1. **(E, K)** When an auditor hires a specialist to assist in corroborating a client estimate (here complex pension calculations), and that specialist's findings are reasonably close to those of the client, no report modification is required or permitted. Since the specialist's findings support the financial statements in this situation, a standard unmodified audit report is appropriate. When major unresolved differences between the findings of management and the specialist exist, report modification is appropriate.
2. **(A, I)** When the client's financial statements materially depart from generally accepted accounting principles, either a qualified opinion or an adverse opinion is appropriate, depending on the magnitude of the misstatement. The value of the client's note receivable has been impaired and therefore the client should write the note receivable down to its net realizable value. The auditor will consider the pervasiveness of the misstatement to determine whether to issue a qualified opinion or an adverse opinion on the basis of the materiality of the misstatement. A basis for modification paragraph will be included.
3. **(B, H)** A situation where the auditor is unable to obtain sufficient appropriate audit evidence is referred to as a scope limitation. A scope limitation may require the auditor to either qualify his or her opinion or to disclaim an opinion altogether. Since the auditor was unable to observe the inventory count or to obtain evidence through alternative procedures, the auditor will have to decide whether to issue a qualified opinion or a disclaimer of opinion. The decision will be based on the auditor's judgment as to the nature and magnitude of the potential effects of the matters in question and by their significance to the financial statements. A basis for modification paragraph will be added to the report.
4. **(E, K)** An auditor need not modify a report for an immaterial item that the client declines to reflect.
5. **(A, I)** Since the client's financial statements omitted required disclosures on certain long-term lease obligations, they are not prepared in accordance with generally accepted accounting principles. As a result, the auditor should express either a qualified opinion or an adverse opinion. The decision to express either a qualified or adverse opinion is based on the pervasiveness of the misstatement. The audit report, for either opinion, will include a basis for modification paragraph to describe the substantive reasons for the modification.
6. **(E, K)** When a principal auditor decides not to take responsibility for the work of another auditor, the principal auditor should make reference to the work of the other auditor in the audit report, but no additional paragraph is added to the report. The opinion remains unmodified.
7. **(E, H)** When an auditor agrees with a change in accounting principles, a lack of consistency results in an unmodified opinion with an emphasis-of-matter paragraph.
8. **(E, H)** The auditor has substantial doubt about the client's ability to remain a going concern for a reasonable period of time. The audit report should emphasize this concern to the financial statement users. As a result, the auditor's report will include an unmodified opinion with an emphasis-of-matter paragraph following the opinion paragraph.

Task-Based Simulation 3

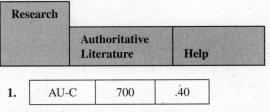

(A) (B) (C) (D) (E) (F) (G) (H)

1. Which section of the Professional Standards addresses this issue and will be helpful in responding to the partner?

● ○ ○ ○ ○ ○ ○ ○

2. Enter the exact section and paragraph with the appropriate guidance.

| 210 | A31 |

Note that the question asks for "the matters that subject to an auditor's inquiry of a predecessor auditor." More general guidance is provided in AU-C 210.11.

Task-Based Simulation 4

1. | AU-C | 700 | .40 |

2. She is not correct; including the location is required.

Task-Based Simulation 5

| Audit Report Details | | |
| Authoritative Literature | Help | |

(A) (B) (C) (D) (E) (F) (G) (I) (J) (K) (L)

1. National's inadequate inventory records precluded White from forming an opinion as to the proper application of generally accepted accounting principles to inventory balances on January 1, 20X2.

○ ● ○ ○ ○ ○ ○ ○ ○ ○ ○

2. Rapid Parts Company, a consolidated subsidiary of National, was audited for the year ended December 31, 20X2, by Green & Co. CPAs.

○ ○ ○ ● ○ ○ ○ ○ ○ ○ ○

3. White has completed its audit procedures on March 28, 20X3, and planned to submit its auditor's report to National on April 4, 20X3.

○ ○ ○ ○ ○ ● ○ ○ ○ ○ ○

4. The most appropriate addressee of the audit report.

○ ○ ○ ○ ○ ○ ○ ● ○ ○ ○

5. National's audit report should be signed by

○ ○ ○ ○ ○ ○ ○ ○ ○ ● ○

Explanations

1. **(B)** The lack of evidence about the beginning inventory affects only the results of operations (the income statement).

2. **(D)** The involvement of the other audit firm results in a division of responsibility because White does not want to take responsibility for the other auditor's work.

3. **(F)** The report should be dated as of the date that all substantive audit evidence has been obtained.

4. **(I)** Ordinarily the report should be addressed to the board of directors, audit committee, or the company itself, not management.

5. **(K)** Only White & Co. will sign the audit report.

Module 6: Accounting and Review Services

Overview

This module presents guidance on engagements performed under the AICPA Statements on Standards for Accounting and Review Services (SSARS—codified with an *AR* prefix). The SSARS apply to unaudited financial statements or other unaudited financial information of a nonpublic entity. Currently the SSARS outline two forms of accountant association with financial statements—compilations and reviews. A compilation is a service in which the accountant assists in the preparation of financial statements; compilation reports provide no assurance. A review is an attest service in which the accountants (1) perform analytical procedures, (2) make inquiries of management and others, and (3) obtain representations from management relating to the financial statements. Review reports include limited (negative) assurance.

Determining the appropriate standards for reviews may be confusing. Make certain that you understand the appropriate standards for reviews performed under the SAS and SSARS, as follows:

- SAS Reviews: These are for interim (ordinarily quarterly) financial statements of either public or nonpublic companies. Public company ("issuer") interim reviews are required by the SEC. Nonpublic company ("nonissuer") interim reviews are ordinarily not required, but are performed for companies that select the service. The public company and nonpublic company standards are very similar and apply to interim reviews of companies that have an annual audit (AU-C 930). The Reporting module presents guidance on these reviews.
- SSARS Reviews: These reviews are only for nonpublic companies. Most frequently they are performed on annual financial statements of companies that choose not to have an audit, although they may also be performed on interim financial statements. This module presents guidance on SSARS (AR) reviews.

The professional standards underlying compilations and reviews have far less quantity than those for audits. Yet, this topic is heavily tested on every exam. The limited quantity of guidance makes this a particularly "manageable" area for candidates, although the need for the exam to include enough questions on this topic to meet the percentages included on the content specification outline requires that it be examined in depth. You might expect a number of multiple-choice questions related to this area, but also, frequently, a research oriented simulation question which requires you to perform research finding an appropriate compilation or review report, or appropriate procedures in a particular situation.

The following sections of Statements on Standards for Accounting and Review Services pertain to this module:

AR 60	Framework for Performing and Reporting on Compilation and Review Engagements
80	Compilation of Financial Statements
90	Review of Financial Statements
110	Compilation of Specified Elements, Accounts or Items of a Financial Statement
120	Compilation of Pro Forma Financial Information
200	Reporting on Comparative Financial Statements
300	Compilation Reports on Financial Statements Included in Certain Prescribed Forms
400	Communications between Predecessor and Successor Accountants
500	Reporting on Compiled Financial Statements
600	Reporting on Personal Financial Statements Included in Written Personal Financial Plans

Virtually all of the information in the ***Overall Objectives and Approach*** section at the beginning of each AR outline is essential. In addition, while material from all of the outlines is examined heavily, make absolutely certain you know virtually all the information presented in the outlines of AR 60, 80, and 90. The remaining sections (110 +) are also important, but ordinarily slightly less thoroughly examined.

The next section of this outline provides you with an introductory summary of some of the very most important points followed by the AR outlines. It can serve to provide you with both introductory and final study information. But you must be very familiar with the guidance in the AR outlines.

FINANCIAL STATEMENT COMPILATIONS

A. Nature of Compilations

1. A compilation involves assisting management in presenting financial information in the form of financial statements. To perform a compilation Statements on Standards for Accounting and Review Services require the accountants to have knowledge of the accounting principles and practices used within the client's industry and a general understanding of the client's business transactions and accounting records.

   a. At a minimum, the accountants must *read* the compiled statements for appropriate format and obvious material misstatement. CPAs performing a compilation must not accept patently unreasonable information.

      (1) If the client's information appears to be incorrect, incomplete, or otherwise unsatisfactory, the CPAs should insist upon revised information. If the client refuses to provide revised information, the CPAs should withdraw from the engagement.

      (2) Beyond these basic requirements, CPAs have no responsibility to perform any investigative procedures to substantiate the client's representations.

   b. Proper CPA reporting on compiled statements is dependent upon whether the financial statements are expected to be used by a third party other than management

      (1) When no such third-party use is expected, an accountant may either (1) issue a compilation report or (2) not issue a compilation report, but document the understanding with the client through use of an engagement letter.

         (a) When not issuing a compilation report, the engagement letter, signed by management, must make clear the services performed and the limitations on the use of the financial statements. A phrase such as "Restricted for Management's Use Only" should be included on each page of the financial statements.

      (2) When the financial statements are to be used by a third party (or reasonably might be expected to be used by a third party) a compilation report must be issued by the CPA. This report disclaims an opinion or any other form of assurance on the financial statements.

2. AR 60 states that a compilation is an attest service, but not an assurance service.

> **NOTE:** Although the professional standards require independence for attest services, an exception to the requirement exists for compilations—a nonindependent CPA may perform a compilation as long as the lack of independence is disclosed in the CPA's report.

B. Planning Compilations

1. The accountant should establish an understanding with management re the compilation and should document the understanding through a written communication with management.

2. The CPAs may, with the permission of management or those charged with governance, decide to make inquiries of the predecessor accountants before accepting a compilation (or review) engagement. These inquiries include questions regarding the integrity of management, disagreements over accounting principles, the willingness of management to provide or to revise information, and the reasons for the change in accountants. The decision of whether to contact the predecessor accountants is left to the judgment of the successor CPAs. Ordinarily the predecessor is expected to respond fully to inquiries. (AR 400 provides guidance on communicating with the predecessor.)

3. A CPA may accept a compilation (or review) engagement in an industry s/he is unfamiliar with if s/he is able to obtain the required level of knowledge before compiling (reviewing) the financial statements.

C. Compilation Procedures

1. Sections A and B of the outline of AR 80 provide guidance on requirements to establish an understanding with the client (note that a written engagement letter should be obtained) and the compilation performance requirements.
2. The accountant is not required to perform other procedures such as making inquiries or performing procedures to verify information supplied by the entity. However, whenever an accountant becomes aware of information that is incorrect, incomplete, or otherwise unsatisfactory, the accountant should obtain additional or revised information. If the entity refuses to provide (or correct) such information, the accountant should withdraw from the compilation. Finally, independence is not required when performing a compilation.

D. Overall Compilation Reporting Issues

1. Standard Report

We have compiled the accompanying balance sheet of XYZ Company as of December 31, 20XX, and the related statements of income, retained earnings, and cash flows for the year then ended. We have not audited or reviewed the accompanying financial statements and, accordingly, do not express an opinion or any assurance about whether the financial statements are in accordance with accounting principles generally accepted in the United States of America.

Management is responsible for the preparation and fair presentation of the financial statements in accordance with accounting principles generally accepted in the United States of America and for designing, implementing, and maintaining internal control relevant to the preparation and fair presentation of the financial statements.

Our responsibility is to conduct the compilation in accordance with Statements on Standards for Accounting and Review Services issued by the American Institute of Certified Public Accountants. The objective of a compilation is to assist management in presenting financial information in the form of financial statements without undertaking to obtain any assurance that there are no material modifications that should be made to the financial statements.

2. Related issues

a. Each page of the unaudited financial statements should be marked "See Accountants' Compilation Report."
b. The compilation report should be dated as of the completion of the compilation.
c. A compilation report may be issued on one or more individual financial statements, without compiling a complete set of statements.
d. Financial statements may be compiled on a special purpose framework (i.e., comprehensive basis of accounting) *other than* generally accepted accounting principles. In this case, the basis of accounting used must be disclosed either in the statements or in the accountants' report.

3. Other compilation reporting circumstances

Circumstance	Resolution
Departures from GAAP	A departure from generally accepted accounting principles requires the accountants to discuss the departure in a separate paragraph in the compilation report.
Lack of consistent application of GAAP, substantial doubt about ability to remain a going concern properly disclosed in financial statements	Compilation report not required to be altered.
Lack of consistent application of GAAP, substantial doubt about ability to remain a going concern **not** properly disclosed in financial statements	Modify the compilation report for a departure from generally accepted accounting principles.

Circumstance	Resolution
Compilations of information that omits substantially all disclosures (e.g., note disclosures omitted)	This is permissible. In such situations the accountants should add the following last paragraph to their report: • Management has elected to omit substantially all of the disclosures (and the statement of cash flows) required by generally accepted accounting principles. If the omitted disclosures were included in the financial statements, they might influence the user's conclusions about the company's financial position, results of operations, and cash flows. Accordingly, these financial statements are not designed for those who are not informed about such matters. The financial statements should also indicate "Selected Information—Substantially All Disclosures Required by Generally Accepted Accounting Principles Are Not Included."
Compilations when the CPAs are not independent	Independence is not required. The following may be added to the compilation report: • We are not independent with respect to XYZ Company. In addition the CPAs may also provide reason(s) for the lack of independence (e.g., a member of the audit team had a direct financial interest in XYZ Company).

FINANCIAL STATEMENT REVIEWS

A. Nature of Reviews

1. A review is a service, the objective of which is to obtain limited assurance (also referred to as negative assurance) that there are no material modifications that should be made to the financial statements in order for the statements to be in conformity with the applicable financial reporting framework.

   a. In a review engagement, the accountant should accumulate review evidence to obtain a limited level of assurance.

2. A review engagement is an assurance engagement as well as an attest engagement.

B. Planning Reviews

1. The CPAs may decide to make inquiries of the predecessor accountants before accepting a compilation or review engagement. These inquiries include questions regarding the integrity of management, disagreements over accounting principles, the willingness of management to provide or to revise information, and the reasons for the change in accountants. The decision of whether to contact the predecessor accountants is left to the judgment of the successor CPAs. However, if inquiries are made with the client's consent, the predecessor accountants are generally required to respond.

2. CPAs must prepare an engagement letter clearly specifying the objectives of the review engagement, management's responsibilities, the accountant's responsibilities, and limitations of the engagement.

C. Review Procedures

1. Sections A and B of the outline of AR 90 provide guidance on requirements to establish an understanding with the client (as is the case with compilations, a written engagement letter should be obtained) and the review performance requirements. Particularly important points include

   a. Overall, the procedures should be sufficient to provide a reasonable basis for obtaining limited assurance that there are no material modifications needed.

   b. As is the case with compilations, the accountant must obtain an understanding of the industry and knowledge of the client (the business itself and accounting principles followed).

   c. Know that the procedures involve primarily analytical procedures, inquiries, and obtaining written representations from management. The inquiries are primarily of management and others within the company and ordinarily do not include inquiries of third parties (e.g., lawyers, confirmations of receivables). The accountant investigates differences from expectations developed when performing analytical procedures.

2. Unexpected results obtained through the use of analytical procedures are followed up by inquiries to management and certain other procedures.

   a. While a review ordinarily does not require accountants to corroborate management's responses with other evidence, they should consider the consistency of management responses in light of the results of other review procedures and their knowledge of the client's business and internal control.

   b. Additional procedures should be performed if the accountants become aware that information may be incorrect, incomplete, or otherwise unsatisfactory. The accountants should perform these procedures to the extent considered necessary to provide limited assurance that there are no material modifications that should be made to the statements.

      (1) For example, if review procedures lead an accountant to question whether a significant sales transaction is recorded in conformity with generally accepted accounting principles, it may become necessary to discuss the terms of the transaction with both senior marketing and accounting personnel and to read the sales contract.

3. Summary of review procedures

Analytical procedures	Inquiries of management members with responsibility for financial and accounting matters about
• Develop *expectations* by identifying and using plausible relationships that are reasonably expected to exist. • Compare recorded amounts or ratios developed from recorded amounts to expectations. • Compare the consistency of management's responses in light of results of other review procedures and knowledge of business and industry. **Obtain written representations from management and perform other procedures such as** • Inquire as to actions taken at shareholder, board of director, and other committees of board of directors. • Read financial statements. • Obtain reports from other accountants, if any, that have reviewed significant components.	• Whether financial statements are prepared in conformity with GAAP. • Whether accounting principles, practices, and methods are applied. • Any unusual or complex situations that might affect the financial statements. • Significant transactions taking place near the end of the period. • Status of uncorrected misstatements identified in a previous engagement. • Questions that have arisen in applying review procedures. • Subsequent events. • Knowledge of potentially material fraud or suspected fraud. • Significant journal entries and other adjustments. • Communications from regulatory agencies.

4. Other procedures performed in a review include reading available minutes of stockholder and director meetings, reading the interim financial information, and obtaining reports from other accountants who have reviewed significant components of the company. Evidence must also be obtained showing that the interim financial information agrees or reconciles with the accounting records.

5. A review does *not* contemplate (a) obtaining an understanding of the entity's internal control, (b) assessing fraud risk, (c) tests of accounting records by obtaining sufficient appropriate audit evidence through inspection, observation, confirmation, (d) the examination of source documents (for example, cancelled checks or bank images); or (e) other procedures ordinarily performed in an audit.

6. A representation letter signed by management should be dated the date of the review report and should include management's acknowledgement of its

   • Responsibility for the financial statements' conformity with generally accepted accounting principles and its belief that it has met this responsibility.

   • Responsibility to prevent and detect fraud, as well as to divulge any knowledge that it has of any actual or suspected fraud that is material.

   • Responsibility to respond fully and truthfully to all inquiries and to provide complete information, including that on subsequent events.

D. Overall Review Reporting Issues

1. Standard review report

   We have reviewed the accompanying balance sheet of XYZ Company as of December 31, 20XX, and the related statements of income, retained earnings, and cash flows for the year then ended. A review includes primarily applying analytical procedures to management's financial data and making inquiries of company management. A review is substantially less in scope than an audit, the objective of which is the expression of an opinion regarding the financial statements as a whole. Accordingly, we do not express such an opinion.

Management is responsible for the preparation and fair presentation of the financial statements in accordance with accounting principles generally accepted in the United States of America and for designing, implementing, and maintaining internal control relevant to the preparation and fair presentation of the financial statements.

Our responsibility is to conduct the review in accordance with Statements on Standards for Accounting and Review Services issued by the American Institute of Certified Public Accountants. Those standards require us to perform procedures to obtain limited assurance that there are no material modifications that should be made to the financial statements. We believe that the results of our procedures provide a reasonable basis for our report.

Based on our review, we are not aware of any material modifications that should be made to the accompanying financial statements in order for them to be in conformity with accounting principles generally accepted in the United States of America.

2. Departures from GAAP. Departures from GAAP, when the accountant concludes that modification of the standard report is appropriate, result in modification of the fourth paragraph and inclusion of an explanatory paragraph; for example

    With the exception of the matter described in the following paragraph, we are not aware of any material modifications....

    As disclosed in Note 6 to the financial statements, generally accepted accounting principles require that land be stated at cost. Management has informed us that the Company has stated its land at appraised value and that, if generally accepted accounting principles had been followed, the land account and stockholders' equity would have been decreased by $500,000.

    Notice that the report is neither "qualified" nor "adverse" in form as would be the case with an audit report in which a departure from GAAP exists. Audit reports, not review reports, result in an opinion, be it unmodified, qualified or adverse. Also, if the accountant believes that modification of the report is not adequate to indicate the deficiencies in the financial statements, the accountant should withdraw from the review engagement and provide no further services with respect to those financial statements.

3. As is the case for compilation reports, review reports are not required to be altered in situations involving a lack of consistent application of generally accepted accounting principles or the existence of major uncertainties (including going-concern uncertainties) that have been properly reported in the financial statements. However, when that information is not properly presented or disclosed in the financial statements, the financial statements contain a departure from generally accepted accounting principles, and the review report should be appropriately modified.

4. Other issues

    a. Because reviews are attest services, an accountant must be independent to perform a review.
    b. Each page of the financial statements should include a reference such as "See Accountant's Review Report."
    c. If the client restricts the scope of review procedures or refuses to provide an accountant with a representation letter, the review is incomplete and no review report may be issued.
    d. When current year financial statements have been reviewed and prior year financial statements were audited, an accountant may either reissue the audit report and issue a review report, *or* may refer to the audit in the review report. In referring to the audit in the review report, an accountant should indicate that the statements were audited, the date of the previous opinion, reasons for any departures from an unqualified form, and that no auditing procedures were performed after the date of the previous report. (When the current year financial statements have been compiled, the same procedures are followed.)
    e. When the current year financial statements have been audited and prior year financial statements were reviewed the audit report should include a statement indicating the type of service performed, the date of the report, a description of any material modifications noted in the report, and a statement that the service was less in scope than an audit and does not provide a basis for the expression of an opinion on the financial statements. (When prior year financial statements have been compiled, the same procedures are followed.)

    f. An audit engagement may be changed to a review engagement (or a review to a compilation) if the reason for the client's request is considered reasonable. In such a situation, this change is not referred to in the report issued.

5. Other communications.

    a. As with annual financial statement audits, the CPAs should communicate to the audit committee the information about significant adjustments found during the review and the acceptability and quality of significant accounting policies and estimates. The audit committee should also be informed about any disagreements with management over accounting principles or review procedures, or any other difficulties encountered in performing the review. These communication responsibilities with respect to an audit were described in detail in the internal control module.

    b. The CPAs should make sure that the audit committee is informed about any instances of fraud or illegal acts that come to their attention, as well as any significant deficiencies and material weaknesses related to the preparation of interim financial statements.

The outlines of the SSARS follow.

STATEMENTS ON STANDARDS FOR ACCOUNTING AND REVIEW SERVICES

The following outlines emphasize the standards as represented by the *Statements on Standards for Accounting and Review Services* (SSARS) Numerous questions related to the SSARS appear on a typical exam. The SSARS have been codified as follows:

Section	Title
AR 60	Framework for Performing and Reporting on Compilation and Review Engagements
AR 80	Compilation of Financial Statements
AR 90	Review of Financial Statements
AR 110	Compilation of Specified Elements, Accounts or Items of a Financial Statement
AR 120	Compilation of Pro Forma Financial Information
AR 200	Reporting on Comparative Financial Statements
AR 300	Compilation Reports on Financial Statements Included in Certain Prescribed Forms
AR 400	Communications between Predecessor and Successor Accountants
AR 500	Reporting on Compiled Financial Statements
AR 600	Reporting on Personal Financial Statements Included in Written Personal Financial Plans

AR 60, 80 and 90 Compilation and Review Engagements

Overall Objectives and Approach—These sections present guidance on appropriate procedures and reporting for **compilation** and **review** engagements of *nonissuer* financial statements. In general terms, a *nonissuer* is one whose securities are *not* registered with the Securities and Exchange Commission—that is, a nonpublic company. AICPA pronouncements apply to *nonissuers* while PCAOB pronouncements apply to *issuers*.

    For nonissuers, in addition to this section (and other AR sections), AU-C 930 provides guidance for reviews. In each circumstance either AU-C 930 *or* the ARs apply. AU-C 930 applies for interim financial information of nonissuers if the following conditions are met:

- Entity's latest annual financial statements have been audited by the accountant or a predecessor;
- Accountant has been engaged to audit the entity's current year financial statements; and
- Client prepares interim financial information in accordance with the same financial reporting framework as that used for annual financial statements.
- In addition, if the interim information involved is condensed

    • It must comply with appropriate accounting standards

- It must include a note that condensed information should be read in conjunction with latest audited annual financial statements
- The audited annual financial statements should accompany it, or be readily available

If the above requirements are not met, AR 100 (and other AR sections) apply.

Important to the section is the concept of "**submitting financial statements,**" defined as presenting to a client or third parties financial statements that the accountant has prepared either manually or through the use of computer software. A CPA should not submit unaudited financial statements of a nonissuer unless he or she, at a minimum, performs a compilation. While performing a compilation is the minimum service, issuance of a compilation report is only required when third-party reliance upon the compiled financial statements is reasonably expected.

Although performance of a compilation is the minimum requirement for submitting financial statements, services such as the following do **not** result in submission and accordingly may be performed without meeting the requirements included in this section.

- Simply reading or typing client-prepared financial statements
- Preparing a working trial balance
- Proposing adjusting or correcting entries
- Providing a client with financial statement format that does not include amounts

A CPA should not consent to the use of his/her name in a document containing unaudited financial statements unless he or she has compiled or reviewed the financial statements, or the financial statements are accompanied by an indication that the accountant has not compiled or reviewed the financial statements and assumes no responsibility for them (e.g., "The accompanying [list the financial statements] were not audited, reviewed, or compiled by us and, accordingly, we do not express an opinion or any other form of assurance on them.") The outline is organized as follows:

- Framework for Performing and Reporting on Compilation and Review Engagements (AR 60)
- Compilation of Financial Statements (AR 80)
- Review of Financial Statements (AR 90)

AR 60 Framework for Performing and Reporting on Compilation and Review Engagements

A. Selected relevant definitions

1. **Assurance engagement.** An engagement in which an accountant expresses a conclusion designed to enhance the degree of confidence of third parties and management about the outcome of an evaluation or measurement of the financial statements (subject matter) against the applicable financial reporting framework (criteria).

> **NOTE:** There must always be subject matter and an applicable financial reporting framework in an assurance or attest engagement.

2. **Attest engagement.** An engagement that requires independence—as independence is defined by the AICPA *Professional Standards*.

> **NOTE:** Independence is defined in ET 100.06 as requiring both independence of mind and independence in appearance.

3. **Financial reporting framework.** A set of criteria used to determine measurement, recognition, presentation, and disclosure of all material items appearing in the financial statements.

   a. **Applicable financial reporting framework**. The financial reporting framework adopted by management and, where appropriate, those charged with governance. (Most frequently this is either GAAP or IFRS—International Financial Reporting Standards.)

   b. **Other comprehensive basis of accounting (OCBOA).** A definite set of criteria, other than GAAP or IFRS, having substantial support underlying the preparation of financial statements prepared pursuant to that basis. Examples include tax and cash basis accounting.

4. **Nonissuer**. In general, nonpublic companies. That is, companies not required to register securities or file reports with the SEC.
5. **Review evidence.** The information used by the accountant to provide a reasonable basis for the obtaining of limited assurance.
6. **Submission of financial statements.** Presenting to management financial statements that the accountant has prepared.

B. Objectives and overall guidance on compilation and review engagements

1. Compilations

   a. Objective—To assist management in presenting financial information in the form of financial statements, information that is the representation of management (owners) without undertaking to obtain any assurance that there are no material modifications that should be made to the financial statements in order for the statements to be in conformity with the applicable financial reporting framework

      (1) The standard states that, although a compilation is not an assurance engagement, it is an attest engagement.

   b. A compilation differs from a review or an audit as follows:

      (1) Review—It does not contemplate performing inquiry, analytical procedures, or other procedures performed in a review.
      (2) Audit—It does not contemplate obtaining an understanding of internal control, assessing fraud risk, tests of accounting records by obtaining sufficient appropriate audit evidence, or other procedure ordinarily performed in an audit.

2. Reviews

   a. Objective of a review—Obtain limited assurance that there are no material modifications that should be made to the financial statements in order for the statements to be in conformity with the applicable financial reporting framework

      (1) In a review the accountant should accumulate review evidence to obtain a limited level of assurance.
      (2) A review engagement is an assurance engagement as well as an attest engagement.

   b. A review differs from an audit in that it does not contemplate obtaining an understanding of internal control, assessing fraud risk, tests of accounting records by obtaining sufficient appropriate audit evidence, or other procedure ordinarily performed in an audit.

      (1) Accordingly, a review only provides limited assurance that there are no material modifications needed.

   c. Materiality considerations for a review engagement are similar to those of an audit.

3. Much like the auditing standards, the SSARS use two categories of professional requirements identified by specific terms to describe the degree of responsibility they impose on accountants:

   a. **Unconditional requirements.** The accountant is required to comply with an unconditional requirement in all cases in which the circumstances exist to which the unconditional requirement applies. SSARS use the words *must* or *is required* to indicate an unconditional requirement.
   b. **Presumptively mandatory requirements.** The accountant is also required to comply with a presumptively mandatory requirement in all cases in which the circumstances exist to which the presumptively mandatory requirement applies; however, in rare circumstances, the accountant may depart from a presumptively mandatory requirement provided that the accountant documents his or her justification for the departure and how the alternative procedures performed in the circumstances were sufficient to achieve the objectives of the presumptively mandatory requirement. SSARS use the word *should* to indicate a presumptively mandatory requirement.
   c. In addition to (a) and (b) above, if a SSARS states that an accountant "should consider" a procedure, the consideration of the procedure is presumptively required, whereas carrying out the procedure is not.

4. Application guidance is defined as the text within a SSARS (excluding appendices and interpretations) that may provide *further explanation and guidance* on professional requirements *or* identify and describe *other procedures* or actions relating to the accountant's activities.

    a. *Further explanation and guidance.* It is descriptive, not imperative (required)—such guidance explains the objective of the requirements, explains why the accountant might consider procedure and additional information to consider in exercising professional judgment.

    b. *Other procedures.* Not intended to impose a professional requirement. Procedures or actions require the accountant's attention and understanding; how and whether accountant carries out such procedures depends upon exercise of professional judgment. The words *may, might,* and *could* are used to describe.

5. If an accountant is not in the practice of public accounting, the issuance of a written communication or report under SSARS would be inappropriate.

C. Hierarchy of compilation and review standards and guidance

1. Levels (In the event of a conflict between levels, the lower numbered level prevails)

    a. Level 1: Compilation and Review Standards (SSARS).

    b. Level 2: Interpretative publications (compilation and review interpretations of the SSARS, appendixes to the SSARS, compilation and review guidance included in AICPA Audit and Accounting Guides, and AICPA Statements of Positions).

    c. Level 3: Other compilation and review publications (e.g., other AICPA accounting and review publications, AICPA annual compilation and review alert, other articles and related programs).

2. AICPA members performing compilations and reviews are governed by the AICPA Code of Professional Conduct and Statements of Quality Control Standards.

D. Elements of a compilation or review engagement

1. A three-party relationship involving the (1) responsible party (management), (2) an accountant, and (3) intended users

    a. Responsible party—Management is responsible for the financial statements.

    b. Accountant—Should possess a level of knowledge of the accounting principles and practices of the industry in which the entity operates that will enable him/her to compile or review financial statements that are appropriate in form for an entity operating in that industry

        (1) In some cases this requirement can be satisfied by the accountant using the work of experts or specialists.

    c. Intended users—Persons who understand the limitations of the compilation or review and of financial statements; the accountant has no responsibility to identify the intended users

        (1) In some cases intended users may impose additional procedures or requirements for a specific purpose—an accountant may comply as long as s/he adheres to the professional standards.

        (2) In some cases, management and the intended users may be the same.

2. An applicable financial reporting framework (e.g., GAAP or International Financial Reporting Standards)

3. Financial statement or financial information

    a. An accountant may compile or review a complete set of financial statements, an individual financial statement (e.g., a balance sheet only) for an annual period or for a shorter or longer period, depending on management's needs.

4. Evidence

    a. Compilations—No responsibility to obtain evidence about accuracy or completeness of financial statement (this is why no assurance is provided)

    b. Reviews—Procedures (analytical procedures and inquiries) designed to accumulate review evidence that will provide a reasonable basis for obtaining limited assurance that there are no material modifications needed

5. Reports

    a. Compilation

        (1) Third-party reliance expected—A report or written communication is required unless the accountant withdraws. If the accountant is not independent, s/he may issue a compilation report provided s/he complies with compilation standards.

        (2) No third-party reliance expected—A report is not required, although one may be issued.

b. Review

(1) A written report is required unless the accountant withdraws from the engagement.

E. Materiality—these requirements are essentially the same as materiality considerations on audits.

AR 80 Compilation of Financial Statements

A. Establishing an understanding for a compilation

1. An accountant should establish an understanding with management regarding services to be performed and should document it through a written communication (in an engagement letter); an understanding should include

a. Objective of compilation is to assist management in presenting financial information in the form of financial statements
b. Accountant uses information that is the representation of management without undertaking to obtain any assurance on its accuracy
c. Management is responsible for

(1) Preparation and fair presentation of financial statements
(2) Designing, implementing and maintaining IC
(3) Preventing and detecting fraud
(4) Entity compliance with laws and regulations
(5) Making all financial records and related information available to the accountant

d. The accountant is responsible for conducting engagement as per Statements on Standards on Accounting and Review Services (SSARS) issued by AICPA
e. Differences between a compilation and a review or an audit
f. Compilation cannot be relied upon to disclose errors, fraud, or illegal acts
g. Accountant will inform management of material misstatements and illegal acts
h. The effect of any independence impairments on the expected compilation report

2. Other matters can be added to the engagement letter (e.g., fees, additional services).
3. If the compilation is not expected to be used by a third party, the accountant should so indicate in the engagement letter.

B. Compilation performance requirements

1. *Understanding of industry*—The accountant should possess such an understanding

a. Yet, an accountant may accept a compilation engagement of an entity in an industry with which the accountant has no previous experience—s/he must obtain the required level of knowledge (e.g., through AICPA guides, industry publications, textbooks, CPE, etc.) so as to be able to perform the engagement competently.

2. *Knowledge of the client*—This includes the client's business and the accounting principles followed by the client.
3. *Reading the financial statements*—Read and consider whether they appear to be appropriate in form and free from material errors.
4. *Other compilation procedures*—The accountant is *not* required to make inquiries or perform other procedures to verify, corroborate, or review information supplied by the entity.

a. However, the accountant may have made inquiries or performed other procedures which revealed misstatements, illegal acts, etc.; in such cases

(1) The accountant should request that management consider the matters.
(2) When accountant believes financial statements are materially misstated, obtain additional, or revised information; if the entity refuses to provide such information the accountant should withdraw from the engagement.

C. Documentation in a compilation engagement should include

1. Signed engagement letter (by management and the accountant)
2. Any findings or issues that, in the accountant's judgment are significant, such as

    a. Results of compilation procedures that indicate financial statements could be misstated, including actions taken to address such findings

    b. To the extent the accountant had questions or concerns as a result of compilation procedures, how they were resolved

3. Communication (oral or written) to the appropriate level of management regarding fraud or illegal acts that came to the accountant's attention

D. Reporting on compiled financial statements—General

1. When the accountant is engaged to report on compiled statements or submits financial statements that are *reasonably expected to be used by a third-party* the financial statements should be accompanied by a compilation report.

2. Basic elements of a compilation report

    a. *Title*, such as "Accountant's Compilation Report"

    b. *Addressee*, as appropriate in the circumstances

    c. *Introductory paragraph:*

        (1) Identify the financial statements and indicate they have been compiled

        (2) Date of each financial statement

        (3) A statement that the financial statements have not been audited or reviewed and, accordingly, no opinion, or any assurance is expressed

    d. Management's responsibility for the financial statements and for IC over financial reporting

    e. Accountant's responsibility

        (1) Conduct compilation in accordance with SSARS issued by AICPA

        (2) Objective of a compilation is to assist management in presenting financial information in the form of financial statements without undertaking to obtain any assurance that there are no material modifications that should be made to the financial statements.

    f. *Signature of the accountant*—manual or printed

    g. *Date of the accountant's report*—Date of completion of the compilation

3. Other

    a. Any procedures that the accountant might have performed before or during the compilation should *not* be described in the report.

    b. Each page of the compiled statements should include a reference, such as "See Accountant's Compilation Report."

    c. Other comprehensive basis of accounting (OCBOA) statements should include a description of the OCBOA and informative disclosures similar to those required by GAAP.

E. Reporting on financial statements—Circumstances resulting in modification of the compilation report

1. Financial statements that omit substantially all disclosures (e.g., the notes)

    a. An accountant may compile and report on such statements if the intent, to the accountant's knowledge, is not to mislead users.

    b. Report modifications—in the report indicate that

        (1) Management has elected to omit substantially all disclosures (and the statement of cash flows, if applicable) required by the applicable financial reporting framework.

        (2) The omitted disclosures might influence the user's conclusions about the company's financial position, results of operations and cash flows.

        (3) The financial statements are not designed for those who are not informed about such matters.

    c. When the entity wishes to include disclosures about only a few matters in the form of notes to the financial statements, such disclosures should be labeled "Selected Information—Substantially All Disclosures Required by [identify applicable financial reporting framework, e.g., GAAP] are not included."

2. Accountant is not independent

    a. The accountant need not provide the reason for a lack of independence, but should add "I am (we are) not independent with respect to XYZ Company" in a final paragraph to the report.

b. However, an accountant may choose to provide the reason for a lack of independence; examples: "I am (we are) not independent with respect to XYZ Company during the year ended December 31, 20XX because

(1) A member of the engagement team had a direct financial interest in XYZ company."
(2) An individual of my immediate family was employed by XYZ company."
(3) We performed certain accounting services [describe] that impaired our independence."

c. If an accountant elects to disclose reasons for a lack of independence, s/he must disclosure all of them.

3. When the financial statements are **not** expected to be used by a third party

a. Accountant is not required to issue a compilation report.
b. This must be so indicated in the engagement letter (returned, signed by management).
c. Add a reference on each page of the financial statements restricting their use, such as "Restricted for Management's Use Only."
d. If accountant finds such financial statements have been distributed to third parties, discuss with client and request that the client have the statements returned.

(1) If the client refuses, notify the known third parties that the financial statements are not intended for third-party use, preferably in consultation with accountant's attorney.

4. Emphasis of a matter

a. Accountant may, in a separate paragraph, emphasize a matter concerning the financial statements; such paragraphs are never required.
b. Examples of matters: uncertainties, entity a component of a larger enterprise, significant transactions with related parties, unusually important subsequent events, accounting matters.

5. Departures from applicable financial reporting framework

a. If accountant believes modification of standard report is appropriate, disclose departure in a separate paragraph of the report, including the effects of such departure if known.

(1) The accountant is not required to determine the effects of a departure if management has not done so, provided the accountant states in the report that such determination has not been made.

b. If the accountant believes modification is not adequate to indicate the deficiencies, withdraw from the engagement and provide no further services with respect to those financial statements.

> **NOTE:** Departures from an applicable financial reporting framework do not result in a "qualified" or "adverse" opinion when one is conducting a compilation or review—opinions only result from audits.

6. Restricting the use of an accountant's compilation report

a. Overall, general use vs. restricted use reports

(1) General use—An accountant's report not restricted to specified parties. Accountants' reports on financial statements prepared in conformity with an applicable financial reporting framework ordinarily are not restricted regarding use.

(a) However, nothing in this section precludes the accountant from restricting the use of any report.

(2) Restricted use—An accountant's report intended only for one or more specified third parties. Use is restricted in a number of circumstances, including

(a) Report may be misunderstood when taken out of context in which it was intended to be used.
(b) Subject matter of the accountant's report or the presentation being reported on is based on measurement or disclosure criteria contained in contractual agreements or regulatory provision that are not in conformity with an applicable financial reporting framework.
(c) As per (1) above, nothing in this section precludes the accountant from restricting the use of any report.

b. Other situations

   (1) When one accountant's report covers both the restricted subject matter and the not restricted subject matter—the accountant's report should indicate that the restricted portion is for the specified parties.

   (2) When required by law, a separate restricted use report may be included in a document that *also contains a general use report*. In this circumstance inclusions of the restricted use report in the document that contains a general use report is acceptable—the restricted use report remains restricted, and the general use report continues for general use.

   (3) Subsequent to completion of the engagement resulting in a restricted use report, the accountant may be asked to consider adding other parties as specified parties—the accountant may agree to this if it seems reasonable. If so, the accountant should

      (a) Obtain affirmative acknowledge, preferably in writing, from the other parties of their understanding of the nature of the engagement, measurement criteria, and related report.

      (b) The accountant may either reissue the report with the new specified party added, or provide written acknowledgement of the fact.

         • If reissued, the report date should not be changed.
         • If written acknowledgement, such acknowledgment should state no procedures have been performed subsequent to the date of the report.

c. The report modification to restrict use should

   (1) State that the report is intended solely for information and use of specified parties
   (2) Identify those specified parties
   (3) Say that report is not intended for and should not be used by anyone other than the specified parties

7. Uncertainty about an entity's ability to continue as a going concern

   a. Request management to consider possible effects on the financial statements, including need for related disclosure.

   b. If accountant determines management's conclusions are unreasonable or the disclosure of uncertainty on going concern is not adequate, it should be treated as a departure from the applicable financial reporting framework.

   c. Accountant may wish to emphasize an uncertainty (emphasis of a matter) concerning going concern; but this emphasis is not required.

8. Subsequent events and subsequent discovery of facts existing at date of report—treated similarly to audits, see AU-C 560.

9. Supplementary information presented
   a. Accountant should clearly indicate degree of responsibility, if any, being taken with respect to such information.

F. Communicating to management and others when performing a compilation

1. When fraud or an illegal act come to the accountant's attention—communicate to an appropriate level of management.

   a. Accountant need not report matters regarding illegal acts that are clearly inconsequential.

   b. Matters involving senior management should be reported to an individual or group higher in the organization (e.g., manager [owner] or those charged with governance).

      (1) Communication may be oral or written; if oral document it.

   c. If owner is involved, consider resigning.

   d. Accountant should consider consulting legal counsel whenever evidence that fraud or an illegal act has occurred comes to his/her attention, unless it is clearly inconsequential.

2. Contacting a party outside the organization is not ordinarily part of the accountant's responsibility and the accountant should not do so. Exceptions are as follows:

   a. To comply with certain legal and regulatory requirements
   b. Response to a successor auditor inquiry
   c. Response to a subpoena

G. Change in engagement from audit or review to a compilation

1. Before agreeing to a change consider

   a. Reasonableness of reason for client's request

      (1) Examples of acceptable reasons:

          (a) Change in circumstances
          (b) Misunderstanding of nature of audit, review, or compilation

   b. Additional audit or review effort needed to complete the engagement—generally, the closer to complete, the less reasonable
   c. Estimated additional cost to complete the audit or review

2. Other
   a. Situations in which an accountant ordinarily cannot change to a compilation

      (1) In an audit, the accountant has been prohibited from corresponding with entity's legal counsel.
      (2) In an audit or review the client does not provide a signed representation letter.

   b. If accountant concludes the change is reasonable, the compilation report should not include reference to the original engagement, procedures performed, scope limitations.

NOW REVIEW MULTIPLE-CHOICE QUESTIONS 1 THROUGH 29

AR 90 Review of Financial Statements

A. Applicability—This section establishes review standards on reviews of financial statements

1. It does not apply when AU-C 930 applies (accountant also audits annual financial statements).
2. An accountant may not perform a review if the accountant's independence is impaired for any reason other than the performance of an internal control service.

B. Establishing an understanding for a review

1. An accountant should establish an understanding with management, and if applicable, those charged with governance regarding services to be performed and should document it in an engagement letter signed by management and the accountant; an understanding should include

   a. Objective of review is to obtain limited assurance that there are no material modifications that should be made to the financial statements in order for the statements to be in conformity with the applicable financial reporting framework.

   NOTE: Make certain that you know the above objective.

   b. Management is responsible for

      (1) Preparation and fair presentation of financial statements
      (2) Designing, implementing, and maintaining IC
      (3) Preventing and detecting fraud
      (4) Complying with laws and regulations
      (5) Making all financial records and related information available to the accountant
      (6) Providing the accountant, at the conclusion of the engagement, a representation letter

   c. The accountant is responsible for conducting engagement as per Statements on Standards for Accounting and Review Services (SSARS) issued by AICPA.

    d. A review

      (1) Consists primarily of inquiries of company personnel and analytical procedures applied to financial data

      (2) Is substantially less in scope than an audit (and then describe how it is different)

      (3) Cannot be relied upon to disclose errors, fraud, or illegal acts

    e. The accountant will inform management of material misstatements and illegal acts that are identified.

2. The understanding should be communicated in the form of an engagement letter, signed by the accountant and management (or, if applicable, those charged with governance).

3. Other matters can be added to the letter (e.g., fees, additional services).

C. Review performance requirements—General

1. Procedures must be sufficient to accumulate review evidence that will provide a reasonable basis for obtaining limited assurance that there are no material modifications needed.

2. Understanding of industry—The accountant should possess such an understanding.

    a. Yet, an accountant may accept a review engagement of an entity in an industry with which the accountant has no previous experience—s/he must obtain the required level of knowledge (e.g., through AICPA guides, industry publications, textbooks, CPE, etc.) so as to be able to perform the engagement competently.

3. Knowledge of the client—this includes the client's business and the accounting principles followed by the client

D. Designing and performing review procedures

1. Based on the accountant's understanding of the industry and client, the accountant designs and performs analytical procedures and makes inquires and performs other procedures as appropriate to obtain limited assurance that there are no needed material modifications.

2. Analytical procedures

    a. Involve comparisons of recorded amounts, or ratios developed from recorded amounts to expectations developed by the accountant. Expectations are developed by identifying and using plausible relationships. Examples of sources of information for developing expectations

      (1) Financial information for comparable prior periods

      (2) Anticipated results (e.g., budgets)

      (3) Relationships among elements of financial information within the period

      (4) Information regarding the industry (e.g., gross margin information)

      (5) Relationships of financial information with relevant nonfinancial information (e.g., payroll costs to number of employees)

    b. When analytical procedures identify unexpected fluctuations or relationships, the accountant should investigate these differences by inquiring of management and performing other procedures as necessary in the circumstances.

      (1) Although the accountant is not required to corroborate management's responses with other evidence, the accountant may need to perform other procedures when, for example, management is unable to provide an explanation, or its explanation is not considered adequate.

3. Inquiries and other review procedures

    a. Inquiries to management concerning

      (1) Whether statements prepared in conformity with applicable financial reporting framework

      (2) Entity's accounting principles followed

      (3) Unusual or complex situations that may have an effect on financial statements

      (4) Significant transactions near end of reporting period

      (5) Status of uncorrected misstatements identified during previous engagement

      (6) Questions that have arisen in the course of applying review procedures

      (7) Events subsequent to date of financial statements

      (8) Knowledge of fraud or suspected fraud affecting entity involving management or others that could have a material effect on financial statements

      (9) Significant journal entries and other adjustments

    (10) Communications with regulatory agencies

  b. Inquiries concerning actions taken at meetings of stockholders, board of directors, etc.

  c. Reading the financial statements to consider whether they appear to conform with the applicable financial reporting framework

  d. Obtaining reports from other accountants, if any, which are involved with significant components

4. The accountant ordinarily is not required to corroborate management's responses with other evidence; however, the accountant should consider the reasonableness and consistency of management's responses in light of the results of other review procedures and the accountant's knowledge of the client's business and the industry in which it operates.

5. Incorrect, incomplete or otherwise unsatisfactory information

  a. Request management to consider the effects of these matters on the financial statements and communicate results to the accountant.

  b. If the accountant believes financial statements may be materially misstated, perform additional procedures to obtain limited assurance there are no material modifications needed. If the accountant concludes the financial statements are materially misstated, follow guidance on reporting departures from the applicable financial reporting framework.

6. Management's representations

  a. Written representations are required from management for all financial statements and periods covered by the review report.

    (1) If current management was not present during all periods covered, the accountant should nevertheless obtain written representations from current management for all such periods.

  b. The accountant should obtain written representations from management on

    (1) Its responsibility for fair presentation of financial statements

    (2) Its belief the financial statements are fairly presented

    (3) Its acknowledgement of its responsibility to design, implement, and maintain IC

    (4) Its knowledge of any fraud or suspected fraud that could have a material effect on the financial statements.

    (5) Its knowledge of any fraud or suspected fraud affecting the entity involving management or others where the fraud could have a material effect on the financial statements

    (6) Its full and truthful response to all inquiries

    (7) Completeness of information

    (8) Information concerning subsequent events

    (9) Other matters specific to the entity's business or industry

  c. Representations should be made as of the date of the accountant's review report.

    (1) Normally the CEO and CFO or others with equivalent positions sign the representation letter.

E Documentation in a review engagement

1. Documentation provides

  a. Principal support that the review was performed in accordance with SSARS

  b. Principal support for conclusion that accountant is not aware of any material modifications needed to financial statements

2. Documentation should include

  a. Engagement letter

  b. Analytical procedures performed, including

    (1) Expectations

    (2) Results of comparison of expectations to recorded amounts/ratios

    (3) Management's responses to accountant's inquires regarding fluctuations

    c. Any additional review procedure performed in response to significant unexpected differences
    d. Significant matters covered in inquiry procedures and responses thereto
    e. Findings that in the accountant's judgment are significant
    f. Significant unusual matters
    g. Evidence from performance of internal control services, if applicable
    h. Communications, whether oral or written, to management concerning fraud or illegal acts
    i. Representation letter

F. Reporting on the Financial Statements—General

1. Objective in reporting: Prevent misinterpretation of the degree of responsibility the accountant is assuming when his/her name is associated with the financial statements
2. Basic elements of a review report

    a. *Title*, such as "Independent Accountant's Review Report"
    b. *Addressee*, as appropriate in the circumstances
    c. *Introductory paragraph*

        (1) Identify the financial statements and indicate that have been reviewed.
        (2) Date of each financial statement.
        (3) A review consists primarily of applying analytical procedures to management's financial data and making inquiries of company management.
        (4) A statement that a review is substantially less in scope than an audit, the objective of which is the expression of an opinion; the accountant does not express such an opinion.

    d. Management's responsibility for the financial statements and for IC over financial reporting
    e. Accountant's responsibility

        (1) Conduct review in accordance with SSARS issued by AICPA.
        (2) Review standards require the accountant to perform the procedures to obtain limited assurance that there are no material modifications needed.
        (3) Accountant believes the results of his/her procedures provide a reasonable basis for the report.

    f. *Results of the engagement*—Accountant is not aware of any material modifications that should be made to the financial statement, other than those modifications (if any) indicated in the report
    g. *Signature of the accountant*—manual or printed
    h. *Date of accountant's report*—Not earlier than the date on which the accountant has accumulated review evidence sufficient to provide a reasonable basis for expressing limited assurance

3. Other

    a. Each page of the financial statements should include a reference such as "See Accountant's Review Report."
    b. When the accountant is unable to perform inquiry and analytical procedures considered necessary, or the client does not provide a representation letter, the review is incomplete—no review report should be issued. The accountant should consider whether it is appropriate to issue a compilation report on the financial statements.
    c. An accountant may review one financial statement (e.g., balance sheet) as long as inquiry and analytical procedures are not restricted.
    d. OCBOA financial statements should include a description of the OCBOA and informative disclosures similar to those required by GAAP.

G. Reporting on financial statements—Circumstances resulting in modification of the review report

1. Emphasis of a matter

    a. Accountant may, in a separate paragraph, emphasize a matter concerning the financial statements.
    b. Such paragraphs are never required.
    c. Examples of matters: uncertainties, entity a component of a larger enterprise, significant transactions with related parties, unusually important subsequent events, accounting matters.

2. Departures from applicable financial reporting framework

    a. If accountant believes modification of standard report is appropriate, disclose departure in a separate paragraph of the report, including the effects of such departure if known.

       (1) The accountant is not required to determine the effects of a departure if management has not done so, provided the accountant states in the report that such determination has not been made.

    b. If the accountant believes modification is not adequate to indicate the deficiencies, withdraw from the engagement and provide no further services with respect to those financial statements.

3. Restricting the use of an accountant's review report—The restrictions are very similar to those for a compilation (see E.6. of outline AR 80 presented earlier).
4. Uncertainty about an entity's ability to continue as a going concern

    a. Request management to consider possible effects on the financial statements, including need for related disclosure.
    b. If accountant determines management's conclusions are unreasonable or the disclosure of uncertainty on going concern is not adequate, it should be treated as a departure from the applicable financial reporting framework.
    c. Accountant may wish to emphasize an uncertainty (emphasis of a matter) concerning going concern; this emphasis is not required.

5. Subsequent events and subsequent discovery of acts existing at date of report—treated similarly to audits, see AU-C 560
6. Supplementary information presented

    a. Accountant should clearly indicate degree of responsibility, if any, being taken with respect to such information

H. Communicating to management and others—The requirements are very similar to that of a compilation— The communications are very similar to those for a compilation (see F. of AR 80 outline) and include

1. When fraud or an illegal act come to the accountant's attention—communicate to an appropriate level of management.

    a. Account need not report matters regarding illegal acts that are clearly inconsequential.
    b. Matters involving senior management should be reported to an individual or group higher in the organization (e.g., manager [owner] or those charged with governance).

       (1) Communication may be oral or written; if oral document it.

    c. If owner is involved, consider resigning.
    d. Accountant should consider consulting legal counsel whenever evidence that fraud or an illegal act has occurred comes to his/her attention, unless it is clearly inconsequential.

2. Contacting a party outside the organization is not ordinarily part of the accountant's responsibility and the accountant should not do so. Exceptions are as follows:

    a. To comply with certain legal and regulatory requirements
    b. Response to a successor auditor inquiry
    c. Response to a subpoena

I. Change in engagement from audit to review

1. Before agreeing to a change consider

    a. Reasonableness of reason for client's request

       (1) Examples of acceptable reasons:

          (a) Change in circumstances
          (b) Misunderstanding of nature of audit or review

    b. Additional audit effort needed to complete the audit—generally, the closer to complete, the less reasonable.
    c. Estimated additional cost to complete the audit

2. Other

    a. In considering the implications of an audit scope restriction, the accountant should evaluate the possibility that information affected by the scope restriction may be incorrect. When in an audit the accountant has been prohibited by the client from corresponding with the entity's legal counsel, the accountant ordinarily would be precluded from issuing a review report.

    b. If accountant concludes the change is reasonable, the review report should not include reference to original engagement, procedures performed, or scope limitations.

AR 110 Compilation of Specified Elements, Accounts, or Items of a Financial Statement

Overall Objectives and Approach—This section expands SSARS to apply to compilations of one or more specified elements, accounts or items of a financial statement (hereafter, specified elements). Examples of specified elements include schedules of rentals, royalties, profit participation, or provision for income taxes. The section outlines the required understanding with the entity that must be obtained, performance requirements, and reporting requirements.

A. The accountant should obtain overall understanding with the entity that includes

1. The engagement cannot be relied upon to disclose errors, fraud or illegal acts
2. The accountant will inform an appropriate level of management of any material errors, fraud or illegal acts that are discovered

B. Performance requirements include adherence to SSARS and, prior to issuance of a compilation report, reading the specified elements and consideration of whether the information appears appropriate in form and free of obvious material misstatements

C. Reporting requirements

1. The report should include

    a. A statement that the specified elements were compiled. If the compilation was performed in conjunction with a compilation of the company's financial statements, indicate this and the date of that compilation report. Any departure from the standard report on the financial statements should be disclosed if it is relevant to the specified element

    b. Compilation performed in accordance with SSARS issued by AICPA

    c. Description of the reporting basis followed if basis is not GAAP (e.g., tax basis)

    d. Financial information that is the representation of management (owners)

    e. Specified elements not audited or reviewed, and no opinion or assurance is provided

    f. Signature of accounting firm or accountant, as appropriate

    g. Date of report (completion of compilation)

2. Each page of compiled specified elements should include a reference such as "See Accountant's Compilation Report"

AR 120 Compilation of Pro Forma Financial Information

Overall Objectives and Approach—This section is very similar to AR 110, but applies to pro forma financial information. The objective of pro forma financial information is to show what the significant effects on historical financial information might have been had a consummated or proposed transaction (or event) occurred at an earlier date. Pro forma information is commonly used to show the effect of transactions such as business combinations, changes in capitalization, disposal of a significant portion of the business, changes in the form of the business, and the proposed sale of securities.

    The overall understanding of the entity and the performance requirements for a compilation of pro forma financial information correspond to those in AR 110 for specified elements, accounts, or items of a financial statement and are not repeated here. The reporting requirements include those as per AR 110, plus

- A reference to the financial statements from which the historical information is derived and a statement as to whether that information was compiled, reviewed or audited
- A separate paragraph explaining the objective of the pro forma financial information and its limitations

AR 200 Reporting on Comparative Financial Statements

Overall Objectives and Approach—This section presents guidance for reporting on comparative statements of a nonissuer, at least a portion of which are not audited (i.e., one or more years is compiled or reviewed). The existence of compiled, reviewed, and audited financial statements, as well as financial statements with which the auditor has had no association, presents a situation in which there are numerous implementation issues related to compiled statements. For example, perhaps the first year's statements have been reviewed, and the second year's compiled.

This section presents and resolves an overwhelming number of situations which may occur in practice. In the outline we attempt to provide information on the most frequent cases which one would expect to see on the CPA exam. You should be aware that several questions on the exam have required candidates either to prepare or to critique comparative reports of this nature.

The outline provides (a) overall guidance as well as (b) enumerating important situations.

A. Overall guidance

1. The accountant's report should cover each period presented as a comparative statement

   a. An entity may include financial information with which the accountant is not associated (e.g., last year's statements) in a report that also includes information with which the accountant is associated (e.g., this year's compiled or reviewed statements)

      (1) When the information is presented on separate pages, the information should clearly indicate that the accountant is not associated
      (2) The accountant should not allow his/her name to be associated with such financial statements (i.e., the year which s/he is not associated) that are presented in columnar form with financial statements on which s/he has reported

         (a) If the entity still intends to use the accountant's name, the accountant should consult with his/her attorney

2. When compiled statements of one year omit most of the disclosures required per GAAP (e.g., do not include footnotes) they should not be presented with another year's which do have such disclosures, and the accountant should **not** issue a report on such comparative statements
3. Each page of comparative financial statements compiled or reviewed by an accountant should include a reference such as "See Accountant's Report"
4. The following is general guidance on the overall form of comparative reports

   a. When both years have been compiled or reviewed, the report uses the standard form, modified to include both years
   b. A continuing accountant who performs the same or a **higher level of service** with respect to financial statements of the current period (e.g., review this year, compilation last year) should update his/her report on the financial statements of a prior period presented with those of the current period

---

EXAMPLE

Issue a standard review report supplemented with the following paragraph:

The accompanying 20X1 financial statements of XYZ were compiled by me. A compilation is limited to representing in the form of financial statements information that is the representation of management. I have not audited or reviewed the 20X1 financial statements and accordingly, do not express an opinion or any other form of assurance on them.

---

   c. A continuing accountant who performs a **lower level of service** with respect to the financial statements of the current period (e.g., compilation this year, review last year) should either

      (1) Include a separate paragraph in his/her report with a description of the responsibility assumed for the prior period statements or
      (2) Reissue his/her report on the financial statements of the prior period

> **EXAMPLE**
>
> Approaches (1) and (2)
>
>   (1) Issue a compilation report on 20X4 which includes a paragraph summarizing the responsibility assumed for the 20X3 financial statements. The description should include the original date of the review report and should state that no procedures have been performed on the review after that date.
>
>   (2) Combine the compilation report on 20X4 with the reissued report on the financial statements of the prior period or print them separately. The combined report should state that the accountant has not performed any procedures in connection with that review engagement after the date of the review report.

B. Other situations

  1. **Existence of a predecessor auditor**—as is the case with audited financial statements, a decision must be made as to whether the predecessor will reissue his/her compilation or review report

> **NOTE:** The situation here is one in which a choice is made as to whether two reports will be associated with the comparative information (20X3 the predecessor's, 20X4 the successor's) **or** one report in which the successor summarizes the predecessor's findings.

    a. Reissuance of the predecessor's report

        (1) The predecessor must determine whether his/her report is appropriate based on

            (a) Current vs. prior period statement format
            (b) Newly discovered subsequent events
            (c) Changes in the financial statements affecting the report

        (2) The predecessor should also perform the following procedures:

            (a) Read the current statements and the successor's report
            (b) Compare prior and current statements
            (c) Obtain representation letter from successor suggesting that s/he is not aware of any matters having a material effect on the prior statements

        (3) If anything comes to the predecessor's attention that affects the report, the predecessor should

            (a) Make any necessary inquiries and perform any necessary procedures
            (b) If necessary insist that the client revise the statements and revise the report as appropriate (normally add an explanatory paragraph)

                1. The report will be "dual dated"—see outline of AU-C 560 on dual dating

    b. No reissuance of predecessor's report (i.e., it is not presented)

        (1) The successor auditor should add a paragraph stating that the

            (a) Prior (comparative) statements were compiled (or reviewed) by another accountant
            (b) Date of the predecessor's report
            (c) Assurance, if any, provided in the predecessor's report
            (d) Reasons for any modification of the predecessor's report

  2. **20X3 reviewed (or compiled) and 20X4 audited**—The situation here is similar to above with a predecessor auditor in that the prior year's report may be reissued, or a summary of it included in the 20X4 report

  3. When an accountant is reporting on financial statements that now omit substantially all disclosures (i.e., notes), which when originally issued did not omit such disclosures, a paragraph is added to the report indicating that the disclosures have been omitted; also, the final paragraph indicates the accountant's prior form of association with the information.

EXAMPLE

20X4 has been reviewed, and now, in 20X5, 20X4 statements have been compiled from the previously reviewed statements. A compilation report is issued on 20X5, with a paragraph on the omitted disclosures (see Section E.1 of AR 80 outline presented earlier) and with a paragraph on the 20X4 statements such as the following:

   The accompanying 20X4 financial statements were compiled by me from financial statements that did not omit substantially all of the disclosures required by generally accepted accounting principles and that I previously reviewed as indicated in my report dated March 1, 20X5.

---

4. When a company changes its status (i.e., nonpublic to public, or vice versa) the proper reporting responsibility is determined by the status at the time of reporting

AR 300 Compilation Reports on Financial Statements Included in Certain Prescribed Forms

Overall Objectives and Approach—This section presents guidance on issuing compilation reports related to information presented on prescribed forms, designed by the bodies with which they filed (e.g., governmental bodies, trade associations, banks). For example, assume that a state governmental body has a balance sheet form which all companies incorporated in that state are required to fill out with appropriate financial information. Also, assume that the state requires that a compilation report be filed with the report. This section deals with the manner in which the auditor should report on such forms. The following outline provides general guidance on the report issued.

A. General guidance on compilation reports for prescribed forms

1. An overall presumption is made that the form is sufficient to meet the needs of the body which has designed or adopted it
2. Departures from GAAP

   a. **Required to appropriately complete the form**—There is **no need** to advise such bodies of this type of departure

   b. **Other departures**—Indicate in second paragraph and add a final paragraph

---

EXAMPLE

If, because of the requirements of the form, inventory is included on the form at cost, rather than the lower of cost and market, no indication would be provided that this departure from GAAP existed.

---

3. Departures from the requirements of the prescribed form—treat in the same manner as 2.b. above
4. When a prescribed form does not conform to the guidance provided in either AR 100 or AR 300, the accountant should not sign it, but should append an appropriate report to the prescribed form

AR 400 Communications between Predecessor and Successor Accountants

Overall Objectives and Approach—This section presents guidance for situations in which a successor accountant **decides to communicate** with a predecessor accountant concerning acceptance of a compilation or a review engagement of a nonissuer (nonpublic) entity; such communication is **not** required.

   The guidance provided is similar to that in AU-C 210, which requires such communication prior to accepting an **audit**. As is the case with that section, inquiries of a predecessor may occur: (a) in conjunction with acceptance of the engagement, and (b) other inquiries, subsequent to acceptance of the engagement. The section also provides guidance for situations in which the successor becomes aware of information indicating the need for revision of the statements with which the predecessor is associated.

A. Inquiries in conjunction with accepting an engagement

1. Circumstances in which a successor might choose to communicate

    a. Information concerning client, principals, and management is limited or appears to be in need of special attention
    b. Change in accountants occurs substantially after end of period for which financial statements are to be compiled or reviewed
    c. There have been frequent changes in accountants

2. An accountant may not disclose confidential information without consent of client

    a. Except as permitted by AICPA Code of Conduct
    b. Successor accountant should request client to

        (1) Permit him/her to make inquiries
        (2) Authorize predecessor to respond completely

    c. If client refuses to comply with request for inquiry, accountant should consider reasons for, and implications of, such denial as they relate to accepting the engagement

3. May be oral or written and typically would include requests for information on

    a. Matters which might affect the integrity of management (owners)
    b. Disagreement about accounting principles or necessity of certain procedures
    c. If necessary, cooperation of management (owners) in providing additional or revised information
    d. Predecessor's understanding of reason for change in accountants

4. The predecessor should respond promptly and completely to requests made in connection with engagements

    a. If, due to unusual circumstances, response must be limited, accountant should so indicate

        (1) For example, unusual circumstances include pending litigation but do not include unpaid fees

B. Other inquiries

1. May be made before/after acceptance of engagement to facilitate a compilation or review
2. Might include questions about prior periods' circumstances such as

    a. Deficiencies in underlying financial data
    b. Necessity of performing other accounting services
    c. Areas requiring inordinate amounts of time

3. May include request for access to predecessor's working papers

    a. Successor should request client authorization
    b. Customary for predecessor to be available for consultation and provide certain of his/her workpapers
    c. Predecessor and successor should agree on which workpapers

        (1) Will be available
        (2) May be copied

    d. Generally, predecessor should provide access to workpapers relating to

        (1) Matters of continuing accounting significance
        (2) Contingencies

    e. Predecessor may refuse for valid business reasons, including but not limited to, unpaid fees
    f. If client is considering several successors

        (1) Predecessor and working papers need not be made available until client names an accountant as successor

    g. Successor should not reference report on work of predecessor in his/her report except when comparative statements are being issued—see outline of AR 200.

C. Predecessor accountant's financial statements

1. If successor becomes aware of information indicating the need for revision of financial statements reported on by predecessor, the successor should

   a. Request that the client inform the predecessor accountant

2. If the client refuses to inform the predecessor or the successor is not satisfied with the predecessor's actions, the successor should consult his/her attorney

AR 500 Reporting on Compiled Financial Statements

(Deleted)

AR 600 Reporting on Personal Financial Statements Included in Written Personal Financial Plans

Overall Objectives and Approach—This section provides an exception to the AR 100 requirement that accountants either compile, review, or audit financial statements with which they are associated. The section allows accountant association with unaudited statements included in written personal financial plans prepared by the accountant. The outline presents related details.

A. Requirements relating to "unaudited" association with personal financial plans

1. Financial statements in personal financial plans need not be compiled, reviewed, or audited if

   a. The accountant establishes an understanding (preferably in writing) with the client that statements will be used solely to assist the client and the client's advisors to develop and achieve personal financial goals and objectives
   b. Nothing came to accountant's attention to cause him/her to believe that the financial statements will be used for other purposes

2. The accountant's report should state that the financial statements

   a. Are for the financial plan
   b. May be incomplete or contain GAAP departures and should not be used for other purposes
   c. Have not been audited, reviewed, or compiled

> **NOW REVIEW MULTIPLE-CHOICE QUESTIONS 30 THROUGH 52**

KEY TERMS

Assurance engagement. An engagement in which an accountant issues a report designed to enhance the degree of confidence of third parties and management about the outcome of an evaluation or measurement of financial statements (subject matter) against an applicable financial reporting framework.

Attest engagement. Defined somewhat differently in the Code of Professional Conduct and the attestation standards. The Code of Professional Conduct defines an attest engagement as an engagement performed by public accountants that requires independence. The attest standards define it as one in which the public accountants issue an examination, a review, or an agreed–upon procedures report on subject matter or on an assertion about subject matter that is the responsibility of another party (ordinarily management).

Compilation of financial statements. An accounting service that involves the preparation of financial statements from client records. No assurance is provided in a compilation. The current professional standards consider compilations to be attest engagements.

Financial reporting framework. A set of criteria used to determine measurement, recognition, presentation and disclosure of all material items appearing in the financial statements; for example, accounting principles generally accepted in the United States of America, International Financial Reporting Standards (IFRS) issued by the International Accounting Standards

Board (IASB). An "applicable financial reporting framework" is the framework adopted by management of the company being audited in a particular situation.

Issuer. A company whose stock is traded on a public market or a company in the process of registering its stock for public sale.

Limited (negative) assurance. A conclusion by CPAs that, after applying limited investigative techniques to certain information, they are not aware of the need to modify the presentation of the information.

Nonissuer. A company whose securities are *not* registered under requirements of the Securities and Exchange Commission; ordinarily, a "nonissuer" is a nonpublic company. This is in contrast to an issuer, a company whose securities are registered under the requirements of the Securities and Exchange Commission. The *Statements on Accounting and Review Services* apply to nonissuers.

Review of financial statement. A form of attestation based on inquiry and analytical procedures applied for the purpose of expressing limited assurance that the historical financial statements are presented in accordance with GAAP or some other appropriate basis.

Multiple-Choice Questions (1–52)

Compilation and Review—General

1. Statements on Standards for Accounting and Review Services establish standards and procedures for which of the following engagements?

   a. Assisting in adjusting the books of account for a partnership.
   b. Reviewing interim financial data required to be filed with the SEC.
   c. Processing financial data for clients of other accounting firms.
   d. Compiling an individual's personal financial statement to be used to obtain a mortgage.

2. The authoritative body designated to promulgate standards concerning an accountant's association with unaudited financial statements of an entity that is not required to file financial statements with an agency regulating the issuance of the entity's securities is the

   a. Financial Accounting Standards Board.
   b. General Accounting Office.
   c. Accounting and Review Services Committee.
   d. Auditing Standards Board.

3. Which of the following accounting services may an accountant perform without being required to issue a compilation or review report under the Statements on Standards for Accounting and Review Services?

   I. Preparing a working trial balance.
   II. Preparing standard monthly journal entries.

   a. I only.
   b. II only.
   c. Both I and II.
   d. Neither I nor II.

4. May an accountant accept an engagement to compile or review the financial statements of a not-for-profit entity if the accountant is unfamiliar with the specialized industry accounting principles, but plans to obtain the required level of knowledge before compiling or reviewing the financial statements?

	Compilation	Review
a.	No	No
b.	Yes	No
c.	No	Yes
d.	Yes	Yes

5. Which of the following statements is correct concerning both an engagement to compile and an engagement to review a nonissuer's financial statements?

   a. The accountant does not contemplate obtaining an understanding of internal control.
   b. The accountant must be independent in fact and appearance.
   c. The accountant expresses no assurance on the financial statements.
   d. The accountant should obtain a written management representation letter.

6. The objective of an accountant's compilation of the financial statements of a nonissuer (nonpublic company) is to provide what type of assurance?

   a. Absolute assurance.
   b. Limited assurance.
   c. No assurance.
   d. Reasonable assurance.

7. A company hires a CPA who has invested in its outstanding bonds payable to issue accounting reports for the company. Assuming any required disclosures are made, which of the following reports may the CPA issue?

   a. Compilations.
   b. Reviews.
   c. Audits.
   d. Agreed-upon procedures.

Compilation—General

8. An accountant is required to comply with the provisions of Statements on Standards for Accounting and Review Services when

   I. Reproducing client-prepared financial statements, without modification, as an accommodation to a client.
   II. Preparing standard monthly journal entries for depreciation and expiration of prepaid expenses.

   a. I only.
   b. II only.
   c. Both I and II.
   d. Neither I nor II.

9. Kell engaged March, CPA, to submit to Kell a written personal financial plan containing unaudited personal financial statements. March anticipates omitting certain disclosures required by GAAP because the engagement's sole purpose is to assist Kell in developing a personal financial plan. For March to be exempt from complying with the requirements of

Statements on Standards for Accounting and Review Services. Kell is required to agree that the

    a. Financial statements will **not** be presented in comparative form with those of the prior period.

    b. Omitted disclosures required by GAAP are **not** material.

    c. Financial statements will **not** be disclosed to a non-CPA financial planner.

    d. Financial statements will **not** be used to obtain credit.

10. Statements on Standards for Accounting and Review Services (SSARS) apply when an accountant has

    a. Typed client-prepared financial statements, without modification, as an accommodation to the client.

    b. Provided a client with a financial statement format that does **not** include dollar amounts, to be used by the client in preparing financial statements.

    c. Proposed correcting journal entries to be recorded by the client that change client-prepared financial statements.

    d. Generated, through the use of computer software, financial statements prepared in accordance with a comprehensive basis of accounting other than GAAP.

11. Davis, CPA, accepted an engagement to audit the financial statements of Tech Resources, a nonissuer. Before the completion of the audit, Tech requested Davis to change the engagement to a compilation of financial statements. Before Davis agrees to change the engagement, Davis is required to consider the

	Additional audit effort necessary to complete the audit	Reason given for Tech's request
a.	No	No
b.	Yes	Yes
c.	Yes	No
d.	No	Yes

12. An accountant may compile a nonissuer's financial statements that omit all of the disclosures required by GAAP only if the omission is

    I. Clearly indicated in the accountant's report.
    II. Not undertaken with the intention of misleading the financial statement users.

    a. I only.
    b. II only.
    c. Both I and II.
    d. Either I or II.

Compilation Procedures

13. When engaged to compile the financial statements of a nonissuer (nonpublic) entity, an accountant is required to possess a level of knowledge of the entity's accounting principles and practices. This requirement most likely will include obtaining a general understanding of the

    a. Stated qualifications of the entity's accounting personnel.

    b. Design of the entity's internal controls placed in operation.

    c. Risk factors relating to misstatements arising from illegal acts.

    d. Internal control awareness of the entity's senior management.

14. Which of the following procedures is ordinarily performed by an accountant in a compilation engagement of a nonissuer (nonpublic) entity?

    a. Reading the financial statements to consider whether they are free of obvious mistakes in the application of accounting principles.

    b. Obtaining written representations from management indicating that the compiled financial statements will **not** be used to obtain credit.

    c. Making inquiries of management concerning actions taken at meetings of the stockholders and the board of directors.

    d. Applying analytical procedures designed to corroborate management's assertions that are embodied in the financial statement components.

Compilation Reporting

15. A CPA is reporting on comparative financial statements of a nonissuer. The CPA audited the prior year's financial statements and compiled those of the current year in accordance with Statements on Standards for Accounting and Review Services (SSARS). The CPA has added a separate paragraph to the review report to describe the responsibility assumed for the prior year's audited financial statements. This separate paragraph should indicate

    a. The type of opinion expressed previously.

    b. That the CPA did **not** update the assessment of control risk.

    c. The reasons for the change from an audit to a review.

    d. That the audit report should **no** longer be relied on.

16. One of the conditions required for an accountant to submit a written personal financial plan containing unaudited financial statements to a client without complying with the requirements of Statements on Standards of Accounting and Review Services, is that the

    a. Client agrees that the financial statements will **not** be used to obtain credit.

    b. Accountant compiled or reviewed the client's financial statements for the immediate prior year.

    c. Engagement letter acknowledges that the financial statements will contain departures from generally accepted accounting principles.

    d. Accountant expresses limited assurance that the financial statements are free of any material misstatements.

17. While performing a compilation of financial statements, information indicating that the entity whose information is being compiled may lack the ability to continue as a going concern has come to the accountant's attention. The client agrees that such a situation does exist, but refuses to add disclosures relating to it. What effect is this most likely to have on the accountant's review report?

    a. No effect, a standard unqualified report is appropriate.

    b. The report should indicate a departure from generally accepted accounting principles, with modification of the report's third paragraph and addition of an explanatory paragraph.

    c. An adverse opinion should be issued, with modification of the opinion paragraph and addition of an explanatory paragraph.

    d. A qualified opinion should be issued, with modification of the opinion paragraph and addition of an explanatory paragraph.

18. When compiled financial statements are accompanied by an accountant's report, that report should state that

    a. A compilation includes assessing the accounting principles used and significant management estimates, as well as evaluating the overall financial statement presentation.

    b. The accountant compiled the financial statements in accordance with Statements on Standards for Accounting and Review Services.

    c. A compilation is substantially less in scope than an audit in accordance with GAAS, the objective of which is the expression of an opinion.

    d. The accountant is not aware of any material modifications that should be made to the financial statements to conform with GAAP.

19. Miller, CPA, is engaged to compile the financial statements of Web Co., a nonissuer (nonpublic) entity, in conformity with the income tax basis of accounting. If Web's financial statements do **not** disclose the basis of accounting used, Miller should

    a. Disclose the basis of accounting in the accountant's compilation report.

    b. Clearly label each page "Distribution Restricted— Material Modifications Required."

    c. Issue a special report describing the effect of the incomplete presentation.

    d. Withdraw from the engagement and provide **no** further services to Web.

20. When an accountant is engaged to compile a nonissuer's financial statements that omit substantially all disclosures required by GAAP, the accountant should indicate in the compilation report that the financial statements are

    a. Not designed for those who are uninformed about the omitted disclosures.

    b. Prepared in conformity with a comprehensive basis of accounting other than GAAP.

    c. Not compiled in accordance with Statements on Standards for Accounting and Review Services.

    d. Special-purpose financial statements that are **not** comparable to those of prior periods.

21. Which of the following is least likely to be included in the understanding with management that an accountant obtains when a compilation is to be performed?

    a. The objective of a compilation is to assist management in presenting financial information in the form of financial statements.

    b. Management is responsible for preventing and detecting fraud.

    c. Management is responsible for identifying and ensuring that the company complies with laws and regulations applicable to its activities.

    d. In a compilation an accountant obtains only limited assurance of detecting misstatements.

22. Clark, CPA, compiled and properly reported on the financial statements of Green Co., a nonissuer, for the year ended March 31, 2008. These financial statements omitted substantially all disclosures required by generally accepted accounting principles (GAAP). Green asked Clark to compile the statements for the year ended March 31, 2009, and to include all GAAP disclosures for the 2009 statements only, but otherwise present both years' financial statements in comparative form. What is Clark's responsibility concerning the proposed engagement?

    a. Clark may **not** report on the comparative financial statements because the 2008 statements are **not** comparable to the 2009 statements that include the GAAP disclosures.

    b. Clark may report on the comparative financial statements provided the 2009 statements do **not** contain any obvious material misstatements.

    c. Clark may report on the comparative financial statements provided an explanatory paragraph is added to Clark's report on the comparative financial statements.

    d. Clark may report on the comparative financial statements provided Clark updates the report on the 2008 statements that do **not** include the GAAP disclosures.

23. Which of the following statements should **not** be included in an accountant's standard report based on the compilation of an entity's financial statements?

    a. A statement that the compilation was performed in accordance with standards established by the American Institute of CPAs.

    b. A statement that the accountant has **not** audited or reviewed the financial statements.

    c. A statement that the accountant does **not** express an opinion but expresses only limited assurance on the financial statements.

    d. A statement that a compilation is limited to presenting, in the form of financial statements, information that is the representation of management.

24. How does an accountant make the following representations when issuing the standard report for the compilation of a nonissuer's financial statements?

	The financial statements have *not* been audited	The accountant has compiled the financial statements
a.	Implicitly	Implicitly
b.	Explicitly	Explicitly
c.	Implicitly	Explicitly
d.	Explicitly	Implicitly

25. An accountant's compilation report should be dated as of the date of

    a. Completion of fieldwork.
    b. Completion of the compilation.
    c. Transmittal of the compilation report.
    d. The latest subsequent event referred to in the notes to the financial statements.

26. An accountant has compiled the financial statements of a nonissuer in accordance with Statements on Standards for Accounting and Review Services (SSARS). Does SSARS require that the compilation report be printed on the accountant's letterhead and that the report be manually signed by the accountant?

	Printed on the accountant's letterhead	Manually signed by the accountant
a.	Yes	Yes
b.	Yes	No
c.	No	Yes
d.	No	No

27. Which of the following is correct relating to compiled financial statements when third-party reliance upon those statements is anticipated?

    a. A compilation report must be issued.
    b. Omission of note disclosures is unacceptable.
    c. A written engagement letter is required.
    d. Each page of the financial statements should have a restriction such as "Restricted for Management's Use Only."

28. Which communication option(s) may be used when an accountant submits compiled financial statements to be used only by management?

	Compilation report	Written engagement letter
a.	Yes	Yes
b.	Yes	No
c.	No	Yes
d.	No	No

29. A compilation report is **not** required when compiled financial statements are expected to be used by

    a. Management only.
    b. Management and third parties.
    c. Third parties only.
    d. A compilation report is required whenever financial statements are compiled.

Review—General

30. If requested to perform a review engagement for a nonissuer in which an accountant has an immaterial direct financial interest, the accountant is

    a. Not independent and, therefore, may not be associated with the financial statements.
    b. Not independent and, therefore, may not issue a review report.
    c. Not independent and, therefore, may issue a review report, but may not issue an auditor's opinion.
    d. Independent because the financial interest is immaterial and, therefore, may issue a review report.

31. Moore, CPA, has been asked to issue a review report on the balance sheet of Dover Co., a nonissuer. Moore will not be reporting on Dover's statements of income, retained earnings, and cash flows. Moore may issue the review report provided the

    a. Balance sheet is presented in a prescribed form of an industry trade association.
    b. Scope of the inquiry and analytical procedures has not been restricted.
    c. Balance sheet is not to be used to obtain credit or distributed to creditors.
    d. Specialized accounting principles and practices of Dover's industry are disclosed.

32. Baker, CPA, was engaged to review the financial statements of Hall Co., a nonissuer. During the engagement Baker uncovered a complex scheme involving client illegal acts that materially affect Hall's financial statements. If Baker believes that modification of the standard review report is **not** adequate to indicate the deficiencies in the financial statements, Baker should

    a. Disclaim an opinion.
    b. Issue an adverse opinion.
    c. Withdraw from the engagement.
    d. Issue a qualified opinion.

Review Procedures

33. Which of the following is not generally considered a procedure followed by an accountant in obtaining a reasonable basis for the expression of limited assurance for a review of financial statements?

    a. Apply analytical procedures.
    b. Assess fraud risk.
    c. Make inquiries of management.
    d. Obtain written representations from management.

34. Which of the following procedures would an accountant **least** likely perform during an engagement to review the financial statements of a nonissuer?

   a. Observing the safeguards over access to and use of assets and records.
   b. Comparing the financial statements with anticipated results in budgets and forecasts.
   c. Inquiring of management about actions taken at the board of directors' meetings.
   d. Studying the relationships of financial statement elements expected to conform to predictable patterns.

35. Which of the following procedures should an accountant perform during an engagement to review the financial statements of a nonissuer?

   a. Communicating significant deficiencies discovered during the assessment of control risk.
   b. Obtaining a client representation letter from members of management.
   c. Sending bank confirmation letters to the entity's financial institutions.
   d. Examining cash disbursements in the subsequent period for unrecorded liabilities.

36. An accountant should perform analytical procedures during an engagement to

	Compile a nonissuer's financial statements	Review a nonissuer's financial statements
a.	No	No
b.	Yes	Yes
c.	Yes	No
d.	No	Yes

37. Which of the following inquiry or analytical procedures ordinarily is performed in an engagement to review a nonissuer's financial statements?

   a. Analytical procedures designed to test the accounting records by obtaining corroborating audit evidence.
   b. Inquiries concerning the entity's procedures for recording and summarizing transactions.
   c. Analytical procedures designed to test management's assertions regarding continued existence.
   d. Inquiries of the entity's attorney concerning contingent liabilities.

38. Which of the following procedures would most likely be included in a review engagement of a nonissuer?

   a. Preparing a bank transfer schedule.
   b. Inquiring about related-party transactions.
   c. Assessing internal control.
   d. Performing cutoff tests on sales and purchases transactions.

39. Which of the following would the accountant most likely investigate during the review of financial statements of a nonissuer if accounts receivable did **not** conform to a predictable pattern during the year?

   a. Sales returns and allowances.
   b. Credit sales.
   c. Sales of consigned goods.
   d. Cash sales.

40. When performing an engagement to review a nonissuer's financial statements, an accountant most likely would

   a. Confirm a sample of significant accounts receivable balances.
   b. Ask about actions taken at board of directors' meetings.
   c. Obtain an understanding of internal control.
   d. Limit the distribution of the accountant's report.

Review Reporting

41. An accountant has been engaged to review a nonissuer's financial statements that contain several departures from GAAP. If the financial statements are **not** revised and modification of the standard review report is **not** adequate to indicate the deficiencies, the accountant should

   a. Withdraw from the engagement and provide **no** further services concerning these financial statements.
   b. Inform management that the engagement can proceed only if distribution of the accountant's report is restricted to internal use.
   c. Determine the effects of the departures from GAAP and issue a special report on the financial statements.
   d. Issue a modified review report provided the entity agrees that the financial statements will **not** be used to obtain credit.

42. When providing limited assurance that the financial statements of a nonissuer (nonpublic entity) require **no** material modifications to be in accordance with generally accepted accounting principles, the accountant should

   a. Assess the risk that a material misstatement could occur in a financial statement assertion.
   b. Confirm with the entity's lawyer that material loss contingencies are disclosed.
   c. Understand the accounting principles of the industry in which the entity operates.
   d. Develop audit programs to determine whether the entity's financial statements are fairly presented.

43. Smith, CPA, has been asked to issue a review report on the balance sheet of Cone Company, a nonissuer, and not on the other related financial statements. Smith may do so only if

   a. Smith compiles and reports on the related statements of income, retained earnings, and cash flows.
   b. Smith is **not** aware of any material modifications needed for the balance sheet to conform with GAAP.
   c. The scope of Smith's inquiry and analytical procedures is **not** restricted.
   d. Cone is a new client and Smith accepts the engagement after the end of Cone's fiscal year.

44. In reviewing the financial statements of a nonissuer, an accountant is required to modify the standard report for which of the following matters?

	Inability to assess the risk of material misstatement due to fraud	Discovery of significant deficiencies in the design of the entity's internal control
a.	Yes	Yes
b.	Yes	No
c.	No	Yes
d.	No	No

45. Each page of a nonissuer's financial statements reviewed by an accountant should include the following reference:

a. See Accompanying Accountant's Footnotes.
b. Reviewed, No Material Modifications Required.
c. See Accountant's Review Report.
d. Reviewed, No Accountant's Assurance Expressed.

46. Financial statements of a nonissuer that have been reviewed by an accountant should be accompanied by a report stating that a review

a. Provides only limited assurance that the financial statements are fairly presented.
b. Includes examining, on a test basis, information that is the representation of management.
c. Consists principally of inquiries of company personnel and analytical procedures applied to financial data.
d. Does **not** contemplate obtaining corroborating evidential matter or applying certain other procedures ordinarily performed during an audit.

47. An accountant who had begun an audit of the financial statements of a nonissuer was asked to change the engagement to a review because of a restriction on the scope of the audit. If there is reasonable justification for the change, the accountant's review report should include reference to the

	Scope limitation that caused the changed engagement	Original engagement that was agreed to
a.	Yes	No
b.	No	Yes
c.	No	No
d.	Yes	Yes

48. Gole, CPA, is engaged to review the 20X8 financial statements of North Co., a nonissuer. Previously, Gole audited North's 20X7 financial statements and expressed an unqualified opinion. Gole decides to include a separate paragraph in the 20X8 review report because North plans to present comparative financial statements for 20X8 and 20X7. This separate paragraph should indicate that

a. The 20X8 review report is intended solely for the information of management and the board of directors.
b. The 20X7 auditor's report may **no** longer be relied on.
c. No auditing procedures were performed after the date of the 20X7 auditor's report.
d. There are justifiable reasons for changing the level of service from an audit to a review.

49. An accountant's standard report on a review of the financial statements of a nonissuer should state that the accountant

a. Does **not** express an opinion or any form of limited assurance on the financial statements.
b. Is **not** aware of any material modifications that should be made to the financial statements for them to conform with GAAP.
c. Obtained reasonable assurance about whether the financial statements are free of material misstatement.
d. Examined evidence, on a test basis, supporting the amounts and disclosures in the financial statements.

50. Financial statements of a nonissuer that have been reviewed by an accountant should be accompanied by a report stating that

a. The scope of the inquiry and analytical procedures performed by the accountant has not been restricted.
b. All information included in the financial statements is the representation of the management of the entity.
c. A review includes examining, on a test basis, evidence supporting the amounts and disclosures in the financial statements.
d. A review is greater in scope than a compilation, the objective of which is to present financial statements that are free of material misstatements.

51. During a review of the financial statements of a nonissuer, an accountant becomes aware of a lack of adequate disclosure that is material to the financial statements. If management refuses to correct the financial statement presentations, the accountant should

a. Issue an adverse opinion.
b. Issue an "except for" qualified opinion.
c. Disclose this departure from generally accepted accounting principles in a separate paragraph of the report.
d. Express only limited assurance on the financial statement presentations.

52. An accountant who reviews the financial statements of a nonissuer should issue a report stating that a review

a. Is substantially less in scope than an audit.
b. Provides negative assurance that internal control is functioning as designed.
c. Provides only limited assurance that the financial statements are fairly presented.
d. Is substantially more in scope than a compilation.

Multiple-Choice Answers and Explanations

Answers

1. d __ __	12. c __ __	23. c __ __	34. a __ __	45. c __ __
2. c __ __	13. a __ __	24. b __ __	35. b __ __	46. c __ __
3. c __ __	14. a __ __	25. b __ __	36. d __ __	47. c __ __
4. d __ __	15. a __ __	26. d __ __	37. b __ __	48. c __ __
5. a __ __	16. a __ __	27. a __ __	38. b __ __	49. b __ __
6. c __ __	17. b __ __	28. a __ __	39. b __ __	50. b __ __
7. a __ __	18. b __ __	29. a __ __	40. b __ __	51. c __ __
8. d __ __	19. a __ __	30. b __ __	41. a __ __	52. a __ __
9. d __ __	20. a __ __	31. b __ __	42. c __ __	
10. d __ __	21. d __ __	32. c __ __	43. c __ __	1st: __/52 = __%
11. b __ __	22. a __ __	33. b __ __	44. d __ __	2nd: __/52 = __%

Explanations

1. (d) The requirement is to identify the engagement for which Statements on Standards for Accounting and Review Services establish standards and procedures. Answer (d) is correct because the Statements apply when a CPA either compiles or reviews the financial statements of a nonissuer. Answer (a) is incorrect because the Statements do not apply when the CPA is assisting in adjusting the books of account for a partnership or other organization. Answer (b) is incorrect because the Statements only apply to nonissuer (nonpublic) entities. Answer (c) is incorrect because the Statements do not apply when processing the financial data for clients of other accounting firms.

2. (c) The requirement is to identify the authoritative body designated to promulgate standards concerning an accountant's association with unaudited financial statements of an entity that is **not** required to file financial statements with an agency regulating the issuance of the entity's securities. Answer (c) is correct because the Accounting and Review Services Committee is so designated. Answer (a) is incorrect because the Financial Accounting Standards Board is the authoritative body designated to promulgate financial accounting standards. Answer (b) is incorrect because Government Accountability Office is not one of the bodies designated by the AICPA to promulgate technical standards. Answer (d) is incorrect because the Auditing Standards Board is the authoritative body designated to promulgate statements on auditing standards. ET Appendix A presents the bodies designated to promulgate technical standards.

3. (c) The requirement is to determine which of the two listed accounting services an accountant may perform **without** being required to issue a compilation or review report under the Statements on Standards for Accounting and Review Services. Answer (c) is correct because the Statements on Standards for Accounting and Review Services do not apply to preparing a working trial balance or to preparing standard monthly journal entries. See SSARS for these and additional circumstances in which the standards do not apply. Accordingly, no compilation or review report needs to be issued when these services are provided.

4. (d) The requirement is to determine whether an accountant can accept a compilation or a review engagement when s/he is unfamiliar with a prospective client's specialized industry accounting principles, but s/he plans to obtain the required level of knowledge prior to the engagement. Answer (d) is correct because an accountant may accept either a compilation or a review engagement in such circumstances.

5. (a) The requirement is to determine the correct statement concerning both an engagement to compile and an engagement to review a nonissuer's financial statements. Answer (a) is correct because neither a compilation nor a review contemplates obtaining an understanding of internal control. Answer (b) is incorrect because when performing a compilation the accountant need not be independent; independence is required for reviews. Answer (c) is incorrect because a review provides limited assurance. Answer (d) is incorrect because the accountant is not required to obtain a written management representation letter for a compilation; a management representation letter is required for a review.

6. (c) The requirement is to identify the type of assurance (if any) provided in a financial statement compilation report. Answer (c) is correct because the objective of a compilation is to present in the form of financial statements information that is the presentation of management (owners) without undertaking to express any assurance on the statements. Answer (a) is incorrect because accountants never provide absolute assurance. Answer (b) is incorrect because reviews result in limited (negative) assurance. Answer (d) is incorrect because audits, not compilations, provided reasonable assurance.

7. (a) The requirement is to identify the type of report that may be issued by a CPA who has invested in a company's outstanding bonds payable. Answer (a) is correct because such an investment impairs independence and compilations allow a nonindependent CPA to perform the service when it is properly disclosed. Answers (b), (c), and (d) are all incorrect because independence is required for reviews, audits, and agreed-upon procedures engagements.

8. (d) The requirement is to determine whether reproducing client-prepared financial statements without modification and preparing standard monthly journal entries are included in the provisions of Statements on Standards for Accounting and Review Services. Answer (d) is correct because AR 100 allows these services as long as the accountant's name is not associated with the financial statements.

9. (d) The requirement is to identify the correct statement about unaudited personal financial statements included in a personal financial plan. Answer (d) is correct because AT 600 requires that the financial statements be used solely to assist the client and the client's advisor and not be used to obtain credit. Answer (a) is incorrect because financial statements may be presented in comparative form. Answer (b) is incorrect because omitted disclosures may be material. Answer (c) is incorrect because such financial statements may be disclosed to a non-CPA financial planner.

10. (d) The requirement is to identify the circumstance in which Statements on Standards for Accounting and Review Services apply. The Standards apply when a CPA submits unaudited financial statements of a nonissuer (nonpublic) entity to his or her client or others. Accordingly, answer (d) is correct. Answers (a), (b), and (c) are all incorrect because they are all included as services that do not constitute a submission of financial statements to a client.

11. (b) The requirement is to determine whether either or both of (1) the additional audit effort necessary to complete the audit and (2) the reason for the change in the engagement should be considered by a CPA whose client has requested that an audit engagement be changed to a compilation. Answer (b) is correct because SSARS states that additional necessary audit effort and the reason for the change—as well as the additional cost to complete the audit—be considered.

12. (c) The requirement is to determine when a CPA may compile and be associated with financial statements that omit disclosures required by GAAP. Answer (c) is correct because the CPA may compile such financial statements provided that the omission of substantially all disclosures (1) is clearly indicated in the audit report and (2) is not, to the CPA's knowledge, undertaken with the intention of misleading those who might reasonably be expected to use the financial statements.

13. (a) The requirement is to determine an accountant's responsibility relating to knowledge of the client's accounting principles and practices when performing a compilation. Answer (a) is correct because to compile financial statements the accountant should possess a general understanding of the nature of the entity's business transactions, the form of its accounting records, the stated qualifications of its accounting personnel, the accounting basis on which the financial statements are to be presented, and the form and content

of the financial statements. Answer (b) is incorrect because the accountant need not have a general understanding of the entity's controls. Answer (c) is incorrect because no such consideration of risk factors is envisioned in a compilation. Answer (d) is incorrect because no such consideration of internal control awareness of senior management is made.

14. (a) The requirement is to identify the procedure an accountant ordinarily performs in a compilation engagement of a nonissuer. Answer (a) is correct because the accountant is required, at a minimum, to read the financial statements to consider whether they are free from obvious material errors.

15. (a) The requirement is to identify a CPA's reporting responsibility when current year financial statements are compiled while the preceding year's financial statements were audited. Answer (a) is correct because a separate paragraph to the report should indicate (1) that the financial statements of the prior period were audited, (2) the date of the previous report, (3) the type of opinion expressed, (4) if the opinion was other than unmodified, the substantive reasons therefor and (5) that no auditing procedures were performed after the date of the previous report. Answer (b) is incorrect because no indication is made concerning updating the assessment of control risk. Answer (c) is incorrect because the CPA does not indicate reasons for changing from an audit to a compilation. Answer (d) is incorrect because the audit report may be relied on for the prior year's financial statements.

16. (a) The requirement is to identify a condition required for an accountant to submit a written personal financial plan containing unaudited financial statements to a client without complying with the compilation and review requirements presented in SSARS. Answer (a) is correct because SSARS allow such an exception when the plan (1) is to be used to assist the client and the client's advisors in developing financial goals and objectives, (2) will not be used to obtain credit, and (3) when nothing comes to the accountant's attention that would lead him/her to believe that the statements will be used for credit or for any other purposes. Answer (b) is incorrect because any work performed on the prior year statements is not applicable to the statements of the current year. Answer (c) is incorrect because the engagement letter need not acknowledge departures from GAAP. Answer (d) is incorrect because no assurance is provided in such reports.

17. (b) The requirement is to identify an accountant's reporting responsibility when performing a compilation and he or she determines that a going concern uncertainty has not been properly disclosed by a client. Answer (b) is correct because this is a departure from GAAP and results in modification of the report's third paragraph and addition of an explanatory paragraph. Answer (a) is incorrect because the information on the client's ability to continue as a going concern should be included in the financial statements; if it is not, a departure from GAAP exists. Answer (c) is incorrect because adverse opinions are not issued based on compilations. Answer (d) is incorrect because qualified opinions are not issued based on compilations.

18. (b) The requirement is to identify the statement that should be included in a compilation report. Answer (b) is correct because compilation reports indicate that the accountant compiled the financial statements in accordance with Statements on Standards for Accounting and Review Services.

19. (a) The requirement is to determine how a CPA should indicate that a client's compiled financial statements were prepared in conformity with the income tax basis of accounting when the financial statements provide no such disclosure. Answer (a) is correct because if the basis of accounting is not disclosed in the financial statements, the accountant should disclose the basis in the compilation report. Answer (b) is incorrect because each page of the financial statements should only include the reference "See Accountant's Compilation Report." Answer (c) is incorrect because the auditor is not required to issue a special report. Answer (d) is incorrect because the auditor does not have to withdraw from the engagement.

20. (a) The requirement is to determine how the compilation report should be modified to indicate that the entity's financial statements do not include all disclosures required by GAAP. Answer (a) is correct because AR 100 states that while the accountant may compile such financial statements, the accountant must clearly indicate in the compilation report that substantially all disclosures required by GAAP have been omitted. Answer (b) is incorrect because the financial statements are not compiled on a comprehensive basis other than GAAP. Answer (c) is incorrect because a compilation may be performed on financial statements lacking such disclosures. Answer (d) is incorrect because these financial statements are not considered "special-purpose financial statements."

21. (d) The requirement is to determine the information least likely to be included in the understanding with management that an accountant obtains when a compilation is to be performed. Answer (d) is correct because in a compilation an accountant obtains no assurance, not limited assurance; limited assurance is related to reviews. Answers (a), (b), and (c) are all items included in the understanding.

22. (a) The requirement is to determine a CPA's responsibility when the first year of compiled comparative financial statements omit substantially all disclosures required by generally accepted accounting principles, while the second year's statements include such disclosures. Answer (a) is correct because the CPA may **not** report on the comparative financial statements because of a lack of comparability. Answers (b), (c), and (d) are all incorrect because they allow such reporting to occur under certain circumstances.

23. (c) The requirement is to identify the statement that should **not** be included in a CPA's financial statement compilation report. Answer (c) is correct because a compilation report provides no assurance on the financial statements.

24. (b) The requirement is to determine the representations made explicitly and implicitly when issuing a standard compilation report on a nonissuer's financial statements. Answer (b) is correct because the report explicitly states that the financial statements have not been audited and that the accountant has compiled them.

25. (b) The requirement is to determine the appropriate date for an auditor's compilation report. SSARS require that the date of completion of the compilation should be used.

26. (d) The requirement is to determine whether an accountant's compilation report must be printed on the accountant's letterhead, manually signed by the accountant, or both. Answer (d) is correct because the professional standards require neither that the report be printed on the accountant's letterhead, nor that it be manually signed by the accountant. Answers (a), (b), and (c) are all incorrect because they include an inappropriate "yes" to one or both issues. See SSARS for information on reporting on a compilation of financial statements.

27. (a) The requirement is to identify the correct statement concerning compiled financial statements that are to be made available to third parties. Answer (a) is correct because a compilation report must be issued when third-party reliance upon compiled financial statements is anticipated. Answer (b) is incorrect because note disclosures may be omitted. Answer (c) is incorrect because while advisable, use of an engagement letter is not required in such circumstances. Answer (d) is incorrect because no such restriction is necessary.

28. (a) The requirement is to identify the correct statement concerning appropriate communication option(s) when compiled financial statements are only going to be used by management. Answer (a) is correct because when an accountant submits to a client compiled financial statements that are not expected to be used by a third party, either a compilation report or a written engagement letter (or both) may be used. Answer (b), (c), and (d) are all incorrect because they suggest that either a compilation report, a written engagement letter, or both are unacceptable.

29. (a) The requirement is to identify the circumstance in which a compilation report is not required. Answer (a) is correct because when financial statements are only for management, no compilation report is required. Answers (b) and (c) are incorrect because when third parties are expected to use compiled financial statements, a compilation report is required. Answer (d) is incorrect because a compilation report is not always required.

30. (b) The requirement is to determine the effect of an immaterial direct financial interest on accountant independence. Answer (b) is correct because even immaterial direct financial interests impair the independence that is required for the performance of reviews. Answer (a) is incorrect because a CPA who lacks independence may compile those financial statements when this lack of independence is disclosed in the compilation report. Answer (c) is incorrect because a review report may not be issued. Answer (d) is incorrect because the CPA is not independent.

31. (b) The requirement is to identify the circumstance in which a CPA may issue a review report on a single financial statement. Answer (b) is correct because an accountant may issue a review report on a financial statement, such as a balance sheet, and not report on the other related financial statements if the scope of his or her inquiry and analytical procedures has not been restricted. Answer (a) is incorrect because the balance sheet need not be presented in pre-scribed form. Answer (c) is incorrect because the balance sheet may be used to obtain credit or to distribute to credi-tors. Answer (d) is incorrect because specialized accounting principles and practices in an industry may or may not need to be disclosed depending upon the circumstances.

32. (c) The requirement is to identify a CPA's responsi-bility when he or she believes that modification of the stan-dard review report is **not** adequate to indicate deficiencies in financial statements affected by illegal acts. Answer (c) is correct because whenever a CPA believes that modification of the standard report is not adequate to indicate the deficiencies in the financial statements, he or she should withdraw from the review engagement and provide no further services with respect to those financial statements.

33. (b) The requirement is to identify the procedure not followed by an accountant in obtaining a reasonable basis for the expression of limited assurance for a review of financial statements. Answer (b) is correct because reviews ordinarily do not include an assessment of the risk of fraud. Answer (a) is incorrect because reviews include analytical procedures. Answer (c) is incorrect because a review includes inquiries of management. Answer (d) is incorrect because auditors obtain written representation from management when performing a review.

34. (a) The requirement is to identify the procedure **least** likely to be performed in a review of the financial statements of a nonissuer. Answer (a) is correct because a review of a nonissuer financial statements does not specifically address observing the safeguards over access to and use of assets and records. Answers (b), (c), and (d) are all incorrect because they are included in the procedures suggested for a review by SSARS.

35. (b) The requirement is to identify the procedures that an accountant would perform during an engagement to review the financial statements of a nonissuer. Answer (b) is correct because AR 100 requires that the CPA obtain a representation letter. Answers (a), (c), and (d) are incorrect because they are not included in SSARS which present a list of procedures per-formed during a review.

36. (d) The requirement is to determine whether analytical procedures need to be performed on a compilation and/or a review engagement. Answer (d) is correct because a com-pilation does not require performance of analytical procedures, while a review does.

37. (b) The requirement is to determine the type of inquiry or analytical procedures ordinarily performed in an engagement to review a nonissuer's financial statements. Answer (b) is correct because an accountant will make inquiries concerning the entity's procedures for recording, classifying, and summarizing transactions, and accumulating information for disclosure in the financial statements. Answer (a) is incorrect because the analytical procedures and other procedures involved in a review do not in general obtain corroborating audit evidence as do the procedures of an audit. Answer (c) is

incorrect because the procedures for reviews are not specially designed to test management's assertion regarding continued existence. Answer (d) is incorrect because inquiries of the entity's attorney are not normally required when a review is being performed.

38. (b) The requirement is to determine the most likely procedures to be included in a review engagement of a non-issuer. Answer (b) is correct because a review consists pri-marily of inquiries and analytical procedures. Answer (a) is incorrect because a bank transfer schedule is generally not prepared for a review engagement. Answer (c) is incorrect because a review does not include assessing the control structure. Answer (d) is incorrect because cutoff tests on sales and purchases are not normally performed on a review. Note that the procedures included in answers (a), (c), and (d) are typically performed in an audit.

39. (b) The requirement is to determine the type of trans-action the accountant is most likely to investigate during a review when the year's accounts receivable did **not** conform to a predictable pattern. Answer (b) is correct because accounts receivable are generated from credit sales and an accountant would therefore investigate them. Answer (a) is incorrect because sales returns and allowances would be less likely to cause large shifts in accounts receivable than credit sales. Answer (c) is incorrect because it is less complete than answer (b) since sales of consigned goods represent only one possible type of sale that might impact accounts receivable. Answer (d) is incorrect because cash sales do not affect accounts receivable.

40. (b) The requirement is to identify the most likely proce-dure to be included in a review of a nonissuer's financial statements. Answer (b) is correct because SSARS state that reviews ordinarily include inquiries concerning actions taken at board of directors' meetings. Answer (a) is incorrect because reviews consist primarily of inquiry and analytical procedures and do not generally include confirmation of accounts receivable. Answer (c) is incorrect because a review of a nonpublic entity does not normally include obtaining an understanding of internal control or assessing control risk. Answer (d) is incorrect because distribution of a review report need not be limited. See SSARS for specific procedures included in reviews.

41. (a) The requirement is to determine a CPA's re-sponsibilities when performing a review of a nonissuer's financial statements that contain uncorrected departures from GAAP and the CPA believes that the review report is not adequate to indicate the deficiencies. Answer (a) is cor-rect because SSARS state that in such circumstances the CPA should withdraw from the engagement and provide no further services with respect to those financial statements. Answers (b) and (d) are incorrect because restricting distri-bution is not adequate or appropriate in such a circumstance. Answer (c) is incorrect because the standards on special reports do not apply in this circumstance.

42. (c) The requirement is to determine the listed require-ment when an accountant is providing limited assurance that the financial statements of a nonissuer require **no** material modifications to be in accordance with generally accepted accounting principles. Accountants perform reviews to provide such limited assurance. Answer (c) is correct because obtaining an understanding of the accounting principles in the industry is required for reviews. See SSARS for this and other requirements. Answer (a) is incorrect because reviews do not require the accountant to assess the risk of material misstatement. Answer (b) is incorrect because reviews generally do not include any communication with the entity's lawyer. Answer (d) is incorrect because an "audit" program is not required since a review is being performed.

43. (c) The requirement is to identify the circumstances in which a CPA may issue a review report on the balance sheet of a nonissuer, and not report on the related financial statements. Answer (c) is correct because an accountant may issue a review report on one financial statement and not on the other related statements if the scope of the inquiry and analytical procedures has not been restricted. Answer (a) is incorrect because the CPA need not compile or report on the related statements of income, retained earnings, and cash flows when reviewing only the balance sheet. Answer (b) is incorrect because, when material modifications are needed, a CPA may still report on the balance sheet, but must indicate the modifications in the review report. Answer (d) is incorrect because the client need not be new.

44. (d) The requirement is to identify whether a review report is modified due to either inability to assess the risk of material misstatement due to fraud, a discovery of internal control deficiencies, or both. Answer (d) is correct because neither of these circumstances requires modification of a review report. Answers (a), (b), and (c) are all incorrect because they suggest that one or the other of these circumstances results in modification of a review report. A departure from GAAP is the primary cause of a review report modification. SSARS provide guidance on review reports.

45. (c) The requirement is to identify the reference that should be included in each page of a nonissuer's reviewed financial statements. SSARS require that each page of the financial statements include a reference such as "See Accountant's Review Report."

46. (c) The requirement is to identify the statement that is included in an accountant's review report on the financial statements of a nonissuer. Answer (c) is correct because a review report includes a statement that a review consists principally of inquires of company personnel and analytical procedures applied to financial data. See SSARS for information that should be included in a review report.

47. (c) The requirement is to determine a CPA's reporting responsibility when an audit engagement for a nonissuer has been changed to a review engagement because of what the CPA believes to be a reasonable restriction on the scope of the audit. Answer (c) is correct because in such circumstances the CPA should neither include reference to the original engagement nor to the scope limitation.

48. (c) The requirement is to identify the correct statement relating to a CPA's report on comparative statements when the current year has been reviewed and the previous year has been audited. Answer (c) is correct because when a separate paragraph is being added to the CPA's review report the CPA should clearly indicate the difference in the levels of assurance for the two years. In this situation, SSARS require the auditor to indicate that the previous year's financial statements were audited, the date of the report, the type of opinion expressed and if the opinion was other than unqualified, the substantive reasons for that opinion, and that no auditing procedures were performed after the date of the previous report. Answer (a) is incorrect because the review report is not solely intended for management or the board of directors. Answer (b) is incorrect because the prior year's audit report may still be appropriate. Answer (d) is incorrect because this statement does not need to be included within the review report.

49. (b) The requirement is to identify the statement included in the standard report issued by an accountant after reviewing the financial statements of a nonissuer. Answer (b) is correct because the report states that the accountant is not aware of any material modifications that should be made to the financial statements in order for them to be in conformity with generally accepted accounting principles. SSARS present the required disclosures for a review report.

50. (b) The requirement is to identify the information presented in a review report of financial statements of a nonissuer. Answer (b) is correct because the report indicates that all information included in the financial statements is the representation of the management of the entity.

51. (c) The requirement is to determine an accountant's reporting responsibility when associated with a nonissuer's reviewed statements which contain a material departure from generally accepted accounting principles. Answer (c) is correct because SSARS require the inclusion of a separate paragraph describing the departure. Answers (a) and (b) are incorrect because an adverse opinion or an "except for" qualified opinion may only be issued when an audit has been performed. Answer (d) is incorrect because expressing limited assurance (as is normally provided in reviews) on the financial statements is not adequate to disclose the departure.

52. (a) The requirement is to identify the reply which is correct concerning the content of a review report. Answer (a) is correct because a review report indicates that a review is substantially less in scope than an audit. Answer (b) is incorrect because a review report provides no information on internal control. Answer (c) is incorrect because while a review report states that the accountant is not aware of any material modifications that should be made to the financial statements, it does not provide limited assurance that the financial statements are fairly presented. Answer (d) is incorrect because while a review report does state that a review is substantially less in scope than an audit, it does not refer to a compilation.

Simulations

Task-Based Simulation 1

Auditors who audit public nonpublic companies must be familiar with professional standards developed by a variety of sources. For each of the types of services below indicate the proper source of professional requirements. Each source may be used once, more than once, or not at all.

Source of Standards

A. Accounting and Review Services committee Statements on Standards for Accounting and Review Services
B. Auditing Standards Board Statements on Auditing Standards
C. PCAOB Auditing Standards

		(A)	(B)	(C)
1.	An annual review of the financial statements of a nonpublic company.	○	○	○
2.	A quarterly review of the financial statements of a nonpublic company that has an annual audit.	○	○	○
3.	A quarterly review of the financial statements of a public company that has an annual audit.	○	○	○
4.	An audit of the financial statements of a nonpublic company.	○	○	○
5.	A compilation of the financial statements of a nonpublic company.	○	○	○
6.	A quarterly review of the financial statements of a nonpublic company that annually has a review of its financial statements. (Note: The question is on the quarterly review.)	○	○	○
7.	A letter to an underwriter of a public company.	○	○	○
8.	A report on summary financial statement of a nonpublic company.	○	○	○
9.	An audit of a public company.	○	○	○

Task-Based Simulation 2

Review Reports

The president of Enright Corporation, a nonpublic client, asked you to perform a review of the financial statements for the current year only. You have now completed your inquiry and other review procedures and find that you can issue a standard review report.

Selections

A. AU-C
B. PCAOB
C. AT
D. AR
E. ET
F. BL
G. CS
H. QC

		(A)	(B)	(C)	(D)	(E)	(F)	(G)	(H)
1.	Which title of the Professional Standards presents a standard review report on one year?	○	○	○	○	○	○	○	○

2. Enter the exact section and paragraph that lists the basic elements of such a review report.

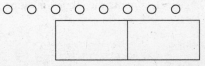

Simulation Solutions

Task-Based Simulation 1

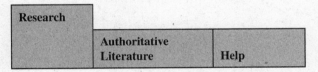

		(A)	(B)	(C)
1.	An annual review of the financial statements of a nonpublic company.	●	○	○
2.	A quarterly review of the financial statements of a nonpublic company that has an annual audit.	○	●	○
3.	A quarterly review of the financial statements of a public company that has an annual audit.	○	○	●
4.	An audit of the financial statements of a nonpublic company.	○	●	○
5.	A compilation of the financial statements of a nonpublic company.	●	○	○
6.	A quarterly review of the financial statements of a nonpublic company that annually has a review of its financial statements. (Note: The question is on the quarterly review.)	●	○	○
7.	A letter to an underwriter of a public company.	○	○	●
8.	A report on summary financial statement of a nonpublic company.	○	●	○
9.	An audit of a public company.	○	○	●

Task-Based Simulation 2

		(A)	(B)	(C)	(D)	(E)	(F)	(G)	(H)
1.	Which title of the Professional Standards presents a standard review report on one year?	○	○	○	●	○	○	○	○

2. Enter the exact section and paragraph that lists the basic elements of such a review report.

90	28

Module 7: Audit Sampling

Overview

Sampling is essential throughout audits as auditors attempt to gather sufficient appropriate audit evidence in a cost efficient manner. The following "Diagram of an Audit" was originally presented in the auditing overview section.

Diagram of an Audit

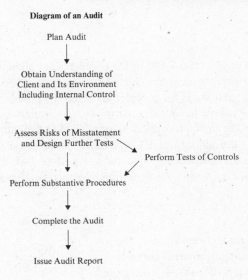

Plan Audit

↓

Obtain Understanding of Client and Its Environment Including Internal Control

↓

Assess Risks of Misstatement and Design Further Tests → Perform Tests of Controls

↓

Perform Substantive Procedures

↓

Complete the Audit

↓

Issue Audit Report

Audit sampling is used for both tests of controls (attributes sampling) and for tests of details of transactions and balances (usually, variables sampling). In both attributes sampling and variables sampling, the plans may be either nonstatistical or statistical. The chart at the bottom of this page summarizes methods of audit sampling.

Audit sampling has been tested on most recent auditing examinations, usually in the form of multiple-choice questions. One might anticipate additional questions dealing with concepts such as sampling risk, nonsampling risk, tolerable misstatement[1], and the projection of sample results to an overall population. Also, as in the past, one might expect exam questions dealing with the relationships between statistical concepts and basic audit concepts such as assessing control risk, materiality, and audit decision making. One might expect a portion of a simulation to require candidates to calculate or interpret statistical results.

---

[1] Tolerable misstatement may be viewed as the application of performance materiality (see Module 2) to a particular sampling procedure. In this module we emphasize tolerable misstatement, the approach taken for audit sampling in the PCAOB, ASB, and international standards.

Detailed Audit Sampling Techniques

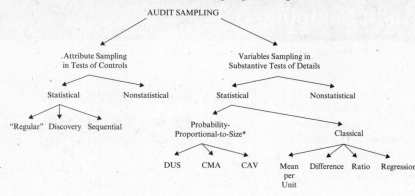

* Probability-proportional-to-size sampling may also be used for attributes sampling. A number of variations of probability-proportional-to-size sampling exist, including dollar-unit sampling and monetary-unit sampling.

The material in this module is primarily structured around both AU-C 530 and the *Audit Sampling* guide. It is presented in outline form to allow an efficient review of the material. Additionally, AU-C 320 on audit risk and materiality relates to this area.

A. Basic Audit Sampling Concepts

1. **Definition of Sampling**

    a. **Audit sampling** is selection of less than 100% of the population of audit relevance, and the evaluation of that sample, such that the auditor expects the items selected (the sample) to be representative of the population, and thus likely to provide a reasonable basis for conclusions about the population. In this context, a **representative sample** is one that will result in conclusions that, subject to the limitations of **sampling risk,** are similar to those that would be drawn if the same procedures were applied to the entire population. Basic to audit sampling is sampling risk, the risk that the auditor's conclusion based on the sample may be different from the conclusion if the entire population were subjected to the same audit procedure. (AU-C 530).

    b. The AICPA Audit and Accounting Guide, *Audit Sampling*, lists procedures that **do not** involve sampling as follows:

        (1) Inquiry and observation

            (a) Interview management and employees
            (b) Obtain an understanding of internal control
            (c) Obtain written representations from management
            (d) Scan accounting records for unusual items
            (e) Observe behavior of personnel and functioning of business operations
            (f) Observe cash-handling procedures
            (g) Inspect land and buildings

        (2) Analytical procedures
        (3) Procedures applied to every item in a population

            (a) For example, some audit plans include the audit of all "large" accounts and a portion of the small accounts. In such situations only the "small" accounts would be subject to sampling.

        (4) Tests of controls where application is not documented

            (a) Procedures that depend on segregation of duties or that otherwise provide no documentary evidence

        (5) Procedures from which the auditor does not intend to extend a conclusion to the remaining items in the account

            (a) For example, tracing several transactions through accounting system to obtain understanding

        (6) Untested balances

2. **General Approaches to Audit Sampling—Nonstatistical and Statistical**

  a. Both involve judgment in planning, executing the sampling plan, and evaluating the results of the sample

  b. Both can provide sufficient appropriate audit evidence

  c. Statistical sampling helps the auditor to

    (1) Design an efficient sample

    (2) Measure the sufficiency of the audit evidence obtained

    (3) Evaluate the sample results

      (a) The auditor can objectively **quantify sampling risk** to limit it to a level considered acceptable. (This has been the proper reply to numerous multiple-choice questions on the advantages of sampling.)

  d. Costs of statistical sampling

    (1) Training auditors

    (2) Designing samples

    (3) Selecting items to be tested

3. **Uncertainty and Audit Sampling**—Eliminating all uncertainty, even if possible, would delay release of audited information and greatly increase audit cost

  a. **Audit risk** is a combination of the risk that a material misstatement will occur and the risk that it will not be detected by the auditor. It consists of (1) the risk (inherent risk and control risk) that the balance or class and related assertions contain misstatements that could be material when aggregated with other misstatements, and (2) the risk (detection risk) that the auditor will not detect such misstatement. Recall our discussion of audit risk in the Engagement Planning Module (Section A.1.a.).

    (1) **Audit risk** may be expressed using the following model:

$$AR = IR \times CR \times DR$$

$$AR = IR \times CR \times AP \times TD$$

where:

AR	=	Audit risk
IR	=	Inherent risk
CR	=	Control risk
DR	=	Detection risk
AP	=	Analytical procedures risk and other relevant substantive tests
TD	=	Test of details allowable risk of incorrect acceptance for this substantive test

> **NOTE:** The second equation is presented in the Appendix to AU-C 530. This model separates detection risk into the two components of AP and TD.

    (2) **Nonsampling risk** includes all aspects of audit risk that are not due to sampling. It is controlled by adequate planning and supervision of audit work and proper adherence to quality control standards. The following are examples of nonsampling risk:

      (a) The failure to select appropriate audit procedures

      (b) The failure to recognize misstatements in documents examined

      (c) Misinterpreting the results of audit tests

    (3) **Sampling risk** is the risk that the auditor's conclusion, based on a sample, might be different from the conclusion that would be reached if the test were applied in the same way to the entire population (AU-C 530).

      (a) Tests of controls sampling risks include the risk of assessing control risk too high and the risk of assessing control risk too low. These risks are discussed in section B.1. of this outline.

(b) Substantive test sampling risks include the risk of incorrect rejection and the risk of incorrect acceptance. These risks are discussed in section C.1. of this outline.

> **NOTE:** A number of exam multiple-choice questions have required candidates to identify the response that is an example of nonsampling risk. For example, illustrations of three of the above sampling risks may be presented with one of nonsampling risk. To identify nonsampling risk, think of it as the risk of "human" type errors (e.g., failure to detect a misstatement).

4. **Types of Audit Tests in Which Sampling May Be Used**

   a. **Tests of controls** are directed toward the design or operation of a control to assess its effectiveness in preventing or detecting material misstatements in a financial statement assertion.
   b. **Substantive tests** are used to obtain evidence about the validity and propriety of the accounting treatment of transactions and balances.
   c. **Dual-purpose tests** are those in which a single sample is used to test a control **and** to serve as a substantive test of a recorded balance or class of transactions. When a dual-purpose test is used, auditors select the sample size as the higher of that required for the two purposes. For example, if the test of control test required thirty-five items, and the substantive test required forty, both tests would be performed using the forty items.

5. **Types of Statistical Sampling Plans**

   a. **Attributes sampling** (used in tests of controls) reaches a conclusion in terms of a rate of occurrence—discussed in section B. below.
   b. **Variables sampling** (used in substantive testing) reaches a conclusion in dollar amounts (or possibly in units).

      (1) **Probability-proportional-to-size (PPS) sampling**—discussion in section C.2
      (2) **Classical variables sampling techniques**—discussed in section C.3

   Below is an outline organized around the audit guide's steps involved in attributes and variables sampling.

AUDIT AND ACCOUNTING GUIDE SAMPLING STEPS

Attributes Sampling (used in Tests of Controls)

1. **Determine** the objectives of the test
2. **Define** the deviation conditions

3. **Define** the population

   a. Define the period covered by the test
   b. Define the sampling unit
   c. Consider the completeness of the population

4. **Determine** the method of selecting the sample

   a. Random-number sampling
   b. Systematic sampling
   c. Other sampling

Attributes Sampling (used in Tests of Controls)

5. **Determine** the sample size

   a. Consider the acceptable risk of assessing control risk too low
   b. Consider the tolerable rate
   c. Consider the expected population deviation rate
   d. Consider the effect of population size
   e. Consider a sequential or a fixed sample-size approach

Variables Sampling (used in Substantive Testing)

Determine the objectives of the test
Define the population

   a. Define the sampling unit
   b. Consider the completeness of the population
   c. Identify individually significant items

Select an audit sampling technique

Determine the sample size

   a. Consider the variation within the population
   b. Consider the acceptable level of risk
   c. Consider the tolerable misstatement
   d. Consider the expected amount of misstatement
   e. Consider the population size

Variables Sampling (used in Substantive Testing)

Determine the method of selecting the sample

6. **Perform** the sampling plan
7. **Evaluate** the sample results

    a. Calculate the deviation rate
    b. Consider sampling risk
    c. Consider the qualitative aspects of the deviations
    d. Reach an overall conclusion

8. **Document** the sampling procedure

Perform the sampling plan
Evaluate the sample results

    a. Project the misstatement to the population and consider sampling risk
    b. Consider the qualitative aspects of the misstatements and reach an overall conclusion

Document the sampling procedure

NOTE: Be familiar with the preceding steps as the CPA exam questions have required candidates to list and explain them.

NOW REVIEW MULTIPLE-CHOICE QUESTIONS 1 THROUGH 19

B. Sampling in Tests of Controls

1. **Sampling Risk**

    a. **Risk of assessing control risk too high (alpha risk, type I error)** is the risk that the assessed level of control risk based on the sample is **greater** than the true operating effectiveness of the control structure policy or procedure. Know that this risk relates to **audit efficiency**. If the auditor assesses control risk too high, substantive tests will consequently be expanded beyond the necessary level, leading to audit inefficiency.

    b. **Risk of assessing control risk too low (beta risk, type II error)** is the risk that the assessed level of control risk based on the sample is **less** than the true operating effectiveness of the control structure policy or procedure. Know that this risk relates to **audit effectiveness**. If the auditor assesses control risk too low, substantive tests will not be expanded to the necessary level to ensure an effective audit. Because materially misstated financial statements may result from this situation, controlling this risk is generally considered of greater audit concern than controlling the risk of assessing control risk too high. The table below illustrates the two aspects of sampling risk for tests of controls.

TRUE OPERATING EFFECTIVENESS OF THE CONTROLS IS

The test of controls sample indicates:	Adequate for planned assessed level of control risk	Inadequate for planned assessed level of control risk
Extent of operating effectiveness is adequate	Correct Decision	Incorrect Decision (risk of assessing control risk too low)
Extent of operating effectiveness is inadequate	Incorrect Decision (risk of assessing control risk too high)	Correct Decision

2. **Statistical (Attributes) Sampling for Tests of Controls**

    a. **Steps involved in attributes sampling**

        (1) **Determine the objectives of the test**—Remember that tests of controls are designed to provide reasonable assurance that internal control is operating effectively. For example, attributes sampling might test controls for voucher processing, billing systems, payroll systems, inventory pricing, fixed-asset additions, and depreciation computations.

        (a) Attributes sampling is generally used when there is a trail of documentary evidence.

(2) **Define the deviation conditions**—An auditor should identify characteristics (attributes) that would indicate operation of the internal control procedures. The auditor next defines the possible deviation conditions. A deviation is a departure from the prescribed internal control policy or procedure.

EXAMPLE

If the prescribed procedure to be tested requires the cancellation of each paid voucher, a paid but uncanceled voucher would constitute a deviation.

---

(3) **Define the population**—For tests of controls, the population is the class of transactions being tested. Conclusions based on sample results can be projected only to the population from which the sample was selected. Three steps are involved in defining the population.

  (a) **Define the period covered by the test**—Ideally, tests of controls should be applied to transactions executed during the entire period under audit. In some cases it is more efficient to test transactions at an interim date and use supplemental procedures to obtain reasonable assurance regarding the remaining period.

  (b) **Define the sampling unit**—The sampling unit is one of the individual elements constituting the population. In our earlier example, the sampling unit is the voucher.

  (c) **Consider the completeness of the population**—The auditor actually selects sampling units from a physical representation of the population (in our example, the recorded paid vouchers). Because subsequent statistical conclusions relate to the physical representation, the auditor should consider whether it includes the entire population.

(4) **Determine the method of selecting the sample**—The sample should be representative of the population. All items in the population should have an opportunity to be selected. Methods include

  (a) **Random-number sampling**—Every sampling unit has the same probability of being selected, and every combination of sampling units of equal size has the same probability of being selected. Random numbers can be generated using a random number table or a computer program.

  (b) **Systematic sampling**—Every nth (population size/sample size) item is selected after a random start. When a random starting point is used, this method provides every sampling unit in the population an equal chance of being selected. If the population is arranged randomly, systematic selection is essentially the same as random number selection.

   1. One problem with systematic sampling is that the population may be systematically ordered; for example, the identification number of all large items ends with a nine. A biased sample may result since nine's may be selected either too frequently **or** never. This limitation may be overcome by using multiple random starts or by using an interval that does not coincide with the pattern in the population.
   2. An advantage of systematic sampling, as compared to random-number sampling, is that the population items do not have to be consecutively numbered for the auditor to use this method.

  (c) **Haphazard sampling**—A sample consisting of units selected without any conscious bias, that is, without any special reason for including or omitting items from the sample. It does not consist of sampling units selected in a "careless" manner, but in a manner that the auditor hopes to be representative of the population. Haphazard sampling is not used for statistical sampling because it does not allow the auditor to measure the probability of selecting a given combination of sampling units.

  (d) **Block sampling**—A sample consisting of contiguous units.

EXAMPLE

An auditor selects three blocks of ten vouchers for examination.

The advantage of block sampling is the ease of sample unit selection. The disadvantage is that the sample selected may not be representative of the overall population. Because of this disadvantage, use of this method is **generally the least desirable** method.

(5) **Determine the sample size**—A series of decisions must be made.

    (a) **Allowable risk of assessing control risk too low.** Since the auditor uses the results of tests of controls as the source of evidence for assessing control risk at levels below the maximum, a low allowable risk is normally selected.

        1. Risk levels between 1% and 10% are normally used.

        2. There is an inverse relationship (e.g., as one increases the other decreases) between the risk of assessing control risk too low and sample size.

    (b) **Tolerable rate (tolerable deviation rate)**—The maximum rate of deviation from a prescribed control structure policy or procedure that an auditor is willing to accept without modifying the planned assessed level of control risk.

        1. The auditor's determination of the tolerable deviation rate is a function of

            a] The planned assessed level of control risk.

            b] The degree of assurance desired by the sample.

        2. When the auditor's planned assessed level of control risk is low, and the degree of assurance desired from the sample is high, the tolerable rate should be low.

            a] This will be the case, for example, when the auditor does not perform other tests of controls for an assertion.

    (c) **Expected population deviation rate (expected rate of occurrence)**—An estimate of the deviation rate in the entire population

        1. If the expected population deviation rate exceeds the tolerable rate, tests (tests of controls/attributes sampling) will not be performed.

        2. Although the risk of assessing control risk too high is often not explicitly controlled when determining attributes sample size, it can be controlled to some extent by specifying a conservative (larger) expected deviation rate.

        3. There is a direct relationship (e.g., as one increases, the other also increases) between the expected deviation rate and sample size.

        4. The expected population deviation rate is

            a. Typically determined by using last year's deviation rate adjusted judgmentally for current year changes in the control procedure, or by determining the deviation rate in a small preliminary sample.

            b. Used only to determine sample size and not to evaluate sample results, so the estimate need not be exact.

        5. Because a deviation from a control procedure does not necessarily result in a misstatement (e.g., an unapproved invoice may still represent a valid business expenditure), the rate of misstatements is generally lower than the deviation rate.

    (d) **Population effect**—Increases in the size of the population normally increase the sample size. However, it is generally appropriate to treat any population of more than 5,000 sample units as if it were infinite.

    (e) When (a) through (d) above have been quantified, the sample size can be easily determined through the use of sample size tables. For the CPA exam **remember the following relationships**:

**ATTRIBUTES SAMPLING
SUMMARY OF RELATIONSHIPS TO SAMPLE SIZE**

Increases in	Effect on Sample Size
Risk of assessing control risk too low	Decrease
Tolerable rate	Decrease
Expected population deviation rate	Increase
Population	Increase (slightly for large samples)

    (f) **Fixed vs. sequential sample size approach**—Audit samples may be designed using either a fixed or a sequential sample size approach. Supplementing traditional attributes (fixed size) sampling approaches are

        1. **Sequential (stop-or-go) sampling**—a sampling plan for which the sample is selected in several steps, with the need to perform each step conditional on the results of the previous steps. That is, the results may either be so poor as to indicate that the control may not be relied upon, or so good as to justify reliance at each step.

        2. **Discovery sampling**—a procedure for determining the sample size required to have a stipulated probability of observing at least one occurrence when the expected population deviation rate is at a designated level. It is most appropriate when the expected deviation rate is zero or near zero. If a deviation is detected, the auditor must either (1) use an alternate approach, or (2) if the deviation is of sufficient importance, audit all transactions.

(6) **Perform the sampling plan**—The auditor should apply the appropriate audit procedures to all items in the sample to determine if there are any deviations from the prescribed control procedures. Each deviation should be analyzed to determine whether it is an isolated or recurring type of occurrence.

    (a) The auditor should select extra sample items (more than the needed sample size) so that voided, unused, or inapplicable documents can be excluded from the sample and be replaced.

    (b) If the auditor is unable to examine a selected item (e.g., a document has been misplaced), it should be considered a deviation for evaluation purposes. Furthermore, the auditor should consider the reasons for this limitation and its implications for the audit.

    (c) In some cases the auditor may find enough deviations early in the sampling process to indicate that a control cannot be relied upon. The auditor need not continue the tests in such circumstances.

(7) **Evaluate the sample results**—Once audit procedures have been performed on all sample items, the sample results must be evaluated and projected to the entire population from which the sample was selected.

    (a) Calculate the sample deviation rate.

        1. $\text{Deviation rate} = \dfrac{\text{Number of observed deviations}}{\text{Sample size}}$

        2. The deviation rate is the auditor's best estimate of the true (but unknown) deviation rate in the population.

    (b) For the risk of assessing control risk too low that is being used, determine the **upper deviation limit** (upper occurrence limit, achieved upper precision limit).

        1. The auditor uses the number of deviations noted, and the appropriate sampling table (not presented here) to calculate the upper deviation limit.

            a. This upper deviation limit represents the sample deviation rate plus an **allowance for sampling risk**.

    (c) Compare the upper deviation limit to the tolerable rate specified in designing the sample.

        1. If the upper deviation limit is less than or equal to the tolerable rate, the sample results support reliance on the control procedure tested.

EXAMPLE

Assume that the auditor established the following criteria for an attributes sampling plan:
    Population size: over 5,000 units
    Allowable risk of assessing control risk too low: 5%
    Tolerable deviation rate: 6%
    Estimated population deviation rate: 2.5%

By referencing the appropriate sample size table (not included here) the auditor determined that the required sample size was 150 units.

The auditor applied appropriate audit procedures to the 150 sample units and found eight deviations.

    a. The sample deviation rate = 8/150 = 5.3%

    b. The upper deviation limit found from the table (not presented) for a 5% risk of assessing control risk too low and eight deviations = 9.5%

    c. The allowance for sampling risk = 9.5 – 5.3 = 4.2%

    d. The conclusions that can be drawn include

        i. There is a 5% chance of the true population deviation rate being greater than or equal to 9.5%.

        ii. Since the upper deviation limit (9.5%) exceeds the tolerable deviation rate (6%), the sample results indicate that control risk for the control procedure being tested is higher than planned, and, therefore, the scope of resulting substantive tests must be increased.

  (d) In addition to the frequency of deviations found, the auditor should consider the qualitative aspects of each deviation.

    1. The nature and cause of each deviation should be analyzed. For example, are the deviations due to a misunderstanding of instructions or to carelessness?

    2. The possible relationship of the deviations to other phases of the audit should be considered. For example, the discovery of fraud ordinarily requires broader consideration than does the discovery of an error.

  (e) Reach an overall conclusion by applying audit judgment

    1. If all evidence obtained, including sample results, supports the auditor's planned assessed level of control risk, the auditor generally does not need to modify planned substantive tests.

    2. If the planned level is not supported, the auditor will

      a. Test other related controls

      b. Modify the related substantive tests to reflect increased control risk assessment

(8) **Document the sampling procedure.** Each of the prior seven steps, as well as the basis for overall conclusions, should be documented in the workpapers.

3. **Nonstatistical Sampling for Tests of Controls**—The steps involved in the design and implementation of a nonstatistical sampling plan are similar to statistical plans. Differences in determining sample size, sample selection, and evaluating sample results are discussed below.

  a. **Determine sample size**—As in statistical sampling, the major factors are the risk of assessing control risk too low, the tolerable rate, and the expected population deviation rate.

    (1) In nonstatistical sampling it is not necessary to quantify these factors.

    (2) The auditor should still consider the effects on sample size as described in section B.2.a.(5).

  b. **Sample selection**—Any of the sample selection methods discussed under statistical sampling (B.2.) may be used (i.e., random-number, systematic, haphazard, or, less desirably, block).

  c. **Evaluate sample results**—In nonstatistical sampling it is impossible to determine an upper deviation limit or to quantify sampling risk.

    (1) The auditor should relate the deviation rate in the sample to the tolerable rate established in the design stage to determine whether an adequate allowance for sampling risk has been provided to draw the conclusion that the sample provides an acceptably low level of risk.

      (a) **Rule of thumb**—If the deviation rate in a properly designed sample does not exceed the expected population deviation rate used in determining sample size, the auditor can generally "accept" the population and conclude that the control is operating effectively.

    (2) As in statistical sampling, the qualitative aspects of deviations should be considered in addition to the frequency of deviations.

    (3) Again the auditor must use his/her professional judgment to reach an overall conclusion as to the assessed level of control risk for the assertion(s) related to the internal control procedure tested.

NOW REVIEW MULTIPLE-CHOICE QUESTIONS 20 THROUGH 38

C. Sampling in Substantive Tests of Details

1. Sampling Risk

a. **Risk of incorrect rejection (alpha risk, type I error)** is the risk that the sample supports the conclusion that the recorded account balance is materially misstated when it is not materially misstated. Know that like the risk of assessing control risk too high, this risk relates to **audit efficiency**. If the sample results incorrectly indicate that an account balance is materially misstated, the performance of additional audit procedures will generally lead to the correct conclusion.

b. **Risk of incorrect acceptance (beta risk, type II error)** is the risk that the sample supports the conclusion that the recorded account balance is not materially misstated when it is materially misstated. Know that like the risk of assessing control risk too low, this risk relates to **audit effectiveness**. If the sample results indicate that an account balance is not misstated, when it is misstated, the auditor will not perform additional procedures and the financial statements may include such misstatements.

c. Although the two risks are mutually exclusive (the auditor cannot incorrectly decide to reject an account balance at the same time s/he incorrectly decides to accept an account balance), both risks may be considered in the sample design stage. The following table illustrates both aspects of sampling risk for substantive tests.

	THE POPULATION ACTUALLY IS	
The Substantive Test Sample Indicates	**Not Materially Misstated**	**Materially Misstated**
The population is not materially misstated	Correct Decision	Incorrect Decision (risk of incorrect acceptance)
The population is materially misstated	Incorrect Decision (risk of incorrect rejection)	Correct Decision

NOTE: The following portions of this outline summarize the steps involved in substantive testing (section C.1.d.), probability- proportional-to-size sampling (section C.2.), and classical variables sampling (section C.3.). Finally, PPS and classical variables sampling are compared (section C.4.).

d. Steps involved in variables sampling

(1) **Determine the objectives of the test**—Remember that variables sampling is used primarily for substantive testing and that its conclusion is generally stated in dollar terms (although conclusions in terms of units [e.g., inventory] are possible). Variables sampling might test, for example, the recorded amount of accounts receivable, inventory quantities and amounts, payroll expense, and fixed asset additions.

(2) **Define the population**—The population consists of the items constituting the account balance or class of transactions of interest. Three areas need to be considered.

(a) **Sampling unit**—The sampling unit is any of the individual elements that constitute the population.

EXAMPLE

If the population to be tested is defined as total accounts receivable, the sampling unit used to confirm the balance of accounts receivable could be each individual account receivable.

(b) **Consider the completeness of the population**—Since sampling units are selected from a physical representation (e.g., a trial balance of receivables), the auditor should consider whether the physical representation includes the entire population.

(c) **Identify individually significant items**—Items that are individually significant for which sampling risk is not justified should be tested separately and not be subjected to sampling. These are items in which potential misstatements could individually equal or exceed tolerable misstatement.

(3) **Select an audit sampling technique**—Either nonstatistical or statistical sampling may be used. If statistical sampling is used, either probability-proportional-to-size sampling (PPS) or classical variables techniques are appropriate.

(4) **Determine the sample size**—Five items need to be considered.

   (a) **Variation within the population**—Increases in variation (standard deviation in classical sampling) result in increases in sample size.

   (b) **Acceptable level of risk**—The risk of incorrect acceptance is related to audit risk (see AU-C 320 outline and Engagement Planning Module Section A.2.). The auditor may also control the risk of incorrect rejection so as to allow an efficiently performed audit. Increases in these risks result in decreases in sample size.

NOTE: The risk of incorrect rejection **is not** typically controlled when using PPS sampling, but **is** controlled when using classical methods.

   (c) **Tolerable misstatement (error)**—An estimate of the maximum monetary misstatement that may exist in an account balance or class of transactions, when combined with misstatements in other accounts, without causing the financial statements to be materially misstated. As tolerable misstatement increases, sample size decreases.

   (d) **Expected amount of misstatement (error)**—Expected misstatement is estimated using an understanding of the business, prior year information, a pilot sample, and/or the results of the review and evaluation of internal control. As expected misstatement increases, a larger sample size is required.

   (e) **Population size**—Sample size increases as population size increases. The effect is more significant in classical variables sampling than PPS sampling.

VARIABLES SAMPLING
SUMMARY OF RELATIONSHIPS TO SAMPLE SIZE

Increases in	Effect on sampling size
Risk—Incorrect Acceptance	Decrease
Risk—Incorrect Rejection	Decrease
Tolerable Misstatement (Error)	Decrease
Expected Misstatement (Error)	Increase
Population	Increase
Variation (standard deviation)	Increase

NOTE: Memorize the above relationships. As an aid remember that, in both variables sampling and attributes sampling, increases in risk and in the "tolerables" (tolerable misstatement and tolerable rate) lead to decreases in sample size. For the risks especially, this result is intuitively appealing in that one expects more risk in many contexts when one does less work. Increases in the other factors increase sample size.

(5) **Determine the method of selecting the sample**—Generally random number or systematic sampling

(6) **Perform the sampling plan**—Perform appropriate audit procedures to determine an audit value for each sample item.

(7) **Evaluate the sample results**—The auditor should project the results of the sample to the population. The total projected misstatement, after any adjustments made by the entity, should be compared with the tolerable misstatement and the auditor should consider whether the risk of misstatement in excess of the tolerable amount is at an acceptably low level. Also, qualitative factors (such as the nature of the misstatements and their relationship to other phases of the audit) should be considered. For example, when fraud has been discovered, a simple projection of them will not in general be sufficient as the auditor will need to obtain a thorough understanding of them and of their likely effects.

(8) **Document the sampling procedure**—Each of the prior seven steps, as well as the basis for overall conclusions, should be documented.

e. **Comments on nonstatistical sampling**—Both statistical and nonstatistical sampling require judgment. The major differences between statistical and nonstatistical sampling in substantive testing are in the steps for determining sample size and evaluating sample results.

(1) **Determination of sample size**—Be aware of the relationships summarized in section C.1.d.(4)(e). Also, know that the statistical tables **may** be used to assist in the determination of sample size.

(2) **Evaluation of sample results**—The auditor should project misstatements found in the sample to the population and consider sampling risk.

(a) Projecting misstatements can be accomplished by

1. Dividing the total dollar amount of misstatement in the sample by the fraction of total dollars from the population included in the sample, or
2. Multiplying the average difference between audit and book values for sample items times the number of units in the population.

(b) If tolerable misstatement exceeds projected misstatement by a large amount, the auditor may be reasonably sure that an acceptably low level of sampling risk exists. Sampling risk increases as projected misstatement approaches tolerable error.

(c) When sampling results do not support the book value, the auditor can

1. Examine additional sampling units,
2. Apply alternative auditing procedures, or
3. Ask the client to investigate and, if appropriate, make necessary adjustments.

(d) Qualitative aspects of misstatements need to be considered as well as frequency and amounts of misstatements.

2. **Probability-Proportional-to-Size (PPS) Sampling [dollar-unit, cumulative monetary amount (CMA) sampling]**

a. Uses attributes sampling theory to express a conclusion in dollar amounts. PPS sampling has gained popularity in practice because it is easier to apply than classical variables sampling.

b. Steps in PPS sampling

(1) **Determine the objectives of the test**—PPS tests the reasonableness of a recorded account balance or class of transactions. PPS is primarily applicable in testing account balances and transactions for **overstatements**.

(2) **Define the population**—The population is the account balance or class of transactions being tested.

(a) **Define the sampling unit**—The sampling units in PPS are the individual dollars in the population. The auditor ordinarily examines each individual account or transaction (called a **logical unit**) that includes a sampled dollar.

(b) **Consider the completeness of the population**—As with other sampling plans, the auditor must assure him/herself that the physical representation of the population being tested includes the entire population.

(c) **Identify individually significant items**—PPS automatically includes in the sample any unit that is individually significant.

(3) **Select an audit sampling technique**—Here we have selected PPS.

(4) **Determine the sample size**—A PPS sample divides the population into sampling intervals and selects a logical unit from each sampling interval.

(a)   Sample size = $\dfrac{\text{Book value of population} \times \text{Reliability factor}}{\text{Tolerable error} - (\text{Expected error} \times \text{Expansion factor})}$

Sampling interval = $\dfrac{\text{Book value of population}}{\text{Sample size}}$

Expansion Factors (from the Audit Sampling guide) for expected misstatements

	Risk of Incorrect Acceptance								
	1%	**5%**	**10%**	**15%**	**20%**	**25%**	**30%**	**37%**	**50%**
Factor	1.9	1.6	1.5	1.4	1.3	1.25	1.2	1.15	1.0

Reliability Factors (from the Audit Sampling guide) for misstatements of overstatement. (Use 0 errors for determining Reliability Factor.)

Number of Overstatements	Risk of Incorrect Acceptance								
	1%	**5%**	**10%**	**15%**	**20%**	**25%**	**30%**	**37%**	**50%**
0	4.61	3.00	2.31	1.90	1.61	1.39	1.21	1.00	.70
1	6.64	4.75	3.89	3.38	3.00	2.70	2.44	2.14	1.68
2	8.41	6.30	5.33	4.72	4.28	3.93	3.62	3.25	2.68
3	10.05	7.76	6.69	6.02	5.52	5.11	4.77	4.34	3.68

(b) Observations

1. The size of the **sampling interval** is related to the risk of incorrect acceptance and tolerable misstatement. The auditor controls the risk of incorrect rejection by making an allowance for expected misstatements. The auditor specifies a planned allowance for sampling risk so that the estimate of projected misstatement plus the allowance for sampling risk will be less than or equal to tolerable misstatement.
2. If no misstatements are expected, the sampling interval is determined by dividing tolerable misstatement by a factor that corresponds to the risk of incorrect acceptance (i.e., the reliability factor).
3. A reliability factor table such as the one above has been included with CPA exam questions.

(5) **Determine the method of selecting the sample**—PPS samples are generally selected using **systematic sampling** with a random start. All logical units (e.g., accounts) with dollar amounts greater than or equal to the sampling interval are certain to be selected.

(6) **Perform the sampling plan**—The auditor must apply appropriate audit procedures to determine an audit value for each logical unit included in the sample.

(7) **Evaluate the sample results**—Misstatements found should be projected to the population and an allowance for sampling risk should be calculated. When the sample contains misstatements, the **upper limit on misstatements** is the total of projected misstatement and the allowance for sampling risk (with its two subcomponents).

Upper limit on misstatements   =   Projected misstatement   +   Allowance for sampling risk

Basic precision

Incremental allowance for projected misstatements

Projected misstatement is calculated for each logical unit containing misstatements and totaled. The approach differs based on whether the book value of the specific logical unit is less than or greater than the size of the sampling interval.

Logical unit less than sampling interval—Multiply the percentage the account is misstated (misstatement/book value, referred to as the "taint") times the sampling interval. For example, an account with a book value of $100 has an audited value of $95, and a sampling interval of $3,000. The tainting percentage of 5% ($5 misstatement/$100) is multiplied times the $3,000 sampling interval, or

$$\$5/\$100 \times \$3,000 = \$150 \text{ projected misstatement}$$

Logical unit greater than sampling interval—The actual amount of misstatement is considered to be the projected misstatement. For example, consider an account with a book value of $4,000, an audited value of $40, and a sampling interval of $3,000; the projected misstatement is $3,960 ($4,000 – $40). Similarly, if the audited value is $3,300, the projected misstatement is $700 ($4,000 – $3,300).

> **NOTE:** Questions have required candidates to calculate a projected misstatement for one or more accounts. If more than one account is involved, the various projected misstatements are simply totaled.
>
> For completeness' sake we also present computations of basic precision and the incremental allowance for projected misstatements. That information has not been heavily examined to this point.

Basic precision is found by multiplying the reliability factor [see section C.2.b.(4)] times the sampling interval.

Incremental allowance for projected misstatements is determined by ranking the misstatements for logical units that are less than the sampling interval from highest to lowest and considering the incremental changes in reliability factors for the actual number of misstatements found. The table of Reliability Factors presented earlier [section C.2.b.(4)] presents values for zero through three misstatements. The *Audit Sampling* guide presents additional values for situations in which more misstatements are detected. One must subtract 1.00 from each incremental change to isolate the incremental allowance for projected misstatements.

(a) **Decision rule:** Compare the upper limit on misstatements to tolerable misstatement.

1. If the upper limit on misstatements is less than or equal to tolerable misstatement, the sample results support the conclusion that the population is not misstated by more than tolerable misstatement at the specified risk of incorrect acceptance.
2. If the upper limit on misstatements is greater than the tolerable misstatement, the sample results do not support the conclusion that the population is not misstated by more than the tolerable misstatement. This may be due to the fact that (a) the population is misstated, (b) the auditor's expectation of misstatement was low and resulted in too small of a sample, or (c) the sample is not representative of the population.
3. The auditor should consider qualitative aspects of errors found as well as quantitative factors.

(b) **Observation:** If no misstatements are found, projected misstatement and the incremental allowance for projected misstatements will equal zero, leaving the basic precision as the only nonzero component of the upper limit on misstatements. No further calculations are needed since the tolerable misstatement will be greater than this amount.

(8) **Document the sampling procedure**—Each of the prior seven steps, as well as the basis for overall conclusions, should be documented.

The following example illustrates the probability-proportional-to-size method:

Probability-Proportional-to-Size Sampling Example

Step 1.   Objective of test—determine reasonableness of accounts receivable
Step 2.   Define population—individual dollars in account
Step 3.   Select sampling technique—probability-proportional-to-size
Step 4.   Determine sample size

Given:

Tolerable misstatement (TM)	$50,000
Risk of incorrect acceptance	.05
Expected misstatement (EM)	$10,000

$$\text{Calculation sample size} = \frac{\text{Book value of population} \times \text{Reliability factor}}{\text{Tolerable misstatement} - (\text{Expected misstatement} \times \text{Expansion factor})}$$

$$= \frac{\$1,000,000 \times 3}{\$50,000 \ (10,000 \times 1.6)} \approx 88$$

$$\text{Sampling interval} = \frac{\text{Book value of population}}{\text{Sample size}}$$

$$= \frac{\$1,000,000}{88} \approx \$11,333.33$$

Step 5.　Determine method of selecting sample—systematic

Step 6.　Perform sampling plan

Step 7.　Evaluate and project results

Projected misstatement—Assume 3 misstatements

Book value	Audited value	Misstatement	Taint %	Sampling interval	Projected misstatement
$ 100	$ 95.00	$ 5.00	5%	$11,333	$ 567
11,700	212.00	11,488.00	--*	NA	11,488
65	58.50	6.50	10%	11,333	1,133
Projected misstatement					$13,188

* Not applicable; book value larger than sampling interval.

NOTE: Make certain that you understand details of the projected misstatement computation as it has been required on various CPA examination questions.

Basic precision	=	Reliability factor	× Sampling interval
	=	3.0	× $11,333.33
	=	$34,000.00	

Incremental allowance for projected misstatements

Reliability factor	Increment	(Increm – 1)	Projected misstatements	Incremental allowance
3.00	—	—	—	—
4.75	1.75	.75	$1,133	$ 850
6.30	1.55	.55	567	312
Incremental allowance for projected misstatements				$1,162

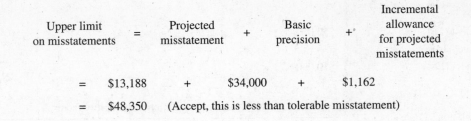

$$
\begin{array}{cccccc}
\text{Upper limit} & = & \text{Projected} & + & \text{Basic} & + & \begin{array}{c}\text{Incremental}\\\text{allowance}\end{array}\\
\text{on misstatements} & & \text{misstatement} & & \text{precision} & & \begin{array}{c}\text{for projected}\\\text{misstatements}\end{array}
\end{array}
$$

$$
= \quad \$13,188 \quad + \quad \$34,000 \quad + \quad \$1,162
$$

$$
= \quad \$48,350 \quad \text{(Accept, this is less than tolerable misstatement)}
$$

3. **Classical Variables Sampling**

   a. **Classical variables sampling models** use normal distribution theory to evaluate selected characteristics of a population on the basis of a sample of the items constituting the population.

      (1) For any normal distribution, the following fixed relationships exist concerning the area under the curve and the distance from the mean in standard deviations. This table assumes a two-tailed approach that is appropriate since classical variables sampling models generally test for both overstatement and understatement.

Distance in Stan. Dev. (Reliability coefficient)	Area under the Curve (Reliability level)	
± 1.0	68%	
1.64	90%	*
1.96	95%	
2.0	95.5%	
2.7	99%	

         * *Most frequently tested on CPA exam*

Example where the mean = 250 and the standard deviation = 10:

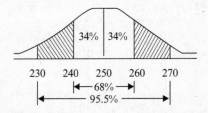

      (2) For large samples (greater than or equal to thirty) the distribution of sample means tends to be normally distributed about its own mean which is equal to the true population mean, even if the population is not normally distributed (Central Limit Theorem). Since many populations sampled in auditing are not normally distributed, this is important.

      (3) **The standard deviation** in the above model measures the dispersion among the respective amounts of a particular characteristic, for all items in the population for which a sample estimate is developed.

   b. **Variations of classical variables sampling**

      (1) **Mean-per-unit estimation** is a classical variables sampling technique that projects the sample average to the total population by multiplying the sample average by the number of items in the population.

         (a) Determine audit values for each sample item.
         (b) Calculate the average audit amount.
         (c) Multiply this average audit amount times the number of units in the population to obtain the estimated population value.

(2) **Difference estimation** is a classical variables sampling technique that uses the average difference between audited amounts and individual recorded amounts to estimate the total audited amount of a population and an allowance for sampling risk.

    (a) Determine audit values for each sample item.
    (b) Calculate the difference between the audit value and book value for each sample item.
    (c) Calculate the average difference.
    (d) Determine the estimated population value by multiplying the average difference by the total population units and adding or subtracting this value from the recorded book value.

(3) **Ratio estimation** is a classical variables sampling technique that uses the ratio of audited amounts to recorded amounts in the sample to estimate the total dollar amount of the population and an allowance for sampling risk.

    (a) Determine audit values for each sample item.
    (b) Calculate the ratio between the sum of sample audit values and sample book values.
    (c) Determine the estimated population value by multiplying the total population book value times this ratio.

(4) **The regression approach** is similar to the difference and ratio approaches. This approach has the effect of using both the average ratio and the average difference in calculating an estimate of the total amount for the population.

(5) **Difference and ratio estimation** are used as alternatives to mean-per-unit estimation. The auditor should use these approaches when applicable because they require a smaller sample size (i.e., they are more efficient than mean-per-unit estimation).

    (a) One factor in the calculation of sample size for classical variables sampling models is the estimated standard deviation. If the standard deviation of differences or ratios is smaller than the standard deviation of audit values, these two methods will produce a smaller sample size.

        1. Difference estimation will be used if the differences between sample audit values and book values are a relatively constant dollar amount, regardless of account size.
        2. Ratio estimation will be used if the differences are a constant percentage of book values.

    (b) In order to use either difference or ratio estimation, the following constraints must be met:

        1. The individual book values must be known and must sum to the total book value.
        2. There must be more than a few differences (twenty is often suggested as a minimum) between audit and book values.

    (c) These two methods will usually be more efficient than mean-per-unit estimation when stratification of the population is not possible.

(6) **Stratification** separates a population into relatively homogeneous groups to reduce the sample size by minimizing the effect of variation of items (i.e., the standard deviation) in the population.

    (a) Although stratification may be applied with any of the classical methods, it is most frequently used with the mean-per-unit estimation method.
    (b) Know that the primary objective of stratification is to decrease the effect of variance in the total population and thereby reduce sample size.

c. Variables sampling steps applied to classical variables sampling

  (1) **Determine the objectives of the test**—Recall that variables sampling models are designed to draw conclusions in dollar amounts.
  (2) **Define the population**—The population consists of the items constituting the account balance or class of transactions.

    (a) **Sampling unit**—As with PPS sampling, the sampling unit is any of the individual elements that constitute the population. For example, the sampling unit in receivables is often an individual customer's account.

(b) **Consider the completeness of the population**—As discussed in PPS, the auditor must consider whether the physical representation includes the entire population.

(c) **Identify individually significant items**—Items which are individually significant for which sampling risk is not justified, should be tested separately and not be subject to sampling. These are items for which potential error could individually equal or exceed tolerable misstatement. Note that in PPS these items were automatically selected.

(3) **Select an audit sampling technique**—Here we would select among mean-per-unit, difference, ratio, and regression estimation.

(4) **Determine the sample size**—The following factors are included in the sample size calculation:

(a) **The population size** is directly related to sample size.

(b) **Estimated standard deviation**—An estimate must be made of the dispersion of audit values for the units constituting the population. This value can be estimated by

1. Calculating the standard deviation of recorded amounts,
2. Auditing a small pilot sample, or
3. Using the standard deviation found in the previous audit.

(c) **Tolerable misstatement**—An estimate of the maximum monetary misstatement that may exist in an account balance or class of transactions, when combined with error in other accounts, without causing the financial statements to be materially misstated.

(d) **Risk of incorrect rejection (alpha risk)**—Since the risk of incorrect rejection is inversely related to sample size, the auditor must weigh the costs of a larger sample size against the potential additional costs associated with expanded audit procedures following the initial rejection resulting from a sample size that was too small.

(e) **Risk of incorrect acceptance (beta risk)**—In specifying an acceptable level of risk of incorrect acceptance, the auditor considers the level of audit risk that s/he is willing to accept. Recall this discussion in section A.1.a. of the Engagement Planning Module.

(f) **Planned allowance for sampling risk (desired precision)**—The allowance is a function of the auditor's estimates of tolerable misstatement, risk of incorrect rejection, and risk of incorrect acceptance. The risk of incorrect acceptance is not explicitly included in the sample size equation, but the allowance for sampling risk controls the level of risk the auditor is assuming.

Various approaches are used to calculate the planned allowance for sampling risk. Since these approaches are not frequently examined, we will not present them. Depending upon the risk assumed (incorrect acceptance and rejection) the planned allowance for sampling risk is either equal to or less than the tolerable misstatement. For example, when a 5% and 10% risk of incorrect acceptance and rejection respectively are established, the planned allowance for sampling risk is established at 1/2 the amount of the tolerable misstatement.

(g) **Sample size equation**

$$n = \left(\frac{N \times SD \times U_R}{A} \right)^2$$

n	=	Sample size
N	=	Population size
SD	=	Estimated population standard deviation
U_R	=	The standard normal deviate for the acceptable risk of incorrect rejection
A	=	Planned allowance for sampling risk

(h) The above formula assumes sampling with replacement and may be adjusted by a finite correction factor (thereby reducing sample size) when sampling without replacement.

$$n' = \frac{n}{1 + n/N} \qquad n' = \text{Sample size adjusted for finite correction factor}$$

(5) **Determine the method of selecting the sample**—Classical samples are generally selected using random sampling or stratified random sampling.
(6) **Perform the sampling plan**—Perform appropriate audit procedures to determine an audit value for each item.
  (a) If the auditor is unable to examine selected items (i.e., accounts receivable confirmations are not returned), s/he should perform alternative procedures that provide sufficient evidence to form a conclusion.
(7) **Evaluate and project the sample results**—As was the case with sample selection, the actual evaluation and projection of sample results is affected by the method used. Additionally, the various auditing textbooks do not agree on the approach for evaluating sample results. We provide a summarized approach. Assume a population of 10,000 accounts with a book value of $1,000,000; this represents an average book value of $100 ($1,000,000/10,000 accounts). Further, assume that a sample has been selected and the following results obtained:

Average book value of items in sample	$101
Average audited value of items in sample	$ 98

Projected misstatement and estimated total audited value (ETAV). As was the case with PPS sampling a projected misstatement may be calculated.

Mean-Per-Unit Method

ETAV = Population size × Average audited value
    = 10,000 × $98 = $980,000

Projected misstatement = $1,000,000 – $980,000 = $20,000 overstatement

Difference Estimation Method

Average difference (in sample): Average BV – Average AV.
$101 – $98 = $3

Projected misstatement: 10,000 accounts × $3 = $30,000 overstatement
ETAV = $1,000,000 – $30,000 = $970,000

Ratio Estimation Method

ETAV = (Sample Avg. AV/Sample Avg. BV) × Population BV
    = ($98 / $101) × $1,000,000 = $970,297

Projected Misstatement = $1,000,000 – $970,297 = $29,703 overstatement

> **NOTE:** The difference and ratio estimation methods use the book value of the sample items in the analysis, while the mean-per-unit method **does not**.

Considering sampling risk. When statistical sampling is used, the auditors utilize statistical formulas to determine whether the account balance should be accepted. In essence, these formulas help the auditor to determine whether the projected misstatement may reveal a materially misstated account. One approach is to construct an adjusted allowance for sampling risk (plus or minus) around the estimated audited population value. (The CPA exam does not generally require such a computation.)

If the book value falls within this interval, the auditors will accept that the population is materially correct. If not, the auditors will conclude that there is an unacceptably high risk that the inventory account is materially misstated. When a conclusion is reached that an account is materially misstated, the auditors may decide to (1) increase the sample size of the test, (2) perform other audit tests of the account, or (3) work with the client's personnel to locate other misstated items in the account.

4. **Comparison of PPS Sampling to Classical Variables Sampling**

   a. Advantages of PPS sampling

      (1) Generally easier to use
      (2) Size of sample not based on variation of audited amounts
      (3) Automatically results in a stratified sample
      (4) Individually significant items are automatically identified.
      (5) Usually results in a smaller sample size if no misstatements are expected
      (6) Can be easily designed and sample selection can begin before the complete population is available

   b. Advantages of classical variables sampling

      (1) May result in a smaller sample size if there are many differences between audited and book values
      (2) Easier to expand sample size if that becomes necessary
      (3) Selection of zero balances does not require special sample design considerations.
      (4) Inclusion of negative balances does not require special sample design considerations.

NOW REVIEW MULTIPLE-CHOICE QUESTIONS 39 THROUGH 58

KEY TERMS

Attributes sampling. A sampling plan enabling the auditors to estimate the deviation rate in a population.

Audit sampling (sampling). The selection of less than 100% of the population of audit relevance, and the evaluation of that sample, such that the auditor expects the items selected (the sample) to be representative of the population, and thus likely to provide a reasonable basis for conclusions about the population. In this context, a **representative sample** is one that will result in conclusions that, subject to the limitations of **sampling risk,** are similar to those that would be drawn if the same procedures were applied to the entire population. Basic to audit sampling is sampling risk, the risk that the auditor's conclusion based on the sample may be different from the conclusion if the entire population were subjected to the same audit procedure.

Deviation rate. A defined rate of departure from prescribed controls. Also referred to as occurrence rate or exception rate.

Difference estimation. A classical variables sampling plan that uses the difference between the audited (correct) values and the book values of items in a sample to calculate the estimated total audited value of the population.

Discovery sampling. A procedure for determining the sample size required to have a stipulated probability of observing at least one occurrence when the expected population deviation rate is at a designated level. It is most appropriate when the expected deviation rate is zero or near zero. If a deviation is detected, the auditor must either (1) use an alternate approach, or (2) if the deviation is of sufficient importance, audit all transactions.

Mean-per-unit estimation. A classical variables sampling plan enabling auditors to estimate the average dollar value of items in a population by determining the average value of items in a sample.

Misstatement. A difference between the amount, classification, presentation, or disclosure of a reported financial statement item and the amount, classification, presentation, or disclosure that is required for the item to be in accordance with the applicable financial reporting framework. Misstatements can arise from error or fraud. Misstatements also include those adjustments of amounts, classifications, presentations, or disclosures that, in the auditor's judgment, are necessary for the financial statements to be presented fairly, in all material respects.

   a. **Factual misstatements**—Misstatements about which there is no doubt.
   b. **Judgmental misstatements.** Differences arising from the judgments of management concerning accounting estimates that the auditor considers unreasonable or the selection or application of accounting policies that the auditor considers inappropriate.
   c. **Projected misstatements.** The auditor's best estimate of misstatements in populations, involving the projection of misstatements identified in audit samples to the entire population from which the samples were drawn. For example, if statistical sampling was used with receivables, the difference between auditor estimated total audited value and the book value of receivables is the projected misstatement.

Nonsampling risk. The risk that the auditor reaches an erroneous conclusion for any reason not related to sampling risk. Examples of nonsampling risk include use of inappropriate audit procedures or misinterpretation of audit evidence and failure to recognize misstatement or deviation.

Performance materiality. The amount (or amounts) set by the auditor at less than materiality for the financial statements as a whole to reduce to an appropriately low level the probability that the aggregate of uncorrected and undetected misstatements exceeds materiality for the financial statements as a whole. It may also refer to the amount or amounts set by the auditor at less than the materiality level or levels for particular classes of transactions, account balances, or disclosures. See also **tolerable misstatement**.

Population. The entire set of data from which a sample is selected and about which the auditor wishes to draw conclusions.

Probability-proportional-to-size (PPS) sampling. A variables sampling procedure that uses attributes theory to express a conclusion in monetary (dollar) amounts.

Ratio estimation. A classical variables sampling plan enabling auditors to use the ratio of audited (correct) values to book values of items in a sample to calculate the estimated total audited value of the population.

Risk of assessing control risk too high. The risk that the assessed level of control risk based on the sample is greater than the true operating effectiveness of the control. That is, the auditor concludes that the system operates less effectively than it actually does.

Risk of assessing control risk too low. This risk is the possibility that the assessed level of control risk based on the sample is less than the true operating effectiveness of the controls. That is, the auditor concludes that the system operates more effectively than it actually does.

Risk of incorrect acceptance. The risk that sample results indicate that a population is not materially misstated when, in fact, it is materially misstated.

Risk of incorrect rejection. The risk that sample results indicate that a population is materially misstated when, in fact, it is not.

Sampling risk. The risk that the auditor's conclusion based on a sample may be different from the conclusion if the entire population was subjected to the same audit procedure.

Sampling unit. The individual items constituting a population.

Statistical sampling. Audit sampling that uses the laws of probability for selecting and evaluating a sample from a population for the purpose of reaching a conclusion about the population.

Stratification. Division of the population into groups.

Tolerable misstatement. A monetary amount set by the auditor in respect of which the auditor seeks to obtain an appropriate level of assurance that the monetary amount set by the auditor is not exceeded by the actual misstatement in the population. Tolerable misstatement is also the application of **performance materiality** to a particular sampling procedure.

Tolerable rate of deviation. A rate of deviation from prescribed internal control procedures set by the auditor in respect of which the auditor seeks to obtain an appropriate level of assurance that that rate of deviation set by the auditor is not exceeded by the actual rate of deviation in the population.

Uncorrected misstatements. Misstatements that the auditor has accumulated during the audit and that have not been corrected.

Variables sampling. Sampling plans designed to estimate a numerical measurement of a population, such as dollar value.

Multiple-Choice Questions (1–58)

A.2. General Approaches to Audit Sampling—Nonstatistical and Statistical

1. An advantage of using statistical over nonstatistical sampling methods in tests of controls is that the statistical methods

     a. Can more easily convert the sample into a dual-purpose test useful for substantive testing.

     b. Eliminate the need to use judgment in determining appropriate sample sizes.

     c. Afford greater assurance than a nonstatistical sample of equal size.

     d. Provide an objective basis for quantitatively evaluating sample risk.

2. An advantage of statistical sampling over nonstatistical sampling is that statistical sampling helps an auditor to

     a. Eliminate the risk of nonsampling errors.

     b. Reduce the level of audit risk and materiality to a relatively low amount.

     c. Measure the sufficiency of the evidential matter obtained.

     d. Minimize the failure to detect errors and fraud.

A.3. Uncertainty and Audit Sampling

3. The likelihood of assessing control risk too high is the risk that the sample selected to test controls

     a. Does **not** support the auditor's planned assessed level of control risk when the true operating effectiveness of the control structure justifies such an assessment.

     b. Contains misstatements that could be material to the financial statements when aggregated with misstatements in other account balances or transactions classes.

     c. Contains proportionately fewer monetary errors or deviations from prescribed controls than exist in the balance or class as a whole.

     d. Does not support the tolerable error for some or all of management's assertions.

4. The risk of incorrect acceptance and the likelihood of assessing control risk too low relate to the

     a. Allowable risk of tolerable misstatement.

     b. Preliminary estimates of materiality levels.

     c. Efficiency of the audit.

     d. Effectiveness of the audit.

5. Which of the following best illustrates the concept of sampling risk?

     a. A randomly chosen sample may **not** be representative of the population as a whole on the characteristic of interest.

     b. An auditor may select audit procedures that are **not** appropriate to achieve the specific objective.

     c. An auditor may fail to recognize errors in the documents examined for the chosen sample.

     d. The documents related to the chosen sample may **not** be available for inspection.

6. In assessing sampling risk, the risk of incorrect rejection and the risk of assessing control risk too high relate to the

     a. Efficiency of the audit.

     b. Effectiveness of the audit.

     c. Selection of the sample.

     d. Audit quality controls.

Items 7 and 8 are based on the following information:

The diagram below depicts the auditor's estimated deviation rate compared with the tolerable rate, and also depicts the true population deviation rate compared with the tolerable rate.

	True State of Population	
	Deviation rate exceeds tolerable rate	Deviation rate is less than tolerable rate
Auditor's estimate based on sample results Deviation rate exceeds tolerable rate	I.	II.
Deviation rate is less than tolerable rate	III.	IV.

7. In which of the situations would the auditor have properly concluded that control risk is at or below the planned assessed level?

     a. I.

     b. II.

     c. III.

     d. IV.

8. As a result of tests of controls, the auditor assesses control risk too high and thereby increases substantive testing. This is illustrated by situation

     a. I.

     b. II.

     c. III.

     d. IV.

9. While performing a test of details during an audit, an auditor determined that the sample results supported the conclusion that the recorded account balance was materially misstated. It was, in fact, not materially misstated. This situation illustrates the risk of

     a. Assessing control risk too high.

     b. Assessing control risk too low.

     c. Incorrect rejection.

     d. Incorrect acceptance.

A.4. Types of Audit Tests in Which Sampling May Be Used

10. The size of a sample designed for dual-purpose testing should be

    a. The larger of the samples that would otherwise have been designed for the two separate purposes.

    b. The smaller of the samples that would otherwise have been designed for the two separate purposes.

    c. The combined total of the samples that would otherwise have been designed for the two separate purposes.

    d. More than the larger of the samples that would otherwise have been designated for the two separate purposes, but less than the combined total of the samples that would otherwise have been designed for the two separate purposes.

A.5. Types of Statistical Sampling Plans

11. The expected population deviation rate of client billing errors is 3%. The auditor has established a tolerable rate of 5%. In the review of client invoices the auditor should use

    a. Stratified sampling.

    b. Variable sampling.

    c. Discovery sampling.

    d. Attribute sampling.

12. Which of the following sampling methods would be used to estimate a numerical measurement of a population, such as a dollar value?

    a. Attribute sampling.

    b. Stop-or-go sampling.

    c. Variables sampling.

    d. Random-number sampling.

13. For which of the following audit tests would an auditor most likely use attribute sampling?

    a. Making an independent estimate of the amount of a LIFO inventory.

    b. Examining invoices in support of the valuation of fixed asset additions.

    c. Selecting accounts receivable for confirmation of account balances.

    d. Inspecting employee time cards for proper approval by supervisors.

14. An underlying feature of random-based selection of items is that each

    a. Stratum of the accounting population be given equal representation in the sample.

    b. Item in the accounting population be randomly ordered.

    c. Item in the accounting population should have an opportunity to be selected.

    d. Item must be systematically selected using replacement.

15. Which of the following statistical selection techniques is **least** desirable for use by an auditor?

    a. Systematic selection.

    b. Stratified selection.

    c. Block selection.

    d. Sequential selection.

16. Which of the following statistical sampling plans does not use a fixed sample size for tests of controls?

    a. Dollar-unit sampling.

    b. Sequential sampling.

    c. PPS sampling.

    d. Variables sampling.

17. If certain forms are not consecutively numbered

    a. Selection of a random sample probably is not possible.

    b. Systematic sampling may be appropriate.

    c. Stratified sampling should be used.

    d. Random number tables cannot be used.

18. When performing a test of a control with respect to control over cash receipts, an auditor may use a systematic sampling technique with a start at any randomly selected item. The biggest disadvantage of this type of sampling is that the items in the population

    a. Must be systematically replaced in the population after sampling.

    b. May systematically occur more than once in the sample.

    c. Must be recorded in a systematic pattern before the sample can be drawn.

    d. May occur in a systematic pattern, thus destroying the sample randomness.

19. What is the primary objective of using stratification as a sampling method in auditing?

    a. To increase the confidence level at which a decision will be reached from the results of the sample selected.

    b. To determine the occurrence rate for a given characteristic in the population being studied.

    c. To decrease the effect of variance in the total population.

    d. To determine the precision range of the sample selected.

B.1. Tests of Controls—Sampling Risk

20. As a result of tests of controls, an auditor assessed control risk too low and decreased substantive testing. This assessment occurred because the true deviation rate in the population was

    a. Less than the risk of assessing control risk too low, based on the auditor's sample.

    b. Less than the deviation rate in the auditor's sample.

    c. More than the risk of assessing control risk too low, based on the auditor's sample.

    d. More than the deviation rate in the auditor's sample.

21. Which of the following factors is(are) considered in determining the sample size for a test of controls?

	Expected deviation rate	Tolerable deviation rate
a.	Yes	Yes
b.	No	No
c.	No	Yes
d.	Yes	No

22. Which of the following statements is correct concerning statistical sampling in tests of controls?

   a. Deviations from control procedures at a given rate usually result in misstatements at a higher rate.
   b. As the population size doubles, the sample size should also double.
   c. The qualitative aspects of deviations are not considered by the auditor.
   d. There is an inverse relationship between the sample size and the tolerable rate.

23. In determining the sample size for a test of controls, an auditor should consider the likely rate of deviations, the allowable risk of assessing control risk too low, and the

   a. Tolerable deviation rate.
   b. Risk of incorrect acceptance.
   c. Nature and cause of deviations.
   d. Population size.

24. Which of the following combinations results in a decrease in sample size in a sample for attributes?

	Risk of assessing control risk too low	Tolerable rate	Expected population deviation rate
a.	Increase	Decrease	Increase
b.	Decrease	Increase	Decrease
c.	Increase	Increase	Decrease
d.	Increase	Increase	Increase

25. An auditor is testing internal control procedures that are evidenced on an entity's vouchers by matching random numbers with voucher numbers. If a random number matches the number of a voided voucher, that voucher ordinarily should be replaced by another voucher in the random sample if the voucher

   a. Constitutes a deviation.
   b. Has been properly voided.
   c. Cannot be located.
   d. Represents an immaterial dollar amount.

26. An auditor plans to examine a sample of twenty purchase orders for proper approvals as prescribed by the client's control procedures. One of the purchase orders in the chosen sample of twenty cannot be found, and the auditor is unable to use alternative procedures to test whether that purchase order was properly approved. The auditor should

   a. Choose another purchase order to replace the missing purchase order in the sample.
   b. Consider this test of control invalid and proceed with substantive tests since internal control cannot be relied upon.
   c. Treat the missing purchase order as a deviation for the purpose of evaluating the sample.
   d. Select a completely new set of twenty purchase orders.

27. When assessing the tolerable rate, the auditor should consider that, while deviations from control procedures increase the risk of material misstatements, such deviations do not necessarily result in errors. This explains why

   a. A recorded disbursement that does not show evidence of required approval may nevertheless be a transaction that is properly authorized and recorded.
   b. Deviations would result in errors in the accounting records only if the deviations and the errors occurred on different transactions.
   c. Deviations from pertinent control procedures at a given rate ordinarily would be expected to result in errors at a higher rate.
   d. A recorded disbursement that is properly authorized may nevertheless be a transaction that contains a material error.

28. The objective of the tolerable rate in sampling for tests of controls of internal control is to

   a. Determine the probability of the auditor's conclusion based upon reliance factors.
   b. Determine that financial statements taken as a whole are not materially in error.
   c. Estimate the reliability of substantive tests.
   d. Estimate the range of procedural deviations in the population.

29. The tolerable rate of deviations for a test of a control is generally

   a. Lower than the expected rate of errors in the related accounting records.
   b. Higher than the expected rate of errors in the related accounting records.
   c. Identical to the expected rate of errors in related accounting records.
   d. Unrelated to the expected rate of errors in the related accounting records.

30. If the auditor is concerned that a population may contain exceptions, the determination of a sample size sufficient to include at least one such exception is a characteristic of

   a. Discovery sampling.
   b. Variables sampling.
   c. Random sampling.
   d. Dollar-unit sampling.

31. In determining the number of documents to select for a test to obtain assurance that all sales have been properly authorized, an auditor should consider the tolerable rate of deviation from the control activity. The auditor should also consider the

I. Likely rate of deviations.
II. Allowable risk of assessing control risk too high.

    a. I only.
    b. II only.
    c. Both I and II.
    d. Either I or II.

32. An auditor should consider the tolerable rate of deviation when determining the number of check requests to select for a test to obtain assurance that all check requests have been properly authorized. The auditor should also consider

	The average dollar value of the check requests	The allowable risk of assessing control risk too low
a.	Yes	Yes
b.	Yes	No
c.	No	Yes
d.	No	No

B.2. Statistical (Attributes) Sampling for Tests of Controls

33. Which of the following statements is correct concerning statistical sampling in tests of controls?

    a. As the population size increases, the sample size should increase proportionately.
    b. Deviations from specific internal control procedures at a given rate ordinarily result in misstatements at a lower rate.
    c. There is an inverse relationship between the expected population deviation rate and the sample size.
    d. In determining tolerable rate, an auditor considers detection risk and the sample size.

34. What is an auditor's evaluation of a statistical sample for attributes when a test of fifty documents results in three deviations if tolerable rate is 7%, the expected population deviation rate is 5%, and the allowance for sampling risk is 2%?

    a. Modify the planned assessed level of control risk because the tolerable rate plus the allowance for sampling risk exceeds the expected population deviation rate.
    b. Accept the sample results as support for the planned assessed level of control risk because the sample deviation rate plus the allowance for sampling risk exceeds the tolerable rate.
    c. Accept the sample results as support for the planned assessed level of control risk because the tolerable rate less the allowance for sampling risk equals the expected population deviation rate.
    d. Modify the planned assessed level of control risk because the sample deviation rate plus the allowance for sampling risk exceeds the tolerable rate.

Items 35 and 36 are based on the following:

An auditor desired to test credit approval on 10,000 sales invoices processed during the year. The auditor designed a statistical sample that would provide 1% risk of assessing control risk too low (99% confidence) that not more than 7% of the sales invoices lacked approval. The auditor estimated from previous experience that about 2 1/2% of the sales invoices lacked approval. A sample of 200 invoices was examined and 7 of them were lacking approval. The auditor then determined the achieved upper precision limit to be 8%.

35. In the evaluation of this sample, the auditor decided to increase the level of the preliminary assessment of control risk because the

    a. Tolerable rate (7%) was less than the achieved upper precision limit (8%).
    b. Expected deviation rate (7%) was more than the percentage of errors in the sample (3 1/2%).
    c. Achieved upper precision limit (8%) was more than the percentage of errors in the sample (3 1/2%).
    d. Expected deviation rate (2 1/2%) was less than the tolerable rate (7%).

36. The allowance for sampling risk was

    a. 5 1/2%
    b. 4 1/2%
    c. 3 1/2%
    d. 1%

37. Which of the following statements is correct concerning statistical sampling in tests of controls?

    a. The population size has little or no effect on determining sample size except for very small populations.
    b. The expected population deviation rate has little or no effect on determining sample size except for very small populations.
    c. As the population size doubles, the sample size also should double.
    d. For a given tolerable rate, a larger sample size should be selected as the expected population deviation rate decreases.

B.3. Nonstatistical Sampling for Tests of Controls

38. When an auditor has chosen a random sample and is using nonstatistical attributes sampling, that auditor

    a. Need not consider the risk of assessing control risk too low.
    b. Has committed a nonsampling error.
    c. Will have to use discovery sampling to evaluate the results.
    d. Should compare the deviation rate of the sample to the tolerable deviation rate.

C.1. Tests of Details—Sampling Risk

39. How would increases in tolerable misstatement and assessed level of control risk affect the sample size in a substantive test of details?

	Increase in tolerable misstatement	Increase in assessed level of control risk
a.	Increase sample size	Increase sample size
b.	Increase sample size	Decrease sample size
c.	Decrease sample size	Increase sample size
d.	Decrease sample size	Decrease sample size

40. Which of the following courses of action would an auditor most likely follow in planning a sample of cash disbursements if the auditor is aware of several unusually large cash disbursements?

    a. Set the tolerable rate of deviation at a lower level than originally planned.
    b. Stratify the cash disbursements population so that the unusually large disbursements are selected.
    c. Increase the sample size to reduce the effect of the unusually large disbursements.
    d. Continue to draw new samples until all the unusually large disbursements appear in the sample.

41. Which of the following sample planning factors would influence the sample size for a substantive test of details for a specific account?

	Expected amount of misstatements	Measure of tolerable misstatement
a.	No	No
b.	Yes	Yes
c.	No	Yes
d.	Yes	No

42. When planning a sample for a substantive test of details, an auditor should consider tolerable misstatement for the sample. This consideration should

    a. Be related to the auditor's business risk.
    b. Not be adjusted for qualitative factors.
    c. Be related to preliminary judgments about materiality levels.
    d. Not be changed during the audit process.

43. A number of factors influences the sample size for a substantive test of details of an account balance. All other factors being equal, which of the following would lead to a larger sample size?

    a. Greater reliance on internal control.
    b. Greater reliance on analytical procedures.
    c. Smaller expected frequency of errors.
    d. Smaller measure of tolerable misstatement.

44. In estimation sampling for variables, which of the following must be known in order to estimate the appropriate sample size required to meet the auditor's needs in a given situation?

    a. The qualitative aspects of errors.
    b. The total dollar amount of the population.
    c. The acceptable level of risk.
    d. The estimated rate of misstatements in the population.

45. An auditor established a $60,000 tolerable misstatement for an asset with an account balance of $1,000,000. The auditor selected a sample of every twentieth item from the population that represented the asset account balance and discovered overstatements of $3,700 and understatements of $200. Under these circumstances, the auditor most likely would conclude that

    a. There is an unacceptably high risk that the actual misstatements in the population exceed the tolerable misstatement because the total projected misstatement is more than the tolerable misstatement.
    b. There is an unacceptably high risk that the tolerable misstatement exceeds the sum of actual overstatements and understatements.
    c. The asset account is fairly stated because the total projected misstatement is less than the tolerable misstatement.
    d. The asset account is fairly stated because the tolerable misstatement exceeds the net of projected actual overstatements and understatements.

C.2. Probability-Proportional-to-Size (PPS) Sampling

46. Which of the following statements is correct concerning probability-proportional-to-size (PPS) sampling, also known as dollar unit sampling?

    a. The sampling distribution should approximate the normal distribution.
    b. Overstated units have a lower probability of sample selection than units that are understated.
    c. The auditor controls the risk of incorrect acceptance by specifying that risk level for the sampling plan.
    d. The sampling interval is calculated by dividing the number of physical units in the population by the sample size.

47. Hill has decided to use probability-proportional-to-size (PPS) sampling, sometimes called dollar-unit sampling, in the audit of a client's accounts receivable balances. Hill plans to use the following PPS sampling table:

TABLE
Reliability Factors for Overstatements

Number of over- statements	Risk of incorrect acceptance				
	1%	5%	10%	15%	20%
0	4.61	3.00	2.31	1.90	1.61
1	6.64	4.75	3.89	3.38	3.00
2	8.41	6.30	5.33	4.72	4.28
3	10.05	7.76	6.69	6.02	5.52
4	11.61	9.16	8.00	7.27	6.73

Additional information

Tolerable misstatements (net of effect of expected misstatements)	$ 24,000
Risk of incorrect acceptance	20%
Number of misstatements	1
Recorded amount of accounts receivable	$240,000
Number of accounts	360

What sample size should Hill use?

a. 120
b. 108
c. 60
d. 30

48. In a probability-proportional-to-size sample with a sampling interval of $5,000, an auditor discovered that a selected account receivable with a recorded amount of $10,000 had an audit amount of $8,000. If this were the only error discovered by the auditor, the projected error of this sample would be

a. $1,000
b. $2,000
c. $4,000
d. $5,000

C.3.　Classical Variables Sampling

49. An auditor is determining the sample size for an inventory observation using mean-per-unit estimation, which is a variables sampling plan. To calculate the required sample size, the auditor usually determines the

	Variability in the dollar amounts of inventory items	Risk of incorrect acceptance
a.	Yes	Yes
b.	Yes	No
c.	No	Yes
d.	No	No

50. In statistical sampling methods used in substantive testing, an auditor most likely would stratify a population into meaningful groups if

a. Probability-proportional-to-size (PPS) sampling is used.
b. The population has highly variable recorded amounts.

c. The auditor's estimated tolerable misstatement is extremely small.
d. The standard deviation of recorded amounts is relatively small.

51. The use of the ratio estimation sampling technique is most effective when

a. The calculated audit amounts are approximately proportional to the client's book amounts.
b. A relatively small number of differences exist in the population.
c. Estimating populations whose records consist of quantities, but not book values.
d. Large overstatement differences and large understatement differences exist in the population.

52. In the application of statistical techniques to the estimation of dollar amounts, a preliminary sample is usually taken primarily for the purpose of estimating the population

a. Variability.
b. Mode.
c. Range.
d. Median.

53. Using statistical sampling to assist in verifying the year-end accounts payable balance, an auditor has accumulated the following data:

	Number of accounts	Book balance	Balance determined by the auditor
Population	4,100	$5,000,000	?
Sample	200	$ 250,000	$300,000

Using the ratio estimation technique, the auditor's estimate of year-end accounts payable balance would be

a. $6,150,000
b. $6,000,000
c. $5,125,000
d. $5,050,000

54. Use of the ratio estimation sampling technique to estimated dollar amounts is inappropriate when

a. The total book value is known and corresponds to the sum of all the individual book values.
b. A book value for each sample item is unknown.
c. There are some observed differences between audited values and book values.
d. The audited values are nearly proportional to the book values.

55. An auditor is performing substantive tests of pricing and extensions of perpetual inventory balances consisting of a large number of items. Past experience indicates numerous pricing and extension errors. Which of the following statistical sampling approaches is most appropriate?

a. Unstratified mean-per-unit.
b. Probability-proportional-to-size.
c. Stop or go.
d. Ratio estimation.

56. The major reason that the difference and ratio estimation methods would be expected to produce audit efficiency is that the

    a. Number of members of the populations of differences or ratios is smaller than the number of members of the population of book values.

    b. Beta risk may be completely ignored.

    c. Calculations required in using difference or ratio estimation are less arduous and fewer than those required when using direct estimation.

    d. Variability of the populations of differences or ratios is less than that of the populations of book values or audited values.

57. Which of the following statements is correct concerning the auditor's use of statistical sampling?

    a. An auditor needs to estimate the dollar amount of the standard deviation of the population to use classical variables sampling.

    b. An assumption of PPS sampling is that the underlying accounting population is normally distributed.

    c. A classical variables sample needs to be designed with special considerations to include negative balances in the sample.

    d. The selection of zero balances usually does not require special sample design considerations when using PPS sampling.

C.4.   *Comparison of PPS Sampling to Classical Variables Sampling*

58. Which of the following most likely would be an advantage in using classical variables sampling rather than probability-proportional-to-size (PPS) sampling?

    a. An estimate of the standard deviation of the population's recorded amounts is not required.

    b. The auditor rarely needs the assistance of a computer program to design an efficient sample.

    c. Inclusion of zero and negative balances generally does not require special design considerations.

    d. Any amount that is individually significant is automatically identified and selected.

Multiple-Choice Answers and Explanations

Answers

1. d	__ __	13. d	__ __	25. b	__ __	37. a	__ __	49. a	__ __
2. c	__ __	14. c	__ __	26. c	__ __	38. d	__ __	50. b	__ __
3. a	__ __	15. c	__ __	27. a	__ __	39. c	__ __	51. a	__ __
4. d	__ __	16. b	__ __	28. d	__ __	40. b	__ __	52. a	__ __
5. a	__ __	17. b	__ __	29. b	__ __	41. b	__ __	53. b	__ __
6. a	__ __	18. d	__ __	30. a	__ __	42. c	__ __	54. b	__ __
7. d	__ __	19. c	__ __	31. a	__ __	43. d	__ __	55. d	__ __
8. b	__ __	20. d	__ __	32. c	__ __	44. c	__ __	56. d	__ __
9. c	__ __	21. a	__ __	33. b	__ __	45. a	__ __	57. a	__ __
10. a	__ __	22. d	__ __	34. d	__ __	46. c	__ __	58. c	__ __
11. d	__ __	23. a	__ __	35. a	__ __	47. d	__ __	1st: __/58 = __%
12. c	__ __	24. c	__ __	36. b	__ __	48. b	__ __	2nd: __/58 = __%

Explanations

1. (d) The requirement is to identify an advantage of statistical sampling over nonstatistical sampling. Answer (d) is correct because statistical sampling helps the auditor to: (1) design an efficient sample, (2) measures the sufficiency of the evidential matter obtained, and (3) evaluate the sample results (AICPA *Audit Sampling Guide*). Answer (a) is incorrect because dual-purpose tests, which both test a control and serve as substantive test, may be performed with either a statistical or a nonstatistical sample. Answer (b) is incorrect because both statistical and nonstatistical sampling require the use of judgment, although that judgment is quantified when statistical sampling is used. Answer (c) is incorrect because either statistical or nonstatistical sampling may provide equal assurance to the auditor.

2. (c) The requirement is to identify an advantage of statistical sampling over nonstatistical sampling. Answer (c) is correct because statistical sampling helps the auditor to: (1) design an efficient sample, (2) measure the sufficiency of the evidential matter obtained, and (3) evaluate the sample results (AICPA *Audit Sampling Guide*). Answer (a) is incorrect because the risk of nonsampling errors is not directly affected by whether statistical or nonstatistical sampling is used. Answer (b) is incorrect because either statistical or nonstatistical sampling can be used to reduce the level of audit risk to a low level; the materiality level should not be affected by the type of sampling used. Answer (d) is incorrect because either statistical or nonstatistical sampling may be used to minimize the failure to detect errors and fraud.

3. (a) The requirement is to determine the meaning of the likelihood of assessing control risk too high in a test of controls. Answer (a) is correct because the risk of assessing control risk too high is the risk that the sample does **not** support the auditor's planned assessed level of control risk when the true operating effectiveness of the control structure justifies such an assessment. Answer (b) is incorrect because the risk of assessing control risk too high relates to the deviation rate from a control procedure in a population, not to monetary misstatements. Answer (c) is incorrect because the risk of assessing control risk too high does not directly relate to monetary misstatements. Answer (d) is incorrect because tolerable error (misstatement) relates to variables sampling applied to substantive testing and not to tests of controls and because the meaning of "support the tolerable error" is uncertain.

4. (d) The requirement is to determine the nature of the risk of incorrect acceptance and the risk of assessing control risk too low. Answer (d) is correct because the risk of incorrect acceptance and the risk of assessing control risk too low relate to the effectiveness of an audit in detecting an existing material misstatement or deviation. Answer (a) is incorrect because the term "allowable risk of tolerable misstatement" is not used in the professional standards. Answer (b) is incorrect because preliminary estimates of materiality levels relate most directly to the risk of incorrect acceptance, and only indirectly to the risk of assessing control risk too low. Answer (c) is incorrect because the risk of incorrect rejection and the risk of assessing control risk too high relate to the efficiency of the audit.

5. (a) The requirement is to determine which answer represents the concept of sampling risk. Sampling risk arises from the possibility that an auditor's conclusions based upon a sample would differ from the conclusions which would be drawn from examining the entire population (i.e., the risk that the sample examined is not representative of the population). Answers (b), (c), and (d) are all incorrect because they relate to errors which could occur even if 100% of the population were examined, that is, nonsampling risk.

6. (a) The requirement is to determine what is related to the risk of incorrect rejection and the risk of assessing control risk too high. Answer (a) is correct because AU-C 530 states that the risk of incorrect rejection and the risk of assessing control risk too high relate to the efficiency of the audit. These two errors generally result in an auditor performing unnecessary additional procedures. Answer (b) is incorrect because the risk of incorrect acceptance and the risk of assessing control risk too low relate to the effectiveness of an audit. Answer (c) is incorrect because the risks do not relate directly to the actual selection of the sample. Answer (d) is incorrect because the audit quality controls do not directly mention either of these risks.

7. (d) The requirement is to determine the situation in which an auditor has properly concluded that control risk is at or below the planned assessed level. Answer (d) is correct because to support the planned level, the deviation rate must be less than the tolerable rate and the auditor must conclude that the deviation rate is less than the tolerable rate. Answer (a) is incorrect because it represents a situation in which the auditor appropriately decides that the deviation rate exceeds the tolerable rate. Answer (b) is incorrect because it represents a situation in which an auditor erroneously concludes that the deviation rate exceeds the tolerable rate when it actually does not. Answer (c) is incorrect because the auditor erroneously concludes that the deviation rate is less than the tolerable rate when it actually exceeds it.

8. (b) The requirement is to determine the situation in which the auditor assesses control risk too high and thereby increases substantive testing. Answer (b) is correct because to assess control risk too high, an auditor must estimate that the deviation rate exceeds the tolerable rate when it actually is less than the tolerable rate. Answer (a) is incorrect because it represents a situation in which the auditor appropriately decides that the deviation rate exceeds the tolerable rate. Answer (c) is incorrect because the auditor erroneously concludes that the deviation rate is less than the tolerable rate when it actually exceeds the tolerable rate. Answer (d) is incorrect because to properly rely on internal control, the deviation rate must be less than the tolerable rate and the auditor must conclude that the deviation rate is less than the tolerable rate.

9. (c) The requirement is to determine the type of risk demonstrated when an auditor concludes that an account is misstated when in fact it is not. Answer (c) is correct because the risk of incorrect rejection is the risk that the sample supports the conclusion that the recorded account balance is materially misstated when the account is not misstated. Answers (a) and (b) are incorrect because the risk of assessing control risk too high and the risk of assessing control risk too low relate to tests of controls, and not to substantive tests of details. Answer (d) is incorrect because the risk of incorrect acceptance is the risk that the sample support the conclusion that the account is not misstated when in fact it is misstated.

10. (a) The requirement is to identify the correct statement with respect to the size of a sample required for dual purpose testing. Answer (a) is correct because the auditor should select the larger of the required sample sizes.

11. (d) The requirement is to identify the type of sampling involved in a review of client invoices in which an expected population deviation rate and an established tolerable rate are provided. Answer (d) is correct because attribute sampling is used to reach a conclusion about a population in terms of a rate of occurrence (*Audit Sampling Guide*). Answer (a) is incorrect because stratified sampling is generally used to reach a dollar-based conclusion in variables sampling approaches. Answer (b) is incorrect because, as indicated, variables sampling deals with a dollar amount conclusion, not deviation rates. Answer (c) is incorrect because discovery sampling is only used in cases in which the auditor expects deviation rates to be extremely low (approaching zero).

12. (c) The requirement is to identify the sampling method that would be used to estimate a numerical measurement such as a dollar value of a population. Answer (c) is correct because sampling for variables addresses such numerical measurements. Answer (a) is incorrect because attributes sampling deals with deviation rates. Answer (b) is incorrect because stop-or-go sampling (also referred to as sequential sampling) is a form of attributes sampling. Answer (d) is incorrect because random-number sampling is simply a sample selection technique that may be used with either an attributes or a variables form of sampling; accordingly, a numerical measurement such as a dollar value is not necessary for random-number sampling.

13. (d) The requirement is to determine the audit test for which an auditor would most likely use attribute sampling. Answer (d) is correct because attribute sampling is used to reach a conclusion about a population in terms of a rate of occurrence. Here the rate of occurrence will be the rate of (un) approved time cards. Answers (a), (b), and (c) are all incorrect because they all relate more directly to variables sampling which is generally used to reach conclusion about a population in terms of a dollar amount. See the AICPA Audit and Accounting Guide, *Audit Sampling,* and AU-C 530 for more information on audit sampling.

14. (c) The requirement is to determine the correct statement with respect to random sampling. Answer (c) is correct because every item in the accounting population should have an opportunity to be selected. Answer (a) is incorrect because with stratified random sampling, each stratum need not be given equal representation. Answer (b) is incorrect because while sample units should be randomly selected, there is no requirement that the accounting population be randomly ordered. Answer (d) is incorrect because random sampling, by its very nature, is not systematic. Additionally, random sampling may be performed without replacement.

15. (c) The requirement is to determine the least desirable statistical selection technique. Answer (c), block selection, is correct because, ideally, a sample should be selected from the entire set of data to which the resulting conclusions are to be applied. When block sampling is used, the selection of blocks often precludes items from being so selected. In most cases, systematic [answer (a)], stratified [answer (b)], and sequential [answer (d)] selection techniques all provide a better representation of the entire population than does block selection.

16. (b) The requirement is to identify the type of sampling plan that does **not** use a fixed sample size for tests of controls. Answer (b) is correct because sequential sampling results in the selection of a sample in several steps, with each step conditional on the result of the previous steps. Therefore, sample size will vary depending upon the number of stages that prove necessary. Answers (a), (c), and (d) are all incorrect because dollar-unit sampling, PPS sampling, and variables sampling all use a fixed sample size.

17. (b) The requirement is to identify the correct statement concerning a statistical sampling application where the population consists of forms which are not consecutively numbered. Answer (b) is correct because systematic sampling is a procedure where a random start is obtained and then every n*th* item is selected. For example, a sample of forty from a population of a thousand would require selecting every 25th item after obtaining a random start between items 1 through 25. Answer (a) is incorrect because selection of a random sample is possible even though the population is not consecutively numbered. Answer (c) is incorrect because there is no special reason for using stratified sampling. Stratified sampling breaks down the population into subpopulations and applies different selection methods to each subpopulation. This selection method is used when the population consists of different types of items (e.g., large balances and small balances). Answer (d) is incorrect because random number tables can be used even though the forms are not consecutively numbered. If random numbers are selected for which there are no forms, they are ignored. This is the same as if there were 86,000 items in a consecutively numbered population and random numbers selected between 86,000 and 99,999 are ignored.

18. (d) Answer (d) is correct because systematic items occurrence in a population **may** destroy a sample's randomness. Answer (a) is incorrect because items need not be replaced in the population, and therefore is not a disadvantage of systematic sampling. Answer (b) is incorrect because an individual item will not occur more than once in a sample when systematic sampling is being used (because the auditor selects every nth item). Answer (c) is incorrect because systematic sampling refers to the type of sampling selection plan used and not the manner in which items in the population are recorded. Also, as indicated in (d) above, a systematic pattern in the population is a hindrance to systematic sampling.

19. (c) Stratified sampling is a technique of breaking the population down into subpopulations and applying different sample selection methods to the subpopulations. Stratified sampling is used to minimize the variance within the overall population [answer (c)]. Recall that as variance increases, so does the required sample size (because of the extreme values). Thus, stratification allows the selection of subpopulations to reduce the effect of dispersion in the population.

20. (d) The requirement is to identify the circumstance that would cause an auditor to assess control risk too low and decrease substantive testing inappropriately. Answer (d) is correct because when the true deviation rate in the population exceeds that in the sample, the auditor may assess control risk too low. The AICPA *Audit Sampling Guide* discusses

tests of controls and attributes sampling in its second chapter. Answers (a) and (c) are incorrect because the true deviation rate and the risk of assessing control risk too low do not have such a relationship, either positive or negative. Answer (b) is incorrect because a deviation rate in the population that is less than the deviation rate in the auditor's sample may lead the auditor to assess control risk too high.

21. (a) The requirement is to determine whether the expected deviation rate, the tolerable deviation rate, or both affect the sample size for a test of controls. Answer (a) is correct because attribute sampling formulas and tables used in auditing generally require the auditor to specify an expected deviation rate, a tolerable deviation rate and the risk of assessing control risk too low. See AICPA *Audit Sampling Guide* and AU-C 530 for more information on audit sampling.

22. (d) The requirement is to identify the correct statement about sampling for attributes. Answer (d) is correct because the sample size increases as the tolerable rate decreases, an inverse relationship. Answer (a) is incorrect because many deviations do not necessarily result in a misstatement. Answer (b) is incorrect because a doubling of the population size will result in less than a doubling of the required sample size. Answer (c) is incorrect because auditors must consider the qualitative aspects of deviations.

23. (a) The requirement is to identify the information needed in addition to the likely rate of deviations and the allowable risk of assessing control risk too low to determine the sample size for a test of controls in an attributes sampling plan. Answer (a) is correct because the tolerable deviation rate is also needed. Answer (b) is incorrect because the risk of incorrect acceptance relates to variables sampling applied to substantive testing, not attributes sampling applied to tests of controls. Answer (c) is incorrect because the auditor will examine the nature and cause of deviations after the sample has been selected. Answer (d) is incorrect because auditors often do not consider population size when performing attributes sampling applied to tests of controls.

24. (c) The requirement is to determine when a sample size would be decreased when sampling for attributes. Answer (c) is correct because the sample size will decrease when the risk of assessing control risk too low is increased, the tolerable rate is increased, and the expected population deviation rate is decreased (Audit and Accounting Guide *Audit Sampling*). Answers (a), (b), and (d) are all incorrect because they include combinations of changes that would not necessarily decrease sample size.

25. (b) The requirement is to identify the correct statement with respect to treatment of a voided voucher that has been selected in a sample. Answer (b) is correct because the AICPA *Audit Sampling Guide* states that the auditor should obtain reasonable assurance that the voucher has been properly voided, and should then replace it with another voucher. Answer (a) is incorrect because the voided voucher is not normally considered to be a deviation. Answer (c) is incorrect because the auditor must obtain reasonable assurance that the misplaced voucher has been voided. Answer (d) is incorrect because the level of materiality normally does not directly affect the decision.

26. (c) The requirement is to determine the proper method of handling a sample item which cannot be located for evaluation purposes. Answer (c) is correct because an auditor would ordinarily consider the selected item to be a deviation. Answers (a) and (d) are incorrect since a possible cause for the missing purchase order could be a breakdown in one of the controls of the system. Thus, in selecting a new sample item(s) the auditor may be ignoring a portion of the population which is in error and may be artificially skewing the results of the tests performed on the sample. Answer (b) is incorrect because there is no reason to believe that the entire test is invalid and cannot be relied upon.

27. (a) The requirement is to determine why deviations from control procedures do not necessarily result in errors. Answer (a) is correct because it provides an example of a situation in which a deviation from a control procedure exists (lack of documentation of transaction approval), although the entry was authorized and proper. Thus, such a deviation does not necessarily result in an error in the financial statements. Answer (b) is incorrect because a deviation from control procedure and an error may occur in the same transaction. Answer (c) is incorrect since the fact that all deviations do not lead to errors will result in a lower error rate. Answer (d) is incorrect because while it represents a correct statement, it does not follow from the point of the question which is based on the idea that deviations do not directly result in errors.

28. (d) The requirement is to determine the objective of the tolerable rate in sampling. Tolerable rate is calculated to determine the range of procedural deviations in the population. Answer (a) is incorrect because probabilities relate more directly to reliability. Answer (b) is incorrect because errors on financial statements in materiality terms relate to variables sampling. Answer (c) is incorrect because the tolerable rate does not relate directly to substantive tests.

29. (b) The requirement is to determine the correct relationship between the tolerable rate of deviations and the expected rate of deviations for a test of a control. The tolerable rate of deviations is the maximum rate of deviations from a prescribed control procedure that an auditor would be willing to accept and, unless the expected error rate is lower, reliance on internal control is not justified. Answer (a) is incorrect because if the tolerable rate of deviations is less than the expected rate, the auditor would not plan to rely on internal control and would therefore omit tests of controls. Answer (c) is incorrect because testing of controls is inappropriate if the expected rate of errors equals the tolerable rate of deviations (mathematically, the precision of zero makes the sample size equal to population size). Answer (d) is incorrect because, as indicated above, to perform tests of controls one must assume that the tolerable rate of deviations is more than the expected error rate.

30. (a) The requirement is to determine the type of sampling which is most directly related to finding at least one exception. Discovery sample sizes and related discovery sampling tables are constructed to measure the probability of at least one error occurring in a sample if the error rate in the population exceeds the tolerable rate. Answer (b) is incorrect because variables sampling need not include at least one exception

(mean per unit sampling, for example, needs no errors). Answer (c) is incorrect since random sampling only deals with the technique used to select items to be included in the sample. Answer (d) is incorrect because dollar-unit sampling results are not directly related to finding at least one exception.

31. (a) The requirement is to determine whether an auditor should consider the likely rate of deviation, the allowable risk of assessing control risk too high, or both, when performing a test of a control. Answer (a) is correct because an auditor will consider the likely rate of deviations, but will not ordinarily consider the allowable risk of assessing control risk too high when following the approach outlined in the AICPA *Audit Sampling Guide*.

32. (c) The requirement is to determine whether an auditor would consider the average dollar value of check requests, the allowable risk of assessing control risk too low, or both, when testing whether check requests have been properly authorized. Answer (c) is correct because a test of authorization such as this is an attributes test which requires the auditor to determine an allowable risk of assessing control risk too low, but does not deal directly with dollar values. Answers (a), (b), and (d) are all incorrect because they include incorrect combinations of the replies. See AU-C 530 and the AICPA *Audit Sampling Guide* for information on sampling.

33. (b) The requirement is to identify the correct statement concerning statistical sampling in tests of controls. Answer (b) is correct because while deviations from pertinent control procedures increase the risk of material misstatements, any specific deviation need not necessarily result in a misstatement. For example, a recorded disbursement that does not show evidence of required approval might nevertheless be a transaction that is properly authorized and recorded (AICPA *Audit Sampling Guide*). Answer (a) is incorrect because increases in population size result in small increases in sample size. Answer (c) is incorrect because a direct relationship, not an inverse relationship, exists between the expected population deviation rate and the sample size—that is, increases in the expected population deviation rate result in an increase in the required sample size. Answer (d) is incorrect because when determining the tolerable rate, the auditor does not yet have the required sample size.

34. (d) The requirement is to determine the proper evaluation of a statistical sample for attributes when a test of 50 documents results in 3 deviations, given a tolerable rate of 7%, an expected population deviation rate of 5%, and an allowance for sampling risk of 2%. Answer (d) is correct because when the deviation rate plus the allowance for sampling risk exceeds the tolerable rate, the assessed level of control risk may increase. Here the deviation rate of 6% (3 deviations/50 documents) plus the allowance for sampling risk of 2% equals 8% and exceeds the tolerable rate of 7%. Answer (a) is incorrect because the tolerable rate plus the allowance for sampling risk will always exceed the expected population deviation rate when tests of controls are being performed. Answer (b) is incorrect because when the sample deviation rate plus the allowance for sampling risk exceeds the tolerable rate the sample results do not support the planned assessed level of control risk. Answer (c) is incorrect because the tolerable rate less the allowance for sampling risk should be compared with the actual deviation rate.

35. (a) The requirement is to determine the circumstance in which an auditor would decide to increase the level of the preliminary assessment of control risk. Answer (a) is correct because the assessment of control risk will increase when the achieved upper precision limit (here 8%) exceeds the tolerable rate (here 7%). Answer (b) is incorrect because the expected deviation rate was 2 1/2%, not 7%. Also, if the expected deviation rate is higher than the percentage of error in the sample, the preliminary assessment does not need to be increased. Answer (c) is incorrect because the achieved upper precision limit will always exceed the percentage of errors in the sample. Answer (d) is incorrect because, in circumstances in which the auditor decides to sample the population, the expected deviation rate will always be less than the tolerable rate.

36. (b) The requirement is to determine the allowance for sampling risk of the presented sample. When considering the allowance for sampling risk, one may consider both the planned allowance for sampling risk or the adjusted allowance based on the sample results. Answer (b) is correct because both the planned and adjusted allowance for sampling risk are 4 1/2% (7% – 2.5% for planning purposes, and 8% – 3.5% [7/200] as adjusted).

37. (a) The requirement is to identify the correct statement concerning statistical sampling for tests of controls. Answer (a) is correct because population size has little or **no** effect on sample size. Answer (b) is incorrect because the population deviation rate has a significant effect on sample size. Answer (c) is incorrect because sample size increases to a much lesser extent than doubling as the population size doubles. Answer (d) is incorrect because for a given tolerable rate, a smaller, and not a larger, sample size should be selected as the expected population deviation rate decreases.

38. (d) The requirement is to identify the proper statement concerning a random sample when nonstatistical attributes sampling is being used. Answer (d) is correct because the deviation rate of the sample should be compared to the tolerable deviation rate regardless of whether statistical or nonstatistical sampling is being used. Answer (a) is incorrect because the risk of assessing control risk too low should be considered, although it may be done judgmentally. Answer (b) is incorrect because nonsampling error relates to "human" type errors such as not identifying a deviation, and not specifically to the use of nonstatistical sampling. Answer (c) is incorrect because discovery sampling will not be used to evaluate the results.

39. (c) The requirement is to determine whether either or both of an increase in tolerable misstatement and an increase in the assessed level of control risk increase sample size in a substantive test of details. Answer (c) is correct because while an increase in tolerable misstatement decreases sample size for a substantive test of details, an increase in the assessed level of control risk increases the sample size for a substantive test of details because a lower level of detection risk is required.

40. (b) The requirement is to determine the proper course of action when an auditor is planning a sample of cash disbursements and he or she is aware of several unusually large cash disbursements. Given the description of the several disbursements as "unusually large," an auditor will generally test them. Answer (b) is therefore correct because stratifying the population will allow the auditor to ensure inclusion of the disbursements. The sampling procedure (selecting less than all items) will then be applied only to the smaller disbursements. Answer (a) is incorrect because the existence of the large disbursements will have no necessary relationship to the tolerable rate of deviation when attributes sampling is being used. Answer (c) is incorrect because while increasing the sample size might be appropriate in some variables sampling applications (we are not told in this problem whether attributes or variables sampling is being followed), the fact that the disbursements are described as "unusually large" leads one to include them. Answer (d) is incorrect because an auditor will not draw numerous samples to assure inclusion of the large disbursements.

41. (b) The requirement is to determine whether either or both of the expected amount of misstatement and the measure of tolerable misstatement influence sample size for a substantive test of details. Answer (b) is correct because both the expected amount of misstatement and the tolerable misstatement affect sample size (AICPA *Audit Sampling Guide*). Increases in the expected amount of misstatements increase sample size, while increases in the tolerable misstatement decrease sample size.

42. (c) The requirement is to determine the correct statement concerning the auditor's consideration of tolerable misstatement. Answer (c) is correct because the consideration of tolerable misstatement is related to preliminary judgments in a manner such that when the auditor's preliminary judgments about tolerable misstatement levels for accounts or transaction types are combined for the entire audit plan, the preliminary judgments about materiality levels for the financial statements are not exceeded. Answer (a) is incorrect because the auditor's judgment of business risk related to a client is not directly related to tolerable misstatement. Answer (b) is incorrect because tolerable misstatement may be adjusted for qualitative factors. Answer (d) is incorrect because tolerable misstatement may be changed during the audit process, especially as misstatements are identified and the auditor considers the nature of the misstatements.

43. (d) The requirement is to determine the factor that would lead to larger sample size in a substantive test of details. Answer (d) is correct because the sample size required to achieve the auditor's objective at a given risk of incorrect acceptance increases as the auditor's assessment of tolerable misstatement for the balance or class decreases. Answer (a) is incorrect because a greater reliance on internal control will lead to a smaller sample size in a substantive test of details. Answer (b) is incorrect because greater reliance upon analytical procedures will result in a need for less reliance on substantive tests of details and therefore will result in a smaller sample. Answer (c) is incorrect because a smaller expected frequency of errors will generally include properly functioning internal control and will therefore result in a smaller sample for substantive tests of details.

44. (c) The requirement is to identify the factor which must be known in order to estimate the appropriate sample size when using variables sampling. Answer (c) is correct because the auditor must set an acceptable level of risk for both variables sampling and attribute sampling. Answer (a) is incorrect because while the auditor will consider the qualitative aspects of errors when evaluating the sample, they need not be considered in determining an appropriate sample size. Answer (b) is incorrect because a primary objective of variables sampling is to estimate the audited dollar amount of the population. Also, in some forms of variables sampling, knowledge of book values is not necessary (e.g., mean-per-unit). Answer (d) is incorrect because a rate of error in the population relates to attribute sampling.

45. (a) The requirement is to identify an auditor's most likely response to a circumstance in which there is a tolerable misstatement of $60,000, and the auditor has discovered misstatement of a net overstatement of $3,500 ($3,700 – $200) when 1/20 of the account has been included in the sample. Because auditors must project the misstatements to the entire population, one would expect a misstatement of approximately $70,000 (20 times the misstatement of $3,500). Since this exceeds the tolerable misstatement, there is little question that the risk of material misstatement is too high and that the misstatement in the population exceeds the tolerable misstatement, therefore answer (a) is correct. Answer (b) is incorrect because it seems that the sum of actual overstatement and understatement is likely to exceed the tolerable misstatement. Also, answer (b) makes little sense since there probably is no such thing as "an unacceptably high risk" that the tolerable misstatement exceeds the sum of actual overstatements and understatements; in such a circumstance the auditor simply accepts the population as being materially correct. Answers (c) and (d) are incorrect because the total projected misstatement must be calculated as indicated above. See AU-C 530 and the *Audit Sampling Guide* for information on sampling.

46. (c) The requirement is to identify the correct statement regarding probability-proportional-to-size (PPS) sampling. Answer (c) is correct because when using PPS sampling, the auditor controls the risk of incorrect acceptance by specifying a risk level when planning the sample. Answer (a) is incorrect because PPS sampling does not assume a normal distribution. Answer (b) is incorrect because the book value of the unit determines how probable it is that it will be included in the sample, not whether it is over or understated. Answer (d) is incorrect because the sampling interval is calculated by dividing the book value of the population by the sample size.

47. (d) The requirement is to determine the sample size that should be used in a probability-proportional-to-size (PPS) sample. One approach is to first calculate a sampling interval and use it to determine an appropriate sample size. Using this approach, when provided with the tolerable misstatement already adjusted for expected misstatements (as is the situation in this problem), one divides that total by the number of

expected misstatements column for the appropriate risk of incorrect acceptance (the fact that some overstatements are expected is not used). Here that computation is $24,000/1.61 = $14,906.83. Sample size is computed by dividing the recorded amount by the sampling interval, here $240,000/14,906.83, for a sample size of 16. An alternate approach is to use the reliability factor for the expected number of overstatements. In that case the computations become $24,000/3.00 = $8,000. Sample size is $240,000/$8,000 = 30. In either case answer (d) is the closest and therefore the correct reply.

48. (b) The requirement is to determine the projected error (misstatement) of a probability-proportional-to-size (PPS) sample with a sampling interval of $5,000, when an auditor has discovered that an account with a recorded amount of $10,000 had an audit amount of $8,000. Answer (b) is correct since, when an account's recorded amount exceeds the sampling interval, the projected error equals the actual misstatement, here $2,000 ($10,000 – $8,000).

49. (a) The requirement is to determine whether an auditor uses the variability in dollar values, the risk of incorrect acceptance, or both, in a mean-per-unit estimation variables sampling plan. Answer (a) is correct because both factors are included in a sampling plan. Answers (b), (c), and (d) are all incorrect because they suggest that one or both factors are not considered. See AU-C 530 and the AICPA *Audit Sampling Guide* for information on sampling.

50. (b) The requirement is to identify the circumstance in which an auditor most likely would stratify a population into meaningful groups. Answer (b) is correct because stratified sampling is used to minimize the effect on sample size of variation within the overall population and results in the largest savings for populations with high variability. Answer (a) is incorrect because while PPS sampling may in essence stratify a population, the items selected, other than those larger than the sampling interval, are not in "meaningful groups." Answer (c) is incorrect because the tolerable misstatement in and of itself will not lead to stratification. Answer (d) is incorrect because stratification is used primarily when there is a relatively large standard deviation, not a relatively small standard deviation.

51. (a) The requirement is to determine when ratio estimation sampling is most effective. The ratio estimation sampling technique uses the ratio between the audited to book amounts as a measure of standard deviation in its sample size computation. Answer (a) is correct because when audit differences are approximately proportional to account size the standard deviation of the ratio is small and this results in a relatively small required sample size. Answer (b) is incorrect because a relatively large number of differences between book and audited values must exist to calculate a reliable standard deviation under the ratio method. Answer (c) is incorrect because while the ratio estimation sampling technique may be used with quantities, it offers no particular advantage over other methods. Answer (b) is incorrect because the absolute size of differences does not make the ratio estimation method most effective.

52. (a) The requirement is to determine the purpose of taking a preliminary sample when one uses statistical techniques. It is necessary to obtain an estimate of a population's standard deviation (variability) when calculating the required sample size and when using sampling techniques. Answers (b), (c), and (d) are incorrect because, in most statistical techniques used by auditors, the mode (most frequent balance), the median (middle balance) and the range (difference between the highest and lowest values) are not used.

53. (b) The requirement is to determine the estimated audited accounts payable balance using the ratio estimation technique. Answer (b) is correct because the ratio estimation technique estimates the audited value by multiplying the audited value/book value of the sample times the population book value. In this case, ($300,000/$250,000) × $5,000,000 = $6,000,000.

54. (b) The ratio estimation sampling technique is based on comparing the ratio of the book value to the audited value of the sampled items. Answer (b) is correct because this method cannot be used when there is no book value to make the comparison. The circumstances described in answers (a) and (c) are necessary for ratio point and interval estimation. Answer (d) describes the circumstances in which the use of ratio estimation will be efficient in terms of required sample size.

55. (d) The requirement is to determine the most appropriate sampling approach for substantive tests of pricing and extensions of perpetual inventory balances consisting of a large number of items for which past experience indicates numerous expected pricing and extension errors. Answer (d) is correct because ratio estimation is appropriate when testing a population for which a large number of errors of this nature is expected (Audit and Accounting Guide, *Audit Sampling*). Answer (a) is incorrect because the unstratified mean-per-unit method will typically provide a larger sample size than the ratio estimation method to achieve the same level of sampling risk. Thus, the ratio estimation method would be more appropriate. Answer (b) is incorrect because probability-proportional-to-size sampling is most efficient for testing populations with relatively low expected error rates. Answer (c) is incorrect because "stop or go" or "sequential" sampling is most frequently used in attribute sampling.

56. (d) Difference and ratio estimation methods are statistical sampling methods. They measure the difference between audit and book values or the ratio of audit to book values. As these differences should not be great, the population of these differences will have little variance. In statistical sampling, the less variation in a population, the smaller the required sample to provide an estimate of the population. In other words, difference and ratio estimation methods are more efficient because the differences between audit and book values are expected to vary less than the actual items in the population. Answer (a) is incorrect because the number of members in the population for differences or ratio methods would be the same as the number of items in the population for a direct estimation method. In difference sampling, many items would be zero because audit and book are the same, and in ratio sampling, many of the members would be one for the same reason. Answer (b) is incorrect because beta risk can never be ignored, as beta risk is the risk of accepting an incorrect (unacceptable) population. Answer (c) is incorrect because the calculations required in difference and ratio sampling are similar to those used in direct estimation sampling.

57. (a) The requirement is to identify the correct statement concerning the auditor's use of statistical sampling. Answer (a) is correct because an estimate of the variation of the population, the standard deviation, is needed to use classical variables sampling (AICPA Audit and Accounting Guide, *Audit Sampling*). Answer (b) is incorrect because PPS sampling does not make an assumption that the underlying population is normally distributed. Answers (c) and (d) are incorrect because classical variables sample selected accounts and therefore need not include special considerations to those with a negative balance.

58. (c) The requirement is to identify an advantage in using classical variables sampling rather than probability-proportional-to-size sampling. Answer (c) is correct because the inclusion of zero and negative balances generally does **not** require special design considerations when using classical sampling, while it does when using probability-proportional-to-size sampling (AICPA *Audit Sampling Guide*). Answer (a) is incorrect because classical variables sampling does require an estimate of the standard deviation of the population's recorded amounts. Answer (b) is incorrect because the computational process involved with classical variables sampling may make use of a computer program desirable. Answer (d) is incorrect because probability-proportional-to-size sampling, not classical sampling, automatically stratifies individually significant items.

Simulations

Task-Based Simulation 1

Analyzing PPS Results		
	Authoritative Literature	Help

The following is a computer printout generated by audit software using probability-proportional-to-size (PPS) sampling:

Winz Corporation
Receivable Sampling Evaluation Results
December 31, 20X2

Population book value = $2,400,000; Tolerable misstatement = $280,000

Projected Misstatement

Book value	Audited value	Misstatement	Tainting percentage	Sampling interval	Projected misstatement
$1,000	$ 0	$1,000	100%	$80,000	$ 80,000
750	600	150	20%	$80,000	16,000
85,000	60,000	25,000	NA	NA	25,000
					$121,000

Basic Precision = 3.0 * $80,000 $240,000

Incremental Allowance

Reliability factor	Increment	(Increment –1)	Projected misstatement	Incremental allowance
3.00				
4.75	1.75	.75	$80,000	$60,000
6.30	1.55	.55	16,000	8,800
				$68,800

The software uses factors from the following PPS sampling table:

TABLE

Reliability Factors for Overstatements

Number of overstatements	Risk of incorrect acceptance				
	1%	5%	10%	15%	20%
0	4.61	3.00	2.31	1.90	1.61
1	6.64	4.75	3.89	3.38	3.00
2	8.41	6.30	5.33	4.72	4.28
3	10.05	7.76	6.69	6.02	5.52
4	11.61	9.16	8.00	7.27	6.73

Answer the following questions relating to the above worksheet:

Answers

1. What was the planned sample size?

2. What is the total misstatement in the sample?

3. What is the most likely total misstatement in the population?

4. Calculate the upper limit on misstatement.

5. Calculate the allowance for sampling risk.

6. Would one "accept" or "reject" the population as being materially correct?

7. What is the risk of incorrect acceptance?

A.	30 items	K.	$240,000
B.	60 items	L.	$308,800
C.	76 items	M.	$361,000
D.	90 items	N.	$429,800
E.	0	O.	Accept
F.	$ 26,150	P.	Reject
G.	$ 68,800	Q.	5%
H.	$ 80,000	R.	20%
I.	$ 121,000	S.	100%
J.	$ 189,800		

Task-Based Simulation 2

PPS Sampling Concepts		
	Authoritative Literature	Help

Reply as to whether you believe the following statements are correct or incorrect concerning PPS sampling:

	Correct	Incorrect
1. Size of a PPS sample is not based on the estimated variation of audited amounts.	O	O
2. PPS sampling results in a stratified sample.	O	O
3. Individually significant items are automatically identified.	O	O
4. PPS sampling results in a smaller sample size when numerous small misstatements are expected.	O	O
5. If no misstatements are expected, PPS sampling will usually result in a smaller sample size than classical variables sampling methods.	O	O
6. One does not need a book value for individual items to evaluate a PPS sample.	O	O
7. A PPS sample eliminates the need to project results to the overall population.	O	O
8. PPS sampling is "preferred" by the professional standards.	O	O

Tolerable misstatement	$ 50,000
Sample size	100
Expected of misstatement	$ 10,000
Recorded amount of accounts receivable	$300,000

	Correct	Incorrect
9. The sampling interval is $500.	O	O
10. Increasing the expected misstatement to $10,000 will increase the sample size.	O	O

Task-Based Simulation 3

Research		
	Authoritative Literature	Help

Sampling vs. nonsampling risk

As a new assistant with Webber & Co. CPAs, you have been asked to perform research on the nature of sampling risk versus nonsampling risk.

Selections
A. AU-C
B. PCAOB
C. AT
D. AR
E. ET
F. BL
G. CS
H. QC

	(A)	(B)	(C)	(D)	(E)	(F)	(G)	(H)
1. Which title of the Professional Standards addresses this issue?	○	○	○	○	○	○	○	○

2. Enter the exact section and paragraph(s) which define sampling risk and nonsampling risk.

Simulation Solutions

Task-Based Simulation 1

Analyzing PPS Results		
	Authoritative Literature	Help

1. **(A)** Thirty items. Calculated by dividing the population book value ($2,400,000) by the sampling interval size ($80,000). Accordingly $2,400,000/80,000 = 30 items.
2. **(G)** $26,150. Calculated by summing the misstatements ($1,000 + $150 + $25,000 = $26,150).
3. **(I)** $121,000. Projected misstatement represents the most likely total misstatement in the population ($121,000).
4. **(N)** $429,800. The upper limit on misstatement is the sum of projected misstatement, basic precision, and the incremental allowance ($121,000 + $240,000 + $68,800 = $429,800).
5. **(L)** $308,800. The allowance for sampling risk is the sum of basic precision and the incremental allowance ($240,000 + $68,800 = $308,800).
6. **(P)** Reject because the upper limit on misstatement ($429,800) exceeds the tolerable misstatement ($280,000).
7. **(5%)** Because basic precision uses a 3.0 factor, the test is being performed at 5%.

Task-Based Simulation 2

PPS Sampling Concepts		
	Authoritative Literature	Help

	Correct	Incorrect
1. Size of a PPS sample is not based on the estimated variation of audited amounts.	●	○
2. PPS sampling results in a stratified sample.	●	○
3. Individually significant items are automatically identified.	●	○
4. PPS sampling results in a smaller sample size when numerous small misstatement are expected.	○	●
5. If no misstatements are expected, PPS sampling will usually result in a smaller sample size than classical variables sampling methods.	●	○
6. One does not need a book value for individual items to evaluate a PPS sample.	○	●
7. A PPS sample eliminates the need to project results to the overall population.	○	●
8. PPS sampling is "preferred" by the professional standards.	○	●
9. The sampling interval is $500.*	○	●
10. Increasing the expected misstatement to $10,000 will increase the sample size.	●	○

---

*It is the recorded amount divided by sample size: $300,000/100 = $3,000

Task-Based Simulation 3

Research		
	Authoritative Literature	**Help**

(A) (B) (C) (D) (E) (F) (G) (H)

●   ○   ○   ○   ○   ○   ○   ○

1. Which title of the Professional Standards addresses this issue?

2. Enter the exact section and paragraph(s) which define sampling and nonsampling risk.

530	05*

---

*Alternatively, the terms are defined in the glossary (AU-C GLO)

Module 8: Auditing with Technology

Overview

Computers have become the primary means used to process financial accounting information and have resulted in a situation in which auditors must be able to use and understand current information technology (IT) to audit a client's financial statements. Accordingly, knowledge of computer terminology, computer systems, and related audit procedures is tested both on the Business Environment and Concepts section and on the Auditing and Attestation section of the CPA exam.

The following "Diagram of an Audit" was first presented and explained in the auditing overview section:

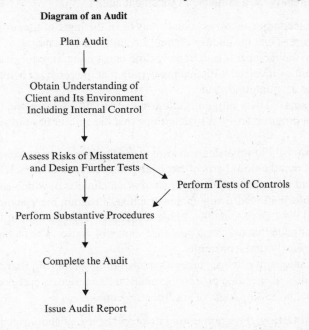

Diagram of an Audit

Plan Audit

↓

Obtain Understanding of
Client and Its Environment
Including Internal Control

↓

Assess Risks of Misstatement
and Design Further Tests

→ Perform Tests of Controls

↓

Perform Substantive Procedures

↓

Complete the Audit

↓

Issue Audit Report

Computer processing (historically referred to as electronic data processing or EDP) does not necessitate modification of the diagram. However, the auditor's consideration of internal control includes an assessment of computerized as well as manual controls. Also, audit procedures may include computerized and manual procedures for considering internal control and for performing substantive tests.

Because much of the IT information you need to know for auditing relates to IT systems, you should refer to the material that appears in Module 41, Information Technology, as a supplement to this volume. The coverage here is limited to audit considerations.

A. The Auditor's Consideration of Internal Control When a Computer Is Present

1. **General**

   The auditor's responsibilities with respect to internal control over computer systems remain the same as with manual systems, that is, to obtain an understanding adequate (1) to aid in planning the remainder of the audit and (2) to assess control risk. Yet the auditor's consideration of internal control may be affected in that computer systems may

   a. Result in transaction trails that exist for a short period of time or only in computer-readable form
   b. Include program errors that cause uniform mishandling of transactions—clerical errors become much less frequent

c. Include computer controls that need to be tested in addition to the segregation of functions

d. Involve increased difficulty in detecting unauthorized access

e. Allow increased management supervisory potential resulting from more timely reports

f. Include less documentation of initiation and execution of transactions

g. Include computer controls that affect the effectiveness of related manual control activities that use computer output

As is the case for all controls, the auditor needs to test operating effectiveness only when control risk is to be assessed below the maximum. General application controls may be tested through inquiry, observation, and inspection techniques. In addition, application controls may be tested using reperformance techniques outlined in the following section. Because general controls affect all computer applications, the auditor's initial focus should be on them since the effectiveness of specific application controls depends upon the effectiveness of the general controls.

2. **Computerized Audit Tools (CAAT) for Tests of Controls**

Tests of controls may be divided into the following categories of techniques: (a) program analysis, (b) program testing, (c) continuous testing, and (d) review of operating systems and other systems software.

a. **Techniques for program analysis.** These techniques allow the auditor to gain an understanding of the client's program. Because these techniques ordinarily are relatively time-consuming and require a high level of computer expertise, they are infrequently used in financial statement audits.

(1) **Code review**—This technique involves actual analysis of the logic of the program's processing routines. The primary advantage is that the auditor obtains a detailed understanding of the program. Difficulties with the approach include the fact that it is extremely time-consuming, it requires a very high level of computer expertise, and difficulties involved with making certain that the program being verified is in fact the program in use throughout the accounting period.

(2) **Comparison programs**—These programs allow the auditor to compare computerized files. For example, they can be used in a program analysis to determine that the auditor has the same version of the program that the client is using.

(3) **Flowcharting software**—Flowcharting software is used to produce a flowchart of a program's logic. A difficulty involved is that the flowcharts of large programs become extremely involved.

(4) **Program tracing and mapping**—Program tracing is a technique in which each instruction executed is listed along with control information affecting that instruction. Program mapping identifies sections of code that can be "entered" and thus are executable. These techniques allow an auditor to recognize logic sequences or dormant section of code that may be a potential source of abuse. The techniques are infrequently used because they are extremely time-consuming.

(5) **Snapshot**—This technique in essence "takes a picture" of the status of program execution, intermediate results, or transaction data at specified processing points in the program processing. This technique helps an auditor to analyze the processing logic of specific programs.

b. **Techniques for program testing.** Program testing involves the use of auditor-controlled actual or simulated data. The approach provides direct evidence about the operation of programs and programmed controls. Historically, knowledge of these techniques has been tested relatively frequently on the CPA exam.

(1) **Test data**—A set of dummy transactions is developed by the auditor and processed by the client's computer programs to determine whether the controls which the auditor intends to test (not necessarily all controls) to restrict control risk are operating effectively. Some of these dummy transactions may include errors to test effectiveness of programmed controls and to determine how transactions are handled (e.g., time tickets with invalid job numbers). When using test data, each control generally need only be tested once. Several possible problems include

(a) Making certain the test data is not included in the client's accounting records

(b) Determining that the program tested is actually used by the client to process data

(c) Adequately developing test data for every possible control

(d) Developing adequate data to test key controls may be extremely time-consuming

(2) **Integrated test facility (ITF)**—This method introduces dummy transactions into a system in the midst of live transactions and is usually built into the system during the original design. One way to accomplish this is to incorporate a simulated or subsidiary into the accounting system with the sole purpose of running test data through it. The test data approach is similar and therefore its limitations are also similar, although the test

data approach does not run simultaneously through the live system. The running of dummy transactions in the midst of live transactions makes the task of keeping the two transaction types separate more difficult.

(3) **Parallel simulation**—Parallel simulation processes actual client data through an **auditor's generalized audit software program** and frequently, although not necessarily, the auditor's computer (generalized audit software is discussed in Section G. of this module). After processing the data the auditor compares the output obtained with output obtained from the client. The method verifies processing of **actual** transactions (as opposed to test data and ITF that use dummy transactions) and allows the auditor to verify actual client results. This method allows an auditor to simply test portions of the system to reduce the overall time and concentrate on key controls. The limitations of this method include

  (a) The time it takes to build an exact duplicate of the client's system
  (b) Incompatibility between auditor and client software
  (c) Tracing differences between the two sets of outputs to differences in the programs may be difficult
  (d) The time involved in processing large quantities of data

(4) **Controlled reprocessing**—Controlled reprocessing, a variation of parallel simulation, processes actual client data through a copy of the **client's application program**. As with parallel simulation, this method uses actual transactions and the auditor compares the output obtained with output obtained from the client. Limitations of this method include

  (a) Determining that the copy of the program is identical to that currently being used by the client
  (b) Keeping current with changes in the program
  (c) The time involved in reprocessing large quantities of data

c. **Techniques for continuous (or concurrent) testing.** Advanced computer systems, particularly those utilizing EDI, sometimes do not retain permanent audit trails, thus requiring capture of audit data as transactions are processed. Such systems may require audit procedures that are able to identify and capture audit data as transactions occur.

(1) **Embedded audit modules and audit hooks**—Embedded audit modules are programmed routines incorporated into an application program that are designed to perform an audit function such as a calculation, or logging activity. Because embedded audit modules require that the auditor be involved in system design of the application to be monitored, this approach is often not practical. An audit hook is an exit point in an application program that allows an auditor to subsequently add an audit module (or particular instructions) by activating the hook to transfer control to an audit module.

(2) **Systems control audit review files (SCARF)**—A SCARF is a log, usually created by an embedded audit module, used to collect information for subsequent review and analysis. The auditor determines the appropriate criteria for review and the SCARF selects that type of transaction, dollar limit, or other characteristic.

(3) **Extended records**—This technique attaches additional data that would not otherwise be saved to regular historic records and thereby helps to provide a more complicated audit trail. The extended record information may subsequently be analyzed.

(4) **Transaction tagging**—Tagging is a technique in which an identifier providing a transaction with a special designation is added to the transaction record. The tag is often used to allow logging of transactions or snapshot of activities.

d. **Techniques for review of operating systems and other systems software.** Systems software may perform controls for computer systems. Related audit techniques range from user-written programs to the use of purchasing operating systems monitoring software.

(1) **Job accounting data/operating systems logs**—These logs, created by either the operating system itself or additional software packages that track particular functions, include reports of the resources used by the computer system. Because these logs provide a record of the activity of the computer system, the auditor may be able to use them to review the work processed, to determine whether unauthorized applications were processed, and to determine that authorized applications were processed properly.

(2) **Library management software**—This software logs changes in programs, program modules, job control language, and other processing activities. Auditors may review these logs.

(3) **Access control and security software**—This software supplements the physical and control measures relating to the computer and is particularly helpful in online environments or in systems with data communications because of difficulties of physically securing computers. Access control and security software restricts access to computers to authorized personnel through techniques such as only allowing certain users with "read-only" access or through use of encryption. An auditor may perform tests of the effectiveness of the use of such software.

3. Information technology (IT) provides potential benefits of effectiveness and efficiency because it enables an entity to

   a. Consistently apply predefined business rules and perform complex calculations on large volumes of transactions
   b. Enhance timeliness, availability, and accuracy of information
   c. Facilitate the additional analysis of information
   d. Enhance the ability to monitor the performance of the entity's activities and its policies and procedures
   e. Reduce risk that controls will be circumvented
   f. Enhance ability to achieve effective segregation of duties by implementing security controls in applications, databases, and operating systems

4. IT poses specific risks to internal control including

   a. Systems or programs may inaccurately process information
   b. Unauthorized access to data may lead to destruction of data or inappropriate changes to data
   c. Unauthorized changes to data in master files
   d. Unauthorized changes to systems or programs
   e. Failure to make necessary changes to systems or programs
   f. Inappropriate manual intervention
   g. Potential loss of data

5. Use of an IT specialist

   a. In determining whether specialized IT skills are needed to design and perform the audit, the auditor considers factors such as

      (1) Complexity of entity's systems and IT controls
      (2) Significance of changes made to existing systems, or implementation of new systems
      (3) Extent to which data is shared among systems
      (4) Extent of entity's participation in electronic commerce
      (5) Entity's use of emerging technologies
      (6) Significance of audit evidence available only in electronic form

   b. Procedures an auditor may assign to a professional possessing IT skills

      (1) Inquiring of entity's IT personnel on how data and transaction are initiated, recorded, processed, and reported, and how IT controls are designed
      (2) Inspecting systems documentation
      (3) Observing operation of IT controls
      (4) Planning and performing of tests of IT controls

6. Documenting the understanding of internal control

   a. For an information system with a large volume of transactions that are electronically initiated, recorded, processed, or reported, may include flowcharts, questionnaires, or decision tables
   b. For an information system with limited or no use of IT, or for which few transactions are processed (e.g., long-term debt) a memorandum may be sufficient
   c. When an auditor is performing only substantive tests to restrict detection risk to an acceptable level, the auditor should obtain evidence about the accuracy and completeness of the information

7. Effects of IT on assessment of control risk

   a. In determining whether to assess control risk at the maximum level or at a lower level, the auditor should consider

    (1) Nature of the assertion

    (2) Volume of transactions

    (3) Nature and complexity of systems, including use of IT

    (4) Nature of available audit evidence, including evidence in electronic form

  b. In designing tests of automated controls

    (1) The inherent consistency of IT processing may allow the auditor to reduce the extent of testing (e.g., use a smaller sample)

    (2) Computer-assisted audit techniques may be needed for automated controls

8. Effects of IT on restriction of detection risk

  a. An auditor may assess control risk at the maximum and perform substantive tests to restrict detection risk when he or she believes that the substantive tests by themselves would be more efficient than performing tests of controls; for example

    (1) Client has only a limited number of transactions related to fixed assets and long-term debt and the auditor can readily obtain corroborating evidence in the form of documents and confirmations.

  b. When evidence is entirely or almost entirely electronic, the auditor in some circumstances may need to perform tests of controls. This is because it may be impossible to design effective substantive tests that by themselves provide sufficient evidence in circumstances such as when the client

    (1) Uses IT to initiate order using predetermined decisions rules and to pay related payables based on system-generating information, and no other documentation is produced

    (2) Provides electronic service to customers (e.g., Internet service provider or telephone company) and uses IT to log service provided, initiate bills, process billing, and automatically record amounts in accounting records

---

NOW REVIEW MULTIPLE-CHOICE QUESTIONS 1 THROUGH 18

B. Computerized Audit Tools

A variety of computerized audit tools (which may also be viewed as computer assisted audit techniques) are available for administering, planning, performing, and reporting of an audit. We present a summary of major types.

1. Generalized Audit Software (GAS)

    The auditor may use various types of software on PCs (or other computers) and may include customized programs, utility software, and generalized audit software for performing tests of controls and substantive tests. Customized programs are written specifically for a client. Commercially produced utility software is used for sorting, merging, and other file maintenance tasks. Generalized audit software also performs such file maintenance tasks but generally requires a more limited understanding of the client's hardware and software features. The following is a list of functions performed by GAS (it is based on the AICPA Auditing Procedure Study *Auditing with Computers*):

  a. Record extraction—Extract (copy) records that meet certain criteria, such as

    (1) Accounts receivable balances over the credit limit

    (2) Inventory items with negative quantities or unreasonably large quantities

    (3) Uncosted inventory items

    (4) Transactions with related parties

  b. Sorting (e.g., ascending or descending order)

  c. Summarization, such as

    (1) By customer account number

    (2) Inventory turnover statistics

    (3) Duplicate sales invoices

   d. Field statistics, such as

      (1) Net value
      (2) Total of all debt (credit values)
      (3) Number of records
      (4) Average value
      (5) Maximum (minimum) value
      (6) Standard deviation

   e. File comparison, such as

      (1) Compare payroll details with personnel records
      (2) Compare current and prior period inventory files

   f. Gap detection/duplicate detection—Find missing or duplicate records
   g. Sampling
   h. Calculation
   i. Exportation—Select an application that has been performed using GAS and export to another file format (for additional analysis)

2. **Electronic Spreadsheets**

Electronic spreadsheets, often included in generalized audit software, may be used for applications such as analytical procedures and performing mathematical procedures; Microsoft's Excel is an electronic spreadsheet. Also, auditors often use electronic spreadsheets to prepare working trial balances, lead, and other schedules. Such spreadsheets may significantly simplify the computational aspects of tasks such as incorporating adjustments and reclassifications on a worksheet and are relatively easy to use, inexpensive, and can be saved and easily modified in the future. Disadvantages include the need for auditor training, and the fact that original spreadsheet development takes a significant amount of time.

3. **Automated Workpaper Software**

Originally used to generate trial balances, lead schedules, and other workpapers, advances in computer technology (e.g., improvements in scanning) make possible an electronic workpaper environment. Ordinarily, this type of software is easy to use and inexpensive. The primary disadvantage is the time required to enter the data for the first year being audited.

4. **Database Management Systems**

We have discussed database management systems in Section C. of this module. Database management software may be used to perform analytical procedures, mathematical calculations, generation of confirmation requests, and to prepare customized automated workpapers. An auditor may, for example, download relevant client files into his or her database and analyze the data as desired. Advantages of this approach include a great opportunity for the auditor to rearrange, edit, analyze, and evaluate a data file in a manner well beyond that possible to be performed manually and the ability to download client data without time-consuming data entry. Disadvantages include auditor training (more than with spreadsheets) and the need for adequate client documentation of applications.

5. **Text Retrieval Software**

Text retrieval software (also referred to as text database software) enables access to such databases as the AICPA Professional Standards and various FASB and SEC pronouncements. This software allows an auditor to research technical issues quickly and requires minimal training. Disadvantages include the fact that some training is required and that some professional literature is not currently available in software form.

6. **Public Databases**

Public databases may be used to obtain accounting information related to particular companies and industries as well as other publicly available information on, for example, electronic bulletin boards, that an auditor may use. Current developments for companies and their industries may be obtained from the Internet. The Internet provides online access to newspaper and journal articles. In addition, many companies and industry associations have World Wide Web home pages that describe current developments and statistics.

7. **Word Processing Software**

Auditors use word processing software (e.g., Microsoft's Word) in a variety of communication-related manners including the consideration of internal control, developing audit programs, and reporting.

> **NOW REVIEW MULTIPLE-CHOICE QUESTIONS 19 THROUGH 32**

KEY TERMS

Computer assisted auditing techniques. The practice of using computers to automate or simplify the audit process. In the broadest sense of the term, they can refer to any use of a computer during the audit.

Controlled reprocessing. A variation of parallel simulation, processes actual client data through a copy of the client's application program. As with parallel simulation, this method uses actual transactions and the auditor compares the output obtained with output obtained from the client.

Generalized audit software. Software designed to read, process, and write data with the help of functions performing specific audit routines and with self-made macros. It is a tool in applying computer assisted auditing techniques. Functions of generalized audit software include importing computerized data; thereafter other functions can be applied (e.g., the data can be browsed, sorted, summarized, stratified, analyzed, taken samples from, and made calculations, conversions, and other operations with).

Integrated test facility (ITF). This method introduces dummy transactions into a system in the midst of live transactions and is usually built into the system during the original design. One way to accomplish this is to incorporate a simulated or subsidiary into the accounting system with the sole purpose of running test data through it. The test data approach is similar and therefore its limitations are also similar, although the test data approach does not run simultaneously through the live system. The running of dummy transactions in the midst of live transactions makes the task of keeping the two transaction types separate more difficult.

Parallel simulation. Parallel simulation processes actual client data through an auditor's generalized audit software program and frequently, although not necessarily, the auditor's computer (generalized audit software is discussed in Section G. of this module). After processing the data the auditor compares the output obtained with output obtained from the client. The method verifies processing of actual transactions (as opposed to test data and ITF that use dummy transactions) and allows the auditor to verify actual client results. This method allows an auditor to simply test portions of the system to reduce the overall time and concentrate on key controls.

Test data. A set of dummy transactions is developed by the auditor and processed by the client's computer programs to determine whether the controls which the auditor intends to test (not necessarily all controls) to restrict control risk are operating effectively. Some of these dummy transactions may include errors to test effectiveness of programmed controls and to determine how transactions are handled (e.g., time tickets with invalid job numbers). When using test data, each control generally need only be tested once.

A. Auditor's Consideration of Internal Control When a Computer Is Present

1. An advantage of using systems flowcharts to document information about internal control instead of using internal control questionnaires is that systems flowcharts

  a. Identify internal control weaknesses more prominently.
  b. Provide a visual depiction of clients' activities.
  c. Indicate whether control procedures are operating effectively.
  d. Reduce the need to observe clients' employees performing routine tasks.

2. A flowchart is most frequently used by an auditor in connection with the

  a. Preparation of generalized computer audit programs.
  b. Review of the client's internal control.
  c. Use of statistical sampling in performing an audit.
  d. Performance of analytical procedures of account balances.

3. Matthews Corp. has changed from a system of recording time worked on clock cards to a computerized payroll system in which employees record time in and out with magnetic cards. The computer system automatically updates all payroll records. Because of this change

  a. A generalized computer audit program must be used.
  b. Part of the audit trail is altered.
  c. The potential for payroll-related fraud is diminished.
  d. Transactions must be processed in batches.

4. Which of the following is correct concerning batch processing of transactions?

  a. Transactions are processed in the order they occur, regardless of type.
  b. It has largely been replaced by online real-time processing in all but legacy systems.
  c. It is more likely to result in an easy-to-follow audit trail than is online transaction processing.
  d. It is used only in non-database applications.

5. An auditor would be most likely to assess control risk at the maximum level in an electronic environment with automated system-generated information when

  a. Sales orders are initiated using predetermined, automated decision rules.
  b. Payables are based on many transactions and large in dollar amount.
  c. Fixed asset transactions are few in number, but large in dollar amount.

  d. Accounts receivable records are based on many transactions and are large in dollar amount.

6. In a highly automated information processing system tests of control

  a. Must be performed in all circumstances.
  b. May be required in some circumstances.
  c. Are never required.
  d. Are required in first year audits.

7. Which of the following is **least** likely to be considered by an auditor considering engagement of an information technology (IT) specialist on an audit?

  a. Complexity of client's systems and IT controls.
  b. Requirements to assess going concern status.
  c. Client's use of emerging technologies.
  d. Extent of entity's participation in electronic commerce.

8. Which of the following strategies would a CPA most likely consider in auditing an entity that processes most of its financial data only in electronic form, such as a paperless system?

  a. Continuous monitoring and analysis of transaction processing with an embedded audit module.
  b. Increased reliance on internal control activities that emphasize the segregation of duties.
  c. Verification of encrypted digital certificates used to monitor the authorization of transactions.
  d. Extensive testing of firewall boundaries that restrict the recording of outside network traffic.

9. Which of the following is **not** a major reason for maintaining an audit trail for a computer system?

  a. Deterrent to fraud.
  b. Monitoring purposes.
  c. Analytical procedures.
  d. Query answering.

10. Computer systems are typically supported by a variety of utility software packages that are important to an auditor because they

  a. May enable unauthorized changes to data files if not properly controlled.
  b. Are very versatile programs that can be used on hardware of many manufacturers.
  c. May be significant components of a client's application programs.
  d. Are written specifically to enable auditors to extract and sort data.

11. An auditor would most likely be concerned with which of the following controls in a distributed data processing system?

    a. Hardware controls.
    b. Systems documentation controls.
    c. Access controls.
    d. Disaster recovery controls.

12. Which of the following types of evidence would an auditor most likely examine to determine whether internal control is operating as designed?

    a. Gross margin information regarding the client's industry.
    b. Confirmations of receivables verifying account balances.
    c. Client records documenting the use of computer programs.
    d. Anticipated results documented in budgets or forecasts.

13. An auditor anticipates assessing control risk at a low level in a computerized environment. Under these circumstances, on which of the following activities would the auditor initially focus?

    a. Programmed control activities.
    b. Application control activities.
    c. Output control activities.
    d. General control activities.

14. After the preliminary phase of the review of a client's computer controls, an auditor may decide not to perform tests of controls related to the controls within the computer portion of the client's internal control. Which of the following would **not** be a valid reason for choosing to omit such tests?

    a. The controls duplicate operative controls existing elsewhere in the structure.
    b. There appear to be major weaknesses that would preclude reliance on the stated procedure.
    c. The time and dollar costs of testing exceed the time and dollar savings in substantive testing if the tests of controls show the controls to be operative.
    d. The controls appear adequate.

15. Auditing by testing the input and output of a computer system instead of the computer program itself will

    a. Not detect program errors which do **not** show up in the output sampled.
    b. Detect all program errors, regardless of the nature of the output.
    c. Provide the auditor with the same type of evidence as tests of application controls.
    d. Not provide the auditor with confidence in the results of the auditing procedures.

16. Which of the following client information technology (IT) systems generally can be audited without examining or directly testing the IT computer programs of the system?

    a. A system that performs relatively uncomplicated processes and produces detailed output.
    b. A system that affects a number of essential master files and produces a limited output.
    c. A system that updates a few essential master files and produces no printed output other than final balances.
    d. A system that performs relatively complicated processing and produces very little detailed output.

17. An auditor who wishes to capture an entity's data as transactions are processed and continuously test the entity's computerized information system most likely would use which of the following techniques?

    a. Snapshot application.
    b. Embedded audit module.
    c. Integrated data check.
    d. Test data generator.

18. Which of the following computer-assisted auditing techniques processes client input data on a controlled program under the auditor's control to test controls in the computer system?

    a. Test data.
    b. Review of program logic.
    c. Integrated test facility.
    d. Parallel simulation.

B. Computerized Audit Tools

19. To obtain evidence that online access controls are properly functioning, an auditor most likely would

    a. Create checkpoints at periodic intervals after live data processing to test for unauthorized use of the system.
    b. Examine the transaction log to discover whether any transactions were lost or entered twice due to a system malfunction.
    c. Enter invalid identification numbers or passwords to ascertain whether the system rejects them.
    d. Vouch a random sample of processed transactions to assure proper authorization.

20. An auditor most likely would introduce test data into a computerized payroll system to test controls related to the

    a. Existence of unclaimed payroll checks held by supervisors.
    b. Early cashing of payroll checks by employees.
    c. Discovery of invalid employee I.D. numbers.
    d. Proper approval of overtime by supervisors.

21. When an auditor tests a computerized accounting system, which of the following is true of the test data approach?

    a. Several transactions of each type must be tested.
    b. Test data are processed by the client's computer programs under the auditor's control.
    c. Test data must consist of all possible valid and invalid conditions.
    d. The program tested is different from the program used throughout the year by the client.

22. Which of the following is **not** among the errors that an auditor might include in the test data when auditing a client's computer system?

    a. Numeric characters in alphanumeric fields.
    b. Authorized code.
    c. Differences in description of units of measure.
    d. Illogical entries in fields whose logic is tested by programmed consistency checks.

23. Which of the following computer-assisted auditing techniques allows fictitious and real transactions to be processed together without client operating personnel being aware of the testing process?

    a. Integrated test facility.
    b. Input controls matrix.
    c. Parallel simulation.
    d. Data entry monitor.

24. Which of the following methods of testing application controls utilizes a generalized audit software package prepared by the auditors?

    a. Parallel simulation.
    b. Integrated testing facility approach.
    c. Test data approach.
    d. Exception report tests.

25. In creating lead schedules for an audit engagement, a CPA often uses automated workpaper software. What client information is needed to begin this process?

    a. Interim financial information such as third quarter sales, net income, and inventory and receivables balances.
    b. Specialized journal information such as the invoice and purchase order numbers of the last few sales and purchases of the year.
    c. General ledger information such as account numbers, prior year account balances, and current year unadjusted information.
    d. Adjusting entry information such as deferrals and accruals, and reclassification journal entries.

26. Using laptop computers in auditing may affect the methods used to review the work of staff assistants because

    a. The generally accepted auditing standards may differ.
    b. Documenting the supervisory review may require assistance of consulting services personnel.
    c. Supervisory personnel may **not** have an understanding of the capabilities and limitations of laptops.
    d. Working paper documentation may not contain readily observable details of calculations.

27. An auditor would **least** likely use computer software to

    a. Access client data files.
    b. Prepare spreadsheets.
    c. Assess computer control risk.
    d. Construct parallel simulations.

28. A primary advantage of using generalized audit software packages to audit the financial statements of a client that uses a computer system is that the auditor may

    a. Access information stored on computer files while having a limited understanding of the client's hardware and software features.
    b. Consider increasing the use of substantive tests of transactions in place of analytical procedures.
    c. Substantiate the accuracy of data through self-checking digits and hash totals.
    d. Reduce the level of required tests of controls to a relatively small amount.

29. Auditors often make use of computer programs that perform routine processing functions such as sorting and merging. These programs are made available by electronic data processing companies and others and are specifically referred to as

    a. Compiler programs.
    b. Supervisory programs.
    c. Utility programs.
    d. User programs.

30. Smith Corporation has numerous customers. A customer file is kept on disk storage. Each customer file contains name, address, credit limit, and account balance. The auditor wishes to test this file to determine whether credit limits are being exceeded. The best procedure for the auditor to follow would be to

    a. Develop test data that would cause some account balances to exceed the credit limit and determine if the system properly detects such situations.
    b. Develop a program to compare credit limits with account balances and print out the details of any account with a balance exceeding its credit limit.
    c. Request a printout of all account balances so they can be manually checked against the credit limits.
    d. Request a printout of a sample of account balances so they can be individually checked against the credit limits.

31. An auditor most likely would test for the presence of unauthorized computer program changes by running a

    a. Program with test data.
    b. Check digit verification program.
    c. Source code comparison program.
    d. Program that computes control totals.

32. An entity has the following invoices in a batch:

Invoice #	Product	Quantity	Unit price
201	F10	150	$ 5.00
202	G15	200	$10.00
203	H20	250	$25.00
204	K35	300	$30.00

Which of the following numbers represents the record count?

    a. 1
    b. 4
    c. 810
    d. 900

Multiple-Choice Answers and Explanations

Answers

1. b	__ __	7. b	__ __	13. d	__ __	19. c	__ __	25. c	__ __	31. c	__ __
2. b	__ __	8. a	__ __	14. d	__ __	20. c	__ __	26. d	__ __	32. b	__ __
3. b	__ __	9. c	__ __	15. a	__ __	21. b	__ __	27. c	__ __		
4. c	__ __	10. a	__ __	16. a	__ __	22. a	__ __	28. a	__ __		
5. c	__ __	11. c	__ __	17. b	__ __	23. a	__ __	29. c	__ __	1st: __/32 = __%
6. b	__ __	12. c	__ __	18. d	__ __	24. a	__ __	30. b	__ __	2nd: __/32 = __%

Explanations

1. (b) The requirement is to identify an advantage of using systems flowcharts to document information about internal control instead of using internal control questionnaires. Answer (b) is correct because flowcharts provide a visual depiction of clients' activities which make it possible for auditors to quickly understand the design of the system. Answer (a) is incorrect because while the flow of operations is visually depicted, internal control weaknesses are not as obvious. Answer (c) is incorrect because while a flowchart describes a system, the flowchart alone does not indicate whether that system is operating effectively. Answer (d) is incorrect because auditors still need to determine whether the system has been placed in operation and therefore the need to observe employees performing routine tasks remains.

2. (b) The requirement is to determine when a flowchart is most frequently used by an auditor. Answer (b) is correct because flowcharts are suggested as being appropriate for documenting the auditor's consideration of internal control. Answer (a) is incorrect because auditors do not frequently write their own generalized computer audit programs, the most likely time a flowchart would be used with respect to such software. Answers (c) and (d) are incorrect because statistical sampling and analytical procedures do not in general require the use of flowcharts.

3. (b) The requirement is to identify the correct statement with respect to a computerized, automatically updating payroll system in which magnetic cards are used instead of a manual payroll system with clock cards. Answer (b) is correct because the automatic updating of payroll records alters the audit trail which, in the past, included steps pertaining to manual updating. Answer (a) is incorrect because although an auditor may choose to use a generalized computer audit program, it is not required. Answer (c) is incorrect because no information is presented that would necessarily indicate a change in the likelihood of fraud. Answer (d) is incorrect because given automatic updating, a large portion of the transactions are not processed in batches.

4. (c) The requirement is to identify the correct statement concerning the batch processing of transactions. Batch processing involves processing transactions through the system in groups of like transactions (batches). Answer (c) is correct because the similar nature of transactions involved with batch processing ordinarily makes it relatively easy to follow the transactions throughout the system. Answer (a) is incorrect

because transactions are processed by type, not in the order they occur regardless of type. Answer (b) is incorrect because many batch applications still exist and might be expected to exist well into the future. Answer (d) is incorrect because batch processing may be used for database applications.

5. (c) The requirement is to determine when an auditor would be most likely to assess control risk at the maximum level in an electronic environment with automated system-generated information. Answer (c) is correct because the few transactions involved in fixed assets make it most likely to be one in which a substantive approach of restricting detection risk is most likely to be effective and efficient. Answer (a) is incorrect because an auditor might be expected to perform tests of controls to assess control risk below the maximum when automated decision rules are involved for an account (sales) which ordinarily has many transactions. Answers (b) and (d) are incorrect because the numerous transactions in payables and receivables make it likely that control risk will be assessed below the maximum.

6. (b) The requirement is to identify the most accurate statement with respect to tests of controls of a highly automated information processing system. Answer (b) is correct because in some such circumstances substantive tests alone will not be sufficient to restrict detection risk to an acceptable level. Answer (a) is incorrect because tests of controls need not be performed in all such circumstances. Answer (c) is incorrect because such tests are sometimes required. Answer (d) is incorrect because tests of controls are not in such circumstances in all first year audits.

7. (b) The requirement is to identify the least likely circumstance in which an auditor would consider engagements of an IT specialist on an audit. Answer (b) is correct because the requirement to assess going concern status remains the same on all audits, and thus does not directly affect engagement of an IT specialist. Answers (a), (c), and (d) are all incorrect because complexity, the use of emerging technologies, and participation in electronic commerce are all factors which make it more likely that an IT specialist will be engaged.

8. (a) The requirement is to identify a strategy that a CPA most likely would consider in auditing an entity that processes most of its financial data only in electronic form. Answer (a) is correct because continuous monitoring and analysis of transaction processing with an embedded audit module might provide an effective way of auditing these processes—although some question exists as to how many embedded audit modules CPAs have actually used in practice. Answer (b) is incorrect because there may well be a decrease in reliance on internal control activities that emphasize this segregation of duties since so many controls are in the hardware and software of the application. Answer (c) is incorrect because digital certificates deal with electronic commerce between companies, a topic not directly addressed by this question, and because such certificates provide limited evidence on authorization. Answer (d) is incorrect because while firewalls do control network traffic, this is not the most significant factor in the audit of electronic form financial data.

9. (c) The requirement is to identify the reply that is **not** a major reason for maintaining an audit trail for a computer system. Answer (c) is correct because analytical procedures use the outputs of the system, and therefore the audit trail is of limited importance. Answer (a) is incorrect because an audit trail may deter fraud since the perpetrator may realize that his or her act may be detected. Answer (b) is incorrect because an audit trail will help management to monitor the computer system. Answer (d) is incorrect because an audit trail will make it much easier to answer queries.

10. (a) The requirement is to identify a reason that utility software packages are important to an auditor. Answer (a) is correct because client use of such packages requires that the auditor include tests to determine that no unplanned interventions using utility routines have taken place during processing (Audit and Accounting Guide, *Computer Assisted Audit Techniques*). Answer (b) is incorrect because a client's use of such programs implies that they are useful on his/her computer hardware, and therefore any flexibility is not of immediate relevance to the auditor. Answer (c) is incorrect because the primary purpose of utility programs is to support the computer user's applications (*Computer Assisted Audit Techniques*). Answer (d) is incorrect because utility software programs have a variety of uses in addition to enabling auditors to extract and sort data (*Computer Assisted Audit Techniques*).

11. (c) The requirement is to identify the types of controls with which an auditor would be most likely to be concerned in a distributed data processing system. A distributed data processing system is one in which there is a network of remote computer sites, each having a computer connected to the main computer system, thus allowing access to the computers by various levels of users. Accordingly, answer (c) is correct because numerous individuals may access the system, thereby making such controls of extreme importance. Answers (a), (b), and (d), while requiring concern, are normally considered less critical than proper access controls for this situation.

12. (c) The requirement is to identify the type of evidence an auditor would examine to determine whether internal control is operating as designed. Answer (c) is correct because the inspection of documents and records such as those related to computer programs represents an approach for obtaining an understanding of internal control. Answer (a) is incorrect because examining gross margin information is more likely to be performed during the performance of analytical procedures.

Answer (b) is incorrect because confirming of receivables is a substantive test. Answer (d) is incorrect because anticipated results documented in budgets or forecasts are much more frequently used in the performance of analytical procedures.

13. (d) The requirement is to determine the procedures on which the auditor would initially focus when anticipating assessing control risk at a low level. Answer (d) is correct because auditors usually begin by considering general control procedures. Since the effectiveness of specific application controls is often dependent on the existence of effective general controls over all computer activities, this is usually an efficient approach. Answers (a), (b), and (c) are all incorrect because they represent controls that are usually tested subsequent to the general controls.

14. (d) The requirement is to determine an **inappropriate** reason for omitting tests of controls related to computer control procedures. Answer (d) is correct because the fact that the controls **appear** adequate is not sufficient justification for reliance; tests of controls must be performed before the auditor can actually rely upon a control procedure to reduce control risk. Answer (a) is incorrect because when controls duplicate other controls the auditor who wishes to rely upon internal control need not test both sets. Answer (b) is incorrect because if weak controls are not to be relied upon, the auditor need not test their effectiveness. Answer (c) is incorrect because tests of controls may be omitted if their cost exceeds the savings from reduced substantive testing resulting from reliance upon the controls.

15. (a) The requirement is to determine the correct statement with respect to testing inputs and outputs of a computer system instead of testing the actual computer program itself. Answer (a) is correct because portions of the program which have errors not reflected on the output will be missed. Thus, if a "loop" in a program is not used in one application, it is not tested. Answer (b) is incorrect because the lack of an understanding of the entire program precludes the detection of all errors. Answer (c) is incorrect because while auditing inputs and outputs can provide valuable evidence, it will often be different than the evidence obtained by testing the program itself. Answer (d) is incorrect because such auditing of inputs and outputs may well satisfy the auditor.

16. (a) The requirement is to identify the type of computer system that can be audited without examining or directly testing computer programs (i.e., auditing around the system). Auditing around the system is possible if the system performs uncomplicated processes and produces detailed output (i.e., is a fancy bookkeeping machine). Answers (b), (c), and (d) all describe more complicated computer systems that produce only limited output. In these more complicated systems, the data and related controls are within the system, and thus the auditor must examine the system itself. Auditors must identify and evaluate the accounting controls in all computer systems. Further, complex computer systems require auditor specialized expertise to perform the necessary procedures.

17. (b) The requirement is to determine an audit technique to determine whether an entity's transactions are processed and to continuously test the computerized information system.

Answer (b) is correct because an embedded audit module is inserted within the client's information system to continuously test the processing of transactions. Answer (a) is incorrect because a snapshot application analyzes the information system at one point in time. Answer (c) is incorrect because an integrated data check simply tests data at one point in time. Answer (d) is incorrect because a test data generator provides a sample of possible circumstances in which data might be improperly processed.

18. (d) The requirement is to identify the computer-assisted audit technique that processes client input data on a controlled program under the auditor's control to test controls in a computer system Answer (d) is correct because parallel simulation processes actual client data through an auditor's generalized audit software program. Answer (a) is incorrect because test data is a set of dummy transactions developed by the auditor and processed by the client's programs to determine whether the controls which the auditor intends to test are operating effectively. Answer (b) is incorrect because a review of program logic is an approach in which an auditor reviews the steps by which the client's program processes data. Answer (c) is incorrect because an integrated test facility introduces dummy transactions into a client's system in the midst of live transactions.

19. (c) The requirement is to determine the best way to obtain evidence that on-line access controls are properly functioning. Answer (c) is correct because entering invalid identification numbers or passwords will provide the auditor with evidence on whether controls are operating as designed. Answer (a) is incorrect because directly testing access controls is more direct than testing data through checkpoints at intervals. Answer (b) is incorrect because a transaction log will not in general, by itself, identify whether transactions were lost or entered twice. Answer (d) is incorrect because vouching proper authorization is only one measure of whether controls are properly functioning.

20. (c) The requirement is to identify the situation in which it is most likely that an auditor would introduce test data into a computerized payroll system. Test data is a set of dummy transactions developed by the auditor and processed by the client's computer programs. These dummy transactions are used to determine whether the controls which the auditor tests are operating effectively. Answer (c) is correct because test data with invalid employee I.D. numbers could be processed to test whether the program detects them. Answer (a) is incorrect because the unclaimed payroll checks are held by the supervisors and no testing of the computer program is involved. Answer (b) is incorrect because no computer processing is generally involved when payroll checks are "cashed early" by employees. Answer (d) is incorrect because to test whether the approval of overtime is proper, one must determine what criteria are used for the decision and must then determine whether supervisors are following those criteria; it is less likely that this will all be included in a computer program than a test for invalid employee ID numbers.

21. (b) The requirement is to identify the correct statement regarding the test data approach. Answer (b) is correct because the test data approach consists of processing a set of

dummy transactions on the client's computer system. The test data approach is used to test the operating effectiveness of controls the auditor intends to rely upon to assess control risk at a level lower than the maximum. Answer (a) is incorrect because only one transaction of each type is generally tested. Answer (c) is incorrect because it is not possible to include **all** possible valid and invalid conditions. Answer (d) is incorrect because the program that should be tested is the client's program which is used throughout the year.

22. (a) The requirement is to determine which reply is not among the errors which are generally detected by test data. An auditor uses test data to determine whether purported controls are actually functioning. Answer (a) is correct because one would not use test data to test numeric characters in alphanumeric fields; numeric characters are accepted in alphanumeric fields and thus do not represent error conditions. Answer (b) is incorrect because authorization codes may be tested by inputting inappropriate codes. Answer (c) is incorrect because differing descriptions of units of measure may be inputted to test whether they are accepted. Answer (d) is incorrect because illogical combinations may be inputted to test whether they are detected by the system.

23. (a) The requirement is to identify the computer-assisted auditing technique which allows fictitious and real transactions to be processed together without client operating personnel being aware of the testing process. Answer (a) is correct because the integrated test facility approach introduces dummy transactions into a system in the midst of live transactions. Accordingly, client operating personnel may not be aware of the testing process. Answer (b) is incorrect because an input control matrix would simply indicate various controls in the form of a matrix. Answer (c) is incorrect because the parallel simulation technique requires the processing of actual client data through an auditor's software program. In this case, the client would be aware of the testing process since the auditor would need to request copies of data run on the actual system so that the data could then be run on the auditor's software program. Additionally, only valid transactions would be tested under parallel simulation. Answer (d) is incorrect because the client would generally be aware of an auditor using a data entry monitor (screen) to input transactions.

24. (a) The requirement is to determine the auditing technique which utilizes generalized audit software. Answer (a) is correct because the parallel simulation method processes the client's data using the CPA's software. Answers (b) and (c) are incorrect because the client's hardware and software are tested using test data designed by the CPA. Answer (d) is incorrect because although a CPA may test a client's exception reports in various manners, generalized software is unlikely to be used. Exception reports are generally tested via CPA-prepared test data containing all the possible error conditions. The test data are then run on the client's hardware and software to ascertain whether the exception reports are "picking up" the CPA's test data.

25. (c) The requirement is to identify the information that must be available to begin creating automated lead schedules. A lead schedule is used to summarize like accounts (e.g., if a client has five cash accounts those accounts may be summarized on a lead schedule). Answer (c) is correct because lead schedules include information such as account numbers, prior year account balances, and current year unadjusted information. Answer (a) is incorrect because interim information is not necessary. Answer (b) is incorrect because invoice and purchase order numbers are not summarized on lead schedules. Answer (d) is incorrect because adjusting entry information is identified subsequent to the creation of lead schedules.

26. (d) The requirement is to identify an effect on audit work review methods of using laptop computers in auditing. Answer (d) is correct because laptops typically produce a number of the "working papers" in computer disk form and because many computations, etc. will be performed directly by the computer with few details of the calculations conveniently available. Answer (a) is incorrect because the generally accepted auditing standards remain the same regardless of whether or not computers are being utilized. Answer (b) is incorrect because one would not normally expect consulting services personnel to help with documentation. Answer (c) is incorrect because supervisory personnel must have an understanding of the capability and limitations of laptops before they are utilized on audits.

27. (c) The requirement is to determine an auditor's **least** likely use of computer software. Answer (c) is correct because an auditor will judgmentally assess control risk related to both the computer and manual systems after having performed the various tests of controls. Answer (a) is incorrect because computer software will be used to access client data files. Answers (b) and (d) are incorrect because software is used to prepare spreadsheets and to perform parallel simulations.

28. (a) The requirement is to identify a primary advantage of using generalized audit software packages to audit the financial statements of a client that uses a computer system. Answer (a) is correct because generalized audit software allows an auditor to perform audits tests on a client's computer files. Answer (b) is incorrect because generalized audit software packages may assist the auditor with either substantive tests of transactions or analytical procedures. Answer (c) is incorrect because while generalized audit software might be used to perform such operations, this is not their primary advantage. Answer (d) is incorrect because generalized audit software packages have no direct relationship to the performance of tests of controls.

29. (c) The requirement is to determine the type of computer programs which auditors use to assist them in functions such as sorting and merging. Answer (c) is correct because a utility program is a standard routine for performing commonly required processing such as sorting, merging, editing, and mathematical routines. Answer (a) is incorrect because compiler programs translate programming languages such as COBOL or FORTRAN to machine language. Answer (b) is incorrect because supervisory programs or "operating systems" consist of a series of programs that perform functions such as scheduling and supervising the application programs, allocating storage, controlling peripheral devices, and handling errors and restarts. Answer (d) is incorrect because user or "application programs" perform specific data processing tasks such as general ledger, accounts payable, accounts receivable, and payroll. Application programs make use of utility routines.

30. (b) The requirement is to determine the best approach for determining whether credit limits **are being exceeded** when accounts receivable information is stored on disk. Answer (b) is correct because a program to compare actual account balances with the predetermined credit limit and thereby prepare a report on whether any actual credit limits are being exceeded will accomplish the stated objective. Answer (a) is incorrect because while test data will indicate whether the client's program **allows** credit limits to be exceeded, it will not indicate whether credit limits **are actually being exceeded**. Answer (c) is incorrect because a manual check of all account balances will be very time consuming. Answer (d) is incorrect because a sample will provide less complete information than the audit of the entire population which is indicated in answer (b).

31. (c) The requirement is to identify how an auditor would test for the presence of unauthorized computer program changes. Answer (c) is correct because comparing source code of the program with a correct version of the program will disclose unauthorized computer program changes. Answer (a) is incorrect because test data is generally used to test specific controls and it will generally be less effective for detecting unauthorized changes than will source code comparison. Answer (b) is incorrect because check digits are primarily used as an input control to determine that input data is proper. Answer (d) is incorrect because properly computing control totals is only one possible unauthorized change that might be made to a program.

32. (b) The requirement is to identify the number that represents the record count. Answer (b) is correct because the record count represents the number of records in a file, in this case 4.

Simulation

Task-Based Simulation 1

Computer Audit Techniques and Terms		
	Authoritative Literature	Help

Computer processing has become the primary means used to process financial accounting information in most businesses. Consistent with this situation, CPAs must have knowledge of audit techniques using computers and of computer terminology.

Select the type of audit technique being described in **items 1 through 5**. Computer audit techniques may be used once, more than once, or not at all.

Computer audit technique

A. Auditing "around" the computer
B. I/O audit approach
C. Integrated test facility
D. Parallel simulation
E. Processing output control
F. Test data
G. Write extract routine

Description	(A)	(B)	(C)	(D)	(E)	(F)	(G)
1. Auditing by manually testing the input and output of a computer system.	O	O	O	O	O	O	O
2. Dummy transactions developed by the auditor and processed by the client's computer programs, generally for a batch processing system.	O	O	O	O	O	O	O
3. Fictitious and real transactions are processed together without the client's operating personnel knowing of the testing process.	O	O	O	O	O	O	O
4. May include a simulated division or subsidiary into the accounting system with the purpose of running fictitious transactions through it.	O	O	O	O	O	O	O
5. Uses a generalized audit software package prepared by the auditors.	O	O	O	O	O	O	O

For **items 6 through 10** select the type of computer control that is described in the definition that is presented. Each control may be used once, more than once, or not at all.

Control

H. Backup and recovery
I. Boundary protection
J. Check digit
K. Control digit
L. File protection ring
M. Hash total
N. Missing data check
O. Personal identification codes
P. Visitor entry logs

Description	(H)	(I)	(J)	(K)	(L)	(M)	(N)	(O)	(P)
6. A control that will detect blanks existing in input data when they should not.	O	O	O	O	O	O	O	O	O
7. A control to ensure that jobs run simultaneously in a multiprogramming environment cannot change the allocated memory of another job.	O	O	O	O	O	O	O	O	O
8. A digit added to an identification number to detect certain types of data transmission or transposition errors.	O	O	O	O	O	O	O	O	O
9. A terminal control to limit access to programs or files to authorized users.	O	O	O	O	O	O	O	O	O
10. A total of one field for all the records of a batch where the total is meaningless for financial purposes.	O	O	O	O	O	O	O	O	O

Simulation Solution

Task-Based Simulation 1

Computer Audit Techniques and Terms		
	Authoritative Literature	Help

Description	(A)	(B)	(C)	(D)	(E)	(F)	(G)
1. Auditing by manually testing the input and output of a computer system.	●	○	○	○	○	○	○
2. Dummy transactions developed by the auditor and processed by the client's computer programs, generally for a batch processing system.	○	○	○	○	○	●	○
3. Fictitious and real transactions are processed together without the client's operating personnel knowing of the testing process.	○	○	●	○	○	○	○
4. May include a simulated division or subsidiary into the accounting system with the purpose of running fictitious transactions through it.	○	○	●	○	○	○	○
5. Uses a generalized audit software package prepared by the auditors.	○	○	○	●	○	○	○

Explanations

1. (**A**) Auditing "around" the computer involves examining inputs into and outputs from the computer while ignoring processing, as contrasted to auditing "through" the computer which in some manner directly utilizes the computer's processing ability.

2. (**F**) Test data is a set of dummy transactions developed by the auditor and processed by the client's computer programs to determine whether the controls that the auditor intends to rely upon are functioning as expected.

3. (**C**) An integrated test facility introduces dummy transactions into a system in the midst of live transactions and is often built into the system during the original design.

4. (**C**) An integrated test facility approach may incorporate a simulated division or subsidiary into the accounting system with the sole purpose of running test data through it.

5. (**D**) Parallel simulation involves processing actual client data through an auditor's software program to determine whether the output equals that obtained when the client processed the data.

Description	(H)	(I)	(J)	(K)	(L)	(M)	(N)	(O)	(P)
6. A control that will detect blanks existing in input data when they should not.	○	○	○	○	○	○	●	○	○
7. A control to ensure that jobs run simultaneously in a multiprogramming environment cannot change the allocated memory of another job.	○	●	○	○	○	○	○	○	○
8. A digit added to an identification number to detect certain types of data transmission or transposition errors.	○	○	●	○	○	○	○	○	○
9. A terminal control to limit access to programs or files to authorized users.	○	○	○	○	○	○	○	●	○
10. A total of one field for all the records of a batch where the total is meaningless for financial purposes.	○	○	○	○	○	●	○	○	○

Explanations

6. (**N**) A missing data check tests whether blanks exist in input data where they should not (e.g., an employee's division number). When the data is missing, an error message is output.

7. (**I**) Boundary protection is necessary because most large computers have more than one job running simultaneously (a multiprogramming environment). To ensure that these simultaneous jobs cannot destroy or change the allocated memory of another job, the systems software contains boundary protection controls.

8. (J) A check digit is an extra digit added to an identification number to detect certain types of data transmission or transposition errors. It is used to verify that the number was entered into the computer system correctly; one approach is using a check digit that is calculated as a mathematical combination of the other digits.

9. (O) Personal identification codes require individuals to in some manner identify themselves to determine that only authorized users access programs or files.

10. (M) A hash total is the total of one field for all the records of a batch where the total is a meaningless total for financial purposes, such as a mathematical sum of employee social security numbers to determine that all employees have been processed.

Outlines of Professional Standards

This section presents outlines of (1) the Statements on Standards for Attestation Engagements, (2) the Statements on Auditing Standards, and (3) the Statements on Standards for Accounting and Review Services. When codified sequence differs from chronological sequence, we have presented the outlines in codified sequence. Study these outlines in conjunction with the related topical material (e.g., ethics, reports, etc.).

STATEMENTS ON STANDARDS FOR ATTESTATION ENGAGEMENTS

Overview. The Statements on Standards for Attestation Engagements are issued by three organizations: (1) the Auditing Standards Board, (2) the Accounting and Review Services Committee, and (3) the Management Advisory Services Executive Committee.

AT 20 Defining Professional Requirements in Statements on Standards for Attestation Engagements (SSAE 13)—This section sets forth the meaning of terms in SSAEs. Similar to Statements on Auditing Standards, SSAEs includes the following type of requirements:

A. **Unconditional requirements**—The accountant is required to comply in all cases in which the circumstances exist. SSAEs use the words *must* or *is required* to indicate an unconditional requirement.

B. **Presumptively mandatory requirements**—The accountant is required to comply in all cases in which the circumstances exist. However, in rare cases the accountant may depart provided that the accountant documents the justification and how alternative procedures performed were adequate. SSAEs use the word *should* to indicate a presumptively mandatory requirement.

AT 50 SSAE Hierarchy (SSAE 14)—This section sets forth the authoritative level of various attestation guidance.

A. **Generally Accepted Attestation Standards and Statements on Standards for Attestation Engagements**

1. An accountant must identify those applicable to the engagement and exercise professional judgment in applying SSAEs.
2. An accountant must document justification for departures and explain how alternative procedures were sufficient.

B. **Attestation Interpretations** consist of Interpretations of SSAEs, appendixes to SSAEs, attestation guidance in AICPA Audit and Accounting Guides, and AICPA Statements of Position.

1. Accountant must be aware of this guidance.
2. Accountant who does not apply should be prepared to explain how s/he complied with the applicable SSAE.

C. **Other attestation publications,** such as articles, textbooks, etc.

1. Have no authoritative status, but may help the accountant apply SSAEs.

AT 101 Attestation Standards

Overall Objectives and Approach—This section is composed of (1) definitions and underlying concepts and (2) the eleven attestation standards with related explanations. This information is the general framework for attest services. Subsequent AT sections take the information included in AT 101 as a starting point and provide additional guidance, generally a particular type of service (e.g., reporting on internal control, or compliance with laws and regulations).

The scope of the section includes engagements in which a CPA is engaged to issue or does issue an examination, a review, or an agreed-upon procedures report on subject matter—or an assertion about the subject matter—that is the responsibility of another party. However, only limited guidance is provided relating to agreed-upon procedures engagements, which are discussed in detail in AT 201. Be aware that services explicitly **excluded** from this section's coverage include services and engagements performed

- Under Statements on Auditing Standards (see the AU outlines)
- Under Statements on Standards for Accounting and Review Services (see the AR outlines)

- Under Statements on Standards for Consulting Services
- Advocating a client's position (e.g., matters being reviewed by the Internal Revenue Service)
- Preparing tax returns or providing tax advice.

The following outline has four sections. Section A defines and provides underlying concepts relating to attest engagements. Sections B, C, and D present the general, fieldwork, and reporting standards, respectively. Note that the attest standards are included in *italics* as numbered subheadings under Sections B, C, and D. Finally, while the standards use the term "practitioner" in most places, we will use the term "CPA."

A. Definitions and underlying concepts

1. **Subject matter**—May take many forms, including

   a. Historical or prospective performance or condition (e.g., prospective financial statements)
   b. Physical characteristics (e.g., narrative descriptions, square footage of facilities)
   c. Historical events (e.g., price of goods at a certain date)
   d. Analyses (e.g., breakeven analyses)
   e. Systems and processes (e.g., internal control)
   f. Behavior (e.g., corporate governance, compliance with laws and regulations, human resource practices)

2. **Assertion**—Any declaration or set of declarations about whether the subject matter is based on or in conformity with the criteria selected

   a. A CPA may report on a written assertion or on the subject matter
   b. When a written assertion is not obtained the use of the report should be restricted

3. **Responsible party**—The party responsible for the subject matter

   a. A CPA should obtain written acknowledgement or other evidence of responsible party's responsibility
   b. Most frequently, the responsible party is top management

B. General standards

1. First general standard—The engagement shall be performed by a practitioner having adequate technical training and proficiency in the attest function
2. Second general standard—The engagement shall be performed by a practitioner having adequate knowledge of the subject matter
3. Third general standard—The practitioner shall perform the engagement only if he or she has reason to believe that the subject matter is capable of reasonably consistent evaluation against criteria that are suitable and available to users

   a. Suitable criteria

      (1) Are the standards or benchmarks used to measure and present the subject matter and against which the CPA evaluates the subject matter

   > **NOTE:** To illustrate the suitable criteria concept, think of financial statements—the suitable criteria are frequently generally accepted accounting pr inciples. We use this illustration because most are familiar with generally accepted accounting principles. Recognize that historical financial statements are not included under the attestation standards.

      (2) Although trade-offs exist, suitable criteria must be

          (a) Objective
          (b) Measurable
          (c) Complete
          (d) Relevant

   b. Guidelines on suitable criteria

      (1) Criteria established or developed by groups composed of experts that follow due process (e.g., FASB) are ordinarily considered suitable
      (2) Criteria established or developed by management, industry associations, or other groups that do not follow due process may or may not be suitable
      (3) Some criteria are suitable only to a limited number of parties who participated in their establishment or have an understanding of them

    (a) In such circumstance use of the report should be restricted to those parties

  c. Criteria should be available in one or more of the following ways

    (1) Publicly
    (2) Inclusion with the subject matter or in the assertion
    (3) Inclusion in CPA's report
    (4) Well understood by most users (e.g., The distance between A and B is twenty feet)
    (5) Available only to specified parties

        (a) In this circumstance the CPA's report should be restricted to those parties

  4. Fourth general standard—In all matters relating to the engagement, an independence in mental attitude shall be maintained by the practitioner

C. Standards of fieldwork

  1. First fieldwork standard—The work shall be adequately planned and assistants, if any, shall be properly supervised
  2. Second fieldwork standard—Sufficient evidence shall be obtained to provide a reasonable basis for the conclusion that is expressed in the report

    a. Presumptions

    (1) Evidence from independent sources provides greater assurance than evidence secured solely from within the entity
    (2) Information obtained from direct personal knowledge is more persuasive than information obtained indirectly
    (3) The more effective the controls over subject matter, the more assurance they provide about the subject matter or assertion

> **NOTE:** Recall that the above presumptions are also presented in AU 326.

  3. Types of attest engagements

    a. **Examination**—CPA selects from all available procedures and provides a high level of assurance to limit attestation risk to an appropriately low level
    b. **Review**—CPA generally limits procedures to inquiries and analytical procedures and provides a moderate level of assurance to limit attestation risk to moderate level
    c. **Agreed-upon procedures**—Presented in AT 201

D. Standards of reporting

  1. First reporting standard—The report shall identify the subject matter or the assertion being reported on and state the character of the engagement
  2. Second reporting standard—The report shall state the practitioner's conclusion about the subject matter or the assertion in relation to the criteria against which the subject matter was evaluated
  3. Third reporting standard—The report shall state all of the practitioner's significant reservations about the engagement, the subject matter, and if applicable, the assertion related thereto
  4. Fourth reporting standard—The report shall state that the use of the report is restricted to specified parties under the following circumstances [abridged]:

    a. Criteria are suitable only for a limited number of parties
    b. Subject matter is available only to specified parties
    c. Written assertion has not been provided by the responsible party
    d. Agreed-upon procedures engagements

  5. An examination report on subject matter [assertion] should include

    a. Title with word "independent"
    b. Identification of subject matter [assertion]
    c. Subject matter [assertion] is the responsibility of the responsible party
    d. CPA's responsibility is to express opinion on subject matter [assertion]
    e. Examination conducted in accordance with attestation standard established by AICPA

    f.   Examination provides reasonable basis for opinion

    g.   Opinion on whether subject matter [assertion] follows criteria

    h.   Statement restricting use of report as per fourth reporting standard (D.4. above)

    i.   Manual or printed signature of firm

    j.   Date of report

6. A review report on subject matter [assertion] should include

    a.   Title with word "independent"

    b.   Identification of subject matter [assertion]

    c.   Subject matter [assertion] is the responsibility of the responsible party

    d.   Review conducted in accordance with attestation standards established by AICPA

    e.   Review substantially less in scope than an examination, the objective of which is expression of an opinion, and accordingly, no such opinion is expressed

    f.   Statement about whether CPA is aware of any material modifications needed for subject matter [assertion] to comply with criteria

    g.   Statement restricting use of report as per fourth reporting standard (D.4. above)

    h.   Manual or printed signature of firm

    i.   Date of report

E.   Attest documentation

1. Purposes

    a.   Principal support for practitioner's report

    b.   Aid in conduct and supervision of engagement

2. Should be sufficient to

    a.   Enable members of engagement team with supervision and review responsibilities to understand nature, timing, extent, and results of attest procedures performed and information obtained

    b.   Indicate who performed and reviewed the work

AT 201 Agreed-Upon Procedures Engagements

Overall Objectives and Approach—This section sets forth attestation requirements and provides guidance for a CPA's performance of agreed-upon procedures (AUP) engagements. Recall that auditors currently perform three types of attestation engagements—examinations and reviews (emphasized in AT 101) and agreed-upon procedures. Because many of the concepts in AT 201 carry over from AT 101, make certain that you are familiar with that information.

A.   An agreed-upon procedures engagement is one in which a CPA is engaged by a client to issue a report of findings based on specific procedures performed on subject matter

1. The client engages the CPA to assist specified parties in evaluating subject matter or an assertion

    a.   Specified parties and the CPA agree upon the procedures that the specified parties believe appropriate

    b.   Specified parties assume responsibility for the sufficiency of the procedures

    c.   CPA's report should indicate that its use is restricted to those specified parties

---

EXAMPLE 1

Assume that representatives of a bank ask that specified procedures be performed on balance sheet accounts that are to serve as collateral for a loan to a CPA's client. Those representatives would ordinarily be considered specified parties.

---

2. A CPA may perform an AUP engagement provided that

    a.   CPA is independent

    b.   Party that wishes to engage CPA is

        (1)   Responsible for subject matter, or has a reasonable basis for providing a written assertion about the subject matter **or**

        (2)   **Not** responsible for the subject matter but is able to provide CPA, or have a third party who is responsible for the subject matter provide evidence of third party's responsibility for the subject matter

    c. CPA and specified parties agree on procedures to be performed

    d. Specified parties take responsibility for sufficiency of procedures

    e. Subject matter involved is subject to reasonably consistent measurement

    f. Criteria used to determine findings are agreed upon between CPA and specified parties

    g. Procedures applied are expected to result in reasonably consistent findings using the criteria

    h. Evidential matter is expected to provide reasonable basis for expressing findings

    i. Where applicable, CPA and specified parties agree on materiality limits

    j. Use of report restricted to specified parties

    k. For AUP engagements on prospective financial information, the statements include a summary of significant findings

  3. A written assertion is generally **not** required

  4. CPA should establish an understanding with client about a variety of matters including—nature of engagement, identification of subject matter, specified parties, use restrictions, etc.

B. Procedures, findings, and working papers

  1. Responsibility

    a. Specified parties—sufficiency of agreed-upon procedures

    b. CPA—perform procedures and report findings in accordance with attest standards and have adequate knowledge of subject matter

  2. Procedures performed may be limited or extensive

    a. But mere reading of an assertion or specified information about subject matter does not constitute a sufficient procedure to report on AUP

    b. CPA should not agree to perform procedures so overly subjective and possibly open to varying interpretations; examples are

      (1) Reading work performed by others solely to describe their findings

      (2) Evaluating competency or objectivity of another party

      (3) Obtaining understanding about a particular subject

      (4) Interpreting documents outside scope of CPA's expertise

    c. In certain circumstances a specialist may be called to assist the CPA in performing one or more procedures

  3. Report should be in form of findings, and should **not** include negative assurance

  4. The concept of materiality limits does not in general apply, unless agreed to by the specified parties

  5. Working papers should indicate that work was adequately planned and supervised and that adequate evidential matter was obtained

C. Reporting

  1. Required elements

    a. Title with word "independent"

    b. Identification of specified parties

    c. Identification of subject matter (or written assertion related thereto) and character of engagement

    d. Subject matter responsibility of responsible party

    e. Procedures performed agreed to by specified parties

    f. AUP engagements conducted in accordance with attestation standards established by AICPA

    g. Sufficiency of procedures responsibility of specified parties

    h. List of procedures performed and related findings

    i. Description of agreed-upon materiality limits (if any)

    j. CPA not engaged to perform examination, disclaimer on subject matter, statement that if additional procedures had been performed other matters might come to CPA's attention

    k. Statement restricting use of report to specified parties

    l. For AUP on prospective financial information, items required under AT 301

    m. Where applicable, description of nature of assistance provided by specialist

    n Manual or printed signature of CPA's firm

    o. Date of report

2. Explanatory language may be included, such as

   a. Stipulated facts, assumptions, interpretations
   b. Condition of records, controls, etc.
   c. Explanation that CPA has no responsibility to update report
   d. Explanation of sampling risk

3. Report should be dated as of date of completion of agreed-upon procedures
4. If CPA's procedures restricted, CPA should describe restrictions in report or withdraw
5. Additional specified parties may be added if they agree to take responsibility for sufficiency of procedures

D. Other

1. CPA may wish to, but is not required to, obtain representation letter from responsible party
2. A CPA who has performed another form of attest or nonattest engagement may be requested to change engagement to AUP engagement

   a. Before changing to AUP, the CPA should consider

      (1) Possibility that procedures performed for other engagement not appropriate for AUP
      (2) Reason for request
      (3) Additional effort required
      (4) If applicable, reasons for changing from general-use report to restricted-use report

   b. In all circumstances, if original engagement substantially complete, CPA should consider propriety of accepting a change in the engagement

3. AUP reports may be combined with reports on other services (e.g., audit of financial statements) providing types of services clearly distinguished and report remains restricted

AT 301 Financial Forecasts and Projections

Overall Objectives and Approach—This section sets forth standards and provides guidance for CPAs who are engaged to issue examination, compilation, or agreed-upon procedures reports on prospective financial information. As a starting point, it is important that you understand the basic information presented in Section A of the outline. That information is used throughout the remainder of the outline. Sections B, C, and D of the outline provide information on the three basic forms of CPA association with prospective financial information—compilations, examinations, and agreed-upon procedures. (CPAs do **not** perform reviews on prospective information.) Recognize that standards for the compilation form of association is not included in AT sections other than AT 301.

A. Definition and basic concepts

1. Prospective financial statements—Partial presentations, financial forecasts, and financial projections

   a. Types

      (1) **Prospective forecasts**—Either financial forecasts or financial projections, including summaries of significant assumptions and accounting policies
      (2) **Partial presentations**—A presentation of prospective financial information that excludes one or more of the items required for prospective financial statements (see b. below)
      (3) **Financial forecasts**—Prospective financial statements that present the responsible party's beliefs about the entity's expected financial position, results of operations, and cash flows
      (4) **Financial projection**—Prospective financial statements that present expected results, to the best of the responsible party's knowledge and belief **given one or more hypothetical assumptions**. A projection is a "what would happen if. . .?" statement.

   b. Minimum disclosures

      (1) **Financial statement information:** sales, gross profit (or cost of goods sold), unusual or infrequently occurring items, provision for income taxes, discontinued operations, extraordinary items, income from continuing operations, net income, earnings per share, and significant cash flows
      (2) **Background information:** purpose of prospective statements, assumptions, and significant accounting policies
      (3) **Assumptions**

> **NOTE:** Omission of group 1 items creates a "partial presentation" not considered in the Statement. Omission of group 2 items in the presence of group 1 items results in a presentation subject to the provisions of this Statement. The accountant should not compile or examine statements lacking disclosure of assumptions (group 3).

    c. **Pro forma statements** (those which show how a hypothetical transaction might have affected historical statements) and accountant financial analysis of a particular project are not included under provisions of this statement

    d. Financial forecasts and projections may both be in the form of single point estimates or ranges (in which case a paragraph discussing the estimates or ranges is added to report)

    e. Uses of prospective financial statements

        (1) **General**—May be used by persons with whom the responsible party is not negotiating directly (e.g., in an offering statement for debt or equity interests). Only a forecast is appropriate for general use

        (2) **Limited**—May only be used by responsible party or by responsible party and third parties with whom responsible party is negotiating directly. A forecast or a projection is appropriate for limited use

2. Accountant independence—an accountant need **not** be independent to perform a compilation, but must be independent to perform an examination or agreed-upon procedures

    a. When the accountant is not independent when performing a compilation, this is indicated in a separate paragraph added to the report. If the accountant elects to disclose a description about the reasons for a lack of independence, he or she should ensure that all reasons are included.

3. The accountant's report should not indicate that engagement included "preparation" of prospective financial statements

B. Compilations of prospective financial statements

1. Compilation procedures

    a. Assemble, to extent necessary, based on responsible party's assumptions

    b. **Perform required compilation procedures**

        (1) Establish understanding with client (preferably in writing) about services to be performed

        (2) Inquire about accounting principles used

        (3) Ask how responsible party identifies key factors and assumptions

        (4) List (or obtain a list of) significant assumptions and consider its completeness

        (5) Consider whether there are obvious inconsistencies in assumptions

        (6) Test mathematical accuracy

        (7) Read statements for conformity with AICPA guidelines and determine that assumptions are not obviously inappropriate

        (8) If a significant portion of prospective period has expired, inquire about actual results

        (9) Obtain written client representation letter (signed by responsible party at highest level of authority)

        (10) Attempt to obtain additional or revised information when above procedures make errors seem likely

2. Compilation reports (see the standard report in the Reporting Module)

    a. A compilation report on prospective financial information should include

        (1) Identification of prospective financial statements

        (2) Statements compiled in accordance with attestation standards established by AICPA

        (3) Compilation limited in scope and does not enable accountant to express opinion or any other form of assurance on prospective financial statements

        (4) Prospective results may not be achieved

        (5) Accountant assumes no responsibility to update the report after its issuance

    b. Circumstances resulting in departure from standard compilation report

        (1) Presentation deficiencies or disclosure omissions, other than a significant assumption (clearly indicate deficiency in report)

        (2) Comprehensive basis statements which do not disclose the basis used (disclose the basis in the report)

        (3) Summary of significant accounting policies omitted (a paragraph is needed which discloses that the policies have been omitted)

C. Examinations of prospective financial statements

1. Examination procedures

    a. Evaluate preparation

    b. Perform examination procedures

        (1) Reach an **understanding with client** (ordinarily confirmed in an engagement letter)

        (2) **Evaluate the support for underlying assumptions** (consider available support, consistency, reliability of underlying historical information, logical arguments or theory)

        (3) **Obtain written representation letter** (signed by responsible party at highest level of authority)

    c. Evaluate presentation for conformity with AICPA presentation guidelines (especially, that presentations reflect assumptions)

2. The examination report on prospective financial statements should include

    a. Title with the word independent

    b. Identification of prospective financial statements

    c. Identification of responsible party

    d. CPA's responsibility is to express opinion on the prospective financial information

    e. Examination conducted in accordance with attestation standards established by AICPA

    f. Examination provides reasonable basis for opinion

    g. Opinion on whether subject matter (assertion) follows criteria

    h. Caveat that prospective results may not be obtained

    i. CPA assumes no responsibility to update report

    j. Manual or printed signature of firm

    k. Date of report

3. Circumstances resulting in departure from standard examination report

    a. Departure from AICPA presentation guidelines (result in a qualified or adverse opinion)

    b. Unreasonable assumptions (adverse opinion)

    c. Scope limitation (disclaimer)

    d. Emphasis of a matter (unqualified)

    e. Evaluation based in part on report of another auditor (unqualified—divided responsibility)

D. Application of agreed-upon procedures to prospective financial statements

1. An accountant engaged to perform agreed-upon procedures on prospective financial statements should follow SSAE 4 guidance (included in outline of AU 622)

2. An agreed-upon procedures engagement may be performed if

    a. The accountant is independent

    b. The accountant and specified users agree on procedures

    c. The specified users take responsibility for sufficiency of the agreed-upon procedures

    d. The prospective financial statements include a summary of significant assumptions

    e. The prospective financial statements to which the procedures are applied are subject to reasonably consistent estimation or measurement

    f. Criteria to be used (accounting principles, policies and assumptions) are agreed upon between the accountant and the specified users

    g. Procedures are expected to result in reasonably consistent findings using the criteria

    h. Evidential matter to which the procedures are applied is expected to exist to provide a reasonable basis for expressing the findings in the accountant's report

    i. Where applicable, there is agreement on any materiality limits

    j. Use of the report is restricted to the specified users (although an accountant may perform an engagement pursuant to which his or her report will be matter of public record)

3. The procedures may be as limited or as extensive as specified users desire, but must exceed mere reading of the prospective financial statements

4. The report on agreed-upon procedures should be in the form of procedures and findings and include

    a. Title with word "independent"

    b. Identification of specified parties

c. Reference to the prospective financial statements and the character of the engagement
d. Statement that procedures were agreed to by specified parties
e. Identification of responsible party
f. Reference to attestation standards established by AICPA
g. Sufficiency of procedures responsibility of specified parties and a disclaimer of responsibility for sufficiency of those procedures
h. List of procedures performed (or reference thereto) and related findings
i. Where applicable, a description of any agreed-upon materiality limits
j. Statement that CPA did not perform an examination of prospective financial statements; a disclaimer of opinion; if the CPA had performed additional procedures, other matters might have come to his or her attention that would have been reported
k. A statement of restriction on the use of report because it is intended to be used solely by the specified parties
l. Various other restrictions
m. A caveat that prospective results may not be achieved
n. A statement that accountant assumes no responsibility to update report
o. Description of nature of assistance provided by a specialist (if applicable)
p. Manual or printed signature of practitioner's firm
q. The report should be dated as of the completion of the agreed-upon procedures

AT 401 Reporting on Pro Forma Financial Information

Overall Objective and Approach—This section presents guidance on appropriate procedures and for reporting on certain pro forma financial information. As a starting point, this section **does not** apply to circumstances in which (1) pro forma information is presented within the same document, but not with financial statements (see the outline of AU 550) or (2) financial statements footnote information includes pro forma information (e.g., to show a revision of debt maturities, or a revision of earnings per share for a stock split).

This section **does** apply to pro forma financial information, presented with the basic financial statements, used to show the effects of an underlying transaction or event (hereafter, simply transaction). Such transactions include possible (1) business combinations, (2) changes in capitalization, (3) disposition of a significant portion of a business, and (4) proposed sale of securities and the application of proceeds. For example, a company which is considering issuing debt might prepare pro forma financial information to indicate what the effect of granting a loan in the prior period would have been. The pro forma financial information must be included with the historical financial statements. Thus, financial statements would generally have a column for historical information, and one for pro forma information.

This section divides much of the procedural and reporting advice into three areas—(1) determining that the assumptions are reasonable, (2) determining that the assumptions lead to the adjustments, and (3) determining that the adjustments have been properly reflected in the "pro forma column." The outline is divided into (a) procedural requirements and (b) reporting requirements.

A. Procedural requirements

1. The overall approach is to apply pro forma adjustments to historical financial information
2. An accountant may agree to report on an **examination** or a **review** of pro forma financial information if the following conditions are met

   a. The document with the pro forma financial information includes (or incorporates by reference) complete financial statements for the most recent period
   b. The historical financial statements on which the pro forma financial information is based have been audited or reviewed

      (1) The level of assurance for the pro forma financial information should be limited to the level of assurance provided on the historical financial statements

---

EXAMPLE

When the historical financial statements have been audited, the pro forma financial information may be examined or reviewed. When the historical financial statements have been reviewed, the pro forma financial information may only be reviewed.

---

   c. The accountant must have an appropriate level of knowledge of the accounting and financial reporting practices of each significant part of the combined entity

---

EXAMPLE

In a business combination between Company A and Company B, the accountant reporting on the pro forma financial information must obtain the knowledge relating to both companies, even if s/he has only audited one of them.

---

3. The objective of an accountant's examination or review procedures relates to whether

   a. Management's assumptions are reasonable
   b. The pro forma adjustments appropriately follow from the assumptions
   c. The pro forma financial information column of numbers reflects proper application of the adjustments

> **NOTE:** When performing an examination, or review, reasonable assurance and negative assurance, respectively, are provided.

4. The following procedures should be applied to assumptions and pro forma adjustments for either an examination or a review

   a. Obtain knowledge of each part of the combined entity in a business combination
   b. Obtain an understanding of the underlying transaction (e.g., read contracts, minutes of meetings, make inquiries)
   c. Procedures applied to the assumptions

      (1) Discuss with management
      (2) Evaluate whether they are presented in a clear and comprehensive manner and are consistent with one another

   d. Procedures applied to the adjustments and their accumulation

      (1) Obtain sufficient evidence in support of adjustments
      (2) Evaluate whether pro forma adjustments are included for all significant effects of the transaction
      (3) Evaluate whether adjustments are consistent with one another and with the data used to develop them
      (4) Determine that computation of pro forma adjustments are mathematically correct and properly accumulated

   e. Obtain written representations from management concerning their

      (1) Responsibility for the assumptions
      (2) Belief that the assumptions are reasonable, that adjustments give effect to the assumptions, and that pro forma column reflects application of those adjustments
      (3) Belief that significant effects attributable to the transactions are properly disclosed

   f. Read the pro forma financial information and determine that the following disclosures are presented

      (1) Underlying transaction, pro forma adjustments, significant assumptions, and significant uncertainties
      (2) The source of the historical financial information on which the pro forma financial information is based has been appropriately identified

B. Reporting on pro forma financial information

1. Overall issues

   a. The report on the pro forma financial information may be added to the accountant's report on the historical financial information, or it may appear separately
   b. The report on pro forma financial information should be dated as of the completion of the appropriate procedures

(1) When the reports on the historical and the pro forma financial information are combined, and when the completion of the pro forma procedures is after the completion of fieldwork for the audit or review of the historical financial information, the report should be dual dated

(a) For example, "March 1, 20X8, except for the paragraphs referring to the pro forma financial information, for which the date is March 20, 20X8"

2. The CPA's report on pro forma financial information should include

  a. Title with word "independent"
  b. Identification of pro forma financial information
  c. Reference to financial statements from which historical information derived
  d. Identification of responsible party
  e. CPA's responsibility is to express opinion on the pro forma financial
  f. Examination conducted in accordance with attestation standards established by AICPA
  g. Examination provides reasonable basis for opinion
  h. Objective of pro forma financial information and limitations
  i. Opinion on whether subject matter (assertion) follows criteria
  j. Manual or printed signature of CPA's firm
  k. Date of the examination report

> **NOTE:** A review report is similar to the above, but presents negative assurance instead of an opinion.

3. The accountant may qualify the opinion, render an adverse opinion, disclaim or withdraw due to circumstances such as scope limitation, uncertainties about the assumptions, conformity with presentation with assumptions or other reservations

AT 501 An Examination of an Entity's Internal Control over Financial Reporting That Is Integrated with an Audit of Its Financial Statements

Overall Objectives and Approach—This section provides guidance for examining and reporting on an entity's internal control over financial reporting. In essence this section is the nonpublic company companion to PCAOB Standard 5's public company requirements for performing the internal control portion integrated audit. Because the procedures and requirements are very similar in the two documents, our approach is to discuss them together in Section C of the Internal Control Module rather than provide separate outlines. Section C provides an outline of PCAOB Standard 5 and a summary of a number of areas where the two documents differ.

AT 601 Compliance Attestation

Overall Objectives and Approach—This section provides guidance on the CPA's (referred to as the "practitioner's") responsibilities with respect to attestation engagements to test compliance with specified requirements which arise through laws, regulations, contracts, rules, or grants. As indicated in part A.2. of the outline, not included in this section are engagements in accordance with *Government Auditing Standards* and various related acts (see AU 801) and several other areas.

The emphasis in this section is upon agreed-upon procedures engagements, although procedures and reporting responsibilities for examination engagements are also presented. Guidance for three types of engagements is provided: (1) agreed-upon procedures engagements on compliance with **specified requirements,** (2) agreed-upon procedures engagements on the effectiveness of an entity's **internal control over compliance,** and (3) examination engagements on compliance with **specified requirements**. (Reviews are not permitted for any of these engagements; general guidance for examinations of the internal control over compliance is in AT 101.)

Section A of the outline presents general information. Sections B and C provide information on agreed-upon procedures and examination engagements respectively. Section D provides guidance on the required management representation letter that must be obtained on all of these engagements.

A. Introduction and general requirements

1. This section provides guidance for engagements related to **management's written assertion** about either

  a. An entity's compliance with requirements of specified laws, regulations, rules, contracts, or grants (hereafter, compliance with specified requirements) or
  b. Effectiveness of internal control over compliance with specified requirements

      (1) Management's assertions may be either financial or nonfinancial in nature

      (2) Engagements should comply with SSAE 1, *Attestation Standards,* which provides the overall attestation "umbrella" under which this more specific guidance exists

2. Section does **not** apply to

   a. GAAS audit responsibility

   b. Auditor reports on compliance based solely on an audit (see AU 623 outline)

   c. *Government Auditing Standards* and other governmental type engagements such as Single Audit Act engagements (see AU 801 outline)

   d. Letters for Underwriter (see AU 634 outline)

   e. Internal control engagements for a broker or dealer required by SEC Act of 1934

3. Allowed scope of services

   a. Three types of engagements are permitted

      (1) Agreed-upon procedures related to management's assertion about compliance with specified requirements

      (2) Agreed-upon procedures related to management's assertion about the effectiveness of an entity's internal control over compliance

> **NOTE:** This type of engagement differs from an AT 501 engagement on internal control in that AT 501 is about management's internal control over financial reporting and this section is on management's internal control over compliance with specified requirements.

      (3) Examination of management's assertion about compliance with specified requirements

   b. Review engagements are **not** permitted

4. Conditions for engagement performance

   a. Overall, management must

      (1) Accept responsibility for compliance with requirements **and** effectiveness of internal control over compliance

      (2) Evaluate compliance with specified requirements (or effectiveness of internal control over compliance)

      (3) Provide to the practitioner its written assertion about compliance with specified requirements (or effectiveness of internal control over compliance)

         (a) The written assertion must be in a separate management report if a general distribution examination report is to be issued (all agreed-upon procedures engagements and examinations with only a representation letter written assertion result in limited distribution reports)

      (4) For examinations

         (a) Assertion must be capable of evaluation against reasonable criteria that are expected to result in findings that are capable of reasonably consistent estimation

         (b) Sufficient evidential matter must support management's evaluation

   b. Management must identify applicable compliance requirements, establish policies to provide reasonable assurance of compliance, evaluate compliance, and produce specific reports that satisfy requirements.

B. Agreed-upon procedures engagements

1. The **objective** of an agreed-upon procedures engagement is to present specific findings to assist users in evaluating management's assertion about an entity's compliance with specified requirements or about the effectiveness of an entity's internal control over compliance based on procedures agreed upon by the users of the report

   a. The practitioner may be engaged to perform agreed-upon procedures about compliance with specified requirements **or** about effectiveness of internal control over compliance

2. Ordinarily the accountant will communicate directly to obtain acknowledgment as to procedures from specified users; when this is not possible accountant may

    a. Compare procedures to written requirements of specified users
    b. Discuss procedures to be applied with representatives of the specified users, and/or
    c. Review relevant contracts or communication from specified users

3. The report on agreed-upon procedures should include

    a. Title with word "independent"
    b. Identification of specified parties
    c. Identification of subject matter (internal control over financial reporting)
    d. Identification of responsible party
    e. Subject matter is responsibility of responsible party
    f. Procedures agreed to by the specified parties
    g. Examination conducted in accordance with attestation standards established by AICPA
    h. Sufficiency of procedures responsibility of specified parties
    i. List of procedures performed and related findings
    j. Where applicable, description of materiality limits
    k. CPA not engaged to perform an examination (and other limitations)
    l. Restriction of use of report to specified parties
    m. Where applicable, reservations or restrictions concerning procedures or findings
    n. Where applicable, description of nature of assistance provided by specialist
    o. Manual or printed signature of CPA's firm
    p. Date of the examination report

C. Examination engagements

1. The audit risk model (AU 312) is adapted to compliance as follows:

    a. Attestation risk—Risk practitioner unknowingly fails to modify opinion on management's assertion, composed of

        (1) Inherent risk—Risk of material noncompliance assuming no internal control
        (2) Control risk—Risk material noncompliance could occur and not be prevented or detected on a timely basis by internal control
        (3) Detection risk—Practitioner's procedures lead to conclusion that material noncompliance does not exist when it does

2. Materiality differs from GAAS audit in that it is affected more by

    a. Nature of assertion and compliance requirements, which may or may not be quantifiable in monetary terms
    b. Nature and frequency of noncompliance identified with appropriate consideration of sampling risk
    c. Qualitative considerations, including needs and expectations of report's users

        (1) In some cases practitioner may provide a supplemental report of all or certain noncompliance discovered

3. Procedures to be followed

    a. Obtain understanding of specified compliance requirements
    b. Plan the engagement

        (1) Testing compliance at every location may be unnecessary
        (2) Practitioner may decide to use work of a specialist and to consider and use work of internal auditors

    c. Consider relevant portions of internal control over compliance

        (1) When control risk to be assessed below maximum, perform tests of controls

    d. Obtain sufficient evidence including testing compliance with specified requirements
    e. Consider subsequent events

        (1) Responsibility similar to that of audits (see outline of AU 560)

    f. Form opinion about whether entity compiled, in all material respects, with specified requirements (or management's assertion abort such compliance is fairly stated in all material respects)

4. Report should include

   a. Title with word "independent"
   b. Identification of compliance requirements
   c. Compliance is the responsibility of management
   d. Practitioner's responsibility is to express an opinion on compliance
   e. Examination was made in accordance with the attestation standards of AICPA, and included examining evidence about compliance
   f. Examination provides reasonable basis for opinion
   g. Examination does not provide a legal determination of compliance
   h. Opinion on whether entity complied, in all material respects, with specified requirements (or whether management's assertion about compliance is fairly stated) based on established or agreed-upon criteria
   i. Limitation on use when prepared in conformity with criteria specified by regulatory agency
   j. Manual or printed signature of firm
   k. Date of examination report

5. Report modifications

   a. Material noncompliance

      (1) Practitioner should state an opinion on compliance with specified requirements, not on management's assertion
      (2) If management discloses noncompliance and appropriately modifies its assertion, practitioner should modify opinion paragraph by including a reference to the noncompliance and add an explanatory paragraph (before the opinion paragraph) that describes the noncompliance
      (3) Depending upon significance either a qualified or an adverse opinion is appropriate

   b. Material uncertainty—may lead to a qualified opinion or a disclaimer of opinion

D. Management's representations

1. On all engagements a representation letter must be obtained from management
2. Management's refusal to furnish a representation letter is a scope limitation sufficient to require withdrawal in an agreed-upon procedures engagement and a qualified opinion or disclaimer in an examination engagement
3. When management's assertion is included in a report with other information the practitioner's only responsibility is to read that other information and consider whether it is materially inconsistent with the information appearing in management's report or whether it contains a material misstatement of fact

AT 701 Management's Discussion and Analysis

Overall Objectives and Approach—This section presents guidance on management's discussion and analysis (MD&A) presented pursuant to the Securities and Exchange Commission's (SEC) rules and regulations (also, nonregistrants may voluntarily choose to present such information). It presents guidance for performing either a review or an examination on such information. The SEC does **not** require registrants to have MD&A information either reviewed or examined—the only current requirement is that an auditor meet the AU 550 requirement by reading all information accompanying the audited financial statements for consistency with those statements. While the section is extremely lengthy, in this outline we present only its most major points. You should be familiar with all of the information in the outline and the accompanying summary tables.

A. Review

1. Overall considerations

   a. Objective is to report whether any information came to practitioner's attention leading him/her to believe

      (1) MD&A presentation does **not** include, in all material respects, the SEC **required elements,** including a discussion of the entity's

         (a) Financial condition
         (b) Changes in financial condition and results of operations
         (c) Liquidity and capital resources

(2) Historical amounts included in MD&A **not** accurately derived from financial statements

(3) Underlying information, determinations, estimates and assumptions do **not** provide a reasonable basis for MD&A disclosures

b. Consists principally of applying analytical procedures and making inquiries of persons responsible for financial accounting and operational matters; does **not** contemplate

(1) Tests of accounting records through inspection, observation, or confirmation

(2) Obtaining corroborative evidential matter

(3) Applications of other examination type procedures

c. A review of annual MD&A may be performed when practitioner has audited the historical financial statements of latest period to which MD&A relates, and other periods have been audited

d. A review of interim information may be performed if a quarterly review (or audit) of interim information has been performed

2. The review approach is similar to that for financial statements (analytical procedures and inquiry emphasis)

3. The review report of an issuer (public) company (or a nonissuer [nonpublic] company that is making a public offering) should be restricted to the use of specified parties

4. See MD&A General and Reporting Summaries at the end of this outline for guidance on planning, internal control, procedures, and reports

B. Examination

1. Overall considerations

a. Objectives are to express an opinion on whether

(1) Presentation includes SEC **required elements,** including a discussion of the entity's

(a) Financial condition

(b) Changes in financial condition and results of operations

(c) Liquidity and capital resources

(2) Historical amounts accurately derived from financial statements

(3) Underlying information, determinations, estimates, and assumptions provide a reasonable basis for MD&A disclosures

b. Engagement may be performed when practitioner has audited the historical financial statements of the latest period to which MD&A relates, and other periods have been audited

2. Practitioner should obtain reasonable assurance of detecting both intentional and unintentional misstatements, and adequately restrict attestation risk and its components—inherent risk, control risk, detection risk

3. The assertions embodied in MD&A include

a. Occurrence

b. Consistency with financial statements

c. Completeness

d. Presentation and disclosure

> **NOTE:** Points 1. and 2. above are the MD&A adaptations of "audit risk" and point 3. is the MD&A adaptation of the financial statement assertions—see AU 312.

4. See MD&A General and Reporting Summaries below for guidance on planning, internal control, procedures, and reports

MD&A SUMMARY—GENERAL SUMMARY

	Review	Examination
Planning	1. Obtain understanding of SEC MD&A rules and regulations 2. Develop an overall strategy for the analytical procedures and inquiries to be performed to provide negative assurance	1. Same as for reviews 2. Develop an overall strategy for the expected scope and performance of the engagement to obtain reasonable assurance to express an opinion
Internal Control	Consider relevant portions to identify types of potential misstatement and to select the inquires and analytical procedures—no tests of controls performed	Obtain understanding to plan the engagement and assess control risk (tests of controls may be performed)
Procedures (test assertions)	1. Read MD&A, compare to financial statements, recompute increases, decreases, and percentages 2. Compare nonfinancial amounts to financial statements or other records 3. Consider consistency of MD&A explanations with information obtained during financial statement review or audit; make any necessary further inquiries 4. Compare MD&A to SEC requirements 5. Obtain and read available prospective financial information, inquire concerning this information 6. Obtain public communications and minutes of meetings and compare to MD&A 7. Make inquiries of officers with responsibility for operating areas and financial accounting matters as to their plans and expectations for the future 8. Inquire as to prior SEC experience 9. Consider whether there are additional matters that should be disclosed in MD&A based on results of preceding procedures	1. Same as review 2. Same as review, but also perform tests on other records 3. Same as review, but investigate further explanations that cannot be substantiated by information in audit working papers 4. Same as review 5. Same as review, plus evaluate whether the underlying information, determinations, estimates, and assumptions provide a reasonable basis for MD&A disclosures 6. Same as review, plus consider obtaining other types of publicly available information for comparison to MD&A 7. Same as review 8. Same as review 9. Test completeness of results 10. Examine documents in support of existence, occurrence, or expected occurrence of events, transactions, etc.
Report	Includes negative assurance	Includes an opinion (reasonable assurance)
Other	1. Must consider events subsequent to balance sheet 2. Must obtain management written representations	1. Same as review 2. Same as review

MD&A SUMMARY—REPORTING SUMMARY

	Review	Examination
Report should include	1. Title with word independent 2. Identification of MD&A and period covered 3. Management responsible for MD&A 4. Reference to audit report on financial statements and, if nonstandard, reasons therefor 5. Review conducted in accordance with attestation standards and description of scope of examination established by AICPA; a description of review procedures 6. Review substantially less in scope than an examination 7. Paragraph stating that preparation of MD&A requires interpretations, and actual future results may vary 8. If nonissuer (nonpublic) entity, MD&A intended to follow SEC rules 9. Statement about whether any information came to practitioner's attention concerning misstatements relating to (1) required elements, (2) historical amounts accurately derived, (3) underlying information provides reasonable basis (negative assurance provided) 10. Restriction on distribution if issuer (public) company 11. Manual or printed signature 12. Date of a review	1. Same as review 2. Same as review 3. Same as review 4. Same as review 5. Examination conducted in accordance with attestation standards established by AICPA and description of scope of examination 6. Practitioner believes examination provides reasonable basis for opinion 7. Same as review 8. Same as review 9. Practitioner's opinion on (1) presentation includes required elements, (2) historical amounts accurately derived, (3) underlying information provides reasonable basis 10. (No such requirement) 11. Same as review 12. Same as review

MD&A SUMMARY—REPORTING SUMMARY

	Review	Examination
Report modified for	1. Exclusion of a material required element 2. Historical financial amounts not accurately derived from financial statements 3. Underlying information has no reasonable basis 4. Practitioner decides to refer to report of another practitioner. 5. Practitioner reviews MD&A after it has already been filed with SEC	1. through 5., same as review, but also when there is a restriction on the scope of the engagement
Other	1. Must consider events subsequent to balance sheet 2. Must obtain management written representations	1. Same as review 2. Same as review

AT 801 Reporting on Controls at a Service Organization

A. Introduction and objectives

1. This section addresses examination engagements undertaken by a service auditor to report on controls at organizations that provide services to user entities when those controls are likely to be part of the user entities' information and communication systems relevant to financial reporting. (Study it in conjunction with your study of AU 324—that section deals with a user auditor using the report of a service auditor).
2. The objectives of the service auditor are to obtain reasonable assurance and report about whether, in all material respects, based on suitable criteria

   a. Management's description of the service organization's system is fairly represented.
   b. The controls are suitably designed to achieve the control objectives stated in management's description of the service organization's system.
   c. When included in the scope of the engagement, the controls operated effectively throughout the specified period to achieve the control objectives.

> **NOTE:** Make certain that you know that in general, the service auditor is engaged to issue one of two types of reports. Type 1 deals with points a. and b. above; this report addresses whether controls have been properly designed and implemented. Type 2 deals with points a., b. and c.; that is, they also address control operating effectiveness. Type 1 reports are as of a specific date, while Type 2 are for a time period.

B. Selected definitions

1. **Complementary user entity controls.** Controls that management of the service organization assumes, in the design of its service, will be implemented by user entities, and which, if necessary to achieve the control objectives stated in management's description of the service organization's system, are identified as such in that description.
2. **Report on management's description of a service organization's system and the suitability of the design of controls** (referred to in this section as a *type 1 report*). A report that comprises

   a. Management's description of the service organization's system, prepared by management of the service organization.
   b. A written assertion by the service organization's management about whether, in all material respects, and based on suitable criteria

      (1) Management's description of the service organization's system fairly presents the service organization's system that was designed and implemented as of a specified date.
      (2) The controls related to the control objectives stated in the description were suitably designed to achieve those control objectives as of the specified date.

   c. A service auditor's report that expresses an opinion on the matters in b(1)-b(2).

3. **Report on management's description of a service organization's system and the suitability of the design and operating effectiveness of controls** (referred to in this section as a *type 2 report*). (Ref: par. A1) A report that comprises

    a.   A description of the service organization's system prepared by management of the service organization.

    b.   A written assertion by the service organization's management, about whether in all material respects and, based on suitable criteria,

      (1)   Management's description of the service organization's system fairly presents the service organization's system that was designed and implemented throughout the specified period.

      (2)   The controls related to the control objectives stated in the description of the service organization's system were suitably designed throughout the specified period to achieve those control objectives.

      (3)   The controls related to the control objectives stated in the description of the service organization's system operated effectively throughout the specified period to achieve those control objectives.

    c.   A service auditor's report that

      (1)   Expresses an opinion about the matters in b(1)-b(3).

      (2)   Includes a description of the service auditor's tests of controls and the results thereof.

> **NOTE:** The difference between a type 1 and type 2 report is that only a type 2 report addresses operating effectiveness. They both address how controls have been designed and implemented.

4. **Service auditor.** A practitioner who reports on controls at a service organization.

5. **Service organization.** An organization or segment of an organization that provides services to user entities that are likely to be relevant to those user entities' internal control over financial reporting.

6. **Subservice organization.** A service organization used by another service organization to perform some of the services provided to user entities that are part of the user entities' information and communication systems relevant to financial reporting.

7. **User auditor.** An auditor who audits and reports on the financial statements of a user entity.

8. **User entity.** An entity that uses a service organization and whose financial statements are being audited.

C.   Requirements—General

1. Acceptance and continuance

    a.   A service auditor should accept or continue an engagement to report on controls at a service organization only if

      (1)   The service auditor has the capabilities and competence to perform the engagement.

      (2)   The service auditor's preliminary knowledge of the engagement circumstance indicates that the criteria to be used will be suitable, sufficient appropriate evidence will be available, and the scope of the engagement will not be restricted.

      (3)   Management agrees to the terms of the engagement by accepting responsibility for

        (a)   Preparing its description of the service organization's system and the accompanying assertion.

        (b)   Having a reasonable basis for the assertion.

        (c)   Selecting criteria used and stating them in the assertion.

        (d)   Specifying control objectives.

        (e)   Identifying risks

        (f)   Providing a written assertion that will be included in, or attached to management's description of the service organization's system and provided to user entities.

2. The service auditor must assess the suitability of the criteria being followed by the service organization

3. When the service organization has an internal audit function, the service auditor should obtain an understanding of that function and may use the work of that function. In such circumstances, the service auditor should make no reference to the internal audit function's work *in the service auditor's opinion.*

    a.   But when a Type 2 report is issued and the internal audit function has been used in performing tests of controls, the service auditor's *description of controls* should include description of the internal auditor's work and the service auditor's procedures with respect to that work.

4. If the service auditor intends to use the work of a specialist, the service auditor should follow procedures similar to those required of a financial statement auditor in such a situation—see AU 336.

D. Requirements—Performance of examination

1. To issue a Type 1 report, the service auditor should

    a. Obtain an understanding of the service organization's system

       (1) When obtaining this understanding, the service auditor should obtain information for use in identifying risks that the service organization's system is not fairly presented (in management's description and assertion) or that the control objectives stated were not achieved.

    b. Obtain evidence regarding the description of the service organization's system.

       (1) The service auditor should obtain and read the description and evaluate accuracy
       (2) The service auditor should determine whether the service organization's system described in management's description has been implemented.

    c. Obtain evidence regarding the design of controls.

       (1) The service auditor should determine which of the controls are necessary to achieve the control objective stated in the description and should assess whether they were suitably designed to achieve those control objectives.

2. To issue a Type 2 report, the service auditor should

    a. Perform the procedures listed above for a Type 1 report.
    b. Obtain evidence regarding the operating effectiveness of controls

       (1) Here the requirements are similar to when a financial statement auditor performs tests of controls performed for a financial statement audit. In essence, the auditor tests controls to determine whether they operate effectively to meet the control objectives in the management's description.

3. A service auditor should ask management to provide written representations

    a. Reaffirming the assertion.
    b. All records were made available.
    c. The following were disclosed to the service auditor

       (1) Any noncompliance with laws or uncorrected errors that affect a user entity.
       (2) Knowledge of overrides of controls or misappropriation of assets.
       (3) Design deficiencies.
       (4) Instances where controls have not operated as described.
       (5) Subsequent events.

4. The service auditor should prepare documentation that would enable an experienced service auditor having no previous connection with the engagement to understand the

    a. Procedures performed.
    b. Results obtained.
    c. Significant matters arising during the engagement, the conclusions reached thereon, and significant professional judgments made in reaching those conclusions.

5. Report issued

    a. The opinion

       (1) Type 1

         (a) The description of the service organization's system fairly presents it.
         (b) The controls related to the control objective stated in the description of the service organization's system were suitably designed to provide reasonable assurance that those control objectives would be achieved if the controls operated effectively.

       (2) Type 2

           (a) Points (1) and (2) above

           (b) The controls the service auditor tested, which were those necessary to provide reasonable assurance that the control objectives stated in the description were achieved, operated effectively throughout the specified period.

   b. Use of service auditor reports is restricted to customers of the service organization.

   c. Modified opinions (generally qualified) result from

        (1) A management description of the system which is not fairly presented in all material respects.

        (2) Controls that are not suitably designed to provide reasonable assurance that the control objectives stated in the description would be achieved if the controls operated as described.

        (3) The service auditor is unable to obtain sufficient, appropriate evidence.

        (4) For a Type 2 report—controls did not operate effectively.

STATEMENTS ON AUDITING STANDARDS (CLARIFIED)

Overview The Statements on Auditing Standards (SAS) are issued by the Auditing Standards Board. The standards in effect for exams after June 30, 2013, are codified in the following **overall** categories:

Section	Title
---	Preface—Principles Underlying an Audit Conducted in Accordance with Generally Accepted Auditing Standards
AU-C 200*	General Principles and Responsibilities
AU-C 300	Risk Assessment and Response to Assessed Risks
AU-C 400	Risk Assessment and Response to Assessed Risks (concluded)
AU-C 500	Audit Evidence
AU-C 600	Using the Work of Others
AU-C 700	Audit Conclusions and Reporting
AU-C 800	Special Considerations
AU-C 900	Special Considerations in the United States

*Currently, 200 is the first numbered section.

Preface to the Codification of Statements on Auditing Standards, *Principles Underlying an Audit Conducted in Accordance with Generally Accepted Auditing Standards*

A. Overview

   1. This preface contains the principles underlying an audit conducted in accordance with GAAS.

   2. The ASB has developed the principles underlying an audit to provide a framework that is helpful in understanding an audit and in explaining what an audit is; the principles are meant to provide a structure for the codification of the SAS and are organized as

      a. Purpose of an audit (B. below).

      b. Personal responsibilities of the auditor (C. below).

      c. Auditor actions (Performance) in performing the audit (D. below).

      d. Reporting (reporting—E. below).

> **NOTE:** These principles replace the 10 generally accepted auditing standards (general standards, fieldwork standards, and reporting standards) long included in the professional standards.

B. Purpose

   1. *Purpose*: Provide financial statement users with an opinion by the auditor on whether the financial statements are prepared, in all material respects, in accordance with the applicable financial reporting framework. An auditor's opinion enhances the degree of confidence that intended users can place in the financial statements.

   2. *Premise of an audit*: Management and, where appropriate, those charged with governance have responsibility

a. For preparation and presentation of the financial statements in accordance with the applicable financial reporting framework; this includes the design, implementation, and maintenance of internal control relevant to the preparation and presentation of financial statements that are free from material misstatement, whether due to fraud or error; and

b. To provide the auditor with

   (1) All information, such as records, documentation, and other matters that are relevant to the preparation and presentation of the financial statements.

   (2) Any additional information that the auditor may request.

   (3) Unrestricted access to those within the entity from whom the auditor determines it necessary to obtain audit evidence.

C. Responsibilities

1. Auditors are responsible for having appropriate competence and capabilities to perform the audit, complying with ethical requirements, maintaining professional skepticism, and exercising professional judgment throughout the audit.

D. Performance

1. To express an opinion, the auditor *obtains reasonable assurance* about whether the financial statements as a whole are free from material misstatement, whether due to fraud or error.

2. *To obtain reasonable assurance*, which is a high but not absolute level of assurance, the auditor

   a. Plans the work and properly supervises any assistants.

   b. Determines and applies appropriate materiality level or levels through the audit.

   c. Identifies and assesses risks of material misstatement, whether due to fraud or error, based on an understanding of the entity and its environment, including the entity's internal control.

   d. Obtains sufficient appropriate audit evidence about whether material misstatements exist, through designing and implementing appropriate responses to the assessed risks.

3. The auditor is unable to obtain absolute assurance that the financial statements are free from material misstatement because of inherent limitations which arise from the

   a. Nature of financial reporting.

   b. Nature of audit procedures.

   c. Need for the audit to be conducted within a reasonable period of time so as to achieve a balance between benefits and costs.

E. Reporting

1. Based on evaluation of the evidence obtained, the auditor expresses an opinion on whether the financial statements are prepared, in all material respects, in accordance with the applicable financial reporting framework, *or* states that an opinion cannot be expressed, in the form of a written report.

> **NOTE:** There currently are no sections numbered lower than AU-C 200.

AU-C 200 Overall Objectives of the Independent Auditor and the Conduct of an Audit in Accordance with Generally Accepted Auditing Standards

A. Introduction

1. This section addresses the independent auditor's overall responsibilities when conducting an audit in accordance with generally accepted auditing standards (GAAS). It sets out overall objectives of the auditor and explains the nature and scope of an audit. It also explains the scope, authority and structure of GAAS and includes requirements for establishing the general responsibilities of the auditor applicable to all audits, including the obligation to comply with GAAS.

2. GAAS are developed and issued in the form of Statements on Auditing Standards (SAS) and codified into AU-C sections.

3. An auditor is associated with financial statements when the auditor has applied procedures sufficient to report on (1) an audit or (2) an interim review.

4. Purpose of an audit of financial statements: Provide financial statement users with an opinion by the auditor on whether the financial statements are prepared, in all material respects, in accordance with an applicable financial reporting framework (e.g., GAAP). An auditor's opinion enhances the degree of confidence that intended users can place in the financial statements.

5. The financial statements subject to audit are prepared and presented by management, with oversight from those charged with governance.

   a.   The auditor may make suggestions about the form or content of the financial statements, or assist management by drafting them, based on information provided by management. Such assistance is a nonattest service to which independence ethical standards apply.

   b.   The financial statements may be prepared in accordance with

      (1)   A general-purpose framework (a financial reporting framework designed to meet the common financial information needs of a wide range of users—e.g., GAAP); or

      (2)   A special-purpose framework (a financial reporting framework, other than GAAP, which is a cash, tax, regulatory, or contractual basis of accounting).

   c.   The requirements of the applicable financial reporting framework determine the form and content of the financial statements.

      (1)   Many, but not all, frameworks provide information about financial position (e.g., balance sheet), financial performance (e.g., income statement), and cash flows (e.g., statement of cash flows) of an entity.

      (2)   The mandates of audits of financial statements of governmental entities and entities that receive government awards may be broader than those of other entities, affecting both management and auditor responsibilities.

   d.   GAAS requires that an auditor obtain *reasonable assurance* about whether the financial statements are free of material misstatement, whether due to fraud or error.

      (1)   Reasonable assurance is a high, but not absolute level of assurance.

      (2)   Reasonable assurance is obtained when the auditor has obtained sufficient appropriate audit evidence to reduce audit risk (the risk that the auditor expresses an inappropriate opinion when the financial statements are materially misstated) to an acceptably low level.

      (3)   Misstatements are considered *material* if, individually or in the aggregate, they could reasonably be expected to influence the economic decisions of users that are taken based on the financial statements.

         (a)   Materiality judgments include both qualitative and quantitative considerations.

         (b)   An audit does *not* include reasonable assurance that immaterial misstatements will be detected.

6. GAAS require that the auditor exercise professional judgment and maintain professional skepticism throughout the planning and performance of the audit and, among other things

   a.   Identify and assess risks of material misstatement, whether due to fraud or error.

   b.   Obtain sufficient appropriate audit evidence about whether material misstatements exist.

   c.   Form an opinion on the financial statements, or determine that an opinion cannot be formed, based on the conclusions drawn from the audit evidence obtained.

7. The opinion by the auditor is on whether the financial statements are prepared, in all material respects, in accordance with the applicable financial reporting framework.

8. The form of the opinion by the auditor depends on the *applicable financial reporting framework* and any applicable laws or regulations. Most financial reporting frameworks include requirements relating to the presentation of the financial statements; for such frameworks, preparation of the financial statements in accordance with the applicable financial reporting framework includes presentation.

B. Overall objectives of the auditor

1. The overall objectives of the auditor are to

   a.   Obtain reasonable assurance about whether the financial statements as a whole are free from material misstatement, whether due to fraud or error, thereby enabling the auditor to express an opinion on whether the financial statements follow an applicable financial reporting framework.

    b. Report on the financial statements, and communicate as required by GAAS, in accordance with the auditor's findings.

2. When reasonable assurance cannot be obtained and a qualified opinion is insufficient in the circumstances of reporting to the intended users, GAAS requires that the auditor disclaim an opinion or withdraw (resign) from the engagement, where withdrawal is possible under applicable law or regulation.

C. Definitions

1. **Applicable financial reporting framework.** The financial reporting framework adopted by management and, where appropriate, those charged with governance in the preparation of the financial statements that is acceptable in view of the nature of the entity and the objective of the financial statements, or that is required by law or regulation.

2. **Audit evidence.** Information used by the auditor in arriving at the conclusions on which the auditor's opinion is based. Audit evidence includes both information contained in the accounting records underlying the financial statements and other information.

    a. Sufficiency of audit evidence is the measure of the quantity of audit evidence. The quantity of the audit evidence needed is affected by the auditor's assessment of the risks of material misstatement and also by the quality of such audit evidence.

    b. Appropriateness of audit evidence is the measure of the quality of audit evidence; that is, its relevance and its reliability in providing support for the conclusions on which the auditor's opinion is based.

3. **Audit risk.** The risk that the auditor expresses an inappropriate audit opinion when the financial statements are materially misstated. Audit risk is a function of the risks of material misstatement and detection risk.

4. **Auditor.** The term used to refer to the person or persons conducting the audit, usually the engagement partner or other members of the engagement team, or, as applicable, the firm. Where an AU-C section expressly intends that a requirement or responsibility be fulfilled by the engagement partner, the term *engagement partner* rather than *auditor* is used. *Engagement partner* and *firm* are to be read as referring to their governmental equivalents where relevant.

5. **Detection risk.** The risk that the procedures performed by the auditor to reduce audit risk to an acceptably low level will not detect a misstatement that exists and that could be material, either individually or when aggregated with other misstatements.

6. **Financial reporting framework.** A set of criteria used to determine measurement, recognition, presentation, and disclosure of all material items appearing in the financial statements; for example, accounting principles generally accepted in the United States of America, International Financial Reporting Standards (IFRS) issued by the International Accounting Standards Board (IASB), or a special-purpose framework. The term *fair presentation framework* is used to refer to a financial reporting framework that requires compliance with the requirements of the framework and

    a. Acknowledges explicitly or implicitly that, to achieve fair presentation of the financial statements, it may be necessary for management to provide disclosures beyond those specifically required by the framework; or to achieve fair presentation of the financial statements. Such departures are expected to be necessary only in extremely rare circumstances.

        A financial reporting framework that requires compliance with the requirements of the framework, but does not contain the acknowledgements in (a) or (b) of the preceding is not a fair presentation framework.

7. **Financial statements.** A structured representation of historical financial information, including related notes, intended to communicate an entity's economic resources or obligations at a point in time or the changes therein for a period of time in accordance with a financial reporting framework. The related notes ordinarily comprise a summary of significant accounting policies and other explanatory information. The term *financial statements* ordinarily refers to a complete set of financial statements as determined by the requirements of the applicable financial reporting framework, but can also refer to a single financial statement.

8. **Historical financial information.** Information expressed in financial terms in relation to a particular entity, derived primarily from that entity's accounting system, about economic events occurring in past time periods or about economic conditions or circumstances at points in time in the past.

9. **Interpretive publications.** Auditing interpretations of GAAS, exhibits to GAAS, auditing guidance included in AICPA Audit and Accounting Guides, and AICPA Auditing Statements of Position.

10. **Management.** The person(s) with executive responsibility for the conduct of the entity's operations. For some entities, management includes some or all of those charged with governance; for example, executive members of a governance board or an owner-manager.

11. **Misstatement.** A difference between the amount, classification, presentation, or disclosure of a reported financial statement item and the amount, classification, presentation, or disclosure that is required for the item to be in

accordance with the applicable financial reporting framework. Misstatements can arise from fraud or error. Where the auditor expresses an opinion on whether the financial statements are presented fairly, in all material respects, misstatements also include those adjustments of amounts, classifications, presentations, or disclosures that, in the auditor's judgment, are necessary for the financial statements to be presented fairly, in all material respects.

12. **Other auditing publications.** Publications other than interpretive publications; these include AICPA auditing publications not defined as interpretive publications; auditing articles in the *Journal of Accountancy* and other professional journals; auditing articles in the AICPA *CPA Letter,* continuing professional education programs and other instruction materials, textbooks, guide books, audit programs, and checklists; and other auditing publications from state CPA societies, other organizations, and individuals.

13. **Premise, relating to the responsibilities of management and, where appropriate, those charged with governance, on which an audit is conducted.** Management and, where appropriate, those charged with governance have the following responsibilities that are fundamental to the conduct of an audit in accordance with GAAS:

   a. For the preparation and presentation of the financial statements in accordance with the applicable financial reporting framework; this includes the design, implementation and maintenance of internal control relevant to the preparation and presentation of financial statements that are free from material misstatements, whether due to fraud or error; and

   b. To provide the auditor with

   (1) All information, such as records and documentation, and other matters that are relevant to the preparation and presentation of the financial statements;

   (2) Any additional information that the auditor may request from management and, where appropriate, those charged with governance; and

   (3) Unrestricted access to those within the entity from whom the auditor determines it necessary to obtain audit evidence.

   In the case of a fair presentation framework, the responsibility is for the preparation and *fair* presentation of financial statements in accordance with the financial reporting framework. This applies to all references to "preparation and presentation of the financial statements" in GAAS.

   The phrase *premise, relating to the responsibilities of management and, where appropriate, those charged with governance, on which an audit is conducted* may also be referred to as the term *premise.*

14. **Professional judgment.** The application of relevant training, knowledge, and experience, within the context provided by auditing, accounting, and ethical standards, in making informed decisions about the courses of action that are appropriate in the circumstances of the audit engagement.

15. **Professional skepticism.** An attitude that includes a questioning mind, being alert to conditions that may indicate possible misstatement due to fraud or error, and a critical assessment of audit evidence.

16. **Reasonable assurance.** In the context of an audit of financial statements, a high, but not absolute, level of assurance.

17. **Risk of material misstatement.** The risk that the financial statements are materially misstated prior to the audit. This consists of two components, described as follows at the assertion level:

   • **Inherent risk.** The susceptibility of an assertion about a class of transaction, account balance, or disclosure to a misstatement that could be material, either individually or when aggregated with other misstatements, before consideration of any related controls.

   • **Control risk.** The risk that a misstatement that could occur in an assertion about a class of transaction, account balance, or disclosure and that could be material, either individually or when aggregated with other misstatements, will not be prevented, or detected and corrected, on a timely basis by the entity's internal control.

18. **Those charged with governance.** The person(s) or organization(s) (for example, a corporate trustee) with responsibility for overseeing the strategic direction of the entity and the obligations related to the accountability of the entity. This includes overseeing the financial reporting process. Those charged with governance may include management personnel; for example, executive members of a governance board or an owner-manager.

D. Requirements, application, and other explanatory material

1. The auditor should be independent (in fact and in appearance) of the entity subject to the audit.

2. Ethical requirements relating to an audit of financial statements

   a. The auditor is subject to relevant ethical requirements, including those pertaining to independence.

    (1) The requirements consist of AICPA Code of Professional Conduct along with rules of state boards of accountancy and applicable regulatory agencies that are more restrictive.

  b. Statements on Quality Control Standards (SQCS) establish firm responsibilities to establish and maintain a system of quality control for audit engagements.

3. Professional skepticism—An audit should be planned and performed with professional skepticism.

> **NOTE:** Make certain that you know the definition of professional skepticism: Professional skepticism is an attitude that includes a questioning mind, being alert to conditions that may indicate possible misstatement due to fraud or error, and a critical assessment of audit evidence.

  a. Professional skepticism includes being alert to, for example,

    (1) Audit evidence that contradicts other audit evidence.
    (2) Information that brings to question the reliability of documents and responses to inquiries to be used as audit evidence.
    (3) Conditions that may indicate possible fraud.
    (4) Circumstances that suggest that need for audit procedures in addition to those required by GAAS.

  b. The auditor may accept records and documents as genuine unless the auditor has reason to believe contrary.

    (1) Nonetheless, the auditor is required to consider the reliability of information used as audit evidence. In cases of doubt, GAAS requires further investigation.

  c. An auditor neither assumes that management is dishonest nor assumes unquestioned honesty. While the auditor cannot be expected to disregard past experience of management (and other) honesty and integrity, there is still a need to maintain professional skepticism.

4. Professional judgment—The auditor should exercise professional judgment in planning and performing an audit of financial statements.

  a. The exercise of professional judgment needs to be appropriately documented in such a way that an experienced auditor, having no previous connection with the audit, could understand the significant professional judgments made in reaching conclusions on significant matters arising during the audit.

5. Sufficient appropriate audit evidence and audit risk

  a. To obtain reasonable assurance, the auditor should obtain sufficient appropriate audit evidence to reduce audit risk to an acceptably low level and thereby enable the auditor to draw reasonable conclusions on which to base the auditor's opinion.

  b. Sufficiency and appropriateness of audit evidence

    (1) Audit evidence is cumulative in nature and is primarily obtained from audit procedures performed during the course of the audit.

      (a) It may, however, also include information obtained from other sources such as previous audits (provided the auditor determines it is still relevant) or a firm's quality control procedures for client acceptance/continuance, as well as other sources.

    (2) Sufficiency is a measure of the quantity of audit evidence.

      (a) The quantity needed is affected by the auditor's assessment of the risks of material misstatement (higher assessed risks ordinarily require more audit evidence) and also by the quality of such audit evidence (the higher the quality, the less may be required). But obtaining more evidence may not compensate for its poor quality.

    (3) Appropriateness is the measure of the quality of the audit evidence, its relevance and reliability in supporting conclusions on which the auditor's opinion is based.

      (a) The reliability of evidence is influenced by its source and by its nature, and is dependent on the circumstances in which it is obtained.

  c. Audit risk—Discussed in detail in Section E. below.

6. Conducting the audit in accordance with GAAS

    a.   An auditor should comply with all AU-C sections relevant to the audit.

    b.   GAAS uses two categories or professional requirements:

        (1) *Unconditional requirements*: The auditor must comply with an unconditional requirement in all cases where such requirement is relevant. GAAS uses the word *must* to indicate an unconditional requirement.

        (2) *Presumptively mandatory requirements*: The auditor must comply with a presumptively mandatory requirement in all cases in which the requirement is relevant except in rare circumstances. GAAS uses the word *should* to indicate a presumptively mandatory requirement.

E. Audit risk

1. Audit risk is a function of the risks of material misstatement (inherent risk and control risk) and detection risk.

    a.   Definition of audit risk: The risk that the auditor expresses an inappropriate audit opinion when the financial statements are materially misstated.

    b.   Audit risk does not include

        (1) The risk that the auditor might express an opinion that the financial statements are materially misstated when they are not (this risk is ordinarily insignificant).

        (2) The auditor's business risks such as loss from litigation, adverse publicity, or other events arising in connection with the audit.

2. Risks of material misstatement

    a.   Exist at two levels

        (1) Overall financial statement level.

        (2) Assertion level for classes of transactions, account balances, and disclosures.

    b.   Risks of misstatement at the overall financial statement level refer to risks of material misstatement that relate pervasively to the financial statements as a whole and potentially affect many assertions.

    c.   Risks of material misstatement at the assertion level are assessed in order to determine the nature, timing, and extent of necessary further audit procedures.

    d.   The risks of material misstatement consist of two components—inherent risk and control risk.

        (1) Inherent risk is higher for some assertions than others (e.g., those subject to complex calculations).

        (2) Control risk is a function of the effectiveness of the design, implementation and maintenance of internal control.

            (a) Internal control can reduce, but not eliminate the risks of material misstatement due to inherent limitations of internal control, including

                1] Possibility of human errors or mistakes.

                2] Circumvention of controls by collusions.

                3] Inappropriate management override.

        (3) The auditor may make separate or combined assessments of inherent and control risk.

            (a) The assessment may be expressed in quantitative terms (e.g., percentages) or in nonquantitative terms (e.g., "high").

    e.   AU-C 315 establishes requirements and provides guidance on identifying and assessing risks of material misstatement at the financial statement and assertion levels.

3. Detection risk

    a.   The acceptable level of detection risk varies inversely to the assessed risks of material misstatement at the assertion level (e.g., the greater the risks of material misstatement the auditor believes exists, the less the deviation risk that can be accepted).

4. Because there are inherent limitations of an audit, the auditor cannot reduce audit risk to zero; principal inherent limitations

    a.   Nature of financial reporting. Financial reporting involves

        (1) Judgments.

        (2) Other subjective decisions or assessments or a degree of uncertainty.

        (3) Estimates based on predications of future events.

   b. Nature of audit procedures. For example

     (1) Management may not provide complete information.
     (2) Fraud may involve sophisticated and carefully organized schemes designed to conceal it.
     (3) Auditors are not given specific legal powers to investigate matters.

   c. Need for the audit to be conducted within a reasonable period of time and at a reasonable cost.

5. Other matters that affect the inherent limitations of an audit

   a. Fraud, particularly fraud involving senior management or collusion.
   b. Existence and completeness of related-party relationships and transactions.
   c. Occurrence of noncompliance with laws and regulations.
   d. Future events and conditions may cause an entity to cease to continue as a going concern.

6. Accordingly, subsequent discovery of a material misstatement does not by itself indicate a failure to conduct an audit in accordance with GAAS.

   a. Whether an auditor performed an audit in accordance with GAAS is determined by the audit procedures performed in the circumstances, the sufficiency and appropriateness of the audit evidence obtained, and the suitability of the auditor's report based on an evaluation of that evidence in light of the overall objectives of the auditor.

AU-C 210 Terms of Engagement

A. Introduction: This section addresses the auditor's responsibilities in agreeing to the terms of the audit engagement with management and, when appropriate, those charged with governance. This includes establishing that certain preconditions for an audit, for which management and, when appropriate, those charged with governance are responsible, are present.

B. Objective

1. The objective of the auditor is to accept or continue an audit engagement only when the basis upon which it is to be performed has been agreed upon through

   a. Establishing whether the preconditions for an audit are present, and
   b. Confirming that a common understanding of the terms of the audit engagement exists between the auditor and management and, when appropriate, those charged with governance.

C. Definition

1. **Preconditions for an audit.** The use by management and, when appropriate, those charged with governance, of an acceptable financial reporting framework in the preparation of the financial statements and the agreement of management and, when appropriate, those charged with governance, to the premise on which an audit is conducted.

D. Requirements, application, and other explanatory material

1. Preconditions for an audit: To establish whether the preconditions are present, the auditor should

   a. Determine whether the financial reporting framework used is acceptable; recall that GAAP, International Financial Reporting Standards, cash basis, etc. are among the acceptable frameworks.
   b. Obtain agreement of management that acknowledges and understands its responsibility

     (1) For preparing financial statements in accordance with applicable financial reporting framework.
     (2) For internal control.
     (3) To provide the auditor with

       (a) Access to all relevant information of which management is aware.
       (b) Additional information the auditor may request from management.
       (c) Unrestricted access to persons within the entity from whom the auditor determines it necessary to obtain audit evidence.

NOTE: Have a general familiarity with the above preconditions.

2. Scope limitation prior to audit engagement acceptance: If management, or those charged with governance, of a company that is not required by law to have an audit imposes a scope limitation that will result in a disclaimer of opinion, the auditor should not accept the engagement as an audit.

    a. Examples of scope limitations that would **not** preclude the auditor from accepting the engagement include

        (1) A restriction imposed by management the auditor believes will result in a qualified opinion (although one expected to result in a disclaimer would preclude the auditor from accepting such an engagement).

        (2) A restriction imposed by circumstances beyond the control of management.

    b. If the limitation is for a company required to have an audit, the auditor is permitted, but is not required, to accept the engagement.

3. Other factors affecting audit engagement acceptance

    a. An auditor (unless required by law) should not accept a proposed audit engagement when the financial reporting framework is unacceptable or management does not agree relating to the information to be provided.

    b. The agreed-upon terms of the audit engagement should be included in an engagement letter or other suitable written agreement, including

        (1) Objective and scope of the audit.

        (2) Responsibilities of the auditor.

        (3) Responsibilities of management.

        (4) Because of inherent limitations of audit and internal control, risk exists that material misstatement may not be detected.

        (5) Identification of the applicable financial reporting framework.

        (6) Reference to the expected form and content of any reports to be issued by the auditor and a statement that there may be circumstances in which a report may differ from its expected form and content.

4. On recurring audits the auditor should assess whether the terms of the audit engagement need to be revised (e.g., they may need to be if ownership and/or senior management has changed); if they do not the auditor should remind the entity of the terms of the engagement and the reminder should be documented.

    a. The reminder may be written or oral, but if oral, it should be documented in the working papers.

> **NOTE:** PCAOB Standard Number 16 requires an engagement letter every year.

5. Before accepting an engagement for an initial audit, including reaudits, the auditor should request management to authorize the predecessor auditor to respond fully to the auditor's inquiries about matters that will assist the auditor in determining whether to accept the engagement.

    a. If management refuses or limits the predecessor's response, the auditor should inquire about the reasons and consider the implications in deciding whether to accept the engagement.

        (1) A predecessor auditor is not expected to be available to respond until an auditor has been selected and has accepted the engagement, subject to the communication with the predecessor (that is, a predecessor is not required to meet with multiple possible successor auditors).

        (2) The communication with the predecessor auditor may be either written or oral, and may include

            (a) Information bearing on management integrity.

            (b) Disagreements with management about accounting policies, auditing procedures, etc.

            (c) Communications to those charged with governance regarding fraud and noncompliance with laws.

            (d) Communications to management and those charged with governance regarding IC significant deficiencies and material weaknesses.

            (e) Predecessor auditor's understanding about the reasons for the change.

    b. For a reaudit (with the original audit performed by the predecessor), before accepting the engagement the auditor should communicate the purpose of the inquires to the predecessor.

    c. The predecessor auditor should respond to the auditor's inquiries promptly, and in the absence of unusual circumstances fully respond on the basis of known facts.

    (1) If the predecessor auditor limits his/her response, due to unusual circumstances (e.g., litigation), he or she should state the response is limited.

    (2) If the predecessor provides no response or a limited response, the auditor should consider the implications in deciding whether to accept the engagement.

6. If prior to completing the audit the auditor is requested to change the audit to an engagement with a lower level of assurance (ordinarily review or compilation), the auditor should determine whether there is reasonable justification for doing so.

    a. If the auditor is unable to agree to a change and management will not allow an audit, the auditor should withdraw from the audit and determine whether any obligation (legal, contractual, or otherwise) exists to report this to other parties.

    b. Examples of reasonable and not reasonable reasons for change

        (1) Reasonable—Misunderstanding of the nature of the service originally requested.

        (2) Not reasonable—Change relates to information that is incorrect, incomplete or otherwise unsatisfactory (e.g., auditor unable to obtain sufficient appropriate evidence regarding receivables).

7. If a law prescribes a specific layout, form, or wording of the auditor's report that significantly differs from GAAS, the auditor should consider whether users might misunderstand the report; if they might misunderstand, the auditor should determine whether s/he is permitted to reword the form or to attach a separate report.

    a. If the auditor determines that rewording or attaching a separate report would not be permitted or would not mitigate the risk, the auditor should not accept the audit engagement unless required by law to do so.

        (1) An audit conducted in accordance with such law does not comply with GAAS, and accordingly, the auditor should not include any reference in the report to GAAS.

AU-C 220 Quality Control for an Audit of Financial Statements

A. Introduction

1. Scope: This section addresses the specific responsibilities of the auditor regarding quality control procedures for an audit of financial statements. It also addresses, where applicable, the responsibilities of the quality control reviewer. It also applies, adapted as necessary, to other engagements, conducted in accordance with GAAS (e.g., review of interim information).

2. Although Statements on Quality Control standards do not apply to auditors in government audit organizations, this SAS does apply to auditors in government audit organizations who perform financial audits in accordance with GAAS.

3. Quality control systems, policies, and procedures are the responsibility of the audit firm. The firm has an obligation to establish a system of quality control to provide reasonable assurance that

    a. The firm and personnel comply with standards.

    b. The reports issued are appropriate in the circumstances.

4. Within the context of the firm's system of quality control, engagement teams have a responsibility to implement quality control procedures applicable to the audit and to provide the firm with relevant information to enable the functioning of that part of the firm's system of quality control relating to independence.

5. Engagement teams are entitled to rely on the firm's system of quality control, unless the engagement partner determines that it is inappropriate to do so based on information provided by the firm or other parties.

B. Objective

1. The objective of the auditor is to implement quality control procedures at the engagement level that provide the auditor with reasonable assurance that

    a. The audit complies with professional standards and applicable legal and regulatory requirements.

    b. The auditor's report issued is appropriate in the circumstances.

C. Requirements

1. The engagement partner should take responsibility for the overall quality on each audit to which that partner is assigned.

2. Relevant ethical requirements

  a. The engagement partner should remain alert for evidence of noncompliance with relevant ethical requirements by the engagement team.

    (1) If such matters arise, the engagement partner, in consultation with others in the firm, should determine the appropriate action.

  b. The engagement partner should form a conclusion on compliance with independence requirements that apply to the audit, including

    (1) Obtaining relevant information from the firm to identify threats to independence.
    (2) Evaluate information on identified breaches, if any.
    (3) Take appropriate action to eliminate such threats or to reduce them to an acceptable level, or if considered appropriate, to withdraw from the audit engagement.

3. The auditor should be satisfied (or take corrective action) concerning

  a. Acceptance/continuance of client relationships.
  b. The engagement team.
  c. Adequate consultation on difficult or contentious matters.

4. For an engagement in which the firm has determined that an engagement quality control review is required, the engagement partner should determine that an engagement quality control reviewer has been appointed, discuss issues with that reviewer, and not release the auditor's report until completion of that review.

  a. The engagement quality control reviewer should perform an objective evaluation of the significant judgments made by the engagement team and conclusions reached.

5. If differences of opinion arise within the engagement team with those consulted or, where applicable, between the engagement partner and the engagement quality control reviewer, the engagement team should follow the firm's policies and procedures for dealing with and resolving differences of opinion.
6. An effective system of quality control includes a monitoring process designed to provide the firm with reasonable assurance that its policies and procedures related to quality control are relevant, adequate, and operating effectively.
7. Documentation requirements

  a. The auditor should document

    (1) Issues identified with respect to ethical requirements and how they were resolved.
    (2) Conclusions on independence.
    (3) Conclusions on acceptance/continuance of the client.
    (4) Nature and scope of, and conclusions resulting from consultation undertaken.

  b. The engagement quality control reviewer should document

    (1) Procedures required by firm have been performed.
    (2) Date the engagement quality control review was completed.
    (3) The reviewer is not aware of any unresolved matters that would cause the reviewer to believe that the significant judgments that the engagement team made and the conclusions they reached were not appropriate.

AU-C 230 Audit Documentation

A. Introduction

1. This section addresses the auditor's responsibility to prepare audit documentation for an audit of financial statements.
2. Audit documentation provides evidence

  a. Of the auditor's basis for a conclusion about the achievement of the overall objectives.
  b. That the audit was planned and performed in accordance with GAAS and applicable legal and regulatory requirements.

B. Purposes of audit documentation include

1. Assisting the engagement team in planning and performing the audit.
2. Assisting those on the engagement team responsible for supervision.

3. Enabling engagement team to demonstrate that it is accountable for its work.
4. Retaining a record of significant matters for future audits.
5. Enabling conduct of quality control reviews and inspections in accordance with Quality Control Standards and appropriate legal, regulatory or other requirements.
6. Assisting an auditor who reviews a predecessor auditor's audit documentation.
7. Assisting current year auditors to understand prior year work to aid in planning.

C. The overall objective of the auditor is to prepare documentation that provides

1. A sufficient and appropriate record of the basis for the auditor's report.
2. Evidence that the audit was planned and performed in accordance with GAAS and applicable legal and regulatory requirements.

D. Definitions

1. **Audit documentation.** The record of audit procedures performed, relevant audit evidence obtained, and conclusions the auditor reached (terms such as working papers or workpapers are also sometimes used.)
2. **Audit file.** One or more folders or other storage media, in physical or electronic form, containing the records that constitute the audit documentation for a specific engagement.
3. **Documentation completion date.** The date, no later than 60 days following the report release date, on which the auditor has assembled for retention a complete and final sets of documentation in an audit file.
4. **Experienced auditor.** An individual (whether internal or external to the firm) who has practical audit experience and a reasonable understanding of audit processes, GAAS, the business environment in which the entity operates, and auditing and financial reporting issues relevant to the industry.

E. Requirements, application, and other explanatory material

1. The auditor should prepare audit documentation on a timely basis.
2. Audit documentation should be sufficient to enable an experienced auditor, having no previous connection with the audit, to understand

   a. Nature, timing and extent of audit procedures performed.
   b. Results of such procedures.
   c. Significant findings and conclusions.

3. The auditor should record

   a. Identifying characteristics of specific items or matters tested.
   b. Who performed the audit work and the date it was completed.
   c. Who reviewed the audit work and the date and extent of such review.
   d. Other

      (1) For inspection of significant contract or agreements, the auditor should include abstracts or copies of the contracts or agreements.
      (2) The auditor should document significant discussions with management, those charged with governance, and others.
      (3) If information inconsistent with the auditor's final conclusion exists the auditor should document how the matter was addressed.

4. Matters arriving after the date of the auditor's report—Document the circumstances, new or additional audit procedures performed, conclusions, date, and who made changes in the documentation.
5. Assembly and retention of the final audit file

   a. Document the report release date.
   b. Assemble the audit documentation no later than 60 days following the report release date.
   c. When audit documentation must be modified subsequently, document the reasons for the changes, when and by whom made.

AU-C 240 Consideration of Fraud in a Financial Statement Audit

A. Introduction

1. Scope: This section addresses the auditor's responsibilities relating to fraud in an audit of financial statements.
2. For purposes of GAAS, the auditor is concerned with fraud that causes a material misstatement in the financial statements—(1) those arising from *fraudulent financial reporting* and (2) those arising from *misappropriation of assets*.

    a. Fraud is intentional, whereas errors (the other cause of misstatements) are unintentional.

    b. To commit fraud, an individual ordinarily has

        (1) An incentive or pressure to commit.
        (2) An opportunity to commit.
        (3) The ability to rationalize committing the act.

    c. Fraudulent financial reporting may be accomplished by

        (1) Manipulation, falsification, or alteration of records.
        (2) Misrepresentation or omission of events, transactions, etc.
        (3) Intentional misapplication of accounting principles.

    d. Misappropriation of assets may be accomplished by

        (1) Embezzling receipts.
        (2) Stealing assets.
        (3) Causing an entity to pay for goods and service not received.
        (4) Using entity assets for personal use.

3. Those charged with governance responsibility and management are responsible for the prevention and detection of fraud.

4. Auditor responsibility with respect to fraud

    a. Conduct audit in accordance with GAAS and thereby obtain reasonable assurance that the financial statements are free of material misstatement, whether caused by fraud or error.

    b. The risk of not detecting a material misstatement from fraud is higher than risk of not detecting an error because

        (1) Fraud may involve sophisticated and carefully organized schemes to conceal it (e.g., forgery).
        (2) Collusion.

    c. The risk of the auditor not detecting a material misstatement relating to management fraud is greater than for employee fraud because management is frequently in a position to directly or indirectly manipulate accounting records, present fraudulent financial information, or override control procedures.

    d. An auditor must maintain an attitude of professional skepticism throughout the audit.

B. **Objectives:** The objectives of the audit are to

1. Identify and assess risks of material misstatement of the financial statement due to fraud.
2. Obtain sufficient appropriate audit evidence regarding the assessed risks of material misstatement due to fraud, through designing and implementing appropriate response.
3. Respond appropriately to fraud or suspected fraud identified during the audit.

C. **Definitions**

1. **Fraud.** An intentional act by one or more individuals among management, those charged with governance, employees, or third parties, involving the use of deception that results in a misstatement in financial statements that are subject of an audit.

2. **Fraud risk factors.** Events or conditions that indicate an incentive or pressure to perpetrate fraud, provide an opportunity to commit fraud, or indicate attitudes or rationalizations to justify a fraudulent action.

D. **Requirements, application, and other explanatory material**

1. Professional skepticism

    a. An attitude of professional skepticism (which includes a questioning mind and a critical assessment of audit evidence) must be maintained throughout the audit.

    b. Unless the auditor has reason to believe the contrary, the auditor may accept records and documents as genuine.

        (1) An audit rarely involves authentication of documents.
        (2) When the auditor identifies conditions that cause the auditor to believe a document may not be authentic (or is authentic but modified), the auditor should obtain additional evidence to address the inconsistencies or unsatisfactory responses; examples are

            (a) Confirming directly with the third party.
            (b) Using the work of a specialist to assess the document's authenticity.

2. Discussion among the engagement team concerning fraud

   a. AU-C 315 requires such a discussion for material misstatements. The discussion here (which may be combined with the AU-C 315 discussion) should include an exchange of ideas or brainstorming among engagement team members about how and where financial statements are susceptible to material misstatement due to fraud, how management could perpetrate and conceal fraudulent financial reporting, and how assets could be misappropriated.

   b. Particular emphasis should be placed on

      (1) Known external and internal factors affecting the entity that may create an incentive or pressure for management or others to commit fraud, provide the opportunity, and indicate a culture that enables rationalization of committing fraud.

      (2) The risk of management override of controls.

      (3) Consideration of circumstances that might indicate earnings management or manipulation of other financial measures.

      (4) The importance of maintaining professional skepticism throughout the audit.

      (5) How the auditor might respond to the susceptibility of the entity's financial statements to material misstatement due to fraud.

3. Risk assessment procedures and related activities—The auditor should perform the following procedures to obtain information for use in identifying the risks of material misstatement due to fraud:

   a. Make inquiries of management and others within the organization

      (1) Management's assessment of the risk that the financial statements may be materially misstated due to fraud.

      (2) Management's process for identifying, responding to, and monitoring the risks of fraud.

      (3) Management's communication, if any, to those charged with governance concerning the risks of fraud.

      (4) Management communication, if any, to employees regarding its views on business practices and ethical behavior.

      (5) Ask management and others within entity if they have knowledge of actual, suspected, or alleged fraud.

         (a) If an internal audit function exists, inquire of them to obtain their views about the risks of fraud, and determine their knowledge concerning fraud and whether management has satisfactorily responded to any internal auditor findings regarding fraud.

      (6) Since management is often in the best position to perpetrate fraud, the auditor may judge it necessary to corroborate their responses.

   b. Those charged with governance (unless all are involved in management)

      (1) The inquiries here should be made of those charged with governance—or the audit committee or, at least, its chair of those charged with governance.

      (2) Obtain an understanding of how they identify and respond to risks of fraud.

      (3) Inquire to determine their views about the risks of fraud and whether they have knowledge of any actual, suspected, or alleged fraud affecting the entity (this inquiry may be made to the audit committee or, at least, its chair).

   c. Unusual or unexpected relationships identified

      (1) Based on analytical procedures performed as a part of risk assessment procedures and as part of substantive procedures, the auditor should evaluate whether unusual or unexpected relationships have been identified.

         (a) For example, analytical procedures relating to revenue may indicate a possible material misstatement due to fraud.

   d. Other information

      (1) In addition to analytical procedures, other sources include the discussion among team members, information obtained during the client acceptance/retention processes and information from other engagements (e.g., review of interim information).

   e. Evaluation of fraud risk factors

(1) Evaluate whether information obtained from other risk assessment procedures indicate one or more fraud risk factors.

(2) Although fraud risk factors ordinarily do not necessarily indicate the existence of fraud with certainty, they have often been present where frauds have occurred and therefore may indicate risks of material misstatement due to fraud.

(3) Some of these factors will be present in entities where the specific conditions do not present risks of material misstatement. The determination of whether a fraud risk factor should be considered in assessing the risks of material misstatement due to fraud requires the exercise of professional judgment.

4. Identification and assessment of the risks of material misstatement due to fraud

   a. The auditor should identify and assess the risks of material misstatement due to fraud at the financial statement level, and at the assertion level for classes of transactions, account balances, and disclosures; this process is ongoing throughout the audit.

   b. Revenue recognition—*The audit should include a presumption that the risk of fraud exists in this area*

      (1) Examples—premature revenue recognition, fictitious revenues, improperly shifting revenues to a later period.
      (2) The presumption may be rebutted (e.g., in a situation in which a single type of simple revenue transaction exists).

   c. The auditor should treat those assessed risks of material misstatement due to fraud as *significant risks* and, accordingly, to the extent not already done so, the auditor should obtain an understanding of related controls.

5. Responses to the assessed risks of material misstatement due to fraud

   a. Overall responses

      (1) Address risks of material misstatement due to fraud

         (a) *Assign personnel with appropriate knowledge, skill and ability* (e.g., IT and/or forensic experts).
         (b) *Evaluate whether the selection and application of accounting principles* by the entity, particularly those related to subjective measurements and complex transactions may indicate fraud.
         (c) *Incorporate an element of unpredictability* in the section of the nature, timing, and extent of audit procedures; examples are

            1] Perform substantive procedures on accounts not otherwise tested due to materiality or risk.
            2] Adjust timing of procedures.
            3] Use different sampling methods.
            4] Perform audit procedures at different locations or at locations on an unannounced basis.

   b. Audit procedures responsive to assessed risks of material misstatement due to fraud at the assertion level

      (1) Nature—May need *more reliable* and relevant corroborative information, for example

         (a) Physical observation or inspection of certain assets may become more important.
         (b) Increase external confirmations and include information on terms of sales in addition to balance.

      (2) Timing—Obtaining information at or *near period end* may be more important (i.e., fewer tests performed at an interim date).
      (3) Extent—*Increase sample sizes* or perform analytical procedures at a more detailed level.

   c. Audit procedures responsive to risks related to management override of controls

      (1) Although the risk of management override of controls will vary from entity to entity, it is present in all entities.
      (2) Even if specific risks of material misstatement due to fraud are not identified by the auditor, there is a possibility that management override of controls could occur. Accordingly, the auditor should address that risk apart from any conclusions regarding the existence of more specifically identifiable risk, by designing and performing audit procedures to

         (a) *Test appropriateness of journal entries* made in the preparation of financial statements, including entries posted directly to financial statement drafts. The auditor should

            1] Make inquiries of individuals involved in financial reporting about inappropriate or unusual activity relating to entries.

2] Consider fraud risk factors, controls, and the nature and complexity of accounts and entries processed outside the normal course of business.

3] Select journal entries and other entries made at the end of a reporting period.

4] Consider the need to test journal entries and other adjustments throughout the period.

(b) *Review accounting estimates* for biases and evaluate whether the circumstances producing the bias, if any, represent a risk of material misstatement due to fraud.

1] Estimates selected for testing should include those that are based on highly sensitive assumptions or otherwise significantly affected by judgments made by management.

6. Evaluation of audit evidence

a. At, or near the end of the audit, the auditor should evaluate whether the results of auditing procedures applied affect the risk of material misstatement due to fraud made earlier in the audit. If not already performed during the overall review stage, analytical procedures relating to revenue should be performed through the end of the reporting period.

b. When the auditor identifies a misstatement, s/he should consider whether it is indicative of fraud. If it may indicate fraud and management is involved (in particular, senior management), the auditor should reevaluate the assessment of the risk of material misstatement due to fraud and the impact on the nature, timing, and extent of audit procedures.

7. Fraud may result in the auditor being unable to continue the engagement

a. If as a result of a misstatement resulting from fraud or suspected fraud, the auditor encounters exceptional circumstances that bring into question his/her ability to continue performing the audit, the auditor should

(1) Determine applicable professional and legal responsibilities.

(2) Consider whether it is appropriate to withdraw from the engagement, where withdrawal is legally permitted.

(3) If the auditor withdraws

(a) Discuss with the appropriate level of management and those charged with governance.

(b) Determine whether a professional or legal requirement exists to report to the person(s) who made the audit appointment, or in some cases, regulatory authorities.

8. The auditor should obtain written representations from management

a. Acknowledging its responsibility for designing internal control over fraud.

b. Disclosing to auditor results of its assessment of the risk of fraud, its knowledge of fraud, and allegations of fraud.

9. Communications to management and with those charged with governance

a. If the auditor has identified fraud or obtained information that indicates fraud may exist—communicate on a timely basis to an appropriate level of management.

b. Unless all those charged with governance are involved in managing the entity, if the auditor has identified or suspects fraud involving (1) management, (2) employees who have significant roles in internal control or (3) others where the fraud results in a material misstatement, communicate these matters to those charged with governance on a timely basis.

c. If the auditor suspects management fraud, communicate suspicions to those charged with governance.

d. Communicate with those charged with governance any matters related to fraud that are, in the auditor's judgment, relevant to their responsibilities.

10. Communications to regulatory and enforcement authorities

a. If a legal responsibility to report identified suspected fraud exists, it should be reported.

11. Documentation

a. Understanding of entity and it environment and the assessment of the risks of material misstatement

(1) Significant decisions reached during the discussion among the engagement team regarding the susceptibility of the financial statements to fraud and how and when the discussion occurred and the audit team members who participated.

(2) The identified and assessed risks of material misstatement due to fraud at the financial statement and assertion level.

b. The auditor should include in audit documentation the overall auditor responses to the assessed risks of material misstatement due to fraud, including the nature, timing and extent of audit procedures, and the linkage of those procedures to the assessed risks of material misstatement due to fraud at the assertion level. Also, results of audit procedures designed to address management override of controls should be documented.

c. The auditor should include in documentation communications about fraud made to management, those charged with governance, regulators, and others.

d. The *auditor should presume a risk of material misstatement due to fraud related to revenue recognition exists on every audit*; where the auditor overcomes this presumption, documentation should include reasons for that conclusion.

(1) Overall responses and the linkage of those procedures to the assessed risks of material misstatement due to fraud at the assertion level.

(2) Results of audit procedures, including those addressing the risk of management override.

(3) Other conditions and analytical relationships that cause the auditor to believe that additional procedures are required, and any further responses.

e. The auditor should document communications about fraud to management and those charged with governance, regulators, and others.

f. When a presumption of material misstatement due to fraud related to revenue recognition is not applicable, the reasons for that conclusion.

AU-C 250 Consideration of Laws and Regulations in an Audit of Financial Statements

A. Introduction

1. Scope: This section addresses the auditor's responsibility to consider laws and regulations (hereafter, laws) when performing an audit of financial statements.

2. *Some laws have a direct effect* on the financial statement reported amounts and disclosures in the financial statements, while *others do not have a direct effect.*

3. It is the responsibility of management, with oversight of those charged with governance, to ensure that the entity's operations are conducted in accordance with the provisions of laws.

a. The auditor is not responsible for preventing noncompliance and cannot be expected to detect noncompliance with all laws. *It is noncompliance with those with a direct effect (would result in an adjusting journal entry and, possibly, related disclosures) that the auditor provides reasonable assurance of detecting.*

4. Limitations on the auditor's ability to detect material misstatements are greater than other inherent limitations of an audit because

a. Many laws do not typically affect the financial statements and are not captured by the entity's information system relevant to financial reporting.

b. Noncompliance may involve conduct designed to conceal it (e.g., collusion, forgery, failure to record transactions, management override of controls, or intentional misrepresentations made to the auditor).

c. Whether an act constitutes noncompliance is ultimately a matter for legal determination by a court of law.

5. Ordinarily, the further removed noncompliance is from the events and transactions in the financial statements, the less likely an auditor is to become aware of noncompliance.

6. This section distinguishes the auditor's responsibilities in relation to compliance with the following two categories of laws and regulations:

a. *Direct effect*—Laws with an effect on the determination of material amounts and disclosures in the financial statements (e.g., tax and pension laws).

b. *Other laws*—Laws that do not have a direct effect on the determination of amounts (and related disclosures) in the financial statement (e.g., complying with the terms of an operating license, compliance with regulatory solvency requirements, compliance with environmental regulations, occupational safety, equal employment, price fixing). Their effect is normally the result of the need to disclose a contingent liability because of the allegation or determination of identified or suspected noncompliance.

7. Auditor responsibility

   a. *Laws with a direct effect*—Undertaking specified audit procedures that may identify noncompliance with those laws that may have a material effect on the financial statements.

   b. *Other laws*—Remain alert to the possibility that other audit procedures applied for the purpose of forming an opinion on the financial statements may bring instances of identified or suspected noncompliance to the auditor's attention and

      (1) Inquire of management (and as appropriate those charged with governance) about whether the entity is in compliance with laws.

      (2) Inspect correspondence, if any, with relevant licensing or regulatory authorities.

B. Objectives: The objectives of the auditor are to

1. Obtain sufficient appropriate audit evidence regarding material amounts and disclosures in the financial statements for those laws with a *direct effect* on their determination.

2. Perform specified audit procedures (A.7. above) that may identify instances of noncompliance with other laws that may have a material effect on the financial statements.

3. Respond appropriately to noncompliance or suspected noncompliance with laws and regulations identified during the audit.

C. Definitions

1. **Noncompliance.** Acts of omission or commission by the entity, either intentional or unintentional, which are contrary to the prevailing laws or regulations. Such acts involve transactions entered into by, or in the name of the entity, or on its behalf, by those charged with governance, management, or employees. Noncompliance does not include personal misconduct (unrelated to the business activities of the entity) by those charged with governance, management, or employees of the entity.

D. Requirements, application, and other explanatory material

1. The auditor's consideration of compliance with laws; the auditor should

   a. Obtain a general understanding of the legal and regulatory framework applicable to the entity and how the entity is complying with that framework.

   b. Obtain sufficient appropriate audit evidence regarding material amounts and disclosures in the financial statements that are determined by laws to have a direct effect on their determination.

   c. Perform the following audit procedures that may identify noncompliance with laws:

      (1) Inquire of management and, where appropriate, those charged with governance, as to whether the entity is in compliance with laws.

      (2) Inspect correspondence, if any, with the relevant licensing or regulatory authorities.

   d. Remain alert to the possibility that other audit procedures may identify instances of noncompliance or suspected noncompliance with laws to the auditor's attention; examples are

      (1) Reading minutes.

      (2) Inquiring of in-house counsel or external legal counsel concerning litigation, claims and assessment.

      (3) Performing substantive tests of details.

2. Audit procedures when noncompliance is identified or suspected

   a. If the auditor is aware of information concerning noncompliance or suspected noncompliance, the auditor should obtain

      (1) An understanding of the nature of the act and circumstances

         (a) Examples

            1] Examining supporting documents.

            2] Confirming significant information.

            3] Determining whether transaction was authorized.

      (2) Further information to evaluate possible effects on the financial statements

        (a) Examples

            1] Quantitative and qualitative materiality of the effect of noncompliance.

            2] Potential financial consequences that may require disclosure.

            3] Seriousness of financial consequences.

    b. Discuss with management (at a level above those involved with noncompliance, if possible) and, where appropriate, those charged with governance; legal advice may also be sought.

    c. If sufficient information cannot be obtained, there is a la ck of sufficient appropriate audit evidence.

3. Reporting of identified or suspected noncompliance

    a. Reporting noncompliance to those charged with governance

      (1) Unless all those charged with governance are involved in management, communicate to those charged with governance.

      (2) If noncompliance is believed to be intentional and material, communicate as soon as practicable.

      (3) If the auditor suspects that management or those charged with governance are involved in noncompliance, communicate to the next higher level of authority, if it exists, such as an audit committee or supervisory board. Consider the need for legal advice.

    b. Reporting noncompliance in the auditor's report

      (1) If noncompliance has not been adequately reflected in the financial statements—qualified or adverse opinion (due to departure from GAAP).

      (2) If the auditor is precluded by management or those charged with governance from obtaining sufficient appropriate audit evidence—qualified opinion or disclaimer (due to scope limitation).

      (3) If auditor is unable to determine whether noncompliance has occurred because of limitations imposed by the circumstances rather than management or those charged with governance—evaluate the effect on the auditor's opinion in accordance with AU-C section 705.

    c. Reporting noncompliance to regulatory and enforcement authorities

      (1) Determine whether there is a responsibility to report the identified or suspected noncompliance to parties outside the entity.

        (a) Example: The auditor of a governmental entity may be required to report on compliance with laws, regulations and provisions of contracts or grant agreements as a part of the audit of the governmental entity's financial statements.

4. Documentation—The auditor should document identified or suspected noncompliance with laws and the results of discussion with management and, where applicable, those charged with governance, and other parties both inside and outside the entity.

AU-C 260 The Auditor's Communication with Those Charged with Governance

A. Introduction

1. This section addresses the auditor's responsibility to communicate with those charged with governance in an audit of financial statements; it does not establish requirements regarding communication with management or owners unless they are also charged with a governance role.

B. The objectives of the auditor are

1. Communicate clearly with those charged with governance the responsibilities of the auditor and an overview of the planned scope and timing of the audit.

2. Obtain from those charged with governance information that is relevant to the audit.

3. Provide those charged with governance timely observations rising in the audit that are significant and relevant to their responsibility to oversee the financial reporting process.

4. Promote effective two-way communication between the auditor and those charged with governance.

C. Definitions

1. **Management.** Persons with executive responsibility for the conduct of the entity's operations. For some entities, management includes some or all of those charged with governance; for example, executive members of a governance board or an owner-manager.

2. **Those charged with governance.** The person(s) or organization(s) with responsibility for overseeing the strategic direction of the entity and the obligations related to the accountability of the entity. This includes overseeing the financial reporting process. Those charged with governance may include management personnel; for example, executive members of a governance board or an owner-manager.

D. **Requirements, application, and other explanatory material**

1. The auditor should determine the appropriate person(s) with corporate governance to communicate with

   a. If the auditor communicates with a subgroup, such as the audit committee or an individual, s/he should determine whether to communicate with the entire governing body.
   b. When all those charged with governance are involved in managing the entity, if a matter is communicated to those individuals in their management roles, this is sufficient.

2. Matters to be communicated to those charged with governance

   a. Auditor responsibilities regarding the audit

      (1) Forming an opinion on the financial statements
      (2) Does not relieve management or those charged with governance of their responsibilities.

   b. Overview of the planned scope and timing of the audit.
   c. Significant findings or issues from the audit

      (1) Qualitative aspects of the entity's significant accounting practices
      (2) Significant difficulties, if any encountered during the audit,
      (3) Disagreements with management, if any.
      (4) Other findings arising from audit that the auditor believes should be communicated.

   d. Uncorrected misstatements and the effect of previous year uncorrected misstatements.
   e. When not all those charged with governance are involved in management

      (1) Material, corrected misstatements identified.
      (2) Significant findings or issues arising from the audit discussed with management.
      (3) Auditor's views about significant matters that were subject of management's consultations with other accountants.
      (4) Written representations the auditor is requesting.

3. The communication process

   a. *Form*—in writing *if* the auditor believes oral communication would not be adequate. If in writing, it need not include matters satisfactory resolved with those charged with governance.
   b. *Restricted use*—communication intended solely for those charged with governance.
   c. *Timing*—Timely basis; some issues may be during planning of the audit, others when difficulties arise, others at the end of the audit.
   d. *Adequacy of process*—The auditor should evaluate the adequacy of the communication.
   e. *Documentation*—Communicated matters should be included in audit documentation, including when and to whom communicated. When in writing, a copy of the written communication should be included.

AU-C 265 Communicating Internal Control Related Matters Identified in an Audit

A. **Scope:** This section addresses the auditor's responsibility to appropriately communicate to those charged with governance and management, deficiencies in internal control that the auditor has identified in an audit of financial statements.

   1. IC deficiencies may be identified during the risk assessment process, but also at any other stage of the audit.

B. **Objective:** The objective of the auditor is to appropriately communicate, to those charged with governance and management, deficiencies in internal control that the auditor has identified during the audit and that, in the auditor's professional judgment, are of sufficient importance to merit attention.

C. **Definitions**

   1. **Deficiency in internal control.** A deficiency in internal control exists when the design or operation of a control does not allow management or employees, in the normal course of performing their assigned functions, to prevent, or detect and correct, misstatements on a timely basis. A *deficiency in design* exists when (a) a control necessary to

meet the control objective is missing or (b) an existing control is not properly designed so that, even if the control operates as designed, the control objective would not be met. A *deficiency in operation* exists when a properly designed control does not operate as designed, or when the person performing the control does not possess the necessary authority or competence to perform the control effectively.

2. **Material weakness.** A deficiency, or a combination of deficiencies, in internal control such that there is a reasonable possibility that a material misstatement of the entity's financial statements will not be prevented, or detected and corrected, on a timely basis.

3. **Significant deficiency.** A deficiency, or a combination of deficiencies, in internal control that is less severe than a material weakness, yet important enough to merit attention by those charged with governance.

D. Requirements, selected application, and other explanatory material

1. The auditor should determine whether, on the basis of audit work performed, s/he has identified one or more deficiencies in IC.

2. Evaluating the severity of identified deficiencies in IC

   a. Determine whether individually or in combination identified deficiencies constitute significant deficiencies or material weaknesses. Think here of 3 types of deficiencies that increase in severity: deficiency that is less than a significant deficiency, a significant deficiency, and a material weakness.

      (1) If the auditor determines that a deficiency is not a material weakness, s/he should consider whether prudent officials, having knowledge of the same facts and circumstances, would likely reach the same conclusion.

      (2) The severity of a deficiency depends not only on whether a misstatement actually occurred, but *also on the magnitude of potential misstatements* resulting from the deficiency and whether there is a reasonable possibility that the entity's controls will fail to prevent or detect and correct a misstatement; significant deficiencies and material weaknesses may exist even when the auditor has not identified misstatements.

         (a) The maximum amount of an account's overstatement is ordinarily the recorded amount, whereas understatements could be larger than the recorded amount.

      (3) The evaluation of whether a deficiency presents a reasonable possibility (more likely than remote) of misstatement may be made without quantifying the probability; this evaluation is important since a reasonable possibility of occurring is required for a material weakness.

   b. The following are indicators of material weaknesses in internal control:

      (1) Identified fraud, whether or not material, by senior management.
      (2) Restatement of previously issued financial statements to reflect a correction of a material misstatement due to fraud or error.
      (3) Identification of a material misstatement in the financial statements under audit when the misstatement would not have been detected by the entity's IC.
      (4) Ineffective oversight of the entity's financial reporting and IC by those charged with governance.

   NOTE: Know the above 4 indicators.

3. Communicating deficiencies in IC

   a. Material weaknesses and significant deficiencies—The auditor should communicate to *those charged with governance* and *management* in *writing* on a timely basis.

      (1) The written communication should include

         (a) Definitions of material weaknesses and, when relevant, significant deficiency.
         (b) Description of significant deficiencies and material weaknesses and explanation of their potential effects.
         (c) Sufficient information to enable those charged with governance and management to understand the context of the communication, including

            1] Purpose of audit was to express an opinion on the financial statements.
            2] Consideration of IC was to design appropriate audit procedures, not to express an IC opinion.

3] The auditor is not expressing an opinion on IC.

4] Consideration of IC not designed to identify all deficiencies in IC.

   (d) Restriction of report to management, those charged with governance, others in the organization, and any specified governmental authority.

b. Other deficiencies in internal control—The auditor should communicate to **management** in **writing or orally** (if they have not been communicated by other parties) if, in the auditor's professional judgment, they are of sufficient importance to merit management's attention.

c. Although ordinarily best communicated by the report release date, it should be communicated no later than 60 days following the report release date.

d. Significant deficiencies and material weaknesses should be communicated even if management and those charged with governance are aware of them (e.g., it may be necessary to re-communicate [or make reference to] a previous year significant deficiency or material weakness that has not been eliminated).

   (1) Absent a rational explanation as to why such a deficiency was not corrected, a failure to act may in itself represent a significant deficiency or material weakness.

e. Other deficiencies that have previously been communicated (not significant deficiencies or material weaknesses) need not be recommunicated.

f. The appropriate level of management to communicate to is the one that has responsibility and authority to evaluate the deficiencies in IC and to take necessary remedial action; for significant deficiencies and material weaknesses this is likely to be the CEO or CFO.

g. If management wishes to (or is required to by a regulator) include a response to the auditor's IC communication in a document that includes that IC communication, the auditor may add a paragraph to his/her IC communication disclaiming an opinion on such information.

4. Reporting issues

a. When no material weaknesses are identified—The auditor may issue a report indicating no material weaknesses were identified.

b. When no significant deficiencies (or material weaknesses) are identified—the auditor should **not** issue a written communication stating that no significant deficiencies were identified.

> **NOTE**: Know the above two rules.

AU-C 300 Planning an Audit

A. Introduction

1. Scope: This section addresses the auditor's responsibility to plan an audit of financial statements.

2. Planning an audit involves establishing the overall audit strategy and developing the audit plan. Adequate planning benefits the audit by helping the auditor to

a. Identify and devote appropriate attention to important areas of the audit.

b. Identify and resolve potential problems on a timely basis.

c. Organize and manage the engagement in an effective and efficient way.

d. Assist in selection of appropriate engagement team members.

e. Facilitate direction and supervision of team members.

f. Assist, where applicable, in coordination of work done by auditors of components and specialists.

3. Planning is not a discrete phase of an audit, but rather a continual iterative process that often starts after completion of the previous audit and continues until completion of the current audit.

4. Planning includes the need to consider, prior to the auditor's identification and assessment of the risks of material misstatement, matters such as

a. Analytical procedures to be applied.

b. Legal and regulatory requirements.

c. Materiality.

d. Involvement of specialists.

e. Performance of other risk assessment procedures.

B. Objective: The objective of the auditor is to plan the audit so that it will be performed in an effective manner.

C. Requirements, application, and other explanatory material

1. Discussion among key engagement team members

    a. The engagement partner and other *key members* of the engagement team should be involved in planning, including participating in the discussion among engagement team members.

    b. The objective of the discussion (required in AU-C 315) is to consider the susceptibility of financial statements to material misstatement. It may also include the required discussion on fraud as per AU-C 240.

2. Preliminary engagement activities

    a. At the beginning of the audit, the auditor should undertake procedures related to quality control on continuance of the client, evaluate compliance with ethical requirements, and establish an understanding of the terms of the engagement as per AU-C 210.

3. Planning activities

    a. An overall audit strategy (which is more general than the audit plan) should be developed to set the scope, timing and direction of the audit and to guide the development of the audit plan.

        (1) In establishing the overall audit strategy the auditor should

            (a) Identify important engagement characteristics.
            (b) Ascertain engagement reporting objectives to plan timing of audit and nature of required communications.
            (c) Consider significant factors.
            (d) Consider result of preliminary engagement activities.
            (e) Ascertain nature, timing and extent of necessary resources.

    b. An audit plan should describe

        (1) Nature, timing and extent of planned risk assessment procedures and further audit procedures.
        (2) Other planned audit procedures that are required.
        (3) The audit strategy and audit plan should be updated as necessary throughout the audit.

4. Determining the extent of involvement of professionals with specialized skills

    a. The auditors should consider whether specialized skills are needed in performing the audit; when they are needed the auditor should have sufficient knowledge to

        (1) Communicate the objectives of the other professional's work.
        (2) Evaluate whether the specified audit procedures meet the auditor's objectives.
        (3) Evaluate the results of the audit procedures as they relate to the nature, timing and extent of further planned audit procedures.

    b. Examples of specialists: valuation experts, appraisers, actuaries, IT professionals.

5. Documentation: should include the overall audit strategy, the audit plan, and significant changes to each.

6. Additional considerations in initial audit engagements

    a. Prior to starting an initial audit the auditor should perform required quality control procedures regarding the acceptance of the client relationship and communicating with the predecessor auditor; such procedures may include

        (1) Arrangement with the predecessor auditor.
        (2) Major issues discussed with management.
        (3) Necessary audit procedures to obtain sufficient appropriate audit evidence regarding open balances.
        (4) Other procedures (e.g., involvement of another partner to review the overall audit strategy).

AU-C 315 Understanding the Entity and Its Environment and Assessing the Risks of Material Misstatement

A. Introduction: This section addresses the auditor's responsibility to identify and assess the risks of material misstatement in the financial statements, through understanding the entity and its environment, including the entity's internal control (IC).

B.   Objective: The objective of the auditor is to identify and assess the risks of material misstatement, whether due to fraud or error, at the financial statement and relevant assertion levels, through understanding the entity and its environment, including the entity's internal control, thereby providing a basis for designing and implementing responses to the assessed risks of material misstatement.

C.   Definitions

1.   **Assertions.** Representations by management, explicit or otherwise, that are embodied in the financial statements, as used by the auditor to consider the different types of potential misstatements that may occur.

2.   **Relevant assertion.** A financial statement assertion that has a reasonable possibility of containing a misstatement or misstatements that would cause the financial statements to be materially misstated. The determination of whether an assertion is a relevant assertion is made without regard to the effect of controls.

3.   **Business risk.** A risk resulting from significant conditions, events, circumstances, actions, or inactions that could adversely affect an entity's ability to achieve its objectives and execute its strategies, or from the setting of inappropriate objectives and strategies.

4.   **Internal control.** A process—effected by those charged with governance, management, and other personnel— designed to provide reasonable assurance about the achievement of the entity's objectives with regard to the reliability of financial reporting, effectiveness and efficiency of operations, and compliance with applicable laws and regulations. Internal control over safeguarding of assets against unauthorized acquisition, use, or disposition may include controls relating to financial reporting and operations objectives.

5.   **Risk assessment procedures.** The audit procedures performed to obtain an understanding of the entity and its environment, including the entity's internal control, to identify and assess the risks of material misstatement, whether due to fraud or error, at the financial statement and assertion levels.

6.   **Significant risk.** An identified and assessed risk of material misstatement that, in the auditor's judgment, requires special audit consideration.

D.   Requirements, application, and other explanatory material

1.   Risk assessment procedures and related activities

a.   These procedures provide a basis for identification and assessment or risks of material misstatements, but by themselves risk assessment procedures do not provide sufficient appropriate audit evidence.

b.   Risk assessment procedures include

(1)   Inquiries of management and others within the organization

(2)   Analytical procedures performed as risk assessment procedures

(a)   May identify aspects of the entity of which the auditor is unaware.

(b)   May help enhance the auditor's understanding of the client's business and significant transactions since the last audit and may help the auditor to auditor identify unusual or unexpected relationships that may lead to identifying risks of material misstatement.

(c)   Yet, these procedures performed at this stage often use highly aggregated data and accordingly only provide a broad initial indication of whether a material misstatement exists.

(d)   Some smaller entities may not have interim or monthly financial information that may be used for analytical procedures. In such circumstance, the auditor may need to plan to perform analytical procedures to identify and assess risks of misstatement when an early draft of the financial statements is available.

(3)   Observation and inspection

(a)   Examples: Observing operations; inspecting documents, reports, and plant facilities.

c.   When information obtained from the auditor's previous experience is used, including that from audit procedures performed on previous audits, the auditor should determine whether changes have occurred since the previous audit that may affect their relevance to the current audit.

(1)   Examples of such information: past misstatements, nature of entity and its IC (including IC deficiencies), significant changes in entity since prior period.

(2)   The auditor may use inquiries and perform other appropriate audit procedures, such as walkthroughs of relevant systems.

d.   Discussion among engagement team: Such a discussion is required to consider the susceptibility of the financial statements to material misstatements. It consists in large part with the more experienced team members exchanging information among themselves and with those with lesser experience.

(1) This discussion may be held concurrently with the AU-C 240 required brainstorming session on fraud.

(2) The engagement partner and other key engagement team members should discuss the susceptibility of the financial statements to material misstatement (a "brainstorming session").

(3) It is not always necessary or practical to include all members in a single discussion (e.g., a multilocation audit), nor is it necessary for all members to be informed of all decisions reached in the discussion.

> **NOTE:** AU-C 240 requires such a discussion relating to fraud; the discussion presented here and the AU-C 240 discussion may be combined.

e. During planning, consider the results of the assessment of the risk of material misstatement due to fraud along with other information to identify risks of material misstatement.

2. Understanding the entity and its environment, including IC

   a. Industry, regulatory and other external factors

      (1) Examples: industry conditions, regulatory environment, relevant accounting pronouncements, legal and political environment, other external factors such as general economic conditions.

   b. Nature of entity

      (1) Refers to entity's operations, ownership, governance, types of investments, etc.
      (2) Entity's selection and application of accounting policies.
      (3) Objectives and strategies related to business risks.
      (4) Measurement and review of entity's financial performance.

3. Internal control

   a. Most, but not all, controls relevant to audit are those related to financial reporting.
   b. The auditor must obtain an understanding of the components of IC—control environment, risk assessment process, information system, control activities, and monitoring of controls.
   c. For the information system this includes

      (1) Significant classes of transactions.
      (2) Procedures (IT and manual) by which transactions are initiated, authorized recorded, processed, corrected (if necessary), transferred to general ledger, and reported in financial statements.
      (3) Related accounting records.
      (4) How information system captures significant events and conditions other than transactions.
      (5) Financial reporting process used to prepare financial statements.
      (6) Controls surrounding journal entries.

   d. For more information on internal control, see point E. later in outline.

4. Identifying and assessing the risks of material misstatement

   a. Risks should be identified at both the financial statement level and the relevant assertion level for each major class of transactions, account balance, and disclosure. To accomplish this, the auditor should

      (1) Identify risks, including relevant controls related to risks.
      (2) Assess identified risks.
      (3) Relate identified risks to what can go wrong at the assertion level.
      (4) Consider the likelihood of misstatement and whether the potential magnitude is material.

   b. For more information on identifying and assessing the risks of material statement, see point F. later in outline.

5. Risks that require special audit consideration

   a. The auditor should determine whether a "significant risk" has been identified (i.e., a risk that requires special audit consideration)

      (1) In exercising this judgment, the auditor should exclude the effects of identified controls related to the risk.
      (2) *Significant risks often relate to significant nonroutine transactions and judgmental matters.*

(a) Nonroutine transactions—transactions that are unusual, either due to size or nature and that therefore occur infrequently.

(b) Judgmental matters—may include the development of accounting estimates for which a significant measurement uncertainty exists.

(3) Routine, noncomplex transactions that are subject to systematic processing are less likely to give rise to significant risks.

b. In exercising judgment about whether a risk is significant, the auditor should consider at least

(1) Whether the risk is a risk of fraud.
(2) Whether risk is related to significant economic, accounting or other developments.
(3) Complexity of transactions.
(4) Whether the risk involves significant transactions with related parties.
(5) Degree of subjectivity of measurement.
(6) Whether risk involves significant transactions outside the normal course of business.

c. *When a significant risk exists, the auditor should obtain an understanding of the entity's relevant controls including control activities relevant to that risk, and based on that understanding, evaluate whether such controls have been suitably designed and implemented to mitigate such risks.*

d. For more information on risks that require special audit consideration see point F. later in this outline.

6. Other

a. Sometimes substantive procedures alone may not provide sufficient appropriate audit evidence—then controls must also be considered.

b. The auditor's assessment of the risks of material misstatement may change during the audit; further audit procedures should be modified as necessary.

c. For more information on identifying the risk of material misstatement see point F. below.

7. Documentation

a. Discussion of engagement team (brainstorming session).
b. Key elements of understanding of entity and its environment.
c. Identified and assessed risks of material misstatements.
d. Risks requiring special audit consideration.

E. **Internal Control** (expansion of point D.3. earlier)

1. Understanding IC assists auditor in identifying types of potential misstatements and factors that affect the risks of material misstatement, and in designing the nature, timing, and extent of further audit procedures; it may be divided into five components

a. Control environment.
b. Entity risk assessment process.
c. Information system.
d. Control activities.
e. Monitoring of controls.

2. General nature and characteristics of IC

a. Definition: A process, effected by those charged with governance, management, and other personnel, designed to provide reasonable assurance about the achievement of the entity's objectives with regard to the reliability of financial reporting, effectiveness and efficiency of operations, and compliance with applicable laws and regulations.

b. Limitations

(1) Limitations of human judgment.
(2) Collusion to circumvent controls.
(3) Management and other employee override of controls.

3. Characteristics of manual and automated elements of internal control relevant to the auditor's risk assessment

a. Benefits of IT

      (1) Consistent application of business rules and performance of complex calculations.

      (2) Enhanced timeliness, availability, and accuracy of information.

      (3) Facilitate additional analysis of information.

      (4) Enhance ability to monitor performance of entity's activities and its policies and procedures.

      (5) Reduce risk that controls will be circumvented.

      (6) Enhance ability to achieve effective segregation of duties.

  b. Risks of IT

      (1) Reliance on systems and programs.

      (2) Unauthorized access to data.

      (3) IT personnel gaining inappropriate access privileges.

      (4) Unauthorized changes to data in master files.

      (5) Unauthorized changes to systems or programs.

      (6) Failure to make necessary changes to systems.

      (7) Inappropriate manual intervention.

      (8) Potential loss of data or inability to access data as required.

  c. Manual controls may be

      (1) More suitable where judgment and discretion are required (e.g., large unusual transactions, circumstances where errors are difficult to define).

      (2) Less suitable when there is a high volume of recurring transactions and where control activities can effectively be automated.

  d. Controls relevant to an audit—*primarily* financial reporting, but operations and compliance objectives may also be relevant.

  e. Nature and extent of the understanding of relevant controls—Whether the control is capable of effectively preventing or detecting and correcting material misstatements.

      (1) Implementation of a control means that the control exists and the entity is using it.

      (2) The auditor first considers the design of the control, and if that seems proper, its implementation.

      (3) The standard then provides a detailed discussion that points out that the understanding of internal control considers all five components of internal control.

4. If the entity has an internal audit function, the auditor should obtain an understanding of its responsibilities, how it fits in the entity's organization structure, and its activities performed.

F. Identifying and Assessing the Risks of Material Misstatement (expansion of point D.4. earlier)

1. Assessment of risks of material misstatement at the financial statement level

  a. These risks relate pervasively to the financial statements as a whole and potentially affect many assertions; they may often relate to

      (1) A weak control environment, for example, sometimes due to management's

         (a) Lack of competence.

         (b) Override of controls.

  b. The auditor's understanding may raise doubts about the auditability of the financial statements, due to, for example, concerns about

      (1) Management's integrity.

      (2) Condition and reliability of entity's records that may cause the auditor to conclude that it is unlikely that sufficient appropriate audit evidence will be available.

2. Assessment of risks of material misstatement at the assertion level

  a. Obtaining an understanding of the entity is a continuous, dynamic process of gathering, updating and analyzing information throughout the audit. The understanding establishes a frame of reference for planning the audit and exercising professional judgment, for example

      (1) Assessing risks of material misstatement.

      (2) Determining materiality.

      (3) Considering appropriateness of accounting policies and financial statement disclosures.

(4) Identifying areas where special audit consideration may be necessary (e.g., related-party transactions, going concern assumption, business purpose of transactions, existence of complex and unusual transactions).

(5) Developing expectations for analytical procedures.

(6) Responding to the risk of material misstatement.

(7) Evaluating sufficiency and appropriateness of audit evidence obtained.

b. The risks of misstatement are related to classes of transactions, account balances, and disclosures

c. Financial statement assertions fit into three categories:

  (1) Assertions about classes of transactions and events for the period under audit

    (a) *Occurrence*—Transactions and events that have been recorded have occurred and pertain to the entity.

    (b) *Completeness*—All transactions and events that should have been recorded have been recorded.

    (c) *Accuracy*—Amounts and other data relating to recorded transactions and events have been recorded appropriately.

    (d) *Cutoff*—Transactions and events have been recorded in the correct accounting period.

    (e) *Classification*—Transactions and events have been recorded in the proper amounts.

  (2) Assertions about account balances at the period end

    (a) *Existence*—Assets, liabilities, and equity interests exist.

    (b) *Rights and obligations*—The entity holds or controls the rights to assets, and liabilities are the obligations of the entity.

    (c) *Completeness*—All assets, liabilities, and equity interests that should have been recorded have been recorded.

    (d) *Valuation and allocation*—Assets, liabilities, and equity interests are included in the financial statements at appropriate amounts, and any resulting valuation or allocation adjustments are appropriately recorded.

  (3) Assertions about presentation and disclosure

    (a) *Occurrence and rights and obligations*—Disclosed events, transactions, and other matters have occurred and pertain to the entity.

    (b) *Completeness*—All disclosures that should have been included in the financial statements have been included.

    (c) *Classification and understandability*—Financial information is appropriately presented and described, and disclosures are clearly expressed.

    (d) *Accuracy and valuation*—Financial and other information is disclosed fairly and in appropriate amounts.

3. *Relevant assertions*—for each material class of transactions, account balance, and presentation, the auditor must determine the relevance of each of the financial statement assertions. Identifying relevant assertions includes determining the source of likely potential misstatements.

4. The risk assessment determines the nature, timing, and extent of further audit procedures to be performed.

5. Relating controls to assertions—In making risk assessments, the auditor identifies controls that are likely to prevent or detect and correct material misstatement in specific assertions.

a. Often, several controls together may be needed to address a risk. Conversely, sometimes one control is adequate for more than one assertion (e.g., control over personnel counting physical inventory addresses existence and completeness).

  (1) Controls may directly or indirectly relate to an assertion. The more indirect, the less effective a control (e.g., a sales manager's review of a summary report may indirectly address completeness and may be less effective than matching shipping documents with billing documents).

b. Significant risks—Significant risks often relate to *nonroutine transactions* and *judgmental matters*. Routine, noncomplex transactions subject to systematic processing are less likely to give rise to significant risks.

  (1) Risks of material misstatement for significant *nonroutine transactions* arise from

    (a) Greater management intervention to specify accounting treatment.

    (b) Greater manual intervention for data collecting.

       (c) Complex calculations or accounting principles.
       (d) Nonroutine transactions may be difficult to control.
       (e) Related-party transactions.

    (2) Risks relating to *judgmental matters*

       (a) Accounting principles for accounting estimates (e.g., allowance for doubtful accounts) may be subject to differing interpretation.
       (b) Required judgment may be subjective or complex.

6. Controls related to significant risks

  a. Risks related to significant nonroutine or judgmental matters are often less likely to be subject to routine controls; the auditor considers whether and how management responds.
  b. If management has not appropriately responded by implementing controls over significant risks, the auditor must communicate to those charged with governance if the auditor believes a significant deficiency or material weakness in internal control exists.

7. Risks for which substantive procedures alone do not provide sufficient appropriate audit evidence

  a. Example: An automated sales system using the Internet.
  b. In such circumstances test of controls may be necessary in addition to substantive procedures.

8. Revision of the risk assessment

  a. During the audit, information may come to the auditor's attention that differs significantly from the information on which the risk assessment was based.
  b. Example: Tests of controls reveal system not operating effectively.
  c. This will ordinarily result in the need to modify the audit program.

9. See AU-C 330 for responses to the risk of misstatement and the financial statement and assertion levels.

G. Appendices

1. Appendix A—Provides details on matters the auditor may consider when obtaining an understanding of the industry, regulatory, and other external factors that affect the entity; the nature of the entity; objectives and strategies and related business risks; and measurement and review of the entity's financial statements.
2. Appendix B—Provides details on the five internal control components—control environment; risk assessment; information and communications systems; control activities; and monitoring.
3. Appendix C—Composed of the following examples that may indicate the existence of risks of material misstatement:

  • Operations in regions that are economically unstable
  • Operations exposed to volatile market (e.g., futures trading)
  • High degree of complex regulation
  • Going concern and liquidity issues
  • Constraints on the availability of capital and credit
  • Changes in the industry in which the entity operates
  • Changes in the supply chain
  • Developing or offering new products or services
  • Expanding into new locations
  • Changes in the entity, such as through acquisitions, etc.
  • Entities or business segments likely to be sold
  • Complex alliances and joint ventures
  • Use of off-balance-sheet finance, special-purpose entities, and other complex financing arrangements
  • Significant transactions with related parties
  • Lack of personnel with appropriate accounting and financial reporting skills
  • Change in key personnel
  • Deficiencies in internal control
  • Inconsistencies between entity's IT strategy and its business strategies
  • Changes in the IT environment and systems

- Installation of significant new IT systems related to financial planning
- Inquiries into entity's operations or financial results by regulators
- Past misstatements, history of errors, or a significant amount of adjustments at period end
- Significant amount of nonroutine or nonsystematic transactions
- Transactions recorded based on management's intent (e.g., debt refinancing, assets to be sold, classification of marketable securities)
- Application of new accounting pronouncements
- Complex processes related to accounting measurements
- Events or transactions that result in significant measurement uncertainty, including accounting estimates
- Pending litigation and contingent liabilities

AU-C 320 Materiality in Planning and Performing an Audit

A. Introduction

1. This section addresses the auditor's responsibility to apply the concept of materiality in planning and performing an audit.
2. Materiality considerations

    a. Misstatements, including omissions, are material if they could reasonably be expected to influence the economic decisions of users taken on the basis of the financial statements.
    b. Judgments about materiality are made in light of the surrounding circumstances and are affected by the size and/or nature of the misstatement.
    c. Judgments about materiality are made based on a consideration of the common financial information needs of users as a group, not specific individual users.

3. Users are assumed to

    a. Have a reasonable knowledge of business, economic activities and accounting and a willingness to study the information in the financial statements.
    b. Understand that financial statements are prepared, presented and audited to levels of materiality.
    c. Recognize the uncertainties in financial statements.
    d. Make reasonable economic decisions based on the information in the financial statements.

4. Materiality is applied by the auditor both in

    a. *Planning*/performing the audit by providing a basis for

        (1) Determining the nature and extent of risk assessment procedures.
        (2) Identifying and assessing the risks of material misstatement.
        (3) Determining the nature, timing, and extent of further audit procedures.

    b. *Evaluating* the effect of uncorrected misstatements on the financial statements and in forming the opinion in the auditor's report.

5. Materiality and audit risk—Audit risk is the risk that the auditor expresses an inappropriate audit opinion when the financial statements are materially misstated. Materiality and audit risk are considered throughout the audit, in particular when

    a. Identifying and assessing the risks of material misstatement.
    b. Determining the nature, timing, and extent of further auditor procedures.
    c. Evaluating the effect of uncorrected misstatements on the financial statements and in forming an opinion on the financial statements.

6. The circumstances related to some misstatements may cause the auditor to evaluate them as material even if they are below materiality since both size and the nature of uncorrected misstatements are considered.

    a. For example, a related-party transaction may be considered material even if the amount involved is less than the amount of materiality determined in planning the audit.

B. Objective: The objective of the auditor is to apply the concept of materiality appropriately in planning and performing the audit.

C. **Definition**

1. **Performance materiality.** The amount or amounts set by the auditor at less than materiality for the financial statements as a whole to reduce to an appropriately low level the probability that the aggregate of uncorrected and undetected misstatements exceeds materiality for the financial statements as a whole. If applicable, planning materiality also refers to the amount or amounts set by the auditor at less than the materiality level or levels for particular classes of transactions, account balances, or disclosures. Performance materiality is to be distinguished from tolerable misstatement (tolerable misstatement is discussed in AU-C 530).

D. **Requirements, application, and explanatory material**

1. The auditor should determine materiality for the financial statements as a whole. If, in a specific circumstance, one or more classes of transactions, account balances of disclosures exists with lesser amounts, also establish that amount.

   a. Using benchmarks in determining materiality—(e.g., x% of income before taxes or of net sales).

      (1) This is acceptable if materiality is based on the auditor's understanding of user needs and expectations.
      (2) The percentage used involves the exercise of professional judgment.
      (3) Example for a governmental entity benchmarks: Based on total cost or net cost relating to program activities.

   b. Materiality for governmental entities—Legislators and regulators are often the primary users of the financial statements; this influences materiality judgments.

      (1) For state or local governments the applicable financial reporting framework is often based on multiple reporting units. These units each represent an opinion unit to the auditor. The auditor is responsible for detection of material misstatements to an opinion unit within a governmental entity, but not for immaterial misstatements.

2. Determine *performance materiality* for purposes of assessing the risks of material misstatement and determine the nature, timing, and extent of further audit procedures.

   a. Performance materiality considers the fact that several individually immaterial misstatements may cause the financial statements to be materially misstated.

      (1) Performance materiality is set at a lower level to limit this risk.
      (2) Performance materiality vs. tolerable misstatements (from AU-C 530). *Performance materiality* is determined in order to address the risk that the aggregate of individually immaterial misstatements may cause the financial statements to be materially misstated and provide a margin for possible undetected misstatements. *Tolerable misstatement* is the application of performance materiality to a particular sampling procedure. Tolerable misstatement may be the same amount or an amount lower than performance materiality (for example, when the sample population is lower than the account balance).

3. As the audit progresses, materiality may be revised.
4. Documentation

   a. Materiality for the financial statements as a whole.
   b. If applicable, materiality for particular classes of transactions, account balances, or disclosures.
   c. Performance materiality.
   d. Any revision of (a) to (c) as the audit progresses.

AU-C 330 Performing Audit Procedures in Response to Assessed Risks and Evaluating the Audit Evidence Obtained

A. **Scope:** This section addresses the auditor's responsibility to design and implement responses to the risks of material misstatement identified and assessed by the auditor in accordance with AU-C 315 (*Understanding the Entity. . .*).
B. **Objective:** The objective of the auditor is to obtain sufficient appropriate audit evidence about the assessed risks of material misstatement through design and implementing appropriate responses to those risks.

C. Definitions

1. **Substantive procedure.** An audit procedure designed to detect material misstatements at the assertion level. Substantive procedures comprise tests of details (classes of transactions, account balances, and disclosures) and substantive analytical procedures.
2. **Tests of controls.** An audit procedure designed to evaluate the operating effectiveness of controls in preventing, or detecting/correcting material misstatements at the assertion level.

D. Requirements, application, and other explanatory material

1. Overall responses to address the assessed risks of material misstatement (see AU-C 315).

   a. The auditor should design and implement overall responses to the assessed risks of material misstatement at the financial statement level.

      (1) These responses may include

          (a) Emphasizing to the audit team the need to maintain professional skepticism.
          (b) Assigning more experienced staff or those with specialized skills or specialists.
          (c) Providing more supervision.
          (d) Incorporating unpredictability in further audit procedures.
          (e) Making other changes in audit procedures.

      (2) Deficiencies in the control environment may lead to high assessed risks of material misstatement at the financial statement level. Auditor responses may include

          (a) More audit procedures as of the period end (rather than interim date).
          (b) More extensive audit evidence from substantive procedures.
          (c) More locations included in the audit scope.

2. Audit procedures responsive to the assessed risks of material misstatement at the relevant assertion level.

   a. Such procedures must be designed

      (1) Examples of approaches

          (a) When risk is high

              1] Perform only substantive procedures for particular assertions (e.g., when no effective controls exist).
              2] Combine tests of controls and substantive procedures

          (b) When risk is low

              1] Substantive analytical procedures alone may provide sufficient appropriate audit evidence.

      (2) Nature, timing and extent of audit procedures

          (a) *Nature* refers to its purpose (tests of controls or substantive procedure) and its type (inspection, observation, inquiry, confirmation, recalculation, reperformance or analytical procedure).
          (b) *Timing* (at the period end or at an interim date)—ordinarily after year-end is best since the entire period can be sampled from

              1] The higher the risk of material misstatement, the more likely the auditor is to perform substantive procedures nearer to or at the period end.
              2] Certain procedures can only be performed at or after period end, including

                  a] Agreeing financial statements to accounting records.
                  b] Examining adjustments made during the course of preparing financial statements.
                  c] Procedures to respond to a risk at period end.

          (c) *Extent* (sample size)—The higher the risk of material misstatement, the greater extent of procedures the auditor is likely to perform.

      (3) Because effective controls generally reduce but do not eliminate the risk of material misstatement, tests of controls reduce but do not eliminate the need for substantive procedures. Also, substantive analytical procedures alone may not be sufficient in some cases.

b. In designing further audit procedures (i.e., tests of controls and substantive procedures) consider the reasons for the assessed risk of material misstatement at the assertion level for each material class of transactions, account balance, and disclosure, including

   (1) *Inherent risk*—the likelihood of material misstatement due to particular characteristics of the class of transactions, account balance, or disclosure.
   (2) *Control risk*—whether the risk assessment takes account of relevant controls.

3. Selecting items for testing to obtain audit evidence—overall

   a. Approaches

      (1) Selecting all items (100 percent examination)

         (a) When?

            1] Small number of large value items.
            2] Significant risk and other means do not provide sufficient appropriate audit evidence.
            3] Other cost effective circumstances.

      (2) Selecting specific items

         (b) Which ones?

            1] High value or key items.
            2] All items over a certain amount.
            3] Other.

      (3) Audit sampling—see AU-C 530.

4. Selecting items for testing to obtain audit evidence—tests of controls

   a. When are tests of controls performed?

      (1) Auditor's assessment includes an expectation that controls operate effectively, or
      (2) Substantive procedures alone cannot provide sufficient appropriate audit evidence.

   b. Nature and extent of tests of controls; the auditor should

      (1) Perform tests of controls in combination with inquiry to obtain information on operating effectiveness of controls, including

         (a) *How* control applied.
         (b) *Consistency with which applied.*
         (c) *By whom* applied, including whether the person performing the control possesses the necessary authority and competence.

      (2) Determine whether the controls tested depend upon other controls (indirect controls), and if so, also test the indirect controls.
      (3) The more an auditor depends upon operating effectiveness of a control, the more persuasive the test of controls performed should be.
      (4) Overall

         (a) Tests of controls are *performed only on controls suitably designed to prevent or detect/correct material misstatement in a relevant assertion.*
         (b) *Inquiry alone is not sufficient to test operating effectiveness of controls*; it can be combined with inspection, recalculation or reperformance to provide more assurance.
         (c) *If documentation of the performance of a control is not available, inquiry and observation* (and perhaps computer assisted audit techniques) may be the only tests available.
         (d) Some risk assessment procedures may not have been designed as test of controls, but may nevertheless provide evidence on operating effectiveness and serve as tests of controls.

            1] Inquiring about management's use of budgets.
            2] Observing management's comparison of monthly budgeted and actual expense.
            3] Inspecting reports pertaining to variances between budgeted and actual amounts.

         (e) A *dual-purpose test* is one which concurrently tests a control and is a test of details (of a transaction, balance, or disclosure).

c. Timing of test of controls

  (1) When the auditor obtains audit evidence about operating effectiveness of controls during an interim period, the auditor should obtain evidence about significant changes subsequent to that period and determine the additional audit evidence to be obtained for the remaining period; relevant factors are

  (a) Significance of the risks.
  (b) Changes in system.
  (c) Length of remaining period.
  (d) Extent auditor intends to reduce further substantive procedures based on control relevance.

d. When determining whether it is appropriate to use audit evidence about operating effectiveness obtained in previous audits, the auditor should consider

  (1) Effectiveness of other elements of IC, including the control environment, monitoring, and risk assessment.
  (2) Risks from the control.
  (3) Effectiveness of general IT controls.
  (4) Others.

e. *When using audit evidence from a previous audit on operating effectiveness, the auditor should perform audit procedures to establish the continuing relevance of that information to the current audit* (inquiry combined with observation or inspection).

  (1) *If there have been changes that matter, the auditor should tests the controls in the current audit.*
  (2) *If there have not been such changes, the auditor should test the controls at least once in every third audit* and should test some controls during each audit to avoid the possibility of testing all controls in a single audit period with no testing of controls in the subsequent two audit periods.

f. When the auditor plans to rely on controls over a *significant risk,* the auditor should test the operating effectiveness of those controls in the current period.

g. When evaluating operating effectiveness of relevant controls, the auditor should evaluate whether misstatements that have been detected by substantive procedures indicate that controls are not operating effectively. But, the absence of misstatements detected by substantive procedures does not provide audit evidence that controls related to the relevant assertion being tested are effective.

5. Selecting items for testing to obtain audit evidence—substantive procedures

a. Irrespective of the assessed risks of material misstatement, the auditor should design and perform substantive procedures for all relevant assertions related to each material class of transactions, account balance and disclosure

  (1) This is because the auditor's assessment is judgmental and may not identify all risks and because of inherent limitations of internal control.
  (2) Depending upon the circumstances, the following *may* reduce audit risk to an acceptably low level:

  (a) Only substantive analytical procedures (generally large volumes of transactions that tend to be predicable).
  (b) Only test of details.
  (c) A combination of substantive analytical procedures and tests of details.

  (3) Substantive procedures related to the financial statement closing process should be included; examples are

  (a) Agreeing or reconciling financial statements to underlying accounting records.
  (b) Examining material journal entries and other adjustments made during financial statement preparation.

  (4) Substantive procedures responsive to *significant risks:* Substantive procedures should be performed for all significant risks. When only substantive procedures are being performed (i.e., no test of controls), the procedures should include tests of details.

  (a) Example of a *significant risk*—Management under pressure to meet earnings expectations. In such a circumstance additional substantive procedures (e.g., confirming not only balances, but details of terms) may be appropriate.

  (5) When substantive procedures are performed at an interim date, the auditor should cover the remaining period by performing substantive procedures, combined with test of controls for the intervening period or further substantive procedures (if appropriate).

(a) In most cases audit evidence from a previous audit's substantive procedures provides little or no audit evidence for the current period; exceptions exist (e.g., a legal opinion in a previous audit related to the structure of a securitization).

(b) In determining whether to perform substantive analytical procedures during the intervening period the auditor should consider predictability of amount of account, relative significance, client controls, etc.

6. The auditor shall consider whether external confirmation procedures are to be performed as substantive audit procedures

   a. Confirmation procedures may be relevant audit evidence responding to assessed risks of material misstatement for

   (1) Bank balances and other information relevant to banking relationships.
   (2) Accounts receivable balances and terms.
   (3) Inventories held by third parties at warehouses or on consignment.
   (4) Property title deeds held by lawyers or financiers.
   (5) Investments held for safekeeping by third parties or purchased from stockbrokers, but not yet delivered.
   (6) Amounts due to lenders, including terms.
   (7) Accounts payable balance and terms.

   b. Confirmations are better for some assertions than others, for example: they provide less relevant audit evidence for recoverability of accounts receivable balances than they do of their existence.

7. At the conclusion of the audit the auditor should consider whether assessments of the risks of material misstatement levels at the relevant assertion level remain appropriate and whether sufficient appropriate evidence has been obtained.

8. Documentation

   a. The auditor should document

   (1) Overall response to assessed risks of material misstatement.
   (2) Linkage of those procedures with the assessed risks at the relevant assertion level.
   (3) Results of audit procedures, including conclusions where they are not otherwise clear.

   b. When audit evidence on operating effectiveness of controls was obtained in previous audits and used in this audit, document conclusions reached about relying on them.

   c. The auditors' documentation should demonstrate that the financial statements agree or reconcile with the underlying accounting records.

AU-C 402 Audit Considerations Relating to an Entity Using a Service Organization

A. Introduction

1. Scope: This section addresses the *user auditor's* responsibilities for obtaining sufficient appropriate audit evidence in an audit of the financial statements of an entity that uses one or more service organizations.

   a. A user auditor audits and reports on the financial statements of an entity that uses a service organization; the issue here is that when a service organization takes over procedures that are relevant to the internal control of the entity being audited, the auditor has certain responsibilities.

   b. This section is on using the report of a service auditor (an auditor that reports on internal controls at a service organization), not on reporting on service organization controls (that guidance is presented in AT 402).

2. Many organizations outsource aspects of business activities to "service organizations."

3. Services provided by a service organization are relevant to an audit of a user entity's financial statements when those services and controls over them affect the user entity's information. A service organization's services are likely to relate to financial reporting, but may also be relevant to other controls (e.g., safeguarding of assets). A service organization's services are part of a user entity's information system relevant to financial reporting if these services affect any of the following:

   a. The classes of transactions in the entity's operations that are significant to the entity's financial statements.

   b. The procedures within both automated and manual systems by which the entity's transactions are initiated, authorized, recorded, processed, corrected as necessary, and reported in the financial statements.

c. The related accounting records (whether electronic or manual); supporting information; and specific accounts in the entity's financial statements involved in initiating, authorizing, recording, processing, and reporting the entity's transactions. This includes the correction of incorrect information.

d. How the entity's information and communication systems capture events and conditions, other than transactions, that are significant to the financial statements.

e. The financial reporting process used to prepare the entity's financial statements, including significant accounting estimates and disclosure.

f. Controls surrounding journal entries.

4. The section does **not** apply to services that are limited to processing transactions that are specifically authorized by the entity, such as processing checking account transactions by a bank or securities transactions by a broker.

B. **Objective:** The objective of the auditor when the user entity uses the services of a service organization are

1. To obtain an understanding of the nature and significance of the services provided by the service organization and their effect on the user entity's internal control relevant to the audit sufficient to identify, assess, and respond to the risks of material misstatement.

2. Design and perform audit procedures responsive to those risks.

C. **Definitions**

1. **Complementary user entity controls.** Controls that the service organization assumes, in the design of its service, will be implemented by user entities, and which, if necessary to achieve the control objectives stated in the description of the service organization's system, are identified as such in that description.

2. **Report on management's description of a service organization's system and the suitability of the design of controls** (referred to in this section as a *type 1 report*). A report that comprises

   a. Management's description of the service organization's system.
   b. A written assertion by management of the service organization about whether, in all material respects, and based on suitable criteria

      (1) Management's description of the service organization's system fairly presents the service organization's system that was designed and implemented as of a specified date.
      (2) The controls related to the control objectives stated in management's description of the service organization's system were suitably designed to achieve those control objectives as of the specified date.

   c. A service auditor's report that expresses an opinion on the matters in b(1)-b(2).

3. **Report on management's description of a service organization's system and the suitability of the design and operating effectiveness of controls** (referred to in this section as a *type 2 report*). A report that comprises

   a. Management's description of the service organization's system.
   b. A written assertion by management of the service organization, about whether in all material respects and, based on suitable criteria,

      (1) The description of the service organization's system fairly presents the service organization's system that was designed and implemented throughout the specified period.
      (2) The controls related to the control objectives stated in the description of the service organization's system were suitably designed throughout the specified period to achieve those control objectives.
      (3) The controls related to the control objectives stated in the description of the service organization's system operated effectively throughout the specified period to achieve those control objectives.

   c. A service auditor's report that

      (1) Expresses an opinion about the matters in b(1)-b(3).
      (2) Includes a description of the service auditor's tests of controls and the results thereof.

> **NOTE:** The two primary differences between a type 1 and type 2 report are that (1) a type 2 report deals with controls over a time period (often a year) while a type 1 report deals with controls at a point in time and (2) only a type 2 report addresses operating effectiveness.

4. **Service auditor.** A practitioner who reports on controls at a service organization.

5. **Service organization.** An organization or segment of an organization that provides services to user entities that are likely to be relevant to user entities' internal control as it relates to financial reporting.

6. **Service organization's system.** The policies and procedures designed, implemented and documented by management of the service organization to provide user entities with the services covered by the service auditor's report. Management's description of the service organization's system identifies the services covered, the period to which the description relates (or in the case of a type 1 report, the date to which the description relates), the control objectives specified by management or an outside party, the party specifying the control objectives (if not specified by management), and the related controls.

7. **Subservice organization.** A service organization used by another service organization to perform some of the services provided to user entities that are relevant to those user entities' internal control over financial reporting.

8. **User auditor.** An auditor who audits and reports on the financial statements of a user entity.

9. **User entity.** An entity that uses a service organization and whose financial statements are being audited.

D. Requirements, application, and explanatory material

1. For either a type 1 and type 2 report (see definitions C.2 and C.3) a user auditor should obtain an understanding of the services provided by the service organization; this should include

   a. The nature and significance of services provided by the service organization, including their effect on the user entity's internal control.
   b. The nature and materiality of the transactions processed by the service organization.
   c. The degree of interaction between the activities of the service organization and those of the user entity.
   d. Also, if considered necessary, one or more of the following procedures:

      (1) Obtaining and reading a type 1 or type 2 report.
      (2) Contacting the service organization to obtain information.
      (3) Requesting that a service auditor be engaged to perform necessary procedures.
      (4) Visiting the service organization and performing such procedures.

2. When the user auditor's risk assessment includes an expectation that service organization controls are operating effectively, the user auditor should obtain audit evidence from one or more of the following:

   a. Obtaining and reading a type 2 report, if available.
   b. Performing appropriate test of controls at the service organization.
   c. Using another auditor to perform test of controls at the service organization on behalf of the user auditor.

3. Using a service auditor's report

   a. If a type 1 or type 2 report is to be used as audit evidence by the user auditor, the user auditor should

      (1) Evaluate whether the description of the service organization's system is as of a date or for a period that is appropriate.
      (2) Evaluate the sufficiency and appropriateness of the evidence provided by the report for understanding the user entity's internal control relevant to the audit.
      (3) Determine whether complementary user entity controls are relevant to the user entity's financial statement assertions, and, if so, whether they have been designed and implemented.

   b. A type 2 report may or may not be useful to any particular user auditor; to make this determination, the user auditor should

      (1) Evaluate whether the service auditor's report on the organization's system seems appropriate for the user auditor's purposes.
      (2) Determine whether complementary user entity controls identified by the service organization are relevant to the user entity, and if so, test their design, implementation, and operating effectiveness.
      (3) Evaluate the adequacy of the period covered by the tests of controls on which the service auditor's report is based.
      (4) Evaluate whether tests of controls performed by the service auditor are relevant to the assertions in the user entity's financial statements.

4. Reporting by the user auditor

   a. The user auditor should modify the opinion in the user auditor's report in accordance with AU-C 705 if the user auditor is unable to obtain sufficient appropriate audit evidence regarding the services provided (i.e., this situation is usually due to a scope limitation).

b. The user auditor should **not** refer to the work of a service auditor in an audit report with an unmodified opinion.

c. If reference to the work of a service auditor is relevant to an understanding of a modification of the user auditor's opinion, the user auditor's report should indicate such reference does not diminish the auditor's responsibility.

5. The user auditor should inquire of management of the user entity about whether the service organization has reported to the user entity, or whether the user entity is otherwise aware of any fraud, noncompliance with laws and regulations, or uncorrected misstatements affecting the financial statements of the entity.

a. If so, the user auditor should evaluate how such matters affected the nature, timing, and extent of further auditor procedures, including the effect on the user auditor's audit report.

AU-C 450 Evaluation of Misstatements Identified During the Audit

A. Introduction

1. Scope: This section addresses the auditor's responsibility to evaluate the effect of identified misstatements on the audit and uncorrected misstatements, if any, on the financial statements.
2. Note that this section deals completely with evaluating misstatements identified during the audit. AU-C 320 presents overall information on materiality and on using materiality for planning purposes.

B. Objective: The objective of the auditor is to evaluate (1) the effect of identified misstatements on the audit and (2) the effect of uncorrected misstatements, if any, on the financial statements.

C. Definitions

1. **Misstatement.** A difference between the amount, classification, presentation, or disclosure of a reported financial statement item and the amount, classification, presentation, or disclosure that is required for the item to be in accordance with the applicable financial reporting framework. Misstatements can arise from error or fraud. Misstatements also include those adjustments of amounts, classifications, presentations, or disclosures that, in the auditor's judgment, are necessary for the financial statements to be presented fairly, in all material respects.

    a. **Factual misstatements.** Misstatements about which there is no doubt.
    b. **Judgmental misstatements.** Differences arising from the judgments of management concerning accounting estimates that the auditor considers unreasonable or the selection or application of accounting policies that the auditor considers inappropriate.
    c. **Projected misstatements.** The auditor's best estimate of misstatements in populations, involving the projection of misstatements identified in audit samples to the entire population from which the samples were drawn. For example, if statistical sampling was used with receivables, the difference between auditor estimated total audited value and the book value of receivables is the projected misstatement.

2. **Uncorrected misstatements.** Misstatements that the auditor has accumulated during the audit and that have not been corrected.

D. Requirements, application, and other explanatory material

1. Accumulation of identified misstatements: The auditor should do this during the audit, except for those that are clearly trivial.

    a. If there is any uncertainty about whether an item is clearly trivial, it is not.

2. The auditor should determine whether the overall audit strategy and audit plan need to be revised based on the nature of identified misstatements and as the aggregate of misstatements accumulated during the audit approaches materiality.
3. Communications and correction of misstatements

    a. On a timely basis the auditor should communicate all misstatements (other than those that are clearly trivial) to an appropriate level of management and ask management to correct them.
    b. If management has corrected misstatements that were detected, the auditor should perform additional audit procedures to determine whether misstatements remain.
    c. If management refuses to correct some or all of the misstatements communicated, the auditor should obtain an understanding of management's reason and should evaluate whether the financial statements as a whole are free from material misstatement.

   d. Other

      (1) A law or regulation may restrict the auditor's communication of certain misstatements (legal advice may need to be sought).

      (2) When an auditor has sampled a population and arrived at a projected misstatement for the population, that auditor may request management to examine the population to find misstatements.

4. Evaluating the effect of uncorrected misstatements

   a. Prior to evaluating the uncorrected misstatements, the auditor should reassess materiality to determine that its level is still considered appropriate.

   b. In evaluating the materiality of uncorrected misstatements individually and in total, the auditor should consider both the *size* and *nature* of the misstatements. The auditor should also consider the effect of uncorrected misstatements from prior periods.

      (1) Evaluating the effect of uncorrected misstatements

         (a) Information obtained during the audit may require the auditor to revise the materiality for the audit.

         (b) If an individual misstatement is material, it is unlikely that it can be offset by other misstatements (e.g., a material overstatement of sales should not be offset against a material overstatement of expenses).

            1] But a classification misstatement on one balance sheet account may be offset by another balance sheet account misstatement if the totals are small in comparison to the balance sheet and the income is not affected (nor any key ratios).

         (c) Determining whether a misstatement is material involves qualitative considerations

            1] The effect on key ratios may be considered.

            2] Circumstances may cause the auditor to evaluate misstatements as material, even if they are lower than materiality of financial statements as a whole. The following are examples (the standard itself provides 20 illustrations):

               a] Affects compliance with regulatory requirements or compliance with debt covenants.

               b] Masks a change in earnings or other trends.

               c] Affects ratios used to evaluate financial position, results of operations, or cash flows.

               d] Has offsetting effects of individually significant, but different misstatements.

               e] Currently immaterial, expected to become material.

               f] Indicates a motivation of management to bias reporting.

      (2) For a governmental entity, the evaluation of whether a misstatement is material is also affected by legislation or regulation and additional responsibilities for the auditor to report other matters, including, for example, fraud.

5. Documentation should include

   a. Amount below which misstatements would be regarded as clearly trivial.

   b. All misstatements accumulated during the audit other than those that are clearly trivial and whether they have been corrected.

   c. The auditor's conclusion about whether uncorrected misstatements are material individually or in aggregate, and the basis for that conclusion; it may take into account.

      (1) Aggregate effect of uncorrected misstatements.

      (2) Whether the material level(s) have been exceeded.

      (3) Effect of uncorrected misstatements on key ratios or trends and compliance with legal, regulatory and contractual requirements (e.g., debt covenants).

AU-C 500 Audit Evidence

A. Introduction

1. This section explains what constitutes audit evidence and addresses the auditor's responsibility to design and perform audit procedures to obtain sufficient appropriate audit evidence to be able to draw reasonable conclusions on which to base the audit opinion. Other sections (e.g., AU-C 570 on going concern) address specific aspects of audit evidence for audits.

B. **Objective:** The objective of the auditor is to design and perform audit procedures in such a way to enable the auditor to obtain sufficient appropriate audit evidence to be able to draw reasonable conclusions on which to base the auditor's opinion.

C. **Definitions**

1. **Accounting records.** The records of initial accounting entries and supporting records, such as checks and records of electronic fund transfers; invoices; contracts; the general and subsidiary ledgers, journal entries and other adjustments to the financial statements that are not reflected in journal entries; and records such as work sheets and spreadsheets supporting cost allocations, computations, reconciliations, and disclosures.

2. **Appropriateness (of audit evidence).** The measure of the quality of audit evidence; that is, its relevance and its reliability in providing support for the conclusions on which the auditor's opinion is based.

3. **Audit evidence.** Information used by the auditor in arriving at the conclusions on which the auditor's opinion is based. Audit evidence includes both information contained in the accounting records underlying the financial statements and other information.

4. **Management's specialist.** An individual or organization possessing expertise in a field other than accounting or auditing, whose work in that field is used by the entity to assist the entity in preparing the financial statements.

5. **Sufficiency (of audit evidence).** The measure of the quantity of audit evidence. The quantity of the audit evidence needed is affected by the auditor's assessment of the risks of material misstatement and also by the quality of such audit evidence.

D. **Requirements, selected application, and other explanatory material**

1. The auditor should design and perform audit procedures that are appropriate in the circumstances for the purpose of obtaining sufficient appropriate audit evidence.

   a. Sufficient appropriate audit evidence

   (1) Audit evidence is cumulative and is primarily obtained from audit procedures performed during the audit.

      (a) It may, however, include information from other sources, such as previous audits when the auditor establishes its continued relevance to the current audit.

      (b) Audit *procedures* to obtain audit *evidence* include inspection, observation, confirmation, recalculation, reperformance, and analytical procedures. Inquiry may provide important audit evidence, but alone ordinarily does not provide sufficient audit evidence.

   (2) Sufficiency is a measure of the quantity of audit evidence and is affected by assessed risks of misstatement (the higher the risks, the more evidence needed) and the quality of audit evidence.

   (3) Appropriateness measures the quality of audit evidence—its relevance and its reliability in providing support for audit conclusion; appropriateness is influenced by its source and nature and is dependent on the individual circumstances.

   b. Sources of audit evidence

   (1) *Accounting records* (e.g., reperforming accounting procedures, reconciling information). Accounting records alone do not provide sufficient appropriate evidence.

   (2) More assurance is ordinarily obtained from consistent audit evidence from different sources or of a different nature than from items of audit evidence considered individually

      (a) Example: Corroborating information from an independent source may increase the assurance the auditor obtains from audit evidence generated internally such as from accounting records, minutes of meetings, or a management representation.

         1] Evidence from independent sources includes confirmations from third parties, analysts' reports, and comparable data about competitors (benchmarking data).

   c. Audit procedures for obtaining audit evidence

   (1) Audit evidence is obtained by performing

      (a) Risk assessment procedures.

      (b) *Further audit procedures—tests of controls, and substantive procedures (tests of details and substantive analytical procedures).*

   (2) Types of procedures

(a) Inspection—records or documents, assets.
(b) Observation—watching a process or procedure (e.g., observing inventory counting or the performance of control activities).
(c) External confirmations.
(d) Recalculation—checking mathematical accuracy.
(e) Reperformance—auditor's independent execution of procedures or controls that were originally performed as part of the entity's IC.
(f) Analytical procedures—evaluations of financial information made by a study of plausible relationships.
(g) Inquiry—written or oral.

2. When designing and performing audit procedures, the auditor should consider the relevance and reliability of the information to be used as audit evidence.

a. Relevance—logical connection with or bearing upon the assertion under consideration.
b. Reliability—Generalizations (for which there are exceptions)

(1) The reliability of audit evidence is increased when it is obtained from *independent sources* outside the entity.
(2) The reliability of audit evidence that is generated internally is increased when the related *controls are effective*, including those over its preparation and maintenance.
(3) Audit evidence *obtained directly by the auditor* (for example, observation of the application of a control) is more reliable than audit evidence obtained indirectly or by inference (for example, inquiry about the application of a control).
(4) Audit evidence in *documentary* form, whether paper, electronic, or other medium, is *more reliable than evidence obtained orally* (for example, a contemporaneously written record of a meeting is more reliable than a subsequent oral representation of the matters discussed).
(5) Audit evidence provided by *original documents* is more reliable than audit evidence provided by photocopies, facsimiles, or documents that have been filmed, digitized, or otherwise transformed into electronic form, the reliability of which may depend on the controls over their preparation and maintenance.

> **NOTE:** Know these five principles that in general make audit evidence more reliable: (1) independent sources, (2) effective controls, (3) directly obtained by auditor, (4) documentary, (5) original documents.

3. If information to be used as audit evidence has been prepared using the work of a *management's specialist*, the auditor should, to the extent necessary, (1) *evaluate that specialist's competence*, capabilities and objectivity, (2) obtain an *understanding of that specialist's work* and (3) evaluate the *appropriateness of that specialist's work* as audit evidence for the relevant assertion.

a. In the auditing standards, the term "specialist" relates to an individual with expertise in a field other than accounting or auditing (e.g., actuarial calculations, valuations or engineering data).
b. For guidance on the auditor's specialist see outline of AU-C 620 (specialists hired by auditors as contrasted to by management). The guidance for management vs. auditor specialist is similar. But note that the auditor must be *particularly concerned about the objectivity of management's specialist*. Also, it is less likely there will be a written agreement between the auditor and management's specialist.

4. If audit evidence from one source is inconsistent with that from another or the auditor doubts the reliability of information to be used as audit evidence, the auditor should determine necessary modifications to audit procedures.

AU-C 501 Audit Evidence—Specific Considerations for Selected Items

A. **Scope:** This section addresses specific considerations by the auditor in obtaining sufficient appropriate audit evidence, including certain aspects of (1) investments in securities and derivative instruments; (2) inventory; (3) litigation, claims, and assessments; and (4) segment information.

B. **Objective:** The objective of the auditor is to obtain sufficient appropriate audit evidence for

1. Valuation of securities and derivative instruments;
2. Existence and condition of inventory;
3. Completeness of litigation, claims and assessments;

4. Presentation and disclosure of segment information in accordance with the applicable financial reporting framework.

C. Requirements, selected application, and other explanatory material

1. Investments in securities and derivative instruments

    a. Valuation of *investments in securities* valued based on investee's financial results (excluding investments accounted for using the equity method of accounting)

        (1) The auditor should obtain sufficient appropriate audit evidence as follows:

            (a) Obtain and read available financial statements of investee and whether the associated audit report is satisfactory for this purpose.

            (b) If investee's financial statements are not audited, or the audit report is not satisfactory, apply or request the investor company to arrange with the investee to have another to apply, appropriate auditing procedures.

            (c) Obtain sufficient appropriate audit evidence to support any amounts that are not recognized in the investee's financial statements or fair values of assets that are materially different from the investee's carrying amounts.

            (d) If the difference between the financial statement period of the company and the investee has or could have a material effect on the financial statements, determine that it has been properly handled.

        (2) If the auditor is unable to obtain sufficient appropriate audit evidence, it may result in a modified audit report (e.g., a scope limitation resulting in either a qualified opinion or a disclaimer may be appropriate).

    b. Investments in *derivative instruments* and securities measured or disclosed at fair value

        (1) The auditor should

            (a) Determine whether the applicable financial reporting framework specifies a method to be used to determine fair value.

            (b) Evaluate whether the determination is consistent with the specified valuation method.

        (2) If estimates of fair value of derivative instruments or securities are obtained from broker-dealers or other third party sources based on proprietary valuation models, the auditor should understand the method used in developing the estimate and consider whether assistance is needed from a specialist or on using a service organization.

        (3) If derivative instruments or securities are valued using a valuation model, the auditor should obtain evidence supporting management's assertions about fair value determined using the model.

        (4) Impairment losses: The auditor should evaluate management's conclusion about the need for impairment loss for a decline in market value and obtain sufficient appropriate audit evidence supporting the amount.

        (5) Unrealized appreciation or depreciation: The auditor should obtain sufficient appropriate audit evidence about the amount of unrealized appreciation or depreciation in the fair value of a derivative that is recognized or disclosed because of the ineffectiveness of a hedge.

2. Inventory

    a. *If inventory is material* to the financial statements, the *auditor should obtain sufficient appropriate audit evidence* regarding the existence and condition of inventory by

        (1) *Attending physical inventory counting* (hereafter, the count), unless impracticable, to

            (a) Evaluate management's instructions and procedures for recording and controlling results of the count.

            (b) Observe the performance of management's count procedures.

            (c) Inspect the inventory.

            (d) Perform test counts.

        (2) Performing audit procedures over final inventory records to determine whether they accurately reflect the count

            (a) If the count is at a date other than the date of financial statements, the auditor should also obtain audit evidence about whether changes in inventory between the count date and the date of the financial statements are recorded properly.

      (b) If the auditor is unable to attend the physical inventory counting due to unforeseen circumstances, the auditor should make or observe some physical counts on an alternative date and perform audit procedures on intervening transactions.

      (c) If attendance at the count is impracticable, the auditor should perform alternative audit procedures regarding existence and condition of inventory; if this is not possible the auditor should modify the auditor's report (e.g., this probably represents a scope limitation, and a qualified opinion or a disclaimer of opinion may be appropriate).

      (d) If inventory under the custody and control of a third party is **material** (e.g., inventory in a public warehouse), the auditor should obtain sufficient appropriate audit evidence regarding existence and condition by performing one or both of the following:

          1] Request confirmation of quantities and condition.
          2] Perform inspection or other appropriate audit procedures.

  b. If an *outside inventory-taking firm* performs the count, the auditor must still obtain sufficient appropriate audit evidence that an accurate count is taken.

3. Litigation, claims and assessments

  a. The auditor should design and perform audit procedures to identify litigation, claims and assessments (hereafter, litigation) that could give rise to a risk of material misstatement, including

    (1) Inquiry of management and where applicable, others within the company, including in-house legal counsel.
    (2) Obtaining from management a description and evaluation of litigation from the date of the financial statements to the date the information is furnished.
    (3) Review minutes of meetings of those charged with governance, and correspondence between the company and its external legal counsel.
    (4) Review legal expense accounts.

  b. For actual or potential litigation identified in a., the auditor should obtain audit evidence on the

    (1) Period in which the underlying cause of legal action occurred.
    (2) Probability of an unfavorable outcome.
    (3) Amount or range of potential loss.

  c. Unless audit procedures required by a. and b. above indicate that no actual or potential material claims or assessments exist, the auditor should, in addition to the procedures required by other SAS, seek direct communication with the company's external legal counsel. This should be done through a letter of inquiry, prepared by management and sent by the auditor, requesting the company's external legal counsel to communicate directly with the auditor.

    (1) When the company's in-house counsel has the primary responsibility for litigation, the auditor should seek direct communication with that counsel through a similar letter of inquiry. Audit evidence obtained from in-house counsel is not, however, a substitute for direct communication with external legal counsel.

  d. The auditor should request the company's legal counsel to inform the auditor of litigation that counsel is aware of, together with an assessment of the outcome of the litigation. The letter of inquiry should include

    (1) Identification of company.
    (2) List prepared by management (or request by management that legal counsel prepare the list) for which counsel has devoted substantive attention.

      (a) Request that legal counsel furnish information relating thereto.

    (3) List prepared by management of unasserted claims probable of assertion and, if asserted, at least a reasonable possibility of an unfavorable of outcome.

      (a) Request that legal counsel comment on items.
      (b) Request that legal counsel confirm its understanding of requests and any reasons for limitations in its request.

(4) Other

    (a) A letter of inquiry to a company's legal counsel is the auditor's primary means of obtaining corroboration of the information furnished by management concerning litigation, claims, assessments and unasserted claims.

    (b) While audit evidence obtained from the company's internal legal counsel or legal department may provide the auditor with the necessary corroboration, it is not a substitute for information external counsel refuses to furnish.

(5) In certain circumstances, the auditor may judge it necessary to *meet with* the company's legal counsel to discuss likely outcomes of litigation or claims; examples are

    (a) The auditor determines that the matter is a significant risk.

    (b) The matter is complex.

    (c) A disagreement exists between management and external legal counsel.

> **NOTE:** Normally such meetings require management's permission and are held with a representative of management in attendance.

e. The auditor should modify the opinion in the auditor's report when external legal counsel refuses to respond appropriately and the auditor is unable to obtain sufficient appropriate audit evidence by performing alternative audit procedures or management refuses to give the auditor permission to communicate with external legal counsel.

(1) This is ordinarily a scope limitation that will result in either a qualified opinion or a disclaimer of opinion.

f. Legal counsel may be unable to respond concerning the likelihood of an unfavorable outcome of litigation, claims, and assessments, or the amount or range of potential loss, because of inherent uncertainties.

(1) In such circumstances, the auditor may conclude that the financial statements are affected by an uncertainty concerning the outcome of a future event (this may result in addition of an emphasis of matter paragraph being added to the audit report).

4. Segment information

a. The auditor should obtain sufficient appropriate audit evidence on segment information in accordance with the applicable financial reporting framework by

(1) Obtaining an understanding of the methods used by management in determining segment information, and

    (a) Evaluating whether such methods are in accordance with the applicable financial reporting framework, and

    (b) Where appropriate, testing the application of such methods.

(2) Performing analytical procedures or other audit procedures appropriate in the circumstances.

AU-C 505 External Confirmations

A. Introduction

1. Scope: This section addresses the auditor's use of external confirmation procedures to obtain audit evidence. It does not address inquiries regarding litigation, claims, and assessments (included in AU-C 501).

2. AU-C 500 indicates that the reliability of audit evidence is influenced by is source and nature and is dependent on the individual circumstances under which it is obtained. It includes the following generalizations:

a. Audit evidence is more reliable when it is obtained from independent sources outside the entity.

b. Audit evidence obtained directly by the auditor is more reliable than audit evidence obtained indirectly or by inference.

c. Audit evidence is more reliable when it exists in documentary form, whether paper, electronic, or other medium.

Accordingly, depending upon the circumstances, external confirmations may be more reliable than evidence generated internally by the entity.

B. Objective: The objective of the auditor, when using external confirmation procedures, is to design and perform such procedures to obtain relevant and reliable audit evidence.

C. Definitions

1. **External confirmation.** Audit evidence obtained as a direct written response to the auditor from a third party (the confirming party), either in paper form or by electronic or other medium (for example, through the auditor's direct access to information held by a third party).

   a. The auditor's direct access to information held by the confirming party may meet the definition of an external confirmation when, for example, the auditor is provided by the confirming party with the electronic access codes or information necessary to access a secure Web site where data that addresses the subject matter of the confirmation is held.

   b. The auditor's access to information held by the confirming party may also be facilitated by a third party provider. Where access codes or information necessary to access data held by a third party is provided to the auditor by management (i.e., not by the confirming party), evidence obtained by the auditor from access to such information does not meet the definition of an external confirmation.

2. **Positive confirmation request.** A request that the confirming party respond directly to the auditor providing the requested information or indicating whether the confirming party agrees or disagrees with the information in the request.

3. **Negative confirmation request.** A request that the confirming party respond directly to the auditor only if the confirming party disagrees with the information provided in the request.

4. **Nonresponse.** A failure of the confirming party to respond, or fully respond, to a positive confirmation request, or a confirmation request returned undelivered.

5. **Exception.** A response that indicates a difference between information requested to be confirmed, or contained in the entity's records, and information provided by the confirming party.

D. Requirements, application, and other explanatory material

1. External confirmation procedures

   a. When using external confirmation procedures, the auditor should maintain control over external confirmation requests by

      (1) Determining the information to be confirmed or requested.

      (2) Selecting the appropriate confirming party.

         (a) An appropriate confirming party is a party the auditor believes is knowledgeable about the information to be confirmed; for example, a financial institution official who is knowledgeable about the transactions (not management in general).

      (3) Designing the confirmation requests, including determining that requests are properly directed to the appropriate confirming party and provide for being responded to directly to the auditor.

         (a) A positive external confirmation request asks the confirming party to reply in all cases (either indicating agreement or disagreement) or by asking the confirming party to provide information.

         (b) Not including the amount (or other information) in a positive external confirmation request and asking the confirming party to fill in the amount may decrease the risk that the confirming party may reply to the confirmation request without verifying that the information is correct. This is a "blank" confirmation request; a limitation is that it may result in lower response rates due to additional effort required from the confirming parties.

         (c) The auditor should determine that requests are properly addressed before they are sent out. For example, the auditor may verify e-mail addresses supplied by management.

      (4) Sending the requests, including follow-up requests when applicable, to the confirming party.

2. Management's refusal to allow the auditor to perform confirmation procedures

   a. If management refuses to allow the auditor to perform external confirmation procedures, the auditor should

(1) Inquire as to reasons.

(2) Evaluate the implications of the refusal, including the risk of fraud and the effect on the nature, timing, and extent of other audit procedures.

(3) Perform alternative audit procedures.

b. If the auditor concludes that management's refusal is unreasonable or the auditor is unable to obtain relevant and reliable evidence from alternative audit procedures, the auditor should communicate this to those charged with governance and also should determine the implications on the audit opinion.

3. Results of the external confirmation procedures

a. Reliability of responses to confirmation requests—If the auditor doubts reliability, the auditor should obtain further audit evidence and evaluate the implications for the assessment of the relevant risks of material misstatement.

b. Risks of the confirmation process

(1) Information obtained not from an authentic source.

(2) Respondent not knowledgeable about information confirmed.

(3) Integrity of information compromised.

c. Responses received electronically (e.g., fax or email) involve risks relating to reliability because the proof of origin or identity of the confirming party may be difficult to establish and alterations difficult to detect.

(1) In some cases the auditor may determine reliability is acceptable by validating the respondent (e.g., by telephone).

d. Nonresponses—The auditor should perform *alternative audit procedures* (e.g., vouch support for receivable). If there are no such adequate alternative procedures the auditor should determine the implications for the audit and auditor's opinion.

e. Exceptions—The auditor should investigate to determine whether they are indicative of misstatements.

4. Negative confirmations

a. Provide less persuasive audit evidence than positive confirmations. The auditor *should not use negative confirmation requests as the sole substantive audit procedure* to address an assessed risk of material misstatement, unless *all* of the following procedures are present:

(1) Assessed risk of material misstatement is low and the auditor has obtained sufficient appropriate audit evidence regarding the operating effectiveness of controls related to the assertion.

(2) Population of items subject to negative confirmation procedures comprises a large number of small, homogeneous account balances, transactions, or conditions.

(3) A very low exception rate is expected.

(4) The auditor is not aware of circumstances or conditions that would cause recipients of negative confirmation requests to disregard such requests.

b. Failure to receive a response to a negative confirmation request does not explicitly indicate receipt by the intended confirming party or verification of the accuracy of the information contained in the request.

5. Evaluating the evidence obtained

a. The auditor may categorize results as

(1) A response by the appropriate confirming party indicating agreement or providing requested information without exception.

(2) A response deemed unreliable.

(3) A nonresponse.

(4) A response indicating an exception.

b. The auditor must determine whether sufficient appropriate audit evidence has been obtained or whether further audit evidence is necessary.

c. Restrictive language in a response does not necessarily invalidate the reliability of the response—it depends on the nature and substance of the restrictive language.

AU-C 510 Opening Balances—Initial Audit Engagements, Including Reaudit Engagements

A. Introduction: This section addresses the auditor's responsibilities relating to opening balances in an initial audit, including a reaudit engagement. In addition to financial statement amounts, opening balances include matters requiring disclosure that existed at the beginning of the period, such as contingencies and commitments.

B. Objective

1. The objective of the auditor in conducting an initial audit, including a reaudit, is to obtain sufficient appropriate audit evidence regarding opening balances about whether

   a. Opening balances contain misstatements that materially affect the current period's financial statements.
   b. Appropriate accounting policies reflected in the opening balances have been consistently applied in the current period's financial statements, or changes thereto are appropriately accounted for and adequately presented.

C. Definitions

1. **Initial audit engagement.** An engagement in which either (1) the financial statements for the prior period were not audited or (2) the financial statements for the prior period were audited by a predecessor auditor.
2. **Opening balances.** Those account balances that exist at the beginning of the period. Opening balances are based upon the closing balances of the prior period and reflect the effects of transactions and events of prior periods and accounting policies applied in the prior period Opening balances also include matters requiring disclosure that existed at the beginning of the period such as contingencies and commitments.
3. **Predecessor auditor.** The auditor from a different audit firm who has reported on the most recent audited financial statements or was engaged to perform but did not complete an audit of the financial statements.
4. **Reaudit.** An initial audit engagement to audit a financial statements that have been previously audited and reported on by a predecessor auditor.

D. Requirements, application, and other explanatory material

1. Audit procedures

   a. The auditor should read the most recent financial statements, if any, and the predecessor auditor's report for information relevant to opening balances, including disclosures and consistency in the application of accounting policies
   b. Consideration when there is a predecessor auditor

      (1) Request management to authorize the predecessor to allow a review of the predecessor auditor's audit documentation and for the predecessor auditor to respond fully to inquires by the auditor to obtain information for planning and performing the engagement

         (a) This may occur either before or after accepting the engagement
         (b) The predecessor may request a consent and acknowledgement letter from the client to reduce misunderstandings about the scope of communications
         (c) The predecessor ordinarily makes himself/herself available to the auditor and makes available for review certain of the working papers.

            • The predecessor determines which working papers are to be made available for review and which may be copied. Ordinarily, the following are made available: documentation of planning, risk assessment procedures, further audit procedures, audit results, and other matters of continuing significance (e.g., uncorrected misstatements, analysis of balance sheet accounts, contingencies).
            • The predecessor decides whether to make available audit documentation. The extent made available, if any, is a matter of judgment. The predecessor's denial or limitation of access may affect the auditor's assessment of risk regarding opening balances, nature, timing and extent of procedures on opening balances and consideration of consistency of accounting principle use.

         (d) Before permitting access to working papers, the predecessor may obtain written communications from the auditor regarding the use of the audit documentation.

   c. Opening balances

(1) The auditor should obtain sufficient appropriate evidence on whether opening balances contain misstatements that could materially affect current financial statements by

    (a) Determining whether prior period's closing balances have been correctly brought forward

    (b) Determining whether opening balances reflect appropriate accounting policies

    (c) Evaluating whether audit procedures performed in the current period provide evidence relevant to the opening balance and performing one or both of

- When prior year financial statements were audited, review predecessor auditor's audit documentation on opening balances
- Performing specific audit procedures to obtain evidence on opening balances

    (d) Example of additional audit procedures the auditor may perform for opening inventory

- Observe a current inventory count and reconcile to opening inventory quantities
- Perform audit procedures on the valuation of opening inventory items.
- Perform audit procedures on gross profit and cutoff.

(2) The auditor should perform additional procedures on opening balances when those opening balances contain misstatements. The auditor should

    (a) Determine the effect on the current period's financial statements

    (b) Communicate the misstatements to management and those charged with governance as per AU-C 260 requirements.

  d. Consistency of accounting policies—The auditor should obtain sufficient appropriate audit evidence about consistency of application of accounting principles

  e. Relevant information in the predecessor auditor's report—consider information if the report was modified

  f. If the auditor becomes aware of information that leads him/her to believe that the financial statements reported upon by the predecessor may require revision, the auditor should request that the client so inform the predecessor and arrange for the three parties to discuss the matter

(1) If the client refuses to inform the predecessor that the prior period financial statements may need revision or if the auditor is not satisfied with the resolution, the auditor should evaluate whether to withdraw from the engagement, but if law or regulation does not allow this, the auditor should disclaim an opinion on the financial statements.

2. Audit conclusions and reporting

  a. The auditor should not make reference to the report or work of the predecessor as the basis, in part, for the auditor's own opinion

  b. Opening balances

(1) If unable to obtain sufficient appropriate audit evidence express a qualified opinion or a disclaimer of opinion (scope limitation)

(2) If the opening balances contain a material misstatement that affects this period's financial statements, the auditor should express a qualified opinion or an adverse opinion, as appropriate (based on pervasiveness of misstatement)

  c. Consistency of accounting principles

(1) If the current period's accounting policies are not consistently applied or accounting policies not properly accounted for express a qualified opinion or an adverse opinion as per AU-C 705

  d. Modification to the opinion in the predecessor auditor's report

(1) If this matter remains relevant to the current period, modify the current opinion as per AU-C 705

AU-C 520 Analytical Procedures

A. Scope: This section addresses

1. The auditor's use of analytical procedures as substantive procedures (substantive analytical procedures).

2. The auditor's responsibility to perform analytical procedures near the end of the audit that assist the auditor when forming an overall conclusion on the financial statements.

NOTE: AU-C 315 and AU-C 330 address the use of analytical procedures as risk assessment procedures (which may be referred to as analytical procedures used to plan the audit).

B. **Objectives:** The objectives of the auditor are to

1. Obtain relevant and reliable audit evidence when using substantive analytical procedures.
2. Design and perform analytical procedures near the end of the audit that assist the auditor in forming an overall conclusion as to whether the financial statements are consistent with the auditor's understanding of the entity.

C. **Definition**

1. **Analytical procedures.** Evaluations of financial information through analysis of plausible relationships among both financial and nonfinancial data. Analytical procedures also encompass such investigation, as is necessary, of identified fluctuations or relationships that are inconsistent with other relevant information or that differ from expected values by a significant amount.

    a. Analytical procedures include comparisons of the entity's financial information with, for example,

        (1) Prior period information (e.g., 20X1 sales with 20X0 sales).
        (2) Anticipated results (e.g., budgets, forecasts).
        (3) Similar industry information (e.g., ratio of sales to accounts receivable compared with industry averages).
        (4) Relationships among elements of financial information (e.g., such as gross margin percentages).
        (5) Financial and *nonfinancial* information (e.g., payroll costs compared to number of employees).

    NOTE: Know the above 5 types of information used for analytical procedures.

    b. A basic premise underlying the application of analytical procedures is that plausible relationships among data may reasonably be expected to exist and continue in the absence of known conditions to the contrary. The presence of an unexpected relationship may provide important evidence when appropriately scrutinized.

2. **Scanning.** A type of analytical procedure involving the auditor's use of professional judgment to review accounting data to identify significant or unusual items.

D. **Requirements, application, and other explanatory material**

1. When performing *substantive* analytical procedures the auditor should

    a. *Determine suitability* of particular analytical procedures for addressing given assertions by considering the assessed risks of material misstatement and tests of details to be performed (if any).

        (1) As more persuasive audit evidence is desired, more predictable relationships are necessary to develop the expectations.

            (a) Expectations that are more predictable

                1] A stable environment rather than a dynamic or unstable environment.
                2] Income statement accounts rather than balance sheet accounts.
                3] Not subject to management discretion rather than those subject to management discretion.

        (2) Substantive analytical procedures are generally more applicable to large volumes of transactions that tend to be predictable over time.
        (3) Substantive analytical procedures may be suitable when tests of details are also performed:

            (a) Example: Aging customers' accounts (analytical procedure) in addition to examining subsequent cash receipts (tests of details) to determine collectability of receivables.

    b. *Evaluate the reliability* of data from which the auditor's expectation of recorded amounts or ratios is developed.
        (1) Both the source and nature need to be considered.

(2) The auditor may consider testing operating effectiveness of controls over the information used for substantive analytical procedures; when controls operate effectively, the auditor may place greater confidence in the reliability of the results of analytical procedures.

(3) When expectations are developed at a detailed level, the auditor generally has a greater chance of detecting misstatements of a given amount than when broad comparisons are used (e.g., monthly amounts may be more effective than annual amounts).

c. *Develop an expectation* of recorded amounts (or ratios) and evaluate whether the expectation is sufficiently precise (considering whether substantive analytical procedures are to be performed alone or in combination with tests of details) to identify a material misstatement.

(1) More precise expectation examples

(a) Comparing gross margins from one period to another vs. comparing discretionary expenses, such as research or advertising.

(b) Analytical procedures applied to financial information on individual sections of an operation or to financial components of a diversified entity vs. the financial statements of the entity as a whole.

d. *Compare the recorded amounts (or ratios) to expectations* and determine the amount of any difference from expected values that is acceptable without further investigation.

(1) The amount is influenced by materiality and the desired level of assurance.

(2) As the assessed risk increases, the amount of difference considered acceptable without investigation decreases in order to achieve the desired level of persuasive evidence.

2. Analytical procedures that assist when *forming an overall conclusion* (those performed near the end of the audit)

a. These are intended to corroborate audit evidence obtained during the audit to assist the auditor in forming an overall conclusion as to whether the financial statements are consistent with the auditor's understanding of the entity.

b. These may include reading the financial statements and considering

(1) The adequacy of evidence gathered in response to unusual or unexpected balances identified during the audit.

(2) Unusual or unexpected balances or relationships that were not previously identified.

c. These procedures may be similar to those that would be used as risk assessment procedures (see AU-C 315 and AU-C 330).

3. Investigating results of analytical procedures

a. If analytical procedures identify fluctuations or relationships that are inconsistent with other relevant information, the auditor should investigate such differences by *inquiring of management* and *obtaining appropriate audit evidence relevant to management responses* and *performing other audit procedures as necessary* in the circumstances.

(1) Audit evidence relevant to management's response may be obtained by evaluating those responses, taking into account the auditor's understanding of the entity and its environment and with other audit evidence.

(2) The need to perform other audit procedures may arise when, for example, management is unable to provide an explanation, or the explanation, together with the audit evidence obtained relevant to management's response, is not considered adequate.

4. Documentation; the auditor should document

a. Expectations.

b. Results of comparison of expectations to recorded amounts (or ratios).

c. Any additional auditing procedures performed relating to fluctuations or relationships that are inconsistent with other relevant information.

AU-C 530 Audit Sampling

A. Scope: This section applies when the auditor has decided to use audit sampling in performing audit procedures. It addresses statistical and nonstatistical sampling. It complements AU-C 500, *Audit Evidence*.

B. Objective: The objective of the auditor when using audit sampling is to provide a reasonable basis for the auditor to draw conclusions about the population from which the sample is selected.

C. Definitions

1. **Audit sampling (sampling).** The selection of less than 100% of a population of audit relevance, and the evaluation of that sample, such that the auditor expects the items selected (the sample) to be representative of the population, and thus likely to provide a reasonable basis for conclusions about the population. In this context, *representative* means that the sample will result in conclusions that, subject to the limitations of sampling risk, are similar to those that would be drawn if the same procedures were applied to the entire population.

2. **Nonsampling risk.** The risk that the auditor reaches an erroneous conclusion for any reason not related to sampling risk. Examples of nonsampling risk include use of inappropriate audit procedures or misinterpretation of audit evidence and failure to recognize a misstatement or deviation.

3. **Population.** The entire set of data from which a sample is selected and about which the auditor wishes to draw conclusions.

4. **Sampling risk.** The risk that the auditor's conclusion based on a sample may be different from the conclusion if the entire population were subjected to the same audit procedure. Sampling risk can lead to two types of erroneous conclusions as follows:

   a. In the case of a test of controls, that controls are more effective than they actually are or, in the case of a test of details, that a material misstatement does not exist when in fact it does. The auditor is primarily concerned with this type of erroneous conclusion because it affects audit effectiveness and is more likely to lead to an inappropriate audit opinion.

   b. In the case of a test of controls, that controls are less effective than they actually are or, in the case of a test of details, that a material misstatement exists when in fact it does not. This type of erroneous conclusion affects audit efficiency as it would usually lead to additional work to establish that initial conclusions were incorrect.

5. **Sampling unit.** The individual items constituting a population.

6. **Statistical sampling.** An approach to sampling that has the following characteristics:

   a. Random selection of the sample items.
   b. The use of an appropriate statistical technique to evaluate sample results.

   A sampling approach that does not have characteristics (a) and (b) is considered nonstatistical sampling.

7. **Stratification.** Division of the population into groups.

8. **Tolerable misstatement.** A monetary amount set by the auditor in respect of which the auditor seeks to obtain an appropriate level of assurance that the monetary amount set by the auditor is not exceeded by the actual misstatement in the population.

   a. The Professional Standards require that the auditor determine performance materiality to reduce to an appropriately low level the probability that the aggregate of uncorrected and undetected misstatements in the fanatical statements exceeds materiality for the financial statements as a whole.

   b. Tolerable misstatement is the application of performance materiality to a particular sampling procedure. Tolerable misstatement may be the same amount or an amount smaller than performance materiality (for example, when the population from which the population is selected is smaller than the account balance).

9. **Tolerable rate of deviation.** A rate of deviation from prescribed internal control procedures set by the auditor in respect of which the auditor seeks to obtain an appropriate level of assurance that that rate of deviation set by the auditor is not exceeded by the actual rate of deviation in the population.

D. Requirements, application, and other explanatory material

1. Sample design, sample size and selection of items for testing

   a. Sample design

(1) The auditor should select items for the sample in such a way that the sample will be representative of the relevant population and likely to provide the auditor a reasonable basis for conclusions about the population.

    (a) Either nonstatistical or statistical sampling approaches are acceptable.

    (b) As detection risk decreases for substantive procedures, the auditor's allowable risk of incorrect acceptance also decreases, and thus the sample size increases.

    (c) The auditor must have a clear understanding of what constitutes a deviation (attributes sampling) or a misstatement (variable sampling).

b. Sample size

    (1) For tests of controls (attributes sampling) the following influence sample size:

        (a) Tolerable rate of deviation (increases result in a decrease in required sample size).

        (b) Expected rate of deviation (increases result in an increase in required sample size).

        (c) Desired level of assurance (increases result in an increase in required sample size).

        (d) Number of sampling units (increase slightly required sample size).

    (2) For substantive tests of details (variables sampling) the following influence sample size).

        (a) Desired level of assurance (increases result in an increase in required sample size).

        (b) Tolerable misstatement (increases result in a decrease in required sample size).

        (c) Expected misstatement for the population (increases result in an increase in required sample size).

        (d) Stratification of the population when performed (this is aimed at decreasing required sample size).

        (e) For some sampling methods, the number of sampling units in each stratum.

    (3) Required sample size is not a valid criterion to decide between statistical and nonstatistical approaches.

    (4) An auditor who applies nonstatistical sampling uses professional judgment to relate the same factors used in statistical sampling.

c. Selection of items for testing

    (1) To be considered representative, an audit sample must be selected in a manner such that the auditor can expect that the sample is free of intentional bias or preference.

    (2) With statistical sampling, sample items are selected in a way that each sampling unit has a known probability of being selected; with nonstatistical sampling, haphazard or random-based selection is used.

    (3) The principal methods of selecting samples are random selection, systematic selection, and haphazard selection.

2. Performing audit procedures—The auditor should perform audit procedures appropriate to the purpose on each item selected.

a. If the audit procedure is not applicable to a selected item, the auditor should perform the procedure on a replacement item.

    (1) Example—An auditor is testing for evidence of payment authorization and a voided check is selected.

        (a) If the auditor is unable to apply the designed audit procedures or suitable alternative procedures to a selected item, the auditor should treat that item as a deviation from the prescribed control (for tests of controls) or as a misstatement (for tests of details); examples are

            1] Unable to apply a designed audit procedure—Client unable to locate supporting documentation.

            2] Suitable alternative procedure—Examination of a subsequent cash receipt and related documentation of the sale when no reply is received in response to a positive confirmation request.

3. Nature and cause of deviations and misstatements—The auditor should investigate and evaluate their possible effect on the purpose of the audit procedure and on other areas of the audit.

a. When identified deviations (misstatements) have a common feature (e.g., type of transaction, location, product line), the auditor may decide to identify all items in the population with the common feature.

b. In addition to the frequency and amounts of material misstatements, the auditor should consider qualitative aspects of misstatements (e.g., nature and cause, possible relationship to other phases of audit).

    c. An auditor may not assume that the observed incidence of misstatements or deviations in the sample is not representative of the population because a misstatement or deviation included in the sample is caused by unusual circumstances (this is sometimes referred to as an anomalous or isolate misstatement or deviation).

4. Projecting misstatements—The auditor should project misstatements or deviations found in the sample to the population.

    a. This is done for misstatements in tests of details (variables sampling); for tests of controls (attributes sampling) no explicit projection is necessary because the sample deviation rate is also the projected deviation rate for the population as a whole.

5. Evaluating results of audit sampling—The auditor should evaluate the results of the sample and whether the use of audit sampling has provided a reasonable basis for the conclusions about the population that has been tested.

    a. In general

        (1) Tests of controls—An unexpectedly high sample deviation rate may lead to an increase in the assessed risks of material misstatement unless further audit evidence substantiating the initial assessment is obtained.

        (2) Tests of details—An unexpectedly high misstatement amount in a sample may cause the auditor to believe that a class of transactions or account balance is materially misstated in the absence of further audit evidence that no material misstatement exists.

    b. In tests of details

        (1) Projected misstatement is the auditor's best estimate of misstatement in the population.

        (2) As projected misstatement approaches or exceeds tolerable misstatement, the more likely it is that actual misstatement in the population may exceed tolerable misstatement; this circumstance is indicative that an unacceptable sampling risk exists.

    c. If the auditor concludes that audit sampling has not provided a reasonable basis for conclusions about the population, the auditor may

        (1) Request management to investigate identified misstatements and the potential for further misstatements and make necessary adjustments, or

        (2) Tailor the nature, timing, and extent of further audit procedures to achieve the required assurance (e.g., extend sample, test an alternative control, or modify related substantive procedures).

AU-C 540 Auditing Accounting Estimates, Including Fair Value Accounting Estimates and Related Disclosures

A. Introduction

1. Scope: This section addresses the auditor's responsibilities relating to accounting estimates, including fair value accounting estimates and related disclosures in an audit of financial statements.

2. Nature of accounting estimates

    a. Accounting estimates are financial statement items that cannot be measured precisely, but can only be estimated.

    b. The measurement objective of accounting estimates can vary depending on the applicable financial reporting framework and the financial item being reported.

    c. A difference between the outcome of an accounting estimate and the amount originally recognized or disclosed in the financial statements does not necessarily represent a misstatement of the financial statements; it could be an outcome of estimation uncertainty.

        (1) In the case of fair value accounting estimates, an observed outcome may be affected by events or conditions subsequent to the date at which the measurements estimated for the financial statements.

    d. Examples of situations where accounting estimates, other than fair value accounting estimates, may be required: allowance for doubtful accounts, inventory obsolescence, and warranty obligations.

    e. Examples of accounting estimates where fair value accounting estimates may be required: complex financial instruments which are not traded on an active and open market, share-based payments, property or equipment held for disposal.

    f. Examples of accounting estimates with relatively high uncertainty when they are based on significant assumptions: outcome of litigation, fair value accounting estimates for derivative financial instruments not publicly traded, fair value accounting estimates of highly specialized entity-developed model-based assumptions that cannot be observed in the marketplace.

B. Objective: The objective of the auditor is to obtain sufficient appropriate audit evidence about whether, in the context of the applicable financial reporting framework:

    1. Accounting estimates, including fair value accounting estimates, in the financial statements, whether recognized or disclosed, are reasonable; and

    2. Related disclosures in the financial statements are adequate.

C. Definitions

    1. **Accounting estimate.** An approximation of a monetary amount in the absence of a precise means of measurement. This term is used for an amount measured at fair value where there is estimation uncertainty, as well as for other amounts that require estimation. Where this section addresses only accounting estimates involving measurement at fair value, the term *fair value accounting estimates* is used.

    2. **Auditor's point estimate or auditor's range.** The amount, or range of amounts, respectively, derived from audit evidence for use in evaluating the recorded amount.

    3. **Estimation uncertainty.** The susceptibility of an accounting estimate and related disclosures to an inherent lack of precision in its measurement.

    4. **Management bias.** A lack of neutrality by management in the preparation and presentation of information.

    5. **Management's point estimate.** The amount selected by management for recognition or disclosure in the financial statements as an accounting estimate.

    6. **Outcome of an accounting estimate.** The actual monetary amount which results from the resolution of the underlying transaction(s), event(s), or condition(s) addressed by the accounting estimate.

D. Requirements, application, and other explanatory material

    1. Risk assessment procedures and related activities

        a. The auditor should obtain an understanding of the following to provide a basis for identifying and assessing the risks of material misstatement for accounting estimates:

           (1) Requirements of the applicable financial reporting framework relevant to accounting estimates, including related disclosures.

           (2) How management identifies transactions, events and conditions that may give rise to accounting estimates; how management makes accounting estimates, including

               (a) The method, and where applicable model used.

               (b) Relevant controls.

               (c) Whether management has used a specialist.

               (d) Assumptions underlying the accounting estimates.

               (e) Whether there has been or ought to have been a change from the prior period in the method(s) for making accounting estimates, and if so, why.

               (f) Whether management has assessed the effect of estimation uncertainty.

        b. The auditor should review the outcome of accounting estimates included in the prior period financial statements or, where applicable, their subsequent re-estimation for the purpose of the current period.

           (1) However, the auditor need not review the outcome of every accounting estimate included in the prior period.

    2. Identifying and 6 the risks of material misstatement: The auditor should

        a. Evaluate the degree of estimation uncertainty associated with an accounting estimate; examples of high estimation uncertainty estimates are

           (1) Highly dependent on judgment (e.g., litigation, timing of future cash flows).

           (2) Estimates not calculated using recognized measurement techniques.

      (3) Estimates whose subsequent year estimated amounts were inaccurate.

      (4) Fair value accounting estimates for which a highly specialized entity-developed model is used or for which there are no observable inputs.

  b. Determine whether any of those accounting estimates that have been identified as having high estimation uncertainty give rise to significant risks.

3. Further substantive procedures to respond to significant risks

  a. Estimation uncertainty—Evaluate

      (1) How management has considered alternative assumptions or outcomes.

      (2) Whether significant assumptions used by management are reasonable.

      (3) Where relevant, management's intent to carry out specific courses of action related to the estimates.

      (4) Where the auditor believes management has not addressed estimation uncertainty adequately, the auditor should, if considered necessary, develop a range with which to evaluate the reasonableness of the accounting estimate.

  b. Recognition and measurement criteria—Obtain sufficient appropriate evidence on

      (1) Management's decision to recognize, or not recognize, the accounting estimate in the financial statements.

      (2) The selected management basis for the accounting estimates.

  c. The auditor should evaluate the reasonableness of accounting estimates and that disclosures are adequate.

  d. The auditor should review the judgments and decisions made by management in making the accounting estimates to identify whether indications of possible management bias exist.

  e. Documentation should include

      (1) For those accounting estimates that give rise to significant risks, the basis for the auditor's conclusions about their reasonableness.

      (2) Indicators of possible management bias, if any.

AU-C 550 Related Parties

A. Introduction

1. Scope: This section addresses the auditor's responsibility relating to related-party relationships and transactions in an audit of financial statements.

  a. GAAP includes specific disclosure requirements for related-party relationships and guidance.

  b. Special-purpose frameworks in some circumstances do not have specific disclosure requirements. Nonetheless, in such a situation the auditor evaluates whether related-party information is disclosed in a manner comparable to GAAP so as to achieve fair presentation.

2. There is nothing illegal or improper in and of itself of a typical related-party transaction.

  a. Many related-party transactions occur in the normal course of business and carry no higher risk of material misstatement than similar transactions with unrelated parties.

3. But in some circumstances related-party transactions may give rise to higher risks of material misstatement than transactions with unrelated parties; higher risks may occur because

  a. Related parties may operate through an extensive and complex range of relationships and structures, with a corresponding increase in the complexity of related-party transactions.

  b. Information systems may be ineffective at identifying and summarizing transactions and outstanding balances between an entity and its related parties.

  c. In some circumstances related-party transactions may

      (1) Not be conducted under normal market terms and conditions.

      (2) Be motivated solely or in large measure to engage in fraudulent financial reporting or to conceal misappropriation of assets.

> **NOTE:** The above two points summarize much of the accounting and auditing problem for auditors.

4. Because related parties are not independent of each other, financial reporting frameworks establish specific accounting and disclosure requirements for related-party relationships, transactions, and balances.

    a. Accounting principles ordinarily do not require transactions with related parties to be accounted for on a basis different from that which would be appropriate if the parties were not related. But with a related-party transaction the substance of a particular transaction may be different from its form. Accordingly, the financial statements would recognize the substance of such transactions rather than merely their legal form.

    b. Examples of transactions that may indicate the existence of related parties are

        (1) Borrowing or lending on an interest-free basis or at a rate of interest significantly different from market rates.
        (2) Selling real estate at a price that differs significantly from its appraised value.
        (3) Exchanging property for similar property in a nonmonetary transaction.
        (4) Making loans with no scheduled terms for repayment.

    c. Examples of circumstances in which related-party transactions may occur are

        (1) Lack of sufficient working capital or credit to continue the business.
        (2) Overly optimistic earning forecast.
        (3) Dependence on a single or relatively few products, customers, or transactions.
        (4) Declining industry.
        (5) Excess capacity.
        (6) Significant litigation.
        (7) Significant obsolescence.

5. Auditor responsibility: To perform audit procedures to identify, assess, and respond to the risks of material misstatement arising from the entity's failure to appropriately account for or disclose related-party transactions.

6. Identifying related-party transactions is particularly difficult because

    a. Management may be unaware of the existence of the related-party relationships and transactions.
    b. Related-party relationships may present a greater opportunity for collusion, concealment, or manipulation by management than do non-related-party relationships.

B. Objectives: The objectives of the auditor are to obtain

1. An understanding of related-party relationships and transactions sufficient to be able to

    a. Recognize fraud risk factors, if any, arising from related-party relationships and transactions that are relevant to the identification and assessment of risks of material misstatement due to fraud.
    b. Conclude, based on the audit evidence obtained, whether the financial statements, insofar as they are affected by those relationships and transactions, achieve fair presentation.

2. Sufficient appropriate audit evidence about whether related-party relationships and transactions have been appropriately identified, accounted for and disclosed in the financial statements.

C. Definitions

1. **Arm's-length transaction.** A transaction conducted on such terms and conditions between a willing buyer and a willing seller who are unrelated and are acting independently of each other and pursuing their own best interests.
2. **Related-party.** A party defined as a related-party in GAAP.

D. Requirements, application, and other explanatory material

1. Risk assessment procedures and related activities

    a. The engagement team discussion ("brainstorming session") should include specific consideration of the susceptibility of the financial statements to material misstatement due to fraud or error from related-party relationships and transactions.

        (1) Matters that may be addressed include

            (a) Nature and extent of entity's relationships/ transactions with related parties.
            (b) Importance of skepticism throughout the audit regarding material misstatement associated with related-party relationships/transactions.
            (c) Conditions of the entity that may indicate related-party relationships/transactions.

       (d) Records or documents that may indicate existence of related-party relationships/transactions.

       (e) Importance that management and those charged with governance attach to identification and accounting for related-party relationships/transactions.

  (2) Specific considerations of how related parties may be involved in fraud; examples are

       (a) Entities formed for specific purposes and controlled by management might facilitate earnings management.

       (b) Transactions between the entity and a known business partner of a key member of management could be arranged to facilitate asset misappropriation.

       (c) The form of related-party transactions may mask its substance.

       (d) Related-party transactions may be subject to period-end window dressing (e.g., stockholder pays a loan shortly before period-end, but obtains a loan again shortly after period end).

       (e) Government and regulated industries may circumvent laws or regulations that restrict them their ability to engage in transactions with related parties.

b. The auditor should inquire of management regarding

  (1) Identity of the entity's related parties.

  (2) Nature of the relationships.

  (3) Whether the entity entered into any transactions with these related parties during the period and, if so, the type and purpose of the transactions.

c. The auditor should inspect the following for indications of related-party relationships or transactions that management has not identified or disclosed:

  (1) Bank and legal confirmations.

  (2) Minutes of shareholder and those charged with governance meetings.

  (3) Other considered necessary in the circumstances.

> **NOTE:** A multiple-choice question might list procedures and ask which is most likely to reveal a related-party transaction. One of the above would likely be the correct reply.

d. When the auditor identifies significant transactions outside the entity's normal course of business (including from the above step), the auditor should inquire of management about

  (1) The nature of the transactions.

  (2) Whether related parties could be involved.

2. Identification and assessment of the risks of material misstatement associated with related-party relationships and transactions

a. The auditor should identify and assess risks of material misstatement associated with related-party relationships and transactions and determine whether any of those risks are significant risks.

  (1) The auditor should treat identified significant related-party transactions *outside the entity's normal course of business* as giving rise to *significant risks.*

b. If fraud risk factors are identified, the auditor should consider them.

3. Responses to the risks of material misstatement associated with related-party transactions

a. The auditor designs and performs further audit procedures (i.e., tests of controls, but particularly substantive procedures) to obtain sufficient appropriate audit evidence about the risks of material misstatement associated with related-party relationships and transactions.

b. Identification of previously identified or undisclosed related parties or significant related-party transactions

  (1) Communicate to other members of engagement team.

  (2) Request management to identify all transactions with the newly identified related parties.

  (3) Inquire why entity's controls failed to enable the identification or disclosure of related-party relationships or transactions.

(4) Perform appropriate audit procedures relating to the newly identified related parties or significant related-party transactions.

(5) Reconsider the risk that other such related parties and transactions exist.

(6) Evaluate the implications for the audit of management's nondisclosure if it appears intentional.

c. Identified significant related-party transactions outside the entity's normal course of business

(1) Inspect the underlying contracts or agreements, if any, and evaluate whether

(a) The business rationale (or lack thereof) of transactions suggest that they may have been entered into to engage in fraudulent financial reporting or to conceal misappropriation of assets.

(b) The terms of the transactions are consistent with management's explanations.

(c) The transactions have been properly accounted for and disclosed.

(2) Obtain audit evidence that the transactions have been appropriately authorized and approved.

d. Assertions that related-party transactions were conducted on terms equivalent to those prevailing in an arm's-length transaction

(1) If management makes this assertion, the auditor should obtain sufficient appropriate audit evidence about the assertion.

4. Evaluation of the accounting for, and disclosure of, identified related-party relationships and transactions; the auditor should evaluate

a. Whether the identified related-party relationships and transactions have been appropriately accounted for and disclosed.

b. Whether the effects of the related-party relationships and transactions prevent the financial statements from achieving fair presentation.

AU-C 560 Subsequent Events and Subsequently Discovered Facts

A. Introduction and objective

1. This section addresses the auditor's responsibilities relating to *subsequent events* and *subsequently discovered facts* in the audit of financial statements (see definitions of these terms below). It also addresses a predecessor auditor's responsibilities for subsequent events and subsequently discovered facts when reissuing the auditor's report on previously issued financial statements of a prior period that are to be presented on a comparative basis with audited financial statements of a subsequent period.

2. Financial reporting frameworks (e.g., GAAP) ordinarily identify two types of events that occur after the date of the financial statements, those that provide evidence of conditions that

a. Existed at the date of the financial statements (subsequently discovered facts).

b. Arose after the date of the financial statements (subsequent events).

3. This section addresses both of the above areas.

B. Objectives

1. The objectives of the auditor are to

a. Obtain sufficient appropriate audit evidence about whether events occurring between the date of the financial statements and the date of the auditor's report that require adjustment of, or disclosure in, the financial statements are appropriately reflected in those financial statements in accordance with the applicable financial reporting framework.

b. Respond appropriately to facts that become known to the auditor after the date of the auditor's report that, had they been known to the auditor at that date, may have caused the auditor to amend the auditor's report.

2. The objective of a predecessor auditor, who is requested to reissue a previously issued auditor's report on financial statements that are to be presented on a comparative basis with audited financial statements of a subsequent period, is to perform specified procedures to determine whether the previously issued auditor's report is still appropriate before such report is reissued.

C. Definitions

1. **Date of the financial statements.** The date of the end of the latest period covered by the financial statements.

2. **Date of the auditor's report.** A date no earlier than the date on which the auditor has obtained sufficient appropriate audit evidence, including evidence that the audit documentation has been reviewed.

3. **Subsequent events.** Events occurring between the date of the financial statements and the date of the auditor's report that require adjustment of, or disclosure in, the financial statements.

4. **Subsequently discovered facts.** Facts that become known to the auditor after the date of the auditor's report that, had they been known to the auditor at that date, may have caused the auditor to amend the auditor's report.

D. Requirements, application, and other explanatory material

1. Subsequent events

   a. The auditor should perform audit procedures to obtain sufficient appropriate audit evidence that all subsequent events that require adjustment of, or disclosure in, the financial statements have been identified; these procedures should include

      (1) Obtaining an understanding of any procedures management has established to identify subsequent events.
      (2) Inquiring of management and, where appropriate, those charged with governance about subsequent events.
      (3) Reading minutes, if any, of the meetings of the entity's owners, management, and those charged with governance.
      (4) Reading the entity's latest subsequent interim financial statements, if any.

2. Situation: Subsequently discovered facts that become known to the auditor before the report release date (the date the auditor grants permission to use the audit report)

   a. The auditor is not required to perform audit procedures after the date of the auditor's report. However, if a subsequently discovered fact becomes known before the report release date, the auditor should

      (1) Discuss with management and, where appropriate, those charged with governance.
      (2) Determine whether the financial statements need amendment and, if so, inquire how management intends to address the matter.

   b. If management amends the financial statements, the auditor should either

      (1) Date the auditor's report as of the later date and extend audit procedures to the new date of the auditor's report on the amended financial statements, or
      (2) Include an additional date in the auditor's report on the amended financial statements limited to the amendment (that is, dual-date the auditor's report for that amendment), for example, "February 3, 20X1, except as to Note Y, which is as of February 6, 20X1."

   c. If management does not amend the financial statements, the auditor should modify the audit report to include a qualified or adverse opinion (due to a lack of following GAAP).

3. Situation: Subsequently discovered facts that become known to the auditor after the report release date

   a. If such facts become available after the report release date the auditor should

      (1) Discuss the matter with management and, where appropriate, those charged with governance.
      (2) Determine whether the financial statements need amendment and, if so, inquire how management intends to address the matter.

   b. If management amends the financial statements, the auditor should

      (1) Apply the necessary audit procedures on the amended financial statements.
      (2) If the audited financial statements (before amendment) have been made available to third parties, assess whether steps taken by management are timely and appropriate to ensure that anyone in receipt of financial statements is informed of the situation and that the audited financial statements should not be relied upon.
      (3) If the new auditor's opinion on the amended financial statements differs from the opinion originally expressed, include an additional paragraph that discloses

         (a) Date of the auditor's previous report.
         (b) The type of opinion previously expressed.
         (c) The substantive reasons for the different opinion.
         (d) That the auditor's opinion on the amended financial statements is different from the auditor's previous opinion.

c. If management **does not** amend the financial statements in circumstances where the auditor believes they need to be amended

   (1) If the financial statements have **not** been made available to third parties: Tell management and those charged with governance not to make the audited financial statements so available before the necessary amendments have been made and a new auditor's report on the amended financial statements has been provided. If this advice is ignored, the auditor should take appropriate action to seek to prevent reliance on the auditor's report.

   (2) If the financial statements have been made available to third parties: Assess whether the steps taken by management are timely and appropriate to ensure that those who received the financial statements are informed of the situation and that the audited financial statements are not to be relied upon. If management does not take the necessary steps, the auditor should notify management and those charged with governance that the auditor will seek to prevent future reliance on the auditor's report. If this advice is ignored, the auditor should take appropriate action to seek to prevent reliance on the auditor's report.

d. Auditor actions to seek to prevent reliance on the auditor's report depend on various factors. Unless the auditor's legal counsel recommends a different course of action, the auditor may

   (1) Notify management and those charged with governance that the auditor's report is not to be associated with the financial statements and is not to be relied upon.
   (2) Notify regulatory agencies.
   (3) Notify anyone known to be relying on the financial statements.

e. If the auditor was unable to determine whether the financial statements need amendment, the notification to anyone in receipt of the financial statements may indicate that information became available to the auditor and that, if the information is true, the auditor believes that the auditor's report is not to be relied upon. The specific matter need not be detailed in the notification.

4. Predecessor auditor's reissuance of the auditor's report in comparative financial statements

a. Background: Assume a company is presenting 20X1 and 20X2 year financial statements in comparative form (two columns of numbers—one for each year). In this situation the predecessor audited 20X1, but is no longer the entity's auditor. Ordinarily when two years of comparative financial statements are presented, as is here the case, the fact that both years have been audited must be communicated. This communication may either be through the predecessor auditor reissuing the auditor's report for 20X1, or by the current auditor (successor auditor) providing the information in his/her report on 20X2. The situation in which the successor auditor summarizes the predecessor's report is addressed in AU-C 706.

b. Before reissuing his/her report, the predecessor should perform procedures to determine whether the previously issued report is still appropriate, including

   (1) Reading the subsequent period financial statements.
   (2) Comparing prior period financial statements with the subsequent financial statements.
   (3) Inquiring of and obtaining a representation letter from management indicating whether any

      (a) Information has come to management's attention that would cause it to believe that any of the previous representations should be modified.
      (b) Events have occurred subsequent to the date of the latest prior period financial statements reported on by the predecessor that would require adjustment to or disclosure in those financial statements.

   (4) Obtaining a representation letter from the successor auditor stating whether the successor auditor's audit revealed any matters that might have a material effect on the financial statements reported on by the predecessor.

c. If the above procedures reveal a subsequently discovered fact, the predecessor auditor should

   (1) As per earlier in the outline discuss with management, etc.
   (2) If management amends the financial statements and predecessor plans to issue a new auditor's report, follow earlier standards in this section.

      (a) If predecessor does not plan to issue a new auditor's report, assess whether management's steps on the matter are timely and appropriate.

(3) If management does not amend the financial statements and the predecessor believes they need to be amended, follow earlier requirements in this section (i.e., those aimed at preventing reliance on the auditor's report).

AU-C 570 The Auditor's Consideration of an Entity's Ability to Continue as a Going Concern

A. Introduction

1. Scope: This section addresses auditor responsibilities for evaluating whether there is *substantial doubt about the entity's ability to continue as a going concern for a reasonable period of time* (hereafter, substantial doubt).

   (a) It applies to all audits that involve various financial reporting frameworks—that is, it not only applies to GAAP-based statements but others (e.g., cash-basis statements)

   (b) It does not apply to financial statements prepared based on the assumption of liquidation. That is, it does not apply when the situation is "beyond" substantial doubt and the company is virtually certain to liquidate.

2. Continuation of an entity as a going concern is assumed in the absence of significant information to the contrary.

   (a) Examples of information to the contrary: Inability to meet obligations as they become due without substantial disposition of assets outside the ordinary course of business, restructuring of debt, externally forced revisions of operations, or similar actions.

3. Responsibilities of the auditor

   (a) Evaluate whether there is substantial doubt about the entity's ability to continue as a going concern for a reasonable period of time, not to exceed one year beyond the date of the financial statements being audited.

      (1) The evaluation is based on conditions and events that exist at, or have occurred prior to the date of the auditor's report.

   (b) Information about such conditions or events is obtained through application of audit procedures planned and performed to achieve audit objectives that are related to financial statement assertions.

   (c) Because the auditor cannot predict future events or conditions, the absence of any reference to substantial doubt in the auditor's report cannot be viewed as a guarantee of the entity's ability to continue as a going concern.

B. Objectives: The objectives of the auditor are to

1. Evaluate and conclude, based on the audit evidence obtained, whether there is substantial doubt about the entity's ability to continue as a going concern for a reasonable period of time.
2. Assess the possible financial effect, including the adequacy of disclosure regarding uncertainties about the entity's ability to continue as a going concern.
3. Determine other implications for the auditor's report.

C. Requirements, application and other explanatory material

1. Evaluating whether substantial doubt exists: Evaluate for a period not to exceed one year beyond the date of the financial statements (a "reasonable period of time"). Auditors consider the results of procedures performed during the audit to identify conditions and events that, when considered in the aggregate, indicate there could be substantial doubt; examples of procedures:

   (a) Analytical procedures.
   (b) Review of subsequent events.
   (c) Review of compliance with the terms of debt and loan agreements.
   (d) Reading stockholder, board of director and important committee minutes.
   (e) Inquiry of legal counsel.
   (f) Confirmation with related and third parties of details of arrangement to provide or maintain financial support.

2. Examples of conditions or events that indicate that there could be substantial doubt

   (a) Negative trends—(e.g., recurring operating losses, working capital deficiencies, negative cash flows from operations, adverse financial ratios).
   (b) Other indications of possible financial difficulties—(e.g., default on loan, arrearages in dividends, denial of trade credit, restructuring of debt, noncompliance with statutory capital requirements, need to seek new sources or methods of financing, need to dispose of substantial assets).

(c) Internal matters—(e.g., work stoppages, other labor difficulties, substantial dependence on success of one project, uneconomic long-term commitments, need to significantly revise operations).

(d) External matters that have occurred—(e.g., legal proceedings, legislation, loss of a key franchise, license or patent, loss of a principal customer or supplier, uninsured losses).

3. If after considering the identified conditions or events the auditor believes there is substantial doubt, the auditor should obtain information about management's plans that are intended to mitigate the adverse effects of such conditions and events. Management's plans include

(a) Plans to dispose of assets
(b) Plans to borrow money or restructure debt
(c) Plans to reduce or delay expenditures.
(d) Plans to increase ownership equity.

4. In considering management's plans the auditor should

(a) Assess whether it is likely the adverse effects will be mitigated for a reasonable period of time.
(b) Identify elements of management's plans that are particularly significant to overcoming the adverse effects of the conditions or events and plan/perform procedures to obtain audit evidence about them, including, where applicable, considering adequacy of support regarding ability to obtain additional financing or disposal of assets.
(c) Assess whether it is likely that such plans can be effectively implemented.

5. When prospective financial information is particularly significant to management's plans, auditor should obtain management's support for significant assumptions and pay particular attention to assumptions that are

(a) Material to the prospective financial information.
(b) Especially sensitive or susceptible to change.
(c) Inconsistent with historical trends.

6. When after considering management's plans the auditor concludes that there is substantial doubt, the auditor should include an emphasis-of-matter paragraph in the audit report. The terms "substantial doubt" and "going concern" should be used.

(a) The report should not use qualifying language such as

(1) "There may be substantial doubt" or
(2) "Unless the company is able to obtain financial support, there is substantial doubt"

(b) Alternatively the auditor may disclaim an opinion on the financial statements.
(c) If management's disclosures relating to going concern are inadequate, a departure from GAAP exists and a qualified or adverse opinion, as appropriate, should be issued.

7. If the auditor believes, before consideration of management's plans, that there is substantial doubt, the auditor should obtain written representations from management

(a) Regarding its plans that are intended to mitigate the adverse effects of conditions or events that indicate there is substantial doubt and the likelihood that those plans can be effectively implemented.
(b) Financial statement disclosure of all relevant information, including conditions and events and management's plans.

8. Communication with those charged with governance when there is substantial doubt includes

(a) Nature of conditions or events identified.
(b) Possible effect on the financial statements and adequacy of disclosures.
(c) Effects on the auditor's report.

9. Situation: The client is presenting comparative financial statements (last year and this year). Last year a going concern emphasis-of-matter paragraph was included in audit report, but this year it has been removed for the current period; resolution: do not repeat the going concern paragraph for last year.

10. Situation: Auditor is requested to reissue an auditor's report and eliminate a going concern emphasis-of-matter paragraph; resolution:

(a) Perform audit procedures related to the event or transactions that prompted the request to reissue.
(b) Perform procedures listed in AU 560 for subsequent events.

(c) Consider management's plans.

(d) Consider whether to reissue as per client request.

11. Documentation: When the auditor concludes there is substantial doubt, document

(a) Conditions or events that led to substantial doubt conclusion.

(b) Elements of management's plans considered particularly significant to overcoming adverse effects of conditions or events.

(c) Audit procedure performed related to management's plans.

(d) Auditor's conclusion as to whether there is substantial doubt or whether it is alleviated.

(1) If substantial doubt remains, document possible effects of conditions or events on financial statements.

(2) If substantial doubt is alleviated, document auditor's conclusion as to the need for and adequacy of disclosures of the principal conditions or events that initially caused the auditor to believe there was substantial doubt.

(e) Auditor's conclusions with respect to effects on audit report.

AU-C 580 Written Representations

A. **Introduction:**

1. This section addresses obtaining written representations (a "representations letter") from management and, when appropriate, those charged with governance.

a. References in this outline to "management" should be read as "management and, when appropriate, those charged with governance."

2. Written representations complement other auditing procedures and do **not** provide sufficient appropriate audit evidence on their own about any of the matters with which they deal.

a. Obtaining written representations does not affect the nature or extent of other procedures performed.

B. **Objectives**

1. Obtain written representations from management that they believe that they have fulfilled their responsibility for the preparation of the financial statements and the completeness of the information provided to the auditor.

2. Support other audit evidence by means of written representations.

3. Respond appropriately to written representations provided by management and when appropriate, those charged with governance.

C. **Definition**

1. **Written representation.** A written statement by management provided to the auditor to confirm certain matters or to support other audit evidence. Written representations, for purposes of this section, do **not** include financial statements, the assertions therein, or supporting books and records.

D. **Requirements, application, and other explanatory material**

1. *Management from whom representations are requested*: Those with overall responsibility for financial and operating matters who are responsible for, and knowledgeable about (directly or through others in the organization) the matters covered by the representations, including the financial statements.

a. Usually the CEO and CFO, although sometimes equivalent persons that do not use such titles.

2. *Management's responsibilities written representations obtained*

a. Preparation of the financial statements

(1) In accordance with applicable financial reporting framework.

(2) Maintaining IC to allow accurate financial statement to be prepared.

b. Has provided auditor with all relevant information and access and all transactions have been recorded.

NOTE: (a) and (b) are particularly important in that, as discussed later in the outline, if the auditor concludes there is sufficient doubt about the integrity of management and such written representations, or management does not provide the above representations, the auditor should disclaim an opinion.

3. *Other written representations obtained*

    a. About fraud—Management

        (1) Is responsible for designing IC to prevent and detect fraud.

        (2) Has disclosed to the auditor results of its assessment of the risk that the financial statements may be materially misstated due to fraud.

        (3) Has disclosed to the auditor knowledge of fraud or suspected fraud affecting the entity involving management, employees with significant IC roles, and others when fraud could have a material effect.

    b. Laws and regulations—All instances of noncompliance with those whose effects should be considered when preparing financial statements have been disclosed to the auditor.

    c. Uncorrected misstatements—Management believes effects are immaterial.

    d. Litigation and claims—All have been disclosed to the auditor.

    e. Estimates—Significant assumptions used are reasonable.

    f. Related-party transactions—Disclosed to auditor and appropriately accounted for.

    g. Subsequent events—Properly adjusted or disclosed.

4. Details of written representations

    a. The auditor may choose to obtain additional written representations.

    b. Date should be the date of the auditor's report.

    c. Should be in form of a representation letter addressed to the auditor.

E. Doubt about the reliability of written representations and representations not provided

1. Doubt about reliability

    a. If possible perform audit procedures to resolve matter (e.g., representation differs from other audit evidence); if still unresolved

        (1) Reconsider assessment of competence, integrity, ethical values and diligence of management.

        (2) If auditor concludes representations not reliable, take appropriate action in determining effect on opinion.

2. Requested representations not provided

    a. Discuss matter with management.

    b. Reevaluate integrity of management and evaluate effect on reliability of representations and audit evidence in general.

    c. Take appropriate actions, including determining possible effect on opinion.

Overall: The auditor should disclaim an opinion or withdraw from the engagement if he or she concludes there is sufficient doubt about integrity of management such that the written representations are not reliable or management does not provide them.

AU-C 585 Consideration of Omitted Procedures after the Report Date

A. Scope: This section addresses auditor responsibilities when subsequent to the release of the auditor's report on financial statements, the auditor becomes aware that one or more auditing procedures considered necessary in the circumstances existing at the time of the audit were omitted from the audit of the financial statements.

1. The provisions of this SAS do not apply to an engagement in which an auditor's work is at issue in a threatened or pending legal proceeding or regulatory investigation.

2. Objective: **The objectives of the auditor are to assess** the effect of omitted procedures of which the auditor becomes aware on the auditor's present ability to support the previously expressed opinion on the financial statements and to respond appropriately.

B. Definition

1. **Omitted procedure.** An auditing procedure that the auditor considered necessary in the circumstances existing at the date of the audit of financial statements, but which was not performed.

C. Requirements, application, and other explanatory material

1. If subsequent to the report release date the auditor becomes aware of an omitted procedure, the auditor should assess the effect of the omitted procedure on the auditor's present ability to support the previously expressed opinion on the financial statements. Procedures may include

    a. Review audit documentation.
    b. Discuss circumstances with engagement personnel and others in firm.
    c. Reevaluate the overall scope of audit.

2. If the auditor concludes that an omitted procedures impairs present ability to support a previously expressed opinion *and* the auditor believes users are currently relying on (or are likely to rely on) the report, the auditor should promptly perform the omitted procedure or alternative procedures as necessary.

    a. If the auditor is unable to apply the omitted procedure or alternative procedures, s/he may decide to contact (1) legal counsel to determine the appropriate course of action, (2) regulatory agencies (if any), and (3) users relying, or likely to rely on the audit report.

3. When such procedures are performed, if the auditor becomes aware of facts regarding the financial statements that existed at the report release date that, had they been known to the auditor at that date, may have caused the auditor to amend the auditor's report, the auditor should apply AU-C 560, *Subsequent Events and Subsequently Discovered Facts.*

AU-C 600 Special Considerations—Audits of Group Financial Statements (Including the Work of Component Auditors)

A. Introduction

1. Scope: This section addresses special considerations that apply to group audits, in particular those that involve component auditors.
2. To think about a group audit consider an example—a parent company that has three subsidiaries.

    a. Parent company is required to have an audit report on its overall consolidated financial statements (assume your firm will issue that report). Parent company is composed of Subsidiaries A, B and C.
    b. Subsidiaries A and B are audited by your firm (the group engagement team or group auditor).
    c. Subsidiary C is audited by another auditor (the component auditor).
    d. The issues here are largely about the group auditor's responsibilities with respect to the work performed by the component auditor and issuing the audit report on the overall parent company financial statements (which include the subsidiaries).

3. The group audit team and component auditors collectively possess the appropriate competence and capabilities. The group engagement partner is responsible for the direction, supervision and performance for the group audit.
4. The overall purpose here is to obtain sufficient appropriate audit evidence on the entire entity.
5. The group engagement partner is responsible for deciding, individually for each component, to either

    a. Assume responsibility for the work of a component auditor.
    b. Not assume responsibility for and accordingly make reference to audit of component auditor in the auditor's report on the group financial statements.

B. Objectives: The objectives of the auditor are to determine whether to act as the auditor of the group financial statements, and, if so,

1. Determine whether to make reference to the audit of a component auditor in the auditor's report on the group financial statements.
2. Communicate clearly with component auditors.
3. Obtain sufficient appropriate audit evidence regarding the financial information of the components and the consolidation process to express an opinion about whether the group financial statements are prepared, in all material respects, in accordance with the applicable financial reporting framework.
4. Determine whether to make reference to the audit of a component auditor in the auditor's report on the group financial statements.

C. Definitions

1. **Component.** An entity or business activity for which group or component management prepares financial information that should be included in the group financial statements.
2. **Component auditor.** An auditor who performs work on the financial information of a component that will be used as audit evidence for the group audit. A component auditor may be part of the group engagement partner's firm, a network firm of the group engagement partner's firm, or an unrelated firm.
3. **Component management.** Management responsible for preparing the financial information of a component.
4. **Component materiality.** The materiality for a component determined by the group engagement team for the purposes of the group audit.
5. **Group.** All the components whose financial information is included in the group financial statements. A group always has more than one component.
6. **Group audit.** The audit of group financial statements.
7. **Group audit opinion.** The audit opinion on the group financial statements.
8. **Group engagement partner.** The partner or other person in the firm who is responsible for the group audit engagement and its performance and for the auditor's report on the group financial statements that is issued on behalf of the firm. When joint auditors conduct the group audit, the joint engagement partners and their engagement teams collectively constitute the group engagement partner and the group engagement team. This SAS does not, however, deal with the relationship between joint auditors or the work that one joint auditor performs in relation to the work of the other joint auditor.
9. **Group engagement team.** Partners, including the group engagement partner, and staff who establish the overall group audit strategy, communicate with component auditors, perform work on the consolidation process, and evaluate the conclusions drawn from the audit evidence as the basis for forming an opinion on the group financial statements.
10. **Group financial statements.** Financial statements that include the financial information of more than one component. The term *group financial statements* also refers to combined financial statements aggregating the financial information prepared by components that have no parent but are under common control.
11. **Group management.** Management responsible for preparing and presenting the group financial statements.
12. **Group-wide controls.** Controls designed, implemented, and maintained by group management over group financial reporting.
13. **Significant component.** A component identified by the group engagement team (a) that is of individual financial significance to the group or (b) that, due to its specific nature or circumstances, is likely to include significant risks of material misstatement of the group financial statements.

D. Responsibilities, application, and other material

1. The group engagement partner is responsible for

   a. Direction and performance of group audit in compliance with professional standards and regulatory and legal requirements.
   b. Determining whether the auditor's report that is issued is appropriate.

2. Acceptance and continuance

   a. The group engagement partner should determine whether sufficient appropriate audit evidence can reasonably be expected to be obtained.
   b. When the group engagement partner concludes that it will not be possible to obtain sufficient appropriate evidence due to restrictions imposed by group management, he or she should

      (1) For potential new audits—not accept engagement.
      (2) For continuing audits—withdraw.

NOTE: When law or regulation prohibits not accepting or withdrawing, disclaim an opinion on the group financial statements

3. Overall audit strategy

    a. The group engagement team is responsible.

    b. The group engagement partner should review and approve the overall group audit strategy and group audit plan.

4. Understanding the component auditor—the group engagement team should obtain an understanding of

    a. Whether component auditor understands and will comply with relevant ethical requirements (e.g., independence).

    b. Component auditor's professional competence.

        (1) Inquiries may be made of AICPA, state board of accountancy, applicable state society of CPAs, or corresponding groups for foreign auditors.

> **NOTE:** When there are concerns about (1) and (2) above due to the component auditor, sufficient appropriate audit evidence should be obtained without using the work of the component auditor and without making reference to the audit of the component auditor in the auditor's report on the group financial statements.

    c. Extent, if any, group engagement team will be able to be involved with component auditor.

    d. Whether group engagement team will be able to obtain needed information affecting consolidation process from component auditor.

    e. Whether component auditor operates in a regulatory environment that actively oversees auditors.

5. Determining whether to make reference to a component auditor in the audit report on the group financial statements

    a. Group engagement partner should not make reference to the audit of a component auditor unless

        (1) The component auditor has performed an audit of the component in accordance with the relevant requirements of GAAS.

        (2) Component auditor has issued an auditor's report that is not restricted as to use.

    b. If the component financial statements are prepared using a different financial reporting framework than the group financial statements, reference to the component auditor should not be made unless

        (1) Criteria similar to group's framework.

        (2) Group auditor has obtained sufficient appropriate evidence for evaluating appropriateness of adjustments needed to convert component's financial statements to group's framework.

    c. When group engagement partners decide to make reference, the group engagement team should obtain sufficient appropriate audit evidence by performing

        (1) Various procedures aimed at determining whether component has been properly audited.

        (2) Reading the component's financial statements and the component auditor's report and when considered necessary, communicating with the component auditor.

    d. Making reference in the group engagement audit report

        (1) Clearly indicate in the introductory, scope, and opinion paragraphs the division of responsibility between the group engagement team and the component auditor concerning that portion of the financial statements covered by the group engagement team's audit and that covered by the component auditor.

        (2) If the group engagement partner decides to name the component auditor

            (a) Obtain component auditor's permission.

            (b) Present component auditor's report together with the group audit report.

        (3) When the component's financial statements are prepared using a different financial reporting framework from that used for the group financial statements, that different framework should be disclosed and the group auditor must take responsibility for evaluating the appropriateness of the adjustments to convert those financial statements to the financial reporting framework used by the group.

        (4) When the component auditor has performed the audit using other than GAAS (or PCAOB standards), the group audit report indicates that the component's financial statements were audited by other auditors in accordance with (describe standards) and that additional audit procedures were performed as necessary by the group auditor to conform with US GAAS (PCAOB standards).

    e. If the group engagement partner decides to assume responsibility for the work of the component auditor, no reference should be made to the component auditor.

6. Materiality—The group engagement team should determine group and component materiality.
7. Responding to assessed risks—The auditor is required to design and implement appropriate responses to address the assessed risks of material misstatement in the financial statements.
8. Consolidation process—The group engagement team must determine this is done properly.
9. Subsequent events—Both group and component auditors have ordinary audit responsibilities (AU-C 560).
10. The communication with the component auditor should include

   a. Request that the component auditor confirm expected use of report and indicate it will cooperate.
   b. Ethical requirements (e.g., independence).
   c. List of related parties prepared by group management and any others identified.
   d. Identified significant risks of material misstatement of the group financial statements that are relevant to the work of the component auditor.

11. The group engagement team should request a component auditor to communicate matters such as

   a. Whether component auditor complied with group engagement team's requirements.
   b. Identification of the financial information of the component on which the component auditor is reporting.
   c. Component auditor's overall findings, conclusions, or opinion.

12. Evaluating the sufficiency and appropriateness of audit evidence obtained

   a. Overall, the group engagement team should evaluate the component auditor's communication and determine whether it is necessary to review other relevant parts of a component auditor's audit documentation.

13. Communication with group management and those charged with governance of the group

   a. As per AU-C 265, significant deficiencies and material weaknesses (identified in the group and component audits) that are relevant to the group (whether identified by the group or component auditor) should be communicated to management and those charged with governance.
   b. Various matters such as fraud identified, nature of involvement of component auditors, etc.

14. Documentation by the group engagement team should include analysis of significant components, written communications with component auditors, etc.
15. Additional requirements when assuming responsibility for the work of a component auditor are appropriateness of performance, materiality at component level, nature of work performed, etc., (there are many detailed requirements here).

610 The Auditor's Consideration of the Internal Audit Function in an Audit of Financial Statements

> **NOTE:** The following outline is the only one not yet modified under the Auditing Standards Board Clarity Project.

Overall Objectives and Approach—This section presents guidance on how CPAs (1) **consider the effect of work** of internal auditors on the nature, timing, and extent of audit procedures and (2) use internal auditors to **provide direct assistance** on the audit. When considering internal auditors' work, the CPA must assess both **competence** and **objectivity**. Internal auditors may affect CPA understanding of internal control, control risk assessment, and substantive tests.

A. Obtaining an understanding of the internal auditing function

1. CPA should obtain an understanding of the internal auditing function sufficient to aid in planning the audit
2. CPA should make inquiries concerning internal auditors'

   a. Organizational status within the entity
   b. Application of professional standards
   c. Audit plan
   d. Access to records, including any scope limitations placed on internal auditors
   e. Charter, mission statement, etc.

3. Consider relevant activities (those pertaining to entity's ability to record, process, summarize, and report financial data) using knowledge from prior-year audits, reviewing internal audit function allocation of its audit resources, and by reading internal auditors' reports

4. If CPA concludes internal auditors' activities are not relevant to audit, those activities need not be considered further unless CPA wishes to obtain internal auditors' direct assistance on audit (part D of this outline)

EXAMPLE

A CPA is not typically interested in internal auditors' evaluation of management decision-making processes.

B. Assessing *competence* and *objectivity* of internal auditors

1. When assessing **competence** CPA should consider internal auditors'

   a. Education and experience
   b. Professional certification and continuing education
   c. Audit policies, programs, and procedures
   d. Practices regarding assignments
   e. Supervision and review activities
   f. Quality of working paper documentation, reports, and recommendations
   g. Evaluation of performance

2. When assessing **objectivity** CPA should consider internal auditors'

   a. Organizational status, including whether

      (1) Internal auditors report to officer of sufficient status
      (2) Internal auditors have direct access to board of directors, audit committee, or owner-manager
      (3) Board of directors, audit committee, or owner/manager oversees internal auditors' employment decisions

   b. Policies to maintain internal auditors' objectivity about areas audited, such as policies prohibiting internal auditors from auditing areas where

      (1) Relatives are employed in important or audit-sensitive positions
      (2) An internal auditor was recently assigned or is scheduled to be assigned

3. Sources of information for assessing competence and objectivity

   a. Previous experience
   b. Discussions with management
   c. Recent external quality review of internal auditors' activities
   d. Professional internal auditing standards

C. Effect of internal auditors' work on the audit

1. Effect of internal auditors' work on the nature, timing, and extent of audit (effect on 3 stages of audit)

   a. **Understanding of internal control**—Internal auditors may have developed useful information for CPA (e.g., flowcharts, evidence on whether controls have been placed in operation)
   b. **Risk assessment**

      (1) **Financial statement level**—May affect many financial statement assertions (e.g., CPA and internal auditors may coordinate work to reduce number of entity's locations CPA performs auditing procedures)
      (2) **Account-balance or class-or-transaction level**—May affect nature, timing, and extent of tests

   c. **Substantive procedures**—CPA has ultimate responsibility for opinion

      (1) Responsibility for opinion cannot be shared with internal auditors
      (2) In determining extent of effect, CPA should consider materiality, risk of misstatement, and subjectivity of evidence
      (3) For assertions with high risk of material misstatement, internal auditors' work cannot alone eliminate need for CPA testing

(a) Examples: Assertion on valuation of accounting estimates, related-party transactions, contingencies, uncertainties, subsequent events

(4) For assertions related to immaterial financial statement amounts where risk of material misstatements is low, CPA in some circumstances may not need to do additional procedures

(a) Examples: Existence of cash, prepaid assets, fixed asset additions

2. Work of internal auditors and CPA should be coordinated through periodic meetings, scheduling audit work, access of internal auditors' working papers, reviewing audit reports, and discussions
3. When evaluating the effectiveness of internal auditors' **work** the CPA should

a. Consider whether

(1) Scope of work appropriate
(2) Audit programs appropriate
(3) Adequate documentation in working papers
(4) Appropriate conclusions in reports
(5) Reports consistent with results of work

b. Test internal auditors' work through examining controls, transactions, or balances either examined by internal auditors or similar to those examined by internal auditors

D. Using internal auditors to *provide direct assistance*, CPA should

1. Consider internal auditors' competence and objectivity
2. Supervise, review, evaluate, and test internal auditors' work performed

AU-C 620 Using the Work of an Auditor's Specialist

A. Introduction

1. Scope: This section addresses the auditor's responsibilities relating to the work of an individual or organization possessing expertise in a field other than accounting or auditing (referred to as the "auditor's specialist) when that work is used to assist the auditor in obtaining sufficient appropriate audit evidence.

a. It does not address consultations related to (1) expertise in a specialized area of accounting or auditing or (2) the auditor's use of the work of a specialist used by management (management's specialist—see AU-C 620 for guidance).

2. The auditor has sole responsibility for the audit opinion expressed, and that responsibility is not reduced by the use of the auditor's specialist; nonetheless, if the auditor follows this section's requirements s/he may accept the auditor's specialist's findings as appropriate audit evidence.

B. Objectives: The objectives of the auditor are

1. To determine whether to use the work of an auditor's specialist.
2. If using the work of an auditor's specialist, to determine whether that work is adequate for the auditor's purposes.

C. Definitions

1. **Auditor's specialist.** An individual or organization possessing expertise in a field other than accounting or auditing, whose work in that field is used by the auditor to assist the auditor in obtaining sufficient appropriate audit evidence. An auditor's specialist may be either an auditor's internal specialist (who is a partner or staff, including temporary staff, of the auditor's firm or a network firm) or an auditor's external specialist.
2. **Expertise.** Skills, knowledge, and experience in a particular field.
3. **Management's specialist.** An individual or organization possessing expertise in a field other than accounting or auditing, whose work in that field is used by the entity in preparing the financial statements. Note that this may be an employee of the entity, or a nonemployee individual or organization providing management with the service.

D. Requirements, selected application, and other explanatory material

1. Determining the need for an auditor's specialist

a. Specialists may be needed in areas such as

       (1) Valuation of complex financial instruments, land and buildings, plant and machinery, jewelry, works of art, antiques, intangible assets, assets acquired and liabilities assumed in business combinations, and assets that may have been impaired.

       (2) Actual calculation of liabilities.

       (3) Estimation of oil and gas reserves.

       (4) Valuation of environmental liabilities and site cleanup costs.

       (5) Interpretation of contracts, laws, and regulations.

       (6) Analysis of complex or unusual tax compliance issues.

    b. In some cases, particularly those involving an emerging area of accounting or auditing expertise, distinguishing between specialized areas of accounting/auditing and another field will be a matter of professional judgment.

    c. When an individual has accounting/auditing expertise, as well as expertise in another area (e.g., an actuary also may be an accountant), the determination of whether that individual is an auditor or a specialist depends on the nature of the work performed for purposes of the audit.

2. Nature, timing, and extent of audit procedures

    a. This will vary with the circumstances; the auditor should consider

       (1) Nature of the matter to which the work of the auditor's specialist relates.

       (2) Risks of material misstatement in the area.

       (3) Significance of the work of the auditor's specialist in context of audit.

       (4) Auditor's knowledge of, and experience with, previous work of the auditor's specialist.

       (5) Whether auditor's specialist is subject to auditor's firm's quality control policies and procedures.

3. The auditor should determine whether the auditor's specialist has the necessary competence, capabilities and objectivity for the auditor's purposes.

4. The auditor should obtain a sufficient understanding of the auditor's specialist's field of expertise to

    a. Determine the nature, scope and objectives of the auditor's specialist's work.

    b. Evaluate the adequacy of that work for the auditor's purposes.

5. The auditor should agree, in writing, when appropriate with the auditor's specialist regarding

    a. Nature, scope, and objectives of the work of the auditor's specialist.

    b. Respective roles and responsibilities of the auditor and auditor's specialist.

    c. Nature, timing, and extent of communication between auditor and auditor's specialist.

    d. Need for the auditor's specialist to observe confidentiality requirements.

6. Evaluating the adequacy of the work of the auditor's specialist

    a. The auditor should evaluate the adequacy of the work of the auditor's specialist for the auditor's purposes, including

       (1) Relevance and reasonableness of the findings and conclusions of the auditor's specialist and their consistency with other audit evidence.

       (2) If the auditor's specialist's work involves use of significant assumptions and methods

          (a) Obtaining an understanding of those methods and assumptions.

          (b) Evaluating the relevance and reasonableness of those assumptions and methods in relation to the auditor's other findings and conclusions.

    b. If the auditor's specialist's work is not adequate, the auditor should

       (1) Agree with that auditor's specialist on the nature and extent of further work, or

       (2) Perform additional audit procedures appropriate in the circumstances.

7. Reference to the auditor's specialist in the auditor's report

    a. The auditor should not refer to the work of an auditor's specialist in an auditor's report containing an unmodified opinion.

    b. It may be appropriate to refer to the auditor's external specialist in an auditor's report containing a modified opinion to explain the nature of the modification; in such circumstances, the auditor may need to obtain the auditor's specialist's permission.

AU-C 700 Forming an Opinion and Reporting on Financial Statements

A. Introduction

1. Scope: This section addresses the auditor's responsibility to form an opinion on the financial statements. It also addresses the form and content of the auditor's report to be issued.

B. Objectives: The objectives of the auditor are to

1. Form an opinion on the financial statements based on an evaluation of the audit evidence obtained, including evidence obtained about comparative financial statements and comparative financial information.
2. Express clearly that opinion on the financial statements through a written report that also describes the basis for that opinion.

C. Definitions

1. **Comparative financial statements.** A complete set of financial statements for one or more prior periods included with current year financial statements of the current period.
2. **Comparative information.** Prior period information presented for purposes of comparison with current period amounts or disclosures that is not in the form of a complete set of financial statements.
3. **Fair presentation framework.** A financial reporting framework that requires compliance with the requirements of the framework and

   a. Acknowledges explicitly or implicitly that, to achieve fair representation of the financial statements, it may be necessary for management to provide disclosures beyond those specifically required by the framework, or
   b. Acknowledges explicitly that it may be necessary for management to depart from a requirement of the framework to achieve fair presentation of the financial statements. Such departures are expected to be necessary only in extremely rare circumstances.

   NOTE: The Auditing Standards Board considers all frameworks in the US fair presentation frameworks.

4. **General-purpose financial statements.** Those prepared in accordance with a general-purpose framework.
5. **General-purpose framework.** A financial reporting framework designed to meet the common financial information needs of a wide range of users.
6. **Unmodified opinion.** The opinion expressed when the auditor concludes that the financial statements are prepared in all material respects, in accordance with the applicable financial reporting framework.

D. Requirements, application, and selected other explanatory material

1. Overall the auditor's procedures are aimed at allowing the auditor to form an opinion on whether financial statements present fairly in all material respects in accordance with the applicable financial reporting framework. The auditor should conclude on whether s/he has obtained reasonable assurance about whether the financial statements as a whole are free from material misstatements (whether due to errors or fraud).

   a. The evaluation should include consideration of the qualitative aspects of the entity's accounting practices, including indicators of possible bias in management's judgments (e.g., it would be inappropriate for a client to only record identified correcting entries that increase earnings when others decrease earnings).
   b. The auditor should evaluate whether, in view of the requirements of the applicable financial reporting framework

      (1) The financial statements disclose significant accounting policies and those policies are consistent with the financial reporting framework.
      (2) Accounting estimates are reasonable.
      (3) Information in the financial statements is relevant, reliable, comparable and understandable.
      (4) The financial statements provide adequate disclosures.
      (5) Terminology in the financial statements is appropriate.

2. Form of opinion

   a. The auditor should express an *unmodified opinion* when the auditor concludes the financial statements present fairly, in all material respects, in accordance with the applicable financial reporting framework.
   b. The auditor should modify the opinion if the auditor

        (1) Concludes that, the financial statements are materially misstated, or

        (2) Is unable to obtain sufficient appropriate audit evidence to conclude that the financial statements are free from material misstatement.

  c. In some situations financial statements prepared in accordance with the requirements of a fair presentation framework may not achieve fair presentation. When this is the case, management may be able to add additional disclosures.

        (1) Rule 203 of the Code of Professional Conduct allows for unusual circumstances when it states that the framework may be departed from in unusual circumstances. In such a situation an emphasis of matter paragraph would be added to a report with an unmodified opinion—it is not anticipated that GAAP-based financial statements will have this occur. One ordinarily expects a departure from GAAP to result in either a qualified or adverse opinion.

3. The auditor's report should be in writing and include

  a. Title that includes the word independent.

  b. Addressee

        (1) Ordinarily to the entity being audited.

        (2) Depending on the circumstances, may be to partners, proprietor and occasionally to an entity that is not the client.

  c. Introductory paragraph should

        (1) Identify the entity being audited.

        (2) State that the financial statements have been audited.

        (3) Identify the title of each statement.

        (4) Specify the date or period covered by each financial statement.

  d. Management's responsibility for the financial statements

        (1) Should include heading with "Management's Responsibility for the Financial Statements."

        (2) Should include that management is responsible for the preparation and fair presentation of financial statements and that this responsibility includes the design, implementation, and maintenance of IC.

        (3) The description should not be further elaborated upon in the auditor's report or referenced to a separate statement by management.

  e. Auditor's responsibility

        (1) Should include a heading with "Auditor's Responsibility."

        (2) To express an opinion on the financial statements based on the audit.

        (3) Audit conducted in accordance with GAAS, and those standards require the auditor to plan and perform the audit to obtain reasonable assurance about whether the financial statements are free from material misstatement.

        (4) An audit involves performing procedures to obtain audit evidence about the amounts and disclosures in the financial statements.

        (5) The procedures selected depend upon the auditor's judgment.

        (6) An audit includes evaluating the appropriateness of accounting policies and the reasonableness of significant accounting estimates, as well as overall presentation.

        (7) The auditor believes that the audit evidence obtained is sufficient and appropriate to provide a basis for an opinion.

  f. Auditor's opinion

        (1) Should include a heading with "Opinion."

        (2) When expressing an unmodified opinion, the auditor's opinion should state that the financial statements present fairly, in all material respects, the financial position, results of operation and cash flows in accordance with the applicable financial reporting framework (name the framework).

  g. Other reporting responsibility

        (1) If other reporting responsibilities exist they should be addressed in a separate section of the auditor's report that should be subtitled "Report on Other Legal and Regulatory Requirements" or otherwise as appropriate.

      (a) If this occurs, the audit report itself (point 3. above) should be included under the subtitle "Report on the Financial Statement" and this section should follow that.

  h. Signature of the auditor—Manual or printed signature of the auditor's firm, including the city and state where the auditor practices.

  i. Date of the auditor's report—No earlier than the date on which the auditor has obtained sufficient appropriate audit evidence, including evidence that

    (1) Audit documentation has been reviewed.

    (2) All statements that comprise the financial statements, including the related notes, have been prepared.

    (3) Management has asserted that they have taken responsibility for the financial statements.

4. Additional reporting issues

  a. If the audit was conducted in accordance with GAAS and another set of auditing standards (e.g., international) the report may so indicate.

  b. When comparative statements are presented, the auditor's report should refer to each period.

  c. If summarized comparative information for the prior period is presented and the entity requests the auditor to express an opinion on all periods presented, the auditor should consider whether the prior period information contains sufficient detail to constitute fair presentation.

    (1) Sufficient appropriate audit evidence should be obtained on the comparative information.

    (2) Written representations should be obtained on all periods referred to in the auditor's opinion.

    (3) If the prior period was audited by a predecessor, and the predecessor auditor's report is not reissued, in addition to expressing an opinion on the current period's financial statements, the auditor should state in an *other matter paragraph*

      (a) Prior period statements audited by a predecessor auditor.

      (b) Type of opinion and if the opinion was modified, the reasons.

      (c) Date of the predecessor's report.

    (4) When comparative statements are presented and prior period statements contain a material misstatement, the auditor should tell management and those charged with governance about this; if the prior period financial statements are amended and the predecessor agrees to issue a new auditor's report on the amended statements of the prior period, the auditor should express an opinion only on the current period.

    (5) When comparative statements are presented, but the prior period is not audited, the auditor should so state in an *other matter paragraph*.

AU-C 705 Modifications to the Opinion in the Independent Auditor's Report

A. Introduction

1. Scope: This section addresses the auditor's responsibility to issue an appropriate report in circumstances when, in forming an opinion, the auditor concludes that a modification to the auditor's opinion on the financial statements is necessary.

2. Types of modified opinions

  a. There are 3 types of modified opinions—qualified, adverse, and disclaimers

  b. The decision of which type of modification to issue depends upon

    (1) The nature of the matter giving rise to the modification (i.e., whether the financial statements are misstated or, in the case of an inability to obtain sufficient appropriate evidence, whether they may be misstated).

    (2) The auditor's judgment about the pervasiveness of the effects or possible effects on the financial statements.

B. Objective: To express clearly an appropriately modified opinion when

1. The auditor concludes, based on the evidence obtained, that the financial statements as a whole are materially misstated, *or*

2. The auditor is unable to obtain sufficient appropriate audit evidence.

C. Definitions

1. **Pervasive.** The effects on financial statements of misstatements or possible effects of misstatements that are undetected due to an inability to obtain sufficient appropriate audit evidence. Pervasive effects on the financial statements are those that, in the auditor's judgment

   a. Are not confined to specific elements, accounts or items of the financial statements, or
   b. If so confined, represent or could represent a substantial proportion of the financial statements, or
   c. In relation to disclosures, are fundamental to users' understanding of the financial statements.

   > **NOTE:** This term is particularly important. When a misstatement's effects are pervasive, an adverse opinion is issued; when material but not pervasive, a qualified opinion is issued. Similarly, when the effects of a scope limitation are pervasive, a disclaimer of opinion is issued; when they are material but not pervasive, a qualified opinion is issued.

2. **Modified opinion.** A qualified opinion, an adverse opinion, or a disclaimer of opinion.

D. Requirements, application, and other explanatory material

1. Circumstances when a modification to the auditor's opinion is required

   a. Financial statements as a whole are materially misstated.
   b. Auditor unable to obtain sufficient appropriate audit evidence to conclude that the financial statements as a whole are free from material misstatement (also referred to as a *limitation on the scope of the audit*—or, *scope limitation* or *scope restriction*).

2. Determining the type of modification to the auditor's report

   a. Qualified opinion—Two distinct circumstances

      (1) Misstatements are material, but not pervasive, to the financial statements.
      (2) Auditor unable to obtain sufficient appropriate evidence, but the possible effects of undetected misstatements, if any, could be material but not pervasive.

   b. Adverse opinion—Misstatements, individually or in aggregate, are both material and pervasive.
   c. Disclaimer of opinion—The auditor is unable to obtain sufficient appropriate audit evidence on which to base an opinion and concludes that the possible effects on the financial statements of undetected misstatements, if any, could be both material and pervasive.

      (1) Limitations on the scope of the audit create the situation in which the auditor is unable to obtain sufficient appropriate audit evidence

         (a) May arise from

            1] *Circumstances beyond the control of the entity* (e.g., accounting records destroyed; accounting records seized by governmental authorities).
            2] *Circumstances relating to the nature or timing of the auditor's work* (e.g., auditor hired after counting of physical inventories; auditor unable to obtain audited financial statements of an investee; auditor determines substantive procedures alone are not sufficient and entity controls are ineffective).
            3] *Limitations imposed by management* (e.g., management prevents auditor from observing the counting of physical inventory or confirming account balances).

         (b) An inability to perform a specific procedure does not constitute a limitation on the scope of the audit if the auditor is able to obtain sufficient appropriate audit evidence by performing alternative procedures.

      (2) Management-imposed scope limitation: If management places a scope limitation likely to result in a qualified opinion or disclaimer of opinion, the auditor should

    (a) Request management to remove scope limitation.

    (b) If management will not remove the scope limitation, communicate the matter to those charged with governance (unless all are members of management) and determine whether it is possible to perform alternative procedures to obtain sufficient appropriate audit evidence.

    (c) If the auditor is unable to obtain sufficient appropriate audit evidence due to a management-imposed scope limitation, and if the auditor believes undetected misstatements could be both material and pervasive, the auditor should either disclaim an opinion or, where practicable, withdraw from the audit.

d. Uncertainties and disclaimers—Conclusive audit evidence concerning the ultimate outcome of uncertainties cannot be expected to exist at the time of the audit because the outcome and related audit evidence are prospective.

    (1) Absence of information related to the outcome of an uncertainty does not necessarily lead to a conclusion that the audit evidence supporting management's assertion is not sufficient. The auditor's judgment regarding sufficiency is based on the audit evidence that is, or should be available.

        (a) If the auditor concludes sufficient appropriate audit evidence supports management's assertions about the uncertainty, an unmodified opinion ordinarily is appropriate.

        (b) Despite (a), in cases involving multiple uncertainties, the auditor may conclude that it is not possible to form an opinion on the financial statements as a whole due to the interaction and cumulative possible effects of the uncertainties.

> **NOTE:** (b) is indicating that multiple uncertainties, in and of themselves, may result in a disclaimer of opinion. The notion here is that the multiple uncertainties create a situation in which it is impossible to obtain sufficient appropriate audit evidence.

e. When either an adverse opinion or a qualified opinion is being issued, the auditor's report should not include an unmodified opinion on a single financial statement or one or more specific elements, accounts or items of a financial statement.

f. Summary table for types of opinions

Nature of matter giving rise to the possible modification	Auditor's judgment about the pervasiveness of the effects or possible effects on the financial statements		
	Not material (accordingly, not pervasive)	Material but not pervasive	Material and pervasive
Financial statements are misstated (GAAP departure)	Unmodified	Qualified	Adverse
Inability to obtain sufficient appropriate audit evidence (scope limitation)	Unmodified	Qualified	Disclaimer

3. Form and content of the auditor's report when the opinion is modified

a. Add a basis for modification paragraph immediately *before* the opinion paragraph with a heading that includes "Basis for Qualified Opinion" etc.

    (1) Material misstatements of accounts or disclosures—the auditor should include in the paragraph a description and quantification of the effects, unless impracticable (if impracticable, so state).

    (2) Omissions of information—describe, including the omitted information if practicable.

    (3) Inability to obtain sufficient appropriate audit evidence (scope limitation)—include the reasons for the inability.

b. Opinion paragraph

    (1) Use the heading "Qualified Opinion" etc.

    (2) Qualified due to a material misstatement—State in the opinion paragraph that, in the auditor's opinion, except for the effects of the matter described in the basis for qualified opinion paragraph, the financial statements are fairly presented, in all material respects, in accordance with the applicable framework.

      (3) Qualified due to inability to obtain sufficient appropriate audit evidence—"Except for the possible effects of the matters. . . ."

      (4) Adverse—"Because of the significance of the matter described in the basis for adverse opinion paragraph, the financial statements are not presented fairly in accordance with the applicable financial reporting framework."

      (5) Disclaimer—"Because of the significance of the matter described in the basis for disclaimer of opinion paragraph, I have not been able to obtain sufficient appropriate audit evidence to provide a basis for an audit opinion and accordingly, I do not express an opinion on the financial statements."

  c. Description of auditor's responsibility when the auditor expresses a

      (1) Qualified or adverse opinion—Amend the paragraph to say that the auditor believes that the audit evidence obtained is sufficient and appropriate to provide a basis for the auditor's modified audit opinion.

      (2) Disclaimer of opinion—Amend the paragraph to state that that the auditor was not able to obtain sufficient appropriate audit evidence to provide a basis for an audit opinion.

  d. When the auditor expects to modify the opinion, the auditor should communicate this with those charged with governance.

AU-C 706 Emphasis-of-Matter Paragraphs and Other Matter Paragraphs

A. Introduction

1. Scope: This section addresses additional communications in the auditor's report when, in the auditor's judgment, the auditor considers it necessary to draw users' attention to

  a. A matter or matters presented or disclosed in the financial statements that are of such importance that they are fundamental to users' understanding of the financial statements (*emphasis-of-matter paragraph*); examples are

      (1) An uncertainty relating to

         (a) The future outcome of exceptional litigation or regulatory action.

         (b) A major catastrophe.

      (2) Going concern modification being issued with an unmodified audit opinion.

      (3) Auditor providing an opinion on supplementary information in relation to the financial statements as a whole.

      (4) A lack of consistency in application of accounting principles.

  b. Any matter or matters other than those presented or disclosed in the financial statements that are relevant to users' understanding of the audit, the auditor's responsibilities, or the auditor's report (*other-matter paragraph*); examples are

      (1) Auditor issues an updated report on financial statements of a prior period that contains an opinion different from the opinion previously expressed.

      (2) Required supplemental information.

      (3) Other information in documents containing audited financial statements.

      (4) Audits prepared in accordance with special-purpose frameworks.

      (5) Compliance with aspects of contractual agreements or regulatory requirements in connection with audited financial statements.

B. Objective: To draw users' attention, when in the auditor's judgment it is necessary to do so, by way of clear additional communication in the auditor's report, to

1. A matter that is appropriately presented or disclosed in the financial statements that is of such importance that it is fundamental to users' understanding of the financial statements; or

2. As appropriate, any other matter that is relevant to users' understanding of the audit, the auditor's responsibilities, or the auditor's report.

C. Definitions

1. **Emphasis-of-a matter paragraph.** A paragraph included in the auditor's report at the auditor's discretion that refers to a *matter appropriately presented or disclosed in the financial statements* that, in the auditor's judgment, is of such importance that it is fundamental to users' understanding of the financial statements.
2. **Other-matter paragraph.** A paragraph include in the auditor's report that refers to a matter *other than those presented or disclosed in the financial statements* that, in the auditor's judgment, is relevant to users' understanding of the audit, the auditor's responsibilities, or the auditor's report.

D. Requirements, application, and selected other explanatory material

1. When the auditor includes an *emphasis-of-matter paragraph*, the auditor should

   a. Include it immediately *after* the opinion paragraph.
   b. Use the heading "Emphasis of Matter" or other appropriate heading.
   c. Include in the paragraph clear reference to the matter emphasized and to where relevant disclosures can be found in the financial statements.
   d. Indicate that the auditor's opinion is not modified with respect to the matter emphasized.

2. Placement of an other matter paragraph

Nature of information communicated	Placement
Draw users' attention to a matter relevant to their understanding of the audit.	Immediately after the opinion paragraph (and after any emphasis of matter paragraph).
Draw users' attention to matter relating to other reporting responsibilities addressed in the auditor's report.	In the section subtitled "Report on Other Legal and Regulatory Requirements."
When relevant to all the auditor's responsibilities or users' understanding of the auditor's report.	As a separate section following the "Report on the Financial Statements" and the "Report on Other Legal and Regulatory Requirements."

> **NOTE:** In considering the above three situations, most CPA exam questions relate to the first situation, drawing attention to a matter relevant to user's understanding of the audit.

3. Overall, make certain that you know

   a. *An emphasis-of-matter paragraph* refers only to matters appropriately presented or disclosed in the financial statements.
   b. *An other-matter paragraph* refers to a matter *other than* those presented or disclosed in the financial statements that, in the auditor's judgment, is relevant to users' understanding of the audit, the auditor's responsibilities, or the auditor's report.

AU-C 708 Consistency of Financial Statements

A. Scope: This section addresses the auditor's evaluation of the consistency of the financial statements between periods, including changes to previously issued financial statements, and the effect of that evaluation on the auditor's report on the financial statements.

B. Objective: The objectives of the auditor are to

1. Evaluate the consistency of the financial statements for the periods presented, and
2. Communicate appropriately in the auditor's report when the comparability of financial statements between periods has been materially affected by a change in accounting principle or by adjustments to correct a material misstatement in previously issued financial statements.

C. Definition

1. **Current period.** The most recent period upon which the auditor is reporting.

D. Requirements, application and other explanatory material

1. The auditor should evaluate whether the comparability of financial statements between periods has been materially affected by a change in accounting principle or by adjustments to correct a material misstatement in previously issued financial statements.

   a. The periods included in the evaluation of consistency depend on the periods covered by the auditor's opinion on the financial statements.

If auditor opinion covers	The auditor should evaluate consistency
Only the current period.	Of the current period financial statements with the preceding period, regardless of whether those of the preceding period are presented.
Two or more periods.	Between such periods and the consistency of the earliest period covered by the auditor's opinion with the period prior thereto, if such period is presented with the financial statements being reported upon.

   b. The above evaluation in a. encompasses previously issued financial statements for the relevant periods, even if those previously statements have been retrospectively adjusted to reflect the change in accounting principle.

   c. When a change in principle is accounted for by applying the principle to prior periods that are presented with the current financial statements, the financial statements will be consistent. However, the originally presented financial statements differ from the restated statements. Accordingly, this sort of change results in an emphasis of matter paragraph on consistency.

2. Change in accounting principle

   a. When a change has occurred, the auditor should evaluate it to determine whether

      (1) The new accounting principles is in accordance with the applicable financial reporting framework.
      (2) The method of accounting for the change is proper.
      (3) Disclosures are adequate.
      (4) The entity has justified that the alternative accounting principle is preferable.

   b. If criteria in a. (immediately above):

      (1) Have been met—the auditor should include an emphasis of matter paragraph (following the opinion paragraph) and refer to the entity's disclosure.
      (2) Have *not* been met—Treat as a departure from GAAP (or other financial reporting framework being used) and issue a report with a qualified or adverse opinion.

   c. The auditor should include an emphasis of matter paragraph the year of the change and until the new accounting principle is applied in all periods presented; for changes with retrospective application, the paragraph is needed only in the period of such change.

   d. When no material effect on comparability results from a change in accounting principle or an adjustment to previously issued financial statements, the auditor need not refer to consistency in the auditor's report.

   e. A change in estimate that is inseparable form a change in principle is treated as a change in principle (e.g., changing both the life and depreciation method of an asset).

   f. A change in reporting entity results in an emphasis of matter paragraph on consistency; examples

      (1) Presenting consolidated or combined f/s in place of individual entity f/s.
      (2) Changing specific subsidiaries that make up the consolidated or combined group.

   g. Example of emphasis of matter paragraph for a change in accounting principle resulting from adoption of a new accounting pronouncement:

Emphasis of matter

As discussed in Note X of the financial statement, in 20X8, the entity adopted new accounting guidance [description of the new accounting guidance]. Our opinion is not modified with respect to this matter.

---

h. Example of emphasis-of-matter paragraph when the entity has made a voluntary change in accounting principle (i.e., other than a change due to the adoption of a new accounting pronouncement).

> **Emphasis of matter**
>
> As discussed in Note X to the financial statements, the entity has elected to change its method of accounting for [describe accounting method change] in 20X0. Our opinion is not modified with respect to this matter.

3. Correction of a material misstatement in previously issued financial statements

   a. Include an emphasis-of-matter paragraph indicating previous statements restated and reference the disclosure of the correction of the misstatements; the paragraph should include

      (1) Statement that previous f/s have been restated for correction of a misstatement.
      (2) Reference to the entity's disclosure of the correction.

   b. If disclosures are *inadequate,* treat it as a departure from GAAP (qualified or adverse opinion).

4. Changes in classification

   a. Changes in classification do not require recognition unless the change represents the correction of a material misstatement or a change in accounting principle

      (1) Example of a correction of error: Reclassifying cash flows from operating activities to financing activities because the item was incorrectly classified in the previously issued financial statements.

AU-C 720 Other Information in Documents Containing Audited Financial Statements

A. Introduction

1. This section addresses the auditor's responsibility in relation to other information in documents containing audited financial statements and the auditor's report thereon. In the absence of any separate requirement in the particular circumstances of the engagement, the auditor's opinion does not cover other information and the auditor has no responsibility for determining whether such information is properly stated. This section establishes the requirement for the auditor to read the other information because the credibility of the audited financial statements may be undermined by material inconsistencies between the audited financial statements and other information.

2. In this section, *documents containing audited financial statements* refers to annual reports (or similar documents) that are issued to owners (or similar stakeholders) and annual reports of governments and organizations for charitable or philanthropic purposes that are available to the public that contain audited financial statements and the auditor's report thereon. This section also may be applied to other documents to which the auditor, at the client's request, devotes attention.

   a. Examples of other information: A report by management on operations, financial summaries or highlights, employment data, financial ratios, names of officer and directors, selected quarterly data

   b. Examples of information not considered "other information:" A press release or cover letter accompanying the document with audited financial statements, information contained in analyst briefings, information contained on the entity's website

B. Objective: The auditor's objective is to respond appropriately when he or she becomes aware that documents containing audited financial statements and the auditor's report thereon include other information that could undermine the credibility of those financial statements and the auditor's report.

C. Definitions

1. **Inconsistency.** Other information that conflicts with information contained in the audited financial statements. A material inconsistency may raise doubt about the audit conclusions drawn from audit evidence previously obtained and, possibly, about the basis for the auditor's opinion on the financial statements.

2. **Other information.** Financial and nonfinancial information (other than the financial statements and the auditor's report thereon) that is included in a document containing audited financial statements and the auditor's report thereon, excluding required supplementary information.

3. **Misstatement of fact.** Other information that is unrelated to matters appearing in the audited financial statements that is incorrectly stated or presented. A material misstatement of fact may undermine the credibility of the document containing audited financial statements.

D. Requirements, application and other explanatory material

1. Reading other information

     a. The auditor should read the other information of which the auditor is aware in order to identify material inconsistencies, if any, with the audited financial statements

     b. The auditor should attempt to obtain the other information prior to the report release date; if this is not possible, the auditor should read other information as soon as possible

         (1) The auditor may delay the report release date until management provides the other information

     c. The auditor should communicate with those charged with governance the auditor responsibility and other procedures performed relating to other information

2. Inconsistencies between the audited information and the other information identified: If the auditor identifies a material inconsistency, the auditor should determine whether the audited financial statements or the other information needs to be revised; when management refuses

     a. If the audited financial statements are incorrect: The auditor should modify the auditor's report for a departure from GAAP (assuming management does not correct the statements).

     b. If the other information is incorrect: the auditor should do one of the following:

         (1) Include an other matter paragraph in the audit report

         (2) Withhold the auditor's report; or

         (3) Where withdrawal is legally permitted, withdraw.

3. If material inconsistencies are identified subsequent to the report release date the auditor should refer to AU-C 560.

4. If the other information includes misstatements of fact, the auditor should

     a. Discuss with management

     b. If still unresolved, request management to consult with a qualified third party (e.g., legal counsel) and the auditor should consider the advice received

     c. If still unresolved, the auditor's reaction depends upon the particular circumstances

         (1) Possible reactions include notifying the client in writing about the auditor's view and consulting legal counsel as to further appropriate action

AU-C 725 Supplementary Information in Relation to the Financial Statements as a Whole

A. Introduction

1. Scope: This section addresses the auditor's responsibility when engaged to report on whether supplementary information is fairly stated, in all material respects, in relation to the financial statements as a whole. The information covered by this section is presented outside the basic financial statements and is not considered necessary for the financial statements to be fairly presented. This SAS also may be applied when the auditor is engaged to report on whether *required* supplementary information is fairly stated, in all material respects, in relation to the financial statements as a whole.

2. This section also may be adapted and applied when engaged to report on whether required supplemental information is fairly stated, in all material respects, in relation to the financial statements.

B. Objective: The objective is to evaluate and report on whether the supplementary information is fairly stated, in all material respects, in relation to the financial statements as a whole.

C. Definition

1. **Supplementary information.** Information outside the basic financial statements (excluding required supplementary information) that is not considered necessary for the financial statements to be fairly presented in accordance with the applicable financial reporting framework. Such information may be presented in a document containing the audited financial statements or separate from the financial statements.

   a. Examples of supplementary information: Additional details on items related to the basic financial statements, consolidating information, historical summaries of financial statement items, statistical data, other material, some of which may be from sources outside the accounting system or outside the entity
   b. Supplementary information may be prepared in accordance with frameworks other than GAAP.

D. Requirements, application and other explanatory material

1. To accept an engagement to apply procedures to determine whether supplementary information is fairly stated, in all material respects, in relation to the financial statements as a whole, the auditor should determine that all of the following conditions are met:

   a. Supplementary information was derived from and relates directly to the underlying accounting and other records used to prepare financial statements.
   b. The other information relates to the same period as the financial statements.
   c. The financial statements were audited and the auditor served as the principal (group) auditor.
   d. Neither an adverse opinion nor a disclaimer of opinion was issued on the financial statements.
   e. The supplementary information will accompany the audited financial statements, or such audited financial statements will be made readily available by the entity (e.g., they are posted on a website).

2. The auditor should obtain the agreement of management that it acknowledges and understands its responsibility

   a. For proper preparation of supplementary information
   b. To provide auditor with written representations on information
   c. To include the auditor's report on the supplementary information in any document that includes that information
   d. To present the supplementary information with the audited financial statements or to make the audited financial statements available

3. Perform the following procedures using the same materiality level used in the audit of the financial statements:

   a. Inquire of management about the purpose of the information and whether it has been prepared in accordance with the applicable financial reporting framework (e.g., GAAP)
   b. Determine form and content of supplementary information complies with applicable criteria
   c. Obtain understanding about methods of preparing information
   d. Compare and reconcile information to underlying accounting and other records
   e. Inquire of management as to significant assumptions, interpretations, etc.
   f. Evaluate appropriateness and completeness of information
   g. Obtain written representations from management
   h. While the auditor has no responsibility for considering subsequent events with respect to supplementary information, if such information comes to his/her attention, AU-C 560 is relevant.

4. Reporting

   a. The auditor should include an other-matter paragraph in the audit report (or a separate report) with the following elements:

      (1) Audit conducted for purposes of forming an opinion on the financial statements as a whole
      (2) Supplementary information is presented for purposes of additional analysis and is not a required part of the financial statements
      (3) Supplementary information is the responsibility of management and was derived from and relates directly to the underlying accounting and other records used to prepare the financial statements
      (4) The other information has been subjected to the auditing procedures applied in the audit of financial statements and certain additional procedures, including reconciling information to the underlying accounting and other records used to prepare the financial statements and additional procedures in accordance with US GAAS
      (5) If the auditor has issued an unmodified opinion on the financial statements, a statement that the supplementary information is fairly stated in all material respects in relation to the financial statements taken as a whole
      (6) If the auditor is issuing a qualified opinion on the financial statements and the qualification has an effect on the supplementary information, a statement that, in the auditor's opinion, except for the effects of the matter referred to, such information is fairly stated in all material respects in relation to the financial statements as a whole

b. When the entity does not present the other information with the financial statements, the auditor should include the required reporting in a separate report on the other information

c. When the auditor's report on the financial statements includes an adverse opinion or a disclaimer of opinion, the auditor is precluded from expressing an opinion on the supplementary information

   (1) When permitted by law, the auditor may withdraw from the engagement

   (2) If the auditor does not withdraw, the auditor's report on the supplementary information should state that because of the significance of the matter described in the auditor's report, it is inappropriate to, and the auditor does not, express an opinion on the supplementary information

d. The date of the auditor's opinion on the other information should not be earlier than the date on which the auditor completed the required procedures

e. If the auditor concludes the supplementary information is materially misstated, discuss with management and proper revisions; if management does not revise

   (1) Modify opinion on supplementary information and describe the misstatement, or

   (2) If a separate report is being issued on the supplementary information, withhold the auditor's report on the supplementary information

AU-C 730 Required Supplementary Information (RSI)

A. Scope: This section addresses the auditor's responsibility in relation to information supplementary to the basic financial statements that is required by a designated accounting standard setter to accompany such financial statements. In the absence of any separate requirement in the circumstances of the engagement, the auditor's opinion on the basic financial statements does not cover this required supplementary information (RSI).

B. Objective: When a designated accounting standard setter requires information to accompany an entity's basic financial statements, the auditor's objectives are to

1. Describe in the auditor's report whether required supplementary information is presented and
2. Communicate when some or all of the required supplementary information has not been prepared in accordance with guidelines established by a designated accounting standard setter or when the auditor has identified material modifications needed to required supplementary information.

C. Selected Definitions

1. **Required supplementary information (RSI).** Information that a designated accounting standard setter requires to accompany an entity's basic financial statements. RSI is not a part of the basic financial statements; however, a designated accounting standard setter considers the information to be an essential part of financial reporting. In addition, authoritative guidelines for measurement and presentation have been established.
2. **Applicable financial reporting framework.** The financial reporting framework adopted by management, and when appropriate, those charged with governance in the preparation of financial statements that is acceptable in view of the nature of the entity and the objective of the financial statements, or that is required by law or regulation (for example, accounting principles generally accepted in the United States of America, International Financial Reporting Standards issued by the International Accounting Standards Board, or comprehensive bases of accounting other than generally accepted accounting principles).

D. Requirements, application and other explanatory material

1. Procedures

   a. The auditor should

     (1) *Inquire* of management about methods of preparing information—including whether it was prepared following prescribed guidelines, whether methods of measurement or presentation have changed from prior period, and whether there were any significant assumptions or interpretations underlying the measurement or presentation of information

     (2) *Compare information* for consistency with

       (a) Management's responses to the inquiries
       (b) The basic financial statements
       (c) Other knowledge obtained during the audit

     (3) *Obtain written representations* from management acknowledging its responsibility that the information is measured within guidelines, methods have not changed, and significant assumptions

b. If the auditor is unable to complete the above procedures, the auditor should consider whether management contributed to the auditor's inability to complete the procedures—if so, inform those charged with governance.

2. Reporting

    a. Overall, add an other-matter paragraph to the auditor's report and, depending upon the circumstances, indicate that

       (1) RSI is included and the auditor has applied the procedures (described earlier)

       (2) RSI is omitted

       (3) Some RSI is missing and some is presented

       (4) The auditor has identified material departures from the applicable financial reporting framework

       (5) The auditor is unable to complete the prescribed procedures

       (6) The auditor has unresolved doubts about whether the RSI conforms to guidelines

    b. If all or some of the RSI is included, the explanatory paragraph in the auditor's report should include the following elements:

       (1) A statement that (identify applicable financial reporting framework, e.g., US GAAP) requires the RSI

       (2) RSI, although not a part of basic financial statements, is required and considered essential.

       (3) If auditor is able to complete prescribed procedures

          (a) Auditor has applied procedures in accordance with GAAS, which consisted of inquires of management and comparing the information for consistency with management's responses, the basic financial statements, and other knowledge the auditor obtained during the audit

          (b) The auditor does not express an opinion or provide any assurance on the information because the limited procedures do not provide sufficient evidence

       (4) If auditor is unable to complete prescribed procedures—indicate and say the auditor does not express an opinion or any other form of assurance on the RSI.

       (5) If some RSI omitted—indicate.

       (6) If RSI departs materially from guidelines, so indicate.

       (7) If auditor has unresolved doubts about whether RSI conforms with guidelines, so indicate.

    c. If all RSI is omitted, the explanatory paragraph should include the following elements:

       (1) Management has elected to omit RSI

       (2) Although not a part of basic financial statements, the RSI is considered essential

       (3) A statements that although the auditor's opinion on the basic financial statements is not affected by the missing information, the entity has not complied with the applicable financial reporting framework

> **NOTE:** Omission or incorrect RSI results in an other-matter paragraph describing the matter—yet it does not result in modification of the auditor's opinion. Also, the auditor does not provide the RSI in the audit report.

AU-C 800 Special Considerations—Audits of Financial Statements Prepared in Accordance with Special-Purpose Frameworks

A. Introduction

1. Scope: This section applies to special considerations in an audit of financial statements that are prepared in accordance with a special-purpose framework (defined below).

2. Realize that an audit of financial statements is involved here—the difference here is that a special-purpose framework is being followed, not GAAP.

B. Objective: The objective of the auditor, when applying GAAS in an audit of financial statements prepared in accordance with a special-purpose framework, is to address appropriately the special considerations that are relevant to

1. Acceptance of the engagement.

2. Planning and performing the engagement.

3. Forming an opinion and reporting on the financial statements.

C. Definitions

1. **Special-purpose financial statements.** Financial statements prepared in accordance with a special-purpose framework.
2. **Special-purpose framework.** A financial reporting framework other than GAAP, which is one of the following bases of accounting:

    a. Cash basis.
    b. Tax basis.
    c. Regulatory basis—A basis of accounting that the entity uses to comply with the requirements or financial reporting provisions of a regulatory agency to whose jurisdiction the entity is subject

        (1) For example, a basis of accounting that insurance companies pursue following the rules of a state insurance commission.
        (2) Some result in general use statements and others in restricted-use statements.

    d. Contractual basis—In accordance with an agreement between the entity and one or more third parties other than the auditor.

> **NOTE:** The cash, tax, and regulatory bases of accounting previously were referred to as "other comprehensive bases of accounting" (OCBOA) by the AICPA; they still have that title in PCAOB standards.

    e. An other basis of accounting.

        (1) It must use a definite set of logical, reasonable criteria that is applied to all material items appearing in financial statements.

D. Requirements, application, and selected other explanatory material

1. Considerations when accepting the engagement.

    a. Obtain an understanding of

        (1) The purpose for which the financial statements are prepared.
        (2) The intended users.
        (3) The steps taken by management to determine that the applicable financial reporting framework is acceptable in the circumstances.

    b. Obtain agreement of management that it acknowledges and understands its responsibility to include all appropriate informative disclosures for the special-purpose framework

2. Considerations when planning and performing the audit

    a. The auditor should follow and adapt AU-C sections as necessary.
    b. For financial statements prepared in accordance with a contractual basis of accounting, the auditor should obtain an understanding of any significant management interpretations of the contract.

3. Forming an opinion and reporting considerations

    a. Overall reporting requirements

        (1) In audits of special-purpose financial statements the auditor should evaluate whether the financial statements are suitably titled, include a summary of significant accounting policies and adequately describe how the special-purpose framework differs from GAAP.
        (2) Contractual basis statements—the auditor should evaluate whether the financial statements adequately describe significant interpretations of the contract.
        (3) For special-purpose financial statements that contain items the same as or similar to those per GAAP, the auditor should evaluate whether informative disclosures similar to those required by GAAP are presented.
        (4) The auditor's report should

    (a) Make reference to management's responsibility for determining that the applicable financial reporting framework is acceptable if a choice of frameworks exists.

    (b) Describe the purpose of the financial statements.

b. Unless the special-purpose financial statements are prepared in accordance with a regulatory basis of accounting and the financial statements together with the auditor's report are intended for general use, the auditor's report should include an emphasis of matter paragraph that

    (1) Alerts users that the financial statements are prepared in accordance with the special-purpose framework.

    (2) Refers to the note in the financial statements that describes the framework.

    (3) States that the special-purpose framework is a basis of accounting other than GAAP.

c. When regulatory basis financial statements are intended for general use, the auditor should not include an emphasis of matter or other matter paragraph as required for other reports in this standard. Instead, the auditor should express two opinions

    (1) On whether financial statements are prepared in accordance with GAAP.

    (2) Whether the financial statements are prepared in accordance with the special-purpose framework.

d. Restricting use of the auditor's report

    (1) For restricted reports, include an other matter paragraph that restricts the use of the auditor's report to those within the entity, the parties to the contract or agreement, or the regulatory agencies to whose jurisdiction the entity is subject.

    (2) When special-purpose financial statements follow regulatory basis and are for general use, the auditor should express opinions on whether they are in accordance with (1) GAAP and (2) separately, in another paragraph, with the special-purpose framework.

Overview of reporting requirements

	Cash basis or tax basis	Contractual basis	Regulatory basis	Regulatory basis (general use)	Other basis
Opinion(s)	Single opinion on special-purpose framework	Single opinion on special-purpose framework	Single opinion on special-purpose framework	Dual opinion on special-purpose framework on GAAP	Single opinion on special-purpose framework
Description of purpose for which special-purpose financial statements are prepared	No	Yes	Yes	Yes	Yes
Emphasis-of-matter paragraph alerting readers re: special-purpose framework	Yes	Yes	Yes	No	Yes
Other-matter paragraph with alert restricting use.	No	Yes	Yes	No	If required by section 905

AU-C 805 Special Considerations—Audits of Single Financial Statements and Specific Elements, Accounts or Items of a Financial Statement

A. Introduction

1. Scope: This section addresses the application of professional standard guidance to an audit of a single financial statement (e.g., a balance sheet) or of a specific element, account or item of a financial statement (e.g., accounts receivable). The single financial statement or account may be prepared in accordance with a general- or special-purpose framework.

B. Objective

1. The objective of the auditor, when applying GAAS in an audit of a single financial statement or element, is to address appropriately the specific considerations that are relevant to

    a. Acceptance of the engagement.
    b. Planning and performing the engagement.
    c. Forming an opinion and reporting on the single financial statement or element.

C. Definitions

1. A single financial statement or a specific element of a financial statement includes the related notes. The related notes ordinarily comprise a summary of significant accounting policies and other explanatory information relative to the financial statement or to the element.
2. For purposes of this section, an element means an element, account or item of a financial statement.

D. Requirements, application, and selected other explanatory material

1. Considerations when accepting the engagement

    a. When auditing a single financial statement or element of a financial statement, the auditor must comply with all AU-C sections relevant to the audit—this holds for planning, performing, and forming an opinion.
    b. When not also auditing the complete set of financial statements, the auditor should determine whether the audit of a single financial statement or a specific element is practicable.

        (1) While this section deals with auditing portions of financial statements less than the complete set of financial statements, there may be situations in which the complete set of financial statements are audited *and* a specific element is also audited.

    c. In an audit of a single financial statement or a specified element, the auditor should obtain an understanding of

        (1) Purpose of the information.
        (2) Intended users.
        (3) Steps by management to determine application of financial reporting framework is acceptable in the circumstances.

    d. The auditor should consider whether application of the financial reporting framework will result in a presentation that provides adequate disclosure to enable intended users to understand the information conveyed in the financial statement or element.

2. Considerations when planning and performing the audit

    a. Many of the elements of financial statements are interrelated. For example, sales and receivables; inventory and payables; buildings and equipment and depreciation. When auditing a single financial statement or a specific element, the auditor may not be able to consider the financial statement or element in isolation. An auditor should perform procedures on interrelated items as necessary to meet the objective of the audit.

        (1) Special considerations are necessary in two areas because of their extreme interrelatedness to other elements:

            (a) Stockholders equity—Obtain evidence to express an opinion on financial position.
            (b) Net income—Obtain evidence to express an opinion on financial position and result of operations.

    b. Materiality considerations

        (1) Single financial statement—materiality for that statement as a whole.
        (2) One or more elements—materiality for each individual element reported; **not** the aggregate of all elements or the complete financial statements as a whole.

3. Forming an opinion and reporting considerations

    a. Situation: Engagement is only on a single financial statement or on a specific element

        (1) The report is similar to that on a complete set of financial statements, but limited throughout to the single financial statement or specific element.

    b. Situation: Two engagements—one on the entity's complete set of financial statements, and one on a single financial statement or a specific element

(1) The auditor should issue a separate report for each engagement. The report on a specific element of a financial statement should include the date of the first engagement's report and the nature of the opinion expressed.

(2) An audited single financial statement or an audited specific element generally may be published together with the entity's audited complete set of financial statements provided the presentations are sufficiently differentiated.

    (a) If the auditor concludes that sufficient differentiation has not occurred

        1] Ask management to remedy the situation.

        2] Do not release auditor's reports on single financial statement (or specific element) until satisfied.

c. Modified Opinion, emphasis of a matter paragraph or other matter paragraphs in the auditor's report on the entity's complete set of financial statements

    (1) Summary of key situations for reporting on an element of the financial statements.

Opinion on complete set of financial statements	Resulting opinion on element
Qualified due to a material misstatement	If relevant to the element, issue an adverse opinion on the element
Qualified due to inability to obtain sufficient appropriate audit evidence	If relevant to the element, issue a disclaimer of opinion on the element
Adverse due to a pervasive material misstatement or disclaimer due to a pervasive lack of sufficient appropriate audit evidence	If relevant to the element, adverse opinion (or disclaimer) on the element. If not relevant, make certain opinion is not published together with the auditor's report containing the adverse opinion. The specific element must not constitute a major portion of the complete set of financial statements and not be based upon the stockholders' equity or net income or the equivalent.*

*A single financial statement is deemed a major portion of a complete set of financial statements. Therefore, the auditor should not express an unmodified opinion on a single financial statement in this situation.

    (2) If the auditor's report on the complete set of financial statements includes an emphasis of a matter paragraph or an other matter paragraph the auditor should

        (a) Determine the effect this may have on the auditor's report on the element, and

        (b) Include an emphasis of matter paragraph or an other matter paragraph in the single element report.

4. Reporting on an incomplete presentation that is otherwise in accordance with GAAP

  a. What is this? Examples are

    (1) A governmental agency may require a schedule of gross income and certain expenses of a company's real estate operation in which income and expenses are measured in accordance with GAAP, but expenses are defined to exclude certain items such as interest, depreciation and income taxes.

    (2) An agreement in which one company is considering acquiring another company may specify a schedule of gross assets and liabilities of the company measured in accordance with GAAP, but limited to the assets to be sold and liabilities to be transferred according to the agreement.

  b. Reporting: The reporting requirements under point 3. above apply, but the auditor also should include an emphasis of matter paragraph in the auditor's report that states the

    (1) Purpose for which the presentation is prepared and refers to a note in the financial statements that describes the basis of presentation, and

    (2) Presentation is not intended to be a complete presentation of the entity's assets, liabilities, revenues or expenses.

AU-C 806 Reporting on Compliance with Aspects of Contractual Agreements or Regulatory Requirements in Connection with Audited Financial Statements

A. Introduction

1. Scope: This section addresses the auditor's responsibility and the form and content of the report when the auditor is requested to provide assurance on the entity's compliance with aspects of contractual agreements or regulatory requirements in connection with the audit of financial statements.

   a. Example: An entity may have a loan agreement that imposes a variety of obligations involving matters such as payments of interest, maintenance of ratios, and restrictions of dividend payments. In some circumstances the lender may request assurance from the auditor that the borrower has complied with certain covenants of the agreements relating to accounting matters. The auditor may satisfy such a request by providing negative assurance relative to the applicable covenants based on the audit of financial statements.

B. Objective: The objective of the auditor is to report appropriately on an entity's compliance with aspects of contractual agreements or regulatory requirements, in connection with the audit of financial statements when the auditor is requested to so report.

C. Requirements, application, and selected other explanatory material

1. The auditor's report on compliance should include negative assurance only when

   a. Auditor has not identified any instance of noncompliance
   b. Auditor has expressed unmodified or qualified opinion on related financial statements.
   c. The applicable covenants relate to accounting matters that have been subjected to the audit procedures applied in the financial statement audit.

2. When the auditor has identified one or more instances of noncompliance, the report on compliance should describe such noncompliance.
3. When an auditor has expressed an adverse opinion or disclaimed an opinion on the financial statements, the auditor should issue a compliance report only when instances of noncompliance are identified.

   a. But whenever required by law to issue such a report (e.g. under Government Auditing Standards), such a report on compliance may be issued.

4. The report should be in writing, either in a separate report or one or more paragraphs added to audit report.
5. Reporting: The report should be in writing, providing negative assurance on compliance either in a separate report or in one or more paragraphs added to the financial statement audit report.

   a. Example of negative assurance: In connection with our audit, nothing came to our attention that caused us to believe that the XYZ Company failed to comply with the accounting provisions of (name agreement). However, our audit was not directed primarily toward obtaining knowledge of such noncompliance.
   b. The report should be restricted to the specified parties (e.g., representatives of the bank involved).
   c. When the auditor has identified one or more items of noncompliance that the auditor believes should be reported, the auditor should identify the instances of noncompliance in the report. When the auditor believes that the nature and extent of instances of noncompliance are pervasive, the auditor should consider whether a negative assurance statement is appropriate.

AU-C 810 Engagements to Report on Summary Financial Statements

A. Introduction

1. Scope: This section addresses the auditor's responsibilities relating to an engagement to report separately on summary financial statements (defined below) derived from financial statements audited in accordance with GAAS by the same auditor. In such an engagement, the auditor expresses an opinion as to whether the summary financial statements are consistent, in all material respects, with the audited financial statements, in accordance with the applied criteria.
2. Summary financial statements may be required by a designated accounting standard setter (e.g., GASB) to accompany the basic financial statements.

B. Objectives: The objectives of the auditor are

1. To determine whether it is appropriate to accept the engagement to report on summary financial statements.
2. If engaged to report on summary financial statements

    a. To form an opinion on the summary financial statements based on an evaluation of the conclusions drawn from the evidence obtained.

    b. To express clearly that opinion through a written report that also describes the basis for that opinion.

C. Definitions

1. **Applied criteria.** The criteria applied by management in the preparation of the summary financial statements.

2. **Summary financial statements.** Historical financial information that is derived from the financial statements but contains less detail, while still providing a structured representation consistent with the financial statements.

D. Requirements, application, and selected other explanatory material

1. Engagement acceptance—Before accepting the engagement the auditor should (1) determine whether the applied criteria are acceptable and (2) obtain agreement of management that it acknowledges and understands its responsibility. If either of these are not accomplished, the auditor should not accept the engagement.

    a. In considering the acceptability of applied criteria, consider

        (1) Nature of the entity.

        (2) Purpose of the summary financial statements.

        (3) Information needs of the intended users of the summary financial statements.

        (4) Whether the applied criteria will result in summary financial statements that are not misleading.

2. Nature of procedures

    a. Evaluate whether summary financial statements adequately disclose their summarized nature and identify the audited financial statements. When audited financial statements are not present with summary financial statements, the summary financial statements should clearly describe where the audited financial statements are available and whether they are readily available.

    b. Evaluate the summary financial statements for adequate disclosure as per applied criteria and compare them with related information in audited financial statements.

    c. Evaluate whether the summary financial statements are prepared in accordance with applied criteria and evaluate whether they contain the necessary information.

3. Representations from management—Should be obtained on management's responsibility, that it will make available audited financial statements to the intended users (when not accompanied by the audited financial statements), and whether management is aware of any information subsequent to the audit that may be relevant (if this report is later than the date of the auditor's report on the audited financial statements). The date of the written representations should be the date of the auditor's report on the summary information.

4. Form of opinion and audit report on summary financial statements

    a. When an unmodified opinion is appropriate, the opinion should state that the summary financial statements are consistent, in all material respects, with the audited financial statements from which they have been derived in accordance with (the applied criteria).

    b. The report should be dated no earlier than the date on which the auditor has obtained sufficient appropriate evidence relating to the summary financial information and the date of the auditor's report on the audited financial statements.

    c. When the audited financial statement report is restricted, so should be the summary financial statement audit report.

    d. When the financial statement audit report includes an adverse opinion or disclaimer, withdraw from engagement on summary financial statements where this is possible under applicable law or regulation.

        (1) If unable to withdraw, report should state

            (a) Audit report on audited financial statements contains an adverse opinion or disclaimer.

            (b) Describe basis for that opinion.

            (c) State that because of this situation, auditor does not express an opinion on summary financial statements.

    e. An adverse opinion is issued on the summary statements when they are not consistent, in all material respects, with the audited financial statements.

    f. When unaudited information is presented with the summary financial statements, the auditor should make certain that it is clearly differentiated from the summary financial statements; if management will not clearly differentiate, the auditor's report on the summary information should make clear that the unaudited information is not covered by that report.

AU-C 905 Alert That Restricts the Use of the Auditor's Written Communication

A. **Scope:** This section addresses the auditor's responsibility, when required or the auditor decides, to include in the audit report or other written communication language that restricts the use of the auditor's written communication. The language referred to is an alert.

1. The following SAS require the auditor to include an alert in the auditor's written communications as to their intended use by specified parties

   a. AU-C 260, *The Auditor's Communication with Those Charged with Governance.*
   b. AU-C 265, *Communicating Internal Control Related Mattes Identified in an Audit.*
   c. AU-C 725, *Supplementary Information in Relation to the Financial Statements as a Whole.*
   d. AU-C 800, *Special Considerations—Audits of Financial Statements Prepared in Accordance with Special-Purpose Frameworks*
   e AU-C 806, *Reporting on Compliance with Aspects of Contractual Agreements or Regulatory Requirements in Connection with Audited Financial Statements.*
   f. AU-C 910, *Financial Statements Prepared in Accordance with a Financial Reporting Framework Generally Accepted in Another Country*
   g. AU-C 915, *Report on the Application of Requirements of an Applicable Financial Reporting Framework*
   h. AU-C 920, *Letters for Underwriters and Certain Other Requesting Parties*

B. **Objective**: The objective of the auditor is to restrict the use of the auditor's written communication by including an alert when the potential exists for the auditor's written communication to be misunderstood if taken out of the context in which the auditor's communication is intended to be used.

C. **Definition**

1. **Specified parties.** The intended users of the auditor' written communication.

D. **Requirements, and selected application and other explanatory material**

1. Alert that restricts the use of the auditor's written communication

   a. An auditor's written communication should include an alert, in a separate paragraph, that restricts its use when the subject matter of the auditor's written communication is based on

      (1) Measurement or disclosure criteria determined by auditor to be suitable only for a limited number of users who can be presumed to understand.
      (2) Measurement or disclosure criteria available only to the specified parties.
      (3) Matters identified by the auditor during the course of the engagement that are not the primary objective of the engagement, commonly referred to as *by-product report* (e.g., IC deficiencies).

   b. The "alert paragraph" should

      (1) State that the written communication is intended solely for the information and use of the specified parties.
      (2) Identify the specified parties; those specified parties should only include

         (a) Management
         (b) Those charged with governance
         (c) Others within the entity
         (d) Parties to the contract agreement
         (e) Regulatory agencies to whose jurisdiction the entity is subject, as appropriate in the circumstances

      (3) State that the written communication is not intended to be and should not be used by anyone other than the specified parties.

      Exception to D.1.b.: When the alert is for engagements performed in accordance with *Government Auditing Standards* and in accord with AU-C 265, AU-C 806, or AU-C 935, the language in point D.1.b should not be used; the auditor should describe the purpose of the written communication and state that the written communication is not suitable for any other purpose

2. When the auditor is requested to add other parties, the auditor should determine whether to agree with the request

   a. When auditor agrees to add, the auditor should obtain affirmative acknowledgement, in writing, from the parties of their understanding of

(1) Engagement nature.

(2) Measurement or disclosure criteria.

(3) Auditor's written communication.

b. If these parties are added *after* the release, in addition to the requirements immediately above, the auditor should *either*

(1) Amend written communication to add other parties (do not change date) *or*

(2) Provide a written acknowledgement to management and the other parties that such parties have been added and state that no procedures were performed subsequent to the date of the written communication or the date the engagement was completed, as appropriate.

3. Although auditors' reports on financial statements prepared in accordance with a general purpose framework ordinarily do not include a paragraph alerting readers as to intended use by specified parties, nothing in GAAS precludes such a paragraph.

AU-C 910 Reporting on Financial Statements Prepared in Accordance with a Financial Reporting Framework Generally Accepted in Another Country

A. Introduction

1. Scope: This section addresses circumstances in which an auditor practicing in the United States is engaged to report on financial statements that have been prepared in accordance with a financial reporting framework generally accepted in another country. Also, the financial reporting framework of the other country is not adopted by a body designated by the council of the AICPA to establish GAAP.

2. The standard is also applicable to audits of financial statements prepared in accordance with a jurisdictional variation of IFRS when the financial statements do **not** contain an explicit and unreserved statement in the notes that the financial statements are in compliance with IFRS issued by the International Accounting Standards Board.

B. Objective:
The objective of the auditor, when engaged to report on financial standards prepared in accordance with a financial reporting framework generally accepted in another country, is to address appropriately the special considerations that are relevant to

1. The acceptance of the engagement.

2. The planning and performance of that engagement.

3. Forming an opinion and reporting on the financial statements.

C. Requirements, application, and selected other explanatory material

1. Considerations when accepting the engagement

a. The auditor should obtain an understanding of the

(1) Purpose for which financial statements are prepared and whether the financial reporting framework is a fair presentation framework.

> **NOTE:** A "fair presentation framework" is a financial reporting framework that requires compliance with its requirements and acknowledges (a) explicitly or implicitly that it may be necessary for management to provide disclosures beyond those specifically required by the framework or (b) acknowledges that it may be necessary (rarely) for management to depart from a requirement of the framework to achieve fair presentation.

(2) Intended users of the financial statements.

(3) Steps taken by management to determine that the applicable financial reporting framework is acceptable in the circumstances.

b. When the auditor plans to issue a standard report of another country, the auditor should obtain an understanding as to whether any additional legal responsibilities are involved.

2. Performance

a. The auditor should comply with GAAS, except for the reporting requirements when financial statements prepared in accordance with a financial reporting framework generally accepted in another country that are intended for use *only outside the US.*

b. The auditor should obtain an understanding of the financial reporting framework generally accepted in the other country.

c. The auditor should obtain an understanding of the other country auditing standards (as well as US GAAS).

3. Reporting

a. When intended for use only outside the US, the auditor should report using either

   (1) The US report reflecting that financial statements prepared in accordance with financial reporting framework of another country, including

      (a) A statement referring to note in financial statements describing basis.

   (2) Standard report of other country, if

      (a) Such report would be issued in other country in similar circumstances.

      (b) Auditor understands and has obtained sufficient appropriate audit evidence.

      (c) Auditor has complied with standards of that country.

b. When also to be used in the US, the auditor may issue two reports

   (1) Use US form report

      (a) Include an emphasis of matter paragraph that identifies the accounting framework used and indicates such framework differs from US GAAP.

   (2) The auditor may (probably will) also issue a second report, one that is per a. above. Thus, two reports often will be issued—one for US use and one for foreign use.

AU-C 915 Reports on Application of Requirements of an Applicable Financial Reporting Framework

A. Introduction:

1. This section addresses the reporting accountant's responsibilities when preparing a written report on the

a. Application of the requirements of an applicable financial reporting framework (e.g., GAAP) to a specific transaction, or

b. Type of report that may be issued on a specific entity's financial statements.

> **NOTE:** It is important to distinguish between the continuing accountant (the CPA that is engaged to report on the financial statements) and the reporting accountant (the one being asked to write the written report on the application above). As an example, assume that a company asks a reporting accountant to submit a proposal on the accounting for a particular transaction. This may occur when management desires a certain method which its continuing accountant does not believe is acceptable. This section is about requirements for the reporting accountant. This situation has sometimes resulted in a situation in which management of the company might "shop" until it finds a CPA that goes along with its desired method and then hires that CPA as its auditor. This becomes problematical when the company's management shops until it finds a CPA who for one reason or another misapplies accounting standards in arriving at its conclusion that management's desired accounting for the transaction is acceptable. This section is meant to control this situation.

2. This section also applies to oral advice that the reporting accountant

a. Concludes is intended to be used as an important factor in reaching a decision on how a specific transaction is treated in an applicable financial reporting framework, or

b. Provides on the type of report that may be issued.

3. This section does **not** apply to

a. The above when it relates to a continuing accountant (although the continuing accountant may find it helpful).

b. Engagements either to assist in litigation or provide expert testimony.

c. Professional advice provided to another accountant in public practice.

d. Communications such as position papers (e.g., newsletters, articles, speeches, lectures).

B. Objective

1. The objective of the reporting accountant, when engaged to issue a written report, or provide oral advice on the application of the requirements of an applicable financial reporting framework to a specific transaction, or on the type of report that may be issued on a specific entity's financial statements, is to address appropriately the following:

   a. The acceptance of the engagement.
   b. The planning and performance of that engagement.
   c. Reporting on the specific transaction or the type of report.

C. Definitions

1. **Continuing accountant.** An accountant who has been engaged to report on the financial statements of a specific entity.
2. **Hypothetical transaction.** A transaction or financial reporting issue that does not involve facts or circumstances of a specific entity.
3. **Reporting accountant.** An accountant, other than a continuing accountant, in the practice of public accounting, as described in ET section 92.25 of the AICPA Code of Professional Conduct, who prepares a written report or provides oral advice on the application of the requirements of an applicable financial reporting framework to a specific transaction, or on the type of report that may be issued on a specific entity's financial statements. (A reporting accountant who is also engaged to provide accounting and reporting advice to a specific entity on a recurring basis is commonly referred to as an advisory accountant.)
4. **Specific transaction.** A completed transaction, proposed transaction, or financial reporting issue involving facts and circumstances of a specific entity.
5. **Written report.** Any written communication that expresses a conclusion on the appropriate application of the requirements of an applicable financial reporting framework to a specific transaction, or on the type of report that may be issued on a specific entity's financial statements.

D. Requirements, application, and other explanatory material

1. Engagement acceptance by reporting accountant—Only accept such an engagement (written or oral) when it involves facts or circumstances of a specific entity; do not accept an engagement to issue a written report on hypothetical transactions.

   a. In determining whether to accept, the reporting accountant should consider

      (1) Circumstances under which the written report or oral advice is requested.
      (2) The purpose of the request.
      (3) The intended use of the written report or oral advice.

   b. If engagement is to be accepted, the reporting accountant should establish an understanding with the entity that

      (1) Responsibility for the proper accounting treatment rests with management, who should consult with its continuing accountant.
      (2) Management acknowledges that the reporting accountant may need to consult with the continuing accountant and will authorize such if requested.
      (3) Management will notify those charged with governance of the engagement.

2. Engagement planning and performance

   a. The reporting accountant should

      (1) Obtain an understanding of the transaction(s).
      (2) Review relevant requirements of the applicable financial reporting framework.
      (3) Consult with other professionals, experts or regulatory authorities as appropriate.
      (4) Perform research as appropriate.

   b. The reporting accountant should consult with continuing accountant to determine whether reporting accountant has all available relevant facts; exception (both (1) and (2) must be met):

      (1) The advice is not on the type of report that may be issued, but is on application of applicable financial reporting framework, and
      (2) The reporting accountant is engaged to provide recurring accounting and reporting advice (e.g., bookkeeping or assistance in formulating accounting positions in selected matters which are services commonly performed by an advisory accountant), and

(a) Does not believe a second opinion is being requested.

(b) Has full access to management.

(c) Believes that relevant information has been obtained.

1] In this exceptional case, the basis for not consulting should be documented in the working papers.

3. Written Report

   a. The reporting accountant's written report should be addressed to the entity (i.e., management or those charged with governance) and should include

      (1) Brief description of nature of engagement and that it was performed following GAAS.

      (2) Identification of the specific identity, description of the transaction(s), and relevant other information.

      (3) Statement on appropriate application of the requirements of an applicable financial reporting framework.

      (4) Statement that responsibility for proper accounting treatment rests with preparers of financial statements, who should consult continuing accountant.

      (5) Statement that any difference in facts, etc. may change report.

      (6) Separate paragraph at end of report that includes

         (a) Report is solely for use of the specified parties.

         (b) An identification of the specified parties.

         (c) A statement that the report is not intended to be and should not be used by anyone other than the specified parties.

AU-C 920 Letters for Underwriters and Certain Other Requesting Parties

> **NOTE:** Historically the CPA exam has asked only a few questions pertaining to letters for underwriters. Accordingly, this outline contains less detail than most other outlines.

A. Introduction

1. Scope: This section addresses the auditor's responsibilities when engaged to issue letters to underwriters and certain other requesting parties (hereafter, underwriters) when a nonissuer is issuing public securities under the Securities Act of 1933

2. These letters are referred to as comfort letters

3. Auditors' services include audits or reviews of financial statements included in securities offerings; auditors are often requested by underwriters and other parties to issue a comfort letter.

4. The auditor is not required by GAAS to accept an engagement to issue a comfort letter.

5. The subjects that may be covered in a comfort letter include

   a. Independence of auditor

   b. Whether financial statements comply with SEC requirements under the 1933 Securities Act

   c. Unaudited financial statements, condensed interim financial information, capsule financial information, pro forma financial information, financial forecasts, management's discussion and analysis, and changes in selected financial statement items during period subsequent to the date and period of the financial statements included in the securities offering

B. Objectives:
The objectives of the auditor are to (1) address appropriately the acceptance of the engagement and the scope of service and (2) issue a letter with the appropriate form and content.

C. Auditor reporting in comfort letters

1. Auditor independence.

   a. Auditor states "We are independent certified public accountants with respect to the company. . . ."

2. Whether audited financial statements in the registration statement comply with SEC requirements.

   a. Since ordinarily the auditor has audited the financial statements, s/he states "In our opinion. . . the financial statements . . . comply as to form in all material respects with the applicable accounting requirements of the Act. . . ."

3. Unaudited financial statements, condensed interim financial information, capsule financial information, pro forma financial information, financial forecasts, management's discussion and analysis, and changes in selected financial statement items during a period subsequent to the date and period of the latest financial statements included in the securities offering.

  a. In general, if the auditor has required background knowledge on the client's internal control and accounting (as would be the case for an audit client), negative assurance may be provided on the information if procedures performed do not reveal likely misstated information.

   (1) Negative assurance consists of a statement that, based on the procedures performed, nothing has come to the auditor's attention that caused the auditor to believe that specified matters do not meet specified criteria.
   (2) The exact form of the negative assurance differs somewhat by the information on which it is being provided.

  b. If the auditor does not have the required background knowledge the comfort letter generally includes procedures performed and findings, with no negative assurance.

4. Tables, statistics, and other financial information in the securities offering.

  a. Only comment on information expressed in dollars (or percentage of dollars) and from accounting records
  b. Provide negative assurance, but only on information obtained or derived from accounting records that is subject to the accounting system of internal control.
  c. The auditor should not

   (1) Use the term *presents fairly* in comments concerning this information.
   (2) Provide positive or negative assurance on nonfinancial data presented in MD&A.

5. Negative assurance about whether certain nonfinancial statement information, in the registration statement complies with SEC requirements.

D. Additional

1. Comfort letters are not required by the SEC, and copies are not filed with the SEC. They have evolved as a common condition of an underwriting agreement for the sale of securities.
2. Comfort letters are signed by the auditor.
3. Comfort letters should only be provided to (addressed to):

  a. Underwriters
  b. Other parties with a statutory due diligence defense

4. A representation letter must be provided

  a. Addressed to the auditor
  b. Stating that the review process applied by the requesting party is, or will be, substantially consistent with the due diligence process that would be performed if securities were offered under the Securities Act of 1933.
  c. Requesting party must sign.

5. Brief summary of auditor reporting in a comfort letter: The auditor affirmatively states that s/he is independent and that the financial statements meet SEC requirements; negative assurance is provided on most of the remaining information (or only a summary of procedures performed and findings in some circumstances).

AU-C 925 Filings with the US Securities and Exchange Commission Under the Securities Act of 1933

A. Introduction

1. Scope: This section addresses the auditor's responsibilities in connection with financial statements of a nonissuer included or incorporated by reference in a registration statement filed with the SEC under the Securities Act of 1933 (hereafter, Securities Act).
2. Know that filings under the Securities Act ordinarily include audited financial statements for the most recent year and, often, unaudited interim results subsequent to year end, and a variety of other disclosures. The auditors ordinarily will have audited the annual financial statements and, often, reviewed interim financial information. Other information they simply read. They also perform a variety of procedures related to identifying possible subsequent events occurring after year-end (also see AU-C 560).

3. There is an "experts section" in a registration statement that describes the auditors' work that has been performed.

B. **Objective:** The objectives of the auditor, in connection with fanatical statements of a nonissuer that are separately included in a registration statement filed with the SEC under the Securities Act is to perform specified procedures at or shortly before the effective date of the registration statement to sustain the burden of proof that the auditor has performed a reasonable investigation as under Securities Act.

C. **Definitions**

1. **Auditor's consent.** A statement signed by the auditor which indicates that the auditor consents to inclusion of the auditor's report in a registration statement filed under the Securities Act (hereafter, registration statement).
2. **Awareness letter.** A letter signed and dated by the auditor acknowledging awareness that the auditor's review report on unaudited interim financial information is being used in a registration statement.
3. **Effective date of registration statement.** The date on which the registration statement becomes effective for purposes of evaluating auditor liability under Section 11 of the Securities Act.

D. **Requirements, and selected application and other explanatory material**

1. The auditor should request management to keep the auditor advised of the progress of the registration proceedings through the effective date.
2. When the auditor's report on audited financial statements is included in a registration statement, the auditor should perform AU-C 720, *Other Information in Documents Containing Audited Financial Statements* procedures (e.g., read that information).
3. Subsequent event procedures

   a. Apply procedures to identify events occurring between date of auditor's report and effective date of registration statement that require adjustment of or disclosure in financial statements; procedures should include

      (1) Obtaining an understanding of procedures management has established to ensure that such events are identified.
      (2) Inquiring of management and those charged with governance (when appropriate) about whether such events have occurred that might affect the financial statements.
      (3) Reading minutes of meetings (e.g., owners management, those charged with governance).
      (4) Reading latest subsequent interim financial statements, if any.

   b. Obtain updated written representation from management

      (1) Information has come to management's attention that would cause previous representations to be modified.
      (2) Any subsequent events requiring adjustment or disclosure of financial statements have occurred.

   c. If a predecessor auditor audited the entity's separate financial statements for a prior period included in the registration statement, but not the most recent financial statements, the predecessor should perform AU-C 560 procedures relating to such a situation.

4. Unaudited financial statements or unaudited financial information

   a. If these statements are not in conformity with requirements of applicable financial reporting framework (e.g., GAAP), request management to revise; if management does not revise and

      (1) If the CPA has issued a review report, refer to AU-C 560.
      (2) If the CPA has not issued a review report or report is not included in registration statement, modify the report on the audited financial statements to describe the unaudited financial statement (or interim statement) departure.
      (3) Consider whether to withhold the auditor's consent and whether to obtain legal advice.

AU-C 930 Interim Financial Information

> **NOTE:** This outline differs from the other outlines because of the similarities between interim financial information reviews under Statements on Auditing Standards (AU-C) and those under Statements on Standards for Accounting and Review Services (AR—outlines included in Module 6). Our basic approach is to ask you to first study the information in Module 6 on accounting and review services to obtain an understanding of the nature of reviews (and compilations). In this outline we compare the two types of reviews, emphasizing differences.

Overview

AU-C reviews involve interim (ordinarily quarterly) information. For a public company, this involves required reviews of its interim information that is included in form 10Q for the first three quarters of the year and of its fourth quarter interim information included in the annual Form 10K. The interim information under AU-C 930 for nonpublic companies relates to those that do have annual audits, but for one reason or another also have a review of their interim financial statements. Public and nonpublic company AU-C reviews are extremely similar.

For nonpublic companies, in addition to AU-C 930, the various *Statements on Standards for Accounting and Review Services* (codified as AR) provide guidance. Reviews performed under either the AU-Cs or the ARs have several differences, although in most areas they are similar. As indicated in the earlier "note," prior to reading the remainder of this outline, study Module 6, or at least the portion on reviews. Then study the following analysis, which primarily emphasizes areas in which interim financial reviews differ from AR reviews.

	AU-C 930	**AR 60, 90**
Objective	Allow the accountant to obtain a basis for reporting whether the auditor is aware of any material modifications that should be made to the financial statements.	Express limited assurance that there are no material modifications that should be made to the financial statements
Information reported on	Interim information. Public company interim information is reviewed following these standards. A nonpublic company's interim information ordinarily falls under this section if that company has an audit of its annual financial statements.	May be interim or annual information, but most frequently annual.
Written review report	Required except for reviews required by an external party and that party does not require a written report.	Required
Important procedures in common	• Based largely on inquiries of management, analytical procedures, and obtaining written representations from management. • Understanding with client should be in writing (engagement letter or other written form).	
Understanding of entity and its environment	The accountant should have sufficient an understanding of the entity and its environment, including internal control to · Identify types of potential misstatements · Select inquiries and analytical procedures to provide a basis for communicating whether he or she is aware of any material modifications that should be made to the interim financial information **NOTE:** The biggest difference here is the required understanding of internal control under AU-C 930.	An AR review does not contemplate obtaining an understanding of the entity's internal control. The accountant should obtain knowledge, including an understanding of · Client's industry, including accounting principles generally used · Client's business. · Accounting principles used by client.
	AU-C 930	**AR 60, 90**

	AU-C 930	AR 60, 90
Written representations by management	Required. AU-C 930 details more overall procedures, but two primary differences are that management must · Acknowledge its responsibility to establish sufficient controls · Disclose all significant deficiencies and material weaknesses	Required, but no representations on internal control
Communicating with management and those charged with governance	Requirements are very similar to those of an audit. For example, the need for material modifications, fraud of which the CPA becomes aware of and internal control matters of AU-C 265 (material weaknesses and significant deficiencies) and AU-C 260 requirements (a variety of disclosures) are required if such information has come to the accountant's attention. The communication may be written or oral	Although communication of any matters coming to the accountant's attention is appropriate, no examples relating to internal control are included. The communication may be written or oral

AU-C 935 Compliance Audits

A. Introduction and applicability

1. Governments frequently establish governmental audit requirements for entities to undergo an audit of their compliance with applicable compliance requirements. This section is applicable when an auditor is engaged to perform a compliance audit in accordance with

    a. GAAS
    b. Government Auditing Standards (generally accepted government auditing standards [GAGAS] or the "Yellow Book")
    c. A governmental audit requirement

2. This section addresses the application of GAAS to a compliance audit. Compliance audits usually are performed in conjunction with a financial statement audit.
3. Management is responsible for the entity's compliance, including

    a. Identifying the entity's government programs and compliance requirements.
    b. Establishing related controls.
    c. Evaluating and monitoring the entity's compliance.
    d. Taking corrective action on audit findings of the compliance audit.

B. Objectives: The objectives of a compliance audit are

1. Obtain sufficient appropriate audit evidence to form an opinion and report at the level specified on the governmental audit requirement on whether the entity complied in all material respects with the applicable compliance requirements
2. Identify audit and reporting requirements specified in the governmental audit requirement that are supplementary to GAAS and Government Auditing Standards (if any) and perform procedures to address those requirements.

C. Requirements: The auditor must

1. Adapt and apply the AU-C sections to the objectives of a compliance audit
2. Establish materiality levels for the audit based on the governmental audit requirement
3. Identify government programs and applicable compliance requirements

    a. Sources an auditor may consult include

    (1) Compliance Supplement issued by the Office of Management and Budget
    (2) Applicable program-specific audit guide information issued by the grantor agency which requires the various compliance requirements

4. Perform risk assessment procedures.
5. Assess the risks of material noncompliance whether due to error or fraud for each applicable compliance requirement; factors include

   a. Complexity of compliance requirements
   b. Susceptibility of compliance requirements to noncompliance
   c. Time entity has been subject to compliance requirements
   d. Auditor's observation about company prior year compliance
   e. Potential effect on the entity of noncompliance
   f. Degree of judgment involved
   g. Auditor's assessment of the risks of material misstatement in the financial statement audit

6. Perform further audit procedures in response to assessed risks.

   a. If the auditor identifies a risk of material noncompliance that is pervasive to the entity's compliance, the auditor should develop an overall response to the assessed risks of material noncompliance

      (1) Examples of risks of noncompliance that are pervasive: An entity experiencing financial difficulty which increase the likelihood of improper diversion of funds, an entity with poor recordkeeping for government programs.

   b. Perform further audit procedures, including test of details, to obtain sufficient appropriate audit evidence about compliance with each applicable requirement in response to the assessed risks of material noncompliance

   c. Adapt and apply requirements from AU-C 330 in designing and performing further audit procedures in response to the assessed risks of noncompliance. Test of controls over compliance should be performed if the auditor's risk assessment

      (1) Includes an expectation of operating effectiveness or
      (2) Substantive procedures alone do not provide sufficient appropriate audit evidence, or
      (3) Such test of controls are required by the governmental audit requirements.

7. Identify audit requirements specified in the governmental audit requirement that are supplemental to GAAS and GAGAS and perform procedures to address these requirements.
8. Obtain written representations from management related to the entity's compliance with applicable compliance requirements.
9. Consider subsequent events
10. Evaluate the sufficiency and appropriateness of audit evidence and form an opinion
11. Forming an opinion and reporting

   a. An auditor's report on compliance includes an opinion as per the governmental audit requirement.

      (1) If noncompliance is identified, that results in an opinion modification.

   b. An auditor's report on compliance may be combined with a report on internal control over compliance, and related information on internal control over compliance should be added.

   c. If a report on internal control over compliance is required and the auditor chooses to issue a separate report on internal control, this is acceptable.

   d. Reports on compliance are modified for

      (1) Scope restrictions.
      (2) Making reference to the report of another auditor.
      (3) Inability to comply with GAAS, GAGAS, or the governmental audit requirement, as well as for noncompliance.

   e. The auditor should document

      (1) Risk assessment procedures performed.
      (2) Responses to assessed risk of material noncompliance, the procedures performed to test compliance with applicable compliance requirements and the results of those procedures, including any tests of controls over compliance.
      (3) Materiality levels and how they were determined.
      (4) How s/he complied with specific governmental audit requirements that are supplemental to GAAS and GAGAS.

STANDARDS OF THE PUBLIC COMPANY ACCOUNTING OVERSIGHT BOARD

Overview. The Public Company Accounting Oversight Board issues its own series of Standards. At this point they have not been codified.

PCAOB Auditing Standard No. 1 (and related reporting guidance)—References in Auditors' Reports to the Standards of the PCAOB

Overall Objectives and Approach—This very brief statement requires auditors to refer to standards of the Public Company Accounting Oversight Board (rather than to generally accepted auditing standards) in their reports on audits of issuer (public) companies.

A. Auditors' reports for audits of issuer (public) company financial statements

1. The PCAOB adopted as interim standards, the AICPA Statements on Auditing Standards and other auditing guidance
2. The financial statement audit report for an issuer (public) client

   a. Refers to "standards of Public Company Accounting Oversight Board (United States)" rather than to generally accepted auditing standards
   b. Has a title of "Report of Independent Registered Public Accounting Firm"
   c. Includes a paragraph referring to the auditor's report on internal control (this requirement was added subsequent to passage of Standard 1)
   d. Includes the city and state (or country) in which the report was issued

3. For reports on interim financial statements

   a. Refers to "standards of the Public Company Accounting Oversight Board (United States)" rather than standards of the AICPA
   b. Has a title of "Report of Independent Registered Public Accounting Firm"
   c. Includes the city and state (or country in which the report was issued

B. Sample audit report for financial statements

Report of Independent Registered Public Accounting Firm

We have audited the accompanying balance sheets of X Company as of December 31, 20X3 and 20X2, and the related statements of operations, stockholders' equity, and cash flows for each of the three years in the period ended December 31, 20X3. These financial statements are the responsibility of the Company's management. Our responsibility is to express an opinion on these financial statements based on our audits.

We conducted our audits in accordance with the standards of the Public Company Accounting Oversight Board (United States). Those standards require that we plan and perform the audit to obtain reasonable assurance about whether the financial statements are free of material misstatement. An audit includes examining, on a test basis, evidence supporting the amounts and disclosures in the financial statements. An audit also includes assessing the accounting principles used and significant estimates made by management, as well as evaluating the overall financial statement presentation. We believe that our audits provide a reasonable basis for our opinion.

In our opinion, the financial statements referred to above present fairly, in all material respects, the financial position of the Company as of [at] December 31, 20X3, and 20X2, and the results of its operations and its cash flows for each of the three years in the period ended December 31, 20X3, in conformity with US generally accepted accounting principles.

We also have audited, in accordance with the standards of the Public Company Accounting Oversight Board (United States), the effectiveness of X Company's internal control over financial reporting as of December 31, 20X3, based on criteria established in Internal Control–Integrated Framework issued by the Committee of Sponsoring Organizations of the Treadway Commission and our report dated February 24, 20X4, expressed an unqualified opinion thereon.

[*Signature*]

[*City and State or Country*]

[*Date*]

PCAOB Auditing Standard No. 2—An Audit of Internal Control over Financial Reporting Performed in Conjunction with an Audit of Financial Statements—Superseded by PCAOB Auditing Standard No. 5

PCAOB Auditing Standard No. 3—Audit Documentation

Overall Objectives and Approach—This standard establishes general guidelines for audit documentation (working papers) that the auditor should prepare and retain in connection with engagements under the PCAOB standards—audits of financial statements, audits of internal control over financial reporting, and reviews of interim financial information.

A. General

1. **Audit documentation**—the written record of the basis for the auditor's conclusion that provides the support for the auditor's representations, whether those representations are contained in the auditor's report or otherwise

   a. Audit documentation also facilitates planning, performance and supervision of the engagement.
   b. It is the basis for the review of the quality of the work because it provides the reviewer with written documentation of the evidence supporting the auditor's significant conclusions

2. Audit documentation should

   a. Demonstrate that the engagement complied with PCAOB standards
   b. Support the auditor's conclusions for every relevant financial statement assertion
   c. Demonstrate that the underlying accounting records agree or reconcile with the financial statements

3. Audit documentation must contain sufficient information to enable an *experienced auditor* having no previous connection with the engagement to

   a. Understand the nature, timing, extent, and results of the procedures performed, evidence obtained, and conclusions reached
   b. Determine who performed the work, the date such work was completed, the person who reviewed the work, and the date of such review

B. The Standard also contains the following specific documentation requirements:

1. Documentation must make it possible to identify the items examined by the auditor in areas such as the inspection of documents, confirmation, tests of details, tests of operating effectiveness of controls, and walk-throughs
2. Significant findings or issues must be documented, including

   a. Significant matters involving accounting principles
   b. Results of auditing procedures that indicate (1) the need to modify planned auditing procedures, (2) the existence of material misstatements, (3) omissions in the financial statements, or (4) the existence of significant deficiencies or material weaknesses in internal control over financial reporting
   c. Audit adjustments
   d. Disagreements among members of the engagement team or others consulted about final conclusions reached on significant accounting or auditing matters
   e. Circumstances causing difficulty in applying auditing procedures
   f. Significant changes in the assessed level of audit risk
   g. Any matters that could result in modification of the auditor's report

   The above information should be included in an *engagement completion document*

3. In addition, the auditor must obtain, review, and retain information from other auditors that are involved in the audit

C. Retention of and subsequent changes to audit documentation

1. Important dates

   a. **Report release date**—The date the auditor grants permission to use the auditor's report. On this date the auditor has

      (1) Completed all necessary auditing procedures, including clearing review notes and providing support for all final conclusions

      (2) Obtained sufficient evidence to support the representations in the auditor's report

  b. **Documentation completion date**—Not more than 45 days after the report release date

2. Audit documentation requirements

  a. Should be retained for 7 years from the report release date, unless a longer period of time is required by law

  b. No deletions or discarding after the documentation completion date, but information may be added (indicating date added, name of person who prepared the additional documentation, and the reason for adding it)

  c. Audit documentation related to the work of other auditors should also be retained

  d. If after the documentation completion date the auditor becomes aware that documentation of necessary audit procedures is lacking, the auditor should investigate whether sufficient procedures were performed

      (1) If "yes," the auditor should consider what additional documentation is needed and add that documentation

      (2) If the auditor is unable to determine whether sufficient procedures were performed, the auditor should comply with AU 390 (consideration of omitted procedures)

PCAOB Auditing Standard No. 4—Reporting on Whether a Previously Reported Material Weakness Continues to Exist

Overall Objectives and Approach—This standard applies when an auditor is engaged to report on whether a previously reported material weakness in internal control continues to exist as of a date specified by management. The situation here is one in which the existence of a material weakness previously led to an adverse opinion in an internal control report. In such a circumstance, the company is ordinarily motivated to eliminate the weakness as quickly as reasonably possible, and may voluntarily engage the auditors to report on whether the material weakness continues to exist.

A. Conditions for CPA engagement performance; management must

1. Accept responsibility for effectiveness of IC
2. Evaluate the effectiveness of the specific controls that address the material weakness using the same control criteria (e.g., COSO)
3. Assert that the control(s) identified is effective in achieving the control objective
4. Support its assertion with sufficient evidence
5. Present a written report that will accompany auditor's report

B. Overall

1. Terminology

  a. A control objective relates to a relevant financial statement assertion and states a criterion for evaluating whether the company's control procedures in a specific area provide reasonable assurance that a misstatement in that relevant assertion is prevented or detected by controls on a timely basis.

  b. If a material weakness has previously been reported, a necessary control objective (or objectives) has not been met

  c. Examples of control objectives and related assertions

      (1) Recorded sales of product are real (existence or occurrence)
      (2) The company has legal title to recorded product X inventory (rights and obligations)

2. The control objective provides management and the auditor with a target against which to evaluate whether the material weakness continues to exist

3. Management and the auditor must be satisfied that the control objective has been achieved (and therefore the material weakness no longer exists)

  a. If management and the auditor have difficulty in identifying all stated control objectives affected by a material weakness (e.g., a weakness related to the control environment), the material weakness probably is not suitable for this engagement

4. An engagement includes

    a. Planning
    b. Obtaining an understanding of IC
    c. Testing and evaluating whether material weakness continues to exist
    d. Forming an opinion on whether previously reported material weakness continues to exist

5. Applying procedures

    a. Consistent with Standard 2, the auditor should evaluate operating effectiveness of a specified control for an adequate period of time
    b. Substantive procedures may be necessary

6. The auditor should evaluate whether to use work performed by others
7. Written representations should be obtained from management

C. Reporting

1. Auditor may issue an opinion only when there have been no restrictions on the scope of work
2. Management's report

    a. Management responsibility for maintaining IC
    b. Control criteria followed (e.g., COSO)
    c. Identification of the material weakness
    d. Identification of control objectives
    e. Statement that material weakness no longer exists

3. Auditor's report

    a. Title with word "independent"
    b. Statement about previous audit and a description of the material weakness
    c. Identification of management's report that includes the assertion that the material weakness no longer exists and a statement that management is responsible for its assertion
    d. Identification of specific controls management asserts address the material weakness and an identification of the company's stated control objective that is achieved by these controls
    e. It is the auditor's responsibility to express an opinion on whether the material weakness continues to exist as of the date of management's assertion
    f. Engagement conducted in accordance with PCAOB standards, standards that require the auditor to plan and perform engagement to obtain evidence that will allow auditor to provide reasonable assurance about whether the material weakness continues to exist
    g. Auditor believes auditing procedures provide a reasonable basis for opinion
    h. Opinion on whether identified material weakness exists (or no longer exists) as of date of management's assertion
    i. An audit of IC was not performed and inherent limitations of IC may not prevent or detect misstatements
    j. Signature of firm, city and state, and date

4. The report is modified if any of the following exist:

    a. Other material weaknesses are not addressed in the auditor's report (that is, if other material weaknesses existed that are not being addressed here, the auditor's report must so indicate)
    b. A subsequent event since the date being reported on (e.g., a change in effectiveness of identified controls)
    c. Management's report includes additional information (auditor should indicate that no opinion or other assurance is provided on that information)

5. If auditor believes material weakness continues to exist, this is so indicated in the audit report
6. If a new material weakness is identified, the auditor must communicate it to the audit committee (but not in this report)

PCAOB Auditing Standard No. 5—An Audit of Internal Control over Financial Reporting That Is Integrated with an Audit of Financial Statements

Overall Objectives and Approach—Section 404 of the Sarbanes-Oxley Act of 2002 requires that company management assess and report on the effectiveness of the company's internal control, and that the company's auditor attest to management's disclosures regarding the effectiveness of internal control. PCAOB Standard 5 (which replaced Standard 2) provides guidance for auditing issuer (public) companies' internal control over financial reporting in conjunction with an audit of the financial statements (i.e., an "integrated audit"). Specifically, the standard requires the auditor to examine the design and operating effectiveness of internal control over financial reporting to provide a sufficient basis to provide an opinion on its effectiveness in preventing or detecting material misstatement of the financial statements. We have integrated the outline of Standard 5 into Module 3, Internal Control, as Section C.

PCAOB Auditing Standard No. 6—Evaluating Consistency of Financial Statements

Overall Objectives and Approach—This Standard addresses when audit reports are modified to reflect a lack of consistency in audits performed in accordance with PCAOB Standards. It is in response to FASB Statement No. 154 which establishes a requirement that, unless impracticable, retrospective application is the required method for reporting a change in accounting principles; for public company audits it replaces AU 420.

A. **Consistency and the auditor's report on financial statements**

    1. The periods covered in the auditor's evaluation of consistency depend on the periods covered by the auditor's report

        a. When the auditor reports only on the current period (e.g., as a successor auditor) s/he should evaluate whether the current period financial statements are consistent with those of the preceding period

        b. When the auditor reports on two or more periods, s/he should evaluate consistency between such periods and the consistency of such periods with the period prior thereto *if* such prior period is presented with the financial statements being reported upon

    2. The following situations, when material, result in a consistency modification (i.e., a paragraph following the opinion paragraph indicating a lack of consistency):

        a. A change in accounting principle

        b. An adjustment to correct a misstatement in previously issued financial statements

B. **Change in accounting principle**

    1. A change in accounting principle that has a material effect on the financial statements should be recognized in the auditor's report

        a. If the change is treated properly in the financial statements (i.e., it and its method of application are generally accepted, disclosures are adequate, the company has justified that it is preferable), an explanatory paragraph indicating the lack of consistency is added following the opinion paragraph of the audit report

        b. If the change is not handled properly, the auditor should treat it as a departure from GAAP (i.e., issue a qualified or adverse opinion)

C. **Correction of a material misstatement in previously issued financial statements**

    1. A correction of a material misstatement in previously issued financial statements should be recognized in the auditor's report

        a. If the change is treated properly in the financial statements, an explanatory paragraph describing the correction and the lack of consistency is added following the opinion paragraph of the audit report

        b. If the correction is not handled properly, the auditor should treat it as a departure from GAAP (i.e., issue a qualified or adverse opinion)

D. **Change in classification**

    1. Does not require recognition in the auditor's report unless the change represents the correction of a material misstatement or a change in accounting principle

a. Examples of a correction of a material misstatement: Reclassification of debt from long-term to short-term or reclassifications of cash flows from operating activities to financing, when those items were incorrectly classified in the previously issued financial statements

   (1) In such situations, the reclassification is also a correction of a misstatement and the audit report is modified for consistency (as per C. above)

PCAOB Standard No. 7—Engagement Quality Review

Overall Objective and Approach—This standard provides guidance relating to engagement quality review which must be completed prior to issuance of an audit report on a public company. An independent quality reviewer in essence reviews the primary areas of the audit and determines whether he or she concurs with the audit as performed and has not identified one or more significant engagement deficiencies. We have integrated coverage of this material into topic D3 of Module 4, Responding to Risk Assessment: Evidence Accumulation and Evaluation.

PCOAB Standards 8 through 16—The Auditor's Assessment of, and Response to, Risk

These standards are similar in most areas to the AICPA and international risk assessment standards. In this manual we emphasize the AICPA risk assessment standards, but, throughout the text, we identify areas in which the various standards differ when we consider it appropriate. The following are the PCAOB brief summaries of its risk assessment standards.

Auditing Standard 8—Audit Risk

This standard discusses the auditor's consideration of audit risk in an audit of financial statements as part of an integrated audit or an audit of financial statements only. It describes the components of audit risk and the auditor's responsibilities for reducing audit risk to an appropriately low level in order to obtain reasonable assurance that the financial statements are free of material misstatement.

Auditing Standard 9—Audit Planning

This standard establishes requirements regarding planning an audit, including assessing matters that are important to the audit, and establishing an appropriate audit strategy and audit plan.

Auditing Standard 10—Supervision of the Audit Engagement

This standard sets forth requirements for supervision of the audit engagement, including, in particular, supervising the work of engagement team members. It applies to the engagement partner and to other engagement team members who assist the engagement partner with supervision.

Auditing Standard 11—Consideration of Materiality in Planning and Performing an Audit

This standard describes the auditor's responsibilities for consideration of materiality in planning and performing an audit.

Auditing Standard 12—Identifying and Assessing Risks of Material Misstatement

This standard establishes requirements regarding the process of identifying and assessing risks of material misstatement of the financial statements. The risk assessment process discussed in the standard includes information-gathering procedures to identify risks and an analysis of the identified risks.

Auditing Standard 13—The Auditor's Responses to the Risks of Material Misstatement

This standard establishes requirements for responding to the risks of material misstatement in financial statements through the general conduct of the audit and performing audit procedures regarding significant accounts and disclosures.

Auditing Standard 14—Evaluating Audit Results

This standard establishes requirements regarding the auditor's evaluation of audit results and determination of whether the auditor has obtained sufficient appropriate audit evidence. The evaluation process set forth in this standard includes, among other things, evaluation of misstatements identified during the audit; the overall presentation of the financial statements, including disclosures; and the potential for management bias in the financial statements.

Auditing Standard 15—Audit Evidence

This standard explains what constitutes audit evidence and establishes requirements for designing and performing audit procedures to obtain sufficient appropriate audit evidence to support the opinion expressed in the auditor's report.

Auditing Standard 16—Communications with Audit Committee

This standard corresponds to clarified AICPA standards AU 210 (*Terms of Engagement*) and AU 260 (*The Auditor's Communication with Those Charged with Governance*). Although it is structured differently, most Standard 16 communications are similar. Following are exceptions in that for each bulleted item the requirements in PCAOB Standard 16 go beyond explicit AU requirements; however, it might be argued that the more general AU requirements also in essence require a number of these communications. PCAOB Standard 16 requires that:

- An annual written engagement letter be used. Note that this differs from AU 210 which requires a written engagement letter or other form of written agreement for a first year audit, but for recurring audits the auditor has the option of reminding management of the terms of the engagement either in writing or orally.
- The auditor inquire about whether the audit committee is aware of matters relevant to the audit, including violations or possible violations of laws.
- The auditor must communicate:

  - An overview of overall audit strategy, including timing of the audit, significant risks the auditor identified, and significant changes in the planned audit strategy or identified risks.
  - Information on the nature and extent of specialized skill or knowledge needed in the audit, the extent of the planned use of internal auditors, company personnel, and third parties working under the direction of management or the audit committee in the audit.
  - Names, locations, and planned responsibilities of other independent public accounting firms or other persons not employed by the auditor.
  - Significant unusual transactions and the auditor's understanding of the business rationale for those transactions.
  - Difficult or contentious matters for which the auditor consulted outside the audit team.
  - When more than one audit firm is involved, the basis on which it determined it can serve as principal (i.e., group) auditor.
  - More information on company going concern status.

- The communication must occur prior to issuance of the auditor's report (AU 260 requires communication on a timely basis).

GOVERNMENT AUDITING STANDARDS (ISSUED BY THE COMPTROLLER GENERAL OF THE UNITED STATES, GENERAL ACCOUNTING OFFICE)

Background—Government Auditing Standards (GAS), also referred to as the "Yellow Book," is a book of standards issued by the Comptroller General of the United States. The standards (referred to as generally accepted government auditing standards—GAGAS) are for the use of auditors of government entities and entities that receive government awards. When studying this information also review the outline of AU 801 on AICPA audit requirements in this area. In this outline we present a brief outline of the information on three types of government audits: (a) financial audits, (b) attestation engagements, and (c) performance audits.

A. Overall

1. All *GAS* audits and attestation engagements begin with objectives, and those objectives determine the type of audit to be performed and the applicable standards to be followed
2. GAGAS requirements apply to the following types of audit and attestation engagements:

   a. Financial audits
   b. Attestation engagements
   c. Performance audits

B. Financial Audits

1. Provide an independent assessment and reasonable assurance about whether an entity's reported financial condition, results, and use of resources are presented fairly in accordance with recognized criteria

2. Reporting on financial audits performed in accordance with GAGAS include an audit report on the financial information, but also reports on

   a. Internal control over financial reporting (hereafter IC).
   b. Compliance with laws and regulations, and provisions of contracts and grant agreements as they relate to financial transactions, systems and processes.

3. There are two types of financial audits

   a. Financial statement audits—The primary purpose is to provide reasonable assurance through an opinion (or a disclaimer) about whether an entity's financial statements are presented fairly in all material respects in conformity with GAAP or with a comprehensive basis of accounting other than GAAP.

   b. Other financial audits—Other types of financial audits under GAGAS provide for different levels of assurance and entail various scopes of work, including

      (1) Special reports (e.g., on specified elements)
      (2) Reviews of interim financial information
      (3) Letters for underwriters and certain other requesting parties
      (4) Reports on the controls over processing of transactions by a service organization
      (5) Compliance with regulations relating to federal award expenditures and other governmental financial assistance in connection with a financial statement audit

4. Require following generally accepted auditing standards reporting standards, plus reporting on

   a. Compliance with GAGAS (report should say auditors performed audit in accordance with GAGAS)
   b. IC *and* compliance with laws, regulations, and provisions of contracts or grant agreements

      (1) The auditors should report on the scope of the auditor's testing of compliance and internal control, and state in the reports whether the tests they performed provided sufficient appropriate evidence to support an opinion on IC over financial reporting and on compliance with laws, regulations, and provisions of contracts or grant agreements.

         (a) Although auditors test compliance with laws and regulations, responsibility for compliance is the responsibility of management

      (2) The reports on IC and compliance may be combined or separate.

   c. A variety of additional matters, including various deficiencies related to

      (1) IC—significant deficiencies and material weaknesses are reported
      (2) Fraud, illegal acts, violations, and abuse

         (a) Under GAAS and GAGAS—Auditors have a responsibility to provide reasonable assurance of detecting fraud and illegal acts with a material effect on the financial statements and to determine that those charged with governance are informed

         (b) Auditors should include in their audit report the following that are discovered during the audit:

            1] Fraud and illegal acts that are more than inconsequential
            2] Violations of provisions of contracts or grant agreements with a material effect on financial statements
            3] Abuse that is material, either quantitatively or qualitatively

         (c) **Auditors should report known or likely fraud, illegal acts, or abuse directly to parties** *outside the audited entity* **in two circumstances:**

            1] When management does not satisfy legal or regulatory requirements to report
            2] When management fails to take timely and appropriate steps to respond to known or likely fraud, illegal acts, violations of contracts, or abuse

   d.   Communicating significant matters in the auditors' report

      (1)   The auditors may emphasize in the report significant matters regarding the financial statements.

> **NOTE:** This is like GAAS "emphasis of a matter" reporting.

   e.   Reporting on the restatement of previously issued financial statements

      (1)   The auditors should update the audit report as appropriate. They should notify those charged with governance if management doesn't timely (a) disclose new information that should be disclosed or (b) restate financial statements when necessary

   f.   Reporting views of responsible officials

      (1)   If the auditors' report discloses deficiencies in IC, fraud, illegal acts, violations of contracts, or abuse, auditors should obtain and report the views of responsible officials concerning the information.

      (2)   When auditors receive written comments from the responsible officials, they should include in their report a copy of them, or a summary. When only oral comments are provided, the auditor should prepare a summary and include in report as appropriate

   g.   Reporting confidential or sensitive information

      (1)   If certain information is prohibited from public disclosure, auditors should disclose in the report that certain information has been omitted and the reason or circumstances that make the omission necessary.

   h.   Distribution of audit reports

      (1)   Distribution depends on the relationship of the auditors to the audited organization and the nature of the information contained in the report. If the subject involves material that is classified for security purposes or contains confidential or sensitive information, the auditors may limit the report distribution. The auditors should document any limitation on report distribution.

C.   Attestation Engagements

1. Can cover a broad range of financial or nonfinancial objectives and may provide different levels of assurance about the subject matter or assertion depending on the users' needs
2. They are examination, review, or agreed-upon procedures engagements
3. Examples of subject matter are similar to those of attestation standards, for example

   a.   Prospective financial or performance information
   b.   Management discussion and analysis
   c.   Internal control over financial reporting
   d.   Effectiveness of internal control over compliance

4. Reporting standards for attestation engagements; AICPA attestation reporting standards *plus* reporting on

   a.   Compliance with GAGAS (report should say auditors performed audit in accordance with GAGAS)
   b.   Reporting deficiencies in IC, fraud, illegal acts, violations of provisions of contracts or grant agreements, and abuse
   c.   Reporting views of responsible officials
   d.   Reporting confidential or sensitive information
   e.   Distribution of reports

> **NOTE:** Overall reporting standards are similar to those for financial audits described earlier in Section B of this outline.

D. Performance audits

1. Engagements that provide assurance or conclusions based on an evaluation of sufficient, appropriate evidence against stated criteria, such as specific requirements, measures, or defined business practices

2. They provide objective analysis so that management and those charged with governance and oversight can use the information to improve program performance and operations, reduce costs, facilitate decision making by parties with responsibility to oversee or initiate corrective action, and contribute to public accountability

3. Performance audits that comply with GAGAS provide reasonable assurance that the auditors have obtained sufficient appropriate evidence to support the conclusions reached

4. Performance audit objectives may vary widely and include assessments of program effectiveness, economy and efficiency, internal control, compliance, and prospective analyses.

5. Audit objectives that focus on economy and efficiency address the costs and resources used to achieve program objectives; examples

   a. Assessing relative ability of alternative approaches to yield better program performance or eliminate factors that inhibit program effectiveness

   b. Analyzing the relative cost-effectiveness of a program or activity

   c. Determining whether a program produced intended results

6. Examples of audit objectives related to internal control include an assessment of whether the IC provides reasonable assurance about whether

   a. Organizational missions, goals, and objectives are achieved effectively and efficiently

   b. Resources are used in compliance with laws, regulations, or other requirements

   c. The integrity of information from computerized systems is achieved

7. Examples of compliance audit objectives include determining whether

   a. The purpose of the program, the manner in which it is to be conducted, the services delivered, the outcomes or the population it serves is in compliance with laws, regulations, contract provisions, grant agreements, and other requirements.

   b. Government services and benefits are distributed to citizens based on the individual's eligibility to obtain those services and benefits.

   c. Incurred or proposed costs are in compliance with applicable laws, regulations, and contracts or grant agreements.

8. Examples of prospective analysis audit objectives include providing conclusions based on

   a. Current or projected trends and future potential impact on government programs and services

   b. Program or policy alternatives, including forecasting program outcomes under various assumptions

   c. Management's assumptions on which prospective information is based

9. Reporting standards for performance audits; auditors should perform audit reports that contain

   a. The objectives, scope, and methodology of the audit

   b. The audit results, including findings, conclusions, and recommendations, as appropriate

   c. A statement about the auditors' compliance with GAGAS

   d. A summary of the views of responsible officials

   e. If applicable, the nature of any confidential or sensitive information

> **NOTE:** Although the overall requirements are similar to those of financial statement audits, the great variety of performance audits results in less specific requirements.

Module 41: Information Technology (Supplement)

Because much of the IT information you need to know for auditing relates to IT systems, we have duplicated the material from *Module 41* as a supplement to this volume.

Overview

Computers have become the primary means used to process financial accounting information and have resulted in a situation in which auditors must be able to use and understand current information technology. Accordingly, knowledge of information technology implications is included in the Business Environment and Concepts section of the CPA exam. In addition, auditing procedures relating to information technology (IT) are included in the Auditing and Attestation portion of the CPA exam.

This module describes various types of information technology and describes the major types of controls that are used to assure the accuracy, completeness, and integrity of technology processed information.

Ideally, to effectively reply to technology-related questions, you should have previously studied or worked in computerized business environments. However, if you do not have this background, we believe that the information in this module should prepare you to perform reasonably well on a typical exam. Keep in mind that the review of these materials cannot make you an expert, and a module such as this cannot cover all possible topics related to information technology. However, this material should help you to understand the complexities introduced by computers in sufficient detail to answer most questions. Before beginning the reading you should review the key terms at the end of the module.

A. Information Systems Within a Business

1. **Definition**—An information system processes data and transactions to provide users with the information they need to plan, control and operate an organization, including

    a. Collecting transaction and other data
    b. Entering it into the information system
    c. Processing the data
    d. Providing users with the information needed
    e. Controlling the process

2. **Manual vs. Computer Systems**

    a. On an overall basis, manual accounting systems have in most circumstances been replaced by computerized accounting information systems of various types, although portions of many systems remain manual.
    b. Computer processing tends to reduce or eliminate processing time, and prevent computational errors and errors in processing routine transactions (when fraud is not involved).

3. **General Types of IT Systems**

    a. **Office automation systems**—Designed to improve productivity by supporting daily work of employees (e.g., word processing, spreadsheets, presentation tools, e-mail, electronic calendars, contact management software)
    b. **Transaction processing systems**—Involve the daily processing of transactions (e.g., airplane reservation systems, payroll recording, cash receipts, cash disbursements)
    c. **Management reporting systems**—Designed to help with the decision making process by providing access to computer data

(1) **Management information systems**—Systems designed to provide past, present and future information for planning, organizing and controlling the operations of the organization

(2) **Decision support systems**—Computer-based information systems that combine models and data to resolve nonstructured problems with extensive user involvement

(3) **Expert systems**—Computer systems that apply reasoning methods to data in a specific relatively structured area to render advice or recommendations, much like a human expert

(4) **Executive information systems**—Computerized systems that are specifically designed to support executive work

> **NOTE:** It is helpful to consider these two distinct roles for systems—that is, (a) recording transactions of various types versus (b) providing support for decision making. These topics are discussed in detail under topic B.2. (Methods of Processing).

4. Systems Design and Process Improvement

Designing and implementing a new information and control system provides an opportunity to reexamine business processes, especially if the new system is an enterprise resource planning (ERP) system. Management can take advantage of the capabilities of the technology to redesign business processes making them more efficient and effective. The traditional methodology for developing information systems is the systems development lifecycle (SDLC). This methodology is characterized by its phases, each representing a specific set of development activities. Typically, the SDLC phases include: planning, analysis, design, development, testing, implementation and maintenance.

a. The Planning Phase

Major activities in the planning phase include

(1) Identify the problem(s) that proposed system will solve.

(2) Define the system to be developed. This involves identifying and selecting the system to be developed based on the strategic goals of the organization.

(3) Determine the project scope. This activity sets the project's boundaries by providing a clear understanding of what the new system will do and how it will be evaluated. A project scope document is used to describe the project scope. During the process of systems design, the scope of the project may be revisited and revised.

(4) Develop a project plan. The project plan defines the activities that will be performed, and the individuals and resources that will be used. A project manager is individual that develops the plan and tracks its progress. The plan establishes project milestones which set forth dates by which certain activities need to be performed.

(5) Evaluate the initial feasibility of the project. Feasibility analysis may involve multiple measures including determining the project's technical, organizational, and economic feasibility.

b. The Analysis Phase

This phase involves teams including end users, information technology specialists, systems analysts, and process design specialists to understand the requirements for the proposed system. Typically, processing, data, and logic models are produced during this phase to help determine the system requirements. A needs assessment may also be performed. A needs assessment involves determining the requirements for the system in terms of processes, data capture, information and reporting. Next, an analysis is performed on the existing system along the same dimensions. Then, a gap analysis is performed to examine the differences (gaps) between the required system and the existing system. Finally priorities will be established for the gaps (requirements) which will be documented in a requirements definition document, which will receive sign-off from the end users. It is during this phase that a company can take advantage of the processes inherent in the new system to improve existing processes. System specification documents contain information on basic requirements which include

(1) Performance levels
(2) Reliability
(3) Quality
(4) Interfaces

(5) Security and privacy

(6) Constraints and limitations

(7) Functional capabilities

(8) Data structures and elements

c. **The Design Phase**

The primary goal of the design phase is to build a technical blueprint of how the proposed system will work. The components that are typically designed during this phase include

(1) Databases

(2) User interfaces for input and output

(3) Required reports

(4) Programs

(5) Infrastructure and controls

d. **The Development Phase**

During the development phase the documents from the design phase are transformed into the actual system. In the design phase the platform on which the system is to operate is built or purchased off-the-shelf and customized and databases are developed.

e. **The Testing Phase**

The testing phase involves verifying that the system works and meets the business requirements as set forth in the analysis phase. The testing phase is obviously critical. The following types of test should be performed:

(1) *Unit testing.* Unit testing involves testing the units or pieces of code.

(2) *System testing.* System testing involves testing of the integration of the units or pieces of code into a system.

(3) *Integration testing.* Integration testing involves testing whether the separate systems can work together.

(4) *User acceptance testing.* User acceptance testing determines whether the system meets the business requirements and enables users to perform their jobs efficiently and effectively.

f. **The Implementation Phase**

The implementation phase involves putting the system in operation by the users. In order to effectively implement the system detailed user documentation must be provided to the users, and the users must be adequately trained. An organization may choose from a number of implementation methods including:

(1) *Parallel implementation.* This method uses both systems until it is determined that the new system is operating properly. This has the advantages of a full operational test of the new system with less risk of a system disaster. The disadvantage of this method is the additional work and cost during the period in which both systems are operating.

(2) *Plunge implementation.* Using this method the organization ceases using the old system and begins using the new system immediately. This method is less costly than the parallel method but it has higher risk of a system breakdown.

(3) *Pilot implementation.* This method involves having a small group of individuals using the new system until it is seen to be working properly. This has the advantage of providing a partial operational test of the new system at a lower cost than parallel implementation.

(4) *Phased implementation.* This method involves installing the system in a series of phases.

g. **The Maintenance Phase**

This phase involves monitoring and supporting the new system. In this phase the organization provides ongoing training, help desk resources, and a system for making authorized and tested changes to the system.

B. Characteristics of IT Systems—General

1. **Types of Computers, Hardware, and Software**

a. **Types of computers (in order of size and power)**

(1) **Supercomputers**—Extremely powerful, high-speed computers used for extremely high-volume and/or complex processing needs.

(2) **Mainframe computers**—Large, powerful, high-speed computers. While less powerful than supercomputers, they have traditionally been used for high-volume transaction processing. Clusters of lower cost, less powerful "servers" are increasingly taking over the processing chores of mainframe computers.

(3) **Servers**—High-powered microcomputers that "serve" applications and data to clients that are connected via a network (e.g., web servers, database servers). Servers typically have greater capacity (faster processors, more RAM, more storage capacity) than their clients (microcomputers) and often act as a central repository for organizational data. Servers today are often configured as a "virtual machine," meaning multiple operating systems can coexist and operate simultaneously on the same machine. Virtual machines are appealing because they lower hardware costs and they create energy savings.

(4) **Microcomputers (e.g., desktop computers, laptop computers)**—Designed to be used by one person at a time, they are often called personal computers. Typically used for word processing, e-mail, spreadsheets, surfing the web, creating and editing graphics, playing music, and gaming.

(5) **Tablets/Smart Phones/Personal Digital Assistants** (e.g., iPad, iPhone, Android, Blackberry). These are typically smaller, handheld wireless devices that depend on WiFi and/or cellular technology for communication. Many of these devices support touch screen input.

b. **Hardware—Physical equipment**

(1) **Central processing unit (CPU)**—The principal hardware components of a computer. It contains an arithmetic/logic unit, primary memory, and a control unit. The major function of the CPU is to fetch stored instructions and data, decode the instructions, and carry out the instructions.

   (a) **Arithmetic/logic unit**—Performs mathematical operations and logical comparisons.
   (b) **Primary memory (storage)**—Active data and program steps that are being processed by the CPU. It may be divided into RAM (random-access memory) and ROM (read-only memory). Application programs and data are stored in the RAM at execution time.
   (c) **Control unit**—Interprets program instructions and coordinates input, output, and storage devices.

(2) **Secondary storage**

   (a) **Storage devices**

      1] **Magnetic tape**—Slowest type of storage available because data is stored sequentially. Primarily used for archiving purposes today.
      2] **Magnetic disks**—The most common storage medium in use on computers today. Magnetic disks are also called "hard disks" or "hard disk drives" (HDD). Data can be accessed directly.
      3] **RAID (Redundant array of independent [previously, inexpensive] disks)**—A way of storing the same data redundantly on multiple magnetic disks

         a] When originally recorded, data is written to multiple disks to decrease the likelihood of loss of data.
         b] If a disk fails, at least one of the other disks has the information and continues operation.

      4] **Compact Discs**—Discs (CDs) and Digital Video Discs (DVDs)—Both are the same physical size and both use optical technology to read and write data to the disc.
      5] **Solid State Drives (SSDs)**—Use microchips to store data and require no moving parts for read/write operations. SSDs are faster and more expensive per gigabyte than CDs, DVDs, and HDDs. SSDs are increasingly being used in place of HDDs in microcomputers but cost and limited capacity have constrained their adoption as a primary storage device. SSDs are more commonly used for auxiliary storage. SSDs that are "pluggable" are often called "thumb drives," "flash drives," or "USB drives" (because they use a USB interface to "plug" into other devices).
      6] **Cloud-Based Storage**—Also called "Storage as a Service" (SaaS). This type of storage is hosted offsite, typically by third parties, and is accessed via the Internet.

   (b) **Manner in which information is represented in a computer**

      1] **Digital**—A series of binary digits (0s and 1s). One binary digit is called a "bit." A series of 8 bits is referred to as a "byte." One byte can form a letter, a number, or a special character (e.g., 00000111 is the binary equivalent of the decimal number 7).
      2] **Analog**—The representation that is produced by the fluctuations of a continuous signal (e.g., speech, temperature, weight, speed, etc.). Rather than using 0s and 1s to represent information, analog signals use electrical, mechanical, hydraulic or pneumatic devices to transmit the fluctuations in the signal itself to represent information.

(c) **Related computer terms**

1] **Online**—Equipment in direct communication with, and under the control of, the CPU. Online also refers to having a connection to the Internet.

2] **Off-line**—Equipment not in direct communication with the CPU; the operator generally must intervene to connect off-line equipment or data to the CPU (e.g., mount a magnetic tape of archival data). Off-line also refers to the absence of an Internet connection.

3] **Console**—A terminal used for communication between the operator and the computer (e.g., the operator of a mainframe computer)

4] **Peripheral equipment**—All non-CPU hardware that may be placed under the control of the central processor. Classified as online or off-line, this equipment consists of input, storage, output, and communication.

5] **Controllers**—Hardware units designed to operate specific input-output units

6] **Buffer**—A temporary storage unit used to hold data during computer operations

7] **MIPS**—Millions of instructions per second; a unit for measuring the execution speed of computers

(3) **Input devices**

(a) **Keying data—Data entry devices**

1] **Key-to-tape** and **key-to-disk** in which data is entered on magnetic tape and/or disk respectively, and then read into a computer

(b) **Online entry**

1] **Visual display terminal/monitors**—Uses keyboard to directly enter data into computer

a] **Input interface**—A program that controls the display for the user (usually on a computer monitor) and that allows the user to interact with the system

b] **Graphical user interface (GUI)** uses icons, pictures, and menus instead of text for inputs (e.g., Windows).

c] **Command line interface**—Uses text-type commands

2] **Mouse, joystick, light pens**—Familiar devices that allow data entry

3] **Touch-sensitive screen**—Allows users to enter data from a menu of items by touching the surface of the monitor

(c) **Turnaround documents**—Documents that are sent to the customer and returned as inputs (e.g., utility bills)

(d) **Automated source data input devices**

1] **Magnetic tape reader**—A device capable of sensing information recorded as magnetic spots on magnetic tape

2] **Magnetic ink character reader (MICR)**—Device that reads characters that have been encoded with a magnetic ink (e.g., bank check readers)

3] **Scanner**—A device that reads characters on printed pages

4] **Automatic teller machine (ATM)**—A machine used to execute and record transactions with financial institutions

5] **Radio Frequency Identification (RFID)**—Uses radio waves to track and input data. Increasingly used for inventory and contactless payment systems. RFID tags can be read wirelessly by RFID readers; does not require line-of-sight access like bar code technology (e.g., Mobil's Speedpass® payment systems, FasTrak® toll collection system).

6] **Point-of-sale (POS) recorders**—Devices that read price and product code data (e.g., recall purchasing groceries—items are frequently passed over a POS recorder). POS recorders ordinarily function as both a terminal and a cash register.

a] POS processing allows one to record and track customer orders, process credit and debit cards, connect to other systems in a network, and manage inventory. Generally, a POS terminal has as its core a personal computer, which is provided with application-specific programs and input/output devices for the particular environment in which it will serve.

b] POS terminals are used in most industries that have a point of sale such as a service desk, including restaurants, lodging, entertainment, and museums. For example, a POS system for a restaurant is likely to have all menu items stored in a database that can be queried for information in a number of ways.

> c] Increasingly, POS terminals are also Web-enabled, which makes remote training and operation possible, as well as inventory tracking across geographically dispersed locations.

> 7] **Voice recognition**—A system that understands spoken words and transmits them into a computer.

(e) **Electronic commerce** and **electronic data interchange**—Involves one company's computer communicating with another's computer. For example, a buyer electronically sending a purchase order to a supplier. Discussed in further detail in section C.5. of this module.

(4) **Output devices**

(a) Many automated source data input devices and electronic commerce/electronic data interchange devices [(3)(d) and (e) above] are capable of outputting data ("writing" in addition to "reading") and therefore become output devices as well as input devices.

(b) **Monitors**—Visually display output

(c) **Printers**—Produce paper output

(d) **Plotters**—Produce paper output of graphs

(e) **Computer output to microfilm or microfiche (COM)**—Makes use of photographic process to store output

c. **Software—Computer programs that control hardware**

(1) **Systems software**

(a) **Operating system**—Manages the input, output, processing and storage devices and operations of a computer (e.g., Windows, Linux, Unix)

> 1] Performs scheduling, resource allocation, and data retrieval based on instructions provided in job control language

(b) **Utility programs**—Handle common file, data manipulation and "housekeeping" tasks

(c) **Communications software**—Controls and supports transmission between computers, computers and monitors, and accesses various databases

(2) **Applications software**—Programs designed for specific uses, or "applications," such as

(a) Word processing, graphics, spreadsheets, email, and database systems

(b) Accounting software

> 1] **Low-end**—All in one package, designed for small organizations
> 2] **High-end**—Ordinarily in modules (e.g., general ledger, receivables)
> 3] **Enterprise Resource Planning (ERP)**—Designed as relatively complete information system "suites" for large and medium size organizations (e.g., human resources, financial applications, manufacturing, distribution). Major vendors are well known—SAP, PeopleSoft, Oracle, and J.D. Edwards.

>> a] Advantages of ERP systems—Integration of various portions of the information system, direct electronic communication with suppliers and customers, increased responsiveness to information requests for decision-making
>> b] Disadvantages of ERP systems—Complexity, costs, integration with supplier and customer systems may be more difficult than anticipated

(3) **Software terms**

(a) **Compiler**—Produces a machine language object program from a source program language

(b) **Multiprocessing**—Simultaneous execution of two or more tasks, usually by two or more CPUs that are part of the same system

(c) **Multitasking**—The simultaneous processing of several jobs on a computer

(d) **Object program**—The converted source program that was changed using a compiler to create a set of machine readable instructions that the CPU understands

(e) **Source program**—A program written in a language from which statements are translated into machine language; computer programming has developed in "generations"

> 1] Machine language (composed of combinations of 1's and 0's that are meaningful to the computer).

2] Assembly language—A low-level programming language that uses words (mnemonics) instead of numbers to perform an operation. Assembly language must be translated to machine language by a utility program called an *assembler*. Generally, an assembly language is specific to a computer architecture and is therefore not portable like most high-level languages.

3] "High-level" programming languages such as COBOL, Basic, Fortran, C++, and Java.

    a] C++ and Java are considered object-oriented programs (OOP) in that they are based on the concept of an "object" which is a data structure that uses a set of routines, called "methods," which operate on the data. The "objects" are efficient in that they often are reusable in other programs.

    b] Object-oriented programs keep together data structures and procedures (methods) through a procedure referred to as encapsulation. Basic to object-oriented programs are the concepts of a class (a set of objects with similar structures) and inheritance (the ability to create new classes from existing classes).

4] An "application-specific" language usually built around database systems. These programs are ordinarily closer to human languages than the first three generations (e.g., SQL, Structured Query Language: an instruction to create a report might be *Extract all Customers where "Name" is Jones*).

5] A relatively new and developing form that includes visual or graphical interfaces used to create source language that is usually compiled with a 3rd or 4th generation language compiler.

  (f) **Virtual memory (storage)**—Online secondary memory that is used as an extension of primary memory, thus giving the appearance of larger, virtually unlimited internal memory

  (g) **Protocol**—Rules determining the required format and methods for transmission of data

(4) Programming terms

  (a) **Desk checking**—Review of a program by the programmer for errors before the program is run and debugged on the computer

  (b) **Debug**—To find and eliminate errors in a computer program. Many compilers assist debugging by listing errors in the program such as invalid commands

  (c) **Edit**—To correct input data prior to processing

  (d) **Loop**—A set of program instructions performed repetitively a predetermined number of times, or until all of a particular type of data has been processed

  (e) **Memory dump**—A listing of the contents of storage

  (f) **Patch**—A section of coding inserted into a program to correct a mistake or to alter a routine

  (g) **Run**—A complete cycle of a program including input, processing and output

2. Methods of Processing

a. Batch or online real-time

(1) Batch

  (a) Transactions flow through the system in groups of like transactions (batches). For example, all cash receipts on accounts receivable for a day may be aggregated and run as a batch.

  (b) Ordinarily leaves a relatively easy-to-follow audit trail.

(2) Online real-time (also referred to as direct access processing)

General: Transactions are processed in the order in which they occur, regardless of type. Data files and programs are stored online so that updating can take place as the edited data flows to the application. System security must be in place to restrict access to programs and data to authorized persons. Online systems are often categorized as being either online transaction processing systems or online analytical processing systems.

  (a) **Online transaction processing (OLTP)**

    1] Databases that support day-to-day operations

    2] Examples: airline reservations systems, bank automatic teller systems, and Internet website sales systems

(b) **Online analytical processing (OLAP)**

　　1] A category of software technology that enables the user to query the system (retrieve data), and conduct an analysis, etc., ordinarily while the user is at a PC. The result is generated in seconds. OLAP systems are primarily used for analytical analysis.

EXAMPLE

An airline's management downloads its OLTP reservation information into another database to allow analysis of that reservation information. At a minimum, this will allow analysis without tying up the OLTP system that is used on a continuous basis; the restructuring of the data into another database is also likely to make a more detailed analysis possible.

　　2] Uses statistical and graphical tools that provide users with various (often multidimensional) views of their data, and allows them to analyze the data in detail.

　　3] These techniques are used as **decision support systems** (computer-based information systems that combine models and data in an attempt to solve relatively unstructured problems with extensive user involvement).

　　4] One approach to OLAP is to periodically download and combine operational databases into a **data warehouse** (a subject-oriented, integrated collection of data used to support management decision-making processes) or a **data mart** (a data warehouse that is limited in scope).

　　　　a] **Data mining**—Using sophisticated techniques from statistics, artificial intelligence and computer graphics to explain, confirm and explore relationships among data (which is often stored in a data warehouse or data mart)

　　　　b] **Business intelligence (BI)**—A combination of systems that help aggregate, access, and analyze business data and assist in the business decision-making process.

　　5] **Artificial intelligence (AI)**—Computer software designed to help humans make decisions. AI may be viewed as an attempt to model aspects of human thought on computers. AI ordinarily deals with decisions that may be made using a relatively structured approach. It frequently involves using a computer to quickly solve a problem that a human could ultimately solve through extremely detailed analysis.

　　6] **Expert system**—One form of AI. A computerized information system that guides decision processes within a well-defined area and allows decisions comparable to those of an expert. Expert knowledge is modeled into a mathematical system.

EXAMPLE

An expert system may be used by a credit card department to authorize credit card purchases so as to minimize fraud and credit losses.

---

b. **Centralized, Decentralized, or Distributed**

(1) **Centralized**

(a) Processing occurs at one location.

(b) Historically, this is the model used in which a mainframe computer processes data submitted to it through terminals.

(c) Today, centralized vs. decentralized processing is often a matter of degree—how much is processed by a centralized computer vs. how much by decentralized computers.

(2) **Decentralized**

(a) Processing (and data) are stored on computers at multiple locations.

(b) Ordinarily the computers involved are not interconnected by a network, so users at various sites cannot share data.

(c) May be viewed as a collection of independent databases, rather than a single database.

(d) End-user computing (topic C.4. below) is relatively decentralized.

(3) **Distributed**

(a) Transactions for a single database are processed at various sites.

EXAMPLE

Payroll is processed for Minneapolis employees in Minneapolis, and for Santa Fe employees in Santa Fe. Yet the overall payroll information is in one database.

(b) Processing may be on either a batch or online real-time basis.

(c) An overall single data base is ordinarily updated for these transactions and available at the various sites.

3. Methods of Data Structure

a. Data organization for computer operations

(1) **Bit**—A binary digit (0 or 1) which is the smallest storage unit in a computer.

(2) **Byte**—A group of adjacent bits (usually 8) that is treated as a single unit, or character, by the computer. Printable alphanumeric characters (e.g., A-Z, a-z, 0-9); special characters (e.g., $, %, !, @, etc.) and unprintable control codes (e.g., those that control peripheral devices such as printers) can be represented by an 8-bit Byte. Character-encoding schemes for computers, such as ASCII and UTF-8, ensure universal interpretation of the 8-bit codes.

(3) **Field**—A group of related characters (e.g., a social security number).

(4) **Record**—An ordered set of logically related fields. For example, all payroll data (including the social security number field and others) relating to a single employee.

(5) **File**—a group of related records (e.g., all the weekly pay records year-to-date), which is usually arranged in sequence.

(6) **Table**—A group of related records in a relational database with a unique identifier (primary key field) in each record.

(7) **Database**—A group of related files or a group of related tables (if a relational database).

(8) **Array**—In a programming language, an aggregate that consists of data objects with attributes, each of which may be uniquely referenced by an index (address). For example, an array may be used to request input of various payroll information for a new employee in one step. Thus an array could include employee name, social security number, withholdings, pay rate, etc.—for example (John Jones, 470-44-5044, 2, $18.32, …). Name would be indexed as 1 (or zero), with each succeeding attribute receiving the next higher number as an address. Also arrays may be multidimensional. They are often used with object-oriented programming such as C++ and Java.

(9) **Master file**—A file containing relatively permanent information used as a source of reference and periodically updated with a detail (transaction) file (e.g., permanent payroll records).

(10) **Detail or transaction file**—A file containing current transaction information used to update the master file (e.g., hours worked by each employee during the current period used to update the payroll master file).

b. Data file structure

(1) **Traditional file processing systems**—These systems focus upon data processing needs of individual departments. Each application program or system is developed to meet the needs of the particular requesting department or user group. For accounting purposes these systems are often similar to traditional accounting systems, with files set up for operations such as purchasing, sales, cash receipts, cash disbursements, etc.

(a) **Advantages of traditional processing systems**

1] Currently operational for many existing (legacy) systems

2] Often cost effective for simple applications

(b) **Disadvantages of traditional processing systems**

1] Data files are dependent upon a particular application program.
2] In complex business situation there is much duplication of data between data files.
3] Each application must be developed individually.
4] Program maintenance is expensive.
5] Data may be isolated and difficult to share between functional areas.

(2) **Database systems**

(a) **Definitions**

1] **Database**—A collection of interrelated files, ordinarily most of which are stored online.

  a] **Normalization**—The process of separating the database into logical tables to avoid certain kinds of updating difficulties (referred to as "anomalies").

2] **Database system**—Computer hardware and software that enables the database(s) to be implemented.

3] **Database management system**—Software that provides a facility for communications between various applications programs (e.g., a payroll preparation program) and the database (e.g., a payroll master file containing the earnings records of the employees).

4] **Data independence**—Basic to database systems is this concept which separates the data from the related application programs.

5] **Data modeling**—Identifying and organizing a database's data, both logically and physically. A data model determines what information is to be contained in a database, how the information will be used, and how the items in the database will be related to each other.

  a] **Entity-relationship modeling**—An approach to data modeling. The model (called the Entity-Relationship diagram, or ERD) divides the database in two logical parts—entities (e.g. "customer," "product") and relations ("buys," "pays for").

  b] **Primary key**—The field(s) that make a record in a relational database table unique.

  c] **Foreign key**—The field(s) that are common to two (or more) related tables in a relational database.

  d] **REA data model**—A data model designed for use in designing accounting information databases. REA is an acronym for the model's basic types of objects: **R**esources—Identifiable objects that have economic value, **E**vents—An organization's business activities, **A**gents—People or organizations about which data is collected.

6] **Data Dictionary** (also referred to as a **data repository** or **data directory** system)—A data structure that stores meta-data.

  a] **Meta-data**—Definitional data that provides information about or documentation of other data managed within an application or environment. For example, data about data elements, records and data structures (length, fields, columns, etc.).

7] **Structured query language (SQL)**—The most common language used for creating and querying relational databases (see (b)3] below), its commands may be classified into three types.

  a] **Data definition language (DDL)**—Used to define a database, including creating, altering, and deleting tables and establishing various constraints.

  b] **Data manipulation language (DML)**—Commands used to maintain and query a database, including updating, inserting in, modifying, and querying (asking for data). For example, a frequent query involves the joining of information from more than one table.

  c] **Data control language (DCL)**—Commands used to control a database, including controlling which users have various privileges (e.g., who is able to read from and write to various portions of the database).

(b) **Database structures**

1] **Hierarchical**—The data elements at one level "own" the data elements at the next lower level (think of an organization chart in which one manager supervises several assistants, who in turn each supervise several lower level employees).

2] **Networked**—Each data element can have several owners and can own several other elements (think of a matrix-type structure in which various relationships can be supported.

3] **Relational**—A database with the logical structure of a group of related spreadsheets. Each row represents a record, which is an accumulation of all the fields related to the same identifier or key; each column represents a field common to all of the records. Relational databases have in many situations largely replaced the earlier developed hierarchical and networked databases.

4] **Object-oriented**—Information (attributes and methods) are included in structures called object classes. This is the newest database management system technology

5] **Object-relational**—Includes both relational and object-oriented features.

6] **Distributed**—A single database that is spread physically across computers in multiple locations that are connected by a data communications link. (The structure of the database is most frequently relational, object-oriented, or object-relational.)

(c) **Database controls**

1] **User department**—Because users directly input data, strict controls over who is authorized to read and/or change the database are necessary.

2] **Access controls**—In addition to the usual controls over terminals and access to the system, database processing also maintains controls within the database itself. These controls limit the user to reading and/or changing (updating) only authorized portions of the database.

a] **Restricting privileges**—This limits the access of users to the database, as well as operations a particular user may be able to perform. For example, certain employees and customers may have only read, and not write, privileges.

b] **Logical views**—Users may be provided with authorized *views* of only the portions of the database for which they have a valid need.

3] **Backup and recovery**—A database is updated on a continuous basis during the day. Three methods of backup and recovery include

a] **Backup of database and logs of transactions** (sometimes referred to as "systems logs"). The approach is to backup the entire database several times per week, generally to magnetic tape. A log of all transactions is also maintained. If there is extensive damage to a major portion of the database due to catastrophic failure, such as disk crash, the recovery method is to restore the most recent past copy of the database and to reconstruct it to a more current state by reapplying or redoing transactions from the log up to the point of failure.

b] **Database replication.** To avoid catastrophic failure, another approach is to replicate the database at one or more locations. Thus, all data may be recorded to both sets of the database.

c] **Backup facility.** Another approach is to maintain a backup facility with a vendor who will process data in case of an emergency.
Further information on backup and recovery is included under Disaster Recovery—D.11 of this module.

4] **Database administrator (DBA)**—Individual responsible for maintaining the database and restricting access to the database to authorized personnel.

5] **Audit software**—Usually used by auditors to test the database; see Auditing with Technology Module.

(d) **Advantages of database systems**

1] **Data independence**—Data can be used relatively easily by differing applications.

2] **Minimal data redundancy**—The manner in which data is structured results in information being recorded in only one place, thus making updating much easier than is the case with traditional file systems.

3] **Data sharing**—The sharing of data between individuals and applications is relatively easy.

4] Reduced program maintenance.

5] Commercial applications are available for modification to a company's needs.

(e) **Disadvantages of database systems**

1] Need for specialized personnel with database expertise

2] Installation of database costly

3] Conversion of traditional file systems (legacy systems) costly

4] Comprehensive backup and recovery procedures are necessary.

C. Characteristics of IT Systems—Specific

1. Types of Networks

a. Background

(1) A network is a group of interconnected computers and terminals.

(2) The development of **telecommunications**—The electronic transmission of information by radio, fiber optics, wire, microwave, laser, and other electromagnetic systems—has made possible the electronic transfer of information between networks of computers. This topic is discussed in detail later in this module.

b. Classified by geographical scope

(1) **Personal area network** (PAN)—A computer network that is centered around an individual and the personal communication devices he/she uses. PANs can be associated with both wireless and wired communication devices (e.g., the Bluetooth devices we use with our mobile phones for driving; the USB devices that we connect to our computers).

(2) **Local area networks** (LAN)—Privately owned networks within a single building or campus of up to a few miles in size. Because this topic has been emphasized in AICPA materials, it is discussed further later in this module.

(3) **Metropolitan area network** (MAN)—A larger version of a LAN. For example, it might include a group of nearby offices within a city.

(4) **Wide area networks** (WAN)—Networks that span a large geographical area, often a country or continent. It is composed of a collection of computers and other hardware and software for running user programs.

c. Classified by ownership

(1) **Private**—One in which network resources are usually dedicated to a small number of applications or a restricted set of users, as in a corporation's network.

    (a) A typical approach is to lease telephone lines that are dedicated to the network's use.

    (b) Also, traditional EDI systems (discussed below) use a private network.

    (c) Advantages: Secure, flexible, performance often exceeds that of public.

    (d) Disadvantage: Costly

(2) **Public**—Resources are owned by third-party companies and leased to users on a usage basis (also referred to as public-switched networks [PSN]).

    (a) Access is typically through dial-up circuits.

    (b) Example: Applications using the Internet.

    (c) Advantages and disadvantage: In general, the opposite of those for private networks, but certainly a significant disadvantage is that they are less secure.

        1] Improvements in Internet communications will decrease the disadvantages and will lead to a dramatic increase in the use of public networks (e.g., rapid increases in the use of Internet-based electronic commerce).

(3) **Cloud computing/cloud services**—The use and access of multiple server-based computational resources via a digital network (WAN, Internet connection using the World Wide Web, etc.). A user accesses the server resources using a computer, netbook, tablet computer, smart phone, or other device. With cloud computing, applications are provided and managed by the cloud server and data is stored remotely in the cloud configuration. Users do not download and install applications on their own device or computer; all processing and storage is maintained by the cloud server. Cloud services may be offered by a cloud provider or by a private organization.

    (a) Risks of cloud computing

        1] Information security and privacy—users must rely on the cloud providers' data access controls.

        2] Continuity of services—user problems may occur if the cloud provider has disruptions in service.

        3] Migration—users may have difficulty in changing cloud providers because there are no data standards.

d. **Classified by use of Internet**

General: The following all use the Internet. They have in common that data communications are ordinarily through **Hypertext Markup Language (HTML)** and/or **Extensible Markup Language (XML)**—languages used to create and format documents, link documents to other Web pages, and communicate between Web browsers. XML is increasingly replacing HTML in Internet applications due to its superior ability to tag (i.e., label) and format documents that are communicated among trading partners.

Extensible Business Reporting Language (XBRL) is an XML-based language being developed specifically for the automation of business information requirements, such as the preparation, sharing, and analysis of financial reports, statements, and audit schedules. XBRL is used in filings with the SEC that are made available on EDGAR, the SEC's Electronic Data Gathering and Retrieval database.

(1) **Internet**—An international collection of networks made up of independently owned computers that operate as a large computing network. Internetwork communication requires the use of a common set of rules, or protocols (TCP), and a shared routing system (IP).

(a) Primary applications of the Internet include

1] E-mail
2] News dissemination
3] Remote log-in of computers
4] File transfer among computers
5] Electronic commerce

(b) Terminology

1] **Hypertext Transfer Protocol (HTTP)**—The primary Internet protocol for data communication on the World Wide Web.
2] **Uniform Resource Locator (URL)**—A standard for finding a document by typing in an address (e.g., www.azdiamondbacks.com). URLs work in much the same way as addresses on mail processed by the postal department.
3] **World Wide Web (the web or WWW)**—A framework for accessing linked resources (e.g., documents, pictures, music files, videos, etc.) spread out over the millions of machines all over the Internet.
4] **Web browser**—Client software (e.g., Internet explorer, Firefox, Chrome, Mosaic, etc.) that provides the user with the ability to locate and display web resources.
5] **Web servers**—The software that "serves," (i.e., makes available) web resources to software clients. web servers (e.g., Apache and Internet Information Server [IIS]) typically run on "server" hardware. However, many computing devices today support their own web server software.
6] **Firewall**—A method for protecting an organization's computers and computer information from outsiders. A firewall consists of security algorithms and router communications protocols that prevent outsiders from tapping into corporate database and e-mail systems.
7] **Router**—A communications interface device that connects two networks and determines the best way for data packets to move forward to their destinations.
8] **Bridge**—A device that divides a LAN into two segments, selectively forwarding traffic across the network boundary it defines; similar to a switch.
9] **Switch**—A device that channels incoming data from any of multiple input ports to the specific output port that will take the data toward its intended destination.
10] **Gateway**—A combination of hardware and software that links to different types of networks. For examples, gateways between e-mail systems allow users of differing e-mail systems to exchange messages.
11] **Proxy server**—A server that saves and serves copies of web pages to those who request them (e.g., potential customers). When a web page is requested, the proxy server is able to access that page either through its cache (reserve of web pages already sent or loaded) or by obtaining it through the original server. A proxy server can both increase efficiency of Internet operations and help assure data security.
12] **Web 2.0**—2nd generation of the web. Refers to era of web-based collaboration and community-generated content via web-based software tools such as

        a] **Blog**—An asynchronous discussion, or web log, led by a moderator that typically focuses on a single topic. Similar to an electronic bulletin board. Blogs are an efficient way to share information, views, and opinions.

        b] **Wiki**—An information-gathering and knowledge-sharing website that is developed collaboratively by a community or group, all of whom can freely add, modify, or delete content.

        c] **Twitter**—A micro-variation of a blog. Restricts input (tweets) to 140 characters. Commonly used to "follow" friends and celebrities. Increasingly companies are using Twitter to inform followers.

        d] **RSS/ATOM Feeds—Really Simple Syndication**—An XML application that facilitates the sharing and syndication of website content by subscription. RSS feeds are automatically checked by RSS-enabled client software (including most browsers and RSS readers) for new website content on a regular basis.

    13] **TCP/IP (Transmission Control Protocol/Internet Protocol)**—The basic communication language or protocol of the Internet. It has two layers. The higher layer assembles messages or files into smaller packets that are transmitted over the Internet. The lower layer assigns IP addresses and insures that messages are delivered to the appropriate computer.

    14] **IP address**—The number that identifies a machine as unique on the Internet.

    15] **ISP (Internet Service Provider)**—An entity that provides access to the Internet.

  (c) The nature of the Internet has resulted in the spread of a series of malicious programs (often through email) that may adversely affect computer operations, including

    1] **Virus**—A program (or piece of code) that requests the computer operating system to perform certain activities not authorized by the computer user. Viruses can be easily transmitted through use of files that contain macros that are sent as attachment to e-mail messages.

        a] **Macro**—A stored set of instructions and functions that are organized to perform a repetitive task and can be easily activated, often by a simple keystroke combination. Most macros serve valid purposes, but those associated with viruses cause problems.

        b] Unexpected changes in, or losses of, data may be an indication of the existence of a virus on one's computer.

        c] E-mail attachments and **public domain software** (generally downloadable from the Internet at no cost to users) are notorious sources of viruses.

    2] **Trojan horse**—A malicious, security-breaking program that is disguised as something benign, such as a game, but actually is intended to cause IT damage.

    3] **Worm**—A program that propagates itself over a network, reproducing itself as it goes.

    4] **Antivirus software**—Is used to attempt to avoid the above types of problems. But the rapid development of new forms of viruses, Trojan horses, and worms results in a situation in which antivirus software developers are always behind the developers.

    5] **Botnet**—A network of computers that are controlled by computer code, called a "bot," that is designed to perform a repetitive task such as sending spam, spreading a virus, or creating a distributed denial of service attack.

  (2) **Intranet**—A local network, usually limited to an organization, that uses internet-based technology to communicate within the organization.

  (3) **Extranet**—Similar to an intranet, but includes an organization's external customers and/or suppliers in the network.

e. **Database client-server architecture**

    General: When considering networks, it is helpful to consider their architecture (design). Bear in mind that the architecture must divide the following responsibilities (1) input, (2) processing, and (3) storage. In general, the client-server model may be viewed as one in which communications ordinarily take the form of a request message from the client to the server asking for some service to be performed. A "client" may be viewed as the computer or **workstation** of an individual user. The server is a high-capacity computer that contains the network software and may provide a variety of services ranging from simply "serving" files to a client to performing analyses.

(1) **Overall client-server systems**—A networked computing model (usually a LAN) in which database software on a server performs database commands sent to it from client computers

Illustration of Client/Server Architecture

(2) **Subtypes of client/server architectures**

(a) **File servers**—The file server manages file operations and is shared by each of the client PCs (ordinarily attached to a LAN). The three responsibilities (input/output, processing, and storage) are divided in a manner in which most input/output, and processing occurs on client computers rather than on the server. The file server acts simply as a shared data storage device, with all data manipulations performed by client PCs.

(b) **Database servers**—Similar to file servers, but the server here contains the database management system and thus performs more of the processing.

> **NOTE:** The above two architectures are referred to as "two-tier" architecture—client tier and server database tier.

(c) **Three-tier architectures**—A client/server configuration that includes three tiers. The change from the above systems is that this architecture includes another server layer in addition to the two tiers discussed above. For example, application programs (e.g., a transaction processing monitor that controls the input of transactions to the database) may reside on the additional server rather than on the individual clients. This system of adding additional servers may generalize to additional tiers and thus become **n-tier** architecture. Examples of other servers that may be added are as follows:

1] **Print server**—Make shared printers available to various clients.
2] **Communications server**—May serve a variety of tasks, such as acting as a gateway (i.e., means of entrance) to the internet or to the corporate intranet.
3] **Fax server**—Allow clients on the network to share the hardware for incoming and outgoing fax transmissions.
4] **Web server**—Stores and serves web pages on request.

(3) **Distributed systems**—These systems connect all company locations to form a distributed network in which each location has its own input/output, processing, and storage capabilities. These local computers also pass data among themselves and possibly to a server (often referred to as a "host" in this context) for further processing. An illustration of this type of system is presented in the database section of this outline.

2. **Local Area Networks (LANs)**—Privately owned networks within a single building or campus of up to a few miles in size.

   a. **Software**

      (1) Software allows devices to function cooperatively and share network resources such as printers and disk storage space.
      (2) Common services

         (a) Network server
         (b) File server
         (c) Print server
         (d) Communications server

   b. **Hardware components**

      (1) **Workstations**—Ordinarily microcomputers.
      (2) **Peripherals**—For example, printers, network attached storage (NAS) devices, optical scanners, fax board.
      (3) **Transmission media**—Physical path that connect components of LAN, ordinarily twisted-pair wire, coaxial cable, or optical fiber. LANs that are connected wirelessly are called WLANs or WiFi networks.
      (4) **Network interface cards**—Connect workstation and transmission media.

   c. **Control implications**

      (1) General controls are often weak (e.g., controls over development and modification of programs, access and computer operations).
      (2) Controls often rely upon end users, who may not be control conscious.
      (3) Often users may not be provided adequate resources for problem resolution, troubleshooting and recovery support.
      (4) Controlling access and gaining accountability through logging of transactions enforces a segregation of duties.
      (5) Good management controls are essential—for example, access codes, passwords.
      (6) LAN software ordinarily does not provide security features available in larger scale environments.

   > **NOTE:** Tests of controls may address whether controls related to the above are effective.

   d. LANs generally make possible the computer audit techniques that may be performed either by internal auditors or external auditors.

3. **Microcomputers**

   a. The proliferation of microcomputers (e.g., personal computers [PC], laptop computers) has had a profound effect on information systems. A small-business client will probably use a PC to run a commercially purchased general ledger package (off-the-shelf software). Segregation of duties becomes especially difficult in such an environment because one individual may perform all recordkeeping (processing) as well as maintain other nonrecordkeeping responsibilities.
   b. A larger client may use a network of PCs that may or may not be linked to a large corporate mainframe computer. In all systems, management policies should be in place regarding the development and modification of programs and data files.
   c. Regardless of the system, the control objectives remain the same. When small computers are involved, the following points need to be considered:

      (1) **Security**—Security over small computers, while still important, may not be as critical as security over the data and any in-house developed software. Most companies can easily replace the hardware, but may suffer a severe setback if the data and/or in-house developed software is lost. Access to the software installation files should be controlled and backup copies should be made. Access to the hard drive must be restricted since anyone turning on the power switch can read the data stored on those files. Also, a control problem may exist because the computer operator often understands the system and also has access to the input data. The management of the company may need to become more directly involved in supervision when a lack of segregation of duties exists in data processing.

(2) **Verification of processing**—Periodically, an independent verification of the applications being processed on the small computer system should be made to prevent the system from being used for personal projects. Also, verification helps prevent errors in internally developed software from going undetected. Controls should be in operation to assure the accuracy of in-house created spreadsheets and databases.

(3) **Personnel**—Centralized authorization to purchase hardware and software should be required to ensure that appropriate purchasing decisions are made, including decisions that minimize software and hardware compatibility difficulties. Software piracy and viruses may be controlled by prohibiting the loading of unauthorized software and data on company-owned computers.

　(a) Software is copyrighted, and violation of copyright laws may result in litigation against the company.

　(b) A company may control possible software piracy (the use of unlicensed software) by employees by procedures such as:

　　1] Establishing a corporate software policy

　　2] Maintaining a log of all software purchase

　　3] Auditing individual computers to identify installed software

4. **End-User Computing (EUC)**—The end user is responsible for the development and execution of the computer application that generates the information used by that same end user.

　a. User substantially eliminates many of the services offered by an MIS department.

　b. Risks include

　　(1) End-user applications are not always adequately tested before implemented.

　　(2) More client personnel need to understand control concepts.

　　(3) Management often does not review the results of applications appropriately.

　　(4) Old or existing applications may not be updated for current applicability and accuracy.

　c. Overall physical access controls become more difficult when companies leave a controlled MIS environment and become more dependent upon individual users for controls.

　d. Control implications

　　(1) Require applications to be adequately tested before they are implemented

　　(2) Require adequate documentation

　　(3) Physical access controls, including

　　　(a) Clamps or chains to prevent removal of hard disks or internal boards

　　　(b) Diskless workstations that require download of files

　　　(c) Regular backup

　　　(d) Security software to limit access to those who know user ID and password

　　　(e) Control over access from outside

　　　(f) Commitment to security matters written into job descriptions, employee contracts, and personnel evaluation procedures

　　(4) Control access to appropriate users

　　　(a) Passwords and user IDs

　　　(b) Menus for EUC access to database

　　　(c) Protect system by restricting user ability to load data

　　　(d) When end user uploads data, require appropriate validation, authorization, and reporting control

　　　(e) Independent review of transactions

　　　(f) Record access to company databases by EUC applications.

　　(5) Control use of incorrect versions of data files.

　　　(a) Use control totals for batch processing of uploaded data.

　　(6) Require backup of files.

　　(7) Provide applications controls (e.g., edit checks, range tests, reasonableness checks).

　　(8) Support programmed or user reconciliations to provide assurance that processing is correct.

> **NOTE:** Since end-user computing relies upon microcomputers, the controls here required for microcomputers and EUC are similar. Also, tests of controls may address whether controls related to the above are effective.

5. **Electronic Commerce**

   a. **General:** Electronic commerce involves individuals and organizations engaging in a variety of electronic transactions with computers and telecommunication networks. The networks involved may be publicly available (e.g., the Internet) or private to the individuals and organizations involved (e.g., through telephone lines privately leased by the parties involved). Wide acceptance of the Internet (more specifically, that portion of the Internet referred to as the World Wide Web, or the web) is currently leading to a great expansion in electronic commerce.

   b. Five areas of risk associated with electronic commerce IT systems (as well as to varying degrees with other IT systems) are (1) security, (2) availability, (3) processing integrity, (4) online privacy, and (5) confidentiality. See section E.1 of this module for a discussion.

   c. Use of the web is growing rapidly as both the number and types of electronic transactions increase. However, many believe that risks such as those listed above are currently impairing its growth.

      (1) As discussed further in the Reporting Module, the AICPA and the Canadian Institute of Chartered Accountants have developed a form of assurance referred to as the "WebTrust Seal of Assurance" that tells potential customers that the firm has evaluated a website's business practices and controls to determine whether they are in conformity with WebTrust principles.

      (2) Digital certificates, also referred to as digital IDs, are a means of assuring data integrity.

         (a) A digital certificate (signature) allows an individual to digitally sign a message so the recipient knows that it actually came from that individual and was not modified in any manner.
         (b) Ordinarily the message is encrypted and the recipient decrypts it and is able to read the contents.

      (3) **Encryption**—The conversion of data into a form called a cipher text, that cannot be easily understood by unauthorized people. **Decryption** is the process of converting encrypted data back into its original form so it can be understood. The conversion is performed using an algorithm and key which only the users control.

         (a) **Algorithm**—A detailed sequence of actions to perform to accomplish some task (in this case to encrypt and/or decode data).
         (b) **Key**—In the content of encryption, a value that must be fed into the algorithm used to decode an encrypted message in order to reproduce the original plain text.
         (c) **Private key system**—An encryption system in which both the sender and receiver have access to the electronic key, but do not allow others access. The primary disadvantage is that both parties must have the key.
         (d) Encryption is important in a variety of contexts, including any time two or more computers are used to communicate with one another, and even to keep private information on one computer.
         (e) The machine instructions necessary to encrypt and decrypt data constitute **system overhead;** that is, they slow down the rate of processing.

      (4) To assure continuity in the event of a natural disaster, firms should establish off-site mirrored Web servers.

   d. **Electronic funds transfer (EFT)**—Making cash payments between two or more organizations or individuals electronically rather than by using checks (or cash).

      (1) Banks first became heavily involved with EFT; it is now a major part of most types of electronic commerce.

      (2) EFT systems are vulnerable to the risk of unauthorized access to proprietary data and to the risk of fraudulent fund transfers; controls include

         (a) Control of physical access to network facilities.
         (b) Electronic identification should be required for all network terminals authorized to use EFT.
         (c) Access should be controlled through passwords.
         (d) Encryption should be used to secure stored data and data being transmitted. See section C.5.c.(3) for more information on encryption.

e. **Electronic data interchange (EDI)**—The electronic exchange of business transactions, in a standard format, from one entity's computer to another entity's computer through an electronic communications network.

(1) Traditionally, the definition of electronic commerce has focused on EDI. Currently, web-based commerce is replacing a portion of these EDI systems.

(2) Risks related to EDI

    (a) EDI is commonly used for sales and purchasing, and related accounts. The speed at which transactions occur often reduces amounts receivable (payables) due to electronic processing of receipts (payments). Another effect is to make preventive controls particularly desirable, since detective controls may be too late.

    (b) In these systems, documents such as purchase orders, invoices, shipping forms, bills of lading, and checks are replaced by electronic transactions.

        1] For example, in electronic funds transfer systems, a form of EDI, electronic transactions replace checks as a means of payment. As discussed below, EDI is often conducted on private networks.

        2] To determine that transactions are properly processed, effective audit trails for both internal auditors and external auditors include activity logs, including processed and failed transactions, network and sender/recipient acknowledgment of receipt of transactions, and proper time sequence of processing.

        3] In some EDI applications, portions of the documentation of transactions are retained for only short period of time; this may require auditors to pay particular attention to controls over the transactions and to test controls on a timely basis when records remain available.

(3) Methods of communication between trading partners

    (a) **Point-to-point**—A direct computer-to-computer private network link

        1] Automakers and governments have traditionally used this method.

        2] Advantages

            a] No reliance on third parties for computer processing.

           b] Organization controls who has access to the network.

           c] Organization can enforce proprietary (its own) software standard in dealings with all trading partners.

           d] Timeliness of delivery may be improved since no third party is involved.

        3] Disadvantages

           a] Must establish connection with each trading partner

           b] High initial cost

           c] Computer scheduling issues

           d] Need for common protocols between partners

           e] Need for hardware and software compatibility

    (b) **Value-added network (VAN)**

        1] A VAN is a privately owned network that routes the EDI transactions between trading partners and in many cases provides translation, storage, and other processing. It is designed and maintained by an independent company that offers specialized support to improve the transmission effectiveness of a network. It alleviates problems related to interorganizational communication that results from the use of differing hardware and software.

        2] A VAN receives data from sender, determines intended recipient, and places data in the recipient's electronic mailbox.

        3] Advantages

           a] Reduces communication and data protocol problems since VANs can deal with differing protocols (eliminating need for trading partners to agree on them).

           b] Partners do not have to establish the numerous point-to-point connections.

           c] Reduces scheduling problems since receiver can request delivery of transactions when it wishes.

           d] In some cases, VAN translates application to a standard format the partner does not have to reformat.

           e] VAN can provide increased security.

   4] Disadvantages

    a] Cost of VAN
    b] Dependence upon VAN's systems and controls
    c] Possible loss of data confidentiality

  (c) **Public networks**—For example, the Internet-based commerce solutions described earlier

   1] Advantages

    a] Avoids cost of proprietary lines
    b] Avoids cost of VAN
    c] Directly communicates transactions to trading partners
    d] Software is being developed which allows communication between differing systems.

   2] Disadvantages

    a] Possible loss of data confidentiality on the Internet
    b] Computer or transmission disruption
    c] Hackers and viruses
    d] Attempted electronic frauds

  (d) **Proprietary networks**—In some circumstances (e.g., health care, banking) organizations have developed their own network for their own transactions. These systems are costly to develop and operate (because of proprietary lines), although they are often extremely reliable.

 (4) Controls required for other network systems are required for EDI systems. In addition, disappearance of "paper transactions" and the direct interrelationship with another organization's computer makes various authentication and encryption controls particularly important for these transactions.

  (a) **Authentication**—Controls must exist over the origin, proper submission, and proper delivery of EDI communications. Receiver of the message must have proof of the origin of the message, as well as its proper submission and delivery.
  (b) **Packets**—A block of data that is transmitted from one computer to another. It contains data and authentication information.
  (c) **Encryption**—The conversion of plain text data into cipher text data used by an algorithm and key which only the users control. See section C.5.c.(3) for more information on encryption.

 (5) The AICPA Auditing Procedures Study, *Audit Implications of EDI,* lists the following benefits and exposures of EDI:

  (a) Benefits

   1] Quick response and access to information
   2] Cost efficiency
   3] Reduced paperwork
   4] Accuracy and reduced errors and error-correction costs
   5] Better communications and customer service
   6] Necessary to remain competitive

  (b) Exposures

   1] Total dependence upon computer system for operation
   2] Possible loss of confidentiality of sensitive information
   3] Increased opportunity for unauthorized transactions and fraud
   4] Concentration of control among a few people involved in EDI
   5] Reliance on third parties (trading partners, VAN)
   6] Data processing, application and communications errors
   7] Potential legal liability due to errors
   8] Potential loss of audit trails and information needed by management due to limited retention policies
   9] Reliance on trading partner's system

6. **Telecommunications**—The electronic transmission of information by radio, wire, fiber optic, coaxial cable, microwave, laser, or other electromagnetic system.

a. Transmitted information—Voice, data, video, fax, other
b. Hardware involved:

(1) Computers for communications control and switching
(2) Transmission facilities such as copper wire, fiber optic cables, microwave stations and communications satellites
(3) Modems may be used to provide compatibility of format, speed, etc.

c. Software controls and monitors the hardware, formats information, adds appropriate control information, performs switching operations, provides security, and supports the management of communications.
d. While telecommunications is **not** an end of itself, it enables technologies such as the following:

(1) Electronic data interchange
(2) Electronic funds transfer
(3) Point of sale systems
(4) Commercial databases
(5) Airline reservation systems

e. Controls needed

(1) System integrity at remote sites
(2) Data entry
(3) Central computer security
(4) Dial-in security
(5) Transmission accuracy and completeness
(6) Physical security over telecommunications facilities

> **NOTE:** Tests of controls may address whether controls related to the above are effective.

7. **Computer Service Organizations (Bureaus, Centers)**—Computer service organizations record and process data for companies. These organizations allow companies (users) to do away with part of the data processing function. While many computer service organizations simply record and process relatively routine transactions for a client (e.g., prepare payroll journals and payroll checks), a VAN is a service organization that takes a broader role of providing network, storing, and forwarding (mailbox) services for the companies involved in an EDI system.

D. Control Objectives for Information and Related Technology (COBIT)

1. The Information Systems Audit and Control Association (ISACA) has developed a framework to assist enterprises in achieving their objectives for governance and management of enterprise IT. The current version of the framework (COBIT 5) is business-oriented in that it provides a systematic way of integrating IT with business strategy and governance. COBIT 5 takes a stakeholder approach to addressing information needs and incorporates the following 5 principles:

a. Meeting stakeholder needs.
b. Covering the enterprise end-to-end.
c. Applying a single integrated framework.
d. Enabling a holistic approach.
e. Separating governance from management.

The factors that individually and collectively influence whether something will work in an organization are referred to as the COBIT 5 enablers. They include:

a. Processes—an organized set of practices and activities to achieve certain objectives.
b. Organizational structures—the key decision-making entities in an organization.
c. Culture, ethics, and behavior of individuals and the organization.
d. Principles, policies and frameworks—the vehicle to translate the desired behavior into guidance for day-to-day management.
e. Information produced and used by the enterprise.
f. Services, infrastructure and applications—the infrastructure, technology, and applications that provide the enterprise with information technology processing and servicers.
g. People, skills, and competencies required for successful completion of all activities and for making correct decisions.

E. Effect of IT on Internal Control

NOTE: We have already discussed the effect of a computer on internal control of several systems under C. (microcomputers, end-user computing, and electronic commerce). In this section we discuss the effect in general terms as presented in the AICPA Audit Guide, **Consideration of Internal Control in a Financial Statement Audit**. This section presents information on controls a company may have. We begin by discussing overall principles of a reliable system and overall risks. We then consider the effect of a computer on internal control using the five components of internal control—control environment, risk assessment, information and communication, monitoring, and control activities.

1. Principles of a Reliable System and Examples of Overall Risks

    a. A reliable system is one that is capable of operating without material error, fault, or failure during a specified period in a specified environment.

    b. One framework for analyzing a reliable system is presented by the AICPA's Trust Services. Trust Services, which provide assurance on information systems, use a framework with five principles of a reliable system—(1) security, (2) availability, (3) processing integrity, (4) online privacy, and (5) confidentiality. Accordingly, when a principle is not met a risk exists.

Principle	Examples of Risks
1. **Security.** The system is protected against unauthorized access (both physical and logical)	Physical access—A lack of physical security allows damage or other loss (e.g., theft) to the system •Weather •Acts of war •Disgruntled employees or others Logical access—A lack of security over access to the system allows •Malicious (or accidental) alteration of, or damage to, files and/or the system •Computer based fraud •Unauthorized access to confidential data
2. **Availability.** The system is available for operation and use as committed or agreed. The system is available for operation and use in conformity with the entity's availability policies.	System failure results in •Interruption of business operations •Loss of data
3. **Processing Integrity.** System processing is complete, accurate, timely, and authorized.	Invalid, incomplete, or inaccurate •Input data •Data processing •Updating of master files •Creation of output
4. **Online Privacy.** Personal information obtained as a result of e-commerce is collected, used, disclosed, and retained as committed or agreed.	Disclosure of customer information (or that of others) such as •Social security numbers •Credit card numbers •Credit rating •Medical conditions
5. **Confidentiality.** Information designated as confidential is protected as committed or agreed.	Examples of confidential data that might be disclosed •Transaction details •Engineering details of products •Business plans •Banking information •Legal documents •Inventory or other account information •Customer lists •Confidential details of operations

NOTE: Make certain that you are familiar not only with the above principles, but are familiar with the nature of the various risks relating to computer processing.

2. **Control Environment**

   a. Recall the seven factors of the control environment:

   I—Integrity and ethical values
   C—Commitment to competence
   H—Human resource policies and practices
   A—Assignment of authority and responsibility
   M—Management's philosophy and operating style
   B—Board of directors or audit committee participation
   O—Organizational structure

   b. Although all seven factors may be affected by computer processing, the organizational structure is modified to include an information systems department (EDP department). It is helpful to keep in mind that the information systems department is involved with two distinct functions—systems development and data processing.

   c. Steps in the **system development lifecycle:**

   (1) Software concept—identify the need for the new system.
   (2) Requirements analysis—determine the needs of the users.
   (3) Architectural design—determining the hardware, software, people, etc. needed.
   (4) Coding and debugging—acquiring and testing the software.
   (5) System testing—testing and evaluating the functionality of the system.

   d. Organizational structure

   (1) **Segregation controls**

       (a) Segregate functions between information systems department and user departments.

           1] User departments are the other departments of the company that utilize the data prepared by the information systems department.

       (b) Do not allow the information systems department to initiate or authorize transactions.
       (c) At a minimum, segregate programming, data entry, operations, and the library function within the information systems department.
       (d) A more complete segregation of key functions within the information systems department may be possible; one way to separate key functions is as follows:

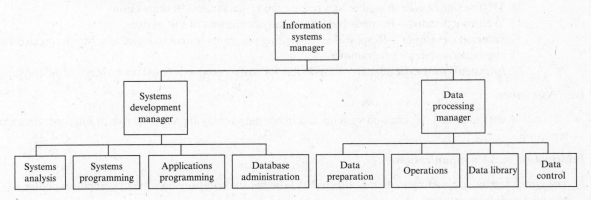

           1] **Systems analysis**—The systems analyst analyzes the present user environment and requirements and may (1) recommend specific changes, (2) recommend the purchase of a new system, or (3) design a new information system. The analyst is in constant contact with user departments and programming staff to ensure the users' actual and ongoing needs are being met. A system flowchart is a tool used by the analyst to define the systems requirements.
           2] **Systems programming**—The systems programmer is responsible for implementing, modifying, and debugging the software necessary for making the hardware work (such as the operating system, telecommunications monitor, and the database management system). For some companies the term "software engineer" is viewed as similar or identical to that of systems programmer. For others, the software engineer is involved with the creation of designs used by programmers.

3] **Applications programming**—The applications programmer is responsible for writing, testing, and debugging the application programs from the specifications (whether general or specific) provided by the systems analyst. A program flowchart is one tool used by the applications programmer to define the program logic.

4] **Database administration**—In a database environment, a database administrator (DBA) is responsible for maintaining the database and restricting access to the database to authorized personnel.

5] **Data preparation**—Data may be prepared by user departments and input by key to storage devices.

6] **Operations**—The operator is responsible for the daily computer operations of both the hardware and the software. The operator supervises operations on the operator's console, accepts any required input, and distributes any generated output. The operator should have adequate documentation available to run the program (a run manual), but should not have detailed program information.

   a] Help desks are usually a responsibility of operations because of the operational nature of their functions (for example, assisting users with systems problems and obtaining technical support/vendor assistance).

7] **Data library**—The librarian is responsible for custody of the removable media (i.e., magnetic tapes or disks) and for the maintenance of program and system documentation. In many systems, much of the library function is maintained and performed electronically by the computer.

8] **Data control**—The control group acts as liaison between users and the processing center. This group records input data in a control log, follows the progress of processing, distributes output, and ensures compliance with control totals.

Ideally, in a large system, all of the above key functions should be segregated; in a small computer environment, many of the key functions are concentrated in a small number of employees. For purposes of the CPA exam remember that, at a minimum, an attempt should be made to segregate **programming, operations,** and the **library** functions. Large organizations typically have a chief information officer (CIO) that oversees all information technology and activities.

(e) Electronic commerce has resulted in a number of new web-related positions, including

1] **Web administrator (web manager)**—Responsible for overseeing the development, planning, and the implementation of a website. Ordinarily a managerial position.

2] **Web master**—Responsible for providing expertise and leadership in the development of a website, including the design, analysis, security, maintenance, content development, and updates.

3] **Web designer**—Responsible for creating the visual content of the website.

4] **Web coordinator**—Responsible for the daily operations of the website.

5] **Internet developer**—Responsible for writing programs for commercial use. Similar to a software engineer or systems programmer.

6] **Intranet/Extranet developer**—Responsible for writing programs based on the needs of the company.

3. **Risk Assessment**

   a. Changes in computerized information systems and in operations may increase the risk of improper financial reporting.

4. **Information and Communication**

   a. The computerized accounting system is affected by whether the company uses small computers and/or a complex mainframe system.

   (1) For small computer systems, purchased commercial "off-the-shelf" software may be used.

       (a) Controls within the software may be well known.

       (b) Analysis of "exception reports" generated during processing is important to determine that exceptions are properly handled.

   (2) For complex mainframe systems a significant portion of the software is ordinarily developed within the company by information systems personnel.

       (a) Controls within the software are unknown to the auditor prior to testing.

       (b) As with small computer systems, analysis of exception reports is important, but controls over the generation of such reports must ordinarily be tested to a greater extent.

5. **Monitoring**

  a. Proper monitoring of a computerized system will require adequate computer skills to evaluate the propriety of processing of computerized applications.

  b. A common method of monitoring for inappropriate access is review of system-access log.

  c. IT can also facilitate monitoring.

    (1) IT can constantly evaluate data and transactions based on established criteria and highlight items that appear to be inconsistent or unusual.

    (2) IT can capture samples of items for audit by internal auditors.

6. **Control Activities—Overall**

  a. Control activities in which a computer is involved may be divided into the following categories:

    (1) Computer **general** control activities.

    (2) Computer **application** control activities.

Programmed application control activities.
Manual follow-up of computer exception reports.

    (3) **User** control activities to test the completeness and accuracy of computer processed controls.

The following illustration, adapted from the AICPA Audit Guide, *Consideration of Internal Control in a Financial Statement Audit*, summarizes the relationships among the controls.

COMPUTER CONTROL ACTIVITIES

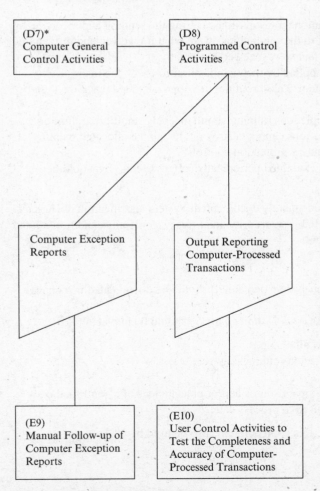

EXPLANATION OF COMPUTER CONTROL ACTIVITIES

Computer General Control Activities control program development, program changes, computer operations, and access to programs and data. These control activities increase the assurance that programmed control activities operate effectively during the period.

Computer Application Control Activities

  Programmed Control Activities relate to specific computer applications and are embedded in the computer program used in the financial reporting system. The concepts presented here related to programmed control activities may also apply to other activities within the computer accounting system.

  Manual Follow-Up of Computer Exception Reports involves employee follow-up of items listed on computer exception reports. The effectiveness of application control activities that involve manual follow-up of computer reports depends on the effectiveness of both the programmed control activities that produce the exception report and the manual follow-up activities.

User Control Activities to Test the Completeness and Accuracy of Computer Processed Transactions represent manual checks of computer output against source document or other input, and thus provide assurance that programmed aspects of the accounting system and control activities have operated effectively.

* Section below in which control discussion is presented.

7. **Computer General Control Activities**

> **NOTE:** General control activities affect all computer applications. There are four types of general controls—
> (a) developing new programs and systems, (b) changing existing programs and systems, (c) controlling access
> to programs and data, and (d) controlling computer operations.

a. **Developing new programs and systems**

(1) **Segregation controls**

(a) User departments participate in systems design.

(b) Both users and information systems personnel test new systems.

(c) Management, users, and information systems personnel approve new systems before they are placed into operation.

(d) All master and transaction file conversions should be controlled to prevent unauthorized changes and to verify the accuracy of the results.

(e) Programs and systems should be properly documented (see Section F. of outline).

(2) **Computer hardware is extremely reliable.** This is primarily due to the chip technology. However, it is also due to the controls built into the hardware and systems software to provide for a self-diagnostic mechanism to detect and prevent equipment failures. The following are examples of such controls:

(a) **Parity check**—A special bit is added to each character that can detect if the hardware loses a bit during the internal movement of a character.

(b) **Echo check**—Primarily used in telecommunications transmissions. During the sending and receiving of characters, the receiving hardware repeats back to the sending hardware what it received and the sending hardware automatically resends any characters that were received incorrectly.

(c) **Diagnostic routines**—Hardware or software supplied by the manufacturer to check the internal operations and devices within the computer system. These routines are often activated when the system is booted up.

(d) **Boundary protection**—Most CPUs have multiple jobs running simultaneously (multiprogramming environment). To ensure that these simultaneous jobs cannot destroy or change the allocated memory of another job, the systems software contains boundary protection controls.

(e) **Periodic maintenance**—The system should be examined periodically (often weekly) by a qualified service technician.

(3) **Documentation.** Systems and programs should be adequately documented. System specification documents should detail such matters as performance levels, reliability, security and privacy, constraints and limitations, functional capabilities, and data structure and elements.

b. **Changing existing programs and systems**

(1) Suggestions for changes (from users and information system personnel) should be documented in a change request log.

(2) Proper *change control* procedures (also referred to as *modification controls*) should be in place.

(a) The information systems manager should review all changes.

(b) The modified program should be appropriately tested (often using test data).

(c) Details of all changes should be documented.

(d) A *code comparison program* may be used to compare source and/or object codes of a controlled copy of a program with the program currently being used to process data.

1] This will identify any unauthorized changes (this approach may also be used by CPAs).

c. **Controlling access to programs and data**

(1) **Segregation controls**

(a) Access to program documentation should be limited to those persons who require it in the performance of their duties.
(b) Access to data files and programs should be limited to those individuals authorized to process data.
(c) Access to computer hardware should be limited to authorized individuals such as computer operators and their supervisors.

(2) **Physical access to computer facility**

(a) **Limited physical access**—The physical facility that houses the computer equipment, files, and documentation should have controls to limit access only to authorized individuals. Possible controls include using a guard, automated key cards, and manual key locks, as well as the new access devices that permit access through fingerprints or palm prints.

(b) **Visitor entry logs**—Used to document those who have had access to the area.

(3) **Hardware and software access controls**

(a) **Access control software** (user identification)—The most used control is a combination of a unique *identification code* and a confidential *password*.

1] Passwords should be made up of a combination of alphabetic, numeric, and symbol elements.
2] Passwords should be changed periodically.
3] Passwords should be disabled promptly when an employee leaves the company.

(b) **Call back**—Call back is a specialized form of user identification in which the user dials the system, identifies him/herself, and is disconnected from the system. Then either (1) an individual manually finds the authorized telephone number or (2) the system automatically finds the authorized telephone number of the individual and calls back.

(c) **Encryption**—Data is encoded when stored in computer files and/or before transmission to or from remote locations (e.g., through use of modems and telephone lines). This coding protects data, since to use the data unauthorized users must not only obtain access, but must also translate the coded form of the data. Encryption performed by physically secure hardware (often special-purpose computers) is ordinarily more secure, but more costly than that performed by software. See section C.5.c.(3) for more information on encryption.

d. **Controlling computer operations**

(1) **Segregation controls**

(a) Operators should have access to an **operations manual** that contains the instructions for processing programs and solving routine operational program issues, but not with detailed program documentation.
(b) The control group should monitor the operator's activities and jobs should be scheduled.

(2) **Other controls**

(a) **Backup and recovery**—Discussed in Section D.11. in this module
(b) **Contingency processing**—Detailed contingency processing plans should be developed to prepare for system failures. The plans should detail the responsibilities of individuals, as well as the alternate processing sites that should be utilized. Backup facilities with a vendor may be used to provide contingent sites in case of an emergency. This topic is discussed further in Section D.11. of this module.
(c) **Internal and external labels**—External labels are gummed-paper labels attached to storage media which identify the file. Internal labels perform the same function through the use of machine readable identification in the first record of a file. The use of labels allows the computer operator to determine whether the correct file has been selected for processing.

8. **Computer Application Control Activities—Programmed Control Activities**

> **NOTE:** Programmed application controls apply to a specific application rather than multiple applications. These controls operate to assure the proper input and processing of data. The input step converts human-readable data into computer-readable data. Ensuring the integrity of the data in the computer is critical during processing. The candidate should be prepared to identify the following common controls in a multiple-choice question.

a. **Input controls**

(1) **Overall controls**

   (a) Inputs should be properly authorized and approved.
   (b) The system should verify all significant data fields used to record information (editing the data).
   (c) Conversion of data into machine-readable form should be controlled and verified for accuracy.

(2) **Input validation (edit) controls**

   (a) **Preprinted form**—Information is preassigned a place and a format on the input form.
   (b) **Check digit**—An extra digit added to an identification number to detect certain types of data transmission errors. For example, a bank may add a check digit to individuals' 7-digit account numbers. The computer will calculate the correct check digit based on performing predetermined mathematical operations on the 7-digit account number and will then compare it to the check digit.
   (c) **Control, batch, or proof total**—A total of one numerical field for all the records of a batch that normally would be added, (e.g., total sales dollars).
   (d) **Hash total**—A control total where the total is meaningless for financial purposes (e.g., a mathematical sum of employee social security numbers).
   (e) **Record count**—A control total of the total records processed.
   (f) **Limit (reasonableness) test**—A test of the reasonableness of a field of data, given a predetermined upper and/or lower limit (e.g., for a field that indicates auditing exam scores, a limit check would test for scores over 100).
   (g) **Menu driven input**—As input is entered, the operator responds to a menu prompting the proper response (e.g., What score did you get on the Auditing part of the CPA Exam [75-100]?).
   (h) **Field check**—A control that limits the types of characters accepted into a specific data field (e.g., a pay rate should include only numerical data).
   (i) **Validity check**—A control that allows only "valid" transactions or data to be entered into the system (e.g., a field indicating sex of an individual where 1 = female and 2 = male—if the field is coded in any other manner it would not be accepted).
   (j) **Missing data check**—A control that searches for blanks inappropriately existing in input data (e.g., if an employee's division number were left blank an error message would result).
   (k) **Field size check**—A control of an exact number of characters to be input (e.g., if part numbers all have 6 digits, an error message would result if more or less than 6 characters were input).
   (l) **Logic check**—Ensures that illogical combinations of input are not accepted (e.g., if the Tuba City branch has no company officers, an error message would result if two fields for a specified employee indicated that the employee worked as an officer in Tuba City).
   (m) **Redundant data check**—Uses two identifiers in each transaction record (e.g., customer account number and the first five letters of customer's name) to confirm that the correct master file record is being updated.
   (n) **Closed-loop verification**—A control that allows data entry personnel to check the accuracy of input data. For example, the system might retrieve an account name of a record that is being updated, and display it on the operator's terminal. This control may be used instead of a redundant data check.

(3) **Processing controls**

Overall: When the input has been accepted by the computer, it usually is processed through multiple steps. Processing controls are essential to ensure the integrity of data. Essentially all of the controls listed for input may also be incorporated during processing. For example, processed information should include limit tests, record counts, and control totals. In addition, external labels should be used on removable media, with internal header and trailer labels used to determine that all information on a file has been read.

> **NOTE:** Previously, the professional standards divided application controls into three categories—input, processing, and output. The current categories of application controls (programmed and manual) and user controls have replaced that breakdown. As an aid to discussing controls we distinguish between input and processing above. User control activities include the essentials of the previous "output" controls.

9. **Application Controls—Manual Follow-Up of Computer Exception Reports**

    a. These controls involve employee (operator and/or control group) follow-up of items listed on computer exception reports. Their effectiveness depends on the effectiveness of both the programmed control activities that produce the reports and the manual follow-up activities.

10. **User Control Activities to Test the Completeness and Accuracy of Computer-Processed Controls**

    a. These manual controls, previously referred to as *output controls,* include

       (1) Checks of computer output against source documents, control totals, or other input to provide assurance that programmed aspects of the financial reporting system and control activities have operated effectively.
       (2) Reviewing computer processing logs to determine that all of the correct computer jobs executed properly.
       (3) Maintaining proper procedures and communications specifying authorized recipients of output.

    b. These procedures are often performed by both the control group and users.
    c. In some systems, user departments evaluate the reliability of output from the computer by extensive review and testing; in others, users merely test the overall reasonableness of the output.

11. **Disaster Recovery and Business Continuity**

    a. A plan should allow the firm to

       (1) Minimize the extent of disruption, damage, and loss.
       (2) Establish an alternate (temporary) method for processing information.
       (3) Resume normal operations as quickly as possible.
       (4) Train and familiarize personnel to perform emergency operations.

    b. A plan should include priorities, insurance, backup approaches, specific assignments, period testing and updating, and documentation, as described below.

       (1) **Priorities**—Which applications are most critical?
       (2) **Insurance to defer costs**
       (3) **Backup approaches**

          (a) Batch systems—The most common approach is the **Grandfather-Father-Son** method. A master file (e.g., accounts receivable) is updated with the day's transaction files (e.g., files of cash receipts and credit sales). After the update, the new file master file is the son. The file from which the father was developed with the transaction files of the appropriate day is the grandfather. The grandfather and son files are stored in different locations. If the son were destroyed, for example, it could be reconstructed by rerunning the father file and the related transaction files.
          (b) Online databases and master files systems

             1] **Checkpoint**—Similar to grandfather-father-son, but at certain points, "checkpoints," the system makes a copy of the database and this "checkpoint" file is stored on a separate disk or tape. If a problem occurs the system is restarted at the last checkpoint and updated with subsequent transactions.

    2] **Rollback**—As a part of recovery, to undo changes made to a database to a point at which it was functioning properly

    3] **Backup facilities**

        a] **Reciprocal agreement**—An agreement between two or more organizations (with compatible computer facilities) to aid each other with their data processing needs in the event of a disaster. This is sometimes referred to as a mutual aid pact.

        b] **Hot site**—A commercial disaster recovery service that allows a business to continue computer operations in the event of computer disaster. For example, if a company's data processing center becomes inoperable, that enterprise can move all processing to a hot site that has all the equipment needed to continue operation. This is also referred to as a recovery operations center (ROC) approach.

        c] **Cold site**—Similar to a hot site, but the customer provides and installs the equipment needed to continue operations. A cold site is less expensive, but takes longer to get in full operation after a disaster. This is sometimes referred to as an "empty shell" in that the "shell" is available and ready to receive whatever hardware the temporary user needs.

        d] **Internal site**—Large organizations with multiple data processing centers sometimes rely upon their own sites for backup in the event of a disaster.

> **NOTE:** Be aware that most approaches to control for catastrophic failures rely upon backup of the entire system in one form or another. Also, various combinations of the above approaches may be used.

        e] **Mirrored web server**—An exact copy of a website which is the best way to back up the website.

(4) **Specific assignments, including having individuals involved with**

    (a) Arranging for new facilities.
    (b) Computer operations.
    (c) Installing software.
    (d) Establishing data communications facilities.
    (e) Recovering vital records.
    (f) Arranging for forms and supplies.

(5) **Periodic testing and updating of plan**
(6) **Documentation of plan**

F. Flowcharting

General: Flowcharts analytically describe some aspect of an information system. Flowcharting is a procedure to graphically show the sequential flow of data and/or operations. The data and operations portrayed include document preparation, authorization, storage, and decision making. The more common flowcharting symbols are illustrated below. Knowledge of them would help with occasional multiple-choice questions and with problems that present a detailed flowchart that must be analyzed.

1. Common Flowcharting Symbols

	Document	This can be a manual form or a computer printout
	Computer Operation	Computer process which transforms input data into useful information
	Manual Operation	Manual (human) process to prepare documents, make entries, check output, etc.
	Decision	Determines which alternative path is followed (IF/THEN/ELSE Conditions)
	Input/Output	General input or output to a process. Often used to represent accounting journals and ledgers on document flowcharts
	Online Storage	Refers to direct access computer storage connected directly to the CPU. Data is available on a random access basis
	Disc Storage	Refers to data stored on a magnetic disk
	Off-Line Storage	Refers to a file or indicates the mailing of a document (i.e., invoices or statements to customers). A letter in the symbol below the line indicates the order in which the file is stored. (N-Numerical, C-Chronological, A-Alphabetical)
	Display	Visual display of data and/or output on a terminal screen
	Batch Total Tape	Manually computed total before processing (such as the number of records to be processed). This total is recomputed by the computer and compared after processing is completed.
	Magnetic Tape	Used for reading, writing, or storage on sequential storage media
	Manual Data Entry	Refers to data entered through a terminal keyboard or key-to-tape or key-to-disk device
	Annotation	Provides additional description or information connected to symbol to which it annotates by a dotted line (not a flowline)
	Flowline	Shows direction of data flow, operations, and documents
	Communication Link	Telecommunication line linking computer system to remote locations
	Start/Termination	Used to begin or end a flowchart. (Not always used or shown in flowcharts on the CPA exam.) May be used to show connections to other procedures or receipt/ sending of documents to/from outsiders
	On Page Connector	Connects parts of flowchart on the same page
	Off Page Connector	Connects parts of flowchart on separate pages

2. **Types and Definitions**

   a. **System flowchart**—A graphic representation of a data processing application that depicts the interaction of all the computer programs for a given system, rather than the logic for an individual computer program.
   b. **Program flowchart**—A graphic representation of the logic (processing steps) of a computer program.
   c. **Internal control (audit) flowchart** or **document flowchart**—A graphic representation of the flow of documents from one department to another, showing the source flow and final disposition of the various copies of all documents. Most flowcharts on the CPA exam have been of this type.

3. **Other Documentation Charting Techniques**

   a. **Decision table**—Decision tables use a matrix format that lists sets of conditions, and the actions that result from various combinations of these conditions. See Module 3 on internal control for an example of a decision table.
   b. **Data flow diagram (DFD)**—Presents logical flows of data and functions in a system. For example, a data flow diagram for the delivery of goods to a customer would include a symbol for the warehouse from which the goods are shipped and a symbol representing the customer. It would not emphasize details such as computer processing and paper outputs.

KEY TERMS

Because the content of this module is largely terminology, a set of key terms is not provided.

APPENDICES

The following appendices provide you with additional practice for the exam.

Appendix A: Auditing and Attestation Sample Examination

Testlet 1

1. Which of the following is ordinarily considered to be a fraud risk factor?

   a. The company's financial statements include a number of last minute material adjustments.

   b. Management regularly informs investors of forecast information.

   c. The company has experienced increasing earnings over the previous five years.

   d. The company's president is included as a member of the board of directors.

2. Which of the following statements **best** describes the primary purpose of Statements on Auditing Standards?

   a. They are guides intended to set forth auditing procedures that are applicable to a variety of situations.

   b. They are procedural outlines that are intended to narrow the areas of inconsistency and divergence of auditor opinion.

   c. They are authoritative statements, enforced through the *Code of Professional Conduct*.

   d. They are interpretive guidance.

3. Independence is required for which of the following types of engagements?

	Agreed-upon procedures	Review
a.	Yes	Yes
b.	Yes	No
c.	No	Yes
d.	No	No

4. Which of the following should an auditor obtain from the predecessor auditor prior to accepting an audit engagement?

   a. Analysis of balance sheet accounts.

   b. Analysis of income statement accounts.

   c. All matters of continuing accounting significance.

   d. Facts that might bear on the integrity of management.

5. Which of the following is correct concerning allowing additions and deletions to audit documentation after the documentation completion date under requirements of the Public Company Accounting Oversight Board?

	Additions	Deletions
a.	Allowed	Allowed
b.	Allowed	Not allowed
c.	Not allowed	Allowed
d.	Not allowed	Not allowed

6. One reason that an auditor only obtains reasonable, and not absolute, assurance that financial statements are free from material misstatement is

   a. Comprehensive basis reporting.

   b. Employee collusion.

   c. Material misstatements.

   d. Professional skepticism.

7. The auditors of a nonissuer (nonpublic) company must perform a test of the operating effectiveness of a significant control

   a. In all audits.

   b. When the control relates to a significant asset.

   c. When substantive procedures alone will not provide sufficient evidence about the related assertion.

   d. When the auditors believe that the control may not be effective.

8. The independent auditor selects several transactions in each functional area and traces them through the entire system, paying special attention to evidence about whether or not the controls are in operation. This is an example of a(n)

   a. Application test.

   b. Test of a controls.

   c. Substantive test.

   d. Test of a function.

9. In obtaining an understanding of a manufacturing entity's internal control over inventory balances, an auditor most likely would

   a. Review the entity's descriptions of inventory policies and procedures.

   b. Perform test counts of inventory during the entity's physical count.

   c. Analyze inventory turnover statistics to identify slow-moving and obsolete items.

   d. Analyze monthly production reports to identify variances and unusual transactions.

10. Further audit procedures consist of which of the following?

	Risk assessment procedures	Substantive procedures	Test of controls
a.	Yes	No	No
b.	Yes	Yes	No
c.	No	Yes	No
d.	No	Yes	Yes

11. Which of the following statements best describes the ethical standard of the profession pertaining to advertising and solicitation?

   a. All forms of advertising and solicitation are prohibited.

   b. There are **no** prohibitions regarding the manner in which CPAs may solicit new business.

   c. A CPA may advertise in any manner that is **not** false, misleading, or deceptive.

   d. A CPA may only solicit new clients through mass mailings.

12. Which is **least** likely to be a question asked of client personnel during a walk-through in an audit of the internal control of an issuer (public) company?

    a. What do you do when you find an error?

    b. Who is most likely to commit fraud among your coworkers?

    c. What kind of errors have you found?

    d. Have you ever been asked to override the process or controls?

13. Which of the following matters is an auditor required to communicate to an entity's audit committee?

	Significant audit adjustments	Changes in significant accounting policies
a.	Yes	Yes
b.	Yes	No
c.	No	Yes
d.	No	No

14. An abnormal fluctuation in gross profit that might suggest the need for extended audit procedures for sales and inventories would most likely be identified in the planning phase of the audit by the use of

    a. Tests of transactions and balances.

    b. A preliminary review of internal control.

    c. Specialized audit programs.

    d. Analytical procedures.

15. When auditing merchandise inventory at year-end, the auditor performs a purchase cutoff test to obtain evidence that

    a. All goods purchased before year-end are received before the physical inventory count.

    b. No goods held on consignment for customers are included in the inventory balance.

    c. No goods observed during the physical count are pledged or sold.

    d. All goods owned at year-end are included in the inventory balance.

16. An auditor who uses the work of a specialist may refer to and identify the specialist in the auditor's report if the

    a. Specialist is also considered to be a related party.

    b. Auditor indicates a division of responsibility related to the work of the specialist.

    c. Specialist's work provides the auditor greater assurance of reliability.

    d. Auditor expresses an "except for" qualified opinion or an adverse opinion related to the work of the specialist.

17. Which of the following statements concerning audit evidence is correct?

    a. Appropriate evidence supporting management's assertions should be convincing rather than merely persuasive.

    b. Effective internal control contributes little to the reliability of the evidence created within the entity.

    c. The cost of obtaining evidence is **not** an important consideration to an auditor in deciding what evidence should be obtained.

    d. A client's accounting data **cannot** be considered sufficient audit evidence to support the financial statements.

18. Burrow & Co., CPAs, have provided annual audit and tax compliance services to Mare Corp. for several years. Mare has been unable to pay Burrow in full for services Burrow rendered nineteen months ago. Burrow is ready to begin fieldwork for the current year's audit. Under the ethical standards of the profession, which of the following arrangements will permit Burrow to begin the fieldwork on Mare's audit?

    a. Mare sets up a two-year payment plan with Burrow to settle the unpaid fee balance.

    b. Mare commits to pay the past due fee in full before the audit report is issued.

    c. Mare gives Burrow an eighteen-month note payable for the full amount of the past due fees before Burrow begins the audit.

    d. Mare engages another firm to perform the fieldwork, and Burrow is limited to reviewing the workpapers and issuing the audit report.

19. A note to the financial statements of the First Security Bank indicates that all of the records relating to the bank's business operations are stored on magnetic disks, and that there are no emergency back-up systems or duplicate disks stored since the First Security Bank and their auditors consider the occurrence of a catastrophe to be remote. Based upon this, one would expect the auditor's report to express

    a. An adverse opinion.

    b. An "except for" opinion.

    c. An unmodified (unqualified) opinion.

    d. A qualified opinion.

20. A company has changed its method of inventory valuation from an unacceptable one to one in conformity with generally accepted accounting principles. The auditor's report on the financial statements of the year of the change should include

    a. No reference to consistency.

    b. A reference to a prior period adjustment in the opinion paragraph.

    c. An emphasis-of-matter paragraph explaining the change.

    d. A justification for making the change and the impact of the change on reported net income.

21. When an auditor reissues in 20X7 the auditor's report on the 20X5 financial statements at the request of the client without revising the 20X5 wording, the auditor should

    a. Use the date of the original report.

    b. Use the date of the client's request.

    c. Use the date of the current period report.

    d. Dual date the report.

22. Which of the following is not a covered member for purposes of application of the independence requirements of the AICPA Code of Professional Conduct?

    a. A staff person on the attest team.

    b. A staff person that performs tax services for the attest client.

    c. The partner in charge of the firm office that performs the attest engagement.

    d. A partner that performs extensive consulting services for the attest client.

23. Accounting control procedures within computer processing may leave no visible evidence indicating that the procedures were performed. In such instances, the auditor should test these controls by

a. Making corroborative inquiries.
b. Observing the separation of duties of personnel.
c. Reviewing transactions submitted for processing and comparing them to related output.
d. Reviewing the run manual.

24. Which is **least** likely to be a response when an auditor has obtained evidence indicating a risk of material misstatement in the area of inventory?

a. Discuss questions of inventory valuation with any other auditors involved with the audit.
b. Make oral inquiries of major suppliers in addition to written confirmations.
c. Perform inventory observations on an unannounced basis.
d. Request inventory counts at the end of each month.

25. Confirmations of accounts receivable address which assertion most directly?

a. Completeness.
b. Existence.
c. Valuation.
d. Classification.

26. Which of the following is always present in an attestation engagement?

a. Assertion about the subject matter.
b. Generally accepted assurance principles.
c. Subject matter.
d. An examination report.

27. Which of the following is not typically performed when accountants are performing a review of the financial statements of a nonissuer?

a. Analytical procedures applied to financial data.
b. Inquiries about significant subsequent events.
c. Inquiries of the client's attorney about legal matters.
d. Obtaining an understanding of the accounting principles followed by the client's industry.

28. If information is for management's use only, which of the following forms of CPA association with financial information is most likely to result in no report being issued?

a. An agreed-upon procedures engagement.
b. An audit.
c. A compilation.
d. A review.

29. A CPA who is not independent may perform which of the following services for a nonissuer company?

	Compilation	Review
a.	Yes	Yes
b.	Yes	No
c.	No	Yes
d.	No	No

30. When performing a review of an issuer company, which is least likely to be included in the CPA's inquires of management members with responsibility for financial and accounting matters?

a. Subsequent events.
b. Significant journal entries and other adjustments.
c. Communications with related parties.
d. Unusual or complex situations affecting the financial statements

Hints for Testlet 1

1. Which factor deals most directly with expected intentional misstatements?

2. The SAS provide authoritative guidance.

3. Independence is required for performing attest engagements.

4. The auditor wants to minimize the likelihood of association with a client whose management lacks integrity.

5. Remember that audits may sometimes be affected by subsequent discovery of facts existing at the date of the audit report.

6. What real world difficulty makes detecting misstatements difficult?

7. For most assertions tests of controls are not required.

8. The auditor is trying to determine the effectiveness of internal control.

9. The auditor is not evaluating the effectiveness of internal control.

10. Which set of procedures is used to design the others?

11. Advertising must be appropriate.

12. Which question seems too aggressive?

13. The audit committee that has responsibility for the oversight of the client's financial reporting process, should be kept informed about the scope and results of the audit.

14. Which substantive test relies on the premise that plausible relationships among data may reasonably be expected to exist and continue in the absence of known conditions to the contrary?

15. The purchase cutoff test verifies that the purchasing transactions are recorded in the proper period.

16. The auditor refers to the specialist if the auditor issues a qualified, adverse, or disclaimer as a result of the specialist's work.

17. In addition to the accounting data, the auditor must obtain corroborating audit evidence.

18. Prior year past due fees impair independence.

19. The financial statements are presented fairly in conformity with GAAP.

20. The audit report should disclose the lack of consistency.

21. Nothing has changed with regard to the 20X5 report.

22. Only managers or partners performing nonattest services for an attest client may become covered members.

23. The auditor wants to see the effects of the controls on the transactions.

24. Think of procedures that are likely to provide additional evidence relating to the financial statements being reported upon.

25. Does a confirmation assure that the account will be collected?

26. A report may ordinarily be on two of these—but one of them is always present.

27. Confirmation with outside parties is not required.

28. Which situation is most likely to result in a report that only management will use?

29. Compilations do not provide assurance.

30. Inquiries are general in nature.

Answers to Testlet 1

1.	a	6.	b	11.	c	16.	d	21.	a	26.	c
2.	c	7.	c	12.	b	17.	d	22.	b	27.	c
3.	c	8.	b	13.	a	18.	b	23.	c	28.	c
4.	d	9.	a	14.	d	19.	c	24.	d	29.	b
5.	b	10.	d	15.	d	20.	c	25.	b	30.	c

Explanations to Testlet 1

1. (a) Last minute material adjustments is a situation that has been found to be associated with fraudulent financial reporting.

2. (c) The Statements on Auditing Standards are authoritative statements that are enforced through the AICPA Code of Professional Conduct.

3. (c) Independence is required for audits, reviews and agreed-upon procedure engagements.

4. (d) Prior to accepting the engagement, the successor auditor should obtain information to assist in deciding whether to accept the engagement, including facts that might bear on the integrity of management. All of the other items might be obtained but need not be obtained prior to acceptance.

5. (b) Under PCAOB standards, after the documentation completion date additions are allowed but deletions are not allowed.

6. (b) Employee collusion is a limitation of internal control. It may render internal control ineffective.

7. (c) Internal control must be tested when substantive procedures alone will not provide sufficient evidence.

8. (b) This describes a test of control using audit sampling.

9. (a) To obtain an understanding of internal control, the auditor would review the company's documentation of policies and procedures. Items (b), (c), and (d) are substantive tests of balances or transactions.

10. (d) After assessing risk by performing risk assessment procedures, the auditor designs further audit procedures, which include tests of controls and substantive procedures.

11. (c) The AICPA Code of Professional Conduct allows advertising providing it is not false, misleading or deceptive.

12. (b) "Who is most likely to commit fraud among your coworkers?" is a confrontational question that is not likely to get a meaningful response.

13. (a) The audit committee should be informed about both significant audit adjustments and changes in significant accounting policies.

14. (d) Analytical procedures involve the use of comparisons of financial and nonfinancial information to identify fluctuations that increase risk or may need investigation.

15. (d) Cutoff tests are used to determine that items are recorded in the proper accounting period.

16. (d) The auditor may refer to the specialist only when the specialist's work affects the auditor's opinion.

17. (d) A client's accounting data cannot be considered sufficient audit evidence. Responses (a), (b) and (c) are not true.

18. (b) Independence is impaired when prior year fees for professional services remain unpaid for more than one year prior to the date of the report.

19. (c) The lack of a back-up system does not affect the fairness of the financial statements. Therefore, an unmodified (unqualified) opinion would be appropriate.

20. (c) The auditors must refer to the change in an emphasis-of-matter paragraph.

21. (a) If the auditor reissues a previously issued report at the request of the client, it would normally be dated its original date. To change the date would require the auditor to perform audit procedures up to the new date.

22. (b) Covered members include members of the attest engagement team, an individual in a position to influence the attest engagement, a partner who provides nonattest services to the attest client, a partner in the office in which the lead attest engagement partner practices, and the firm. A staff person that performs tax services for the attest client is not a covered member.

23. (c) An approach to testing computer controls is comparing input to the computer output.

24. (d) Requesting inventory counts at the end of each month is least likely to be an effective procedure in this case.

25. (b) Confirmation provides evidence of the existence of recorded transactions or balance sheet amounts.

26. (c) An attestation engagement always involves comparison of a subject matter to a set of criteria.

27. (c) Inquiries of the client's attorney are not required.

28. (c) If there is no need for any assurance to a third party, the information should most likely be compiled by the CPA.

29. (b) Compilations may be performed by an accountant that lacks independence but reviews may not.

30. (c) Inquiry about communications with related parties is not part of the required inquiries.

Testlet 2

1. Which of the following is least likely to be a test of a control?

  a. Inquiries of appropriate personnel.
  b. Inspection of management's engagement letter.
  c. Observation of the application of a policy.
  d. Reperformance of the application of a policy.

2. When one auditor succeeds another, the successor auditor should request the

  a. Client to instruct its attorney to send a letter of audit inquiry concerning the status of the prior year's litigation, claims, and assessments.
  b. Predecessor auditor to submit a list of internal control weaknesses that have **not** been corrected.
  c. Client to authorize the predecessor auditor to respond to inquiries.
  d. Predecessor auditor to update the prior year's report to the date of the change of auditors.

3. A difference of opinion concerning accounting and auditing matters relative to a particular phase of the audit arises between an assistant auditor and the auditor responsible for the engagement. After appropriate consultation, the assistant auditor asks to be disassociated from the resolution of the matter. The working papers would probably be

  a. Silent on the matter since it is an internal matter of the auditing firm.
  b. Expanded to note that the assistant auditor is completely disassociated from responsibility for the auditor's opinion.
  c. Expanded to document the additional work required, since all disagreements of this type will require expanded substantive testing.
  d. Expanded to document the assistant auditor's position, and how the difference of opinion was resolved.

4. On the audit of a nonissuer (nonpublic) company, the purpose of performing risk assessment procedures is to

  a. Obtain an understanding of the entity and its environment.
  b. Reduce detection risk.
  c. Evaluate management ability.
  d. Determine the operating effectiveness of controls.

5. Under the ethical standards of the profession, which of the following situations involving independent members of an auditor's family is most likely to impair the auditor's independence?

  a. A parent's immaterial investment in a client.
  b. A first cousin's loan from a client.
  c. A spouse's employment as CEO of a client.
  d. A sibling's loan to a director of a client.

6. Which of the following controls may prevent the failure to bill customers for some shipments?

  a. Each shipment should be supported by a prenumbered sales invoice that is accounted for.

  b. Each sales order should be approved by authorized personnel.
  c. Sales journal entries should be reconciled to daily sales summaries.
  d. Each sales invoice should be supported by a shipping document.

7. Which of the following is a control weakness for a company whose inventory of supplies consists of a large number of individual items?

  a. Supplies of relatively little value are expensed when purchased.
  b. The cycle basis is used for physical counts.
  c. The storekeeper is responsible for maintenance of perpetual inventory records.
  d. Perpetual inventory records are maintained only for items of significant value.

8. The accounts payable department receives the purchase order form to accomplish all of the following **except:**

  a. Compare invoice price to purchase order price.
  b. Ensure the purchase had been properly authorized.
  c. Ensure the goods had been received by the party requesting the goods.
  d. Compare quantity ordered to quantity purchased.

9. Before applying substantive tests to the details of asset and liability accounts at an interim date, the auditor should

  a. Assess the difficulty in controlling incremental audit risk.
  b. Investigate significant fluctuations that have occurred in the asset and liability accounts since the previous balance sheet date.
  c. Select only those accounts that can effectively be sampled during year-end audit work.
  d. Consider the tests of controls that must be applied at the balance-sheet date to extend the audit conclusions reached at the interim date.

10. Which of the following situations would **most** likely require special audit planning by the auditor?

  a. Some items of factory and office equipment do **not** bear identification numbers.
  b. Depreciation methods used on the client's tax return differ from those used on the books.
  c. Assets costing less than $500 are expensed even though the expected life exceeds one year.
  d. Inventory is comprised of precious stones.

11. What body has the responsibility for issuing auditing standards for auditors of issuer (public) companies?

  a. The AICPA's Auditing Standards Board.
  b. The Chief Accountant of the Securities and Exchange Commission.
  c. The Public Company Accounting Oversight Board.
  d. The Financial Accounting Standards Board.

12. Morgan, CPA, is the group engagement partner (principal auditor) for the audit of a nonpublic corporation. Jones, CPA, has audited and reported on the financial statements of a significant subsidiary of the corporation. Morgan is satisfied with the independence and professional reputation of Jones, as well as the quality of Jones' audit. With respect to Morgan's report on the consolidated financial statements, taken as a whole, Morgan

    a. Must **not** refer to the audit of Jones.
    b. Must refer to the audit of Jones.
    c. May refer to the audit of Jones.
    d. May refer to the audit of Jones, in which case Morgan must include in the auditor's report on the consolidated financial statements a qualified opinion with respect to the examination of Jones.

13. If the objective of a test of details is to detect overstatements of sales, the auditor should trace transactions from the

    a. Cash receipts journal to the sales journal.
    b. Sales journal to the cash receipts journal.
    c. Source documents to the accounting records.
    d. Accounting records to the source documents.

14. The auditor's program for the examination of long-term debt should include steps that require the

    a. Verification of the existence of the bondholders.
    b. Examination of any bond trust indenture.
    c. Inspection of the accounts payable subsidiary ledger.
    d. Investigation of credits to the bond interest income account.

15. All corporate capital stock transactions should ultimately be traced to the

    a. Minutes of the Board of Directors.
    b. Cash receipts journal.
    c. Cash disbursements journal.
    d. Numbered stock certificates.

16. According to the ethical standards for the profession, which of the following would impair the independence of an auditor in providing an audit for First State Bank, a nonpublic financial institution?

    a. The accountant has an automobile loan with the bank collateralized by the automobile.
    b. The accountant has a credit card with the bank with an outstanding balance of $12,000.
    c. The accountant has a $20,000 loan at the bank collateralized by a certificate of deposit.
    d. The accountant has a demand deposit account of $25,000 with the bank.

17. When the audited financial statements of the prior year are presented together with those of the current year, the continuing auditor's report should cover

    a. Both years.
    b. Only the current year.
    c. Only the current year, but the prior year's report should be presented.
    d. Only the current year, but the prior year's report should be referred to.

18. Information accompanying the basic financial statements should **not** include

    a. An analysis of inventory by location.
    b. A statement that the allowance for doubtful accounts is adequate.
    c. A statement that the depreciable life of a new asset is twenty years.
    d. An analysis of revenue by product line.

19. The objective of auditing procedures applied to segment information is to provide the auditor with a reasonable basis for concluding whether

    a. The information is useful for comparing a segment of one enterprise with a similar segment of another enterprise.
    b. Sufficient evidential matter has been obtained to allow the auditor to be associated with the segment information.
    c. A separate opinion on the segment information is necessary due to inconsistent application of accounting principles.
    d. The information is presented in conformity with the FASB guidance on segment information in relation to the financial statements taken as a whole.

20. An accountant has been asked to issue a review report on the balance sheet of a nonissuer (nonpublic) company but not to report on the other basic financial statements. The accountant may **not** do so

    a. Because compliance with this request would result in an incomplete review.
    b. Because compliance with this request would result in a violation of the ethical standards of the profession.
    c. If the scope of the inquiry and analytical procedures has been restricted.
    d. If the review of the balance sheet discloses material departures from generally accepted accounting principles.

21. An auditor was unable to obtain audited financial statements or other evidence supporting an entity's investment in a foreign subsidiary. Between which of the following opinions should the entity's auditor choose?

    a. Adverse and unmodified (unqualified) with an emphasis-of-matter paragraph added.
    b. Disclaimer and unmodified (unqualified) with an emphasis-of-matter paragraph added.
    c. Qualified and adverse.
    d. Qualified and disclaimer.

22. In which of the following cases would the auditor be most likely to conclude that all of the items in an account under consideration should be examined rather than tested on a sample basis?

	The measure of tolerable misstatement is	Misstatement frequency is expected to be
a.	Large	Low
b.	Small	High
c.	Large	High
d.	Small	Low

23. Which of the following factors is generally **not** considered in determining the sample size for a test of controls?

    a. Risk of incorrect acceptance.
    b. Tolerable rate.
    c. Risk of assessing control risk too low.
    d. Expected population deviation rate.

24. Hart, CPA, is concerned about the type of fee arrangements that are permissible under the profession's ethical standards. Which of the following professional services may be performed for a contingent fee?

    a. A review of financial statements.
    b. An examination of prospective financial statements.
    c. Preparation of a tax return.
    d. Information technology consulting.

25. A limitation on the scope of an auditor's procedures is likely to result in a report with a(n)

	Qualified opinion	Adverse opinion
a.	Yes	Yes
b.	Yes	No
c.	No	Yes
d.	No	No

26. Which of the following is least likely to be considered when assessing inherent risk?

    a. Nonroutine transactions.
    b. Estimation transactions.
    c. Susceptibility to theft.
    d. Expected effectiveness of controls.

27. A proper report on the compilation of the financial statements that omit notes disclosure

    a. Includes an adverse opinion.
    b. Indicates that management has omitted such note disclosures.

    c. Includes a qualification or disclaimer of opinion on the accuracy of such note disclosures.
    d. Indicates that note disclosures are not necessary for those not informed about such matters.

28. Which of the following is most likely to result in modification of a compilation report?

    a. A departure from generally accepted accounting principles.
    b. A lack of consistency in application of generally accepted accounting principles.
    c. A question concerning an entity's ability to continue as a going concern.
    d. A major uncertainty facing the financial statements.

29. Which of the following is an accurate statement of the nature of the modification of report on a compilation of financial statements of nonissuer company when the accountant is not independent?

    a. The report need not be modified.
    b. The report must include a statement that the accountant is not independent but cannot indicate the reason for the lack of independence.
    c. The report must include a statement that the accountant is not independent and may indicate the reason for the lack of independence.
    d. A report may not be issued when the accountant is not independent.

30. Which of the following is used to obtain evidence that the client's equipment accounts are **not** understated?

    a. Analyzing repairs and maintenance expense accounts.
    b. Vouching purchases of plant and equipment.
    c. Recomputing depreciation expense.
    d. Analyzing the miscellaneous revenue account.

Hints for Testlet 2

1. Which reply relates to an auditor-prepared item?

2. The predecessor auditor has a confidential relationship with the ex-client.

3. Working papers document the audit procedures applied, the information obtained, and the conclusions reached during the engagement.

4. Audit risk often relates to business risk.

5. Which is a close relative?

6. A control should be present which readily shows a missing sales invoice.

7. Where is it most likely that control will be lost because of information overload?

8. The accounts payable department is responsible for the recordkeeping function.

9. The auditor needs to be assured that the assessed level of control risk is the same at the balance sheet date as it is at the interim date.

10. Which situation would require the auditor to use the work of a specialist?

11. What body was created by the Sarbanes-Oxley Act of 2002?

12. The group (principal) auditor must decide whether or not to assume responsibility for the work of the component (other) auditor.

13. The auditor is testing for existence.

14. The audit program should include procedures to ensure that the debt is properly presented on the balance sheet.

15. Where does authorization for these transactions originate?

16. Which loan is unsecured?

17. The auditor's opinion regarding the financial statement should apply to the financial statements as a whole.

18. Which information is the auditor required to determine when auditing the financial statements?

19. The auditor normally considers segment information when performing an audit of financial statement in accordance with generally accepted auditing standards.

20. Limited reporting objectives is not the same as limiting the available procedures.

21. How does the auditor report a scope limitation?

22. Where does the auditor have the greatest risk of a material misstatement?

23. One reply deals with variables sampling, while three deal with attributes sampling.

24. Which services are performed only for the client?

25. A scope limitation may lead to a situation in which an auditor does not know whether the financial statements follow GAAP.

26. Remember the auditor also assesses control risk.

27. Opinions are only issued based on audits.

28. Reporting of which seems most essential to the CPA's role?

29. Report must be modified.

30. Which reply is most likely to find an equipment purchase that has not been capitalized?

Answers to Testlet 2

1.	b	**6.**	a	**11.**	c	**16.**	b	**21.**	d	**26.**	d
2.	c	**7.**	c	**12.**	c	**17.**	a	**22.**	b	**27.**	b
3.	d	**8.**	c	**13.**	d	**18.**	b	**23.**	a	**28.**	a
4.	a	**9.**	a	**14.**	b	**19.**	d	**24.**	d	**29.**	c
5.	c	**10.**	d	**15.**	a	**20.**	c	**25.**	b	**30.**	a

Explanations to Testlet 2

1. (b) The engagement letter has no relationship to internal control.

2. (c) The auditor should obtain permission from the client to communicate and get information from the predecessor auditor.

3. (d) In this situation, the documentation should be expanded to include the assistant's position and how the difference of opinion was resolved.

4. (a) Risk assessment procedures are performed to obtain an understanding of the entity and its environment to provide a basis to assess the risk of material misstatement and design further audit procedures.

5. (c) The spouse is a member of the CPA's immediate family and is employed in a key position.

6. (a) Requiring prenumbered sales invoices to support each shipment is an effective way to ensure that all shipments are billed.

7. (c) The individual with custody of an asset should not maintain the records.

8. (c) The purchase order would not have information about receipt of goods. A receiving report should also be obtained by accounts payable and would provide evidence of receipt of the goods.

9. (a) When a balance is audited at an interim date there is incremental audit risk that must be controlled by the auditor.

10. (d) The auditor normally does not have the requisite skills to determine the value of precious stones.

11. (c) The Public Company Accounting Oversight Board is the body responsible for issuing standards for auditors of public (issuer) companies.

12. (c) It is optional as to whether the group (principal) auditor refers to the other auditor in the report.

13. (d) To detect overstatement the auditor would normally trace transactions from the accounting records to the source documents.

14. (b) In auditing long-term debt the auditor should examine the bond trust indenture to assure that covenants in the indenture are adequately disclosed in the financial statements.

15. (a) To determine that they are authorized, capital stock transactions should be traced to authorization in the minutes of board of director or shareholder meetings.

16. (b) An interpretation of the independence rule prohibits credit card accounts in excess of $10,000.

17. (a) A continuing auditor's report should cover both years.

18. (b) If the allowance for doubtful accounts is inadequate, this fact should result in a qualification of the auditor's opinion.

19. (d) The procedures are performed to determine that the information is presented in conformity with the FASB requirements in relation to the financial statements taken as a whole.

20. (c) An accountant may review a balance sheet providing the scope of the procedures is not limited.

21. (d) If the auditor cannot obtain sufficient evidence, he or she must choose between a qualified opinion and a disclaimer, depending on the significance of the limitation.

22. (b) The auditor would most likely decide not to sample when the tolerable misstatement is small and the expected misstatement rate is high. In this case it would be more appropriate to examine all or most of the items in the population.

23. (a) The risk of incorrect acceptance is a consideration when sampling is used for a substantive procedure.

24. (d) Rule 302 prohibits contingent fees for audits or reviews of financial statements, examinations of prospective financial information, and preparation of tax returns.

25. (b) A significant limitation in the scope of audit procedures would result in a qualified opinion or a disclaimer of opinion depending on its significance.

26. (d) The effectiveness of internal control is a consideration regarding control risk.

27. (b) The professional standards require that the CPA clearly indicate in the accountants' report the omission.

28. (a) Compilation reports are modified for departures from generally accepted accounting principles. The other items do not affect compilation reports.

29. (c) The accountant must modify the report and may indicate the reason for lack of independence.

30. (a) Analyzing repairs and maintenance expense may result in the discovery of property and plant expenditures that were erroneously expensed.

Testlet 3

1. The risk that an auditor's procedures will lead to the conclusion that a material misstatement does **not** exist in an account balance when, in fact, such misstatement does exist is referred to as

- a. Audit risk.
- b. Inherent risk.
- c. Control risk.
- d. Detection risk.

2. Which of the following is an audit **least** likely to detect?

- a. Theft of cash received from collection of accounts receivable.
- b. Intentional omission of transactions relating to equipment purchases.
- c. Intentional violations of occupational safety and health laws.
- d. Misapplication of accounting principles relating to inventory.

3. Prior to beginning the fieldwork on a new audit engagement in which a CPA does **not** possess expertise in the industry in which the client operates, the CPA should

- a. Reduce audit risk by lowering the preliminary levels of materiality.
- b. Design special substantive tests to compensate for the lack of industry expertise.
- c. Engage financial experts familiar with the nature of the industry.
- d. Obtain a knowledge of matters that relate to the nature of the entity's business.

4. For purposes of an audit of internal control performed under Public Company Accounting Oversight Board standards, a significant deficiency is a control deficiency that

- a. Is at least as severe as a material weakness.
- b. Is probable of occurring in an amount that is material.
- c. Must be communicated to those responsible for oversight of the company's financial reporting.
- d. Remains unresolved at the date of completion of final internal control analysis procedures.

5. Under the ethical standards of the profession, which of the following investments in a client is not considered to be a direct financial interest?

- a. An investment held through a nonclient regulated mutual fund.
- b. An investment held through a nonclient investment club.
- c. An investment held in a blind trust.
- d. An investment held by the trustee of a trust.

6. Audit evidence on the proper segregation of duties ordinarily is best obtained by

- a. Preparation of a flowchart of duties performed by available personnel.
- b. Inquiring whether control activities operated consistently throughout the period.
- c. Reviewing job descriptions prepared by the personnel department.
- d. Direct personal observation of the employees who apply control activities.

7. In considering internal control, the auditor is basically concerned that it provides reasonable assurance that

- a. Operational efficiency has been achieved in accordance with management plans.
- b. Material misstatements due to errors and fraud have been prevented or detected.
- c. Controls have **not** been circumvented by collusion.
- d. Management **cannot** override the system.

8. In properly designed internal control, the same employee should **not** be permitted to

- a. Sign checks and cancel supporting documents.
- b. Receive merchandise and prepare a receiving report.
- c. Prepare disbursement vouchers and sign checks.
- d. Initiate a request to order merchandise and approve merchandise received.

9. Which of the following is an effective control over cash payments?

- a. Signed checks should be mailed under the supervision of the check signer.
- b. Spoiled checks that have been voided should be disposed of immediately.
- c. Checks should be prepared only by persons responsible for cash receipts and cash disbursements.
- d. A check-signing machine with two signatures should be utilized.

10. Inquiries of warehouse personnel concerning possible obsolete or slow-moving inventory items provide assurance about management's assertion of

- a. Completeness.
- b. Existence.
- c. Presentation.
- d. Valuation.

11. The primary reason an auditor requests letters of inquiry be sent to a client's attorneys is to provide the auditor with

- a. A description and evaluation of litigation, claims, and assessments that existed at the date of the balance sheet.
- b. An expert opinion as to whether a loss is possible, probable, or remote.
- c. The opportunity to examine the documentation concerning litigation, claims, and assessments.
- d. Corroboration of the information furnished by management concerning litigation, claims, and assessments.

12. Lott and Lott, CPAs, recently acquired a public company as an audit client. With respect to this client, the Sarbanes-Oxley Act of 2002 requires

- a. Rotation of accounting firms every five years.
- b. Joint audits by two auditing firms.
- c. Rotation of the partner in charge of the audit every five years.
- d. Joint management of the audit by two or more partners.

13. When providing limited assurance that the financial statements of a nonissuer (nonpublic) entity require **no** material modifications to be in accordance with generally accepted accounting principles, the accountant should

- a. Understand internal control.
- b. Test the accounting records that identify inconsistencies with the prior year's financial statements.
- c. Understand the accounting principles of the industry in which the entity operates.
- d. Develop audit programs to determine whether the entity's financial statements are fairly presented.

14. According to the ethical standards for the profession, which of the following fee arrangements is prohibited?

- a. A fee for a review of financial statements that is based on time spent on the engagement.
- b. A fee for a review of financial statements that is based on time spent and a premium for the risk involved.
- c. A fee for a review engagement that is based on a fixed fee of $5,000.
- d. A fee for a review engagement that varies depending on the amount of financing that the company may obtain.

15. Which of the following procedures is **not** included in a review engagement of a nonissuer (nonpublic) entity?

- a. Inquiries of management.
- b. Inquiries regarding events subsequent to the balance sheet date.
- c. Any procedures designed to identify relationships among data that appear to be unusual.
- d. Tests of internal control.

16. Which of the following is not considered by the PCAOB as an indicator of the existence of a material weakness in internal control?

- a. Identification of a material fraud committed by senior management in the areas of sales.
- b. Restatement of previously issued financial statements to reflect correction of a material misstatement relating to improper inventory valuation.
- c. Identification by the auditor of a material misstatement in cost of goods sold in circumstances that indicate that the misstatement would not have been detected by the company's internal control.
- d. Lack of oversight by the audit committee of details of raw material purchases.

17. Kane, CPA, concludes that there is substantial doubt about Lima Co.'s ability to continue as a going concern for a reasonable period of time. If Lima's financial statements adequately disclose its financial difficulties, Kane's auditor's report is required to include a paragraph that specifically uses the phrase(s)

	"Possible discontinuance of operations"	"Reasonable period of time, not to exceed 1 year"
a.	Yes	Yes
b.	Yes	No
c.	No	Yes
d.	No	No

18. How are management's responsibility and the auditor's responsibility represented in the standard auditor's report?

	Management's responsibility	Auditor's responsibility
a.	Explicitly	Explicitly
b.	Implicitly	Implicitly
c.	Implicitly	Explicitly
d.	Explicitly	Implicitly

19. In estimation sampling for attributes, which one of the following must be known in order to appraise the results of the auditor's sample?

- a. Estimated dollar value of the population.
- b. Standard deviation of the values in the population.
- c. Actual occurrence rate of the attribute in the population.
- d. Sample size.

20. Processing data through the use of simulated files provides an auditor with information about the reliability of controls. One of the techniques involved in this approach makes use of

- a. Controlled reprocessing.
- b. Integrated test facility.
- c. Input validation.
- d. Program code checking

21. After the audit documentation completion date, the auditor

- a. May not delete any audit documentation.
- b. May not make changes in audit documentation.
- c. May not add new information to audit documentation.
- d. May make changes or deletions to audit documentation providing that the fact that alterations were made is documented.

22. Prior to or in conjunction with obtaining information to identify risks of fraud, which of the following is required?

- a. A brainstorming session among team members about where financial statements may be susceptible to fraud.
- b. A discussion with the client's legal counsel as to contingent liabilities likely to affect the financial statements.
- c. Indirect verification of significant financial statement assertions.
- d. Professional skepticism concerning illegal acts that do not have an effect on financial statement amounts.

23. Which of the following is **not** ordinarily performed in response to the risk of management override?

- a. Evaluating the rationale for significant unusual transactions.
- b. Observe counts of inventory at all locations.

c. Review accounting estimates for bias.

d. Test appropriateness of journal entries and adjustments.

24. When an auditor has a question concerning a client's ability to continue as a going concern, the auditor considers management's plans for dealing with the situation. That consideration is most likely to include consideration of management's plans to

a. Decrease ownership equity.

b. Dispose of assets.

c. Increase expenditures on key products.

d. Invest in derivative securities.

25. A change from one accounting principle to another with which the auditor concurs is likely to result in a report with a(n)

	Qualified opinion	Adverse opinion
a.	Yes	Yes
b.	Yes	No
c.	No	Yes
d.	No	No

26. A significant circumstance-caused scope limitation in a Sarbanes/Oxley 404 internal control audit is more likely to result in a(n)

a. Adverse opinion.

b. Qualified opinion.

c. Unmodified (unqualified) opinion with an emphasis-of-matter paragraph.

d. Scope reduction opinion.

27. According to the ethical standards for the profession, which of the following is **not** acceptable advertising content?

a. The fees for services.

b. The qualifications of professional staff.

c. Implications regarding the ability to influence regulatory bodies.

d. Implications regarding the value of the services.

28. An accountant should establish an understanding with management regarding the services to be performed and document in writing for a

	Compilation	Review
a.	Yes	Yes
b.	Yes	No
c.	No	Yes
d.	No	No

29. Wilson, CPA, has been engaged to review the financial statements of Roland Company, a nonissuer company. The management of Roland Company has refused to sign a representation letter for the engagement. What should be Wilson's response?

a. Not issue a review report.

b. Issue a standard review report providing all other review procedures were performed.

c. Issue a review report modified for a scope restriction.

d. Issue a review report modified for a possible departure from generally accepted accounting principles.

30. Violation of which of the following is most likely to be considered a "direct effect" illegal act?

a. Environmental protection laws.

b. Occupational safety and health law violations.

c. Securities trading laws.

d. Tax laws.

Hints for Testlet 3

1. The auditor performs audit procedures to detect material misstatements in the account balance.

2. Which is least likely to misstate financial statement amounts?

3. The CPA must understand the business issues of the company and industry.

4. Think about control deficiencies, significant deficiencies, and material weaknesses.

5. What is an indirect financial interest?

6. Which control gives the auditor the best idea about the daily operation of the company?

7. Which area does the auditor have the most control over?

8. Segregate recordkeeping from authorization.

9. Which control helps the client maintain accountability for the cash payments?

10. Obsolete or slow moving inventory may never be sold and so the amount of inventory presented on the balance sheet may be overstated.

11. The client has primary responsibility for the fair presentation of the financial statements.

12. Partner rotation helps assure independence.

13. A requirement for any engagement is for the auditor to understand the environment they are working in.

14. Which fee is contingent?

15. A review engagement provides only limited assurance.

16. Think carefully about the indicators provided by the PCAOB.

17. Mentally "write" an emphasis-of-matter paragraph and consider whether it is likely that these items would be required.

18. The standard audit report should give the reader a clear understanding about responsibilities.

19. The auditor wants to determine a deviation rate for the sample.

20. Which technique places the simulated files into the midst of live transactions?

21. Documentation should be as accurate as possible.

22. One of these is intended to get the audit team "up to speed" in the area.

23. Which procedure may not be practical in some situations?

24. Consider a reply that will provide resources to the company.

25. Client's are able to change accounting principles.

26. Scope limitations may result in two types of opinion—only one is listed.

27. Which is false, misleading, or deceptive?

28. For both types of association a CPA attempts to avoid misunderstandings.

29. Scope limitation reports are not allowed.

30. Which is most likely to result in direct misstatement of a financial statement account balance?

Answers to Testlet 3

1.	d	6.	d	11.	d	16.	d	21.	d	26.	b
2.	c	7.	b	12.	c	17.	d	22.	a	27.	c
3.	d	8.	c	13.	c	18.	a	23.	b	28.	a
4.	c	9.	a	14.	d	19.	d	24.	b	29.	a
5.	a	10.	d	15.	d	20.	b	25.	d	30.	d

Explanations to Testlet 3

1. (d) Detection risk is the risk that the auditor's procedures will fail to detect a material misstatement if it exists.

2. (c) Intentional violations of occupational safety and health laws are the most difficult to detect because they are not related to financial statement numbers and they are not within the auditor's expertise.

3. (d) If the auditor does not have an understanding of the client's industry, he or she should obtain that understanding.

4. (c) A significant deficiency is a matter that must be communicated to those responsible for oversight of the company's financial reporting process because it should be of interest to those individuals.

5. (a) An investment in a mutual fund that holds an investment in a client is considered to be an indirect financial interest.

6. (d) Direct personal observations of employees performing activities is the best test of segregation of duties.

7. (b) Internal control should be designed to provide reasonable assurance that material errors or fraud are prevented, or detected and corrected.

8. (c) In a properly designed system of internal control an individual should not have custody of assets (be able to sign checks) and also keep accounting records (prepare disbursement vouchers).

9. (a) For appropriate internal control the check signer should supervise the mailing of the checks.

10. (d) Inquiries of warehouse personnel about obsolete or slow-moving inventory items is designed to identify items that may be overvalued.

11. (d) The attorney's letter corroborates the information about litigation, claims, and assessments provided by management.

12. (c) The Sarbanes-Oxley Act requires rotation of the partner in charge of the audit every five years.

13. (c) Statements on Standards for Accounting and Review Services requires the accountant to understand the accounting principles of the industry in which the entity operates. All the other items are not required.

14. (d) A fee that varies depending on the amount of financing obtained is a contingent fee that is not allowed for a review engagement.

15. (d) A review of the financial statements of a nonissuer company does not involve tests of the effectiveness of internal control.

16. (d) The audit committee would not be expected to oversee the details of raw material purchases.

17. (d) Neither of these phrases is required in the auditor's emphasis-of-matter paragraph.

18. (a) The auditor's report explicitly describes management's responsibility and the auditor's responsibility.

19. (d) The sample size and the occurrence rate in the sample are the items that must be known to evaluate the sample results.

20. (b) An integrated test facility introduces test (dummy) transactions with live transactions to test the effectiveness of IT controls.

21. (d) The auditor may make changes or deletions to audit documentation providing the fact that the changes were made is documented.

22. (a) Auditing standards require a brainstorming session among audit team members regarding where the financial statements may be susceptible to fraud.

23. (b) Observation of inventory is not ordinarily a procedure performed in response to the risk of management override of internal control.

24. (b) Management plans to deal with a going concern issue usually involves disposition of assets or obtaining additional financing.

25. (d) A change from one acceptable accounting principle to another acceptable principle does not result in either a qualified opinion or an adverse opinion. An unmodified (unqualified) opinion with emphasis-of-matter language is appropriate.

26. (b) A circumstance-caused scope limitation would normally result in a qualified opinion.

27. (c) Advertising content that implies the ability to influence regulatory bodies would be considered false, misleading, or deceptive.

28. (a) Both types of engagements require such a written communication.

29. (a) If the scope is restricted by management, the accountant should not issue a report.

30. (d) Direct-effect illegal acts affect the numbers in the financial statements. An important example is the violation of a tax law.

Testlet 4

Task-Based Simulation 1

TSQ Risks		
	Authoritative Literature	Help

Assume you are performing the 20X8 audit of Tommi Stone and Quarry.

Company Information

In 20X1 Jill Tommi founded Tommi Stone and Quarry (TSQ). Within its first year of existence, the company completed initial development of the extraction pit area and constructed an aggregate processing plant which is equipped to crush, screen, and wash aggregate products. By 20X3 the sand and gravel operation was profitable, and growing market conditions justified modifications and expansion. Currently, at the conclusion of 20X8, TSQ produces a wide range of sand and stone products from its pit near Albuquerque, New Mexico. The materials it develops range from various sand and stone materials for residential and commercial construction and highway projects. TSQ sells to a wide variety of residential, commercial and governmental customers, with no one customer accounting for more than 5% of its total sales.

TSQ has worked closely with stucco manufacturers and plastering contractors in the Albuquerque plastering industry to produce a plaster sand ("Plasand") that exceeds normal specifications and produces a superior ingredient which improves stucco and plastering finished products. Plasand has been increasingly widely accepted as superior to products offered by competitors, and now accounts for approximately 10% of the company's sales, and 12% of its profits. TSQ is currently working closely with sport complexes and golf course architects in conjunction with test laboratories to develop a superior sand for use in the construction and top dressing of golf courses and sport complex playing fields.

The company experienced a level of profitability in 20X8 of about the same as that of 20X7—but this is well below the net incomes of the preceding several years. Jill suggested to you that, surprisingly, intense price competition from several smaller competitors in the Albuquerque area caused the somewhat low level of profitability. But, she added, she didn't expect the problem to last for long because she doubted that those companies could continue to operate selling at these lower prices. Jill had hoped for a more profitable year in 20X8 as a significant amount of the company's long-term debt is payable in 20X9. TSQ is currently involved in discussions with the bank on refinancing.

TSQ added significant additional crushing and washing plants and equipment during 20X8 to increase production in the future by more than 100% while expanding capabilities to produce custom specification materials.

Until 20X7 and 20X8, most of earnings were distributed through dividends to TSQ's five shareholders—CEO and Chair of the Board of Directors Jill Tommi, her husband Mort Tommi, CFO Googlo Permasi and two college friends of Jill's who invested in the company, Jian Zhang and Kendra Kovano. These five individuals make up the company's Board of Directors.

This year, in reaction to pressure from a bank that provides a significant portion of the financing, TSQ established an audit committee composed of Mort Tommi, Googlo Permasi, and Jian Zhang.

You are working on your firm's fifth audit of TSQ. The previous audits have all resulted in standard unmodified (unqualified) audit reports.

Industry Information

The industry consists of preparation for the mining and extraction of sand and rock products. These include the activities of cleaning, separating and sorting of quarried sand, and the crushing of rocks. The products are in the form of sand used in making concrete; sand used in laying bricks (contains little soil); sand used for fill (contains lots of soil, and quartz sand); and excluding the products of gravel quarrying (sandstone, gravel stone, and iron sand).

While sales within the industry are relatively unaffected by changes in technology, or obsolescence, sales rely heavily upon both the residential and commercial construction markets as well as government spending. During the past five years construction has performed well and that trend is expected to continue at least for the coming several years. Sand and gravel production has increased at approximately 3% per year during this time period, as has construction within the Albuquerque.

The sand and gravel market in central New Mexico has been particularly healthy due in large part to the growth of Albuquerque into a major metropolitan area. The most significant question facing the industry is whether the strong construction will continue as expected. During the past two years the economy of the United States has been in a recovery period, yet unemployment remains high as compared to previous periods of recovery. Thus, the questions concerning the continuing construction demand.

	(A)	(B)	(C)	(D)
	○	○	○	○

1. A risk factor relating to misstatements arising from fraudulent financial reporting is

   A. Earnings this year are lower than management had hoped.
   B. Fewer competitors exist than in the past, and this places the company in a position in which it is easier to manipulate earnings.
   C. Sales are made to residential, commercial, and governmental purchasers.
   D. The industry faces great technological changes in almost all of its products.

	(A)	(B)	(C)	(D)
	○	○	○	○

2. Which of the following correctly identifies a risk facing TSQ that might adversely affect sales during the coming years?

   A. A general slowdown in the economy.
   B. Sales to many different types of customers.
   C. Increased attention to developing new products.
   D. A board of directors dominated by management.

	(A)	(B)	(C)	(D)
	○	○	○	○

3. Which of the following correctly identifies a risk facing TSQ that might affect its ability to continue as a going concern over the long run?

   A. Competition from several competitors.
   B. Customer satisfaction with the quality of TSQ's current products.
   C. The nature of inventory items—small in size, high in value.
   D. Obsolescence of all major products due to rapid changes in technology in the industry.

	(A)	(B)	(C)	(D)
	○	○	○	○

4. The most significant risk factor relating to the misstatement arising from fraudulent financial reporting for TSQ is that the company

   A. Operates in the Albuquerque area.
   B. Officers serve on the board of directors.
   C. Must refinance a significant portion of its debt.
   D. Paid no dividend this year.

Task-Based Simulation 2

An assistant has been working in the revenue cycle area and has compiled a list of possible errors and fraud that may result in the misstatement of Model Company's financial statements, and a corresponding list of controls that, if properly designed and implemented, could assist in preventing or detecting the errors and fraud.

For each possible error and fraud numbered **1** through **15**, select one internal control from the answer list below that, if properly designed and implemented, most likely could assist management in preventing or detecting the errors and fraud. Each response in the list of controls may be selected once, more than once, or not at all.

Controls

A. Shipping clerks compare goods received from the warehouse with the details on the shipping documents.
B. Approved sales orders are required for goods to be released from the warehouse.
C. Monthly statements are mailed to all customers with outstanding balances.
D. Shipping clerks compare goods received from the warehouse with approved sales orders.

E. Customer orders are compared with the inventory master file to determine whether items ordered are in stock.
F. Daily sales summaries are compared with control totals of invoices.
G. Shipping documents are compared with sales invoices when goods are shipped.
H. Sales invoices are compared with the master price file.
I. Customer orders are compared with an approved customer list.

J. Sales orders are prepared for each customer order.

K. Control amounts posted to the accounts receivable ledger are compared with control totals of invoices.

L. Sales invoices are compared with shipping documents and approved customer orders before invoices are mailed.

M. Prenumbered credit memos are used for granting credit for goods returned.

N. Goods returned for credit are approved by the supervisor of the sales department.

O. Remittance advices are separated from the checks in the mailroom and forwarded to the accounting department.

P. Total amounts posted to the accounts receivable ledger from remittance advices are compared with the validated bank deposit slip.

Q. The cashier examines each check for proper endorsement.

R. Validated deposit slips are compared with the cashier's daily cash summaries.

S. An employee, other than the bookkeeper, periodically prepares a bank reconciliation.

T. Sales returns are approved by the same employee who issues receiving reports evidencing actual return of goods.

Possible Errors and Fraud

1. Invoices for goods sold are posted to incorrect customer accounts.
2. Goods ordered by customers are shipped, but are **not** billed to anyone.
3. Invoices are sent for shipped goods, but are **not** recorded in the sales journal.
4. Invoices are sent for shipped goods and are recorded in the sales journal, but are **not** posted to any customer account.
5. Credit sales are made to individuals with unsatisfactory credit ratings.
6. Goods are removed from inventory for unauthorized orders.
7. Goods shipped to customers do **not** agree with goods ordered by customers.
8. Invoices are sent to allies in a fraudulent scheme and sales are recorded for fictitious transactions.
9. Customers' checks are received for less than the customers' full account balances, but the customers' full account balances are credited.
10. Customers' checks are misappropriated before being forwarded to the cashier for deposit.
11. Customers' checks are credited to incorrect customer accounts.
12. Different customer accounts are each credited for the same cash receipt.
13. Customers' checks are properly credited to customer accounts and are properly deposited, but errors are made in recording receipts in the cash receipts journal.
14. Customers' checks are misappropriated after being forwarded to the cashier for deposit.
15. Invalid transactions granting credit for sales returns are recorded.

Task-Based Simulation 3

Auditors often find it necessary to sample only selected items from populations as contrasted to auditing entire populations. The sampling process introduces a number of terms into auditing. For each term in the first column below identify its definition (or partial definition). Each definition may be used once or not at all.

Definition (or partial definition)

A. A classical variables sampling plan enabling the auditors to estimate the average dollar value (or other variable) of items in a population by determining the average value of items in a sample.

B. A defined rate of departure from prescribed controls. Also referred to as *occurrence rate* or *exception rate*.

C. A sampling plan enabling the auditors to estimate the rate of deviation (occurrence) in a population.

D. A sampling plan for locating at least 1 deviation, providing that the deviation occurs in the population with a specified frequency.

E. A sampling plan in which the sample is selected in stages, with the need for each subsequent stage being conditional on the results of the previous stage.

F. Also referred to as *precision*, an interval around the sample results in which the true population characteristic is expected to lie.

G. An estimate of the most likely amount of monetary misstatement in a population.

H. The complement of the risk of incorrect acceptance.

I. The maximum population rate of deviations from a prescribed control that the auditor will accept without modifying the planned assessment of control risk.

J. The possibility that the assessed level of control risk based on the sample is less than the true operating effectiveness of the controls.

K. The possibility that the assessed level of control risk based on the sample is greater than the true operating effectiveness of the control.

L. The risk that sample results will indicate that a population is materially misstated when, in fact, it is not.

M. The risk that sample results will indicate that a population is not materially misstated when, in fact, it is materially misstated.

N. The risk that the auditors' conclusion based on a sample might be different from the conclusion they would reach if the test were applied to the entire population.

Term	(A)	(B)	(C)	(D)	(E)	(F)	(G)	(H)	(I)	(J)	(K)	(L)	(M)	(N)
1. Allowance for sampling risk	O	O	O	O	O	O	O	O	O	O	O	O	O	O
2. Deviation rate	O	O	O	O	O	O	O	O	O	O	O	O	O	O
3. Discovery sampling	O	O	O	O	O	O	O	O	O	O	O	O	O	O
4. Projected misstatement	O	O	O	O	O	O	O	O	O	O	O	O	O	O
5. Reliability	O	O	O	O	O	O	O	O	O	O	O	O	O	O
6. Risk of assessing control risk too low	O	O	O	O	O	O	O	O	O	O	O	O	O	O
7. Risk of incorrect acceptance	O	O	O	O	O	O	O	O	O	O	O	O	O	O
8. Sampling risk	O	O	O	O	O	O	O	O	O	O	O	O	O	O
9. Tolerable deviation rate	O	O	O	O	O	O	O	O	O	O	O	O	O	O

Task-Based Simulation 4

Accounts Payable Misstatements		
	Authoritative Literature	Help

The year under audit is year 2. During the audit of accounts payable, you detected misstatements previously undetected by the client. All misstatements were related to year 2. For each of the liability misstatements shown below, double-click on the shaded cell and select the most appropriate item from the list provided.

- In column B, indicate the audit procedure that was most likely used to detect the misstatement.
- In column C, select the internal control that most likely could prevent or detect this type of misstatement in the future.

Audit procedures and internal controls may be selected once, more than once, or not at all.

Misstatement	Column B — Audit procedure used to detect misstatement	Column C — Internal control that could prevent or detect misstatement in the future
1. An accounts payable clerk misplaces year-end invoices for raw materials that were received on December 21, year 2, and therefore liabilities were not recorded.		
2. The company tends to be careless in recording payables in the correct period.		
3. The company has the same person approving pay requests and cutting checks.		
4. The company's receiving department misplaces receiving reports for purchases of raw materials at year-end and therefore liabilities were not recorded.		

Column B selection list

1. From the January, year 3, cash disbursements journal, select payments and match to corresponding invoices.
2. Review the cash disbursements journal for the month of December, year 2.
3. On a surprise basis, review the receiving department's filing system, and test check quantities entered on December, year 2, receiving reports to packing slips.
4. Identify open purchase orders and vendors' invoices at December 31, year 2, and investigate their disposition.
5. Request written confirmation from the accounts payable supervisor that all vendor invoices have been recorded in the accounts payable subsidiary ledger.
6. Investigate unmatched receiving reports dated prior to January 1, year 3.
7. Compare the balances for selected vendors at the end of year 2 and year 1.
8. Determine that credit memos received 10 days after the balance sheet date have been recorded in the proper period.
9. Select an unpaid invoice and ask to be walked through the invoice payment process.

Column C selection list

1. The purchasing department supervisor forwards a monthly listing of matched purchase orders and receiving reports to the accounts payable supervisor for comparison to a listing of vouched invoices.
2. The accounts payable supervisor reviews a monthly listing of open purchase orders and vendors' invoices for follow-up with the receiving department.
3. Copies of all vendor invoices received during the year are filed in an outside storage facility.
4. All vendor invoices are reviewed for mathematical accuracy.
5. On a daily basis, the receiving department independently counts all merchandise received.
6. All vendor invoices with supporting documentation are canceled when paid.
7. At the end of each month, the purchasing department confirms terms of delivery with selected vendors.
8. Accounts payable personnel are assigned different responsibilities each quarter within the department.
9. A clerk is responsible for matching purchase orders with receiving reports and making certain they are included in the proper month.

Task-Based Simulation 5

Your firm has become aware of the following situations relating to five of its clients. Use the following possibilities to indicate what type of opinions are appropriate in the circumstances (assume all are material).

Opinion Types

    A. Standard unmodified (unqualified).
    B. Unmodified (unqualified) with a matter.
    C. Qualified.
    D. Adverse.
    E. Disclaimer.
    F. Either qualified or adverse.
    G. Either qualified or disclaimer.
    H. Either adverse or disclaimer.

	(A)	(B)	(C)	(D)	(E)	(F)	(G)	(H)
1. Bowles Company is engaged in a hazardous trade and has obtained insurance coverage related to the hazard. Although the likelihood is remote, a material portion of the company's assets could be destroyed by a serious accident.	O	O	O	O	O	O	O	O
2. Draves Company owns substantial properties that have appreciated significantly in value since the date of purchase. The properties were appraised and are reported in the balance sheet at the appraised values with full disclosure. The CPAs believe that the appraised values reported in the balance sheet reasonably estimate the assets' current values.	O	O	O	O	O	O	O	O

3. During the audit of Eagle Company the CPA firm has encountered a significant scope limitation relating to inventory record availability and is unable to obtain sufficient appropriate audit evidence in that area.   ○ ○ ○ ○ ○ ○ ○ ○ ○

4. London Company has material investments in stocks of subsidiary companies. Stocks of the subsidiary companies are not actively traded in the market, and the CPA firm's engagement does not extend to any subsidiary company. The CPA firm is able to determine that all investments are carried at original cost, and the auditors have no reason to suspect that the amounts are not stated fairly.   ○ ○ ○ ○ ○ ○ ○ ○ ○

5. Slade Company has material investments in stocks of subsidiary companies. Stocks of the subsidiary companies are actively traded in the market, but the CPA firm's engagement does not extend to any subsidiary company. Management insists that all investments shall be carried at original costs, and the CPA firm is satisfied that the original costs are accurate. The CPA firm believes that the client will never ultimately realize a substantial portion of the investments, and the client has fully disclosed the facts in notes to the financial statements.   ○ ○ ○ ○ ○ ○ ○ ○

Task-Based Simulation 6

The table below presents ratios that the company uses to track its performance. During fieldwork, the auditors determined that the ratios were inaccurate due to significant errors, described below, made by the company in year 2. The company has agreed to make adjusting journal entries for year 2 to correct the errors.

After you have determined the appropriate adjusting journal entry (entries) to correct each error, double-click the shaded cell and select the impact, if any, that the adjusting journal entry (entries) would have on the erroneous ratio.

Selection list
Increases
Decreases
No impact

Ratio	Year 2 Erroneous ratio	Ratio	Year 2 Erroneous ratio
Inventory turnover	4.38	Return on equity	17.53%

Impact of adjusting journal entries on the inventory turnover ratio	Company errors	Impact of adjusting journal entries on the return on equity ratio
	1. Inventory stored at a distribution center on December 31, year 2, was inadvertently omitted during the year 2 physical inventory count, to which the general ledger was adjusted.	
	2. During the physical inventory, the company included inventory that it was holding on consignment.	
	3. The company failed to record the materials in transit accrual for late supplier/vendor invoices.	
	4. The company declared and paid a cash dividend on December 30, year 2, but failed to record the transaction in year 2.	

Task-Based Simulation 7

Misstated Audited Financial Statements

You and your staff have completed an audit of a nonissuer for the calendar year ended December 31, year 2. The audit report date of the financial statement was March 11, year 3, and on March 26, year 3, the client issued the financial statements.

On April 15, year 3, as you are ascertaining that the workpapers and related audit programs are complete and properly signed off, you notice that the financial statements include a material misstatement subsequent to the issuance of an unmodified (unqualified) report. The misstatement was determined to be the inclusion of nonexistent sales.

Your audit team issued the financial statements. Information regarding nonexistent sales was not known at the date of the audit report. The auditors find the subsequently discovered information is both reliable and existed at the date of the auditor's report. Management has revised the financial statements and the auditor will reissue the audit report.

Selections
A. AU-C
B. PCAOB
C. AT
D. AR
E. ET
F. BL
G. CS
H. QC

	(A)	(B)	(C)	(D)	(E)	(F)	(G)	(H)
1. Which section of the Professional Standards addresses this issue and will be helpful in responding to the CEO?	○	○	○	○	○	○	○	○

2. Enter the exact section and paragraph with helpful information on dating of the audit report.

Answers to Testlet 4

Solution to Task-Based Simulation 1

TSQ Risks		
	Authoritative Literature	Help

1. (A) The requirement is to identify a risk factor relating to misstatements arising from fraudulent financial reporting. Answer (A) is correct because historically low levels of earnings may have created pressure on management to at least exceed the previous year's net income. Answer (B) is incorrect because there are not fewer competitors. Answer (C) is incorrect because selling to residential, commercial, and governmental purchasers presents no particular risk. Answer (D) is incorrect because there is no indication that the company is involved with overly complex transactions (maintaining lien rights on inventory is not complex) and the industry does not face great technological changes in products.

2. (A) The requirement is to identify the correct statement relating to a risk that might adversely affect TSQ's sales. Answer (A) is correct because the simulation emphasizes the fact that sales are dependent upon economic growth. Answer (B) is incorrect because selling to different types of customers diversifies away some of the risk of declining sales. Answer (C) is incorrect because increased attention to developing new products may help the company increase future sales. Answer (D) is incorrect because while the board of directors may be dominated by management, it is uncertain that such lack of independence would lead to a decline in sales.

3. (A) The requirement is to identify the risk facing TSQ that might affect its ability to continue as a going concern over the long run. Answer (A) is correct because the competition that has led to decreased sales prices may ultimately create a difficult situation for TSW. Answer (B) is incorrect because customers are satisfied with the quality of TSQ's products. Answer (C) is incorrect because sand and gravel is not generally small in size and high in value in the quantities sold. Answer (D) is incorrect because obsolescence is not a problem.

4. (C) The requirement is to identify the most significant risk factor relating to misstatements arising from fraudulent financial reporting. Answer (C) is correct because the pressure to obtain the refinancing creates pressure on management. Answer (A) is incorrect because operating in the Albuquerque area presents no particular problem. Answer (B) is incorrect because company officers ordinarily serve on the board of directors. Answer (D) is incorrect because the lack of a dividend bears no particular relationship with fraudulent financial reporting.

Solution to Task-Based Simulation 2

Sales and Collections Controls		
	Authoritative Literature	Help

1. (C) Invoices posted to incorrect customer accounts will be detected by analyzing customer responses to monthly statements that include errors, particularly statements with errors not in favor of the customer.

2. (G) The comparison of shipping documents with sales invoices will detect goods that have been shipped but not billed when no sales invoice is located for a particular shipping document.

3. (F) To provide assurance that all invoiced goods that have been shipped are recorded as sales, daily sales summaries should be compared with invoices. For example, a sale that has not been recorded will result in a sales summary that does not include certain sales invoices.

4. (K) A comparison of the amounts posted to the accounts receivable ledger with the control total for invoices will provide assurance that all invoices have been posted to a customer account.

5. (I) Comparing customer orders with an approved customer list will provide assurance that credit sales are made only to customers that have been granted credit.

6. (B) Requiring an approved sales order before goods are released from the warehouse will provide assurance that goods are not removed for unauthorized orders.

7. (D) A comparison by shipping clerks of goods received from the warehouse with the approved sales orders will provide assurance that goods shipped to customers agree with goods ordered by customers.

8. (L) A comparison of sales invoices with shipping documents and approved sales orders will detect invoices that do not have the proper support. Accordingly, it will help prevent the recording of fictitious transactions.

9. (P) Comparing amounts posted to the accounts receivable ledger with the validated bank deposit will detect improper postings to accounts receivable since any differences in amounts will be investigated.

10. (C) Misappropriations of customers' checks will be detected when customers indicate that they have made payments for items shown as payable on their monthly statement. Note that replies O and P will only detect this misappropriation in the unlikely event that the perpetrator does not dispose of the remittance advice.

11. (C) Mispostings of payments made will be detected when customers indicate that they have made payments for items shown as payable on their monthly statement.

12. (P) Crediting more than one account for a cash receipt will be detected when the total of amounts posted to the accounts receivable ledger is compared with the validated bank deposit slip.

13. (S) An independent reconciliation of the bank account will reveal improper total recording of receipts in the cash receipts journal because unlocated differences between bank and book balances will occur and be investigated.

14. (P) Comparing total amounts posted to the accounts receivable ledger with the validated bank deposit slip will detect a difference between total cash receipts and the amount credited to the accounts receivable ledger.

15. (N) Requiring the approval of the supervisor of the sales department for goods received will provide assurance that invalid transactions granting credit for sales returns are not recorded. Note that using prenumbered credit memos (reply M) will only be effective if the sequence is accounted for and if credit memos may be compared in some form to actual returns.

Solution to Task-Based Simulation 3

Sampling Terminology		
	Authoritative Literature	**Help**

	(A)	(B)	(C)	(D)	(E)	(F)	(G)	(H)	(I)	(J)	(K)	(L)	(M)	(N)
1. Allowance for sampling risk	○	○	○	○	○	●	○	○	○	○	○	○	○	○
2. Deviation rate	○	●	○	○	○	○	○	○	○	○	○	○	○	○
3. Discovery sampling	○	○	○	●	○	○	○	○	○	○	○	○	○	○
4. Projected misstatement	○	○	○	○	○	○	●	○	○	○	○	○	○	○
5. Reliability	○	○	○	○	○	○	○	●	○	○	○	○	○	○
6. Risk of assessing control risk too low	○	○	○	○	○	○	○	○	○	●	○	○	○	○
7. Risk of incorrect acceptance	○	○	○	○	○	○	○	○	○	○	○	○	●	○
8. Sampling risk	○	○	○	○	○	○	○	○	○	○	○	○	○	●
9. Tolerable deviation rate	○	○	○	○	○	○	○	○	●	○	○	○	○	○

Solution to Task-Based Simulation 4

Accounts Payable Misstatements		
	Authoritative Literature	**Help**

Misstatement	Column B Audit procedure used to detect misstatement	Column C Internal control that could prevent or detect misstatement in the future
1. An accounts payable clerk misplaces year-end invoices for raw materials that were received on December 21, year 2, and therefore liabilities were not recorded.	6	1
2. The company tends to be careless in recording payables in the correct period.	1	9
3. The company has the same person approving pay requests and cutting checks.	9	8
4. The company's receiving department misplaces receiving reports for purchases of raw materials at year-end and therefore liabilities were not recorded.	4	2

Explanations

1. (6,1) *Audit procedure.* The audit procedure must identify situations in which there should be invoices, but are not. Item 6 will accomplish this since one would expect that when a receiving report has been prepared, an invoice will either be available or will soon be available from the supplier. When one is not present, it may have been misplaced.

Internal control. The monthly list will include the purchase order and receiving reports and will lead to question as to why an invoice is not present.

2. (1,9) *Audit procedure.* An examination of disbursements after year-end will reveal situations in which payables that should have been recorded prior to year-end were not recorded until subsequent to year-end.

Internal control. A clerk that effectively matches purchase orders with receiving reports should make certain that purchases are recorded on a timely basis. Information on the purchase orders (shipping details) and receiving reports (the date for FOB destination items) will allow the clerk to determine which period the accounting entry should be reported in.

3. (9,8)

> NOTE: Although it is possible that the control deficiency described here will lead to a misstatement, such misstatement is not obvious here based on the description.

Audit procedure (to identify the control deficiency). The auditor may identify a situation such as this by performing a walk-through of transactions as it will become obvious that both functions are performed by the same individual.

Internal control. Rotating responsibilities, and having individuals perform the different responsibilities is an effective control.

4. (4,2) *Audit procedure.* Identifying open purchase orders and vendors' invoices will reveal a situation in which one would expect a receiving report to have been prepared. Note that misplacement of a receiving report might result in no preparation of a sales invoice, thus the open purchase order might also identify this situation.

Internal control. The accounts payable supervisor's review of open purchase orders and vendors' invoices should detect this through follow-up with the receiving department.

Solution to Task-Based Simulation 5

Report Types		
	Authoritative Literature	Help

1. **(A)** A standard unmodified (unqualified) audit report should be issued.

2. (**F**) Either a qualified or an adverse opinion is required. Valuation of assets at appraised values is not in accordance with generally accepted accounting principles. Since the difference between appraised value and cost is significant, an unmodified (unqualified) opinion would not be appropriate.

3. (**G**) A scope limitation results in either a qualified opinion or a disclaimer of opinion.

4. (**G**) As is (c), this is a scope limitation and either a qualified opinion or a disclaimer of opinion is appropriate.

5. (**F**) An adverse or a qualified opinion is necessary. The CPA firm has acquired sufficient competent evidence to the effect that the investments in stock of subsidiary companies are overstated. Note disclosure does not compensate for improper balance sheet presentation.

Solution to Task-Based Simulation 6

Impact of Adjusting Entries		
	Authoritative Literature	Help

Impact of adjusting journal entries on the inventory turnover ratio	Company errors	Impact of adjusting journal entries on the return on equity ratio
Decreases	1. Inventory stored at a distribution center on December 31, year 2, was inadvertently omitted during the year 2 physical inventory count, to which the general ledger was adjusted.	Increases
Increases	2. During the physical inventory, the company included inventory that it was holding on consignment.	Decreases
Decreases	3. The company failed to record the materials in transit accrual for late supplier/vendor invoices.	Increases
No impact	4. The company declared and paid a cash dividend on December 30, year 2, but failed to record the transaction in year 2.	Increases

The ratios involved are

$$\text{Inventory Turnover} = \frac{\text{Cost of goods sold}}{\text{Inventory}}$$

$$\text{Return on Equity} = \frac{\text{Net income}}{\text{Owners' equity}}$$

1. Appropriate journal entry:

Inventory
    Cost of goods sold

Inventory turnover. The ratio will decrease because the journal entry decreases the numerator and increases the denominator. Solely for illustrative purposes, assume that cost of goods sold was 438, and inventory 100 to obtain the 4.38 ratio provided. If the misstatement is for 20, the ratio will become $(438 - 20) / (100 + 20) = 418 / 120 = 3.48$. Note that any numbers which approximate the beginning ratio that was provided may be used; similarly, any reasonable adjustment may be used to adjust those numbers (e.g., unreasonable would be an adjustment resulting in a ratio with negative numbers).

Return on equity. In this situation both the numerator (net income) and the denominator (owners' equity) increase by the same amount. An equal increase in the numerator and denominator of a ratio that is less than one results in an increase in the overall ratio. For example, rounding the ratio to 17%, assume the ratio is 17 / 100. If the same number is added to the ratio (say, 10) the ratio increases as ® $(17 + 10) / (100 + 10) = 27 / 100$ @ 25%).

2. Appropriate journal entry

> Cost of Goods Sold
>> Inventory

Inventory turnover. Increases because the numerator increases and the denominator decreases.

Return on equity. Decreases because net income decreases (through an increase in cost of goods sold) and the denominator decreases by the same amount. An equal decrease in the numerator and denominator of a ratio that is less than one results in a decrease in the overall ratio. You may wish to convince yourself of this through use of an example.

3. As presented, this question is subject to interpretation as it is unclear whether goods had been received and included in the year-end count, and whether the process resulted in recording or modification of any journal entry. We include three possible interpretations, only the first of which provides the two answers that were released by the AICPA.

Assumed Situation 1: Inventory not received or included in count, but an entry recording inventory (purchases) and accounts payable was recorded. In this situation the company in essence debited purchases (inventory) and credited accounts payable. The inventory count did not include the goods since they were in transit and in essence was reduced to those on hand, with the payable remaining recorded. If this is the case, the appropriate journal entry is

> Inventory
>> Cost of goods sold

Inventory turnover. Decreases because the numerator decreases and the denominator increases.

Return on equity. Increases because both numerator increases and the denominator increase by the amount of the increase in income.

Assumed Situation 2: Inventory not received or included in count, no entry recorded. In this situation the correcting entry is

> Inventory
>> Accounts payable

Inventory turnover. Decreases because the denominator increases.

Return on equity. No impact because neither net income nor owners' equity changes.

Assumed Situation 3: Inventory received and included in count, no entry recorded. In this situation the correcting entry is

> Cost of goods sold
>> Accounts payable

Inventory turnover. Increases because the numerator increases.

Return on equity. Decreases because the numerator and denominator decrease by the same amount.

4. Appropriate journal entry

> Retained earnings
>> Dividends payable

Inventory turnover. No impact because neither the numerator nor the denominator is affected.

Return on equity. Increases because the denominator decreases (retained earnings decreases).

Solution to Task-Based Simulation 7

	(A) (B) (C) (D) (E) (F) (G) (H)
1. Which section of the Professional Standards addresses this issue and will be helpful in responding to the CEO?	● ○ ○ ○ ○ ○ ○ ○

2. Enter the exact section and paragraph with helpful information.

AU	560	13

Appendix B: Sample Auditing and Attestation Testlet Released by AICPA

1. According to the profession's ethical standards, an auditor would be considered independent in which of the following instances?

   a. The auditor is the officially appointed stock transfer agent of a client.

   b. The auditor's checking account that is fully insured by a federal agency is held at a client financial institution.

   c. The client owes the auditor fees for more than two years prior to the issuance of the audit report.

   d. The client is the only tenant in a commercial building owned by the auditor.

1. **(b)** The requirement is to identify the instance in which an auditor would be considered independent. Answer (b) is correct because per ET 191.140–.141 the auditor's independence would not be impaired, provided the checking accounts, etc. are fully insured by an appropriate deposit insurance agency. Answer (a) is incorrect because per ET 191.077–.078 an auditor's independence would be impaired since the function of a transfer agent is considered equivalent to that of a member of management. Answer (c) is incorrect because per ET 191.103–.104 an auditor's independence is considered to be impaired if, when the report on the client's current year is issued, fees remain unpaid, whether billed or unbilled, for professional services provided more than one year prior to the date of the report. Answer (d) is incorrect because per ET 191.58 leasing property to a client results in an indirect financial interest in that client. Therefore, an auditor's independence would be considered to be impaired if the indirect financial interest in a client is material to the auditor.

2. Which of the following characteristics most likely would heighten an auditor's concern about the risk of material misstatements in an entity's financial statements?

   a. The entity's industry is experiencing declining customer demand.

   b. Employees who handle cash receipts are **not** bonded.

   c. Bank reconciliations usually include in-transit deposits.

   d. Equipment is often sold at a loss before being fully depreciated.

2. **(a)** The requirement is to identify the characteristic that would likely heighten an auditor's concern about the risk of material misstatements in an entity's financial statements. Answer (a) is correct because the professional standards indicate that a declining industry with increasing business failures and significant declines in customer demand is a risk factor relating to misstatements arising from fraudulent financial reporting. Answer (b) is incorrect because bonding will not necessarily affect the risk of material misstatements. Answer (c) is incorrect because many bank reconciliations ordinarily include in-transit deposits and this does not necessarily increase the risk of material misstatement. Answer (d) is incorrect because equipment sold at a loss may often occur (as may gains) and not necessarily affect the risk of material misstatement.

3. Which of the following fraudulent activities most likely could be perpetrated due to the lack of effective internal controls in the revenue cycle?

   a. Fictitious transactions may be recorded that cause an understatement of revenues and an overstatement of receivables.

   b. Claims received from customers for goods returned may be intentionally recorded in other customers' accounts.

   c. Authorization of credit memos by personnel who receive cash may permit the misappropriation of cash.

   d. The failure to prepare shipping documents may cause an overstatement of inventory balances.

3. **(c)** The requirement is to identify the fraudulent activity most likely to be perpetrated due to the lack of effective internal control over the revenue cycle. Answer (c) is correct because the authorization of credit memos by personnel who receive cash presents a situation in which those individuals may issue fraudulent credit memos and misappropriate the cash. Answer (a) is incorrect because one would expect such fictitious transactions to overstate both revenues and receivables; note that the situation described in answer (a) with an understatement of revenues and an overstatement of receivables results in two debits and no credits. Answer (b) is incorrect because recording such claims in the wrong account is likely to be quickly detected when customers who have not received the credit complain. Answer (d) is incorrect because such an overstatement of inventory balances is likely to be detected through an inventory observation.

4. In planning an audit, the auditor's knowledge about the design of relevant controls should be used to

a. Identify the types of potential misstatements that could occur.
b. Assess the operational efficiency of internal control.
c. Determine whether controls have been circumvented by collusion.
d. Document the assessed level of control risk.

4. **(a)** The requirement is to determine how the auditor's knowledge about the design of relevant controls is used in planning an audit. Answer (a) is correct because such knowledge is used to (1) identify types of potential misstatements, (2) consider factors that affect the risk of material misstatements, and (3) design substantive tests. Answer (b) is incorrect because auditors are more concerned with identifying types of potential misstatements not detected by internal control rather than with assessing its operational efficiency. Answer (c) is incorrect because while auditors are concerned with whether controls are circumvented by collusion, this is not the primary emphasis during planning and is less complete than answer (a). Answer (d) is incorrect because documentation during planning emphasizes the auditor's understanding of the entity's internal control.

5. Which of the following information discovered during an audit most likely would raise a question concerning possible illegal acts?

a. Related-party transactions, although properly disclosed, were pervasive during the year.
b. The entity prepared several large checks payable to cash during the year.
c. Material internal control weaknesses previously reported to management were **not** corrected.
d. The entity was a campaign contributor to several local political candidates during the year.

5. **(b)** The requirement is to identify the information that most likely would raise a question concerning possible illegal acts. Answer (b) is correct because such large checks payable to cash raise a question as to their actual business purpose. Answer (a) is incorrect because the mere existence of **properly disclosed** related-party transactions is less likely to indicate an illegal act than are checks written to cash. Answer (c) is incorrect because management may, for valid reasons, choose to not correct material internal control weaknesses. Answer (d) is incorrect because such campaign contributions may well be legal.

6. During an engagement to review the financial statements of a nonissuer (nonpublic) entity, an accountant becomes aware that several leases that should be capitalized are not capitalized. The accountant considers these leases to be material to the financial statements. The accountant decides to modify the standard review report because management will not capitalize the leases. Under these circumstances, the accountant should

a. Issue an adverse opinion because of the departure from GAAP.
b. Express **no** assurance of any kind on the entity's financial statements.
c. Emphasize that the financial statements are for limited use only.
d. Disclose the departure from GAAP in a separate paragraph of the accountant's report.

6. **(d)** The requirement is to determine an accountant's reporting responsibility when associated with a nonissuer (nonpublic) entity's **reviewed** statements which contain a material departure from generally accepted accounting principles. Answer (d) is correct because AR 100 requires the inclusion of a separate paragraph describing the departure. Answer (a) is incorrect because an adverse opinion may only be issued when an audit has been performed. Answer (b) is incorrect because a review report provides negative assurance, not **no** assurance. Answer (c) is incorrect because a review report is ordinarily available for general distribution, and need not emphasize that the financial statements are for limited use only.

Task-Based Simulation 1

Enright Corporation is a **nonissuer (nonpublic)** manufacturer of golf balls, golf clubs, and other golf-related equipment. The company has been in business for over fifty years and has its headquarters in San Diego, California.

Enright is divided into two divisions, which represent the major markets for the company's products. One division focuses on new golf clubs and resorts, and providing them with all of the necessary golf equipment to begin operations. The other division focuses on new product development and helps existing golf clubs and resorts to upgrade their existing equipment. Currently, each division accounts for approximately equal amounts of Enright's revenues and net income.

The company experienced its second most profitable year in 20X2. However, the financial results did not meet management's expectations. Total reported revenues for the year decreased three percent compared to the prior year. Management recognizes the fact that domestic sales growth has slowed significantly in recent years. As a result, the company is now adopting a global focus for marketing its products and is looking to open up new markets in Australia and Japan.

In order to be competitive in world markets, as well as to improve their domestic market share, management believes that they must strictly control costs and make their overall operations more efficient. At the end of 20X2, Enright announced it would make a series of restructuring changes as part of its overall business plan for the future.

Senior management at the company has experienced a significant turnover in recent years. The CEO has been with the company for only two years. He was hired from a major competitor after the prior CEO left to take a position with a large manufacturing company in the Northeast. In addition, the company's long-time CFO retired after twenty-five years of service. The current CFO was hired six months ago. She is a former audit manager from the office that works on Enright's annual audit.

Enright has engaged the same auditing firm for its annual audits for the past decade. There have been no disagreements over accounting issues in any of the past three years.

Financial Statements

Enright Corporation
BALANCE SHEET
December 31, 20X2 and 20X1

	12/31/X2	12/31/X1
Assets		
Current assets		
Cash and cash equivalents	$300,000	$235,000
Receivables—net	750,000	816,000
Investments	600,000	545,000
Inventory	1,000,000	1,171,000
Total current assets	2,650,000	2,767,000
Plant and equipment—net	850,000	876,000
Total assets	$3,500,000	$3,643,000
Liabilities and Stockholders' Equity		
Current liabilities		
Accounts payable	$390,000	$410,000
Current portion of long-term debt	620,000	620,000
Other current liabilities	315,000	298,000
Total current liabilities	1,325,000	1,328,000
Long-term debt	475,000	1,095,000
Total liabilities	1,800,000	2,423,000
Stockholders' equity		
Common stock	1,000,000	1,000,000
Retained earnings	700,000	220,000
Total stockholders' equity	1,700,000	1,220,000
Total liabilities and stockholders' equity	$3,500,000	$3,643,000

Enright Corporation
INCOME STATEMENT
For the Years Ended December 31, 20X2 and 20X1

	12/31/X2	12/31/X1
Sales	$5,250,000	$5,450,000
Cost of goods sold:	2,100,000	2,209,000
Gross profits on sales	3,150,000	3,241,000
Expenses		
Selling expenses	$1,050,000	$1,124,000
General and administrative	1,070,000	1,215,000
Other operating expenses		
Depreciation	30,000	35,000
Interest expense	200,000	227,000
Total expenses	$2,350,000	$2,601,000
Income before taxes	$800,000	$640,000
Provision for income taxes	320,000	256,000
Net income	$ 480,000	$ 384,000

Enright Corporation
STATEMENT OF CASH FLOWS
For the Year Ended December 31, 20X2

Cash flows from operating activities:	
Net income (loss)	$480,000
Adjustments to reconcile net income (loss) to cash provided by (used for) operating activities	
Depreciation and amortization	30,000
Changes in certain assets and liabilities:	
Decrease (increase) in receivables	66,000
Decrease (increase) in inventory	171,000
Increase (decrease) in accounts payable	(20,000)
Increase (decrease) in other current liabilities	17,000
Net cash provided by (used for) operating activities	744,000
Cash flows from investing activities:	
Purchase of property, plant, and equipment	(4,000)
Change in short-term investments	(55,000)
Net cash provided by (used for) investing activities	(59,000)
Cash flows from financing activities:	
Principal payments on long-term debt	(620,000)
Net cash provided by (used for) financing activities	(620,000)
Net increase (decrease) in cash and cash equivalents	65,000
Cash and cash equivalents at beginning of year	235,000
Cash and cash equivalents at end of year	$300,000

Industry Information

Market Forecasts

    In 20X7, the USA sports equipment market is forecast to reach $47 million, an increase of 19.3% since 20X2.
The compounded annual growth rate of the global sports equipment market over the period 20X2–20X7 is predicted to be 3.5%.

Table 4: USA Sports Equipment Market Value Forecasts: $Mn (20X1 Prices), 20X2–20X7

Market value	$Mn (20X1 prices)	% Growth
20X2	$40,133	2.9%
20X3	$41,398	3.2%
20X4	$42,936	3.7%
20X5	$44,389	3.4%
20X6	$46,232	4.2%
20X7	$46,892	3.6%

    Sales of golf clubs and related equipment declined about 6% in wholesale dollars in 20X1, with most of the decease being due to a decrease in the sales of irons. The country's weak economy which began in 20X1, continues to be weak in 20X2 and is expected to result in further slight sales declines.

    The total number of golfers grew by 5%, from 28.9 million for the period ending on 20X0. New course development was flat in 20X1, with approximately 200 construction projects completed through the first nine months, compared to approximately 400 in each of the preceding two years.

    Some experienced golfers are trying to increase the number of very young players. A small but national tournament for players aged four to twelve was first offered in 20X1 and has met with moderate success. Major equipment manufacturers are marketing youth-sized clubs and a few facilities are developing training programs for children once considered too young to play the game.

(A) (B) (C) (D)

1.   Which of the following correctly identifies an aspect of the company's business model, strategies,   ○ ○ ○ ○
   and operating environment that is most likely to increase audit risk?

    A. Attracting very young players.
    B. The turnover of senior management in recent years.

C. The company's result in the current year of its second most profitable year in over fifty years of operations.

D. The company's organization into two divisions, which represent the major markets for the company's products.

The table below presents several ratios that were identified as significant in the current and prior year's audits of Enright. Compare the values for each ratio. Then double-click on each of the shaded spaces in the table and select a possible audit finding that could account for the 20X2 value. For each ratio, you should select an audit finding that is consistent with these metrics. Each audit finding may be used once, more than once, or not at all. (Turnover ratios are based on year-end balances.)

Audit findings

A. The company uses a periodic inventory system for determining the balance sheet amount of inventory.

B. The company accumulated excess inventories that are physically deteriorating or are becoming obsolete.

C. Merchandise was received, placed in the stockroom, and counted, but not included in the year-end count.

D. A smaller percentage of sales occurred during the last month of the year, as compared to the prior year.

E. A dividend declared prior to the end of the year was not recorded in the general ledger.

F. A dividend declared prior to the end of the year was recorded twice in the general ledger.

	Ratio	20X2	20X1	(A)	(B)	(C)	(D)	(E)	(F)
1.	Inventory turnover	2.1	1.9	○	○	○	○	○	○
2.	Return on equity	28.2%	31.5%	○	○	○	○	○	○

Solution to Task-Based Simulation 1

Risk and Audit Findings		
	Authoritative Literature	Help

		(A)	(B)	(C)	(D)
1.	Which of the following correctly identifies an aspect of the company's business model, strategies, and operating environment that is most likely to increase audit risk?	○	●	○	○

Explanation

1. (B) The requirement is to identify the aspect of a company's business that is most likely to increase audit risk. Answer (B) is correct because turnover of senior management frequently signals a higher level of audit risk both because in some circumstances the reasons for turnover raise questions, and because of inexperience of new top management. Answer (A) is incorrect because attracting very young players is likely to increase sales through purchases made by young people and has no necessary tie to audit risk. Answer (C) is incorrect because simply having the second most profitable year doesn't make the information seem likely to indicate a misstatement. Answer (D) is incorrect because an organization with two divisions represents no major difficulty for the audit, and does not ordinarily increase audit risk.

Industry Information

	Ratio	20X2	20X1	(A)	(B)	(C)	(D)	(E)	(F)
1.	Inventory turnover	2.1	1.9	○	○	●	○	○	○
2.	Return on equity	28.2%	31.5%	○	○	○	○	●	○

Explanations

1. (C) The requirement is to identify an explanation for an increase in the inventory turnover—the ratio of cost of goods sold to inventory. Answer (C) is correct because while the inventory was received, it was not included in the final inventory count and the purchase was not recorded. Thus, the denominator of the ratio decreases, increasing the overall turnover.

2. (E) The requirement is to identify a possible reason for a decrease in the return on equity—net income divided by stockholders' equity. Answer (E) is correct because not recording a dividend that has been declared has the effect of overstating the denominator (owner's equity) and thereby reducing the overall return rate.

Task-Based Simulation 2

Audit Procedures		
	Authoritative Literature	Help

The auditor determines that each of the following objectives will be part of Enright's audit. For each audit objective, select a substantive procedure that would help to achieve the audit objectives by double-clicking on each shaded space and selecting a procedure. Each of the procedures may be used once, more than once, or not at all.

Substantive procedures

A. Review minutes of board of director's meetings and contracts, and make inquiries of management.
B. Test inventory transactions between a preliminary physical inventory date and the balance sheet date.
C. Obtain confirmation of inventories pledged under loan agreement.
D. Review perpetual inventory records, production records, and purchasing records for indication of current activity.
E. Reconcile physical counts to perpetual records and general ledger balances and investigate significant fluctuation.
F. Examine sales after year-end and open purchase order commitments.
G. Examine paid vendors' invoices, consignment agreements, and contracts.
H. Analytically review and compare the relationship of inventory balance to recent purchasing, production, and sales activity.

Objective	(A)	(B)	(C)	(D)	(E)	(F)	(G)	(H)
1. Confirm that inventories represent items held for sale or use in the normal course of business.	O	O	O	O	O	O	O	O
2. Confirm that the inventory listing is accurately completed and the totals are properly included in the inventory accounts.	O	O	O	O	O	O	O	O

Solution to Task-Based Simulation 2

Audit Procedures		
	Authoritative Literature	Help

	(A)	(B)	(C)	(D)	(E)	(F)	(G)	(H)
1. Confirm that inventories represent items held for sale or use in the normal course of business.	O	O	O	●	O	O	O	O
2. Confirm that the inventory listing is accurately completed and the totals are properly included in the inventory accounts.	O	O	O	O	●	O	O	O

Explanations

1. (D) The requirement is to identify the best substantive procedure to confirm that inventories represent items held for sale or use in the normal course of business. Answer (D) is best because a review of perpetual inventory records, production records, and purchasing records for indication of current activity will reveal whether those items are being sold.

2. (E) The requirement is to identify the best substantive procedure to confirm that the inventory listing is accurately completed and the totals are properly included in the inventory counts. Answer (E) is correct because reconciling physical counts to perpetual records and general ledgers balances and investigating significant fluctuations will identify errors in totals.

Appendix C: 2013 Released AICPA Questions for Auditing and Attestation

1. Which of the following types of audit evidence provides the **least** assurance of reliability?

   a. Receivable confirmations received from the client's customers.

   b. Prenumbered receiving reports completed by the client's employees.

   c. Prior months' bank statements obtained from the client.

   d. Municipal property tax bills prepared in the client's name.

2. An auditor is considering whether the omission of the confirmation of investments impairs the auditor's ability to support a previously expressed unmodified opinion. The auditor need **not** perform this omitted procedure if

   a. The results of alternative procedures that were performed compensate for the omission.

   b. The auditor's assessed level of detection risk is low.

   c. The omission is documented in a communication with the audit committee.

   d. No individual investment is material to the financial statements taken as a whole.

3. Which of the following explanations most likely would satisfy an auditor who questions management about significant debits to accumulated depreciation accounts in the current year?

   a. Prior years' depreciation expenses were erroneously understated.

   b. Current year's depreciation expense was erroneously understated.

   c. The estimated remaining useful lives of plant assets were revised upward.

   d. Plant assets were retired during the current year.

1. **(b)** The requirement is to identify the type of audit evidence that provides the least assurance of reliability. Answer (b) is correct because audit evidence obtained from nonindependent employees of the client is ordinarily considered to provide a lower level of evidence, as compared to the other replies. Answer (a) is incorrect because audit evidence obtained from knowledgeable independent sources outside the client's company is ordinarily considered more reliable than evidence obtained from nonindependent sources (e.g., client employees). Answer (c) is incorrect because bank statements are prepared externally, and such externally generated documents are ordinarily considered more reliable than internally generated documents or inquiries of nonindependent sources. Answer (d) is incorrect because a property tax bill is prepared externally and considered more reliable than internally created documents or inquiries of nonindependent sources.

2. **(a)** The requirement is to identify the situation in which an auditor need not perform an omitted audit procedure when an audit report has been issued. Answer (a) is correct because in such a circumstance an auditor will first assess the importance of the omitted procedure(s) to the audit opinion that was issued: here, since appropriate alternative procedures were performed, the confirmation of investments is unnecessary. Answer (b) is incorrect because it is less precise than answer (a) and it does not make clear whether the assessed level of detection risk is appropriate given the omission of the confirmation of investments. Answer (c) is incorrect because communication to the audit committee, in and of itself, is inadequate. Answer (d) is incorrect because the combination of all of the investments may be material.

3. **(d)** The requirement is to identify the most satisfactory explanation relating to significant debits to accumulated depreciation accounts in the current year. Answer (d) is correct because when plant assets are retired, the accumulated depreciation is closed to zero with a debit equal to its credit balance. Answer (a) is incorrect because a debit to the account would decrease accumulated depreciation and although this might be appropriate when depreciation expense is overstated, it is not when depreciation expense is understated. Answer (b) is incorrect because, as is the case with answer (a), a credit to accumulated depreciation would be appropriate. Answer (c) in incorrect because no adjustment to accumulated depreciation will occur for a change in useful life of the plant assets.

4. An auditor has substantial doubt about the entity's ability to continue as a going concern for a reasonable period of time because of negative cash flows and working capital deficiencies. Under these circumstances, the auditor would be most concerned about the

a. Control environment factors that affect the organizational structure.
b. Correlation of detection risk and inherent risk.
c. Effectiveness of the entity's internal control activities.
d. Possible effects on the entity's financial statements.

4. **(d)** The requirement is to identify what an auditor would be most concerned about when that auditor has substantial doubt about an entity's ability to continue as a going concern because of negative cash flows and working capital deficiencies. Answer (d) is correct because when the auditor has concluded that such substantial doubt exists, the auditor should determine whether the entity's financial statement's disclosures are adequate—if not, a departure from GAAP exists. Answers (a) and (c) are incorrect because the difficulty here is the negative cash flows and working capital deficiencies more than concern over internal control. Answer (b) is incorrect because any correlation between detection risk and inherent risk is unlikely to directly affect the going concern judgment.

5. Subsequent to issuing a report on audited financial statements, a CPA discovers that the accounts receivable confirmation process omitted a number of accounts that are material, in the aggregate. Which of the following actions should the CPA take immediately?

a. Bring the matter to the attention of the board of directors or audit committee.
b. Withdraw the auditor's report from those persons currently relying on it.
c. Perform alternative procedures to verify account balances.
d. Discuss the potential financial statement adjustments with client management.

5. **(c)** The requirement is to determine a CPA's responsibility when, subsequent to issuing a report on audited financial statements, that CPA discovers that the accounts receivable confirmation process omitted a number of accounts that, in aggregate, are material. Answer (c) is correct because the CPA should assess the importance of the omitted procedures to the audit opinion, and if considered important, should attempt to perform the omitted procedures or appropriate alternative procedures. Answer (a) is incorrect because while bringing the matter to the attention of the board of directors or audit committee is ordinarily appropriate, it generally would occur subsequent to attempting to perform alternative procedures. Answer (b) is incorrect because any decision to withdraw the auditor's report would occur subsequent to an attempt to perform alternative procedures. Answer (d) is incorrect because there is, at this point, no evidence that financial statement adjustments are necessary.

6. An entity engaged an accountant to review its financial statements in accordance with Statements on Standards for Accounting and Review Services. The accountant determined that the entity maintained its accounts on a comprehensive basis of accounting other than generally accepted accounting principles (GAAP). In this situation, the accountant most likely would have taken which of the following actions?

a. Withdrawn from the engagement because the entity has **not** been following GAAP.
b. Advised management to make the adjustments necessary for the account balances to conform with GAAP.
c. Modified the review report to reflect the fact that the financial statements were presented on another comprehensive basis of accounting.
d. Requested that management justify the use of the other comprehensive basis of accounting in the management representation letter.

6. **(c)** The requirement is to identify an auditor's responsibility when reviewing financial statements prepared in accordance with a basis of accounting other than GAAP. Answer (c) is correct because a client may follow such a basis (e.g., cost basis or tax basis) and an accountant may report on whether those financial statements follow that basis: the review report should include a disclosure that a basis of accounting other than GAAP is being followed. Answer (a) is incorrect since such an engagement may be performed. Answer (b) is incorrect because management may follow such a basis in the preparation of its financial statements and need not adjust them to GAAP. Answer (d) is incorrect because no such justification is necessary.

7. Which of the following factors should an external auditor obtain updated information about when assessing an internal auditor's competence?

    a. The reporting status of the internal auditor within the organization.

    b. The educational level and professional experiences of the internal auditor.

    c. Whether policies prohibit the internal auditor from auditing areas where relatives are employed.

    d. Whether the board of directors, audit committee, or owner-manager oversees employment decisions related to the internal auditor.

7. **(b)** The requirement is to identify the information an external auditor should consider when assessing an internal auditor's competence. Answer (b) is correct because in assessing competence, the external auditors consider the educational level, professional experience, and professional certifications of the internal audit staff; they may also investigate internal auditors' policies, programs, procedures, working papers, etc. Answer (a) is incorrect because reporting status of the internal auditor relates more to internal auditor independence than competence. Answer (c) is incorrect because policies on internal auditor relatives relate to internal auditor independence. Answer (d) is incorrect because the overseeing of employment decisions is likely to have an effect on the competence of internal auditors hired; it is a less complete answer than (b).

8. An auditor traces the serial numbers on equipment to a nonissuer's subledger. Which of the following management assertions is supported by this test?

    a. Valuation and allocation.

    b. Completeness.

    c. Rights and obligations.

    d. Presentation and disclosure.

8. **(b)** The requirement is to identify the management assertion addressed when an auditor traces the serial numbers on equipment to a client's equipment subledger. Answer (b) is correct because completeness addresses whether "all" equipment was properly recorded; here, if the equipment is on hand, it should be recorded as an asset if the client owns it. Answer (a) is incorrect because valuation addresses the value of the equipment, which is not directly addressed here. Answer (c) is incorrect because rights and obligations would be tested by vouching in the opposite direction to support ownership—vouching from the subledger to source documents. Answer (d) is incorrect because presentation and disclosure relates to classification and adequate disclosure issues.

9. Which of the following should a practitioner perform as part of an engagement for agreed-upon procedures in accordance with Statements on Standards for Attestation Engagements?

    a. Issue a report on findings based on specified procedures performed.

    b. Assess whether the procedures meet the needs of the parties.

    c. Express negative assurance on findings of work performed.

    d. Report the differences between agreed-upon and audit procedures.

9. **(a)** The requirement is to identify the correct practitioner responsibility with respect to an agreed-upon procedures (AUP) engagement. Answer (a) is correct because a list of procedures performed and findings is included in an AUP engagement. Answer (b) is incorrect because the specified parties involved in the engagement determine the procedures they believe necessary to meet their needs, not the practitioner. Answer (c) is incorrect because a summary of findings, not negative assurance, is included in the report. Answer (d) is incorrect because no indication of the differences between agreed-upon procedures and audit procedures is included.

10. When the operating effectiveness of a control is **not** evidenced by written documentation, an auditor should obtain evidence about the control's effectiveness by

    a. Mailing confirmations.

    b. Inquiry and other procedures such as observation.

    c. Analytical procedures.

    d. Recalculating the balance in related accounts.

10. **(b)** The requirement is to identify the type of evidence on operating effectiveness that an auditor may gather when a control does not provide written documentation of having been performed. Answer (b) is correct because the professional standards indicate that procedures such as inquiry and observation are possible in such a situation. Answer (a) is incorrect because the confirmation process is ordinarily related to substantive procedures and not operating effectiveness of a control. Answer (c) is incorrect because analytical procedures ordinarily do not directly address operating effectiveness. Answer (d) is incorrect because recalculation often will not be possible as a test of a control—it will often be performed as a substantive procedure.

11. An auditor is evaluating a client's internal controls. Which of the following situations would be the most difficult internal control issue for an auditor to detect?

    a. The accounting staff neglects the control, due to increased transactions to be processed.

    b. The technology department writes a program that does **not** properly implement the control, due to a lack of understanding.

    c. Two employees, who work in different departments, are circumventing an internal control.

    d. Someone erroneously disables edit checks in a software program designed to identify control exceptions.

11. (c) The requirement is to identify a breakdown in internal control that would be difficult for the auditor to detect. Answer (c) is correct because collusion is often difficult to detect and when between two employees in different departments it may be even more so. Answer (a) is incorrect because while an auditor considers whether controls have been implemented such neglect may be identified; also, resulting errors in processing may become obvious throughout the audit. Answer (b) is incorrect because auditors must address implementation of controls. Answer (d) is incorrect because the auditor may identify resulting errors throughout the audit.

12. Inherent risk and control risk differ from detection risk in which of the following ways?

    a. Inherent risk and control risk are calculated by the client.

    b. Inherent risk and control risk exist independently of the audit.

    c. Inherent risk and control risk are controlled by the auditor.

    d. Inherent risk and control risk exist as a result of the auditor's judgment about materiality.

12. (b) The requirement is to identify a difference between inherent and control risk when compared to detection risk. Answer (b) is correct because inherent risk and control risk (their combination is referred to as the risk of material misstatement) are attributes of the client's environment while detection risk relates to the risk that an auditor's procedures will not detect a material misstatement. Answer (a) is incorrect because the auditor assesses inherent risk and control risk and then appropriately limits detection risk. Answer (c) is incorrect because inherent risk and control risk are assessed by the auditor, not controlled. Answer (d) is incorrect because inherent risk and control risk exist independently of the auditor.

13. Which of the following matters does an auditor usually include in the engagement letter?

    a. Arrangements regarding fees and billing.

    b. Analytical procedures that the auditor plans to perform.

    c. Indications of negative cash flows from operating activities.

    d. Identification of working capital deficiencies.

13. (a) The requirement is to identify the information ordinarily included in an engagement letter. Answer (a) is correct because an engagement letter will include information on fees and billing since that letter is in essence the contract for the audit. Overall, engagement letters should include (1) the objective and scope of the audit, (2) auditor and management responsibilities, (3) inherent limitations of an audit, (4) the applicable financial reporting framework (e.g., GAAP) and (5) the expected reports to be issued. Answer (b) is incorrect because such details on analytical procedures are not ordinarily included in an engagement letter. Answer (c) is incorrect because an engagement letter ordinarily will not include an analysis of cash flows. Answer (d) is incorrect because an engagement letter will not ordinarily include any discussion of working capital deficiencies.

14. Which of the following is an important consideration when deciding the nature of tests to use in a financial statement audit?

    a. Tests of details typically provide a low level of assurance.

    b. Analytical procedures are an inefficient means of obtaining assurance.

    c. The procedures to be applied on a particular engagement are a matter of the auditor's professional judgment.

    d. The use of tests of controls should be considered without regard to the level of assurance required.

14. (c) The requirement is to identify an important consideration in designing audit tests. Answer (c) is correct because differences between clients makes the exercise of professional judgment particularly important in auditing. Answer (a) is incorrect because tests of details will often provide a high level of assurance. Answer (b) is incorrect because analytical procedures may be particularly efficient in certain circumstances. Answer (d) is incorrect because tests of controls are performed when the auditor wishes to obtain audit evidence on the operating effectiveness of controls.

15. Which of the following procedures would an auditor most likely complete to test the existence assertion of property, plant and equipment?

    a. Obtaining a listing of all current-year additions, vouching significant additions to original invoices, and determining that they have been placed in service.

    b. Obtaining a detailed fixed-asset register and ensuring items are appropriately capitalized.

    c. Obtaining a listing of current-year additions and verifying that items are recorded in the proper period.

    d. Obtaining a detailed fixed-asset register and ensuring depreciation methods are applied consistently.

16. Which of the following is correct regarding a compilation of financial statements engagement in accordance with Statements on Standards for Accounting and Review Services?

    a. If the accountant's independence is impaired, a qualified opinion must be issued.

    b. The accountant may **not** base the report on information obtained from prior engagements with the same client.

    c. The accountant is **not** required to make inquiries **nor** perform procedures to corroborate the information provided by the client.

    d. The accountant should perform analytical procedures to financial data.

17. What is the primary objective of the fraud brainstorming session?

    a. Determine audit risk and materiality.

    b. Identify whether analytical procedures should be applied to the revenue accounts.

    c. Assess the potential for material misstatement due to fraud.

    d. Determine whether the planned procedures in the audit program will satisfy the general audit objectives.

18. While performing an audit of the financial statements of a company for the year ended December 31, year 1, the auditor notes that the company's sales increased substantially in December, year 1, with a corresponding decrease in January, year 2. In assessing the risk of fraudulent financial reporting or misappropriation of assets, what should be the auditor's initial indication about the potential for fraud in sales revenue?

    a. There is a broad indication of misappropriation of assets.

    b. There is an indication of theft of the entity's assets.

    c. There is an indication of embezzling receipts.

    d. There is a broad indication of financial reporting fraud.

15. **(a)** The requirement is to identify the audit procedure an auditor would perform to address the existence assertion of property, plant and equipment. Answer (a) is correct because vouching significant recorded additions to original invoices addresses whether those recorded additions actually exist. Answer (b) is incorrect because determining whether items are properly capitalized addresses valuation more than existence. Answer (c) is incorrect because while determining that additions are recorded in the proper period does address existence, it is a less complete answer than (a). Answer (d) is incorrect because the consistency of use of depreciation methods addresses valuation.

16. **(c)** The requirement is to identify the correct statement with respect to a compilation of financial statements. Answer (c) is correct because in a compilation an auditor is not required to make inquiries nor perform procedures to corroborate the information provided by the client; however, in circumstances when the accountant believes that the financial statements are materially misstated, the accountant should obtain additional or revised information. Answer (a) is incorrect because an accountant lacking independence so indicates in the compilation report—no opinion, qualified or otherwise, is included in a compilation report. Answer (b) is incorrect because in appropriate circumstances information obtained from prior engagements with that client may be used. Answer (d) is incorrect because analytical procedures are not required while performing a compilation.

17. **(c)** The requirement is to identify the primary objective of the fraud brainstorming session of an audit. Answer (c) is correct because the session is held to identify and assess the potential risks of material misstatement due to fraud. Answer (a) is incorrect because the session is aimed at fraud more directly than the overall topics of audit risk and materiality, although these issues may arise in the meeting. Answer (b) is incorrect as analytical procedures related to revenue accounts are required in all audits, and this is not the emphasis of the session. Answer (d) is incorrect because the session is aimed at fraud more than general audit objectives.

18. **(d)** The requirement is to determine an initial indication of potential fraud related to sales revenues which increase in December of year 1 and decrease in January of year 2. Answer (d) is correct because such a pattern may indicate that sales occurring in year 2 have fraudulently been included in year 1 totals. Answers (a), (b), and (c) are all incorrect because they all relate less directly to the unexpected relationship between recorded December and January sales revenue, the basis of the question. Also, given that one month seems overstated while the other understated, financial reporting fraud is more likely than misappropriation of assets [which (a), (b), and (c) are examples of].

19. According to the Sarbanes-Oxley Act of 2002, which of the following nonaudit services can be provided by a registered public accounting firm to the client contemporaneously with the audit when preapproval is granted by audit committee action?

    a. Internal audit outsourcing services.
    b. Tax services.
    c. Actuarial services related to the audit.
    d. Advice on financial information system design.

20. Which of the following situations would **not** impair objectivity, integrity, or independence with respect to an audit client?

    a. An auditor takes the client's audit committee to Las Vegas for the weekend.
    b. An out-of-town client takes the audit engagement team out to dinner at a renowned local restaurant.
    c. An auditor provides client management with box seats for the season at a major league baseball franchise.
    d. A client takes the audit engagement team on a two-day ski trip after the audit team worked for two consecutive weekends.

21. When a PCAOB auditing standard indicates that an auditor "could" perform a specific procedure, how should the auditor decide whether and how to perform the procedure?

    a. By comparing the PCAOB standard with related AICPA auditing standards.
    b. By exercising professional judgment in the circumstances.
    c. By soliciting input from the issuer's audit committee.
    d. By evaluating whether the audit is likely to be subject to inspection by the PCAOB.

22. While performing certain nonaudit services for an insurance company, a professional accountant is asked to recommend the appropriate accounting treatment for a weather hedge transaction. The accountant has worked with financial hedges but has no experience with weather hedges. Which of the following actions by the accountant would be in compliance with the IFAC Code of Ethics for Professional Accountants?

    a. Agree to recommend the appropriate accounting treatment after performing sufficient research on weather hedges.
    b. Refuse to conduct the research and make a recommendation, because of insufficient experience.
    c. Refuse to conduct the research and make a recommendation, because of a conflict of interest.
    d. Agree with the accounting treatment recommended by the company's hedge fund trader.

23. According to the SEC, members of an issuer's audit committee may **not**

    a. Establish procedures for employees to anonymously report fraud.
    b. Be responsible for the compensation of any registered public accounting firm employed by the registrant to provide an audit report.
    c. Accept any consulting, advisory, or other compensatory fee from the registrant for services other than as a member of the board.
    d. Engage independent counsel as deemed necessary to carry out their duties.

19. (b) The requirement is to identify the nonaudit service allowed under the Sarbanes-Oxley Act of 2002. Answer (b) is correct because tax services are allowed. Section 201 of the Act prohibits internal audit outsourcing services [answer (a)], actuarial services [answer (c)] and advice on financial information system design [answer (d)].

20. (b) The requirement is to identify the situation that would not impair auditor objectivity, integrity or independence with respect to a client. Answer (b) is correct because a "reasonable gift" is permissible, and dinner is likely to be considered reasonable. Answer (a) is incorrect since it seems a costly, unreasonable gift. Answer (c) is incorrect because while box seats for a baseball game may be a reasonable gift, box seats for an entire season seems costly and unreasonable. Answer (d) is incorrect; this does not seem a reasonable gift for the audit engagement team to accept, particularly given its likely cost.

21. (b) The requirement is to identify auditor responsibility when a PCAOB auditing standard indicates that an auditor "could" perform a specific procedure. Answer (b) is correct because when the word "could" is used the auditor should use judgment to consider whether performing the procedure. Answer (a) is incorrect because such comparison of PCAOB and AICPA standards is not required. Answer (c) is incorrect because an auditor ordinarily will not solicit input from the issuer's audit committee on audit procedures to be followed. Answer (d) is incorrect because whether the audit is likely to be subject to inspection does not determine the meaning of "could."

22. (a) The requirement is to identify an auditor's responsibility under international ethical standards when asked to recommend an accounting treatment. Answer (a) is correct because the auditor may recommend the appropriate accounting treatment once he or she has conducted adequate research. Answers (b) and (c) are incorrect because the auditor need not refuse to conduct research or make a recommendation. Answer (d) is incorrect because the company's hedge fund trader may recommend inappropriate accounting.

23. (c) The requirement is to identify a restriction on members of an issuer's audit committee. Answer (c) is correct because members of the audit committee may not accept any consulting, advisory, or other compensatory fee from the registrant for service other than as a member of the board. Answer (a) is incorrect because audit committee members are charged with establishing or determining that the company has appropriate procedures for anonymously reporting fraud. Answer (b) is incorrect because audit committees are responsible for engagement and compensation of a company's public accounting firm. Answer (d) is incorrect because audit committee members may engage independent counsel.

24. Which of the following would **not** be included in an accountant's documentation of a compilation of a client's financial statements?

    a. Discussion with the client regarding the proper presentation of gross cash flows for investment purchases.

    b. An engagement letter.

    c. A memo to the CFO about a potentially significant fraud revealed during compilation procedures.

    d. A review of the segregation of duties in the cash disbursement process.

25. If requested to perform a compilation engagement for a nonissuer in which an accountant has an immaterial direct financial interest, the accountant is

    a. Independent because the financial interest in the nonissuer is immaterial.

    b. Not independent and, therefore, may **not** be associated with the financial statements.

    c. Not independent and, therefore, may **not** issue a compilation report.

    d. Not independent and, therefore, may issue a compilation report, but may **not** issue a review report.

26. When there has been a change in accounting principles, but the effect of the change on the comparability of the financial statements is **not** material, the auditor should

    a. Not refer to the change in the auditor's report.

    b. Refer to the note in the financial statements that discusses the change.

    c. Refer to the change in an emphasis-of-matter paragraph.

    d. Explicitly state whether the change conforms with GAAP.

27. An entity prepares its financial statements on the income tax basis. A description of how that basis differs from GAAP should be included in the

    a. Notes to the financial statements.

    b. Auditor's engagement letter.

    c. Management representation letter.

    d. Introductory paragraph of the auditor's report.

28. When an accountant compiles projected financial statements, the accountant's report should include a separate paragraph that

    a. Disclaims any form of assurance on the historical financial statements.

    b. Expresses limited assurance that the results will be within the projected range.

    c. Describes the limitations on the usefulness of the projection.

    d. Evaluates the hypothetical assumptions used to prepare the projection.

24. (d) The requirement is to identify the item that would not be documented in a compilation engagement letter. Answer (d) is correct because a compilation does not require a review of the segregation of duties. Answer (a) is incorrect because issues of proper presentation are discussed with the client. Answer (b) is incorrect because an engagement letter is required. Answer (c) is incorrect because suspected fraud must be revealed to management.

25. (d) The requirement is to determine the correct statement concerning an immaterial direct financial interest when performing a compilation. Answer (d) is correct because while the accountant is not independent, that accountant may perform a compilation, but not a review. Answer (a) is incorrect because even an immaterial direct financial interest impairs independence. Answers (b) and (c) are incorrect because an accountant who is not independent may perform a compilation.

26. (a) The requirement is to identify the effect on an audit report of a change in accounting principles with an immaterial effect on the financial statements. Answer (a) is correct because an accounting change with an immaterial effect need not be referred to in the audit report. Answer (b) is incorrect because the note is not referred to in the audit report. Answer (c) is incorrect because no emphasis-of-matter paragraph is added to the audit report. Answer (d) is incorrect because the change is not referred to.

27. (a) The requirement is to identify where a description of how the income tax basis of accounting differs from GAAP should be included. Answer (a) is correct because any such discussion will be in the notes to the financial statements. Answer (b) is incorrect because such a description is not ordinarily included in an engagement letter. Answer (c) is incorrect because the management representation letter will not ordinarily include such a discussion. Answer (d) is incorrect because while the auditor's report will refer to the basis, it will not discuss differences between it and GAAP.

28. (c) The requirement is to determine the information that leads to a separate paragraph in a compilation report on projected financial statements. Answer (c) is correct because the report requires a paragraph on limitations of the usefulness of the projection. Answer (a) is incorrect because no such paragraph is required relating to the historical financial statements. Answer (b) is incorrect because no assurance is provided in a compilation. Answer (d) is incorrect because the hypothetical assumptions are not evaluated in a separate paragraph to the compilation report.

29. Which of the following would be considered an analytical procedure?

    a. Testing purchasing, shipping, and receiving cutoff activities.

    b. Comparing inventory balances to recent sales activities.

    c. Projecting the deviation rate of a statistical sample to the population.

    d. Reconciling physical count to perpetual records and general ledger balances.

29. (b) The requirement is to identify an analytical procedure. Answer (b) is correct because analytical procedures involve evaluations of financial statement information by a study of relationships among financial and nonfinancial data—here the comparison of inventory balances with sales. Answer (a) is incorrect because procedures such as testing of purchasing, shipping and receiving are ordinarily considered tests of controls or substantive tests of details of transactions and balances. Answer (c) is incorrect because projecting a deviation rate is not an analytical procedure but a procedure used in summarizing the results of tests of controls. Answer (d) is incorrect because reconciling such counts to general ledger balances is most likely a substantive procedure.

30. Which of the following statements should be included in a practitioner's report on the application of agreed-upon procedures?

    a. A statement that the practitioner performed an examination of prospective financial statements.

    b. A statement of scope limitation that will qualify the practitioner's opinion.

    c. A statement referring to standards established by the AICPA.

    d. A statement of negative assurance based on procedures performed.

30. (c) The requirement is to identify the statement included in an agreed-upon procedures (AUP) report. Answer (c) is correct because such reports include a statement on the practitioner having followed standards established by the AICPA. Answer (a) is incorrect because the engagement is an AUP engagement, not an examination. Answer (b) is incorrect because no scope limitation is involved and because auditors only express an opinion as a result of an examination (audit). Answer (d) is incorrect because a summary of findings with no negative assurance is provided.

31. Which of the following documents the procedures that are applied and the conclusions reached in an audit engagement?

    a. Management representation letter.

    b. Audit guide.

    c. Auditor's report.

    d. Working papers.

31. (d) The requirement is to identify the document that includes the procedures that are applied and the conclusions reached in an audit engagement. Answer (d) is correct because audit working papers include that information. Answer (a) is incorrect because management's representation letter does not include audit procedures applied. Answer (b) is incorrect because while an audit guide may include discussion of various audit procedures, it does not relate to a particular audit engagement. Answer (c) is incorrect because the auditor's report does not include detailed information on the procedures applied.

32. When reviewing the financial statements of a nonissuer in accordance with Statements on Standards for Accounting and Review Services, an accountant's procedures should include

    a. Obtaining an understanding of internal control.

    b. Assessing fraud risk.

    c. Applying substantive tests of transactions.

    d. Inquiring into actions taken at meetings of the board of directors.

32. (d) The requirement is to identify the procedure included in a review. Answer (d) is correct because a review includes inquiry of actions taken at meetings of the board of directors as well as a variety of other inquiries and analytical procedures. Answer (a) is incorrect because a review under Statements on Standards for Accounting and Review Services does not include obtaining an understanding of internal control; note, however, that an interim review following either PCAOB or Statements on Auditing Standards does include such an understanding. Answer (b) is incorrect because a review does not include assessing fraud risk. Answer (c) is incorrect because reviews include inquiries and analytical procedures, not applying substantive test of transactions.

33. Which of the following rules of the AICPA Code of Professional Conduct must be observed even by a member who is **not** in public practice?

    a. Independence in Fact and Appearance.
    b. Integrity and Objectivity.
    c. Professional Competence.
    d. Compliance with Standards.

33. (b) The requirement is to identify the rule of the AICPA Code of Professional Conduct that must be observed even by a member who is not in public practice. Answer (b) is correct because integrity and objectivity are required in the performance of any professional service. Answer (a) is incorrect because independence is only required for engagements that result in a report which provides assurance (e.g., engagements performed under the attestation and auditing standards). Answer (c) is incorrect because the AICPA Code of Professional Conduct only requires professional competence for providing professional services, with professional services defined as all services performed by a member while holding out a CPA. Answer (d) is incorrect because the compliance with standards section applies to members who perform auditing, review, compilation, management consulting, tax or other professional services related to standards promulgated by bodies designated by AICPA Council.

34. A practitioner is engaged to express an opinion on management's assertion that the square footage of a warehouse offered for sale is 150,000 square feet. The practitioner should refer to which of the following sources for professional guidance?

    a. Statements on Auditing Standards.
    b. Statements on Standards for Attestation Engagements.
    c. Statements on Standards for Accounting and Review Services.
    d. Statements on Standards for Consulting Services.

34. (b) The requirement is to identify the source on standards relating to management's assertion that the square footage of a warehouse offered for sale is 150,000 square feet. Answer (b) is correct because the Statements on Standards for Attestation Engagements relate to such nonfinancial statement information. Answer (a) is incorrect because Statements on Auditing Standards relate to audits of historical financial statements on nonissuers. Answer (c) is incorrect because Statements on Standards for Accounting and Review Services relate to compilations and reviews of nonissuer historical financial statements. Answer (d) is incorrect because Statements on Standards for Consulting Services relate to consulting services.

35. Which of the following would a successor auditor ask the predecessor auditor to provide after accepting an audit engagement?

    a. Disagreements between the predecessor auditor and management as to significant accounting policies and principles.
    b. The predecessor auditor's understanding of the reasons for the change of auditors.
    c. Facts known to the predecessor auditor that might bear on the integrity of management.
    d. Matters that may facilitate the evaluation of financial reporting consistency between the current and prior years.

35. (d) The requirement is to identify the information a successor auditor would ask of a predecessor auditor after accepting an audit engagement. Answer (d) is correct because, after the engagement is accepted, the inquiry will focus upon such matters as a review of working papers related to opening balances and the consistency of application of accounting principles. Answers (a), (b), and (c) are all incorrect because they relate to a potential successor's inquiries prior to accepting the engagement.

36. Which of the following procedures should a user auditor include in the audit plan to create that most efficient audit when an audit client uses a service organization for several processes?

    a. Review that service auditor's report on controls placed in operations.
    b. Review the service auditor's report and outline the accounting system in a memo to the working papers
    c. Audit the service organization's controls, assess risk, and prepare the audit plan.
    d. Audit the service organization's controls to test the work of the service auditor.

36. (a) The requirement is to identify the procedure a user auditor should include in the audit plan to create the most efficient audit when an audit client uses a service organization for several processes. Answer (a) is correct because a user auditor will review the service auditor's report on controls placed in operation (implemented) to obtain information on the processes. Answer (b) is incorrect because the user auditor will not ordinarily outline the accounting system when a service auditor is involved—although it would be acceptable to do so. Answer (c) is incorrect because ordinarily the user auditor will use the service auditor's report rather than audit the service organization's controls. Answer (d) is incorrect because the user auditor ordinarily will not audit the service organization's controls to test the work of the service auditor.

37. Which of the following is a management assertion regarding account balances at the period end?

   a. Transactions and events that have been recorded have occurred and pertain to the entity.

   b. Transactions and events have been recorded in the proper accounts.

   c. The entity holds or controls the rights to assets, and liabilities are obligations of the entity.

   d. Amounts and other data related to transactions and events have been recorded appropriately.

37. (c) The requirement is to identify a management assertion regarding account balances. Answer (c) is correct because rights and obligations represents one of the account balance assertions (the other three are existence, completeness and valuation). Answer (a) is incorrect because transactions and events having been recorded is a transactions and events assertion. Answer (b) is incorrect because transactions and events having been recorded in the proper accounts (classification) is a transactions and events assertion. Answer (d) is incorrect because amounts and other data related to transactions and events having been recorded appropriately (accuracy) is a transaction and events assertion.

38. While performing interim audit procedures of accounts receivable, numerous unexpected errors are found resulting in a change of risk assessment. Which of the following audit responses would be most appropriate?

   a. Move detailed analytical procedures from year-end to interim.

   b. Increase the dollar threshold of vouching customer invoices.

   c. Send negative accounts receivable confirmations instead of positive accounts receivable confirmations.

   d. Use more experienced audit team members to perform year-end testing.

38. (d) The requirement is to identify the most appropriate response when numerous unexpected errors are found resulting in a change of the risk assessment relating to accounts receivable. Answer (d) is correct because more experienced team members performing year-end testing are likely to control the increased risk involved. Answer (a) is incorrect because performing tests at year-end is more likely to provide reliable evidence in such a situation. Answer (b) is incorrect because increasing the threshold of vouching customer invoices does not seem appropriate given the increased risks. Answer (c) is incorrect because negative accounts receivable are more appropriate under circumstances of good internal control and when small accounts are involved.

39. Which of the following types of risk increases when an auditor performs substantive analytical audit procedures for financial statement accounts at an interim date?

   a. Inherent.

   b. Control.

   c. Detection.

   d. Sampling.

39. (c) The requirement is to identify the type of risk that increases when an auditor performs substantive analytical procedures at an interim (rather than year-end) date. Answer (c) is correct since such procedures affect detection risk and performing them at an interim date increases that risk. Answer (a) is incorrect because inherent risk is not directly related to substantive procedures. Answer (b) is incorrect because the control risk assessment is affected by tests of controls, not substantive procedures. Answer (d) is incorrect because sampling risk is not involved here since no sample is being selected.

40. Which of the following matters relating to an entity's operations would an auditor most likely consider as an inherent risk factor in planning an audit?

   a. The entity's fiscal year ends on June 30.

   b. The entity enters into derivative transactions as hedges.

   c. The entity's financial statements are generated at an outside service center.

   d. The entity's financial data are available only in computer-readable form.

40. (b) The requirement is to determine which reply an auditor most likely would consider as an inherent risk factor in planning the audit. Answer (b) is correct since the nature of such derivative transactions is complex and subject to misstatement. Answer (a) is incorrect because the date of the fiscal year-end should not increase inherent risk. Answer (c) is incorrect because any risk related to use of an outside service center has more of an effect on control risk than inherent risk. Answer (d) is incorrect because availability of data in only a computer-readable form does not necessarily increase inherent risk.

41. Which of the following is a factor in the control environment?

   a. Segregation of duties.

   b. Information processing.

   c. Performance reviews.

   d. Management's philosophy and operating style.

41. (d) The requirement is to identify a factor in the control environment. Answer (d) is correct because under the Committee of Sponsoring Organizations' concept of internal control management's philosophy and operating style is encompassed. Answers (a), (b) and (c) are all incorrect because segregation of duties, information processing controls, and performance reviews are all included as control activities—a different component of the control environment.

42. Which of the following statements about audit sampling risks is correct for a nonissuer?

   a. Nonsampling risk arises from the possibility that, when a substantive test is restricted to a sample, conclusions might be different than if the auditor had tested each item in the population.

   b. Nonsampling risk can arise because an auditor failed to recognize misstatements.

   c. Sampling risk is derived from the uncertainty in applying audit procedures to specific risks.

   d. Sampling risk includes the possibility of selecting audit procedures that are **not** appropriate to achieve the specific objective.

43. An auditor of a nonissuer should design tests of details to ensure that sufficient audit evidence supports which of the following?

   a. The planned level of control risk.

   b. Management's assertions that internal controls exist and are operating efficiently.

   c. The effectiveness of internal controls.

   d. The planned level of assurance at the relevant assertion level.

44. Providing more supervision during an audit of a nonissuer in response to assessed risks of material misstatement at the financial statement level is an example of

   a. A substantive response.

   b. Further audit procedures.

   c. Tests of controls.

   d. An overall response.

45. The Public Company Accounting Oversight Board was established by which of the following?

   a. The Financial Accounting Standards Board.

   b. The American Institute of Certified Public Accountants.

   c. The Sarbanes-Oxley Act of 2002.

   d. The International Accounting Standards Board.

46. Which of the following applies to an accountant conducting a review of interim financial information?

   a. The accountant must indicate in the report those circumstances in which generally accepted accounting principles have **not** been consistently observed in the current period in relation to the preceding period.

   b. The accountant must express an opinion on the financial statements taken as a whole.

   c. The accountant must maintain independence in mental attitude in all matters relating to the engagement.

   d. The accountant must obtain sufficient appropriate evidence by performing procedures to afford a reasonable basis for an opinion.

42. (b) The requirement it to identify the correct statement regarding audit sampling risks. Answer (b) is correct because nonsampling risks relate to "human errors" such as an auditor's failure to recognize a misstatement. Answer (a) is incorrect because it is describing sampling risk, not nonsampling risk, that arises from the possibility that a substantive procedure is restricted to a sample. Answer (c) is incorrect because sampling risk is a part of the overall sampling process and not a result of uncertainty in applying audit procedures. Answer (d) is incorrect because selecting the wrong procedures is an example of nonsampling risk, not sampling risk.

43. (d) The requirement is to identify the purpose of an auditor designing tests of details. Answer (d) is correct because tests of details are used to limit detection risk and provide assurance at the relevant assertion and account level. Answer (a) is incorrect because tests of controls relate to the planed level of control risk, not tests of details. Answer (b) is incorrect because it is tests of controls that address whether controls operate effectively (not efficiently). Answer (c) is incorrect because tests of controls address the effectiveness of controls.

44. (d) The requirement is to identify what providing more supervision during an audit in response to assessed risks of material misstatement is an example of. Answer (d) is correct because it is an example of an overall response; other overall responses are (1) using more experienced staff, (2) increasing unpredictability of further audit procedures and (3) increasing the scope of audit procedures. Answer (a) is incorrect because "a substantive response" is a vague term not ordinarily used in the audit standards. Answer (b) is incorrect because tests of details of transactions, balances and disclosures and tests of controls are further audit procedures. Answer (c) is incorrect because tests of controls are performed to limit the assessed level of control risk.

45. (c) The requirement is to identify the organization or act that established the Public Company Accounting Oversight Board (PCAOB). Answer (c) is correct because the Sarbanes-Oxley Act of 2002 established the PCAOB. Answer (a) is incorrect because the Financial Accounting Standards Board did not establish the PCAOB. Answer (b) is incorrect because the American Institute of Certified Public Accountants did not establish the PCAOB. Answer (d) is incorrect because the International Accounting Standards Board did not establish the PCAOB.

46. (c) The requirement is to identify the reply that applies to an accountant conducting a review of interim financial information. Answer (c) is correct because independence is required for all reviews services. Answer (a) is incorrect because consistency need not be reported upon in a review report. Answer (b) is incorrect because negative (limited) assurance, not an opinion, is provided. Answer (d) is incorrect because the evidence obtained in a review is short of that for providing an opinion on the financial statements.

47. Which of the following circumstances would be inappropriate for the auditor to communicate to those charged with governance?

    a. A material misstatement was noted by the auditor and corrected by management.

    b. No significant deficiencies in internal control exist that would affect the financial statements.

    c. The auditor is requesting representations regarding the financial statements from management.

    d. Management has consulted with other accountants about accounting and auditing matters during the period under audit.

48. An auditor may provide an issuer client any of the following nonaudit services without impairing independence and without obtaining the preapproval of the audit committee, **except**

    a. Nonaudit services with revenues in aggregate of **less** than 5% of the total revenues paid by the issuer to the auditor during the fiscal year in which the nonaudit services are provided.

    b. Nonaudit services that were promptly brought to the attention of, and approved by, the audit committee prior to the completion of the audit.

    c. Nonaudit services to perform financial information systems design and implementation.

    d. Services that the issuer did **not** recognize as nonaudit services at the time of the engagement.

49. An accountant compiles the financial statements of a nonissuer and issues the standard compilation report. Although **not** specifically stated in this report, it is implied that

    a. The accountant has **not** audited or reviewed the financial statements.

    b. Substantially all disclosures required by GAAP are included in the financial statements.

    c. The financial statements should **not** be used to obtain credit.

    d. The compilation is limited to presenting information that is the representation of management.

50. According to the Sarbanes-Oxley Act of 2002, what is the maximum number of years an audit partner can perform audit services for an issuer before the auditor rotation is required?

    a. 2 years.

    b. 3 years.

    c. 4 years.

    d. 5 years.

47. (b) The requirement is to identify the matter that should not be communicated to those charged with governance. Answer (b) is correct since a statement that no significant deficiencies exist should not be issued, although a statement that no material weaknesses were identified may be communicated. Answers (a), (c), and (d) all represent matters communicated to those charged with governance.

48. (c) The requirement is to identify the nonaudit service that will impair auditor independence with respect to an issuer. Answer (c) is correct because under the requirements of the Sarbanes-Oxley Act financial information systems design and implementations may not be performed for an audit client—independence is impaired. Answer (a) is incorrect because less than 5% of total revenues is acceptable. Answer (b) is incorrect because such services may be allowed (if they do not relate to prohibited types of services). Answer (d) is incorrect because such services, depending upon their nature, may be allowable.

49. (b) The requirement is to identify what is implied in a compilation report. Answer (b) is correct since, when disclosures are omitted, the report so indicates. Answer (a) is incorrect because the report explicitly states that the accountant has not audited or reviewed the financial statements. Answer (c) is incorrect because such statements may be used to obtain credit (if acceptable to the credit granting organization). Answer (d) is incorrect because the statement that a compilation is limited to presenting information that is the representation of management is included in a compilation report.

50. (d) The requirement is to determine the maximum number of years an audit partner can perform audit services for an issuer before auditor rotation is required. Answer (d) is correct because Section 204 of the Sarbanes-Oxley Act makes it unlawful for an audit partner having primary responsibility for the audit or the audit partner responsible for reviewing the audit to perform the service for more than five years. Answers (a), (b), and (c) are all incorrect because the rotation requirement is for 5 years, not for 2, 3, or 4 years.

Task-Based Simulation 1

For each of the account balances and associated assertions below, double-click on the associated shaded cell and select from the list provided the procedure that provides the most appropriate audit evidence for the assertion with respect to the account.

	A	B	C
1	**Account balances**	**Assertion**	**Procedure**
2	Accounts receivable	Completeness	
3	Inventory	Valuation and allocation	
4	Fixed assets	Rights and obligations	
5	Accounts payable	Completeness	
6	Cash	Existence	

Select Item

Column 2C	Column 3C	Column 4C	Column 5C	Column 6C
Review confirmation of accounts receivable balances and agreed to accounts receivable subledger	Examine invoices from suppliers	Interview plant manager regarding fixed asset additions during the year	Compare aging of accounts payable to prior periods	Agree bank statement to the subsidiary ledger
Review list of accounts written off during year	Examine invoices paid subsequent to year-end and trance to subsidiary ledger	Recalculate partial year depreciation for fixed asset acquisitions	Confirm accounts payable balance with suppliers	Agree cash balance per the bank reconciliation to the year-end bank statement
Review schedule of bad debt expense	Select items from inventory listing and locate the items in the warehouse	Trace fixed asset item to fixed asset master control listing	Examine invoices paid subsequent to year-end and trace to subsidiary ledger	Agree cash balance to online year-end bank statement
Trace individual customer account transactions to sales invoice	Select items located in the inventory warehouse and trace to inventory listing	Vouch fixed asset acquisitions to purchase invoices	Trace individual payable transactions to purchase order	Recalculate bank statement balance, including interest receivable
Trace sales invoice and shipping documents just before year-end to customer account transactions	Trace sales invoice and shipping documents just before year-end to customer accounts	Vouch fixed asset acquisitions to related cash disbursement	Vouch invoices for the purchase of supplies to receiving documents	Trace deposit per the bank statement to the cash subsidiary ledger

Solution to Task-Based Simulation 1

Internal Control Reporting	Authoritative Literature	Help

	A	B	C
1	**Account balances**	**Assertion**	**Procedure**
2	Accounts receivable	Completeness	Trace sales invoice and shipping documents just before year-end to customer account transactions
3	Inventory	Valuation and allocation	Examine invoices from suppliers
4	Fixed assets	Rights and obligations	Vouch fixed asset acquisitions to purchase invoices
5	Accounts payable	Completeness	Examine invoices paid subsequent to year-end and trace to subsidiary ledger
6	Cash	Existence	Agree cash balance per the bank reconciliation to the year-end bank statement

Task-Based Simulation 2

Possible Ratio Explanations	Analytics Definitions	Authoritative Literature	Help

During the audit of a dealership selling only new luxury automobiles, the auditors calculated the year 2 and year 1 ratios in the table below. Double-click on the associated shaded cells and select from the list provided the most reasonable explanation the controller will provide for the change. An explanation may be used once, more than once, or not at all. Consider each ratio independently.

	A	B	C	D
1	**Ratios**	**Year 2**	**Year 1**	**Explanations**
2	Days sales in accounts receivable	32	20	
3	Inventory turnover	4.01	6.32	
4	Debt to equity	3.2	4.3	
5	Return on assets	10.5%	12%	
6	Net fixed assets to equity	19%	23.2%	

Select Item
Due to an economic downturn, buyers have shifted to economy cars.
In October of year 1, the company hired additional collection clerks.
In year 1, the company removed some fully depreciated machinery from its books.
In year 2, the board of directors decided to begin a buyback of company stock.
In year 2, the company began accounting for inventory using the last in, first out method from the first in, first out.
In year 2, the company increased the annual dividend to shareholders.
In year 2, the company instituted more stringent collection policies.
In year 2, the company made a required principal payment on its long-term debt.
In year 2, the company reclassified its international production factories to held-for-sale.
Positive consumer reviews have caused increased movements of cars.
Sales managers are recording fraudulent sales to receive larger commissions.

Solution to Task-Based Simulation 2

	A	B	C	D
1	**Ratios**	**Year 2**	**Year 1**	**Explanations**
2	Days sales in accounts receivable	32	20	Sales managers are recording fraudulent sales to receive larger commissions.
3	Inventory turnover	4.01	6.32	Due to an economic downturn, buyers have shifted to economy cars.
4	Debt to equity	3.2	4.3	In year 2, the company made a required principal payment on its long-term debt.
5	Return on assets	10.5%	12%	Due to an economic downturn, buyers have shifted to economy cars.
6	Net fixed assets to equity	19%	23.2%	In year 2, the company reclassified its international production factories to held-for-sale.

Task-Based Simulation 3

In preparation for a meeting on the firm's ethics policy, a manager wants to include a segment on the questions a CPA should ask when confronted with ethical dilemmas affecting integrity for which there is no specific authoritative guidance. Which section of the professional standards provides guidance for the manager's presentation on the decision-making process?

Enter your response in the answer fields below. Guidance on correctly structuring your response appears above and below the answer fields.

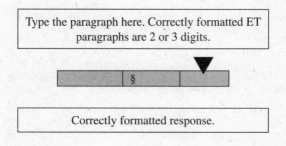

Solution to Task-Based Simulation 3

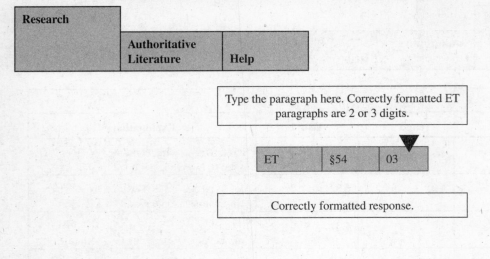

Index